THE
WESTERN HERITAGE

THE WESTERN HERITAGE

Brief Edition

COMBINED VOLUME
Third Edition

Donald Kagan
YALE UNIVERSITY

Steven Ozment
HARVARD UNIVERSITY

Frank M. Turner
YALE UNIVERSITY

A. Daniel Frankforter
PENNSYLVANIA STATE UNIVERSITY, BEHREND COLLEGE

Prentice
Hall

UPPER SADDLE RIVER, NEW JERSEY 07458

Library of Congress Cataloging-in-Publication Data

Kagan, Donald.
  The western heritage/Donald Kagan, Steven Ozment, Frank M. Turner; with the assistance of A. Daniel Frankforter.—3rd ed., brief ed.
    p. cm.
  "Combined volume."
  Includes bibliographical references and index.
  ISBN 0-13-041578-2 (pbk.)
    1. Civilization, Western. I. Ozment, Steven E. II. Turner, Frank M. (Frank Miller), 1944- III. Title
  CB245.K28 2001b
  909'.09812—dc21   00-066895

Editorial Director: Charlyce Jones Owen
Acquisitions Editor: Charles Cavaliere
Associate Editor: Emsal Hasan
Director of Production and Manufacturing: Barbara Kittle
Production Editor: Louise Rothman
Prepress and Manufacturing Manager: Nick Sklitsis
Prepress and Manufacturing Buyer: Lynn Pearlman
Creative Design Director: Leslie Osher
Interior and Cover Designer: Nancy Wells and Laura Gardner

Cover Art: Ferdinard George Waldmuller (1793–1865) Austrian, *Lower Austrian Farm Wedding* 1843, Austrian Gallery in Belvedere, Vienna/A.K.G., Berlin/SuperStock

This book was set in 10/12 Trump Mediaeval by Carlisle Communications and was printed and bound by Webcrafters.
The cover was printed by Phoenix Color Corp.

 © 2002, 1999, 1996 by Pearson Education, Inc.
Upper Saddle River, New Jersey 07458

Printed in the United States of America

10 9 8 7 6 5 4 3 2 1

0-13-041578-2

Prentice-Hall International (UK) Limited, *London*
Prentice-Hall of Australia Pty. Limited, *Sydney*
Prentice-Hall Canada Inc., *Toronto*
Prentice-Hall Hispanoamerica, S.A., *Mexico*
Prentice-Hall of India Private Limited, *New Delhi*
Prentice-Hall of Japan, Inc., *Tokyo*
Pearson Education Asia Pte. Ltd., *Singapore*
Editora Prentice-Hall do Brasil, Ltda., *Rio de Janeiro*

Brief Contents

PART 5   TOWARD THE MODERN WORLD

PART 6   GLOBAL CONFLICT, COLD WAR, AND NEW DIRECTIONS

Detailed Contents

PART 3   EUROPE IN TRANSITION, 1300–1750

PART 5   TOWARD THE MODERN WORLD

Maps

Preface

The heritage of Western civilization is a major point of departure for an understanding of the modern world. The global context in which we now conduct our daily lives is unprecedented, and it has been shaped in large measure by Western technologies, economic systems, and political ideologies. From the sixteenth through the twentieth centuries the West had a tremendous influence, for both good and ill, on cultures scattered around the globe, and we live today in the wake of that impact. It is the goal of this book to help students become better informed and more culturally sensitive citizens of the emerging global age by introducing them to the West's legacy.

Since *The Western Heritage* first appeared, its authors have sought to provide their readers with a work that does justice to the scope of Western civilization. Their expectation is that accurate understanding of the West will foster useful debates about the West's character, values, institutions, and global influence. Since the authors believe that a critical attitude toward their own culture has always been a characteristic of Western peoples, it is hoped that this new brief edition of *The Western Heritage* will contribute to the on-going debate about the strengths and weaknesses of the West that has been a persistent feature of Western intellectual life.

In this edition as in earlier ones, the goal has been to present Western civilization fairly, accurately, and in a way that does justice to the immense diversity of the human enterprise. Since history is made, experienced, and recorded by a multiplicity of peoples, history has many facets, no one of which can account for all the others. Any attempt to tell the story of the West from a single overarching perspective, no matter how timely, is bound to neglect or suppress some important part of that story. The authors have had to make selections to bring the story of the West within the compass of an introductory text, but they have also tried to provide the broadest possible coverage of their subject.

They also believe that any book that addresses the experience of the West must look beyond Europe's borders. The students who will read this book are drawn from a wide variety of social contexts, and they live in a world characterized by highly interconnected economies and instant communication across cultural boundaries. It is important, therefore, to recognize the ways in which Western civilization has, throughout its history, engaged other cultures and been influenced by them. Examples of the two-way interaction between Western and non-Western societies appear throughout the text and are highlighted in a series of comparative essays entitled "The West & the World."

Goals of the Text

The primary goal of *The Western Heritage* is to present a strong, clear narrative that surveys key developments in Western history while paying special attention to several critical themes:

- The capacity of Western civilization to generate transforming self-criticism.

- The development of political freedom, constitutional government, and concern for the rule of law and the rights of individuals.

- The shifting relations among religion, society, and the state.

- The development of science and technology and their expanding impact on thought, social institutions, and everyday life.

- The major religious and intellectual influences that have shaped Western culture.

FLEXIBLE PRESENTATION   *The Western Heritage* is designed to accommodate a variety of approaches to a course in Western civilization and to allow instructors to stress what is most important to them. The last two chapters (30 and 31) have been specifically reorganized and rewritten so that courses can conclude by emphasizing either social or political developments.

INTEGRATED SOCIAL, CULTURAL, AND POLITICAL
HISTORY   *The Western Heritage* provides one of
the richest accounts of Western social history
found in any current textbook. It provides strong
coverage of family life, the changing roles of
women, and the place of the family in relation to
broader economic, political, and social developments. This reflects the explosive growth that has
taken place in social historical research in the past
quarter century and which has enriched virtually
all areas of historical study. But the authors, while
strongly believing in the value of social history,
have also been sensitive to the needs of teachers
who have repeatedly said that they believe that a
political narrative provides students with the most
effective tool for constructing an initial understanding of the past.

No other survey text presents so full an account
of the religious and intellectual development of the
West. People may be political and social animals,
but they are also reasoning and spiritual beings.
What past generations thought and believed are
among the most important things we can know
about them, and we cannot fully understand ourselves without understanding the intellectual currents of the past that have shaped our thoughts and
conceptual categories.

CLARITY AND ACCESSIBILITY   Good narrative history requires clear, vigorous prose. The goal of the
authors was to produce a fully accessible text without condescending to readers by compromising vocabulary or conceptual level.

Changes in the Current Edition

ART & THE WEST   A beautiful and important new
feature enhances students' understanding of the
artistic heritage of the West. In each chapter a work
of art or architecture is highlighted to illustrate key
developments from the era of its creation.

THE WEST & THE WORLD   Sections of the text are
supplemented by a series of extended essays that
compare various Western institutions with those
from other parts of the world or which discuss the
ways in which developments in the West have influenced non-Western cultures.

RECENT SCHOLARSHIP   The new edition has been
revised to incorporate the most recent developments

in historical scholarship and to address the current
concerns of professional historians. Of particular interest are expanded discussions of:

- **Women in the history of the West** (see, especially, chapters 3, 4, 5, 7, 14, 30.)

- **The Scientific Revolution** (chapter 14 has been
  wholly revised and rewritten to explain the scientific theories that arose from the Copernican
  revolution, the current interpretation of the
  Galileo case, the role played by pioneering female
  scientists, and the social context for the development of early science).

- **The Dutch Golden Age** (chapter 15 contains a
  new section discussing the United Netherlands
  during the seventeenth and eighteenth centuries).

- **Africa and the transatlantic economy** (chapter 17
  extensively explores the relationship of Africa to
  the transatlantic economy of the sixteenth
  through the eighteenth centuries, focusing on: the
  role of African society and politics in the slave
  trade, the experience of Africans forcibly transported to the Americas, and the incorporation of
  African elements in New World cultures).

- **Jewish thinkers in the Enlightenment** (chapter 18
  contains a new section discussing the thought of
  Spinoza and Moses Mendelsohn as they relate to
  the role of Jewish religion and society in the wider
  European culture).

- **The Holocaust** (chapter 29 provides more analysis of the causes of the Holocaust, and chapter 30
  includes an extensive new section on the destruction of the Jews of Poland).

- **Twentieth century social history** (*The Western
  Heritage* presents the most extensive treatment
  of modern social history available in a survey
  text; of particular significance is chapter 30
  which treats the experiences of women under authoritarian governments, the collectivization of
  Soviet agriculture, the destruction of the Polish
  Jews, European migration, and the impact of
  computers and new technology on European life).

- **The history of the Cold War and Europe at the
  start of the twenty-first century** (chapter 31,
  which deals with the Soviet–American rivalry and
  the collapse of communism, has been wholly
  rewritten). Chapters 30 and 31 are designed so
  that instructors, though teaching both chapters,
  may choose to close their course with either one.
  Those who want to emphasize social history

might end with chapter 30 and those who wish to emphasize political developments may choose to conclude with chapter 31.

MAPS AND ILLUSTRATIONS   To help students understand the relationship between geography and history, relief features have been added to many of the maps. The text also contains numerous color illustrations.

PEDAGOGICAL FEATURES   These include chronological tables, a list of key topics at the beginning of each chapter, chapter summaries, review questions, and bibliographies. This edition continues the practice of using B.C.E. (before the common era) and C.E. (common era) instead of B.C. (before Christ) and A.D. (anno domini, the year of the Lord) to designate dates. It also utilizes the most accurate currently accepted English transliterations of Arabic words.

Ancillary Instructional Materials

The ancillary instructional materials that accompany *The Western Heritage* include print and multimedia supplements that are designed to reinforce and enliven the richness of the past and inspire students with the excitement of studying the history of Western civilization.

Print Supplements for the Instructor

INSTRUCTOR'S MANUAL WITH TEST ITEMS   The Instructor's Manual contains chapter summaries, key points and vital concepts, and information on audiovisual resources that can be used in developing and preparing lecture presentations. Also included is a test item file that offers multiple-choice, identification, and essay test questions.

PRENTICE HALL CUSTOM TEST   This commercial-quality computerized test management program, for Windows and Macintosh environments, allows users to create their own tests using items from the printed Test Item File. The program allows users to edit the items in the Test Item File and to add their own questions. Online testing is also available.

TRANSPARENCY PACKAGE   This collection of full-color transparency acetates provides the maps, charts, and graphs from the text for use in classroom presentations.

Print Supplements for the Student

STUDY GUIDE, VOLUMES I AND II   The study guide includes commentaries, definitions, and a variety of exercises designed to reinforce the concepts in the chapter. These exercises include: identification, map exercises, and short-answer and essay questions.

DOCUMENTS SET, VOLUMES I AND II   This carefully selected and edited set of documents provides over 100 additional primary source readings. Each document includes a brief introduction as well as questions to encourage critical analysis of the reading and to relate it to the content of the text.

MAP WORKBOOK   This brief workbook gives students the opportunity to increase their knowledge of geography through identification and other map exercises. It is available free to students when shrink-wrapped with the text.

HISTORICAL ATLAS OF THE WORLD   This four-color historical atlas provides additional map resources to reinforce concepts in the text. It is available for a nominal fee when shrink-wrapped with the text.

UNDERSTANDING AND ANSWERING ESSAY QUESTIONS   Prepared by Mary L. Kelley, San Antonio College. This brief guide suggests helpful study techniques as well as specific analytical tools for understanding different types of essay questions and provides precise guidelines for preparing well-crafted essay answers. This guide is available free to students when shrink-wrapped with the text.

READING CRITICALLY ABOUT HISTORY: A GUIDE TO ACTIVE READING   Prepared by Rose Wassman and Lee Ann Rinsky. This guide focuses on the skills needed to learn the essential information presented in college history textbooks. Material covered includes vocabulary skills, recognizing organizational patterns, critical thinking skills, understanding visual aids, and practice sections. This guide is available free to students when shrink-wrapped with the text.

THEMES OF THE TIMES   *The New York Times* and Prentice Hall are sponsoring *Themes of the Times*, a

program designed to enhance student access to current information of relevance in the classroom. Through this program, the core subject matter provided in the text is supplemented by a collection of current articles from one of the world's most distinguished newspapers, *The New York Times*. These articles demonstrate the vital, ongoing connection between what is learned in the classroom and what is happening in the world around us. To enjoy the wealth of information of *The New York Times* daily, a reduced subscription rate is available. For information call toll-free: 1-800-631-1222.

Prentice Hall and *The New York Times* are proud to co-sponsor *Themes of the Times*. We hope it will make the reading of both textbooks and newspapers a more dynamic, involving process.

Multimedia Supplements

HISTORY ON THE INTERNET This guide focuses on developing the critical thinking skills necessary to evaluate and use online sources. The guide also provides a brief introduction to navigating the Internet, along with complete references related specifically to the History discipline and how to use the *Companion Website™* available for *The Western Heritage*. This supplementary book is free to students when shrink-wrapped with the text.

COMPANION WEBSITE™
ADDRESS: WWW.PRENHALL.COM/KAGAN
Students can now take full advantage of the World Wide Web to enrich their study of Western Civilization through *The Western Heritage Companion Website™*. Features of the website include, for each chapter in the text, objectives, study questions, map labeling exercises, related links, and document exercises. A faculty module provides material from the Instructor's Manual and the maps and charts from the text in Powerpoint™ format.

POWERPOINT™ IMAGES CD ROM Available for Windows and Macintosh environments, this resource includes the maps, charts, and graphs from the text for use in Powerpoint™. Organized by chapters in the text, this collection of images is useful for classroom presentations and lectures.

IRC WESTERN CIVILIZATION CD ROM Available for Windows 95 and 3.1, this lecture and presentation resource includes a library of over 3000 images, each with a descriptive caption, plus film clips, maps, and sound recordings. A correlation guide lists the images as they correspond to the chapters of *The Western Heritage*. Contact your local Prentice Hall representative for information about the adoption requirements for this resource.

DOCUMENTS CD ROM Functional in both Windows and Macintosh environments, this resource contains all the primary source readings from the print Documents Set in easy-to-read Adobe Acrobat™. Additionally, all the document questions are linked directly to the *Companion Website™*, enhancing an already useful study tool. This CD ROM comes packaged free with all new copies of *The Western Heritage, Brief Third Edition*.

Acknowledgments

We are grateful to the scholars and teachers whose thoughtful and often detailed comments helped shape this revision:

Lenard R. Berlanstein, University of Virginia, Charlottesville
Stephanie Christelow, Idaho State University
Samuel Willard Crompton, Holyoke Community College
Robert L. Ervin, San Jacinto Community College
Benjamin Foster, Yale University
Joseph Gonzales, Moorpark College
Victor Davis Hanson, California State University, Fresno
James Halverson, Judson College
Mark C. Herman, Edison Community College
William I. Hitchcock, Wellesley College
Pardaic Kenny, University of Colorado, Boulder
Raymond F. Kierstead, Reed College
David Lindberg, University of Wisconsin, Madison
Eleanor McCluskey, Palm Beach Atlantic College and Broward Community College
Robert J. Mueller, Hastings College
John Nicols, University of Oregon, Eugene
Sandra J. Peacock, State University of New York, Binghamton
John Powell, Cumberland College
Robert A. Schneider, Catholic University
Hugo Schwyzer, Pasadena City College
Sidney R. Sherter, Long Island University
Roger P. Snow, College of Great Falls

Finally, we would like to thank the dedicated people who helped produce this revision. Our acquisitions team of Charlyce Jones Owen, Charles Cavaliere, and Emsal Hasan; our development editor, Roberta Meyer; our production editor, Louise Rothman; Nancy Wells and Laura Gardner, who created the handsome new design of this edition; Lynn Pearlman, our manufacturing buyer; and Barbara Salz, photo researcher.

D.K.
S.O.
F.M.T.

About the Authors

DONALD KAGAN is Hillhouse Professor of History and Classics at Yale University, where he has taught since 1969. He received the A.B. degree in history from Brooklyn College, the M.A. in classics from Brown University, and the Ph.D. in history from Ohio State University. During 1958–1959 he studied at the American School of Classical Studies as a Fulbright Scholar. He has received three awards for undergraduate teaching at Cornell and Yale. He is the author of a history of Greek political thought, *The Great Dialogue* (1965); a four-volume history of the Peloponnesian war, *The Origins of the Peloponnesian War* (1969); *The Archidamian War* (1974); *The Peace of Nicias and the Sicilian Expedition* (1981); *The Fall of the Athenian Empire* (1987); and a biography of Pericles, *Pericles of Athens and the Birth of Democracy* (1991); and *On the Origins of War* (1995). He is coauthor, with Frederick W. Kagan of *While America Sleeps* (2000). With Brian Tierney and L. Pearce Williams, he is the editor of *Great Issues in Western Civilization*, a collection of readings.

STEVEN OZMENT is McLean Professor of Ancient and Modern History at Harvard University. He has taught Western Civilization at Yale, Stanford, and Harvard. He is the author of ten books. *The Age of Reform, 1250–1550* (1980) won the Schaff Prize and was nominated for the 1981 American Book Award. *Magdalena and Balthasar: An Intimate Portrait of Life in Sixteenth Century Europe* (1986), *Three Behaim Boys: Growing Up in Early Modern Germany* (1990), *Protestants: The Birth of a Revolution* (1992), and *The Burgermeister's Daughter: Scandal in a Sixteenth Century German Town* (1996) were selections of the History Book Club, as is his most recent book, *Flesh and Spirit: Private Life in Early Modern Germany* (1999).

FRANK M. TURNER is John Hay Whitney Professor of History at Yale University, where he served as University Provost from 1988 to 1992. He received his B.A. degree at the College of William and Mary and his Ph.D. from Yale. He has received the Yale College Award for Distinguished Undergraduate Teaching. He has directed a National Endowment for the Humanities Summer Institute. His scholarly research has received the support of fellowships from the National Endowment for the Humanities and the Guggenheim Foundation and the Woodrow Wilson Center. He is the author of *Between Science and Religion: The Reaction to Scientific Naturalism in Late Victorian England* (1974), *The Greek Heritage in Victorian Britain* (1981), which received the British Council Prize of the Conference on British Studies and the Yale Press Governors Award, and *Contesting Cultural Authority: Essays in Victorian Intellectual Life* (1993). He has also contributed numerous articles to journals and has served on the editorial advisory boards of *The Journal of Modern History*, *Isis*, and *Victorian Studies*. He edited *The Idea of a University*, by John Henry Newman (1996). Since 1996 he has served as a Trustee of Connecticut College.

A. DANIEL FRANKFORTER is Professor of Medieval History at the Pennsylvania State University. He holds degrees from Franklin and Marshall College, Drew University, and the Pennsylvania State University, where he has taught since 1970. His books include: *A History of the Christian Movement; Civilization and Survival; The Shakespeare Name Dictionary, The Medieval Millennium, An Introduction;* an edition and translation of Françoise Poullain de la Barre's *De l'Égalité des Deux Sexes,* and *Stones for Bread: A Critique of Contemporary Worship*. He has received four awards for excellence in teaching and research from the Pennsylvania State University.

THE
WESTERN HERITAGE

Chapter 1

The Birth of Civilization

K E Y   T O P I C S

- The earliest history of humanity, the origins of human culture in the Paleolithic Age, the shift from food gathering to food production, and the emergence of civilizations in the Middle East and Africa
- The ancient civilizations of Mesopotamia and Egypt
- The great Middle Eastern empires, 1500–539 B.C.E.[1]
- The emergence of Judaism
- The different outlooks of the ancient Middle Eastern and Greek civilizations

For hundreds of thousands of years, human beings lived by hunting and gathering what nature provided. Only about 10,000 years ago did they begin to cultivate plants and domesticate animals. As they turned from harvesting food to producing it, settled life became possible. About 5,000 years ago the Sumerians, who lived near the confluence of the Tigris and Euphrates Rivers (a region the Greeks named "Mesopotamia," i.e., "between-rivers"), and the Egyptians, who dwelt in the Nile Valley, pioneered civilization. By the

[1]This book substitutes B.C.E. ("before the common era") and C.E. ("common era") for B.C. and A.D.

fourteenth century B.C.E. *powerful empires had arisen and were struggling for dominance of the civilized world. But one of the region's smaller states, Israel, made the ancient Middle East's greatest contribution to civilization. It began the evolution of the modern West's major religions: Judaism, Christianity, and Islam.*

Early Humans and Their Culture

Scientists estimate that Earth may be 6 billion years old and that its human inhabitants have been developing for 3 to 5 million years. Some 1 to 2 million years ago, erect, tool-using beings spread from their probable place of origin in Africa to Europe and Asia. Our own species, *Homo sapiens*, is about 200,000 years old, and fully modern humans have existed for about 90,000 years.

Humans are distinguished by a unique capacity to construct cultures. A *culture* may be defined as a way of life invented by a group and passed on by teaching. It includes both material things (tools, clothing, and shelter) and ideas, institutions, and beliefs. Because cultural behaviors are guided by learning rather than instinct, they can be altered at will to enable human beings to adapt rapidly to different environments and changing conditions.

The Paleolithic Age

Anthropologists identify prehistoric human cultures by the styles of their most durable and plentiful artifacts—stone tools. The earliest period in cultural development—the Paleolithic (Greek for "old stone") era—began with the first use of stone tools some 1 million years ago. It continued until about 10,000 B.C.E. Throughout this immensely long period of time, people were nomadic hunters and gatherers who depended for their food on what nature spontaneously offered. An uncertain food supply and vulnerability to wild beasts, accidents, and environmental disasters persuaded early humans that they occupied a world governed by superhuman powers. Cave art, ritual burial practices, and other evidences of religious or magical belief that appeared during the Paleolithic era bear witness to a suspicion as old as humanity itself that there is more to the world than meets the eye.

Human society in the Paleolithic Age was probably based on a division of labor by sex. Males ranged far afield on the hunt. Females, who were less mobile because of the burdens of childbearing and nursing, gathered edibles of various kinds in the vicinity of a base camp. The knowledge that people acquired as hunters and gatherers enabled them to develop agriculture and herding, food-producing technologies that drastically changed the human lifestyle.

The Neolithic Age

About 10,000 years ago people living in some parts of the Middle (or Near) East began to shift from hunting and gathering to agriculture. Only a few societies initially made the change, and anthropologists and archaeologists disagree as to what motivated them. Since the shift coincided with advances that promoted greater precision in chipping and grinding new styles of stone tools, this period is called the Neolithic (i.e., "new stone") Age. Neolithic peoples, who lived in the mountain foothills to which wild species of sheep, goats, wheat, and barley were native, began to domesticate these food sources. Once domesticated, species could then be transplanted to areas where they did not naturally occur.

Hunters and gatherers must wander from place to place to find food, but farmers have to stay with the fields they cultivate. Agriculture necessitated village life. That prompted the invention of techniques for constructing more permanent dwellings, and it encouraged the use of new materials such as pottery (in which to cook and store agricultural products). The earliest Neolithic dwellings were small, circular huts that clustered around a central storage facility. Later Neolithic people built larger rectangular homes with private storage places and enclosures for livestock. The similarity in size and equipment of these structures suggests that there were only minor differences in wealth and social status within Neolithic communities. There was some trade among them, but they were largely self-sufficient.

The two most exceptional Neolithic sites that have come to light are at Jericho (near the Dead Sea) and Çatal Hüyük (about 150 miles south of the capital of modern Turkey). Jericho was occupied as early as 12,000 B.C.E., and by 8000 B.C.E. it had a massive stone wall enclosing a space of more

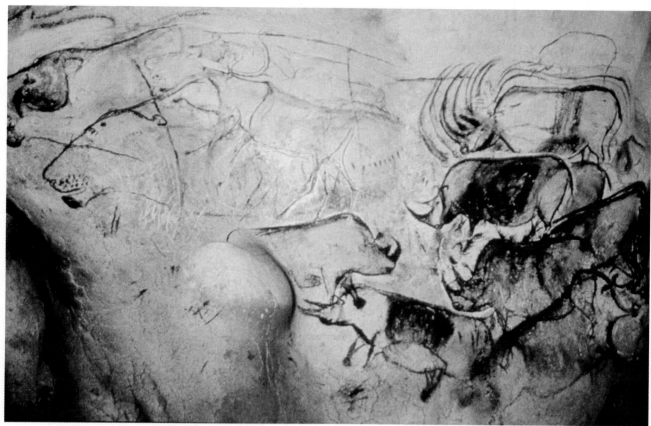

In Chauvet cave, near Avignon, France, Paleolithic artists decorated the walls with exquisite drawings of animals. Jean Clottes/Corbis Sygma Photo News

than eight acres. (No other Neolithic site is known to have been fortified.) Çatal Hüyük was a somewhat later and larger community with a population well over 6,000. Its mud-brick dwellings were packed so tightly together that there were no streets between them and people entered them from ladders through roofs. Many interiors were elaborately and mysteriously decorated with sculptures and paintings that are assumed to have ritual significance.

In regions where agriculture and animal husbandry appeared, the relationship between human beings and nature was changed forever. Human population grew at an unprecedented rate, and people began to try to control nature, not just respond to what it offered. This was a vital prerequisite for the development of civilization, but it was not without cost. Farmers had to work harder and longer than hunters and gatherers. They faced health threats from accumulating wastes, and they had to figure out ways to live to-

gether permanently in one place. The earliest Neolithic communities appeared in the Middle East about 8000 B.C.E., in China about 4000 B.C.E., and in India about 3600 B.C.E.

The Bronze Age and the Birth of Civilization

As Neolithic villages and herding cultures were spreading over much of the world, another major shift in human lifestyles began on the plains along the Tigris and Euphrates Rivers and in the valley of the Nile River. Some villages grew into towns and cities and began to dominate the regions in which they evolved. These new urban centers usually had some monumental structures that could have been built only by the sustained effort of hundreds or thousands of people over many years. Social stratification appeared, and people were assigned to classes on the basis of wealth, family lineage, and religious and political authority. Writing was invented, probably to deal with urban problems of management and record keeping. Elaborate artwork was produced, and an important new technology for manufacturing tools and weapons appeared. It involved techniques for smelting metal ores and combining tin with copper to make a hard alloy called bronze. The prevalence of bronze has led scholars to call the period from 3100 B.C.E. to 1200 B.C.E. in the Middle East the Bronze Age. The characteristics of Bronze Age cultures (i.e., urbanism; technological, industrial, and social change; long-distance trade; and writing systems) are the hallmarks of *civilization.*

Early Civilizations to About 1000 B.C.E.

During the fourth millennium, populations of unprecedented density began to develop along Mesopotamia's Tigris and Euphrates Rivers and Egypt's Nile River. By about 3000 B.C.E., when the invention of writing gave birth to history, urban life had spread throughout these regions and centralized states had begun to develop. Since city-dwellers do not grow their own food, they need to establish some system to promote, collect, and disburse surpluses produced by rural farmers and herders. The arid climates of Mesopotamia and Egypt meant that farmers could meet the demands of urban populations for their products only with the help of extensive irrigation systems. Irrigation technology was more elaborate in Mesopotamia than in Egypt. In Egypt the Nile flooded at the right moment for cultivation, and irrigation simply involved channeling water to the fields. In Mesopotamia, however, the floods came at the wrong season. Dikes were needed to protect fields where crops were already growing and to store water for future use. Mesopotamian towns and villages were strung along rivers, streams, and canals. These were their lifelines, and control of the water they supplied was a contentious issue that could lead to war. Mesopotamia was a flat plain. The terrain provided little protection from floods and allowed swollen rivers and streams to carve new channels and change their courses. Cities were sometimes severely damaged or even forced to relocate. Archaeologists once believed that the

This statue of Gudea, city ruler of Lagash after the fall of the Akkadian empire, shows him as a pious Sumerian ruler. It was carved of very hard imported black stone. A brief historical inscription is visible on his cloak. Gudea built a major temple to a local deity at Lagash, Ningirsu, and describes the work, step by step, in one of the longest Sumerian poems known today. Scala/Art Resource, NY

need to construct and manage irrigation systems caused the development of cities and centralized states, but they now know that large-scale irrigation appeared long after urban civilization was established.

Mesopotamian Civilization

Civilization probably made its first appearance in Mesopotamia in Babylonia, a zone of arid ecology that stretches from modern Baghdad to the Persian Gulf. The first cities seem to have been founded in Sumer, the southern half of Babylo-

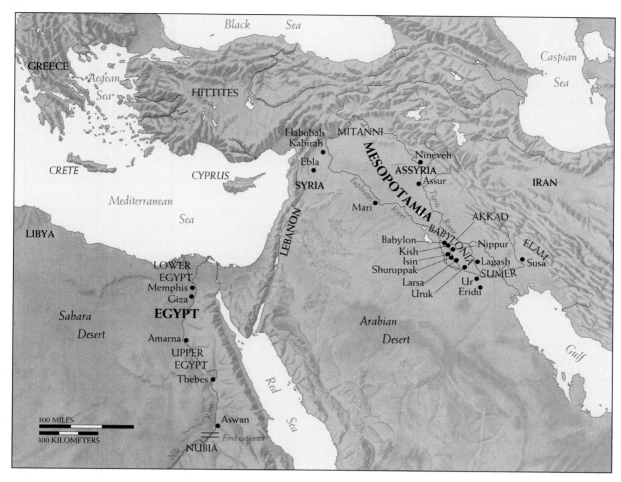

MAP 1–1 THE ANCIENT MIDDLE EAST   *The West's two premier civilizations were both dependent on unique, annually flooding rivers. Egypt was united as a single state at a very early period, but Mesopotamia was long divided into a number of city-states.*

nia, during the fourth millennium B.C.E. The earliest urban center may have been at Uruk, a city that established outposts of its culture as far afield as Syria and southern Anatolia. During the Early Dynastic Period (i.e., 2800–2370 B.C.E.), Uruk was joined by a number of other city-states scattered along the banks of the Tigris and Euphrates. Competition for water and land led to wars among them. Leagues and alliances were formed, and the weaker cities became subject to kingdoms built by the stronger. Legend claims that history's first monarchs reigned in the city of Kish.

The Sumerian language is not related to any known language, and most of the Sumerians' neighbors spoke Semitic tongues (i.e., languages belonging to the same family as Hebrew and Arabic). Many of the Semitic peoples were influenced by Sumerian civilization and adapted the Sumerian writing system for their own use. Among these were the Akkadians, a people whose first king, Sargon, established his seat at Akkade (near Baghdad). Sargon created history's first empire by conquering all the Sumerian city-states and extending his authority into southwestern Iran and northern Syria. Memory of the dynasty's splendor led later Mesopotamians to think of the reign of Naram-Sin, his grandson, as the high point of their history. (See "Art and the West.")

External attack and internal weakness eventually combined to destroy the Akkadian state, but about 2125 B.C.E. the kings of the Third Dynasty of the ancient Sumerian city of Ur restored unity to a part of the old empire. Under the leadership of the Third Dynasty of Ur, Sumerian civilization had its final flowering. Great monuments were built, epic poems were composed to celebrate the deeds of ancient heroes, and thousands of surviving documents witness to the existence of a highly centralized administrative system. Ur survived, however, for little more than a century. An extended period of agricultural failure may have produced a famine that undercut its ability to defend itself. The Elamites invaded Sumer from the east and the Amorites invaded from the north. They brought an end to Sumerian rule and eventually absorbed the Sumerian peoples. The Sumerian language survived but only as a learned tongue studied by priests and scholars—much like Latin in the modern West.

New Amorite dynasties seated themselves at Isin and Larsa, but they were soon brought under the control of a powerful new dynasty that founded the famous city of Babylon. Babylon extended its control over most of Mesopotamia. Its empire and culture reached their peaks during the reign of Hammurabi (r. ca. 1792–1750 B.C.E.), a ruler who is best remembered for the collection of laws that was issued during his reign. Earlier kings had compiled lists of laws, but the so-called Code of Hammurabi is the earliest major collection to survive. It provides its readers with uniquely intimate insights into the values and institutions of an early civilization.

Amorite society was divided into classes of nobles, commoners, and slaves, each one of which was treated differently by the law. Crimes against highly ranked individuals were punished more severely than those against inferior persons, but even the poor and humble had some protection under the law. The principle of justice was retribution: "an eye for an eye, a tooth for a tooth." Professionally trained judges decided cases on the basis of evidence and the testimony of witnesses. When that was unavailable, accused persons might be compelled to prove their innocence by taking sacred oaths or undergoing physical ordeals.

Hammurabi's dynasty survived until about 1600 B.C.E. It collapsed in the face of invasions from the north that brought new peoples (i.e., the Hittites, Hurrians, and Kassites) into Mesopotamia.

GOVERNMENT   The earliest historical records document the existence of monarchy in ancient Mesopotamia. The type of monarchy, however, varied according to time and place. Early Sumerian art depicts kings leading armies, executing captives, and making offerings to gods. In the northern district of Assyria kings served as chief priests, but in the south, in Babylonia, the roles of kings and priests were kept separate. Kings often appointed their sons and daughters to priesthoods. Enheduanna, daughter of the Akkadian emperor Sargon, was one of these. She is remembered for the poetry she wrote, some of which has survived to make her history's first identifiable author.

The royal and priestly establishments were supported by income from large landed estates. Some of this land was worked by low-ranking laborers in exchange for food rations, and some of it was leased to citizen entrepreneurs who paid rent or farmed it for a share of the crop. The government and the temples also maintained large herds of animals, which supported, among other things, the large-scale manufacture of textiles. Exports of wool and textiles were needed to pay for metals that were not available in Mesopotamia. Priests and kings did not own all the land in a Sumerian city-state. Some was in the hands of private individuals who bought and sold it freely.

WRITING AND MATHEMATICS   The challenge of administrating a Sumerian city promoted the invention of the world's first system of writing. Modern scholars have named it *cuneiform* (from Latin *cuneus*, "wedge") after the wedge-shaped marks that the Sumerian scribe made by pressing a reed stylus into the common writing material, a clay tablet. Writing began with a few signs intended to help the reader remember something that he already knew. Gradually the system evolved to record all the elements of speech so that authors could use it to pass on new information to their readers. Sumerian scribes had to learn several thousand characters, some of which stood for words and others for sounds. Since it took considerable time and training to learn how to write, the skill was restricted to a tiny elite whose services were much in demand.

Before 3000 B.C.E. no one seems to have conceived of the concept of a number apart from the act of counting specific things. Scribes used different numerals for counting different things, and a single sign could mean, for example, either 10 or 18 depending on what was being counted.

A Monument to a King's Triumph: The Victory Stele of Naram-Sin

The Victory Stele of Naram-Sin King of Akkad, over the mountain-dwelling Lullubi, Mesopotamian, Akkadian Period, c. 2230 B.C.E. (pink sandstone). Louvre, Paris, France. The Bridgeman Art Library International Ltd.

*T*he Akkadian ruler Naram-Sin erected a pillar (i.e., stele) to commemorate a victory over the Lullubi, a people who lived in the Zagros Mountains on Mesopotamia's eastern frontier. Steles were erected in temples to record the deeds of kings and on frontiers to frighten off potential invaders by advertising a king's military prowess. Naram-Sin's stele is a six-foot-high slab of limestone that was carted off as war booty in the twelfth century B.C.E. by the Elamites. Modern archaeologists discovered it (along with the stele on which the Code of Hammurabi was inscribed) in the ruins of the Elamite capital at Susa.

Naram-Sin's stele is one of the finest extant Akkadian sculptures, and it illustrates the novel imperialistic point of view that distinguished the Akkadians from the Sumerians. The figure of the king is larger than all the others in testimony to his dominance. He wears a horned helmet to symbolize his divine power, and he tramples on the bodies of his enemies. The composition strides diagonally up the stele, creating a sense of mounting, conquering energy. Landscape appears for the first time in Mesopotamian art, and figures are naturalistically modeled with the exception of the gods. They are symbolized by stars to prevent them from competing with the deified king for dominance of the scene.

Once numbers began to be thought of as entities in themselves, development was rapid. Sumerian mathematicians developed a sexagesimal system (i.e., based on the number 60). It survives today in our convention of the 60-minute hour and the circle divided into 360 degrees. Mathematics enabled the Mesopotamians to make great strides in the study of astronomy and to develop accurate calendars.

RELIGION The Mesopotamians produced a large body of sacred literature, some of which influenced the composition of the Hebrew Bible. They worshiped many gods and goddesses, most of whom were deified natural phenomena (e.g., the powers behind storms, earthquakes, and the fecundity of nature). The Mesopotamians were religiously tolerant and accepted the fact that different people might have different gods. They assumed that the gods, although immortal and much greater in power than themselves, had the same needs as they did. Myths claimed that the gods had created humanity to do the work of food raising and housekeeping that otherwise the gods would have had to do for themselves. A temple served literally as a god's home. The image of the deity that it housed was provided with meals, draped in clothing, offered entertainment, and honored with ritual and ceremony. A garden was maintained for the god's pleasure and a bed for its nightly repose. Deities had universal authority, but each major god or goddess laid exclusive claim to a city of his or her own. The greater temples in the Sumerian cities were erected on the tops of huge terraced mounds of mudbrick called *ziggurats*. Poets sometimes described these structures as mountains linking earth with heaven, but their precise purpose and symbolism remain uncertain.

The gods were grouped into families, and heaven was assumed to be organized much like a human community. Each deity had its own area of responsibility. Gods presided not only over the processes of nature but also over human skills and crafts. The great gods who dominated heaven, like the kings who governed human affairs, were too remote to be approached by common people. Ordinary men and women took their concerns to minor deities whom they hoped would intercede for them in the courts of heaven.

Intercession was needed. The Mesopotamians had a keen sense of the fragility of human existence, and religion provided some of their most important tools for coping with life's crises and uncertainties. Mesopotamians believed that their world was full of omens that, if properly understood, would reveal the future. Knowledge of the future was important, for it was assumed that unfavorable developments could be headed off by appropriate rituals and careful planning. The Mesopotamians developed an elaborate science of divination that found meaning in everything from chance events to the shapes of the entrails of animals sacrificed to the gods. Temples kept extensive records of omens to enable priests to hone their skills at divining the meanings of portents. The Mesopotamians also believed that many of life's reverses could be blamed on black magic, and there were many rituals to provide protection against witchcraft.

The Mesopotamians did not hold out any hope for a better life after death. Death doomed spirits to a glum existence in a dusty, dark netherworld where they suffered hunger and thirst unless their living relatives continued to supply them with offerings. There was no reward in death for those who had led virtuous lives and no punishment for the wicked. Everyone was equally miserable. Since the desperate spirits of the dead might escape confinement to haunt the living, families took the precaution of burying their dead with offerings and holding ceremonies from time to time to placate departed kin. At the funerals of some of the early rulers, large numbers of their servants were sacrificed to provide them with retinues in the underworld.

SOCIETY Hundreds of thousands of cuneiform texts, dating from the early third millennium to the third century B.C.E., provide us with a detailed picture of life in ancient Mesopotamia. Evidence from the reign of Hammurabi is particularly abundant. In addition to his famous law code, there are numerous administrative documents and royal and private letters. The amount of space given to various topics in Hammurabi's code suggests the issues that were of chief concern to his subjects.

The code's third largest category of laws deals with commerce. Regulations governing debts, rates of interest, security, default, and the conduct of professionals (e.g., contractors, surgeons, etc.) testify to the complexity of Babylonian economic life. The second largest group of laws relates to land tenure and suggests that individual landholders feared that powerful officials would try to take their property from them. The largest collection of laws is devoted to family issues, that is, marriage, inheritance, and adoption. Parents arranged marriages for their children. The groom made a payment for his bride and her family provided her with a dowry. A marriage was expected to be monogamous unless it failed to produce offspring. In that case, a man whose wife was barren or sickly could take a second wife to provide him with the children he needed to care for them in their old age. Husbands were permitted extramarital affairs with concubines, slaves, and prostitutes, but wives were not granted comparable license. A married woman's place was assumed to be in the home, but wives could own property and run their own businesses—so long as they did not neglect the duties they owed to their husbands and families. A woman could initiate divorce and reclaim her dowry so long as her husband could not convict her of any wrongdoing. Single women sometimes supported themselves as tavern owners, moneylenders, midwives, nurses, priestesses, or temple servants.

SLAVERY: CHATTEL SLAVES AND DEBT SLAVES
There were two kinds of slavery in ancient Mesopotamia: chattel slaves and persons enslaved for debt. Chattel slaves were treated like pieces of property. They had no legal rights, for they were usually foreigners—prisoners of war or aliens bought from slave merchants. They were expensive luxuries and were used primarily as domestic servants. Debt slavery was more common. Individuals could pledge themselves or members of their families as security for loans, and extremely high interest rates made repayment difficult. Debtors who defaulted on their loans were enslaved to work off their debts, but they could not be sold. They could regain their freedom if they repaid their loan, and they could conduct businesses, own property, and marry free persons.

Egyptian Civilization

While Mesopotamian civilization evolved along the banks of the Tigris and Euphrates Rivers, another great civilization appeared in Egypt. It depended on the Nile, a river that flows from its source in central Africa some 4,000 miles north to the Mediterranean. The Nile divided Egypt into two geographically distinct districts. Upper (i.e., upstream) Egypt occupied a narrow valley and extended 650 miles from Aswan to Lower (downstream) Egypt, the Nile's 100-mile deep, triangularly shaped delta. Without the Nile, agriculture would have been impossible in Egypt's arid environment. Annually, rains in central Africa caused the river to flood, soaking Egypt's fields and depositing a new layer of fertile silt just in time for the autumn planting season. As the waters retreated, farmers sowed their crops, and relatively simple irrigation techniques were adequate to guarantee a level of prosperity that was unmatched in the ancient world.

Egypt was a long, narrow country. But since no one was ever far from the Nile, the river served as a kind of highway to tie the Egyptians together. As early as 3100 B.C.E., when the cities of Mesopotamia were still fighting among themselves, Upper and Lower Egypt had become a single state. It enjoyed remarkable stability, thanks in part to the security provided by its location. The cliffs and deserts that surrounded Egypt protected it from invasion. The valley sheltered its inhabitants from the violent storms that swept the Mesopotamian plain, and the river's annual flooding was predictable and minimally destructive. The peace and order that characterized life in Egypt produced an optimistic outlook that contrasts markedly with the pessimistic tone of so much Mesopotamian literature.

Events in the more than 3,000-year span of ancient Egyptian history are traditionally dated by reference to the reigns of thirty-one dynasties of pharaohs beginning with Menes, the king who united Upper and Lower Egypt, and ending with the death of Cleopatra (30 B.C.E.), the last ruler from a dynasty founded by one of Alexander the Great's Greek generals. Egypt was then absorbed into the Roman empire and ruled by a Roman provincial governor. This very long history spans three lengthy eras of stability and creativity (the Old, Middle, and New Kingdoms) separated by relatively brief episodes of confusion (the Intermediate Periods).

THE OLD KINGDOM (2700–2200 B.C.E.) Egypt's first two dynasties, the rulers of the Early Dynastic

Period (3100–2700 B.C.E.), unified the country and paved the way for the brilliant achievements of the Old Kingdom. The Old Kingdom provided Egypt with over 400 years of stability and prosperity and fostered the development of many of the institutions, monuments, and arts that are most characteristic of Egyptian civilization.

The land and people of Egypt were the property of an absolute ruler, the pharaoh (i.e., "the great house"). He was considered to be a god on whom the safety and prosperity of his people depended. By building temples and honoring his fellow gods with rituals and offerings he maintained *maat*, the equilibrium of the universe. His word was law, and an elaborate bureaucracy of officials existed to help him enforce it. Pharaoh's officials exercised centralized control over granaries, land surveys, assessments, tax collections, and disbursements from the royal treasury. In addition to these agents of the central government, there were also governors of regional districts (i.e., *nomes*) called *nomarchs* who dealt with important local issues such as water management.

The power and resources of the Old Kingdom pharaohs are clearly revealed by their greatest monuments, the pyramids, which were built to serve as their tombs. The first experiments in pyramid construction were carried out by Djoser, a pharaoh of the Third Dynasty. He erected history's first major stone building, a great solid pyramid composed of six layers, or steps, and surrounded by an elaborate funeral complex. Snefru, founder of the Fourth Dynasty, built the first true (i.e., smooth-sided) pyramid, and his son Khufu (Cheops, in Greek sources) commissioned the largest pyramid every constructed. It rose on the desert plateau of Giza opposite Memphis, the Old Kingdom capital on the border between Upper and Lower Egypt. It covered 13.1 acres, soared to a height of 481 feet, and was composed of 2.3 million blocks of stone, each averaging 2.5 tons. It is extraordinary not only for its size, but for the precision of its engineering. Khufu's successors built additional pyramids at Giza, and the pharaoh Khafre added the famous Sphinx, a huge version of the enigmatic half-lion, half-human creature that was a common subject for Egyptian sculptors. The pyramids and their temples were originally provided with lavish offerings to support

the pharaoh in the afterlife, but they were stripped of their contents by ancient grave robbers. The only major artifacts the thieves missed were two full-sized wooden boats that were buried at the base of the pyramids. These were intended to convey the pharaoh on his journeys in the next world.

THE FIRST INTERMEDIATE PERIOD AND THE MIDDLE KINGDOM (2200–1630 B.C.E.) The Old Kingdom came apart when, for political and economic reasons, the power of the pharaohs declined and the nomarchs and other officials established their independence. Decentralization introduced an era of confusion and disorder (i.e., the First Intermediate Period) that lasted until about 2025 B.C.E. At that point, Amunemhet I, a vizier (i.e., chief minister) to a dynasty of pharaohs seated in the Upper Egyptian city of Thebes, seized control, reunited Egypt, and inaugurated the Middle Kingdom.

The confusion of the First Intermediate Period may have undercut some of the traditions that supported the pharaoh's authority. The rulers of the Middle Kingdom were regarded as less distant and godlike than their predecessors, and they seem to have been more directly concerned with the affairs of their subjects. The nomarchs who served them had more autonomy, and to secure an uncontested succession to the throne pharaohs found it wise to establish their heirs as co-regents during their lifetimes.

Egypt began to emerge from its isolation during the Middle Kingdom and to pay more attention to foreign affairs. The pharaohs pushed up the Nile into Nubia and built fortresses to guard the trade routes that brought African goods to Egypt. Syria and Palestine also became areas of concern, and fortifications were built to staunch the flow of eastern migrants into the delta.

THE SECOND INTERMEDIATE PERIOD AND THE NEW KINGDOM (1630–1075 B.C.E.) For unknown reasons the crown passed rapidly from hand to hand during the Thirteenth Dynasty, and weak pharaohs were unable to prevent the rise of rivals in the western delta. In the eastern delta, Asiatic migration continued, and the region passed into the hands of pharaohs whom the native Egyptians called the Hyksos (i.e., "chiefs of foreign lands"). Archaeological remains suggest that these rulers were probably Amorites who had infiltrated the

Major Periods in Mesopotamian and Egyptian History

Mesopotamia

ca. 3500 B.C.E.	Cities appear
ca. 2800–2370 B.C.E.	First Dynasties
2370–2205 B.C.E.	Sargon's empire
2125–2027 B.C.E.	III Dynasty of Ur
Hammurabi (r. 1792–1750 B.C.E.)	
ca. 1600, fall of Amoritic Babylon	

Egypt

ca. 3100–2700 B.C.E.	Early Dynastic Period (dynasties I–II)
ca. 2700–2200 B.C.E.	The Old Kingdom (dynasties III–VI)
2200–2025 B.C.E.	I Intermediate Period (dynasties VII–XI)
2025–1630 B.C.E.	The Middle Kingdom (dynasties XII–XIII)
1630–1550 B.C.E.	II Intermediate Period (dynasties XIV–XVII)
1550–1075 B.C.E.	The New Kingdom (dynasties XVIII–XX)

delta during the Middle Kingdom. They became the dominant power in Egypt for about a century until they were driven out by Ahmose, first king of the Eighteenth Dynasty and founder of the New Kingdom.

The pharaohs of the New Kingdom had imperialistic aspirations. Their armies reached the Euphrates in the east and drove deep into Africa—extending Egyptian influence 1,300 miles south from Memphis. The Egyptian empire provided the pharaohs with unprecedented wealth and subjected them to numerous foreign influences. The result was the establishment in Thebes of a cosmopolitan court of extraordinary splendor and sophistication and a spate, throughout Egypt, of monumental building projects. The pharaohs of this era, hoping perhaps to safeguard the vast treasures they accumulated for the afterlife, ceased to erect pyramids that advertised the sites of their graves. They chose instead to be buried in cave-like tombs cut into the walls of the desolate "Valley of the Kings" near Thebes. Despite elaborate precautions, however, they failed to secure their final resting places. Only one pharaonic tomb (that of a young Eighteenth Dynasty ruler named

Tutankhamun) escaped looting by ancient grave robbers. He was a fairly minor king who died prematurely and was buried in haste. His grave was doubtless less lavishly equipped than those of the more prominent pharaohs, but its treasures are truly awe-inspiring.

Tutankhamun was succeeded by a line of solider-pharaohs who erected some of Egypt's most imposing monuments. They fought numerous battles in Syria and Palestine where their chief opponents were the Hittites whose powerful empire was based in Asia Minor. The later New Kingdom pharaohs fended off attacks on the delta from the Libyans and from Mediterranean raiders called the Sea Peoples, but an increasingly volatile international situation gradually eroded their position. By 1075, Egypt was no longer an imperial power. It was weakened by internal divisions and succumbed to a succession of foreign conquerors—Assyrian, Persian, Greek, and ultimately Roman.

LANGUAGE AND LITERATURE The Egyptians began to write about 3000 B.C.E. They may have been inspired by the example of Mesopotamia, but they invented their own writing systems. The Greeks called formal Egyptian writing *hieroglyphs* (i.e., "sacred carving"), for it was used to engrave holy texts on monuments. For business and general purposes there was an alternative cursive script that could be written much more rapidly and easily. It used pen and ink and a sheet of paperlike material made from the papyrus reed. Texts were usually written horizontally from right to left, but they could also be written from left to right and up and down in horizontal columns. The Egyptian writing system was very complex, for some hieroglyphic symbols represented syllables, others words, and still others categories of words.

The Egyptians produced a large and varied body of literature encompassing religious myths, entertaining stories, collections of proverbs, how-to advice for aspiring bureaucrats, love poems, personal letters, medical texts, astronomical observations, calendars, autobiographies, judicial records, and administrative documents. Curiously missing are any traces of epic poetry or of dramas, although the latter, at least, are known to have been performed as parts of some cult rituals.

RELIGION: GODS, TEMPLES, AND THE AFTERLIFE The Egyptians never found it necessary to impose consistency on their religious beliefs. Three different myths arose in different parts of Egypt to explain the creation of the world, and each credited that achievement to a different god. Since gods sometimes had overlapping functions, they tended to blend into one another. Some were known by a variety of names. Gods were usually depicted as having human or animal form or an animal head on a human body. As in Mesopotamia they were believed literally to inhabit their temples. These structures became increasingly elaborate as time passed. The sacred complex at Karnak (near Thebes) was under construction for over 2,000 years. Armies of full-time priests tended the gods with elaborate rituals and managed their temple endowments. Ordinary people did not worship in the great temples, but they did attend festivals in which the images of the gods were brought out for the public to view.

Egyptian religion was the product of very ancient, enduring traditions. But during the reign of the Eighteenth Dynasty, a pharaoh named Amunhotep IV attempted suddenly to impose a new faith on his people. Amunhotep declared an aspect of the sun, the Aten (i.e., "disk"), to be the supreme god. He claimed that the Aten was the creator and sustainer of life and that he and his queen Nefertiti were the sole mediators between the Aten and the Egyptian people. To honor his god, Amunhotep changed his name to Akhenaten (i.e., "the effective spirit of the Aten") and built a new capital called Akhetaten (i.e., "the horizon of the Aten") near Amarna north of Thebes. Akhenaten's religious reforms failed to take hold, and after his death the court returned to Thebes. Akhetaten was dismantled. The Aten cult was suppressed, and the worship of the older sun-god, Amun, was restored. Alone among the Egyptian gods, the Aten was represented by an abstract symbol, not a human or animal form. The art of the Amarna period is also noteworthy for a degree of abstraction that marked a radical, if brief, departure from the traditional conventions of Egyptian painting and sculpture.

Most Egyptians worshiped at small local shrines, and many householders had private collections of sacred objects. Belief in magic, oracles, and amulets to ward off evil was strong, and magic was the primary tool on which the Egyptians relied for coping with the dangers that the soul presumably faced as it made its transition to the afterlife. Originally only the pharaoh was assumed to be able to survive death and join the immortal gods, but gradually the belief spread that all persons who could make the necessary preparations might enjoy this privilege. The spells needed to pass the various tests and fend off the monsters of the underworld were preserved in the *Book of the Dead,* which was often inscribed on tombs. The dead were assumed to want and need the same things as the living, and persons who could afford to do so loaded their tombs with provisions and equipment for life after death. It was the duty of their descendants to make occasional offerings at their tombs to replenish their supplies.

WOMEN IN EGYPTIAN SOCIETY   The Egyptian woman's primary duty was the management of a household. She could not study in scribal schools, become an artisan, or hold a government office, but she could own and manage property, sue for divorce, and claim the same legal protections as a man. Royal women were, of course, an exception. They often wielded considerable influence, and a few, such as Thutmosis I's daughter Hatshepsut, governed either as regents for dependent males or in their own names. Women are often depicted in art in scenes in which they make and receive offerings and enjoy the pleasures of banqueting and hunting with their husbands.

SLAVES   Slaves did not become common in Egypt until the foreign campaigns of the pharaohs of the Middle Kingdom began to produce Nubian and Asian prisoners of war. The successful imperialistic ventures of the New Kingdom vastly increased the number of captives who became slaves. Sometimes entire peoples were enslaved.

Slaves were assigned all kinds of tasks. Some worked in the fields alongside the native peasants. Some were domestic servants. Some were trained as artisans. A few even exercised authority as police or soldiers. They could be freed, but manumission was rare. There were no racial or other obstacles, however, to their gradual assimilation into the mass of the population.

Ancient Middle Eastern Empires

While Egypt was organizing the New Kingdom, new states and peoples were carving out domains for themselves in the Middle East.

This painting from the Theban tomb of a high-ranking Eighteenth Dynasty official shows him, accompanied by his wife and daughter, on a hunting trip through the papyrus marshes, an activity the family enjoyed during their lives on earth and would continue in the afterlife. Courtesy of the Trustees of the British Museum. Copyright The British Museum

The Hittites

The Hittites were an Indo-European people. That is, their language (which belonged to the same family as Greek, Latin, and Indian Sanskrit) set them apart from the older Middle Eastern peoples, most of whom favored Semitic tongues. The Hittites built a strong, centralized kingdom with its seat at Hattusas (near modern Turkey's capital, Ankara). From 1400 to 1200 B.C.E. they grew to become the dominant power in the Middle East. They destroyed their neighbors, the Mitannians, and contested control of Syria and Palestine with Egypt. An indecisive battle in 1285 B.C.E. culminated in a truce between these two superpowers. About 1200, the Hittite kingdom collapsed. It was one of the many victims of the confusion created by the invaders whom the Egyptians called the Sea Peoples.

The Hittites adopted the cuneiform script and many aspects of Mesopotamian culture, but their political institutions were their own. Their kings did not claim to be divine or even to be representatives of the gods. The king was advised by a council of nobles who limited his power, and an heir's succession to the throne required ratification by the army. One thing that may have contributed to Hittite success was the development in their region (a bit before the rise of their kingdom) of techniques for smelting iron and forging it into weapons. Iron was more plentiful and, therefore, more economical than bronze, and its spreading use merits designating the period after 1100 B.C.E. the Iron Age. Clay tablets from the Hittite archives are particularly interesting because they provide the earliest information about the Greeks, the Hittites' western neighbors.

The Kassites

The Kassites emerged from obscure origins to replace the Amorites as the rulers of Babylonia and to found a dynasty that endured for nearly half a millennium. They adopted, preserved, and promoted Babylonian culture and made Babylonia one of the major nation-states of the late Bronze Age. Their kingdom was tribally organized and supported by a military aristocracy skilled in the use of the most prestigious military equipment of the day, the horse and chariot. The Kassites engaged in frequent, but usually inconclusive, wars with their neighbors on a variety of fronts and were treated with respect by both the Hittites and Egyptians.

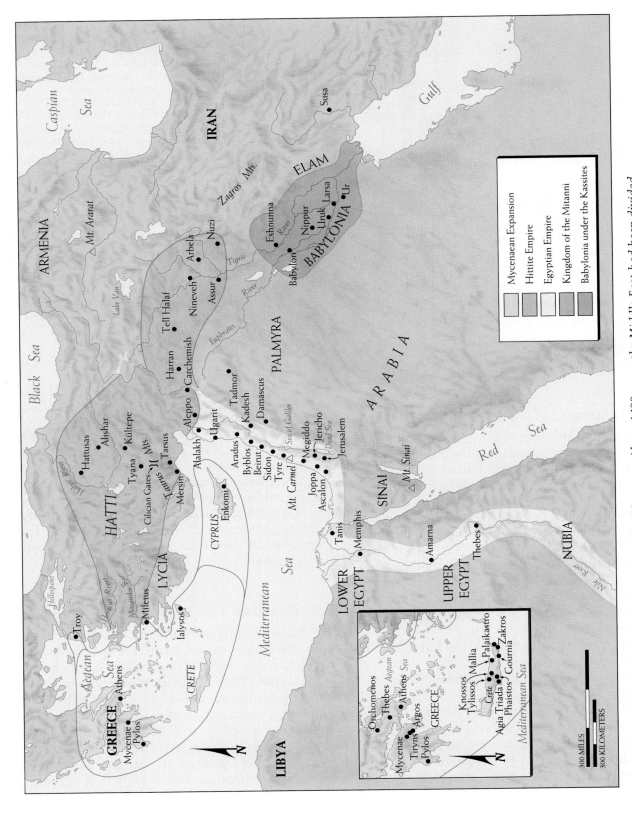

MAP 1–2   THE MIDDLE EAST AND GREECE ABOUT 1400 B.C.E.   *About 1400 B.C.E., the Middle East had been divided among four empires: Egypt, which extended south to Nubia and north to Phoenicia, Kassite Babylonia, Hittite Asia Minor, and Mitannian Assyria. Much of the Aegean was under the control of an assortment of Mycenaean Greek kingdoms.*

The Mitannians

The Mitannians were part of a large group of people called the Hurrians whose Mesopotamian roots went back to the era of Akkad and the Third Dynasty of Ur. They remain something of a mystery, for their language is imperfectly understood and the location of their capital is unknown. They provided an important service by helping to spread Mesopotamian civilization throughout Syria and into Anatolia. They were masters of chariot warfare and used their military skills to build a large state between the Euphrates and the mountains of Iran. It was eventually overwhelmed by the Hittites.

The Assyrians

The Assyrian homeland was centered at Assur, a city on the Tigris River in northern Mesopotamia. The Assyrians spoke a Semitic language related to Babylonian and ancient trading ties with Babylonia imbued them with its cultural influences. When the Mitannian kingdom collapsed during the fourteenth century B.C.E., Assyria began to push out its northern and western frontiers. In the general confusion that descended on the Middle East at the end of the second millennium, an invasion by the Arameans brought an end to this first Assyrian empire. The Arameans originated in northern Syria, and they spread widely throughout the Middle East. Their language, Aramaic, is still a living language, and it played a role in the development of the biblical tradition.

About 1000 B.C.E. the Assyrians recovered and began to expand again. By 665 B.C.E. they had won control of Mesopotamia, southern Asia Minor, Syria, Palestine, and Egypt. They were famous for their innovative military technology and their willingness to commit atrocities to frighten their opponents into submission. The Assyrian empire was divided into provinces headed by military governors and kept in line by garrisons. Defeated peoples were often evicted from their homes and resettled elsewhere in order to break up potential pockets of resistance to Assyrian rule. Agricultural colonies were established to populate unused land and to maintain caches of supplies for the army. Great palaces were erected at Nineveh and Nimrud and ornamented with superb stone carvings in bas relief. They were meant to intimidate the vassal kings who annually brought their tribute to the Assyrian capital.

The Assyrian empire may have been a victim of its own success—becoming too large, given the communications available, to govern. Squabbling among its leaders also set it up for disaster, particularly once the Medes, an Indo-European people who settled in Iran, perfected a lethal, new style of fighting utilizing mounted archers. When the Medes attacked Assyria, the Babylonians seized the opportunity to rebel, and by 612 B.C.E., the Assyrian empire had collapsed.

This eighth-century B.C.E. relief of a hero gripping a lion formed part of the decoration of an Assyrian palace. The immense size of the figure and his powerful limbs and muscles may well have suggested the might of the Assyrian king. Giraudon/Art Resource, NY

The Neo-Babylonians

The Medes failed to exploit their victory, and this gave Nebuchadnezzar, king of Babylon, the chance to extend his authority over much of the old Assyrian empire. Babylon became a center of world trade and quickly developed into a city filled with monuments and wonders. Nebuchadnezzar's dynasty was, however, short-lived. The throne passed rapidly through a number of hands, and its last heir alienated his subjects by permitting graft and gross mismanagement and by imposing a new religion. They failed to put up much resistance when a conqueror from Persia descended on them in 539 B.C.E., and Babylon survived to enjoy even greater prosperity as a province within his empire.

Palestine

Many great kingdoms rose and fell in the ancient Middle East, but none had as much influence on Western civilization as a tiny state that began to develop in Palestine about 1200 B.C.E. Three of the world's great religions (Judaism, Christianity, and Islam) trace their origins, at least in part, to this region, and the history of its peoples inspired the Hebrew Bible.

The Canaanites and the Phoenicians

The original inhabitants of Palestine spoke a Semitic language called Canaanite. They lived in walled cities and were farmers and seafarers. Their most influential achievement was a highly simplified writing system. Instead of the hundreds of characters found in cuneiform and hieroglyphic scripts, it used a brief alphabet of twenty to thirty symbols. This made learning to read and write much easier and allowed the skill to spread more broadly.

The Canaanites of the Palestinian interior were forced out or absorbed by invading tribes of Israelites, but those on the northern coast, the Phoenicians, hung on to their territory. They became a seafaring people and developed a trade network that spanned the length of the Mediterranean Sea. They scattered colonies as far west as Spain, the most famous of which was the north African port of Carthage (near modern Tunis). Phoenician trade spread culture as well as goods. It acquainted the Greeks with the alphabet, which they adopted and passed on to us.

The Israelites

Since there are few references to the Israelites in records compiled by their neighbors, knowledge of them must be inferred from their chief literary monument: the Bible. Although the Bible contains some historical narratives (as well as collections of laws, ritual instructions, wisdom literature, poetry, and prophecy), it was not meant to be read simply as history. Scholars have developed all sorts of techniques to extract objective information from it, and there are many disputes about their findings.

According to tradition, the family of Abraham, the patriarch (i.e., founding father) of the Hebrew (or Israelite) nation, originated in Ur. He himself was, however, a homeless nomad who, about 1900 B.C.E., wandered into the land of the Canaanites. Some of his descendants later drifted into Egypt, perhaps in the wake of the Hyksos who were their fellow Semites. By the thirteenth century B.C.E., they had left Egypt under the leadership of a man named Moses. They spent some time wandering in the Sinai desert and then returned to Canaan where they settled down. They conquered their neighbors and established a monarchy that reached its peak in the tenth century B.C.E. under King David and his son and heir Solomon. At Solomon's death, the kingdom split in two. Israel, the northern section, was the larger and more advanced. Judah, the southern portion, was less populous and more rural, but it was the location of the old capital of Jerusalem, the site of the Israelites' most important temple.

In 722 B.C.E. Assyria conquered Israel and dispersed its people. The disappearance of the "ten lost tribes of Israel" left only the people of Judah (i.e., the Jews) to maintain their country's traditions, culture, and literature. But in 586 B.C.E. Judah was conquered by the Neo-Babylonian ruler Nebuchadnezzar II. He destroyed Jerusalem and its temple and resettled many of the Jews in distant lands. This period of exile or Babylonian captivity did not last long. When Babylon fell to Persia in 539 B.C.E., the new emperor permitted some Jews to return to rebuild Jerusalem and the temple. With only brief exceptions, the tiny Jewish homeland remained under the dominance of foreign powers until 70 C.E., when the Romans once again destroyed Jerusalem and dispersed its people. The Jews did not return to reestablish a state of Israel until 1948 C.E.

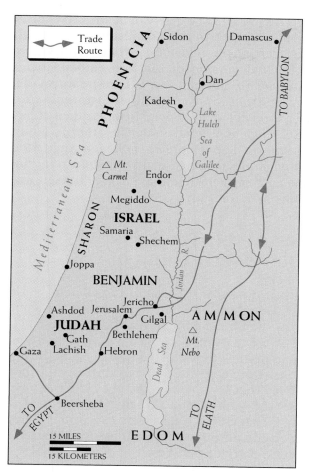

MAP 1–3   ANCIENT PALESTINE   *The Hebrews established a unified kingdom in Palestine under Kings David and Solomon in the tenth century B.C.E. After the death of Solomon, however, the kingdom was divided into two parts—Israel in the north and Judah, with its capital, Jerusalem, in the south. Along the coast, especially to the north, were the great commercial cities of the Phoenicians, such as Sidon and Tyre.*

The Jewish Religion

The fate of the tiny nation of Israel would be of little interest were it not for its unique religious achievement. The Jews' belief in a single universal God—in an all-powerful creator who loves humankind but demands righteousness and obedience to his laws—may be as old as Moses' generation and certainly dates back to the preaching of the major prophets in the eighth century B.C.E. The Jewish God is not thought of as a force of nature or a superhuman being. He is so transcendent that He cannot be pictured in any way. These beliefs have become fundamental to the religions that helped form the Western heritage.

Unlike most other ancient peoples, the Jews believed that there was a link between ethics and religion. They were a unique people because their ancestor Abraham had made a covenant (i.e., a contract) with God. God promised to preserve them so long as they accepted the burden of revealing Him by living according to the principles He established. The Jewish prophets described God as a severe but just judge who was not content with mere ritual and sacrifice. God is righteous and expects His people to live righteously. Although the prophets assured their followers that God dealt mercifully with repentant sinners, they explained the misfortunes that befell their country as a just God's necessary interventions in history to correct the people when they went astray. Confidence that God would fulfill His promise to deliver them from their enemies gradually persuaded the Jews that God intended to send them a special leader, a messiah (i.e., "annointed one") who would have the power to enable them fulfill their mission in history. Christianity diverges from Judaism in maintaining that Jesus of Nazareth was that messiah.

General Outlook of Middle Eastern Cultures

There were differences among the various cultures of the Middle East, but all of them taken together contrast significantly with the outlook of the ancient people who exerted the greatest influence on the Western tradition, the Greeks. This becomes clear when we compare the assumptions that the Greeks and other ancient peoples made about fundamental human concerns.

HUMANS AND NATURE   The peoples of the Middle East did not envision an absolute gulf between animate beings and inanimate objects. They believed that all things took part in life and the spirit and that the universe was an arena for a war of supernatural wills. They concluded that because nature seemed chaotic from the human perspective, the gods who governed it must be capricious. The Babylonian creation myth claimed that humanity's chief purpose was to serve the gods. In a world that powerful deities ran for their own benefit and with little concern for their human servants, existence was precarious. Even disasters, like wars, which we would see as the result of human decisions, were assumed to be the products of divine wills.

The helplessness of humankind in the face of irrational divine powers is the point of the story of a great primeval flood that is found in one form or another in Babylonian, Egyptian, and Hebrew sources. In the Egyptian tale the god Re, who created human beings, comes to believe that they are plotting against him and sends the vicious goddess Sekhmet to destroy them. Humanity is saved only when the god has a last minute, unexplained change of heart. In the Babylonian version of the story it is the noise made by an increasing human population that annoys the gods and determines them to destroy humanity. The species is saved only because one man wins the favor of the god Enki who helps him and his wife survive. In a world governed by such quixotic principles, human beings could not hope to control events by understanding them. At best, they might try to pit one mysterious force against another by means of magical spells.

Humans and the Gods, Law, and Justice

Since the gods could destroy humankind—and might do so at any time for no apparent reason—people tried to win the gods over by offering prayer and sacrifice. There was, however, no guarantee of success, for gods were capricious beings who were not bound by reason or conscience.

In areas that were more or less under human control, people attempted to establish more orderly and consistent principles to guide their lives. In the earliest civilized societies rulers decreed laws to govern human relations. The problem was to find some justification that would impart authority to laws. Why, apart from a lawgiver's power to coerce obedience, should anyone obey the law? The Egyptians simply assumed that since the king was a god, he had the right to establish whatever rules seemed best to him at the moment. The Mesopotamians believed that the gods commissioned their kings and gave them divine authority to keep order among the human herd. The Hebrews had a more subtle understanding of

law. Their God was capable of destructive rages, but He was open to rational discussion and imposed certain moral standards on Himself. In the biblical version of the flood story God is wrathful but not arbitrary. His creatures deserve destruction as punishment for their sins. When God decides to save Noah, He does so because Noah is a good man who merits God's protection. The Hebrews believed that God wanted human beings to live in just relationships with one another and that He Himself was an advocate for human justice.

Toward the Greeks and Western Thought

Many, if not most, Greeks in the ancient world must have thought about life in much the same way as their neighbors in the Middle East. Their gods were assumed to behave like Mesopotamian deities; they trusted in magic and incantations to manage life's uncertainties; and they believed that laws were to be obeyed simply because the gods decreed them. The surprising thing is that some Greeks were exceptions. They conceived strikingly original ideas that charted a different path for the West.

As early as the sixth century B.C.E., an intellectual revolution had begun among thinkers who lived on the Aegean coast of Asia Minor. Thales, the first Greek philosopher, taught his followers to explain natural events by referring them to other natural events, not to unknowable supernatural causes. His search for naturalistic explanations for phenomena launched Western science.

Rationalism of this kind characterized the approach major Greek thinkers took to exploring all kinds of issues. Xenophanes of Colophon, Thales's contemporary, pointed out that people had no grounds for imagining gods in human form. He argued that if oxen could draw, they would sketch gods who looked like oxen. Comments like this might promote skepticism, but they could also produce valuable insights. In the fifth century B.C.E., Thucydides of Athens wrote a history that made no reference to the gods, but explained events as the result of human decisions and chance. Similarly, Hippocrates of Cos founded a school of medicine that diagnosed and treated disease without invoking the supernatural. The same absence of interest in divine causality characterized Greek attitudes toward law and justice.

In Perspective

Although the Greeks' original insights account for much of the uniqueness of Western civilization, we should not forget that they were built on a foundation of lore that people in the Middle East had accumulated over millennia. Phoenicia gave the Greeks a writing system, and from ancient Mesopotamia and Egypt the Greeks acquired vital technical information and models that stimulated the development of mathematics, astronomy, art, and literature. The discontinuities between the cultures of the Greeks and their eastern neighbors are, however, more striking than the continuities.

A secular, reasoned quest for an understanding of the world that proceeded by seeking explanations for events in the natures of things rather than in the supernatures of gods was not characteristic of pre-Greek cultures. Nor would it appear in similar societies at other times in other parts of the world. This raises the issue of whether there was something special in the Greek experience that caused fundamental questions to be pondered in strikingly original ways.

REVIEW QUESTIONS

1. How was life during the Paleolithic Age different from life during the Neolithic Age? What advances account for the difference? Were there advances so major that they warrant referring to the Neolithic as a revolutionary era?
2. What differences do you see in the political and intellectual outlooks of the Egyptian and Mesopotamian civilizations? How do their religious views compare? What influence did geography have on religious outlooks?
3. How did religious faith help to bind the Hebrews together politically? Why did Middle Eastern civilizations regard the concept of monotheism as a radical idea?
4. Why were the Assyrians so successful in building an empire? How did their empire differ from those of the Egyptians and Hittites? What caused its failure? What might it have contributed to the civilization of the Middle East?
5. How did Greek thinkers depart from the assumptions that guided the work of Middle Eastern intellectuals?

SUGGESTED READINGS

M. EHRENBERG, *Women in Prehistory* (1989). An account of the role of women in early times.

H. FRANKFORT ET AL., *Before Philosophy* (1949). A brilliant examination of the mind of the ancients from the Stone Age to the Greeks.

O. R. GURNEY, *The Hittites* (1954). A good general survey.

W. W. HALLO AND L. YOUNGER, EDS. *The Context of Scripture, Canonical Compositions from the Biblical World* (1997). A good collection of literary works translated from ancient Middle Eastern sources, complete with introductions and explanatory notes.

G. HART, *Egyptian Myths* (1990). A clear presentation of major myths and religious literature.

D. C. JOHNSON AND M. R. EDEY, *Lucy: The Beginnings of Mankind* (1981). A study of the first human creatures based on remains found in Africa.

B. J. KEMP, *Ancient Egypt: Anatomy of a Civilization* (1989). A thought-provoking assessment of Egypt's social and intellectual history.

A. KUHRT, *The Ancient Near East, c. 3000–330 B.C.* (1995). The best compact and reliable history of the ancient Middle East, including Egypt and Israel.

S. LLOYD, *The Archaeology of Mesopotamia*, rev. ed. (1984). An account of the material remains of Mesopotamia and their meaning from the Paleolithic Age to the Persian Conquest.

K. R. NEMET-NEJAT, *Daily Life in Ancient Mesopotamia* (1998). An excellent introduction for the general reader.

J. N. POSTGATE, *Early Mesopotamia* (1992). An excellent study of Mesopotamian economy and society from the earliest times to about 1500 B.C.E.

D. B. REDFORD, *Akhenaten* (1987). A new study of the controversial pharaoh.

G. ROBINS, *Women in Ancient Egypt* (1993). A comprehensive study of the role of women in Egyptian society.

D. C. SNELL, *Life in the Ancient Near East, 3100–332 B.C.E.* (1997). Imaginative study focusing on social and economic history.

A. J. SPENCER, *Early Egypt: The Rise of Civilization in the Nile Valley* (1993). An up-to-date account of the latest research on the Predynastic and Early Dynastic periods.

M. VAN DE MIEROOP, *The Ancient Mesopotamian City* (1997). A concise survey of Mesopotamian urban life.

Chapter 2

The Rise of Greek Civilization

KEY TOPICS

- The Bronze Age civilizations that ruled the Aegean area before the development of Hellenic civilization
- The rise, development, and expansion of the *polis,* the characteristic political unit of Hellenic Greece
- The early history of Sparta and Athens
- The wars between the Greeks and the Persians

A bout 2000 B.C.E., *Greek-speaking peoples settled the lands surrounding the Aegean Sea and established a culture that became one of the most powerful forces shaping Western heritage. The Greeks' location at the eastern end of the Mediterranean put them in touch, early in their history, with Mesopotamia, Egypt, Asia Minor, and Syria-Palestine. The Greeks acknowledged a debt to the cultures of these regions but were well aware of the uniqueness of their own contributions to civilization.*

The Bronze Age on Crete and on the Mainland to About 1150 B.C.E.

Bronze Age civilizations developed in three parts of the Aegean world—on the island of Crete, on the smaller islands of the Aegean Sea, and on the mainland of Greece. Crete provided the bridge that linked these new cultural centers with the older civilizations of the East.

The Minoans

Historians have named the Aegean's first civilization—that of Crete—for Minos, a legendary king of the island. From 2100 to 1150 B.C.E. (the Middle and Late Minoan periods) Crete evolved a unique way of life. The palace sites that modern archaeologists have excavated at Phaestus, Haghia Triada, and especially Cnossus are its most striking remains. Cnossus was a labyrinth of rooms organized around great courtyards and rising in sections to a height of four stories. The main and upper floors contained living quarters as well as workshops for making pottery and jewelry, and the cellars had elaborate storage facilities for oil and grain. There were richly decorated reception rooms and even bathrooms to which water was piped. Roofs were supported by columns of a unique design that tapered from broad capitals down to narrow bases. Murals depicting landscapes, seascapes, festivals, and sports in a unique style reflected some Eastern influences.

The Minoan-period Palace at Cnossus on the island of Crete. D. A. Harissiadis Photography, Benaki Museum, Photographic Department.

Chronology of the Rise of Greece	
ca. 2900–1150 B.C.E.	Minoan period
ca. 1900 B.C.E.	Arrival of the Greeks on the mainland
ca. 1600–1150 B.C.E.	Mycenaean period
ca. 1250 B.C.E.	Sack of Troy
ca. 1200–1150 B.C.E.	Fall of the Mycenaean kingdoms
ca. 1150–750 B.C.E.	The Greek Dark Ages
ca. 750–500 B.C.E.	Greek colonial expansion
ca. 725 B.C.E.	Homer flourished
ca. 700 B.C.E.	Hesiod flourished
ca. 700–500 B.C.E.	Ascendancy of the tyrants

Since Minoan palaces and settlements were wealthy, they would have been attractive targets for raiders. It is surprising, therefore, that the great Minoan structures lacked defensive walls. Minoan command of the sea may have made the fortification of buildings on Crete unnecessary.

The Minoans wrote on clay tablets similar to those found in Mesopotamia. Many of the extant specimens were preserved accidentally when they were baked into tiles by a great fire that destroyed the palace at Cnossus. The Cnossus tablets are inscribed with three distinct kinds of writing: hieroglyphic (picture writing) and two different linear scripts (A and B). Only Linear B, which records an early form of Greek, has been deciphered.

The Linear B tablets found at Cnossus are pedestrian documents. Most are inventories, the working papers of the kind of elaborate bureaucracy that was characteristic of the ancient Middle Eastern monarchies. However, they raise an intriguing question. The Minoans were not Greeks, so why were records at Cnossus being written in Greek?

The Mycenaeans

During the third millennium B.C.E. (the Early Helladic Period) the Greek mainland was occupied by non-Greek peoples. Some of the names they gave to places have survived, and these names do not fit the phonetic patterns of the Indo-European family of languages to which Greek belongs. Sometime after 2000 B.C.E., many of the Early Helladic sites were destroyed, abandoned, or occupied by a new people who were probably the Greeks. During the Late Helladic era (1580–1150 B.C.E.), the newcomers ruled the mainland and developed a civilization that historians have named for Mycenae, one of its cities. The Greek Linear B tablets found at Cnossus suggest that at the height of Mycenaean power (ca. 1400–1200 B.C.E.) the Mycenaeans conquered Crete.

The Mycenaean world contained a number of independent, powerful, and well-organized kingdoms. Their archaeological remains are those of a civilization that was influenced by, but very different from, that of the Minoans. Unlike the Minoans, the Mycenaeans were preoccupied with war. The walls of their palaces were decorated with paintings depicting scenes of battle and hunting, and they chose defensible sites for their cities. A need for protection probably promoted the development of strong, centralized monarchies.

By 1500 B.C.E. Mycenaean kings were constructing monumental *tholos* tombs that testify to the wealth and power of their governments. These great domed chambers were built of enormous blocks of dressed stones. They resembled

MAP 2–1 THE AEGEAN AREA IN THE BRONZE AGE *Two civilizations flourished in the Aegean during its Bronze Age (1900–1100 B.C.E.): the Minoan (1900–1400 B.C.E.) and the Mycenaean (1600–1200 B.C.E.).*

beehives buried beneath artificial mountains. The wealth needed to finance the construction of such monuments probably came from raids and trade. Mycenaean ships visited the islands of the Aegean, the coast of Asia Minor, the cities of Syria, Egypt, and Crete, and ventured as far west as Italy and Sicily.

The Mycenaeans reached the height of their power from 1400 to 1200 B.C.E. They expanded their trade, established commercial colonies in the East, and began to be mentioned in Hittite and Egyptian archives. About 1250 B.C.E. the Mycenaeans probably sacked the city of Troy on the coast of northwestern Asia Minor. This campaign may have been the Mycenaeans' last great adventure, for by 1200 B.C.E. their world was in trouble, and by 1100 B.C.E. it was gone. Some memory of them survived, however, to give rise to the earliest monuments of Greek literature, Homer's epics, the *Iliad* and the *Odyssey*.

THE DORIAN INVASION   Many Mycenaean towns fell about 1200 B.C.E., but some flourished for another century, and some were never destroyed or abandoned. Ancient Greek legends imply that there may have been an attack on the Peloponnesus (the southern Greek peninsula) by Dorians, a rude people from the north whose Greek dialect was different from that of the Mycenaeans. Perhaps this set in motion a chain of events that undermined Mycenaean civilization. The development of rigid bureaucracies probably limited the flexibility of the Mycenaean kingdoms and increased their vulnerability to invasion. It is impossible, however, to say with any certainty what happened at the end of the Aegean Bronze Age.

The Greek "Middle Ages" to About 750 B.C.E.

The collapse of the Mycenaean world inaugurated a long period of depopulation, impoverishment, and cultural decline in the Aegean. The palaces of the kings and the bureaucratic governments of which they were the seats were destroyed. The wealth and social order that supported civilized life were swept away, and many villages were abandoned and never resettled.

Greek Migrations

The confusion that attended the Mycenaean decline caused many Greeks (including the Dorians who invaded the Peloponnesus) to emigrate from the mainland to the Aegean islands and the coast of Asia Minor. This turned the Aegean into a Greek lake, but trade and travel diminished with the fading of civilization. Each community was left largely to its own devices, and people turned inward. At the time, the Middle East was also in disarray, so no great foreign power was poised to take advantage of the Aegean's situation. The Greeks, therefore, had a chance to recover and the freedom to evolve a unique way of life. Little is known about this crucial era, for writing disappeared with the Mycenaeans. It was not reinvented until after 750 B.C.E., when architecture, sculpture, and painting also resume. This is for historians, therefore, a "dark age."

The Age of Homer

The *Iliad* and the *Odyssey* are our best sources of information about the Greek Dark Ages. They are the end products of a long tradition of oral poetry with roots in the Mycenaean era. For generations bards passed on tales of the heroes who fought at Troy. Since they used rhythmic formulas to aid the accurate memorization of their verses, some very old material was preserved. The poems, in the form in which they were ultimately written down, date from the eighth century B.C.E. and are attributed to an individual named Homer.

Although the poems narrate the adventures of Mycenaean heroes, the society they describe is not purely Mycenaean. Homer's warriors are not buried in *tholos* tombs but are cremated; they worship gods in temples, whereas no Mycenaean temples have been found; they have chariots but do not know their proper use in warfare. These inconsistencies arise because Homer's epics combine memories of the ancient Mycenaeans with material drawn from the very different world in which the poets of the tenth and ninth centuries B.C.E. lived.

GOVERNMENT AND SOCIETY   The kings Homer describes had much less power than Mycenaean monarchs. Homeric kings had to arrive at decisions in consultation with their nobles, and their nobles felt free to debate vigorously and to oppose a king's wishes. In the *Iliad,* Achilles does not hesitate to accuse Agamemnon, the "most kingly" commander of the Trojan expedition, of having "a dog's face and a deer's heart." This was impolite but apparently not treasonous.

The right to speak before a royal council was limited to noblemen, but the common people could not be ignored. If a king planned a war or a major change of policy, he would call all his soldiers together and explain his intentions. They expressed their feelings by acclamation, but they could not debate or propose ideas of their own. At a very early date, the Greeks seemed to have been accustomed to a very limited form of popular government.

Homeric society was sharply divided into classes. A hereditary aristocracy presided over three kinds of commoners: *thetes,* landless laborers, and slaves. The *thetes* may have owned the land they worked, or their fields may have been the property of their family clans and could not be sold. The landless agricultural laborer had the worst lot in life. Slaves who were attached to a household were guaranteed protection and food, but free workers were desperately vulnerable. They were loners in a society in which the only safety lay in belonging to a group that looked out for its members. There were few slaves. Most were women who served as maids and concubines. Some male slaves worked as shepherds, but throughout Greek history most farmers were free men.

HOMERIC VALUES   The Homeric poems celebrated an aristocratic code that influenced all later Greek thinkers, for Greek education was based on Homer's works. The Greeks memorized Homer's texts and internalized respect for his values: physical prowess; courage; fierce protection of family, friends, and property; and, above all, defense of honor. The *Iliad* is the story of a dispute about honor. Agamemnon, the king who presides over the Greek army besieging Troy, wounds the honor of Achilles, his most important warrior. Achilles then refuses to fight and persuades the gods to avenge him by heaping defeat on the Greeks. When Achilles finally returns to the battlefield, he is brought back by a

personal obligation to avenge the death of a friend, not by a sense of duty to his country.

The highest virtue in Homeric society was *arete*—the manliness, courage, and excellence that enabled a hero to acquire and defend honor. Men demonstrated this quality by engaging in contests with worthy opponents. Homeric battles were usually single combats between matched competitors, and most Homeric festivals (even the funeral of Achilles' friend Patroclos, which ends the *Iliad*) featured athletic competitions.

Homer's view of life is summed up by the advice Achilles' father gave him when the young man left for the Trojan war: "Always be the best and distinguished above others." The father of another Homeric hero added a codicil to this prescription: "Do not bring shame on the family of your fathers." These admonitions articulated the ultimate concerns of the Homeric aristocrat: to vie for individual supremacy in *arete* and to enhance the honor of the family.

WOMEN IN HOMERIC SOCIETY   The male-oriented warrior society that Homer describes relegated women to domestic roles. Their chief functions were to bear and raise children and to manage and safeguard their husbands' estates when the men were called away to battle. A husband might have sexual adventures, but a wife was expected to be unswervingly faithful. Homer's ideal woman was Penelope, Odysseus' wife. Her husband disappears for twenty years, but she does not give him up for dead. She refuses the many suitors who seek her hand (and his estate) and lives in chaste seclusion with her maids. She fills her days with the labor that Greeks associated with women of all classes: spinning and weaving. Penelope's opposite, the epitome of female evil, was Agamemnon's wife, Clytemnestra. While her husband leads the war at Troy, she takes a lover, and the two of them assassinate Agamemnon when he returns home. Homer's upper-class females were free to come and go as they wished. They attended banquets with their husbands and conversed with other men. No such privileges were enjoyed by their aristocratic sisters in later periods in Greek history. These women were expected to confine themselves to special women's quarters in their family homes.

The *Polis*

Classical Greek civilization emerged from an institution called the *polis* (plural *poleis*) that evolved during the Dark Ages. *Polis* is usually translated as "city-state," but that implies too much and too little. All Greek *poleis* began as agricultural villages, and many never grew large enough to be considered cities. All of them, however, were states in the sense that they were self-governing, but they were more than political institutions. The citizens of a *polis* viewed themselves as a kind of extended family based on descent from a common legendary ancestor, shared religious cults, and membership in a variety of hereditary subgroups (i.e., clans, tribes, and *phratries*—military fraternities).

In the fourth century B.C.E., hundreds of years after the *polis* came into existence, the philosopher Aristotle outlined the assumptions on which it was based. He argued that the human being was by nature "an animal who lives in a *polis*," for the attributes that define humanity—the power of speech and the ability to distinguish right from wrong—can be developed only when people live together.

Development of the Polis

Originally the word *polis* referred to a citadel, a defensible high ground to which the farmers of an area could retreat when attacked. (The most famous example is the Acropolis at the center of the city of Athens.) Unplanned, unfortified towns tended to evolve spontaneously at such sites. In contrast to Mesopotamian city-states, rivers or trade routes did not determine the location of Greek *poleis*. Proximity of farmland to a natural fortress was the decisive factor. Spots well back from the coast were popular, for they minimized the danger of pirate raids. Eventually an *agora*—a place for markets and political assemblies—would evolve beside the citadel to provide a center for community life.

Poleis probably appeared early in the eighth century B.C.E. and spread widely and quickly. All the colonies that the Greeks established in the years after 750 B.C.E. were *poleis*. Monarchy tended to disappear wherever *poleis* evolved. Sometimes vestigial kings survived as politically powerless figures whose functions were ceremonial. A *polis* was often founded as a republic dominated by an aristocratic class, but over time political participation tended to broaden. About 750 B.C.E., coincident with the development of the *polis*, there were other significant changes in Greek culture. A new style of pottery appeared, and the Greeks borrowed a script from the Phoenicians. By adding vowels to it, they created the first complete alphabet and invented a method of writing that was easy for the common person to learn. This empowered the ordinary man at a time when changes in military technology were also enhancing his importance.

The Hoplite Phalanx

Early Greek warfare was a disorganized free-for-all. Small troops of cavalry led by aristocratic "champions" cast spears at their enemies and then engaged individual opponents with swords at close quarters. Late in the eighth century B.C.E., a true infantry soldier called a *hoplite* began to dominate the battlefield. He was a heavily armed foot soldier, equipped with a spear and a large round shield (a *hoplon*), who fought in a tight formation called a *phalanx*—a company of men at least eight ranks deep. A phalanx that preserved its order on the field of battle could withstand cavalry charges and rout much larger armies consisting of less disciplined men. The phalanx reigned supreme in the ancient Mediterranean world until the more flexible Roman legion appeared.

A phalanx was effective only when all its members kept themselves in top physical condition, maintained their courage, and worked together as a team. *Hoplite* warfare favored brief, violent battles that resolved disputes quickly with minimal risk to the property on which citizen families depended for their survival. Its goal was to kill or drive off an enemy, not enslave him or hold him for ransom.

Greeks had traditionally thought of war as an aristocratic profession, but in the era of the *hoplite* no *polis* could afford to limit recruitment to a small group of nobles. The strength of an infantry depended on numbers. Farmers working relatively small holdings had to join aristocrats in defending their cities and could afford to do so. When they did, shared military responsibilities led inevitably to demands for shared political privileges.

A Funeral Scene in Eighth Century B.C.E. Greece: The Dipylon Vase

The Dipylon Vase, c. 750 B.C.E. The Metropolitan Museum of Art, Rogers Fund, 1914. [14.130.14] Photograph © 1996 The Metropolitan Museum of Art. Sources: Janson, *History of Art*, (New York: Prentice Hall and Harry N. Abrams, 1997), 110–112; Marilyn Stokstad, *Art History*, rev. ed. (Upper Saddle River, NJ: Prentice Hall, 1999), pp. 152–161.

From 1100 to 700 B.C.E., a uniquely Hellenic civilization emerged from the more generally Mediterranean Bronze Age cultures of the Minoan and Mycenaean periods. Since writing had disappeared, this development is best documented by what happened in the arts—particularly the craft of pottery painting.

The potters and vase painters of this period broke with the past both in the shape and decoration of their work. The style they pioneered is called Geometric, for it is dominated by abstract forms (e.g., circles, rectangles, and triangles) arranged in parallel bands running around their vases. The earliest examples used simple schemes, but as the style developed designs became more complicated, and ultimately human and animal figures were added to the geometric patterns.

The *Dipylon Vase*, which was made about the time when Homer's poems were taking shape (ca. 750 B.C.E.), is an excellent example of the fully developed style. It is about 3 1/2 feet tall and was made to serve as a funeral monument in a graveyard outside Athens' Dipylon gate. It depicts a funeral. The top band or register shows the body of the deceased displayed on a high platform and surrounded by mourners. The lower register describes a funeral procession featuring horse-drawn chariots and soldiers equipped with shields. The vase was made with holes in its base to allow the libations that were poured into it to seep into the ground, but the Greeks did not share the Egyptian belief in an afterlife where the dead enjoyed the pleasures of this existence. The Greek view of what lay beyond the grave was much more grim.

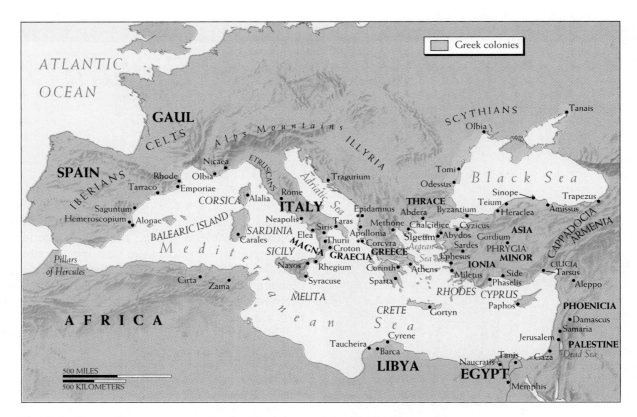

MAP 2–2   GREEK COLONIZATION   *Greek colonizing activity reached its peak between 750 and 550 B.C.E. and scattered colonies from the Black Sea and Asia Minor across Italy and Sicily to France and Spain.*

Expansion of the Greek World

About the middle of the eighth century B.C.E., the Greeks launched a colonization movement that planted *poleis* from Spain to the Black Sea. They avoided the eastern end of the Mediterranean, which was well populated and defended, and searched for western sites that were sparsely settled or whose natives were not well organized to resist. So many Greek colonies were established in southern Italy and Sicily that the Romans named the region *Magna Graecia,* "Great Greece."

The Greek Colony

The pressures of overpopulation probably explain why thousands of Greeks left the cities of their birth to found new *poleis.* Emigration was difficult but potentially rewarding. Colonies were carefully planned, and most had excellent prospects as centers of trade. Many copied the constitutions and the religious rites of the cities that founded them, but they were not controlled or exploited by those cities and their wealth was not siphoned off for the homeland. Colonies governed themselves. They usually maintained friendly relations with their mother-cities and each might ask the other for help. Occasionally, a city might try to impose its will on one of its colonies, and this could provoke a war.

Colonization added greatly to the material and cultural resources of Greek civilization. Over 1,000 *poleis* were established. This helped the Greeks of the mainland maintain peace among themselves by providing outlets for excess population. It also heightened the Greeks' sense of their unique identity by bringing them into contact with different cultures. *Poleis* across the Mediterranean sponsored festivals such as the Olympic Games to promote and keep alive their memory of their common heritage.

The colonies transformed life in the Greek homeland. The new markets they created had great economic and sociopolitical impact. Farmers on the Greek mainland began to concentrate less on local consumption and more on producing specialized crops (e.g., olives and wine) for export. Demand also increased for manufactured goods such as pottery, tools, weapons, and fine artistic metalwork. Expanding commercial opportunities enlarged the class of independent commoners, and their increasing prosperity led them to resent the aristocrats' traditional monopoly of governmental authority. The political turmoil this generated brought tyrants to power in some *poleis*.

The Tyrants (ca. 700–500 B.C.E.)

A tyrant, in the ancient Greek sense, was a ruler who ignored legal niceties and simply seized power. He often did so with widespread popular support. A typical tyrant was an aristocrat who broke with his class and took control of a city by appealing to the masses of its poor and politically disenfranchised. He usually expelled his aristocratic opponents, distributed their land among his followers, and instituted economic programs that benefitted the city at large.

A tyrant's authority was backed up by a personal bodyguard and troops of mercenary soldiers, but his rule was not necessarily oppressive. Tyrants preferred to concentrate on domestic development and to avoid wars. Aggression against a neighboring state would require fielding a citizen army that might turn on its tyrant. Tyrants courted the masses by financing public works projects that were popular and provided employment for the poor. They also promoted civic pride by sponsoring festivals and supporting the arts.

Despite the positive effect tyranny had on the evolution of some *poleis*, tyrannies faded away during the sixth century B.C.E. There was something about tyranny that was inconsistent with the forces that created the *polis*. The institutions of a *polis* were shaped by the responsibility all its citizens bore for its defense. Since they shared this traditional responsibility of the military aristocracy, they felt entitled also to share the customary aristocratic political prerogatives. The rule of a tyrant, no matter how beneficent, was unacceptable, for it was arbitrary and could not be held accountable. Tyranny did, however, contribute to the growth of popular government by breaking the monopoly aristocracies had on political power.

The Major States

There were many *poleis* and much diversity in their organization, but two—Sparta and Athens—were of such importance that they merit special attention.

Sparta

About 725 B.C.E., Sparta embarked on a path that made it Greece's most respected military power. It invaded Messenia, its western neighbor, to acquire more land to support its growing population. The conquest and enslavement of the Messenians solved Sparta's economic problems but created a difficulty of a different kind. The Spartans found themselves outnumbered ten to one by Helots, the Spartan term for slaves. A crisis was reached about 650 B.C.E. when a slave revolt nearly destroyed Sparta. The Spartans concluded that in order to survive they had to live constantly in a state of total military mobilization.

SPARTAN SOCIETY   The Spartan system subordinated the natural feelings of devotion to self and family interests to the needs of the state. The state needed all its men to be superb soldiers, and it persuaded them to sacrifice privacy and comfort to physical conditioning, military training, and discipline. The Spartans allowed nothing to distract them from their goal of becoming the best warriors in the world.

The Spartan *polis* controlled the life of each of its members from birth to death. Only infants whom officials of the state judged to be physically fit were raised. At the age of seven boys left their mothers to begin training at military camps. They learned to fight, to endure privation, to bear physical pain, and to live off the land. At twenty they joined the army in the field, and they lived in barracks until the age of thirty. They were allowed to marry but not to live at home. Young Spartan husbands had to steal away from camp to visit their wives. Only after a man acquired full citizen rights at the age of thirty could he maintain a home. But even then he took his meals at a public mess with other members of his military unit. His sparse diet included little meat or wine, and he eschewed all luxuries. His financial future was, however, secure, for he was supported by a grant from the state—a plot of land worked by Helots.

He remained on active military duty until the age of sixty.

Sparta prepared its females as well as its males to serve the state. Female infants were examined for fitness in the same way as males, and young girls, like boys, were given athletic training. Because Spartan men concentrated on military affairs and were often absent from home, Spartan women had much greater freedom and responsibility than other Greek females.

SPARTAN GOVERNMENT   The Spartan constitution mixed elements of monarchy, oligarchy, and democracy. Sparta acknowledged two royal families; the functions of the kings who headed them were chiefly religious and military. The Spartan army was usually commanded by one of its kings when it was in the field, but kings did not govern Sparta. An oligarchic council composed of the kings and twenty-eight men (aged sixty or more and elected for life) devised policy and sat as a high court. All Spartan males over the age of thirty could take part in a democratic assembly that, in theory, had final authority. The assembly, however, could only consider proposals referred to it by the council. Since it voted by acclamation rather than by counting ballots, it was limited to ratifying decisions already taken or deciding between alternative proposals.

The administration of Sparta's government was the duty of a board of five executives called *ephors*. The ephors were elected annually by the assembly. They controlled foreign policy, oversaw the generalship of the kings, presided at the assembly, and policed the Helots.

THE PELOPONNESIAN LEAGUE   Suppression of the Helots required all the energy Sparta had, and the Spartans did not want to overextend themselves by conquering and assimilating potentially troublesome neighbors. They preferred to force these people into alliances that left them free internally but subservient to Sparta's foreign policy. Sparta eventually enrolled every southern Greek state except Argos in its Peloponnesian League and became the most powerful *polis* on the Greek mainland before the rise of Athens.

Athens

Athens evolved more slowly than Sparta. Since Attica, the region Athens dominated, was large

Aristogeiton and Harmodius were Athenian aristocrats slain in 1514 B.C.E. after assassinating Hipparchus, brother of the tyrant Hippias. After the overthrow of the Pisistratus in 510 B.C.E., the Athenians erected a statue to honor their memory. This is a Roman copy.
Scala/Art Resource, NY

by Greek standards (about 1,000 square miles), it was able to absorb a growing population. But size slowed its consolidation as a *polis* until the seventh century B.C.E., and its economic development was hampered by the fact that it was not situated on the trade routes most traveled during the eighth and seventh centuries B.C.E.

POLITICAL TENSIONS   In the seventh century B.C.E., aristocratic families held the most and the best land around Athens. They also dominated Attica by controlling the tribes, clans, and military fraternities that structured Athenian society. Athens' government was headed by the

Council of the Areopagus, a group of nobles that annually chose the city's nine *archons*, the magistrates who administered the *polis*. Since there was no formal law, leaders were guided primarily by custom and tradition.

Athens' political evolution was accelerated by an agrarian crisis that developed during the seventh century B.C.E. Many Athenians depended on small family farms that grew wheat, the staple of the ancient diet. Years of consistent cultivation diminished the fertility of their fields and the size of their harvests, but few could afford to shift to more profitable crops such as olives (for oil) and grapes (for wine). A lot of capital was needed to bring a vineyard or olive grove into production. In bad years the poorer farmers were forced to borrow from their wealthier neighbors—mortgaging future crops and, therefore, their own labor as surety for their loans. Eventually this reduced them to slavery, and some of them were even exported for sale outside Attica. The poor came to resent this and began to agitate for the abolition of debts and the redistribution of the land.

In 632 B.C.E., a nobleman named Cylon tried to exploit this situation to establish a tyranny. He failed, but his attempt frightened Athens' aristocratic leaders into taking steps to head off future coups. In 621 B.C.E., they commissioned a man named Draco to codify and publish Athens' laws. Draco decreed extremely hard punishments for crimes in hopes of deterring the blood feuds that resulted when victims sought revenge for wrongs done them. The establishment of a common standard of justice for all Athenians was meant to dissuade individuals from taking things into their own hands.

In the year 594 B.C.E., the Athenians instituted a more radical reform. They empowered a single *archon* (a man named Solon) to reorganize the *polis* as he saw fit. Solon attacked agrarian problems by canceling debts and forbidding loans secured by the freedom of the borrower. He emancipated people who had been enslaved for debt and brought home many of the Athenians who had been sold abroad. Instead of alienating the rich by redistributing their land to the poor, he tried to expand Athens' economy to create more opportunities of employment for the poor. He forbade the export of wheat (which might create shortages and drive up the price of the common person's food) but not olive oil (one of Attica's

cash crops). He facilitated trade by conforming Athenian weights and measures to standards used by Corinth, Euboea, and other commercial centers. And he developed industries by offering citizenship to foreign artisans who agreed to set up shop in Athens.

Solon also reformed Athenian political institutions. He divided Athens' citizens into four classes on the basis of wealth. Members of the two richest classes qualified for *archonships* and membership in the Council of the Areopagus. Men of the third class could serve as *hoplites* and be elected to a council of 400 chosen by the citizens. Solon intended this council to serve as a check on the Council of the Areopagus, and he gave it the power to decide what business was to be set before the popular assembly, the political organization to which all adult male citizens belonged. The poorest class, the *thetes*, voted in this assembly, participated in the election of *archons*, and sat on a popular new court that heard appeals from other jurisdictions. Women from citizen families were granted no role in the political process.

THE TYRANNIES Since the beneficial effects of Solon's reforms were slow to be felt, tensions continued to mount in Athens. On several occasions fighting was so bad that no *archons* could be elected. Twice (in 560 B.C.E. and 556 B.C.E.) a military hero named Pisistratus tried and failed to establish a tyranny, but in 546 B.C.E. his third attempt succeeded. Pisisitratus remained in power until his death in 527 B.C.E., and his son Hippias continued the tyranny until a competitor drove him from the city in 510 B.C.E.

Like the tyrants of other Greek cities, Pisistratus dominated his subjects by courting them. He sponsored public works programs, urban development, and civic festivals. He employed poets and artists to add luster to his court. And he secured his power by hiding it behind the facade of Solon's constitution. All the councils, assemblies, and courts continued to meet, and all the magistrates were elected. Pisistratus merely saw to it that his supporters won the key offices and dominated the important meetings. The constitutional cloak he spread over his tyranny won him a reputation as a popular, gentle ruler, but it also gave his people more experience with (and a greater appetite for) self-government.

Pisistratus's elder son, Hippias, began by imitating his father's gentle style, but in 514 B.C.E., the murder of his brother, Hipparchus, made him fearful for his own saftey. He began to impose harsh measures that lessened popular support for his rule and created opportunities for his opponents. In 510 B.C.E. the Alcmaeonids, a noble family that had been exiled from Athens, persuaded the Spartans to help them overthrow Hippias. Hippias fled, and the Spartans set a man named Isagoras over Athens. Isagoras believed that returning aristocrats to power would stabilize Athens, and he purged the citizen lists to remove the commoners whom Solon and Pisistratus had enfranchised. This was unpopular, and it created an opportunity for the Alcmaeonid leader, Clisthenes.

Clisthenes mobilized the masses against his political opponents, and Isagoras responded by calling on his Spartan allies. This time the Athenians resisted Spartan intervention in their affairs and helped Clisthenes drive out Isagoras.

DEMOCRACY   Clisthenes set about destroying the regional political machines that were the bases for the aristocracy's power. In 508 B.C.E., he divided Attica into small political units called *demes.* The demes were then grouped together to create the tribes that composed Athens' army and elected its government. Care was taken to make sure that each tribe was made up of demes from different parts of Attica. This prevented the wealthy aristocratic families, whose large estates gave them control of local governments, from dominating the new tribal organizations. Aristocrats now found themselves voting with men who were strangers to them and not economically dependent on them.

Clisthenes increased Solon's council from 400 to 500 members and gave it authority to receive foreign emissaries and manage some fiscal affairs. Its chief responsibility was to prepare legislative proposals for discussion by the popular assembly in which ultimate authority was vested. All adult male Athenians were members of this assembly and had the right to propose legislation, to offer amendments, and to debate freely. Thanks to Solon, Pisistratus, and Clisthenes, Athens entered the fifth century B.C.E. well down the path to prosperity and democracy and prepared to claim a place among Greece's leading *poleis.*

Life in Archaic Greece

Society

Greek society's unique features began to become visible at the end of the Dark Ages. The vast majority of Greeks made their living from the land, but artisans and merchants acquired greater importance as contact with the non-Hellenic (i.e., non-Greek) world increased.

FARMERS   Ordinary country folk rarely leave any record of their thoughts or activities, but the poet Hesiod (ca. 700 B.C.E.), who claimed in his *Works and Days* to be a small farmer, described what life was like for members of his class in ancient Greece. The crops farmers usually cultivated were barley, wheat, grapes for wine, olives for oil (for cooking, lighting, and lubrication), green vegetables, beans, and fruit. Sheep and goats provided milk and cheese. Since land that was fertile enough to grow fodder for cattle was better used to grow grain for human consumption, most people only dined on meat at religious festivals where they feasted on the animals sacrificed to the gods.

Hesiod had the help of oxen and mules and occasional hired laborers, but his life was one of continuous toil. The toughest season began with October's rains, the time for the first plowing. Plows were iron-tipped but light and fragile. Even with the aid of a team of animals it was difficult to break the sod. During autumn and winter, wood was cut and repairs were made to buildings and equipment. Vines needed attention in late winter. Grain was harvested in May. At the height of summer's heat there was time for a little rest. In September grapes had to be harvested and pressed, and then the round of yearly tasks began again. Hesiod says nothing about pleasures or entertainments, but the existence of his poetry witnesses to the presence in Greece of a more dynamic rural population than we know of anywhere else in the ancient world.

ARISTOCRATS   Wealthy aristocrats worked their extensive lands with hired laborers, sharecroppers, and slaves. This gave them leisure for other kinds of activities. The centerpiece of aristocratic social life was the symposium, a men's drinking party. A symposium was sometimes only a pursuit of inebriation, but it could be

The ruins of the sanctuary of Apollo at Delphi, dating from the sixth century B.C.E. Greeks and foreigners traveled great distances to worship Apollo and to consult the famous Delphic oracle for clues to the future. Josè Fuste Raga/The Stock Market

more. It began with prayers and libations to the gods. There were usually games such as dice or *kottabos* (a contest in which wine was flicked from cups at a target). Sometimes dancing girls or flute girls offered entertainment. Frequently guests amused themselves with songs, poetry, or philosophical discussions. These activities were structured as contests, for aristocratic values put a premium on competition and the need to excel.

Athletic contests spread widely early in the sixth century B.C.E. They usually included foot races, long jumps, discus and javelin events, boxing, wrestling, and chariot races. Since the rich were the only ones who could afford horses, the chariot race was the special preserve of the nobility. Wrestling was also favored by the upper classes, and the *palaestra* where they practiced was an important gathering place. There was a great contrast between the drab lives of simple farmers and the cultivated pursuits of leisured aristocrats.

Religion

OLYMPIAN Religion permeated every aspect of Greek life. The Greeks were polytheists whose official pantheon centered on the twelve major deities who resided on Mount Olympus. Zeus, a sky god, exercised a kind of patriarchal authority over the other gods. He had three sisters: Hera, who was also his wife; Hestia, goddess of the hearth; and Demeter, goddess of agriculture and marriage. Zeus's brother Poseidon was god of the seas and earthquakes. By various mates he had an assortment of children: Aphrodite, goddess of love and beauty; Apollo, god of the sun, music, poetry, and prophecy; Ares, god of strife; Artemis, goddess of the moon and the hunt; Athena, goddess of wisdom and the arts; Hephaestus, god of fire and metallurgy; and Hermes, a cunning messenger-god who was the patron of traders.

Gods were believed, apart from their superhuman strength and immortality, to resemble mortals. Zeus, the defender of justice, presided over the cosmos, but he and the other gods were not omnipotent. They operated within limits set by the Fates who personified the inviolable order of the universe. Olympian religion was Panhellenic (i.e., shared by all the Greeks), but each *polis* chose one of the gods as its special guardian, and in the eighth and seventh centuries B.C.E., shrines honored by all Greeks were established at Olympia (to Zeus), Delphi (to Apollo), Corinth (to Poseidon), and Nemea (also to Zeus). Each of these sanctuaries staged athletic games in honor of its god, and all Greeks were invited to attend them. During the games, sacred truces suspended wars so that all parties could safely participate.

In the sixth century B.C.E., the shrine of Apollo at Delphi became famous for its oracle, the most important of several that the Greeks looked to for guidance. Delphian Apollo endorsed the pursuit of self-knowledge and self-control. "Know thyself" and "Nothing in excess" were Apollo's mottos. *Hubris,* the arrogance produced by excessive wealth or good fortune, was believed to be the most dangerous of human failings. It created moral blindness and tempted the gods to take vengeance. The moral order the gods enforced was simple. Virtue consisted of paying one's debts, doing good to one's friends, and attacking one's enemies. Civic responsibility involved taking part in the cult of the state deities, performing public service, and fighting in the state's army.

THE DIONYSIAN AND ORPHIC CULTS   The worship of the Olympian gods was a state religion that was not meant to address the concerns of private individuals. For their personal needs the Greeks practiced a religion of a different kind. They worshiped countless lesser deities associated with local shrines. Some were human heroes, both real and legendary, whose deeds had won them divine status. Ordinary people had no such grandiose aspirations. The cults that appealed to them offered divine help for this life.

The worship of Dionysus, a fertility deity associated with the growing of grapes, was very popular—particularly with women. Dionysus was a god of drunkenness and sexual abandon. His female devotees (the *maenads*) cavorted by night and were reputed, when possessed by their god, to tear to pieces and devour any creatures they encountered. The cult of Orpheus, a mythical poet, taught respect for life and offered the

prospect of some kind of triumph over the grave—perhaps a transmigration of souls.

Poetry

A shift from epic to lyric poetry reflected the great changes that swept through the Greek world in the sixth century B.C.E. The poems of Sappho of Lesbos, Anacreon of Teos, and Simonides of Cos were intimately personal—often describing the pleasure and agony of love. Alcaeus of Mytilene, an aristocrat driven from his city by a tyrant, wrote bitter invectives, and from a political point of view the most interesting poet of the century may be Theonis of Megara. He spoke for the aristocrats whose power over most *poleis* was waning. He insisted that only nobles could aspire to true virtue, for only nobles possessed the crucial sense of honor. Honor, he claimed, could not be taught; it was innate, and noble families lost it if they debased their lines by marrying commoners. Although the political privileges of the old nobility were reduced in most Greek states, traditional assumptions of aristocratic superiority continued to influence important thinkers such as Plato.

The Persian Wars

The Greeks' era of freedom from interference from the outside world came to an end in the middle of the sixth century B.C.E. First, the Greek colonies, which had flourished on the coast of Asia Minor since the eleventh century B.C.E., came under the control of Croesus (ca. 560–546 B.C.E.), king of the Anatolian nation of Lydia. Then in 546 B.C.E., Lydia and its dependencies passed into the hands of the Persians.

The Persian Empire

The Persian Empire was created in a single generation by Cyrus the Great, founder of the Achaemenid dynasty. When Cyrus became the ruler of Persia in 559 B.C.E., it was a small kingdom well to the east of lower Mesopotamia. He steadily expanded his domain in all directions, conquered Babylon, and ultimately reached Asia Minor where he defeated Croesus and occupied Lydia. Most of the Greek cities of Asia Minor resisted the Persians, but by 540 B.C.E. they had all been subdued.

The Ionian Rebellion

The Greeks of Ionia (i.e., the western coast of Asia Minor) had been developing democratic governments, and they were restive under Persian rule. But the Persians were clever empire builders. They appointed Greek tyrants to govern Greek cities. Since these native leaders usually governed benignly and Persian tribute was not excessive, many Greeks were soon reconciled to life in Persia's empire. Neither the death of Cyrus in 530 B.C.E., nor the suicide of his successor Cambyses, nor the civil war that followed that event in 522–521 B.C.E. prompted the Greeks to revolt. In 521 B.C.E. when Darius became Great King (the Persian royal title), Ionia submitted to him as to his predecessors.

Aristagoras, an ambitious tyrant of Miletus, was responsible for ending the era of peaceful cooperation between Ionia and Persia. To escape punishment for having committed the Persians to an unsuccessful campaign against the island of Naxos, he persuaded the Ionian cities to join him in a rebellion in 499 B.C.E. He won support by helping to overthrow unpopular fellow tyrants and by endorsing democratic constitutions for some cities. He also sought help from the mainland states. The Spartans declined to become involved. They had no ties with the Ionians, no national interest in the region, and could not risk weakening their hold over their slaves by sending their army abroad.

The Athenians were more sympathetic toward Aristagoras. They were related to the Ionians and had reasons of their own to fear the Persians. Hippias, the deposed tyrant of Athens, was an honored guest at Darius's court, and the Great King supported Hippias's plans to restore his tyranny in Athens. The Persians also held both shores of the Hellespont, Athens' route to the grain fields surrounding the Black Sea. For all these reasons, the Athenian assembly decided to send a fleet of twenty ships to help the rebels.

In 498 B.C.E. the Athenian and Ionian armies overwhelmed Sardis, the capital of Lydia and the seat of the Persian *satrap* (i.e., governor). The sack of Sardis encouraged others to join the rebellion, but the Greeks did not follow up their victory. Athens withdrew, and the Persians gradually recovered the ground they had lost. In 495 B.C.E. they defeated the Ionian fleet at Lade, and a year later they leveled Miletus.

A Greek hoplite attacks a Persian soldier. The contrast between the Greek's metal body armor, large shield, and long spear and the Persian's cloth and leather garments indicates one reason the Greeks won. This Attic vase was found on Rhodes and dates from ca. 475 B.C.E. Greek vase, Red-figured. Attic.ca. 480–470 B.C. Neck amphora, Nolan type. Side 1: Greek warrior attacking a Persian. Said to be from Rhodes. Terracotta H. 13–11/16 in. The Metropolitan Museum of Art, Rogers Fund, 1906. (06.1021.117) Photograph © 1986 The Metropolitan Museum of Art.

The War in Greece

In 490 B.C.E. the Persians launched an expedition to punish Athens, to restore Hippias, and to gain control of the Aegean Sea. They first attacked Naxos and destroyed it as punishment for its resistance in 499 B.C.E. Then they conquered Eretria and deported its people, for the Eretrians had sent help to Miletus.

Despite the failure of their neighbors to withstand Persia's assault, the Athenians refused to submit to the invader. They chose Miltiades, an Athenian with a personal grudge against the Persians, to lead them and marched out to Marathon, the plain north of Athens where the Persians had made their landing. Although the odds were against them, the Athenians defeated the Persians and forced them to retreat. Victory

The Rise of the *Polis*

ca. 725 B.C.E.	Sparta conquers Messenia
ca. 650 B.C.E.	Spartan constitution militarizes the state
594 B.C.E.	Solon reforms the Athenian constitution
546–510 B.C.E.	Athenian tyranny of Pisistratus and Hippias
521 B.C.E.	Ionia submits to Persian rule
508 B.C.E.	Clisthenes inaugurates Athenian democracy
499 B.C.E.	Miletus rebels against Persia
490 B.C.E.	Darius's invasion, the battle of Marathon
480 B.C.E.	Xerxes' invasion, the battles of Thermopylae and Salamis
479 B.C.E.	Battles of Plataea and Mycale, Greek victory over Persia

enhanced their pride in themselves and their confidence in the fledgling democracy they had recently invented to govern their *polis.*

THE GREAT INVASION Internal troubles prevented the Persians from taking swift revenge for their loss at Marathon. Almost ten years elapsed before Darius's successor, Xerxes, turned his attention to the Greeks. In 481 B.C.E. he assembled an army of at least 150,000 men and a navy of more than 600 ships and set out to conquer the Aegean.

By then Athens had changed significantly. Themistocles, the city's leading politician, had begun to turn the *polis* into a naval power. During his *archonship* in 493 B.C.E., Athens built a fortified port at Piraeus, and a decade later the Athenians used the income from a rich vein of silver discovered in the state mines to finance the construction of a fleet. By 480 B.C.E., Athens had over 200 ships. They proved to be the salvation of Greece.

Of the hundreds of Greek states, only thirty-one (led by Sparta, Athens, Corinth, and Aegina) were willing to commit to fighting the vast Persian army that gathered south of the Hellespont in the spring of 480 B.C.E. Xerxes' strategy was to overwhelm the Greeks with superior numbers,

but Themistocles perceived a weakness in the emperor's plan. The Persian army had to stay in touch with the fleet that carried its supplies. If the Persian ships were destroyed, the army would have to retreat. Themistocles, therefore, argued that a naval engagement could win the war for the Greeks.

The Greek League, which was organized specifically to deal with the Persian invasion, met at Corinth as the Persians prepared to cross the Hellespont. Sparta was chosen to lead the Greeks, and the Greeks decided to take their stand at Thermopylae (i.e., the "hot gates"). The Persian army had to stay near the coast to maintain contact with its fleet, and at Thermopylae the coast was extremely narrow for the mountains came nearly to the sea. It was possible for a small force to stop the Persians here by blocking the narrow strip of beach at the foot of the mountains. The Greek army with which the Spartan king, Leonidas, hoped to hold this spot numbered only about 9,000—of which 300 were Spartans.

The Greeks had some luck, for storms wrecked a large number of Persians ships before Xerxes attacked Thermopylae. For two days the Greeks stood their ground and butchered the troops he threw at them. On the third day, however, a Greek traitor showed the Persians a trail through the mountains, and a company of Xerxes' men outflanked the Greek army and attacked it from the rear. Leonidas realized that the situation was hopeless. He discharged his Greek allies, but he and his 300 Spartans chose to stay and to die fighting. The way was now clear for the Persian army to invade Attica and burn Athens. If an inscription discovered in 1959 is authentic, Themistocles had foreseen this possibility and begun the evacuation of the city while the Greek army was still at Thermopylae.

The fate of Greece was decided by a sea battle fought in the narrow straits between Attica and the island of Salamis. The Spartans wanted the Athenian fleet to retreat from Salamis and move south to guard the coast of the Peloponnese, but Themistocles forced them to change their minds by threatening to abandon the war and use the fleet to carry the Athenians to new homes in Italy. In the battle that followed at Salamis the Persians lost more than half their ships. This forced Xerxes to return to Persia, but he left a large portion of his army behind to continue the war under a general named Mardonius.

While Mardonius went into winter camp in central Greece, Pausanias, a Spartan leader, assembled the largest army the Greeks had ever fielded. In the summer of 479 B.C.E. it decisively defeated Mardonius's forces at a battle near Plataea in Boeotia. At the same time, the Ionian Greeks persuaded Leotychidas, the Spartan commander of the Greek fleet, to take the offensive against a key Persian naval base at Mycale on the coast of Asia Minor. Leotychidas routed the enemy, and the Persians retreated from the Aegean and Ionia. Greece was safe, but no one knew for how long.

In Perspective

The Hellenic civilization that has so powerfully influenced the modern West was itself influenced by the Bronze Age cultures of Minoan Crete and Mycenae. But these early Aegean states more closely resembled Egypt, Mesopotamia, and Palestine-Syria than the Hellenic poleis. They were urbanized societies with systems of writing, centralized monarchies, large administrative bureaucracies, hierarchical social systems, professional standing armies, and systems of taxation. The Hellenic civilization that slowly emerged from the rubble of the Mycenaean kingdoms was quite different.

The Mycenaean collapse inaugurated an era of cultural decline for the Greeks. Villages replaced cities. Trade all but ended. Communication was curtailed. The art of writing was lost, and a "dark age" descended on the Aegean during which the Greeks were largely forgotten by the outside world. During this period (1100–750 B.C.E.), however, the Greeks laid foundations for a new civilization based on the polis, the Hellenic city-state.

Monarchy faded with the passing of the Mycenaean kingdoms, and several factors encouraged the development of republican governments in the new poleis. Because Greece was poor, distinctions of wealth between social classes were less dramatic than in other societies. Reliance on infantry—the hoplite phalanx—further narrowed the gap between aristocrat and commoner. A city that depended on its citizen-soldiers for its defense could hardly deny them some role in its government. Most poleis also had

no need to impose regular taxation, for they did not have to hire professional soldiers or administrators. These services were duties citizens were expected to volunteer to the state. There were, therefore, no professional bureaucracies to stifle individual initiatives and no castes of priests to enforce religious orthodoxy. A polis was a dynamic, secular, and remarkably free community that created the kind of cultural environment in which speculative thinking (the basis of science) could thrive.

REVIEW QUESTIONS

1. What are the similarities and the differences between the Minoan and the Mycenaean civilizations?
2. What are the sources from which historians can derive information about the Aegean Bronze Age? What is Linear B and what can be learned from it? What are the difficulties in using the Homeric epics as historical sources?
3. What was a Greek *polis*? What role did geography play in the development of the Greek *poleis*? What contribution did the *polis* make to the development of Hellenic civilization?
4. How did the political, social, and economic institutions of Athens and Sparta compare around 500 B.C.E.? What explains Sparta's uniqueness?
5. What transpired in Athens between 600 and 500 B.C.E. to help it make the transition from aristocracy to democracy? What did Draco, Solon, Pisistratus, and Clisthenes each contribute to the process?
6. Why did the Greeks and Persians go to war in 490 and 480 B.C.E.? What motivated the Persian attempt to conquer Greece? Why were the Greeks victorious over the Persians? What were the effects of victory on the victors?

SUGGESTED READINGS

J. CHADWICK, *The Mycenaean World* (1976). A readable account by a man who helped decipher Mycenaean writing.

J. M. COOK, *The Persian Empire* (1983). A valuable study of Persian history based on archaeological and literary evidence.

O. DICKINSON, *The Aegean Bronze Age* (1994). A fine survey of Bronze Age culture in the Aegean region.

R. DREWS, *The End of the Bronze Age: Changes in Warfare and Catastrophes ca. 1200 B.C.* (1993). An examination of the theories explaining the fall of the late Bronze Age civilizations.

V. EHRENBERG, *From Solon to Socrates* (1968). An interpretive history that uses literature to illuminate politics.

J. V. A. FINE, *The Ancient Greeks* (1983). An excellent survey that discusses historical problems and the evidence that gives rise to them.

M. I. FINLEY, *World of Odysseus*, 2nd. ed. (1978). A fascinating attempt to reconstruct Homeric society.

W. G. FORREST, *The Emergence of Greek Democracy* (1966). An interpretation of social and political developments in the archaic period.

P. GREEN, *The Greco-Persian Wars* (1998). A stimulating history of the Persian wars.

V. D. HANSON, *The Western Way of War* (1989). A brilliant description of the *hoplite* phalanx and its influence on Greek society.

V. D. HANSON, *The Other Greeks* (1995). A revolutionary account of the invention of the family farm by the Greeks and the role of agrarianism in the *polis*.

J. M. HURWIT, *The Art and Culture of Early Greece* (1985). A fascinating study of the art of early Greece in its cultural context.

D. KAGAN, *The Great Dialogue: A History of Greek Political Thought from Homer to Polybius* (1965). A discussion of the relationship between historical experience and political theory.

P. B. MANVILLE, *The Origins of Citizenship in Ancient Athens* (1990). An examination of the concept of citizenship in Solon's generation.

L. G. MITCHELL and P. J. RHODES, eds., *The Development of the* Polis *in Archaic Greece* (1997). A collection of articles on the early development of the *polis*.

R. SALLARES, *The Ecology of the Ancient Greek World* (1991). A valuable study of the Greeks and their environment.

Chapter 3

Classical and Hellenistic Greece

KEY TOPICS

- The Peloponnesian War and the struggle between Athens and Sparta
- Democracy and empire in fifth-century B.C.E. Athens
- Culture and society in Classical Greece
- The struggle for dominance in Greece after the Peloponnesian War
- The Hellenistic world

The Greeks' victory over the Persians in 489–479 B.C.E. marked the start of an era of great achievement. Fear of another Persian incursion into the Aegean led the Greeks to contemplate some kind of cooperative defense. The Spartans refused to make commitments that would take them away from their homeland, but the Athenians were eager for opportunities to increase their influence. They negotiated a military alliance called the Delian League. As it developed into an Athenian empire, fear of Athenian expansion led *other states to ally with Sparta. The polarized Greek world erupted in a civil war that weakened everyone, and in 338 B.C.E. Philip of Macedon imposed his will on the Greeks and brought the era of the* polis *to an end.*

Aftermath of Victory

The Greek *poleis* had found it hard to cooperate even in the face of Persian invasions of their homeland. Within two years of Persia's retreat, divisions had emerged among the Greeks that threatened to involve them in serious civil conflict.

The Delian League

The Spartans led the Greeks to victory against the Persian invaders of the Greek mainland, but they were not prepared to assume responsibility for de-

fending the Aegean against the return of the Persians. Sparta could not risk stationing its troops far from home for long periods lest its slaves rebel. A *polis* with a navy was also better equipped to defend the Aegean than the Spartan army.

Athens was Greece's leading naval power, and it was an Ionian state with ties to the Greeks whom the Persians still threatened on the Aegean islands and the coasts of Asia Minor. In the winter of 478–477 B.C.E., the Athenians joined other Greeks on the sacred island of Delos to swear oaths of mutual assistance in a continuing struggle with Persia. The purpose of the Delian League they formed was to free Greeks still under Persian rule, to defend against a Persian return, and to obtain compensation from the Persians by raiding their lands.

The league succeeded in driving back the Persians and clearing the Aegean of pirates. In 467 B.C.E., it won a great victory over the Persians at

MAP 3–1 CLASSICAL GREECE *The history of Greece in the Classical Period (ca. 480–338 B.C.E.) centers on the Aegean, although Greek cities in Italy, Sicily, and the Black Sea also made important contributions.*

the Eurymedon River in Asia Minor, and some cities concluded that the alliance had served its purpose. When they tried to withdraw from the league, however, Athens forced them to continue their contributions. What had begun as a voluntary association of free states became an empire dominated by Athens.

The Rise of Cimon

Themistocles fell from power at the end of the Persian Wars, and for two decades leadership of Athens was exercised by Cimon, son of Miltiades, the general who triumphed at Marathon. At home, Cimon defended a limited version of Clisthenes' democratic constitution. Abroad he maintained pressure on Persia and cultivated friendly relations with Sparta.

The First Peloponnesian War: Athens Against Sparta

The Thasian Rebellion

In 465 B.C.E. the island of Thasos rebelled against the Delian League. During the two years it took to put down the revolt, Cimon was absent from Athens. When he returned, his political opponents tried to bring him down by charging him with taking bribes. He was acquitted, but a radically democratic faction led by a man named Ephialtes (and his young protégé, Pericles) continued to attack Cimon for his pro-Spartan, proaristocratic policies.

The Breach with Sparta

At the start of the Thasian rebellion, Thasos had asked Sparta to assist it by invading Athens. Sparta agreed, but an earthquake sparked a Helot revolt that kept the Spartan army tied up at home. Instead of attacking Athens, Sparta asked the Athenians for help. Cimon's fatal mistake was to talk the Athenians into sending it. The Spartans soon reconsidered the wisdom of letting an Athenian army into their land and ordered Cimon to retreat. The humiliated Athenians blamed Cimon, exiled him (461 B.C.E.), and allied with Argos, Sparta's enemy. A radical democratic faction under the leadership of Pericles emerged triumphant in Athens.

The Division of Greece

Since Sparta had been willing to help Thasos break up the Delian League by rebelling from Athens, Pericles persuaded Athens to back the city of Megara when it withdrew from Sparta's Peloponnesian League. (Since Megara was a key spot on the road that linked Attica with the Peloponnesus, Athens also understood the strategic importance of an alliance with Megara.) Sparta's vigorous objection led to the outbreak of the First Peloponnesian War. The Athenians maintained the upper hand until about 455 B.C.E., when they lost a fleet that they had sent to Egypt to harrass the Persians. Some members of Athens' empire seized the opportunity this gave them to rebel, and Athens was compelled to disentangle itself from war with Sparta. A truce was arranged, and in 449 B.C.E. Athens also made peace with Persia.

In 446 B.C.E., war again broke out between Sparta and Athens, but Pericles soon ended it by negotiation. Sparta recognized the Athenian empire in exchange for Athens ending its drive to win control of more of the Greek mainland, and the two *poleis* pledged to keep the peace for thirty years. This effectively divided Greece into two power blocs: Sparta dominating the Greek mainland and Athens ruling the Aegean Sea.

Classical Greece

The Athenian Empire

The Athenians used the failure of their Egyptian campaign as an excuse to move the league's treasury from the island of Delos to the greater security of Athens, and they began to keep one-sixtieth of its annual revenues for themselves. By 445 B.C.E. only Chios, Lesbos, and Samos maintained a semblance of equality with Athens by contributing their own ships to the league's navy. All the other states paid tribute like subject states, and they resented doing so. The fading of the Persian threat had removed the rationale for the league, but Athens profited too much from it to allow it to dissolve. Although the league became an Athenian empire, it was not unpopular with everyone. Democratic factions in its subject cities supported it, and Athens did what it could not to look like an oppressor but like a mother-city to

The Acropolis was both the religious and civic center of Athens. In its final form it is the work of Pericles and his successors in the late fifth century B.C.E. This photograph shows the Parthenon and to its left the Erechtheum. Meredith Pillon, Greek National

which allies were bound, like colonies, by ties of good feelings and shared religion.

Athenian Democracy

DEMOCRATIC LEGISLATION The Athenians sensed no inconsistency in demanding more democratic privileges for themselves while they pursued greater imperial dominance over others. The property qualification for holding high office was virtually suspended, and the Athenian *hoplite* class became eligible for the *archonship*. Pericles sponsored a law providing pay for jury members, which made it possible for the poor, who could not afford to take unpaid leave from their jobs, to serve. He revived the custom of sending circuit judges into the countryside to make justice readily available to the rural poor. He also persuaded the electorate to limit citizenship to men whose parents both descended from citizen families. Democracy made citizenship a valuable commodity, and it was in the self-interest of the electorate to increase the value of each vote by limiting the number of voters. All the Greek states denied participation in government to large segments of their populations—resident aliens, women, and slaves.

HOW DID THE DEMOCRACY WORK? Athenian democracy gave citizens extensive powers. Every decision of the state had to be approved by the popular assembly—by the voters themselves, not their representatives. Every judicial decision was subject to appeal to a popular court composed of not fewer than 51 and possibly as many as 1,501 citizens selected from the Athenian population at large. Most officials were chosen by casting lots, and their class status was unimportant. Successful candidates for the chief offices—for example, the imperial treasurers and the city's ten generals (who had both political and military authority)—were usually wealthy aristocrats. But the voters could, in theory, elect anyone. All public officials had to submit to examination before taking office. They could be removed from office and were called to account at the end of their term for the uses they had made of their authority. Since there was no standing army and no police force (public or secret), the city's leaders could not coerce or intimidate voters.

Pericles was elected to the generalship fifteen years in a row and thirty times in all, not because he was a dictator but because he was a persuasive speaker and a respected leader. On the few occasions when he lost the people's confidence, they did not hesitate to remove him from office. Pericles had been an imperialist, but after the defeat of the fleet Athens sent to Egypt and the failure of Athens' plans to win control over more of the mainland, he advocated a more conservative policy that was designed to preserve the empire Athens already had and peace with Sparta. By 443. B.C.E., when the First Peloponnesian War ended, he was at the height of his power as the guardian of Athens' imperial democracy.

Athenian Women: Legal Status and Everyday Life

Greek society, like most others throughout history, was dominated by men, and democratic Athens was no exception. Women from citizen families were excluded from most aspects of public life. They could not debate, vote, or hold office and were subject all their lives to the authority of a male guardian—a father, a husband, or other male relative. They married young, usually between the ages of twelve and eighteen. Since men often did not marry until they were in their thirties, husbands probably treated wives like dependent children. Marriages were arranged—often without consulting the bride. Woman were assigned dowries, but they had no control over them or any other property. Divorce was difficult for a woman to obtain, for she had to find a male relative who was willing to take responsibility for her after the dissolution of her marriage.

The chief function of an Athenian woman from a citizen family was the production of male heirs to perpetuate her husband's *oikos* (i.e., "household"). If a woman's father died without leaving a male heir, she became an *epikleros*, an heiress. If such a woman was married, she was required to separate from her husband and wed one of her father's relatives to bear a son who would reestablish the male line for her father's *oikos*.

Because citizenship was inherited, the legitimacy of children was important. Athenian males consorted freely with prostitutes and concubines, but citizen women were denied contact with any men but close relatives. Women spent their days confined to special women's quarters in their homes raising children, cooking, weaving, and managing their households. Occasionally they emerged in public to take part in the state religion. But for the most part, Athenian women were expected to be invisible. In a frequently quoted speech, Pericles declared that

Greek Women at Leisure. Most Greek women of the upper classes appear to have led a secluded and confined existence, but there is some evidence that suggests a somewhat richer social and cultural life. The picture of these women comes from a water-jar of the mid-fifth century B.C.E. Women used them to bring water into the house from wells or fountains, where ancient comedies portray them as gathering and conversing. This scene, however, is indoors, in the women's quarters of the house. The seated woman reads from a scroll; another holds a chest containing other works of literature on scrolls while the remaining two listen attentively. The British Museum

"the greatest glory of women is to be least talked about by men, whether for good or bad."

Evidence from myths and from the works of the great Athenian dramatists (who often featured women in their plays) suggests that the roles played by Athenian women may have been more complex than their legal status implies. Only the rich could have afforded to lock their women up at home. The poor needed the labor of their women in fields and shops, and such women had often to move about in public. Fetching water from the town wells and fountains was also women's work, and vase paintings and literature depict women gathering at these places. The opinions historians form about the place of women in Greek society depend on the kinds of sources they choose to emphasize. Consequently, woman's place in the Greek world remains a topic for debate.

AN EXCEPTIONAL WOMAN: ASPASIA   The woman Pericles cared most for did not cultivate the invisibility that he said was "the greatest glory of women." Her name was Aspasia, and she was a *hetaira*, a high-class courtesan. Aspasia was not an Athenian. She came from Miletus, where Greek philosophy got its start. She was evidently very intelligent and apparently well educated. Socrates enjoyed her conversation, and in one of his dialogues Plato jokingly credits her with writing Pericles' speeches. There is no doubt that Pericles loved her. After divorcing his first wife, he took Aspasia into his home and treated her better than many Athenian men may have treated their wives. He lavished affection on her, involved her in conversations with his friends, discussed important issues with her, and respected her opinions. Athens was scandalized—not because Pericles kept a *hetaira* but because he held one in such high regard.

Slavery

The Greeks always had some form of slavery, but the earliest forms of bondage resembled serfdom more than chattel slavery. When the Spartans, for instance, conquered a people, they reduced them to the status of Helots—peasants who were bound to the state-owned farms that supported the Spartan soldiers. Until Solon put an end to the practice in Athens about 600 B.C.E., default on a debt could lead to temporary bondage for an Athenian citizen or even sale into permanent slavery outside Attica.

Chattel slavery proper began to increase about 500 B.C.E. and remained important to Greek society thereafter. Most slaves were prisoners of war or persons abducted by pirates. Like other ancient peoples, the Greeks regarded foreigners as inferior, and most slaves were foreigners. They were sometimes employed as shepherds, but Greek farms were often too small to support more than one enslaved agricultural worker. The upper class had more land, but it was usually worked by free tenant farmers. The estates of wealthy men usually consisted of small farms scattered about the *polis* rather than large, consolidated plantations. They had no use for the hordes of slaves associated with plantation economies. Slaves were used in greater numbers in some industries, especially mining. They worked as craftsmen in almost every trade, where, like slaves on small farms, they labored alongside their masters. Slaves were also used as domestic servants, and publicly owned slaves served as prison attendants, clerks, and secretaries.

The numbers of slaves and their importance to ancient Greek society are debated issues. Reliable statistics are hard to come by. During the fifth and fourth centuries B.C.E., there may have been anywhere from 20,000 to 100,000 slaves in Athens. If the accurate number is the mean between these extremes—60,000—and the city had about 40,000 households, there were fewer than two slaves per family. Only a quarter to a third of free Athenians may have owned slaves. This is comparable to the situation that existed in the American South prior to the Civil War, but unlike the South the Athenian economy did not depend on a single cash crop produced by slave labor. Greek slaves also did not differ from their masters in skin color, and slaves walked the streets of Athens with such ease as to offend class-conscious Athenians. The emancipation of slaves was rare in America but common in Greece.

The Great Peloponnesian War

The thirty years of peace that Sparta and Athens pledged to maintain in 445 B.C.E. ended prematurely. About 435 B.C.E., a dispute began in a remote part of the Greek world that escalated into a war that shook the foundations of Greek civilization.

Causes

The conflict began with a quarrel between Corinth and Corcyra, an island at the entrance to the Adriatic Sea. The Athenians decided to intervene because the Corcyraean fleet was second in size only to that of Athens. Its capture by Corinth would have upset the balance of power and threatened Athens' interests. This infuriated Corinth, a member of Sparta's Peloponnesian League. Corinth appealed to Sparta for help, and in the summer of 432 B.C.E., the Spartans convened a meeting of their allies to discuss the situation. The Corinthians persuaded the league to declare war on Athens, and in the spring of 431 B.C.E. Sparta marched into Attica.

Strategic Stalemate

The Spartan strategy was traditional—invade the enemy's territory, threaten his crops, and force him to defend them in a *hoplite* battle. Since the Spartans and their allies had the better army and outnumbered the Athenians by more than two to one, they were confident of victory.

Any ordinary *polis* would have yielded, but Athens had unique resources—the income from an empire, a vast reserve fund, and the Long Walls (a fortified highway that connected the inland city to its port at Piraeus). So long as the Athenians maintained their enormous navy, they could ride out a siege by supplying themselves from the sea. And if they remained secure behind their walls and ignored the Spartan invasion, they could demonstrate to the world that the Spartan army was no threat to them. Meanwhile the Athenian fleet could raid the Peloponnesian coast to frighten Sparta's allies. Pericles believed that this strategy would force the Peloponnesians to recognize the hopelessness of the situation and sue for peace. The plan was intelligent but difficult to implement. It required Athens' voters to exercise great self-control while Sparta destroyed their farms and taunted them, but Pericles' inspired leadership helped the democracy stay the course. In 429 B.C.E., however, plague swept the crowded city. Pericles died, and the politicians who succeeded him were unable to stick to a consistent plan of action.

Two factions appeared. The one led by a man named Nicias wanted to continue Pericles' defensive strategy; the other, which was headed by a certain Cleon, favored launching an offensive. In 425 B.C.E. Athens captured 400 Spartans in a skirmish in the Peloponnese, and Sparta offered peace in exchange for the return of its men. Cleon's party persuaded the Athenians to pass up this opportunity and to continue the war. The failure of two campaigns the following year shook the Athenian electorate's confidence in his aggressive policy—particularly after the Spartan general, Brasidas, captured Amphipolis, a port on which Athens depended for the protection of its grain imports. In 422 B.C.E., Cleon led an assault on Amphipolis in which both he and Brasidas were killed. The deaths of the leaders of the aggressive factions paved the way in the spring of 421 B.C.E. for a truce. There was also another outcome of the struggle over Amphipolis.

The Athenian admiral who failed to arrive in time to save the city was named Thucydides. Athens punished him with exile, and he used his enforced leisure to write a masterful account of the war—which, as it turned out, was far from over.

The Fall of Athens

The agreement between Athens and Sparta (the Peace of Nicias) was supposed to guarantee peace for fifty years, but neither side honored all its commitments. Despite the likelihood that hostilities would break out again, in 415 B.C.E. an ambitious young politician named Alcibiades persuaded the Athenians to send an army to intervene in the complicated affairs of Sicily. Two years later the entire expedition was destroyed. Athens lost 200 ships and 4,500 men, and the huge loss borne by its allies sparked rebellion in its empire. Persia sized up the situation and saw an opportunity to help the Greeks destroy themselves. It offered aide to Sparta.

Remarkably, the Athenians found the strength to continue fighting, but their resources were no match for the support Spartans received from Persia. In 405 B.C.E., Athens' fleet was caught at Aegospotami and destroyed. Since the city could not afford to replace it, Lysander, the Spartan commander, was able to cut off Athens' food supply and starve the city into submission (404 B.C.E.). Athens was allowed to survive but was stripped of its fleet and empire.

Competition for Leadership in the Fourth Century B.C.E.

Sparta tried, but failed, to take Athens' place as leader of the Greek world. Its limited population, restive slaves, conservative traditions, and indebtedness to Persia prevented it from devising means to govern and protect the Aegean. From 404 B.C.E. until 338 B.C.E., the Greeks squandered their resources fighting among themselves.

The Hegemony of Sparta

Sparta quickly alienated the Greeks by ceding the cities of Ionia to Persia as repayment for the help it had received during the war. Lysander then made a mockery of Sparta's claim to have freed the Greeks from Athenian dominance by attempting to make them part of a new Spartan empire. He installed oligarchies that were loyal to him in the Greek cities and deployed Spartan garrisons to back up his puppet governments. The tribute he demanded was no less than what Athens had collected.

In 404 B.C.E. Lysander installed an oligarchic government in Athens. It became so unpopular that its members were known as the Thirty Tyrants. When persecution prompted Athens' democratic leaders to flee to Thebes and Corinth and to begin to raise an army with which to retake their city, Sparta's cautious king, Pausanias, intervened. He prevented an outbreak of fighting by recalling Lysander and allowing Athens to revert to democracy. So long as Athenian foreign policy remained under Spartan control, Sparta could afford to allow Athens to have any kind of government it wanted.

Persia was distracted from further intervention in Greek affairs by an internal power struggle. In 405 B.C.E. the emperor Darius II died, and a young prince named Cyrus recruited a Greek mercenary army to contest the succession to the throne of his brother, Artaxerxes II. In 401 B.C.E., the Greeks defeated the Persians at Cunaxa in Mesopotamia, but Cyrus was killed in that battle. The Greeks suddenly found themselves stranded without a leader or a purpose deep in enemy territory. They succeeded in fighting their way back to the Black Sea and safety, but the cities of Asia Minor that had supported Cyrus now faced the threat of Artaxerxes' revenge.

In 396 B.C.E. the Spartans sent an army under the command of their king, Agesilaus, to defend Greek interests in Asia Minor. The Persians countered by offering aid to any Greek state willing to rebel against Sparta. Thebes was willing, and in 395 B.C.E. it created an alliance that included Argos, Corinth, and a resurgent Athens. The Corinthian War (395–387 B.C.E.) that ensued forced the Spartan army to evacuate Asia Minor, and in 394 B.C.E. the Persian fleet destroyed Sparta's navy. The Athenians seized the opportunity to rebuild their walls, enlarge their navy, and recover some of their foreign possessions.

The Persians believed that Athens was potentially a greater threat than Sparta, and they were willing to support Sparta so long as its ambitions were confined to the Greek mainland. In 382 B.C.E. Agesilaus seized Thebes in a surprise at-

tack. A Spartan attempt to occupy Athens failed, and by 379 B.C.E. the Thebans had regained their independence. In 371 B.C.E. the great Theban general, Epaminondas, gave the Spartans a crushing defeat at Leuctra. He then freed the Helots and helped them found a city of their own. This deprived Sparta of much of its land and its slave labor force and hemmed it in with hostile neighbors. Sparta was never again to be a major power.

The Hegemony of Thebes: The Second Athenian Empire

Epaminondas's victory over Sparta opened the way for Thebes to become the dominant power in Greece, and Thebes took control of all the Greek states north of Athens and along the Corinthian Gulf. Theban expansion, however, threatened many Greeks, and Athens was able to recruit their help in opposing it. In 362 B.C.E. Epaminondas led an army into the Peloponnesus to confront Athens and its allies. His men routed their opponents at the battle of Mantinea, but he was killed. When no comparable leader arose to

The Competition for Leadership of Greece	
479 B.C.E.	Battles of Plataea and Mycale
478–477 B.C.E.	Formation of Delian League
465–463 B.C.E.	Thasos attempts to leave the league
462 B.C.E.	Pericles begins to lead Athens
460–445 B.C.E.	First Peloponnesian War
454 B.C.E.	Athens defeated in Egypt
449 B.C.E.	Peace with Persia
435 B.C.E.	Corinth attacks Corcyra
432–404 B.C.E.	Great Peloponnesian War
421 B.C.E.	Peace of Nicias
415–413 B.C.E.	Athens' Sicilian campaign
404 B.C.E.	Sparta victorious over Athens
404–403 B.C.E.	Thirty Tyrants govern Athens
382 B.C.E.	Sparta seizes Thebes
378 B.C.E.	Second Athenian Confederation
371 B.C.E.	Thebes defeats Sparta at Leuctra
362 B.C.E	End of Theban hegemony
338 B.C.E.	Philip of Macedon dominates Greece
336–323 B.C.E.	Reign of Alexander the Great

take his place, the era of Theban dominance came to an end.

Sixteen years earlier (in 378 B.C.E.), an alliance known as the Second Athenian Confederation had been organized to guard against Spartan aggression in the Aegean. Although its constitution was designed to prevent Athens from exploiting this alliance as it had the Delian League, Athens soon alienated its confederates. The collapse of Sparta and Thebes and Persia's lack of aggressive behavior convinced some of Athens' allies that the confederation was unnecessary. They rebelled, and by 355 B.C.E., Athens had once again lost an empire. Two centuries of almost continuous warfare had failed to bring order to the Greek world.

The Culture of Classical Greece

The Greeks' early victories in the Persian Wars inspired them with tremendous self-confidence and unleashed a flood of creative activity that was rarely, if ever, matched anywhere at any time. The result was the development of the Classical Period in the history of Western civilization.

The Fifth Century B.C.E.

The term *classical* often invokes the idea of calm and serenity, but the products of Greece's Classical Period are filled with tension. There were two reasons for this. One was the incompatibility between the private ambitions of individuals and the self-restraint imposed by the duties of *polis* citizenship. The other was the conflict between the Greeks' competitive drive and their fear that the gods punished excessive striving. The Greeks' faith in themselves had been strengthened by their victory over Persia, but they knew that they were not exempt from the kind of punishment Xerxes had received for his overreaching ambition. The Greek playwrights pondered this just as Athens and Sparta teetered on the brink of self-destructive war.

ATTIC TRAGEDY Greek plays were staged as competitions among playwrights at festivals honoring the god Dionysus. Poets competed by submitting three tragedies (which might or might not have a common subject) and a satyr play (a concluding comic choral dialogue with Dionysus). An *archon* chose three competitors for each festival and assigned each of them three actors and a chorus. The actors were paid by the state, and the chorus was sponsored by a donation from a wealthy citizen. Most plays were performed in the temple of Dionysus, an amphitheater of 30,000 seats on the south side of the Acropolis. A jury of Athenians, chosen by lot, awarded prizes for the best author, actor, and sponsor.

Attic theater provided poets with opportunities to challenge their fellow citizens to ponder vital issues of the day. On rare occasions the subject of a play might be a contemporary or historical event, but usually a playwright chose a tale from mythology that illuminated current affairs. The plays of Aeschylus and Sophocles, our earliest extant examples, deal with religion, politics, and ethics. The plays of Euripides, which were written a little later, show a greater interest in exploring the psychology of the individual.

OLD COMEDY Comedies were added to the Dionysian festival early in the fifth century B.C.E. The only complete comic plays to survive are those of Aristophanes (ca. 450–385 B.C.E.), who wrote humorously about serious political issues. He employed scathing invective and satire to lampoon his contemporaries—even powerful politicians such as Pericles and Cleon.

ARCHITECTURE AND SCULPTURE Like the plays that members of Pericles' generation witnessed, the buildings the city erected during this period reflect creative tension. In 448 B.C.E., Pericles inaugurated a great building program on the Acropolis (using income from the Delian League). The plan included new temples to honor the city's gods and an imposing gateway for the sacred precinct. Pericles' intent was to represent visually the political power and intellectual greatness of Athens—to make Athens, in his words, "the school of Hellas."

PHILOSOPHY The art of the fifth century B.C.E. tried to define humanity and illustrate its place in the natural world order. Similar concerns prompted the invention of philosophy in the sixth century B.C.E. Thales, the first philosopher, proposed a theory to explain how a world filled with

Victory and Nobility in Bronze:
The Charioteer of Delphi

The Charioteer of Delphi. c. 470 B.C.E.
Nimatallah/Art Resource, NY

This statue is one of the few full-scale bronze sculptures to survive from the fifth century B.C.E. It was a gift to the god Apollo at Delphi from Polyzalus, tyrant of Gela in Sicily, a thank offering for his victory in the chariot race at Delphi's Pythian games in 478 or 474 B.C.E. A victory in one of the greater Greek games (i.e., at Olympia, Delphi, Corinth, or Nemea) was one of the highest honors to which a Greek could aspire, and the deeds of such athletes were memorialized by major poets such as Pindar.

The statue represents the driver of a chariot sponsored by Polyzalus, not Polyzalus himself. It is the only surviving piece from a tableau that once included the chariot, horses, and possibly Polyzalus riding in a victory procession. It is an example of the "severe style" that characterized Greek art in the period after the Persian invasion (i.e., 480–479 B.C.E.). In contrast to earlier work, it is simple, serious, and austere. The expression on the charioteer's face is not the rigid smile typical of archaic sculpture. It projects a moody inwardness—the *ethos* (i.e., character) of a nobleman who takes justifiable pride in his achievements but eschews the arrogance that offends the gods.

Sources: J. J. Pollitt, *Art and Experience in Classical Greece* (Cambridge: Cambridge University Press, 1972), pp. 15–63. H. W. Janson and Anthony F. Janson, *History of Art*, 5th ed., rev. (Upper Saddle River, NJ: Prentice Hall, 1997), pp. 139–151.

changing phenomena could hang together as a stable, coherent whole. He suggested that the changes we see are nothing but alterations in the state of a single underlying universal substance. When attempts to identify this substance failed, later thinkers concluded that Thales had been naive in assuming that change and permanence could both exist in the same world.

Heraclitus argued that permanence was an illusion produced by our inability to perceive change that was very slow. Parmenides of Elea and his pupil Zeno countered that the concept of change was a logical absurdity, for it implied that something arose from nothing. Empedocles of Acragas suggested a compromise between these opposing points of view. He said that the world was composed of unchanging elements (e.g., fire, water, earth, and air) whose combinations changed. Similarly, Leucippus of Miletus and Democritus of Abdera imagined the world to be made up of innumerable tiny, solid, indivisible particles (*atomoi*, in Greek) that clump together and spin apart in the void of space. These philosophies endorsed materialism. That is, they assumed that spirit (or mind) was composed of matter and that physical laws, therefore, could explain everything. Anaxagoras of Clazomenae agreed that the universe was composed of tiny fundamental particles he called "seeds," but he claimed that it also contained another reality—a rational force, *nous* (i.e., "mind"), which controlled everything. These Greek thinkers began a debate between materialism and idealism that has yet to be resolved.

Most philosophical speculations were too abstract to interest many people, but the Sophists, a group of professional teachers who flourished in the mid-fifth century B.C.E., attracted a popular following. They were paid to develop and teach a practical skill: rhetoric. The arts of rhetorical persuasion were much valued in democracies in which many issues were resolved through public debate. Some Sophists also claimed to teach wisdom and virtue. They refrained from speculations about the physical universe but used reason to critique human beliefs and institutions. This led them to ponder a central issue of social life: the conflict between nature and custom. The more traditional among them argued that laws were of divine origin and in accord with nature, but others argued that laws were merely conventions—arbitrary agreements among people. The most extreme Sophists maintained that law was contrary to nature—a device to reverse the natural order and enable the weak to dominate the strong. Critias, an Athenian oligarch, went so far as to claim that the gods themselves had been invented to deter people from doing what they wanted to do. Such speculations undermined the concept of justice on which the *polis* was founded, and the later giants of philosophy, Plato and Aristotle, worked hard to refute them.

HISTORY Herodotus—"the father of history," as he has been deservedly called—was born shortly before the outbreak of the Persian Wars. The account he wrote of those wars far exceeded attempts by earlier prose writers to explain human actions. Although his *History* was completed about 425 B.C.E. and shows a few traces of Sophist influence, its spirit is that of an earlier time. Herodotus accepted, although not uncritically, information taken from legends and oracles, and he often explained events as the result of divine intervention. But his work is typical of its time in celebrating the crucial role of human intelligence in determining the course of history. Herodotus was also aware of the importance of institutions. He credited Greece's victory over Persia to the love of liberty the *polis* instilled in its citizens.

Thucydides, the historian of the Peloponnesian War, was born about 460 B.C.E. and died a few years after the end of the war he spent his life studying. His thought was influenced by the secular, human-centered, skeptical rationalism of the Sophists of the late fifth century B.C.E., and he shared the scientific attitudes that characterized the work of contemporaries such as the physician Hippocrates of Cos. Thucydides took great pains to achieve factual accuracy, and he searched his evidence for significant patterns of human behavior. He hoped that by discovering these patterns people would be able to foresee events. Since human nature was, he believed, essentially unchanging, similar circumstances ought to produce similar responses. But Thucydides admitted that the lessons of history were not always enough to guarantee success. He believed that an element of randomness (i.e., chance) helps to shape human destiny.

The Fourth Century B.C.E.

The Peloponnesian War marked the passing of the *polis* as an effective form of government. The Greeks of the fourth century B.C.E. may not fully have grasped this fact, but they did realize that their traditional way of life was threatened. Some tried to shore up the weakened structure of the *polis*; others looked for alternatives to it; and still others averted their gaze from the public arena altogether.

DRAMA   The poetry of the fourth century B.C.E. reveals the disillusionment some Greeks felt with the *polis*. Its subjects are no longer drawn from politics and public life but from the private concerns of ordinary people—the family and the interior life of the individual. Old Comedy had focused on political issues and matters of public policy. Middle and New Comedy was devoted to a humorous-realistic depiction of daily life, to intrigue, and to mild satire of domestic situations. The role of the chorus, which in a way had represented the *polis* in the drama, was very much diminished. Menander (342–291 B.C.E.), the pioneer of New Comedy, wrote domestic tragicomedy: gentle satires of the foibles of ordinary people and tales of temporarily thwarted lovers—material such as is found in modern situation comedies.

Tragedy, which drew its inspiration from the robust political life of the *polis*, declined during the fourth century B.C.E. No plays from the period have survived. Theatrical producers may have sensed a decline in qualilty, for they began to revive the plays of the previous century. Euripides' tragedies, which had rarely won top honors when first produced, finally found their audiences. More than the other great playwrights of his age, Euripides had explored the interior lives of individual human beings, and some of his late plays are more like fairy tales, fantasy adventures, or love stories than tragedies.

SCULPTURE   The same movement away from the grand, the ideal, and the general—and toward the ordinary, the real, and the individual—is apparent in the evolution of Greek sculpture. This becomes obvious when the work of Polycleitus (ca. 450–440 B.C.E.) is compared with that of Praxiteles (ca. 340–330 B.C.E.) or Lysippus (ca. 330 B.C.E.).

The striding god from Artemisium is a bronze statue dating from about 460 B.C.E. It was found in the sea near Artemisium, the northern tip of the large Greek island of Euboea, and is now on display in the Athens archaeological museum. Exactly whom he represents is not known. Some have thought him to be Poseidon holding a trident; others believe that he is Zeus hurling a thunderbolt. In either case, he is a splendid representative of the early Classical period of Greek sculpture.   National Archaeological Museum, Athens

Philosophy and the Crisis of the *Polis*

SOCRATES   The life and teachings of Socrates (469–399 B.C.E.) reflect an early awareness of the crises that were developing for the *polis*. Socrates recognized the difficulties and criticized the shortcomings of the *polis*. He did not take an active role in politics, but he did not abandon the *polis* ideal. He fought as a soldier to defend Athens, obeyed its laws, and sought a sound, rational foundation for its values.

Since Socrates wrote nothing, our knowledge of him depends on the reports of his disciples, Plato and Xenophon, and on the work of later commentators. As a young man, he supposedly took an interest in the theories about the physical world developed by the first philosophers, but his concern soon shifted to the interior world—

to the explication of the processes of human understanding and decision making. Unlike some Sophists, he believed in the existence of truth and the power of reason to search it out.

Socrates sought truth by cross-examining people who were reputed to have it: that is, those who knew something—craftsmen, poets, and politicians. His conversations with them always ended the same way—by demonstrating that, apart from technical information and skills, they had little knowledge of the fundamental principles of human behavior. It is not surprising that Athenians, whose opinions were challenged by his rigorous logical critiques, concluded that he was trying to undermine their confidence in the beliefs and values on which the *polis* was based. Socrates also made enemies by failing to conceal his contempt for democracy—a system of government that he believed empowered the ignorant to make important decisions about things of which they knew nothing.

In 399 B.C.E. Athens, its confidence shaken by the loss of the Peloponnesian War, decided that it could no longer tolerate Socrates. He was condemned to death on charges that implied that he was undercutting the traditions on which the survival of the *polis* depended. He was given a chance to escape, but Plato says that he refused because of his respect for the laws of the city. In taking this stand Socrates demonstrated that he was not a Sophist or an irresponsible skeptic. He accepted that the laws of the *polis* were more than arbitrary human conventions that could be ignored whenever they proved inconvenient. What he had been unable to prove by rational argument he witnessed to by powerful example.

THE CYNICS Socrates had advocated concern with personal morality and the state of one's soul, disdain of worldly pleasure and wealth, and withdrawal from political life. After his death these ideas were developed as a program for a group of extremist philosophers called Cynics. Antisthenes (ca. 455–360 B.C.E.), a follower of Socrates, was the first, but the most famous was Diogenes of Sinope (ca. 400–325 B.C.E.), whom Plato described as Socrates gone mad.

Diogenes believed that happiness was achieved by satisfying natural needs in the simplest and most direct way. He dismissed all the constraints of civilized behavior as nothing more than arbitrary social convention and reveled in conduct that illustrated his contempt for the artifice of civilization and society. He begged for his bread, wore rags, lived in a tub, performed intimate acts of personal hygiene in public, and ridiculed religious observances.

Although the Cynics claimed to follow Socrates, they contradicted some of his beliefs. Socrates said that virtue was a matter of knowledge—that people do wrong only through ignorance of what is right. The Cynics, on the other hand, argued that wisdom and happiness derived from habits of living, not from knowledge. Where Socrates had criticized but ultimately defended the *polis*, the Cynics abandoned it. When Diogenes was asked about his citizenship, he answered that he was *kosmopolites*, "a citizen of the world."

PLATO Plato (429–347 B.C.E.), the most important of Socrates' associates, is the prime example of the pupil who becomes greater than his master. Plato was the first systematic philosopher—the first to lay out a consistent worldview that provided a context for all fundamental questions. He was also a brilliant writer. His twenty-six philosophical discussions—most cast in the form of dialogues—are artistic masterpieces that make the analysis of complicated philosophical ideas dramatic and entertaining.

Plato, like other members of his aristocratic Athenian family, planned a career in politics, but Socrates' execution discouraged him. He made two trips to Sicily, where he hoped that the tyrants of Syracuse (Dionysius I and II) would allow him to guide them in building a model state. When this project failed, he returned to Athens to found the Academy (386 B.C.E.), a center for research and a school for training statesmen and citizens. The Academy survived until a Christian government closed it in the sixth century C.E.

Like Socrates and unlike the radical Sophists, Plato believed in the *polis*. He thought that it was consistent with human nature and was an instrument for creating good people. Socrates' insistence that virtue was a kind of knowledge led Plato, however, to reject democracy as an ideal form of government for a *polis*. Justice, Plato said, consists in each man doing that to which he is best suited by nature. The true knowledge on which virtue is based is beyond most people. It is *episteme* (i.e., science), a wisdom achieved by only a few highly trained and specially gifted individuals. Plato believed that these persons should serve society as "philosopher kings." Only they could be trusted with political power, for only they were capable of subordinating private interests to the good of the community. Only they could restore harmony to the *polis* by eliminating the causes of strife: private property, the family, and every personal concern that distracts individuals from the public good.

Concern for the redemption of the *polis* was central to Plato's philosophy. Since he believed that the survival of the *polis* depended on its ability to produce good citizens, he felt that he had to define goodness—and since he believed that goodness was a kind of knowledge, he had to work out a theory of knowledge. This led him into the realm of metaphysics and culminated in the birth of systematic philosophy.

ARISTOTLE   Aristotle (384–322 B.C.E.) was born at Stagirus in the Chalcidice, the son of the physician to the court of Macedon. As a youth he studied in Plato's Academy and remained in Athens until Plato's death. He then went to Assos and Mytilene in Asia Minor to conduct research in marine biology. In 342 B.C.E., he accepted an appointment as tutor to Alexander, son of King Philip of Macedon, and in 336 B.C.E., he returned to Athens to found his own school, the Lyceum or the *Peripatos*, a reference to a covered walkway on its grounds. (It was this that caused Aristotle's disciples to be dubbed the Peripatetics). After Alexander's death in 323 B.C.E., the Greeks turned against the Macedonians, and Aristotle found it wise to leave Athens. He died at Chalcis in Euboea a year later.

The program of the Lyceum was different from that of the Academy. Plato's students were preoccupied with mathematics; Aristotle was interested in gathering, ordering, and analyzing data relating to all fields of human knowledge. He and his students assembled collections of materials to support various scientific studies. The range of his interests is astonishing. He wrote on logic, physics, astronomy, biology, ethics, rhetoric, literary criticism, and politics.

Aristotle began the study of every subject the same way—by collecting empirical evidence. Sometimes the evidence was physical; sometimes it was anecdotal—a garnering of common opinions. The evidence was then rationally analyzed to see if it could be consistently explained and if it revealed any general principles. Like Plato, Aristotle viewed things teleologically; that is, he explained things in terms of their ultimate ends or purposes. Plato described these ends as universal ideas or forms—transcendent realities that shaped the world but which people could not directly experience. Aristotle, however, inferred the purposes of most things from their behavior in the world. The most striking characteristic of his philosophy is its common sense. In his view, matter existed to achieve an end, and it evolved until it fully realized the form (i.e., the idea) that made it intelligible as what it was. Being was a constant process of moving from matter to form, from potentiality to actuality.

This metaphysical model is at the heart of Aristotle's thinking about the *polis*. He rejected the Sophists' claim that social life was a convention that frustrated the true nature of individuals. He believed that the *polis* was natural because it was necessary for the realization of human potential—that is, life as a social being. Since human survival and happiness depended on group life, the fundamental purpose of the *polis* was not economic or military. It was moral. It made life good.

Aristotle was less interested in theorizing about the perfect state than in designing the best state practically possible. To determine what this was, he assembled a collection of 158 constitutions. (Only the *Constitution of the Athenians* has come down to us.) He concluded that a *politeia*—not the best constitution but the one best suited to most states—was characterized by moderation. It was dominated neither by the rich nor the poor but the middle class. A large middle class was essential for political stability, for this class was not tempted to the arrogance of the rich nor infected by the malice that resentment of their circumstances creates in the poor. Stable constitutions were also usually "mixed"—that is, they blended aspects of democracy and oligarchy.

All the political thinkers of the fourth century B.C.E. recognized that the *polis* was in danger, and all hoped to save it. All recognized the economic and social troubles that threatened it, but few made such realistic proposals for its reform as Aristotle. It is ironic that the ablest defense of the *polis* came on the eve of its demise.

The Hellenistic World

The term *Hellenistic* was coined in the nineteenth century to describe the period in Greek history that began when a Macedonian dynasty conquered both Greece and the Persian Empire. This event brought elements of Greek and Middle Eastern cultures together to create a new, more cosmopolitan civilization.

The Macedonian Conquest

The quarrels among the Greeks made them vulnerable to conquest by Macedon, the northernmost of the mainland Greek states. By Greek standards Macedon was a backward, semibarbaric land. It had no *poleis* but was ruled by a king who, like Homer's Agamemnon, depended upon the cooperation of his nation's powerful aristocratic families. Hampered by constant wars with barbarian tribes on its northern frontier, internal strife, loose organization, and lack of money, Macedon played no great part in Greek affairs until the fourth century B.C.E.

PHILIP OF MACEDON The Macedonian king who conquered Greece was Philip II (359–336 B.C.E.). As a youth, Philip had spent several years (367–364 B.C.E.) as a hostage in Thebes. There he learned much about Greek politics and warfare under the tutelage of Epaminondas, the general who defeated Sparta. Philip's talent and training made him the ablest king in Macedonian history. He solidified his hold on his throne, pacified the tribes on his frontiers, and challenged Athens' dominance of the northern Aegean. When the conquest of Amphipolis gave him control of the gold and silver mines of Mount Pangaeus, he used this wealth to elevate the level of Macedonian culture. He founded new cities, won friends abroad, and turned his army into the world's finest fighting force.

THE MACEDONIAN ARMY Philip's army was more professional than the amateur armies of citizen-soldiers who fought for the individual *poleis*. Its infantry was recruited from Macedon's sturdy farming class and feisty hill people. Infantrymen were armed with thirteen-foot pikes instead of the *hoplite's* more common nine-foot weapon. This enabled them to spread out and form a more open, flexible phalanx than was customary. The Macedonian cavalry was recruited from the aristocracy. Its members, the "Companions," lived with the king and developed a special loyalty to him. Philip also employed mercenaries who knew the latest tactics and were familiar with the most sophisticated siege machinery. Altogether, he could field an army of about 40,000 men.

THE INVASION OF GREECE The Greeks themselves gave Philip the excuse he needed to intervene in their affairs. The people of Thessaly invited Philip to assist them in a war against the Phocians. Philip won the war, treacherously occupied Thessaly, and marched on Thrace to take control of the Aegean's northern coast and the Hellespont.

These actions threatened the vital interests of Athens, but although Athens had a formidable fleet of 300 ships, it was not the Athens of 350 B.C.E. or the Athens of Pericles. Its population was smaller than in the fifth century B.C.E., and it had no empire from which to draw funds to support a major war. Consequently, the Athenians were uncertain how to respond to Philip.

Eubulus, a financial official and conservative political leader, favored a cautious policy of cooperation with Philip in the hope that his aims were limited and posed no real threat to Athens. Isocrates (436–338 B.C.E.), the head of an important rhetorical school in Athens, saw Philip as the savior of Greece. He believed that Philip could provide the unity and leadership the Greeks needed to launch a Panhellenic campaign against Persia and solve the economic, social, and political problems that had brought poverty and civil strife to Greece since the end of the Peloponnesian War. The leading opponent to appeasement of Macedon was Demosthenes (384–322 B.C.E.), one of the greatest orators in Greek history. He was convinced that Philip was a danger to Greece, and he ultimately persuaded Athens to join Thebes in opposing Macedonian expansion. In 338 B.C.E., a cavalry charge that Philip's eighteen-year-old son Alexander led in the battle of Chaeronea defeated the allied forces and made Philip master of Greece.

THE MACEDONIAN GOVERNMENT OF GREECE The Macedonian settlement of Greek affairs was not as harsh as many had feared. Athens was spared on condition that it accept Macedonian leadership, and Macedonian garrisons were stationed around Greece to guard against rebellions. In 338 B.C.E. Philip called representatives of the Greek states to Corinth where he announced the formation of a federation, the League of Corinth. The constitution of the league promised autonomy, freedom from tribute and garrisons, and cooperation in suppressing piracy and civil war. This was an arrangement that enabled the Greeks to submit with dignity to Macedonian occupation. The defeat at Chaeronea had ended Greek freedom and the autonomy of the *polis.*

Philip chose Corinth as the seat of his new confederacy because it was at Corinth that the Greeks had gathered almost 150 years earlier to plan their strategy for the Persian Wars. It was there also, in 337 B.C.E., that Philip announced his intent to restore the glory of Greece by renewing war with Persia. This was a promise he failed to keep, for in the spring of 336 B.C.E., as he was about to launch this campaign, he was assassinated.

Alexander the Great

THE CONQUEST OF THE PERSIAN EMPIRE   Alexander III (356–323 B.C.E.), who came to be known as "the Great," was only twenty when he ascended his father's throne, but he was determined to carry out his father's plan for invading Persia. The Persian Empire was vast and its resources enormous, but it was not an impossible target. Its size and the diversity of its subjects made it hard to control, and its rulers struggled constantly with threats to their far-flung frontiers and intrigues within their court. At the time of Philip II's death in 336 B.C.E., Persia's new king, Darius III, was inexperienced. But with a navy that dominated the sea, a huge army, and vast wealth, Darius was a formidable opponent.

In 334 B.C.E. Alexander crossed the Hellespont into Asia. His army consisted of only about 30,000 infantry and 5,000 cavalry. He had little money, and his opponents had command of the sea. He could not risk heading far inland until he had neutralized the Persian navy, but he needed a quick victory to inspire his men with confidence in his leadership and to win the booty needed to pay them. Memnon, the commander of the Persian navy, proposed an excellent strategy for defeating the Greeks: retreat, scorch the earth, avoid all but guerrilla engagements, and deprive the enemy of supplies. Pride, however, led the Persians to reject his advice and give Alexander what he hoped for.

The Persians offered Alexander battle at the Granicus River on the coast of Asia Minor. Alexander led a cavalry charge across the river into the teeth of the enemy and nearly lost his life. His courage, however, inspired his soldiers, and the victory opened all of Asia Minor to conquest by the Greeks.

In 333 B.C.E., Alexander marched out of Asia Minor into Syria to meet the main Persian army under Darius. At Issus, Alexander led a cavalry charge that broke the Persian line, but instead of pursuing Darius as he retreated inland, Alexander continued south along the coast, taking Persia's naval bases. When he arrived in Egypt, he was greeted as liberator and proclaimed pharaoh. Like all of Egypt's divine kings, he was proclaimed a son of Re, the god who, as head of the Egyptian pantheon, the Greeks equated with Zeus.

In the spring of 331 B.C.E., Alexander marched into Mesopotamia to confront an army Darius had assembled at Gaugamela (near the ancient Assyrian city of Nineveh). Once again the Persian line broke, and Darius was forced to flee. Alexander occupied Babylon, and in January 330 B.C.E., he entered Persepolis, the Persian capital. Conquest of Persia's treasure cities ended Alexander's financial problems, and the gold he showered on his troops put vast sums of money into circulation—a development whose economic effects were felt for centuries.

Since the new regime could not be secure while Darius was at large, Alexander again set out to capture him. But the Persian nobles deprived the Greeks of that prize. Having lost faith in Darius, they killed him and proclaimed Bessus, one of his relatives, his successor. Alexander pursued Bessus into the east, captured him, and pushed on to the frontiers of India.

Near Samarkand, in the land of the Scythians, he founded the city of Alexandria Eschate ("Farthest Alexandria"), one of many cities Alexander created as part of a plan to secure the future of the empire. Alexander hoped to hold the empire he was winning by scattering Greeks through it and amalgamating its diverse peoples. To set an example, he took his first wife, a princess named Roxane from a remote province called Bactria. He also added 30,000 of her young countrymen to his army.

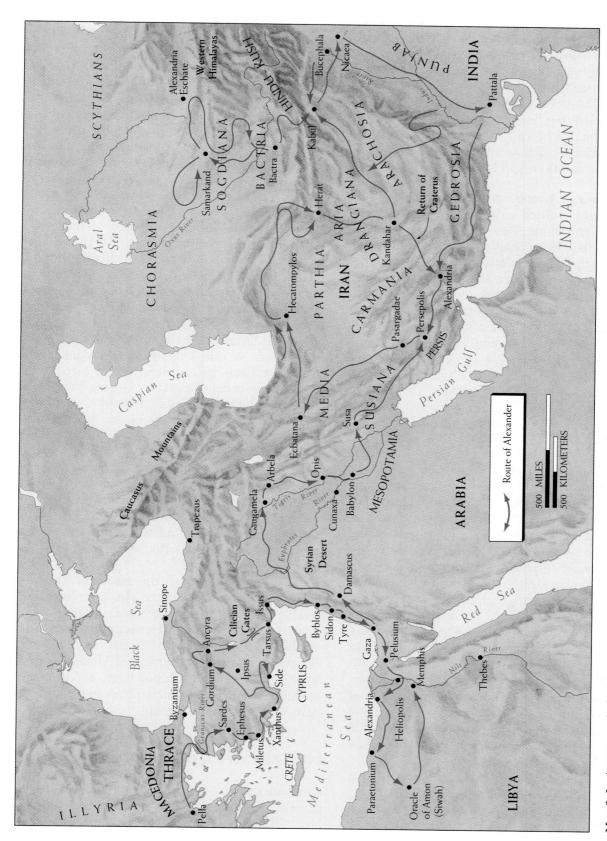

MAP 3–2 ALEXANDER'S CAMPAIGNS *Starting from the Macedonian capital at Pella, Alexander marched his army to the Indus Valley before they persuaded him to return to Babylon where he died.*

55

In 327 B.C.E., the Greeks crossed the Khyber Pass and entered the territory of modern Pakistan. Porus, the native king, was subdued, but Alexander still was not content. He ordered the army farther east to find the river called Ocean that Greek geographers believed encircled the world. At this point his exhausted men mutinied and demanded that he take them home for a rest. By the spring of 324 B.C.E., they were back at the Persian Gulf and celebrating, in true Macedonian style, with a drunken spree.

THE DEATH OF ALEXANDER Alexander, at age thirty-three, was filled with plans for the future, but in Babylon in June 323 B.C.E., he succumbed to a fever and died. He quickly became the subject of myth, legend, romance, and controversy among historians. Some have seen him as a man of grand and noble vision who transcended the narrow limits of Greek and Macedonian ethnocentrism, a visionary who sought to create a great world state based on the common humanity all peoples share. Others have depicted him as a calculating despot, given to drunken brawls, brutality, and murder. The truth probably lies in between.

The Successors

Nobody was prepared for Alexander's sudden death, and he had no obvious successor. He was one of history's greatest generals and a man of rare organizational talent, but even he would have had difficulty holding together the vast empire he had created. His nearest adult male relative, a weak-minded half-brother, could never have filled his shoes. Although Roxane, his queen, bore him a son soon after his death, an infant heir could not administer Alexander's legacy. The Macedonian generals, therefore, divided up responsibility for ruling the empire—allegedly only until the boy came of age. Conflicting ambitions soon had them at each other's throats, and in the battles that followed all of the direct members of the Macedonian royal house were destroyed. The deaths of Roxane and her son in 310 B.C.E. removed the last restraints on the surviving governors, and in 306 B.C.E. and 305 B.C.E. they declared the lands they ruled independent kingdoms.

Three Macedonian dynasties divided up Alexander's empire. Ptolemy I (ca. 367–283 B.C.E.) claimed Egypt and founded its thirty-first dynasty. (The famous queen Cleopatra, who died in 30 B.C.E., was the last of the Ptolemies.) Seleucus I (ca. 358–280 B.C.E.) created the Seleucid dynasty that ruled Mesopotamia, and Antigonus I (382–301 B.C.E.) established the Antigonid family that reigned over Asia Minor and Macedon.

For about seventy-five years after Alexander's death the world economy expanded. The money that Alexander had loosed to circulate increased the level of economic activity, and the opening of vast new territories to Greek trade, the increased demand for Greek products, the enhanced availability of goods, and the enlightened economic policies of the Hellenistic kings all helped the growth of commerce. Problems of overpopulation on the Greek mainland were also solved by opportunities to emigrate to new cities in the east.

The new prosperity was not evenly distributed. Urban Greeks, Macedonians, and Hellenized natives—the upper and middle classes—lived comfortable, even luxurious, lives, while the standard of living for rural laborers declined. The independent small farmers who had built the early *poleis* disappeared. Arable land was consolidated into large plantations, and farmers were reduced to the status of dependent peasants. During prosperous times their lot was bearable, but the costs of continuing wars and the effects of the inflation produced by the influx of Persian gold steadily eroded their position. Kings bore down heavily on the middle class, which shifted the burden to the peasants and the city laborers. These people responded by slowing their work and by striking. In parts of Greece, where economic pressures brought clashes between rich and poor and demands for the abolition of debt and the redistribution of land, civil war returned.

Internal tensions and the strain of endemic warfare rendered the Hellenistic kingdoms vulnerable to invasion. By the middle of the second century B.C.E. they had all, except for Egypt, succumbed to conquest by the Italian city of Rome. The two centuries that separated Alexander from the Roman Empire had, however, not been unproductive. A powerful new phase in Greek civilization had begun to unfold.

Hellenistic Culture

Alexander the Great's life marked a turning point in the history of Greek literature, philosophy, religion, and art. His empire and its successor kingdoms ended the role that the *polis* had played in shaping Greek culture. *Poleis* continued to exist throughout the Hellenistic period, but they were mere shadows of the vital *poleis* of the Hellenic era. Hellenistic cities were not free, sovereign states but municipal towns submerged within great military empires.

As the freedoms central to the life of the *polis* faded, Greeks lost interest in finding political solutions for their problems. They abandoned public affairs and resorted to religion, philosophy, and magic for help in dealing with their private hopes and fears. The confident humanism of the fifth century B.C.E. gave way to a kind of resignation to fate, a recognition of helplessness before forces too great for humans to manage.

Philosophy

Athens survived as the center of philosophical studies during the Hellenistic era. Plato's Academy and Aristotle's Lyceum continued to operate and were joined by new schools advocating the popular new philosophies of Epicureanism and Stoicism.

The Lyceum abandoned the scientific interests of its founder and became a center for literary and historical studies. The Academy was even more radically transformed. It endorsed Skepticism, a critique of the weaknesses of all schools of philosophy that led to the conclusion that nothing could be known. Skeptics urged their students, in lieu of better options, to accept conventional morality and not to try to change the world. The Cynics drew a more radical conclusion from the inevitability of human ignorance. They denounced convention and advocated a life in accordance with nature's cruder impulses. Neither of these views appealed much to the middle-class city-dwellers of the third century B.C.E. who were searching for the kind of dignity and meaning that the *polis* had provided for the lives of their ancestors.

THE EPICUREANS Like many thinkers of his day, Epicurus of Athens (342–271 B.C.E.) doubted that human beings could obtain knowledge. The atomists, Democritus and Leucippus, convinced him that the world was nothing more than a swirl of physical particles continually falling through a void. Knowledge was nothing more than a stream of impressions that atoms left on human sense organs. Since Epicurus believed that the atoms did not obey any laws of motion but swerved in arbitrary, unpredictable ways, he concluded that experience of their movements could not help anyone find truth or certainty. Philosophers, he argued, should abandon pursuit of knowledge of the world and seek insights that would promote human happiness. Epicurus believed that philosophy could free people from things like the fear of death. If people were helped to understand that death was merely the dispersal of the atoms of a body and soul, they would realize that nothing of themselves survived to suffer pain or loss. The proper pursuit of humankind, Epicurus argued, was pleasure—in the sense of *ataraxia*, a state of being undisturbed by any extreme feeling, either good or bad. The happiest people were those who withdrew from the world, avoided business concerns, and stayed free of the duties of family and public life. Epicurus's ideal was the genteel, disciplined selfishness of intellectual men of means. It was a dream not calculated to be widely attractive.

THE STOICS Soon after Epicurus began teaching in Athens, Zeno of Citium (335–263 B.C.E.) established the Stoic school, which was named for the *stoa poikile,* the Painted Portico in the Athenian marketplace where Zeno taught his disciples. Zeno and his successors owed much, by way of the Cynics, to Socrates and to Eastern thinkers.

Like the Epicureans, the Stoics sought the happiness of the individual, but Stoic philosophy relied more on religious images. Stoics believed that human fulfillment lay in living in harmony with nature, and Stoics claimed that nature was a manifestation of divine *logos,* an eternal principle of reason. Every human being had a spark of this divine "fire," and at death it returned to its source in the eternal spirit. Like individual living beings, the whole world was alive and faced periodic destruction and rebirth.

Stoics held that humans experienced happiness when they lived virtuous lives. A sense of fulfillment was produced by living in accordance with natural law. This required one to understand which things in life were good and evil and which were morally "indifferent." Things such as prudence, justice, courage, and temperance were good. Things such as folly, injustice, and cowardice were evil. Some things—such as life, health, pleasure, beauty, strength, and wealth—

were morally neutral, for by themselves they did not produce either happiness or misery. Misery was the result of passion, a disease of the soul that arose from attaching the self to the wrong things. Happy people achieved *apatheia*, freedom from passion.

The Stoics saw the world as a single *polis* in which all people were equally children of God. Despite the fact that politics invited preoccupation with things that were morally indifferent, many Stoics led active public lives. Their intent was to live in accordance with the divine will by fatalistically accepting their places in life and dispassionately playing out the roles in which they found themselves. This fit well with the reality of post-Alexandrian societies in which docile submission was more important than active participation.

Literature

Alexandria became the center of literary production in the third and second centuries B.C.E. Its intellectuals, unlike the creative thinkers who were citizens of a *polis*, were more preoccupied with past than current affairs, for they understood that they had little political influence. The Ptolemies supported a "museum," a great research institute that collected Greek literature of every kind for scholars to edit and interpret. Some of this work was dry and petty, but it helped to preserve the monuments of classical literature.

Architecture and Sculpture

Hellenistic kings could afford to be lavish patrons of artists and architects as well as scholars. They built many new cities and rebuilt old ones, usually on the efficient grid plan introduced in the fifth century B.C.E. by Hippodamus of Miletus. The famous artists who traveled the world, fulfilling royal commissions, created a kind of uniform international style. It featured sentimental, emotional realism rather than the idealism that had been popular during the age of the *polis*.

Mathematics and Science

The most spectacular and remarkable intellectual achievements of the Hellenistic age were in mathematics and science. The scholars of Alexandria amassed the greater part of the scientific knowledge available to the Western world

This is a Roman copy of one of the masterpieces of Hellenistic sculpture, the Laocoon. According to legend, Laocoon was a priest who warned the Trojans not to take the Greeks' wooden horse within their city. This sculpture depicts his punishment. Great serpents sent by the goddess Athena, who was on the side of the Greeks, devoured Laocoon and his sons before the horrified people of Troy.   Musei Vaticani

until the scientific revolution of the sixteenth and seventeenth centuries B.C.E.

Euclid's *Elements*, which was written early in the third century B.C.E., remained the standard textbook of plane and solid geometry until recent times. Archimedes of Syracuse (ca. 287–212 B.C.E.) explored the principles of the lever in mechanics and invented hydrostatics. Heraclides of Pontus (ca. 390–310 B.C.E.) advanced a heliocentric theory of the universe that was fully developed by Aristarchus of Samos (ca. 310–230 B.C.E.). Unfortunately, however, since Hellenistic technology could not provide data to confirm their intuitions, they did not take hold. A geocentric model advanced by Hipparchus of Nicaea (born ca. 190 B.C.E.) and refined by Ptolemy of Alexandria (second century C.E.) acquired currency and remained dominant until the work of Copernicus in the sixteenth century

C.E. The scholars of the age knew that Earth was round, and Eratosthenes of Cyrene (ca. 275–195 B.C.E.) calculated its circumference within about 200 miles. His maps were more accurate than those that were standard in the Middle Ages.

In Perspective

The achievements of Greece's Classical Period were unparalleled. To a great degree they sprang from the unique social environment created by the poleis, *the independent city-states. Democratic imperial Athens nurtured the greatest artists and intellectuals. The freedoms Athens gave its citizens bred respect for the human individual and curiosity about human potential. Philosophy, science, drama, and history were invented to explore this potential, and a naturalistic style of art was developed to celebrate the ideal human form.*

The Classical Period ended when the polis *was replaced by the great empires of the Hellenistic Age. Hellenistic civilization spread, assimilated influences from other cultures, and became a cosmopolitan phenomenon. By bringing diverse peoples together it prepared the way for Rome's empire.*

REVIEW QUESTIONS

1. How did Athens acquire an empire during the fifth century B.C.E.? Did Athens' empire offer any advantages to its subjects? Why was there resistance to Athens' efforts to unify the Greek world in the fifth and fourth centuries B.C.E.?
2. What caused the Great Peloponnesian War? What strategies did Athens and Sparta hope would bring them victory? Why did Sparta win?
3. What were the tensions that characterized Greek life in the Classical Period, and how were they reflected in its art, literature, and philosophy? How does Hellenistic art differ from art of the Classical Period?
4. Although Athens, Sparta, and Thebes each in turn tried to unite and rule the city-states of Greece, each failed. Why? What can you conclude from their examples that successful government requires?
5. How and why did Philip II conquer Greece? Why was Athens unable to stop him? Was his success due to Macedon's strength or to the weaknesses of the Greek city-states?
6. What were the consequences of Alexander the Great's early death? What were his lasting achievements? Did he consciously promote Greek civilization, or was he only an egomaniac devoted to endless conquest?

SUGGESTED READINGS

A. B. BOSWORTH, *Conquest and Empire: The Reign of Alexander the Great* (1988). An excellent, tough-minded account.

J. BUCKLER, *The Theban Hegemony, 371–362 B.C.E.* (1980). A study of Thebes at the height of its power.

W. BURKERT, *Greek Religion* (1985). A fine general study.

E. FANTHAM, H. FOLEY, N. KAMPEN, S. POMEROY, and H. A. SHAPIRO, *Women in the Classical World* (1994). A valuable survey based on written and visual evidence.

Y. GARLAN, *Slavery in Ancient Greece* (1988). An up-to-date survey.

P. GREEN, *From Alexander to Actium* (1990). A brilliant new synthesis of the Hellenistic period.

D. KAGAN, *Pericles of Athens and the Birth of Athenian Democracy* (1991). An account of the life and times of the great Athenian statesman.

D. KAGAN, *The Outbreak of the Peloponnesian War* (1969). A study of the period from the foundation of the Delian League to the coming of the Peloponnesian War that argues that war could have been avoided.

J. J. POLLITT, *Art in the Hellenistic Age* (1986). An extraordinary analysis that places the art in its historical and intellectual context.

S. POMERY, *Families in Classical and Hellenistic Greece* (1998). A valuable and thorough study of the Greek family.

B. S. STRAUSS, *Athens after the Peloponnesian War* (1987). An excellent discussion of Athens' recovery and history in the fourth century B.C.E.

G. VLASTOS, *Socrates: Ironist and Moral Philosopher* (1991). A study of the father of Western ethical philosophy.

F. W. WALBANK, *The Hellenistic World* (1981). A solid history.

Chapter 4

Rome: From Republic to Empire

Prehistoric Italy

The Etruscans
Dominion
Cultural Influences

Royal Rome
Government
The Family
Women
Clientage
Patricians and Plebeians

The Republic
Constitution
The Conquest of Italy
Rome and Carthage
The Republic's Conquest of the
    Hellenistic World

**Civilization in the Early
Roman Republic**
Religion
Education
Slavery

**Roman Imperialism:
The Late Republic**
The Aftermath of Conquest
The Gracchi
Marius and Sulla

The Fall of the Republic
Pompey, Crassus, Caesar, and Cicero
Formation of the First Triumvirate
Julius Caesar and His Government
    of Rome
The Second Triumvirate and the
    Emergence of Octavian

KEY TOPICS

- The emergence of the Roman Republic
- The development of the republican constitution
- Roman expansion and imperialism
- The character of Roman society in the republican era
- The fall of the republic

The Romans, who started with nothing but a small village in central Italy, achieved remarkable things. They united the peoples of the Western world and maintained the longest period of peace in Western history. By adapting and spreading aspects of Greek culture through their empire, the Romans created a universal Graeco-Roman tradition that remains at the heart of Western civilization to this day.

Much of what we know of the Etruscans comes from their funerary art. This sculpture of an Etruscan couple is part of a sarcophagus. Erich Lessing/Art Resource, N.Y.

Prehistoric Italy

Italy's cultural evolution began slowly. The Paleolithic era lingered in Italy until 2500 B.C.E., and Italy did not feel the effects of the Bronze Age until 1500 B.C.E. About 1000 B.C.E., the Umbrians, Sabines, Samnites, and Latins—immigrants from the East whose Italic languages gave the peninsula its name—pioneered Italy's Iron Age. By 800 B.C.E., they had occupied the highland pastures of the Apennines, the mountain range that runs the length of Italy, and had begun to challenge earlier settlers for control of the western coastal plains.

The Etruscans

About 800 B.C.E., a mysterious people whose language was not Italic settled in Etruria (modern Tuscany) on a plain west of the Apennines between the Arno and Tiber Rivers. Although the origin of the Etruscan people is unknown, aspects of their civilization suggest Eastern roots. They had a powerful influence on the development of Rome.

Dominion

Etruscan communities were independent, self-governing city-states loosely linked in a religious confederation. Aristocratic landowners replaced kings in most cities and set up governments run by councils and annually elected magistrates. The Etruscans subjugated the peoples they conquered in Italy and became the militarized ruling class of their nation. They took to the sea as traders and pirates and competed with the other maritime powers of the western Mediterranean, the Carthaginians of north Africa and Italy's Greek colonists.

In the seventh and sixth centuries B.C.E., the Etruscans extended their power north to Italy's Po Valley and overseas to the islands of Corsica and Elba. They also moved south into Latium (a region that included the small town of Rome) and Campania (a plain that the Greeks of Naples had begun to colonize). These conquests were the work of independent Etruscan chieftains who rarely supported each other. As a result, they were short-lived.

Etruscan power peaked before 500 B.C.E. By 400 B.C.E., Celts from Gaul (modern France) had driven the Etruscans from the Po Valley, an area the Romans later called Cisalpine Gaul (i.e., "This-side-of-the-Alps" Gaul). Gradually the cities of Etruria lost their independence. Their language ceased to be a living tongue, but their culture was not forgotten. It had a profound effect on Rome.

Cultural Influences

Roman religion was powerfully influenced by Etruscan culture. The Romans, like the Etruscans, believed that innumerable supernatural beings had the power to intervene in human affairs. The Romans were convinced that human survival depended on understanding and placating these spirits—many of whom were evil. To divine the wills of these mysterious forces, they relied on Etruscan rites for interpreting the omens of the gods.

Roman society contrasted with Greek society in the greater freedom that it accorded women. This, too, may have been the result of Etruscan influences. Unlike Greek women, Etruscan wives appeared in public. They were guests at banquets with their husbands. They attended and participated in athletic contests. Many could read and write. Tomb inscriptions mention the mother as well as the father of the deceased, and Etruscan art depicts husbands and wives in poses that suggest respectful, loving relationships.

MAP 4–1 ANCIENT ITALY   *This map indicates the geographical positions of Rome and its neighbors in the period before Roman expansion.*

Royal Rome

The Latin peoples who settled Rome may have been attracted by its location. Rome was established fifteen miles from the sea at the point where the Tiber River emerges from the foothills of the Apennines. Many trails converged here, for just southwest of Rome's Capitoline Hill an island made the Tiber fordable. Rome's site destined the city to become the center for Italy's inland communication and trade.

Government

Rome's potential was not realized until the sixth century B.C.E., when Etruscan kings established themselves in Rome and conquered most of Latium. Although one family monopolized the royal office, Roman kingship was technically elective. The Roman Senate, an aristocratic council, had to approve a candidate for the throne, and only the assembly of the Roman people could bestow on him his unique power—the *imperium*, the right to enforce commands by fines, arrests, and corporal or capital punishment. The king was Rome's chief priest, high judge, and supreme military leader.

According to legend, Rome's Senate originated when Romulus, Rome's founder, chose 100 of Rome's leading men to advise him. The early Senate had no formal executive or legislative authority. It met only when the king convened it to ask for advice. In practice, however, the Senate was very influential. It was composed of the most powerful men in the state—men a king could not safely ignore.

The curiate assembly, an organization to which all citizens belonged, was the third organ of government. It met only when summoned by the king, and he set its agenda and decided who could address it. Its job was to listen to and ratify the king's decrees. Romans voted, not as individuals, but as members of groups. Citizens were registered in thirty groups, and each group had a single vote that was cast according to the will of its majority.

The Family

Family organizations were the basic units of Roman society. The head of a family was its "king" in the sense that he held *imperium* over

Busts of a Roman couple from the period of the Republic. Although some have identified the individuals as Cato the Younger and his daughter Porcia, no solid evidence confirms this claim. Bust of Cato and Porcia. Roman sculpture. Vatican Museums, Vatican State. Scala/Art Resource NY

all its members. Like the king who presided over the state cult, a father supervised his family's most important religious rites, the daily worship of its ancestors. Like the king, a father had the power to execute his dependents (even his adult children) or sell them into slavery. The male head of a household had less authority over his wife, for she was protected by the family of her birth and could not be divorced unless convicted of certain serious offenses by a court of her male blood relatives. A Roman wife was greatly respected as the administrator of her husband's household. She controlled access to its storerooms, kept its accounts, supervised its slaves, and reared its children. She was also a respected adviser on all questions concerning the family.

Women

Roman society was male dominated and hierarchical. Throughout their lives women were required to have male guardians to conduct legal business on their behalf. Women could own and dispose of property and enter into contracts but only with the approval of these guardians. There were two forms of marriage in early Rome that transferred a woman from the *manus* (i.e., "hand") of her father to that of her husband. Gradually a third kind of marriage developed in which a bride's father retained his power of *manus* over her after her wedding. This gave a

woman more freedom from her husband and more inheritance rights from her father. To preserve the arrangement a woman had to spend at least three consecutive nights a year outside her husband's home.

Clientage

The head of a wealthy family could extend its influence by providing patronage to dependents called clients. Roman clientage was a formal, legally recognized institution. A patron provided a client with physical and legal protection and often with economic assistance. A client might subsist on daily handouts, receive a grant of land, become a tenant farmer, or labor on his patron's estate. In return a client fought for his patron, voted as his patron ordered, and did any jobs that were requested of him. Ambitious members of the upper classes might even become clients of great families with powerful political machines in order to further their careers.

Patricians and Plebeians

From the start of Rome's history, Roman families were divided into two hereditary classes. The patricians were the upper class, and they originally monopolized political authority. Only they could serve as priests, sit in the Senate, and hold office. The lower plebeian class may have sprung from families of small farmers, laborers, and artisans who were clients of the patricians. Wealth alone did not define the classes. Some plebeians were rich, and incompetence and bad luck sometimes impoverished patricians.

The Republic

According to Roman tradition, in 509 B.C.E. an atrocity committed by a member of the royal family sparked a revolt that drove the last Etruscan king from the city. The patricians chose not to appoint another king but to establish a republic.

Constitution

THE CONSULS   The Roman Republic had a very conservative unwritten constitution. At the start, it did little more than transfer many of the duties and trappings of monarchy to elected magistrates. Two patricians were annually chosen to be consuls and vested with *imperium*. Like the former kings, they led the army, oversaw the state religion, and sat as judges. They even used the traditional symbols of royalty—purple robes, ivory chairs, and lictors (guards who accompanied them bearing *fasces,* bundles of rods wrapped around an axe to signify the power to discipline and execute). A consul was, however, not a king, for he remained in office for only a year and had an equal, a colleague who could prevent him from taking independent action. Consular *imperium* was also limited. Consuls could execute citizens who were serving with the army outside the city, but in Rome citizens had the right to appeal all cases involving capital punishment to the popular assembly.

The checks on the consular office discouraged initiative, swift action, and change. This was what a conservative, aristocratic republic wanted. But since a divided command could create serious problems for an army in the field, the Romans usually sent only one consul into battle or assigned consuls sole command on alternate days. If this did not work, the consuls could, with the advice of the Senate, step down and appoint a single dictator. His term of office was limited to six months, but his *imperium* was valid everywhere and unlimited by any right of appeal.

These devices worked well enough for a small city whose wars were short skirmishes fought near home. But as Rome's wars grew longer and more difficult, adaptations had to be made. In 325 B.C.E. proconsulships were invented to extend the terms of consuls serving in the field. This maintained continuity of command during a long war, but it ran the risk of allowing ambitious men to monopolize political authority.

Consuls were assisted by financial officers called quaestors, and a need for more military commanders led to the introduction of other aides called praetors. A praetor's primary function was judicial, but he could also be granted a general's *imperium* and have his term of service in the field extended beyond a year. In the second half of the fifth century B.C.E., the consuls' responsibility for enrolling and keeping track of citizens was delegated to new officials, two censors. Since they determined the status and the tax liability of each citizen, they had to be men of unimpeachable reputation. They were usually senior senators who viewed the censorship as the pinnacle of their careers. By the fourth century B.C.E. censors had the right to expel from the Senate members whose conduct disgraced senatorial dignity.

THE SENATE AND THE ASSEMBLY   The Senate was the only deliberative body continuously in session in the Roman Republic. Senators were prominent patricians, often leaders of clans and patrons with many clients. The Senate controlled the state's finances and foreign policy, and its advice was not lightly ignored by magistrates or by popular assemblies.

The centuriate assembly—the name for the Roman army when it was convened to deliberate rather than fight—was the early republic's most important popular assembly. It elected the consuls and several other magistrates, voted on bills the Senate put before it, made decisions of war and peace, and served as a court of appeal for citizens convicted of serious offenses. The centuriate assembly was named for the "centuries" in which its members voted. A century was, in theory, a unit of 100 soldiers. Because each man bought his own equipment, centuries grouped citizens into classes according to wealth (i.e., according to the kind of weapons they could afford to buy). Each century cast a single vote, and votes were tallied beginning with the centuries that had the most expensive equipment, those of the cavalry.

Family Honor: A Roman Patrician with the Busts of His Ancestors

A Roman Patrician with the busts of his ancestors. First century C.E. Musei Capitolini, Rome/Scala/Art Resource NY

*N*o large Roman sculptures survive much before the first century B.C.E., but literary sources suggest that long before then it was the custom to honor leaders by erecting statues of them in public places. This statue from the late first century C.E. is of an unknown aristocrat depicted with what are probably the busts of his father and grandfather.

When a nobleman died, his heirs had a likeness of his face made in wax. At funerals men marched in processions wearing all the masks in a family's collection so that the deceased's ancestors seemed literally to attend his burial rites. The oration at the funeral praised the achievements of each famous member of the departed's family in order to inspire the young men present to strive to equal the deeds of early generations.

Since wax images did not last, by the first century B.C.E. it was customary to have them copied in marble. Roman sculptors were heavily influenced by the Etruscans and later the Hellenistic Greeks, but these commemorative statues had a style of their own. They did not depict individual character and psychology but conformed to a cultural ideal of a stern, serious nobleman who was a responsible family man and a dutiful citizen.

Sources: Polybius 6.53, Janson; *Art History,* pp. 188–190. D. Kleiner, *Roman Sculpture* (New Haven: Yale University Press, 1992).

THE STRUGGLE OF THE ORDERS   Plebeians were barred from all political and religious offices in the early days of the republic. They could not serve as judges. They did not even know the law, for the law was an oral tradition maintained by patrician magistrates. When Rome acquired new land by conquest, patricians were situated to reward themselves most generously. They dominated the assemblies and the Senate, and they refused to sanction marriages outside their caste that would have permitted at least the most wealthy plebeian families to share their privileges.

The plebeians responded to the intransigence of the patricians by launching the "struggle of the orders," a fight for political, legal, and social equality that lasted for 200 years. Plebeians had a strong position from which to negotiate with the patricians, for plebeians made up a large part of the republic's army. According to tradition, the plebeians discovered early in the republic's history how to use this to their advantage. When danger threatened, they simply withdrew from the city and refused to fight until the patricians granted them concessions.

The plebeians made progress one step at a time. They won the right to form a political organization of their own, the plebeian tribal assembly, and to elect "tribunes," officials with the power to protect plebeians from abuse by patrician magistrates. Tribunes could veto any action of a magistrate or any bill in a Roman assembly or the Senate. The protection of plebeian rights required that Rome's laws be fixed and published, and in 450 B.C.E. the first attempt to codify Rome's harsh customs resulted in something called the Twelve Tables. In 445 B.C.E. plebeians won the right to marry patricians, but they were still barred from many public offices. It was not until 367 B.C.E. that one of the consuls was allowed to be of plebeian rank. Gradually other offices, even the dictatorship and the censorship, were opened to them, and in 300 B.C.E. they were admitted to the most important priesthoods. In 287 B.C.E. the plebeians completed their triumph by securing passage of a law that made decisions of the plebeian assembly binding on all Romans.

The plebeians' victory did not make Rome a democracy. It simply cleared the way for wealthy plebeian families to enter politics and share the privileges of the patrician aristocracy. The *nobiles*, a small group of rich and powerful families of both patrician and plebeian rank, monopolized the republic's highest offices. Since there was no secret ballot, the numerous clients of the wealthy *nobiles* could easily be intimidated into voting as their patrons ordered. This permitted the great families to build political machines and maintain their holds on offices. From 233 to 133 B.C.E. twenty-six families produced 80 percent of the consuls, and ten of those families accounted for almost 50 percent of the successful candidates. Since the politically dominant families were all represented in the Senate, the Senate became the republic's chief deliberative body. The product of the struggle of the orders was, therefore, a republican constitution dominated by a senatorial aristocracy. Most Romans accepted it, for it led Rome well in the wars that won Rome an empire.

The Conquest of Italy

Not long after the birth of the republic in 509 B.C.E., a coalition of Romans, Latins, and Greeks defeated the Etruscans and drove them out of Latium. Rome's neighbor, the Etruscan city of Veii, continued to be a problem until 392 B.C.E. when Rome destroyed Veii and doubled its size by annexing Veii's territory.

Romans used both inducements and threats to come to terms with their foes and increase their military strength. If enemies could be turned into allies, their soldiers could be added to Rome's army. If they could not, their land could be annexed and redistributed to the Roman poor. This enabled them to equip themselves for military service and join the army. Thus, the Roman poor had a stake in their republic's success, which reconciled them to its aristocratic regime. When the long siege of Veii, which kept soldiers from working their farms, prompted the Romans to begin paying men for military service, this too pleased the poor and improved the quality of the army.

GALLIC INVASION OF ITALY AND ROMAN REACTION
Early in the fourth century B.C.E. Rome suffered a dramatic setback. In 387 B.C.E. the Gauls marched south from the Po Valley, defeated the Roman army, and burned Rome. The Romans, who had fled their city, had to pay a ransom to the Gauls to obtain its return. Rome quickly recovered from this humiliation, but in 340 B.C.E.

the city's Latin neighbors formed the Latin League to try to block its expansion. In 338 B.C.E. Rome defeated and dissolved the league. The terms Rome offered set a precedent for the eventual reorganization of Italy.

ROMAN POLICY TOWARD THE CONQUERED The Romans did not destroy any of the Latin cities, nor did they treat them all alike. Some were given full Roman citizenship. Others were granted municipal privileges (i.e., internal self-government, the right to intermarry and trade with Romans—but not to take part in Roman politics unless they moved to Rome and applied for citizenship). The treaties by which other states became allies of Rome differed from city to city. Some were given rights of intermarriage and commerce with Romans; some were not. (Allied states were always forbidden to exercise these rights with one another.) Some states, but not all, were allowed local autonomy. Land was taken from some but not from others. All allies supplied troops to serve in Rome's army under Roman officers, but they did not pay taxes to Rome.

The Romans planted colonies of veteran soldiers on some of the land they annexed. The colonists retained Roman citizenship and served as a permanent garrison to deter rebellion. A network of military roads was built to connect the colonies with Rome and guarantee that a Roman army could swiftly reinforce an embattled colony should it face an uprising.

The Roman settlement of Latium illustrates the strategy that led ultimately to Rome's dominance of Italy. Rome used diplomacy and force to separate enemies. It cultivated a reputation for harsh, speedy punishment of rebels. But it was also generous to those who submitted, and the status given a newly conquered city was not a permanent sentence. Loyal allies could improve their prospects and even achieve full Roman citizenship. This gave Rome's allies a sense of being colleagues rather than subjects. Consequently, most of them remained loyal even when put to severe tests.

DEFEAT OF THE SAMNITES After the struggle with the Latin League, Rome's next challenge was a series of wars with the tough mountain people of the southern Apennines, the Samnites. Some of Rome's allies joined the Samnites, as did various

Etruscans and Gauls. But most of the allies remained loyal, and by 280 B.C.E. Rome's victories over these assorted opponents had won the city mastery of central Italy.

Rome's newly expanded territory brought it into direct contact with the Greek cities of southern Italy where Roman intervention in a quarrel between two of these cities led to a war with a Greek mercenary, Pyrrhus, king of Epirus. Pyrrhus, who was probably the best general of the day, defeated the Romans twice but suffered so many casualties that he decided that he could not afford to see the war through to its conclusion. Judging his a "Pyrrhic victory" (i.e., one not worth its cost), he withdrew, leaving his Greek employers no choice but to join the Roman confederation. By 265 B.C.E. Rome ruled all of Italy south of the Po River, an area of 47,200 square miles, and its defeat of Pyrrhus had won it international recognition as a power in the Hellenistic world.

Rome and Carthage

Late in the ninth century B.C.E. the Phoenician city of Tyre had planted a colony called Carthage ("New City") on the coast of northern Africa near modern Tunis. In the sixth century B.C.E. the conquest of Tyre by the Assyrians liberated the Carthaginians to develop the opportunities offered by their strategic location. Carthage had an excellent harbor and rich lands, which it worked with slave labor.

In the sixth century B.C.E. Carthage's domain expanded westward along the coast of northern Africa past Gibraltar and eastward into Libya. Parts of southern Spain, Sardinia, Corsica, Malta, the Balearic Islands, and western Sicily were also brought into the Carthaginian Empire. Their native peoples served in the Carthaginian army and navy and paid tribute to Carthage. Carthage also claimed exclusive rights to trade in the western Mediterranean.

Rome and Carthage became entangled when Hiero, tyrant of Syracuse, attacked the Sicilian city of Messana. Messana was strategically important, for it commanded the straits between Italy and Sicily. A band of Italian mercenaries who called themselves Mamertines ("Sons of Mars") had seized the city, and Hiero wanted to evict them. The Mamertines asked Carthage for help in fending him off, and Carthage agreed. But

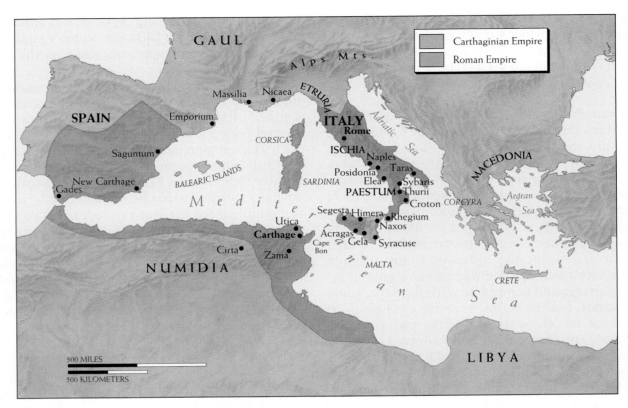

MAP 4–2   THE WESTERN MEDITERRANEAN AREA DURING THE RISE OF ROME   *This map illustrates the theater of conflict between Rome and Carthage in the third century* B.C.E.

the Mamertines then tried to check Carthage by also inviting the Romans to send them aid. Rome realized that if it did not intervene, it was ceding control of the straits and of Sicily to Carthage. Consequently, in 264 B.C.E. the assembly voted to send an army to Messana. Since the Roman term for the Carthaginians was *Poeni* or *Puni* (Latin for "Phoenician"), the ensuing conflict came to be known as the Punic War.

THE FIRST PUNIC WAR (264–241 B.C.E.)   The Romans made no progress against Carthage until they built a fleet to blockade the Carthaginian ports at the western end of Sicily. In 241 B.C.E., after a long war of attrition, Carthage capitulated. It surrendered Sicily and the islands between Italy and Sicily to Rome and agreed to pay a war indemnity. In 238 B.C.E., while Carthage struggled to put down a revolt led by mercenary soldiers whom it had failed to pay, Rome seized Sardinia and Corsica and demanded an additional indemnity. This was a provocative action that was to cost Rome a second war with Carthage.

It is hard to understand why Rome sought more territory, for the administration of lands outside of Italy created serious problems. Sicily, Sardinia, and Corsica became the first provinces in a Roman empire, for the Romans did not feel that it was possible to continue their traditional policy of extending citizenship or alliances beyond the borders of Italy. Rome turned its provinces over to military governors. And since there was no way to oversee the behavior of magistrates outside the city, there was nothing to prevent them from abusing their offices. The residents of the provinces were neither Roman citizens nor allies; they were subjects who paid tribute in lieu of serving in the army. Rome collected this tribute by "farming" out the right to gather money in the provinces to the highest bidder. Provincial governments soon became a source of corruption that undermined the machinery of the Roman Republic.

While Rome struggled to adjust to its new situation, Hamilcar Barca, the Carthaginian governor of Spain (237–229 B.C.E.), put Carthage on the road to recovery. His plan was to build a Punic empire in Spain that would make up for the lands Carthage had lost to Rome. Hasdrubal, Hamilcar's son-in-law and successor, continued his policies with such success that he alarmed the Romans. Rome reacted by imposing a treaty that obligated Carthage not to expand north of Spain's Ebro River. Hasdrubal doubtless assumed that if Carthage accepted the Ebro as its northern frontier, Rome would grant Carthage a free hand in the south. He was wrong. Within a few years the Romans had violated the Ebro treaty (at least in spirit) by accepting an offer of an alliance from the people of Saguntum, a town 100 miles south of the Ebro.

THE SECOND PUNIC WAR (218–202 B.C.E.) Hasdrubal was assassinated in 221 B.C.E., and the army chose Hannibal, the twenty-five-year-old son of Hamilcar Barca, to succeed him. Hannibal quickly consolidated and extended the Punic empire in Spain. At first, he avoided any action against Saguntum, but the Saguntines, confident of Rome's protection, began to stir up trouble for him. When Hannibal besieged and captured the town, the Romans sent an ultimatum to Carthage demanding Hannibal's surrender. Carthage refused, and Rome declared war (218 B.C.E.).

Rome had repeatedly provoked Carthage but had taken no steps to prevent Carthage from rebuilding its empire and made no plans to defend itself against a Punic attack. Hannibal exacted a high price for these blunders. In the fall of 218 B.C.E. he crossed the Alps into Italy with an army that the Gauls were eager to join. Hannibal first defeated the Romans at the Ticinus River and then crushed the joint consular armies at the Trebia River. In 217 B.C.E. he outmaneuvered and trapped another army at Lake Trasimene. He could not take Rome, however, without persuading its allies to abandon it. Despite his efforts to court them, most of them remained loyal.

Sobered by their defeats, the Romans suspended consular government and chose a dictator, Quintus Fabius Maximus. Since time and supplies were on Rome's side, his plan was to avoid pitched battles and wear Hannibal's army down by harassing its flanks. In 216 B.C.E. Hannibal tempted the Romans to abandon this strategy by attacking a grain depot at Cannae in Apulia. They took the bait, met him on the field, and suffered the worst defeat in their history. Eighty thousand Roman soldiers were killed.

The disaster at Cannae shattered Rome's prestige, and most of the allies in southern Italy (the crucial port of Syracuse in Sicily) went over to Hannibal. For the next decade no Roman army dared confront Hannibal directly. But Hannibal had neither the numbers nor the supplies to blockade walled cities, nor did he have the equipment to storm them. If the Romans refused to fight, there was little he could do to bring the war to an end.

The Romans devised a plan to defeat Hannibal by fighting him outside of Italy. Publius Cornelius Scipio (237–183 B.C.E.), whose Carthaginian victories earned him the title Africanus, set out to conquer Spain to deprive Hannibal of reinforcements from that quarter. Scipio was not yet twenty-five, but he was almost as talented a general as Hannibal. Within a few years he had taken Spain and won the Senate's permission to open a front in Africa. In 204 B.C.E. Scipio landed in Africa, defeated the Carthaginians, and forced them to order Hannibal to withdraw from Italy. Hannibal had won every battle but lost the war. His fatal error was to underestimate the determination of Rome and the loyalty of its allies. When Hannibal returned to Carthage, hostilities flared up again. In 202 B.C.E. he and Scipio met at the battle of Zama, and the day was decided by Scipio's generalship and the desertion of Hannibal's mercenaries. Rome, now the undisputed ruler of the western Mediterranean, reduced Carthage to the status of a dependent ally.

The Republic's Conquest of the Hellenistic World

THE EAST By the middle of the third century B.C.E. the three great Hellenistic kingdoms that dominated the eastern Mediterranean had achieved equilibrium. The balance of power among them was threatened, however, by the efforts of Philip V of Macedon (221–179 B.C.E.) and Antiochus III, the Seleucid ruler (223–187 B.C.E.), to expand their domains. Philip had allied himself with Carthage during the Second Punic War—provoking Rome to stir up a conflict in the Aegean called the First Macedonian War (215–205 B.C.E.). Once the Second Punic War was over, Rome determined to make sure that Macedon did not succeed Carthage as a threat to Italy. In 200 B.C.E. the Romans challenged Philip by ordering him to cease preying on the

Greek cities. Two years later the Romans demanded that Philip withdraw from Greece entirely. When Philip refused, Rome declared the Second Macedonian War. In 197 B.C.E. Flamininus, a gifted young Roman general, defeated Philip at Cynoscephalae in Thessaly, and the following year (196 B.C.E.) Flamininus surprised the Greeks by restoring the autonomy of the city-states and pulling Rome's troops out of Greece.

Philip's retreat offered Antiochus an opportunity to advance. On the pretext of freeing the Greeks from Roman domination, he invaded the Greek mainland. The Romans quickly drove him from Greece, and in 189 B.C.E., they crushed his army at Magnesia in Asia Minor. Antiochus was forced to relinquish his war-elephants and his navy and to pay a huge indemnity. Although the Romans again annexed no territory, they treated Greece and Asia Minor as protectorates in whose affairs they could freely intervene. This benign policy was to change as the influence of Cato, a conservative and ruthlessly businesslike censor, increased in Rome.

In 179 B.C.E. Perseus succeeded Philip V as king of Macedon. His popularity with democratic, revolutionary elements in the Greek cities convinced the Romans that he was a threat to the stability of the Aegean. The result was the Third Macedonian War (172–168 B.C.E.) and a harsher Roman policy. Macedon was divided into four separate republics whose citizens were forbidden to intermarry or do business with each other, and leaders of anti-Roman factions in the Greek cities were punished severely. Aemilius Paullus, the Roman general who defeated Perseus, brought so much booty home that Rome abolished some taxes on its citizens. Romans discovered that foreign campaigns could be profitable for the state, its soldiers, and its generals.

THE WEST   Rome's worst abuses of power were directed not against the Greeks but against the people of the Iberian Peninsula whom the Romans considered barbarians. In 154 B.C.E. the natives of Iberia launched a fierce guerrilla campaign against their oppressors. By the time Scipio Aemilianus brought the war to a conclusion in 134 B.C.E. by taking the city of Numantia, Rome was having difficulty finding soldiers willing to go to Spain.

Significant Dates in Rome's Rise to Empire

509 B.C.E.	Republic founded
387 B.C.E.	Gauls sack Rome
338 B.C.E.	Rome defeats the Latin League
295 B.C.E.	Rome defeats the Samnites
287 B.C.E.	"Struggle of the Orders" ends
275 B.C.E.	Pyrrhus abandons Italy to Rome
264–241 B.C.E.	First Punic War
218–202 B.C.E.	Second Punic War
215–205 B.C.E.	First Macedonian War
200–197 B.C.E.	Second Macedonian War
189 B.C.E.	Rome defeats Antiochus
172–168 B.C.E.	Third Macedonian War
149–146 B.C.E.	Third Punic War
154–133 B.C.E.	Roman wars in Spain

Carthage fared much worse. Carthage scrupulously observed the terms of its treaty with Rome and posed no threat to Rome, but fear and hatred of Carthage were deeply ingrained in some Romans. Cato is said to have ended all his speeches in the Senate with a stern warning: "Besides, I think that Carthage must be destroyed." The Romans finally took advantage of a technical breach of the peace to declare war on Carthage, and in 146 B.C.E. Scipio Aemilianus destroyed the city. A province of Africa was then added to the five existing Roman provinces in Sicily, Sardinia-Corsica, Macedonia, Hither Spain, and Further Spain.

Civilization in the Early Roman Republic

The Roman attitude toward the Greeks ranged from admiration for their culture to contempt for their political squabbling and money grubbing. Conservatives such as Cato spoke contemptuously of the Greeks, but, as Roman life was transformed by association with the Greeks, even he learned Greek. The education of the Roman upper classes became bilingual, and young Roman nobles studied Greek rhetoric, literature, and sometimes philosophy. Greek refined the Latin language, and Greek literature provided models that inspired the birth and guided the development of Latin literature.

Religion

The Romans identified their ancestral gods with the Greek deities and worked Greek mythology into their own traditions. But Roman religious practice was little affected until new Eastern cults arrived in the third century B.C.E. In 205 B.C.E. the Senate approved the public worship of Cybele, the Great Mother goddess from Phrygia. But Cybele's cult involved rites that shocked and outraged conservative Romans, and the Senate soon reversed itself. For similar reasons, it banned the worship of Dionysus (i.e., Bacchus) in 186 B.C.E., and in 139 B.C.E. the Senate exiled Babylonian astrologers from Rome.

Education

In the early centuries of the Roman Republic, education was entirely the responsibility of the family. Fathers taught their sons at home. Daughters may not originally have been schooled, but they were at a later period in Rome's history. The curriculum was designed to provide males with vocational skills, to elevate their moral standards, and to inspire them with respect for Roman tradition. Boys were taught to read, write, calculate, and farm. They memorized the laws of the Twelve Tables, practiced religious rites, learned the legendary accounts of Rome's origin, and trained for military service.

HELLENIZED EDUCATION Contact with the Greeks of southern Italy in the third century B.C.E. produced momentous changes in Roman education. Greek teachers introduced the Romans to the study of language, literature, and philosophy—and to what the Romans called *humanitas*, the broad training and instruction in the critical habits of mind that are the characteristics of a liberal education.

Since Rome did not yet have a literature of its own, elementary education involved learning Greek as a preparation for the advanced study of rhetoric—the art of speaking and writing well. Philosophy was at the heart of Greek education, but the practical Romans preferred rhetoric. It was of great use in legal disputes and political life. Some important Romans were powerful advocates of Greek literature and philosophy. Scipio Aemilianus, the man who destroyed Carthage, was a patron of important Greek intellectuals—particularly the historian Polybius and the philosopher Panaetius. Conservative Romans, such as Cato the Elder, feared that Greek learning would weaken Roman moral fiber. On occasion the Senate was persuaded to expel philosophers and teachers of rhetoric from Rome, but Rome could not return to its simple agrarian past. If Romans were to deal with the sophisticated world of the Hellenistic Greeks, which they had come to dominate, they needed the new education.

In the late republic, Roman education, though still entirely private, became more formal and organized. From the ages of seven to twelve, boys went to elementary school accompanied by a Greek slave called a *paedagogus* (hence, our term *pedagogue*). He looked after them and helped them learn Greek by conversing with them. Boys learned to read, to write (on a waxed tablet with a stylus), and to do simple arithmetic with the aid of an abacus and pebbles (*calculi*, in Latin). From twelve to sixteen, boys studied Greek and Latin literature with a *grammaticus*. He gave them a liberal education that included dialectic, arithmetic, geometry, astronomy, music, and some elements of rhetoric. Some boys pursued advanced study in rhetoric. A few, such as the great orator Cicero, undertook what we might

This wall painting from the first century B.C.E. comes from the villa of Publius Fannius Synistor at Pompeii and shows a woman playing a cithera. Fresco on lime plaster. H. 6 ft. 1 1/2 in. W. 6ft. 1 1/2 in. (187 × 187 cm.) The Metropolitan Museum of Art, Rogers Fund, 1903. (03.14.5) Photograph © 1986 The Metropolitan Museum of Art

call postgraduate study by traveling abroad to work with the great teachers of the Greek world.

EDUCATION FOR WOMEN   Though the evidence is limited, it is certain that girls of the upper classes received an education equivalent at least to the early stages of a boy's education. They were probably taught at home by tutors and not sent out to school as was increasingly common for their brothers in the late republican period. Young women did not study with philosophers and rhetoricians, for they were usually married by the age at which a man began this phase of his education. Still, some women found ways to continue their studies, and some became prose writers and poets. By the first century C.E. there were women in aristocratic circles who were famous or—as conservative males saw it—infamous for their learning.

Slavery

The Romans, like most ancient peoples, had always had slaves. But the simple family-farmers of early Rome owned few. Slavery became fundamental to the Roman way of life only during the second century B.C.E. in the wake of Rome's conquests. Between 264 B.C.E. and 133 B.C.E. the Romans enslaved some 250,000 prisoners of war. Slaves could marry, and their children increased the slave population.

In Rome as in Greece, domestic slaves and those engaged in crafts and commerce were allowed to earn money with which to purchase their freedom. The freeing of slaves was very common among the Romans. After a time, a considerable portion of the Roman population consisted of people who had been slaves or whose ancestors had been slaves. It was not uncommon to see a son or grandson of a slave become wealthy as a freedman and the slave himself or his son become a Roman citizen. By importing slaves from all over the Mediterranean world and freeing them, the Romans transformed the ethnic composition of their population.

Rome's unique contribution to slavery was the invention of an agricultural system employing vast numbers of unfree workers. At the end of the republic there were 2 to 3 million slaves in Italy, about 35 percent to 40 percent of the total population. Most belonged to great slave gangs working vast plantations called *latifundia*. These estates produced capital-intensive cash crops (wool, wine, olive oil, cattle) rather than the grain that small farmers raised. The lives of agricultural workers were harder than those of other kinds of slaves, for *latifundia* were designed to produce maximum profits. Slaves, who were simply a means to that end, were fed cheaply, treated like machines, and discarded when they were no longer productive.

Harsh treatment spawned slave rebellions of a kind unknown in other ancient societies. A rebellion in Sicily in 134 B.C.E. kept that island in turmoil for over two years. In 73 B.C.E. a gladiator named Spartacus raised an army of 70,000 fugitive slaves from the Italian countryside and repeatedly defeated the Roman legions. When the Romans finally subdued him, they crucified 6,000 of his men along the road from Capua to Rome.

Roman Imperialism: The Late Republic

Rome had no plan for building an empire. Territories were acquired as a result of wars that the Romans believed were either defensive or preventive. Roman foreign policy was designed to provide security for Rome on Rome's terms, not to acquire land. Since these terms were often unacceptable to other nations, conflicts arose—and, intentionally or not, Rome expanded.

The empire undercut the very republic it was built to protect. The constitution of the republic had been designed for a city-state. It could be adapted to rule Italy but not to handle the responsibility of governing an empire beyond the seas.

The Aftermath of Conquest

Before the Punic Wars most Italians owned their own farms and were largely self-sufficient. Some families had larger holdings than others, but they grew the same crops (mostly grain) and used free laborers rather than slaves. The Punic Wars changed this. For fourteen years Hannibal marauded through Italy, doing terrible damage to its farmland. Many veterans returned from the wars to find that they did not have enough capital to get their devastated farms back into production. Some moved to Rome seeking work as day laborers. Most stayed in the country and became ten-

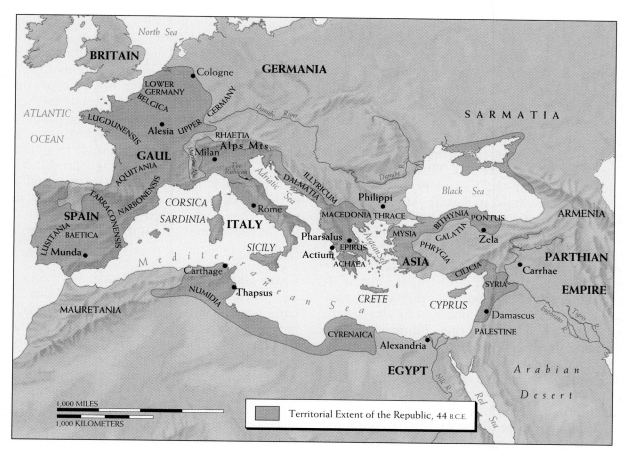

MAP 4–3 ROMAN DOMINIONS OF THE LATE ROMAN REPUBLIC   *Depicted here are the Roman Republic's conquests until the death of Julius Caesar. Areas acquired before the tribunate of Tiberius Gracchus (133 B.C.E.) are distinguished from later conquests and client states.*

ant farmers or hired hands. The land they abandoned was gathered into large parcels by the wealthy who had the capital to convert it to the crops (olives, grapes, and cattle) that were profitable on a world market. The upper classes had plenty of capital to invest, for the political offices they monopolized enabled them to win the governorships that allowed them to exploit Rome's new provinces. The economy that evolved within the empire separated the people of Rome and Italy more sharply into classes of rich and poor, landed and landless, privileged and deprived. The result was an increasingly tense situation that threatened the survival of the republic.

The Gracchi

By the middle of the second century B.C.E., perceptive Roman nobles were aware that institutions fundamental to the republic were collaps-

ing. The decline of the peasant farmer was shrinking the class from which Rome drew its soldiers, and the patron-client organizations that had structured Roman society were weakening. Patrons found it hard to control clients once the latter were no longer tied to the land. The introduction of the secret ballot in the 130s B.C.E. further weakened the traditional ties of clientage.

TIBERIUS GRACCHUS   In 133 B.C.E. Tiberius Gracchus, a tribune, tried to solve these problems by proposing a program of land reform. He suggested reclaiming public land that was being held illegally. Current holders of this land were to be allowed to retain as many as 300 acres in clear title as private property, but the state would take the rest and redistribute it, at low rents and in small lots, to the poor. Those who received farms were not to be allowed to sell them.

There was much opposition to Tiberius's proposal. Many wealthy senators would be hurt by its passage. Others worried about the precedent set by any interference with property rights. Still others feared the political gains that Tiberius would make if the beneficiaries of his legislation were properly grateful to its drafter. When Tiberius put his land reform bill before the tribal assembly, one of his fellow tribunes, M. Octavius, vetoed it. This left Tiberius with the choice of dropping the matter or attempting a maneuver that would undercut the checks and balances of Rome's constitution. Tiberius opted for the later. He persuaded the assembly to remove the veto blocking discussion of his proposal by removing Octavius from office. At this point many of Tiberius's powerful senatorial allies deserted him. If the assembly could pass laws after they had been opposed by the Senate and vetoed by a tribune, then Rome would no longer be an oligarchical republic but a direct democracy (such as Athens).

Tiberius gave up hope of conciliating the Senate and passed a second bill that was harsher than the first one he had proposed—and, therefore, more appealing to the masses. It contained a scheme for funding a commission to carry out land redistribution. King Attalus of Pergamum had just died and left his kingdom to Rome. Tiberius's suggestion that revenue from this source be used to finance implementation of land reform was a second assault on the constitution. It ignored the Senate's traditional control of finances and foreign affairs.

Tiberius knew that he would be in great personal danger once he lost the protection of his tribunal office, so he announced his candidacy for a second successive term. This was another violation of custom, and his opponents feared that if he succeeded, he might hold office indefinitely and rule Rome as a demagogic tyrant. At the elections a riot broke out, and a mob of senators and their clients killed Tiberius and some 300 of his followers. The Senate had beaten back the threat to its rule but at the price of the first internal bloodshed in Rome's political history.

The tribunate of Tiberius Gracchus permanently changed the thinking of Roman politicians. Heretofore Roman politics had been a struggle among great families for honor and reputation. Fundamental issues were rarely at stake. Tiberius's revolutionary proposals and the sena-

torial resort to bloodshed created a new situation. Tiberius, despite his failure, had shown how the tribunate could be used to challenge senatorial dominance. He had demonstrated that a man could acquire power, not by courting the aristocracy, but by appealing directly to the people with a popular issue. Politicians who took this route came to be known as *populares*. Their opponents, who defended the traditional prerogatives of the Senate, were the *optimates* (i.e., "the best men"). These groups were not political parties with formal programs and party discipline. They represented strategies and alliances for winning and holding political power in Rome.

GAIUS GRACCHUS In 123 B.C.E., ten years after the death of Tiberius, his brother Gaius Gracchus became a tribune. Gaius kept himself in power by putting together packages of legislation that formed alliances among disparate groups of voters. He revived efforts to redistribute public land; when supplies of land proved insufficient, he proposed new colonies; and he put through a law stabilizing the price of grain in Rome. Gaius also weakened the rich by pitting the republic's two wealthiest classes (the senatorial and the equestrian) against each other. The equestrians—the men who could afford to equip themselves for the most expensive form of military service, the cavalry—were businessmen with interests in the provinces. In 129 B.C.E., Gaius allowed them, but not senators, to serve on the courts that tried provincial governors. This prevented senators from sitting in judgment on themselves, but it did not improve the administration of the provinces. No senator now dared interfere with the equestrian tax collectors in his province lest he find himself dragged before their court.

In 122 B.C.E., Gaius celebrated reelection to the tribunate—which was now legal—by proposing that Rome's Italian allies be given citizens' rights. The allies had not received a fair share of the profits from the empire they had helped Rome win, and their resentment was threatening Italy's stability. Ordinary Romans, however, did not want to dilute the power of their votes by creating more citizens. This issue cost Gaius support, and he lost the election of 121 B.C.E. The Senate then trumped up a charge against him and killed him—and some 3,000 of his followers. Once again, the senatorial oligarchy triumphed over the *populares,* but the struggle was by no means over. Gaius's death simply taught the *populares* that they would have to resort to violence to oppose the Senate's violence. Marius, an officer who rose to prominence in the Jugurthine War, showed them the way.

Marius and Sulla

In 111 B.C.E. a group of Italian businessmen who were working in Numidia, a client kingdom in Africa, were caught and killed in the crossfire of a dispute over succession to the throne. The Roman electorate promptly declared war against Jugurtha, the perpetrator of this insult to their nation's honor. When the war dragged on longer than expected, rumors circulated that Rome's generals were being bought off.

In 107 B.C.E. the assembly elected C. Marius (157–86 B.C.E.) to a consulship and (usurping the Senate's right to control foreign policy) commissioned him to end the Jugurthine War. Marius was a *novus homo,* a "new man" (i.e., the first of his family to hold a consulship), not a member of the old Roman aristocracy. Marius quickly defeated Jugurtha, and the grateful Romans elected him to a second consulship to deal with another problem. In 105 B.C.E., two barbaric tribes, the Cimbri and the Teutones, had crushed a Roman army in the Rhone Valley. The long struggle to contain them kept Marius in office for five consecutive terms.

Marius won battles because he persuaded Rome to make changes in recruitment that enabled him to put larger armies in the field. He convinced the assembly to drop the property qualification for military service. This was a popular idea for it opened the way to a career for impoverished citizens such as those whom the Gracchi had tried to help. Marius's reforms built a strong army, but they also altered the balance of power in Roman politics. Marius's soldiers were semiprofessional clients of their general. They were dependent on him for their pay and for the grants of land on which they retired as veterans. Since they thought of themselves as his men more than the state's, he was able to use them to frighten the Senate into giving him whatever he needed to keep them happy.

Marius's example inspired imitation, and competitors soon challenged him. The most successful was L. Cornelius Sulla (138–78 B.C.E.), an impoverished aristocrat who had served under Marius in the Jugurthine War. Sulla made his mark in a campaign that Gaius Gracchus had tried to prevent: a war between Rome and its Italian allies. In 90 B.C.E. the allies gave up hope of receiving fair treatment from Rome and established a separate confederation with its own capital and coinage. Rome tried to undercut this by offering citizenship to cities that remained loyal and to rebels who laid down their arms. Despite this, hard fighting was still needed to put down the uprising. By 88 B.C.E. the war was over, and all the Italians became Roman citizens.

Sulla's performance in the war brought him the consulship for 88 B.C.E. and command of a war against Mithridates, a native king who was leading an uprising in Asia Minor. Marius, at the age of seventy, suddenly emerged from obscurity to demand this assignment for himself. When the assembly acquiesced, Sulla loosed the army he had been recruiting against Rome. Marius had used the army as a kind of political party, but now a Roman general used it to directly threaten his fellow citizens. Sulla regained his command. But when he left for the east, Marius and the consul Cinna occupied Rome with their armies. Marius died soon after his election to a seventh consulship in 86 B.C.E., and Cinna became the leader of Marius's party. In 83 B.C.E. Sulla, who had forced Mithridates to retreat and agree to a truce, returned to Rome. He drove Marius's followers from Italy and assumed dictatorial powers.

His first step was to wipe out his opponents. He posted lists of names of men whom he proscribed as enemies of the state. Proscribed individuals could be executed by anyone who found them, and their executioners could claim rewards from the state. Sulla confiscated their property and gave it to his supporters. As many as 100,000 Romans may have died in Sulla's purge.

Sulla could have made himself the permanent ruler of Rome, but he saw himself as the Republic's savior, not its enemy. His intent was to restructure and restore traditional senatorial government. The Senate's political privileges were reaffirmed, and the powers of the office of tribune, which the Gracchi had used to attack senatorial rule, were severely curtailed. In 79 B.C.E. Sulla declared his work complete and retired from public life. The example of what he had done long outlived the political arrangements he had made. It led to a civil war that destroyed the republic.

The Fall of the Republic

Pompey, Crassus, Caesar, and Cicero

Within a year of Sulla's death in 78 B.C.E. the Senate had to begin making exceptions to the very rules Sulla had designed to safeguard its power. The Senate discovered that the only way to deal with emergencies was to create "special commands," which were special because they were free of the constitutional limitations within which ordinary magistrates had to work. The most important of these commands went to a young general named Pompey (106–48 B.C.E.) who had never been elected to any office.

Pompey spent several years subduing a Marian army that had occupied Spain. In 73 B.C.E. the Senate sent him and Marcus Licinius Crassus, a wealthy senator, to put down a slave rebellion led by a gladiator called Spartacus. Crassus and Pompey used their growing influence to repeal most of Sulla's constitution so that ambitious generals and demagogic tribunes could undercut the Senate by appealing directly to the people.

In 67 B.C.E. a special law aimed at the suppression of piracy gave Pompey *imperium* for three years over the entire Mediterranean and its coast inland for fifty miles. In three months Pompey cleared the seas of pirates. The assembly then authorized Pompey to deal with a new war that had broken out with Mithridates. Pompey defeated Mithridates, drove him to suicide, and pushed Rome's frontier to the Euphrates River.

When Pompey returned to Rome in 62 B.C.E., he had more power than any Roman in history. The Senate suspected that he would emulate Sulla and establish a dictatorship. Crassus had most to fear. Although rich and influential, he did not have the kind of military backing Pompey enjoyed. He, therefore, sought alliances with popular political leaders. The ablest of these was Gaius Julius Caesar (100–44 B.C.E.), a descendant of an old but obscure patrician family. Despite noble lineage, Caesar was connected to the popular party. His aunt had been Marius's wife, and he had married Cinna's daughter. Caesar's rhetorical skill made him a valuable ally for

Crassus, for he could rally the people to the cause of the *populares.* Each man needed the help of the other to win the military commands they had to have to build armies to compete with Pompey's.

Cicero (106–43 B.C.E.), a "new man" from Marius's home town of Arpinum, marshaled the opposition to Crassus and Caesar. Although he was an outsider to the senatorial aristocracy, he was no fan of the *populares.* He hoped to create a "harmony of the orders" between the Senate and the equestrians that would consolidate the power of the properted classes. The Senate supported him primarily to block a bid for office made by an extremist named Catiline.

Cicero defeated Catiline for the consulship in 63 B.C.E., but Catiline refused to accept the verdict and hatched a plot to take over the state. News of it leaked to Cicero who speedily suppressed the plot and thereby annoyed Pompey.

A bust of Julius Caesar. Alinari/Art Resource, NY

Formation of the First Triumvirate

Toward the end of 62 B.C.E. Pompey landed at Brundisium. He had delayed his return, hoping to find Italy facing some crisis that would justify his keeping his army. But Cicero's quick suppression of Catiline deprived him of a pretext, and Pompey had to disband his army to avoid the appearance of treason.

Pompey had achieved amazing things for Rome, and he expected the Senate to show its gratitude by deferring to him. He wanted the Senate to approve the treaties he had negotiated in the East and to give him land for his veterans. The Senate should have prudently granted his requests, which were reasonable, but it chose instead to try to curtail his power and influence. This forced him to ally with his natural enemies, Crassus and Caesar. They joined him in an informal political arrangement called the First Triumvirate. By working together they were able to control the republic.

Julius Caesar and His Government of Rome

With the aid of his colleagues, Caesar was elected to the consulship for 59 B.C.E., and he used the office to make sure that each of the triumvirs got what he wanted. Pompey obtained land for his veterans and confirmation of his treaties. Crassus won tax concessions for the equestrians who were his chief supporters. Caesar got a special military command that gave him a chance to rival Pompey. When Caesar's consulship ended, the triumvirs secured their gains by arranging for the election of friendly consuls and by forcing their enemies to leave Rome.

Caesar's special command gave him authority, for five years, over Cisalpine Gaul in the Po Valley and Narbonese Gaul on the other side of the Alps. From these provinces, he set about conquering the rest of Gaul. In 56 B.C.E. he bought himself additional time by persuading Crassus and Pompey to renew the triumvirate. By 50 B.C.E. Caesar had completed the conquest of Gaul and acquired the wealth, fame, and military power he needed to compete against Pompey.

The triumvirate dissolved in 53 B.C.E. when Crassus died leading an army into Parthia, the successor to the Persian Empire, and Pompey saw no reason to sit by while Caesar's star continued to rise. In the late 50s B.C.E. the Senate appointed Pompey sole consul, for it concluded that Pompey was less of a threat than Caesar—and it hoped to help Pompey bring Caesar down. Caesar searched for some way to retain an office that would allow him to keep his army, but the Senate refused to extend his term in Gaul. In January 49 B.C.E. it ordered him to lay down his command. Caesar knew that this meant exile or death. Preferring treason, he ordered his legions to cross the Rubicon River, the boundary of his province, and march on Rome. A civil war ensued that Caesar won in 45 B.C.E.

Caesar made few changes in Rome's government. In theory, the Senate continued to play its role. But Caesar increased its size and packed it with his supporters. His monopoly of military power made a sham of senatorial decrees. In 46 B.C.E. Caesar was appointed dictator for ten years, and a year later his term was extended for life. His enemies concluded that he was aiming at monarchy, and they began to plot his destruction. Gaius Cassius Longinus and Marcus Junius Brutus recruited some sixty senators who helped them assassinate Caesar at a meeting of the Senate on March 15, 44 B.C.E. The assassins expected that once Caesar was dead the republic would automatically flourish. Instead, civil war returned, and it raged for thirteen more years. The assassins had not saved the republic but doomed it.

The Second Triumvirate and the Emergence of Octavian

Caesar had designated his eighteen-year-old grandnephew Gaius Octavian (63 B.C.E.–14 C.E.) his heir. The Senate hoped to use the sickly, inexperienced young man to block Mark Antony, the second-in-command to whom Caesar's men had spontaneously turned for leadership. But Octavian broke with the Senate, marched on Rome, assumed the consulship for 43 B.C.E., and declared war on Caesar's assassins. Mark Antony and another of Caesar's officers, M. Aemilius Lepidus, joined him in the Second Triumvirate, a legally established shared dictatorship charged, ostensibly, with the restoration of the republic.

In 42 B.C.E. the triumvirs defeated Brutus and Cassius at Philippi in Macedonia. Each of the victors rewarded himself with a command. The weakest member, Lepidus, was given Africa.

Octavian took the West—and the troubles that went with it (i.e., a war with one of Pompey's sons, the settlement of some 100,000 veterans, and the restoration of order in Italy). Antony received the most promising assignment: command of the East. This gave him a chance to invade Parthia and build an army large enough to sweep his fellow triumvirs aside.

In 36 B.C.E. Antony attacked Parthia, and the result was disastrous. His soldiers' faith in him was further undercut by a propaganda campaign that Octavian mounted. It convinced them that Antony had fallen under the spell of Egypt's queen, Cleopatra. By 32 B.C.E. all pretense of cooperation came to an end. Lepidus had already been shoved aside, and at Actium in western Greece in 31 B.C.E. Octavian defeated Antony.

The suicides of Antony and Cleopatra ended the civil war and left Octavian, at the age of thirty-two, absolute master of the Mediterranean world. His power was enormous, but so was the task that faced him. To restore peace, prosperity, and stability to Rome he needed to create a form of government that could handle the empire without violating the republican traditions to which the Romans were passionately attached.

In Perspective

The Roman Republic, at its start, resembled the early Greek poleis, *but Rome long remained a nation of simple farmers and herdsmen. As Rome organized itself for war, the traditional distinctions between Rome's patrician and plebeian castes became less important than the wealth that determined how well a man could equip himself for battle. The republic needed a strong army, for it was engaged in virtually continuous warfare in defense of its lands and allies. Rome created something unique: an empire ruled not by a king or bureaucracy but by a republic. Rome acquired and managed its territory as a state guided by an aristocratic Senate and governed by magistrates elected annually by its citizens.*

The temptations and responsibilities of governing an empire proved too much for the republican constitution. As trade increased, a class of merchants and financiers (the equestrians) grew strong enough to inject their commercial interests into Roman politics. Masses of slaves captured in war undermined the small farmers who had been the backbone of the Roman state and its army. Many impoverished citizens moved to Rome and survived by selling their only asset, their vote. Rome's armies of self-supporting farmers were then replaced by volunteer armies of landless men who made careers of being soldiers. They expected to be paid for their service with gifts of land or money and gave the generals who rewarded them the power to ignore constitutional restraints. When their leaders began to jockey among themselves for the upper hand, a long civil war sent the republic down the path to destruction. Despite itself, Rome drifted toward a form of monarchical government similar to those of the ancient states of Egypt and Mesopotamia.

REVIEW QUESTIONS

1. How did the institutions of family and clientage and the establishment of patrician and plebeian classes contribute to the stability of the early Roman Republic? How important was education to the success of the republic? How essential was the institution of slavery?

2. What was "the struggle of the orders"? What methods did plebeians use to get what they wanted? How was Roman society different after the struggle ended?

3. Until 265 B.C.E., how and why did Rome expand its territory? How was Rome able to conquer and to control Italy? How did Rome's desires for security, wealth, power, and fame shape its relations with Greece and Asia Minor in the second century B.C.E.?

4. Why did Romans and Carthaginians clash in the First and Second Punic Wars? Could the wars have been avoided? How did Rome profit from its victory over Carthage? What problems did the victory create for Rome?

5. What social, economic, and political problems did Italy have in the second century B.C.E.? How did Tiberius and Gaius Gracchus propose to solve them? What were the political implications of the Gracchan reform program? Why did reform fail?

6. What were the problems that plagued the Roman Republic in the last century B.C.E.? What

caused these problems, and how did the Romans try to solve them? To what extent were ambitious, power-hungry generals responsible for the destruction of the republic?

SUGGESTED READINGS

R. A. BAUMAN, *Women and Politics in Ancient Rome* (1992). A useful study of women's role in Roman public life.

J. BOARDMAN, J. GRIFFIN, and O. MURRAY, *The Oxford History of the Roman World* (1990). An encyclopedic approach to the varieties of the Roman experience.

T. J. CORNELL, *The Beginnings of Rome: Italy and Rome from the Bronze Age to the Punic Wars* (1995). A fine new study of early Rome.

T. CORNELL and J. MATTHEWS, *Atlas of the Roman World* (1982). Much more than the title indicates, this book presents a comprehensive view of the Roman world in its physical and cultural setting.

E. S. GRUEN, *The Hellenistic World and the Coming of Rome* (1984). A new interpretation of Rome's conquest of the eastern Mediterranean.

S. LANCEL, *Carthage, a History* (1995). A good account of Rome's great competitor.

C. NICOLET, *The World of the Citizen in Republican Rome* (1980). A valuable study of the meaning of Roman citizenship.

J. RICH and G. SHIPLEY, *War and Society in the Roman World* (1993). A useful collection of essays on military topics.

E. T. SALMON, *The Making of Roman Italy* (1980). The story of Roman expansion on the Italian peninsula.

H. H. SCULLARD, *A History of the Roman World 753–146 B.C.E.*, 4th ed. (1980). An unusually fine narrative history with useful critical notes.

G. WILLIAMS, *The Nature of Roman Poetry* (1970). An unusually graceful and perceptive literary study.

Chapter 5

The Roman Empire

KEY TOPICS

- The Augustan constitution
- The organization and government of the Roman Empire
- Culture and civilization from the late republican through the imperial period
- The early history of Christianity
- The decline and fall of Rome

The victory of Octavian over Mark Antony at Actium ended a century of civil strife that had begun with the murder of Tiberius Gracchus. Octavian (subsequently known as Augustus) brought peace to Rome by establishing a monarchy hidden behind a republican facade. The unification of the Mediterranean world improved its government and facilitated economic expansion. The spread of Latin and Greek as the empire's official languages promoted growth of a common "classical" tradition, which had a great

This statue of Emperor Augustus (r. 27 B.C.E.–14 C.E.), now in the Vatican, stood in the villa of Augustus's wife Livia. The figures on the elaborate breastplate are all of symbolic significance. At the top, for example, Dawn in her chariot brings in a new day under the protective mantle of the sky god; in the center, Tiberius, Augustus's future successor, accepts the return of captured Roman army standards from a barbarian prince; and at the bottom, Mother Earth offers a horn of plenty. Charitable Foundation/Gemeinnutzige Stiftung Leonard von Matt

influence on the development of Christianity. Christianity appeared in the first century C.E. as one of the empire's many competing eastern cults.

In the third century C.E. Rome's institutions began to fail. Some emperors resorted to drastic measures to try to restore order. The result was growing centralization and militarization of an increasingly authoritarian government. A wave of barbarian attacks in the second half of the fifth century finally initiated the empire's collapse.

The Augustan Principate

The memory of Julius Caesar's fate was fresh in Octavian's mind in 31 B.C.E. as he pondered what to do with the empire he had won. Octavian had gained control of all of Rome's armies, and he had loyal, capable assistants. The confiscation of Egypt's treasury brought him ample capital. He had the means to be the strong ruler who could end the civil war and restore order, but he knew that it would be dangerous to appear to threaten the republican traditions to which the Romans were so passionately devoted.

Slowly Octavian pieced together a constitution that was acceptable to the Romans and capable of running an empire. It inaugurated a long era of stability and order called the *pax Romana* (i.e., "Roman peace"). Despite republican trappings and an apparent sharing of authority with the Senate, it was a monarchy. All real power, both civil and military, lay with the ruler. Octavian disguised this fact by referring to himself simply as *princeps* ("first citizen") or *imperator* ("commander-in-chief"), but these titles soon acquired connotations of royalty that accurately reflected the power of his office.

During the civil war Octavian's legal authority derived from the triumvirate, a temporary dictatorship set up to restore the republic. After his victory in the civil war terminated the triumvirate, Octavian governed by holding consecutive consulships. This was an unpopular violation of Roman tradition, and he sought an alternative to it. On January 13, 27 B.C.E., at a dramatic Senate meeting, he resigned most of his offices—except for the governorships of Spain, Gaul, and Syria—and returned command of the other provinces to the Senate. This was less risky than it seems, for Octavian's provinces were the border lands that contained twenty of Rome's twenty-six legions. The Senate, however, declared this to be the restoration of the republic and thanked Octavian by granting him the surname "Augustus" (i.e., "revered"). Historians use this title to indicate Octavian's role as founder of Rome's first truly imperial government, the "Principate." In 23 B.C.E. Octavian Augustus made another republican gesture. He resigned the consulship. Henceforth his authority rested on two special powers: proconsular *imperium maius* (supreme military command) and the political privileges of an honorary tribune.

Administration

The Romans were willing to go along with Augustus, for they benefitted from his administration. He weeded out inefficient and corrupt magistrates. He blocked ambitious politicians and generals who might otherwise have disturbed the peace. He eased tension among classes and between Romans and provincials. And he fostered rapid economic development.

The Senate took over most of the political functions of the assemblies, but it became a less parochial institution. Augustus manipulated elections to offices and saw to it that promising young men, whatever their origin, had opportunities to serve the state. Those who did well were rewarded with appointments to the Senate. This allowed equestrians and Italians who had no connection with the old Roman aristocracy to earn Senate membership, and it ensured a Senate composed of talented, experienced statesmen.

Augustus was careful to court the politically volatile residents of Rome. He founded the city's first public fire department and police force. He organized grain distribution for the poor and set up an office to oversee the municipal water supply. The empire's rapidly expanding economy enabled him to fund a vast, popular program of public works.

The provinces, too, benefitted from Augustus's union of political and military power. For the first time, Rome had a central government that was able to oversee the conduct of the men who administered its provinces. Good governors were appointed. Those who abused their power were disciplined, and the provincials themselves were granted a greater degree of political autonomy.

The Army and Defense

Augustus professionalized the military and reduced its numbers to about 300,000 men—a force barely adequate to hold the frontiers. The legions were recruited from Italians, but auxiliary companies admitted provincials. The term of enlistment was twenty years. Pay was good, with occasional bonuses and the promise of a pension on retirement. Armies were permanently based in the provinces where they were likely to be needed, and their presence helped acquaint native peoples with Roman culture. Soldiers married local women and settled new towns. Eventually, provincials qualified for Roman citizenship and developed a commitment to the empire that strengthened its defenses.

Augustus's chief military problem was the defense of the empire's northern frontier. Since very little Roman territory protected Italy from invasion by the barbarians who wandered about Germany, Augustus wanted to expand the empire eastward to a new shorter and more defensible border. But in 9 C.E., when a German tribal leader called Herrmann (or Arminius, in Latin) ambushed and destroyed three Roman legions, the aged Augustus was forced to abandon the campaign.

Religion and Morality

Augustus tried to repair the damage that a century of strife had done to Rome's fundamental institutions. He devised a program to restore traditional values of family and religion. He passed laws to curb adultery and divorce and encourage early marriage and large families. His own austere behavior set a personal example for his subjects, and he banished his only child (Julia) to punish her flagrant immorality.

Augustus restored the dignity of formal Roman religion. He built many temples, revived old cults, invigorated the priestly colleges, and banned the worship of some foreign gods. He did not accept divine honors during his lifetime, but, like his stepfather, Julius Caesar, he was deified after his death.

Civilization of the Ciceronian and Augustan Ages

Roman civilization reached its pinnacle in the last century of the republic and during the principate of Augustus. Hellenistic Greek influences were strong, but the spirit and sometimes the form of Roman art and literature were unique.

The Late Republic

CICERO   Cicero (106–43 B.C.E.) was the most important literary figure of the late Republic. He wrote treatises on rhetoric, ethics, and politics, and developed Latin as an instrument for philosophical disputation. But it is the orations he delivered in the law courts and in the Senate and his private letters (which survive in large numbers) that are his most interesting works. They provide us with better insight into him than we have into any other figure from antiquity.

Ruins of the Roman Forum. From the earliest days of the city, the Forum was the center of Roman life. Augustus had it rebuilt, and it was frequently rebuilt and refurbished by his successors, so most of the surviving buildings date to the imperial period. Corbis

Cicero's thinking was pragmatic and conservative. He believed that the world was governed by a divine natural law that human reason could comprehend and use to guide the development of civilized institutions. His respect for law, custom, and tradition as guarantors of stability and liberty led him to champion the Senate against *populares* leaders such as Mark Antony. When the Second Triumvirate seized power and began its purges, it marked Cicero for execution.

HISTORY Much of the work of the historians who wrote during the last century of the republic has been lost. A few pamphlets on the Jugurthine War and the Catilinarian conspiracy of 63 B.C.E. are all that survive from the pen of the man reputed to be the greatest historian of his generation, Sallust (86–35 B.C.E.). Julius Caesar wrote treatises on the Gallic and civil wars. They are military narratives that Caesar developed for use as political propaganda. Since their direct, simple, and vigorous style still makes them persuasive reading, they must have been most effective with their intended audience.

LAW Before the generation of the Gracchi, Roman law evolved case by case from juridical decisions. However, contact with foreign peoples and the influence of Greek ideas forced a change. The edicts of praetors began to expand the Roman legal code, and the decisions of the magistrates who dealt with foreigners spawned the idea of the *jus gentium*—the law of all peoples as opposed to the law that reflected only Roman practice. In the first century B.C.E. Greek thought promoted the concept of the *jus naturale*, a natural law that lay behind the customary laws of different nations. This law reflected the principles of divine reason that Cicero and the Stoics believed to be at work in the world.

POETRY Two of Rome's greatest poets, Lucretius (ca. 99–ca. 55 B.C.E.) and Catullus (ca. 84–ca. 54 B.C.E.), were Cicero's contemporaries. Each represented a different aspect of Rome's poetic tradition. Hellenistic literary theory maintained that poets ought to be both entertainers and educators, and that was what Lucretius attempted in his epic poem, *De Rerum Natura* (*On the Nature of Things*). Lucretius hoped to save his generation from fear and superstition by converting it to the materialistic philosophies of Epicurus and Democritus. They had claimed that if living beings accepted that they were nothing more than temporary agglomerations of lumps of matter, they would cease to be anxious about death.

Catullus's poems were personal, even autobiographical, descriptions of the joys and pains of love. He hurled invective at important contemporaries such as Julius Caesar, and he amused himself in witty poetic exchanges, but he offered no moral lessons. He celebrated himself—an affirmation of the importance of the individual that was one of the characteristics of Hellenistic art.

The Age of Augustus

The age of Augustus was the golden age of Roman literature. The great poets of the era relied on the patronage of the *princeps,* and their dependence on him limited their freedom of expression. But although their work served his political agenda, they were not mere propagandists. They were sincerely grateful for what he had done for Rome.

VERGIL   The early works (the *Eclogues* or *Bucolics*) of Vergil (70–19 B.C.E.), the most important of the Augustan poets, were somewhat artificial pastoral idylls. Maecenas, Augustus's chief cultural adviser, seems to have suggested the subject for Vergil's *Georgics,* a reworking of Hesiod's *Works and Days.* Vergil transformed the early Greek poet's praise of simple labor into a hymn to heroic human effort—the struggle to wrest civilization from the brutal world of nature. Vergil's celebration of the greatness of Italy's cults and institutions became the theme of his most important poem, the *Aeneid.*

During the civil war, Augustus rallied the Romans to his side by persuading them that Mark Antony had succumbed to alien Eastern influences. Augustus had won the war by depicting himself as the guardian of Italy's culture. He was committed, therefore, to granting Italy special status within his empire. The *Aeneid* helped justify this. It explained Rome's origin and greatness by grounding its history in the founding myth of Hellenic civilization, the *Iliad*'s account of the Trojan War. Vergil's hero, the Trojan prince Aeneas, is not motivated by Homeric lust for personal honor and excellence. He personifies Roman qualities: duty, responsibility, and patriotism—the civic virtues of men such as Augustus who maintain the peace and prosperity of the empire.

HORACE   Horace (65–8 B.C.E.), the son of a freedman, was a highly skillful lyric poet. His *Satires* are genial and humorous. His *Odes,* which ingeniously adapt Latin to the forms of Greek verse, glorify the new Augustan order.

PROPERTIUS   Sextus Propertius was, with Vergil and Horace, a member of the poetic circle favored by Augustus's friend Maecenas. He wrote elegies that were renowned for their grace and wit.

OVID   Ovid (43 B.C.E.–18 C.E.), who wrote light love elegies, was the only one of the great poets to run spectacularly afoul of Augustus's program. His celebration of the loose sexual mores of certain sophisticated Roman aristocrats was not consistent with the serious, family-centered life Augustus was advocating, and Ovid's poetic textbook on the art of seduction, *Ars Amatoria,* confirmed Augustus's decision to exile the poet in 8 C.E. Ovid tried, but failed, to recover favor by switching to less sensitive themes. His *Fasti* was a poetic essay on Roman religious festivals, and his most popular work, the *Metamorphoses,* was a charming survey of Greek mythology.

HISTORY   Augustus's emphasis on tradition and his desire to increase Rome's reverence for its unique cultural traditions encouraged the writing of history. The most important of the Roman historians was Livy (59 B.C.E.–17 C.E.), although only a quarter of his monumental *History of Rome* survives. It treats the period from the legendary origins of Rome until 9 B.C.E. Livy based his history on secondary accounts and did little original research, but he was a gifted narrator. His sketches of historical figures have become perennially popular illustrations of good and bad behavior and models of patriotism.

ARCHITECTURE AND SCULPTURE   Augustus embarked on a building program designed to make Rome worthy of its history. The Campus Martius and the Roman Forum were reconstructed. Augustus donated a new forum of his own to celebrate his victory in the civil war. A splendid temple to his patron god, Apollo, rose on Rome's Palatine Hill. Most of the new building conformed to the Greek classical style, which emphasized serenity and order. The same attributes are visible in the best surviving portrait sculpture of Augustus and his family: the reliefs carved for the Altar of Peace, which Augustus dedicated in 9 B.C.E.

Imperial Rome 14–180 c.e.

The Emperors

Because Augustus was ostensibly only the "first citizen" of a restored republic, he had no public office to which he could openly appoint an heir.

Tiberius (r. 14–37 C.E.), his stepson and immediate successor, at first tried to follow Augustus's example and hide the monarchical nature of his government. But as the Romans became accustomed to the new order, there was less reason to conceal its reality. The terms *imperator* and *Caesar* began to be used as titles for men whose connection with Julius Caesar's family brought them the military power that enabled them to run the Roman world.

Tiberius was followed by his nephew, Gaius Caligula (r. 37–41 C.E.). Caligula was succeeded by his uncle Claudius (r. 41–54 C.E.), and Claudius left the throne to his stepson Nero (r. 54– 68 C.E.). Nero, who was not equal to the responsibility of his job, committed suicide when a rebellion in Gaul convinced him that he had lost control of the army. He was the last of the Julio-Claudians, the descendants of Augustus or of his wife Livia.

The year 69 C.E. saw four different emperors assume power in quick succession as different Roman armies marched on Rome. The victor, Vespasian (r. 69–79 C.E.), and his sons, Titus (r. 79– 81 C.E.) and Domitian (r. 81–96 C.E.), composed the Flavian dynasty. Vespasian was the first emperor who had no connection with the old Roman nobility. He was a tough Italian soldier from the middle class. His sons inherited his excellent administrative talents, but Domitian may have succumbed to paranoia. His increasingly tyrannical behavior frightened his intimates into assassinating him.

Domitian had no close relative to succeed him, and those who killed him were not foolish enough to try to turn the clock back to the days of the republic. They appealed to the Senate to restore order by choosing a new emperor. The Senate elected one of its own, Nerva (r. 96–98 C.E.), the first of the "good emperors:" Trajan (r. 98–117 C.E.), Hadrian (r. 117–138 C.E.), Antoninus Pius (r. 138–161 C.E.), and Marcus Aurelius (r. 161–180 C.E.). None of the first four men had a son to succeed him, so each followed an example set by Nerva—each adopted an heir. This system of succession was a fortunate historical accident, for it guaranteed that worthy men were promoted to power. It produced a century of peaceful, competent government that ended when Marcus Aurelius allowed his unworthy son, Commodus (r. 180–192 C.E.), to follow him to the throne.

The Administration of the Empire

Although some of the emperors tried to enlist the cooperation of the senatorial class—as counselors, judges, and department heads—in running the empire, the imperial government was largely staffed by professionals. These career bureaucrats were in many ways an improvement over the amateurs who had annually exchanged offices in the republic.

The provinces especially benefitted from imperial government. Once exploitation by governors was curbed, they discovered the economic advantages of being part of a huge empire. Rome strove to both unify the empire and respect local customs and differences. By 212 C.E. citizenship had been extended to almost every inhabitant of the empire. The spread of *Romanitas* ("Romanness") was more than nominal, for senators and even emperors began to be chosen from provincial families.

LOCAL MUNICIPALITIES Administratively, the empire was structured as a federation of cities and towns. The typical city had about 20,000 inhabitants. Only three or four had a population of more than 75,000. Rome, however, certainly had more than 500,000 residents—perhaps more than a million. The central government dealt with city governments and had little contact with people who lived in the countryside. A municipal charter left much responsibility in the hands of local councils and magistrates. The holding of a magistracy or, at a later period, a seat on a municipal council earned a man Roman citizenship. In this way the Romans brought the upper classes of the provinces into their own government, spread Roman law and culture, and won the loyalty of influential people. Rome's policy of assimilation did not succeed everywhere. Jews, who on religious grounds refused to compromise with Rome, rebelled in 66–70, 115–117, and 132–135 C.E. and were savagely suppressed. Egypt's peasants were exploited with exceptional ruthlessness and not offered the opportunity to integrate.

The emperors took a broad view of their responsibility for the welfare of their subjects. Nerva conceived and Trajan introduced the *alimenta*, a program of public assistance for children of indigent parents. More and more the emperors intervened when municipalities got into

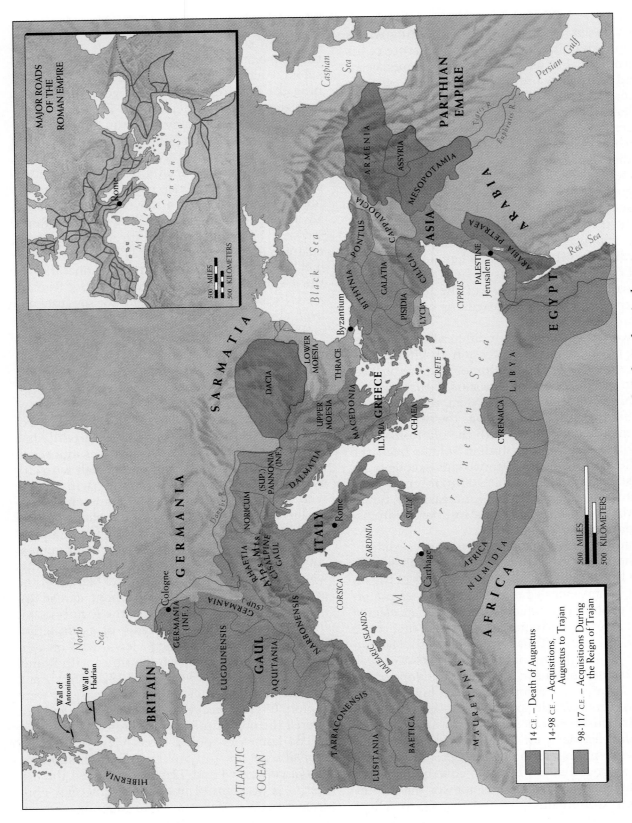

MAP 5–1 PROVINCES OF THE ROMAN EMPIRE TO 117 C.E. *The empire's growth is shown here in three stages: to Augustus's death in 14 C.E., to Nerva's death in 98 C.E., and to Trajan's death in 117 C.E.*

difficulties—sending imperial troubleshooters to deal with problems that were usually financial. As a result, the autonomy of the municipalities declined, and the central administration took on more and more functions. This caused the provincial aristocracy to lose interest in public service and to regard it as a burden rather than an opportunity. The price paid for increased efficiency was a loss of vitality by the empire's local governments.

FOREIGN POLICY Augustus's successors, for the most part, continued his conservative, defensive foreign policy. Trajan was the first to take the offensive. He crossed the Danube and mounted a campaign (101–106 C.E.) that added a new province (Dacia) to the empire. His intent was probably to secure the empire by driving wedges into territory occupied by threatening barbarians. The same reasoning justified an invasion of the Parthian Empire in the East (113–117 C.E.) and the establishment of three more eastern provinces: Armenia, Assyria, and Mesopotamia. Trajan's lines, however, were overextended, and rebellions forced him to retreat. He died on his way back to Rome.

Hadrian, Trajan's successor, developed a new policy for the defense of Rome's frontiers. Heretofore, the Romans had taken the initiative against the barbarians. Although they rarely sought new territory, they conducted frequent military maneuvers to chastise and pacify troublesome tribes. Hadrian hardened Rome's defenses, building a stone wall in the south of Scotland and a wooden one across the Rhine-Danube triangle. As Rome's defensive strategy grew rigid, initiative passed to the barbarians. Marcus Aurelius had to spend most of his reign fending off dangerous attacks in the East and on the Danube frontier.

AGRICULTURE: THE DECLINE OF SLAVE LABOR AND THE RISE OF *COLONI* The defense of the empire's frontiers made enormous demands on its resources, but the effect was not immediately felt. Economic growth continued well into the reigns of the "good emperors." Internal peace and efficient administration benefitted agriculture, as well as trade and industry, by making it easier to market products at a distance.

Small farms continued to exist, but more and more large estates, managed by absentee owners

Significant Dates from the Imperial Period	
The Julio-Claudian Dynasty	
27 B.C.E.–14 C.E.	Augustus
(ca. 4 B.C.E.–30 C.E.)	(Jesus of Nazareth)
14–37 C.E.	Tiberius
37–41 C.E.	Gaius "Caligula"
41–54 C.E.	Claudius
54–68 C.E.	Nero
69 C.E.	(Year of the Four Emperors)
The Flavian Dynasty	
69–79 C.E.	Vespasian
79–81 C.E.	Titus
81–96 C.E.	Domitian
(ca. 70–100 C.E.)	(Composition of the Gospels)
The Antonine Dynasty (the "Good Emperors")	
96–98 C.E.	Nerva
98–117 C.E.	Trajan
117–138 C.E.	Hadrian
138–161 C.E.	Antoninus Pius
161–180 C.E.	Marcus Aurelius

and growing cash crops, dominated agriculture. At first, these estates were worked by slaves, but in the first century C.E. this began to change. Economic pressures forced many members of the lower classes to become *coloni* (i.e., tenant farmers), and *coloni* steadily replaced slaves as the mainstay of agricultural labor. *Coloni* were sharecroppers who paid rent in cash, in labor, or in kind. Ultimately, their movements were restricted, and they were tied to the land they worked. Thanks to the *coloni*, the economic importance of slavery declined in the second century, but slavery survived the fall of Rome's empire.

Women of the Upper Classes

By the time the republic was drawing to its end, upper-class women in Rome were acquiring wealth, education, and political influence. The form of marriage that left a wife free of a husband's *manus* became popular, divorce was common, and some women conducted their sexual lives as freely as men. Privileged women were reluctant to have children and increasingly em-

Portrait of a Young Woman
from Pompeii

$\mathcal{I}$n 79 C.E. a volcanic eruption buried the Roman city of Pompeii (near Naples) and preserved its homes and their contents for excavation by modern archaeologists. This painting of a young woman comes from a modest two-story house whose residents were evidently educated and moderately well off. The woman holds a stylus and wax-coated tablets, common writing materials, and her husband (in a companion portrait) holds a volume of Plato. Her gold hair net and earrings (examples of which have been found at Pompeii) suggest that she was a fashionable lady of some means.

The paintings illustrate contemporary social values. The dual portraits suggest that women were thought of as worthy partners in marriage. Beauty is obviously an important female characteristic, but so, in this case, is pride in literacy. Pompeii was home to many competent women who owned property, conducted businesses, held religious offices, and received public honors for their various services and benefactions. There is no reason to assume that the town was unique in this regard.

Sources: Marilyn Stokstad, *Art History*, revised edition, Harry N. Abrams and Prentice Hall, New York, 1999, pp. 258–259; E. Fantham, H. P. Foley, N. B. Kampen, S. B. Pomeroy and H. A. Shapiro, *Women in the Classical World*, Oxford University Press, Oxford and New York, 1994, pages 340–341

Young Woman Writing, detail of a wall painting from Pompeii. Late 1st century C.E. Diameter 14 ⅝" Museo Archeologico Nazionale, Naples, Italy/Art Resource. © Photograph by Erich Lessing.

ployed contraception and abortion to avoid off-spring. Augustus was concerned about falling birthrates and issued decrees that were intended to encourage procreation, restore moral standards, and protect the integrity of the family. His laws seem to have had little effect. Women defended their freedoms, and in the fourth century C.E., the emperor Diocletian liberated them from the need for male guardians and allowed them to conduct their own legal affairs.

Several of the women who belonged to the imperial family exercised great political influence, if only unofficially. Augustus's wife and adviser Livia was honored with the title "Augusta" and survived him to be a force to be reckoned with in the reign of his heir, Tiberius. Claudius's wife, Messalina, attempted to overthrow him, and Nero may have owed his ascension to the throne to his mother, Agrippina.

Life in Imperial Rome: The Apartment House

The typical Roman city had about 20,000 inhabitants. Only three or four had more than 75,000, although Rome itself may have approached a million. Crowding, noise, and bustle were inescapable features of city life. In Rome the rich lived in large, elegantly decorated single-storyed homes built around courtyards. These occupied about a third of the city's space. Since public buildings (e.g., temples, markets, baths, theaters, and forums) took up another quarter, this forced the vast majority of Romans to squeeze into less than half the city's territory. Ordinary folks found housing in *insulae,* apartment houses that soared to five, six, or more stories. Shortage of space kept rents high even though these buildings were as uncomfortable as they were dangerous. They had neither central heating nor plumbing. Water had to be carried up from public fountains and sewage toted down (or dumped out a window). Heating and cooking relied on smokey stoves, and light was provided by torches, candles, and oil lamps. All these open fires created a great risk of conflagration, for *insulae* were constructed, in part, of flammable materials. They were also cheaply built and kept in poor repair, which meant that collapse was not uncommon. Little wonder that the people of Rome spent most of their time out of doors.

The Culture of the Early Empire

LITERATURE The years between the death of Augustus and the reign of Marcus Aurelius (14–180 C.E.) are known as the silver age of Latin literature. In contrast to the hopeful, optimistic

This is a reconstruction of a typical Roman apartment house found at Ostia, Rome's port. The ground floor contained shops, and the stories above it held many apartments. Museo della Civitá Romana, Rome, Italy. Scala/Art Resource, NY

outlook of the Augustan authors, the writers of the silver age were gloomy and pessimistic. Their works are freighted with complaints and satires that reflect hostility to the growing power and personal excesses of the emperors. Writers also avoided commenting on contemporary affairs and events in recent history that might irritate their emperors. Historical writing about remote periods was safe, as were scholarly studies, but little poetry was produced. In the third century C.E., Greek romances became popular. They suggest that the readers of the age sought entertainment and escape from contemporary realities.

ARCHITECTURE   Advances in engineering enabled Rome's architects to design new kinds of buildings—great public baths (e.g., those of Diocletian and Caracalla), and huge free-standing amphitheaters (e.g., the Flavian Colosseum). Romans continued the tradition of post-and-lintel construction pioneered by the Greeks but supplemented it with the semicircular arch developed by the Etruscans. Romans were also the first to exploit fully a Hellenistic invention: concrete. The Pantheon, the only major Roman temple to survive intact, combines all these elements. They are also visible in multitudes of mundane but useful structures, such as bridges and aqueducts.

SOCIETY   The Roman Empire was at its peak during the first two centuries C.E., but by the second century C.E. it was clear that difficult times lay ahead. The literature of the era expresses a desire to flee the present—to retreat from reality and public life to the remote past, to romance, and to private concerns.

The age's declining interest in public affairs correlates with a loss of vitality in the government of the empire's cities. In the first century C.E., members of the upper classes vied with one another for election to municipal office and for the honor of serving their communities. By the second century C.E., the emperors had to intervene to force unwilling citizens to accept public office. Reluctance to serve was understandable, for the central government had begun to hold local magistrates personally responsible for the revenues due from their towns. Men sometimes fled to avoid an office that might lead to their

property being confiscated to make up for arrears in the collection of a community's taxes.

The central government's extreme fiscal measures were a response to a declining economy. Initially, Rome had prospered from the end of civil war and the influx of wealth looted from the East, but the impact of these developments diminished in the first half of the second century C.E. For reasons that are unknown, population also seems to have declined. The cost of government, however, kept rising. An ever-increasing need for money compelled the emperors to raise taxes and to ignite inflation by debasing the coinage. These policies precipitated crises that finally overwhelmed the empire.

The Rise of Christianity

The triumph of Christianity in the West was most improbable. The faith originated among poor people in an unimportant, remote province of the empire, where it faced opposition from native religious institutions. It had to compete with numerous cults and philosophies throughout the Roman Empire, and it had to survive persecution by the imperial government.

Jesus of Nazareth

Christianity was one of the most important developments of the imperial era. It appeared in Judaea, a remote eastern province of the empire, in response to the life of an obscure Jew, Jesus of Nazareth. The Gospels tell us all we know about him. The Gospel of Mark, which is the earliest, is dated about 70 C.E. (perhaps forty years after Jesus' death), and the latest, the Gospel of John, is dated about 100 C.E. The Gospels were never intended to be read as objective historical narratives of a man's life. They were written to proclaim the faith that Jesus was the Son of God who had come into the world to redeem humanity and to bring immortality to those who believed in him.

Jesus was born during Augustus's reign. He was an effective teacher in the tradition of the early Hebrew prophets. Some of the prophets had predicted the coming of the Messiah, a redeemer who would help Israel triumph over its enemies and who would establish the kingdom of God on earth. Jesus modified this message by claiming that the Messiah would not establish an earthly kingdom but would end the world as human beings knew it at the Day of Judgment. God would then reward the righteous with immortality and happiness in heaven and condemn the wicked to eternal suffering in hell. While the faithful awaited the apocalyptic event, which they believed was imminent, Jesus advised them to forget worldly concerns, to trust in him, and to practice love, charity, and humility.

Jesus won a considerable following, but his criticism of the cultic practices associated with the temple in Jerusalem provoked the hostility of the Jewish religious authorities. The Roman governor of Judaea concluded that Jesus was a threat to peace and ordered his crucifixion (probably in 30 C.E.). Jesus' followers believed that he was resurrected on the third day after his death and that resurrection proved him to have been the Christ (*christos*, the Greek term for "Messiah," the "anointed").

Paul of Tarsus

The most important missionary at work in the generation that founded the Christian church was a Jew named Paul (born Saul), a Roman citizen and native of the city of Tarsus in Asia Minor. Paul was originally a Pharisee, a member of a Jewish sect known for strict adherence to the Jewish law. He began his career as an ardent opponent of Christianity, but about 35 C.E. he experienced a mysterious, precipitous conversion while traveling from Jerusalem to Damascus.

To define themselves the early Christians had to define their relationship to Judaism. James, the brother of Jesus, led those Christians who believed that the new faith was a version of Judaism and that its members had to adhere to the Jewish law. The less conservative Hellenized Jews, like Paul, saw Christianity as a new universal religion. They feared that the imposition of the Jewish law—with its many technicalities, dietary prohibitions, and painful rite of circumcision—would be a tremendous and unnecessary deterrent to conversion. Paul had great success making converts among the gentiles, and the triumph of his point of view in the church greatly facilitated the work of its missionaries.

Paul inaugurated Christian theology. He believed that the followers of Jesus had to spread the gospel, the "good news" of God's gift of the Messiah. But he warned that faith in Jesus as the Christ

was a necessary but not sufficient agent of salvation. Salvation was a gift of God's grace that could not be earned by an act of will or by good deeds.

Organization

Christianity had a unique appeal that enabled it to spread throughout the Roman Empire and beyond Rome's borders. Christ's declaration of the spiritual importance of love and charity focused the Christian community's attention on the needs of the weak, the sick, and the unprotected. Consequently, early churches were characterized by a warmth and a human appeal that stood in marked contrast to the coldness and impersonality of the pagan cults. The Christian promise of salvation, which confirmed the importance of each individual human soul to God, also implied the spiritual equality of all believers, no matter what their social class or gender.

At first, Christianity appealed most to the uneducated urban poor, and its early rites were simple ceremonies congruent with the poverty of its people. Baptism by water brought converts into the community by cleansing them of original sin (i.e., the state of alienation from God into which they had been born). The central ritual of the church was a common meal, the *agape* or "love feast," followed by a *eucharist* (Greek for "thanksgiving"), a celebration of the Lord's Supper in which bread and wine were blessed and consumed. Prayers, hymns, and readings from the Gospels were also part of worship.

The church owed its success in part to the unique organization it evolved. At first, Christian groups had little formal structure, and Christianity was in danger of dissolving into a gaggle of tiny sects. But the need to support missionary preachers and to administer charities prompted churches to elect officers: presbyters (i.e., "elders") and deacons (i.e., "servers"). By the second century C.E., when converts had increased to the point where a city was likely to have many churches, a bishop (from the Greek word *episkopos*, "overseer") was chosen to coordinate their activities. Bishops then extended their authority over the Christian communities in outlying towns and the countryside. Bishops acting together in councils could resolve disputes and preserve the unity of the church, and it was soon accepted that the powers that Jesus had given his original disciples were passed on in the church from one generation of bishops to another. (This is called the doctrine of apostolic succession.) It is unlikely that Christianity could have survived the travails of its early years without the strong government provided by its bishops.

The Persecution of Christians

The Roman authorities could not at first distinguish Christians from Jews and, therefore, gave Christians the same protection under the law as Jews. It soon became clear, however, that Christians were different in potentially dangerous ways. Christians and Jews both incurred suspicion by their hostility to aspects of Roman tradition. (Both, for instance, denied the existence of the pagan gods and refused to take part in the state cult of the emperor.) But although the Jews were not eager to spread their ancient faith, Christians were ardent missionaries, proclaiming an imminent end to the Roman world. They had a network of local associations spreading across the empire, and they were oddly secretive about the rituals they practiced.

Romans were traditionally suspicious of secret organizations, particularly those of a religious nature. Claudius expelled Christians from the city of Rome, and Nero made them scapegoats for the great fire that struck the city in 64 C.E. But for the most part the Roman government did not take the initiative in attacking Christians in the first two centuries. Most of the persecutions in this period were the work of mobs, not governmental officials. Christians alarmed their pagan neighbors by ridiculing the ancient cults on which the state had always depended for its security. When misfortunes befell communities, Christians were blamed for having angered the gods. Persecution was not all bad for the church. It weeded out weaklings, united the faithful, and created the martyrs who became the heroes of Christian legend.

The Emergence of Catholicism

The survival of the church was threatened as much by internal disputes as by external persecution. The simple beliefs held by the great majority of Christians were open to a wide range of interpretations and left many questions unanswered. As a result, differences of opinion about the content of orthodox (i.e., "correct") faith developed. Minorities who disagreed with the catholic (i.e., "universal") majority were branded heretics (i.e., "takers" of unique positions) and driven out of the church.

The need to combat heretics compelled the orthodox to formulate their own views more clearly. By the end of the second century C.E., the church had agreed upon the core of a canon (i.e., a "standard," a collection of holy writings): the Old Testament, the Gospels, and the Epistles of Paul. It took at least two more centuries before consensus was reached on the rest of the Scriptures. The church also drew up creeds, brief statements of faith to which true Christians were expected to adhere, and empowered its bishops to enforce conformity of opinion. Whatever the shortcomings of this development, it ensured the clarity of doctrine, unity of purpose, and discipline needed for the church's survival.

Rome as a Center of the Early Church

During this period, when the church's administrative structures were evolving, the bishop of the city of Rome began to lay claim to "primacy" (highest rank among bishops). Rome was, after all, the capital of the empire, and it had the largest number of Christians of any city. Rome also claimed to be the place where Peter and Paul, the two most important missionaries of the early church, were martyred. Peter, who was said to have been the first bishop of Rome, was an especially important figure. The Gospel of Matthew (16:18) claims that Peter was the first of the apostles to recognize Jesus as the Messiah and that Jesus acknowledged Peter's faith by saying: "Thou art Peter [*Petros*, in Greek] and upon this rock [*petra*] I will build my church." Eventually the bishops of Rome would come to interpret this passage as granting Peter—and his episcopal successors in Rome—supremacy over the church.

The Crisis of the Third Century

Signs of serious trouble for the Roman Empire began during the reign of Commodus, the son and heir of Marcus Aurelius. Unlike his predecessors, the "good emperors" of the Antonine Dynasty, he was incompetent and autocratic.

Barbarian Invasions

The pressure on Rome's frontiers, already serious in the time of Marcus Aurelius (d. 180 C.E.), reached massive proportions in the third century C.E. The eastern frontiers were threatened by a new power arising in the lands that had belonged to the Persians and their successors, the Parthians. In 224 C.E. a new Iranian dynasty, the Sassanians, replaced the Parthians and began to make raids deep into Roman provinces. In 260 C.E. they captured and imprisoned a Roman emperor named Valerian.

On the western and northern frontiers the pressure came from an ever-increasing number of seminomadic German tribes. Though they had been in contact with the Romans since the second century B.C.E., they had not been much affected by civilization. German males were hunters, fighters, and carousers. The limited farming Germans engaged in was done by women and slaves. Tribes were led by chiefs, usually elected from the princes of a royal family by an assembly of fighting men. A chief headed a *comitatus* ("fraternity," in Latin) of warriors pledged by oath to his personal service. Eager for plunder, these career raiders were attracted by the delights they knew to exist in the civilized lands across the Rhine and Danube Rivers.

The most aggressive of the Germans were the Goths. By the third century C.E., they had wandered from the coast of the Baltic Sea, their original home, into southern Russia. From there they launched attacks on Rome's Danube frontier, and, about 250 C.E., they overran the Balkan provinces. To meet the threats posed by the Goths and the Persian Sassanids, the Romans transferred soldiers from their western to their eastern armies. This weakened the defenses of the West and made it easier for the tribes of the Franks and the Alemanni to cross the Rhine frontier.

Rome's internal weakness invited an unprecedented number of simultaneous attacks. A manpower shortage, brought on by a plague, had forced Marcus Aurelius to resort to the conscription of slaves, gladiators, barbarians, and brigands. By the second century C.E., the Roman army was made up mostly of Roman-

ized provincials, and the training, discipline, and professionalism of Rome's forces had begun to decline.

Septimius Severus, who followed Marcus Aurelius's son Commodus to the throne (r. 193–211 C.E.), played a crucial role in the transformation of the character of the Roman army. Septimius was a military usurper who owed everything to the support of his soldiers, many of whom were peasants from the less civilized provinces. He was prepared to make Rome into an undisguised military dictatorship.

Economic Difficulties

The financial crisis exacerbated by the barbarian attacks also forced changes in Rome's military. Inflation had forced Commodus to raise the soldiers' pay, and the Severan emperors had to double it to keep up with prices. This increased the imperial budget by as much as 25 percent. To raise money, emperors resorted to new taxes, debased the coinage, and even sold the palace furniture. To attract men into the army, Septimius relaxed its discipline and made military service the path to social advancement.

The same developments that caused problems for the army did damage to other parts of society. As emperors devoted their attention to the defense of the empire's frontiers, they were less able to preserve internal order. Piracy, brigandage, and the neglect of roads and harbors all hampered trade—as did the debasement of the coinage and inflation. Taxation confiscated property that was badly needed as capital for commercial enterprises, and a shortage of workers reduced agricultural production.

More and more the government had to compel people to provide the food, supplies, money, and labor needed to sustain the armies. As the state began to demand that urban magistrates meet deficits in tax revenue out of their own pockets, the upper classes fled the cities. In the countryside, peasants abandoned farms made unprofitable by excessive taxation.

The Social Order

The new political and economic conditions led to changes in the social order. The senatorial and ruling classes were decimated by attacks from hostile emperors and by economic losses, and their ranks were filled by men coming up through the army. As a result, the state was increasingly militarized. Classes had been distinguished by dress since the days of the republic, but in the third and fourth centuries C.E. the people's everyday clothing became a kind of uniform that precisely declared their status. Titles were assigned to ranks in society just as in the army. Septimius Severus drew a sharp line between the *honestiores* (i.e., the senators, equestrians, municipal aristocrats, and all soldiers) and the lower classes, the *humiliores*. The *honestiores* enjoyed legal privileges: lighter punishments for crimes, immunity from torture, and a right of appeal to the emperor. As time passed, it became more difficult to move from the lower order to the higher. Peasants were tied to their lands, artisans to their crafts, soldiers to the army, and merchants and shipowners to the service of the state. Freedom and private initiative declined as the state strengthened control over its citizens.

Civil Disorder

In 235 C.E. the death of Alexander Severus, the last member of the dynasty founded by Septimius Severus, brought on a half-century of internal anarchy that invited foreign invasion. The empire teetered on the brink of collapse as conspirators overthrew and replaced emperors in rapid succession. A few able men appeared. Claudius II Gothicus (r. 268–270 C.E.) and Aurelian (r. 270–275 C.E.) drove back the barbarians and restored some discipline. But the soldiers who followed Aurelian on the throne employed strategies for defending the empire that acknowledged that it was losing ground. They built walls around Rome, Athens, and other cities and drew back their best troops from the frontiers. Their armies were mobile infantry and heavy cavalry that functioned as a kind of expanded imperial bodyguard. They recruited their soldiers from the least civilized provinces and even from the German tribes. Military power made these men the empire's new aristocrats. They dominated its government and monopolized its throne. In effect, the Roman people succumbed to an army of foreign mercenaries they had hired to protect them.

The Late Empire

As Roman emperors sought to mobilize resources to meet the mounting problems of the empire, they instituted policies that smothered individuality, freedom, and initiative. The state became ever more autocratic, centralized, and intrusive.

The Fourth Century and Imperial Reorganization

At the start of the fourth century C.E. an effort was made to save the empire by extensively reorganizing it. Emperor Diocletian (r. 284–305 C.E.), a native of the Balkan province of Illyria, was a man of undistinguished birth who rose through the ranks of the army. Recent history convinced him that the job of defending and governing the empire was too great for one man. Therefore, he set up a tetrarchy—a committee of four rulers, each of whom had responsibility for a different part of the empire. Diocletian administered the provinces of Thrace, Asia, and Egypt. He assigned Italy, Africa, and Spain to his friend, Maximian. Those two men were the senior members of the tetrarchy and shared the title "Augustus." Their subordinates, the "Caesars" Galerius and Constantius, were given responsibilities, respectively, for the provinces of the Danube-Balkan region and Britain with Gaul.

The tetrarchy stabilized the empire by giving four powerful men a stake in the status quo and by providing for an orderly process of succession to the throne. The Augusti recognized the Caesars whom they appointed as their successors and enhanced their loyalty by dynastic marriages. The system was a return, in a way, to the precedent set by the "good emperors" of 96–180 C.E., who adopted their successors from the pool of ablest men.

Each tetrarch established a residence at a place convenient for frontier defense. No one chose Rome, for it was too remote from the centers of military activity. Maximian's base at Milan commanded the Alpine passes and functioned as the effective capital of Italy. Diocletian donated monumental baths to Rome, but he visited the city only once and resided at Nicomedia in Bithynia.

In 305 C.E. Diocletian retired and compelled Maximian to do the same, but the hope for a smooth succession faded when Constantius died prematurely and his son, Constantine, claimed his father's throne. Other pretenders followed his example, and by 310 C.E. there were five Augusti and no Caesars. Constantine (r. 306–337 C.E.), who began the confusion, was responsible for ending it. In 324 C.E., he defeated his last opponent and made himself sole emperor. He continued Diocletian's policies—with one exception. Where Diocletian had tried to stamp out Christianity, Constantine became the patron of the church.

DEVELOPMENT OF AUTOCRACY The mounting crises facing the government encouraged a drift toward total military mobilization. In the name of efficiency, the government stifled the individuality, freedom, and initiative of its citizens. Traditions of popular government were forgotten. More and more emperors ruled by decree, consulting only a few high officials whom they themselves appointed. They protected themselves from assassination by distancing themselves from their people and becoming unapproachable, remote figures surrounded by elaborate courts. Their subjects prostrated themselves before them and kissed the hems of their purple robes. The emperor's new title, *dominus* ("lord"), asserted a claim to an authority that derived not from the Roman people but from the gods.

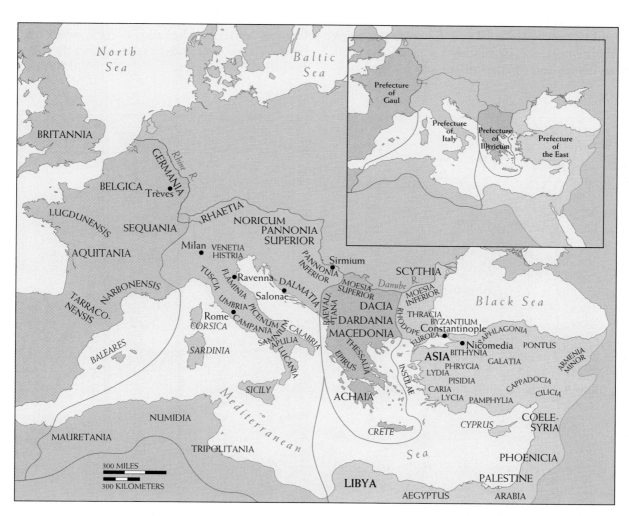

MAP 5–2 DIVISIONS OF THE ROMAN EMPIRE UNDER DIOCLETIAN *Diocletian divided the empire into four prefectures. The inset map shows their boundaries, and the larger map details regions and provinces.*

Constantine gave the empire a new capital. He chose the district of Byzantium on the Bosporus as the location for "Constantinople" (modern Istanbul) because it was midway between the eastern and Danubian frontiers. The site was also easy to defend, for it was surrounded on three sides by water. The dedication of the city of Constantinople in 330 C.E. marked the start of a new empire that repudiated Rome's pagan and republican traditions and embraced Christian autocracy.

The Byzantine emperors of Constantinople secured their position by keeping the civilian and military bureaucracies separate. This reduced the chance that someone might combine both kinds of power and mount a coup. An elaborate administrative hierarchy was set up to divide responsibility and prevent anyone from having very much power, and the entire system was kept under surveillance by a network of spies and secret police. This created a situation that was an invitation to corruption and inefficiency.

The cost of a 400,000-man army, a vast civilian bureaucracy, an imperial court, and the splendid buildings the government erected was more than the empire's already weak economy could sustain. The fiscal experiments that Diocletian began and Constantine continued only made things worse. In 301 C.E., Diocletian had instituted price controls to deal with inflation, but his Edict of Maximum Prices, which set legal limits for the costs of goods and services, simply drove commerce underground. When the peasants who could not pay their taxes and the officials who could not collect them tried to escape, Diocletian had used force to keep them in their places. Peasants, faced with enslavement by their government, often sought protection on a villa, the country estate of a powerful landowner. He protected them from the tax collectors, and they became *coloni*, working his land. Their descendants increasingly became tied to these estates.

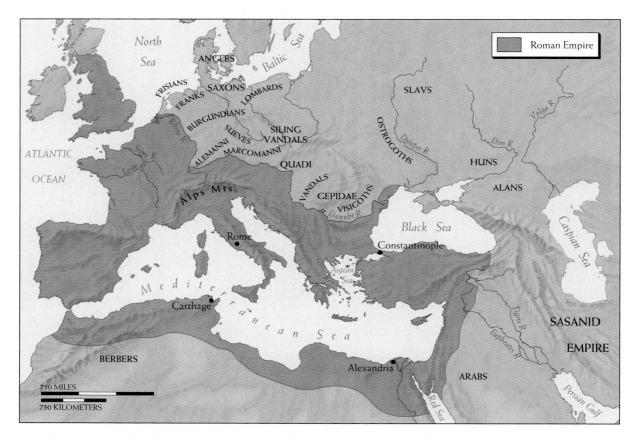

MAP 5–3 THE EMPIRE'S NEIGHBORS   *The map identifies the location of the various peoples who began to put pressure on the frontiers of the Roman Empire in the fourth century C.E.*

DIVISION OF THE EMPIRE Constantine's death was followed by a struggle for succession among his sons. Constantius II (r. 337–361 C.E.), the victor, reunited the empire and bequeathed it to his cousin Julian (r. 361–363 C.E.). The new emperor, whom Christian historians dubbed "the Apostate," concluded that Constantine's pro-Christian policy had caused more strife within the empire than it had resolved, and he set about reviving Rome's traditional cults. His reign, however, was too short to permit his ideas to take root. When he died in battle against Persia, the pagan renaissance died with him.

By the time that Emperor Valentinian (r. 364–375 C.E.) came to the throne, there were so many trouble spots that he concluded that he could not defend the empire alone. He appointed his brother Valens (r. 364–378 C.E.) as co-ruler. Valentinian resided at Milan and spent his reign defending the West against the German tribes of the Franks and Alemanni.

Valens was posted to the East, where he was confronted by a different kind of threat from another group of Germans. In 376 C.E., the Visigoths asked permission to enter the empire to escape the Huns, a fierce tribe migrating out of central Asia. Valens acquiesced but was unable to provide for the huge number of refugees who fled into the empire. In desperation the Goths began to plunder the Balkan provinces. Valens confronted the Goths at Adrianople in Thrace in 378 C.E., and he and his army were destroyed.

Theodosius (r. 379–395 C.E.), an able general, was then named co-ruler for the East. He pacified the Goths, enrolling many of them in his army. After the death of his colleague in the West, Theodosius united the empire for the last time.

THE RURAL WEST The disintegration of the empire was encouraged not just by wars and politics, but by the divergence of the cultures of its eastern and western halves. The West, which had fewer and younger cities, was increasingly rural. The institution of the villa, a fortified country estate, reorganized its society. The *coloni* who lived on a villa served its owner in return for economic assistance and protection from both barbarian invaders and imperial officials. As the upper classes moved to the country and slipped from the control of the imperial authorities, the central government lost its ability to provide fundamental services such as the maintenance and policing of roads. This hastened the decline of trade and communications, depressed the standard of living, and forced regions to become self-sufficient. By the fifth century C.E., the western empire had dissolved into isolated estates belonging to rural aristocrats who dominated a large class of dependent laborers. Only the Christian church kept alive a memory of imperial unity.

THE BYZANTINE EAST In the East the situation was quite different. The loss of the West enabled Constantinople to concentrate on its own affairs. A vital and flourishing hybrid of Christian and classical culture emerged, and the East entered the "Byzantine" phase in its civilization. Because of its defensible location and the relative health of its economy, Constantinople was able to divert most of the barbarians into the West. Eastern cities continued to prosper, and the East's central government retained its power. Christian emperors reigned in Constantinople until the Turks conquered the city in 1453. For a thousand years Constantinople saw itself as chief heir to the cultural legacy of ancient Greece and Rome.

The Triumph of Christianity

Christianity's rise to dominance over the empire was connected with the political and cultural developments that were causing it to be transformed in other ways. Pagan religions lost much of their appeal as the old Roman cities declined. People still took some comfort in traditional rites, but the deities worshiped in these cults seemed less and less effective as the problems of the fourth and fifth centuries C.E. mounted. Worshipers sought more powerful, personal gods who could offer them safety and prosperity in this world and immortality in the next. Consequently, new religions appeared and old ones were combined and interpreted in new ways.

Manichaeism, named for Mani, a Persian prophet who lived in the third century C.E., was an especially potent rival for early Christianity. The Manichaeans saw human history as a war between forces of light and darkness, good and evil. The human body was a material prison for the element of light that was the human soul. To achieve salvation, humans had to free the light by mastering the desires of the flesh. Manichaeans led ascetic lives, worshiped simply, and sustained a sophisticated religious organization. Their faith persisted into the Middle Ages. Christianity drew much from the cults with which it competed for converts. But none had its universal appeal, and none was as great a threat as the ancient philosophies and the state religion.

IMPERIAL PERSECUTION   Until the middle of the third century C.E., Rome's emperors generally ignored Christianity. But as the empire's problems increased and Christians became more numerous and visible, government policy changed. A growing sense of insecurity made rulers less willing to tolerate dissent.

Serious trouble erupted in 250, when Emperor Decius (r. 249–251 C.E.) invoked the aid of the gods in his war against the Goths. He ordered all citizens to sacrifice to the state gods. True Christians could not obey, and Decius launched a major persecution to uphold his law. Valerian (r. 253– 260 C.E.) continued the policy, partly in order to confiscate the wealth of rich Christians. His successors, however, were preoccupied by other more pressing matters, and persecution lapsed until the end of the century.

By Diocletian's day the number of Christians had grown still greater—as had hostility to Christians. Diocletian, who was struggling to hold the empire together, was not tolerant of unorthodox movements. In 303, he launched the most serious persecution Rome ever inflicted on the church. The policy was self-defeating. Christians were, by then, too familiar to seem threatening to most people, and the government's extreme actions horrified many pagans. The courageous demeanor of Christian martyrs also aroused sympathy and made new converts.

In 311 C.E. the Eastern emperor Galerius, who had been one of the most vigorous persecutors, was persuaded, perhaps by his Christian wife, to issue an edict of toleration permitting Christian worship. Constantine concurred, and his support began Christianity's rise to the status of the empire's sole legal religion.

EMERGENCE OF CHRISTIANITY AS THE STATE RELIGION   Constantine's son supported the new religion, but the succession of Julian the Apostate posed a brief threat. Julian was a student of Neoplatonism, a religious philosophy devised by Plotinus (205–270 C.E.). It combined rational speculation and mysticism and was harshly critical of the church's lack of intellectual sophistication. Julian refrained from persecuting the church, but he withdrew its privileges, removed Christians from high offices, and introduced new forms of pagan worship. His reform lasted only as long as his brief reign.

In 394 C.E. Theodosius forbade the celebration of pagan cults, and Christianity became the official religion of the empire. Its victory ended some of the church's problems but created others. As the church acquired prestige and influence, it began to attract converts for the wrong reasons and to lose its spiritual fervor. It also had to work out a relationship with the state. In the East the state was strong enough to subordinate the church. But in the West imperial power faded, and church leaders exercised remarkable independence.

ARIANISM AND THE COUNCIL OF NICAEA   As Christianity matured, doctrinal disputes arose among Christians. These created factions that struggled for control of the state church, and the threat they posed to the social order forced governments to intervene to preserve the peace. Christians, as it turned out, could persecute Christians with as much zeal as pagan fanatics.

The most disruptive of the doctrinal controversies was the fight over Arianism, an explanation of Christ's role advanced by a priest named Arius of Alexandria (ca. 280–336 C.E.). Arius argued that Jesus was a unique being created by God the Father through whom the Father created all other beings. For Arius, Jesus was neither fully man nor fully God but something in between. In Arius's opinion, proponents of the doctrine of the Trinity, which asserts that God is a unity of three persons (Father, Son, and Holy Spirit), were indistinguishable from polytheists. Arian theology had the advantage of seeming simple and rational, but Athanasius (ca. 293–373 C.E.), bishop of Alexandria, objected that the Arian view of Christ destroyed Christ's effectiveness as an agent of human salvation. Athanasius believed that only a fully human and fully divine Christ could have the power to turn humanity into divinity and, thus, bestow eternal life on his followers.

In 325 C.E., Constantine tried to resolve the issue by inviting all the Christian bishops to a meeting at Nicaea, not far from Constantinople. Athanasius's arguments prevailed and were enshrined in the council's Nicene Creed. Arianism, however, continued to spread. Some later emperors were Arians, and some of the most successful missionaries to the barbarians were Arians. Many of the German tribes that overran the empire were Arian Christians. Christianity was a unifying force for the late Roman Empire, but it was also a source of new conflicts.

Arts and Letters in the Late Empire

The art and literature of the late empire reflect the confluence of pagan and Christian ideas and the changing tastes of the aristocracy. Much of the literature of the period is polemical, and much of its art is propagandist. The men who came to power as the empire declined were soldiers from the provinces whose roots were in the lower classes. By restoring and absorbing classical culture they hoped to stabilize their world and confirm their credentials as aristocrats.

The Preservation of Classical Culture

Acquisition of classical culture by the newly arrived ruling class was facilitated in several ways. Works by great authors were reproduced in many copies and were transferred from inconvenient papyrus rolls to sturdier codices (with separate pages stitched together like modern books). Scholars also condensed long works into shorter versions and wrote commentaries to make them more intelligible. Grammars for the classical languages also had to be compiled, for various native tongues were replacing Latin and Greek in many of the provinces.

This late-Roman ivory plaque shows a scene from Christ's Passion. The art of the late empire was transitional between the classical past and the medieval future. Crucifixion, carving, c. 420 A.D. (ivory). British Museum, London, UK/Bridgeman Art Library, London/New York

Christian Writers

Original works by pagan writers of the late empire were neither numerous nor especially distinguished. But the late empire saw a great outpouring of Christian writings. Christian "apologists" (authors who explained Christian practices to pagans) produced much poetry and prose. There were also sermons, hymns, and biblical commentaries designed for use by Christians.

The church was served by several important scholars in this period of its history. Jerome (348–420 C.E.), who was thoroughly trained in classical Latin literature and rhetoric as well as Hebrew, produced a Latin translation of the Bible—the Vulgate (i.e., "common use"). It became the standard text for the Roman Catholic Church. Eusebius of Caesarea (ca. 260–ca. 340 C.E.) wrote an idealized biography of Constantine and an *Ecclesiastical History* that set forth a Christian view of history as a process whereby God's will is revealed. But it is the work of Augustine (354–430 C.E.), bishop of Hippo in North Africa, that best illustrates the complexity of the relationship between classical culture and Christian faith.

Augustine was born at Carthage and trained as a teacher of rhetoric. His father was a pagan, but his mother was a Christian and hers was ultimately the stronger influence. He had a difficult intellectual journey that carried him through Manichaeism, skepticism, and Neoplatonism before he was converted to Christianity. His skill in pagan rhetoric and his gifts as a philosopher made him peerless among his contemporaries as a defender of Christianity. Augustine reconciled Christianity and classical culture by arguing that reason prepares people to receive what is revealed by faith.

Augustine's greatest works are his *Confessions*, an autobiography describing his path to faith, and *The City of God*, a response to the pagan charge that a sack of Rome by the Goths in 410 C.E. took place because Rome had abandoned its old gods. Augustine separated the destiny of the church from that of the Roman Empire. He contrasted the evil secular world, the "City of Man," with the spiritual realm represented by the church, the "City of God." The former was fated to be destroyed on the Day of Judgment, and there was no reason to expect that its conditions would improve before that. The fall of Rome was, therefore, neither surprising nor important. All states, even a Christian Rome, were part of the City of Man and were, therefore, corrupt and mortal. Only the City of God was immortal, and it, home to all the saints on earth and in heaven, was untouched by earthly calamities.

The Problem of the Decline and Fall of the Empire in the West

Whether important to Augustine or not, the massive barbarian invasions of the fifth century C.E. terminated imperial government in the West. Since that time, people have speculated about the causes of the collapse of the ancient world. Theories have been advanced that cite soil exhaustion, plague, climatic change, and even poisoning caused by lead water pipes. Some scholars blame the institution of slavery for Rome's failure to make the advances in science and technology that might have solved its economic problems. Others target excessive governmental interference in the economic life of the empire, and still others point out the significance of the destruction of the urban middle class—the carrier of classical culture.

Although all these things may have been contributing factors, a simpler explanation for Rome's failure can be found. The growth of Rome's empire was fueled by conquests that provided the Romans with the means to continue to expand. Ultimately, there were not enough Romans to conquer and govern any more territory. When pressure from outsiders grew, the overextended Romans could not expand their territory to acquire the additional resources they needed to defeat yet another enemy. Still, their tenacity and success in holding out for so long were remarkable. To blame the ancients for their failure to end slavery and bring on industrial and economic revolutions is no help, for no one has yet satisfactorily explained why those revolutions took place in the modern era. The real question may not be why Rome fell but how it managed to last so long.

In Perspective

Augustus ended the civil wars that plagued the republic and created an era of unity, peace, order, and prosperity. As a result, he was regarded with almost religious awe and was, at his death, able to pass his power down through his family, the Julio-Claudians. For almost 200 years, with a few brief interruptions, the empire was prosperous, peaceful, and well run.

Problems developed when the government assumed numerous responsibilities that promoted the growth of a large, expensive bureaucracy. The costs of government also grew as pressure on the frontiers from barbarian tribes forced Rome to maintain a great standing army. Higher taxes and bureaucratic control combined to stifle civic spirit and private enterprise.

Rome's rulers developed numerous schemes for dealing with the empire's difficulties. More and more, their power and their safety came to depend on the loyalty of the army. To win that, they courted the soldiers with gifts that increased the burden of taxes. The rich and powerful succeeded in avoiding many of their obligations, but this forced the government to bear down ever more heavily on vulnerable ordinary people. Ultimately, even extreme measures failed, and the Roman Empire fell. Something of its culture survived, however, to lay a foundation for the modern West.

REVIEW QUESTIONS

1. How did Augustus alter Rome's constitution and government? How did his innovations solve the problems that had plagued the republic? Why were the Romans willing to accept him?
2. How was the Roman Empire organized, and what enabled it to function smoothly? What role did the emperor play in maintaining its stability?
3. How did the literature of the "golden age" differ from that of the "silver age"? What did poets contribute to the success of Augustus's reforms?
4. Why were Christians persecuted by the Roman authorities? What enabled them to acquire such an enormous following by the fourth century C.E.?
5. What were the political, social, and economic problems that beset Rome in the third and fourth centuries C.E.? How did Diocletian and Constantine deal with them? Were these men able to halt Rome's decline? Were there problems they could not solve?
6. What are the difficulties involved in explaining the fall of the Roman Empire? What sorts of theories have scholars advanced to explain Rome's decline? Which explanations do you find most convincing? Why?

SUGGESTED READINGS

T. BARNES, *The New Empire of Diocletian and Constantine* (1982). A study of the character of the late empire.

A. R. BIRLEY, *Hadrian the Restless Emperor* (1997). A biography of an important emperor.

P. BROWN, *The World of Late Antiquity, C.E. 150–750* (1971). A brilliant and readable essay.

A. FERRILL, *The Fall of the Roman Empire, The Military Explanation* (1986). An interpretation that emphasizes the decline in the quality of the Roman army.

M. GRANT, *The Fall of the Roman Empire* (1990). A lively, well-written account.

A. H. M. JONES, *The Later Roman Empire*, 3 vols. (1964). A comprehensive study of the period.

J. LEBRETON and J. ZEILLER, *History of the Primitive Church*, 3 vols. (1962) The Catholic viewpoint.

H. LIETZMANN, *History of the Early Church*, 2 vols. (1961). From the Protestant viewpoint.

F. G. B. MILLAR, *The Roman Near East, 31 B.C.–A.D. 337* (1993). A valuable study of Rome's relations with an important part of its empire.

H. M. D. PARKER, *A History of the Roman World from A.D. 138 to 337* (1969). A good survey.

G. E. M. DE STE. CROIX, *The Class Struggle in the Ancient World* (1981). A Marxist perspective on classical civilization.

R. SYME, *The Roman Revolution* (1960). A brilliant study of Augustus, his supporters, and their rise to power.

Ancient Warfare

The Causes of War

War has an extremely ancient and enduring lineage. There may be evidence of organized warfare as early as the late Paleolithic era, and war was clearly a preoccupation of the first civilizations of Egypt, Mesopotamia, India, and China. In 1968, Will and Ariel Durant calculated that of the previous 3,421 years, only 268 had been free of war. None has since.

Various explanations have been offered for the persistence of the human species' inclination to make war. Ancient philosophers, such as Plato and Aristotle, simply took it for granted that men were naturally aggressive and acquisitive and that governments had been invented to curb humanity's disruptive inclinations. Thucydides, an ancient Greek historian who described his people's experiences during a catastrophic civil war, concluded that men were driven to fight for three reasons: fear of an enemy, greed for personal gain, and the need to defend honor (i.e., one's sense of duty and of personal integrity). At most times in history, there has been general agreement that some things are worth fighting for—namely, freedom, religious allegiance, and the pursuit of wealth.

Wars are not launched by blind instinct. They are the results of choices that people make. Those who start wars always believe that they have good reasons for doing so and usually make rational cases for their decision. Fundamentally, however, all the arguments for war may boil down to one concern: access to power—the source of security, reputation, and privilege.

War and Technology

From the earliest times war and technology have had a mutually stimulating effect. Warriors' needs inspire the invention of new weapons, and changes in weapons alter the characteristics of war.

Fortress Walls

About 7000 B.C.E. (several millennia before the appearance of the earliest Western civilizations), the Neolithic people who settled at Jericho felt so threatened by war that they surrounded their homes with a thirteen-foot-high stone wall and a ten-foot-deep moat. Their example was followed by the Sumerians who pioneered civilization in Mesopotamia about 3000 B.C.E. By 2000 B.C.E. Egypt's southern border was guarded by a string of forts. A paucity of stone and wood prevented early Chinese communities from being fortified, but by the era of the Shang dynasty (ca. 1766–1050 B.C.E.) walls of hard-packed earth were being erected around settlements in China.

The history of warfare is the story of an interplay between defense and offense. The development of fortified stongholds encouraged the invention of new devices and techniques for besieging them. The ancient Mesopotamians and Egyptians employed scaling ladders, battering rams, and mobile siege towers, and they burrowed beneath walls to undermine them. By the fourth century B.C.E., Greeks were using catapults to hurl stones at enemy fortresses. Until the invention of gunpowder and cannons, however, the most effective means for taking a walled city was to blockade it and starve it into submission.

Army Against Army

Combat did not always involve an assault on a defended position. As early as the Stone Age, groups of men had begun to engage each other in the open field with clubs, spears, axes, and bows and arrows. The Bronze Age saw the appearance of sharper, sturdier weapons and metal body armor. These weapons, when combined with techniques of fortification and large supplies of manpower, enabled the rulers of ancient Mesopotamia and Egypt to extend their authority over vast areas.

This mound marks the ancient city of Jericho. Thought by some to be the earliest Neolithic site in the Middle East, it sprang up around an oasis about 7000 B.C.E. The thick stone walls and moat that surround it show that it was meant to be a fortress that could resist sieges, showing that warfare was common at least as early as the construction of this city. © Zev Radovan, Jerusalem, Israel

The Chariot and the Bow

The next great revolution in warfare came about 1800 B.C.E. with the invention of the chariot and the composite bow. The chariot was a light, two-wheeled, horse-drawn vehicle capable of carrying two men—a driver and a warrior. By gluing together strips of wood and horn, a bow could be made that was small enough to wield from a chariot but powerful enough to fell an enemy at long range. From a rapidly wheeling chariot, an archer could devastate a company of foot soldiers, hitting as many as six a minute.

Beginning about 1800 B.C.E., peoples who spoke Indo-European languages began to descend on the Middle East with chariot-equipped armies. One group of them, the Aryans, destroyed the indigenous Indus civilization. China's Shang dynasty used the new fighting techniques in its rise to power. The nation that brought this form of ancient military technology to its peak was Assyria. By the eighth century B.C.E, the Assyrian kings had discovered how to exploit the full potentials of the new weapons by training companies of men to use them cooperatively and strategically.

Mounted Cavalry

By 612 B.C.E, when the Assyrian empire fell, something new was appearing on ancient battlefields: mounted cavalry. A cavalryman had to learn to control a horse with his knees so as to leave both his hands free to shoot his bow. The first people to become proficient at this were the nomads from the steppes of northern Eurasia. About 690 B.C.E., they began to prey on the civilized lands to the south. They invaded Asia Minor and contributed to Assyria's fall. There is

This carving in low relief from the seventh century B.C.E. shows an Assyrian war-chariot and its charioteer. It comes from the palace of King Ashurbanipal at Nineveh, the capital of the mighty Assyrian Empire that dominated the Middle East in his time. Erich Lessing/Art Resource, NY

no clear evidence of their attacks on China before the fourth century B.C.E., but they may have brought down the western Chou dynasty in 771 B.C.E. Persian and Chinese rulers usually protected their frontiers by paying one group of nomads to fend off another. The Ch'in dynasty (256–206 B.C.E.) constructed China's Great Wall as a defense against the horse warriors from the steppes, but it was not very effective. Mobility and inexpensive weapons gave the men of the grasslands an enduring advantage over the men of the plowlands and produced a pattern of recurrent nomad conquests of civilized regions.

Iron-Wielding Warriors

Since horses were expensive to maintain and the tin needed to make bronze was rare, armies that relied on horses and bronze weapons tended to be small. They were recruited from the members of wealthy warrior aristocracies whose monopoly of weapons made them the ruling classes of their societies. About 1400 B.C.E., however, techniques for manufacturing iron tools and weapons were invented in Asia Minor. Iron is an abundant metal, and its availability made weapons affordable by common people. This enabled them to challenge the power of older aristocratic govern-

ments and progress toward a more democratic order.

The Shield and the Phalanx

Hellenic, or classical, Greek civilization was the product of the *polis,* a city-state defended by an army of yeoman farmers. These were common men who could afford to equip themselves with iron weapons. The methods they developed to employ these weapons restored infantry as the dominant fighting force. Greek infantrymen were equipped with helmets, body armor, round shields, short swords, and iron-tipped pikes, but the chief source of their power was the formation in which they fought—a compact company called a *phalanx.* These disciplined units of highly motivated freemen remained supreme on the battlefield until they were confronted by the more flexible Roman legion in the second century B.C.E.

Trireme Warfare

The Greeks achieved supremacy at sea as well as on land. Oared galleys had appeared about 1000 B.C.E., and the Phoenicians had improved them by adding up to three banks of rowers. The Greeks adapted these *triremes* and employed them in new ways. The earliest form of naval combat entailed coming aside an enemy's ship and boarding it. The Greeks, however, attached rams to the prows of their warships and charged into the hulls of enemy vessels.

Roman Legions

After the development of the phalanx and the trireme, the great success enjoyed by the Greek armies of the Hellenistic era owed more to the discipline of their men and the skill of their generals than to further innovation. In the third and second centuries, military dominance of the Mediterranean world passed to the Roman infantry. The Romans abandoned the phalanx for a more open order of battle. Rome's legions were composed of small, self-sufficient units that could be utilized in a variety of ways. The army attacked by first hurling heavy iron javelins into

The Great Wall of China was originally built during the Ch'in dynasty (256–206 B.C.E.), but what we see today is the wall as it was completely rebuilt during the Ming dynasty (1368–1644 C.E.). Paolo Koch/Photo Researchers, Inc.

the enemy's ranks and then engaging at close quarters with short, double-edged swords. As the ancient world neared its end, the Romans developed a horse soldier called the *cataphract*. He was a heavily armored man on horseback who charged his opponents with a lance. His appearance marked the start of another revolution in the history of warfare, a revolution that passed military supremacy to the medieval knight.

❖ *How early is the evidence for warfare among human beings? Why did Thucydides think that people went to war? Can you think of any good reasons for fighting a war? How did war and technology affect one another in the ancient world?*

Chapter 6
The Early Middle Ages (476–1000): The Birth of Europe

KEY TOPICS

- How the fusion of Germanic and Roman cultures laid the foundation for a distinctively European society following the collapse of the Roman Empire
- The Byzantine and Islamic empires and their impact on the West
- The role of the church in Western society during the early Middle Ages
- The political and economic features of Europe under the Franks
- The characteristics of feudal society

The collapse of Roman civilization forced the peoples of the Mediterranean world to experiment with new ideas and institutions. In what had been the northern and western provinces of the Roman Empire, aspects of Greco-Roman and German cultures combined with Christianity to create a uniquely European way of life. In the East, two other medieval civilizations appeared: Byzantium and Islam.

On the Eve of the Frankish Ascendancy

The attempts made to save the Roman Empire in the late third century influenced how it fell. Diocletian (r. 284–305) dealt with simultaneous threats to the empire in the East and the West by sharing leadership with a colleague, Maximian. His division of the central government set the stage for the halves of the empire to evolve separately. Imperial rule gradually faded from the West, but in the East it grew increasingly autocratic.

Constantine the Great (r. 306–337) reunited the empire and, in 324, relocated its capital to Constantinople, a new city he built in Byzantium on the border between Europe and Asia Minor. The "new Rome" flourished as the old one declined. The city of Milan, which had direct communications with the Rhine and Danube frontiers, assumed Rome's place as the seat of government for the western empire. In 402 Milan itself was judged too exposed to barbarian invasions, and the western court relocated to Ravenna on the Adriatic coast. By the late fourth century, the West was in political disarray, the city of Rome was no longer of much political significance, and imperial power and prestige had shifted decisively to Constantinople.

Germanic Migrations

The German tribes did not burst on the West all of a sudden. Roman and Germanic cultures had commingled peacefully for centuries, thanks to trade and Roman "imports" of barbarian domestics, slaves, and soldiers. Some Germans even rose to command posts in Roman legions. The arrival of the Visigoths (i.e., the "West Goths") in 376, however, signaled the start of an accelerated

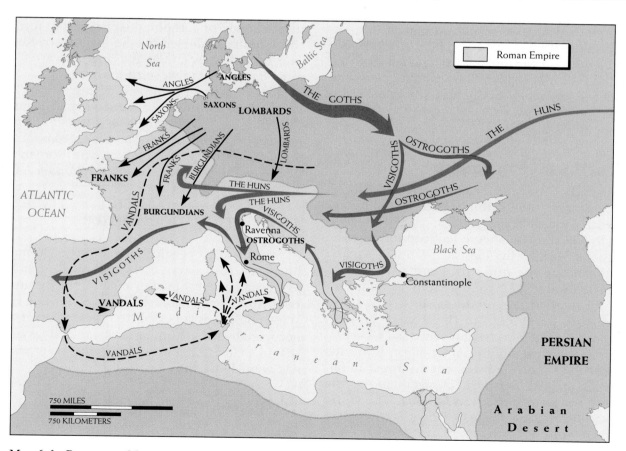

MAP 6–1 BARBARIAN MIGRATIONS INTO THE WEST IN THE FOURTH AND FIFTH CENTURIES
The intrusion of barbarians into the empire created a constantly shifting pattern of migration. The map shows the routes taken by the newcomers and the areas most affected.

rate of barbarian migration that would over-whelm the western half of the empire. The Visigoths were pushed into the empire by the notoriously violent Huns of Mongolia. The eastern emperor Valens (r. 364–378) admitted the Visigoths to the empire in exchange for their promise to help defend its eastern frontier. They became the first *foederati*—the first allied alien nation resident within the empire.

The Visigoths entered the empire as impoverished refugees. Exploitation of their misery by Roman profiteers caused them to rebel, and in 378, at the battle of Adrianople, they destroyed Valens and his army. Constantinople defended itself by persuading the Visigoths to move west. The western government responded by withdrawing troops from the frontiers to guard Italy, and this cleared the way for other German tribes to cross those frontiers unopposed.

It may seem surprising that there was so little resistance in the West to the migration of the Germanic tribes. The largest tribe probably numbered no more than 100,000 people, a small group compared to the Roman population. But the western empire was badly overextended, divided by struggles among ambitious military commanders, and weakened physically by decades of famine, pestilence, and overtaxation.

Fall of the Roman Empire

In the early fifth century, Italy suffered a series of devastating blows. Rome was sacked by the Visigoths and their king Alaric (ca. 370–410) in 410. In 452 the Huns were led into Italy by the infamous Attila. In 455 the Vandals sacked Rome, and by the mid-fifth century, power in western Europe had passed from Roman emperors to barbarian chieftains. In 476, a traditional date for the fall of the Roman Empire, the barbarian general Odovacer (ca. 434–493) deposed the West's nominal emperor, Romulus Augustulus, and ruled without an imperial figurehead. In 493, with encouragement by the eastern emperor Zeno (r. 474–491), Theodoric (ca. 454–526), king of the Ostrogoths (the "East Goths"), took Odovacer's place. By that time barbarians had thoroughly overrun the West. The Ostrogoths settled in Italy, the Franks in northern Gaul, the Burgundians in Provence, the Visigoths in southern Gaul and Spain, the

Vandals in Africa and the western Mediterranean, and the Angles and Saxons in England.

Despite the rise of barbarian leaders, western Europe did not become a savage land. The Germans respected Roman culture and were willing to learn from the people they had conquered. Except in Britain and northern Gaul, Roman language, law, and government coexisted with Germanic institutions. Only the Vandals and the Anglo-Saxons—and, after 466, the Visigoths—refused to profess at least titular obedience to the emperor in Constantinople.

Religion was a potential link between the Romans and their new rulers. The Visigoths, the Ostrogoths, and the Vandals had converted to Christianity before entering the West. Unfortunately, western Christians considered them heretics. Many of the missionaries to the Germans were followers of Arius, the heretical theologian who argued that Christ was a creature subordinate to God the Father. This problem was resolved about 500 when the Franks converted to the orthodox or catholic (i.e., universal) form of Christianity endorsed by the bishops of Rome. The Franks then conquered and converted the other barbarians in western Europe.

Despite Rome's military defeat, Goths and Franks became more Romanized than Romans Germanized. Latin language, orthodox Christianity (i.e., the kind based on the creed issued by the Council of Nicaea in 325), and Roman law triumphed in the West during the Middle Ages.

The Byzantine Empire

As western Europe succumbed to the Germanic invasions, the eastern part of the old Roman Empire became a new medieval state, the Byzantine Empire of Constantinople. From 324, when Constantinople was founded, to 1453, when it was occupied by the Ottoman Turks, the city was the seat of a Christian government. Its power waxed and waned, but the city itself endured.

The Reign of Justinian

The Byzantine Empire reached a territorial and cultural peak during the reign of the emperor Justinian (r. 527–565). Although urban institutions were disappearing in the West, Justinian's domain boasted more than 1,500 cities. The largest (with perhaps

Empress Theodora and her attendants. The union of political and spiritual authority in the person of the empress is shown by the depiction on Theodora's mantle of three magi carrying gifts to the Virgin and Jesus.
Scala/Art Resource, NY

350,000 inhabitants) was Constantinople—the center of Western commerce and communications. The greater provincial cities of the empire had populations of about 50,000 and sustained thriving economies.

Justinian's most important counselor was his brilliant wife Theodora (d. 548). If the controversial *Secret History* by Procopius, Justinian's court historian, is to be believed, Theodora, the daughter of a bear trainer in the circus, began her career as a prostitute. Her background may have given her a toughness that was useful to her husband, for she guided him through crises that might have overwhelmed his government. She was particularly useful in dealing with the religious quarrels that troubled the peace of the empire. Whereas Justinian was a strictly orthodox Christian, Theodora's patronage pacified a powerful faction of Christian heretics, the Monophysites. The Monophysites believed that Jesus had a single nature that was partially human and divine, whereas the orthodox church claimed that he had two distinct natures: one fully human and the other fully divine. The Monophysites were strong enough to form a separate church in the eastern provinces of the empire. After Theodora's death, the imperial government made the mistake of trying to stamp them out. As a result, a few years later when Persian and Arab armies invaded, the resentful Monophysites offered little resistance.

LAW Byzantine policy was to centralize government and enforce legal and doctrinal conformity throughout the empire: "one God, one empire, one religion." One of Justinian's major achievements was the codification of Roman law, the *Corpus Juris Civilis (Body of Civil Law)*. It contained four parts. The *Code,* which appeared in 533, revised imperial edicts issued since the reign of Hadrian (117–138). The *Novellae (New Things)* consisted of Justinian's decrees—which were added to by his successors. The *Digest* was a summary of the opinions of famous legal experts. The *Institutes* was a textbook for young lawyers. It spelled out the principles of law implied by the *Code* and the *Digest.* These works had little immediate effect on medieval common law, but from the Renaissance on they greatly influenced the development of law in Europe.

RELIGION Like law, religion was used to promote the centralization of the Byzantine Empire. Christianity was proclaimed the official religion of the eastern empire in 380. The coronation of emperors became a Christian religious ceremony presided over by the "patriarch" (i.e., the chief bishop) of Constantinople. And as the great churches of Constantinople, Alexandria, Antioch, and Jerusalem acquired enormous wealth, they took on the functions of state welfare agencies.

Paganism was curtailed by persecution and the absorption of some of its practices into popular

Hagia Sophia: A Temple Surpassing That of Solomon

Hagia Sophia, interior. Erich Lessing/Art Resource, NY

The greatest extant monument to the reign of the emperor Justinian is also one of the greatest achievements of all Byzantine art and architecture, the Church of the Holy Wisdom (i.e., *Hagia Sophia*). In 532 Justinian was nearly driven from the throne by rioting mobs, and in the confusion the church that served his court was destroyed. When order was restored, Justinian commissioned two architects (Anthemius of Tralles and Isidore of Miletus) to build a splendid new imperial chapel. With the help of a team of engineers and master masons and 10,000 laborers, they completed the project in about five years.

The new church employed a novel system of domes and pendentives to roof a huge rectangular space. Its most awe-inspiring feature was a central dome 112 feet in diameter that soared to a height of 184 feet. A row of windows circled the base of the crowning cupola to flood the room with light and illuminate the acres of brilliantly colored mosaics that covered the sanctuary's walls. The result was a monumental open, airy, luminous hall that proclaimed the majesty of God and God's illustrious servant, the emperor.

Two decades after the church was completed, Justinian's court historian, Procopius, published an account of its construction. He claimed that Justinian conceived the church in a divine vision and helped to solve the engineering challenges its construction posed. Justinian's chief contribution to the project was, however, probably financial, for the building allegedly cost 320,000 pounds of gold. Justinian doubtless concluded that the money was well spent. A ninth-century source claims that the emperor's intent was to build a church that would surpass the legendary splendor of the temple King Solomon had built for the ancient Jews in Jerusalem. Although the story is fictional, it describes the effect the building still has on its visitors.

When the Turks conquered Constantinople in 1453, *Hagia Sophia* was transformed into a Muslim mosque. Four minarets were added to the building and its mosaics were covered with paint. Muslim faith regarded the efforts of Byzantine artists to depict God as blasphemy.

Sources: H. W. Janson and A. F. Janson, *History of Art*, 5th ed. (Upper Saddle River, NJ: Prentice Hall, 1997), pp. 252–254; Cyril Mango, "Byzantine Writers on the Fabric of Hagia Sophia," in *Hagia Sophia from the Age of Justinian to the Present*, ed. R. Mark and A. S. Cakmak (Cambridge, U.K.: Cambridge University Press, 1992). pp. 41–50.

Christianity, but orthodox Christianity never succeeded in stamping out all the heresies that proliferated throughout the empire. Large numbers of Jews had also to be accommodated. Under Roman law Jews had legal protection so long as they did not proselytize Christians, build new synagogues, or attempt to enter sensitive public offices or professions. Justinian pressured Jews to convert, and later emperors both ordered Jews to be baptized and granted tax breaks to those who voluntarily complied. Neither policy was very successful.

Eastern Influences

Justinian tried but failed to conquer Italy and reestablish the old Roman Empire. His successors were much too preoccupied by developments in the East to devote any thought to the West. Under the emperor Heraclius (610–641), the Byzantine Empire took a decidedly Eastern turn. Heraclius spoke Greek, not Latin, and spent his entire reign struggling with Persians and Muslims. He fought the Persians to a draw, but after 632 Islamic armies advanced relentlessly into his territory. They overran Asia Minor, and in 677 they besieged Constantinople for the first, but not the last, time. Not until the reign of Leo III (717–740), founder of the Isaurian dynasty, were they driven back and Asia Minor recovered.

Leo's relations with western Christians worsened when he outlawed the use of images in Christian worship. Islam equated image veneration with idolatry, and this may have had some influence on Leo and his successors. Be that as it may, western Christians were deeply affronted by the East's iconoclasm, for they had great affection for holy images of Jesus, Mary, and the saints. Leo's assumption that secular rulers have the right to legislate religious practices—a doctrine called Caesaro-papism—was also rejected by the Western church. The ban on images in the East was ultimately lifted in the late eighth century, but in the interim it worsened the divisions in Christendom and destroyed much religious art.

In 1071 the Byzantines were defeated in a battle at Manzikert, and the Muslim Seljuk Turks overran the eastern provinces of the empire. This was the beginning of a long, slow decline for the eastern empire. In 1092 the Byzantine emperor Alexius I Comnenus (r. 1081–1118) appealed to the West for help, and three years later the West responded with the first of the great Crusades. The First Crusade enabled Constantinople to recover some territory, but a century later (in 1204) the Fourth Crusade overwhelmed Constantinople itself and did more damage to the city than all previous Muslim attacks.

Despite its vicissitudes, the Byzantine Empire maintained a protective barrier between Europe and its non-Christian enemies in the East until 1453. Byzantine civilization was also, for much of this time, more advanced than European civilization and the source of much of the classical learning that filtered through to the West.

Islam and the Islamic World

A new religion called Islam arose in Arabia in the sixth century in response to the work of the Prophet Muhammad. It sparked the creation of a third medieval civilization and a rapidly expanding empire that quickly became a threat to Byzantium's Greek emperors and Europe's German kings.

Muhammad's Religion

Muhammad (570–632) was orphaned at a young age and raised by relatives in modest circumstances. As a youth, Muhammad worked on caravans as a merchant's assistant. At the age of twenty-five, he married a wealthy Meccan widow and with her support became a kind of social activist. He opposed the materialism of Meccan society and some of his people's pagan practices. When he was about forty, he had a deep religious experience in which he received visitations from the angel Gabriel. Muhammad then began (and continued for the rest of his life) to recite what his followers believe literally to be God's words. Between 650 and 651, the revealed texts that God had chosen him to convey were collected in a sacred book, the Qur'an ("reciting"). At the heart of Muhammad's message was a call for all Arabs to submit to God's will as revealed through "the Prophet." The terms *Islam* and *Muslim* both imply "submission" or "surrender."

Muhammad did not claim that his message was new—only that it was final and definitive. What he taught was consistent with what a long line of Jewish prophets, from Noah to Jesus Christ, had taught. His special role was to be the last of the prophets that God would send. Islam, like Judaism, was a strictly monotheistic and theocentric religion, and it concurred with Judaism in rejecting Christianity's trinitarian view of God and concept of God's incarnation in the person of Jesus.

Muhammad's birthplace, the community of Mecca, was the location of the Ka'ba, one of Arabia's most holy shrines. The Ka'ba was a simple, rectangular building containing a sacred black stone and various other holy objects. Muhammad's attack on the idols of the Ka'ba was not only an offense to traditional Arab religion. It threatened to diminish Mecca's appeal as a center for trade. In 622 the Meccan authorities forced Muhammad and his followers to flee to Medina, 240 miles to the north. This event, the *Hegira*, has been chosen as the pivotal date for the Islamic calendar, for it marks the moment when Muhammad founded the first Muslim community.

Muhammad and his followers prospered in Medina by raiding the caravans that went to and from Mecca. Success brought him throngs of converts, and by 624 he was powerful enough to persuade Mecca to submit to his authority. He returned in triumph, cleansed the Ka'ba of its idols, and designated it the chief shrine for his new religion. Islam, like Christianity, eased life for its converts by making some compromises with their cherished pagan customs.

Muhammad stressed practice more than doctrine, and, as Islam matured, it evolved characteristic customs and values: (1) to be honest and modest in all dealings and behavior, (2) to be absolutely loyal to the Islamic community, (3) to abstain from pork and alcohol, (4) to pray facing Mecca five times a day, (5) to contribute to the support of the poor and needy, (6) to fast during daylight hours for one month each year, and (7) to make a pilgrimage to the Ka'ba at least once in a lifetime. Muslim men were allowed as many as four wives—provided they were able to treat them all justly and equally. A man could divorce a wife with a simple declaration of his intent. A wife could also initiate divorce, although the procedure was more complicated for her. She was expected to be totally loyal and devoted to her husband, and only her husband was to be allowed to see her face.

Islam made no rigid distinction between clergy and laity. It had no priesthood, but looked for leadership to a scholarly elite of laymen, the *ulema* ("persons with correct knowledge"). The authority of these men derived from their reputations for great piety and learning, and their opinions had the force of law in Muslim society. They also kept a critical eye on Muslim rulers to ensure that they adhered to the letter of the Qur'an.

Islamic Diversity

Islam was very successful in unifying the Arab tribes and various pagan peoples, for it appealed to the pride of groups that had been marginalized in a world dominated by Judaism and Christianity. Islam proclaimed Muhammad to be history's most important religious figure and his followers to be the people God chose to receive his most significant revelation.

Passionate faith in Muhammad did not prevent divisions from emerging within Islam. Factions contested who had the best right to the caliphate, the office held by the men who succeeded to Muhammad's leadership of the Muslim community. Doctrinal differences were debated, as was the issue of the extent to which Islam was meant to be a religion only for Arabs.

The most radical positions were taken by the Kharijites. Their leaders seceded from the camp of the fourth caliph, Ali (r. 656–661). In their opinion, he sacrificed important principles for political advantage, and in 661 one of their members assassinated him. The Kharijites were "Puritans" who excluded from Islam all but rigorously virtuous Muslims.

More influential were the Shi'a, or "partisans" of Ali. The Shi'a regarded Ali and his descendants as the only rightful successors to Muhammad—not only by virtue of their kinship with the Prophet but also by his expressed will. To the Shi'a, Ali's assassination represented a basic truth of devout Muslim life: a true imam ("ruler") and his followers should expect to suffer unjustly even unto death. A theology of martyrdom is the mark of Shi'a teaching, and the Shi'a are still an embattled minority within Islam.

A third group, which has been dominant for most of Islamic history, is the majority centrist party, the Sunnis (i.e., the followers of *sunna*, "tradition"). Sunnis emphasize loyalty to the

Muslims are enjoined to live by the divine law, or Shari'a, *and have a right to have disputes settled by an arbiter of the* Shari'a. *Here we see a husband complaining about his wife before the state-appointed judge, or* qadi. *The wife, backed up by two other women, points an accusing finger at the husband. In such cases, the first duty of the* qadi, *who should be a learned person of faith, is to try to effect a reconciliation before the husband divorces his wife, or the wife herself seeks a divorce.* Cliche Bibliothèque Nationale de France, Paris

fundamental principles of Islam more than to the particular issues that cause the Kharijites and the Shi'a to exclude various people from the Muslim community.

Islamic Empires

Muhammad's first three successors, the caliphs Abu Bakr (r. 632–634), Umar (r. 634–644), and Uthman (r. 644–656), won control of the southern and eastern rim of the Mediterranean. Islam's capital shifted from Mecca to the more centrally located Damascus, and by the eighth century the caliphs ruled an empire that stretched from Spain to India. In 750 the Abbasid family overthrew the Umayyad caliphs of Damascus and moved the seat of their government to Baghdad. Shortly thereafter, their huge domain began to break up into separate states, and rival caliphs contested their authority.

The Muslim conquests proceeded rapidly because the Arabs' opponents, the Byzantines and Persians, had exhausted themselves in a long war. The Arabs struck just as the Byzantine emperor Heraclius drove the Persians out of Egypt, Palestine, Syria, and Asia Minor. Before Heraclius died in 641, Arab armies had taken all these conquests, except for Asia Minor, from him. By 643 they had overrun what remained of the Persian Empire, and by the end of the century the last Byzantine outpost in North Africa had fallen to them.

Most of the inhabitants of the Byzantine lands the Muslims occupied were Christians, but many were also Semitic peoples with links to the Arabs. Heraclius's efforts to stamp out heresy and impose Greek orthodoxy on the Monophysite communities of Egypt and Syria led many of them to welcome the Islamic invaders as liberators from Byzantine oppression.

Islam won control of Christian territories in North Africa and Spain, but its thrust into the European heart of Christendom was rebuffed in 732 by Charles Martel, ruler of the Franks. His defeat of an Arab raiding party at Poitiers (in central France) marked the point at which the Muslim advance in the West began to be reversed. The Isaurian dynasty, which Leo III (r. 717–740) established in Constantinople, defended Asia Minor from Islamic aggression and blocked Muslim access to Europe from the east.

The Western Debt to Islamic Culture

The Christian West was very hostile to Islam, but it profited a great deal from contact with the Muslims. Arab cultures of the early medieval period were far superior to those of Christian Europe. Europe learned important technologies from the Muslims, and Muslim scholars made major works of Greek science and philosophy available to the West in Latin translation. As late as the sixteenth century, in addition to the works of the ancient world's physicians, Hippocrates and Galen, the basic gynecological and child care manuals in use in the West were those of a Baghdad physician, Al-Razi, and the philosophers Avicenna (980–1037) and Averröes (1126–1198), Islam's great authorities on Aristotle. The works

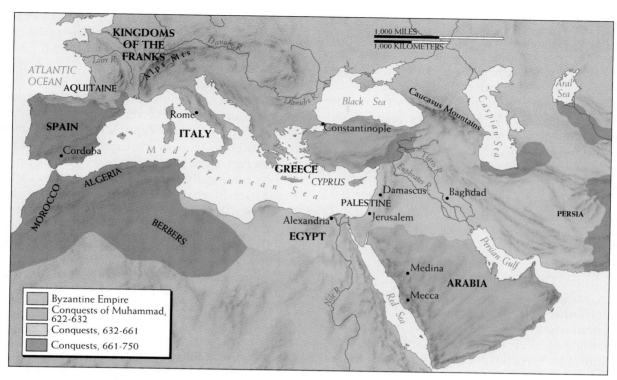

MAP 6–2 MUSLIM CONQUESTS AND DOMINATION OF THE MEDITERRANEAN TO ABOUT 750 C.E.
*Within 125 years of Muhammad's rise, Muslims came to dominate Spain and all areas
south and east of the Mediterranean.*

of multilingual Jewish scholars also helped create bridges between the Muslim and Christian worlds.

Western Society and the Developing Christian Church

Europe, overrun by barbarians from the north and east and threatened in the south by a vigorous and expansive Islam, declined during the fifth and sixth centuries. As trade waned in the increasing chaos, the West lost the urban centers where exchanges of goods and ideas promoted cultural growth. The beleaguered westerners had no help from the East, for the Byzantine emperors of the seventh century were preoccupied with the Islamic threat to their domains. As the Muslims conquered Mediterranean islands and ports and strangled Christian shipping, Europe's communications with the East declined even further. Forced by these developments to rely on their own resources, westerners drew on their Germanic and Greco-Roman heritages to create distinctive new cultures.

As western cities and governments declined, people sought employment and protection on the self-sufficient estates of the great landholders. Peasants made up 90 percent of the population of medieval Europe. Some were free and owned their own land. Some surrendered their land to a more powerful man in exchange for assistance and became serfs. Serfs were bound to the land they worked. They were not free to leave it, but, on the other hand, custom protected them from being separated from it and sold as slaves.

As trade declined, agricultural districts became insular and self-contained. Barter sufficed for exchanging goods among the great estates that were the basic political and economic units of medieval society. Producers adjusted their output to local need. And since there was no way to turn excess goods into profit, there was little incentive to experiment with more efficient techniques or expand production. This was the background for the evolution of the characteristic medieval institutions: an economic system called manorialism and a political system called feudalism.

The Christian church kept some of medieval Europe's fading urban centers alive. During the period of the late empire the church had modeled itself on Rome's imperial government and had located its administrative offices in cities, the empire's centers of power. As the western empire crumbled and secular magistrates disappeared, many of their functions were transferred to bishops, the only Roman officials still available. The local cathedral (a church served by a bishop) became the center of urban life and its bishop the effective governor of his city. The church thus preserved some of the skills and procedures of Roman government.

The church was forced by Rome's decline and the loss of the state's protection to involve itself in politics. The struggle to survive the period of the German and Islamic invasions cost the church some of its spiritual integrity but did not diminish its effectiveness as a civilizing and unifying force. Its rituals and creeds united people across barriers of social class, education, and gender, and its clergy—the best-educated minds in Europe—had knowledge that was invaluable to the German kings who were trying to reestablish order.

Monastic Culture

The early medieval church drew much of its strength from religious institutions called monasteries. The first monks were hermits who protested the relaxation of standards of Christian discipline that followed Constantine's popularization of Christianity in the fourth century. They fled to remote areas to find the freedom to practice the extreme ascetic disciplines that they believed were the mark of true Christian commitment. They became the new Christian heroes—the successors to the martyrs that the Roman government no longer persecuted.

Medieval Christians viewed monastic life—governed, as it was, by the biblical "counsels of perfection" (chastity, poverty, and obedience)—as humanity's highest calling. Monks and the secular (i.e., parish) clergy (whom popular opinion forced to adopt some monastic disciplines) were expected to meet a more demanding spiritual standard than ordinary believers. Consequently, clergy appeared superior to laity, a belief that served the papacy well in struggles with secular rulers.

Although early monasticism was modeled on the lives of hermits such as Anthony of Egypt (ca. 251–356), it soon evolved communal institutions. In the first quarter of the fourth century, Pachomius (ca. 286–346), another Egyptian recluse, set up a highly regimented community in which hundreds of monks lived in accordance with a strict penal code. Such monastic communities tried to become "cities of God," isolating themselves from the collapsing Roman Empire and its nominally Christian society. The form of monasticism that spread throughout the East, however, was that championed by Basil the Great (329–379). It put less stress on personal asceticism and urged monks to care for the needy outside their communities.

Athanasius (ca. 293–373) and Martin of Tours (ca. 315–ca. 399) introduced the West to the monastic practices that were evolving in the East. But in 529 Benedict of Nursia (ca. 480–547) wrote a rule (i.e., a constitution) for a monastery he established at Monte Cassino near Naples, Italy, which defined a uniquely Western style of monasticism and became standard throughout Europe. Benedict's Rule governed a monk's every activity, including sleep. It discouraged the kind of flamboyant asceticism that was popular in the East. Benedict insisted that monks have adequate food, some wine, serviceable clothing, and proper amounts of sleep and relaxation. Periods of time were set aside each day for prayer, communal worship, and study—and for the manual labor by which monks supported themselves. The program was designed to create autonomous religious communities that were economically, spiritually, and intellectually self-sufficient. Benedictine monks did not turn their backs on the world. They were chiefly responsible for the missionary work that converted England and Germany to Christianity, and their discipline and devotion to hard work made them both an economic and a spiritual force wherever they went.

The Doctrine of Papal Primacy

Constantine and the eastern emperors treated the church like a department of state. They intervened in its theological debates and legislated its doctrine. The bishops of Rome, however, acquired independence as imperial power faded in the West. The doctrine of "papal primacy" that they proclaimed asserted their right to undisputed leadership of a church that was totally independent of the state.

Papal primacy was a response to the decline of imperial Rome and the increasing pretensions of Constantinople. In 381 when the ecumenical Council of Constantinople declared the patriarch of Constantinople to be first in rank after the bishop of Rome, Pope Damasus I (366–384) objected. He claimed that Rome had a unique "apostolic" primacy, for its bishops were heirs to the Apostle Peter and his personal legacy as the "rock" on which Jesus had said (Matthew 16:18) that the church was to be built. After the Council of Chalcedon (451) accorded the Byzantine patriarch the same primacy over the East that Rome traditionally had in the West, Pope Leo I (440–461) assumed the title *pontifex maximus* ("supreme priest") to assert his claim to supremacy over all bishops everywhere. At the end of the fifth century, Pope Gelasius I (492–496) further clarified the nature of papal authority by declaring it to be "more weighty" than that of the state—his reason being that the church was responsible for the means of salvation, the most serious human concern.

The Germanic and Islamic invasions prevented Constantinople from exercising much control over the popes and the Western church. When the Lombard tribes invaded Italy late in the sixth century, Pope Gregory I, "the Great" (590–604), ignored the imperial authorities and assumed the right to negotiate with the barbarians as the chief representative of the Italian people.

The Division of Christendom

By the time Gregory became pope, the patriarch of Constantinople was using the title "universal" patriarch to imply a claim to supremacy over Rome. Since he had no authority in the West, this was really an admission that separate churches were functioning in the East and West. The division of the church was apparent in language, doctrine, disciplinary codes, and liturgies. The Greek Byzantine church had a mystical, other-worldly orientation that contrasted with the more practical Christianity of the West's Latin church. Ecclesiastical organization in the East more closely paralleled the hierarchy of imperial government than did the structure of the Western church. But the power of the Byzantine patriarch over the clergy was limited by the

power the emperor had over him. Where the Western church tried to impose monastic celibacy on all clergy, parish priests in the Eastern church (except for bishops) were allowed to marry. The Eastern church used leavened bread in the Eucharist; Rome mandated unleavened bread. The Byzantines rejected the Catholic doctrine of purgatory. They also permitted divorce and, unlike the Catholics, performed their liturgies in the vernacular of the laity.

From time to time, Eastern and Western Christians differed markedly on doctrine. Where the Latin church looked to the Roman pope to define doctrine, the Greek church relied on the authority of the Bible and ecumenical councils. Disputes over the right to define doctrine became acute when the East endorsed iconoclasm (i.e., repudiating the veneration of holy images) and when the West added the word *filioque* ("and from the Son") to the Nicene Creed. The latter was the West's attempt to subvert compromises the East had made with Arianism. It was meant to make it clear that the Holy Spirit proceeded from the Father and the Son as equal partners in the Godhead and not from the Father alone. The claims of Roman popes to a primacy of authority over the whole church were dismissed in the East, for eastern Christianity evolved not as a single organization but as a communion of independent national churches. In the ninth century, when the crucial issue of authority over the universal church came to a head, Pope Nicholas I and Patriarch Photius excommunicated each other. In 1054 Pope Leo IX and Patriarch Michael Cerularius again officially divided the church by repeating the mutual condemnation.

Rome took a risk in quarreling with Constantinople, for popes looked to the eastern empire to defend them from barbarian invaders. But as help declined from that quarter and Christianity spread to the invaders, the popes sought new allies among the Germans. They correctly intuited that the Franks of northern Gaul were Europe's ascendant power and the church's most promising potential protectors. In 754, Pope Stephen II (752–757) took the dramatic step of throwing in his lot with the Germans. He persuaded Pepin III, ruler of the Franks, to defend Rome from the Lombards. This acknowledged the end of the old empire and the transfer of the West to new hands.

The Kingdom of the Franks

Merovingians and Carolingians: From Clovis to Charlemagne

A warrior chieftain named Clovis (ca. 466?–511) founded the first Frankish dynasty. It is called Merovingian after Merovich, an early tribal leader. Clovis and his successors united the Salian and Ripuarian Franks, subdued the Burgundians and Visigoths, won the support of the Gallo-Romans by converting to orthodox Christianity, and turned the Roman province of Gaul into France (i.e., "land of the Franks").

GOVERNING THE FRANKS The Merovingians struggled with the perennial problem of medieval politics: the competing claims of the "one" and the "many." As kings worked to centralize governments, powerful local magnates fought to preserve their regional autonomy. The result was a battle between forces that tried to unify society and those that promoted fragmentation.

The Merovingian kings hoped to pull their nation together by making pacts with the landed nobility and by relying for help in running their domain on a new kind of royal official, the count. Counts were sent out to manage districts in which they had no hereditary estates. Kings hoped that counts would be easier to control than landed aristocrats, for the people the counts governed would have no tradition of loyalty to the counts' families. But as time passed, kings found it impossible to prevent counts from establishing hereditary claims to their offices and becoming as independent as the older nobility. The unification of the Frankish state was also impeded by Frankish inheritance customs, which gave all a king's legitimate male heirs a right to a share in his kingdom.

By the seventh century the Merovingian king was king in title only. Real executive authority had devolved on one of his officials, the "mayor of the palace." The family of Pepin I of Austrasia (d. 639) monopolized this post until 751, when, with the connivance of the pope, one of its members shoved the Merovingians aside, expropriated the Frankish crown, and founded the Carolingian dynasty.

Pepin I's descendent, Pepin II (d. 714), who had ruled the Frankish kingdom in fact but not in title, bequeathed that anomalous situation to his illegitimate son, Charles "Martel" (Charles "the Hammer"). Martel (d. 741) created a great cavalry by bestowing lands as fiefs or benefices ("provisional" grants) on powerful noblemen on condition that they use the income to equip themselves to fight for him. His army proved its worth at Poitiers in 732, when it broke the momentum of the Muslim advance and secured the Pyrenees as the border of western Europe.

Much of the land that Martel distributed as fiefs to create his army came from the church. The church was dependent on the protection of the Franks, and it could do little to prevent the confiscation of property that was used to fund its own defense. Eventually, however, the church was partially compensated for its losses.

Where the Merovingians had tried to weaken the aristocrats by raising landless men to power, the Carolingians forged an alliance with the landed aristocracy and staffed their government almost entirely from its ranks. By playing to strength rather than challenging it, the Carolingians secured their position in the short run.

THE FRANKISH CHURCH The church played a major role in the Frankish government, for its monasteries were the intellectual centers of Carolingian society. In Merovingian times the higher clergy were employed in tandem with counts as royal agents, and the Carolingians—particularly Charles Martel and his successors, Pepin III, "the Short" (d. 768), and Charlemagne (r. 768–814)—relied on Christian missionaries to pacify the barbarian lands that they conquered. Conversion to Nicene Christianity was an essential part of the process of assimilating new subjects. The cavalry broke their bodies, and the clergy reworked their hearts and minds.

The missions of the church and state tended to be confused when the king appointed Christian bishops to govern the lands they were converting. An event from the career of Boniface (born Wynfrith, 680?–754), an Anglo-Saxon monk who was the most famous of the Carolingian missionaries, illustrates how deeply involved in politics the church became. In 751 Pope Zacharias (741–752) sanctioned Pepin the Short's bid for the Frankish throne. Pepin was proclaimed king by the nobility in council, and the last of the Merovingians, the puppet king Childeric III, was hustled off to a monastery where enforced celibacy guaranteed the extermination of his line. Boniface may have anointed Pepin at his coronation. Since anointing was part of the ritual of priestly ordination, the rite was apparently intended to give the Carolingian monarchy a sacral character.

In 753 Pope Stephen II (752–757), Zacharias's successor, asked for a favor in return. He came to Pepin's court to ask the Franks to defend Rome from the Lombards and confirm papal claims to central Italy. In 755 the Franks defeated the Lombards and turned over to the pope the lands surrounding Rome, including some to which the eastern emperor had title. This confirmed the pope's secular authority over a region known as the Papal States.

About this time (750–800) a document called the *Donation of Constantine* began to be circulated to support the church in its dealings with the Franks. It said that Constantine had given the papacy title to the western half of his empire. If so, this implied that the papacy had the right to pass judgment on the legitimacy of western governments. The *Donation* was exposed as a forgery in the fifteenth century, but initially it gave the popes some leverage in dealing with their potentially overwhelming protectors. The Franks drew almost as slight a boundary between state and church as did the eastern emperors, and the church had to fight hard to avoid being subordinated to the Frankish monarchy.

The Reign of Charlemagne (768–814)

In 774 Charlemagne, the son of Pepin the Short, completed his father's work by conquering Italy's Lombards and assuming their crown. He devoted the rest of his reign to expanding the size of the kingdom he had inherited. The Saxons of northern Germany were brutally subdued and pacified by being evicted from their homes for resettlement elsewhere. The Muslims were chased beyond the Pyrenees, and the Avars (a tribe related to the Huns) were practically annihilated—bringing the Danubian plains into the Frankish orbit. By the time of Charlemagne's death on January 28, 814, his kingdom embraced modern France, Belgium, Holland, Switzerland, almost the whole of western Germany, much of Italy, a portion of Spain, and the island of Corsica—an area about equal to the nations of the European Economic Community (EEC).

An equestrian figure of Charlemagne (or possibly one of his sons) from the early ninth century. Giraudon/Art Resource, NY

THE NEW EMPIRE Charlemagne believed that his huge domain entitled him to an imperial title, and to win support for assuming it he tried to look as imperial as possible. Since eastern emperors ruled from a fixed capital, he constructed a palace city for himself at Aachen (or Aix-la-Chapelle), and he turned to the church for help.

Charlemagne's imperial pretensions were confirmed on Christmas Day, 800, when Pope Leo III (795–816) crowned him emperor. The ceremony, which established a fateful link between German kings and Roman Italy, was in part an effort by

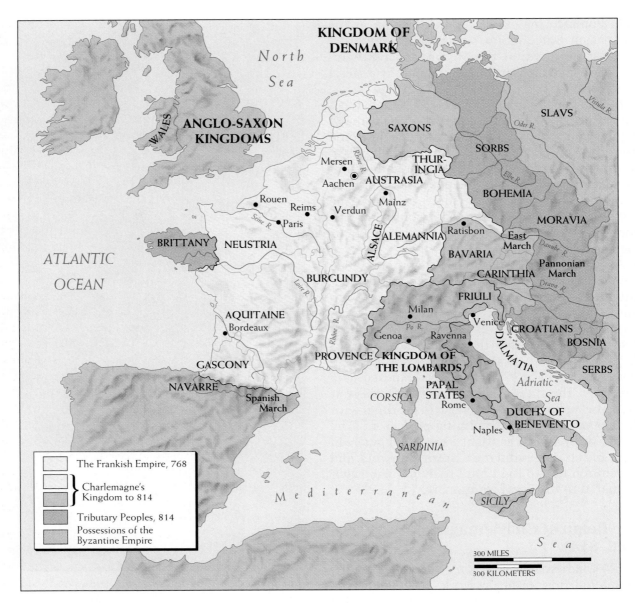

Map 6–3   THE EMPIRE OF CHARLEMAGNE TO 814   *Building on the successes of his predecessors, Charlemagne greatly increased the Frankish domains.*

the pope to gain some leverage over a powerful king. By arranging for the emperor to receive the crown from the hands of the pope, a precedent was set that was useful for the church in its future dealings with the state. At the time, however, the coronation in no way diminished Charlemagne's power over the church, and it strengthened him abroad by confronting the eastern emperors with a *fait accompli.* They reluctantly acknowledged his title once he disclaimed any ambition to move into their lands.

THE NEW EMPEROR   Charlemagne stood a majestic six feet three and one-half inches tall. (His tomb was opened in 1861, and exact measurements of his remains were made.) He was restless, informal, and gregarious—ever ready for a hunt or for a swim with his friends in Aachen's hot springs. He was widely known for his practical jokes, lusty good humor, and warm hospitality. Aachen was a festive court to which visitors and gifts came from all over the world. In 802 the caliph of Baghdad, Harun-al-Rashid, even sent

Charlemagne a white elephant, the transport of which was as great a wonder as the creature itself.

Charlemagne had five official wives (in succession), many mistresses and concubines, and numerous children. This connubial variety caused some political upheavals when Pepin, his oldest son by his first marriage, grew jealous of the attention the emperor showed the sons of his second wife. Pepin joined some nobles in an ill-fated conspiracy against Charlemagne and spent the rest of his life confined to a monastery.

PROBLEMS OF GOVERNMENT Charlemagne relied on counts for help in governing his empire. There may have been as many as 250 deployed to strategic locations. A Carolingian count was usually a local magnate who had soldiers and who was persuaded by royal generosity to put them at the service of his king. He maintained a local army, collected tribute and dues, and administered justice—all in the name of the king.

A count presided over a district law court called the *mallus*. Its job was to hear testimony and to pass judgment based less on evidence than on the character or believability of each party to a quarrel. In situations in which such testimony was insufficient, recourse was had to duels or to various tests or ordeals. A defendant's hand might be immersed in boiling water and his innocence determined by the way his wounds healed. Or a suspect might be bound with ropes and thrown into a river or pond that had been blessed by a priest. If the sacred water rejected him and he floated, he was assumed to be guilty. God was believed to render the verdict in an ordeal. Once guilt was determined, the *mallus* ordered monetary compensation to be paid to injured parties. This settled grievances that otherwise might have caused bloody vendettas.

Charlemagne never solved the problem of creating a loyal bureaucracy to govern his kingdom. The counts he appointed, like their Merovingian predecessors, tended to become little despots within their districts. Charlemagne issued "capitularies" (i.e., royal decrees) to establish policies he wanted his administrators to implement. He tried to exercise some oversight by sending envoys called *missi dominici* to check up on the counts and report back on their behavior. When the *missi*'s infrequent inspections had little impact, Charlemagne created provincial governors

(e.g., prefects, dukes, and margraves) to keep permanent watch over the counts. They, however, proved no more trustworthy than the counts.

Charlemagne often appointed churchmen to government offices, for bishops, like counts, were considered royal servants. This, however, did little to improve the situation. The higher clergy shared the secular lifestyles and aspirations of the counts and were generally indistinguishable from the lay nobility. To be a Christian at this difficult period in the history of Europe was largely a matter of submitting to rituals such as baptism and assenting to creeds. Both clergy and laity were too preoccupied with the struggle to survive to worry much about elevated ethical issues.

ALCUIN AND THE CAROLINGIAN RENAISSANCE Charlemagne tried to improve the government of his empire by making an intensive effort to advance the education of the aristocratic boys who were destined for offices in the church and state. His conquests brought him a great deal of wealth, and he used some of it to attract Europe's best scholars to Aachen—men such as Theodulf of Orleans, Angilbert, Einhard (Charlemagne's biographer), and Alcuin of York (735–804), a famous Anglo-Saxon educator who became director of the king's palace school. The school provided basic instruction in the seven liberal arts with special concentration on grammar, logic, rhetoric, and simple mathematics.

The curriculum was designed to give bureaucrats the simple tools of their trade, but it accomplished more than that. It improved the accuracy of the Latin used in official documents, and it spread a new and much more legible style of handwriting throughout the empire. This Carolingian "minuscule" made reading far easier and more pleasurable than the Merovingian scripts. A modest renaissance or rebirth of interest in antiquity also took place at the palace school as its scholars collected and copied ancient manuscripts. Alcuin worked on the text of the Bible and made editions of the works of Gregory the Great and the Rule of Saint Benedict. Most scholarly projects aimed at concrete reforms. They helped to establish uniformity in church law and liturgy, to educate the clergy, and to raise personal and professional standards for monks and priests.

THE CAROLINGIAN MANOR   Early medieval Europe's chief economic institution was a kind of communal farm called a manor. Medieval farmers often preferred to cluster in villages rather than to live on individual farms. This increased security and enabled them to share labor and expensive agricultural implements such as plows and oxen. But instead of dividing harvests equally among all a manor's workers, each family on the manor had its own strips of land and lived from what they produced.

The status of peasants was determined by the nature of their holdings. A freeman had allodial property (i.e., land free from the claims of an overlord). If he surrendered this to an overlord in exchange for protection, he became a serf and received his land back from his lord with a new set of rights and obligations. Although the land was no longer his property, he had full use of it and could not be separated from it. His chief duty to his lord was to work his lord's *demesne,* the fields on the manor that produced the crops meant for the lord's table. Peasants who entered the service of a lord with little real property (e.g., only a few farm implements and animals) became unfree serfs. Such serfs were much more vulnerable to a lord's demands, often spending up to three days a week working their lord's fields. Truly impoverished peasants, those who had nothing to offer except their hands, had the lowest status and were the least protected from excessive demands.

By Charlemagne's day, a new type of plow was coming into use. It was heavy enough to break up the dense, waterlogged soils of northern Europe and open to cultivation lands that had defeated Roman farmers. Unlike the ancient "scratch" plow (a pointed stick), it cut deeply into the soil and had a moldboard that turned earth over to utilize more of its fertility. Ancient farmers had maintained the fertility of their fields by using a two-field system of crop rotation. That is, they simply alternated fallow and planted fields annually. A fallow field was plowed to keep down weeds but was not planted. The medieval three-field system left only one-third of a farm fallow in a given year. This decreased the amount of unproductive land that had to be plowed and used crop rotation to help maintain fertility. In the fall, one field was planted with winter crops of wheat or rye, which were harvested in early summer. In late spring, a second field was planted

with summer crops of oats, barley, lentils, and legumes, which were harvested in August or September. The third field was left fallow.

RELIGION AND THE CLERGY   Religion had an intrinsic appeal for the masses of ordinary men and women who were burdened, fearful, and had little hope of improving their lots this side of eternity. The privileged upper classes were, however, no less pious. Charlemagne frequented the Church of Saint Mary in Aachen several times a day and decreed on his deathbed that all but a fraction of his great treasure be spent to endow masses and prayers for his soul.

The priests who served the people (the lower clergy as opposed to the ecclesiastical administrators) were poorly prepared to provide spiritual leadership. They were recruited from the ranks of the serfs and fared no better than other peasants. Lords owned the churches on their lands and often staffed them with their own serfs. The church expected a lord to liberate a serf who entered the clergy, but many "serf priests" said mass on Sunday and toiled as peasants during the rest of the week.

Because priests on most manors were no better educated than their congregations, religious instruction barely existed. For most people religion was more a matter of practice than doctrine. They baptized their children, attended mass, tried to learn the Lord's Prayer and the Apostles' Creed, and received the last rites when death approached. They were in awe of sacred relics and devoted to an army of saints who they hoped would intercede for them with their divine overlord in the court of heaven. Simple faith had little need for understanding.

Breakup of the Carolingian Kingdom

As Charlemagne aged, his empire became progressively ungovernable, for there was no way to prevent his nobles from doing what they wanted with the lands they held. In feudal society the intensity of one's loyalty to one's lord diminished as one's distance from that lord increased, and local people obeyed local leaders more readily than distant kings. Charlemagne had to appoint powerful men if he hoped to keep the far-flung regions of his empire under control, but their power always diminished his. In the Carolingian as in the Merovingian kingdom, the noble tail increasingly wagged the royal dog.

LOUIS THE PIOUS   The Carolingians did not give up easily. Charlemagne's successor was his only surviving son, Louis the Pious (r. 814–840). During Charlemagne's last years the emperor shared the imperial title with Louis, for it symbolized the Carolingian hope of consolidating the kingdom by persuading its subjects to transcend regional and tribal loyalties. Unfortunately, in the next generation Louis's fertility undercut this objective. Louis had three sons by his first wife, and, according to Salic (i.e., Salian Frankish) law, each was entitled to a share of his kingdom. Louis tried to break with tradition by making his eldest son, Lothar (d. 855), co-regent and sole imperial heir (817). In 823, however, Louis's second wife bore him a fourth son, Charles "the Bald" (d. 877). In the interest of securing an inheritance for her boy, the queen incited her stepsons, Pepin and Louis the German, to rebel. Supported by the pope, they joined forces and defeated their father in a battle near Colmar in 833.

THE TREATY OF VERDUN AND ITS AFTERMATH   Pepin's death in 838 and his father's in 840 helped clear the field of contenders. In 843 the Treaty of Verdun divided the empire among the three remaining Carolingian princes. Lothar retained the meaningless imperial title and authority over a region called Lotharingia (equivalent to modern Holland, Belgium, Switzerland, Alsace-Lorraine, and Italy). Charles the Bald reigned over much of what was to become France, and Louis the German over Germany.

The Treaty of Verdun was only the start of the division of the Carolingian lands. When Lothar died in 855, his "middle kingdom" was split up among his three sons. This upset the balance of power and tempted the larger eastern and western Frankish kingdoms of France and Germany to stake claims to portions of Lothar's diminished legacy. The decline of the Carolingian Empire in Italy created a political vacuum the popes tried to fill. But both popes and kings became pawns in the hands of the landed nobility. It is at this juncture in European history (i.e., the last quarter of the ninth and the first half of the tenth centuries) that one may speak accurately of a "dark age." Historical record keeping declined not only because the empire and papacy deteri-

The tenth-century crown of the Holy Roman Emperor (the title applied to rulers who succeeded to the remains of Charlemagne's empire) reveals the close alliance between church and throne. The crown is surmounted by a cross, and it includes panels depicting the great kings of the Bible, David and Solomon. Kunsthistorisches Museum, Vienna

rated politically but because barbarian attacks on Europe were renewed. Successive waves of Vikings (i.e., "North-men" or Normans) from Scandinavia, Magyars (i.e., Hungarians from the plains of Russia), and Muslims (from Sicily and Africa) simultaneously invaded Europe from different directions.

The Vikings were the most serious threat. Thanks to their unique skills as seamen, they were able to raid Europe's coasts and use its rivers to reach targets deep inland. Since they moved rapidly and randomly, there was little defense against them. The Franks built fortified towns and castles to serve as refuges. Sometimes they bought off the invaders with silver or grants of land. France even created a duchy of "Normandy" for the newcomers. Since there was little that the central governments of kings could do against myriad bands of raiders descending from multiple directions, communities looked to resident local strongmen for protection.

Feudal Society

In the absence of effective central governments that were able to protect them, medieval people resorted to feudal arrangements. The weaker submitted to the stronger, and those who could guarantee security from rapine and starvation ruled. Medieval feudalism emerged from a world dominated by warlords.

Feudal society was held together by the oaths that individuals made—that is, by promises to provide subordinates with protection or maintenance in exchange for their pledge of service. Men who were equipped as soldiers became vassals and formed a professional military class with its own code of knightly conduct. Networks of personal relationships among members of this class created regional military organizations. The leaders of these organizations, whether or not they had a legal right, assumed responsibility for governing the people who lived under their protection.

Origins

The roots of feudal government go back to the sixth and seventh centuries, when the weakness of the West's governments made it necessary for freemen who were unable to fend for themselves to seek alliances with more powerful neighbors. Freemen who entered into various kinds of contractual relations of dependence on superiors were known as *vassi* or vassals (i.e., "those who serve"). Owners of large estates tried to acquire as many vassals as they could afford to equip as soldiers for their private armies. Originally, such men were maintained as part of their lord's household. But as their numbers grew, this became impractical. Since the collapsing economy was taking money out of circulation, there was no way to pay vassals salaries. Hence, the custom developed of granting them benefices or fiefs (i.e., the right to use a piece of their lord's land to maintain themselves for his service). Vassals lived on their fiefs and were responsible for the peasants who farmed them.

Vassalage and the Fief

A vassal swore fealty to his lord. That meant that he promised to serve his lord and to refrain from actions contrary to his lord's interests. His chief obligation was military. He served as a mounted knight. Bargaining might take place over terms of service, but custom limited the number of days a lord could keep a vassal in the field. (In France in the eleventh century, forty days was standard.) In addition to military duty a vassal was expected to attend his lord's court when summoned and to render his lord financial assistance at times of special need, especially (1) to ransom him from his enemies, (2) to outfit him for a major military campaign, or (3) to defray the costs of the festivities at the marriage of a daughter or the knighting of a son.

Louis the Pious extended vassalage beyond the lay nobility to the higher clergy by requiring bishops and abbots to swear fealty and to accept their appointments on the same terms as royal benefices. He formally "invested" clerics with the rings and staffs that were the symbols of their spiritual offices. This practice was offensive to the church, for it implied the subservience of the church to the state. In the late tenth and eleventh centuries, reform-minded clergy rebelled against the ceremonies of vassalage and "lay investiture," but the reformers never suggested surrendering the grants of land that were the rewards for oaths of homage.

A lord's obligations to his vassals were very specific. He had to protect the vassal from physical harm, to stand as his advocate in court, and to provide for his maintenance by giving him a fief. In Carolingian times a fief varied in size from one or more small villas to several *mansi* (a unit of twenty-five to forty-eight acres). Royal vassals might receive fiefs ranging from 30 to 200 *mansi*. With prizes like this in the offing, vassalage was acceptable to the highest classes of Carolingian society. In the short run the policy marshaled the nobility behind the king, but in the long run the granting of fiefs undercut royal power. Kings found it difficult or impossible to reclaim land once it was granted to vassals. A vassal whom a king enriched sufficiently could then create vassals of his own.

Fragmentation and Divided Loyalty

Since it was possible for a vassal to accept fiefs from more than one lord, all kinds of conflicts of interest might arise. The ninth century developed the concept of the "liege lord," the master to whom a vassal owed primary duty, but this did not halt progressive fragmentation of land and loyalty.

Kings were further weakened by the fact that the fiefs they granted tended to become the real property of their vassals. Although title to a fief remained with the lord who granted it, it was hard for him to prevent his vassal from passing the fief on to an heir. In the ninth century, hereditary possession became a legally recognized principle and laid the basis for claims to outright ownership. In this way, the nobility gradually appropriated much of the royal domain.

Lay society was illiterate. Consequently, the feudal era used symbols and ceremonies to seal the contracts involved in vassalage. A freeman became a vassal by a secular act of "commendation." In the mid-eighth century, a religious oath of fealty was added to increase the solemnity of the act. A vassal reinforced his promise of fidelity to a lord by swearing an oath with his hand on a sacred relic or a Bible. In the tenth and eleventh centuries, paying homage to the lord involved not only the swearing of such an oath but also the placement of the vassal's hands between his lord's hands and the sealing of the ritual with a kiss.

Despite feudalism's obvious vulnerability to abuse and confusion, it created social stability in early medieval Europe and helped restore political centralization during the High Middle Ages. The genius of feudal government lay in its adaptability. Contracts of different kinds could be made with almost anybody to serve almost any purpose. The foundations of the modern nation-state were laid in France and England as kings compromised with vassals and fine-tuned feudal arrangements to reconstruct centralized government.

In Perspective

Between 476 and 1000 the eastern and western halves of the old Roman Empire lost contact with each other and developed in different directions. Classical civilization faded, and three new medieval civilizations took its place. In the East the Byzantine Empire, with its capital at Constantinople, preserved classical literature but used it to nourish a passion- *ately Christian culture. Religion also provided the means for uniting the Arabs and sending them forth to conquer an empire that soon stretched from Spain to China. Islamic culture, as well as the Islamic state, reached its creative peak during the earlier medieval centuries while the West was still recovering from the barbarian invasions and the collapse of the ancient economy. In the West, cities diminished, and society became largely agrarian. Although the Latin church preserved some classical literature and some shreds of Roman institutions, the West was slow to reclaim its classical heritage.*

The West's "renaissances" began with the reign of the Frankish emperor Charlemagne and continued through the sixteenth century. They produced a uniquely European way of life that was a mixture of barbarian customs, Christian faith, and remnants of classical culture. But early medieval Europe made slow progress in that direction, for its society was primitive and fragmented. Its people were preoccupied with the pursuit of basic needs—food, which was supplied by manorialism, and public order, which was maintained by feudalism. Europe could not yet aspire to a civilization as elaborate as those of Byzantium and Islam.

REVIEW QUESTIONS

1. What changes took place in Christianity between its founding and the coronation of the Emperor Charlemagne in 800? What were the distinctive features of the early church? What role did the church play in the Western world after the fall of the Roman Empire?

2. What changes took place in the Frankish kingdom between its foundation and the end of Charlemagne's reign? What were the characteristics of Charlemagne's government? Why did Charlemagne encourage learning at his court? Could the Carolingian renaissance have endangered his authority? Why did his empire break apart?

3. How and why was the history of the eastern half of the former Roman Empire so different from that of its western half? Did Justinian strengthen or weaken the Byzantine Empire? How does his reign compare to Charlemagne's?

4. What were the tenets of Islam? How were the Muslims able to build an empire so quickly? What contributions did the Muslims make to the development of Western Europe?
5. How and why did feudal society begin? What were the essential features of feudalism? Do you think that modern society could "slip back" into a feudal pattern?

SUGGESTED READINGS

G. BARRACLOUGH, *The Crucible of Europe: The Ninth and Tenth Centuries* (1976). Sweeping survey of political history.

H. CHADWICK, *The Early Church* (1967). Among the best treatments of early Christianity.

F. L. GANSHOF, *Feudalism*, trans. by Philip Grierson (1964). The most profound brief analysis of the subject.

R. HODGES and D. WHITEHOUSE, *Mohammed, Charlemagne and the Origins of Europe* (1982). For the social and economic history of early medieval Europe.

A. HOURANI, *A History of the Arab Peoples* (1991). A comprehensive text that includes an excellent overview of the origins and early history of Islam.

B. LEWIS, *The Muslim Discovery of Europe* (1982). Authoritative account from the Muslim perspective.

C. MANGO, *Byzantium: The Empire of New Rome* (1980). Perhaps the most readable account.

R. MCKITTERICK, *The Frankish Kingdoms under the Carolingians, 751–987* (1983). The fate of Carolingian government.

R. W. SOUTHERN, *The Making of the Middle Ages* (1973). Originally published in 1953 but still a fresh account by an imaginative historian.

W. WALTHER, *Woman in Islam* (1981). One hour spent with this book teaches more about the social import of Islam than days spent with others.

S. WEMPLE, *Women in Frankish Society: Marriage and the Cloister, 500–900* (1981). What marriage and the cloister meant to women in these early centuries.

L. WHITE, JR., *Medieval Technology and Social Change* (1962). Often fascinating account of the way primitive technology changed life.

Chapter 7
The High Middle Ages: The Rise of European Empires and States (1000–1300)

KEY TOPICS

- Germany's Saxon dynasty and the Holy Roman Empire
- A movement to reform the church and free it from political domination by kings and emperors
- The emergence of strong national monarchies in England and France
- The fragmentation of Germany, the conclusion of a struggle for supremacy between the Hohenstaufen dynasty and the papacy

The High Middle Ages (1000–1300) was a period of political expansion and consolidation and of intellectual flowering and synthesis. With respect to the development of Western institutions, this may have been a more creative era than the Italian Renaissance or the German Reformation.

The borders of western Europe were secured against foreign invaders, and Europeans, who had long been the prey of foreign powers, mounted a military and economic offensive against the East. The rulers of England and France established nuclei for nation-states by *adapting feudal principles of government to the creation of centralized political realms. Parliaments and popular assemblies emerged in some places to enable the propertied classes to influence the development of the new monarchies. Germany and Italy (i.e., the Holy Roman Empire) were the great exceptions to the trend toward political consolidation. They remained fragmented until the nineteenth century.*

The High Middle Ages also saw the establishment of the distinctive Western custom of separating church and state. By asserting monarchical authority over the church, the popes prevented it from being split up by and absorbed into Europe's emerging states. The cost to the papacy was the charge that it was diverting the church from its spiritual mission into the murky world of politics.

Otto I and the Revival of the Empire

The fortunes of both the empire and the papacy began to revive in the early tenth century, bringing an end to the medieval "dark ages."

Unifying Germany

In 918 the duke of Saxony, Henry I "the Fowler" (d. 936), founded the Saxon dynasty, Germany's first non-Frankish monarchy. Henry reversed the process of political fragmentation that had set in with the decline of the Carolingian Empire. He consolidated the duchies of Swabia, Bavaria, Saxony, Franconia, and Lotharingia and checked the invasions of the Hungarians and the Danes.

The German state that Henry bequeathed to his son Otto I "the Great" (r. 936–973) was the strongest kingdom in Europe. In 951 Otto invaded Italy and proclaimed himself its king. In 955 he defeated the Hungarians at Lechfeld. This secured German borders against barbarian attack and established the frontiers of western Europe.

Embracing the Church

Otto secured the power of the throne by refusing to allow Germany's dukes to turn their duchies into hereditary properties. He also diminished the role powerful lay lords played in his government by appointing bishops and abbots of monasteries to administer his lands and be his agents. Clergy were more likely than laymen to be sympathetic to his plans to restore imperial authority, and, unlike laymen, they could not marry and pass on to their sons the lands they held from the king. The church sensed no conflict between its spiritual and political duties and eagerly embraced the wealth and power Otto pressed on it.

In 961 Otto rescued Pope John XII (955–964) from a scuffle with the Italian nobility, and on February 2, 962, the pope bestowed the lapsed imperial title on Germany's king. Otto's intervention in Italian politics increased his power over the church. Otto appointed the higher clergy and declared himself special "protector" of the Papal States. When Pope John belatedly recognized the royal web in which he had become entangled, he joined a plot against the new emperor. Otto promptly ordered an ecclesiastical synod to depose John and to decree that no pope take office without first swearing allegiance to the emperor. Otto's popes ruled at his pleasure.

The Italian interests that Otto bequeathed to his successors, Otto II (r. 973–983) and Otto III (r. 983–1002), distracted them from events in Germany, and they allowed their German base to disintegrate. It had been unwise to dream of empire before monarchy was firmly in place. As the fledgling empire began to crumble in the first quarter of the eleventh century, the papacy seized the opportunity to reassert its independence.

The Reviving Catholic Church

The papacy was fortunate in that the weakening of Germany's overextended empire corresponded with the rise within the church of a reform movement that restored respect for the authority of the clergy.

The Cluny Reform Movement

In the tenth century a campaign designed to reform the church by liberating the clergy from the control of the feudal nobility was launched from a monastery in east central France. Since the last days of the Roman Empire, monks, who were the least worldly of the clergy, had been the church's most popular representatives. Their educations were the best available, the relics and rituals they

The central nave of the Romanesque abbey of St. Faith (Foy) in Conques, France, where the female saint's relics lie. Roasted alive and beheaded in third-century Gaul, she became widely revered in France, England, Italy, and Spain, and was later a popular South American saint. The interior of the abbey reveals bulky and tightly built pillars, uniform rounded arches, and the restricted lighting that are characteristic of classic Romanesque architecture. Compare and contrast the abbey of St. Faith with the Gothic cathedral of Salisbury, England, on page 138.
Scala/Art Resource, NY

maintained were believed to have magical potency, and the religious ideals embodied in their way of life set the standard for Christian society.

In 910 William the Pious, duke of Aquitaine, founded a new monastery at Cluny that was pledged to maintaining the strictest observance of the Benedictine Rule and to restoring the purest liturgical practices. The Cluniac reformers claimed that the church could not reach its full spiritual potential so long as laymen had the power to appoint and dominate clerics. The lords who endowed the Cluniac houses gave them complete independence, and the abbots who ran them were sincere churchmen who enforced the strictest religious discipline.

Cluniac ideals spread from the monastery to the parish, for the reformers argued that the "sec-ular clergy" (i.e., those serving the *saeculum*, the "world") ought to adopt the ascetic lifestyle of the "regular" clergy (i.e., those living by a *regula*, a monastic "rule"). They also insisted that bishops be freed from the authority of feudal governments and made accountable only to an independent papacy.

Men trained at Cluny were dispatched to reform monasteries throughout France and Italy. Thanks to aggressive abbots, such as Saint Odo (926–946), Cluny acquired nearly 1,500 dependent cloisters and took the lead in various social reform movements. In the late ninth and early tenth centuries, Cluny inspired the "Peace of God" movement. This was an attempt to ease the suffering caused by the endemic warfare that plagued medieval society. It threatened excommunication for all soldiers who attacked members of noncombatant groups (e.g., women, peasants, merchants, and clergy). A "Truce of God" was subsequently proclaimed. It prohibited combat during part of each week (Wednesday night to Monday morning) and in all holy seasons.

During the reign of Emperor Henry III (r. 1039–1056), Cluniac reformers won high offices in the church. Pope Leo IX (1049–1054) appointed them to key administrative posts in Rome, and they encouraged him to suppress simony (i.e., the selling of church offices) and to enforce celibacy among parish priests. The papacy itself, however, continued to be dominated by powerful laymen. Leo IX was himself appointed by Henry III. In the course of his reign, Henry deposed three popes who were pawns of the Roman aristocracy.

When Henry died, he left the empire to an underage son, Henry IV (r. 1056–1106). Reform-minded popes took advantage of the weakness of the boy-king's regents to assert their independence. Pope Stephen IX (1057–1058) reigned without seeking imperial confirmation of his title, and in 1059 Pope Nicholas II (1059–1061) decreed that a body of high church officials (the College of Cardinals) would henceforth choose the popes. The procedures that were developed (and which are still followed) were designed to prevent the Italian nobles and the German kings from interfering in papal elections. The reformers made the papacy an independent, self-perpetuating ecclesiastical monarchy.

The Investiture Struggle: Gregory VII and Henry IV

The German monarchy did not react to the church's new policies until the reign of Pope Gregory VII (1073–1085), a fierce advocate of Cluny's reforms. In 1075 Gregory condemned "lay investiture," the appointment of a clergyman to a church office by a layman. The pope's decree attacked the foundations of imperial government. Since the days of Otto I, German kings had preferred to use bishops rather than lay nobles to administer state lands. If the king lost the right to appoint men to ecclesiastical office, he lost the power to choose some of the most important agents of his government. By prohibiting lay investiture the pope proclaimed the spiritual nature of the episcopacy, but he failed to recognize that the church's religious offices had long since become entwined with the secular offices of the state.

Henry opposed Gregory's action on the grounds that it violated a well-founded tradition on which imperial authority rested. But the pope had important allies. The German nobles were eager for opportunities to undercut their king, for his strength threatened their independence. When German bishops loyal to Henry assembled at Worms in January 1076 to repudiate Gregory, Gregory excommunicated Henry and absolved his subjects from their oaths of allegiance to him. This gave the German magnates an excuse to rebel against Henry and forced Henry to come to terms with Gregory. Henry crossed the Alps in midwinter to reach Gregory's castle at Canossa. There he reportedly stood barefoot in the snow for three days until the pope agreed to absolve him. The pope only appeared to win, for Henry's absolution deprived his nobles of their excuse for continuing their rebellion. The king regrouped his forces and regained much of his power. In March 1080, Gregory excommunicated Henry once again, but this time the German nobles refused to rise to the bait. Four years later Henry drove Gregory into exile and placed his own man, Clement III, on the papal throne.

The investiture controversy ended in 1122 with a compromise spelled out by the Concordat of Worms. Emperor Henry V (r. 1106–1125) agreed to cease investing bishops with the ring and staff that symbolized spiritual office. In return, Pope Calixtus II (1119–1124) recognized the emperor's right to be present at episcopal consecrations and to preside at the ceremonies that bestowed fiefs on bishops. The old church-state "back scratching" continued, but now on a basis that made the church at least look like an independent organization. The pope's attempts to weaken the emperor did little to promote freedom for the church. As the power of emperors declined, Germany's feudal nobles grew stronger and better able to impose their wills on the clergy.

The First Crusades

What the Cluny reform was to the clergy the Crusades to the Holy Land were to the laity—that is, an outlet for the religious zeal and self-confidence that invigorated Europe in the High Middle Ages.

Late in the eleventh century, Alexius I Comnenus, emperor of Constantinople, appealed to the Christian West for help against the Seljuk Turks. At the council of Clermont in 1095, Pope Urban II answered this appeal by proclaiming the First Crusade. The Crusade was popular with different people for different reasons. By calling the Crusade, the pope was able to show that he truly was the West's spiritual leader and to gain leverage in dealing with the Eastern church. The departure of large numbers of warring nobles eased the task of maintaining the peace in Europe, and hordes of restless young knights were enthralled by the opportunity to enrich themselves from foreign conquests. Many were the younger sons of noblemen who, in an age of growing population and limited land, had few prospects of obtaining fiefs at home.

Although motives were mixed, the First Crusade owed more to genuine piety than the mercenary ventures organized by the later Crusaders. Popes recruited Crusaders by promising those who died in battle a plenary indulgence—a complete remission of punishment for their unrepented mortal sins and from all suffering in purgatory. The Crusaders were driven by the passions of a Holy War, a struggle against a hated infidel who had seized control of the most sacred Christian shrines. The Crusade was also the ultimate pilgrimage to the Holy Land. The desire to be part of it even affected those who did not go East. They crusaded at home by launching the first massacres of Europe's Jews.

THE FIRST VICTORY   Three great armies, which mustered perhaps 100,000 men, gathered in France, Germany, and Italy. In 1097 they converged on Constantinople by different routes. They were not the disciplined, professional force the East had hoped to enlist. The Eastern

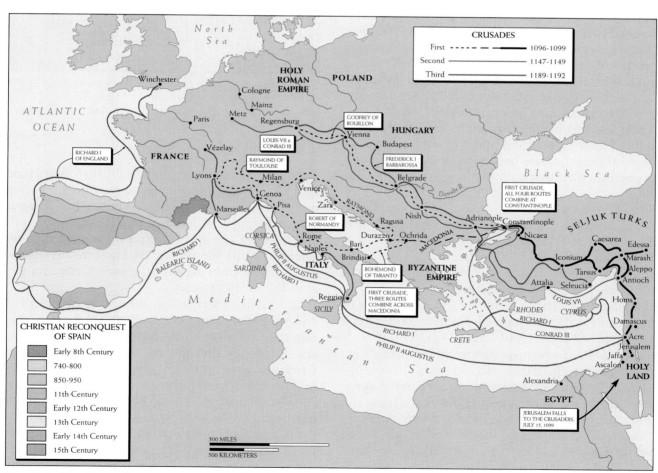

MAP 7–1   THE EARLY CRUSADES   *Routes taken by some of the major leaders of the early Crusades are shown, as is the pattern Christian reconquest took in Spain.*

emperor was suspicious of their motives, and the common people whom they pillaged along the route of their march hardly considered them Christian brothers. Nonetheless, these fanatical Crusaders accomplished what no Eastern army had ever done. They defeated one Seljuk army after another and, on July 15, 1099, captured Jerusalem. The Crusaders' success was due to the superior military technology the West had evolved and to the inability of the Muslim states to cooperate in mounting an effective resistance.

The Crusaders set up governments in Jerusalem, Edessa, and Antioch. Godfrey of Bouillon (and after him his brother Baldwin) was chosen to rule a new kingdom of Jerusalem. The pretentious claims of the "Crusader States" ignored the fact that they were little more than precarious European outposts in a Muslim world. This became clear as the Muslims rallied and took the offensive against the "savages" who had invaded their lands. The Crusaders erected castles and hunkered down in a state of perpetual siege. The once fierce warriors became international businessmen promoting trade between East and West. Some, such as the Knights Templars, built huge fortunes. The Templars were an order of soldier-monks devoted to protecting pilgrims to the Holy Land. Their services to travelers led them into the profitable fields of banking and money-lending and made their monastic order one of Europe's greatest commercial institutions.

THE ULTIMATE DEFEAT After forty years the Latin hold on the East began to weaken. When Edessa fell to Islamic armies in 1144, Bernard of Clairvaux (1091–1153), Christendom's most influential monastic leader, called for a Second Crusade. It was a dismal failure.

In October 1187 Saladin (r. 1138–1193), king of Egypt and Syria, conquered Jerusalem, and Europe responded with a Third Crusade (1189–1192). It enlisted the most powerful western rulers: Emperor Frederick Barbarossa; Richard "the Lion-Hearted," king of England; and Philip Augustus, king of France. Despite its resources, the Third Crusade degenerated into a tragicomedy. Frederick Barbarossa accidentally drowned while fording a stream in Asia Minor. Richard and Philip Augustus reached the outskirts of Jerusalem, but their intense personal rivalry

The crusaders capture the city of Antioch in 1098 during the First Crusade. From Le Miroir Historial *(fifteenth century) by Vincent de Beauvais.* Musée Conde Chantilly. E. T. Archive, London.

doomed their campaign. Philip Augustus quickly returned to France to prey on Richard's continental possessions. When this forced Richard finally to head home, he was captured and held for ransom by the Emperor Henry VI. England's bill for its king's Eastern adventure was greatly increased by the sum Germany demanded for his release.

The Crusades failed to achieve their political and religious objectives, and the Holy Land remained under Muslim control into the modern era. Economically and culturally, however, the Crusades were more constructive. They stimulated trade between the East and the West, and the merchants of Venice, Pisa, and Genoa, who followed the Crusaders, succeeded at sea where the Crusades failed on land at challenging Islamic domination. Wherever trading centers sprang up, cultural as well as economic exchanges were made.

The Pontificate of Innocent III (1198–1216)

The pope who inaugurated the Crusades hoped that they would unite Europe behind the leader of its church. The papal dream of establishing some kind of supremacy over the nations that were emerging in Europe during the High Middle Ages reached its apogee during the reign of Pope Innocent III.

THE NEW PAPAL MONARCHY Under Innocent, the papacy became a great secular power with a treasury and a bureaucracy equal to that of any king. Innocent increased ecclesiastical taxation—both in amount and in effectiveness of collection. A tax known as Peter's pence was imposed on all but the poorest laymen. The clergy paid the pope an income tax of 2.5 percent—as well as annates (i.e., the forfeiture to the papacy by an appointee of the first year's income from his benefice) and fees for the bestowal of things such as the pallium, the stole that was the archbishop's symbol of office. Innocent also reserved to the pope the right to grant absolution for many kinds of sins and religious crimes. The penalties imposed were frequently monetary payments to the papacy.

CRUSADES IN FRANCE AND THE EAST Innocent did not shrink from using the Crusade, the church's weapon against Islam, to suppress dissent in Europe. Protests were raised against the church as it became increasingly secular and materialistic, and the papacy accused some of its critics of heresy. Heresy was often the laity's response to clerical greed and negligence.

In 1209 Innocent launched a Crusade to exterminate heretics called either the Albigensians (from the French town of Albi) or the Cathars ("pure ones"). These people advocated a simple, pious way of life modeled on the New Testament's description of Jesus and his apostles. But they rejected important Christian doctrines. They were dualists. They denied that the wrathful deity of the Old Testament who created the sinful material world was the same god as the heavenly Father to whom Jesus prayed. Their belief that the flesh was the source of sin and a threat to the spirit led them to reject the Christian claim that God was incarnate in Jesus and to

	Significant Dates from the Period of the High Middle Ages	
910	Cluniac reform begins	
955	Otto I defeats Magyars	
1059	College of Cardinals empowered to elect popes	
1066	Norman conquest of England	
1075–1122	Investiture Controversy	
1095–1099	First Crusade	
1144	Edessa falls; Second Crusade	
1152	Hohenstaufen dynasty founded	
1154	Plantagenet dynasty founded	
1187	Jerusalem falls to Saladin	
1189–1192	Third Crusade	
1202	Fourth Crusade sacks Constantinople	
1209	Albigensian Crusade	
1210	Franciscan Order founded	
1215	Fourth Lateran Council; Magna Carta	
1250	Death of Frederick II	

assert that the true church was an invisible, spiritual entity and not the worldly institution headed by the pope. The more radical Cathars recommended celibacy, contraception, or abortion to prevent more immortal souls from being captured and imprisoned in sinful matter. (The Catholic Church's current positions on social issues such as contraception and abortion were shaped in this environment.) Paradoxically, the Cathars' dualism might also be used to justify moral laxity. If the flesh and the spirit are fundamentally different and separate realities, it matters little what the former does.

Since the Albigensian lands were wealthy, knights from northern France were eager to enlist in the pope's Crusade. The church gave them an excuse to seize their neighbors' lands. After a succession of massacres and a special campaign that King Louis VIII of France headed in 1226 utterly devastated the prosperous Albigensian districts, Pope Gregory IX (1227–1241) sent in the Inquisition to root out any heretics who remained. An inquisition was a formal ecclesiastical tribunal set up to detect and punish heresy. Bishops had used inquisitions in their dioceses since the mid-twelfth century, but Innocent III created a centralized court of inquisition that dispatched papal legates to preside at trials and executions throughout Europe.

Innocent also called the fourth of the Crusades intended for the Holy Land. In 1202 some 30,000 Crusaders gathered in Venice, planning to sail for Egypt. Many were poor soldiers of fortune who were unable to pay the price the Venetians demanded for their transport. Venice persuaded them to work off their passage by conquering Zara, a Christian city that was one of Venice's commercial rivals. To the shock of Pope Innocent III, the Crusaders obliged and then allowed Venice to seduce them into storming the most important Christian city in the East, Constantinople.

Although the assault on Constantinople in 1204 was an embarrassment to the pope, the papacy came to terms with the Venetians and shared the spoils. One of Innocent's confidants was appointed patriarch of Constantinople and ordered to win the Greeks and the Slavs to the Roman church. Westerners retained control of Constantinople until 1261 when the Genoese, who envied Venice's coup, helped the exiled Eastern emperor, Michael Paleologus, recapture the city. The half-century of occupation did nothing to reunite the church or improve relations between East and West.

THE FOURTH LATERAN COUNCIL   At the Fourth Lateran Council, which met in 1215, Innocent defined crucial disciplines and doctrines that the church was to enforce throughout Europe. Most significant for the development of Catholicism was the council's endorsement of the doctrine of transubstantiation as the church's explanation of the miracle of the Eucharist. Transubstantiation is the belief that at the moment of priestly consecration the bread and wine of the Lord's Supper become the body and blood of Christ. This idea was consistent with the popular piety of the twelfth century. But since the power to perform this miracle was reserved to priests, it also helped Innocent achieve his goal of enhancing the power of the clergy over the laity. This was also the effect of the council's formalization of the sacrament of penance and its order to every adult Christian to confess and take communion at least once a year (usually at Easter).

FRANCISCANS AND DOMINICANS   The laity's interest in religious devotion surged at the turn of the twelfth century and won recruits for new movements that preached a life of poverty in imitation of Christ. Idealization of poverty was not necessarily heretical, but it could promote criticism of the church that caused groups such as the Waldensians, Beguines, and Beghards to fall under suspicion of heresy.

By licensing two new religious orders (the Franciscans and the Dominicans) Innocent fought fire with fire. Unlike the regular monks, these orders of friars (i.e., "brothers") were mendicants (i.e., "beggars"). Refusing to accept land and endowments, they devoted themselves to preaching and caring for the poor and supported themselves by begging and working. Their saintly behavior did much to refute the heretics who argued that Christian unworldliness was incompatible with obedience to the orthodox church. The tertiaries, or "Third Orders," created by the friars provided refuges for pious laypersons whose desire to live according to high religious ideals might otherwise have led them into heresies.

The Franciscan Order was founded in 1210 by Saint Francis of Assisi (1182–1226), the son of a rich cloth merchant. The Dominican Order (the Order of Preachers) was founded in 1216 by Saint Dominic (1170–1221), a well-educated Spanish cleric. Since both orders reported directly to the pope and not to any local bishops, they provided the central government of the church with an army of dedicated servants who could be dispatched on special missions.

Pope Gregory IX (1227–1241) canonized Saint Francis only two years after Francis's death. But the pope also turned the Franciscans from the path their founder had charted for them. The pope declared that a nomadic life of strict poverty and extreme asceticism was both impractical and unbiblical. Most Franciscans accepted the pope's modification of their order's rule, but a radical branch, the Spiritual Franciscans, resisted and drifted into heresy.

The Dominicans were dedicated to combating heresy. They preached, staffed the offices of the Inquisition, and taught at universities. The man who most furthered their mission was the great theologian, Thomas Aquinas (d. 1274). His synthesis of faith and reason has been embraced by the Catholic Church as the definitive statement of its beliefs.

William the Conqueror on horseback urging his troops into combat with the English at the Battle of Hastings (October 14, 1066). Detail from the Bayeux Tapestry, scene 51, about 1073–1083. Musée de la Tapisserie, Bayeux, France. Giraudon/Art Resource, NY

England and France: Hastings (1066) to Bouvines (1214)

While Germany and Italy were engaged in struggles between popes and emperors, new dynasties were establishing themselves in England and France. They laid the foundations for medieval Europe's strongest nations.

The old Roman province of Britain became England (i.e., "Anglo-land") as Germans from the tribes of the Angles and Saxons took it over at the start of the Middle Ages. When the last of their kings, Edward the Confessor, died childless in 1066, the English throne was claimed by his distant relative, Duke William of Normandy (d. 1087). The Anglo-Saxon assembly—which, in accordance with the ancient traditions of the German tribes, had the right to enthrone kings—preferred a native son, Harold Godwinsson. William invaded England, and at Hastings on October 14, 1066, he destroyed Harold and decimated the Anglo-Saxon nobility.

William the Conqueror

By judiciously combining continental feudalism and Anglo-Saxon custom, William constructed the most effective monarchy in Europe. To discover what the country he had conquered was worth, he carried out a county-by-county survey of its people, animals, and implements. The results, which were compiled as the *Domesday Book* (1080–1086), offer a uniquely detailed description of a medieval kingdom. William compelled every man of property to become his vassal and to hold all land in fief from the king. The Norman nobles who replaced the Anglo-Saxon magnates had no following among their new subjects. They realized, therefore, that they needed the help of a strong leader, and they rarely challenged their king. William's government was further strengthened by unique Anglo-Saxon tax and court systems, and the king honored the Anglo-Saxon tradition of "parleying"—that is, of holding conferences with people who had vested interests in royal policies. By consulting with his nobles on affairs of state, William kept England on track toward the creation of the parliamentary traditions that have shaped the constitutions of so many modern states.

Henry II

The English monarchy continued strong under William's sons and heirs, William Rufus (r. 1087–1100) and Henry I (r. 1100–1135). When Henry died without a male heir, a civil war erupted that threatened to undo the Conqueror's work. But a compromise between the factions resulted in the accession of Henry II (r. 1154–1189), son of the duke of Anjou and Matilda, daughter of Henry I. Henry II established the Plantagenet dynasty, the family name of the Angevin (or Anjouan) kings who ruled England until the death of Richard III in 1485. Henry, by his own rights of inheritance and those of his wife, Eleanor of Aquitaine (ca. 1122–1204), controlled much more of France than did the king of France. Henry also conquered a part of Ireland and made the king of Scotland take an oath of homage to him. The French king, Louis VII, who had good reason to fear these developments, tried to contain the English. French efforts to drive them from the continent were ultimately successful but not until the mid-fifteenth century and the end of the Hundred Years' War.

Eleanor of Aquitaine and Court Culture

Eleanor of Aquitaine had been married to King Louis VII of France before she wed King Henry II of England in 1152, and she was a powerful influence on the politics and culture of both nations. Women of Eleanor's generation were beginning to venture into the masculine fields of politics and business, and she blazed the way. She insisted on accompanying her first husband on the Second Crusade, and she stirred up so much trouble for her second husband that from 1179 until his death in 1189 he kept her under house arrest.

After marrying Henry, Eleanor established a court in Angers, the chief town of Anjou, that became a center of patronage for musicians and poets. The troubadour Bernart de Ventadorn composed many of the popular love songs of the period in her honor. From 1154 to 1170, the queen resided in England, but then she separated from Henry and moved to Poitiers to live with her daughter Marie, the countess of Champagne. Poitiers popularized a new fad among the aristocracy. It was called "courtly love." The troubadours who elaborated the rules of game composed erotic stories to satirize physical passion. They contrasted carnal love with "courteous" love, a spiritual passion for a lady that ennobled her lover. Chrétien de Troyes's stories of King Arthur and the Knights of the Round Table—and of Sir Lancelot's tragic, illicit love for Arthur's wife, Guinevere—are the most famous products of the movement.

Popular Rebellion and Magna Carta

Henry II was a strong king who believed in autocratic monarchy. He insisted that the church operate within parameters set by the state, and he spelled these out in 1164 in the Constitutions of Clarendon. The Constitutions limited the right to appeal cases from England to the papal court, subjected clergy to the king's courts, and gave the king control over the election of bishops. The archbishop of Canterbury, Thomas à Becket (1118?–1170), who was once Henry's compliant chancellor, fled England rather than accept the Constitutions. He was induced to return in 1170, but his continued opposition to the king prompted some of Henry's men to assassinate him. The church leapt at the opportunity to canonize Becket (1172) and to use his martyrdom to bolster its case for freedom from state control.

Henry was followed on the throne by two of his sons: Richard the Lion-Hearted (r. 1189–1199) and John (r. 1199–1216). Neither was a success. Richard imposed ruinous taxation to fund the disastrous Third Crusade and died fighting to recover lands the French had taken from him while he was in the East. In 1209 Pope Innocent III excommunicated Richard's successor, John, in a dispute over the appointment of an archbishop for Canterbury. To extricate himself from a mess of his own making and to win support for a war with France, John surrendered to the pope and declared his kingdom a papal fief. John's efforts to restore his father's Angevin empire foundered, however, when the French defeated him at Bouvines in 1214. England's disillusioned barons then rebelled and forced their king to accept limitations on royal authority.

A document known simply as the Magna Carta (i.e., "Great Charter") spelled out the terms that John and his subjects agreed to in 1215. Among other things, the king promised not to arrest and hold people without giving his reasons, and he acknowledged the necessity of consulting with representatives of the propertied classes before imposing new taxes. Magna Carta was designed to put some constraints on monarchy without fatally weakening it. In the short run, it had little effect, for John's successors largely ignored it. But Magna Carta helped keep alive the traditions that undergird modern English law.

Philip II Augustus

In England during the High Middle Ages, the propertied classes had to fight a strong monarchy to secure their rights. In France the shoe was on the other foot. There, weak kings were confronted by powerful subjects who opposed the growth of monarchy.

In 987 when the Carolingian line came to an end in France, the French nobles chose Hugh Capet, count of Paris, to be king. Although his descendants managed to hang on to the title and to create a Capetian dynasty, for the next two centuries the great feudal princes were France's real rulers. The early Capetian kings even had a struggle to control their own royal domain, the area around Paris and the Île-de-France to the northeast. By the time Philip II (1180–1223) came to the throne, the Capetians had secured hereditary rights to the crown. Only then was it possible for them to begin to impose their will on their vassals and made Paris the center of French government and culture.

In a way the Norman conquest of England in 1066 helped the Capetian kings to unify France and build a true national monarchy. As the Plantagenet dynasty extended its control over French territory, the Capetians were able to enlist support from powerful nobles who considered the English king the greater threat to their independence. The Capetians also won the help of the wealthy merchant class that was beginning to appear in France's reviving cities.

The king of England was at a disadvantage in dealing with the king of France, for, as duke of Normandy, he was a vassal of the French king. A skillful politician such as Philip II Augustus was able to exploit the ambiguity of this relationship. By accusing his English rival of violating the duties of vassalage, Philip could enlist his other vassals in campaigns to repossess the English king's French fiefs. During the reigns of Richard the Lion-Hearted and John, France's armies seized all the territories the English had occupied in France (with the exception of part of Aquitaine).

King John of England enlisted the help of the German emperor Otto IV (r. 1198–1215) against France in what became Europe's first multinational war. France won decisively at the battle at Bouvines in Flanders on July 27, 1214. The victory helped the French king to unite his people, and it greatly weakened his opponents. Otto IV fell from power, and John's subjects welcomed him home with the rebellion that culminated in Magna Carta.

France in the Thirteenth Century: The Reign of Louis IX

The growth of Capetian royal power under Philip Augustus seemed to receive divine confirmation during the reign of his grandson Louis IX (r. 1226–1270). Louis embodied the medieval view of the perfect ruler, and he was canonized shortly after his death. The saintly king was an ascetic whose ethics were far superior to those of his royal and papal contemporaries. But he was also what his generation expected a king to be, a decisive leader and an enthusiastic soldier.

Generosity Abroad

Some of Louis's decisions suggest naiveté or an overly scrupulous conscience. Although he could have driven the English off the continent, he refused to take advantage of King Henry III's weakness. In 1259 he negotiated a generous compromise, the Treaty of Paris, to end the long-simmering dispute between England and France. Had he been more ruthless and confiscated English territories in France, he might have prevented the resumption of hostilities between the two nations and spared Europe the bloodshed of the Hundred Years' War.

King Louis IX (1226–1270) giving justice. Louis, who was canonized in 1297, was the medieval ideal of a perfect ruler. From "Justiniani in Fortiatum," fol. 34. France, 14th C. Biblioteca Real, El Escorial, Madrid, Spain. Giraudon/Art Resource, NY

Salisbury Cathedral: A Church Filled with Light

Salisbury Cathedral, England. © Christopher Cormack/Corbis

$\mathcal{B}$etween 1050 and 1150 the fortress-like Romanesque style dominated European architecture. Thick walls were needed to support the weight of the round Roman arches that composed its stone vaulting. The small windows that could be cut through these walls admitted little light and made the interiors of Romanesque churches dim. About 1140, a new style called Gothic began to evolve in France. It turned the next century into the "Age of Great Cathedrals" as magnificent churches were raised throughout Europe.

Gothic designs sought a mathematical harmony that builders hoped would illustrate the divine laws fundamental to the universe and philosophers' theories about the nature of beauty. Architects strove hard to find ways to flood sanctuaries with light to symbolize the divine presence. The use of broken or pointed arches allowed them to erect vaults of unprecedented height. The development of flying buttresses (i.e., buttresses set away from the walls and linked to them by arches) enabled masons to cut away large portions of walls to make space for great windows. These were filled with pictures executed in a colored glass that filled churches with a mysterious light.

Salisbury Cathedral is a prime example of English Gothic. Built between 1220 and 1226, its construction required 60,000 tons of stone. Soaring arches and rib vaulting, however, impart lightness to its interior, and flying buttresses and intricate carving give its exterior an airy, lacy grace.

Salisbury Cathedral, England. The Image Works.

Louis remained officially aloof while the papacy fought with Frederick II, an emperor from Germany's Hohenstaufen dynasty. But after Frederick's death, Louis's brother, Charles of Anjou, entered the fray on the pope's side, exterminated Frederick's dynasty, and seized its lands in Italy and Sicily. The pope rewarded him by crowning him king of Sicily.

Order and Excellence at Home

Louis's greatest achievement was to improve the government of France. He used the efficient bureaucracy that his predecessors had developed to exploit their subjects to provide his people with more secure order and justice. He sent out *enquêteurs* (i.e., auditors) to monitor royal officials—especially the *baillis* and *prévôts* whom Philip Augustus had appointed to run the government's grass-roots offices. He abolished private warfare among the nobles and serfdom on the lands of the royal domain. He gave his subjects the judicial right of appeal from local to higher courts, and he made the tax system more equitable. The services the French people received from their king generated enthusiasm for the monarchy and for the nationhood it symbolized.

Developments of other kinds helped to shape a French national identity during Louis's reign. His was the golden age of Scholasticism, a time when thinkers such as Thomas Aquinas and the Franciscan scholar Bonaventure made the University of Paris Europe's intellectual center. France became the showcase for monastic reform, chivalry, and the new Gothic style in art and architecture that had been pioneered by Suger, abbot of St. Denis and adviser to Louis IX's great-grandfather, Louis VII. France began to set the cultural standard for Europe, a pattern that continued into the modern era.

Louis's virtues reflected medieval ideals of kingship. He was something of a religious fanatic. He supported the work of the Inquisition, and he personally led the last two of the great Crusades for the Holy Land. Both were failures, but Louis's death of a fever during the second of his holy wars only enhanced his reputation as a saintly king. His successors pointed to him to confirm their claim that God had bestowed a divine right to rule on the Capetians.

The Hohenstaufen Empire (1152–1272)

During the twelfth and thirteenth centuries, while stable governments were developing in both England and France, something quite different happened within the Holy Roman Empire (Germany, Burgundy, and northern Italy). There disunity and feuding created a legacy of political fragmentation that endured into modern times.

Frederick I Barbarossa

The Investiture Controversy, in which the popes had challenged the right of emperors to appoint the higher clergy, had weakened Germany's kings and strengthened its barons. The church was unable to prevent the German princes from dominating episcopal appointments and appropriating their rich endowments.

Imperial authority revived with the accession to the throne of Frederick I Barbarossa (r. 1152–1190), founder of the Hohenstaufen dynasty. Frederick had some help in laying a strong foundation for a new empire. Disaffection with the incessant squabbling of the feudal princes was widespread, and there was growing resentment of the theocratic pretensions of the papacy. At the University of Bologna a scholar named Irnerius (d. 1125) was also reviving the study of Roman law (i.e., Justinian's Code). Frederick found this useful, for Roman law promoted the centralization of states and provided a secular foundation for imperial power that minimized the significance of papal coronation.

From Frederick's base of operation in Switzerland, the bridge between Germany and Italy, he conducted a relatively successful campaign to regain control over the German nobility. In 1180 his strongest rival, Henry the Lion (d. 1195), duke of Saxony, fell from power and was exiled to Normandy. Although Frederick was not strong enough to intervene in the internal affairs of Germany's great duchies, he was vigilant in enforcing his rights as their feudal overlord. This kept memories of royal authority alive until the king was strong enough to risk a showdown with his greater vassals.

Italy proved to be the major obstacle to the realization of Frederick's imperial dreams. In

1155 Frederick restored Rome to Pope Adrian IV (1154–1159) after a religious revolutionary, Arnold of Brescia (d. 1155), had wrested control of the city from the papacy. Frederick's reward was a papal coronation, which he believed gave him title to Italy. Although the imperial Diet of Roncaglia in 1158 officially sanctioned Frederick's claim to Italy, the Italian people, particularly those of Lombardy, refused to accept the governors he appointed.

Just as this challenge to royal authority was being mounted, one of Europe's most skilled lawyers, Cardinal Roland, was elected Pope Alexander III (1159–1181). Frederick soon found himself at war with the pope, the city of Milan, and the kingdom of Sicily. In 1167, the combined forces of the northern Italian cities drove him back into Germany, and a decade later (1176) an Italian army soundly defeated him at Legnano. In the Peace of Constance in 1183 Frederick recognized the claims of the Lombard cities to rights of self-rule.

Henry VI and the Sicilian Connection

Frederick's reign ended with stalemate in Germany and defeat in Italy. But in the last years of his life, he discovered a new opportunity for his dynasty. The Norman ruler of the kingdom of Sicily, William II (r. 1166–1189), asked Frederick for help in launching a campaign for the conquest of Constantinople. In 1186 an alliance was sealed by a marriage between Frederick's son, the future Henry VI (r. 1190–1197), and Constance, heiress to Sicily.

Sicily was a fatal acquisition for the Hohenstaufen kings, for it tempted them to sacrifice their territorial base in northern Europe for projects in Italy. It also stirred up greater resistance to them in Italy. By encircling Rome the Hohenstaufens convinced the papacy that the church's survival hinged on the empire's destruction.

When Henry VI came to the throne in 1190, he faced a multitude of enemies: a hostile papacy; independent German princes; and an England whose adventurous king, Richard the Lion-Hearted, was encouraged to plot against Henry by the exiled duke of Saxony, Henry the Lion. In 1194, Constance bore her husband a son, the future Frederick II. To strengthen his dynasty, Henry campaigned vigorously for recognition of the boy's hereditary right to the imperial throne. The German princes were reluctant to abandon the custom of electing emperors, and the encircled papacy was determined to prevent anything that might secure Hohenstaufen power.

Otto IV and the Welf Interregnum

After Henry's premature death in September 1197, his widow tried to save her young son's Sicilian legacy by arranging for him to become a ward of the papacy. The boy's uncle, Philip of Swabia, claimed the title of German king, but the Welf family, which opposed the Hohenstaufens, backed a rival—Otto of Brunswick, the son of the troublesome Henry the Lion. Richard of England supported Otto; the French supported the Hohenstaufens; and the papacy switched its allegiance back and forth to prevent anyone from surrounding Rome. The result was anarchy and civil war.

Otto outlasted Philip and won general recognition in Germany and coronation as emperor by Pope Innocent III (1198–1215). Within four months of his coronation (October 1209), the wind suddenly changed. Otto attacked Sicily, and this convinced Innocent that he was a threat to Rome. The pope excommunicated him and raised up a rival for his throne.

Frederick II

Pope Innocent's ward, the Hohenstaufen prince Frederick, was now of age, and unlike Otto he had a hereditary claim to the throne. In December 1212 the pope, Philip Augustus of France, and Otto's German enemies arranged for Frederick to be crowned king of the Romans in Mainz. When Philip Augustus defeated the armies of Otto and John of England at the battle of Bouvines in 1214, the way was cleared for Frederick II to mount the imperial throne in Charlemagne's city of Aachen (1215). The young ruler's allies probably expected him to be their puppet, but he quickly demonstrated an independent streak.

Frederick, who had grown up in Sicily, disliked Germany. He spent only nine of the thirty-eight years of his reign in Germany, and he wanted only one thing from the German princes: the imperial title for himself and his sons. To secure it,

he was willing to grant Germany's feudal nobility absolute authority over their domains. Frederick's lack of interest in building a centralized monarchy for Germany halted the development of the nation and condemned it to six centuries of chaotic disunity.

Frederick's policy with respect to the papacy was equally disastrous. The popes excommunicated Frederick four times and came to view him as the Antichrist, the biblical beast of the Apocalypse whose persecution of the faithful signaled the end of the world. Although Frederick abandoned Germany, he was determined to win control over Lombardy, unite it with his Sicilian kingdom, and surround Rome. This the popes were determined to prevent.

The popes won the fight with the Hohenstaufens, but their victory was Pyrrhic. The contest led Pope Innocent IV (1243–1254) to immerse the church more deeply in European politics than ever before. Wholesale secularization increased criticism of the church by religious reformers and by the patriotic champions of national monarchies. Innocent organized and led the German princes against Frederick, and German and Italian resistance kept Frederick on the defensive throughout his last years.

When Frederick died in 1250, the German monarchy died with him. The German nobility repudiated the idea of hereditary succession to the throne, and in 1257 the barons formed an electoral college that claimed the right to bestow the title "king of the Romans." This ensured that the kings they created would be their puppets.

Manfred, Frederick's illegitimate son, fought hard to save something of the Hohenstaufen legacy, but he was defeated in 1266. In 1286 Charles of Anjou, the adventurous brother of the saintly Louis IX, destroyed the last of the Hohenstaufens (Frederick's grandson Conradin). Germany temporarily ceased to meddle in Italy's affairs, but this did not free Italy from the threat of outside interference. France and, to a lesser extent, England aspired to the role Germany had tried to play in Italy.

In Perspective

With borders that were finally secured at the start of the High Middle Ages, western Europe began to develop its characteristic cultural and political institutions. The map of Europe as it appears today began to take shape. England and France built centralized monarchies that unified them as modern nation-states. Germany and Italy, however, failed to overcome the forces of feudal fragmentation.

The dream of creating a Holy Roman Empire tempted German rulers into Italy, where they made enemies of the popes and the rising commercial cities. The result was an unprecedented contest between church and state that promoted the growth of a powerful papal monarchy. The church's involvement with politics alienated kings, secularized the papacy, and increased the church's vulnerability to attack on the grounds that it was failing in its spiritual mission.

REVIEW QUESTIONS

1. How did the Saxon king Otto I rebuild the German Empire? How did he establish control over the various German duchies? How did he use the church to achieve his political goals? Does he deserve to be called "the Great"?

2. What were the main reasons for the Cluny reform movement? How do you account for its success? What was the impact of the reform on the subsequent history of the medieval church and state?

3. In the dispute between Pope Gregory VII and King Henry IV over the issue of lay investiture, what were the causes of the controversy, the actions of the contending parties, and the outcome of the struggle? What was at stake for each of the disputants, and what were the ramifications of the conflict?

4. What did Voltaire, the eighteenth-century French intellectual, mean when he said that the Holy Roman Empire was neither holy nor Roman? Do you agree with him?

5. What developments in western and eastern Europe promoted the crusading movement? Why did the Crusaders fail to establish lasting political and religious control over the Holy Land? What impact did the Crusaders have on the West's politics, religion, and economies? Which of its outcomes do you consider most important? Why?

6. Why does Hohenstaufen rule deserve to be remembered as a disaster for Germany? What

factors prevented German consolidation during the Hohenstaufen era? If France and England could coalesce into reasonably strong states, why was Germany not able to do the same?

SUGGESTED READINGS

J. W. BALDWIN, *The Government of Philip Augustus* (1986). An important scholarly work.

G. BARRACLOUGH, *The Origins of Modern Germany* (1946). Dated but penetrating political narrative setting modern Germany in the perspective of the Middle Ages.

G. BARRACLOUGH, *The Medieval Papacy* (1968). Brief survey with pictures.

H. E. J. COWDREY, *Popes, Monks, and Crusaders* (1984). Re-creation of the atmosphere that gave birth to the Crusades.

E. M. HALLAM, *Capetian France, 987–1328* (1980). Very good on politics and heretics.

J. C. HOLT, *Magna Carta*, 2nd ed. (1992). The famous document and its interpretation by succeeding generations.

H. E. MAYER, *The Crusades*, trans. by John Gilligham (1972). Extremely detailed; the best one-volume account.

J. B. MORRALL, *Political Thought in Medieval Times* (1962). Readable and illuminating account.

C. PETIT-DUTAILLIS, *The Feudal Monarchy in France and England from the Tenth to the Thirteenth Century*, trans. by E. D. Hunt (1964). Political narrative in great detail.

S. REYNOLDS, *Kingdoms and Communities in Western Europe, 900–1300* (1984). For the medieval origins of Western political and cultural traditions.

J. RILEY-SMITH, *The Crusades: A Short History* (1987). Up-to-date, lucid, and readable.

W. ROESENER, *Peasants in the Middle Ages* (1992). Up-to-date overview.

Chapter 8
Medieval Society: Hierarchies, Towns, Universities, and Families (1000–1300)

The Traditional Order of Life
Nobles
Clergy
Peasants

Towns and Townspeople
The Chartering of Towns
The Rise of Merchants
Challenging the Old Lords
New Models of Government
Towns and Kings
Jews in Christian Society

Schools and Universities
University of Bologna
Cathedral Schools
University of Paris
The Curriculum

Women in Medieval Society

The Lives of Children

KEY TOPICS

- The major groups composing medieval society
- The rise of towns and a new merchant class
- The founding of universities and educational curriculum
- How women and children fared in the Middle Ages

From the tenth to the twelfth centuries, the effects of increasing political stability were felt in Europe. Agricultural production increased, population exploded, and trade and urban life revived. Crusades promoted contacts with foreign lands that stimulated both economic and cultural development. A new merchant class, the ancestors of modern capitalists, appeared to serve the West's growing markets, and an urban proletariat developed.

Guided by Muslim intellectuals, Western scholars began again to study classical literature. Schools and universities opened. Literacy increased among the laity, and the twelfth century witnessed a true renaissance. The creative vigor of the new European civilization was proclaimed by the awesome Gothic churches that were the supreme products of its art and science.

The Traditional Order of Life

Medieval political theorists identified three activities that were essential for society's functioning and assigned each to a separate class: protection by knights and landed nobility, prayer by clergy, and production of supplies by peasants and village artisans. The revival of towns in the eleventh century created a fourth class: traders and merchants. They were thought of as a "middle" class, for their lifestyle combined aspects of the roles of the peasantry and aristocracy. They were economically productive like peasants, but they did not work the land. They had wealth like nobles and clergy, but they were not integrated into the institutions of feudal government. Their appearance unbalanced the old social order and ultimately caused it to collapse.

Nobles

As medieval society evolved, a landed aristocracy with special social and legal status emerged from the ranks of the feudal vassals and warrior knights. In the late Middle Ages the aristocratic class was composed of a higher and lower nobility. The higher were the great landowners and territorial magnates; the lower were petty knights with fiefs, newly rich merchants who bought country estates, and wealthy farmers whose prosperity raised them from serfdom. Land ownership was important, for it was the special mark of the nobility that they lived off the labor of others. Nobles were lords of manors. They neither tilled the soil nor engaged in commerce—activities considered beneath the dignity of aristocrats.

WARRIORS   In the eighth century, European warfare changed dramatically. The appearance of the stirrup enabled cavalry to rout the infantry that had dominated ancient battlefields. The stirrup gave a rider a firm mount so that he could charge an enemy and strike a blow without lofting himself off his horse. Cavalry equipment and training were expensive, so lords divided their lands up to create fiefs to support the vassals who staffed their armies. Thus, arms became the nobleman's profession and war the justification for his way of life.

The code by which the nobility lived exalted strength, honor, and aggression. Nobles welcomed war as an opportunity to increase their fortunes by plunder and their reputations by acts of courage. Peace threatened them with economic stagnation and boredom. Peasants and townspeople, on the other hand, needed peace in order to prosper. Consequently, the interests of the classes conflicted, and the nobility looked down on the commoners as cowards.

The quasi-sacramental dubbing ceremony that bestowed knighthood marked a man's entrance into the noble class. A candidate for knighthood took a bath of ritual purification, confessed, communed, and maintained a night-long prayer vigil. A priest then blessed his standard, lance, and sword and girded him with the weapons he was to use in the defense of the church and the service of his lord. Dubbing (i.e., striking) on the shoulders with a sword by a senior knight raised the candidate to a state as sacred in his sphere as clerical ordination made the priest in his.

In the twelfth century, knighthood was legally restricted to men of high birth. The closing of the ranks of the nobility was a reaction to the growing wealth and power of the social-climbing commercial classes. Kings, however, maintained some social mobility by reserving the right to bestow knighthood on anyone. The sale of titles to wealthy merchants was an important source of royal revenue.

WAY OF LIFE   When not warring, noblemen honed their military skills at hunts and tournaments. Their passion for hunting was so great that they forbade commoners to take game from the forests. Peasants greatly resented being deprived of this source of free food, and anger at the nobility's hunting monopoly contributed to peasant uprisings in the late medieval period.

Tournaments sowed seeds of social disruption of a different kind. Mock battles provided military training, but they tended to get out of hand—leading to serious bloodshed and animosity among the combatants. The church opposed tournaments as occasions for pagan revelry and senseless violence, and kings and princes finally agreed that they were a danger to public order. Henry II of England proscribed tournaments in the twelfth century, but they continued in France until the mid-sixteenth century.

During the twelfth century, distinctive standards for courtesy (i.e., "conduct at court") began

A lady and her knight going hunting. Bildarchiv
Preussischer Kulturbesitz

to be imposed on vassals when they attended their lords. Thanks to the influence of powerful women such as Henry II's queen, Eleanor of Aquitaine, knowledge of court etiquette became almost as important for a nobleman as battlefield expertise.

Knights were expected to be literate gentlemen, capable of praising ladies in lyric poetry. The poetry of courtly love was sprinkled with frank eroticism, and courtly poets wrote rapturously of women married to other men. But the love that ennobled a knight was usually not assumed to be the kind consummated by sexual intercourse. Court poets warned that illicit carnal love led to suffering, and the courtly love movement may actually have been an attempt to curtail the notorious philandering of the noble classes.

SOCIAL DIVISIONS   The noble class was composed of many different kinds of noblemen, and some were superior to others. Status within the nobility was a function of how much authority one had over others; a chief with many vassals obviously far outranked the small country nobleman who was lord over none but himself.

In the late Middle Ages there were shifts in wealth and power that sent the landed nobility into a decline from which it never recovered. Climatic changes depressed the agricultural economy that was the source of its wealth, and famines and plagues caused massive demographic dislocations. Changing military tactics rendered noble cavalry nearly obsolete. And wealthy towns helped kings curtail the power of the nobles in local government. After the fourteenth century, possession of land and wealth counted far more than family tree as a qualification for entrance into the highest social class.

Clergy

Unlike the nobility and the peasantry, the rank of clergy was acquired by training and ordination, not by birth. Consequently, people of talent could climb the clerical hierarchy, and the church provided a ladder of social mobility for gifted individuals.

SECULAR AND REGULAR CLERICS   There were two clerical vocations: secular and regular. The secular clergy lived and worked among the laity in the *saeculum* (i.e., the world). The most prestigious among them were the wealthy cardinals, archbishops, and bishops who were recruited almost exclusively from noble families. Below them in rank were the urban priests, the cathedral canons, and the court clerks. At the bottom of the clerical hierarchy was the great mass of poor parish priests, who were neither financially nor intellectually superior to the laypeople they served. Until the eleventh century, parish priests routinely lived with women in a relationship akin to marriage, and they stretched their meager incomes by "moonlighting" as teachers, artisans, and farmers. This practice was accepted and even admired by their parishioners.

Regular clergy were monks and nuns—although women were not, strictly speaking, entitled to clerical status—who lived under the *regula* (i.e., rule) of a cloister. By retreating from the world and adopting rigorous ascetic disciplines, monks and nuns emulated the suffering of Christ and practiced what their contemporaries believed to be the ideal Christian way of life. This

Art & the West

Illuminated Manuscripts:
The Luttrell Psalter

Sir Geoffrey Luttrell on Horseback. From *The Luttrell Psalter,* by permission of the British Library.

M edieval people combined religious and secular interests much more than most modern people tend to. The illustrations reproduced here ornament a Psalter (i.e., a collection of Psalms used in personal devotions), but the events they depict have little to do with the practice of religion. They celebrate the noble lifestyle of a late thirteenth-century English knight, Sir Geoffrey Luttrell. They show him feasting and receiving a token from his lady as he prepares for a tournament.

An illuminated manuscript supplemented a written text with pictures and ornamentation. (When gold leaf was combined with brilliant paints, a manuscript was literally "illuminated," i.e., "filled with light.") It was prized not only for

[Top] *The Lord of the Manor Dining.* From *The Luttrell Psalter,* by permission of The British Library. *[Bottom] Kitchen Scene; Chopping Meat.* From The Luttrell Psalter, by permission of the British Library.

its literary content, but for its materials and workmanship. Its pages were made from parchment—a thin, bleached leather that was labor-intensive to produce. Early medieval manuscripts were usually made by monks for clergy. But in the thirteenth century the market for such items changed. Laypeople began to commission them, and secular workshops were established to produce them. In addition to religious themes, lay readers also wanted stories, romances, legal and medical texts, and genealogical records. Each manuscript was specially made for an individual customer. Expensive editions, such as *The Luttrell Psalter,* might be designed to commemorate events in the lives of their owners, but there were also shops that produced cheap copies that university students could afford. The development of the printing press in the 1480s brought this industry and its arts to an end.

Sources: Alexander, J. J. G. *Medieval Illuminators and Their Methods of Work.* New Haven: Yale University Press, 1992. Backhouse, Janet. *The Luttrell Psalter.* London: British Library, 1989. Camille, M. *Mirror in Parchment: The Luttrell Psalter and the Making of Medieval England.* Chicago: University of Chicago Press, 1998. De Hamel, C. *A History of Illuminated Manuscripts.* (7th–16th centuries) London: Phaidon, 1986. Sandler, L. F. *Gothic Manuscripts, 1285–1385* (A Survey of Manuscripts Illuminated in the British Isles, General editor J. J. G. Alexander, Vol. 6), 2 vols. (London: University of Toronto Press, 1996).

earned them respect and influence. The regular clergy were never completely cut off from the secular world. They maintained contact with the laity through charitable activities (such as feeding the destitute and tending the sick), as instructors in monastic schools, and as supplemental preachers and confessors in parish churches. Some monks of great learning and rhetorical skill rose to prominence as secretaries and private confessors to kings and queens. Nunneries produced famous female scholars, and monasticism inspired many of the religious and social reform movements of the medieval era.

The Benedictine rule had been adopted by most Western monasteries by the end of the Carolingian era, but during the High Middle Ages numerous new orders appeared. Saint Benedict had designed a monastic lifestyle that pursued economic self-sufficiency through hard physical labor more than rigorous ascetic discipline. Thanks, however, to generations of bequests and careful husbandry of resources, many Benedictine houses, like the famous Cluny, grew wealthy and self-preoccupied. They devoted much of their time to creating ever more elaborate liturgies for their elegantly appointed sanctuaries. The new orders rejected Benedictine "luxury." They modeled their rules on the example of poverty and self-sacrifice set by Christ and the apostles in the New Testament.

The Carthusians, who were founded in 1084, were the strictest of the new orders. Carthusian monks lived in isolation, fasted three days a week, observed long periods of silence, and disciplined their flesh by acts of self-flagellation.

The Cistercians, who were established in 1098 at Cîteaux in Burgundy, claimed to restore what they believed was the original intent of the Benedictine rule. They condemned materialism and stressed cultivation of the inner life and the spiritual goals of monasticism. To avoid contamination by the secular world and the temptations of wealth, they located their houses in remote areas where there were few worldly comforts.

The monastic ideal was so popular in the eleventh century that many secular clergy (and some laypersons) chose to live as Canons Regular. These people stayed in the world to serve the laity but lived according to a rule that was credited to Saint Augustine. They merged the spiritual disciplines of the cloister with traditional pastoral duties. Early in the thirteenth century,

the desire to combine the virtues of the secular and regular clerical professions inspired another innovation: the mendicant friars—the Dominicans and Franciscans. And during the late thirteenth and fourteenth centuries, laymen and laywomen set up satellite convents known as Begard (male) and Beguine (female) houses. These were religious communes formed by people who worked in the world but lived together under a quasi-monastic rule. The church was uncomfortable with them, for their religious enthusiasm sometimes blossomed into heresy. The Franciscans and Dominicans often assumed responsibility for directing spiritual practices in these establishments.

PROMINENCE OF THE CLERGY   The clergy were far more numerous in medieval than in modern society. Estimates suggest that 1.5 percent of fourteenth-century Europe was in clerical garb. The clergy as a whole, like the nobility, lived on the labor of others. Their income came from tithes, church taxes, and endowments. The church was a major landowner that collected huge sums in rents and fees, and monastic communities and high prelates acquired great fortunes and immense secular power.

Respect for clergy as members of society's "first estate" derived in large part from their role as mediators between God and humankind. When the priest celebrated the Eucharist, he brought the very Son of God down to earth in tangible form. The priest alone had the power to extend God's forgiveness to sinners or to block their access to it by imposing excommunication—a decree that cut a sinner off from the sacraments that were the only avenue to salvation.

Since the priest was the agent of an authority far superior to any earthly magistrate, it was considered inappropriate for him to be subservient to the laymen who ran the state. Clergy, therefore, had special privileges and immunities. They were not to be taxed by secular governments without approval from the church. Clerical crimes were under the jurisdiction of special ecclesiastical tribunals, not the secular courts. The churches and monasteries where clergy worked were also deemed to be outside the legal jurisdiction of the state. People who took refuge in them received asylum and could not be apprehended by officials of secular governments.

By the late Middle Ages laypeople came increasingly to resent the special privileges of the clergy. The anticlerical sentiments that developed during the medieval era contributed to the success of the Reformation of the sixteenth century. The Protestant theologians insisted that clergy and laity had equal spiritual standing before God.

Peasants

The largest and lowest class in medieval society was the one on whose labor the welfare of all the others depended: the agrarian peasantry. Many peasants lived and worked on manors, the primitive cells of rural social life. When the Frankish tribes moved into Europe at the start of the Middle Ages, individuals divided up the lands belonging to farming villages. They became the lords of these estates or "manors," and those who lived on them became their property. A manor was a kind of rural plantation supporting a lord. It was not necessarily equated with a village, for a single village could be home to serfs who belonged to different manors.

THE DUTIES OF TENANCY A lord was given a manor to support him as a soldier, not a farmer. The peasants who lived on his land worked it for him. They were free to divide the labor as they wished, and any products they raised above and beyond what they owed their lord they could keep for themselves. No set rules governed the size of manors, nor the number a lord could hold.

There were both servile and free manors. The tenants of free manors were descendants of Roman *coloni,* free persons who had traded their land and freedom for a guarantee of protection by their lord. Tenancy obligations on free manors were limited because their residents had some leverage in negotiating terms. Tenants of servile manors were, by comparison, far more vulnerable to the whims of their landlords. Time, however, tended to obscure differences between the two types of manors. Free, self-governing peasant communities that acknowledged no lords also survived in many regions.

The lord was the supreme authority on his manor. Cultivation of his *demesne,* the plots of land producing his income, took precedence over those of his tenants. He could impress his tenants into labor gangs for special projects or lead them

The livelihood of towns and castles depended on the labor of peasants. Here a peasant family collects the September grape harvest outside a fortified castle in France, most likely for the making of wine. Limbourg Brothers. The Month of September Grape Harvest. From Les Tres Riches Heures du Duc de Berry, Chateau de Saumur, Musée Condé, Chantilly, France. Giraudon/Art Resource, NY

out as foot soldiers when he went to war. He owned and leased to his peasants some of the instruments and facilities they used to raise and process food. His income was fattened by petty taxes and monopolies called banalities (e.g., the requirement that all his tenants grind their grain in his mill or bake their bread in his oven). The lord also collected an inheritance tax—usually the best animal from a deceased serf's estate. A serf who wished to travel or to marry outside his manor also had to obtain (i.e., buy) his lord's permission.

THE LIFE OF A SERF Burdened as a serf's life was, it was superior to chattel slavery. Serfs had their own dwellings and modest strips of land. They managed their own labor. They were permitted to market surpluses for their own profit. They were free to choose spouses from the local village community. Their marriages were protected by the church. They could pass on property to their children. And they could not be sold away from their land.

Serfs seldom ventured far from the villages where they were born. Since the church was the only show in town, life on the manor was organized around religion. But poverty of religious instruction meant that beliefs and practices were by no means unambiguously Christian. Although there were social and economic distinctions among the peasants, common dependence on the soil forced them to work together to survive. The ratio of seed to grain yield was poor; about two bushels of seed were required to produce six to ten bushels of grain in good times. There was rarely an abundance of bread and ale, the staple peasant foods. Two crops on which the modern West depends, potatoes and corn (maize), were unknown in Europe until the sixteenth century. Pork was the major source of animal protein, for pigs, unlike cattle, could forage for themselves in the forests. Excess plow teams were also slaughtered when winter set in. Survival hinged on the grain crops. When they failed or fell short, famine threatened.

CHANGES IN THE MANOR As the medieval era waned, the manor and serfdom gave way to the free single-family farm. Many things contributed to the change. Technological advances such as the collar harness (ca. 800), the horseshoe (ca. 900), and the three-field system of crop rotation improved agricultural productivity. To meet the demand of the new markets created by the towns that sprang up during the High Middle Ages, peasants brought more fields into production. They used the surplus income they produced to buy their freedom from the obligation of labor services. As the towns revived trade and brought back a money-based economy, lords found it more profitable to lease their holdings to tenant farmers than to work them with serfs. Although tenants thereby gained greater personal freedom, they were not necessarily better off materially. In hard times serfs might expect assistance from their lords, for their lords viewed them as valuable personal resources. But independent, rent-paying workers were expected to take care of themselves.

As the medieval economy expanded and costs of living rose, the landed aristocracy found it hard to make ends meet. The incomes they drew from their manors were fixed by tradition. In the mid-fourteenth century the nobles in England and France tried to increase taxes on the peasants and limit their freedom of movement. The result was often a mass revolt. Although such uprisings were brutally crushed, they revealed that traditional medieval society was breaking up.

Towns and Townspeople

In the eleventh and twelfth centuries, only about 5 percent of western Europe's population lived in towns. Most urban communities were small. Of Germany's 3,000 towns, 2,800 had populations under 1,000. Only 15 exceeded 10,000, and the largest (Cologne) had a mere 30,000. London was the only English city greater than 10,000. Paris was bigger than London, but not by much. Europe's most populous towns were in Italy. Florence and Milan approached 100,000.

The Chartering of Towns

Despite their comparatively small size, towns were where the action was. In the beginning, they tended to be dominated by the feudal lords who granted the land on which they were built, but most acquired political independence. The charter that a lord issued to the residents of a town gave them much greater freedom than rural workers enjoyed. Freedom was a requirement of life for men and women who lived by invention and audacious commercial enterprise, and lords and bishops were willing to grant it to them in exchange for the products that they made available in their markets.

The oases of freedom from lordship that developed in towns hastened the disintegration of feudal society by providing serfs with options. A serf who fled a manor could find refuge in a town. It offered a chance for a better life, for skill and industry could lift a craftsperson into a higher social class. The mere threat of migration of serfs to towns also forced lords to offer them more favorable terms of tenure to keep them on the land. The growth of towns, therefore, improved the lot of all peasants—both those who stayed in the countryside and those who left.

The Rise of Merchants

The first merchants were probably enterprising serfs or outcasts who found no place in the feudal system. Only men who had nothing to lose and everything to gain would have been tempted by the enormous risks and dangers of foreign trade. Merchants traveled together in armed caravans and convoys, buying goods and products as cheaply as possible at the source, and selling them elsewhere for all they could get. The greed and daring of these rough-hewn men, more than anything else, created our modern urban lifestyle.

Merchants were considered an oddity, for they did not fit into the three classes that theoretically constituted feudal society (i.e., the nobility, the clergy, and the peasantry). As late as the fifteenth century, nobles were still snubbing the urban "patriciate" (the hereditary ruling class that arose in some cities). Over time, however, the politically powerful grew to respect the merchants as much as the weak aspired to imitate them, for wherever merchants went, they left a trail of wealth behind.

Challenging the Old Lords

As the traders established themselves in towns and grew in wealth and numbers, they organized to challenge the feudal authorities. They wanted to end the tolls and tariffs demanded by the myriad of nobles through whose domains their caravans traveled. Wherever merchants settled, they opposed all the tolls, tariffs, and petty restrictions that hampered the flow of goods. Merchant guilds (i.e., unions or protective associations) sprang up in the eleventh century, and they were followed in the twelfth century by guilds of craftsmen. These groups worked together to change what the feudal classes had assumed to be a natural and static social order.

Townspeople wanted simple, uniform laws that were valid over large areas. They objected to the fortress mentality that led feudal lords to split up the countryside into tiny jurisdictions. City-dwellers set up independent communes to wrest control of their towns from the nobles, and they began to try to overcome the political fragmentation created by feudalism. Both the church and the king were eager, for reasons of their own, to join the townspeople in a fight to weaken local magnates.

The Rue du Matelas, a French street in Rouen, Normandy, was preserved intact from the Middle Ages to World War II. Note the narrowness of the street and the open sewer running down its center. The houses were built of rough cast stone, mud, and timber.
H. Roger Viollet/Liaison Agency, Inc.

New Models of Government

By 1100 the old urban nobility and the new burgher upper class had merged in many cities. The wealthiest citizens cooperated to create town councils that became the chief organs of municipal government. Small artisans and craftsmen formed their own associations and won political representation for them on town councils. Townspeople thought of themselves as citizens with basic rights, not as subjects liable to a master's whim. The urban poor certainly knew economic hardship and political exploitation, but so long as there was some social mobility, they had a stake in a system and a reason to support it.

SOCIAL TENSIONS Despite democratic tendencies, class distinctions were prominent in towns.

The wealthiest urban groups aped the lifestyle of the old landed nobility. They acquired coats of arms, castles, and country estates. Once businesses had set up lines of communication and worked out banking procedures for moving funds around, their managers left most traveling to underlings. Investors could settle down on country manors and still run companies. The departure from town of social-climbing entrepreneurs was an economic loss for the communities that had given these people their starts.

A need to be socially distinguished and distinct was not confined to the rich. Towns tried to restrain competition by defining grades of luxury in dress and residence for each social group and vocation. Overly conspicuous consumption was a kind of indecent exposure punishable by "sumptuary" laws—regulations that restricted the type of clothing one might wear or the decoration of one's home. These rules were meant to maintain order by keeping everyone clearly and peacefully in place.

The need for laws to limit competition among classes suggests that medieval towns were not internally harmonious. They were collections of self-centered groups, each seeking to advance its own interests. Conflict between haves and have-nots was inevitable. The poorest workers in the export trades (usually the weavers and woolcombers) were distinct from the economically better off and socially ascending independent artisans and small shopkeepers. The interests of these latter also differed from those of the merchants who brought foreign goods into the city to compete with domestic products. Theoretically, poor men could work their way up this hierarchy, and some lucky ones succeeded. But until they did, they were excluded from the city council. Only property-owning families of long standing had full rights of citizenship. Urban self-government, therefore, tended to become inbred and aristocratic.

Artisans formed guilds to gain the clout needed to win a direct voice in government. Guilds empowered the more successful among them but curtailed the social mobility of poor laborers. The guilds' representatives on city councils worked to monopolize the local market for their members by discouraging imports. They protected the health of that market by ensuring that those who served it produced ac-

ceptable products at fair prices. On the other hand, guilds discouraged improvements in techniques of production for fear that this might give some persons advantages over others. They were also often reluctant to license new producers. This infuriated the journeymen who trained in guild shops, for it prevented them from setting up in business for themselves. It condemned them to the status of politically disenfranchised workers who had no hope of advancement, a true urban proletariat. The protectionism practiced by guild-dominated urban governments ultimately depressed the economy for everyone.

Towns and Kings

A natural alliance developed between the governments of towns and the centralized nation-states that medieval kings labored to build. Towns supplied royal governments with experienced bureaucrats and lawyers who knew Roman law, the tool for designing kingdoms and empires. Towns provided the money that kings needed to hire professional armies and free themselves from dependence on the feudal nobility. Towns, in short, had the human, financial, and technological resources to empower kings.

Towns wanted strong monarchs because national governments provided the best support for commerce. A powerful king could control the local despots whose tolls and petty wars disrupted trade. Unlike a local magnate, kings also tended to keep their distance and allow towns to exercise autonomy. Kings could provide security for large areas, create standardized currencies to ease buying and selling, and simplify the payment of dues and taxes.

The relationship between kings and towns fluctuated with the fate of monarchy in various nations. In France, where the Capetian dynasty flourished, towns were integrated into royal government. In England, towns supported the barons against unpopular kings like John but cooperated with more effective monarchs in subduing the nobility. In Germany, where the feudal magnates triumphed over their kings, towns came under the control of territorial princes. Italy offered towns unique opportunities. Italy had no native royal family for towns to support against the nobility, and a shared opposition to the political ambitions of German kings and Roman popes encouraged Italy's town-dwellers and nobles to work together. As the two classes fused, town governments extended their authority into the countryside and revived the ancient institution of the city-state.

Between the eleventh and fourteenth centuries, towns enjoyed considerable autonomy and once again became the centers of Western civilization. But when true nations began to appear in the fourteenth century, both towns and the church tended to come under the control of kings. By the seventeenth century, few had escaped integration into the larger purposes of the "state."

Jews in Christian Society

The Jews who survived in medieval Europe tended to congregate in towns. Since they could not take Christian oaths of homage, they were excluded from feudal land tenure and forced to earn their livings from trade. For reasons of protection and the practice of their religion, they gathered together in tight communities. The church forbade them to employ Christians, and efforts to keep the two peoples apart promoted mutual suspicion. Ignorance of Jewish practices, resentment of the wealth acquired by some Jews, and a popular tendency to hold the Jews responsible for Christ's crucifixion, fueled baseless rumors of Jewish plots against Christian society. These sparked periodic mob violence against Jews and decisions by church and state authorities to exile them or penalize them in some way.

Schools and Universities

In the twelfth century, European scholars discovered Aristotle's treatises on logic, the writings of Euclid and Ptolemy, Roman law, and the basic works of Greek physicians and Arab mathematicians. Islamic scholars living in Spain were chiefly responsible for the translations and commentaries that made these ancient texts accessible to Westerners. The result was a cultural renaissance and the invention of a new center of intellectual activity, the university.

University of Bologna

When the term *university* was first used, all it implied was a corporation of individuals who "united" for mutual protection. Schools attracted students and teachers from great distances, and many were foreigners who had no civil rights in the towns where they worked. Unless they organized to protect themselves—like the members of an urban trade guild—they could be exploited by the townspeople on whom they were dependent for food and lodging.

The first of the great medieval universities was chartered in Bologna, Italy, by Emperor Frederick Barbarossa in 1158. Bologna, which became a model for schools in Italy, Spain, and southern France, was organized by its students. They "unionized" to guarantee fair rents and prices and high-quality teaching from their masters. They hired their teachers, set pay scales, and assigned lecture topics. Masters who did not live up to student expectations were boycotted, and price-gouging by townspeople was countered by threats to take the university and its profitable business to another town.

Bologna was most famous for the courses in law it offered advanced students. In the late eleventh century, Western scholars discovered the *Corpus Juris Civilis*, the collection of ancient Roman law made by the Byzantine emperor Justinian in the sixth century. In the early twelfth century, Irnerius of Bologna began to use the Roman law to create "glosses" (i.e., commentaries) on current laws. Around 1140, another resident of Bologna, a monk named Gratian, wrote the standard legal text in church (i.e., canon) law, the *Concordance of Discordant Canons* (known simply as the *Decretum*).

Masters, as well as students, formed protective associations, and their guilds dominated the universities of northern Europe, among which Paris was preeminent. Masters' guilds had a monopoly on teaching, and their tests for admission set standards for certification of teachers. The licenses to teach that medieval guilds awarded were the predecessors of modern academic degrees.

Cathedral Schools

The basic course of study at all medieval universities was the liberal arts program. It consisted of the *trivium* (grammar, rhetoric, and logic) and the *quadrivium* (arithmetic, geometry, astronomy, and music). This amounted to instruction in reading, writing, and computation. Students usually entered the university between the ages of twelve and fifteen. Since all books and all instruction were in Latin, they were expected to arrive knowing how to read and speak that language. The first four years of their course of study were devoted to the *trivium*, which polished their Latin and earned them a bachelor of arts degree. A master's degree entailed an additional three or four years of work on the *quadrivium*, the study of classical texts dealing with mathematics, natural science, and philosophy. Doctoral degrees were available in a few fields such as law, medicine, and theology. It could take twenty or more years to earn a degree in theology at the University of Paris.

The liberal arts curriculum evolved in the cathedral and monastery schools that trained clergy. In the early Middle Ages these were the only schools that existed, and the clergy were the only literate class. But by the late eleventh century, students who had no interest in clerical vocations, but who needed Latin and related intellectual disciplines for careers as notaries or merchants, began to frequent the church's schools. In 1179 a papal decree ordered cathedrals to provide teachers gratis for laity who wanted to learn. By the thirteenth century, the demand for literate men to staff the growing urban and territorial governments and expanding merchant firms gave rise to schools offering secular vocational education.

University of Paris

The University of Paris, which provided the model for the schools of northern Europe, evolved, in part, from the cathedral school of Notre Dame. King Philip Augustus and Pope Innocent III chartered Paris in 1200 and gave its students protections and privileges denied ordinary citizens. Only in self-defense, for instance, might a citizen strike a student, and all citizens were obligated to testify against anyone seen abusing a student. University regulations required teachers to be carefully examined before being licensed to teach. French law, in short, recognized students as a valuable and a vulnerable resource.

Paris originated the college or house system. The first colleges were charitable hospices providing room and board for poor students who would not otherwise be able to afford to study. The university soon discovered that these insti-

tutions were useful for overseeing students, and it encouraged all students to enroll in them. The most famous of the Parisian colleges was the Sorbonne, which was founded around 1257 by a royal chaplain named Robert de Sorbon. Early universities had been highly mobile institutions that used rented or borrowed space. But the buildings provided by endowed colleges rooted a university to a particular spot. This reduced the university's leverage in negotiating with townspeople, for it could no longer threaten to move to another place.

The Curriculum

The education provided by cathedral and monastery schools was limited to grammar, rhetoric, and some elementary geometry and astronomy. The standard texts were the Latin grammars of Donatus and Priscian, Saint Augustine's *On Christian Doctrine*, Cassiodorus's *On Divine and Secular Learning*, Boethius's treatises on arithmetic and music, and a few of Aristotle's logical works. The books that entered Europe from Muslim lands in the early twelfth century vastly expanded libraries and made possible the more elaborate curricula of universities. The most revolutionary of the new texts were works by Aristotle, which had previously been unknown in Europe. They were in general circulation by the mid-thirteenth century, and they shaped the dominant intellectual movement of the day: Scholasticism.

In the High Middle Ages scholars assumed that truth was not something one had to go out and find for oneself. It was already enshrined in the works of the great authorities of the past—men such as Aristotle and the fathers of the church. It had only to be apprehended and absorbed. Teachers did not encourage students to strive independently for undiscovered truth. They taught them rather to use logic and dialectic to organize and harmonize the accepted truths of tradition. Dialectic, the art of discovering a truth by finding the contradictions in arguments against it, reigned supreme in all disciplines. Instead of observing phenomena for themselves, students read the traditional authorities in their fields, made short summaries of their teaching, disputed interpretations by elaborating arguments pro and con, and then took positions based on logical cogency.

Because printing with movable type did not yet exist, only a few expensive, hand-copied books were available. Few students could afford texts for quiet, private study. Most had to learn from discussions, lectures, and debates. They memorized the information with which they worked, and they were required to think on their feet. Rhetorical skill, the ability to make an eloquent defense of the points one had clarified by logic and dialectic, was the goal of an education. To win debates, students had to become walking encyclopedias filled with information they could regurgitate as needed.

THE SUMMA The *summa*, a summary of all that was known about a particular subject, was the characteristic intellectual product of the High Middle Ages. The *summa*'s chief purpose was to clarify all that was known about a subject by reconciling apparent contradictions among authorities.

Medieval scholars labored to produce universal summaries for all disciplines, but the most influential were those that appeared in theology, the "queen of the sciences." About 1122 Peter Abelard (1079–1142) published *Sic et Non*, a book that facilitated scholastic debate by juxtaposing seemingly contradictory statements from the works of sacred authorities. A few years later (1155–1157), Peter Lombard (1100–1169) worked this material into his *Four Books of Sentences*, which became the standard theological textbook of the Middle Ages. About 1265 Thomas Aquinas entered the field with the *Summa Theologiae*. It was, in the opinion of Catholic theologians, the epitome of what the *summa* aspired to be: the last word.

CRITICS OF SCHOLASTICISM Even in its heyday Scholasticism had opponents. Some complained that the regimen of the schools was heartless and potentially damaging to Christian faith. The *dictatores*, the professional grammarians and rhetoricians who taught good writing and speaking rather than the highly abstract dialectic of Scholasticism, urged students to go directly to sources (in their original languages) and draw their own conclusions. Their point of view was championed by the humanists of the sixteenth-century Renaissance, and it still informs modern liberal arts curricula.

The church, too, was not completely at ease with Scholasticism. Scholastic thinkers relied heavily on Aristotelian logic to develop their arguments, and there were obvious conflicts between Christian doctrine and ideas that Aristotle defended. For example, since logic cannot account for why there is something rather than nothing or deal with an infinite regression of causes, Aristotle claimed that the world was not created but was eternal. Christianity, however, affirmed the Jewish concept of creation found in the book of Genesis. Aristotle also taught that since logic was the same in all minds, intellect or mind was ultimately the same in all people. This obliterated individuality and threatened Christian ideas about personal responsibility and immortality.

Some of the early Scholastics were inclined to question Christian doctrines that could not be reconciled with Aristotle's teachings. Berengar of Tours (d. 1088), for example, concluded that the church's claim that the bread and wine of the Eucharist became the body and blood of Christ was logically indefensible. Peter Abelard attempted a reinterpretation of the Trinity that preserved a premise of Aristotle's logic, namely, that three could not be one and one could not be three. The boldness of the new logicians shocked conservatives, who concluded that the love of learning at the universities had clearly got in the way of the love of God.

A century of suspicion that Aristotle was undermining Christian theology culminated in 1277, when the bishop of Paris condemned 219 philosophical propositions. The condemnation was a warning to scholars who were more interested in secular philosophy than in Christian truth, and it chilled the relationship between learning and religion. Thinkers ceased to look for ways to reconcile reason and revelation. William of Ockham (d. 1349), for instance, denied that theological truths could be dealt with as if they were of the same order as the truths that came from empirical experience of natural phenomena. Knowledge of God, he insisted, was available only through biblical revelation.

Women in Medieval Society

The concept of femininity developed by medieval scholars was at odds with the lives of the real women of the era. Christian theologians concluded from the evidence contained in Greco-Roman medical, philosophical, and legal

A fifteenth-century rendering of an eleventh- or twelfth-century marketplace. Medieval women were active in all trades, but especially in the food and clothing industries.
Scala/Art Resource, NY

texts—and the Bible—that women were physically, mentally, and morally inferior to men. The Bible clearly taught that a female was a "weaker vessel" who required protection and guidance from a male. Wives were to submit to their husbands and accept corrective beatings from them. The celibate Christian clergy felt that women were debased by marriage and that virgins and chaste widows were more to be honored than wives.

Contrary forces shaped the roles women played in medieval society. The church reinforced many traditional negative assumptions about women, but it condemned bawdy literature that denigrated women and it insisted on the female's spiritual equality with the male. The learned churchman Peter Lombard argued, for instance, that God took Eve from Adam's side because he wanted woman neither to rule over nor to be enslaved by man. She was to stand beside him as his partner in a marriage characterized by mutual aid and trust. In chivalric romances, in courtly love literature, and in the cult of the Virgin Mary that swept Europe in the twelfth and thirteenth centuries, female traits of gentleness, compassion, and grace were exalted over the rougher male virtues. In these traditions, women were put on pedestals and praised as superior to men in the delicate arts of self-control and civilized life.

Germanic traditions tended to moderate Roman customs. They gave medieval women basic rights that prevented their being treated as mere chattel. Roman women in their teens married men much older than themselves, but German women married later in life and took husbands who were their own age. In German lands a groom provided a dowry for his bride to hold as her own property, and all the Germanic law codes granted women economic freedom. They could inherit, administer, dispose of, and confer on their children family property and personal possessions. They could also prosecute men in court for bodily injury and rape.

In the ninth century, the Carolingians, who had tolerated polygyny, concubinage, and divorce, were influenced by Christianity to make monogamous marriage official policy. The result was both a gain and a loss for women. On the one hand, the choice of a wife became a very serious matter, and wives gained greater dignity and legal security. But on the other hand, a woman's burden as household manager and bearer of children greatly increased. Where previously several women may have shared the tasks of running a nobleman's estate and providing heirs to continue his line, now all these duties rested on the shoulders of one woman. After the ninth century, mortality rates for Frankish women rose and their longevity decreased.

LIFE CHOICES   The demands placed on wives explain the cloister's appeal as a refuge for women, but few women were able to choose the celibate life. (There may, for instance, have been no more than 3,500 nuns in all of England at the end of the Middle Ages.) Entrance into a nunnery was contingent on a woman's ability to bring the house a sizable donation as a dowry. Only a few upper-class women could afford the price of admission. Those who did could acquire educations, rise to positions of leadership, and enjoy economic and political power beyond the reach of their sisters in secular life.

Most medieval women were neither aristocratic housewives nor nuns. They were laboring family women who were as prominent and as creative a part of a community's work force as its men. They could not attend the universities and were excluded from the learned professions of scholarship, medicine, and law. They were, however, admitted to the blue-collar trades. Between the ages of ten and fifteen, girls, like boys, held apprenticeships, and many learned to be skilled workers. When they married, they might continue their trades, operating bake shops or dress shops next to a husband's business, or they might become assistants and partners in a husband's line of work. Women held virtually every job from butcher to goldsmith, and they were especially prominent in the food and clothing industries and in domestic service. Women, as well as men, earned membership in guilds and were accorded the rank of master, but they often found that their opportunities were more restricted than a man's. Women's wages for comparable work averaged 25 percent less than men's. Townswomen had opportunities to go to school and acquire literacy in the vernacular, but peasant women, who tilled the fields, had no such chance for self-improvement.

The Lives of Children

With children, as with women in the Middle Ages, image diverged from life's realities. In medieval art children are rarely portrayed as different from adults, and some historians have questioned whether people in the Middle Ages thought of childhood as a distinct period of life requiring special treatment. The same historians have also noted that infant and child mortality was extremely high, and they have speculated that a parent could not have risked becoming emotionally attached to a child who had a 30 to 50 percent chance of dying before the age of five.

The practice of infanticide, which continued despite its condemnation by the church, suggests that children were held in low esteem in ancient and early medieval society. The Romans regulated family size by exposing unwanted children, but showered attention and affection on the offspring they chose to raise. The Germans, on the other hand, had large families but tended to neglect their children. Among the German tribes one paid a much lower *wergild*, or compensatory fine, for injury to a child than for injury to an adult.

It is possible that instead of distancing parents from children, high rates of infant and child mortality increased attachment to offspring. Evidence of special attention being paid to children is found in the great variety of children's toys and child-rearing equipment (e.g., walkers and potty chairs) that existed in the Middle Ages. Medieval medical authorities also offered advice on postnatal care and childhood diseases—cautioning against abuse and recommending moderation in discipline. The church urged parents to love children as Mary loved Jesus. And evidence from medieval art and literature suggests that when infants and children died in the Middle Ages, parents grieved as pitiably then as now.

Childhood was brief in the Middle Ages, for very young children shared adult responsibilities. Peasant children joined their parents in the fields as soon as they could physically manage the labor. The urban working class sent children as young as eight away from home to begin apprenticeships. The church allowed boys to marry at fourteen and girls at twelve. The pressure put on children to mature and learn may have been a sign of concern for them, for no parental responsibility was deemed greater than that of equipping a child for useful employment.

In Perspective

The economic expansion of the High Middle Ages revived urban life in Europe. As cities grew, new social groups—most notably the merchant-artisan classes—rose to prominence. They successfully challenged the old feudal nobility and brought European communities the blessings and problems of nascent capitalism. The seeds of social conflict and class struggle were sown, but a potentially significant alliance was also struck between the urban classes and the kings who were struggling to reverse the fragmenting influences of feudalism. Together they defeated feudalism and began to consolidate Europe's nations.

The new wealth of towns provided patronage for education and culture. The first universities appeared in the eleventh century and, with them, a new way of thinking (Scholasticism) and a revival of art and science. The creativity of the era testifies to the vitality of the rising "middle" class and its determination to reshape the social and political institutions of the Western world.

REVIEW QUESTIONS

1. How did the responsibilities of the nobility differ from those of the clergy and peasantry during the High Middle Ages? In what ways did each social class contribute to the stability of society?

2. What led to the revival of trade and the growth of towns in the twelfth century? What political and social conditions were essential for a revival of trade? How did towns change medieval society?

3. What were the strengths and weaknesses of the educations provided by medieval universities? How would you evaluate the standard curriculum?

4. How would you define Scholasticism? What was the Scholastic program and method of study? Who were the main critics of Scholasticism and what were their complaints?

5. Do Germanic law and Roman law reflect different understandings of the position of women in society? How did options and responsibilities differ for women in each of the social classes? What are the theories concerning the concept of childhood in the Middle Ages?

SUGGESTED READINGS

P. ARIÈS, *Centuries of Childhood: A Social History of Family Life* (1962). Pioneer effort on the subject.

J. W. BALDWIN, *The Scholastic Culture of the Middle Ages: 1000–1300* (1971). Best brief synthesis available.

M. BLOCH, *French Rural History*, trans. by J. Sondheimer (1966). A classic by a great modern historian.

J. GOODY, *The Development of the Family and Marriage in Europe* (1983). Interesting effort to explain the church's stake in regulating family and marriage.

B. A. HANAWALT, *The Ties That Bound: Peasant Families in Medieval England* (1986). Elucidating demographic and economic study of rural life.

B. A. HANAWALT, *Growing Up in Medieval London* (1993). Positive portrayal of parental and societal treatment of children.

C. H. HASKINS, *The Renaissance of the Twelfth Century* (1927). Still the standard account.

C. H. HASKINS, *The Rise of Universities* (1972). A short, minor classic.

D. HERLIHY, *Medieval Households* (1985). Bread-and-butter account of household structure in antiquity and the Middle Ages.

G. KÜNSTLER, *Romanesque Art in Europe* (1973). Standard survey.

E. MÂLE, *The Gothic Image: Religious Art in France in the Thirteenth Century* (1913). An enduring classic.

A. MURRAY, *Reason and Society in the Middle Ages* (1978). A view of the Middle Ages as an age of reason as well as of faith.

E. PANOFSKY, *Gothic Architecture and Scholasticism* (1951). A controversial classic.

H. PIRENNE, *Medieval Cities: Their Origins and the Revival of Trade,* trans. by Frank D. Halsey (1970). A minor classic.

I. S. ROBINSON, *The Papacy, 1073–1198: Continuity and Innovation* (1990). A fresh look at the papacy in a period of reform and independence.

S. SHAHAR, *The Fourth Estate: A History of Women in the Middle Ages* (1983). A comprehensive survey, making clear the great variety of women's work.

B. STOCK, *The Implications of Literacy* (1983). How the ability to read changed medieval society.

L. THORNDIKE, *University Records and Life in the Middle Ages* (1975). Rich primary sources for curricular and extracurricular life.

The Invention of Printing in China and Europe

It was the desire of rulers to govern more effectively—that is, to shape and control the course of events—that brought the printing press into existence both in China and in Europe. Before there was a printing technology there were governors, religious leaders, and merchants who were eager for ways to disperse their laws, scriptures, and goods more widely and more effectively. To train the skilled help they needed, they promoted education. This spread literacy through the middle and upper urban classes and created a broad market for reading materials. Literacy came more slowly to the lower classes, for authorities feared that it might promote their discontent with the status quo. Even after the invention of printing, many people remained illiterate and acquired their information orally.

Resources and Technology: Paper and Ink

The invention of printing would have been impossible without other inventions that supplied sizable quantities of inexpensive, durable paper and a reliable ink. A water-based soot and gum ink was in use across Asia as early as the Shang period (1776–1122 B.C.E.). Europe did not have anything comparable until the early Middle Ages. Shang officials used their ink to authenticate documents by stamping them with images carved on seals. Similar seals were made in ancient Mesopotamia and Egypt, where they were reserved for religious uses.

The chief print medium in the East was silk. In the West it was parchment. Both were expensive. In the second century B.C.E., the Chinese began to manufacture a crude paper from hemp fibers. It was used as wrapping material. In 105 C.E., a man named Ts'ia Lun developed a blend of ingredients that produced a paper on which one could write. By the Tang period (618–907), paper manufacturing had become a major industry in China, and knowledge of its techniques began to make its way to the West. By the ninth century, Samarkand (in Turkestan) had become the East's leading supplier of paper, and a century later fine paper was being shipped to Europe from Baghdad and Damascus. Italy became the major western center of manufacture in the thirteenth century and Germany in the fourteenth century.

Early Printing Techniques

By the seventh century C.E., copies of Confucian scriptures were being made by taking rubbings from stone and metal engravings. At the same time, the West was inching toward the invention of moveable type thanks to improvements in the arts of engraving and in techniques for striking coins. The Chinese were printing with blocks of carved wood as early as the eighth century, and they outpaced the West in inventing moveable type (i.e., printing with individual characters that could be arranged by hand to compose a page of text). Pi Scheng developed this in the 1040s, four hundred years before Johann Gutenberg set up the first press in Europe.

The earliest moveable type was composed of ceramic characters that were bound together by wax or resin to form a printing plate. When a print job was finished, the plate could be heated to melt the wax and free the characters for reuse. Ceramic was, however, fragile, and it and later metal characters did not hold water-based Chinese inks very well. Wooden blocks created clearer imprints, but carving an adequate supply of them to print Chinese texts was difficult. The Chinese script numbered 10,000 individual characters.

Printing Comes of Age

In 952, a quarter century of preparation was crowned by a large-scale printing of a standardized edition of the Confucian Classics. These

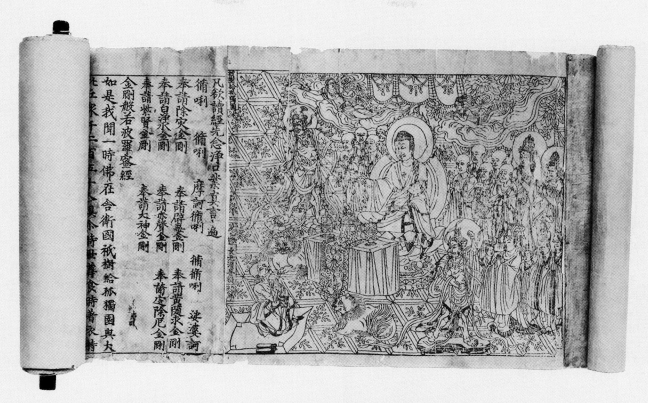

The Diamond Sutra. This Chinese translation of a Sanskrit Buddhist work was printed in 868 and found at Tunhuang. It is the earliest dated piece of block printing yet discovered. The Granger Collection

scrolls were the chief reading material of the elite and the basis for the examinations that qualified candidates for government offices. Their appearance was an epochal event. The Sung period (960–1278) witnessed the first sustained output of block printing. It completed three monumental projects: the histories of the earlier Chinese dynasties and both the Buddhist and the Taoist scriptures. Numerous manuals on medicine and agriculture also became available, and paper money made its first appearance (in Szechwan).

Europeans acquired the knowledge of papermaking from the East, but there is no certain evidence that they learned printing from the same source. Europe seems to have invented its inks, types, and presses independently. This may reflect the fact that the different writing systems in use in the East and the West encouraged different approaches to printing. Carved wood blocks suited the Chinese ideographic script in which a single character expressed a complete concept. European writing systems utilized a brief phonetic alphabet, the characters of which had to be combined to make intelligible words and sentences. This was most efficiently done with moveable type. China's complex script was best reproduced by the simpler machinery of block printing whereas the West's far simpler script required the more complicated machinery of moveable type.

Society and Printing

Cultural and emotional factors help to explain the advent of printing. In the East Buddhists believed that salvation could be earned by copying and disseminating sacred writings. Taoists wanted sacred texts that could be worn as charms.

A European Printshop. This 1568 woodcut by Hans Sachs shows typesetting (rear) and printing (front) underway in an early printshop. Printing made it possible to reproduce exactly and in quantity both text and illustrations, leading to the distribution of scientific and technical information on a scale unimaginable in the preprint world. Houghton Library, Harvard University

Confucianists were concerned to find methods to preserve their sacred writing from the mistakes that crept in when they were copied by hand. In the West the religious orders of monks and friars promoted the printing of standardized, orthodox editions of the Bible and other religious materials. The spread of literacy among the laity created a demand for such things as calendars, newssheets, and how-to pamphlets, but the large-print runs in Europe, as in China, tended to be texts dealing with religious and moral topics.

By 1500 (fifty years after Gutenberg made his invention) there were two hundred presses operating in Europe, and with them came concerns about intellectual property, copyright, and censorship. The increasing availability of books increased the anxiety of governmental and church leaders about the circulation of materials that they considered dangerous. In 1527, the first publisher was executed for printing a book that the church had banned, and in 1559 the pope established an Index of Forbidden Books. For society's authorities, the growing numbers of literate citizens made changes and reforms both easier and more difficult. As a tool of propaganda, the press could work both for and against the state and its favored institutions.

❖ *Why did the invention of printing occur earlier in the East than in the West? Did the West inherit all its knowledge of printing from the East? How do Chinese and European writing systems differ, and what problems do their differences pose for printers? What was the impact of printing on societies?*

Sources: Thomas F. Carter, *The Invention of Printing in China and Its Spread Westward* (1925). Elisabeth L. Eisensrein, *The Printing Press as an Agent of Change,* I–II (1979). Rudolf Hirsch, *Printing, Selling and Reading 1450–1550* (1967). Constance R. Miller, *Technical and Cultural Prerequisites for the Invention of Printing in China and the West* (1983). Denis Twitchett, *Printing and Publishing in Medieval China* (1983).

Chapter 9
The Late Middle Ages: Social and Political Breakdown (1300–1527)

KEY TOPICS

- The Hundred Years' War between England and France
- The effects of the bubonic plague on population and society
- The growing power of secular rulers over the papacy
- Schism, heresy, and reform of the church

During the late Middle Ages, the West endured so many calamities that European civilization seemed in imminent danger of collapse. From 1337 to 1453, France and England waged an increasingly bloody conflict known as the Hundred Years' War. Between 1348 and 1350, the first wave of the bubonic plague (the Black Death) swept over Europe, carrying off a third of its population. In 1378 a quarrel between competing candidates for the papacy tore the church apart and inaugurated a schism that endured for thirty-seven years. And in 1453, the Turks overran Constantinople and charged up the Danube valley toward the heart of Europe.

These crises were accompanied by intellectual developments that undercut assumptions (e.g., about God, mankind, and the social order) that had given comfort to earlier generations. Some philosophers came to the conclusion that human reason was much more limited in scope than the Scholastics had imagined. Feudal institutions, which had been assumed to be divinely ordained, were assaulted by kings who aspired to absolute monarchy. Claims to absolute authority were made by both kings and popes—and challenged by political theorists who argued that subjects could hold rulers accountable for their actions.

The Hundred Years' War and the Rise of National Sentiment

Late medieval rulers practiced the art of feudal government but on a grander scale and with greater sophistication than their predecessors. The Norman kings of England and the Capetian kings of France centralized royal power by fine-tuning feudal relationships by stressing the duties of lesser magnates to greater ones and the unquestioning loyalty of all vassals to the king. They also carefully negotiated alliances with powerful factions within their domains: the feudal nobility, the church, and the towns. These strategies fostered a sense of "national" consciousness that equipped both kingdoms for war on an unprecedented scale.

The Causes of the War

The Hundred Years' War began in May 1337 as a fight over the right of succession to the French throne. In 1328 Charles IV of France died without male issue. This extinguished the senior branch of the Capetian royal house. Edward III (r. 1327–1377), king of England, claimed France's throne by right of his mother, Charles IV's sister. But the French barons had no intention of turning themselves over to England's king. They pledged their allegiance to a cadet branch of the Capetian house, to Charles IV's cousin, Philip VI, duke of Valois (1328–1350). Philip inaugurated the Valois dynasty that ruled France into the sixteenth century.

England and France had long been on a collision course, and the English king's assertion of a claim to the French throne was more a justification than a cause for war. Since the days of the Norman conquest, the king of England had held fiefs on the continent as a vassal of the king of France. English possession of French land hampered attempts by the French kings to centralize the government of their nation. England and France also had competing economic interests in Flanders and on the high seas. The Hundred Years' War was, in light of its many causes, a struggle for national identity as much as for territory.

FRENCH WEAKNESS France should have had no difficulty in winning the war. It had three times the population of England, far greater resources, and the advantage of fighting on its own soil. Yet, until 1415, the major battles were stunning victories for the English.

Internal disunity prevented France from marshaling all its forces against the English, and powerful feudal traditions slowed France's adaptation to new military strategies employed by the English. England's infantry was more disciplined than France's, and English archers wielded a formidable weapon, the longbow. It was capable of firing six arrows a minute and could pierce the armor of a knight at 200 yards.

Progress of the War

The war unfolded in three stages.

THE CONFLICT DURING THE REIGN OF EDWARD III The war began when Edward stirred up rebellions against France in the cities of Flanders by placing an embargo on the English wool that fed Flemish mills. In 1340 the Flemish cities decided that their economic interests lay with England and acknowledged Edward's claim to be king of France and, therefore, overlord of Flanders. On June 23 of that same year, Edward defeated the French fleet in the Bay of Sluys, the first great battle of the war.

In 1346 Edward attacked Normandy. After a series of easy victories that culminated at the battle of Crécy, he seized the port of Calais. Exhaustion and the onset of the Black Death forced a truce in late 1347. There was no further action until 1356, when the English won their greatest victory. Near Poitiers, they routed France's feudal nobles and captured the French king, John II, "the Good" (1350–1364). The loss of king and vassals led to a breakdown of government in France.

Power in France shifted momentarily to the Estates General, a body (resembling England's Parliament) that represented the propertied classes. The powerful merchants of Paris, led by Étienne Marcel, demanded rights similar to those granted the English privileged classes by Magna Carta. But unlike the English Parliament, which expressed the will of a comparatively unified island people, the French Estates General was too divided to be an instrument for effective government. It took time for the leaders of the far-flung regions of a large nation such as France to come to know and trust each other.

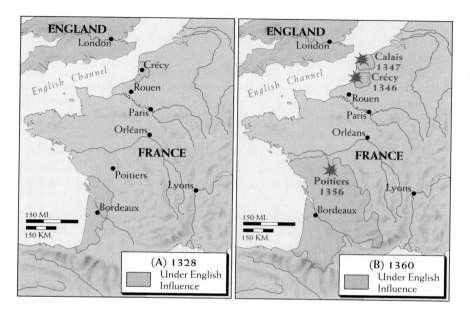

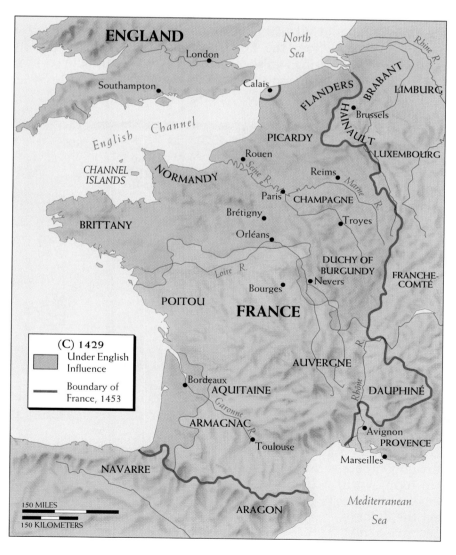

MAP 9–1   THE HUNDRED YEARS' WAR   *These maps show English territorial gains up to the point when Joan of Arc turned the tide of battle in favor of the French in 1429.*

The French privileged classes were able to avoid taxation by foisting the costs of the war onto the backs of the peasants. Beginning in 1358, the desperate peasants launched a series of bloody rebellions called the Jacquerie (from "Jacques Bonhomme," a peasant caricature). The nobility restored order by matching the rebels atrocity for atrocity.

On May 9, 1360, England compelled France to accept terms spelled out in the Peace of Brétigny. Edward renounced his claim to the French throne, but he demanded an end to his vassalage to the king of France and confirmation of his sovereignty over the lands he held in France (including Gascony, Guyenne, Poitou, and Calais). France was also required to pay a ransom of 3 million gold crowns for the return of King John. The treaty was completely unrealistic, and sober observers on both sides knew that the peace it brought could not last long. Within a few years France had reopened hostilities, and by the time of Edward's death in 1377, the English possessed only a few coastal enclaves and the territory around Bordeaux.

FRENCH DEFEAT AND THE TREATY OF TROYES After Edward's death, domestic problems caused England to lose interest in war with France. During the reign of Edward's grandson and successor, Richard II (r. 1377–1399), England experienced its own version of the Jacquerie. In June 1381, John Ball, a secular priest, and Wat Tyler, a journeyman, led a mob of peasants and artisans in an assault on London. The revolt was quickly put down, but it left scars that took decades to heal.

Richard's autocratic behavior turned his nobles against him, and he was replaced on the throne by his cousin, Henry IV. Henry spent his reign confirming his hold on England. His son and heir, Henry V (r. 1413–1422), revived the war with France as a strategy for uniting his people behind their king.

Henry's moment was well chosen, for antagonistic factions had split the French nobility. When Henry V invaded Normandy, the duke of Burgundy's party refused to assist its opponents, the Armagnacs, in defending France. After Henry routed the Armagnacs at Agincourt on October 25, 1415, the Burgundians came to terms with the Armagnacs. But their fragile alliance was shattered in September 1419, when the duke of Burgundy was assassinated by an Armagnac.

Burgundy's son and heir decided to avenge his father's death by helping the English invade Armagnac territory.

With Burgundian assistance Henry V took Paris, captured the French king (Charles VI), and married his daughter. In 1420 the Treaty of Troyes disinherited the French king's son and proclaimed Henry V heir to the French throne. When Henry and Charles died within months of one another in 1422, Henry's infant son, Henry VI, was declared king of both France and England.

JOAN OF ARC AND THE WAR'S CONCLUSION Charles VI's son, the future Charles VII, escaped the English and asserted his right to his father's throne. But the success of the campaign that won him that prize owed less to him than to a remarkable young woman called Joan of Arc (1412–1431). Joan was a peasant from Domrémy who informed Charles VII, in March 1429, that God had commissioned her to deliver Orléans from the English armies that besieged it. The king was skeptical, but he was willing to try anything to reverse French fortunes.

A contemporary portrait of Joan of Arc (1412–1431) in the National Archives in Paris. 15th c. Franco-Flemish miniature. Archives Nationales, Paris, France. Giraudon/Art Resource, NY

Circumstances worked to Joan's advantage. The siege of Orléans had gone on for six months, and the exhausted English troops were at the point of withdrawal when Joan arrived with a fresh French army. The English retreat from Orléans was followed by a succession of victories popularly attributed to Joan. She deserved credit but not for military leadership. Joan's talent lay in inspiring her men with self-confidence and a sense of commitment to a nation. Within a few months of the liberation of Orléans, Charles VII had recovered the city of Rheims and been anointed king in its cathedral—the traditional place for French coronations.

Charles showed little gratitude to his unconventional female ally. When the Burgundians captured Joan in May 1430, Charles abandoned her. The Burgundians and the English, hoping to demoralize their opponents by discrediting Joan, accused her of heresy and turned her over to the Inquisition. After ten weeks of interrogation, the "Maid of Orléans" was executed as a relapsed heretic (May 30, 1431). Twenty-five years later (1456), Charles reopened her trial and had her cleared of all charges, but it was not until 1920 that she was canonized and became Saint Joan.

Once France was united behind its king, the English had no hope of clinging to their continental possessions. In 1435 the duke of Burgundy recognized the inevitable and came to terms with Charles. By the time the war ended in 1453, the English held only a little territory around the port of Calais.

Once separated, England and France had to adjust to their new situation. The war had awakened French nationalism and hastened France's transition from a feudal monarchy to a powerfully centralized state. The loss of England's continental empire, on the other hand, disillusioned the English people with their government and set them on the path to civil war. It ended the medieval phase in the history of their monarchy.

The Black Death

Preconditions and Causes

European society in the late Middle Ages was still thoroughly agrarian. Nine-tenths of the population worked the land. The three-field system of seasonal planting and crop rotation had increased food production, but population growth

Significant Dates from the Period of the Late Middle Ages	
1309–1377	Avignon papacy
1340	Sluys: first major battle of Hundred Years' War
1346	Battle of Crécy and seizure of Calais
1347	Black Death strikes
1356	Battle of Poitiers
1358	Jacquerie disrupts France
1360	Peace of Brétigny
1378–1417	Great Schism
1381	English Peasants' Revolt
1414–1417	Council of Constance
1415	Battle of Agincourt
1422	Treaty of Troyes
1431	Joan of Arc executed as a heretic
1431–1449	Council of Basel
1453	End of Hundred Years' War

kept pace with the food supply. The number of people living in Europe doubled between 1000 and 1300—until there were more mouths than could be fed. The average European probably faced extreme hunger at least once during a life span that averaged only thirty-five years.

Between 1315 and 1317, crop failures contributed to the worst famines of the Middle Ages. Starvation undermined health and increased vulnerability to a virulent bubonic plague that struck in 1348. This "Black Death" (so called because of the way it discolored the bodies of its victims) followed the trade routes from Asia into Europe. Appearing first in Sicily, it entered Europe through the ports of Venice, Genoa, and Pisa. Some places such as Bohemia, which lay outside the major trade routes, were virtually unaffected, but by the early fifteenth century the plague may have reduced the population of western Europe by two-fifths.

The plague bacilli were injected into an individual's bloodstream by flea bites. Pneumonic infection—from a victim's sneezing—was also possible. Medieval physicians had no understanding of these processes and could offer no explanation, defense, or cure. Consequently, the plague inspired deep pessimism, panicky superstition, and an obsession with death and dying.

Images of Death
in the Late Middle Ages

The medieval church taught that life is doomed to end in death but that death is a transition to new life. To make this point, the church's artists represented death from both realistic and religious perspectives. The sculpture shown here, *The Prince of the World*, depicts a healthy young man—when viewed from the front. From the rear, however, the youth's earthly vigor is seen to be impermanent. His body is eaten by worms and frogs, and a serpent (a biblical symbol for sin) spirals up his left leg and enters his back. The church used art and sermons to give the laity graphic lessons in the "art of dying" and urged people to meditate on death, expose themselves to dying people, and often visit graves. In 1424, in the Church of the Holy Innocents in Paris, a new theme appeared that was to become very common in late medieval art: the "dance of death." It represented death as a living skeleton in the

The Prince of the World in the Church of St. Sebald, Nürnberg, 1320–1330. Germnisches Nationalmuseum, Nürnberg.

company of everyone from popes and kings to humble workers. Its point was that no one, no matter how exalted, escaped death.

The point of meditating on death was to strengthen resolves to resist the temptations of sin and, thus, become eligible for rewards rather than punishments in the afterlife. The church promised its obedient sons and daughters that they could share the resplendent glory of the Christ who triumphed over the grave. The *Isenheim Altarpiece* (1509/10–1515) depicted death from the positive perspective of resurrection to an eternal life of blessedness.

Sources: Alberto Tenenti, "Death in History," in *Life and Death in Fifteenth Century Florence*, ed. M. Tetel et al. (Durham, NC: Duke University Press, 1989); Donald Wenstein, "The Art of Dying Well and Popular Piety in the Preaching and Thought of Girolamo Savonarola," in *ibid.*, 88–104; and James M. Clark, *The Dance of Death in the Middle Ages and the Renaissance* (Glasgow: Jackson, Son, and Col, 1950), pp. 1–4, 22–24, 106–110. Joseph L. Koerner, *The Moment of Self-Portraiture in German Renaissance Art* (Chicago, University of Chicago Press, 1993), pp. 199–200. H. W. Janson et al., *History of Art* (Upper Saddle River, NJ: Prentice Hall, 1997), p. 528.

Gruenwald, Mathias (1460–1528), *The Resurrection.* A panel from the Isenheim Altar. Limewood (around 1515), 250 × 650 cm. Musée d'Unterlinden, Colmar, France.

The Apparition of the Knight of Death, an allegory of the plague approaching a city, whose defenses against it are all too unsure. From the *Tres Riches Heures du Duc de Berry* (1284), Limbourg Brothers. Ms. 65/1284, fol. 90v. Musée Conde, Chantilly, France. Giraudon/Art Resource, NY

Amulets and folk remedies abounded. Some people recommended a temperate, disciplined regimen. Others hastened to enjoy as many of life's pleasures as possible before it was too late. Troops of flagellants, religious fanatics who whipped themselves in ritual penance, paraded through the countryside stirring up mass panic. Sometimes unpopular minorities, such as the Jews, were accused of spreading the disease and were murdered.

Social and Economic Consequences

FARMS DECLINE   The plague was most virulent in places where people lived close together. Whole villages and urban districts were some-

times wiped out. As the number of laborers decreased, the wages of those who survived increased. This tempted serfs to abandon farming and seek more rewarding jobs in towns. Agricultural prices fell because of lowered demand, and the price of luxury and manufactured goods—the work of scarce, skilled artisans—rose. These economic developments hurt the nobility. Without workers, the value of their estates declined. To keep workers on their manors, landowners had to offer them better deals. As a result, incomes from rents declined steadily after the plague.

The church was insulated from some of the problems that afflicted the nobility. As a great landholder, it suffered economic losses. But these were offset by an increased demand for masses for the dead and by a flood of gifts and bequests.

To recoup their losses, some landowners converted arable land to sheep pasture. Herding required far fewer expensive laborers than the cultivation of grain. The nobility also used their monopoly of political power to reverse their declining fortunes. They passed laws ordering peasants to stay on the land and freezing wages at low levels. Resentment of such legislation helped fuel the Jacquerie in France and in England a similar rebellion known as the Peasants' Revolt.

CITIES REBOUND   Although the plague hit urban populations especially hard, cities ultimately prospered from its effects. Cities carefully controlled immigration and limited competition in their markets. The omnipresence of death whetted the appetite for pleasure and for the luxuries produced by cities. Initially the demand for manufactured goods could not be met, for craft guilds purposely kept the numbers of masters and apprentices low. The first wave of plague drastically reduced the already restricted supply of artisans, and this caused the prices of manufactured and luxury items to rise to new heights. As high prices for manufactured goods caused wealth to pour into cities, reduced demand for agricultural products (caused by the fall in the numbers of consumers) lowered the cost of living for urban dwellers and the value of investments in farm land. The forces that enriched townspeople impoverished the landed nobility. This enabled cities to extend their influence into the countryside, and the rural gentry began to be absorbed into the ranks of the urban patriciate.

The rapidly changing economic conditions created by the plague were not an unmixed blessing for towns. They increased some of the tensions that had long seethed within urban communities. The merchant classes found it difficult to maintain their traditional dominance over the prospering artisans' guilds. The guilds used their growing political clout to enact restrictive legislation designed to protect local industries. Master artisans kept demand for their products high by limiting the number of shops licensed to share their market. This frustrated many journeymen who were eager to set up in business for themselves, and it created strife within the guilds.

Ecclesiastical Breakdown and Revival: The Late Medieval Church

Kings took full advantage of the rising power of the towns and the declining status of the feudal nobility to centralize governments and economies. The church, which might have resisted the royal drift toward nationalism, faltered just as the new monarchies began to flex their muscles. The plague had weakened the church by killing large numbers of clergy, but the church owed its most serious problems to its own leaders.

The Thirteenth-Century Papacy

In the latter half of the thirteenth century the papacy appeared to be in a strong position. Frederick II had been vanquished. Imperial pressure on Rome had been removed. The saintly French king, Louis IX, was an enthusiastic supporter of the church. The Eastern orthodox clergy even accepted reunion with Rome in 1274 in an attempt to persuade the West to send Constantinople help against the Turks.

But as early as the reign of Pope Innocent III (1198–1216), when papal power reached its height, there were signs of trouble. By creating a centralized papal monarchy with a clearly political mission, Innocent had increased the church's secular power but diminished its spiritual authority. The thirteenth-century papacy became a powerful political institution. It legislated its own laws and enforced them in its own courts. It presided over an efficient international bureaucracy and was preoccupied with finances and the pursuit of secular influence. The papacy thought more in terms of its own needs than those of the church at large.

Many observers noted how far the papacy had departed from the simplicity and other-worldliness of the New Testament apostolic community. In the minds of some, a crucial distinction began to be made between the papal monarchy and the "true" church of faithful Christians.

POLITICAL FRAGMENTATION The papacy was undermined by its own success. The demise of imperial power meant that popes could no longer appeal for support as leaders of Italian resistance to German kings. As external threats from Germany retreated, political intrigues swept the Italian states, and the papacy became just another prize up for grabs.

Pope Gregory X (1271–1276) tried to guarantee the freedom of papal elections by ordering the cardinals to be sequestered when choosing successors to the papal throne. He hoped that physical isolation would prevent outsiders from promoting candidates simply for political reasons, but the College of Cardinals was already too politicized for this to have much effect. Infighting was so great that from 1292 to 1294 the college was unable to elect a pope. In frustration, the cardinals finally chose a compromise candidate—a saintly but inept Calabrian hermit, Celestine V. Celestine shocked Europe by abdicating under suspicious circumstances after only a few weeks in office. His death, which soon followed, led to rumors that he had been murdered to guarantee that his successor had a clear title to office. The new pope, Boniface VIII (1294–1303), was as worldly wise as Celestine had been naively innocent.

Boniface VIII and Philip the Fair

Boniface won the papacy just as England and France were forming nation-states. France's Philip IV, "the Fair" (r. 1285–1314), was a ruthless politician who taught Boniface that the pope's inheritance from Innocent III was not the reality, but only the illusion, of power. Papal monarchy was no match for a king at the helm of one of Europe's new nations.

THE ROYAL CHALLENGE TO PAPAL AUTHORITY If Edward I (r. 1272–1307) of England had been able to resolve problems with Scotland, the Hundred Years' War might have been underway by the time Boniface became pope. France and England were both mobilizing resources for a war they considered inevitable, and their preparations created a problem for Boniface. Both states were levying extraordinary taxes on their clergy. Since Pope Innocent III had decreed in 1215 that rulers had no right to tax the clergy without papal approval, Boniface had to take a strong stand in defense of papal prerogatives. On February 5, 1296, he issued a bull (*Clericis Laicos*) forbidding lay taxation of the clergy.

Edward I retaliated by denying the clergy the protection of the state's laws and courts, and Philip the Fair cunningly deprived the papacy of the bulk of its income by forbidding the exportation of money from France to Rome. Boniface, who had no choice but to come to terms, issued a second bull that conceded the right of a king to tax clergy "during an emergency." To smooth things over, he also agreed to canonize Philip's grandfather, Louis IX.

For much of his reign Boniface was besieged by powerful enemies in Italy. The Colonnas—rivals of Boniface's family, the Gaetani—joined the Spiritual Franciscans in a campaign to invalidate Boniface's election. They alleged that Boniface had forced his predecessor (Celestine V) from office, murdered him, and won the papacy by bribing the cardinals. Boniface fought back, and his fortunes slowly improved. In 1300 Rome celebrated a jubilee, an occasion on which pilgrims to the city received an especially generous indulgence (remission of sin). Tens of thousands flocked to Rome in what the papacy took to be a show of support.

This emboldened Boniface to reassert the papacy's claim to leadership in international politics. He infuriated Edward by supporting the Scots against the English. But his most serious confrontation was with Philip. Philip had arrested Boniface's Parisian legate, Bishop Bernard Saisset of Pamiers, and convicted him in the royal courts of heresy and treason. Philip demanded that Boniface recognize the legitimacy of the proceedings, but to do so would have been to relinquish the pope's jurisdiction over the French clergy. Boniface demanded Saisset's unconditional release and revoked his previous concessions on the matter of clerical taxation. In December 1301, Boniface sent Philip another

bull: *Ausculta Fili (Listen, My Son)*. It pointedly informed the king that "God has set popes over kings and kingdoms."

Philip responded with a ruthless antipapal campaign that forced Boniface to justify the papacy's claim that it and not the state should control the churches within a nation's boundaries. On November 18, 1302, the bull *Unam Sanctam* declared that the temporal authority of kings was "subject" to the spiritual power of the church. Philip viewed the pope's letter as a declaration of war.

Guillaume de Nogaret, Philip's chief minister, denounced Boniface to the French clergy and led an army into Italy to take the pope prisoner. In mid-August 1303, Nogaret surprised Boniface in his retreat at Anagni. The pope was badly beaten and

A book illustration of the Palace of the Popes in Avignon in 1409, the year in which Christendom found itself confronted by three duly elected popes. The "keys" to the kingdom of God, which the pope held on Earth as the vicar of Christ, decorate the three turret flags of the palace. In the foreground, the French poet Pierre Salmon, then journeying via Avignon to Rome, commiserates with a monk over the sad state of the church and France, then at war with England. Book illustration, French, 1409. Paris, Bibliotheque Nationale. AKG Photo.

nearly killed before the people of Anagni rescued him. He returned to Rome, but the ordeal was too much for an aged man. He died in October 1303.

Boniface's successor, Benedict XI (1303–1304), excommunicated Nogaret, but he was in no position to retaliate against the French government. His successor, Clement V (1305–1314), a Frenchman and former archbishop of Bordeaux, utterly capitulated. He lifted Nogaret's excommunication and explained that *Unam Sanctam* was not intended to diminish royal authority in any way. He also gave in to Philip's demand that the Crusading order, the Knights Templars, be condemned for heresy and dissolved—so that Philip could confiscate its wealth. France's victory seemed complete in 1309, when Clement, pleading safety and convenience, moved the papal court to Avignon. Avignon was an independent city situated on land that belonged to the pope, but it was in the southeast corner of territory that was culturally French. The papacy was to remain in Avignon for almost seventy years (until 1377), and no pope was ever again seriously to threaten a king.

The Avignon Papacy (1309–1377)

The Avignon popes were in appearance, although not always in fact, dominated by the French king, and during Clement V's pontificate Frenchmen flooded into the College of Cardinals. Cut off from their Roman estates, the popes at Avignon had to find new sources of income. Their ingenuity and success quickly earned them unfortunate reputations as greedy materialists. Clement V expanded papal taxes on the clergy. Clement VI (1342–1352) began selling indulgences (releases from penance for sin). The doctrine of purgatory—a place of punishment where souls ultimately destined for heaven atoned for venial sins—developed as part of this campaign. By the fifteenth century, the church was urging the living to buy reduced sentences in purgatory for deceased loved ones.

POPE JOHN XXII By the time Pope John XXII (1316–1334) ascended the throne, the popes were well enough established in Avignon to reenter the field of international politics. The result was a quarrel with the German emperor, Louis IV, that inspired an important debate about the nature of legitimate authority.

John backed a candidate who lost the imperial election of 1314 to Louis, and he obstinately—and without legal justification—refused to confirm Louis's title. Louis retaliated by accusing John of heresy and declaring him deposed in favor of an antipope. Two outstanding pamphleteers made the case for the king: William of Ockham, whom John excommunicated in 1328, and Marsilius of Padua (ca. 1290–1342), whose teaching John declared heretical in 1327.

William of Ockham (d. 1349) was a brilliant logician and critic of the "realist" philosophers who claimed that general terms, such as *church*, corresponded to transcendent realities that actually existed. Ockham, a nominalist, insisted that such words were only names the human mind gave to abstract ideas it invented. This position led Ockham to conclude that the real church was the historical human community, not some supernatural entity. The pope was only one of its members and, as such, had no special powers that made him infallible. The church was best guided not by popes, he believed, but by scripture and by councils representing all Christians.

In *Defender of Peace* (1324), Marsilius of Padua argued that clergy were limited to purely spiritual functions and had no right to coerce laity. The spiritual crimes over which the pope had jurisdiction would be punished in the next life, not in this one. An exception might be made if a secular ruler declared a divine law also a law of the state, for God had given the state exclusive authority to maintain secular order by force. A true pope lived according to the strictest apostolic ideals and presumed to lead only by spiritual example.

NATIONAL OPPOSITION TO THE AVIGNON PAPACY John's successor, Benedict XII (1334–1342), began construction of a great palace at Avignon, and his high-living French successor, Clement VI (1342–1352), presided over a splendid, worldly court. The cardinals became lobbyists for various secular patrons, and Avignon's fiscal tentacles spread farther and farther afield.

Secular governments responded by passing legislation restricting papal jurisdiction and taxation. The English had no intention of supporting a papacy that they believed was the puppet of their French enemy. The French monarchy insisted upon its "Gallican liberties," a well-founded tradition that granted the king control of ecclesiastical appointments and taxation. German and Swiss cities also took the initiative to limit and even to overturn traditional clerical privileges and immunities.

JOHN WYCLIFFE AND JOHN HUSS Discontent with the worldly clergy and politicized papacy was expressed not only in government legislation, but in popular lay religious movements. The most significant were the Lollards in England and the Hussites in Bohemia. The Lollards drew their ideas from the writings of John Wycliffe (d. 1384)—as did John Huss (d. 1415), the martyr of the Hussite movement. Neither man would have approved, however, of all that his alleged followers did in his name.

Wycliffe was an Oxford theologian and a major intellectual spokesman for the rights of royalty against the secular pretensions of popes. Wycliffe strongly supported the actions English kings took from 1350 on to reduce the power of the Avignon papacy over the church in England. Like the Franciscans, he believed that clergy "ought to be content with food and clothing," and his arguments for clerical poverty provided justification for confiscations of ecclesiastical property by the state.

Wycliffe maintained that since all authority came from God, only leaders who lived pious lives could lay claim to legitimacy. He believed that faithful laypeople had the right to pass judgment on corrupt ecclesiastics and undertake the reform of the church. This argument could also be used to justify resistance to secular rulers whose immoral lives proved that they held no mandate from God. Wycliffe anticipated some positions that Protestants would eventually take—challenging papal infallibility, the dogma of transubstantiation that gave the priesthood power over the laity, and policies that restricted the laity's access to the Scriptures.

The Lollards, English advocates of Wycliffe's teaching, preached in the vernacular, disseminated translations of Holy Scripture, and championed clerical poverty. So long as they restricted their attention to religious matters, the English government tolerated them. But after the Peasants' Revolt of 1381 popularized egalitarian notions that were linked to Wycliffe's works, the state decided that Lollardy was subversive. In 1401 it was declared a capital offense.

Heresy was not so easily dealt with in Bohemia where government was weak. The University of Prague, founded in 1348, became the center for a Czech nationalistic movement opposing German encroachments on Bohemia. John Huss, the leader of the movement, became rector of the university in 1403. He believed that a reformed religion would help the Czechs develop a national identity.

The Czech reformers advocated vernacular translations of the Bible and rejected practices they labeled superstitions (particularly some customs associated with the Eucharist). Like the Lollards, they doubted that a priest guilty of mortal sin could perform a valid sacrament. They repudiated the Catholic rubric that reserved the cup at communion to the priest. By offering both the wine and the bread to the laity, they removed any suggestion that the clergy were spiritually superior to the people. Hussites also rejected the doctrine of transubstantiation and asserted that bread and wine remained bread and wine after priestly consecration.

Wycliffe's teaching was partly responsible for the Hussite movement. After Anne of Bohemia married King Richard II of England in 1381, Czech students enrolled at Oxford and sent copies of Wycliffe's works home. Huss was the leader of the Wycliffe faction at the University of Prague.

Huss was excommunicated in 1410, and in 1414 he successfully petitioned for a hearing before an international church council that was assembling at Constance, Switzerland. Although he was guaranteed safe conduct by Emperor Sigismund, he was imprisoned and executed for heresy on July 6, 1415. The reaction in Bohemia to his execution and that of his colleague, Jerome of Prague, a few months later was fierce. The Taborites, a militant branch of the Hussites, took up arms under John Ziska and declared their intention to transform Bohemia into a religious and social paradise. Within a decade, they had won control of the Bohemian church.

The Great Schism (1378–1417) and the Conciliar Movement to 1449

In January 1377, Pope Gregory XI (1370–1378) yielded to international pressure and announced that the papacy would leave Avignon and return to Rome. Europe rejoiced—prematurely, as it turned out—at the end of the church's "Babylonian Captivity" (a reference to the exile of the ancient Israelites from their homeland).

URBAN VI AND CLEMENT VII Gregory died soon after returning to Rome, and the cardinals elected an Italian archbishop, Pope Urban VI (1378–1389). When Urban announced his intention to reform the Curia (the church's central administration), the cardinals, most of whom were French, sensed a challenge to their power and insisted on returning the papacy to their base of operation in Avignon. Five months after Urban's enthronement, a group of thirteen cardinals announced that Urban's election was invalid because it had been forced on them by the Roman mob. They then proceeded to elect a "true" pope, Clement VII (1378–1397), a cousin of the French king. Urban denied their allegations and appointed new cardinals to replace them in his college.

Europe, confronted with two papal courts, distributed its support along political lines: England and its allies (the Holy Roman Empire, Hungary, Bohemia, and Poland) acknowledged Urban VI, whereas France and those in its orbit (Naples, Scotland, Castile, and Aragon) supported Clement VII. (The Roman Catholic Church has subsequently decided that the Roman line of popes was the legitimate one.)

Since the schism threatened the survival of the church in its traditional form, responsible leaders hoped to end it quickly. The easiest solution would have been for one or both of the popes to resign for the good of all, but neither was willing to sacrifice himself.

CONCILIAR THEORY OF CHURCH GOVERNMENT Europe's leaders, seeing no other option, began to listen to scholars who argued that an ecumenical church council was needed to end the schism. There were problems: Only a pope could call a legitimate council, and none of the popes wanted to summon a council that might depose him. Also, since a pope's authority derived directly from God and not from his people, it was not at all certain that a council could depose a pope.

To make their argument for a council, the conciliarists had to examine medieval assumptions about the nature of authority. This led them to develop a rationale for popular government. The conciliarists defined the church as the whole body of the faithful and argued that, therefore, ultimate authority rested with all the people. Since popes were chosen to care for the people's church, they were accountable to the people and served at the people's pleasure.

THE COUNCIL OF PISA (1409–1410) In 1409, thirty-one years after the schism began, cardinals from both sides who embraced the conciliarists' position attempted to resolve the problem. They met in Pisa, deposed their respective popes, and agreed on a single new one. To their consternation, neither of the two competing popes accepted their action, and the result was the establishment of a third pope.

THE COUNCIL OF CONSTANCE (1414–1417) Emperor Sigismund finally prevailed on John XXIII, the Pisan pope, to summon a council to meet in the Swiss city of Constance in 1414. Deprived of all support, the competing popes either came to terms or were abandoned. The cardinals at the council then chose a new pope whom everyone agreed to acknowledge, Martin V (1417–1431). Before the council disbanded, it passed a resolution (*Sacrosancta*) that stated that the council was the true government of the church and supreme over popes. Provisions were also made for councils to meet at regular intervals.

THE COUNCIL OF BASEL (R. 1431–1449) Conciliar power peaked when a council meeting at Basel presumed to negotiate church doctrine with the heretic Hussites of Bohemia. In November 1433, it granted the Bohemians jurisdiction over their church (similar to that held by the French and the English), a unique liturgy, and an exalted role for the laity.

The pope believed that these actions trespassed on his jurisdiction, and in 1438 he upstaged the council by negotiating reunion with the Eastern church. The agreement signed in Florence in 1439 was short-lived, but at the time it enhanced papal prestige. When Basel responded by threatening the pope with deposition, the kings of Europe, fearing a return to schism, withdrew their support for the conciliar movement. A decade later the papal bull *Execrabilis* (1460) condemned conciliarism. The movement had, however, achieved something. It had planted the thought that the role of the leader of an institution was to care for the well-being of its members. This idea had wide-ranging ramifications for the state as well as the church.

Medieval Russia

According to legend, Vladimir (972–1015), prince of Kiev (early Russia's greatest city), decided to modernize his people by converting them to one of the world's great religions. He invited delegations from Muslims, Roman Catholics, Jews, and Greek Orthodox Christians to come to his court to make cases for their faiths. After viewing what each had to offer, Vladimir chose the Greek option. Given Kiev's proximity to Constantinople and Russia's commercial ties with the Byzantine Empire, his decision must have been a foregone conclusion.

Politics and Society

Vladimir's successor, Yaroslav the Wise (1016–1054), turned Kiev into a magnificent political and cultural center that rivaled Constantinople. After his death, however, rivalry among the Russian princes split their people into three groups: the Great Russians, the White Russians, and the Little Russians (Ukrainians). Kiev was reduced to being simply one principality among many.

The governments of the Russian states combined monarchy (a prince), aristocracy (a council of noblemen), and democracy (a popular assembly of all adult males). The broadest social division was between freemen and slaves. Freemen included clergy, army officers, boyars (wealthy landowners), townsmen, and peasants. Slaves were mostly prisoners of war. There was also a large semifree group composed of debtors who were working off their obligations.

Mongol Rule (1243–1480)

In the thirteenth century, Mongol (or Tatar) armies swept over China, much of the Islamic world, and Russia. Ghengis Khan's forces (1155–1227) invaded Russia in 1223, and Kiev fell to the Mongol general Batu Khan in 1240. When the Mongols divided their empire, a group called the Golden Horde (a name derived from the Tatar words for the color of Batu Khan's tent) exacted tribute from the Russian cities. The Golden Horde established its seat at Sarai on the lower Volga and ruled the steppe region of what

Genghis Khan holding an audience. This Persian miniature shows the great conqueror and founder of the Mongol empire with members of his army and entourage as well as an apparent supplicant (lower right). E. T. Archive

is now southern Russia. Its agents were stationed in all the principal Russian towns to oversee taxation and the conscription of soldiers.

Mongol rule distanced the Russians from Western culture. Russian women who married Mongols were influenced by Islam, the religion adopted by the Golden Horde. They began to wear veils and to lead secluded lives. But the Mongols interfered little with the political institutions and religion of their Russian subjects, and the peace they maintained brought Russia economic benefits.

Liberation

The princes of Moscow assisted the Mongols with the collection of tribute and grew wealthy in the service of their masters. When Mongol rule began to weaken, the princes added to the territory Moscow controlled. In pursuit of a policy called "the gathering of the Russian Land," they expanded the principality of Moscow by purchase, colonization, and conquest.

In 1380 Grand Duke Dimitri of Moscow (1350–1389) defeated Tatar forces at Kulikov Meadow. His victory precipitated the decline of Mongol hegemony. Another century passed before Ivan III, "the Great," (d. 1505) brought all of northern Russia under Moscow's control and ended Mongol rule (1480). By the last quarter of the fourteenth century, Moscow had become the political and religious center of Russia. In 1453, when Constantinople fell to the Turks, Moscow took on a new role. It proclaimed itself the "third Rome" and the guardian of Orthodox civilization.

In Perspective

War, plague, and schism convulsed Europe in the late Middle Ages. Even God's house became a shambles as competing popes fought over it. William of Ockham, the leading intellectual of the day, embraced philosophical skepticism and acknowledged the limits of human reason. As the leadership of traditional institutions failed, ordinary men and women endeavored to take things into their own hands. But there was more to the age than loss, doubt, and desperation. The fourteenth century saw the birth of humanism, an explosion of lay education, and artistic and cultural movements that heralded Italy's great Renaissance.

REVIEW QUESTIONS

1. What were the causes of the Hundred Years' War? What advantages did each side have? Why were the French ultimately victorious?
2. What were the causes of the Black Death? Why did it spread so quickly? What were its effects on European society? How important do you think disease is in changing the course of history?
3. What was at issue in the struggle between Pope Boniface VIII and King Philip the Fair? Why was Boniface unable to put up a stronger fight? How had political conditions changed since the reign of Pope Innocent III? What did the changes mean for the future of the papacy?
4. What changes took place in the church and in its relationship to secular society between 1200 and 1450? How did it respond to political threats from increasingly powerful monarchs? How great an influence did the church have on secular events?
5. What is meant by the term *Avignon Papacy?* How did this period in the church's history shape the development of the papacy? What caused the Great Schism? How was it resolved? Why was the conciliar movement a threat to the papacy?
6. Why did kings in the late thirteenth and early fourteenth centuries have more power over the church than it had over them? What had changed to make this era different from earlier ones in which popes dominated rulers? What did kings hope to achieve through their struggles with the church?

SUGGESTED READINGS

C. ALLMAND, *The Hundred Years' War: England and France at War, c. 1300–ca. 1450* (1988). Good overview of the war's development and consequences.

P. ARIÈS, *The Hour of Our Death* (1983). People's familiarity with and philosophy of death in the Middle Ages.

J. Huizinga, *The Waning of the Middle Ages: A Study of the Forms of Life, Thought, and Art in France and the Netherlands in the Dawn of the Renaissance* (1924). A classic study of "mentality" at the end of the Middle Ages. Exaggerated but engrossing.

W. H. McNeill, *Plagues and Peoples* (1976). The Black Death in a broader context.

F. Oakley, *The Western Church in the Later Middle Ages* (1979). Eloquent, sympathetic survey.

E. Perroy, *The Hundred Years' War,* trans. by W. B. Wells (1965). Still the most comprehensive one-volume account.

Y. Renovard, *The Avignon Papacy 1305–1403,* trans. by D. Bethell (1970). The standard narrative account.

B. Tierney, *Foundations of the Conciliar Theory* (1955). Important study showing the origins of conciliar theory in canon law.

P. Ziegler, *The Black Death* (1969). Highly readable account.

Chapter 10

Renaissance and Discovery

KEY TOPICS

- ⟳ The politics, culture, and art of the Italian Renaissance
- ⟳ Political struggle and foreign intervention in Italy
- ⟳ The powerful new monarchies of northern Europe
- ⟳ The thought and culture of the northern Renaissance

The late medieval period was an era of creative disruption. The social order that had persisted in Europe for a thousand years failed, but Europe did not decline. It merely changed direction. By the late fifteenth century, Europe's population was recovering from the losses inflicted by the plagues, famines, and wars of the fourteenth century. In many places, able rulers were establishing stable, centralized governments. The city-states of Italy were doing especially well. Italy's strategic location permitted it to dominate world trade, which still centered on the Mediterranean. The great wealth that trade brought Italy's rulers and merchants allowed them to become patrons of government, education, *and the arts. The result was a cultural Renaissance led by Italians.*

Renaissance humanists revived the study of Greek and Latin and recovered the classical literary heritage. They reformed education and, thanks to the invention of the printing press, became the first scholars able to reach out to the general public. In their eagerness to educate ordinary men and women, they championed the development of vernacular languages as vehicles for art and serious thought.

During the late fifteenth and sixteenth centuries, powerful nations arose in western Europe and inaugurated an era of unprecedented territorial expansion. The colonies they planted around the world yielded a flood of gold and exotic new products that transformed the Western way of life.

The Renaissance in Italy (1375–1527)

The Renaissance was a time of transition from the medieval to the modern world. Medieval Europe, especially before the twelfth century, was a fragmented feudal society with a marginal agrarian economy. Intellectually, it was dominated by the church. Renaissance Europe, especially after the fourteenth century, was characterized by growing national consciousness and political centralization, an urban economy based on commerce and capitalism, and an increasingly secular culture. These changes appeared first in Italy.

The Italian City-State

Italy had always had a cultural advantage over the rest of Europe, for its location made it the link between East and West. Trade with the Middle East, which continued uninterrupted throughout the Middle Ages, supported a vibrant urban culture in Italy. During the thirteenth and fourteenth centuries, Italy's cities extended their influence into the countryside and became great city-states.

GROWTH OF CITY-STATES   The growth of Italy's cities and urban culture was promoted by the endemic warfare between Guelf (pro-papal) and Ghibelline (pro-imperial) political factions. Either the pope or the emperor might have brought

MAP 10–1   RENAISSANCE ITALY   *The city-states of Renaissance Italy were self-contained principalities characterized by internal strife and external aggression.*

the cities under control if either had been free to concentrate on the task. Instead, each tried to weaken the other, and the merchant oligarchies that governed the cities were the winners. Free from dominance by kings or territorial princes, the Italian cities expanded into the surrounding countryside and assimilated the rural nobility. The five greatest were the duchy of Milan, the republics of Florence and Venice, the Papal States, and the kingdom of Naples.

SOCIAL CLASS AND CONFLICT   Social strife and competition for power were intense within Italy's city-states. By the fifteenth century, most had concluded that they could preserve order only by turning themselves over to despots. Venice was a notable exception; it remained an oligarchic republic controlled by a small group of merchant families. Florence, on the other hand, was fairly typical of the forces that contended within Italian urban governments.

There were four politically active groups in Florence: the old rich (the *grandi,* the nobles and merchants who were traditional leaders), an emergent newly rich merchant class (capitalists and bankers known as the *popolo grosso* or "fat people"), the middle-burgher ranks (guildmasters, shop owners, and professionals), and the *popolo minuto* (the "little people" of the lower middle classes). In 1457 about 30,000 Florentines, one-third of the population, were listed as paupers.

DESPOTISM AND DIPLOMACY In 1378 the economic dislocation of the Black Death prompted the Ciompi Revolt, a great uprising of the poor in Florence. Stability was not restored until Cosimo dé Medici (1389–1464) took over in 1434. Cosimo dé Medici, in addition to being the richest man in Florence, was an astute statesman. He controlled the city from behind the scenes, skillfully manipulating the constitution and influencing elections. Florence was governed by a council of six (later, eight) men, the *Signoria,* elected from the most powerful guilds. Through informal, cordial relations with the electoral committee, Cosimo saw to it that the members of the *Signoria* were his men. His grandson, Lorenzo the Magnificent (1449–1492), had absolute control of Florence. After 1478, when the pope and a rival Florentine family (the Pazzi) assassinated Lorenzo's brother, Lorenzo ruled with a firm hand. But he was careful to court popular support.

Despotism was less subtle elsewhere. When internal fighting and foreign intrigue got so bad that city governments were paralyzed, warring factions agreed to the appointment of a *podestà.* He was a neutral outsider, a hired strongman who was empowered to do whatever was necessary to maintain law and order and foster a good climate for business. Because a despot could not depend on everyone's cooperation, he policed and protected his town with a mercenary army hired from military brokers called *condottieri.*

The *podestà's* job was hazardous. He could be dismissed by the oligarchy that hired him or assassinated by those whom he offended. The potential spoils of such a career were, however, tempting, for a *podestà* might establish a dynasty. The Visconti family that came to power in Milan in 1278 and the Sforza family that followed them in 1450 both had such roots.

No matter what kind of government it had, a disciplined Italian city provided a congenial climate for intellectual and artistic pursuits. Despots promoted Renaissance culture as enthusiastically as republicans, and spiritually minded popes were no less generous than worldly vicars of Christ.

Humanism

The Florentine Leonardo Bruni (1374–1444) was the first to describe the scholarship of the Renaissance as the study of *humanitas* (i.e., "humanity"). Modern authorities do not agree on how to define the term. For some, humanism is an un-Christian philosophy that exalts human dignity, individualism, and secular values. There were, however, Christian humanists who defended faith from attack by extreme rationalists. Humanism, for many, may have been less a philosophical position than an educational program emphasizing rhetoric and sound scholarship. It championed the study of Latin and Greek classics and Christian church fathers as an end in itself and as a guide to reforming society. The first humanists were orators and poets. Some taught at universities, but many worked as secretaries, speech writers, and diplomats at princely and papal courts.

The humanists were not the first Europeans to take an interest in the study of classical and Christian antiquities. There had been a Carolingian renaissance in the ninth century. Another was led by the cathedral school of Chartres in the twelfth century. The University of Paris in the thirteenth century was transformed by the study of Aristotle, and the works of Saint Augustine reinvigorated intellectual life in the fourteenth century. These earlier scholarly revivals pale, however, in comparison with Italy's late medieval Renaissance.

Humanists did not use the same techniques of debate as those on which the medieval Scholastics relied. Instead of summarizing and reconciling the views of respected commentators on a topic, they went directly to original sources. Avidly searching out neglected manuscripts, Italian humanists recovered all that remained of Greek and Latin literature and made it generally

*Dante Alighieri (1265–1321)
portrayed with scenes of hell,
purgatory, and paradise from the*
Divine Comedy, *his classic epic
poem.* Scala/Art Resource, NY

available to all scholars. They so assimilated the classics and so identified with the ancients that they came to think of the previous centuries as a hiatus, a dark "middle age" separating ancient civilization from its rebirth in their day.

PETRARCH, DANTE, AND BOCCACCIO Francesco Petrarch (1304–1374), "the father of humanism," tried to write like one of the giants of Roman literature. His *Letters to the Ancient Dead* was an imagined correspondence with Cicero, Livy, Vergil, and Horace. His epic poem *Africa* (a tribute to the Roman general Scipio Africanus) continued Vergil's *Aeneid*. His biographies of famous Romans, *Lives of Illustrious Men*, were modeled on those of Plutarch, but his most popular work was more original and not in a classical language. It was a collection of highly introspective Italian love sonnets, which he addressed to a married woman named Laura. He admired her as a courtly lover—from a safe distance.

Classical and Christian values coexist in Petrarch's work. He rejected scholastic learning as sterile and useless, but published tracts refuting Aristotelian arguments that undercut faith in personal immortality. His imagined dialogues with Saint Augustine bear witness to his acceptance of many traditional medieval Christian beliefs.

Petrarch's point of view was more secular than that of his famous near-contemporary, Dante Alighieri (1265–1321). Dante's *Vita Nuova* and *Divine Comedy* rank with Petrarch's sonnets as cornerstones of Italian vernacular literature. They are also moving testimonies to medieval piety. Petrarch's student, Giovanni Boccaccio (1313–1375) created bridges of another kind between medieval literature and humanism. His *Decameron* consists of 100 (often bawdy) tales—many of which are retold from medieval sources.

EDUCATIONAL REFORMS AND GOALS Humanists were activists who treated the magnificent manuscript collections they assembled as if books were potent medicines for the ills of society. The goal of their studies was to discover the good and to practice virtue. Humanist learning was intended to ennoble people by fitting them for the free use of their gifts of mind and body.

Traditional methods of education had to be reformed to nurture the kind of well-rounded people the humanists wanted to produce. The rediscovery in 1416 of the complete text of Quintilian's *Education of the Orator* provided humanists with a classical guide for the revision of curricula. Mentors, such as Vittorino da Feltre (d. 1446), articulated the goals and methods of the reform. Vittorino required his students to master difficult works by Pliny, Ptolemy, Terence, Plautus, Livy, and Plutarch, and to undergo vigorous physical training.

Humanist learning was not confined to the classroom. Baldassare Castiglione's (1478–1529) influential *Book of the Courtier* was written as a practical guide for the nobility at the court of Urbino. It urged them to combine the study of ancient languages and history with the practice of athletic, military, and musical skills. In addition to these accomplishments, a courtier was to have good manners and an exemplary moral character.

Women, most notably Christine de Pisan (1363?–1434), helped shape and profit from educational reform. Christine's father was physician and astrologer to the court of King Charles V of France. At the French court she received as fine an education as any man and became an expert in classical, French, and Italian languages and literature. Married at fifteen and widowed with three children at twenty-seven, she turned to writing lyric poetry to support herself. Her works were soon being read at all the European courts. Her most famous book, *The City of Ladies*, chronicles the accomplishments of the great women of history.

THE FLORENTINE "ACADEMY" AND THE REVIVAL OF PLATONISM The revival of the study of ancient Greek literature, particularly the works of Plato, was the most important of the Renaissance's renewed contacts with the past. Interest in the Greek language led Florence, in 1397, to invite a Byzantine scholar, Manuel Chrysoloras, to immigrate and open a school. The Council of Ferrara-Florence, which met in 1439 to negotiate the reunion of the Eastern and Western churches, brought more Greek scholars and manuscripts to Italy. Their numbers increased greatly when Turks overwhelmed the city of Constantinople in 1453.

Medieval Scholastics were preoccupied with Aristotle's logic and science, but Renaissance thinkers were enthralled by Plato's poetry and mysticism. Platonism's appeal lay in its flattering view of human nature and its apparent congruence with Christianity. Platonism posited the existence of a realm of eternal ideas that were the prototypes for the imperfect, perishable things of the world in which humans lived. Plato argued that the presence in the human mind of an innate knowledge of mathematical truths and moral standards proved that a part of a human being was rooted in the eternal.

To encourage the study of Plato and the Neoplatonic philosophers, Cosimo dé Medici (1389–1464) funded a Platonic Academy, a gathering of influential Florentine humanists headed first by Marsilio Ficino (1433–1499) and later by Pico della Mirandola (1463–1494). From Florence Plato's work circulated throughout the West to promote a new, more optimistic view of human nature. Pico's *Oration on the Dignity of Man* succinctly articulated the Renaissance's faith in human potential. Published in Rome in December 1486, the *Oration* was a preface to a collection of 900 theses proposed for a public debate on all of life's important issues. It lauded human beings as the only creatures in the world possessed of the freedom to become whatever they wanted—angels or pigs.

CRITICAL WORK OF THE HUMANISTS: LORENZO VALLA The careful study of classical languages conducted by humanist scholars sometimes led to conclusions that had wide-ranging ramifications. The leader in this field was Lorenzo Valla (1406–1457), a papal secretary who wrote the era's standard text for the study of Latin philology, *Elegances of the Latin Language*. Valla's linguistic skills enabled him to carry out a devastating critique of *The Donation of Constantine*, a document that popes had used since the eighth century to bolster their claims to power. By pointing out the use of anachronistic terms in the *Donation*, Valla proved that it was a forgery and not an authentic charter from the period of the Emperor Constantine (i.e., the fourth century). Valla also pointed out errors in the Vulgate, the church's authorized Latin Bible. Such historical-critical work helped pave the way for the Protestant Reformation.

CIVIC HUMANISM Although some humanists were clubbish snobs—an intellectual elite with narrow, antiquarian interests—others preached a "civil humanism," an education that promoted virtue and equipped one for public service. They entered politics, produced art and literature to celebrate the cities where they lived, promoted the use of vernacular languages so that ordinary people could profit from their work, and wrote histories of contemporary events.

Renaissance Art

In Renaissance Italy—and in Reformation Europe—the interests of the laity triumphed over those of the clergy. As people began to value the secular world, secular learning, and purely human pursuits as ends in themselves, medieval Christian attitudes adjusted to accommodate a more this-worldly spirit. This development owed something to the crises within the papacy that cost the late medieval church much of its power and prestige. It was also encouraged by the rise of patriotic nationalism, the creation of governmental bureaucracies staffed by laypersons rather than clerics, and the rapid growth of lay education during the fourteenth and fifteenth centuries.

The new perspective on life can be perceived in the painting and sculpture of the "High" or mature Renaissance (the late fifteenth and early sixteenth centuries). Whereas medieval art was abstract and formulaic, Renaissance art focused on describing the natural world and communicating human emotions. It displayed a rational (chiefly mathematical) order, a symmetry and proportionality that reflected a humanistic faith in the harmony and intelligibility of the universe.

During the fifteenth century, artists developed new technical skills. Slow-drying oil-based paints were invented, and new methods of drafting were devised. *Chiaroscuro*, the use of shading, and linear perspective, the adjustment of the size of figures to create the illusion of depth, permitted artists to paint a more natural world. Whereas flat Byzantine and Gothic paintings were intended to be read like pages in a book, Renaissance paintings were windows on a three-dimensional world filled with life.

Giotto (1266–1336), the father of Renaissance painting, was the first to intuit what could be done with the new techniques. Though still filled with religious seriousness, his work was less abstract and more naturalistic than that of a medieval painter. The Black Death of 1340 slowed the development of art, but ideas such as Giotto's emerged again in the fifteenth century in the work of the painter Masaccio (1401–1428) and the sculptor Donatello (1386–1466). The heights were reached by the great masters of the High Renaissance: Leonardo da Vinci (1452–1519), Raphael (1483–1520), and Michelangelo Buonarroti (1475–1564).

LEONARDO DA VINCI   Leonardo came closer than anyone to achieving the Renaissance ideal of universal competence. He was one of the greatest painters of all time—as is demonstrated by his famous portrait of Mona Lisa. Kings and dukes employed him as a military engineer. As an early advocate of scientific experimentation, he defied the church by dissecting corpses to study human anatomy. He also did significant descriptive work in botany. Leonardo's sketch books were filled with designs for such modern machines as airplanes and submarines. He had so many ideas that it was difficult for him to concentrate long on any one of them.

RAPHAEL   Raphael, an unusually sensitive man, was loved for both his work and his kindly personality. He is best known for his tender depictions of madonnas. Art historians consider his fresco *The School of Athens*, a group portrait of the great Western philosophers, a perfect example of Renaissance technique.

MICHELANGELO   Michelangelo was a more melancholy genius, but he also excelled in several fields. His David, an eighteen-foot-high sculpture of a biblical hero in the guise of a Greek god, splendidly illustrates the Renaissance artist's devotion to harmony, symmetry, and proportion—and to the glorification of the human form. Four different popes commissioned works from Michelangelo. The most famous are the frescoes that Pope Julius II (1503–1513) ordered for the Vatican's Sistine Chapel. They originally covered 10,000 square feet and featured 343 figures—most of which Michelangelo executed himself with minimal help from his assistants. It took him four years to complete the extraordinarily original images that have become the best-known icons of the Christian faith.

Michelangelo lived to be nearly ninety, and his later works illustrate the passing of the High Renaissance and the advent of a new style known as mannerism. Mannerism was a reaction against the simplicity and symmetry of High Renaissance art. It made room for the strange, even the abnormal, and gave free reign to the subjectivity of the artist. The name reflects a tendency by artists to employ "mannered" or "affected" techniques—distortions that expressed individual perceptions and feelings. The Venetian Tintoretto (d. 1594) and the Spanish El Greco (d. 1614) represent mannerism at its best.

The frescoes of Michelangelo on the west wall ceiling of the Sistine Chapel in the Vatican Palace. Above the altar is his Last Judgment. Brett Froomer/The Image Bank

Slavery in the Renaissance

The vision of innate human nobility that inspired the Renaissance was marred by what modern observers would consider a major blind spot. Slavery flourished in Italy as extravagantly as art and culture. The slave market developed as early as the twelfth century when Spaniards began to sell Muslim war captives to wealthy Italians. Many of these slaves were employed as domestic servants, but collective plantation slavery also appeared in the eastern Mediterranean during the High Middle Ages. Venetian sugar cane plantations were models for later west Mediterranean and New World slavery.

The demand for slaves soared after the Black Death (1348–1350) reduced the supply of laborers throughout western Europe. A strong, young slave cost the equivalent of the wages paid a free servant over several years. But given the prospect of a lifetime of free service, slaves were considered good bargains. Owners could also dispose of them like any other pieces of property. Slaves of all races were imported from Africa, the Balkans, Constantinople, Cyprus, Crete, and the lands surrounding the Black Sea. Most well-to-do Italian households had slaves, and even clergy kept them.

As in ancient Greece and Rome, slaves of the Renaissance era were often integrated into households like family members. Some female slaves became mothers of their masters' children, and quite a few of these children were adopted and raised as legitimate heirs. It was clearly in the self-interest of owners to protect their investments by keeping slaves healthy and happy, but slaves remained an uprooted and resentful people—a threat to social stability.

Italy's Political Decline: The French Invasions (1494–1527)

The Treaty of Lodi

The protection of Italy from foreign invasion depended on the ability of its independent city-states

An Unprecedented Self-Portrait

Dürer, Albrecht (1471–1528). *Self-portrait at Age 28 with Fur Coat.* 1500. Oil on wood, 67 × 49 cm. Alte Pinakothek, Munich, Germany. Scala/Art Resource, NY

The greatest German painter of the Renaissance was Albrecht Dürer (1471–1528), son of a Nuremberg goldsmith. Dürer studied in Venice where he honed his skills as a painter of extraordinarily realistic scenes. He claimed that one of his self-portraits was so realistic that his dog mistook it for the man himself and gave it an affectionate lick.

The self-portrait depicted here dates from 1500 and is one of about thirty that Dürer painted. His interest in minutely and frequently describing himself witnesses to the new spirit of the age in which he lived. Instead of divine or regal images, the artist turned his attention to exploring and celebrating his own individuality. Here he represented himself in a pose that utilized conventions traditionally reserved for pictures of Christ, and he signed his work with a bold assertion of his own importance: "I, Albrecht Dürer, divinely inspired artist." The power of the picture derives from its strict geometric proportionality and its painstaking attention to detail. It asserts and validates the artist's claim to be a divinely inspired individual who is capable of great deeds.

Sources: Jane Campbell Hutchison, *Albrecht Dürer: A Biography* (Princeton: Princeton University Press, 1990); Joseph Leo Koerner, *The Moment of Self-Portraiture in German Renaissance Art* (Chicago, 1993), esp. pp. xviii, 8–9, 40–42.

to cooperate. During the last half of the fifteenth century, the Treaty of Lodi (1454–1455) brought Milan and Naples, traditional enemies, into alliance with Florence against Venice and the Papal States. This created a balance of power within Italy and a united front against external enemies.

The peace established by the Treaty of Lodi ended in 1494 when Naples, Florence, and Pope Alexander VI prepared to attack Milan. Ludovico il Moro, the despot of Milan, asked France for help. He urged the French to revive their claim to Naples, which they had ruled from 1266 to 1435. He did not pause to consider that France also had a claim on Milan.

Charles VIII's March Through Italy

Charles VIII (r. 1483–1498) was an eager youth in his twenties, and he responded to Ludovico's call with lightning speed. It took him only five months to cross the Alps (August 1495) and march through Florentine territory and the Papal States to Naples. Piero dé Medici, ruler of Florence, tried to placate him by handing over Pisa and other Florentine possessions. This angered his people, and the radical preacher Girolamo Savonarola (1452–1498) persuaded them to rebel and drive him into exile. Savonarola told the Florentines that France's invasion was God's punishment for their sins, and they paid Charles a large ransom to spare the city. Savonarola remained in power for four years. The Florentines then tired of his puritanical tyranny and pro-French policy and executed him (May 1498).

Charles's lightning march through Italy alarmed Ferdinand of Aragon, who believed that a French-Italian axis constituted a threat to his homeland. Ferdinand proposed an alliance (the League of Venice) to unite Aragon, Venice, the Papal States, and the Emperor Maximilian I against the French. When Milan, which regretted inviting the French into Italy, joined the league, Charles was forced to retreat.

Pope Alexander VI and the Borgia Family

Louis XII (r. 1498–1515), Charles's successor, was able to return to Italy, for he made an ally of Pope Alexander VI (1492–1503). Alexander was a member of the infamous Borgia family and probably the church's most corrupt pope.

Alexander's goal was to use the power of the papacy to recover Romagna, a district on the Adriatic coast northeast of Rome that had broken free from the Papal States during the Avignon papacy. His intent was to turn it over to his children, Cesare and Lucrezia, as a hereditary duchy. Venice's opposition to this plan led the pope to break with the League of Venice and ally with France. The dissolution of the league allowed the French to reconquer Milan, and the pope claimed as his reward the hand of the sister of the king of Navarre for his son and the promise of French military aid in Romagna. In 1500 Louis and Ferdinand of Aragon divided up Naples while the pope and Cesare completed the conquest of Romagna.

Pope Julius II

When Cardinal Giuliano della Rovere became Pope Julius II (1503–1513), he suppressed the Borgias and restored Romagna to Rome's control. Julius, the "warrior pope," brought the Renaissance papacy to a peak of military prowess and diplomatic intrigue. Once he had driven the Venetians out of Romagna (1509) and fully secured the Papal States, he set about ridding Italy of his former allies, the French. Julius, Ferdinand of Aragon, and Venice formed a second Holy League in October 1511. Emperor Maximilian I and the Swiss joined them, and by 1512 the French were in full retreat.

The French were nothing if not persistent. Louis's successor, Francis I (r. 1515–1547), led yet another assault on Italy. The Holy League weakened after French armies massacred its Swiss allies at Marignano in September 1515, but the Habsburg emperor then took up the cause. Four Habsburg-Valois wars finally ended in defeat for France.

Francis was more successful in dealing with the pope. The Concordat of Bologna (August 1516) gave the French king control over the French clergy in exchange for France's recognition of the pope's supremacy over church councils and his right to collect certain fees from clergy in France. This virtually nationalized the French Catholic church, thereby undercutting any appeal the Reformation might have had for France's kings.

Significant Dates from the Italian Renaissance (1375–1527)	
1434	Medici rule established in Florence
1454–1455	Treaty of Lodi
1494	Charles VIII of France invades Italy
1495	League of Venice
1499	Louis XII invades Italy
1500	The Borgias conquer Romagna
1512–1513	The Holy League defeats the French
1515	Francis I invades Italy
1527	Sack of Rome by imperial soldiers

Niccolò Machiavelli

As the armies of France, Spain, and Germany made a shambles of Italy, Niccolò Machiavelli (1469–1527), a Florentine scholar, struggled to make sense of the tragedy befalling his homeland. The lesson it taught him was that political ends—the maintenance of peace and order—are justified by any means.

Machiavelli's humanist education had included a close, if somewhat romanticized, study of the history of ancient Rome. He was impressed by the apparent ability of the Romans to act decisively and heroically for the good of their country, and he lamented the absence of such traits among his compatriots. He believed that if the Italians could cease their internal feuding and unite in defense of their nation, they could drive out the invaders. Machiavelli was devoted to republican ideals, but the realities of political life in Italy convinced him that only a strongman could rescue the Italians from the consequences of their own short-sightedness. The salvation of Italy required a cunning dictator who was willing to use "Machiavellian" techniques to manipulate his people.

Machiavelli may have intended *The Prince*, which he wrote in 1513, to be a satire on politics, not a serious justification for despotism. But he seems to have been in earnest when he advised rulers to consider fraud and brutality necessary means to the higher end of unifying Italy.

Machiavelli hoped that the Medici family might produce the leader Italy needed. In 1513 its members controlled both the papacy—Leo X (1513–1521)—and the powerful territorial state of Florence. *The Prince* was dedicated to Lorenzo dé Medici, duke of Urbino and grandson of Lorenzo the Magnificent. The Medicis, however, failed to rise to the challenge Machiavelli set them. In the year he died (1527), a second Medici pope, Clement VII (1523–1534), watched helplessly as Rome was sacked by the army of Emperor Charles V.

Revival of Monarchy in Northern Europe

The feudal monarchies of the High Middle Ages divided the powers of government between kings and their vassals. The nobility and the towns—through representative assemblies such as the English Parliament, the French Estates General, and the Spanish *Cortes*—tried to thwart the growth of royal authority. But by 1450, territorial magnates in many parts of Europe were being brought under the control of centralized national monarchies.

Towns were the crucial factor in this political transition. With the help of townspeople, kings could escape the limitations feudalism imposed on them. Townspeople made the nobility anachronistic by taking their place as royal officials. They helped kings reclaim the powers of taxation, war making, and law enforcement that under the feudal system were the prerogatives of semiautonomous vassals. As the vassals ceded these functions to centralized governments, the regions they had ruled combined to form true nations. Unlike the nobility who were identified with certain districts, the careers of professional civil servants—the Spanish *corregidores*, the English justices of the peace, and the French bailiffs—depended on advancing national, not regional, issues.

As kings acquired the bureaucratic machinery needed to enforce their decrees, they were able to bypass feudal councils and representative assemblies. Ferdinand and Isabella of Spain rarely called the *Cortes* into session. The French Estates General did not meet from 1484 to 1560. And after 1485, when England's Parliament granted Henry VII (r. 1485–1509) the right to collect the customs revenues he needed to cover the costs of government, the king summoned no more parliaments.

By the fifteenth century, monarchies had also begun to create standing national armies that ended the nobles' traditional military monopoly. Changing technologies—such as artillery—enhanced the importance of the common man's infantry and diminished the significance of the noble cavalry. Professional soldiers—even foreign mercenaries—who fought for pay and booty were far more efficient than feudal vassals who fought for honor's sake.

Since the strength of infantry is dependent upon numbers, monarchs wanted large armies. Professional soldiers tend to mutiny, however, if payrolls are not met. Fifteenth- and sixteenth-century governments had, therefore, to find new sources of income to meet the rising costs of warfare. Efforts to expand royal revenues were hampered by the upper classes' determined resistance to taxation. The nobles believed that their king should live as they did—from the income of personal estates. They considered taxation demeaning. In light of their opposition, kings usually found it easier to levy taxes on those who were least able to resist and least able to pay.

Monarchs had several sources of income. As feudal lords, they collected rents from the royal domain. They could levy national taxes on basic food and clothing. (France, for instance, had a tax on salt, and Spain had a 10 percent sales tax.) Rulers could also, with the approval of parliamentary bodies that did not represent the lower classes, levy direct taxes on the peasantry. (France's king relied heavily on such a tax: the *taille*.) Some governments sold public offices and issued high-interest bonds. But instead of taxing the nobility, they turned to them and to bankers for loans. A king's most powerful subjects were often also his creditors.

France

Charles VII (r. 1422–1461) was a king made great by those who served him. His ministers created a permanent professional army, which—thanks to the inspiration of Joan of Arc—drove the English out of France. An enterprising merchant banker, Jacques Coeur, devised policies to strengthen France's economy, diplomatic corps, and national administration. These tools helped the ruthless Louis XI (r. 1461–1483), Charles's son, make France a great power.

The rise of France in the fifteenth century depended on the defeat of two opponents: the king of England, and the duke of Burgundy. The Hundred Years' War cost England its continental possessions. But Burgundy, England's sometime ally in that war, emerged in the mid-fifteenth century as Europe's strongest state. Burgundy's duke, Charles the Bold, hoped to pull together his scattered family domains to create a new "middle" kingdom between France and Germany. It required a coalition of continental powers to stop him.

When Charles the Bold died in battle in 1477, the dream of a Burgundian empire died with him. Louis XI and the Habsburg emperor, Maximilian I, divided up Burgundy's lands. The Habsburgs got the better parts, but the dissolution of Burgundy freed Louis XI to concentrate on France's internal affairs. Louis harnessed France's nobility, fostered its trade and industry, and ended his reign with a kingdom almost twice the size of that with which he had started.

Louis's successors failed to build on the excellent foundation he laid. Their invasions of Italy in the 1490s and the long series of losing wars with the Habsburgs that resulted left France, by the mid-sixteenth century, almost as divided internally as it had been during the Hundred Years' War.

Spain

In 1469 the marriage of Isabella of Castile (r. 1474–1504) and Ferdinand of Aragon (r. 1479–1516) greatly accelerated the process of creating a unified Spanish monarchy. Castile was the richer and more populous of the two states, having about 5 million inhabitants to Aragon's 1 million. Castile also had a lucrative, centrally managed sheep-farming industry managed by a state-backed agency called the *Mesta*. Although both kingdoms shared a dynasty (Ferdinand and Isabella's family), each retained its own government agencies, laws, armies, coinage, taxation, and cultural traditions.

Together, Ferdinand and Isabella were able to do what neither could do alone: that is, bring the nobility under control, secure the borders of their realms, launch wars of conquest, and enforce a common Christian faith among all their subjects. In 1492 they conquered the last Muslim state on the Iberian peninsula, Granada. Naples became a Spanish possession in 1504, and by

1512 Ferdinand had acquired the kingdom of Navarre.

Ferdinand and Isabella relied on the *Hermandad,* a league of cities and towns, for help in subduing the powerful landowners who dominated the countryside. Townspeople replaced the nobility within the royal administration, and the monarchy circumscribed the power of the nobility by extending its authority over wealthy chivalric orders.

Spain had long been remarkable among European lands as a place where three religions—Islam, Judaism, and Christianity—coexisted with a certain degree of toleration. Ferdinand and Isabella ended this by imposing a state-controlled Christianity on all their subjects. They ran the church and used it to promote national unity. Of particular utility was the Inquisition, the ecclesiastical court that tried cases of heresy. In 1479 the Inquisition, run by Isabella's confessor Tomás de Torquemada (d. 1498), was assigned the task of monitoring the activities of the converted Spanish Jews (*conversos*) and Muslims (*Moriscos*). In 1492 the Jews who refused to convert were exiled and their properties were confiscated. In 1502 the same fate befell the Moors of Granada. The state's rigorous enforcement of orthodoxy kept Spain a loyal Catholic country and made it a base of operation for the Counter-Reformation, the Catholic response to the Protestant Reformation of the sixteenth century.

The marriages arranged for Ferdinand and Isabella's children were part of a grand plan to contain France, and they set the stage for Europe's politics in the sixteenth century. In 1496 their eldest daughter and heir, Joanna (later known as "the Mad") wed Archduke Philip, the son of Emperor Maximilian I. Charles, the child of this union, inherited a united Spain from his grandparents. This, augmented by his Habsburg patrimony and election as emperor in 1519, created a European kingdom almost as large as Charlemagne's. Ferdinand and Isabella's second daughter, Catherine of Aragon, wed Arthur, heir to England's King Henry VII. After Arthur's premature death, Catherine was betrothed to his brother, the future King Henry VIII. Henry's desire to end this marriage forced him to break with the papacy and declare England a Protestant nation.

Spain's power was also enhanced by the overseas explorations that Ferdinand and Isabella sponsored. The discoveries made in their names by the Genoese adventurer Christopher Columbus (1451–1506) founded Spain's empire in Mexico and Peru. Gold and silver from this "new world" enabled Spain to dominate Europe during the sixteenth century.

England

The last half of the fifteenth century was an especially difficult period for the English. While they were adjusting to their loss of the Hundred Years' War, a fight broke out between branches of their royal family, the House of York and the House of Lancaster. For thirty years (1455–1485) a dynastic struggle—the Wars of the Roses (York's heraldic emblem was a white rose and Lancaster's a red one)—kept England in a state of turmoil.

Henry VI (r. 1422–1461), a weak king from the Lancastrian house, was challenged by his cousin, the duke of York, who had supporters in England's prosperous southern towns. In 1461 the duke of York's son seized power as Edward IV (r. 1461–1483). Although his reign was interrupted in 1470–1471, by a short-lived restoration of Henry VI, Edward retained the upper hand and greatly increased the power and wealth of the monarchy.

Edward's brother, Richard III (r. 1483–1485), usurped the throne from Edward's young son. He was, in turn, overthrown by Henry Tudor, a distant royal relation who had inherited the leadership of the Lancastrian faction. Henry established England's Tudor dynasty. Shakespeare's powerful play *Richard III* reflects the influence of Tudor propaganda in its portrayal of Richard as an unprincipled villain.

Henry Tudor, Henry VII (r. 1485–1509), married Edward IV's daughter (Elizabeth of York) to unite the rival branches of the royal family and create an uncontestable claim to the throne for their offspring. Henry also devised something called the Court of Star Chamber to bring the English nobility under tighter royal control. Created with the sanction of Parliament in 1487, the court was granted jurisdiction over cases involving the nobility. Since it was staffed by the king's chief councillors, the nobles could not use the tactics of intimidation and bribery that had enabled them to make a mockery of courts staffed by more vulnerable men. Henry construed legal precedents to the advantage of the crown, and he confiscated so much property from the nobility that he did not have to convene Parliament to raise the money he needed to govern. Henry shaped a monarchy that, during the reign of his granddaughter (Elizabeth I), became one of the most effective in early modern Europe.

The Holy Roman Empire

Germany and Italy were exceptions to the general trend toward political centralization seen in the histories of other European nations during the last half of the fifteenth century. Germany's rulers maintained the ancient practice of partitioning lands among all their sons. As a result, by the end of the Middle Ages Germany was divided into some 300 autonomous entities, and its fragmented authorities were powerless to halt the development of revolutionary movements such as the Reformation.

German princes and cities worked together to maintain law and order, if not unity, within the Holy Roman Empire. In 1356 the emperor and the major German territorial rulers issued the *Golden Bull* and created a system that encouraged cooperation among regions of the empire. It allotted choice of an emperor to a seven-member electoral college: the archbishops of Mainz, Trier, and Cologne; the duke of Saxony; the margrave of Brandenburg; the count Palatine; and the king of Bohemia.

The emperor reigned more than ruled, for the extent of his powers, especially over the seven electors, was renegotiated with every imperial election. In the fifteenth century an effort was made to create some unity of purpose among the principalities. A regular national meeting— the imperial diet or *Reichstag* (composed of the seven electors, the nonelectoral princes, and the sixty-five imperial free cities)—began to be held.

In 1495 the diet won concessions from Maximilian I (r. 1493–1519) that were intended to promote order in the nation. Private warfare was banned. A court (the *Reichskammergericht*) was established to enforce internal peace, and an imperial Council of Regency (the *Reichsregiment*) was appointed to coordinate the development of policy. Although these reforms were important, they fell far short of the creation of a centralized state. During the sixteenth and seventeenth centuries, the territorial princes were virtually sovereign rulers in their domains.

The Northern Renaissance

The humanist scholars of the Renaissance were responsible for the development of a climate in Europe favorable to religious and educational reform. Humanism spread to northern Europe from Italy through such intermediaries as students who studied in Italy and merchants who traded there. Reform was also promoted by the Brothers of the Common Life, an influential lay religious movement that began in the Netherlands and permitted men and women to live a shared religious life without making formal vows of poverty, chastity, and obedience.

The northern humanists developed a distinctive culture. They tended to come from more diverse social backgrounds and to be more interested in religious reform than their Italian counterparts. They were also more willing to write for lay audiences. This latter was a crucial factor, for the invention of printing with movable type was about to create a world in which intellectual elites could argue their cases before the public and spark mass movements.

The Printing Press

Since the days of Charlemagne, kings and princes had encouraged literacy. Without people who could read, think critically, and write reliable reports, no kingdom, large or small, could be properly governed. During the late Middle Ages new schools spread literacy far beyond the ranks of the clergy, and the number of universities in Europe tripled from twenty to sixty.

Medieval scribes had written books on expensive sheets of leather called vellum. Since it required 170 calfskins or 300 sheepskins to make a single vellum Bible, few people could afford the complete text. Whole pages were sometimes carved on wooden blocks for printing, but the production of such blocks was difficult and did not much reduce cost.

In the mid-fifteenth century Johann Gutenberg (d. 1468) of Mainz was stimulated by the growing market for books to invent printing with movable type. The development of a process of cheap paper manufacture also helped

This portrait of Katharina, by Albrecht Dürer, provides evidence of African slavery in Europe during the sixteenth century. Katharina was in the service of one João Bradao, a Portuguese economic minister living in Antwerp, then the financial center of Europe. Dürer became friends with Bradao during his stay in the Low Countries in the winter of 1520–1521. Albrecht Dürer, "Portrait of the Moorish Woman Katharina". Uffizi Florence, Italy. Foto Marburg/Art Resource, NY

to bring down the costs of production and make books on subjects ranging from theology to farming and child-rearing available in all price ranges. The new technology generated a great demand, and the number of presses exploded. By 1500, about fifty years after Gutenberg opened his shop, printers were operating in over 200 European cities.

Literacy deeply affected people everywhere, nurturing self-esteem and a critical frame of mind. By standardizing texts and prompting discussions, the print revolution made anyone who could read an authority. As a result, ordinary men and women became less credulous and docile than their ancestors. But print also gave their rulers a powerful tool for manipulating their beliefs.

Erasmus

The career of Desiderius Erasmus (1466?–1536), the most famous of the northern humanists, illustrates the impact of the printing press. Erasmus was both an educational and a religious reformer—a man whose career proves that many loyal Catholics advocated religious reform long before the Reformation erupted.

Erasmus published short Latin dialogues that were intended to teach students how to live as well as how to speak. In their later editions, these pieces (entitled *Colloquies*) included anticlerical dialogues and satires of religious superstitions that were designed to prompt reforms. Erasmus also published a collection of proverbs, the *Adages*. It grew from a first edition containing 800 examples to a final edition composed of over 5,000. It popularized common expressions that are still in use (e.g., "to leave no stone unturned," and "where there is smoke, there is fire").

Erasmus wanted to unite the classical ideals of humanity and civic virtue with the Christian virtues of love and piety. He believed that disciplined study of the classics and the Bible offered the best hope for reforming individuals and society. He taught the *philosophia Christi*—the philosophy of Christ: a simple, ethical piety modeled on Christ's life. Erasmus opposed anyone, Catholic or Protestant, who let doctrine and disputation overshadow humble piety and Christian practice.

Erasmus used his knowledge of classical languages to produce an improved version of the Bible based on the best manuscript sources available at the time. He believed that true reform was possible only if people were guided by a pure, unadulterated source. His Greek edition of the New Testament in 1516 made possible a more accurate Latin translation in 1519.

The church authorities were unhappy with Erasmus's "improvements" on their traditional Bible, the Latin Vulgate, and his popular anticlerical satires. At one point in the mid-sixteenth century all of Erasmus's works were placed on the Catholic church's *Index of Forbidden Books*. Luther, the Protestant leader, also condemned some of Erasmus's views. But friends and foes in both camps used the scholarly tools that Erasmus had created to promote reform.

Humanism and Reform

The work of the humanists encouraged educational and religious reform.

GERMANY Rudolf Agricola (1443–1485) introduced Italian learning to Germany. Conrad Celtis (d. 1508), the first German poet laureate, and Ulrich von Hutten (1488–1523), a knight, promoted a nationalistic version of humanism that was hostile to non-German cultures and especially antagonistic to papal Rome. Hutten, who attacked indulgences and published an edition of Valla's exposé of the *Donation of Constantine*, died in 1523 fighting in a hopeless revolt of the German knights against their princes.

A *cause célèbre* helped to unite reform-minded German humanists. About 1506 a converted Jew named Pfefferkorn, assisted by the Dominican friars of Cologne, launched a campaign to suppress Jewish literature. Johann Reuchlin (1455–1522) was, at the time, Europe's foremost Christian authority on Hebrew and Jewish learning. He was the first Christian scholar to compile a reliable Hebrew grammar, and he was personally attracted to Jewish mysticism. When Pfefferkorn attacked Reuchlin, many German humanists (motivated by a love of academic freedom rather than Judaism) rushed to Reuchlin's defense. The controversy produced one of the great books of the period, the *Letters of Obscure Men* (1515), a merciless satire of monks and Scholastics. It also predisposed the humanists to rally around Martin Luther, for in 1517 some of the same people who attacked Reuchlin attacked Luther for publishing arguments challenging the validity of indulgences.

ENGLAND English scholars and merchants and touring Italian prelates brought Italy's learning to England. Erasmus lectured at Cambridge, and his close friend, Thomas More (1478–1535), became the most famous of the English humanists. More's *Utopia* (1516), a critique of contemporary values, rivals the plays of Shakespeare as the most-read English work from the sixteenth century. Utopia described an imaginary society that overcame social and political injustice by holding all property and goods in common and requiring all persons to earn their bread by their own labor.

Humanism in England, as in Germany, paved the way for the Reformation, but some humanists, such as More and Erasmus, remained steadfastly loyal to the Roman Catholic Church. When More, one of Henry VIII's chief councillors, refused to accept the king's divorce of Catherine of Aragon and England's break with the papacy, Henry ordered his execution (July 1535).

FRANCE When France invaded Italy, Italian learning invaded France. Guillaume Budé (1468–1540), an accomplished Greek scholar, and Jacques Lefèvre d'Étaples (1454–1536), a biblical authority, were the leaders of French humanism. Lefèvre's scholarly works exemplified the new critical scholarship that was to stimulate Martin Luther's thinking and bring on the Reformation. Marguerite d'Angoulême (1492–1549), sister of King Francis I and queen of Navarre, was a noted spiritual writer. She also provided patronage for a generation of young reform-minded humanists that numbered among its members the Protestant reformer John Calvin.

SPAIN In Spain humanism was enlisted to defend the Catholic faith, not promote reform. Francisco Jiménez de Cisneros (1437–1517), confessor to Queen Isabella and (after 1508) the Grand Inquisitor and chief defender of orthodoxy, was the country's leading humanist. In 1509 he founded the University of Alcalá near Madrid. He printed a Greek edition of the New Testament, and he translated many religious tracts that were used to reform clerical life and improve the clergy's direction of the piety of the laity. His greatest achievement was the *Complutensian Polyglot Bible*, a six-volume edition of the Hebrew, Greek, and Latin texts of the Bible in parallel columns.

Voyages of Discovery and the New Empire in the West

The intellectual restlessness that marked the Renaissance and the Reformation was accompanied by a literal restlessness. In the fifteenth century, the Atlantic ceased to be regarded as a wall closing Europe in and began to be explored as a highway to global adventure.

Gold and Spices

Henry the Navigator (r. 1394–1460), prince of Portugal, took the lead by sponsoring exploration of the African coast. By the last decades of the fifteenth century, the Portuguese were importing gold from Guinea by sea and competing with the land routes controlled by Arab traders.

The rush for Africa's gold became a search for India's spices. Spices, especially pepper and cloves, were in great demand in Europe. They were used to preserve food as well as to enhance its taste. In 1487 Bartholomew Dias (d. 1500) rounded the Cape of Good Hope at the tip of Africa. In 1498, Vasco da Gama (d. 1524) reached India, and the cargo he brought back to Portugal was worth sixty times the cost of his voyage. The Portuguese quickly built an empire in the East that gave them control of the European spice trade.

While Portugal explored the Indian Ocean, Spain attacked the Atlantic. Christopher Columbus (1451–1506) dreamed of finding a short route to the spice islands of the East Indies, but he blundered onto something much greater. On October 12, 1492, after a thirty-three-day voyage from the Canary Islands, he landed in San Salvador (Watlings Island) in the eastern Bahamas. He thought he was near Japan. Not until his third voyage to the Caribbean did Columbus realize that the island of Cuba was not Japan and that the South American continent beyond it was not China. Amerigo Vespucci (1451–1512) and Ferdinand Magellan (1480–1521) proved that the lands Columbus found were not, as he died believing, the edge of the Orient. They were a new continent separated from the East by an ocean even greater than the Atlantic. Magellan ventured onto this Pacific Ocean and died in the Philippines.

The Spanish Empire in the New World

Columbus's voyage in 1492 began more than three centuries of Spanish exploitation of a vast American empire. That empire transformed cultures on both sides of the Atlantic. As Europeans and their technologies entered the Americas, American goods and bullion flooded Europe's markets. In neither place was life ever again the same. In parts of both South and North America, Spain established a Roman Catholic faith, a system of economic dependence, and a hierarchical social structure that has endured to the present day.

A Conquered World

Since Columbus was convinced that he had landed in the East Indies, he called the peoples he encountered "Indians." The name persisted even after it was clear that America was not the Indies. The ancestors of the Native Americans had migrated across the Bering Strait from Asia many thousands of years before the European voyages of discovery. As early as the first millennium B.C.E., those who lived in Mesoamerica (i.e., central Mexico to the Yucatan and Guatemala) and the Andean region (Peru and Bolivia) were pioneering advanced civilizations.

The earliest of the Mesoamerican civilizations was the Olmec, which dates from about 1200 B.C.E. By the first millennium C.E., its city of Teotihuacán was one of the largest urban centers in the world. The first millennium C.E. also saw the flowering of the civilization of the Mayas in the Yucatan region. The Mayans acquired considerable knowledge of mathematics and astronomy and built great cities centered on huge pyramids.

The first great interregional civilization in Andean South America, the Chavín, emerged during the first millennium B.C.E. Between 100 C.E. to 600 C.E., regional cultures, the Nazca on the southern coast of Peru and the Moche on the northern coast, appeared. The Huari-Tiahuanco culture again imposed interregional conformity from 600 to 1000, and the Chimu Empire flourished on Peru's northern coast from 800 to 1400. These early Andean societies built great ceremonial centers throughout the Andes; constructed elaborate irrigation systems, canals, and highways; and created exquisite pottery, textiles, and metalwork.

THE AZTECS When the Spanish explorers arrived, Mesoamerica was dominated by the Aztecs and Andean America by the Incas. The forebears of the Aztecs entered the Valley of Mexico early in the twelfth century. In 1428 a chief named Itzcoatl inaugurated an era of Aztec conquest that reached its climax just after 1500. The Aztec state, which centered on Tenochtitlán (modern-day Mexico City), was a collection of enslaved and terrorized tribes. Aztec religion involved the sacrifice of thousands of people a year to the gods of the sun and the soil. By extorting this grim tribute, the Aztecs nourished resentment among their subjects and caused them to dream of liberation.

Armored Spanish soldiers, under the command of Pedro de Alvarado (d. 1541) and bearing crossbows, engage unprotected and crudely armed Aztecs, who are nonetheless portrayed as larger than life by Spanish artist Diego Duran (16th century). Codex Duran: Pedro de Alvarado (c. 1485–1541), companion-at-arms of Hernando Cortés (1485–1547) besieged by Aztec warriors. Biblioteca Nacional, Madrid, Spain. The Bridgeman Art Library International Ltd.

In 1519 Hernán Cortés landed on the coast of Mexico with a mere 600 men. Montezuma, the Aztec ruler, initially believed Cortés to be a god, for an Aztec legend claimed that a priest named Quetzalcoatl, who had been driven into exile four centuries earlier, would return about the time that Cortés appeared. Montezuma tried to appease Cortés with gold, for the Aztecs, who had recently been ravaged by epidemics of European origin (principally smallpox), were in no condition to fight. Gold only stimulated the Spaniards' appetites. Cortés's forces marched on Tenochtitlán and captured Montezuma, who died under unexplained circumstances. The Aztecs rose up to defend themselves. But by 1521 they were defeated, and Cortés was proclaiming the former Aztec Empire "New Spain."

THE INCAS The Incas of the highlands of Peru, like the Aztecs, had conquered many tribes. By the early sixteenth century they ruled harshly over several million subjects—using impressed labor to build roads and cities, to farm, and to fight. In 1531 Francisco Pizarro, who was inspired by Cortés's example, invaded the Inca Empire. His army of 200 men was equipped with guns, swords, and horses—the military potential of which escaped the Incas. Pizarro lured the Inca chief Atahualpa to a conference where he captured him and killed several thousand Indians. Atahualpa raised a huge ransom in gold, but in 1533 Pizarro executed him. Division within the ranks of the Spaniards prevented them from es-

tablishing control of the sprawling Inca territories until the late 1560s.

The conquests of Mexico and Peru are among the most brutal episodes in modern Western history. In addition to loss of life, they prevented the Indian civilizations from having significant impact on Western civilization. The Spaniards and the Indians made some accommodations to each other, but in the end European values, religion, economic goals, and language dominated. South America became Latin America.

The Economy of Exploitation

The native peoples of America and their homelands were immediately drawn into the Atlantic economy and the world of competitive European commercialism. For the Indians of Latin America—and later the blacks of Africa—that meant various forms of forced labor. The colonial economy of Latin America had three components: mining, agriculture, and shipping.

MINING The early *conquistadores* ("conquerors") were primarily interested in gold, but by the middle of the sixteenth century, silver mining had become more profitable. The chief mining centers were Potosí in Peru and various smaller sites in northern Mexico. The Spanish crown received one-fifth (the *quinto*) of all mining revenues and monopolized the production and sale of the mercury that was required in the silver-mining process. Mining by native forced labor for the benefit of Spaniards epitomized the extractive economy that was fundamental to colonial life.

AGRICULTURE The West Indies (i.e., Cuba, Hispaniola, Puerto Rico, and other islands) evolved a plantation system that used the labor of black slaves from Africa to produce sugar for the European market. But the agricultural institution that characterized most of the Spanish colonies was the *hacienda,* a large landed estate owned by persons born in Spain (*peninsulares*) or persons of Spanish descent born in America (*creoles*). The *hacienda* economy was subordinate to the mining economy, for its major products (food and leather) were consumed by American mining communities. Laborers on the *hacienda* were usually bound to the land and prevented from moving from the service of one landowner to another.

LABOR SERVITUDE The Spaniards initially developed a number of ways to use the Indian population to supply the labor needed for mining and agriculture in the New World. The earliest was the *encomienda,* a grant of the right to the labor of a specific number of Indians for a particular period of time. Spain's monarchs were suspicious of this arrangement, for they feared that the holders of *encomienda* might become a powerful independent nobility in the New World. The *encomienda* was phased out in favor of the *repartimiento,* a kind of tax paid in labor. All adult male Indians were required to devote a certain number of working days annually to Spanish economic enterprises. Although this sounded more humane than the servitude of the *encomienda, repartimiento* service was often extremely harsh. The term limitation for laborers led some Spanish managers to work them to death on the assumption that new men were always scheduled to replace those currently employed. Eventually a shortage of workers and the crown's opposition to extreme kinds of forced labor promoted the use of free labor. But the freedom of Indian workers was more apparent than real. They had to purchase the goods they needed from the landowners or mine owners for whom they worked. This created debts that bound them to their employers, a form of exploitation known as debt peonage.

The enslavement of Africans was introduced to the New World on the sugar plantations of the West Indies. It was an extension of a system of forced labor that the Spanish and the Portuguese had previously used in Europe.

Deaths in combat, by forced labor, and from European diseases had devastating demographic consequences for the Indian population. Europeans lived in a far more complex human and animal environment than did Native Americans. Their interaction, over a long period, with different ethnic groups and animal species helped them develop strong immune systems that enabled them to survive the ravages of measles, smallpox, and typhoid. Native Americans evolved in a simpler, more sterile environment, and they were defenseless against Europe's diseases. Within a generation of the conquest, the Indian population of New Spain (Mexico) was reduced by 92 percent—from 25 million to 2 million.

The Impact on Europe

The loss of life and destruction of cultures in the New World was a mixed blessing for the Old World. The bullion that flowed into Europe through Spain vastly increased the amount of money in circulation and created an inflation rate of 2 percent a year. Prices doubled in Spain by 1550 and quadrupled by 1600. In Luther's Wittenberg, the cost of basic food and clothing increased almost 100 percent between 1519 and 1540. Wages and rents, on the other hand, lagged well behind the rise in prices.

The new money enabled governments and private entrepreneurs to sponsor basic research and industrial expansion and to promote the growth of capitalism. The economic thinking of the age favored the creation of monopolies, the charging of high interest for loans, and the free and efficient accumulation of wealth. The late fifteenth and the sixteenth centuries saw the maturation of this type of capitalism and its attendant social problems. Those who owned the means of production were ever more clearly separated from the workers who operated them. The new wealth raised the expectations of the poor and encouraged reactionary behavior by the rich. Social distinctions became ever more visible in the new economic system, and this prepared the way for the upheaval of the Reformation. Columbus's discoveries also encouraged rebels by increasing scepticism about the wisdom of the ancients and the obvious rightness of traditional modes of thought. Europe's explorers proved that there was much more to the world than their ancestors had imagined. This encouraged criticism of traditional institutions and sparked and appetite for new ideas—especially innovations that promised freedom and a chance at a better life.

In Perspective

During the late Middle Ages, previously divided lands came together as nations, and the foundations of modern France, Spain, England, Germany, and Italy were laid. Byzantine and Islamic scholars made ancient Greek science and scholarship available to the West, and Europeans reclaimed a classical cultural heritage from which they had been separated for almost eight centuries. This prompted renaissances of intellectual and artistic activity in both southern and northern Europe.

The new political unity spurred national ambition, and by the late fifteenth century Europeans were venturing far afield—to the shores of Africa, to the southern and eastern coasts of Asia, and to the New World of the Americas. For the first time, they confronted truly non-European civilizations. The savage exploitation of the peoples and lands of the New World revealed the dark side of Europe's culture, and the influx of New World gold and silver exacerbated Europe's economic and social problems. Some Europeans were driven by what they saw to question their traditional values.

REVIEW QUESTIONS

1. In what senses was what happened in Italy in the fifteenth and sixteenth centuries a "renaissance"?
2. How would you define Renaissance humanism? In what ways was the Renaissance a break with the Middle Ages? In what ways was it indebted to medieval civilization?
3. Who were the leading, or most characteristic, literary and artistic figures of the Italian Renaissance? What was "the spirit of the Renaissance" that they all shared?
4. Why did the French invade Italy in 1494? How did this event trigger Italy's political decline?

In what ways do the actions of Pope Julius II and the ideas of Niccolò Machiavelli signify the start of a new era for Italy?
5. Does the history of Renaissance Italy support or refute the common assumption that creative work proceeds best in periods of calm and peace?
6. How did the northern Renaissance differ from the Italian Renaissance? In what ways was Erasmus the embodiment of the northern Renaissance?
7. What prompted the voyages of discovery? How did the Spanish establish their empire in the Americas? What did native peoples experience during and after the conquest?

SUGGESTED READINGS

H. BARON, *The Crisis of the Early Italian Renaissance*, vols. 1 and 2 (1966). A major work, setting forth the civic dimension of Italian humanism.

B. BERENSON, *Italian Painters of the Renaissance* (1957). Eloquent and authoritative.

G. A. BRUCKER, *Renaissance Florence* (1969). Comprehensive survey of all facets of Florentine life.

J. BURCKHARDT, *The Civilization of the Renaissance in Italy* (1867). The old classic that still has as many defenders as detractors.

R. E. CONRAD, *Children of God's Fire: A Documentary History of Black Slavery in Brazil* (1983). Not for the squeamish.

A. W. CROSBY, *The Columbian Exchange: Biological and Cultural Consequences of 1492* (1973). A study of the epidemiological disaster that Columbus visited upon Native Americans.

E. L. EISENSTEIN, *The Printing Press as an Agent of Change: Communications and Cultural Transformations in Early Modern Europe*, 2 vols. (1979). Bold, stimulating account of the centrality of printing to all progress in the period.

W. K. FERGUSON, *Europe in Transition, 1300–1520* (1962). A major survey that deals with the transition from medieval society to Renaissance society.

D. HERLIHY and C. KLAPISCH-ZUBER, *Tuscans and Their Families* (1985). Important work based on quantitative data; excellent specimen of quantitative history.

D. L. Jensen, *Renaissance Europe: Age of Recovery and Reconciliation* (1981). Comprehensive survey.

F. Katz, *The Ancient American Civilizations* (1972). An excellent introduction.

P. O. Kristeller, *Renaissance Thought: The Classic, Scholastic, and Humanist Strains* (1961). A master shows the many sides of Renaissance thought.

I. Maclean, *The Renaissance Notion of Women* (1980). An account of the views of Renaissance intellectuals and their sources in antiquity.

L. Martines, *Power and Imagination: City States in Renaissance Italy* (1980). Stimulating account of cultural and political history.

E. Panofsky, *Meaning in the Visual Arts* (1955). Eloquent treatment of Renaissance art.

J. H. Parry, *The Age of Reconnaissance* (1964). A comprehensive account of exploration in the years 1450 to 1650.

I. A. Richter (ed.), *The Notebooks of Leonardo da Vinci* (1985). The master in his own words.

Q. Skinner, *The Foundations of Modern Political Thought; I: The Renaissance* (1978). Broad survey, including every known political theorist.

Chapter 11
The Age of Reformation

KEY TOPICS

- The social and religious background to the Reformation
- Martin Luther's challenge to the church and the course of the Reformation in Germany
- The Reformation in Switzerland, France, and England
- Transitions in family life between medieval and modern times

In the second decade of the sixteenth century a powerful religious movement began in northern Germany. Protestant reformers, attacking what they believed to be burdensome superstitions that robbed people of money and peace of mind, led a revolt against the medieval church. The Protestant Reformation opposed aspects of the Renaissance, especially the optimistic view of human nature that humanist scholars derived from classical literature. But the Reformation embraced some Renaissance ideas—particularly educational reform and training in ancient languages that equipped scholars to go to the original sources of important texts. Protestant challenges to Catholic practices originated in the study of the Hebrew and Greek Scriptures.

Society and Religion

A struggle between two political foes set the stage for the Reformation: the monarchies that were centralizing governments of nation-states, and the towns and regions that were fighting to preserve their traditional autonomy. Since the fourteenth century, the king's law and custom had been superseding local law and custom almost everywhere. Many townspeople and village folk viewed religious revolt as a part of a wider fight to limit this encroachment on their liberties.

The Reformation began in the free cities of Germany and Switzerland. There were about sixty-five of them, most of which developed Protestant movements even if they did not ultimately come under Protestant control. These cities were troubled by more than a desire to defend themselves against intervention by princes. They suffered deep internal social and political divisions, and some of their factions favored the Reformation more than others. Guilds whose members were prospering and rising in social status were often in the forefront of the Reformation, but less distinguished groups were also attracted to the Protestant revolt. People who felt pushed around by either local or distant authorities tended, at least initially, to find an ally in the Protestant movement. The peasants on the land responded as much as the townsfolk, for their freedoms, too, were eroded by princely governments.

For many converts to Protestantism, religion and politics seemed to be two sides of the same coin. When Protestant preachers scorned the authority of ecclesiastical landlords and ridiculed papal laws as arbitrary human inventions, they raised issues of political as well as religious liberty. An attack on the legitimacy of the one kind of authority translated easily into a critique of the other.

Popular Religious Movements and Criticism of the Church

The Protestant Reformation was, in part, a response to the crises that afflicted the late medieval church: the papacy's "exile" in Avignon, the Great Schism, the conciliar movement, and the flagrant worldliness of the Renaissance popes. These things led many clergy and laity to become increasingly critical of the traditional teaching and spiritual practice of the church. The late Middle Ages were marked by calls for reform and by widespread experimentation with new religious practices.

The laypeople of the late medieval period were less subservient to the clergy than their ancestors. The residents of cities had grown increasingly knowledgeable about the world and politics. As soldiers, pilgrims, explorers, and traders, they traveled widely. The establishment of postal systems and printing presses increased the information at their disposal. Improved access to books and libraries raised the rate of literacy among them and heightened their curiosity. Education equipped them to take the initiative in shaping the cultural lives of their communities.

The lay religious movements that preceded the Reformation all advocated religious simplicity in imitation of Jesus. They were inspired by an ideal of apostolic poverty that they saw in the Gospels' descriptions of the lives of Jesus and his disciples. They wanted a more egalitarian church that gave a voice to its members, not just its head. They wanted a more spiritual church, one that emulated the New Testament model.

THE MODERN DEVOTION   One of the most constructive lay religious movements of the period was led by the Brothers of the Common Life, advocates for the "Modern Devotion." The brothers urged ordinary people to adapt for their own uses the spiritual disciplines of monasticism.

They took no formal vows and held no church offices. They supported themselves by working at secular jobs.

After Gerard Groote (1340–1384) began the movement in the Netherlands, the brother and (less numerous) sister houses spread rapidly throughout northern Europe. The Modern Devotion brought clerics and laity together to share a common life that stressed individual piety and practical religion. Thomas à Kempis (d. 1471) summarized the philosophy of the movement in what became the most popular devotional tract of the period, the *Imitation of Christ*. This guide to the inner life was intended primarily for monks and nuns, but it spoke also to the many laity who sought spiritual growth through the practice of ascetic disciplines.

The Brothers of the Common Life flourished during an age in which the laity wanted instruction from good preachers and were even taking the initiative to create endowments to provide this service. The brothers served the public's desire for better education by opening schools, working as copyists, sponsoring publications, and running hospices for poor students. Some famous scholars, such as Erasmus and Reuchlin, began their training with the brothers.

The Modern Devotion has been credited with inspiring humanist, Protestant, and Catholic reform movements in the sixteenth century, but it was actually a very conservative movement. By integrating traditional clerical doctrines and values with an active common life, the brothers met the need of late medieval people for a more personal religion and a better-informed faith. The Modern Devotion helped laypersons develop fuller religious lives without turning their backs on the world.

LAY CONTROL OVER RELIGIOUS LIFE The medieval papacy's successful campaign to win control over the appointment of candidates to church offices did not improve the administration of the church. The popes sold ecclesiastical posts to the highest bidders. The purchasers were entitled to the income from their offices, but they were not required personally to carry out the duties attached to the offices they bought. They hired inexpensive, often poorly trained and motivated substitutes to do their work while they resided elsewhere. Rare was the late medieval German town that did not complain about clerical malfeasance or dereliction of duty.

City governments sometimes took the initiative in trying to improve religious life by endowing preacherships. These positions provided for well-trained, dedicated pastors who could provide regular preaching and pastoral care superior to the perfunctory services offered by other clergy. In many instances these preacherships became platforms for Protestant reformers.

Because medieval churches and monasteries were holy places, they had been exempted from secular taxes and laws. It was also considered inappropriate for holy persons (clergy) to do "dirty jobs" such as military service, compulsory labor, standing watch at city gates, and other obligations of citizenship. Nor was it thought right that the laity, of whatever rank, should sit in judgment over God's priestly intermediaries. On the eve of the Reformation, however, secular governments were beginning to take steps to curtail clerical privileges that seemed undeserved.

Long before 1520, when Luther published a famous summary of economic grievances (*Address to the Christian Nobility of the German Nation*), communities were loudly protesting the financial abuses of the medieval church. Prominent among these was the sale of indulgences (i.e., papal letters that guaranteed sinners released time from purgatory). If rulers and magistrates were given a share of the profits, they usually did not object. But it was a different matter if local revenues were siphoned off for projects far from home. The state did not join the campaign against financial exactions such as indulgences until rulers recognized how they themselves might profit from religion. The financial appeal of Protestantism lay in its rationale for the state's dissolution of monasteries and confiscation of ecclesiastical properties.

Martin Luther and German Reformation to 1525

The kings of France and England were able to limit ecclesiastical taxation and papal jurisdiction over their churches. But Germany lacked the political unity needed to enforce "national" religious reforms. The restraints imposed on the church on a universal level in England and France were enacted locally and piecemeal in Germany as popular resentment of ecclesiastical abuses spread. By 1517 mass discontent was pervasive enough to win Martin Luther a widespread, sympathetic audience.

Luther (1483–1546) was the son of a successful Thüringian miner. He received his early education in a school run by the Brothers of the Common Life. Between 1501 and 1505, he attended the University of Erfurt where the nominalist teachings of William of Ockham and Gabriel Biel (d. 1495) prevailed. After receiving his master of arts degree in 1505, Luther obeyed his parents and registered with the law faculty. But he never began the study of law. To the disappointment of his family, he entered the Order of the Hermits of Saint Augustine in Erfurt on July 17, 1505. This decision was an attempt to resolve a long-standing spiritual struggle. It came to a head during a lightning storm in which a terrified Luther promised Saint Anne, the patron of travelers in distress, that he would enter a monastery if he escaped death.

Luther was ordained in 1507 and led a conventional monastic life. In 1510 he went to Rome on business for his order and saw firsthand some of the things that were raising doubts about the church. In 1511 he moved to the Augustinian monastery in Wittenberg. A year later, he earned his doctorate in theology from Wittenberg's university and joined its faculty.

Justification by Faith Alone

Reformation theology was a response to the failure of traditional medieval religion to provide many laypeople and clergy with personal or intellectual satisfaction. Luther was especially plagued by his inability to achieve the perfect righteousness that medieval theology taught that God required for salvation. The church's teachings and sacrament of penance failed to console Luther and give him hope. The church seemed to demand of him a perfection he knew neither he nor any other human being could achieve.

The study of St. Paul's letters eventually brought Luther an insight into the process of salvation that quieted his fears. Luther concluded from his reading of the Scriptures that the righteousness that God demanded was not the product of religious works and ceremonies. It was a gift God gives to those who believe and trust in Jesus Christ—who alone is perfectly righteous. To believe in Christ meant to stand before God

clothed in Christ's righteousness—to be justified solely by faith in him, not by confidence in one's record of good works.

The Attack on Indulgences

The doctrine of justification by faith was incompatible with the church's practice of issuing indulgences, which remitted the obligation to perform a "work of satisfaction" for a sin. According to medieval theology, after the priest absolved a penitent of guilt, the penitent still had to pay the penalty for sin. The penitent could discharge the penalty here and now by prayers, fasting, almsgiving, retreats, and pilgrimages. But penitents whose works of satisfaction were inadequate could expect to suffer for them in purgatory.

Indulgences had originally been devised for Crusaders who fell in battle with the enemies of the church without an opportunity to do penance for their sins. Gradually, they were offered to laypeople who were anxious about the consequences of neglected penances or unrepented sins. In 1343 Pope Clement VI (1342–1352) declared the existence of a "treasury of merit," an infinite reservoir of excess good works that the saints had earned and that the pope could appropriate for others. Papal "letters of indulgence" were drafts on this treasury to cover the works of satisfaction owed by penitents. In 1476 Pope Sixtus IV (1471–1484) greatly expanded the market for these letters by proclaiming the church's power to grant indulgences not only to the living but also to souls in purgatory.

Originally, indulgences had been granted only for significant services to the church, but by Luther's day their price had been significantly discounted to encourage mass marketing. Pope Julius II (1503–1513) excited considerable interest by declaring a special Jubilee indulgence (to be sold in 1517) to raise funds for rebuilding Saint Peter's in Rome. In 1517 Archbishop Albrecht of Mainz was in debt to the Fugger bank of Augsburg for a loan he had taken out to pay the pope for permission to ignore church law and hold three profitable ecclesiastical offices—the archbishoprics of Mainz and Magdeburg and the bishopric of Halberstadt. In exchange for Albrecht's help in promoting sale of the Jubilee indulgence, Pope Leo X agreed to share the proceeds. A famous preacher, John Tetzel (d. 1519), was sent to drum up business in Luther's neighborhood.

A contemporary caricature depicts John Tetzel, the famous indulgence preacher. The last lines of the jingle read: "As soon as gold in the basin rings, right then the soul to Heaven springs." It was Tetzel's preaching that spurred Luther to publish his ninety-five theses.
Courtesy Stiftung Luthergedenkstaten in Sachsen-Anhalt/Lutherhalle Wittenberg

According to tradition, Luther posted his ninety-five theses opposing the sale of indulgences on the door of Castle Church in Wittenberg on October 31, 1517. Luther especially protested Tetzel's insinuation that indulgences remitted sins and released the dead from punishment in purgatory. Luther believed Tetzel's claims went far beyond traditional practice and made salvation something that could be bought and sold.

Election of Charles V

The ninety-five theses made Luther famous overnight and prompted official proceedings against him. In April 1518, he was summoned to appear before the general chapter of his order in Heidelberg, and the following October he was called to Augsburg to be examined by the papal legate and general of the Dominican Order, Cardinal Cajetan. Then the death of the Holy Roman Emperor Maximilian I on January 12, 1519, diverted attention from Luther's case to the contest for a new emperor.

Charles I of Spain, a youth of nineteen, succeeded his grandfather and became Emperor Charles V. But the electors, who constantly sought to enhance their power, exacted a price for the office. They forced Charles to agree to consult with a diet of the empire on all major domestic and foreign issues. This ruled out unilateral imperial action in Germany—something for which Luther was soon to be thankful.

Luther's Excommunication and the Diet of Worms

While the imperial election was being held, Luther was in Leipzig (June 27, 1519) to debate an Ingolstadt professor, John Eck. This contest led Luther to question the infallibility of the pope and the inerrancy of church councils and, for the first time, to appeal to the Scripture as the sole authority governing faith.

In 1520 Luther described his position in three famous pamphlets. His *Address to the Christian Nobility of the German Nation* urged the German princes forcefully to reform the Roman

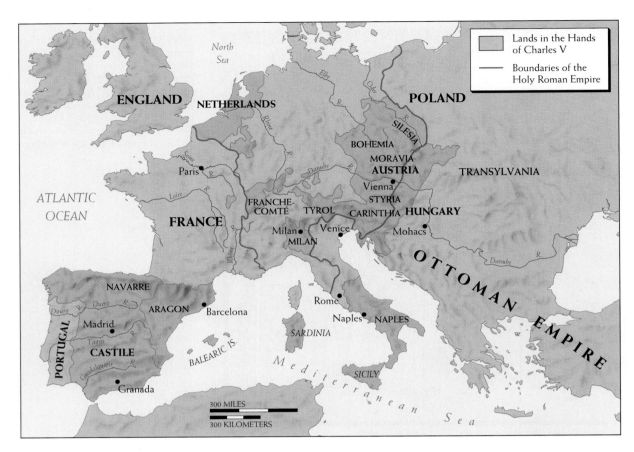

MAP 11–1   THE EMPIRE OF CHARLES V   *Dynastic marriages and simple chance
delivered large, if scattered, portions of Europe (as well as Spain's overseas
possessions) into Charles's hands. Election as emperor increased his responsibilities.*

Catholic Church and curtail its political and economic power. *The Babylonian Captivity of the Church* examined the sacraments, arguing that only two of the church's seven (Baptism and the Eucharist) were authentic. The pamphlet also claimed that the Scriptures, decrees of church councils, and decisions of secular princes were superior to the authority of a pope. The eloquent *Freedom of a Christian* explained Luther's key theological insight, salvation by faith alone.

On June 15, 1520, a papal bull, *Exsurge Domine,* condemned Luther for heresy and gave him sixty days to retract. The final bull of excommunication, *Decet Pontificem Romanum,* was issued on January 3, 1521. In April of that year, Luther appeared before a diet of the empire in Worms (over which the newly elected Charles V presided). Ordered to recant, Luther refused, for such an act, he claimed, would violate Scripture, reason, and conscience. On May 26, 1521, Luther was placed under the imperial ban. This meant that his heresy became a crime punishable by the state. Friends

protected Luther by hiding him in Wartburg Castle. The year (April 1521 to March 1522) he spent in seclusion was put to good use. At Wartburg Luther produced one of the essential tools of Reformation: a German translation of Erasmus's Greek text of the New Testament.

Imperial Distractions: France and the Turks

Charles V was too preoccupied with military ventures to pay much attention to the Reformation that erupted in Wittenberg following Luther's trial. France wanted to move into Italy to drive a wedge through Charles's empire, and the Ottoman Turks were advancing on eastern Europe. Charles needed friendly relations with the German princes in order to recruit German troops for his armies.

In 1526 the Turks overran Hungary at the Battle of Mohacs, and in western Europe the French organized the League of Cognac in preparation for the second of four wars between the Habsburg and Valois dynasties (1521–1559). Thus preoccupied, the emperor, at the Diet of Speyer (1526), granted each German prince the right to deal as he saw fit with the situation Luther had created. This cleared the way for the Reformation to put down roots in places where the princes sympathized with it, and it inaugurated a tradition of princely control over religion that was to be enshrined in law by the Peace of Augsburg in 1555.

How the Reformation Spread

In the 1520s and 1530s, leadership of the Reformation passed from theologians and pamphleteers to magistrates and princes. City governments acted on the proposals of Protestant preachers and their growing flocks and mandated religious reforms. Reform ceased to be a matter of slogans and passed into law binding on all a town's residents. Like urban magistrates, some regional princes (e.g., the elector of Saxony and the prince of Hesse) implemented the reform in large states. They recognized political and economic advantages to themselves in the overthrow of the Roman Catholic Church and urged their neighbors to join them. Powerful alliances were negotiated, and Protestant leaders prepared for war with their Catholic emperor.

The Peasants' Revolt

In its first decade the Protestant movement suffered more from internal division than from imperial interference. By 1525, Luther had become as controversial a figure in Germany as the pope, and many of his early supporters had broken with him. Germany's peasants, who had welcomed Luther as an ally, had a particular reason for losing faith in him. Since the late fifteenth century, their leaders had been struggling to prevent the territorial princes from ignoring traditional restraints and imposing new regulations and taxes. Many peasants saw Luther's proclamation of Christian freedom and criticism of monastic landowners as a declaration of support for their cause.

Luther and his followers sympathized with the peasants, but Lutherans were not social revolutionaries. Luther's freedom of the Christian individual was an inner release from guilt and anxiety, not a restructuring of society by violent revolution. When the peasants rebelled against their masters from 1524 to 1525, Luther condemned them in the strongest possible terms and urged the princes to crush the revolt. Tens of thousands of peasants (possibly 100,000) died in the struggle. Had Luther supported the Peasants' Revolt, he would have contradicted his own teaching and would also probably have ended any chance for his reform to survive beyond the 1520s.

The Reformation Elsewhere

Luther was the first to rebel against the church, but independent reform movements soon developed in France and Switzerland.

Zwingli and the Swiss Reformation

Switzerland's political environment was as favorable to the success of a religious revolt as Germany's. Switzerland was a loose confederacy of thirteen autonomous cantons (states) and allied areas. Some (e.g., Zurich, Bern, Basel, and Schaffhausen) became Protestant, some (especially in the heartland around Lucerne) remained Catholic, and a few effected a compromise. Two developments prepared the ground for the Swiss Reformation: (1) a growth of national sentiment created by opposition to the practice of impressing Swiss soldiers into mercenary service outside their homeland, and (2) an interest in church reform that had been stimulated by the convocation of famous church councils in the Swiss cities of Constance (1414–1417) and Basel (1431–1449).

THE REFORMATION IN ZURICH Ulrich Zwingli (1484–1531), the leader of the Swiss Reformation, received a humanist education and credited Erasmus for sparking his interest in reform. He was chaplain to Swiss mercenaries in Italy in 1515, and his experiences at a disastrous battle at Marignano prompted him to become an ardent critic of mercenary service. By 1518 he was also widely known for opposing the sale of indulgences and for denouncing religious superstitions.

In 1519 Zwingli applied for the post of people's priest in Zurich's main church. His fitness was questioned because of his acknowledged fornication with a barber's daughter. Many of

Art & the West

A Royal Stag Hunt

Lucas Cranach, German, 1472–1553. *Hunting Near Hartenfels Castle*, 1540. Oil on wood, 116.8 × 170.2 cm. © The Cleveland Museum of Art, 2001, John L. Severance Fund, 1958.425.

*L*ucas Cranach the Elder (1472–1553), court painter to the Elector of Saxony, was a close friend of Martin Luther. His employer was one of the most powerful noblemen in Germany, and Cranach was responsible for making sure that the elector's residences reflected his status. He painted interiors and exteriors for five of his lord's dozen residences. He outfitted rooms with portraits, tapestries, furniture, and utensils. He designed decorations for celebrations and even provided tailors with sketches of clothing to be worn at court.

Royal hunts were important social and political occasions, and Cranach's paintings of them were popular. Depicted here is a hunt that took place at Castle Torgau in 1540. Hunts were carefully choreographed. The animals to be hunted were kept in pens until it was time to drive them toward the places where the hunters had stationed themselves. Cranach's picture depicts three hunts: stags in the foreground, a bear in the upper left, and a boar in the upper right. The Elector John Frederick is shown, dressed in green and arming a crossbow, near the center of the painting's bottom edge.

Source: *Lucas Cranach: Ein Maler-Unternehmer aus Franken*, ed. by Claus Grimm, et al. (Verlag Friedrich Pustet, Regensburg, 1994), pp. 311–313.

his contemporaries, however, sympathized with the plight of celibate clergy, and Zwingli defended himself forcefully. Later he led the fight to abolish clerical celibacy and to establish the right of clergy to marry.

Zwingli's post as the people's priest in Zurich gave him a pulpit from which to campaign for reform. His reform program was simple: Whatever lacked literal support in Scripture was to be neither believed nor practiced. Application of that standard led him, as it did Luther, to question many traditional teachings and practices: fasting, transubstantiation, the worship of saints, pilgrimages, purgatory, clerical celibacy, and some of the sacraments. A public debate, held on January 29, 1523, ended with the city government endorsing Zwingli's ideas. Zurich took the lead in the Swiss Reformation and pioneered the kind of Protestantism that came to be called "puritanical."

THE MARBURG COLLOQUY Landgrave Philip of Hesse (1504–1567) believed that Protestants had to cooperate if they hoped to fend off attacks from Catholics, and he tried to unite the Swiss and German reformations. He brought Luther and Zwingli together in his castle in Marburg in early October 1529. But theological disagreements over the nature of Christ's presence in the Eucharist prevented the two leaders from forming a political alliance. Luther concluded that Zwingli was a dangerous fanatic, and Zwingli believed that Luther was irrationally in thrall to medieval ideas.

The disagreement splintered the Protestant movement. Separate credal statements were issued, and separate defense leagues were formed. Semi-Zwinglian views were embodied in the *Confessio Tetrapolitana* prepared by the Strasbourg reformers Martin Bucer and Caspar Hedio. In 1530 this was presented to the Diet of Augsburg as an alternative to the *Augsburg Confession*, which the Lutherans proposed as a basis for unity.

SWISS CIVIL WARS. As Protestants and Catholics divided up the Swiss cantons, civil wars began. There were two major battles—both at Kappel (one in June 1529, the second in October 1531). The first was a clear victory for the Protestants. The Catholic cantons were forced to repudiate their foreign alliances and recognize the rights of

Protestants. The second battle cost Zwingli his life, but the treaty that ended the fighting confirmed the right of each canton to determine its own religion. Thereafter, things settled down. Heinrich Bullinger (1504–1575), Zwingli's protégé, assumed leadership of the Swiss Reformation and guided it toward the status of an established religion.

Anabaptists and Radical Protestants

The seeming failure of the Lutheran and Zwinglian reformations to elevate standards of ethical conduct and the slow pace of change discontented many people. Those who wanted a more rapid and thorough restoration of "primitive Christianity" (the church described in the New Testament) accused the reformers of going only halfway. These people formed radical Protestant movements, chief among which was that of the Anabaptists (among whom were the founders of the Mennonite and Amish communities). The Anabaptists ("rebaptizers") took their name from their rejection of infant baptism and their insistence on rebaptizing adults who had been baptized as infants.

Conrad Grebel (1498–1526) symbolically inaugurated Anabaptism by performing the first adult rebaptism in Zurich in January 1525. In October 1523, Grebel's passion for biblical literalism had caused him to break with his mentor, Zwingli. He opposed Zwingli's support for the government's plea to proceed slowly in altering traditional religious practices. In 1527 Grebel's followers, the Swiss Brethren, published a statement of their principles, the *Schleitheim Confession*. They practiced adult baptism, opposed the swearing of oaths, committed themselves to pacifism, and refused to condone secular governments. Anabaptists literally withdrew from society to be free to live as they believed the first Christians had lived. State authorities interpreted their conduct as an attack on society's bonds.

THE ANABAPTIST REIGN IN MÜNSTER Lutherans and Zwinglians joined Catholics in persecuting the Anabaptists. In 1529 rebaptism became a capital offense throughout the Holy Roman Empire, and from 1525 to 1618 somewhere between 1,000 and 5,000 people were executed for undergoing rebaptism. Brutal punishments for nonconformists increased after state authorities witnessed the behavior of a group of Anabaptist extremists who took over the German city of Münster in 1534 to 1535.

Anabaptists converted the majority of the citizens of Münster and set up a town government that forced Lutherans and Catholics to convert or emigrate. Münster became an Old Testament theocracy—replete with charismatic leaders and the practice of polygamy. The latter was an attempt to provide for the women (widowed or deserted) who greatly outnumbered the men of the city.

The outside world was shocked, and Protestant and Catholic armies united to crush the radicals. After this bloody episode, Anabaptism reasserted its commitment to pacifism, and the movement spread largely among rural populations. Later Anabaptist leaders—such as Menno Simons (1496–1561), the founder of the Mennonites—were moderates.

OTHER NONCONFORMISTS   The Anabaptists were not the only Protestant radicals. The Spiritualists were extreme individualists who believed that the only religious authority one ought to obey was the voice of God's spirit in one's heart. Thomas Müntzer (d. 1525), an early convert to Lutheranism and a leader of a peasants' revolt, belonged to this camp—as did Sebastian Franck (d. 1541), a freelance critic of all dogmatic religion, and Caspar Schwenckfeld (d. 1561), a prolific author for whom the tiny Schwenckfeldian denomination is named.

At the other extreme, the Reformation's critique of religious superstition led some people to embrace rationalism. The most prominent exponents of commonsense, rational, ethical religion were the Antitrinitarians. Their most famous spokesman, a Spaniard named Michael Servetus (1511–1553), was executed by the Protestant government of Geneva for rejecting the doctrine of the Trinity. Italian reformers, Lelio (d. 1562) and Faustus Sozzini (d. 1604), founded Socinianism, a humanistic faith that opposed the emerging Protestant orthodoxies and advocated religious toleration.

John Calvin and the Genevan Reformation

In the second half of the sixteenth century Calvinism replaced Lutheranism as the domi-

A portrait of the young John Calvin.   Bibliotheque Publique et Universitaire, Geneva

nant Protestant force in Europe. Although Calvinists believed strongly in divine predestination, they also believed that Christians ought to reorder society according to God's plan. They were zealous reformers who used the machinery of government to compel men and women to live according to codes of conduct that they believed were set forth in the Scriptures.

Calvinism's founder, John Calvin (1509–1564), was the son of a well-to-do secretary to the bishop of Noyon in Picardy. The church *benefices* the boy was given at age twelve paid for the excellent education he received at Parisian colleges and the law school at Orléans. Young Calvin associated with a group of Catholic humanists (led by Jacques Lefèvre d'Étaples and Marguerite d'Angoulême, the queen of Navarre) who advocated reform. Calvin eventually concluded that these people were ineffectual, but they helped awaken his interest in the Reformation.

It was probably in the spring of 1534 that Calvin converted to Protestantism, an experience he described as God's making his "long stubborn heart . . . teachable." In May 1534, he dramatically surrendered the *benefices* that had long supported him and joined the Reformation.

POLITICAL REVOLT AND RELIGIOUS REFORM IN GENEVA In Luther's Saxony, religious reform paved the way for political revolution. In Calvin's Geneva, political revolution awakened an appetite for religious reform. The Genevans, assisted by the city-states of Fribourg and Bern, won their independence from the House of Savoy in 1527 and drove out their resident prince-bishop. The city councils assumed his legal and political powers. Late in 1533 Bern sent the Protestant reformers Guillaume Farel (1489–1565) and Antoine Froment (1508–1581) to Geneva. In the summer of 1535, after much internal turmoil, the Genevans discontinued the traditional Mass and other Catholic religious practices. On May 21, 1536, Geneva officially joined the Reformation.

Calvin arrived in Geneva in July 1536. He had been forced to flee France to avoid persecution for his religious beliefs, and he was intending to seek refuge in Strasbourg. The third Habsburg-Valois war forced him to detour to Geneva, where Farel persuaded him to stay. Before a year had passed, Calvin had drawn up articles for the governance of Geneva's new church as well as a catechism to guide its people. Both were presented for approval to the city councils in early 1537. Because of the strong measures they proposed for governing the moral conduct of Genevans, the reformers were accused of creating a "new papacy." Both within Geneva and outside it, opponents attacked the attempt to impose a new orthodoxy. Bern, which had adopted a more moderate Protestant reform, pressured Geneva to restore ceremonies and holidays that Calvin and Farel opposed. In February 1538, the four syndics (the leading city magistrates) turned against the reformers and drove them out.

Calvin went to Strasbourg to became pastor to a group of French exiles. During his long stay in Strasbourg, he wrote a second edition of his masterful *Institutes of the Christian Religion.* Many scholars consider this to be the definitive theological explication of Protestant faith. Calvin married, took part in ecumenical discussions, and learned important lessons in practical politics from the Strasbourg reformer Martin Bucer.

CALVIN'S GENEVA In 1540 Geneva elected syndics who were eager to establish the city's independence from Bern. They believed that Calvin would be a valuable ally and invited him to re-turn. Within months of his arrival in September 1540, the city implemented new ecclesiastical ordinances. Civil magistrates were pledged to work with the clergy to maintain discipline within the city.

The church Calvin designed was administered by four kinds of officials: (1) five presiding pastors; (2) various teachers or doctors who handled religious instruction; (3) twelve elders, laymen chosen by and from the Genevan councils to "oversee the life of everybody"; and (4) deacons, also laymen, who managed the church's charitable disbursements. Calvin believed that a strong church government was needed to maintain the highest moral standards for the community, for no Christian city could tolerate conduct that was not pleasing to God. The consistory, a committee composed of the elders and the pastors of the church and presided over by one of the four syndics, was given this responsibility. It meted out punishments for a broad range of moral and religious transgressions—from missing church services (a fine of 3 sous) to fornication (six days on bread and water and a fine of 60 sous). The making of statements critical of Calvin and the consistory was listed among the sins meriting punishment. Calvin branded his opponents wanton "Libertines" and showed them little mercy. His most prominent victim was the Antitrinitarian Michael Servetus. Servetus fled to Geneva in 1553, seeking refuge from the Spanish Inquisition—only to be indicted by Calvin for heresy and burned at the stake.

After 1555 the city's syndics were all solidly behind Calvin, and he began to attract disciples from across Europe. Geneva welcomed the thousands of Protestants who were driven out of France, England, and Scotland, and at one point more than a third of the population of the city consisted of refugees (over 5,000 of them). They were utterly loyal to Calvin, for in their experience Geneva was Europe's only "free" city. Whenever they were allowed to return to their homes, they ardently championed Calvinistic reforms.

Political Consolidation of the Lutheran Reformation

By 1530 the Reformation had become irreversible, but it took several decades for that fact to be accepted throughout Europe.

The Expansion of the Reformation

Charles V, who spent most of his time in Spain and Italy, visited the empire in 1530 to convene a diet at Augsburg. The purpose of the meeting was to resolve the religious conflicts that had developed following Luther's break with the papacy in 1520. Charles adjourned the meeting with a blunt order to all Lutherans to revert to Catholicism.

The Reformation was too far advanced by that time to be halted by such a peremptory gesture. The emperor's mandate only served to persuade Lutherans that they needed to form a defensive alliance, which they called the Schmalkaldic League. The league endorsed a common statement of faith, the *Augsburg Confession,* and followed this in 1538 with Luther's more strongly worded *Schmalkaldic Articles.* Regional consistories (i.e., judicial bodies composed of theologians and lawyers) were set up by Lutheran governments to replace the bishops who had formerly administered their churches. Charles was prevented from doing much about this by the outbreak of new hostilities with France and with the Turks. Consequently, the league's leaders, Landgrave Philip of Hesse and Elector John Frederick of Saxony, were, for the time being, able to hold him at bay as Lutheranism spread.

Christian II (r. 1513–1523) introduced Lutheranism to Denmark, where it became the state religion. In Sweden in 1527, Gustavus Vasa (r. 1523–1560) persuaded a Swedish nobility that was eager to confiscate church property to embrace the reform. Poland, primarily because of the absence of a central political authority, became a model of religious pluralism and toleration. In the second half of the sixteenth century, it sheltered Lutherans, Anabaptists, Calvinists, and even Antitrinitarians.

Reaction and Resolution

In 1547 the armies of Charles V crushed the Schmalkaldic League, and the emperor issued the *Augsburg Interim.* It ordered Protestants to return to Catholic beliefs and practices but made a few concessions to Protestant tastes. Clerical marriage was permitted in individual cases when the pope approved, and laypeople were allowed to receive both the bread and the wine at communion. Many Protestant leaders chose exile rather than comply with the terms of the *In-*

terim, and the Reformation was too entrenched by 1547 to be ended by such an imperial fiat.

Maurice of Saxony, whom Charles V handpicked to replace Elector John Frederick as ruler of Saxony, recognized the inevitable and shifted his allegiance to the Protestants. Wearied by three decades of war, the emperor, too, finally surrendered his lifelong quest for the restoration of religious unity in Europe. In 1552 Charles reinstated John Frederick and Philip of Hesse and issued the Peace of Passau (August 1552), guaranteeing religious freedom for Lutherans. The Peace of Augsburg in September 1555 made the division of Christendom permanent. It legalized a principle well established in practice: *cuius regio, eius religio*—meaning that the ruler of a land determines the religion of that land. A subject who was discontented with the religion chosen by his ruler was permitted to migrate to a district that practiced his preferred faith, but diverse faiths were not permitted within a state.

The English Reformation to 1553

The king of England was the only major European monarch to break with the papacy, but England's Reformation owed more to nationalism than to sympathy with Lutheran or Calvinistic theology.

The Preconditions of Reform

England had a long history of maintaining the rights of the crown against the pope. Edward I (d. 1307) defeated Pope Boniface VIII's attempt to deny kings the right to tax their clergy. In the mid-fourteenth century, the English Parliament passed the first Statutes of Provisors and *Praemunire.* These curtailed the right of the pope to appoint candidates to church offices in England, limited the amount of money that could be sent out of England to Rome, and restricted the number of court cases that could be appealed to Rome from English jurisdictions.

In the late Middle Ages, Wycliffe and the Lollards fanned anticlerical sentiment among the English of all classes, and by the early 1520s advocates of reform were smuggling Lutheran writings into England. From 1524 to 1525 William Tyndale (ca. 1492–1536) translated the New Testament into English and had it published in Cologne and Worms. It began to circulate in England in 1526. Access to a Bible in the language of the people became the centerpiece of the English Reformation.

The King's Affair

Henry VIII (r. 1509–1547), the king who severed England's ties with the papacy, initially opposed the Reformation. When Luther's ideas began to circulate, Henry's chief ministers, Cardinal Thomas Wolsey (ca. 1475–1530) and, later, Sir Thomas More (1478–1535), urged him to rush to the pope's defense. Henry declared his Catholic convictions by publishing a treatise justifying the seven sacraments. It earned him a contemptuous response from Luther and the grant of a title, "Defender of the Faith," from Pope Leo X.

It was the king's unhappy marriage, not his doubts about theology, that allowed the seeds of reform to take root in English soil. Henry had married Catherine of Aragon (d. 1536), daughter of Ferdinand and Isabella of Spain and the aunt of Emperor Charles V. By 1527 the union had produced only one surviving child, a daughter, Mary. Since the precedent for women rulers was weak and the practice controversial, Henry feared that civil war would break out if he left his throne to a daughter.

Henry had wed Catherine in 1509 under unusual circumstances that had required a papal dispensation. Catherine had been the wife of Henry's elder brother, Arthur, the heir to their father's throne. When Arthur died, Catherine was betrothed to Henry, the new heir. This preserved England's alliance with Spain. Catherine's numerous miscarriages and stillbirths convinced Henry that their union, despite papal permission, had been a sin and had violated God's prohibition of incest in Leviticus 18:16, 20:21.

By 1527, Henry was thoroughly enamored of Anne Boleyn, one of the aging Catherine's young ladies in waiting. In order to wed Anne, who he believed would be a more fruitful mate, he needed a papal annulment of his marriage to Catherine. Legally, it would have been difficult for the pope to justify an annulment of a marriage that had been approved by a papal dispensation, and in practical terms it was impossible. The soldiers of the Holy Roman Empire had just mutinied and sacked Rome, and Pope Clement VII was a prisoner of Catherine's nephew, Charles V.

Cardinal Wolsey, Henry's Lord Chancellor and a papal legate who had aspirations to become pope, was given the job of securing the annulment. After two years of profitless diplomatic maneuvering, Henry concluded that Wolsey had failed and dismissed him in disgrace (1529). Thomas Cranmer (1489–1556) and Thomas Cromwell (1485–1540), both of whom harbored Lutheran sympathies, then became the king's chief advisers. They proposed a different course: Why not simply declare the king supreme in England's spiritual affairs as he was in England's temporal government? Once that was done, no foreign permission would be needed to legalize a new marriage for the king.

The "Reformation Parliament"

In 1529 Parliament convened for a seven-year session and began to issue a flood of legislation to establish the king's authority over the clergy. In January 1531, Convocation (a legislative assembly representing the English clergy) recognized Henry as head of the church in England "as far as the law of Christ allows." In 1532 Parliament passed a decree (the Submission of the Clergy) that gave the king jurisdiction over the clergy and canon law. Another act (the Conditional Restraint of Annates) recognized the king's power to withhold from Rome the payment of dues traditionally owed the pope.

In January 1533, Thomas Cranmer secretly wed Henry to the pregnant Anne Boleyn. In February 1533, Parliament's Act for the Restraint of Appeals forbade appeals from the king's courts to those of the pope. In March 1533, Cranmer became archbishop of Canterbury, England's primate (i.e., highest-ranking clergyman) and declared that the king had never been validly married to Catherine. In 1534 Parliament ended all payments by the English clergy and laity to Rome and gave Henry sole jurisdiction over high ecclesiastical appointments. The Act of Succession in the same year declared Anne Boleyn's children legitimate heirs to the throne, and the Act of Supremacy proclaimed Henry "the only supreme head on earth of the Church of England." In 1536 the first Act for Dissolution of Monasteries closed the smaller houses, and three years later all English monasteries were shut and their endowments confiscated by the king.

Not all of Henry's subjects approved of the nationalization of their church, but Henry encouraged compliance by making examples of two of his most prominent critics. When Thomas More and John Fisher, bishop of Rochester, refused to accept the Act of Succession and the Act of Supremacy, Henry had them executed.

Wives of Henry VIII

Henry was more successful as a politician than as a husband. In 1536 Anne Boleyn, who had disappointed Henry by bearing him another daughter (Elizabeth), was executed for alleged treason and adultery. Henry married four more times. His third wife, Jane Seymour, died in 1537, shortly after giving birth to the long-desired male heir, Edward VI. Henry then wed Anne of Cleves as part of a plan that Cromwell promoted to forge an alliance among Protestant princes. Neither the alliance nor Anne—whom Henry found to have a remarkable resemblance to a horse—proved worth the trouble. The marriage was annulled by Parliament, and Cromwell was executed. Catherine Howard, Henry's fifth wife, was beheaded for adultery in 1542. His last wife, Catherine Parr, was a patron of humanists and reformers. Henry was her third husband, and she survived him to marry a fourth time.

The King's Religious Conservatism

Henry was far bolder in politics than in piety. Except for his break with Rome and his approval of the use of English Bibles in English churches, Henry opposed changes in doctrine and practice. The Ten Articles of 1536, a program for England's nationalized church, made only mild concessions to Protestant tenets. In 1539 the king issued the Six Articles, which were intended to stem a rising tide of enthusiasm for Protestantism. These reaffirmed transubstantiation, denied the Eucharistic cup to the laity, preserved mandatory celibacy for the clergy, authorized private masses, and ordered the continuation of auricular confession. England had to await Henry's death before it could become a genuinely Protestant country.

The Protestant Reformation Under Edward VI

When Henry died, his son, Edward VI (r. 1547–1553), was only ten years old. The young king's regents gave him a Protestant education—enlivened by correspondence with John Calvin. Edward's pro-Protestant government repealed Henry's Six Articles and laws against heresy, and it sanctioned clerical marriage and lay communion with both cup and bread. In 1547 the chantries, endowments supporting priests who said masses for the dead, were dissolved. In 1549 the Act of Uniformity imposed Thomas Cranmer's *Book of Common Prayer* on all English churches, and a year later images and altars were ordered removed from churches.

The Second Act of Uniformity, passed in 1552, revised the *Book of Common Prayer* and published a forty-two-article confession of faith written by Thomas Cranmer. The confession endorsed the Protestant doctrines of justification by faith and supremacy of Holy Scripture. It recognized only two sacraments and rejected transubstantiation—although it affirmed the real presence of Christ in the Eucharistic elements.

The turn toward Protestantism that took place during Edward's reign was reversed by his heir, Catherine of Aragon's fervently Catholic daughter, Mary. In 1553 Mary succeeded her teenaged half-brother and made it her mission, as queen, to restore England to the Catholic community. Despite a bloody persecution of Protestants, she was unable completely to undo the work her father and brother had begun. When she died childless in 1558, Anne Boleyn's daughter, Elizabeth (d. 1603), inherited her throne and engineered a religious compromise. The Elizabethan "settlement" left England with a stable, moderately Protestant national church.

Catholic Reform and Counter-Reformation

Before Luther spoke out, proposals had already been made for reforming the Roman Catholic Church. One of the boldest came on the eve of the last church council that met before the Reformation, the Fifth Lateran Council (1513–1517). But the pope, remembering how the councils of Constance and Basel had usurped the authority of his predecessors, squelched the initiative.

Sources of Catholic Reform

The Modern Devotion inspired many of the Catholic laity and clergy who pushed for reform.

The Ecstasy of Saint Teresa of Avila, *by Gianlorenzo Bernini (1598–1680). Mystics like Saint Teresa and Saint John of the Cross helped revive the traditional piety of medieval monasticism.* S. Maria della Vittoria, Rome. Scala/Art Resource, NY

In 1517 it prompted the foundation of a new kind of religious organization in Rome, the Oratory of Divine Love. The Oratory encouraged cooperation among learned laity and clergy who were deeply committed to the cultivation of inner piety, the promotion of Christian living, and the reform of the church.

The fervent Catholic faith of the sixteenth century generated many new religious orders. The Theatines were founded in 1524 to groom devout, reform-minded leaders for the higher levels of the church hierarchy. The Capuchins were established in 1528 to minister to ordinary people by returning to the ideals of Saint Francis. The Somaschi, in the mid-1520s, and the Barnabites, in 1530, dedicated themselves to caring for the residents of war-torn areas of Italy. The Ursulines, founded in 1535, undertook the religious education of girls from all social classes.

The Oratorians, established in 1575, promoted religious literature and church music—the great hymnist and musician Giovanni Palestrina (1526–1594) was one of them. And, thanks to the inspiration of the Spanish mystics, Saint Teresa of Avila (1515–1582) and Saint John of the Cross (1542–1591), older monastic orders also underwent renewal.

Ignatius of Loyola and the Jesuits

The most influential of the new orders, the Society of Jesus, was organized in the 1530s by Ignatius of Loyola (1491–1556). Ignatius, a dashing courtier and *caballero,* began his spiritual pilgrimage in 1521 when he was seriously wounded in battle. He passed a lengthy and painful convalescence reading Christian classics and studying the techniques developed by the church's saints for overcoming mental anguish and pain. A dramatic conversion experience determined him to do whatever was necessary to become a "soldier of Christ." The lessons Ignatius learned from his struggles with himself evolved into a program for personal individual renewal. Ignatius believed that a person could create a new self through study and discipline, and he wrote a devotional guide (*Spiritual Exercises*) to teach techniques for achieving spiritual self-mastery.

The Protestant reformers of Ignatius's day made a virtue of opposing the authority of the traditional church. Ignatius, however, urged Catholics to deny themselves and submit without question to the church. Perfect discipline and self-control were to be cultivated—as were enthusiasm for traditional spirituality, mystical experience, and willingness to subordinate all personal goals to those of the church. People imbued with these qualities were well equipped to counter the Reformation. Within a century the ten original "Jesuits" were joined by more than 15,000 ardent recruits. They recovered districts initially lost to Protestantism in Austria, Bavaria, and the Rhineland, and staffed missions as far afield as India, Japan, and the Americas.

The Council of Trent (1545–1563)

Pope Paul III (1534–1549), in response to pressure from Emperor Charles V, finally called a general council to address the crisis created by the Reformation. The commission, appointed by the pope to prepare for the council, was chaired by

Caspar Contarini (1483–1542), a member of the Oratory of Divine Love. Contarini was such an advocate of reform that his critics branded him a "semi-Lutheran." The report he presented to the pope in February 1537 was so blunt an indictment of the papal curia that Protestants circulated it to justify their break with the papacy.

The opening of the council, which met in Trent in northern Italy, was delayed until 1545, and its three sessions spread over eighteen years (1545–1563). Long interruptions were caused by war, plague, and politics. Unlike the late medieval councils, Trent was strictly under papal control—and dominated by Italian clergy. Only high-ranking churchmen could vote. Theologians from the universities, the lower clergy, and laypersons did not have a voice in the council's decisions.

The council focused on the restoration of internal church discipline. It curtailed the selling of church offices and other religious goods. It ordered bishops who resided outside their dioceses

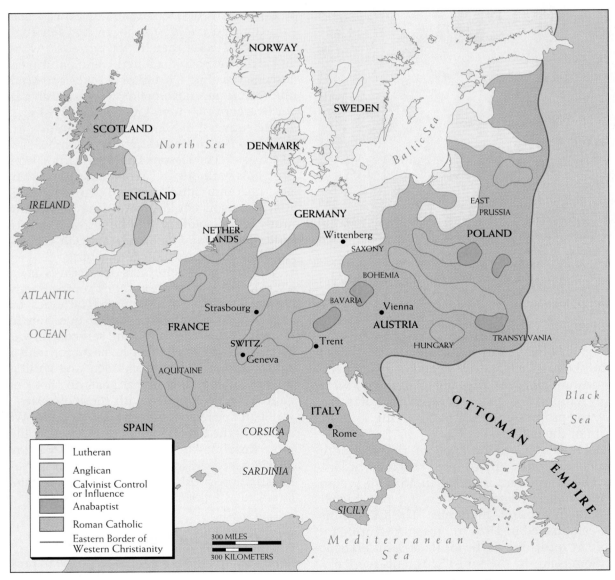

MAP 11–2   THE RELIGIOUS SITUATION ABOUT 1560   *By 1560 Luther, Zwingli, and Loyola were dead, Calvin was near the end of his life, England had separated from Rome, and the last session of the Council of Trent was about to assemble. The religious fragmentation of Europe was well underway.*

to return home and to take steps to elevate the conduct of their charges. Bishops were enjoined to preach and to conduct frequent tours of inspection of the clergy. Trent also sought to increase respect for the parish priest by requiring him to be neatly dressed, better educated, strictly celibate, and active among his parishioners. To achieve these ends Trent called for the construction of a seminary in every diocese.

Trent made no doctrinal concessions to Protestantism. On the contrary, it ringingly affirmed most of the things to which Protestants objected: traditional scholastic education; the role of good works in salvation; the authority of tradition; the seven sacraments; transubstantiation; the withholding of the Eucharistic cup from the laity; clerical celibacy; purgatory; indulgences; and the veneration of saints, relics, and sacred images.

Trent was not designed to heal the rifts that had developed within Christendom but to strengthen the Roman Catholic Church in opposition to Protestantism. Some secular rulers were initially leery of Trent's assertion of papal authority, but they were reassured as the new legislation took hold and parish life revived under the guidance of a devout and better-trained clergy. The increasing religious polarization of Europe was, however, a source for anxiety.

The Church in Spanish America

The Roman Catholic priests who accompanied the expeditions that explored and conquered the Americas were imbued with the Christian humanism that flourished in sixteenth-century Spain. They wanted to convert the Indians not only to Christianity but to European civilization as well.

The early Spanish conquerors and the mendicant friars who worked among the Indians were often at odds. Many priests believed that conquest was a necessary prerequisite for the conversion of the Indians, but they deplored exploitation of native peoples and tried to defend them. Bartolomé de Las Casas, a Dominican, contended that conquest was not necessary for conversion. The campaign he began in 1550 for royal legislation to regulate conquest was successful, but his rhetoric encouraged the growth of the "Black Legend"—a condemnation of all Spanish colonists for inhumanity toward the In-

Significant Dates from the Period of the Protestant Reformation	
1517	Luther posts ninety-five theses against indulgences
1519	Charles V becomes Holy Roman Emperor
1521	Diet of Worms condemns Luther
1524–1525	Peasants' Revolt in Germany
1527	The Schleitheim Confession of the Anabaptists
1529	Marburg Colloquy between Luther and Zwingli
1529	England's Reformation Parliament convenes
1531	Formation of Protestant Schmalkaldic League
1533	Henry VIII weds Anne Boleyn
1534	England's Act of Supremacy
1534–1535	Anabaptists take over Münster
1536	Calvin arrives in Geneva
1540	Jesuits, founded by Ignatius of Loyola, recognized as order by pope
1546	Luther dies
1547	Armies of Charles V crush Schmalkaldic League
1547–1553	Edward VI, king of England
1555	Peace of Augsburg
1553–1558	Mary Tudor, queen of England
1545–1563	Council of Trent
1558–1603	Elizabeth I, queen of England; the Anglican settlement

dians. Although the "Black Legend" contained elements of truth, it exaggerated the case against Spain. The Aztec demands for human sacrifice prove that Indian rulers could also be exceedingly cruel. Had the Aztecs discovered Spain and won the upper hand, they would have dealt with Europeans much as Spaniards dealt with Indians.

By the end of the sixteenth century, the church in Spanish America had made peace with colonialism. On numerous occasions, individual priests defended the rights of Indian tribes, but the church also profited from the growing prosperity of the Spanish colonists. As a great landowner with a stake in the colonial status quo, it did not challenge Spanish domination or any but the most extreme modes of economic exploitation. By the time the colonial era drew to a close in the late eighteenth century, the Roman Catholic Church had become one of the strongest and most conservative institutions in Latin America.

The Social Significance of the Reformation in Western Europe

Luther, Zwingli, and Calvin believed that Christians were called not to separate themselves from the world but to take up their Christian duties as citizens of the state. Consequently, they have been called "magisterial reformers," meaning not only that they were leaders of major Protestant movements but also that they were willing to use the magistrate's sword to advance their causes.

To some modern observers this looks like a compromise of the highest religious principles, but the reformers did not see it that way. They assumed that their reforms had to conform to the realities of the societies of which they were members. The reformers were so sensitive to what they believed was politically and socially possible that some scholars claim that they encouraged acceptance of the status quo. But despite this political conservatism, the Reformation, in some places, contributed to radical changes in traditional religious practices and institutions.

The Revolution in Religious Practices and Institutions

RELIGION IN FIFTEENTH–CENTURY LIFE   On the eve of the Reformation, the clergy and the religious made up 6 to 8 percent of the total population of the central European cities that were about to become Protestant. In addition to their spiritual authority, they exercised considerable political power. They legislated, taxed, tried cases in special church courts, and enforced laws with threats of excommunication. The church calendar regulated the daily life of the city. About one-third of the year was given over to some kind of religious observance, fast, or celebration. Cloisters, which educated the children of prominent citizens and enjoyed the patronage of powerful aristocratic families, had great influence. There was booming business at religious shrines, where

pilgrims gathered by the hundreds or thousands. Begging friars constantly worked the streets, and several times each year special preachers arrived to sell letters of indulgence.

The conduct of many of the religious was a source of concern. Despite the fact that clergy were sworn to celibacy and forbidden legal marriages, many had concubines and children. Society's response to these relationships was mixed, but the church tolerated them upon payment of penitential fines. Everywhere there were complaints about the clergy's exemption from taxation and immunity from prosecution in civil courts, and people grumbled about having to support church offices whose occupants lived and worked elsewhere.

RELIGION IN SIXTEENTH-CENTURY LIFE   The Reformation made few changes in the politics or class structures of the cities where it triumphed. The same aristocratic families governed as before, and the same people were rich and poor. The Reformation did, however, have a profound impact on the clergy. Their numbers fell by two-thirds; religious holidays shrank by one-third. Monasteries and nunneries nearly disappeared— transformed into hospices or educational institutions. Parish churches were reduced in number by at least one-third. Worship was conducted in the vernacular. In some places, particularly those influenced by the Zwinglian reform, the walls of sanctuaries were stripped bare and whitewashed.

The laity observed no obligatory fasts. Local shrines were closed down, and anyone found venerating saints, relics, and images was subject to punishment. Copies of Luther's translation of the New Testament or excerpts from it could be found in private homes. Instead of controlling access to the Scriptures, the new clergy encouraged laypersons to study them. Protestant clergy could marry, and many did. They paid taxes and were punished for their crimes in civil courts. The moral life of the community was supervised by committees composed of equal numbers of laity and clergy, and secular magistrates had the last word in resolving disputes. Not all Protestant clergy were enthusiastic about lay authority in religion. The laity complained about "new papists" among the Protestant preachers—men who sought the strict control over the lives of the laity that the Catholic clergy enjoyed.

The laity themselves were no less ambivalent about certain aspects of the Reformation, and they could be just as reactionary as some clergy. Over half of the original converts returned to the Catholic fold before the end of the sixteenth century.

The Reformation and Education

The Reformation's implementation of humanistic educational theories in new Protestant schools and universities had significant cultural impact. Even when the reformers' views on doctrine and human nature separated them from the humanists, they shared the humanists' belief in the unity of wisdom, eloquence, and action. The humanist program of study, which emphasized language skills and a reliance on original sources, was essential for the practice of a Protestant faith that acknowledged no authority higher than that of Scripture.

When, in August 1518, Philip Melanchthon (1497–1560), a young professor of Greek, joined Luther at the University of Wittenberg, his first act was to champion humanist curricular reforms. In his inaugural address, *On Improving the Studies of the Young*, Melanchthon defended classical studies against medieval scholasticism, and he and Luther completely restructured the University of Wittenberg's program of study. Canon law and commentaries on Lombard's *Sentences* were dropped. Old-fashioned scholastic lectures on Aristotle were replaced by a straightforward historical approach. Students read primary sources directly, not as interpreted by scholastic commentators. Candidates for theological degrees relied on exegesis of the Bible, not the citation of "authorities," to defend their theses. New chairs of Greek and Hebrew were created. Luther and Melanchthon also pressed for universal compulsory education so that both boys and girls could learn to read the Bible in vernacular translation.

In Geneva, John Calvin and his successor, Theodore Beza, founded an academy that developed into the University of Geneva. Their school, which concentrated on training Calvinist ministers, developed a program similar to the one designed by Luther and Melanchthon. Calvinist refugees trained in the academy carried Protestant educational reforms to France, Scotland, England, and the New World. Thanks to them, a working knowledge of Greek and Hebrew became commonplace in educated circles in the sixteenth and seventeenth centuries.

Some contemporaries complained that the original humanist program narrowed its focus as Protestants took it over, but humanist culture and learning profited from the Reformation. Protestant schools and universities consolidated and preserved for the modern world many of the basic pedagogical achievements of humanism.

The Reformation and the Changing Role of Women

The Protestant reformers rejected ascetic disciplines, such as celibacy, as vain attempts to earn salvation, and they urged clergy to marry to dispel the belief that the lives of clergy were spiritually more meritorious than those of laypersons. The development of a more positive attitude toward marriage translated into a more positive attitude toward women.

Medieval thinkers often degraded sexually active women as temptresses (such as Eve) and exalted virginal women as saints (such as Mary). Protestants praised woman in her own right but especially in her biblical vocation as mother and housewife. The reformers acknowledged the contribution their wives made to their ministries, and Protestants stressed as no religious movement before them had the sacredness of home and family. The ideal of companionate marriage—that is, of husband and wife as coworkers in a special God-ordained community of the family—greatly improved women's legal status. Since Protestant marriage was not a sacrament, divorce was easier, and women had the right to leave husbands who flagrantly violated marriage contracts. Although from a modern perspective, Protestant women remained subject to men, new marriage laws gave them greater security and protection.

Because they wanted women to become pious housewives modeling their lives on biblical precepts, Protestants encouraged vernacular literacy for girls. Some women became authors and contributed to the literature of the Reformation. Many, in the course of their studies, pondered the significance of biblical passages that suggested they were equal to men in the presence of God. The discussion of the role of women that Protestant theology encouraged inched society marginally closer to the emancipation of women.

Family Life in Early Modern Europe

Many changes took place in the sixteenth and seventeenth centuries in the customs influencing marriage and family life. The Reformation was only one of many factors shaping these developments.

Later Marriages

Men and women began to delay first marriages to later ages than they had in previous centuries. Grooms tended to be in their mid- to late twenties rather than in their late teens and early twenties, and brides in their early to mid-twenties rather than in their teens. The church-sanctioned minimum age for marriage remained fourteen for men and twelve for women. Betrothal could still occur at these young ages if parents approved.

Later marriages were a reflection of the difficulty couples encountered in amassing enough capital to establish an independent household. Family size and population increased in the fifteenth and early sixteenth centuries. That meant that property tended to be divided among more heirs, and an average couple had to work longer to prepare materially for marriage. Many—possibly 20 percent of all women in the sixteenth century—never married. Single women often grew increasingly impoverished as they aged without the support of a husband or children.

Arranged Marriages

Marriages tended to be "arranged" in the sense that the male heads of two families met and discussed the terms of a marriage before they informed the prospective bride and bridegroom. It was rare, however, for the two people involved not to know each other in advance or to have no prior relationship. Children had a legal right to protest and resist an unwanted marriage. A forced marriage was, by definition, invalid, and no one believed an unwanted marriage would last. The best marriage was one desired by both parties and approved by their families.

Later marriages to older partners shortened the length of the average marriage and elevated the rate of remarriage. Maternal mortality increased with late marriage and, as the rapid growth of orphanages and foundling homes between 1600 and 1800 testifies, so did out-of-wedlock pregnancies.

Family Size

The early modern family was conjugal or nuclear. It consisted of a father and a mother and an average of two to four surviving children. A wife endured a pregnancy about every two years. About one-third of the children born died by age five, and one-half were gone by age twenty. Rare was the family at any social level that did not suffer the loss of children. Martin Luther fathered six children, two of whom died—one at eight months and another at thirteen years.

Birth Control

Birth control methods of limited effectiveness had been available since antiquity: acidic ointments, sponges, and *coitus interruptus.* The church's growing condemnation of contraception in the thirteenth and fourteenth centuries suggests that its use was increasing. St. Thomas Aquinas defended the church's position by asserting that a natural act, such as sex, was moral only when it served the end for which it was created—in this case, the production of children and their subsequent rearing to the glory of God. Christian moral teachings may, however, have increased some couples' use of contraception by encouraging husbands to empathize with the burden frequent pregnancies placed on their wives.

Wet Nursing

Theologians and physicians joined in condemning the widespread custom of putting newborn children out to wet nurses. Wet nurses were mothers who made money by suckling other women's children. Wet nursing often exposed an infant to great risks from disease or neglect, but nursing a child was a chore many upper-class women found distasteful. Husbands also disliked it, for the church forbade sexual intercourse while a woman was lactating on the theory that sexual intercourse spoiled a woman's milk. Nursing also has a contraceptive effect, and there is evidence that some women prolonged nursing to fend off new pregnancy. For wealthy burghers and noblemen who wanted an abundance of male heirs, time spent nursing was time wasted.

Loving Families?

In addition to wet nursing, other practices common to early modern families cause them to appear cold and unloving. A child who spent the first year of his life with a wet nurse might, between the ages of nine and fourteen, find himself sent away from home again for an apprenticeship or employment. Also, the gap in ages between husband and wife was often great, and a widower or widow sometimes remarried very quickly.

The forms love and affection take, however, are as relative to time and culture as other values. Depending on the options that are available, a kindness in one historical period can seem a cruelty in another. Primitive living conditions, which made single life difficult, necessitated quick remarriages. A competitive economic environment with limited opportunities for vocational education encouraged early apprenticeships if children were to have jobs. There is no convincing evidence that people of the Reformation era were less capable of loving one another than modern people are.

Literary Imagination in Transition

As Europe approached the seventeenth century, it was no longer medieval, but it was also not yet modern. The intellectual life of the period may have been so remarkably rich and vital because it issued from the interplay of both points of view. The great literary figures of the era were capable of defending traditional values while exploring alternatives that encouraged people to develop a fresh perspective on life's potentials.

Miguel de Cervantes Saavedra: Rejection of Idealism

There was religious reform in Spain but no Protestant Reformation. The Spanish state empowered the Inquisition to enforce uniformity of opinion in Spain, and the religion of which the state approved was the mystical, ascetic piety of the early Middle Ages. It was this that colored Spain's literature.

For centuries Spain had been a nation of crusaders, and the union of Catholic piety with sec-

Miguel de Cervantes Saavedra (1547–1616), the author of Don Quixote, *considered by many to be Spain's greatest writer.* Art Resource, NY

ular power, which is characteristic of a crusade, shaped a culture based on the ideals of medieval chivalry—particularly, honor and loyalty. The novels and plays of the period are almost all devoted to stories in which these virtues are tested.

Miguel de Cervantes Saavedra (1547–1616), who is generally acknowledged to be the greatest writer Spain has produced, devoted himself to exploring the strengths and weaknesses of religious idealism. Cervantes was self-educated—reading widely and immersing himself in the "school of life." As a youth, he worked in Rome for a Spanish cardinal. He entered the army and was decorated for gallantry in the Battle of Lepanto (1571). He was also captured by pirates and enslaved in Algiers for five years. He later found work as a tax collector and was imprisoned for padding his accounts. It was in prison in 1603 that he began to write his most famous work, *Don Quixote.*

Cervantes set out to satirize the chivalric romances popular in Spain in his day, but he developed a deep affection for Don Quixote, the deluded knight whose story he tells. *Don Quixote* is satire only on the surface. The work raises serious questions about the things that give meaning to human lives. Cervantes's Don Quixote is a none-too-stable, middle-aged man who is driven mad by reading too many chivalric romances. He aspires to become the knight of his own imagination and sets out to prove his worthiness by performing brave deeds. He dedicates himself as a courtly lover to the service of Dulcinea, a quite unworthy peasant girl whom he imagines to be a refined and noble lady. Sancho Panza, a clever, worldly-wise peasant, accompanies him as his squire and watches with bemused skepticism as the Don repeatedly makes a fool of himself. The story ends tragically when a well-meaning friend tries to restore Don Quixote's reason by defeating him in battle and forcing him to renounce his quest for knighthood. Stripped of the delusion that gave meaning to his life, the Don returns to his village to die a shamed and broken-hearted old man.

Don Quixote examines side by side the modern realism of Sancho Panza and the old-fashioned religious idealism of the Don. It comes to the conclusion that both are respectable and both are necessary for human fulfillment.

William Shakespeare: Dramatist of the Age

Little is known about William Shakespeare (1564–1616), the greatest playwright in the English language. He married young (at age eighteen), and by 1585 he and his wife, Anne Hathaway, had three children. He may have worked for a time as a schoolteacher. The wide but erratic knowledge of history and classical literature that informs his plays suggests that he was not schooled as a professional scholar.

Once he could afford it, Shakespeare chose to live the life of a country gentleman. He entered eagerly into the commercialism and the bawdy pleasures of the Elizabethan Age, and his work shows no trace of Puritan anxiety about worldliness. He was radical in neither politics nor religion, and his few allusions to Puritans are more critical than complimentary. By modern standards he was a political conservative, accepting the social rankings and the power structure of his day and demonstrating unquestioned patriotism.

Shakespeare experienced every aspect of life in the theater—as playwright, actor, and owner-producer. He wrote and performed for a famous company of actors, the King's Men, and, between 1590 and 1610, many of his plays were staged at Elizabeth's court. Although the French drama of the period was dominated by classical models, the Elizabethan audience that Shakespeare wanted to please welcomed a mixture of styles: classical comedies and tragedies, medieval morality plays, and contemporary Italian short stories.

Shakespeare wrote all kinds of plays that synthesized the best from the past and from the work of his contemporaries. The most original of Shakespeare's tragedies may be *Romeo and Juliet* (1597), but four of his greatest were the products of one short period in his career: *Hamlet* (1603), *Othello* (1604), *King Lear* (1605), and *Macbeth* (1606). Shakespeare also wrote comedies and plays based on real historical events. The latter were strongly colored by the propaganda that served the Tudor monarchy, but almost all of Shakespeare's plays have demonstrated a remarkable ability to transcend the limits of the world for which they were written. Their keen analyses of human motivation, stirring evocations of human emotion, and stunning poetry keep them alive and capable of filling theaters.

In Perspective

The Lutheran Reformation, which made pluralism a fact of Western religious life, was the product of an age of widespread discontent. People at all levels of society had come to resent a church that failed to hold clergy accountable for their spiritual conduct while exempting them from many burdens imposed on the laity. Spiritual and secular grievances combined to fuel a revolution that restructured both the church and the state.

Luther's declaration that Scripture was the only authority governing faith opened a Pandora's box, for people proved to have very different ideas about what Scripture taught. Lutheran, Zwinglian, Anabaptist, Spiritualist, Calvinist, and Anglican versions of biblical religion appeared in rapid succession, and Protestants had difficulty containing their revolution.

A move to reform the Catholic church was underway long before the Reformation broke out in Germany, but, lacking papal support, it made little progress until the mid-sixteenth century. Catholic reform, when it came, was doctrinally reactionary but administratively and spiritually innovative. The church demanded strict obedience and conformity, but it also provided the laity with a better-educated and disciplined clergy. The result was a smaller but more vigorous church, prepared to fight for its place in an increasingly pluralistic culture.

REVIEW QUESTIONS

1. What were the main problems of the church that contributed to the Protestant Reformation? Why was the church unable to suppress dissent as it had earlier?
2. On what did Luther and Zwingli agree? On what did they disagree? What about Luther and Calvin? Did differences and splits within the ranks lessen the effectiveness of the Protestant movement?
3. Why did the Reformation begin in Germany? How did the political context Germany provided for a reform movement differ from the situation in France or Italy?
4. What was the Catholic Reformation? What were the major reforms instituted by the Council of Trent? Did the Protestant Reformation have a healthy effect on the Catholic church?
5. Why did Henry VIII break with the Catholic church? Did he establish a truly Protestant religion in England? What problems did his successors face as a result of his religious policies?
6. What impact did the Reformation have on women in the sixteenth and seventeenth centuries? What new factors and pressures affected relations between men and women, family size, and child care during this period?

SUGGESTED READINGS

HAROLD BLOOM, *Shakespeare: The Invention of the Human* (1998). A modern master's complete analysis of the greatest writer in the English language.

W. BOUWSMA, *John Calvin: A Sixteenth Century Portrait* (1988). Interpretation of Calvin against the background of Renaissance intellectual history.

J. DELUMEAU, *Catholicism Between Luther and Voltaire: A New View of the Counter Reformation* (1977). Programmatic essay on a social history of the Counter-Reformation.

A. G. DICKENS, *The English Reformation* (1974). The best one-volume account.

M. DURAN, *Cervantes* (1974). Detailed biography.

H. O. EVENNETT, *The Spirit of the Counter Reformation* (1968). Essay on the continuity of Catholic reform and its independence from the Protestant Reformation.

B. GOTTLIEB, *The Family in the Western World* (1992). Accessible overview, with up-to-date annotated bibliographies.

R. HOULBROOKE, *Death, Religion and Family in England, 1480–1758* (1998). How death was met in the early modern English family.

J. L. IRWIN, ed., *Womanhood in Radical Protestantism, 1525–1675* (1979). Sources illustrating images of women in sectarian Protestant thought.

S. MARSHALL, ed., *Women in Reformation and Counter Reformation Europe: Private and Public Worlds* (1989). Lucid and authoritative presentations.

J. F. MCNEILL, *The History and Character of Calvinism* (1954). The most comprehensive account, and very readable.

H. A. OBERMAN, *Luther: Man Between God and the Devil* (1989). Perhaps the best account of Luther's life, by a Dutch master.

J. O'MALLEY, *The First Jesuits* (1993). Extremely detailed account of the creation of the Society of Jesus and its original purposes.

S. OZMENT, *The Age of Reform, 1250–1550: An Intellectual and Religious History of Late Medieval and Reformation Europe* (1980). A broad survey of major religious ideas and beliefs.

S. OZMENT, *Flesh and Spirit: Private Life in Early Modern Germany* (1999).

D. STARKEY, *The Reign of Henry VIII* (1985). Portrayal of the king as in control of neither his life nor his court.

F. WENDEL, *Calvin: The Origins and Development of His Religious Thought*, trans. by Philip Mairet (1963). The best treatment of Calvin's theology.

Chapter 12

The Age of Religious Wars

KEY TOPICS

- The war between Calvinists and Catholics in France
- The Spanish occupation of the Netherlands
- The struggle for supremacy between England and Spain
- The devastation of central Europe during the Thirty Years' War

Political rivalries and religious conflicts combined to make the late sixteenth and the early seventeenth centuries an "age of religious wars." The era was plagued both by civil conflicts within nations and by battles among nations. Catholic and Protestant factions struggled for advantage within France, the Netherlands, and England. The Catholic monarchies of France and Spain attacked Protestant regimes in England and the Netherlands. Ultimately, every major nation in Europe was drawn into a conflict that devastated Germany, the Thirty Years' War (1618–1648).

Renewed Religious Struggle

During the first half of the sixteenth century, religious war was confined to central Europe—to parts of the empire where Lutherans fought for recognition. In the second half of the sixteenth century, the battles shifted to western Europe (France, the Netherlands, England, and Scotland) as Calvinists struggled for their cause.

The Peace of Augsburg (1555) ended the first phase of the war in central Europe by granting each ruler of a region of the empire the right to determine the religion of his subjects. The only kind of Protestantism that Augsburg recognized, however, was Lutheranism. Lutherans and Catholics joined forces to oppose Anabaptists and other sectarians, and Calvinists were not yet strong enough to demand legal standing.

By the time the Council of Trent adjourned in 1563 the Roman Catholic Church had been reinvigorated, and the Jesuits were spearheading a counteroffensive to recover regions lost to Protestantism in western Europe. John Calvin, who died in 1564, made Geneva both a refuge for Protestants fleeing persecution and a school to equip them to meet the Catholic challenge.

Genevan Calvinism and Tridentine Catholicism were equally dogmatic and aggressive—and mutually incompatible. Calvinism mandated a presbyterian organization that distributed authority among local governments. Boards of presbyters (elders), composed of both clergy and laity and representing individual congregations, set policy for the church at large. The Roman Catholic Church was, by contrast, a centralized, hierarchical system that stressed absolute obedience to the pope. The pope and bishops ruled supreme without the necessity of consulting with the laity. Calvinism attracted people who favored the decentralization and distribution of political power and who opposed authoritarian rule, whereas Catholicism was preferred by advocates of absolute monarchy—those who favored "one king, one church, one law."

As religious wars engulfed Europe, intellectuals perceived the wisdom of religious pluralism and toleration. Skepticism, relativism, and individualism in religion increasingly came to be seen as virtues. Valentin Weigel (1533–1588), a Lutheran who surveyed a half-century of religious strife in Germany, spoke for many when he advised people to look within themselves for religious truth and not to churches and creeds.

Politicians were slower than intellectuals to embrace principles of toleration. The rulers who succeeded best at holding religious strife and civil war in check were those who did so—the *politiques*, pragmatic monarchs such as Elizabeth I of England who urged moderation and compromise in religious matters. Governments led by people who took religion with utmost seriousness (e.g., Mary I of England, Philip II of Spain, and England's Oliver Cromwell) failed to maintain stability.

The French Wars of Religion (1562–1598)

Anti-Protestant Measures and the Struggle for Political Power

In the 1520s Lutheran ideas began to circulate in Paris and to excite the suspicions of the French government. French Protestants were dubbed "Huguenots"—after Besançon Hugues, the leader of the revolt that won Geneva its freedom at that time.

In 1525, when Emperor Charles V captured King Francis I of France at the Battle of Pavia, the French authorities began actively to prosecute Protestants. They hoped that by cooperating with Charles's anti-Protestant campaign they might win favorable terms for the king's release. A second crackdown followed a decade later. It was a response to a major Protestant publicity campaign that (on October 18, 1534) plastered Paris and other cities with anti-Catholic placards. The government's reaction convinced some that the monarchy was committing itself to exterminating Protestantism, and John Calvin and other members of the French reform decided to leave France.

Hostilities between the French and the empire (the Habsburg-Valois wars) ended with the Treaty of Cateau-Cambrésis in 1559. The treaty marked a shift in the European balance of power from France to Spain, and it was a prelude to an outbreak of civil conflict within France. Both these developments began with an accident. In 1559 the French king, Henry II, was mortally wounded in a tournament, and his sickly fifteen-year-old son, Francis II, ascended the throne. The queen mother, Catherine de Médicis, governed France as the boy-king's regent. The weakness of her administration tempted three powerful families to struggle for leadership of France: the Bourbons, whose power lay in the south and west; the Montmorency-Chatillons, who controlled the center of France; and the Guises, whose lands were in the east.

The Guises were initially the strongest, and they dominated the young king. Francis, duke of Guise, had commanded Henry II's army, and his brothers, Charles and Louis, were cardinals of the church. They arranged for their niece, Mary Stuart, Queen of Scotland, to marry Francis II. Since the Guise family championed a militant, reactionary Catholicism, France's Protestants rallied behind its opponents—the Bourbon prince of Condé,

Warring Architectural Styles: Baroque vs. Plain Churches

Interior of "Asamkirche," *Asam Cosmas Damian (1686–1739). Saint Nepomit Church in Munich designed by the brothers Cosmas Damian and Egid Quirin Asam in 1733. The church stands next to the house the brothers built for themselves. Asamkirche (St. Johann-Nepomuk).* Erich Lessing/Art Resource, NY

Art and architecture reflect religious beliefs as clearly as creeds and laws. Congregations that embraced the Reformed Protestant doctrines of Calvin and Zwingli and the various nonconformist sects (e.g., Anabaptists and Quakers) believed that traditional ecclesiastical art and music—which Lutherans as well as Catholics endorsed—distracted worshipers from the Word of God. Finding no biblical support for the use of ornament in worship, these groups stripped their sanctuaries bare and confined music to the chanting of psalms. In Catholic districts the Counter-Reformation encouraged the opposite tendency, that is, reliance on an exuberant baroque style of art and architecture that was meant to be emotionally overwhelming. It strove to appeal to worshipers' senses and fill them with awe and wonder at the power of faith. In the hands of the Jesuits, baroque art was an effective tool for strengthening the Catholic community and reclaiming people who had been lost to Protestantism. Both the plain and baroque traditions inspired great artists. The painter Peter Paul Rubens (1571–1640) and the sculptor Gianlorenzo Bernini (1598–1680) were Catholics, but Protestantism could boast artists of equal stature: for example, the architect Christopher Wren (1632– 1723) and the painter Rembrandt van Rijn (1606–1669).

Temple de Lyon. Bibliotheque Publique et Universitaire, Geneve

The interiors of the churches from Munich and Lyon, which are depicted here, dramatically illustrate the contrast between the baroque and Protestant Reform styles. The former dazzles, explodes with energy, and urges worshipers to emotional flights of self-transcendence. The latter removes all distraction, creates an atmosphere conducive to quiet introspection, and assists worshipers in reflecting on God's Word and their individual spiritual lives.

Louis I (d. 1569), and the Montmorency-Chatillons admiral, Gaspard de Coligny (1519–1572).

Appeal of Calvinism

Ambitious aristocrats and discontented towns-people had different reasons for joining Calvinist churches in opposing the Guise-dominated French monarchy. Although there were more than 2,000 Huguenot congregations in France by 1561, Huguenots were a majority of the population in only two regions: Dauphiné and Languedoc. Huguenots made up only about one-fifteenth of France's population, but they controlled important districts and were heavily represented among the more powerful segments of French society. Over two-fifths of the country's aristocracy became Huguenots. Many probably saw Protestantism as a way to strengthen their authority over their domains. They hoped to establish within France a principle of territorial sovereignty akin to that endorsed for the Holy Roman Empire by the Peace of Augsburg.

The military organization of Condé and Coligny progressively merged with the Huguenot churches. Each side had much to gain from the other. Calvinism provided both a theological justification and a practical motive for political resistance to the Catholic monarchy. Armed strength was essential if Calvinism hoped to become a viable religion in France, but the confluence of secular and religious motives cast suspicion on the sincerity of some Calvinist leaders. Religious conviction was neither the only nor always the main reason for their conversion to Protestantism.

Catherine de Médicis and the Guises

Francis II died in 1560, but his mother, Catherine de Médicis, continued to rule France as regent for her second son, Charles IX (r. 1560–1574). Catherine's first concern was always to preserve the monarchy. Hoping to balance the power of the Guises, she sought allies among the Protestants. In 1562, after conversations with Coligny and Theodore Beza, Calvin's successor, she issued the January Edict. This granted Protestants freedom to hold public worship services outside towns—but only private meetings within them. Royal efforts to promote toleration ended abruptly in March 1562, when the duke of Guise massacred a Protestant congregation at Vassy and began a war with the Huguenots.

Had Condé and the Huguenot armies rushed immediately to the queen's side after this attack, they might have secured an alliance with Catherine, who feared the powerful Guises. But the Protestant leaders hesitated, and the Guises won control of the young king and his mother.

THE PEACE OF SAINT-GERMAIN-EN-LAYE During the first French war of religion (April 1562 to March 1563), the duke of Guise was assassinated. A brief resumption of hostilities from 1567 to 1568 was followed from September 1568 to August 1570 by the bloodiest phase in the conflict. Condé was killed, and Huguenot leadership passed to Coligny, who was far the better military strategist. He negotiated the Peace of Saint-Germain-en-Laye in 1570, which won Huguenots religious freedoms within their territories and the right to fortify their cities.

Queen Catherine tried to survive by balancing the fanatical Huguenot and Guise extremes. Like the Guises, she preferred a Catholic France and tolerated Protestants only as a counter to Guise domination of the monarchy. But after the Peace of Saint-Germain-en-Laye strengthened the Huguenots, Catherine switched sides. She began to plot with the Guises to prevent the Protestants from winning over her son. Catherine had reason to fear Coligny. He was on the verge of persuading the young king to invade the Netherlands to help the Dutch Protestants against their Catholic Habsburg ruler. Such a move would have set France on a collision course with Spain, and Catherine knew that France stood little chance in such a contest.

THE SAINT BARTHOLOMEW'S DAY MASSACRE On August 18, 1572, the French nobility gathered in Paris for the wedding of the king's sister, Marguerite of Valois, to Henry of Navarre, a Huguenot leader. Four days later an attempt was made on Coligny's life. Catherine had apparently been party to a plot by the Guises to eliminate Coligny, and when it failed, she panicked. She feared both the king's reaction to her complicity with the Guises and what the Huguenots and Coligny might do in seeking revenge. In desperation she convinced Charles that a Huguenot coup was afoot and that only the swift execution of the Protestant leaders could save the crown.

On Saint Bartholomew's Day, August 24, 1572, Coligny and 3,000 fellow Huguenots were ambushed in Paris and butchered. Within three

The massacre of worshiping Protestants at Vassy, France (March 1, 1562), which began the French wars of religion. An engraving by an unidentified seventeenth-century artist. The Granger Collection

days an estimated 20,000 Huguenots were executed in coordinated attacks throughout France. Protestants across Europe were horrified, while Pope Gregory XIII and Philip II of Spain greeted the news of the Protestant deaths with special religious celebrations.

Catholics came to regret the slaughter of the French Protestants, for Saint Bartholomew's Day changed the nature of the struggle between Protestants and Catholics everywhere. The disastrous outcome of France's internal squabbling over political power and religious freedom convinced Protestants in many lands that they were engaged in an international war for survival—a fight to the death with an adversary whose cruelty justified any means of resistance.

PROTESTANT RESISTANCE THEORY At the start of the Reformation, Protestants tried to honor the biblical mandate (in Romans 13:1) that directed subjects to obey the rulers God placed over them. Luther only grudgingly approved resistance to Charles V after the emperor ordered Protestants to return to Catholicism in 1530. Calvin, secure in his control of Geneva, had always condemned willful disobedience and rebellion against lawfully constituted governments. But he also taught that lower magistrates, as part of legally constituted governments, had the duty to oppose higher authorities if these became tyrannical.

An early Calvinist rationale for revolution was developed by John Knox, a Scot driven into exile by the Catholic regent for Scotland, Mary of Guise. Knox's *First Blast of the Trumpet Against the Terrible Regiment of Women* (1558) declared that the removal of a heathen (i.e., Catholic) tyrant was not only permissible but a Christian duty. The Saint Bartholomew's Day massacre persuaded other Calvinists to adopt a similar point of view. François Hotman's *Franco-Gallia* (1573) argued that France's representative assembly, the Estates General, was an authority superior to the crown. Theodore Beza's *On the Right of Magistrates over Their Subjects* (1574) justified the overthrow of tyrants by lower authorities. And Philippe du Plessis Mornay's *Defense of Liberty Against Tyrants* (1579) urged princes, nobles, and magistrates to cooperate in rooting out tyranny in any land where it appeared.

The Rise to Power of Henry of Navarre

Henry III (r. 1574–1589), the last of Henry II's sons to wear the French crown, was caught between the vengeful Huguenots and the radical Catholic League formed in 1576 by Henry of Guise. Like his mother Catherine, Henry sought a middle course and appealed to the neutral Catholics and Huguenots who put the political survival of France above its religious unity. In May 1576, Henry, in the Peace of Beaulieu, promised the Huguenots almost complete religious and civil freedom. The move was premature, for the Catholic League was able to force Henry to reverse himself. In October 1577, the Edict of Poitiers again restricted Huguenots to limited areas.

By the mid-1580s the Catholic League, with Spanish help, was supreme in Paris. In 1588 Henry III launched a surprise attack (known as the "Day of the Barricades") to rout the league. The coup failed, and the king had to flee. News of the English victory over the Spanish Armada then emboldened him to order the assassinations of both the duke and the cardinal of Guise. These murders enraged the Catholic League, which was led by another Guise brother, Charles, duke of Mayenne. By April 1589, the king was left with no choice but to seek an alliance with the Protestant leader, Henry of Navarre, the Bourbon heir to his throne.

As the two Henrys prepared to attack the Guise stronghold in Paris, a fanatical Jacobin friar assassinated Henry III and cleared the way for Henry of Navarre to become King Henry IV (r. 1589–1610) of France. Pope Sixtus V and King Philip II of Spain were aghast at the prospect of France suddenly becoming a Protestant nation. Philip dispatched troops to support the Catholic League and to claim the throne of France for his daughter, Isabella, Henry II's granddaughter.

The threat of Spanish intervention in their affairs rallied the people of France to Henry IV's side and strengthened his hold on the crown. Henry was a popular man who had the wit and charm to neutralize any enemy in a face-to-face meeting. He was also a *politique*, a leader who considered religion less important than peace. Henry concluded that since most of his subjects were Catholics, he could best rule as a Catholic who was committed to protecting Protestants. Consequently, on July 25, 1593, he embraced Catholicism—reputedly claiming that "Paris is worth a Mass." The Huguenots were horrified, and Pope Clement VIII remained skeptical. But the majority of the French people, both clergy and laity, were relieved. They had had enough of war.

The Edict of Nantes

On April 13, 1598, Henry issued the Edict of Nantes to end the civil wars of religion, and on May 2, 1598, the Treaty of Vervins made peace between France and Spain. The Edict of Nantes confirmed a promise of toleration that Henry IV had made the Huguenots at the start of his reign. By granting some religious rights to a dissenting Protestant minority within what was to remain an officially Catholic country, Nantes came close to creating a state within a state. It designated certain towns and territories as places where Huguenots, who by this time numbered well over a million, could openly conduct worship, hold public offices, enter universities, and maintain forts. Nantes was a truce more than a peace. It turned a hot war into a cold one—a war that eventually claimed Henry IV as a victim. In May 1610, he was assassinated by a Catholic fanatic.

Imperial Spain and the Reign of Philip II (r. 1556–1598)

Pillars of Spanish Power

Philip II of Spain dominated international politics for much of the latter half of the sixteenth century.

Bitter experience had led his father, Charles V, to conclude that the Habsburg family lands were too extensive to be governed by one man. He, therefore, divided them between his son and his brother. Philip inherited the intensely Catholic and militarily supreme western half. The eastern portion (Austria, Bohemia, and Hungary) went to Philip's uncle, Emperor Ferdinand I. The imperial title, thereafter, remained with the Austrian Habsburgs.

Philip was a reclusive man who preferred to rule as the remote executive manager of a great national bureaucracy. His character is reflected in the unique residence he built outside Madrid, the Escorial. A combination palace, church, tomb, and monastery, it was a home for a monkish king. Philip was a learned and pious Catholic, a regal ascetic with a powerful sense of duty to his office. He may even have arranged the death of his son Don Carlos (1568), when he concluded that the prince was too mad and treacherous to be entrusted with the power of the crown.

NEW WORLD RICHES   Philip's home base was Spain's populous and prosperous district of Castile. The wealth of the New World that flowed through the port of Seville gave Philip great sums with which to fight wars and underwrite international intrigues. Despite this flood of bullion, Philip's expenses exceeded his income. Near the end of his life he destroyed one of Europe's great banks, the house founded by the Fuggers of Augsburg, by defaulting on his loans.

The American wealth that entered Europe through Spain had a dramatic impact on society. Increased prosperity led to increased population. By the early seventeenth century, the towns of France, England, and the Netherlands had tripled and quadrupled in size, and Europe's population had reached about 100 million. Growth in wealth and numbers of consumers triggered inflation—a steady 2 percent a year rise in prices. More people with more currency to spend meant more competition for food and jobs, and that caused prices to double and triple while wages stagnated. This was especially the case in Spain, where the new wealth was concentrated in the hands of a few. Nowhere did the underprivileged suffer more than in Spain. The Castilian peasants, the backbone of Philip II's great empire, were the most heavily taxed people in Europe.

SUPREMACY IN THE MEDITERRANEAN   At the start of Philip's reign, his attention focused al-

Titian's portrait of Philip II of Spain (r. 1556–1598), the most powerful ruler of his time. Alinari/Art Resource, NY

naval battle of the sixteenth century and a clear victory for the Christians. Thirty thousand Turks died and over one-third of the Turkish fleet was sunk or captured. The Mediterranean, for the moment, belonged to Spain.

In 1580 Philip confirmed his dominance of the south by annexing Portugal. This augmented Spanish sea power and brought the magnificent Portuguese overseas empire in Africa, India, and the Americas into the Spanish orbit.

The Revolt in the Netherlands

Philip was far less successful in northern Europe than he was in the Mediterranean, and a rebellion in the Netherlands, the richest district in Europe, set in motion a chain of events that ended Spain's dreams of world empire. The Netherlands was governed for Philip by his half-sister, Margaret of Parma. She was assisted by a council headed by Cardinal Granvelle (1517–1586). Granvelle hoped to check the advance of Protestantism in the Netherlands by promoting church reform. He also planned to reduce the autonomy of the seventeen Netherlands provinces and to create a centralized royal government directed from Madrid. The merchant towns of the Netherlands were, however, accustomed to their independence, and many, such as magnificent Antwerp, had become Calvinist strongholds. Two members of the royal council opposed their Spanish overlords: the Count of Egmont (1522–1568) and William of Nassau, the Prince of Orange (1533–1584), surnamed "the Silent" because of his small circle of confidants.

William of Orange was a *politique* who placed the political autonomy and well-being of the Netherlands above religious creeds. In 1561 he married Anne of Saxony, the daughter of the Lutheran Elector Maurice and the granddaughter of the late Landgrave Philip of Hesse, but he remained a Catholic until his conversion to Lutheranism in 1567. After the Saint Bartholomew's Day massacre in 1572, Orange became a Calvinist.

In 1561 Cardinal Granvelle began an ecclesiastical reorganization of the Netherlands that was intended to tighten the Catholic hierarchy's control over the country and to accelerate its assimilation as a Spanish dependency. Orange and Egmont, with the support of the Dutch nobility, succeeded in engineering Granvelle's removal from office in 1564. But when the aristocrats who took Granvelle's place proved inept at running the government, popular unrest mounted.

most exclusively on a struggle with the Turks in the Mediterranean. During the 1560s, the Turks had advanced deep into Austria, and their fleets had spread out across the Mediterranean. Between 1568 and 1570, armies under Philip's half-brother, Don John of Austria, the illegitimate son of Charles V, suppressed and dispersed the Moors in Granada. In May 1571, Spain, Venice, and the pope formed the Holy League—again under Don John's command—to counter Turkish maneuvers in the Mediterranean. On October 7, 1571, Don John's fleet engaged the Ottoman navy under Ali Pasha off Lepanto in the Gulf of Corinth. The result was the largest

In 1564 Philip unwisely insisted that the decrees of the Council of Trent be enforced throughout the Netherlands. Opposition materialized under the leadership of William of Orange's younger brother, Louis of Nassau, who had been raised a Lutheran. The Calvinist-inclined lesser nobility and townspeople joined him in a national covenant, the *Compromise,* a solemn pledge to oppose Trent and the Inquisition. In 1566, when Margaret's government spurned the protesters as "beggars," Calvinists rioted, and Louis called for help from French Huguenots and German Lutherans. A full-scale rebellion against the Spanish regency seemed about to erupt.

THE DUKE OF ALBA   A revolt failed to materialize, for the Netherlands' higher nobility were repelled by the behavior of Calvinist extremists and unwilling to join their rebellion. Philip dispatched the duke of Alba to restore order and make an example of the would-be revolutionaries. In 1567 an army of 10,000 was transferred from Milan, and responsibility for the Netherlands was delegated to a special tribunal, the Council of Troubles (as Spain called it) or the Council of Blood (as it was known in the Netherlands). The new government inaugurated a reign of terror. It executed the counts of Egmont and Horn and several thousand suspected heretics, and it imposed high taxes to force the Netherlanders to pay the costs for the suppression of their revolt. Persecution and taxation drove tens of thousands of refugees from the Netherlands during Alba's cruel six-year rule, and the duke came to be more hated than Granvelle or the radical Calvinists.

RESISTANCE AND UNIFICATION   William of Orange, who was an exile in Germany during these turbulent years, now emerged as the leader of an independence movement in the Netherlands. The northern, Calvinist-inclined provinces of Holland, Zeeland, and Utrecht, of which Orange was the *stadholder* (i.e., governor), became his base. Here, as elsewhere, a fight for political independence was combined with a struggle for religious liberty.

The uprising in the Netherlands was a true popular revolt that enlisted all kinds of people. William even endorsed the raids of the "Sea Beggars," an international group of anti-Spanish exiles and criminals who were brazen pirates. In 1572 the Beggars captured Brill and other seaports in Zeeland and Holland. They incited the native popula-

tion to join the rebellion, and resistance spread steadily southward. In 1574 the people of Leiden heroically withstood a long Spanish siege, and the Dutch opened the dikes and flooded their country to repulse the hated Spanish. The faltering Alba had by that time ceded power to Don Luis de Requesens, who replaced him as commander of Spanish forces in the Netherlands in November 1573.

The greatest atrocity of the war followed Requesens's death in 1576. Leaderless and unpaid Spanish mercenaries ran amok in Antwerp on November 4, 1576. Seven thousand people lay dead in the streets as a result of what came to be called "the Spanish Fury." This brief event did more to unify the Netherlanders than all previous appeals to religion and patriotism. The ten largely Catholic southern provinces (approximating modern Belgium) joined the seven largely Protestant northern provinces (roughly the modern Netherlands) in opposing Spain.

The Pacification of Ghent declared the unification of the Netherlands on November 8, 1576. The Netherlanders resolved religious differences by agreeing to a territorial settlement such as the one that the Peace of Augsburg had defined for the Holy Roman Empire in 1555. In January 1577, the last four provinces joined the all-embracing Union of Brussels, and for the next two years the Spanish faced a unified and determined Netherlands.

In November 1576, Don John, the victor over the Turks at Lepanto, took command of Spain's land forces and promptly suffered his first defeat. In February 1577, he signed the Perpetual Edict, a humiliating treaty that promised the removal of all Spanish troops from the Netherlands within twenty days.

The Spanish were, however, nothing if not persistent. The nobility's fear of Calvinist extremism caused a breakup of the Union of Brussels, and Don John and Alessandro Farnese of Parma, the regent Margaret's son, reestablished Spanish control in the southern provinces. In January 1579, the southern provinces formed the Union of Arras and made peace with Spain. The northern provinces responded by organizing the Union of Utrecht.

NETHERLANDS' INDEPENDENCE   Seizing the opportunity to break the back of the Netherlands' resistance, Philip II declared William of Orange an outlaw and placed a bounty of 25,000 crowns on his head. This stiffened the resistance of the northern provinces, and in a famous speech to the Estates General of Holland in December 1580 (the *Apology*),

Orange denounced Philip as a heathen tyrant whom the Netherlands need no longer obey.

On July 22, 1581, most of the northern provinces belonging to the Union of Utrecht formally repudiated Philip's authority and pledged themselves to the French duke of Alençon, Catherine de Médicis's youngest son. Alençon was seen as a compromise between the extremes of Spanish Catholicism and Calvinism, and he was expected to aspire to nothing more than titular authority over the provinces. When he rashly attempted to impose his will on them in 1583, he was deposed and sent back to France.

When William of Orange was assassinated in July 1584, his son, Maurice (1567–1625), became leader of the Dutch resistance. Fortunately for him and his cause, Philip II overextended himself by meddling in the affairs of France and England. Spain's power waned after England defeated Philip's great Armada in 1588. By 1593 the northern provinces had driven out all Spanish soldiers, and in 1596 France and England formally recognized the independence of these provinces. Peace with Spain was concluded in 1609, and full international recognition came in the Peace of Westphalia in 1648.

England and Spain (1553–1603)

Mary I

In an effort to protect England's Reformation, Edward VI (d. 1553) sought to disinherit his Catholic half-sister, Mary Tudor (r. 1553–1558). As heir to his throne he named, not his sister, but his cousin—Lady Jane Grey, a grandniece of Henry VIII's. The people of England felt, however, that Mary was clearly the rightful heir, and they rose up to support her. Jane Grey lost both the crown and her head.

As queen, Mary exceeded the worst fears of the Protestants. Her Parliaments repealed Edward's Protestant statutes and reverted to the strict Catholic religious practice of her father, Henry VIII. She executed as heretics the great Protestant leaders who had served her brother: John Hooper, Hugh Latimer, and Thomas Cranmer. The names of 282 Protestants whom she burned at the stake are recorded. Many others avoided martyrdom by fleeing to the continent. These "Marian exiles" settled in Germany and Switzerland, where they established communities of worship, wrote tracts justifying armed resistance, and waited for the

time when a Protestant counteroffensive could be launched in their homelands. Many absorbed religious beliefs that were much more radical than those they had brought from England.

In 1554 Mary chose a highly unpopular husband, Prince Philip (later King Philip II) of Spain. She favored him because he was the leader of the militant Catholicism that Mary hoped to establish in England, but many of Mary's subjects feared that the marriage would lead to Spain's dominance of England. The politically troublesome marriage was childless, and Mary died knowing that her half-sister, Elizabeth, the daughter of her father's first Protestant marriage, would follow her to the throne.

Elizabeth I

Elizabeth I (r. 1558–1603), the daughter of Henry VIII and Anne Boleyn, was perhaps the most astute politician of the sixteenth century. Assisted by a shrewd adviser, Sir William Cecil (1520–1598), she built a true kingdom on the ruins of Mary's reign. Between 1559 and 1563, she and Cecil guided a religious settlement through Parliament. It merged a centralized episcopal system, which the queen controlled, with broadly defined Protestant doctrine and traditional Catholic ritual. The resulting Anglican church avoided inflexible religious extremes and spared England the religious conflicts that were bloodying continental nations.

CATHOLIC AND PROTESTANT EXTREMISTS Religious compromises were unacceptable to zealots of both persuasions, and subversive groups worked to undermine Elizabeth. When she ascended the throne, most of her subjects were Catholics. The extremists among them, encouraged by the Jesuits, plotted to replace her with Mary Stuart, Queen of Scots. Unlike Elizabeth, whose father had declared her illegitimate, Mary Stuart had an unblemished claim to the throne inherited from her grandmother Margaret, sister of Henry VIII. Elizabeth responded swiftly to Catholic assassination plots but rarely let emotion override her political instincts. Despite proven cases of Catholic treason and even attempted regicide, she executed fewer Catholics during her forty-five years on the throne than Mary Tudor had executed Protestants during her brief five-year reign.

Elizabeth dealt cautiously with the extreme Protestants—the "Puritans" who wanted to "purify" the national church of every vestige of

Elizabeth I (r. 1558–1603) standing on a map of England in 1592. An astute politician in both foreign and domestic policy, Elizabeth was perhaps the most successful ruler of the sixteenth century.   National Portrait Gallery, London

"popery." The Puritans had two major grievances: (1) the retention of Catholic ceremony and vestments within the Church of England, which made it appear to the casual observer that no Reformation had occurred, and (2) the continuation of the episcopal system of governance, which enabled the queen to take the pope's place in dominating the church.

The more extreme Puritans, the Congregationalists, wanted every congregation to be autonomous, a law unto itself, with neither higher episcopal nor presbyterian control. But most sixteenth-century Puritans were not separatists. They campaigned in Parliament for an alternative national church of semiautonomous congregations governed by representative presbyteries (hence, their name "Presbyterians"). Their model was the system Calvin had established in Geneva. Elizabeth conceded nothing that lessened the hierarchical unity of the Church of England and her control over it. The Conventicle Act of 1593 gave separatists

the option of either conforming to the practices of the Church of England or facing exile or death.

DETERIORATION OF RELATIONS WITH SPAIN   Despite the sincerest desires on the part of both Philip II and Elizabeth to avoid a direct confrontation, events led inexorably to war between England and Spain. In 1567, when the Spanish duke of Alba marched his army into the Netherlands, many in England feared that Spain intended to use the Netherlands as a base for an invasion of England. In 1570 Pope Pius V (1566–1572) branded Elizabeth a heretic and proposed a military expedition to recover England for Catholicism. His mischievous act only complicated a difficult situation.

Following Don John's demonstration of Spain's awesome sea power at the battle of Lepanto in 1571, England signed a mutual defense pact with France. Throughout the 1570s, Elizabeth's famous seamen, John Hawkins (1532–1595) and Sir Francis Drake (1545?–1596), preyed on Spanish shipping in the Americas. Drake's circumnavigation of the globe between 1577 and 1580 was one in a series of dramatic demonstrations of England's growing ascendancy on the high seas.

The Saint Bartholomew's Day Massacre forced a change in Elizabeth's foreign policy. Protestants in France and the Netherlands appealed to her as their only protector. In 1585 she signed the Treaty of Nonsuch, which sent English soldiers to the Netherlands. Funds she had previously funneled covertly to Henry of Navarre's army in France now flowed openly. These developments strained relations between England and Spain, but the event that brought on war was Elizabeth's decision to execute Mary, Queen of Scots (1542–1587).

MARY, QUEEN OF SCOTS   Mary Stuart, the daughter of King James V of Scotland and Mary of Guise, had resided in France from the time she was six years old—training for her role as the future wife of King Francis II. The death of her young husband in 1561 sent Mary back to Scotland to rule a land she barely knew. A year earlier, a fervent Protestant Reformation had won legal recognition in the Treaty of Edinburgh. Mary, who had been raised a Catholic in France, had no sympathy with Scotland's new religion or with its dour morality. She wanted to replicate in Scotland the gaiety and sophistication of French court life.

John Knox, the leader of the Scottish Reformation, railed openly about the queen's private Mass and Catholic practices (which Scottish law made capital offenses for everyone else). Although Queen Elizabeth personally despised Knox, she recognized that his defense of Protestantism served her foreign policy. It limited Mary's ability to persuade the Scots to cooperate with France against England.

In 1568 a scandal cost Mary her throne. Mary had married Lord Darnley, a youth with connections to the royal houses of both England and Scotland. She had a son by him (the James who was eventually to inherit both Scotland and England), but Darnley proved an impossible husband. Mary reputedly took the earl of Bothwell as her lover, and he, allegedly, murdered Darnley. Acquitted of this crime, Bothwell abducted Mary and married her. This amounted to usurpation of the throne. Outraged Protestant nobles forced Mary to abdicate in favor of her infant son and to flee Scotland.

Mary unwisely entered England seeking refuge from her cousin Elizabeth. Elizabeth distrusted Mary, for in the opinion of Catholics, Mary had the superior claim to the English throne. Elizabeth, therefore, held Mary under house arrest—for nineteen years. In 1583 Elizabeth's vigilant secretary, Sir Francis Walsingham, uncovered a plot against Elizabeth involving the Spanish ambassador Bernardino de Mendoza. In 1586 Walsingham exposed still another Spanish scheme to unseat Elizabeth, and this time he had proof of Mary's involvement. Elizabeth was loath to execute Mary. She feared that such an act would diminish the aura of divine right that was one of the props of monarchy, and she knew that it would raise a storm of protest among Catholics. In the end, however, she concluded that she had no choice, and Mary was beheaded on February 18, 1587. Mary's death dashed Catholic hopes for a bloodless reconversion of England and persuaded Philip II that the time had come for a military assault on the Protestant nation.

THE ARMADA   Spain's preparations for war were interrupted in the spring of 1587 by the successful raids Sir Francis Drake led on the port city of Cadiz and the coast of Portugal. These strikes forced Philip to postpone his invasion of England until the spring of 1588.

On May 30, 1588, the ill-fated armada of 130 ships, bearing 25,000 sailors and soldiers under the command of the duke of Medina-Sidonia, set to sea. The barges that were to transport Spanish soldiers from their galleons onto England's shores were prevented from leaving Calais and Dunkirk to rendezvous with the fleet. While the Spanish vessels waited, an "English wind" sprang up and helped the swifter English and Dutch ships scatter the Spanish forces.

Spain never fully recovered from this defeat, and by the time of Philip's death on September 13, 1598, its armies had suffered reversals on all fronts. Philip's successors, Philip III (r. 1598–1621), Philip IV (r. 1621–1665), and Charles II (r. 1665–1700), were all inadequate men. They allowed the French to emerge as the leading continental power and the Dutch and English to nibble away at Spain's empire.

When Elizabeth died on March 23, 1603, she left behind a strong nation poised on the brink of acquiring a global empire. Since Elizabeth had never married (choosing instead to use the hope of winning her hand as a tool for English diplomacy), her death ended the Tudor dynasty. Ironically, her heir, James I of England, was Mary's son, James VI of Scotland.

The Thirty Years' War (1618–1648)

The Thirty Years' War in the Holy Roman Empire was the last and most destructive of the wars of religion, and it was unusually devastating. Religious passions escalated to the point where the combatants seemed willing to sacrifice everything in pursuit of victories that were increasingly less worth winning. Virtually every major European land was drawn into the conflict. When the hostilities ended in 1648, the agreements among the victorious nations shaped the map of northern Europe as we know it today.

Preconditions for War

FRAGMENTED GERMANY   In the second half of the sixteenth century, Germany was a collection of about 360 autonomous political entities: secular principalities (duchies, landgraviates, and marches), ecclesiastical principalities (archbishoprics, bishoprics, and abbeys), free cities, and regions dominated by knights with castles. The Peace of Augsburg (1555) had given each a degree of sovereignty within its borders. Since each levied its own tolls and tariffs and coined its own money, travel and trade were difficult. Many little states also had pretensions that exceeded their powers.

During the Thirty Years' War, Germany, which was Europe's crossroads, became Europe's stomping ground. The great conflict had many causes. Most stemmed from a fear of German unification. The Council of Trent raised Protestant suspicions about an imperial-papal conspiracy to use the Holy Roman Empire to restore Catholic dominance throughout Europe. The imperial diet, which was controlled by the German magnates, was leery of any attempt to consolidate the empire at the expense of the liberties of the territorial princes. It countered every move by the emperor to impose his will in the empire, and individual German rulers called on allies outside of Germany for help in defending their rights. Allies were eager to help, for even the Catholic nations of Europe feared what might happen to the balance of power if Germany was brought under the control of a Catholic emperor.

Religious Division By 1600, there may have been slightly more Protestants than Catholics in the Holy Roman Empire. The territorial principle proclaimed by the Peace of Augsburg in 1555 was designed to freeze Lutherans and Catholics in place by forcing each territory to declare its faith. But as time passed, there were troublesome shifts of jurisdiction. Lutherans gained control in some Catholic areas and Catholics in a few places designated as Lutheran. Lutherans were more successful in securing rights to worship in Catholic lands than Catholics were in securing such rights from Lutherans. Catholic rulers who had been weakened by the Reformation had no choice but to make concessions to Protestant communities within their territories, and these Protestant enclaves became constant sources of tension. Protestants were also reluctant to enforce the "Ecclesiastical Reservation" provision of the Peace of Augsburg, which called for the restoration to Catholic control of ecclesiastical property in places where rulers converted to Protestantism.

Protestant and Catholic antipathies were not the only sources of religious strife. Warring factions emerged among Protestants in the second half of the sixteenth century. Liberal and conservative branches of Lutheranism opposed each other, and Calvinists failed to come to terms with either of these.

Calvinism had not been recognized as a legal religion by the Peace of Augsburg, but it won a foothold in the empire when Frederick III (r. 1559–1576), Elector Palatine (ruler within the Palatinate), made it the official religion of his domain. His royal city of Heidelberg became the German "Geneva," an intellectual center for Calvinism and a staging area for Calvinist penetration of the empire. The Lutherans came to fear the Calvinists almost as much as they did the Catholics, for the bold missionary forays of the Palatine Calvinists threatened

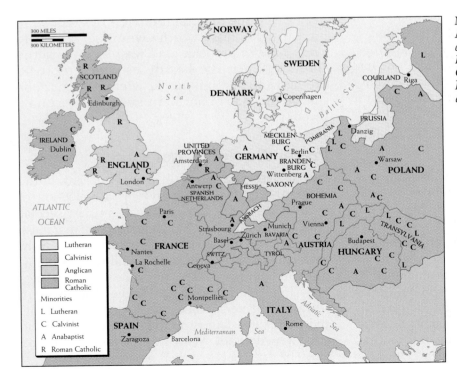

MAP 12–1 RELIGIOUS DIVISIONS ABOUT 1600 *By 1600, with the exception of Spain and southern Italy, which remained thoroughly Catholic, large religious minorities had rooted themselves in almost every European state.*

to undo what the Peace of Augsburg had done to stabilize the empire. Some Lutherans were also shocked by outspoken Calvinist criticism of their doctrines (e.g., Lutheran faith in Christ's real presence in the Eucharist).

Like the Calvinists, the Jesuits also undermined the Peace of Augsburg. Catholic Bavaria, led by Duke Maximilian and supported by Spain, did for the Counter-Reformation what the Palatinate did for Calvinism. Jesuit missionaries, operating from Bavaria, returned major cities (e.g., Strasbourg and Osnabrück) to the Catholic fold. In 1609 Maximilian organized a Catholic League to counter a Protestant alliance formed in the same year by the Calvinist Elector Palatine, Frederick IV (r. 1583–1610). The army the league assembled under the command of Count Johann von Tilly tipped Germany into war.

Four Periods of War

THE BOHEMIAN PERIOD (1618–1625) The war broke out in Bohemia after the ascent to the Bohemian throne in 1618 of Ferdinand, Habsburg archduke of Styria and heir to the empire. Ferdinand, who had been educated by Jesuits, was determined to restore Catholicism to the Habsburg lands. No sooner had he become king of Bohemia than he revoked the religious freedoms of Bohemia's Protestants. The Protestant nobility responded in May 1618 by literally throwing his regents out a window—an event known as the "defenestration of Prague." A year later, when Ferdinand (II) became Holy Roman Emperor, the Bohemians refused to recognize his jurisdiction and declared their allegiance to the Calvinist Elector Palatine, Frederick V (r. 1616–1623).

The Bohemian revolt escalated into an international war. Spain, Maximilian of Bavaria, and the Lutheran Elector John George I of Saxony (r. 1611–1656)—who saw a chance to expand his domains at the expense of the Calvinist Elector Palatine—sided with Ferdinand. Tilly, the empire's general, routed Frederick V's troops at the Battle of White Mountain in 1620, and by 1622 Ferdinand had subdued Bohemia and conquered the Palatinate. As the remnants of Frederick's army retreated north, Duke Maximilian of Bavaria followed—claiming land as he went.

THE DANISH PERIOD (1625–1629) Maximilian's forays into northwestern Germany raised fears of a Catholic consolidation of the empire. Christian IV (r. 1588–1648), the Lutheran king of Denmark and duke of the German duchy of Holstein, was urged by the English, French, and Dutch to undertake the defense of Protestantism. He invaded Germany in 1626 but was quickly forced to retreat by Duke Maximilian.

Fearing Maximilian's growing power, Emperor Ferdinand turned the conduct of the war over to a mercenary whom he had employed against the Bohemians, Albrecht of Wallenstein (1583–1634). A brilliant and ruthless military strategist, Wallenstein became a law unto himself, but he so effectively broke the back of Protestant resistance that Ferdinand was able to issue an Edict of Restitution in 1629. It outlawed Calvinism and ordered

The horror of the Thirty Years' War is captured in this painting by Jan Brueghel (1568–1625) and Sebastien Vranx (1573–1647). During the breaks in fighting, marauding armies ravaged the countryside, destroying villages and massacring the rural population. Kunsthistorisches Museum, Vienna

MAP 12–2 THE HOLY ROMAN EMPIRE ABOUT 1618 *On the eve of the Thirty Years' War, the empire was thoroughly fragmented. Lutherans dominated the north, Catholics the south, and Calvinists controlled the United Provinces, the Palatinate, Brandenburg, and parts of Switzerland.*

the surrender to Catholics of all church lands acquired by the Lutherans since 1552. Compliance would have meant Protestant concession of sixteen bishoprics and twenty-eight cities and towns to Catholic governors. The edict struck panic in the hearts of the Habsburgs' opponents and reignited resistance.

THE SWEDISH PERIOD (1630–1635) Gustavus Adolphus of Sweden (r. 1611–1632), a deeply pious Lutheran monarch and a military genius, took up the gauntlet for Protestantism. He was handsomely bankrolled by two very interested bystanders: Cardinal Richelieu, the minister of the Catholic king of France who wanted to prevent a powerful Habsburg empire from materializing on France's border; and the Dutch—long-standing Protestant opponents of the Habsburgs. The Swedish king won a stunning victory at Breitenfeld in 1630 that suddenly reversed the course of the war. The battle was significant, but far from final—and the Protestant cause faltered when Gustavus Adolphus died fighting Wallenstein's forces at the Battle of Lützen in November 1632. Two years later Ferdinand arranged for Wallenstein, who had outlived his usefulness, to be assassinated. The German Protestant states then reached a compromise agreement with Ferdinand (the Peace of Prague of 1635). But when the Swedes (with encouragement

from France and the Netherlands) refused to join them, hostilities resumed.

THE SWEDISH-FRENCH PERIOD (1635–1648) The French openly entered the war in 1635 and prolonged it for thirteen more years. French, Swedish, and Spanish soldiers looted the length and breadth of Germany. The Germans, who were too disunited to repulse the foreign armies, simply watched and suffered. By the time peace talks began in the Westphalian cities of Münster and Osnabrück in 1644, an estimated one-third of the German population had died. It was the worst catastrophe in Europe since the Black Death of the fourteenth century.

The Treaty of Westphalia

The Treaty of Westphalia ended hostilities in 1648 by ensuring the continued fragmentation of Germany. The territorial principle proclaimed by the Peace of Augsburg in 1555 was reasserted to confirm rulers in their right to determine the religions of their subjects. Calvinism was added to the list of legal religious options, and the German princes were acknowledged supreme over their principalities. Bavaria was elevated to the rank of an elector state, and Brandenburg-Prussia emerged as the most powerful north German

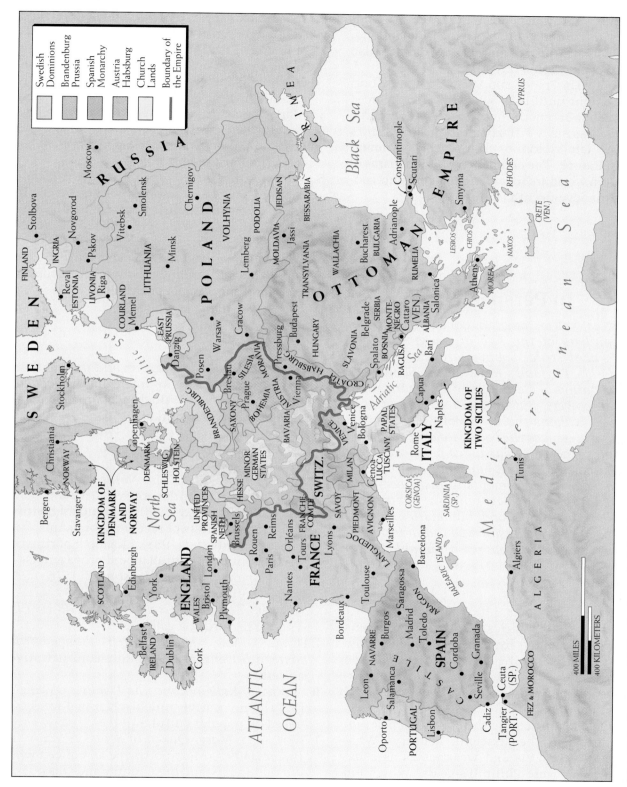

MAP 12–3 EUROPE IN 1648 At the end of the Thirty Years' War, Spain still had extensive possessions, Austria and Brandenburg-Prussia were prominent, the United Provinces and Switzerland were recognized as independent, and Sweden held important north German ports.

principality. The independence of the Swiss Confederacy and of the United Provinces of Holland, long a fact, was proclaimed in law. France also acquired considerable territory.

War between France and Spain continued outside the empire until 1659, when the French forced the Spanish to accept the humiliating Treaty of the Pyrenees. Germany's fragmentation and Spain's humbling left victorious France the dominant power in Europe. The competitive nationalisms of the modern world are rooted in these religious conflicts of the seventeenth century.

In Perspective

Politics, as well as religion, contributed to the great conflicts of the Age of Religious Wars: France's civil strife, Spain's struggle with the Netherlands, England's resistance to Spain, and the devastation of Germany by a consortium of European powers. But neither religion nor politics alone explains the course of the wars. The religious differences that occasioned a war were sometimes ignored in pursuit of political objectives shared by Catholics and Protestants, and wars ended with agreements to disagree—with the recognition of minority religious rights and a guarantee of the traditional boundaries of political sovereignty. The result was that at midcentury Europe had a real but unsustainable peace.

REVIEW QUESTIONS

1. What part did politics play in the religious positions adopted by France's leaders? How did the French king (or his regent) decide which side to favor? What led to the infamous Saint Bartholomew's Day Massacre? What did it achieve?

2. How did Spain acquire the dominant position in Europe in the sixteenth century? What were its strengths and weaknesses as a nation? What were Philip II's goals? Which did he fail to achieve? Why?

3. What made a leader a *politique?* How well does the term describe Henry of Navarre (Henry IV of France), Elizabeth I, and William of Orange?

4. What changes occurred in the religious policies of England's government in the process of establishing the Anglican church? What were Mary I's political objectives? What was Elizabeth I's "settlement"? How was it imposed on England? Who were her opponents? What were their criticisms of her?

5. Why was the Thirty Years' War fought? Could matters have been resolved without war? To what extent did politics determine the outcome of the war? What were the terms and objectives of the Treaty of Westphalia?

6. Was, as some have claimed, the Thirty Years' War "the outstanding example in European history of meaningless conflict"?

SUGGESTED READINGS

F. BRAUDEL, *The Mediterranean and the Mediterranean World in the Age of Philip the Second,* vols. 1 and 2 (1976). Widely acclaimed work of a French master historian.

R. DUNN, *The Age of Religious Wars, 1559–1689* (1979). Excellent brief survey of every major conflict.

P. GEYL, *The Revolt of the Netherlands, 1555–1609* (1958). The authoritative survey.

J. GUY, *Tudor England* (1990). A standard history and good synthesis of recent scholarship.

C. HAIGH, *Elizabeth I* (1988). Elizabeth portrayed as a magnificent politician and propagandist.

J. LYNCH, *Spain under the Hapsburg I: 1516–1598* (1964). Political narrative.

G. PARKER, *Europe in Crisis, 1598–1648* (1979). The big picture at a gallop.

J. H. M. SALMON, *Society in Crisis: France in the Sixteenth Century* (1976). Standard narrative account.

K. THOMAS, *Religion and the Decline of Magic* (1971). Provocative, much-acclaimed work focused on popular culture.

J. WORMALD, *Mary, Queen of Scots: A Study in Failure* (1991). Mary portrayed as a queen who did not understand her country and was out of touch with the times.

Chapter 13
Paths to Constitutionalism and Absolutism: England and France in the Seventeenth Century

Two Models of European Political Development

Constitutional Crisis and Settlement in Stuart England
James I
Charles I
Oliver Cromwell and the Puritan Republic
Charles II and the Restoration of the Monarchy
James II and Renewed Fears of a Catholic England
The "Glorious Revolution"

Rise of Absolute Monarchy in France
Henry IV and Sully
Louis XIII and Richelieu
Young Louis XIV and Mazarin

The Years of Louis's Personal Rule
King by Divine Right
Versailles
Suppression of the Jansenists
Government Geared for Warfare
Louis's Early Wars
Revocation of the Edict of Nantes
Louis's Later Wars
Louis XIV's Legacy

KEY TOPICS

- The factors behind the divergent political paths taken by England and France in the seventeenth century
- The conflict between Parliament and the king over taxation and religion in early Stuart England, the English Civil War, and the abolition of the monarchy
- The Restoration of the English monarchy and the development of Parliament's supremacy over the throne after the "Glorious Revolution"
- The establishment of an absolutist monarchy in France under Louis XIV
- Religious policies of Louis XIV
- The wars of Louis XIV

During the seventeenth century, England and France evolved contrasting political systems. England became a parliamentary monarchy with a policy of religious toleration. France developed an absolutist, highly centralized monarchy that enforced religious conformity. Both systems defy simple description. English monarchs did not share all power with Parliament, and the kings of France were not free of all institutional or customary restraints on their authority.

Two Models of European Political Development

In the second half of the sixteenth century, changes in military technology sharply increased the cost of warfare and forced governments to look for new sources of revenue. Monarchs who, like France's kings, developed sources of income that were not controlled by nobles or by assemblies representing their wealthy subjects achieved absolute power. In places such as England, where rulers had insufficient funds and limited powers of taxation, royal authority was compromised. Kings had to negotiate policy with groups on which they depended for financial support.

The contrast between the French and English political systems was visible by the end of the seventeenth century, but not in 1603 when England's Elizabeth I died. The much revered queen had broad support, and Parliaments met during her reign only to approve taxes. The Stuart kings who succeeded to Elizabeth's throne had a different experience. They pursued fiscal and religious policies that alienated their nation's propertied classes and united them against the crown.

Elizabeth's contemporary, Henry IV (r. 1589–1610) of France, struggled with a divided nation emerging from the turmoil of religious war. His successor, Louis XIII (r. 1610–1643), began to reassert the crown's authority, and in the second half of the seventeenth century, Louis XIV brought the French nobles under control. The aristocratic *Parlement* of Paris won the right to register royal decrees to give them the authority of law, and the king allowed regional *parlements* considerable latitude to deal with local issues. But when the nobles discovered that a strong king was a source of patronage and a guardian of their privileged place in society, they lost interest in organizing anything resembling England's Parliament. An Estates General had developed in France in the late Middle Ages, but once the monarchy won control over taxation, there was little reason for it to meet. No sessions were held from 1614 until the eve of the French Revolution in 1789.

Constitutional Crisis and Settlement in Stuart England

James I

When the childless Elizabeth died in 1603, no one contested the right of James VI of Scotland (the son of Mary Stuart, Queen of Scots) to claim her throne and become James I of England. But a formidable task lay ahead of him. As a Scot, James was an outsider who had no native constituency to help him deal with England's religious factions and substantial national debt. James's advocacy of the divine right of kings, a subject on which he had written a book (*A Trew Law of Free Monarchies*) in 1598, also set him on a collision course with English tradition.

England's Parliament, the country's chief check on royal power, met only when summoned by the monarch to authorize tax levies. James hoped to develop alternative resources that would enable him to fund his government without calling Parliament. Relying on the authority of ill-defined privileges that he alleged were royal prerogatives, James created new customs duties called *impositions*. Members of Parliament resented these, but they preferred to wrangle and negotiate behind the scenes rather than risk serious confrontation.

Religious problems added to political tensions during James's reign. Puritans within the Church of England had hoped that James's upbringing as a Scottish Presbyterian would dispose him to support the reformation of the English church. They wanted to eliminate elaborate priestly rituals and end government of the church by bishops—establishing in their places simple services of worship and congregations run by presbyters elected by the people. James, however, had no intention of using his national church to promote representative government, which he regarded as an infringement on the divine right of kings.

In January 1604, James responded to a list of Puritan grievances (the so-called Millenary Petition) by pledging to maintain and even enhance the Anglican episcopacy. As he explained: "A Scottish presbytery agreeth as well with monarchy as God and the devil. No bishops, no king." James did, however, accept the Protestant demand for the use of vernacular Scriptures, and in 1611 the royal commission he appointed issued an eloquent new translation of the Bible. For generations the Authorized (i.e., King James) Version remained the standard English text.

James had no sympathy with the moral agenda implicit in English Puritanism. The recreations and sports of which the Puritans disapproved were, to the king, innocent activities that were good for people. James also believed that Puritan rigidity about such things discouraged Roman Catholics from converting to the Church of England. Consequently, in 1618 James tried to force a change by ordering the clergy to read his *Book of Sports*—a royal decree that legalized playing games on Sunday—from their pulpits. When they refused, he backed down.

James's lifestyle also seemed designed to give offense to the Puritans, for the royal court was a center of scandal and corruption. James was strongly influenced by a few court favorites, the most powerful of whom, the duke of Buckingham, was rumored to be the king's homosexual lover. Buckingham controlled royal patronage and openly sold peerages and titles to the highest bidders. There had always been royal favorites, but never before had a single person so controlled access to England's monarch.

Disappointment and disgust with James led some Puritans voluntarily to leave England for the New World. In 1620 Puritan separatists founded Plymouth Colony in Cape Cod Bay. Later in the same decade another larger and better-financed group founded the Massachusetts Bay Colony.

In addition to James's domestic policy, his conduct of foreign affairs also roused opposition. James preferred peace to war, for he feared that wars would generate debts that would force him to beg assistance from Parliament. The treaty he signed with Spain in 1604 was long overdue, but some of his subjects viewed it as evidence of his pro-Catholic sentiments. Their suspicions increased when the king tried unsuccessfully to relax the penal laws against Catholics. The situation further deteriorated in 1618, when James wisely hesitated to rush English troops to the aid of German Protestants in the Thirty Years'

War—and when he suggested that his son Charles marry the Infanta, the daughter of the king of Spain.

As James aged and his health failed, the reins of government passed to Charles (and to Buckingham), and parliamentary opposition and Protestant sentiment combined to undo his pro-Spanish foreign policy. The marriage alliance was rejected, and in 1624, shortly before James's death, Parliament pushed England into a war with Spain.

Charles I governed England from 1625 to 1649. His attempts to establish an absolutist government in matters of both church and state provoked clashes with the English Parliament and the outbreak of the Civil War in 1642. He was executed in 1649. Daniel Mytens/The Granger Collection

Charles I

Although Parliament supported war with Spain, distrust of Buckingham undercut its willingness to finance the venture. This forced Charles I (r. 1625–1649), with the help of the unpopular Buckingham, to pursue the same fiscal strategy as his father. Without consulting parliament, he imposed new tariffs and duties, collected discontinued taxes, and subjected people of property (under threat of imprisonment) to the "forced loayn"—a tax that the government, theoretically, was supposed eventually to refund. Soldiers in transit to war zones were also quartered in English homes.

When Parliament met in 1628, its members were furious. They refused to acquiesce to the king's request for funds unless he agreed to abide by terms they set forth in a Petition of Right: (1) no more forced loans or taxation without the consent of Parliament, (2) no imprisonment of citizens without due cause, and (3) an end to billeting troops in private homes. Though Charles promised what was demanded, Parliament did not trust him to keep his word.

Years of Personal Rule   In August 1628, Buckingham, Charles's chief minister, was assassinated. Although his death caused some rejoicing, it was not enough to reconcile king and Parliament. In January 1629, Parliament issued more decrees critical of the king. The levying of taxes without parliamentary consent and Charles's high-church policies were declared acts of treason. Charles responded by dissolving Parliament, and it did not reconvene until a war with Scotland created a fiscal crisis in 1640.

Without funds from Parliament, Charles could not continue his foreign wars. But when he made peace with France in 1629 and Spain in 1630, some of his subjects accused him of wanting to strengthen his ties with Roman Catholic nations. Many Protestant leaders feared that Catholics were establishing ascendancy over their king. Charles had wed a French princess whose marriage contract gave her the right to hear Mass daily at the English court. Charles also favored a movement within the Church of England (the Arminians) that opposed some Puritan doctrines and advocated elaborate services of worship.

To allow Charles to rule without having to negotiate with Parliament for money, the king's chief minister, Thomas Wentworth, earl of Stafford (after 1640), instituted the policy of *thorough*. This was a plan to establish absolute royal control over England by promoting strict efficiency and administrative centralization. Toward this end, Charles's men exploited every legal fund-raising device. They enforced previously neglected laws and extended existing taxes into new areas. Charles won challenges to his policies in the courts but at the cost of alienating the propertied men who would sit in any future Parliament he might be forced to call.

During his years of personal rule, Charles lived expensively. He surrounded himself with an elaborate court and patronized some of the greatest artists of the day. Like his father, he sold titles of nobility to raise money—and to diminish the prestige of the aristocracy. Nobles and great landowners, who saw their fortunes, their local influence, and their social standing diminishing, began to fear that Charles would avoid ever having to call another Parliament.

Charles might have ruled indefinitely without Parliament had he not departed from the tolerant example set by his father and tried to impose religious conformity within England and Scotland. William Laud (1573–1645), Charles's religious adviser and archbishop of Canterbury (after 1633), encouraged the king's preference for high-church Anglicanism. This "Anglo-Catholicism" favored a state-supported church with a powerful episcopacy and elaborate liturgies instead of the preaching-centered worship of the Puritans. In 1637 Charles and Laud, over objections by English Puritans and the Scots, attempted to impose the English episcopal system and prayer book on Scotland. The Scots rebelled, and Charles, having insufficient resources for a war, had to convene Parliament.

The members of Parliament were in the peculiar position of wanting to oppose their king's policies while crushing the rebellion against him. Led by John Pym (1584–1643), they refused to discuss funding for the war until Charles agreed to redress their list of grievances. The king responded by dissolving what came, for obvious reasons, to be known as the Short Parliament (April–May 1640). However, when the Presbyterian Scots invaded England and defeated an English army at the Battle of Newburn in the summer of 1640, Charles had no choice but to recall Parliament on its own terms for a long, fateful session.

THE LONG PARLIAMENT The landowners and the merchant classes whom Parliament represented resented the king's financial exactions and paternalistic rule. Those who were Puritans also disliked his religious policies. The Long Parliament (1640–1660), therefore, enjoyed support from many important factions.

The House of Commons began by impeaching the king's chief advisers, the earl of Stafford and Archbishop Laud. (Stafford was executed for treason in 1641 and Laud in 1645.) Parliament then abolished the instruments the king used to implement the political and religious policy of *thorough*, the Court of Star Chamber and the Court of High Commission. The levying of new taxes without consent of Parliament was declared illegal, and Parliament declared itself a permanent branch of England's government. It claimed that it could not be dissolved without its own consent and that no more than three years could elapse between its meetings.

Members of Parliament were united on the subject of curtailing the powers of the monarchy but divided on the issue of religious reform. Moderate Puritans (Presbyterians) and extreme Puritans (Independents) wanted to abolish the episcopal system and end use of the *Book of Common Prayer*. The Presbyterian majority also hoped to impose a Calvinist system in which the church would be governed by presbyteries, committees composed of representatives from local congregations. The Independents wanted a radical decentralization of the church that would allow each congregation to govern itself. A considerable number of conservatives in both houses of Parliament, however, did not want any changes at all.

These divisions intensified in October 1641, when a rebellion erupted in Ireland and Parliament was asked to raise funds for a royal army to suppress it. Pym and his followers argued that Charles could not be trusted with an army and that Parliament should take command of England's armed forces. Conservatives in Parliament were appalled at the thought of such a radical departure from tradition.

ERUPTION OF CIVIL WAR Charles saw the division within Parliament as a chance to regain the upper hand. On December 1, 1641, Parliament presented him with the Grand Remonstrance, a summary of over 200 grievances against the crown. In January 1642, he responded by sending soldiers into Parliament to arrest Pym and other leaders. When they escaped, Charles withdrew from London and began to raise an army against Parliament. The House of Commons hastened to pass the Militia Ordinance, giving Parliament authority to raise its own army, and for the next four years (1642–1646) civil war engulfed England.

The royal forces, the Cavaliers, were based in the northwestern half of England. They fought for a strong monarchy and an Anglican church presided over by bishops. Their parliamentary opponents, the Roundheads (so-called from their unfashionable short haircuts), had their stronghold in the southeastern half of the country. They wanted parliamentary government and a decentralized church with a presbyterian government.

Oliver Cromwell and the Puritan Republic

Two things contributed to Parliament's victory. The first was an alliance struck between Parliament and Scotland in 1643. It was made possible by Parliament's acceptance of the Scots' presbyterian system of church government. The second was the reorganization of the parliamentary army under Oliver Cromwell (1599–1658), a middle-aged country squire who favored the Independents. Cromwell and his "godly men" wanted neither the king's episcopal system nor the presbyterian organization endorsed by Parliament's Solemn League and Covenant with Scotland. The only established state church they would accept was one that granted freedom of worship to Protestant dissenters.

In 1644 Parliament won the largest engagement of the war, the Battle of Marston Moor, and in June 1645, Cromwell's newly reorganized and fanatical forces, the New Model Army, defeated the king at Naseby. Charles tried to exploit the divisions within Parliament by winning the Presbyterians and the Scots over to his side, but Cromwell foiled him. In December 1648, Colonel Thomas Pride used Cromwell's soldiers to prevent the Presbyterians, who had a majority in Parliament, from taking their seats. After "Pride's Purge," only a "rump" of fewer than fifty members remained. This Rump Parliament was dominated by Independents who did not shy away from bold action. On January 30, 1649, after trial by a special court, the Rump Parliament executed the king and abolished the monarchy, the House of Lords, and the Anglican Church. Civil war had become revolution.

From 1649 to 1660 England was officially a Puritan republic. In reality, Cromwell ruled. On the military front, his achievements were impressive. His army conquered Ireland and Scotland and unified what we know today as Great Britain. Cromwell was, however, a much better general than a politician. He was easily frustrated by the necessity of working with the dawdling members of Parliament. When in 1653 the House of Commons entertained a motion to disband his expensive army of 50,000 men, he marched in and disbanded Parliament.

Calling himself "Lord Protector," Cromwell established a military dictatorship that had minimal popular support. His army and foreign ad- ventures cost taxpayers three times what they had owed to Charles's government, and he was still unable to prevent near chaos from erupting in many parts of England. Commerce suffered, and people chafed under Cromwell's rigorous enforcement of Puritan codes of conduct. The Lord Protector was as intolerant of Anglicans as the king had been of Puritans.

Cromwell failed to build a political system that provided a workable alternative to the monarchy and Parliament. He tried various arrangements, none of which succeeded. By the time he died in 1658, a majority of the English were ready to end the Puritan republican experiments and return to traditional institutions of government. In 1660 the exiled Charles II (r. 1660–1685), son of Charles I, was invited home to restore the Stuart monarchy.

Charles II (r. 1660–1685) was a person of considerable charm and political skill. Here he is portrayed as the founder of the Royal Society. Robert Harding Picture Library

Charles II and the Restoration of the Monarchy

Charles II, a man of considerable charm and political skill, ascended the throne amid great rejoicing, and England returned to the institutions it had abandoned in 1642: a hereditary monarchy that had no obligation to consult with Parliaments, and an Anglican Church with bishops and an official prayer book. Since Charles had secret Catholic sympathies, he favored a policy of religious toleration—which was the best that Catholics could hope for in England. Few in Parliament, however, believed that patriotism and religion could be separated. Between 1661 and 1665, Parliament enacted the Clarendon Code, which excluded Roman Catholics, Presbyterians, and Independents from religious and political offices. Penalties were also imposed for attending non-Anglican worship services. Adherence to the *Book of Common Prayer* and the *Thirty-nine Articles* (the Anglican Church's statement of faith) was demanded, and oaths of allegiance to the Church of England were required of persons who wished to serve in local government. Charles also tried to tighten his grip on the rich English colonies in North America and the Caribbean, many of which had been developed by separatists who wanted independence from English rule.

Charles's foreign policy was dominated by a series of naval wars with Holland that were caused by England's Navigation Acts. These acts required that goods brought to England be carried either in English ships or in ships registered to the country in which their cargo originated. Since Dutch vessels carried goods from many nations, this was a direct attack on Holland's shipping industry. In 1670 Charles allied with the French, who were also at war with Holland, and received French aid to underwrite the cost of his campaign. In exchange for the promise of a substantial subsidy from Louis XIV of France, Charles also secretly pledged to announce, at some propitious moment, his conversion to Catholicism. The time to fulfill that pledge never came.

To unite the English people behind the war with Holland and to show good faith with Louis XIV, Charles issued a Declaration of Indulgence (1672) that suspended all laws against Roman Catholics and Protestant nonconformists. But again, Parliament blocked the king's efforts to promote religious tolerance by refusing to grant money for the war until Charles rescinded the Declaration. Parliament then passed the Test Act, which excluded Roman Catholics from public office by requiring all royal officials to swear an oath repudiating the doctrine of transubstantiation.

The Test Act was aimed in large measure at the king's brother, James, duke of York, heir to the throne and a recent, devout convert to Catholicism. In 1678 a notorious liar, Titus Oates, accused Charles's Catholic wife of plotting with Jesuits and Irishmen to kill her husband and bring his Catholic brother to the throne. Parliament was caught up in the hysteria of Oates's alleged "Popish Plot." Several people were executed, and a faction in Parliament, the Whigs, nearly won passage for a bill excluding James from the succession.

Chronically short of money and having little hope of adequate grants from Parliament, Charles II increased customs duties and extracted more financial aid from Louis XIV. This allowed him to avoid convening a Parliament after 1681. By the time of his death in 1685 (following a deathbed conversion to Catholicism), he had cowed his opponents and positioned James to call a Parliament filled with royal friends.

James II and Renewed Fears of a Catholic England

James II (r. 1685–1688) did not know how to use his opportunities. He alienated Parliament by insisting on the repeal of the Test Act. When Parliament balked, he dissolved it and flaunted the Test Act by openly appointing known Catholics to high offices. In 1687 he issued a Declaration of Indulgence that suspended religious tests and permitted free worship. Candidates for Parliament who opposed the Declaration were evicted by the king's soldiers and replaced by Catholics. In June 1688, James imprisoned seven Anglican bishops who had refused to publicize his suspension of laws against Catholics.

James's policy of toleration was actually a drive to bring England under tighter royal control. His goal was absolutism, and even conservative, loyalist "Tories" (as the monarchy's allies were called) could not abide this. The English had reason to fear that James hoped to establish in England the kind of monarchy that Louis XIV had created in France. (In the year James came to the throne Louis had revoked the Edict of Nantes and used soldiers to suppress Protestant worship in France.)

A birth galvanized James's enemies into action against him. They had hoped that he would die without a male heir and that the throne would pass to Mary, his eldest daughter. She was a Protestant and the wife of William III of Orange, *stadtholder* of the Protestant Netherlands, great-grandson of William the Silent, and the leader of the European states that were threatened by Louis XIV's plots to expand France's power. On June 20, 1688, James's second wife alarmed England's Protestants by giving birth to a son, a Catholic heir to their throne. Within days of the boy's birth, Whig and Tory members of Parliament had agreed to invite William and Mary to invade England to preserve "traditional liberties."

The "Glorious Revolution"

When the English people failed to oppose the landing that William of Orange's army made in November 1688, James accepted defeat and fled to France. Parliament completed the bloodless "Glorious Revolution" by declaring the throne vacant and proclaiming William and Mary its heirs. They, in turn, issued a Bill of Rights that limited the powers of the monarchy and guaranteed the civil liberties of England's privileged classes. Henceforth, the English monarch would be subject to law and would govern with the consent of a Parliament that met regularly. The Bill of Rights also prohibited Roman Catholics from occupying the English throne. The Toleration Act of 1689 legalized all forms of Protestantism—save those that denied the Trinity—and outlawed Roman Catholicism.

In 1701 the Act of Settlement closed the "century of strife" (as the seventeenth century came to be known in England) by providing for the English crown to go to the Protestant House of Hanover in Germany if none of the children of Queen Anne (r. 1702–1714), the second daughter of James II and the last of the Stuart monarchs, survived her. Since she did outlive her children, the Elector of Hanover became King George I of England and the third foreigner to occupy the English throne in just over a century.

Although the "Glorious Revolution" of 1688 was not a popular revolution such as those that erupted in America and France a hundred years later, it established a framework for a government by and for the governed—a permanent check on monarchical power by the classes represented in Parliament. English philosopher John Locke's *Second Treatise of Government* (1690), which was written prior to the revolution, came to be read as a justification for the new system. Locke claimed that the relationship between a king and his people was a bilateral contract. If the king broke that contract, the people (by whom Locke meant those with property) had the right to depose him. Locke's political theory and England's parliamentary monarchy were destined to have wide appeal.

Rise of Absolute Monarchy in France

In seventeenth-century France, unlike England, absolute monarchy established itself, limited the freedom of the nobility, and enforced religious conformity. The dictum of Louis XIV (r. 1643–1715) was "one king, one law, one faith."

Louis's predecessors had provoked a rebellion among the nobles by trying to impose direct rule on the nation at all levels. Louis chose, instead, to work through established social and political institutions rather than to destroy them. His genius lay in his ability to make the monarchy the most powerful political institution in France while assuring the nobles and other wealthy groups that it posed no threat to their private power bases and their standing. Once nobles understood that the king would protect their local authority, they supported his central authority. The king and the nobles agreed that they needed each other but that Louis XIV was the senior partner in the relationship.

Henry IV and Sully

Louis XIV learned much from his predecessors. Henry IV (r. 1589–1610), who came to the throne at the end of the French wars of religion, had tried to rein in the French nobility—particularly the provincial governors, the regional *parlements*, and the powerful *Parlement* of Paris. These groups were divisive elements within the state, for their chief interest was the protection of their privileges. Since the war-weary French were eager for the restoration of order, Henry and his finance minister, the duke of Sully (1560–1641), were able to expand governmental authority. They established royal monopolies on gunpowder, mines, and salt. They began construction of a canal system that linked France's rivers to create a waterway from the Atlantic to the Mediterranean. They introduced the *corvée,* a labor tax that drafted workers to build and maintain roads. Sully even dreamed of joining the whole of Europe in a kind of common market.

Louis XIII and Richelieu

Henry IV was assassinated in 1610, and the following year Sully retired. Louis XIII (r. 1610–1643), Henry's son, was only nine years old at the time, so the task of governing fell to the queen mother, Marie de Médicis (d. 1642). Sensing a lack of support from the French nobility, Marie sought to make a friend of France's archrival, Spain. In 1611 she negotiated the Treaty of Fontainebleau. It provided for a ten-year mutual defense pact and for marriage alliances between the royal houses of the two nations. Louis XIII was to wed the Spanish Infanta, and his sister, Elizabeth, was engaged to the heir to the Spanish throne. The queen's best move was the appointment of Cardinal Richelieu (1585–1642) as the king's chief adviser. The loyal, shrewd Richelieu was the architect of the success the French monarchy enjoyed in the first half of the seventeenth century.

Richelieu was a devout Catholic, but he believed that France's interests were best served by curbing the power of the Catholic Habsburgs. Although he endorsed the queen's treaty with Catholic Spain and encouraged conformity to Catholic practices in France, Richelieu was determined to contain Spain—even if that meant aiding Protestants. In the Thirty Years' War, Richelieu helped to fund the Protestant army of Gustavus Adolphus. His influence with Sweden saved Catholic Bavaria from attack and won freedom of religion for Catholics in places his Protestant allies conquered. Thanks to Richelieu, France emerged from the war with substantial gains in land and political influence.

At home, Richelieu implemented a rigorous centralization of royal government. Supported by a king, who let him make most decisions of state, Richelieu stepped up the campaign Henry IV had begun against separatist provincial governors and *parlements.* He appointed civil servants called *intendants* to guard against abuses in the sale of royal privileges—such as the right to collect taxes or sell licenses. He made it clear to everyone that there was only one law in France. If noblemen disobeyed the king's edicts, they were imprisoned or executed. Such treatment of the nobility won Richelieu much enmity—even from his patron, the queen mother.

In 1629 Richelieu began a campaign against the Huguenots. Royal armies occupied important Huguenot cities and imposed the Peace of Alais. It truncated the Edict of Nantes by denying Protestants the right to maintain garrisoned cities, separate political organizations, and independent law courts. Richelieu was prevented from doing more to limit religious freedoms by France's alliances with Protestant powers in the Thirty Years' War. But in 1685 Louis XIV completed his work by revoking the Edict of Nantes.

Richelieu was a modern politician in the sense that he understood the use of propaganda and the importance of mobilizing popular support for government policies. He employed the arts and the printing press to defend his actions and to persuade the French people to accept things done for *raisons d'état* ("reasons of state"). Louis XIV's masterful use of propaganda to develop royal power was a tribute to Richelieu's example.

Young Louis XIV and Mazarin

Louis XIII survived Richelieu by only five months. Since his heir, Louis XIV (r. 1643–1715), was five years old, the son's reign began, as the father's had, with a regency government. The queen mother, Anne of Austria (d. 1666), entrusted the monarchy to Cardinal Mazarin (1602–1661), Richelieu's protégé.

Since many members of the aristocracy and the wealthy commercial classes had deeply resented Richelieu's efforts to build a strong, centralized monarchy, Mazarin was confronted by a violent political backlash. From 1649 to 1652, there were widespread rebellions, which are known collectively as the *Fronde* (after the name of a slingshot used by street ruffians). The uprisings were exploited by nobles and townspeople who wanted to reverse the drift toward absolute monarchy and to preserve local autonomy.

When the *Parlement* of Paris initiated the *Fronde* in 1649, "the many" (i.e., the nobles) briefly triumphed over "the one" (i.e., the king). Mazarin released some aristocratic prisoners in February 1651, and he and Louis XIV went briefly into exile. (Mazarin left France and Louis fled Paris.) When the nobles failed to restore order and near anarchy ensued, support for the young king materialized and Louis and Mazarin returned in October 1652. The *Fronde* convinced most French people that a strong king was preferable to the chaos created by many competing regional powers. On the other hand, Louis XIV and his later advisers concluded that heavy-handed policies (such as those of Richelieu and Mazarin) might endanger the monarchy.

The Years of Louis's Personal Rule

On the death of Mazarin in 1661, Louis XIV assumed personal control of the government. Unlike his royal predecessors, he appointed no single chief minister. This had the advantage of making revolt more difficult to rationalize. Rebellious nobles could no longer claim that they were opposing their king's wicked ministers but not the crown itself. Mazarin had prepared Louis well for the duties of government, and the young king's experiences during the *Fronde* had stiffened his resolve to be a strong ruler. Louis wrote in his memoirs that the *Fronde* caused him to loathe "kings of straw."

Louis devised two successful strategies for enhancing the power of the monarchy. First, he became a master of propaganda and political image-making. Louis never missed an opportunity to remind the French people of the grandeur of the crown. Second, Louis made sure that the French nobles and other major social groups benefitted from the growth of his authority. Although he maintained control over foreign affairs, he usually conferred informally with regional *parlements* before making rulings that would affect them. Likewise, he rarely enacted economic regulations without consulting local opinion, and local *parlements* were given considerable latitude in regional matters.

King by Divine Right

Reverence for the king, the personification of government, had been nurtured in France since Capetian times, and it was widely accepted that the king's wish was the law of the land. Louis XIV transformed this traditional respect for the crown into a belief in the king's divine right to absolute authority.

Bishop Jacques-Bénigne Bossuet (1627–1704), the king's tutor, provided the theoretical rationale for Louis's concept of the royal office. Bossuet was an ardent champion of the so-called "Gallican liberties," traditional exemptions the French clergy claimed from interference in their affairs by the papacy. (The theory of the "divine right of kings" that Bossuet outlined gave kings spiritual legitimacy as caretakers of national churches.) Bossuet based his theory of monarchy on the example set by the rulers in the Old Testament who had been appointed by and were answerable only to God. Just as medieval popes had insisted that only God could judge a pope, so Bossuet argued that none save God could judge a king. Kings were duty-bound to honor God's will, but as God's regents on earth they were not accountable to mere princes and *parlements*. A king could claim, as Louis was alleged to, "*L'état, c'est moi*" ("I am the state").

Versailles

One of the most successful instruments of Louis XIV's propaganda was the splendid palace he built to house his court at Versailles on the outskirts of Paris (1682). Versailles was a temple to royalty and a proclamation of the glory of France's "Sun King." It was also home to Louis and thousands of his subjects: France's more important nobles and numerous royal officials and servants. The maintenance of Versailles and its expansion and elaboration, which continued throughout Louis's lifetime, consumed over half the royal income. The political dividends Versailles paid, however, proved well worth the investment.

By organizing life at court around his personal routine, Louis demonstrated that he alone was the sole source of power and privilege in France. Nobles scrambled for the honor of being present at intimate moments in the king's day—his rising,

Versailles, as painted in 1668 by Pierre Patel the Elder (1605–1676). The central building is the hunting lodge built for Louis XII earlier in the century. The wings that appear here were some of Louis XIV's first expansions.   Pierre Patel, *Perspective View of Versailles,* Chateau, Versailles, France. Giraudon/Art Resource, NY

dressing, or retiring—in hopes of having a chance to whisper special requests in his ear. Like menial servants, the most distinguished of aristocrats fought for the privilege of holding the king's candle or assisting him with the left sleeve of his nightshirt. These duties were choreographed by an extraordinarily elaborate court etiquette, which was designed to domesticate and trivialize the nobility. Barred by law from high government positions, the nobles were kept busy with ritual and play that left them little time to plot revolt. Luxurious dress codes and high-stakes gambling drove them into debt and financial dependency on the king. Members of the court spent the afternoons hunting, riding, or strolling about the lush gardens of Versailles. Evenings were given over to plays, concerts, gambling, and the like—followed by supper at 10:00 P.M.

The real business of government was handled by Louis and members of councils charged with responsibility for foreign affairs, domestic relations, and the economy. The chief ministers of these councils were talented self-made men or members of families with long histories of loyal service to the crown. Louis trusted them with power, for, unlike the nobility, they had no independent bases in the provinces and relied solely on the king for their places in government and society.

Suppression of the Jansenists

Like Richelieu before him, Louis believed that political stability required religious conformity. The first deviant religious groups to attract his attention were not Protestants but Roman

Rigaud's Louis XIV: The State Portrait

Hyacinthe Rigaud, *Louis XIV*, 1701. Giraudon/Art Resource, NY

Sources: Peter Burke, *The Fabrication of Louis XIV* (New Haven, CT: Yale University Press, 1992); Daniel Roche, *France in the Age of the Enlightenment* (Cambridge, Ma: Harvard University Press, 1998), pp. 273–277; Germain Bazin, *Baroque and Rococo Art* (New York: Praeger, 1966); Marilyn Stockstad, *Art History* (New York: Harry N. Abrams, Inc., and Prentice Hall, Inc., Publishers, 1999), pp. 750–751.

The portrait that Hyacinthe Rigaud painted of the sixty-three-year-old Louis XIV in 1701 broke new ground. The many previous likenesses of the king had placed him in allegorical or historical settings that equated him with mythical heroes and Roman emperors. This picture cloaked the king in images of his own majesty and thereby established the model for what came to be regarded as "the state portrait."

A mature Louis is depicted in coronation robes decorated with the *fleurs-de-lis* symbols of his dynasty. The crown rests beside him, and the throne is in the background. He holds the royal scepter, the staff with which he maintains the social order, and the sword of state, the symbol of his military might and a reminder of his many wars, hangs half concealed at his side. A figure representing justice ornaments the base of the column that rises behind the crown and scepter.

As was the custom, the painting magnified its subject without resorting to absurd flattery. The king's face reflects something of the wisdom (and burden) of his years, but his athletic legs and luxuriant wig imply a youthfulness and vigor that the aging, gout-afflicted monarch may not have felt. The portrait's air of gravity suited a man who was growing more devout, conservative, and restrained in his personal life as he aged. So well did Louis believe that the portrait captured his spirit that he had it copied for distribution and even sent it to represent the crown at council and ministerial meetings he could not attend in person.

Catholics called Jansenists. Catherine de Médicis had prevented the Catholic Jesuits from working in France because of their close connections to Spain, but following Henry IV's conversion to Catholicism, this ban was lifted (1603). Jesuits who swore an oath of allegiance to the king and acquired special licenses were permitted to set up a limited number of colleges and conduct various public activities. The Jesuits soon became the royal confessors and dominated the education of the upper classes. Their commitment was to the enforcement of the decrees of the Council of Trent throughout France.

Jansenism, which appeared in the 1630s, was a Catholic movement named for a Flemish theologian and bishop who was critical of the Jesuits, Cornelius Jansen (d. 1638). Jansenists followed the teachings of Saint Augustine, who emphasized the role divine grace played in human salvation. They objected to the Jesuits' emphasis on free will and good works, for they believed with Saint Augustine that original sin so corrupted humankind that individuals could do nothing good nor secure their own salvation without divine grace. Jansenist emphasis on salvation by grace led the Jesuits to accuse the Jansenists of being crypto-Protestants.

The fight between the Jansenists and the Jesuits had political as well as theological dimensions. Jansen had ties with a prominent Parisian family, the Arnaulds, who, like many others in France, believed that the Jesuits had arranged the assassination of Henry IV in 1610. The Arnaulds dominated Jansenist communities at Port-Royal and Paris during the 1640s. In 1643 a book *(On Frequent Communion)* by Antoine Arnauld attracted attention by charging that the Jesuits' use of the confessional allowed people easily to escape responsibility for their sins.

On May 31, 1653, Pope Innocent X declared that five Jansenist theological propositions concerning grace and salvation were heresies. In 1656 the pope banned a book by Cornelius Jansen (*Augustinus,* 1640), and the Sorbonne censured Antoine Arnauld. In the same year Antoine's friend, Blaise Pascal (d. 1662), published a defense of Jansenism, the first of his *Provincial Letters.* Pascal was a deeply religious man who objected to Jesuit moral theology not only because it was lax, but also because its rationalism failed to do justice to the profound mysteries of religious experience.

In 1660 Louis banned Jansenism and closed down the Port-Royal community. This drove Jansenism underground, where it apparently continued to thrive. In 1710 Louis ordered a more thorough purge of Jansenist sympathizers. His suppression of Jansenism, which was a kind of Catholicism broad enough to appeal to Huguenots, eliminated the best hope for peacefully unifying France's religions.

Government Geared for War

Louis saw himself as a warrior king, and his many campaigns led his neighbors to fear French aggression and form coalitions against him. He, however, probably did not aspire to European domination but only to the defense of what he regarded as France's interests. These centered on achieving a secure northern border (with the Spanish Netherlands, the Franche-Comté, Alsace, and Lorraine), frustrating the ambitions of the Habsburgs, and dealing with problems of succession to the thrones of various states.

COLBERT AND THE FRENCH ECONOMY   The economy of France was overwhelmingly agrarian, as was true of other nations in Louis's day. But Jean-Baptiste Colbert (1619–1683), Louis's brilliant financial adviser, managed it so skillfully that France was able to support a huge standing army. Colbert centralized the French economy just as Louis centralized French government. The kind of economic policy Colbert instituted has been called *mercantilism.* Its aim was to maximize exports, minimize imports, and thus conserve the bullion foreign sales brought to an exporting nation. Colbert relied on state supervision of industries and tariffs to regulate the flow of imports and exports. He established new national industries and imposed a strict regimen for workers in state-run factories. He simplified the administrative bureaucracy; reduced the number of tax-exempt nobles; and increased the *taille,* the direct tax on the peasantry that provided much of the king's income.

LOUVOIS, VAUBAN, AND THE FRENCH MILITARY   Thanks to Colbert, Louis was able to afford an army of about 250,000 men. It was created for him by a father-son team of war ministers: Michel Le Tellier (minister to 1666) and Tellier's son, the marquis of Louvois (minister from 1667 to his death in 1691). Before Louvois, the French army had been an amalgam of local companies of recruits and mercenaries who supplemented their irregular pay by pillaging the countryside. Louvois made soldiering a respectable profession. He improved discipline, established a system of promotion by merit, restricted enlistment to single men, and paid them well. The conduct of the military at all levels was also monitored by civil servants.

New technology was provided for Louvois's new army by a brilliant military engineer, Sebastien Vauban (1633–1707). He perfected the arts of fortifying and besieging towns, invented trench warfare, and developed the concept of the defensive frontier—an idea that remained basic to military tactics through World War I.

Louis's Early Wars

THE WAR OF DEVOLUTION   Louis's first great foreign adventure was the War of Devolution (1667–1668). Like the later War of the Spanish Succession, it was fought to press a claim Louis's wife, Marie Thérèse (1638–1683), had to Spain's Belgian provinces. In 1659 Marie had surrendered her place in the line of succession to the Spanish throne in exchange for a huge dowry to be paid to Louis. The dowry was never paid, but Philip IV of Spain, who died in September 1665, left a will disinheriting Marie in favor of a sickly four-year-old son by a second marriage, Charles II (r. 1665–1700). Louis decided to contest the will, and the legal grounds he chose gave the war its name. Louis argued that in certain regions of Brabant and Flanders, which were part of Philip's estate, property "devolved" to the children of a first marriage rather than to those of a second. Therefore, Marie had a better claim to these districts than Charles. In 1667 Louis sent his armies into Flanders and the Franche-Comté, and England, Sweden, and the United Provinces of Holland reacted by forming the Triple Alliance. In 1668 Louis signed the Treaty of Aix-la-Chapelle and agreed to a peace that gave him control of some towns bordering the Spanish Netherlands.

INVASION OF THE NETHERLANDS   In 1670 France persuaded England to join an alliance against the Dutch. The Triple Alliance crumbled, and in 1672 Louis struck directly at Holland, the power that had organized the Triple Alliance. Without neutralizing Holland, Louis knew he could make

no progress in the Spanish Netherlands, nor could he fulfill his dream of winning European hegemony. Louis's attack on the United Provinces of Holland was countered by the young Prince of Orange, the future William III of England. Orange was the great-grandson of William the Silent, the native leader who had repulsed Philip II and established the independence of Holland. Orange persuaded the Holy Roman Emperor, Spain, Lorraine, and Brandenburg to join him in stopping the "Christian Turk," the voracious French king who was becoming a menace to the whole of western Europe. In 1676 a victory over the Dutch fleet gave France control of the Mediterranean. The United Netherlands, however, lost no territory, and the war ended in 1679 with no clear winner.

Revocation of the Edict of Nantes

Following the Peace of Nijmwegen, which ended the war in the Netherlands and halted (for the moment) France's aggression in Europe, Louis imposed religious conformity on his subjects. The Edict of Nantes of 1598 had established a legal Protestant minority in France, but the Huguenots' relations with the Catholic majority (nine-tenths of the French population) were never good. The French Catholic Church denounced Calvinists as heretics and traitors and declared their persecution a pious, patriotic duty.

Louis hounded the Huguenots from public life by banning them from government office and excluding them from the professions. He raised their taxes, quartered his troops in their towns, and in October 1685, he outlawed their faith by revoking the Edict of Nantes. Protestant churches and schools closed. Protestant clergy went into exile. Nonconverting laity were enslaved on the galleys, and Protestant children were turned over to Catholic priests for baptism.

Louis's flaunting of religious intolerance was a major blunder, for it persuaded Protestant countries that he had to be stopped at all costs. More than a quarter-million French people fled their homeland to stiffen opposition to France in England, Germany, Holland, and the New World. Many of the Huguenots who remained in France formed guerilla bands to fight the king. But Louis, to his death, was persuaded that the revocation of Nantes was his most pious act—one that put God in his debt.

MAP 13–1 THE WARS OF LOUIS XIV *This maps illustrates the territorial changes that resulted from Louis's first three major wars prior to the War of the Spanish Succession.*

Louis's Later Wars

THE LEAGUE OF AUGSBURG AND THE NINE YEARS' WAR In 1681 Louis's forces conquered the free city of Strasbourg, prompting new defensive coalitions to form against him. One of these, the League of Augsburg, expanded to include England, Spain, Sweden, the United Provinces, the electorates of Bavaria, Saxony, and the Palatinate, and the Emperor Leopold. From 1689 to 1697, the league and France fought the Nine Years' War, while in North America England and France fought King William's War, a struggle for the colonies. In 1697 mutual exhaustion forced an interim settlement, the Peace of Ryswick. The treaty was a triumph for William of Orange,

The foreign policy of Louis XIV brought warfare to all of Europe. This eighteenth-century painting by Benjamin West memorializes the British victory over France in the battle of La Hogue in 1692. © 1778, oil on canvas, 1.527 × 2.143 (60 1/8 × 84 3/8); framed: 1.803 × 2.410 (71 × 94 7/8). Andrew W. Mellon Fund. © Board of Trustees, National Gallery of Art, Washington.

now William III of England, and the Emperor Leopold. It secured Holland's borders and thwarted Louis's expansion into Germany.

WAR OF THE SPANISH SUCCESSION: TREATIES OF UTRECHT AND RASTADT Louis tried a fourth time to win dominance over Europe. Charles II of Spain (surnamed "the Sufferer" because of his genetic deformities and lingering illnesses) died on November 1, 1700. Louis and the Austrian Emperor Leopold each claimed the Spanish inheritance for a grandson. Louis's grandson, Philip of Anjou, had the better claim, for his grandmother, Marie Thérèse was the older sister of the Spanish princess, Margaret Thérèse, who had married Leopold. But Marie Thérèse had renounced her right to the Spanish throne when she married Louis.

Louis feared that the Habsburgs would dominate Europe if they ruled both Spain and the Holy Roman Empire. Most of the nations of Europe,

however, feared France more than the Habsburgs. As a result, even before Charles II died, international negotiations were underway to partition his inheritance in a way that would preserve the balance of power. Charles II upset these negotiations by bequeathing his estate to Philip of Anjou. Louis, finding himself the unexpected winner, ignored partition agreements, sent his grandson to Madrid to become Philip V of Spain, and invaded Flanders. In September 1701, England, Holland, and the Holy Roman Empire formed the Grand Alliance. They hoped to secure Flanders as a neutral barrier between Holland and France and to gain a share of the Spanish inheritance for the Habsburgs. The result was the War of the Spanish Succession (1701–1714), another total war enveloping all of western Europe.

In this campaign the French army was poorly financed, poorly equipped, and poorly led. England, on the other hand, had advanced weaponry, superior tactics, and a splendid general—John Churchill, the duke of Marlborough. Marlborough routed French armies in two decisive engagements: Blenheim in August 1704, and Ramillies in 1706. From 1708 to 1709 famine and excessive taxation spawned revolts that tore France apart, and Louis wondered aloud how God could forsake a king who had done so much for Him.

Louis could not bring himself to accept the stiff terms the alliance demanded for peace, and hostilities continued. A clash at Malplaquet (September 1709) created carnage unsurpassed until mod-

ern times. France and England finally declared an armistice at Utrecht in July 1712 and in March 1714 came to an agreement with Holland and the emperor (the Treaty of Rastadt). Philip V remained king of Spain, but England won Gibraltar and a chance to become a Mediterranean power. Spain continued to decline following the war because Philip was distracted by efforts to secure thrones in Italy for the sons of his second wife, Elizabeth Farnese. The sixteenth century had belonged to Spain and the seventeenth to France, but England was to have the eighteenth.

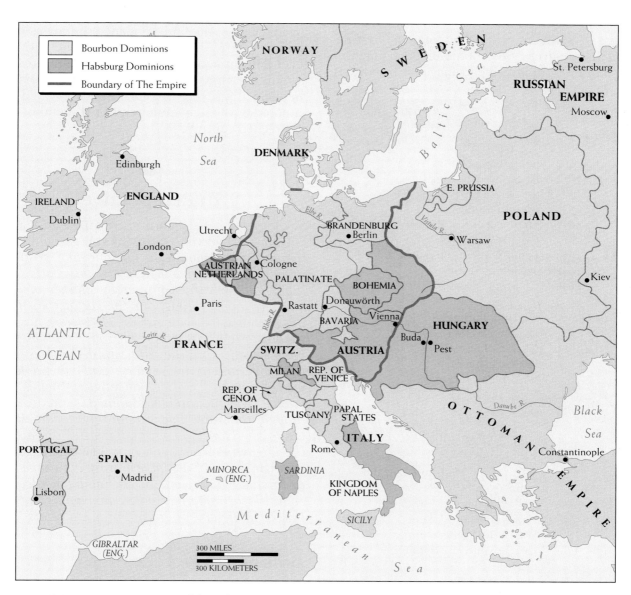

MAP 13–2   Europe in 1714.   *Although France and Spain remained separate countries, the War of the Spanish Succession established Bourbon kings on both their thrones. It also cost Spain its non-Iberian possessions.*

Louis XIV's Legacy

Louis XIV left France a mixed legacy. Although the monarchy was still strong when he died, it was more feared than admired. Its finances were insecure, and its debts great. Its tightly centralized control of political and economic life had suppressed the development of representative institutions, and its use of Versailles to trivialize the lives of aristocrats had diminished their capacity to provide the nation with effective leadership. Louis's wars had also imbued the army and the aristocracy with a thirst for military glory, and the wars that France continued to fight during the eighteenth century doomed efforts to put the government on a sound financial footing.

On the positive side, Louis erected magnificent buildings, provided patronage for important artists, and brought a new majesty to France. He skillfully handled the fractious French aristocracy and bourgeoisie. He appointed talented ministers, councillors, and *intendants*. And he created a French empire by expanding trade with Asia and by colonizing North America.

The Sun King's rule was not so absolute as to oppress the daily lives of his subjects. Louis's France was not a modern police state. His interests were those that traditionally had been assumed to be the responsibilities of kings: the making of war and peace, the regulation of religion, and the oversight of economic activity. Even at the height of his power, local elites enjoyed considerable independence so long as they did not interfere with his plans on the national level. The French people showed little interest in pursuing a more representative form of government until a severe financial crisis revealed the impotency of their monarchy at the end of the eighteenth century.

In Perspective

In the seventeenth century, England and France developed divergent forms of government: parliamentary monarchy in England and absolute monarchy in France. The politically active nobility and wealthy commercial classes of England struggled throughout the century to limit the authority of their rulers. They were not advocates of democracy or religious freedom in a modern sense, but they did establish representative government in England and extend legal recognition to a variety of religious beliefs. In France, the monarchy remained supreme. Although the king had to mollify local elites, France developed no national institution such as the English Parliament. Louis XIV was able, on his own, to build the largest army in Europe and to crush religious dissent. The model of effective centralized monarchy he created had great appeal to later generations of European rulers.

REVIEW QUESTIONS

1. What similarities and differences do you see between the systems of government and religious policies in place in England and France

Significant Dates from the Seventeenth Century	
1603	James I, king of England
1611	Authorized, or King James, Version of the Bible
1625	Charles I, king of England
1642	Outbreak of the English Civil War
1643	Louis XIV, king of France
1648	Treaty of Westphalia
1649	Charles I executed
1649–1652	The *Fronde*
1649–1660	England, Puritan Commonwealth
1660	Charles II restores the English monarchy
1667–1668	War of Devolution
1685	James II, king of England
1685	Louis XIV revokes Edict of Nantes
1688	England's "Glorious Revolution"
1689	William and Mary rule England
1689–1697	Nine Years' War
1701	Act of Settlement, the Hanoverian Succession
1701–1714	War of the Spanish Succession
1702	Queen Anne, the last of the Stuarts
1714	Death of Queen Anne of England
1715	Death of Louis XIV of France

at the end of the seventeenth century? What accounts for the path each nation took?

2. Why did the English king and Parliament come into conflict in the 1640s? Does one of them bear more responsibility than the other for the war that broke out? What role did religion play in the struggle?

3. What was the "Glorious Revolution"? Why did it take place? What were James II's mistakes? What were the issues involved in the events of 1688? What kind of settlement emerged from the revolution? How did England in 1700 differ from England in 1600?

4. By what stages did absolutism develop in France? How did the policies of Henry IV and Louis XIII contribute to the creation of absolute monarchy?

5. How did Louis XIV consolidate his monarchy? What limits were there on his authority? What was Louis's religious policy?

6. How successful was Louis XIV's foreign policy? What were its aims? Were they realistic? To what extent were they attained?

SUGGESTED READINGS

R. ASHTON, *Counter-Revolution: The Second Civil War and Its Origin, 1646–1648* (1995). A major examination of the resumption of civil conflict in England that ended with the abolition of the monarchy.

W. BEIK, *Absolutism and Society in Seventeenth-Century France* (1985). An important study that questions the extent of royal power.

R. BONNEY, *Political Change in France Under Richelieu and Mazarin, 1624–1661* (1978). A careful examination of the manner in which these two cardinals laid the foundation for Louis XIV's absolutism.

G. BURGESS, *Absolute Monarchy and the Stuart Constitution* (1996). A new study that challenges traditional interpretations.

P. BURKE, *The Fabrication of Louis XIV* (1992). Examines the manner in which the public image of Louis XIV was forged in art.

P. COLLINSON, *The Religion of Protestants: The Church in English Society, 1559–1625* (1982). The best recent introduction to Puritanism.

T. ERTMAN, *Birth of the Leviathan: Building States and Regimes in Medieval and Early Modern Europe* (1997). An extensive survey by a sociologist.

R. HUTTON, *Charles the Second, King of England, Scotland, and Ireland* (1989). Replaces all previous biographies.

P. K. MONOD, *The Power of Kings: Monarchy and Religion in Europe, 1589–1715* (1999). An innovative examination of the roots of royal authority.

C. RUSSELL, *The Causes of the English Civil War* (1990). A major revisionist account, which should be read with Stone below.

L. STONE, *The Causes of the English Revolution, 1529–1642* (1972). Brief survey stressing social history and ruminating over historians and historical method.

D. J. STURDY, *Louis XIV* (1998). An excellent overview.

D. UNDERDOWN, *Revel, Riot, and Rebellion* (1985). On popular culture and the English civil war.

J. B. WOLF, *Louis XIV* (1968). Very detailed political biography.

Chapter 14
New Directions in Thought and Culture in the Sixteenth and Seventeenth Centuries

KEY TOPICS

- The astronomical theories of Copernicus, Brahe, Kepler, Galileo, and Newton, and the emergence of the scientific worldview
- Impact of the new science on philosophy
- Social setting of early modern science
- Women and the Scientific Revolution
- Approaches to science and religion
- Witchcraft and witch hunts

During *the sixteenth and seventeenth centuries, science created a new view of the universe that challenged many previously held beliefs. Earth moved from the center of things to become only one of several planets orbiting a sun that was only one of countless stars. This new cosmology forced people to rethink humanity's place in the larger scheme of things. Traditional religion and the new science came into an apparent conflict that raised questions about the received grounds for faith and morality. Europeans discovered that the world was a much more complex place than their ancestors had imagined. The telescope opened the heavens to them while the microscope disclosed the exis-*

tence of a realm of microorganisms. A spate of scientific discoveries added to the intellectual dislocation that had already been created by the Reformation (which challenged many medieval religious and social institutions) and contact with the New World (which confronted Europeans with places, things, and peoples they had never known to exist).

The Scientific Revolution

The intellectual breakthroughs of the sixteenth and seventeenth centuries have been described as the Scientific Revolution, but that metaphor may be misleading if it is assumed to imply a rapid, widespread transformation of culture. The development of science was a slow process that never involved more than a few hundred people. These pioneers thought of themselves as "natural philosophers," not *scientists*—a term that was not invented until the 1830s. Progress in science depended on the inventiveness of artisans and craftspeople as well as a few brilliant minds. Some individuals worked at universities or had the patronage of kings, but many pursued their studies informally from their homes or private workshops. It was not until the second half of the seventeenth century that learned societies and academies were established to promote research.

Despite this rather casual approach to scientific work, by the end of the seventeenth century the new scientific concepts and methods that were emerging were so impressive that they were setting the standard for assessing the validity of all knowledge in the West. Science was already achieving the cultural supremacy over other forms of intellectual activity that it still enjoys and was establishing itself as one of the defining characteristics of modern Western civilization. The discipline that did most to initiate these developments was astronomy.

Nicolaus Copernicus Rejects an Earth-centered Universe

Nicolaus Copernicus (1473–1543), a respected Italian-educated Polish astronomer, had a reputation as a fairly conventional thinker until he published, in the year of his death (1543), a book entitled *On the Revolutions of the Heavenly Spheres*. The book did not so much create a

revolution as lay the groundwork for one by providing Copernicus's successors with an intellectual springboard for a criticism of the previously accepted view of the position of Earth in the universe.

THE PTOLEMAIC SYSTEM   The maps of the universe commonly accepted in Copernicus's day were variants of one found in the ancient Greek astronomer Ptolemy's *Almagest* (c. 150 C.E.). They assumed that Earth was the center point of a ball-shaped universe composed of concentric, rotating crystalline spheres to which the heavenly bodies were attached. At the outer regions of these spheres lay the realm of God and the angels. The assumptions about the laws of physics, which the Greek philosopher Aristotle had popularized, lay behind Ptolemy's model. Earth was at the center of the universe because it was presumed to be the heaviest of objects. Since rest was thought to be the natural state of all objects, an explanation had to be proposed for the motion of the heavenly bodies. They were said to be attached to invisible rotating spheres that transferred motion down from the highest level where a "prime mover" imparted motion to the system. Christians, of course, identified Aristotle's "prime mover" with God.

Medieval astronomers were aware of problems with Ptolemy's system. Chief among these was the fact that the planets did not appear to move in circular orbits. Sometimes they actually seemed to go backward. Ptolemy and his disciples explained this by advancing a theory of epicycles, that is, planets moving in short circular cycles which travel the orbits of much larger cycles. This accounted fairly well with what astronomers observed, but it produced a very cluttered model for the universe.

COPERNICUS'S UNIVERSE   Copernicus's *On the Revolutions of the Heavenly Spheres* was meant not to refute Ptolemy's theory but to propose a refinement that would provide a more elegant solution to some of the mathematical problems it raised. Copernicus suggested that if Earth were assumed to rotate about the sun in a circular orbit, the epicycles could be—if not eliminated—at least reduced in size and the apparent retrograde motion of the planets could be explained as an illusion created by astronomers viewing them from a planet that was itself in motion. Except for modifying the position of Earth, Copernicus maintained most of the other assumptions of Ptolemaic astronomy (e.g., circular orbits, epicycles, etc.), and his system was no more accurate than older ones in predicting the movements of the planets. The Copernican model of the universe was, therefore, slow to attract adherents, and the importance of his work originally lay primarily in the encouragement it gave people to think in new ways about scientific problems.

Tycho Brahe and Johannes Kepler Make New Scientific Observations

Tycho Brahe (1546–1601), a Danish astronomer, spent most of his life trying to refute Copernicus and defending a revised version of Ptolemy's Earth-centered model for the universe. He thought that the moon and the sun revolved around Earth and that the other planets revolved around the sun. To make his case, Brahe collected the most accurate astronomical data that had ever been acquired by observation with the naked eye.

When Brahe died, his astronomical tables passed to Johannes Kepler (1571–1630), a German astronomer and a convinced Copernican. After much work, Kepler discovered that if the planets were described as moving in elliptical, not circular, orbits, Brahe's data supported the Copernican theory that Earth revolved about the sun. Kepler published his findings in 1609 in a book entitled *The New Astronomy*, but their acceptance was hampered by the fact that no one could explain why planets were locked in orbits of any shape rather than spinning out into space. The solution to that puzzle had to await Isaac Newton and his theories about gravitation.

Galileo Galilei Argues for a Universe of Mathematical Laws

By Kepler's day little was known about the universe that could not have been known to Ptolemy, for all data had been gathered with the naked eye. But in the year that Kepler published his work, an Italian scientist, Galileo Galilei (1564–1642), turned a Dutch invention called a telescope on the heavens and saw things that had never been seen before. Unknown stars appeared, mountains were discovered on the moon, spots passed across the face of the sun, and moons

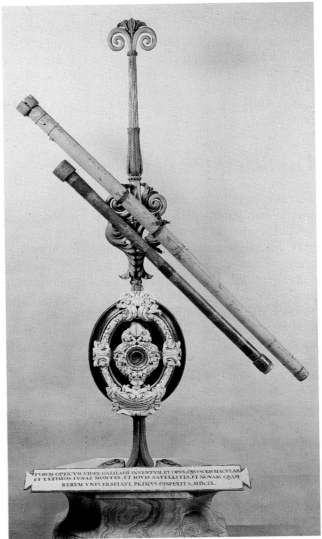

The telescope with which Galileo worked after 1609. He observed Earth's moon and the cyclical phases of the planet Venus and discovered the most prominent moons of Jupiter. These observations had revolutionary intellectual and theological implications in the seventeenth century. Muséo della Scienza, Florence, Italy. Scala/Art Resource, NY

were seen to orbit the planet Jupiter. Galileo argued that a Copernican model of the universe provided the simplest explanation for much of what the telescope revealed.

Galileo did not pursue science in the seclusion of an ivory tower. He worked at the court of the Medici Grand Duke of Tuscany, and his livelihood depended on promoting his discoveries in ways that enhanced the reputation of his noble patron. Galileo, therefore, publicized his findings in literate, accessible treatises. This made him appear to be the leading advocate for the Copernican model of the universe and caused problems for him with the Roman Catholic Church (discussed later).

Galileo not only popularized Copernicanism, he also fostered belief in a universe governed by rational laws stated in mathematical formulas. The mathematical regularity that Copernicus saw in the heavens, Galileo believed, was characteristic of all nature. This conviction encouraged scientists to look for explanations for things by focusing primarily on phenomena that could be quantified. They sought mathematical models to account for qualities such as color, beauty, and taste—and even to explain such things as social relationships and political systems. When viewed from this perspective, nature appeared to be a cold, mechanistic system. Only things that were mathematically measurable seemed real and of lasting significance. This attitude portended a major intellectual shift for Western civilization.

Isaac Newton Discovers the Laws of Gravitation

The puzzle that Copernicus, Kepler, and Galileo left unsolved was why the heavenly bodies moved in the orderly fashion described by the new astronomy. It was an interest in the mystery that lay behind the laws of planetary motion that led Isaac Newton (1642–1727), an English mathematician, to make the discoveries that established a basis for physics that endured for over two centuries.

In 1687 Newton published *The Mathematical Principles of Natural Philosophy* (or *Principia Mathematica*, its Latin title). Newton shared Galileo's faith that reality could be described mathematically, and he was influenced by Galileo's theory of inertia. Earlier scientists had assumed that rest (motionlessness) was an object's natural state and that movement had to be explained. Galileo proposed instead that what the physicist ought to ask is not why there is motion instead of rest, but why there is a change in an existing state—be it rest or movement.

Newton theorized that the revolutions of the heavenly bodies were controlled by gravity, a pull that every physical object exerts on the objects around it. Since the strength of this attrac-

Sir Isaac Newton discovered the mathematical and physical laws governing the force of gravity. Newton believed that religion and science were compatible and mutually supportive, and that the study of nature gave one a better understanding of the Creator. This portrait of Newton is by Sir Godfrey Kneller. Sir Godfrey Kneller, *Sir Isaac Newton.* Bildarchiv Preussicher Kulturbesitz

tion is proportional to the mass and proximity of each object, the order that exists among the planets can be explained as the balance they have achieved among their mutual forces. Newton demonstrated the effects of gravity mathematically, but he made no attempt to explain what gravity was in itself.

Newton believed that mathematics held the key to understanding nature, but, like the other advocates of the new science, he also believed that the ultimate test of a theory was its ability to explain empirical data and observation. The final test of any hypothesis was whether it described what could be observed. Science began and ended with empirical observation of what was actually in nature, not with a rational argument about what ought to be there. Consequently, religious dogma could not dictate conclusions to science.

Philosophy Responds to Changing Science

The revolution taking place in science prompted a major rethinking of the Western philosophical tradition. The religious beliefs of the medieval Scholastics were abandoned in favor of a world described in terms of mechanical metaphors and the language of machinery. The new model for the universe was to imagine it not as a living thing but as a kind of gigantic clock. This dispelled much of the mystery of existence and reduced God to the role of an observer—a great mechanic who had constructed the machinery of the universe but did not participate in its operation. Philosophers had previously assumed that an understanding of the natural order would reveal divine mysteries and yield transcendent insights, but now they concluded that knowledge of nature revealed nothing beyond itself. Such knowledge might lead to physical improvements for living beings, but it could not disclose a divine purpose for life.

Francis Bacon: The Empirical Method

Francis Bacon (1561–1626), the English lawyer, statesman, and author who is often honored as the father of the scientific method of research, was not himself a scientist. His contribution to science was to help create an intellectual climate conducive to its growth. In books such as *The Advancement of Learning* (1605), the *Novum Organum* (1620), and the *New Atlantis* (1627), Bacon attacked medieval Scholasticism's reverence for authority, that is, its belief that most truth had already been discovered and only needed to be explicated. He urged his contemporaries to strike out on their own to search for a new understanding of nature. Bacon was a leader among the early European writers who defended the desirability of innovation and change.

Bacon believed that knowledge was not just an end in itself but that it should produce useful results. It should improve the human condition. He claimed that Scholasticism had nothing more to contribute toward this end, for its practitioners did nothing but rearrange old ideas. If any real progress was to be made, philosophers had to go back and reexamine the foundations of their thought. If they relied on empirical observation more than logical speculation, Bacon promised that they would discover new information that would open new possibilities for humankind.

Bacon's rejection of past methods of inquiry sprang from his awareness that the world was becoming a much more complicated place than it had been for his medieval forebears. Like Columbus, and partially because of him, Bacon claimed that he had to chart a new route to intellectual discovery. The new territories that were being explored on the globe were opening new vistas for the mind. Most people in Bacon's day assumed that the best era in human history lay in antiquity, but Bacon disagreed. He anticipated a future of material improvement and more effective government achieved through the empirical examination of nature.

René Descartes: The Method of Rational Deduction

René Descartes (1596–1650), the gifted French mathematician who invented analytic geometry, popularized a scientific method that relied more on deduction than empirical observation and induction. Thinkers all over Europe eagerly applied his techniques to all kinds of subject matters.

Descartes's *Discourse on Method* (1637) tried to put all human thought on a secure mathematical footing. In order to arrive at truth, Descartes said that it was necessary to doubt all ideas except those that were clear and distinct. An idea was worthy of trust not because some authority vouched for it but because all rational beings could intuit its validity for themselves. Descartes began his search for truth by seeing if he had any ideas he could not doubt, that is, any ideas that were self-substantiating. He concluded that it was not possible to question his own act of thinking without assuming that he existed. To doubt doubting, one could not doubt the existence of the doubter. With this clear and distinct idea as his premise, Descartes was able to construct arguments deducing the existence of God and a real world external to the human mind.

Descartes divided existing things into two basic categories: things in thought and things in space. Thinking was characteristic of the mind, and extension (i.e., things occupying space) of the body. Since space was measurable by mathematical means, mathematical laws governed the world of extension. Its laws were discoverable by reason, for mathematical truths form coherent systems in which each part can be deduced from some other part. Spirits, divinities, or immaterial things have no place in the world of extension. That realm belongs exclusively to the scientist who explains it by using mathematical reason to discover the mechanical properties of matter.

Natural scientists eventually abandoned Descartes's deductive method for induction, the process of formulating a hypothesis by generalizing from discrete bits of empirical data. Deduction, however, remained popular with people who pondered subjects for which little empirical data was available, for example, political theory, psychology, ethics, and theology.

Thomas Hobbes: Apologist for Absolutism

Nowhere did the new science have a greater impact on political thought than in the work of Thomas Hobbes (1588–1679), the most original political philosopher of the seventeenth century. Hobbes was an urbane and much-traveled man who enthusiastically supported the new scientific movement. He visited Paris and made Descartes's acquaintance. He spent time in Italy with Galileo, and he was interested in the work of William Harvey (1578–1657), the man who discovered that blood circulated through the human body. Hobbes was also a superb classicist. His translation of Thucydides' *History of the Peloponnesian War*, the first in English, is still read, and his dark view on human nature probably owed something to Thucydides.

The English Civil War made Hobbes a political philosopher and inspired him in 1651 to publish a book entitled *Leviathan*. It offered a thoroughly materialistic, mechanistic explanation for human behavior. Hobbes theorized that all psychological processes derive from sensation and that all motivations are egoistical. The driving force in each human life is to increase pleasure and minimize pain. Human beings exist for no higher spiritual ends and serve no great moral purpose. They simply strive to meet the needs of daily life,

and to do so they have to form a government. A sovereign commonwealth is all that prevents a society of egotists from tearing itself apart.

The key to Hobbes's political philosophy is found in a brilliant myth he devised to explain humanity's original state. Hobbes claimed that nature inclines people to a "perpetual and restless desire" for power. Because all people want, and in the state of nature possess, a right to everything, their equality breeds enmity, competition, diffidence, and perpetual quarreling—"a war of every man against every man." Whereas earlier and later philosophers saw the original human condition as a paradise from which people had fallen, Hobbes described it as a corrupt environment from which people could be delivered only by the establishment of a politically organized society. Unlike Aristotle and Christian thinkers such as Thomas Aquinas, Hobbes did not believe human beings were naturally sociable. He claimed that they were self-centered beasts who were utterly without discipline unless it was imposed on them by force.

People escape their terrible natural state by entering a social contract, that is, by agreeing to live in a commonwealth ruled by law. It is their desire for "commodious living" and their fear of death that drive them to accept the constraints of communal life. The social contract obliges every person, for the sake of peace and self-defense, to agree to set aside his or her right to all things and be content with as much liberty against others as he or she would allow others against himself or herself. Because words and promises are insufficient to guarantee this agreement, the social contract also authorizes the coercive use of force to compel compliance.

Believing the dangers of anarchy to be greater than those of tyranny, Hobbes thought that rulers should have unlimited power. He did not think that it mattered much what form governments took (e.g., monarchies or legislative bodies). The crucial factor was that there could be no challenge to their authority. There is little room in Hobbes's political philosophy for protest in the name of individual conscience or for a spiritual authority distinct from secular government. Both Catholics and Puritans criticized these features of *Leviathan*, but Hobbes insisted that loss of rights for some individuals was clearly preferable to the suffering everyone experienced in a civil war.

John Locke: Defender of Moderate Liberty and Toleration

The most influential critic of political absolutism was another Englishman, John Locke (1632–1704). Locke's sympathies were with the leaders of popular revolutions. His father fought with the parliamentary army during the English Civil War, and in 1682 Locke himself joined a rebellion against Charles II led by Anthony Ashley Cooper, the earl of Shaftesbury. Its failure forced him to seek asylum in Holland.

During the reign of Charles II, Locke wrote two *Treatises of Government*. The first was a devastating critique of the traditional arguments for absolutism. These tried to justify the power of rulers by comparing it to the role fathers play in patriarchal families. Locke argued that both fathers and rulers are bound by the law of nature that creates everyone equal and independent. In his *Second Treatise of Government* he made the case for government's obligation to be responsive to the wishes of the governed. He disagreed with Hobbes's assumption that people were driven only by passion and selfish interests and argued that they were endowed by nature with reason and goodwill. They are able to cooperate and live together in peace on their own, but they established governments to solve problems and facilitate social life. Governments are based on social contracts that are meant to protect the liberty of the state of nature, not restrain it. Rulers who fail to honor the terms of such contracts can legitimately be replaced by their subjects.

Locke believed that governments should limit themselves to protecting property and should not make religious decisions for their people. In his *Letter Concerning Toleration* (1689) he argued that each individual was responsible for working out his or her own salvation. Differences of opinion were likely, but uniformity could not be imposed because faith was a matter of conscience. Locke denied religious liberty to two groups—to atheists on the ground that their oaths (lacking any divine sanction) could not be trusted, and to Roman Catholics on the ground that they were pledged to serve a foreign prince (i.e., the pope).

Locke's most immediately influential book was his *Essay Concerning Human Understanding* (1690). It offered a scientific explanation for human psychology. Locke claimed that the mind of a newborn was a blank tablet on which no ideas had yet been inscribed. No knowledge was innate. It all came from sensory experience. This meant that human beings were products of their environments and that they could be reformed and perfected by transforming the world that shaped them. Locke claimed that religious knowledge was acquired like other kinds of knowledge. It came from studying the Scriptures and observing the natural order, not from private revelations. These, he believed, were the source of fanaticism and superstition.

The New Institutions of Expanding Natural Knowledge

Medieval scholars assumed that learning was a process of recovering what had already been discovered by ancient philosophers (such as Aristotle) or revealed to the authors of the Bible and the founders of the church. Even the Protestant reformers saw themselves only as restoring the original Christian message and not as discovering something new in it. As science took root, however, confidence grew that genuinely new discoveries about nature and humanity were possible. Learning could advance by creating new knowledge.

The new intellectual faith that science fostered had wide-ranging social implications. The universities, where traditional scholastic and Aristotelian modes of thought were deeply entrenched, became a frequent target of criticism by advocates of the new science. This was not always entirely fair, for the new ideas did penetrate the universities and some of them provided support for natural philosophers (e.g., Newton). The slowness of the schools to assimilate scientific advances, however, persuaded scientists that they needed to establish new kinds of institutions to advance their work.

Most prominent among these was the Royal Society of London, which was founded in 1660 to promote research and the sharing of scientific information. Similar organizations on both the local and national level sprang up in most European countries. Members of these societies met to hear papers and witness experiments. The high social standing of many society "fellows" lent credibility to reports of scientific discoveries, and their polite exchange of ideas helped promote a culture of civility that elevated science above the religious and political conflicts of the day.

The sixteenth and seventeenth centuries saw Europeans expanding their knowledge into the ancient past, into the New World, and into the starry heavens. In this painting, **The Sciences and the Arts,** *the artist depicts recent paintings that connect contemporary culture with the ancient world and the Bible. In the same room, he sets globes depicting the New World and astronomical instruments used by natural philosophers exploring the heavens, according to the theories of Copernicus, Kepler, and Galileo. Yet throughout all of the expansion of mind and geographical knowledge, women were generally excluded as they are in this painting. For example, only on the rarest occasion were women permitted to visit the Royal Society of London.* Adriaen Stalbent, *The Sciences and the Arts.* Wood, 93 × 114 cm. Inv. 1405. Museo del Prado, Madrid, Spain. Erich Lessing/Art Resource, NY

Members of these societies were drawn from the intellectual elite, but their interests led them to cooperate with laborers, craftspersons, and sailors whose skills, work experience, and travels made them invaluable sources of aid and information. Learned societies were eager to demonstrate what science could do to solve practical problems—and, thus, to advance the aims of government and enrich economic life. Persons who had ideas for improvements in things such as navigation, agriculture, engineering, and military technology turned to the societies for support, and the patrons of the new science sought to apply knowledge to practical ends, to urge religious toleration, and to promote political liberty. They were the harbingers of a confident, optimistic future.

Women in the World of the Scientific Revolution

Traditions that had long excluded women from intellectual activities continued to block them from doing scientific work. With a very few exceptions, women were not admitted to medieval or early modern universities—a situation that prevailed until the end of the nineteenth century. Women were also not welcomed into the new scientific societies and academies. A few women from the noble and artisan classes managed, however, with the help of male members of their families, to do some scientific work.

Margaret Cavendish (1623–1673), Duchess of Newcastle, was introduced by her husband to a circle of natural philosophers where she debated the theories of Descartes and Hobbes and criticized the Royal Society for doing too little to explore the practical applications of science. She was the only woman allowed to attend a meeting of the society. Her most important scientific publications were *Observations upon Experimental Philosophy* (1666) and *Grounds of Natural Philosophy* (1668). She also wrote a text intended primarily to introduce women to the study of science: *Description of a New World, Called the Blazing World* (1666). A few men similarly wrote popularizations of scientific theories for female audiences.

Women from the artisan classes had more opportunities to pursue science than other females, for they were traditionally trained to work in their families' businesses. Several German astronomers were assisted by their wives and daughters, and some of these women (e.g., Maria Cunitz, Elisabetha Hevelius, and Maria Winkelmann) wrote books or made notable discoveries on their own. After the death of her husband in 1710, Maria Winkelmann (who had discovered a comet in 1702) applied to the Berlin Academy of Sciences for permission to continue her husband's work. She was denied on the basis of her gender. Years later she tried to return as an assistant to her son, but she was ultimately forced to abandon astronomy.

In the 1730s the French philosopher Voltaire relied on the mathematical expertise of Emilie du Châtelet for help in writing a book on Newton, but few women were admitted to the fields of science and medicine before the late nineteenth century. Allegedly scientific arguments were even developed to explain how differences between male and female brains made women intellectual inferiors who were incapable of scientific work. The pursuit of natural knowledge was said to be a male vocation.

The New Science and Religious Faith

Many people believed that the new science posed a challenge to religion. Three issues were most troublesome: (1) disagreements between the biblical descriptions of the heavens and scientific discoveries, (2) the relative authority of clergymen versus scientists, and (3) the tendency of science to promote an exclusively materialistic view of the universe.

The Case of Galileo

The Roman Catholic Church was going through a particularly difficult period in its history when, in 1633, it took the infamous step of condemning the Copernican theory and Galileo. The Council of Trent asserted that the church alone had the authority to interpret the Bible, and in order to counter Protestant accusations that Catholicism had strayed from the Scriptures the church's interpretations had become narrowly literal. Galileo's views on biblical interpretation, which he published in 1615 (*Letter to the Grand Duchess Christina*), sounded suspiciously Protestant to some Catholic leaders, and the astronomer's discoveries seemed to support the Copernican view of the universe, which the church officially condemned as unbiblical in 1616.

Galileo apparently won the church's permission to write about Copernicanism so long as he did not assert its truthfulness but only entertained it as a theoretical possibility. In 1623 a new pope, who was an acquaintance of Galileo's, took office and allowed him to publish his research. The result was a book, *Dialogue on the Two Chief World Systems* (1632), which clearly asserted the correctness of the Copernican model of the heavens. Pope Urban VIII felt betrayed and mocked by Galileo's work and ordered it investigated. Galileo was forced to repudiate his theories, and he spent the last nine years of his life under house arrest. The incident cast a shadow that troubled the relationship between science and Catholic faith for a very long time. Pope John II eventually reopened the case, and in 1992 the church admitted that errors had been made.

Blaise Pascal: Reason and Faith

Blaise Pascal (1623–1662), a French mathematician and physical scientist, made the most influential attempt to reconcile faith with the new science. Pascal was a deeply religious man who surrendered his wealth to pursue a life of austerity, but he opposed the religious dogmatism of people such as the Jesuits as much as the skepticism of atheists and rationalists. Personally, he sided with the Jansenists, the French Catholics who endorsed the Augustinian doctrines of original sin, predestination, and total dependence on grace for salvation and knowledge of God. Unfortunately, he was never able to turn his insights into a fully integrated system. Instead, he published them as a collection of provocative reflections on the human condition, which he entitled *Pensées*.

Pascal believed that reason could reveal humanity's utter corruption, but that it was too weak to resolve the problems of human nature or disclose the meaning of human life. For these purposes, religion was required, and religion operated outside the domain of reason. It required a "leap of faith" that accepted one's total reliance on divine grace. Pascal proposed an ingenious "wager" to demonstrate the unreasonableness of skepticism. He noted that it is a better bet to believe that God exists than to doubt. If God does exist, the believer wins everything. If it turns out that God does not exist, the believer has not lost much by believing. Furthermore, Pascal argued that religious faith is valuable in and of itself apart from the issue of God's existence. It provides motivation for self-discipline and strengthens moral character. Pascal urged people to pursue self-awareness through "learned ignorance" (i.e., through contemplation of the significance of human limitations). This, he hoped, would counter what he saw as the false optimism promoted by the new scientific rationalism.

The English Approach to Science and Religion

Francis Bacon sought to reconcile religion and science by suggesting that the Bible and nature were both sources of divine revelation. Since both were created by God, it was logical to assume that the knowledge they produced would ultimately be discovered not to be incompatible with itself. One could be expected to illuminate the other.

As science promoted a progressively mechanistic view of the universe, men such as Newton came to believe that the rational laws that governed nature implied that nature's Creator was also characterized by rationality. To study nature was to study the Creator and to move gradually from knowledge of phenomena to knowledge of their ultimate cause. Such faith promoted a popular ideology called *physico-theology*. At a time when Europeans were tiring of wars sparked by religious disputes, it held out the hope that science might end such conflicts by developing a new understanding of God on which all parties could agree. Faith in a rational God also encouraged faith in human rationality and humanity's ability to overcome the errors of its past. The new way of life that began to emerge from the new science was increasingly justified as part of a divine plan. It seemed obvious that God had placed rational beings in a rational world so that they should master it. Scientific advance and economic enterprise, thus, became religious missions.

Continuing Superstition

Despite the optimistic confidence certain European intellectuals had in the ultimate triumph of reason, many Europeans of the sixteenth and seventeenth centuries continued to believe in magic and the occult. Almost all Europeans believed to some degree in the Devil and the power of his demons.

Witch Hunts and Panic

Loss of faith in traditional certainties drove some thinkers to seek a new grounding for truth in reason and science, but there was a darker alternative. Many people responded to the intellectual challenges of the age with fear and suspicion, and in their desperate search for security, they crossed the line that divides religion from superstition. This was as true for the learned as for the less educated. Between 1400 and 1700, an estimated 70,000 to 100,000 people were sentenced to death in the West for practicing harmful magic (*malificium*) and diabolical witchcraft. Between episodes of persecuting their neighbors, witches were said to fly off to conventions called *sabbats* where they engaged in sexual orgies with the Devil and practiced every indecency imaginable. The Reformation may have unintentionally contributed to this development by emphasizing the power of demons and the Devil while eliminating many of the traditional sacraments and rituals that had once offered a defense against these powers of darkness.

Vermeer's The Geographer and The Astronomer: *Painting and the New Knowledge*

The Netherlands stood at the center of the developments that were transforming the intellectual life of Europe in the sixteenth and seventeenth centuries. Dutch opticians and metal workers produced the instruments used in the new science, and Dutch sailors plied the shipping lanes that flooded Europe with information about areas of the world that had previously been unknown to the West. Furthermore, a tradition of religious tolerance, open immigration, and freedom of the press created an atmosphere in the Netherlands that stimulated intellectual activity.

Two paintings by the Dutch artist Jan Vermeer (1632–1675) illustrate the spirit that pervaded the Netherlands. They were intended to be hung side by side and to give meaning to each other. Their subjects, astronomy and geography, were important to the sea-faring Dutch because of the contributions these disciplines made to techniques of navigation. The new maps of the geographer, who gazes out his window onto a world of increasing wonder, acquainted ordinary Europeans with distant, exotic locales and enabled sailors to conduct the trade on which Dutch prosperity depended. The astronomer contemplates a globe that depicts the constellations of the night sky. A chart containing additional astronomical information hangs on his wall, and an instrument for observing the heavens lies on his table. Plainly working with the data of observation and mathematical theorizing was as important to him as peering at the heavens. The most curious element in the picture is the painting that hangs on the wall at the astronomer's back. It depicts the finding of the infant Moses, a subject that symbolizes God's divine providence. Vermeer may have included it to suggest that the new natural knowledge was a part of God's providential plan for humanity.

Mariet Westermann, *A Worldly Art: The Dutch Republic 1585–1718* (New York: Prentice Hall/Abrams, 1996); Arthur K. Wheelock, Jr., *Vermeer and the Art of Painting* (New Haven: Yale University Press, 1995); J. M. Montias, *Vermeer and His Milieu: A Web of Social History* (Princeton: Princeton University Press, 1989); Arthur K. Wheelock, Jr., *Perspective, Optics, and Delft Artists Around 1650* (New York: Garland Press, 1997)

Vermeer van Delft, Jan, *The Geographer* (1668–1669). Oil on canvas. Staedelsches Kunstinstitute, Frankfurt am Main. The Granger Collection

Vermeer van Delft, Jan (1632–1675), *The Astronomer* (1668). Oil on canvas 31.5 × 45.5 cm. Louvre, Dep. des Peintures, Paris, France. Erich Lessing, Art Resource, NY

Three witches suspected of practicing harmful magic are burned alive on a pyre in Bade. On the left, two of them are shown feasting and cavorting with demons at a Sabbat. Bildarchiv, Preussischer Kulturbesitz

Village Origins

Belief in witchcraft pervaded elite as well as popular cultures, but it had deep roots in rural areas. Village societies have customarily dealt with the threats and terrors of life by turning for help to "cunning folk," to people who are believed to have special powers to avert or mitigate natural disasters and ease problems caused by disease and infertility. The witch cultures of medieval and early modern village societies also probably thrived as a form of peasant self-assertion. If they perpetuated ancient, pre-Christian religious practices, their devotees may have seen them as a means for rebelling against the oppressive authority of urban Christian society.

Since a reputation for possession of magical powers gave a person standing in a village society, such claims were often made by people who were most in need of influence—the elderly, the impoverished, and single or widowed women. Should any of their neighbors claim, however, that they used their powers for evil rather than good, they were also the element in society least able to defend itself.

Influence of the Clergy

Widespread faith in magic was the essential precondition for the great witch hunts of the sixteenth and seventeenth centuries, and such belief was not limited to ordinary people. It was shared by intellectuals and the Christian clergy whose sacramental powers were a form of magic. The church promoted fear of demons and the Devil in its efforts to persuade people to accept its discipline, and exorcism of demons was a traditional function of priests.

In the late thirteenth century the church declared that its priests were the only possessors of legitimate magical power. Inasmuch as such power was not human, theologians reasoned that it had to come either from God or from the Devil. Since the only people empowered to act for God were the church's priests, it followed that all other wonder workers must have made pacts with the Devil in order to acquire their magic. The church sincerely believed that it was its duty to root out the servants of the Devil, but by destroying the "cunning folk" it also cleansed village communities of the people who competed with its priests for spiritual authority.

Why Women?

A good 80 percent of the victims of witch hunts were women, most of whom were single and between forty-five and sixty years of age. It is possible that persecution of witches provided a male-dominated society with a means for ridding itself of unconventional women who were not under some man's control. Or it may simply be that older single women were attacked not because of their gender but because they were perceived to be, with other poor people, burdens on society. Some female professions, such as midwifery and nursing, exposed women to suspicion of malfeasance by associating them with mysterious deaths. Economic need may also have driven more women than men to take the risk of claiming supernatural powers as healers and casters of spells.

End of the Witch Hunts

The great witch panics occurred in the second half of the sixteenth and early seventeenth centuries. They were, in part, a response to the suffering caused by the religious divisions and wars that ravaged European society at that time. Increasing levels of violence exacerbated fear and hatred and inspired a search for scapegoats on which to vent these emotions. Witch hunts also helped church and state enforce conformity and eliminate competition for the loyalty of their subjects.

By the end of the seventeenth century, however, authorities began to fear that things were getting out of hand. When it became evident that witch hunting was doing more to destabilize society than to impose order and unanimity, the witch trials ceased. The emergence of the new scientific worldview also undercut belief in witches, and improvements in things such as medicine gave people greater confidence in their ability to solve problems without supernatural assistance. The Reformation may also have helped to end the witch craze by ridiculing the sacramental magic of the old church and by preaching faith in a God who was absolutely sovereign. Ultimately, for Protestants, God was the only significant spiritual force in the universe, and his freely offered grace, not magic, was the only defense against the power of evil.

In Perspective

The Scientific Revolution and the thought of writers whose work was contemporaneous with it mark a major turning point in history. During the seventeenth century, many of the fundamental premises of the medieval worldview were abandoned. The earth was displaced from the center of the universe, and the universe seemed much larger and more complex than had previously been imagined. New knowledge of the physical universe called into question dogmas that rested on the authority of the church and Scripture. Theology and metaphysics yielded to mathematics as the preferred discipline for exploring nature. Political thought became much less concerned with religious issues and much less in awe of traditional authorities. Arguments were developed to promote greater freedom of religious and political expression. People began to comprehend the influence of environment on human character and action. Life on Earth became the chief preoccupation of Western intellectuals, and they demonstrated greater self-confidence in their capacity to realize its potentials.

REVIEW QUESTIONS

1. What contributions to the Scientific Revolution were made by Copernicus, Brahe, Kepler, Galileo, and Newton? What did Bacon contribute to the foundation of scientific thought? Who do you think made the most important contribution? Why?
2. Was the Scientific Revolution truly a revolution? Which has a greater impact on history, a political or an intellectual revolution?
3. How do the political philosophies of Hobbes and Locke compare? How did each view human nature? Would you rather live under a government designed by Hobbes or by Locke? Why?
4. What prevented women from playing a greater role in the development of the new science? How did family connections enable some women to contribute to the advance of natural philosophy?
5. What things account for the church's condemnation of Galileo? How did Pascal try to reconcile faith and reason? How did English natural theology encourage economic expansion?
6. How do you explain the fact that witchcraft and witch hunts flourished during an age of scientific enlightenment? Why did the witch panics occur in the late sixteenth and seventeenth centuries? How might the Reformation have affected them?

SUGGESTED READINGS

R. Ashcraft, *Revolutionary Politics and Locke's Two Treatises of Government* (1986). The most important study of Locke to appear in recent years.

J. Barry, M. Hester, and G. Roberts, eds. *Witchcraft in Early Modern Europe: Studies in Culture and Belief* (1998). A collection of recent essays.

H. Butterfield, *The Origins of Modern Science, 1300–1800* (1949). A classic survey.

H. F. Cohen, *The Scientific Revolution: A Historiographical Inquiry* (1994). Supplants all previous discussions of the history and concept of the Scientific Revolution.

M. A. Finocchiaro, *The Galileo Affair: A Documentary History* (1989). A collection of all the relevant documents and introductory commentary.

S. Gaukroger, *Descartes: An Intellectual Biography* (1995). A major work that explores both the science and philosophy in Descartes's work.

A. Goldgar, *Impolite Learning: Conduct and Community in the Republic of Letters, 1680–1750* (1995). A lively survey of the structure of the European intellectual community.

I. Harris, *The Mind of John Locke: A Study of Political Theory in Its Intellectual Setting* (1994). The most comprehensive recent treatment.

A. Johns, *The Nature of the Book: Print and Knowledge in the Making* (1998). A brilliant study of the role of printing in the intellectual life of early modern Europe.

R. Kieckhefer, *European Witch Trials: Their Foundations in Popular and Learned Culture, 1300–1500* (1976). Excellent background for understanding the great witch panic.

T. S. Kuhn, *The Copernican Revolution* (1957). A scholarly treatment.

B. Levack, *The Witch Hunt in Early Modern Europe* (1986). Lucid up-to-date survey of research.

D. Lindberg and R. L. Numbers, eds., *God and Nature: Historical Essays on the Encounter Between Christianity and Science* (1986). An excellent collection of essays.

L. Pyenson and S. Sheets-Pyenson, *Servants of Nature: A History of Scientific Institutions, Enterprises, and Sensibilities* (1999). A history of the settings in which the creation and diffusion of scientific knowledge have occurred.

E. Reeves, *Painting the Heavens: Art and Science in the Age of Galileo* (1997). An exploration of the impact of Galileo's thought on the visual arts.

L. Schiebinger, *The Mind Has No Sex: Women in the Origins of Modern Science* (1989). A major study of the subject.

S. Shapin, *The Scientific Revolution* (1996). The best brief introduction.

K. Thomas, *Religion and the Decline of Magic* (1971). Provocative, much-acclaimed work focused on popular culture.

R. Tuck, *Philosophy and Government 1572–1651* (1993). A continent-wide survey.

R. S. Westfall, *Never at Rest: A Biography of Isaac Newton* (1981). An important major study.

P. Zagorin, *Francis Bacon* (1998). A comprehensive treatment.

Chapter 15
Successful and Unsuccessful Paths to Power (1686–1740)

KEY TOPICS

- The Dutch Golden Age
- French aristocratic resistance to the monarchy
- Early eighteenth-century political stability
- The efforts of the Habsburgs to secure their holdings
- The emergence of Prussia as a major power under the Hohenzollerns
- The efforts of Peter the Great to transform Russia into a powerful, centralized nation along Western lines

The late seventeenth and early eighteenth centuries witnessed significant shifts of power within Europe. Great Britain, France, Austria, Russia, and Prussia emerged as the dominant states, while Spain, the United Netherlands, Poland, Sweden, and the Holy Roman and Ottoman empires declined. The most successful countries were those that developed strong central governments. During the seventeenth century, the turmoil created by the English civil wars and the Fronde in France had impressed people with the value of a monarch as a guarantor of domestic tranquility. On the continent, this created support for the kind of absolutist government pioneered by France's Louis XIV. The path a nation took was often a function of the character, personality, and energy of its ruler.

The Maritime Powers

Spain and the United Netherlands had been major powers during the sixteenth and seventeenth centuries, but during the eighteenth century they became politically and militarily marginal as England and France took the lead. Both, however, retained considerable economic power and influence.

The Netherlands: Golden Age to Decline

The seven provinces that became the United Provinces of the Netherlands formed the only genuinely new state to appear in Europe during the early modern period. They first asserted their independence in a revolt against Spain in 1572. In the 1580s they won recognition from the other European powers, and Spain acknowledged their autonomy in 1609 and their formal independence in 1648.

While rising powers such as France and England chose to develop strongly centralized governments, the Dutch opted for a republic in which each of their provinces retained considerable authority. The States General, the central government seated in the Hague, tended to be dominated by the prosperous, populous province of Holland. From time to time when war demanded a more powerful executive, the Dutch would permit a member of the noble House of Orange to assume leadership. William III, the *stadtholder* of Holland, led a European coalition against Louis XIV of France and ultimately shared the throne of England with his wife, Mary. Following his death in 1702 and the conclusion of peace with France in 1714, the Dutch returned to republican government.

The official church of the Netherlands stood in the Calvinist Reform tradition, but allegiance to it was not enforced. The population remained religiously mixed, and the Netherlands enjoyed a reputation for tolerance that made it a haven for Jews driven out of other countries. Tolerance proved a workable policy that spared the Netherlands the internal strife that plagued so many other European states.

URBAN PROSPERITY The Dutch were remarkable to their contemporaries as much for their prosperity as their spirit of tolerance. While other states squandered resources on religious wars, the Dutch concentrated on economic development. They transformed agriculture, promoted trade and finance, and built an overseas commercial empire. The Netherlands became the most urbanized region in Europe, boasting a percentage of urban dwellers in its population that other countries did not reach until the industrial era.

The concentration of the Dutch in cities was made possible by innovations in agriculture that were copied throughout Europe. During the seventeenth century Dutch farmers drained and reclaimed a great deal of land from the sea. Since Dutch shipping dominated trade with the Baltic, the Netherlands was able to feed itself with cheap grain from that region. This enabled Dutch farmers to devote their land to more profitable cash crops (e.g., dairy products, meat, and even tulip bulbs). Dutch fishing fleets supplied much of the

In the mid-eighteenth century, when this picture of the Amsterdam Exchange was painted, Amsterdam had replaced the cities of Italy and south Germany as the leading banking center of Europe. Amsterdam retained this position until the late eighteenth century. Painting by Hiob A. Berckheyde, *The Amsterdam Exchange.* Canvas 85 × 105 cm. Coll. Museum Boijmans Van Beuningen, Rotterdam, The Netherlands

herring (a major source of inexpensive protein) consumed on the continent, and Dutch mills provided textiles to many parts of Europe. Dutch ships were found in every European port transporting all kinds of goods, and ship building itself constituted a highly profitable industry for the Netherlands. Profits from these enterprises provided capital for banks, and the Dutch boasted the most advanced financial system of their day. Shareholders funded ventures such as the Dutch East Indies Company, which won control of the East Asian spice trade from the Portuguese. The Netherlands retained a colonial presence in Indonesia until after World War II.

ECONOMIC DECLINE   For a variety of reasons, the Dutch economy began to weaken in the eighteenth century. After the death of William III in 1702, the provinces blocked the rise of another powerful *stadtholder* who could provide unified political leadership. Naval supremacy began to pass to England, the fishing industry declined, and the Dutch lost the technological lead in shipbuilding. Countries developed their own fleets to carry their own goods rather than relying on Dutch shipping, and Dutch manufacturing began to stagnate. The absence of vigorous leadership handicapped efforts to confront these challenges, but the Netherlands still managed to retain considerable influence thanks to its banks and stock exchange.

France after Louis XIV

France, although less strong in 1715 than in 1680, was still a great power. It had a large population, an advanced economy, and a highly developed administrative structure. Its resources were drained by the last of Louis XIV's wars, but these conflicts had similarly debilitated the other major European states. All that France needed in order to recover economically was intelligent leadership and a less ambitious foreign policy.

France did begin to recover, but not because of an improvement in the quality of its leadership. The prestige of the monarchy was already faltering when Louis XIV passed the crown to his five-year-old great-grandson Louis XV (r. 1715–1774). The young king's regent—his uncle, the duke of Orléans—made a deteriorating situation worse. Orléans was a gambler who turned over the financial management of the government to a Scottish speculator, John Law (1671–1729). Law believed

that an increase in the money supply would stimulate postwar economic recovery, so he established a bank to issue paper money. Law transferred responsibility for managing the national debt that this money represented to the Mississippi Company, a corporation that had a monopoly on trading privileges with France's Louisiana colony in North America. The company issued shares of its stock in exchange for government bonds and relied on profits from stock speculation to redeem those bonds. Initially the price of the stock rose handsomely, but smart investors took their profits and exchanged the paper currency from Law's bank for gold. Since the bank lacked sufficient bullion to back up the money it printed, in February 1720, the government had to halt gold trading in France. Law fled the country, and the "Mississippi Bubble" (as the affair was called) burst. The fiasco brought disgrace on the government and cast a shadow over economic activity in France for the rest of the century.

RENEWED AUTHORITY OF THE *PARLEMENTS*   The duke of Orléans further weakened the monarchy by trying to recreate a role for the French nobility in the decision-making processes of the government. Louis XIV had filled governmental offices with commoners and kept aristocrats distracted and competing for meaningless honors at Versailles. The regent was pressured by the aristocrats to restore their influence, and he set up a system of administrative councils on which nobles served with bureaucrats. The experiment failed, for the nobles, whom Louis had thoroughly domesticated, lacked both the talent and the will to govern.

The great French families were not, however, prepared to yield ground in their ancient fight to limit the power of the monarchy over their landed domains. Their most effective weapons in this struggle were the *parlements*, the aristocratically dominated courts. The French *parlements* were different from the English Parliament. They did not have the power to legislate, but as courts that enforced the law, their formal approval was required to make a royal law valid. Louis XIV had curtailed the authority of stubborn, uncooperative *parlements*, but the duke of Orléans restored their right to register laws. For the rest of the century, until the revolution that overthrew the monarchy in 1790, the aristocrats used the *parlements* to resist royal authority.

Rachel Ruysch, Flower Still Life: Flowers, Commerce, and Morality

*P*aintings often contain symbols that give them a deeper meaning than is apparent to the casual observer. This is most obvious when a painter develops an allegorical scene employing mythological figures, but it can also be a characteristic of a still life—a painting of objects. Rachel Ruysch (1664–1750), a female artist working in Amsterdam, chose elaborate floral arrangements as her favorite subject. Several decades before Ruysch completed this painting (*Flower Still Life*) a peculiar mania had swept Holland for wild financial speculation in rare tulip bulbs. This picture and the hundreds of similar ones that were produced in the seventeenth and eighteenth centuries would have reminded people of that event. Flowers represented work and commerce, not just the aesthetic beauties of nature. Commercial growers dealt in exotic plants brought to the Netherlands from its overseas empire, and they symbolized the country's global trade. The flowers depicted here were valuable varieties, not humble blooms. As such, they were emblematic of wealth and abundance.

Paintings such as this one helped the Dutch reconcile life in Europe's richest society with the frugality and abstinence that were the values of their Calvinistic faith. The melancholy atmosphere that hovers over these lush blossoms reminds the viewer that all rare and lovely things soon decay. Shadows surround the flowers' riotous display of beauty, and the empty snail shells on the table hint at death and the transitory nature of existence. The artist's extraordinary attention to detail witnesses, however, to the interests of a scientifically inclined age in accurately describing and cataloguing the transitory things of this world. She probably worked from botanical manuals rather than

Rachel Ruysch, Dutch, 1664–1750, *Flower Still Life* (1956.57). The Toledo Museum of Art, Toledo, Ohio. Purchased with funds from the Libbey Endowment, Gift of Edward Drummond Libbey

from real floral arrangements, for the flowers she depicts did not all bloom in the same season.

Sources: Norman Bryson, *Looking at the Overlooked: Four Essays on Still Life Painting* (Cambridge, MA: Harvard University Press, 1990); Mariët Westermann, *A Worldly Art: The Dutch Republic, 1585–1718* (Upper Saddle River, NJ and New York: Prentice Hall Publishers, Inc., and Harry N. Abrams, Inc., 1990); Marilyn Stokstad, *Art History*, rev. ed. (Upper Saddle River, NJ and New York: Prentice Hall Publishers, Inc., and Harry N. Abrams, Inc., 1999), pp. 798–801.

ADMINISTRATION OF CARDINAL FLEURY   After 1726 things briefly improved for the monarchy thanks to a seventy-three-year-old churchman, Cardinal Fleury (1653–1743), who became the king's chief minister. Like his seventeenth-century predecessors, the cardinals Richelieu and Mazarin, Fleury was a political realist who understood that the nobles were both politically ambitious and irresponsible. He believed that steps had to be taken to enable France to recover economically. To this end, he avoided expensive military ventures, repudiated part of the national debt, built roads and bridges, and encouraged the growth of new industries. He was never able, however, to impose sufficient taxes on the nobles or the church to put the state on a stable financial footing.

Following Fleury's death in 1743, his work was speedily undone. Despite the cardinal's best efforts to train Louis XV for the responsibilities of office, the king possessed all the vices and none of the virtues of his great-grandfather. He wanted absolute power but would not work the long hours required to use it. He became a pawn of the intrigues of his court, and his personal life was scandalous. Louis XV was too mediocre a man to be evil, but in a monarch mediocrity could do as much damage as wickedness.

Despite its lack of able leadership, France remained a major power. At midcentury its army was still the largest and strongest on the continent. Its commerce and production were expanding. Its colonies were producing wealth and spurring the growth of domestic industries. France had great potential, but it lacked a head capable of exploiting its opportunities.

Great Britain: The Age of Walpole

THE HANOVERIAN DYNASTY   The British monarchy was not as degraded as the French, but it was not entirely stable. In 1701 Parliament's Act of Settlement had positioned the German house of Hanover to inherit the throne. But a challenge was mounted to the ascension of the first member of the dynasty, George I (r. 1714–1727). In December 1715, James II's son, James Edward, the "Stuart pretender" (1688–1766), landed in Scotland and began to rally an army. His men were soon dispersed, but the experience alerted the new dynasty to the necessity of consolidating its position.

WHIGS AND TORIES   During the seventeenth century, England had been one of the most politically restive countries in Europe, and as Queen Anne's reign (1702–1714) came to a close, there were sharp clashes between political factions called Whigs and Tories. Neither group was organized like a modern political party. Each was a network of like-minded local politicians whose points of view were articulated by a few national spokesmen. The Tories favored a strong monarchy, low taxes for landowners, and the Anglican Church. The Whigs believed that the monarchy should acknowledge the sovereignty of Parliament. They defended urban commercial interests and rural landowners, and they advocated religious toleration for Protestant nonconformists. Both groups were conservative in that they defended the status quo.

The Tories wanted peace with France, but the Elector of Hanover, who was to succeed Queen

Madame de Pompadour (1721–1764) was the mistress of Louis XV. She exercised considerable political influence at the court and was a notable patron of artists, craftspeople, and writers. This 1763 portrait is by Hubert Drouais (1727–1775).   Liaison Agency, Inc.

Anne as George I, believed that it was in Hanover's interest to keep France at war. The Whigs sought his support, and in the final months of Anne's reign, some Tories opened channels of communication with the Stuart pretender. Given this, it was little wonder that the Whigs won the confidence of the new king. For the forty years following his succession, the chief difference between Whigs and Tories was that the former were given public offices and patronage and the latter were not.

THE LEADERSHIP OF ROBERT WALPOLE English politics remained in a state of flux until Robert Walpole (1676–1745) persuaded the king to redesign the nation's government. Walpole, a Norfolk squire, had been active in the House of Commons and had served as a cabinet minister. A British financial scandal similar to France's Mississippi Bubble scheme brought him to the king's attention.

Management of Britain's national debt had been assigned to the South Sea Company. The company exchanged government bonds for its stock, and, as in the French case, the price of its stock soared until speculators began to sell their holdings. Parliament intervened in 1720 to prevent a crash and, under Walpole's leadership, adopted measures to honor the national debt. Walpole's contemporaries credited him with saving the financial integrity of the nation.

Walpole has often been described as the first prime minister of Great Britain. He originated England's system of administration by a cabinet of ministers—each of whom had responsibility for a separate branch of government. But unlike a modern prime minister, he was not chosen by the House of Commons. His power depended on his ability to manipulate the House while retaining the favor of his kings, George I and George II (r. 1727–1760).

Walpole's slogan, "Let sleeping dogs lie," summarized his policy of maintaining peace abroad while promoting the status quo at home. Corruption was the glue that held his government together, for politicians quickly learned that to oppose him was to risk the almost certain loss of government patronage for self, family, and friends.

THE STRUCTURE OF PARLIAMENT The eighteenth-century British House of Commons was neither a democratic nor a representative body. Members of Parliament were chosen by property owners and expected to protect their economic and social interests. Each county elected two members. But if the more powerful landed families in a county agreed on the candidates, there was no contest. Other members were chosen by units called boroughs. A few boroughs were large enough to hold truly democratic elections, but most boroughs had a very small number of electors. A rich family could buy up most of the property to which the votes of a borough were attached and, in effect, own a seat in Parliament.

Members of Parliament did not pretend to represent the people at large, but they provided England with unified government. Owners of property were suspicious of the bureaucrats who worked for the crown and preferred to bear the burdens of local administration themselves (e.g., as judges, militia commanders, tax collectors). In this sense Britain's nobles and substantial landowners governed the nation. Since Parliament represented their interests, they acknowledged its sovereignty as a central political authority. Parliament, thus, provided Britain with the kind of unity that was possible elsewhere in Europe only under an absolutist monarchy.

Parliament also provided the British government with a sound financial base. Continental kings could impose taxes unilaterally, but the British monarch could do so only with the consent of Parliament. Since the property owners represented in Parliament levied taxes on themselves, in England, unlike France, there were virtually no exemptions from taxation. Consequently, vast sums could be raised to fight the wars that Parliament endorsed. By 1693, when the Bank of England was set up to regulate credit, financial policies were in place that enabled Britain to become a great power.

The British people enjoyed more political freedom than the citizens of continental states. Patronage did not stifle divergent points of view among members of the government. Newspapers and public debate flourished. Free speech and freedom of association were possible, and there was no standing army to intimidate the populace. Rights that the English regarded as traditional raised a real barrier to the government's arbitrary use of power. If public outcry was loud enough, Parliament would rescind unpopular measures or allow itself to be persuaded to begin or end wars. Despite manifest corruption, Britain became a European power of the first order with a form of government and an economy that inspired progressive thinkers across Europe.

Central and Eastern Europe

The maritime nations of western Europe had well-defined borders and strong central governments. Their battles were more often fought on the high seas and in their overseas empires than on European territory. East of the Elbe River, however, political organization was "soft." Economies were largely agrarian. Serfdom persisted. Cities were few. No states had overseas empires or much overseas trade. Wars were fought out at home rather than abroad and accustomed people to frequently shifting political loyalties. The rulers of the region's numerous small states and principalities resisted the development of any centralized monarchy.

In the last half of the seventeenth century, political and social institutions emerged that were to characterize eastern and central Europe for the next 200 years. Following the Peace of Westphalia, the Austrian Habsburgs resigned themselves to the weakness of Germany's Holy Roman Empire and turned their attention to developing a base of power farther east. At the same time in northern Germany, Prussia evolved as a challenger to Habsburg domination. By the start of the eighteenth century, Russia, too, was becoming a major military power. As Sweden, Poland, and the Ottoman Empire faded, Austria, Prussia, and Russia began to flourish.

Sweden: The Ambitions of Charles XII

Sweden had seized the opportunity of the Thirty Years' War to make a bid for empire. During the seventeenth century, it won control of the Baltic and permitted Russia and Germany access to the sea only on its terms. Sweden's economy was not strong enough, however, to sustain its political success.

In 1697 a headstrong (possibly insane) king, Charles XII (r. 1697–1718), ascended Sweden's throne. Three years later Russia launched the Great Northern War (1700–1721) to win a foothold on the Baltic. Charles XII fought vigorously and often brilliantly, but he mismanaged the campaign. After an initial victory and a distracting foray into Poland, he invaded Russia. His army bogged down in the brutal winter weather and suffered decisive defeat at Poltava in 1709. The war ended in 1721, when Sweden ran out of resources. Russia occupied a large section of the eastern Baltic coast and broke Sweden's monopoly of the sea. After Charles XII's death, the Swedish nobles limited the

William Hogarth produced a series of etchings to satirize the notoriously corrupt English electoral system. In this one he shows voters being offered bribes and free gin before they headed off to the polls. Voting was public, for the secret ballot was not introduced in England until 1872. William Hogarth, *An Election Entertainment,* Print. The Metropolitan Museum of Art, Harris Brisbane Dick Fund, 1932. 32.35(212)

power of the monarchy, and Sweden abandoned foreign adventures.

The Ottoman Empire

The Ottoman Empire was the chief barrier to expansion of Europe's major southeastern states: the Austrian Habsburg domain and Russia. Late in the seventeenth century the Ottomans still controlled most of the Balkan peninsula and the entire coastline of the Black Sea.

Although officially Islamic, the Ottoman Empire contained an ethnically and religiously diverse population. Its government worked through religiously defined political entities called *millets*. Laws and regulations applied to people according to the *millets* to which they belonged rather than to the districts in which they lived. The non-Islamic residents of the empire (the *zimmis*) could practice their faiths, but they were second-class citizens who could not rise in the service of the empire. This arrangement limited interaction among—and integration of—people of different faiths.

From its beginnings in the fifteenth century, the Ottoman Empire had been an aggressive power pressing westward from Istanbul (Constantinople) into Europe. By 1683 it was besieging the city of Vienna and forcing Christians in the Balkan peninsula and on the islands of the eastern Mediterranean to convert to Islam. Many of these people had previously been compelled by the Venetians to accept Roman Catholicism, and they welcomed the Turks as liberators.

By the end of the seventeenth century, the Ottomans were overextending themselves. Since military campaigns left Ottoman sultans little time to attend to civilian affairs, political factions in the capital acquired considerable independence. They resisted attempts to strengthen the central government, and rivalries among them weakened the effectiveness of the empire's administration. Control of distant provinces came to depend on the goodwill of native rulers, and commercial agents representing foreign nations dominated the empire's trade and its economy.

By the early eighteenth century, the weakness of the Ottoman Empire was creating a political vacuum on the southeastern perimeter of Europe. For the next two centuries European states probed and appropriated parts of the empire. In 1699 the Turks surrendered Hungary, Transylvania, Croatia, and Slavonia to the Habsburgs. Russia also moved into Ottoman territory, and early in the nineteenth century many of the peoples who lived in the Balkans and around the Black Sea launched campaigns to establish independent states. The result was political and ethnic turmoil that has yet to end.

Poland: Absence of Strong Central Authority

In no other part of Europe was the failure to maintain a competitive political position so complete as in Poland. The fault lay with the Polish nobility, who defeated all attempts to establish an effective central government—even one of their own making.

The Polish monarchy was elective, and divisions among the noble families prevented them from choosing one of their own to be king. Most of Poland's monarchs, therefore, were outsiders and puppets of foreign powers. The Polish nobles belonged to a central legislative body called the *Sejm* (i.e., Diet). It was an aristocratic assembly that excluded representatives from corporate bodies, such as towns. The Diet was virtually powerless. Its rule of *liberum veto* permitted any one of its members unilaterally to disband its meetings—a practice known as "exploding" the Diet. The need to achieve unanimity on every issue made it extremely difficult for the Diet to do much. Government as it was developing elsewhere in Europe simply was not tolerated in Poland. Consequently, during the last half of the eighteenth century, Poland disappeared from the map of Europe.

The Habsburg Empire and the Pragmatic Sanction

The Thirty Years' War was a turning point for the Austrian Habsburgs. It ended their dream of winning control over Germany and returning it to the Catholic fold. The decline of the Spanish branch of the family freed the Austrian Habsburgs to strike out in a new direction of their own.

The Treaty of Westphalia had legalized Protestantism and recognized the autonomy of more than 300 political entities within the Holy Roman Empire. The Habsburg family retained its hold on the imperial title, but the effectiveness of the title depended on the emperor's ability to

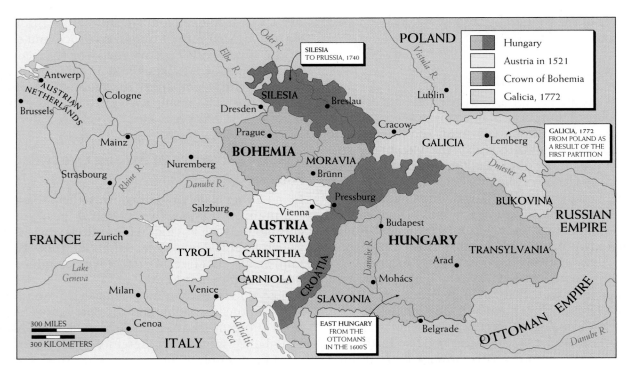

MAP 15–1   THE AUSTRIAN HABSBURG EMPIRE, 1522–1772   *The empire's three chief units were Austria, Bohemia, and Hungary. Expansion was mainly eastward, acquiring East Hungary from the Ottomans in the seventeenth century and Galacia from Poland in 1772. Silesia was lost, but the imperial title preserved some influence for the Habsburgs in Germany.*

elicit cooperation from the members of the imperial Diet. Although the post-Westphalian Holy Roman Empire resembled Poland in its lack of central authority, the Diet (which met at Regensburg from 1663 until its final dissolution in 1806) achieved some coordination of economic and political interests. The Habsburgs' domains and the emerging Prussian state also helped stabilize Germany.

CONSOLIDATION OF AUSTRIAN POWER   The Habsburgs began by consolidating their power within their hereditary possessions. These consisted of the Crown of Saint Wenceslas (i.e., the kingdom of Bohemia in what was until recently Czechoslovakia and the duchies of Moravia and Silesia) and the Crown of Saint Stephen (i.e., Hungary, Croatia, and Transylvania). In the early eighteenth century the family acquired the former Spanish (thereafter Austrian) Netherlands, Lombardy in northern Italy, and, for a brief time, the Kingdom of Naples in southern Italy. For most of the eighteenth and nineteenth centuries, the Habsburgs' power derived from lands outside Germany.

The Habsburgs' possessions were extremely difficult to rule. The various properties that composed the empire were held by different titles, and in most areas the Habsburgs could govern only with the cooperation of the local nobles. Geographical barriers and differences of language and custom prevented the Habsburgs' subjects from developing a common identity. Even the Habsburg zeal for Roman Catholicism was no bond for unity, for many of the Magyar nobles of Hungary were zealous Calvinists. The Habsburgs tried to chart common policies for their far-flung domains, but they repeatedly found it necessary to make concessions to nobles in one part of Europe to maintain their position in another.

Despite these difficulties, Leopold I (r. 1657–1705) was able to keep both the Turks and France's Louis XIV at bay. In 1699 the Ottomans recognized his sovereignty over Hungary, and Leopold's increasing strength in the East enhanced his political leverage in Germany. He began to bring his Magyar subjects under control and to extend his reach into the Balkan peninsula and western Romania. These new possessions

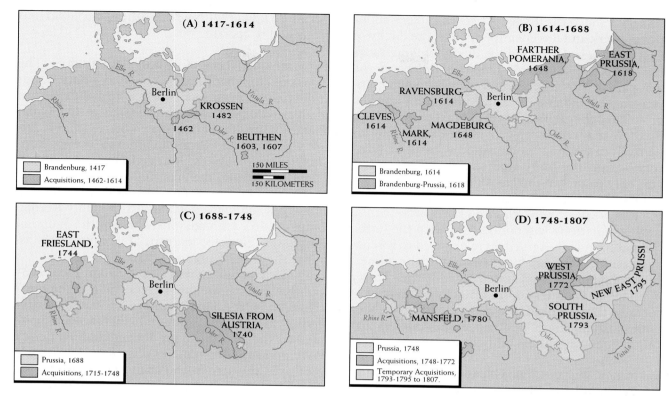

MAP 15–2   EXPANSION OF BRANDENBURG-PRUSSIA   *Brandenburg-Prussia expanded during the seventeenth century by acquiring dynastic titles to geographically separated lands. In the eighteenth century it resorted to aggression, seizing Silesia in 1740 and parts of Poland in 1772, 1793, and 1795.*

made it possible for him to turn the port of Trieste into a base for Habsburg power in the Mediterranean.

THE HABSBURG DYNASTIC PROBLEM   Leopold was succeeded by Joseph I (r. 1705–1711) and Charles VI (r. 1711–1740). Charles, who had no male heir, feared that after his death the European powers would intervene in the Austrian Habsburg lands just as they had in the Spanish Habsburgs' domains in 1700. To prevent this and to provide his realm with a semblance of legal unity, he devoted most of his reign to winning the approval of his family, the various diets representing his subjects, and Europe's chief nations for a document called the Pragmatic Sanction. It recognized a single line of inheritance for the Habsburg dynasty through Charles VI's daughter Maria Theresa (r. 1740–1780).

Charles succeeded in establishing a clear line of succession and a basis for legal bonds among the Habsburg holdings, but he could not prevent other nations from attacking his daughter. Less

than two months after his death, the fragility of his foreign agreements became clear. In December 1740, Frederick II of Prussia invaded the Habsburg province of Silesia, and Maria Theresa had to fight to defend her inheritance.

Prussia and the Hohenzollerns

Like the Habsburgs, the Hohenzollerns of Prussia held a scattered collection of lands by a variety of different feudal titles. But the Hohenzollerns were more successful than the Habsburgs in forging their diverse properties into a centrally administered state. They constructed a powerful bureaucratic machine to mobilize every social class and most economic pursuits in support of the institution on which the state was founded: the army. As a result, *Prussian* has become synonymous with administrative rigor and military discipline.

A STATE OF DISCONNECTED TERRITORIES   The Hohenzollern family rose to prominence in 1417 as rulers of the German territory of Brandenburg. To this they added the duchy of Cleves and the counties of Mark and Ravensburg in 1609, the duchy of East Prussia in 1618, and the duchy of Pomerania in 1637. At Westphalia in 1648 the Hohenzollerns lost part of Pomerania to Sweden but were compensated by the grant of three bishoprics and the promise of the archbishopric of Magdeburg (1680). By the late seventeenth century the scattered Hohenzollern holdings constituted a block of territory within the Holy Roman Empire second in size only to that of the Habsburgs.

Despite its size, the Hohenzollern conglomerate was weak. Except for Pomerania, none of the new acquisitions was contiguous with the home base in Brandenburg. All were exposed to foreign aggression. All were poor in natural resources. Many had been devastated during the Thirty Years' War. Each was dominated by a native aristocracy that limited the power of the Hohenzollern ruler. They shared no single concern that might encourage their unification.

FREDERICK WILLIAM, THE GREAT ELECTOR Frederick William (r. 1640–1688), "the Great Elector," transformed this unlikely mix of possessions into a powerful modern state. His instruments were a tightly centralized bureaucracy and a rigorously disciplined army. The threat of invasion by Sweden or Poland helped persuade his subjects to cooperate in the creation of these institutions.

The army with which Frederick William began his reign was too small to intimidate his neighbors. In 1655, when the Brandenburg estates refused his request for taxes to finance a larger force, he used the soldiers at his disposal to collect the money he needed to employ more. He also skillfully co-opted potential opponents. In exchange for supporting the Hohenzollerns, the Prussian nobles, the Junkers, were granted complete control over the serfs on their estates. Frederick William also used the Junkers to collect his taxes, which fell most heavily not on the nobility, but on the peasants and the urban classes. The privilege of joining the army officer corps became an honor reserved to men of aristocratic lineage.

Since the army was the one institution that drew members from all the Hohenzollern territories and all its soldiers and civilian personnel took an oath of loyalty to the elector, the army defined the state. Total mobilization of the state's resources enabled Frederick William to build a military machine far larger than that usually sustained by a small country. Prussia, thus,

became a power with which other (and larger) nations had to reckon.

FREDERICK WILLIAM I, KING OF PRUSSIA The house of Hohenzollern had created a nation, but it did not yet possess a crown. The acquisition of a royal title was the achievement of the Great Elector's son, Frederick I (r. 1688–1713). Frederick was the least "Prussian" member of his family. He built palaces, founded Halle University (1694), supported the arts, and lived luxuriously. In 1700, when the War of the Spanish Succession broke out, he made a deal with the Holy Roman Emperor. In exchange for the use of the Prussian army, the emperor permitted Frederick to assume the title "King in Prussia."

Frederick's heir, Frederick William I (r. 1713–1740), was both the most eccentric and the most effective of the Hohenzollern monarchs. After giving his father a funeral that would have pleased the luxury-loving Frederick I, Frederick William I imposed policies of strict austerity. He increased the size of the army and consolidated an obedient, compliant bureaucracy. He ruled alone without the assistance of ministers. His officials submitted reports in writing to him in his office, his *Kabinett*. Then he alone studied the papers, made decisions, and issued orders.

Frederick William's civilian bureaucrats worked under military discipline. All departments were centrally managed by the General Directory, the *General-Ober Finanz-Kriegs-und-Domänen- Direktorium*. The nobility were subjected to taxation, and most remaining feudal dues were transformed into money payments. Service to the state and the monarch became an automatic impersonal reflex—a mechanical and unquestioning recognition of a duty to a public office, not a loyalty engendered by any feeling for the unique qualities of the individual who held that office.

THE PRUSSIAN ARMY Frederick William was a near fanatic where his army was concerned. He required each district in his kingdom to provide him with a certain number of men. They were trained with rigorous discipline, and a show regiment composed of the tallest men in Europe was recruited. There were different laws for soldiers and for civilians, and royal patronage made the officer corps society's highest class. Frederick William merged the army, the Junker nobility, and the monarchy into a single political entity.

In 1725 he began the practice of always appearing in military uniform in order to publicize his concept of the state. Frederick William's military force grew from about 39,000 in 1713 to over 80,000 in 1740. Prussia was only the thirteenth most populous nation in Europe, but it fielded Europe's third or fourth largest army. Military priorities and values dominated Prussian government, society, and daily life as no place else in Europe. Other nations possessed armies, but Prussia was possessed by its army.

Having built the best army in Europe, Frederick William avoided using it. He enjoyed drilling his soldiers but not sending them into battle. He was capable of terrorizing his family and associates—occasionally knocking out teeth with his walking stick. But he did not pursue aggressive foreign policies. He regarded the army as a symbol of Prussian power and unity, not an instrument to be used for foreign adventures.

Frederick II, "the Great" (r. 1740–1786) inherited his father's superb military machine, but not his father's self-restraint. He celebrated his ascension to the throne by invading Silesia and challenging Austria for control of Germany. The struggle dominated central European affairs for over a century.

Russia Enters the European Political Arena

The rise of Prussia and the consolidation of the Austrian Habsburg domains doubtless seemed to many at the time only one more shift in the ancient game of German politics. But the entrance of Russia into European affairs was something wholly new. Russia had long been considered a part of Europe only by courtesy. Hemmed in by Sweden on the Baltic and by the Ottoman Empire on the Black Sea, it had no warm-water ports. Archangel, a port on the White Sea, was its chief outlet to the West, but it was closed by ice during part of the year. Russia was a land of vast but unfocused potential.

Birth of the Romanov Dynasty

The reign of Ivan IV, "the Terrible" (1533–1584), the first Muscovite prince to use the title "Tsar of Russia," was followed by a period of anarchy and civil war. In 1613 an assembly of nobles tried to end the confusion of this "Time of Troubles" by recognizing the seventeen-year-old Michael Romanov (r. 1613–1654) as their tsar. He founded the dynasty that ruled Russia until 1917.

Michael Romanov and his two successors, Alexis I (r. 1654–1676) and Theodore III (r. 1676–1682), stabilized Russia's government, but their nation remained weak and poor. Russia's administrative bureaucracy was dominated by the old nobility (the *boyars*), and it was only barely capable of maintaining order. The chief sources of instability were peasant revolts, raids by cossacks (horsemen who lived on the steppe frontier), and the potentially mutinous *streltsy*, Moscow's garrison.

Peter the Great

In 1682 two boys ascended Russia's fragile throne: Peter I, "the Great" (r. 1682–1725), and Ivan V. The succession was bloodily disputed, and the *streltsy* decided the outcome. Sophia, the boys' elder sister, served as regent until Peter's followers overthrew her in 1689. Peter then ruled personally, although in theory he shared the crown with the sickly Ivan until Ivan's death in 1696.

Like Louis XIV of France, whose youthful development had also been shaped by the experience of social upheaval, Peter resolved to establish a strong central monarchy. For ideas about how this could be done, he turned to the West. Products and workers from the West had filtered into Russia, and Europe's culture, particularly its military science, intrigued Peter.

In 1697 Peter made a famous tour of Europe. For convenience, he traveled officially incognito rather than as a head of state. (This minimized ceremonial functions.) The European leaders whom he visited found their almost seven-foot-tall guest both crude and rude. But Peter was thoroughly at home in their shipyards and munitions factories. They offered him what he had come to find.

Peter returned to Moscow determined to Westernize Russia. He set himself four objectives that he pursued ruthlessly: taming the *boyars* and the *streltsy*, extending royal authority over the church, reorganizing governmental administration, and developing the economy. Policy in each of these areas was intended to strengthen the military power of the nation and the authority of the monarchy.

TAMING THE *BOYARS* AND *STRELTSY* In 1698, immediately on his return from abroad, Peter launched an attack on the *boyars*. He personally shaved their long beards and sheared off the dangling sleeves of their shirts and coats—Russian peculiarities that western Europeans mocked. More important, he pressed the *boyars* into government service. In 1722 he published a Table of Ranks that pegged a person's social status to his position in the bureaucracy or the army. This induced boyars to submit to the service of the state, but the Russian nobility was never as thoroughly domesticated as the Prussian aristocracy.

The *streltsy* fared less well than the *boyars.* They rebelled while Peter was on his European tour. When he returned, he brutally suppressed their revolt and executed about 1,200 of them. Their corpses were publicly displayed to demonstrate the consequences of disloyalty to the tsar.

Achieving Secular Control of the Church

Peter was similarly ruthless in his dealings with the Russian Orthodox Church, which was firmly opposed to westernization. In 1667 Patriarch Nikon had attempted to reform the church by introducing some changes into its texts and ceremonies. Since the Russian church had always claimed to be the protector of the most ancient and authentic Christian rituals, these reforms met with a great deal of resistance. A group known as the Old Believers refused to accept the patriarch's mandates, and late in the century thousands of them committed suicide rather than submit to the new liturgies. The tragedy dissuaded the church hierarchy from making any further substantial moves toward modernization. To ensure that the clergy did not blunder into an-

other Old Believer schism or organize to oppose westernization, Peter abolished the office of patriarch in 1721 and ceded its power over the church to a synod headed by a layman, the Procurator General. This was the most radical of Peter's breaks with tradition.

Reorganizing Domestic Administration

Peter modeled his domestic administration on Sweden's government. Rather than set up departments under a single minister to handle things such as tax collection, foreign affairs, wars, and the economy, he established "colleges" with numerous members. In 1711 Peter created a central senate of nine members who were to run the government when the tsar was in the field with the army. The chief purpose of Peter's reforms, like those of Prussia's kings, was to construct a bureaucracy that would support an efficient army.

Developing the Economy and Waging War

The economic projects Peter sponsored were those that served the military. To get the men needed to staff them, young Russians were sent abroad for training and western European craftsmen were invited to immigrate. Although few of Peter's enterprises met with much success, the iron industry he began in the Ural Mountains had by midcentury made Russia the largest iron producer in Europe.

Peter believed that Russia's economic development and its future political power depended on the acquisition of warm-water ports that

Peter the Great built Saint Petersburg on the Gulf of Finland to provide Russia with better contact with western Europe. He moved Russia's capital there from Moscow in 1703. This is an eighteenth-century view of the city. The Granger Collection

would allow Russia to communicate with the West. To acquire these, the tsar built Russia's first navy and went to war with the Ottoman Empire in the Black Sea and with Sweden in the Baltic. In 1696 he drove the Turks from Azov on the Black Sea but held this prize only until 1711.

Achievements on the Swedish front were more lasting. In 1700 Russia invaded Swedish territory on the Baltic. When Charles XII, the erratic king of Sweden, failed to follow up a victory over Peter at Narva, Peter was able to regroup. In 1709 Charles renewed the war, and Peter defeated him at the Battle of Poltava. In 1721 the Peace of Nystad ended the Great Northern War and confirmed Russia's conquest of Estonia, Livonia, and part of Finland. By 1720 the Russian fleet was larger than those of Sweden and Denmark, and Russia's newly won ports were giving it access to the mar-

kets and capitals of western Europe. By then Peter had also assembled an army of about 300,000 men and established a College of War to maintain westernized military discipline.

Peter moved the capital of Russia to a new city he built on the Gulf of Finland, Saint Petersburg. Like other monarchs of his day, he followed the example of Louis XIV and constructed a kind of Versailles. The Russian aristocrats were compelled to move to Saint Petersburg so that the tsar could keep an eye on them. The city filled with lavish buildings modeled on those that housed the courts of western Europe. It was intended to stake Russia's claim to a place among Western nations. But since it looked so different from Russia's other cities, many Russians viewed it as a western intrusion that symbolized Peter's assault on their traditions.

Despite Peter's determination to strengthen the Russian monarchy, he could not bring himself to secure its future. After he quarreled with his only son Alexis, the heir to the throne died mysteriously in his father's prison. Although Peter claimed the right to name a successor, he had not done so by the time he died in 1725. Consequently, for the next thirty years soldiers and nobles struggled to thrust their candidates onto the throne. Peter had made Russia a modern state but not a stable one.

Events and Reigns	
1533–1584	Ivan the Terrible
1584–1613	Time of Troubles
1613	Michael Romanov becomes tsar
1640–1688	Frederick William, the Great Elector
1648	Independence of the Netherlands recognized
1682–1725	Peter the Great
1683	Turkish siege of Vienna
1688–1713	Frederick I of Prussia
1697	Peter the Great's European tour
1700–1721	The Great Northern War
1703	Saint Petersburg founded
1711–1740	Charles VI, the Pragmatic Sanction
1713	War of the Spanish Succession ends
1713–1740	Frederick William I of Prussia
1714	George I founds the Hanoverian dynasty
1715	Louis XV becomes king of France
1720–1742	Robert Walpole dominates British politics
1726–1743	Cardinal Fleury
1727	George II
1740	Maria Theresa succeeds to the Habsburg throne
1740	Frederick II invades Silesia

In Perspective

By the second quarter of the eighteenth century, the major European powers were not yet nation-states in which citizens were united by a shared sense of community, culture, language, and history. They were still monarchies in which the cohesion of the state was a function of the personality of the ruler and personal relationships among great noble families. Monarchs had generally grown stronger, but nobles were still able to resist or obstruct the policies of their rulers.

In foreign affairs there were two long-term conflicts. In central Europe, Austria and Prussia contested leadership of Germany. In western Europe, France and Great Britain fought on two fronts. During the reign of Louis XIV, the French bid for dominance in Europe was at the heart of the struggle. But throughout the eighteenth century, their duel was for control of overseas commerce.

These wars were accompanied by economic and social developments that, in the long run, made more significant contributions to the transformations that were taking place in Europe.

REVIEW QUESTIONS

1. Why did Britain and France remain leading powers while the United Netherlands declined?
2. How did the structure of British government change under the political leadership of Walpole? What were the chief sources of Walpole's political strength?
3. How was the Hohenzollern family able to forge a conglomerate of diverse land holdings into the state of Prussia? Who were the major personalities involved in this process, and what were their individual contributions? Why was the military so important in Prussia?
4. How do the Hohenzollerns and the Habsburgs compare with respect to their approach to dealing with the problems that confronted their domains? Which family was more successful? Why? Why were the rulers of Sweden, the Ottoman Empire, and Poland less successful?
5. How did Russia become a great power? Why? How would you describe the character of Peter the Great? What were Russia's domestic problems before he came to power? What were his methods of reform? To what extent did he succeed? How were his reforms related to his military ambitions?

SUGGESTED READINGS

J. BLACK, *Eighteenth Century Europe, 1700–1789* (1990). An excellent survey.

C. R. BOXER, *The Dutch Seaborne Empire* (1965). Remains the best treatment of the subject.

J. BREWER, *The Sinews of Power: War, Money and the English State, 1688–1783* (1989). An extremely important study of the financial basis of English power.

F. L. CARSTEN, *The Origins of Prussia* (1954). Discusses the groundwork laid by the Great Elector in the seventeenth century.

J. C. D. CLARK, *English Society, 1688–1832: Social Structure and Political Practice During the Ancien Regime* (1985). An important, controversial work that emphasizes the role of religion in English political life.

A. COBBAN, *A History of Modern France*, 2nd ed., vol. 1 (1961). A lively and opinionated volume.

N. DAVIS, *God's Playground*, vol. 1 (1991). Excellent on prepartition Poland.

W. DOYLE, *The Old European Order, 1660–1800* (1992). The most thoughtful treatment of the subject.

R. J. W. EVANS, *The Making of the Habsburg Monarchy, 1550–1700: An Interpretation* (1979). Places much emphasis on intellectual factors and the role of religion.

F. FORD, *Robe and Sword: The Regrouping of the French Aristocracy After Louis XIV* (1953). An important book for political, social, and intellectual history.

L. HUGHES, *Russia in the Age of Peter the Great* (1998). Will likely stand for some time as the standard work.

C. J. INGRAO, *The Habsburg Monarchy, 1618–1815* (1994). The best recent survey.

J. I. ISRAEL, *The Dutch Republic, Its Rise, Greatness, and Fall, 1477–1806* (1995). The major survey of the subject.

R. A. KANN and Z. V. DAVID, *The Peoples of the Eastern Habsburg Lands 1526–1918* (1984). A helpful overview of the subject.

R. K. MASSIE, *Peter the Great: His Life and His World* (1980). A good popular biography.

D. McKAY and H. M. SCOTT, *The Rise of the Great Powers, 1648–1815* (1983). Now the standard survey.

J. H. PLUMB, *The Growth of Political Stability in England, 1675–1725* (1969). An important interpretive work.

S. SCHAMA, *An Embarrassment of Riches: An Interpretation of Dutch Culture in the Golden Age* (1987). Lively and controversial.

P. F. SUGAR, *Southeastern Europe Under Ottoman Rule, 1354–1804* (1977). An extremely clear presentation.

Chapter 16
Society and Economy Under the Old Regime in the Eighteenth Century

KEY TOPICS

- The varied privileges and powers of Europe's aristocracies in the Old Regime and their efforts to increase their wealth
- The plight of rural peasants
- Family structure and family economy
- The transformation of Europe's economy by the agricultural and industrial revolutions
- Urban growth and the social tensions that accompanied it
- The strains on the institutions of the Old Regime brought about by social change

The French Revolution of 1789 was a turning point in European history. The era that led up to it—which later came to be called the ancien régime (i.e., the "Old Regime")—was characterized by absolutist monarchies and agrarian economies that struggled to provide for the general population. Tradition, hierarchy, corporateness, and privilege were the dominant attributes of society during this era. Men and women *thought of themselves less as individuals than as members of groups. The social order seemed fixed and rigid, but there was change. Population grew, and standards of living increased. As farming was slowly commercialized, food became more abundant, and as the Industrial Revolution took hold, consumer goods became more plentiful. The spirit of rationality that had fostered the Scientific Revolution of the seventeenth century thrived in the eighteenth—the "Age of Reason" or the "Enlightenment." In many ways, the Old Regime nourished the very changes that brought its way of life to an end.*

Major Features of Life in the Old Regime

Maintenance of Tradition

Prerevolutionary Europe was dominated by aristocratic elites with numerous inherited privileges and by established churches that were allied with the aristocracy and the state. At the other end of the social scale were an urban labor force that was usually regulated by guilds and a rural peasantry that was burdened by high taxes and feudal dues. Most people believed that the past provided the best guide for planning the future. Innovation was considered undesirable—especially if it altered social relationships. When there was trouble, both nobles and peasants claimed not to be seeking a new order but only the restoration of their traditional rights. The nobles defended their power over local government from intrusion by centralized royal government, and the peasants wanted to maintain or revive customary manorial privileges (such as access to common lands, courts, and grievance procedures).

Hierarchy and Privilege

The traditional view of society that everyone claimed to be defending featured a hierarchical class structure that had been established during the Middle Ages. In the eighteenth century medieval distinctions of rank and degree not only persisted but became more rigid. States or societies were believed to unite "communities of people," not individual citizens. People had few rights as individuals. Their rights were those of the communities to which they belonged (i.e., their villages, municipalities, noble families, clergy, guilds, universities, and parishes). Each of these entities had its own set of privileges—such as a license to practice a trade, an opportunity to educate children for a particular occupation, entitlement to a certain kind of income, or exemption from taxation or from some especially humiliating punishment for crime.

With the exception of Britain, where there was some early industrial development, the economies of eighteenth-century nations remained as tradition-bound as their social systems. The quality and quantity of the grain harvest were the most important facts of life for everyone.

The Aristocracy

The eighteenth century was the great age for aristocracy. In most nations, aristocrats accounted for only 1 to 5 percent of the population, but they were the wealthiest and most influential of the social classes. Land was considered to be the most respectable investment for their money. But, over the century, aristocrats' investments became more diversified. Their chief occupations were the management of local governments and their estates. In most countries they also had their own house in a parliament, estate, or diet, and their lives at royal courts defined high culture and set standards of artistic taste and polite behavior for the rest of society. Although aristocratic lifestyles differed from nation to nation, aristocratic status everywhere was a matter of birth and inherited privilege.

Varieties of Aristocratic Privilege

BRITISH NOBILITY   Great Britain had the smallest, wealthiest, best-defined, and most socially responsible aristocracy. It numbered about 400 families, the male heads of which sat in Parliament's House of Lords. Through use of patronage and local influence, aristocrats also dominated elections to the Commons. British nobles, however, had few exemptions or legal privileges. This meant that the landowners who levied the taxes in Parliament also paid them.

Direct or indirect control of local government gave noble families immense influence, and they augmented this by entering business and the pro-

The foundation of aristocratic life was the possession of land. English aristocrats and large landowners controlled local government as well as the English Parliament. This painting of Robert Andrews and his wife by Thomas Gainsborough (1728–1788) shows an aristocratic couple on their estate. The gun and the hunting dog in this portrait suggest the importance landowners assigned to the virtually exclusive hunting privileges they enjoyed on their land. © National Gallery, London

fessions. The landed estates from which British aristocrats drew rents ranged from a few thousand to 50,000 acres and accounted for about one-fourth of the country's arable land. Nobles also invested in commerce, canals, urban real estate, mines, and industries. Since the eldest sons of aristocratic families inherited their titles and lands, younger sons had to find other careers in business, the army, the professions, and the church. Thus, most positions of leadership in society were occupied by men with noble connections.

FRENCH NOBILITY   The class structures of large continental nations such as France were more complex than those of Britain. France had approximately 400,000 nobles. They were divided into two groups: nobles of the sword and nobles of the robe. The former derived their status from military service; the latter purchased their titles or earned them by serving in the bureaucracy. Nobles were further distinguished between those who belonged to the royal court at Versailles and those who did not. The court nobility reaped immense wealth from government posts and came to monopolize appointments to the church and the military officer corps. The provincial nobility (the *hobereaux*) could not compete, and they were often little better off than wealthy peasants.

Despite these differences, hereditary privileges set all aristocrats off from everyone else in French society. There were many feudal dues that nobles could collect from their tenants, and nobles enjoyed exclusive hunting and fishing rights. The nobles were liable for payment of a kind of income tax, the *vingtième* (the "twentieth"), but they were exempt from many other duties. They did not pay the *taille* (the levy on land that was the basic tax of the Old Regime), and they could not be called up for the royal *corvées* (the forced labor on public works required of peasants).

EASTERN EUROPEAN NOBILITIES   East of the Elbe River, the customs associated with nobility were more complicated and more repressive. Here aristocracy was linked with the military. In Poland, there were thousands of nobles (i.e., *szlachta*), and most of them were relatively poor. After 1741 they were exempt from taxes, and until 1768 they had the right of life and death over their serfs. Political power was the prerogative of the few wealthy nobles who had immense estates.

In Austria and Hungary, the nobles exercised judicial authority over the peasantry through manorial courts. They enjoyed various degrees of exemption from taxation, and a few—such as the Hungarian Prince Esterhazy who owned 10 million acres of land—were extraordinarily rich.

In Prussia, Frederick the Great helped to elevate the status of the Junker nobles. Frederick drew his officers almost wholly from the Junker class, and he needed their enthusiastic support for his wars. The nation's bureaucracy was, like its army, managed by nobles, and here, as elsewhere in eastern Europe, nobles had extensive power over the serfs who lived on their estates.

In Russia in the eighteenth century nobility was reinvented. Peter the Great (r. 1682–1725) hoped to unify and control the aristocracy by giving it a new purpose and identity. He tried to link noble status to state service. The nobles, however, resisted royal demands for compulsory service, and in 1736 Empress Anna (r. 1730–1740) reduced the term for such service to twenty-five years. In 1762 Peter III (r. 1762) exempted the greater nobles, and in 1785 Catherine the Great (r. 1762–1796) legally confirmed the rights of the nobility in exchange for the assurance that nobles would serve the state voluntarily. Aristocratic privilege included the power to transmit noble status to one's wife and children, judicial protection of position and property, power over serfs, and exemption from personal taxes.

Aristocratic Resurgence

As the eighteenth century unfolded, nobles across Europe concluded that the growth of national monarchies was threatening the privileges that defined their caste. The steps they took to defend themselves resulted in what is called the "aristocratic resurgence." They protected their exclusiveness by making it more difficult to become a noble. They monopolized appointments to positions of power (e.g., the army's officer corps, the state bureaucracy, the government ministry, and the church). They used aristocratically controlled institutions (e.g., the British Parliament, the French *parlements*, and the diets of Germany and the Habsburg Empire) to limit royal power. And they improved their financial position by further exempting themselves from taxation and by increasing their power over the peasantry.

The Land and Its Tillers

Land was the economic basis of eighteenth-century life. Well over three-fourths of all Europeans lived in the country, and few people ever traveled more than a few miles from their birthplaces. Except for the wealthier landowners, most people who lived on the land were poor and vulnerable to exploitation.

Peasants and Serfs

Europe's rural classes were subject to different degrees of social dependency. English tenants and most French cultivators were free persons. The serfs of Germany, Austria, and Russia were not. They were legally bound to particular plots of land and particular lords. Everywhere, by controlling local government and courts, the class that owned the land dominated the class that tilled it.

OBLIGATIONS OF PEASANTS The power of landlords increased as one moved across Europe from west to east. Although there were some serfs in eastern France, most French peasants owned a bit of land. Few possessed enough to support their families, and most had to rent land from a lord and pay feudal dues. Nearly all French peasants were subject to *banalités*—obligations that forced them to rent their lord's mill to grind their grain and his oven to bake their bread. Their lord could also requisition a number of days of their labor each year.

In Prussia and the Habsburg Empire, despite attempts by the monarchies late in the century to enact reforms, landlords exercised almost complete control over serfs. In parts of southeastern Europe dominated by the Ottoman Empire, peasants were technically free but were, in practice, dependent on their lords. An estate's owner was often an absentee landlord whose property was managed by an overseer. During the seventeenth and eighteenth centuries, these estates began more and more to be run as commercial enterprises specializing in cash crops. Scarcity of labor more than legal rights gave peasants some independence, for oppressed peasants could always migrate from one landlord to another who offered them better conditions. In the seventeenth century, however, when political disorder began to spread from the capital at Istanbul into the Balkan peninsula, peasants had to turn to their landlords for protection from bandits and rebels. As in medieval times, the manor house of the local landowner became the peasants' refuge. Landlords also controlled the housing and tools peasants needed and furnished their seed grain. Thus, despite their legal freedoms, Balkan peasants became increasingly dependent on their landlords.

Serfs were worst off in Russia. Russian nobles reckoned their wealth by the number of "souls" (i.e., male serfs) they owned rather than by the acreage they possessed. Serfs were mere economic commodities. Landlords could demand as many as six days a week of labor from them, and lords had the right to punish serfs as they saw fit. Serfs had no legal recourse against the whims of lords, and there was little to distinguish Russian serfdom from slavery.

PEASANT REBELLIONS   The tsars contributed to the degradation of Russia's serfs. Peter the Great gave whole villages to favored nobles, and Catherine the Great confirmed the authority of the nobles over their serfs in exchange for the nobles' political cooperation. Between 1762 and 1769, abuse of serfs spawned over fifty peasant revolts. The brutal suppression of the greatest of these uprisings, Pugachev's Rebellion—a conflict (1773–1775) named for its instigator, Emelyan Pugachev (1726–1775)—doomed for a generation any attempt to improve the condition of the serfs. Pugachev's was the largest peasant uprising of the century, but smaller disturbances took place in Bohemia in 1775, in Transylvania in 1784, in Moravia in 1786, and in Austria in 1789. There were almost no revolts in western Europe—except for England where there were numerous rural riots.

The goals of the peasant uprisings were conservative. Rural laborers directed their wrath more against property than persons, and they fought to defend traditional customs against practices they considered innovations—such

things as unfair pricing, new or increased feudal dues, changes in methods of payment or land use, corrupt officials, or brutal overseers and landlords. No one advocated a radical restructuring of society to abolish the traditional classes.

Family Structures and the Family Economy

Households

In preindustrial Europe, the family household was the basic unit of production and consumption. Since few shops or farms employed more than a handful of people who did not belong to the families of their owners, the structure of the family determined the structure of the economy.

NORTHWESTERN EUROPE   Different forms of family organization evolved in different parts of Europe. In northwestern Europe, the household centered on the nuclear family: a married couple, their younger children, and their servants. Except for a few wealthy families, households were small (five or six members). High mortality and late marriage meant that three generations seldom survived to share the same home. Children lived with their parents only until their early teens. Then they left home to enter the work force—usually as servants who lived and worked in another household. A child of a skilled artisan might remain with his or her parents to learn a valuable skill, but only rarely would more than one child do so. Children's labor was more remunerative outside the home.

The word *servant* in this context may be misleading. It does not refer to someone who provides personal services for the wealthy. A servant in preindustrial Europe was a person hired to work for a household in exchange for room, board, and wages. The servant was usually young and by no means socially inferior to his or her employer. Normally the servant was an integral part of the household and ate with the family. Being a servant for several years—often as many as eight or ten—made it possible for young people to acquire training in productive skills and to accumulate the savings needed to strike out on their own.

The young men and women who had left their parental households to find work did not return once they got married. They set up independent homes in new places, a marriage pattern called *neolocalism*. Since it took them some time to amass the property needed to fund a household, they married late—men after age twenty-six and women after twenty-three. The new couple usually had children as soon after marriage as possible. Premarital sexual relations were common and brides were often pregnant, but births out of wedlock were rare.

EASTERN EUROPE   As one moved eastward across the continent, the structure of the household and the pattern of marriage changed. Eastern European households, which averaged from nine to twenty members, tended to be larger than those of the west, for young couples moved in with their parents rather than setting up on their own. This enabled men and women to marry at a much younger age—usually before twenty. It was not unusual, especially among Russian serfs, for wives to be older than their husbands and for three or perhaps four generations of family members to live together.

Landholding patterns in eastern Europe contributed to the district's characteristic family organization. Lords who wanted to ensure an adequate labor force to work their lands shaped peasant families. In Poland, for example, landlords could forbid marriage between their own serfs and those from another estate, and they could require widows and widowers to remarry. Polish landlords frowned on the hiring of free laborers, the West's "servants." This prevented individuals from finding employment that might have allowed them to acquire the capital needed to set up independent households. In Russia, landlords ordered the families of young people to arrange early marriages for them within their villages. Single-generation households were discouraged, for a death or serious illness in such a household might mean that the land assigned to it would go out of cultivation.

Throughout Europe, almost everyone lived in a household, for it was virtually impossible for ordinary people to support themselves on their own. People living outside a household were viewed with suspicion. Some were considered a disruptive—possibly criminal—element in society. Others were resented as potential beggars and drains on community resources.

The Family Economy

Everyone in a household worked. Since frequent poor harvests and economic slumps prevented most households from accumulating a surplus to fall back on, they could not afford idle members. The income family members produced was used to sustain the household, not to profit individuals. Since few families in western Europe had farms large enough to sustain them, one or more of their members usually worked elsewhere and sent wages home. Fathers of peasant families often became migrant workers and left the burden of tilling the family farm to their wives and younger children.

A family economy also characterized life for skilled urban artisans. The father of the household was usually its chief craftsman. He might employ one or more servants but would expect his children to work also. His eldest child was usually trained in his trade. His wife often sold his wares or opened a small shop of her own. Wives of merchants might run their husbands' businesses, especially when their husbands were traveling. If business was poor, family members would look for outside employment—not to support themselves as individuals but to ensure the survival of the family unit.

In western Europe, the death of a father could mean disaster for a household, for its economic life centered on his land or skills. Sometimes a widow or children were prepared to take over a farm or business, but widows generally kept their households from foundering by remarrying quickly. High mortality rates meant that many households were composed of a mix of spouses and children who had survived the breakup of earlier families. They were the lucky ones, for households often simply dissolved. Widows who could not remarry or support themselves became dependent on charity or on relatives. Their children entered the work force at an unusually early age or resorted to crime and begging.

The family economy of eastern Europe provided greater security. There were fewer artisan and merchant households and far less geographical mobility in the East than in the West. Also, serfdom, rural village structures, and multigen-

During the eighteenth century, most goods were produced in small workshops, such as this iron forge painted by Joseph Wright of Derby (1734–1797), or in the homes of artisans. Not until very late in the century, with the early stages of industrialization, did a few factories appear. In the small early workshops, it would not have been uncommon for the family of the owner to visit, as portrayed in this painting. The Iron Forge, 1772 (oil on canvas) by Joseph Wright of Derby (1734–1797). Broadlands Trust, Hants/Bridgeman Art Library, London

erational families created a broader base of support for households.

Women and the Family Economy

Marriage was an economic necessity for most women. Except for aristocrats and members of religious orders, few women could support themselves. A woman helped to maintain her parents' household until she devised a means of getting a household of her own. The bearing and rearing of children were the chief means to this end.

By the age of seven, a girl would have begun to help with household work. She would remain in her parents' home as long as her labor elsewhere was not more remunerative to her family. An artisan's daughter who was learning and practicing a valuable skill might stay with her parents until marriage. But a farm girl, whose tasks could be assumed by her parents and brothers, usually left home between the ages of twelve and fourteen. She might find employment on another farm, but more often she would migrate to a nearby town to become a servant. A young woman's chief goal was to accumulate sufficient capital for a dowry. Marriage within the family economy was a joint economic undertaking. Both brides and grooms were expected to contribute capital toward the establishment of their new households. It might take a young woman ten years or more to save a dowry.

Once married, a woman's chief concern was not homemaking or child rearing but coping with economic pressures. She and her husband were engaged in a constant struggle to ensure an adequate food supply for their household. Couples practiced birth control to limit family size, and infants were often turned over to wet-nurses so that their mothers could return to work.

The Breakfast *and* The Return from the Market: *Two Scenes of Domestic Life*

*P*aintings that depict scenes from everyday life are called *genre* paintings. They were a Dutch invention that became popular throughout Europe in the eighteenth century. They did not intend to convey serious messages but only to depict domestic scenes that everyone could understand and enjoy. French genre painters concentrated on the "woman's sphere," the home. This was a rich subject, for domestic organization was complex and varied with social class.

François Boucher's *The Breakfast*, which was painted in 1739, depicts a wealthy, but probably

F. Boucher. *The Breakfast.* 1739.
Paris. Louvre. Scala/Art Resource, NY

not aristocratic, family at breakfast in a room filled with expensive consumer goods. A Chinese porcelain figure on a shelf represents the exotic items that Paris shops imported from around the world, but the picture makes no political or social comment. It simply represents the feminine domain of domestic consumption and child rearing.

Jean Baptiste Chardin's *The Return from the Market* (1738) describes the domestic environment from quite a different perspective—that of the servant. The woman here appears to be in the employ of a person of moderate means. Chardin avoided depictions of conspicuous consumption and preferred simple interiors that projected order and tranquility. The servants he described have a quiet dignity, but the painter did not moralize or insert social commentary into his work. He viewed himself as a craftsman and painting as a kind of dignified, everyday work akin to that of the woman he depicted in this painting.

Sources: Albert Boime, *Art in an Age of Revolution, 1750–1800* (Chicago: University of Chicago Press, 1987); Norman Bryson, *Looking at the Overlooked: Four Essays on Still Life Painting* (Cambridge, MA.: Harvard University Press, 1990); Richard Rand, *Intimate Encounters: Love and Domesticity in Eighteenth Century France* (Princeton, NJ: Princeton University Press, 1997).

Jean Baptiste Chardin, 1699–1799. *The Return from the Market (La Pourvoyeuse).* (1738). French. Musée Du Louvre, Paris/SuperStock

The work of a married woman was in many ways a function of her husband's occupation. In the few peasant households that possessed enough land to support themselves, wives were their husbands' chief assistants. In most cases, however, men had to find outside employment to supplement the income from their land, and women had to assume primary responsibility for plowing, planting, and harvesting. An artisan or merchant's wife might actively participate in her husband's trade or manufacturing enterprise. If her husband died, she might take over the business or hire an artisan to work under her management. Despite the essential economic contributions women made to their households, many occupations and professions were closed to them because of their gender. Women at all levels of society had fewer opportunities for education than men, and they usually received lower wages than men for the same work. As mechanization of agriculture and the textile industry set in during the eighteenth century, employment opportunities for women were increasingly curtailed.

Children and the World of the Family Economy

For all women, childbirth was a time of fear and personal vulnerability. Contagious diseases endangered both mother and child, and midwives were not universally skillful. Most mothers and newborn infants faced the challenges of immense poverty and wretched housing. Some women nursed their own infants, but many surrendered them at birth to wet-nurses who took them away and kept them for months or years. Convenience encouraged this practice among the wealthy, but economic necessity dictated it for the poor. The demands of the family economy did not give a woman the freedom to devote herself entirely to rearing a child.

The birth of a child was not always welcome. It might be born to an unwed mother, or it might represent another economic burden on an already hard-pressed household. In some places, records show a clear relationship between rising food prices and increasing numbers of abandoned children.

Unwanted births sometimes led to infanticide, but during the eighteenth century society developed an increased sense of responsibility for abandoned children. This expressed itself in the growing size and number of foundling hospitals. Early in the century, an average of 1,700 children a year were being admitted to the Paris Foundling Hospital, but in 1772, the peak year, the orphanage accepted 7,676 children. There was not enough space in institutions to care for all who were in need. In some cases hospitals held lotteries to choose the children they admitted. Parents who had to abandon a baby would sometimes leave personal tokens with it in the vain hope that they might one day be able to reclaim it. Leaving a child at a foundling hospital did not guarantee its survival. Only about 10 percent of children survived to the age of ten in Paris's hospital.

The eighteenth century marked the beginning of the modern awareness of the importance of childhood and gave unprecedented attention to the education of children. Although the increasing demands of the job market made literacy more valuable and literacy rates improved during the century, most Europeans were still unable to read and write. Not until the late nineteenth century, when nations became aware of the importance of a trained citizenry, did formal schooling become a routine childhood experience.

The Revolution in Agriculture

The chief concern of traditional peasant society was the maintenance of stable conditions that would ensure the food supply. Across Europe, the tillers of the soil resisted change. Traditional methods of cultivation were proven to work, and new means entailed risks that few were prepared to take. Failure of a harvest meant not mere hardship but death from outright starvation or protracted debility. Even small increases in the cost of food could exert heavy pressure on peasant or artisan families.

As the eighteenth century progressed, population growth slowly but steadily drove up the price of bread, the staple food of the poor. The rise in grain prices benefitted landowners and the wealthier peasants who had surplus grain to sell. Inflation put serious pressure on consumers, the urban laborers, and the peasants with small farms, but rising grain prices also encouraged an agricultural revolution by motivating landlords to experiment with techniques to increase yields. The new commercialized agricultural methods that were proposed frightened the peasants by challenging the traditional means of production on which they relied. Whenever the rural poor rebelled, governments that were hungry for taxes and dominated by aristocratic landed entrepreneurs called out armies to defend the agents of change.

NEW CROPS AND NEW METHODS　A growing population and a shortage of land motivated a search for ways to improve agricultural production in the Low Countries. During the sixteenth and seventeenth centuries, Dutch agriculturalists improved methods for building dikes and draining land and experimented with new crops that would increase the supply of animal fodder and restore the soil.

In the eighteenth century, English landlords took the lead in sponsoring agricultural development. They popularized ideas developed in the Low Countries and originated a few new farming methods. They increased yields by using iron plows that turned earth deeply and by planting wheat with a drill rather than by wasteful casting. They developed fertilizers to make sandy soil productive and crop rotation methods—involving wheat, turnips, barley, and clover—to replace the fallow-field system of cultivation. Instead of "resting" a plot of land, it was planted with a crop that restored the soil and produced animal fodder. By enabling more livestock to be raised and fed through the winter, this ensured a year-round supply of meat. Larger herds also meant increased quantities of manure that could be used as fertilizer to improve grain production.

ENCLOSURE REPLACES OPEN-FIELD METHOD　Many of the era's agricultural innovations were incompatible with the way land had traditionally been used in England. Most farming was done by small cultivators who lived in villages, and each of them tilled an assortment of strips scattered about the fields belonging to their village. Much of the land was left fallow and unproductive each year in order to maintain its fertility. Animals grazed on common land in the summer and on the stubble of the harvest in the winter. Since decisions about farming were made communally, the system discouraged innovation and favored the poorer farmers who needed the common land and stubble fields to maintain their animals. The methods of traditional production were intended to maintain a steady supply of food, not create large surpluses.

In 1700 approximately half the arable land in England was farmed by this method. But during the second half of the century, the rising price of wheat encouraged landlords to consolidate or "enclose" their lands in order to use the new and more efficient means of cultivation. Enclosure was a more rational, commercial approach to land use, but it entailed the fencing of common lands, reclaiming untilled waste, and combining strips into block fields. These procedures created turmoil in the economic and social life of the countryside and prompted riots.

Because many English farmers either owned their strips or rented them with traditional rights that amounted to ownership, the great landlords had to resort to parliamentary acts to legalize the enclosure of the land that their families had long leased to tenant farmers. Between 1761 and 1792, almost 500,000 acres were enclosed through acts of Parliament, and in 1801 a general enclosure act streamlined the process. The enclosures permitted the expansion of farming and encouraged innovation. This increased food production, but it also disrupted small traditional communities. Although some people were forced off the land, enclosures did not depopulate the countryside. In some counties, where new soil came into production and services subsidiary to farming expanded, population increased.

The enclosure movement did not create the labor force needed for the British Industrial Revolution, but it did demonstrate the new entrepreneurial or capitalistic attitude that was emerging in English society. Commercialization of agriculture, which spread from Britain slowly across the continent during the next century, strained the paternal relationship that had long existed between the governing and governed classes. In the past, landlords had looked after the welfare of the lower orders by accepting price controls or waiving rents during depressed periods. But as landlords became increasingly concerned about profits, they abandoned the peasants to the mercy of the marketplace.

LIMITED IMPROVEMENTS IN EASTERN EUROPE　The Agricultural Revolution had its greatest impact west of the Elbe. To the east—in Prussia, Austria, Poland, and Russia—few improvements were made in farming, for nothing in the relationship of the serfs to their lords encouraged innovation. Landlords or their agents, not village councils, directed farm management. The great landowners sought to squeeze more labor from their serfs rather than greater productivity from their soil. Their chief method of increasing production was to bring previously untilled lands under the plow. The only change in agriculture that improved nutrition was the introduction of maize and the potato.

Population Expansion

The population explosion with which the world contends today began in the eighteenth century. Previously when Europe experienced dramatic increases in population, balance was restored by plagues, wars, or famine. But beginning in the second quarter of the eighteenth century, population started to increase despite these calamities.

In 1700 Europe's population, excluding the European provinces of the Ottoman Empire, was probably between 100 million and 120 million. By 1800 there were almost 190 million, and by 1850, 260 million. The population of England and Wales rose from 6 million in 1750 to over 10 million in 1800. France grew from 18 million in 1715 to approximately 26 million in 1789. Russia's population increased from 19 million in 1722 to 29 million in 1766. Such extraordinary sustained growth put new demands on all resources and considerable pressure on existing social organization.

Population expanded across the continent in both rural and urban districts, and no one is certain what caused its growth. There was a decline in the death rate, for there were relatively few wars and epidemics during the eighteenth century. Hygiene and sanitation improved. But the most important factor may have been changes in the food supply. Grain production expanded, and, more important, the potato began to be cultivated. The potato was a New World vegetable that came into widespread European production during the eighteenth century. It was a significant new product, for a single acre of land could produce enough potatoes to feed a peasant family for an entire year. More food meant that more children survived to adulthood to rear children of their own.

The impact of the population explosion can hardly be overestimated. It increased demands for food, goods, labor, and services. It provided a larger pool of workers. It forced traditional modes of production and life to be revised. It prompted migration as economies were reorganized, and it caused more people to become socially and politically discontent. The world of the Old Regime literally outgrew its traditional bounds.

The Industrial Revolution of the Eighteenth Century

The industrialization of Europe's economy began in the second half of the eighteenth century. Early in the nineteenth century the movement, which was led by Britain, expanded to become the *Industrial Revolution* and the economic equivalent of the great political revolution that took place in France in the 1790s.

Industrialization wrought numerous revolutionary changes. It increased humanity's control over the forces of nature and made possible the production of more goods and services than ever before. It met existing consumer demands while creating new ones. It raised standards of living, and it ended the widespread poverty that Europeans had always taken for granted. It inaugurated an era of unprecedented, sustained economic growth. Previously, periods of growth alternated with periods of stagnation. Since the late eighteenth century, the expansion of the Western economy has been relatively uninterrupted, but the process of industrializing it has exacted a high social cost. New means of production demanded new skills, new discipline in work, and a large labor force. By the middle of the nineteenth century, it was also apparent that industrialization caused unanticipated problems with the environment.

A Revolution in Consumption

The most visible aspect of the Industrial Revolution was the invention of machinery, the establishment of factories, and the creation of a new kind of work force. But intangible changes in attitudes and expectations also lay behind these developments. Early in the eighteenth century, an unprecedented demand for the relatively humble goods of everyday life (e.g., clothing, buttons, toys, china, furniture, rugs, kitchen utensils, candlesticks, brassware, silverware, pewterware, glassware, watches, jewelry, soap, beer, wines, and foodstuffs) encouraged ingenuity on the part of designers and inventors. As each consumer expectation was met, a new one took its place, and the demands of the market drove the development of an ever more productive industrialized economy.

Numerous factors contributed to the growth of a new, consumer-driven economy. During the seventeenth century, the Dutch had enjoyed enormous prosperity that enabled them to pioneer a society centered on consumption. In the eighteenth century, increasing numbers of people acquired more disposable income—possibly because of the improvements taking place in agriculture. More income allowed them to buy more consumer goods than previous generations and to create an economy that grew by expanding domestic markets in Europe, not by exporting things abroad.

These changes were not entirely spontaneous. People had to be persuaded that they needed or wanted new consumer goods, and entrepreneurs did this by developing new methods of marketing. The strategy followed by the porcelain manufacturer Josiah Wedgwood (1730–1795) was typical. He first produced luxury goods that appealed to the royal family and the aristocracy. Once their patronage built his reputation, he began to make less expensive versions of his chinaware for middle-class customers. He opened showrooms and sent out traveling salesmen with samples and catalogs of his wares. He advertised and discovered that there was no limit to the market for consumer goods that could be created by pandering to the desire of the masses to emulate their social superiors. Manufacturers also discovered that by changing styles they could increase demand. The desire to have the latest in fashions and inventions prompted people to return to the market again and again.

Increasing consumption quietly, but steadily, blurred the edges of social distinctions. As people saw what others were consuming, human nature led them to imitate their neighbors. Fashion publications made all levels of society aware of new styles that could be quickly and inexpensively copied. Even servants began to dress well if not luxuriously. New foods and beverages created a demand for new kinds of dishware for the home. New modes of leisure became popular and necessitated new items for their enjoyment. New standards for polite living were described in print and quickly disseminated through nations, and people were encouraged to define their status by the quality and quantity of the goods they consumed.

The consumer economy has always had its critics. Yet ever-increasing consumption has become a hallmark of modern life. It would be difficult to overestimate the importance of the desire for consumer goods and an increasing material standard of living in modern societies. Availability of consumer goods has become the hallmark of a nation's prosperity, and the lack of these things—as much as the absence of civil liberties—lies behind the increasing social tensions that today plague many countries.

Industrial Leadership of Great Britain

Great Britain inaugurated the Industrial Revolution and maintained industrial leadership in Europe into the middle of the nineteenth century. Its industrialization was made possible by a fortunate combination of factors, among which were an increasing domestic demand for goods and the markets that existed in Britain's North American colonies.

England took the lead in inventing the consumer society. The newspapers that thrived in Britain facilitated the advertising that spurred consumer demand. Eighteenth-century London, the largest city in Europe, set the standards for fashion and taste, and the structure of British society allowed people to imitate the lifestyles of their superiors. As a result, the British were the first to develop the love affair with fads and fashions that creates insatiable appetites for new goods.

Britain, the single largest free-trade area in Europe, had an excellent infrastructure: good roads and waterways without internal tolls or other trade barriers. The country was endowed with natural resources: fertile land, coal, and iron ore. It was politically stable. The property rights of its citizens were secure. Sound systems of banking and credit maintained a stable climate for investment. Taxes were high, but collection was efficient and fair. Parliament regulated taxation so that all social classes and regions of the nation paid the same dues. British society was also relatively mobile. The aristocracy accepted into its ranks entrepreneurs who amassed large fortunes. Even persons of wealth who were not admitted to the aristocracy enjoyed social prominence and political influence.

New Methods of Textile Production

Textile manufacturers spearheaded the Industrial Revolution. Their industry began its development in the country, not in cities. Eighteenth-century society was primarily agricultural, and the peasant family was the basic unit of economic production. Although peasants were primarily agricultural workers, they could combine farming with other kinds of labor. They tilled the land in spring and summer and spun thread or wove textiles in the winter. Under what is termed the *domestic* or *putting-out* system, urban textile merchants bought wool or other unfinished fiber and sent it to the homes of peasants to be spun into thread. Other peasants wove that thread into cloth and returned it to the merchants who marketed it. A spinning wheel or hand loom was standard equipment in thousands of peasant cottages from Ireland to Austria. Sometimes peasants owned wheels and looms, but by the middle of the century the merchant capitalist usually provided the machinery as well as the raw material. Textiles remained part of the family economy in Britain and on the continent well into the nineteenth century. By the middle of the eighteenth century, however, the demand for cotton cloth had begun to outstrip home production and to prompt the invention of machines that transformed the industry.

THE SPINNING JENNY   Thanks to the invention of the flying shuttle in the 1730s, weavers had the technical capacity to produce the quantity of cotton fabric demanded. Spinners, however, could not provide weavers with enough thread—until 1765, when James Hargreaves (d. 1778) invented the spinning jenny. This device originally spun 16 spindles of thread simultaneously. By the close of the century its capacity had increased to 120 spindles.

THE WATER FRAME   The spinning jenny broke the bottleneck between the productive capacity of spinners and weavers, but it was still a ma-

chine intended for use in a cottage. The invention that took cotton textile manufacture out of the home and put it into the factory was the water frame, which Richard Arkwright (1732–1792) patented in 1769. This was a water-powered device that produced a 100 percent cotton fabric rather than the standard earlier blend of cotton and linen. When Arkwright lost his patent rights, other manufacturers hastened to appropriate his invention. Domestic production decreased as factories sprang up in the countryside near the streams that provided waterpower for the machines. Cotton output increased by 800 percent between 1780 and 1800. By 1815 cotton composed 40 percent of the value of British domestic exports. By 1830 it was just over 50 percent.

The Industrial Revolution had commenced in earnest by the 1780s, but the full economic and social ramifications of the productive capacity it unleashed were not felt until the early nineteenth century. The expansion of industry and the incorporation of new inventions took place slowly. For example, although Edmund Cartwright (1743–1822) invented the power loom in the late 1780s, it was not until the 1830s that there were more power-loom weavers than hand-loom weavers in Britain. Nor did all of the social ramifications of industrialism appear immediately. The first cotton mills used waterpower, were located in the country, and rarely employed more than two dozen workers. Not until late in the century, after James Watt (1736–1819) perfected the steam engine (1769) and adapted it to textile machinery, could factories be located in cities. The steam engine made possible the modern combination of urbanization with industrialization.

The Steam Engine

The steam engine permitted almost all areas of production to be industrialized because it provided a new source of energy. For the first time in history, people had at their disposal a steady and essentially unlimited source of inanimate power. Unlike engines moved by water, wind, animals, and people, the coal or wood-fed steam engine was portable, dependable, and inexhaustible. Its potential uses were legion.

Early in the eighteenth century, Thomas Newcomen had invented the first engine using steam power. It was driven by injecting steam into a cylinder to push up a piston that fell back as the steam condensed. The machine was heavy and energy inefficient, but it was widely used in Britain to pump water out of coal and tin mines. During the 1760s James Watt, a Scottish engineer, experimented with the Newcomen machine and achieved much greater efficiency by separating the condenser from the piston and the cylinder. His design, however, required precise metalwork, a technical challenge that Matthew Boulton, a successful toy and button maker, and John Wilkinson, a cannon manufacturer, helped him meet. In 1776, a Watt steam engine found its first commercial application: pumping water from mines in Cornwall.

Watt retained exclusive patent rights until 1800 and was reluctant to make changes in his invention. This slowed the development of applications for the steam engine until Boulton finally persuaded him to make improvements that allowed the engines to be used not only for pumping but also for running cotton mills. By the early nineteenth century, the steam engine had become the prime mover in every industry and had begun to transform transportation.

Iron Production

The manufacture of high-quality iron has been basic to modern industrial development. It is the chief material used in all heavy industry and transportation. In the early eighteenth century, British ironmakers produced somewhat less than 25,000 tons annually. Technical problems limited their output. They used charcoal to smelt ore, and charcoal, which came from Britain's diminishing forests, was expensive and hard to burn at ideal temperatures. It was also difficult to produce the blasts of air needed to generate the intense heats of a smelting furnace. Things improved once ironmakers switched to coke, a charcoal-like derivative of coal, and once the steam engine was adapted to power blast furnaces. Since Britain had large coal deposits, coke was cheap, and the steam engine had the felicitous effect of both improving the production of iron and increasing demand for it.

In 1784 Henry Cort (1740–1800) introduced a new "puddling" process (i.e., a new method for melting and stirring ore). By removing more slag (the mix of impurities that bubbles to the top of a pot of molten ore), Cort's technique produced better iron. Cort also developed a rolling mill that formed molten metal into continuous bars, rails, or sheets. Previously, metal had to be shaped by pounding. The result was a better, more versatile product at a lower cost. By the early nineteenth century, Britain was producing over a million tons annually.

The Impact of the Agricultural and Industrial Revolutions on Working Women

The agricultural and industrial revolutions diminished roles for women who had traditionally been part of Europe's work force. Women had always worked the land with men, and farm women often managed industries related to farming (e.g., dairy production, brewing, etc.). When increasing commercialization and mechanization began to transform farming methods, men and machines took over many tasks that had previously been assigned to women. Since women's opportunities to earn livings from the land were consequently constricted, women tended to oppose changes. Many proponents of the new agricultural techniques saw women as impediments to reform.

A similar development took place in the textile industry. The spinning of thread had been a female occupation from time immemorial, but the development of large spinning jennies in factory settings made this a job for men. If women found employment in such factories, they were assigned duties that required less skill and received lower pay than the work made available to men. Many women turned instead to cottage industries—to the manufacture of goods (e.g., buttons, knitted items, baskets, gloves, etc.) that they could make at home. Since this work was very poorly paid, these women were sometimes forced into crime and prostitution. This damaged the reputations and depressed the social standing of working women in general.

The alternative for many women was domestic service in the homes of landed or commercial families. During the nineteenth century this was the largest area of female employment. It was respectable but did not provide women with opportunities to develop the skills they needed to enter the technologically advanced world of factory manufacture and transport. This led many people to assume that women were incapable of being trained for industrial work.

By the end of the eighteenth century the work and workplaces of men and women were becoming separate and distinct. Women's work—whether in cottage industries or domestic service—was associated with the home and men's with the factory. Europeans also tended to assume that a woman worked only to supplement the income of some male who was chiefly responsible for her support. This became a justification for paying female workers less than males and for imposing restrictions on their employment in factories. It was assumed that women belonged in domestic settings and should be discouraged from seeking factory work, which was inherently unsuitable for members of their sex.

The Growth of Cities

Remarkable changes occurred in urban areas between 1500 and 1800. In 1500 Europe (excluding Hungary and Russia) had only 156 cities whose populations reached or exceeded 10,000. Only four of these (Paris, Milan, Venice, and Naples) were larger than 100,000. By 1800 there were about 363 cities of 10,000 or more inhabitants, and seventeen had populations larger than 100,000. The percentage of Europe's people living in urban areas had risen from about 5 percent to 9 percent, and urban concentration in northern Europe had surpassed that of Southern Europe.

Patterns of Preindustrial Urbanization

Growth in towns was particularly rapid in the eighteenth century—a phenomenon that was not unrelated to the political and social upheavals of the era. London in 1700 had about 700,000 inhabitants. By 1800 it had almost 1 million. At the time, Paris had over 500,000 inhabitants. Berlin's population tripled during the century, reaching 170,000. Warsaw had almost 120,000 in 1794, and Saint Petersburg, which did not exist until 1703, grew to over 250,000 inhabitants by the end of the century.

These raw figures conceal significant changes in the ways that cities grew and population distributed itself. Even in France and Great Britain, probably somewhat less than 20 percent of the population lived in cities, and the town of 10,000 inhabitants was much more common than the giant urban center. From 1500 to 1750, most urban expansion took place within the major cities that were already established. After 1750 the pattern changed. New cities were founded, and there was rapid growth of the smaller older cities.

GROWTH OF CAPITALS AND PORTS   The cities that grew most vigorously from 1600 to 1750 were capitals and ports. They profited from the development of the monarchical state and the burgeoning of its bureaucracies, armies, courts, and support personnel. The growth of port cities reflected the expansion of Europe's overseas trade—most especially the Atlantic routes. Except for Manchester in England and Lyons in France, the great urban conglomerates were not centers of industrial manufacture.

During this period (1600 to 1750), cities with populations of fewer than 40,000 inhabitants declined. Rural labor was cheaper than urban labor, and expansion of the putting-out system transferred to the countryside much production that had occurred in medieval cities.

In the middle of the eighteenth century, a new pattern emerged and continued into the nineteenth century. The growth of existing large cities slowed while new cities appeared and smaller cities expanded. Several factors account for this. There was the general overall population increase. The Industrial Revolution was at its start a rural phenomenon that fostered the growth of smaller towns and cities. Factory organization accounted for some concentrations of population in new places, and even where there was little industrialization, the increasing prosperity of European agriculture prompted urban development.

Urban Classes

The urban rich and poor were visibly segregated. The moneyed classes lived in fashionable townhouses arranged around parks. The poorest town dwellers usually congregated along the rivers. Small merchants and craftsmen lived above their shops, and whole families might share a single room. There was little pure water. Sanitary facilities that are now taken for granted were still unknown. Cattle, pigs, goats, and other animals wandered the streets. All the contemporary descriptions of Europe's eighteenth-century cities emphasize the grace and beauty of the homes of the wealthy and the dirt and stench that prevailed elsewhere. It did not require the factories of the Industrial Revolution to make cities into hellholes for the poor and the dispossessed.

Poverty was usually worse in the countryside, but its effects—crime, prostitution, vagrancy, begging, and alcoholism—were more visible in cities. So were its punishments. Public tortures and executions of criminals were frequent spectacles in all of Europe's cities. Many a young person from the countryside migrated to a city in search of a better life, only to find degradation and death. The harsh reality of the drama of London's streets at midcentury has been graphically recorded by a keen observer, the artist William Hogarth (1697–1764).

THE UPPER CLASSES At the top of the urban social scale stood a small group of nobles, great merchants, bankers, financiers, clergy, and government officials. These men (and they were always men) controlled the town. Rights of self-government enshrined in a royal charter usually gave a city corporation or town council authority to select its own members. In a few cities on the Continent, artisan guilds controlled town councils, but it was more common for city governments to be run by self-perpetuating oligarchies, the nobles and the wealthiest commercial families.

THE MIDDLE CLASS A city's most dynamic residents were the persons traditionally regarded as middle class, the *bourgeoisie*—the smaller merchants, tradesmen, bankers, and professional people. The middle class was much less clearly defined than the nobility, for it was not a single, cohesive entity. Several diverse "middling" groups occupied the middle, and some were at odds with others. Professionals, for instance, might resent those who drew their incomes from commerce. Less wealthy bourgeoisie envied richer colleagues who aspired to mix with the nobility.

Middle-class people did not draw their incomes from the land. As merchants, lawyers, or small factory owners, they were the beneficiaries of their era's expanding trade and commerce. They concentrated on amassing capital and using it to improve their social standing. They saw themselves as energetic, productive workers who supported reform, change, and legislation that fostered economic growth. They were both contemptuous and envious of the "idle" aristocracy whose manners they imitated.

The middle class led the revolution in consumption. As owners of factories and of wholesale and retail businesses, they produced and sold goods for a consumer market in which they were the chief customers. They might not enjoy the titles and social prestige of the nobility, but they could emulate the material comfort and prosperity of the aristocratic lifestyle.

The relationship between the middle class and the aristocracy was complicated. Nobles, especially in England and France, augmented their inherited wealth by embracing the commercial spirit. Like good businesspersons, they improved the cultivation of their lands and invested in entrepreneurial ventures. Wealthy members of the middle class, on the other hand, imitated the early customs of the nobility by putting their money into landed estates. There was, however, much tension between the two groups. What was at issue between them was not a clash of values or social ideals but a quarrel about sharing power. The upward social mobility of the bourgeoisie threatened the exclusive privileges of the nobles who defended themselves by using their control of government bureaucracies and government patronage to frustrate the schemes of traders, bankers, manufacturers, and lawyers.

If the urban middle class envied the nobility, it feared the lower orders. The poor were a potentially violent element in society, a threat to property, and—as objects of charity—a drain on community resources.

ARTISANS The lower classes were much more varied than either the aristocracy or the middle class cared to admit. Shopkeepers, artisans, and wage earners composed the single largest group in any city. They had their own culture, values, and institutions, and, like the peasants, they were in many respects conservative. Their economic position was very vulnerable, but they also contributed to the revolution in consumption. They could buy more goods than the poor of earlier generations, and many of them tried to copy the domestic consumption of the middle class.

The lives of artisans and shopkeepers centered on their work and their neighborhoods. They usually lived near or at their places of employment, which were usually workshops with fewer

This engraving illustrates a metalworking shop such as might have been found in almost any town of significance in Europe. Most of the people employed in the shop probably belonged to the same family. Note that two women are also working. The wife may very well have been the person in charge of keeping the accounts of the business. The two younger boys might be children of the owner or apprentices in the trade, or both.
Bildarchiv Preussischer Kulturbesitz

than a half-dozen laborers. The medieval guild system still existed, but it had lost much of its power. Guilds endorsed conservative policies. Rather than promoting economic growth or innovation, they tried to preserve the jobs of their members by reducing competition and preventing too many people from entering a particular trade. The guilds were the artisans' chief protection against the operation of the commercial market, and they were particularly strong in central Europe.

The Urban Riot

The conservative outlook of the artisan class shaped its understanding of social and economic justice. The poor accepted grim conditions that appeared to be established and inevitable, but they opposed any change that threatened to increase their burdens and reduce their already scant opportunities. Often the only means they had to make their voices heard by town governments was to riot in the streets.

Changes in the price of bread, the staple food of the poor, were most likely to spark urban dis-

order. Since the fear of provoking a riot was the chief thing that restrained the greed of merchants, riots were a collective method for maintaining a socially acceptable "just price." Bread riots were not the irrational acts of desperate people but customary behaviors that helped to regulate the Old Regime's economy of scarcity.

Since the riot was a way in which people who were excluded from the political processes could make their wills known, riots of all kinds were common in the eighteenth century. Religious bigotry incited some conflict, but violence was normally directed against property more than people. The rioters were usually not "riff-raff" but small shopkeepers, freeholders, craftsmen, and wage earners. Their intent was not to overthrow the social order but to restore some traditional right or practice that they feared was endangered.

During the last half of the century, urban riots were often manipulated by politicians for private ends. The angry crowds that tore up the streets of eighteenth-century towns could become tools of warring factions within the upper classes. Paris's aristocratic *Parlement* often urged people to riot to strengthen its hand in dealing with the monarchy. In Great Britain in 1792 the government incited mobs to attack people who sympathized with the French Revolution.

The Jewish Population: The Age of the Ghetto

There were Jewish communities that produced famous intellectuals in Amsterdam and other Western cities, but in the eighteenth century the vast majority of Europe's Jews lived in eastern Europe. About 3 million resided in Poland, Lithuania, and the Ukraine. Fewer than 100,000 lived in Germany, approximately 40,000 in France, and only about 10,000 in either England or Holland.

In most nations, unless rights were specifically granted to Jews, they did not enjoy the same privileges as a monarch's Christian subjects. Jews were treated as resident aliens whose right to remain might be revoked at any moment. They lived apart from Christians in ghettos. These were separate districts in cities or whole villages in the countryside. In Poland for much of the century, Jewish communities were virtually self-governing. In other places, Jews struggled under the burden of discriminatory legislation.

Since Jews were often prevented from owning land, many were driven into trade and commerce. Some became very successful bankers, and during the seventeenth century a few of them helped nations finance wars. The loans they made to monarchs were often not repaid, but the "court Jews" became famous for their financial acumen and influence. They formed a tiny network of closely intermarried, exclusive families whose situations were hardly characteristic of those of other Jews.

Most of Europe's Jews lived in poverty. They occupied the most undesirable sections of cities or poor rural villages and worked at the lowest occupations. Their religious beliefs, rituals, and the laws of most communities kept them apart from their Christian neighbors and relegated them to positions of social inferiority. Those who converted to Christianity were welcomed, if not always warmly, into gentile society. But until the last two decades of the eighteenth century, those who remained loyal to their faith suffered discrimination and persecution. They were barred from some professions, restricted in their freedom of movement, deprived of political representation and protection under the law, subjected to exile and confiscation of their property, and generally regarded as lesser beings. Sometimes force was used to persuade them to convert or their children were taken away from them for Christian indoctrination.

During the Old Regime, European Jews were separated from non-Jews, typically in districts known as ghettos. Relegated to the least desirable section of a city or to rural villages, most lived in poverty. This water-color painting depicts a street in Kazimlesz, the Jewish quarter of Cracow, Poland. Judaica Collection, Max Berger, Vienna, Austria

In Perspective

By the end of the eighteenth century, European society had reached the brink of a new era. The commercial spirit was not new, but it was given much freer play than ever before. It encouraged human beings to think of themselves as competing individuals rather than as members of communities struggling to survive together in an economy of scarcity. Agricultural and industrial revolutions, spurred on by growing consumer appetites, overcame scarcity and caused changes in landholding and production that transformed society. Population expanded. Cities grew. Birth became less significant than wealth in determining social relationships. Class structures and hierarchies remained, but their boundaries blurred. The diverse middle class, which was growing richer from trade, commerce, and the practice of the professions, wanted social prestige and influence equal to its wealth. To win this, it was willing to innovate and to challenge tradition, and this helped bring on a new era in European history.

REVIEW QUESTIONS

1. How did the lives of English aristocrats change during the course of the eighteenth century? How did the situation of the English aristocracy differ from that of the French? What kind of privileges distinguished European aristocrats from other social groups?

2. How would you define the family economy? How did the northwestern European household differ from the households common to eastern Europe? In what ways were the lives of women in preindustrial Europe constrained by the family economy?

3. What caused the agricultural revolution? How did technological innovations transform European agriculture? To what extent did the English aristocracy contribute to the Agricultural Revolution? What were some of the reasons for peasant revolts in Europe in the eighteenth century?

4. What factors explain the increase in Europe's population in the eighteenth century? What were the effects of the population explosion?

How did population growth contribute to changes in consumption?

5. What caused the Industrial Revolution of the eighteenth century? What were its major technological innovations? What impacts did these innovations have? Why did Great Britain take the lead in the Industrial Revolution? How did the consumer contribute to the Industrial Revolution?

6. What was city life like during the eighteenth century? Were all European cities fundamentally the same? What changes took place during the century in the distribution of population in cities and towns? How did the lifestyle of the upper class differ from that of the middle and lower classes? What were some of the causes of urban riots?

SUGGESTED READINGS

J. Blum, *The End of the Old Order in Rural Europe* (1978). The most comprehensive treatment of life in rural Europe, especially central and eastern, from the early eighteenth through the mid-nineteenth centuries.

F. Braudel, *The Structures of Everyday Life: The Limits of the Possible,* trans. by M. Kochan (1982). A magisterial survey.

J. Brewer and R. Potter, *Consumption and the World of Goods* (1993). A large, wide-ranging collection of essays.

J. Cannon, *Aristocratic Century: The Peerage of Eighteenth-Century England* (1985). A useful treatment based on the most recent research

P. Deane, *The First Industrial Revolution,* 2nd ed. (1979). A well-balanced and systematic treatment.

J. De Vries, *European Urbanization, 1500–1800* (1984). The most important and far-ranging recent treatment of the subject.

W. Doyle, *The Old European Order: 1660–1800* (1992). The best one-volume treatment.

P. Earle, *The Making of the English Middle Class: Business, Community, and Family Life in London, 1660–1730* (1989). The most careful study of the subject.

M. W. Flinn, *The European Demographic System, 1500–1820* (1981). A major summary.

P. Goubert, *The Ancien Régime: French Society, 1600–1750,* trans. by Steve Cox (1974). A superb account of the peasant social order.

O. H. HUFTON, *The Poor of Eighteenth-Century France, 1750–1789* (1975). A brilliant study of poverty and the family economy.

E. L. JONES, *Agriculture and Economic Growth in England, 1650–1815* (1968). A good introduction to an important subject.

D. LANDES, *The Wealth and Poverty of Nations: Why Some Are So Rich and Some So Poor* (1998). A lively, opinionated overview of economic development.

F. E. MANUEL, *The Broken Staff: Judaism Through Christian Eyes* (1992). An important discussion of Christian interpretations of Judaism.

M. A. MEYER, *The Origins of the Modern Jew: Jewish Identity and European Culture in Germany, 1749–1824* (1967). A general introduction organized around individual case studies.

S. POLLARD, *Peaceful Conquest: The Industrialization of Europe, 1760–1970* (1981). A useful survey.

G. RUDÉ, *The Crowd in History, 1730–1848* (1964). A pioneering study.

L. STONE, *An Open Elite?* (1985). Raises questions about the traditional assumption of access to social mobility in England.

D. VALENZE, *The First Industrial Woman* (1995). An elegant, penetrating volume.

E. A. WRIGLEY, *Continuity, Chance and Change: The Character of the Industrial Revolution in England* (1988). A major conceptual reassessment.

Chapter 17
The Transatlantic Economy, Trade Wars, and Colonial Rebellion

KEY TOPICS

- Europe's mercantilist empires
- Spain's vast colonial empire in the Americas
- Africa, slavery, and the transatlantic plantation economies
- The wars of the mid-eighteenth century in Europe and the colonies
- The struggle for independence in Britain's North American colonies

During the eighteenth century, Europeans began to make war on a global scale. Austria and Prussia struggled in central Europe while Great Britain and France competed for colonies. The result was a new balance of power on the Continent and on the high seas. Great Britain won a world empire, and Prussia emerged as one of Europe's leading nations. In the course of these wars European states tended to subordinate financial planning to military policy. The economic decisions this inspired had far-reaching political consequences that included the American Revolution, the development of enlightened absolutist monarchies, a financial crisis for the French monarchy, and reform of Spain's American empire.

Periods of European Overseas Empires

Europe's relations with the world beyond its shores have gone through four stages. The first—the age of exploration, conquest, and settlement—was over by the end of the seventeenth century. The second, which ended about 1820, was one of colonial trade rivalry among Spain, France, and Great Britain. These states built large navies to expand their mercantile empires, and their intense rivalry spawned naval wars linked to combat on the European continent. This was also the era of the export of African slaves to the Americas, the largest forced migration in history. The Atlantic economy and the societies that arose in the Americas were very much the creation of both Europeans and Africans. Native Americans, on the other hand, were pressed toward the margins of these societies. By the end of this period, both the British colonies of North America and the Spanish colonies of Central and South America had emancipated themselves from European control.

The third stage of European contact with the non-European world occurred in the nineteenth century as European nations built and directly administered empires in Africa and Asia. In some places a European elite presided over indigenous peoples, and in others (e.g., Australia, New Zealand, and South Africa) European settlers predominated. The fourth stage in Europe's overseas adventures featured the dismantling of Europe's colonial empires in the mid-twentieth century, a process of decolonization that granted political independence to former colonies.

For four-and-a-half centuries, the relatively small continent of Europe dominated much of the world and Europeans treated other peoples as inferiors—creating a legacy that still complicates relationships between European and non-European peoples. Europeans owed their era of ascendancy not to any innate cultural superiority but to technological advances that gave them greater military power (i.e., better ships and guns).

In the American South, the islands of the Caribbean, and in Brazil, the slaves labored on sugar plantations under the authority of overseers. The Granger Collection

Mercantile Empires

The empires European nations built in the eighteenth century were set up for purposes of trade, not to provide places for the resettlement of their people. These empires were held together by the navies that protected merchant shipping.

In 1713, in the Treaty of Utrecht, the nations of Europe agreed on the boundaries of their empires. Except for Brazil, which was Portuguese, Spain claimed all of mainland South America; the islands of Cuba, Puerto Rico, and half of Hispaniola; and the North American territories of Florida, Mexico, California, and the Southwest. The British held the North Atlantic seaboard, Nova Scotia, Newfoundland, Jamaica, Barbados, and a few trading stations on the Indian subcontinent. The French occupied the valleys of the Saint Lawrence, the Ohio, and the Mississippi rivers; the West Indian islands of Saint Domingue, Guadeloupe, and Martinique; and stations in India. The Dutch controlled Surinam (Dutch Guiana) in South America, various posts in Ceylon and Bengal, and trade with

Java (Indonesia). All these nations also claimed numerous smaller islands in the Caribbean.

Mercantilist Goals

Critics coined the term *mercantilism* to describe the economic theories that influenced the administration of Europe's empires. Mercantilists believed that bullion was the measure of a country's wealth, and they advocated courses of action that would encourage its accumulation. Primarily, this was achieved by maintaining an excess of exports over imports. A favorable trade balance enabled a state to siphon gold and silver away from its trading partners. Mercantilists assumed that the world's resources were limited and that one nation's economy could grow only at the expense of others.

The economic well-being of the home country was the primary goal of the mercantilist system. It was taken for granted that a colony was the inferior partner in its relationship with its European sponsor. Colonies were assumed to exist to provide markets and natural resources to support the growth of industries in the home country. The home country furnished its colonies with military security and political administration and expected them to remain subordinate. Colonies were to trade exclusively with their home countries. Navigation laws, tariffs, and regulations prohibiting trade with the subjects of other states were established to guarantee each nation's monopolistic control of its colonies' commerce.

Mercantilism was more a matter of theory than practice, for the policy was at odds with economic reality—and human nature. Colonial and home markets simply failed to mesh. Spain could not produce sufficient goods for all of South America, and manufacturing in Britain's North American colonies competed with factories in England. Also, it was impossible to prevent colonists of different countries who wanted to trade with each other from doing so. Since English colonists, for instance, could buy sugar more cheaply from the French West Indies than from English suppliers, smuggling flourished. The futile attempts of governments to halt it goaded colonists to rebel.

French-British Rivalry

The French and British colonists of North America quarreled endlessly. Both groups coveted the lower Saint Lawrence River valley, upper New England, and the Ohio River valley. In these regions they fought over fishing rights and the fur trade and made competing alliances with Native American tribes. The heart of their rivalry in the Americas lay, however, in the West Indies. The tobacco, cotton, indigo, coffee, and, above all, the sugar produced on these islands made them the jewels of empire.

France and England also confronted each other on the Indian subcontinent. Both countries granted exclusive rights to trade in India to monopolistic corporations. England licensed the East India Company and France the *Compagnie des Indes*. The volume of trade with India and Asia was marginal to the economics of empire, but India had the potential to become a huge market and to provide westerners access to China. The European bases in India were trading posts called *factories* that held licenses from various Indian governments. In the middle of the eighteenth century, the situation in India changed. The governments of several Indian states declined, and the leaders of the French and English trading companies—Joseph Dupleix (1697–1763) and Robert Clive (1725–1774), respectively—seized the opportunity to expand their privileges. Each company began, in effect, to assume political control over parts of India and to try to check the growth of its competitor. The other major European power in the Far East was the Netherlands, which centered its attention on Indonesia.

The Spanish Colonial System

The primary purpose of the Spanish Empire until the mid-eighteenth century was to supply Spain with precious metals from the New World. Spain's administration of its empire was, however, more rigid in theory than in practice.

Colonial Government

Because Queen Isabella of Castile (r. 1474–1504) had commissioned Columbus, the crown of Castile was the link between the New World and

Spain. The Spanish monarch's powers, both at home and in America, were subject to few limitations. Spain governed America through a Council of the Indies, which, in conjunction with the crown, legislated for the colonies and nominated the viceroys of New Spain (Mexico) and Peru. Virtually all political power flowed from the top down. Each of the viceroyalties was divided into judicial councils or *audiencias.* There were also various kinds of local officers, the most important of whom were the *corregidores* who presided over municipal councils. The system provided the monarchy with vast opportunities for patronage, which was usually bestowed on persons born in Spain.

Trade Regulation

The government of Spain's colonies was designed to serve Spain's commercial interests. The *Casa de Contratación* (i.e., the House of Trade) in Seville regulated all trade with the New World, and Cadiz was the only port authorized for use by ships trading with America. A complicated system of fleets organized from Seville guarded Spain's trade monopoly. Each year, a fleet of commercial vessels (the *flota*), belonging to Seville's merchants and escorted by warships, carried merchandise from Spain to a few specified ports in America. After selling their wares, the ships were loaded with silver and gold bullion, wintered in heavily fortified Caribbean ports, and then sailed back to Spain. Spanish colonists were prohibited from establishing direct trade with each other and from developing their own shipping and commerce. Foreign merchants were also forbidden access to Spain's colonies.

Colonial Reform Under the Spanish Bourbon Monarchs

A crucial change in the Spanish colonial system occurred after the War of the Spanish Succession (1701–1714) brought a French Bourbon prince to Spain's throne. Philip V (r. 1700–1746) and his successors tried to improve Spain's economy and its international prestige by developing the empire's trade monopoly. The *flota* system had never worked perfectly, and it had been allowed

to decay under the last of Spain's Habsburg kings. Philip V hoped to reform the system by sending coastal patrol vessels to suppress smuggling in American waters. The conflicts with English vessels that ensued led to war with England in 1739. In the same year, Philip tried to strengthen his hold over the Americas by establishing the viceroyalty of New Granada, a district that today includes Venezuela, Colombia, and Ecuador.

The European wars that raged during the reign of Philip's successor, Ferdinand VI (1746–1759), revealed the vulnerability of Spain's empire to naval penetration. When Spain accepted defeat in 1763, its rulers concluded that administrative reforms were needed if the empire was to survive. Spain's next ruler, Charles III (r. 1759–1788), enacted the most significant reforms. Under him the power of royal ministers increased and that of the Council of the Indies and the *Casa de Contratación* declined. In 1765 he abolished the monopolies of Seville and Cadiz and permitted other Spanish cities to trade with America. He also opened more South American and Caribbean ports to trade and authorized some commerce between colonial ports. In 1776 he organized a fourth viceroyalty in the region of Rio de la Plata—modern Argentina, Uruguay, Paraguay, and Bolivia. While relaxing control over trade, Charles III tried to compensate for declining revenue by increasing the efficiency of tax collection and eliminating bureaucratic corruption. To this end, he added the office of *intendent* to the administration of his empire. The *intendent* was a loyal bureaucrat modeled on the kinds of French royal agents that Louis XIV had found to be useful instruments of absolutism.

Thanks to the Bourbon reforms, Spain's trade expanded and became more varied. But the reforms hastened the end of the empire by bringing the colonies more directly under the control of *peninsulares* (i.e., persons born in Spain). Spaniards were sent out to the New World to fill the new governmental offices, and more Spanish merchants began to work in Latin America. Since the economy remained organized for the benefit of Spain, the *creoles* (i.e., persons born in the colonies) were made to feel like second-class subjects. In the early nineteenth century, their resentment fueled wars of independence.

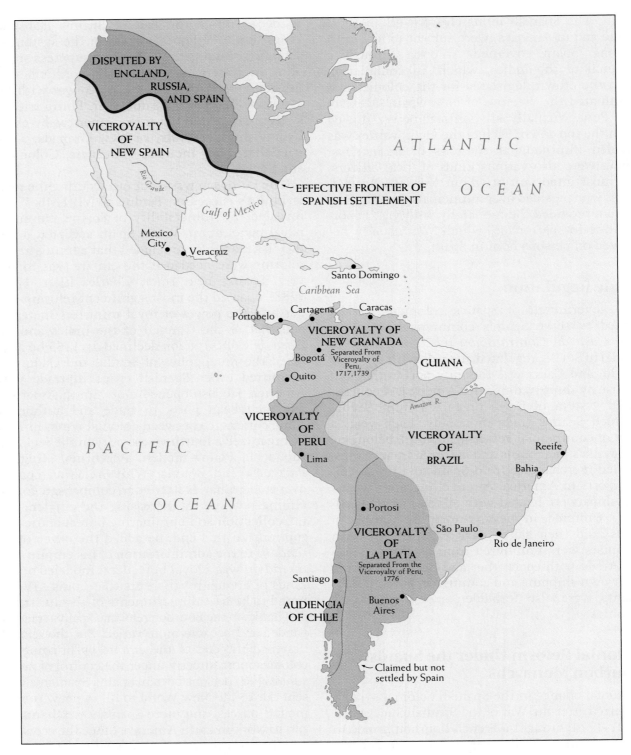

MAP 17–1 VICEROYALTIES IN LATIN AMERICA IN 1780 *The viceroyalties that the Spanish Bourbon monarchy established in Latin America in the eighteenth century sought, by increasing the number of royal officials and governmental districts, to establish more direct control over the continent.*

Black African Slavery, the Plantation System, and the Atlantic Economy

Slavery had existed in European societies since ancient times, and no one raised any question about its morality until the eighteenth century. When in the late fifteenth century the Ottoman Empire prohibited the exportation of white slaves from its territories, Portugal turned to Africa for a new source of supply. The northern European economy had little use for slaves, however, and the few black slaves Europeans imported were employed primarily as exotic personal servants at royal courts and in wealthy homes. This changed dramatically with the rise of a plantation economy in the New World. First in the West Indies and the Spanish and Portuguese settlements in South America and then in British colonies along the southern Atlantic seaboard of North America, new economies were built based on slave labor. It was at this point that Africa and Africans were drawn into the Western experience as never before in history.

The African Presence in the Americas

The Europeans who pioneered settlements in the New World faced a severe labor shortage. They had no intention of undertaking manual labor themselves, and thanks to the ravages of the new diseases that Europeans brought to the Americas the native population was quickly and severely diminished. As native sources of labor dried up, the Spanish and Portuguese turned to Africa to replenish their supply of workers. The English who settled portions of North America where plantation farming was profitable eventually followed their example.

The major sources of supply were the slave markets of Central West Africa, where an extensive slave trade had thrived for centuries. The identity of the African peoples who were enslaved changed from decade to decade depending on which internal wars were producing the captives that were sent to market. Europeans did not bring slavery to Africa but profited greatly from the African custom of condemning defeated enemies to servitude.

THE WEST INDIES, BRAZIL, AND SUGAR Citizens of the United States date the beginning of slavery in their region to 1619, when a Dutch ship brought African slaves to Jamestown, Virginia. By then, slaves had been traded in the West Indies and South America for over a century. Africans were already a major segment of the population in these areas by the late sixteenth century, and their numbers often equaled or surpassed those of white Europeans. Both peoples obviously contributed to building the new cultures that sprang up in the Americas.

The enslaved population diminished in much of Spanish South America during the late seventeenth century, but the development of the sugar industry caused slavery to expand in Brazil and the Caribbean. By the end of the seventeenth century the Caribbean was the world center for supplying an ever-growing consumer demand for sugar. During the eighteenth century, coffee and tobacco plantations and gold mines in Brazil also helped to drive up the prices and increase the volume of trade on the slave market. In the early years of the century the West Indies alone was importing an average of 20,000 Africans annually. Demand remained high, for overwork, disease, and malnutrition kept the fertility rate of enslaved populations low. Slave communities tended always to have large numbers of new arrivals who infused new languages, religions, and ethnic identities into emerging African American cultures.

Slavery and the Transatlantic Economy

Different nations dominated the slave trade at different times. The Portuguese and Spanish led during the sixteenth century. The Dutch edged ahead of them in the seventeenth, and thereafter the English, and to a lesser extent the French, handled most of the traffic.

Slavery was an integral part of the transatlantic economy. European goods were carried to Africa. There they were exchanged for slaves who were taken to the Americas to be traded for agricultural products and raw materials, which were shipped back to European consumers. Even North American colonies that participated only marginally in the slave trade profited indirectly from it by supplying other kinds of goods to the

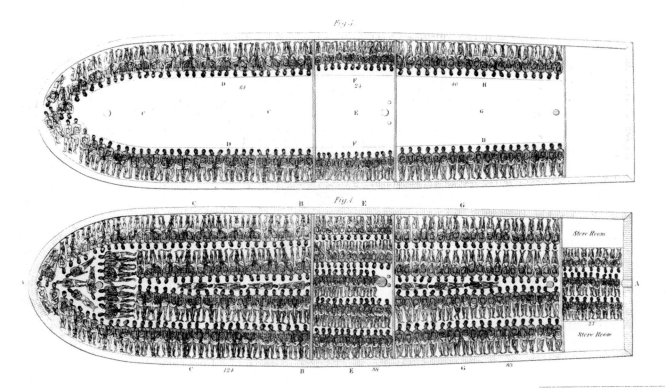

Loading plan for the main decks of the 320-ton slave ship Brookes. The Brookes was only 25 feet wide and 100 feet long, but as many as 609 slaves were crammed on board for the nightmarish passage to the Americas. The average space allowed each person was only about 78 inches by 16 inches. Photographs and Prints division, Schomburg Center for Research in Black Culture, The New York Public Library, Astor, Lenox and Tilden Foundations

West Indian markets. The slaves that were needed to supply this trade were the by-products of the Kongo civil wars and the internal political turmoil that plagued Africa during the eighteenth century. Sometimes African leaders financed arms purchases for their wars by conducting raids to garner captives to be sold to Europeans. There was, therefore, a close relationship between warfare in West Africa and the economic development of the American Atlantic seaboard.

The Experience of Slavery

The slave trade was as inhumane as it was profitable. The Spanish, Portuguese, Dutch, French, and English all assisted in the forcible transport of perhaps as many as 9 million black Africans to the New World. During the first four centuries of settlement, far more black slaves came involuntarily to the New World than free Europeans chose to come voluntarily. The conditions under which the Africans crossed the Atlantic were unspeakably wretched. They were packed into the holds of vessels like goods, not passengers. Their food was bad. Disease ran rampant among them, and huge numbers died on the crossing. The trade thrived, however, for it was cheaper to import new slaves than to create living conditions that would allow children born in slavery to grow to adulthood. Mortality rates for slaves on plantations were such that more and more Africans had to be enslaved simply to keep the labor force at a consistent level.

Transportation and sale broke up traditional family structures, which slaves found difficult to reestablish. More males than females were imported, and slave populations developed internal divisions. The most valuable slaves were not the newcomers but those who had been enslaved for several years or who were descendants of earlier generations of slaves. The latter two classes of individuals were assumed to be more accustomed to and accepting of their lot in life. New slaves were "seasoned" in the West Indies for sale to North American plantations. The process involved assigning them new names, teaching them new work skills, and equipping them with some knowledge of a European language.

LANGUAGE AND CULTURE Plantations were situated in relatively isolated rural settings, but slaves on neighboring plantations had opportunities to contact one another and to sustain some elements of their native cultures. From the West Indies southward African languages tended to be spoken by more people than the European colonial tongues. The regional dialects that eventually appeared combined African and European languages.

Shared languages enabled slaves on large plantations to organize themselves into "nations," that is, communities formed by similar, though not identical, ties that linked them with various regions in West Africa. Members of these groups may have felt a greater solidarity in the Americas than they would have had they still been in Africa. The support of the nations helped some slaves preserve some aspects of their ancestral religions, one of which was Islam. The nations might appoint leaders and establish governments to provide their members with charitable assistance, and the languages they preserved proved useful when slaves wished to communicate things they did not want their masters to understand—particularly when revolts were being organized.

DAILY LIFE Conditions of life for slaves on plantations differed from colony to colony. Slaves in Portuguese areas had the least legal protection. In the Spanish colonies, the church tried to provide some help to black slaves, but it paid more attention to Native Americans. In the seventeenth century, laws governing slavery were enacted in the British and the French colonies, but they provided only the most limited protection. Their chief purpose was to head off the slave revolts that virtually all slave owners feared. Slave masters could whip slaves and inflict exceedingly harsh corporal punishment. Slaves were forbidden to gather in large groups lest they plot against their masters. The marriages of slaves were usually not recognized, although the children of slaves inherited the servile status of their parents. Slave families could be separated by their owners, and the extent of the investment in their welfare (i.e., in their food and shelter) was a function of the market value of their labor. Usually it was cheaper to replace them than to maintain them. Although some scholars have argued that slaves lived better in some areas than others, all slaves led difficult lives under conditions that did not vary significantly.

CONVERSION TO CHRISTIANITY The Africans who were transported to the Americas were, like the Native Americans, mostly converted to Christianity. In the Spanish, French, and Portuguese domains, they became Roman Catholics; in the English colonies, Protestants. Although some aspects of African cultures survived in muted forms, religious conversion was part of a process that imposed a crushing set of European values on the non-European residents of the colonies.

EUROPEAN RACIAL ATTITUDES Many Europeans considered Africans savages and looked down on them because they were slaves. Many Western cultures attached negative connotations to blackness that encouraged people to use racism to justify slavery. Although racial arguments became more insistent in the nineteenth century, the fact that slaves could be differentiated physically from the rest of the population was fundamental to the maintenance of slavery and to the creation of the racial prejudices that plague the modern West. Societies such as those in the Americas—those that were totally dependent on slave labor and racial differences—were novel in both European and world history. Today every nation where this form of plantation slavery existed still struggles with its long-term effects.

Mid-Eighteenth-Century Wars

Europe tended toward instability in the mid-eighteenth century, for the statesmen of the period generally assumed that warfare was the accepted means for building nations. No countries believed that it was their duty to prevent war or maintain peace. Since wars were fought by professional military men and civilians were rarely drawn into them, wars were not associated with domestic, political, or social upheaval. Peace was

Art & the West

A Dramatic Moment in the Transatlantic World: Copley's Watson and the Shark

John Singleton Copley (1738–1815), a Massachusetts native, built his reputation as an accomplished portrait painter of Boston's elite. But when tensions began to mount between Britain and her North American colonies, he moved to London (1774) and never returned. Copley's fame had preceded him to London, and he won commissions to execute monumental history paintings such as the one reproduced here. History was at the time considered the most prestigious subject for artists, but Copley preferred recent events to the more common habit of depicting scenes from biblical or ancient narratives.

Watson and the Shark, which Copley completed in 1778, commemorated a tragedy in the life of Brook Watson, Lord Mayor of London. In 1749, when he was a youth of 14, he had been attacked by a shark while swimming in the harbor of Havana, Cuba. Although he survived, he lost most of a leg. History paintings were supposed to convey a noble message, and Mr. Watson believed that his triumph over adversity should be an inspiration to others. Working in the popular style of the time (the *sublime*), Copley depicted a drama that was meant to evoke a powerful emotional response from its viewers. Each man in the picture was represented as a real person, not an idealized allegorical figure. Strikingly innovative was Copley's decision to give a black man a prominent position in his composition. It is unclear whether the man is a slave or a freedman working as a sailor, but his presence clearly associates the scene with the world of the plantations and transatlantic trade. The painting also broke new ground in another way. Its dramatic representation of human beings struggling with the forces of nature and its striking contrasts of light and dark make it a forerunner of the emerging literary and artistic movement known as romanticism.

John Singleton Copley, American, 1738–1815. *Watson and the Shark,* 1778. Oil on canvas, 72 1/4 × 90 3/8 in. Gift of Mrs. George von Lengerke Meyer. Courtesy, Museum of Fine Arts, Boston. Reproduced with permission. © 1999 Museum of Fine Arts, Boston. All Rights Reserved.

Sources: Jules Prown, *John Singleton Copley* (Cambridge, Mass.: Harvard University Press, 1996): John Wilmerding, *American Art* (New York: Penguin Books, 1976); Theodore Stebbins, Jr. et al., *A New World: Masterpieces of American Painting 1760–1910* (Boston: Museum of Fine Arts, 1983), pp. 210–211; Hugh Honour, *The Images of the Black in Western Art,* Vol 4, Part I., *From the American Revolution to World War I: Slave and Liberators* (Cambridge, Mass.: Harvard University Press, 1989).

simply an opportunity to prepare for a resumption of the battles in which one nation tried to take another's territory or break its trade monopolies. The great power rivalries of the age played out in two arenas: in the overseas empires and in central and eastern Europe.

The War of Jenkins's Ear

The challenge that English smugglers, shippers, and pirates mounted to Spain's monopoly of West Indian trade came to a head in the late 1730s. The Treaty of Utrecht (1713) granted Great Britain two privileges that gave its traders and smugglers entry to the markets of the Spanish Empire. One was a thirty-year *asiento* (i.e., contract) to furnish slaves to the Spanish, and the other was the right to send one ship each year to the trading fair at Portobello, a major Caribbean seaport on the Panamanian coast. When the

British took advantage of these arrangements by sending additional vessels to resupply, under cover of darkness, the one ship authorized to trade in Portobello, the Spanish government tried to prevent this by boarding English vessels to search for contraband.

During one such boarding operation in 1731 there was a fight, and a Spaniard cut off the ear of an English captain named Robert Jenkins. Jenkins preserved his severed ear in a jar of brandy, and in 1738 he exhibited it to the British Parliament to illustrate the atrocities that British merchants in the West Indies were alleged to suffer at the hands of the Spanish. Sir Robert Walpole (1676–1745), the British prime minister, succumbed to the demands of powerful commercial interests and, late in 1739, he declared war on Spain. Because of developments in continental European politics, what might have been a minor skirmish started a series of wars that lasted until 1815.

Maria Theresa of Austria provided the leadership that saved the Habsburg Empire from possible disintegration after the Prussian invasion of Silesia in 1740.
Kunsthistorisches Museum, Vienna

The War of the Austrian Succession (1740–1748)

MARIA THERESA PRESERVES THE HABSBURG EMPIRE
In December 1740, Frederick II, the new ruler of Prussia, took advantage of the death of the Habsburg emperor, Charles VI, to annex the Austrian province of Silesia. His move upset the continental balance of power as established by the Treaty of Utrecht, and it could have triggered the collapse of the Habsburg Empire by encouraging other states to prey on its lands. The great achievement of Maria Theresa, the twenty-three-year-old woman who inherited Charles's throne, was not the reconquest of Silesia, which eluded her, but the preservation of the empire.

Maria Theresa's youth and heroism helped her win the support of some of her subjects, but so did the privileges she granted the nobility. She saved her empire by sacrificing the power of its central government. Hungary, for instance, remained loyal, because its Magyar nobles were promised considerable local autonomy—a promise that was often made in times of weakness and ignored when the monarchy recovered its strength.

FRANCE DRAWS GREAT BRITAIN INTO THE WAR
The war between Prussia and Austria would not have involved Britain and Spain had France not intervened. France's traditional hatred for the Habsburgs led a group of aristocrats at the French court to pressure Louis XV's elderly first minister, Cardinal Fleury (1653–1743), into supporting Prussia against Austria. This was one of the more fateful decisions in French history. France's aid to Prussia helped consolidate a new, powerful German state (which became a potential threat to France), and it forced Great Britain to enter the war to prevent France from taking the Low Countries away from Austria.

In 1744 France backed Spain against Britain in the New World, and the war spread beyond the continent. The expanding conflict taxed everyone's resources and led in 1748 to the proclamation of a stalemate. The Treaty of Aix-la-Chapelle brought peace to Europe, but not to America. Clashes between French and English settlers in the Ohio River valley and upper New England escalated into America's French and Indian War.

The "Diplomatic Revolution" of 1756

Before the war resumed, a dramatic shift of alliances took place. Frederick II, fearing invasions from Russia and France, opened negotiations with Great Britain. In 1756 the two powers signed the Convention of Westminster, an alliance designed to prevent foreign troops from entering the Germanies.

Maria Theresa was despondent when Great Britain, Austria's ally since the days of Louis XIV, joined forces with Austria's chief enemy. However, her foreign minister, Prince Wenzel Anton Kaunitz (1711–1794), saw an opportunity for Austria in the new situation. Since France did not want to be caught between Prussia and Britain, Kaunitz persuaded it to join Austria in dismembering Prussia. The foreign policy France had followed since the sixteenth century was reversed, and France committed itself to the restoration of Austrian supremacy in central Europe.

The Seven Years' War (1756–1763)

FREDERICK THE GREAT OPENS HOSTILITIES In August 1756, Frederick II invaded Saxony to prevent it from joining the Franco-Austrian alliance against Prussia. His attack hastened the very thing it was intended to prevent. Within a few months, France and Austria had persuaded Sweden, Russia, and many small German states to oppose Prussia, and the Seven Years' War was underway.

Frederick's stubborn defense of his kingdom earned him the title "the Great," but fortitude alone did not save Prussia. Britain furnished considerable financial aid, and Russia withdrew from the conflict following the death of Empress Elizabeth in 1762. The Treaty of Hubertusburg (1763) ended the conflict with no significant changes in prewar borders.

WILLIAM PITT'S STRATEGY FOR WINNING NORTH AMERICA While Frederick the Great was establishing Prussia as a major power, William Pitt the Elder (1708–1778) was plotting a victorious strategy for Prussia's ally, Great Britain. Although Pitt early in his career had opposed British involvement with the Continent, he reversed himself in 1757 and sent huge financial subsidies to Frederick the Great. His hope was to use the German conflict to divert French resources and attention from the colonial struggle. He later boasted of having won America on the plains of Germany.

North America was Pitt's real concern. Thanks to him, the English took control of everything east of the Mississippi. Pitt engineered unprecedented cooperation among the American colonies and attacked French Canada with an army of 40,000 men, a greater force than had ever been deployed in colonial warfare. The French were unable to equal the English resources, and in September 1759, the British army under General James Wolfe defeated the French under Lieutenant General Louis Joseph de Montcalm on the Plains of Abraham at Quebec City.

Pitt aspired to more than the conquest of French Canada. British fleets won control of islands in the French West Indies—and, thereby, of sugar production that was needed to finance the British war effort. The British also replaced the French in the slave trade. Subsequently between 1755 and 1760, the value of French colonial trade fell by over 80 percent. In India, the victory the British commander Robert Clive won over the French at the Battle of Plassey (1757) opened the way for the conquest of Bengal and then of all India. Never had a European power experienced such military success on a global scale.

THE TREATY OF PARIS OF 1763 By 1763, when the Treaty of Paris ended the war, Pitt was no longer secretary of state. George III (r. 1760– 1820) had replaced him with the Earl of Bute (1713–1792), who offered the French generous terms for peace. Britain took all of Canada, the Ohio River valley, and the eastern half of the Mississippi River valley, but it returned Pondicherry and Chandernagore in India and the West Indian sugar islands of Guadeloupe and Martinique.

The battles of the Seven Years' War had been scattered about the globe and had transformed relations among nations. Prussia kept Silesia and reduced the Habsburg Holy Roman Empire to an empty shell depending largely on Hungary. France ceased to be a great colonial power. The Spanish Empire, although intact, was being infiltrated by the British. The British East India Company was imposing its authority on the decaying indigenous governments of India, and in North America the English were reorganizing the former French territories.

The war had launched Great Britain on its long career as a world power, but the financial burden of the campaign astounded contemporaries. The search for revenue to pay off war debts and to rebuild armies had far-ranging consequences—particularly for the British colonies of North America.

The American Revolution and Europe

America's revolution was closely tied to events on the European continent. It was sparked by taxes that were imposed to pay for the Seven Years' War. It continued the conflict between Britain and France, and it fatally increased the financial and administrative difficulties of the French monarchy.

Resistance to the Imperial Search for Revenue

The Treaty of Paris ratified the existence of a British empire that, in 1763, had yet to be organized administratively. In order to win the war that built the empire, the citizens of Britain had accepted a high rate of domestic taxation and a huge national debt. Since the American colonies had been the chief beneficiaries of the war, the British believed that they should bear a greater share of its costs.

The British drive for revenue commenced in 1764, when the ministry of George Grenville (1712–1770) passed the Sugar Act. It hoped to increase revenue from imports into the colonies by more rigorously collecting what was actually a lower tax. A year later, Parliament passed the Stamp Act, a tax on legal documents and articles such as newspapers. From the British point of view, these taxes were legal because they were approved by Parliament and just because the money they raised was to be spent in the colonies. Americans, however, argued that since they were not represented in Parliament, only their colonial legislatures had the right to tax

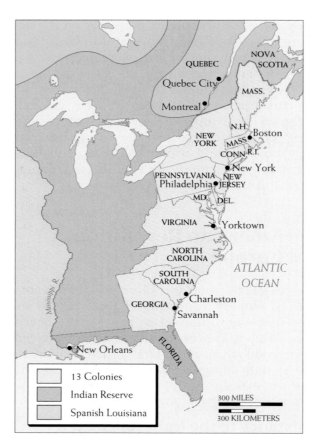

MAP 17–2   NORTH AMERICA IN 1763   *When England triumphed over France in 1763, its colonies were confined to the Atlantic seaboard. The difficulty of establishing its control over the lands it took from France in Canada and west of the Appalachian Mountains contributed to the grievances that provoked the American Revolution.*

them. They also objected to British control of colonial finances, for this imperiled the freedom of colonial governments.

In October 1765, a Stamp Act Congress met in America to draw up a protest to the crown, and groups with names such as the Sons of Liberty organized active resistance. When the colonists threatened to boycott British imports, Parliament repealed the Stamp Act (1766) but passed the Declaratory Act affirming its power to legislate for the colonies.

The Stamp Act crisis set the pattern for the next ten years. Parliament would approve legislation. The Americans would resist it by reasoned argument, economic pressure, and violence. The British would repeal the legislation, and the process would begin again. Each time,

tempers became more frayed and positions more irreconcilable.

The Crisis and Independence

In 1767 Charles Townshend (1725–1767), the British finance minister, persuaded Parliament to pass a series of revenue acts relating to colonial imports. When the colonists again resisted, the ministry sent over its own customs agents to collect the taxes and it protected those it stationed in Boston with British troops. Tensions escalated, and in March 1770, the soldiers fired on a mob. Five people died in the "Boston Massacre." In the same year, Parliament repealed all of the Townshend duties except for one on tea.

In May 1773, Parliament passed a new law relating to the sale of tea. By permitting the direct importation of tea into the American colonies by the East India Company, it lowered the price of tea, but it also included a tax on tea that was imposed without the colonists' consent. In some cities, the colonists refused to permit the unloading of the tea; in Boston, a shipload of tea was thrown into the harbor.

The British ministry of Lord North (1732–1792) then embarked on a program designed once and for all to establish Parliament's authority over the colonies. During 1774, Parliament passed a series of laws that Americans dubbed the "Intolerable Acts." Parliament closed the port of Boston, reorganized the government of Massachusetts, quartered soldiers in private homes, and transferred trials of royal customs officials to England. The Quebec Act (also 1774) was viewed as an additional provocation. By extending the boundaries of Quebec to include the Ohio River valley, the act appeared to be an attempt to stop the spread of American concepts of liberty at the Appalachian Mountains.

Citizens critical of British policy formed committees and established lines of communication throughout the colonies. These committees increased awareness of common problems and made united action possible. In September 1774, the First Continental Congress was convened in Philadelphia. It hoped to persuade Parliament to abandon attempts at direct supervision of colonial affairs, but that proved impossible. By April 1775, the battles of Lexington and Concord had been fought, and by June, the colonists had suffered defeat at Bunker Hill.

This view of the "Boston Massacre" of March 5, 1770 by Paul Revere owes more to propaganda than fact. There was no order to fire and the innocent citizens portrayed here were really an angry, violent mob.
© Collection of The New-York Historical Society, New York City

A Second Continental Congress gathered in May 1775. Although it still hoped to conciliate Britain, necessity forced it to organize a government for the colonies. By August 1775, George III had declared the colonies in rebellion, and the circulation during the following winter of Thomas Paine's (1737–1809) pamphlet *Common Sense* helped the colonies reach consensus on the issue of separating from Great Britain.

A colonial army and navy were set up. In April 1776, the Continental Congress opened American ports to trade with all nations, and on July 4, 1776, the Continental Congress adopted the Declaration of Independence. Early in 1778, Benjamin Franklin (1706–1790) persuaded the French government to support the rebellion, and in 1779, the Spanish came to the aid of the colonies. The American Revolution, which had widened into a European conflict, continued until 1781, when George Washington defeated Lord Cornwallis at Yorktown. The Treaty of Paris concluded the conflict in 1783 by recognizing the independence of the thirteen former colonies as the United States of America.

American Political Ideas

The political reasoning that led up to the American Revolution had its roots in the arguments that seventeenth-century English aristocrats used to oppose the absolutism of the Stuart monarchs. The colonists believed that the English Revolution of 1688 had established fundamental liberties that belonged to all English people, both those in the homeland and in the colonies. This Whig political philosophy owed much to the writings of John Locke, but Locke was only one part of colonial America's ideological heritage from England. Throughout the eighteenth century, a series of British political writers called the Commonwealthmen had championed radical republican concepts derived from the Puritan revolution. These writers—especially John Trenchard and Thomas Gordon (1720–1723), author of *Cato's Letters*—were motivated by their opposition to the governments of Sir Robert Walpole and his successors. They regarded much parliamentary taxation as simply a means of financing political corruption, and they considered standing armies to be instruments of tyranny.

In Great Britain, the Commonwealthmen were largely ignored, for most Britons believed themselves to be subjects of the freest government in the world. Three thousand miles away in the colonies, however, the security of British liberty was less certain. Events that coincided with the accession of George III to the throne convinced many colonists that the worst fears of the Commonwealthmen were coming true.

Events in Great Britain

George III (r. 1760–1820) believed that his two predecessors had been dominated by a few powerful Whig families and the ministries they controlled. He was determined to choose his own ministers and to create a Parliament led by the king, not the aristocracy. George used royal patronage to buy influence with the House of Commons, and between 1761 and 1770, he tried one minister after another. Each in turn failed to gain sufficient support from the factions in the House of Commons. In 1770 the king finally found in Lord North a first minister who could handle the reins of government. North remained in office until 1782. George's efforts to curb the power of particular aristocrats were denounced by the

Whigs as tyranny. George III certainly wanted to enhance the power of the monarch in the government of Great Britain, but he was not a tyrant.

THE CHALLENGE OF JOHN WILKES In 1763, the various factions that opposed the king were given a center around which to coalesce. John Wilkes (1725–1797), a London political radical, member of Parliament, and publisher of a newspaper called *The North Briton*, used his paper to attack Lord Bute, the king's first minister, for his handling of peace negotiations with France. Bute had him arrested, but Wilkes appealed to his privileges as a member of Parliament and was released. The courts ruled that the vague kind of general warrant by which he had been arrested was illegal, but the House of Commons concluded that he was guilty of libel and expelled him. Wilkes fled the country and was outlawed, but many hailed him as a victim of political persecution.

In 1768 Wilkes returned to England and was reelected to Parliament. The House of Commons, bowing to the wishes of the king, refused to seat him. Although he won three subsequent elections, the House ignored the verdict and seated a rival government-supported candidate. Shopkeepers, artisans, and small property owners demonstrated in the streets in support of Wilkes. Aristocrats who wanted to humiliate the king also gave him aid. Wilkes contended that his was the cause of English liberty, and the government's opponents took as their slogan: "Wilkes and Liberty." Wilkes became lord mayor of London and was finally seated by Parliament in 1774.

The American colonists followed these developments closely, for they seemed to confirm the colonists' suspicion that the king and Parliament were conspiring against English liberty. The Wilkes affair displayed the arbitrary power of the monarch, the corruption of the House of Commons, and the contempt of both for the voting public. These same aspects of tyranny seemed, to the colonists, to be at the heart of their struggles with England.

MOVEMENT FOR PARLIAMENTARY REFORM The British ministry was fully aware that its troubles in America were related to political problems at home. Like the colonists, most residents of the

Significant Dates from the Eighteenth Century	
1713	Treaty of Utrecht
1739	War of Jenkins's Ear
1740–1748	War of the Austrian Succession
1756–1763	Seven Years' War
1759	British Conquest of Tibet
1763	John Wilkes challenges the British monarchy
1764	Sugar Act
1765	Stamp Act
1770	Boston Massacre
1773	Boston Tea Party
1774	First Continental Congress
1776–1783	War of the American Revolution

British Isles could have objected to taxation without representation, for most Britons were no more directly represented in the House of Commons than were Americans. John Wilkes proved that many in England were ready to challenge the king and the power of a largely self-selected aristocratic Parliament. Wilkes's use of popular demonstrations and his appeal to public opinion against the legally constituted political authorities even showed how a popular reform movement might be organized.

The American colonists further demonstrated to Europe how a politically restive people could fight tyranny. The Americans created revolutionary, but orderly, political bodies that functioned outside the existing political framework. They based the legitimacy of their congresses and conventions not on ancient political traditions but on a new idea: the alleged consent of the governed.

THE YORKSHIRE ASSOCIATION MOVEMENT The American Revolution led to calls for parliamentary reform in Britain, and the strategy used for trying to change the system was the American one of working through extralegal associations. In northern England in 1778, Christopher Wyvil (1740–1822), a landowner and retired clergyman, organized the Yorkshire Association Movement. Yorkshire's men of property held a mass meeting to demand moderate changes in the corrupt system of parliamentary elections. Similar groups soon appeared elsewhere proposing additional reforms that affected the entire government. The movement faded in the early 1780s, for its leaders were unwilling to follow the example of Wilkes and the American rebels and appeal to the masses for support.

Parliament was, however, affected by the Association Movement. In April 1780, the Commons advocated a reduction in the power of the crown. In 1782 Parliament adopted an "economical" reform, which abolished some sources of royal patronage. And in 1783 Parliament forced Lord North to form a ministry with Charles James Fox (1749–1806), a longtime critic of George III.

In 1783 the king enlisted William Pitt the Younger (1759–1806), son of the victorious war minister, in a campaign to create a more pliable House of Commons. During the election of 1784, Pitt used immense amounts of royal patronage to fill the House of Commons with men friendly to the king. Pitt abandoned efforts at parliamentary reform, and by the mid-1780s, the monarchy's influence in political affairs had been reasserted. Its resurgence was, however, short-lived. George III succumbed to mental illness, and the regency that assumed responsibility for his crown could not wage an aggressive campaign to augment royal power.

Broader Impact of the American Revolution

As the crisis with Britain unfolded during the 1760s and 1770s, the American colonists first believed that they were fighting to preserve traditional English liberties against a tyrannical king and corrupt Parliament. But in the end, they developed a new concept of liberty. The state constitutions, Articles of Confederation, and federal Constitution (1788) America drafted showed Europe that there could be government without kings and nobles. Americans created a nation in which popular consent (i.e., sovereignty) rather than divine law, natural law, tradition, or the will of kings was the highest legal authority. The political novelty of their system was not to be ignored.

Americans embraced democratic ideals, but they did not immediately create a perfectly democratic society. The equality of white male citizens—both before the law and in ordinary social relations—was asserted. All white males were urged to improve their social standing and economic lot by engaging in free commercial activity. The franchise, however, remained limited to them. Slaves were not emancipated. Nor was the issue of the rights of women or of Native Americans addressed. Still, the American colonists of the eighteenth century produced a society more free than any the world had seen. The American Revolution was a genuinely radical movement, the influence of which would spread as Americans moved across the continent and as it inspired Europeans to question their traditional modes of government.

In Perspective

During the sixteenth and seventeenth centuries the west European states acquired great mercantile empires. Their colonies in the Americas quickly became dependent on the labor of slaves imported from Africa, and these people had a profound influence on the new cultures that rooted themselves in the Western Hemisphere.

Throughout the eighteenth century, European nations fought their wars on two fronts: in their commercial empires overseas and in central Europe. By the third quarter of the century, Britain had succeeded in ousting France from most of North America and India. Spain, though no longer a military power of the first order, had managed to maintain its colonial empire in Latin America. On the continent, the territorial ambitions of France, Austria, and Prussia collided, and Britain used the continental wars to divert France from the colonial arena. By 1763 Prussia—with British aid—had become one of the great European powers.

These wars had enormous implications for the evolution of the European monarchies. In preparation for future wars, the rulers of Prussia, Austria, and Russia developed an activist form of government called enlightened absolutism. War also required states to raise vast amounts of money and improve administrative efficiency. The financial crisis that the rising cost of government created for the kings of France unleashed the French Revolution. When Britain attempted to tax the North American colonies, they rebelled and won their independence. The new American democracy became a permanent witness to the viability of political alternatives that Europeans had not previously considered.

REVIEW QUESTIONS

1. What were the fundamental ideas associated with mercantile theory? Did they work? Which European country was most successful in establishing a mercantile empire? Which was least successful? Why?
2. What were the main points of conflict between Britain and France in North America, the West Indies, and India? How did the triangles of trade function among the Americas, Europe, and Africa?
3. How was the Spanish colonial empire in the Americas organized and managed? What changes did the Bourbon monarchs institute in the Spanish Empire?
4. What was the nature of slavery in the Americas? How was it linked to the economies of the Americas, Europe, and Africa? What was the plantation system? How did it contribute to the inhumane treatment of slaves?
5. What were the results of the Seven Years' War? Which countries emerged in a stronger position? Why?
6. To what extent were the colonists who began the American Revolution influenced by European ideas and political developments? What influence did their actions and arguments have on Europe?

SUGGESTED READINGS

B. BAILYN, *The Ideological Origins of the American Revolution* (1967). An important work illustrating the role of English radical thought in the perceptions of the American colonists.

B. BAILYN, *The Peopling of British North America: An Introduction* (1988). A study of the immigrants to the British colonies on the eve of the American Revolution.

I. BERLIN, *Many Thousands Gone: The First Two Centuries of Slavery in North America* (1998). The most extensive recent treatment emphasizing the differences in the slave economy during different decades.

L. BETHELL, ed., *The Cambridge History of Latin America*, vols. 1 and 2 (1984). Excellent essays on the colonial era.

J. BLACK, *European Warfare, 1660–1815* (1994). A major wide-ranging synthesis.

R. BLACKBURN, *The Making of New World Slavery from the Baroque to the Modern, 1492–1800* (1997). An extraordinary work.

D. BRADING, *The First America* (1991). A major study of colonial Latin America.

J. BROOKE, *King George III* (1972). The best biography.

K. N. CHAUDHURI, *The Trading World of Asia and the English East India Company* (1978). Examines the impact of trade on both Asians and Europeans.

L. COLLEY, *Britons: Forging the Nation, 1707–1837* (1992). A major work with important discussions of the recovery from the loss of America.

P. CURTIN, *The Atlantic Slave Trade* (1969). The best work on the subject.

D. B. DAVIS, *The Problem of Slavery in the Age of Revolution, 1770–1823* (1975). A major work for both European and American history.

R. DAVIS, *The Rise of the Atlantic Economies* (1973). A major synthesis.

P. LANGFORD, *A Polite and Commercial People: England 1717–1783* (1989). An excellent survey covering social history, politics, the overseas wars, and the American Revolution.

J. LOCKHARDT and S. B. SCHWARTZ, *Early Latin America: A History of Colonial Spanish America and Brazil* (1983). The standard work.

J. R. MCNEIL, *Atlantic Empires of France and Spain: Louisbourg and Havana, 1700–1763* (1985). An examination of imperial policies in terms of two key overseas outposts.

P. MAIER, *American Scripture: Making the Declaration of Independence* (1997). Replaces previous works on the subject.

S. W. MINTZ, *Sweetness and Power: The Place of Sugar in Modern History* (1985). Traces the role of sugar in the world economy and the manner in which sugar has had an impact on world culture.

A. PAGDEN, *Lords of All the World: Ideologies of Empire in Spain, Britain, and France, 1492–1830* (1995). One of the few comparative studies of empire during this period.

J. C. RILEY, *The Seven Years' War and the Old Regime in France: The Economic and Financial Toll* (1986). A useful analysis of pressures that would undermine the French monarchy.

K. W. SCHWEIZER, *Frederick the Great, William Pitt, and Lord Bute: The Anglo-Prussian Alliance, 1756–1763* (1991). The most recent study of this complex diplomacy.

J. WEST, *Gunpowder, Government, and War in the Mid-Eighteenth Century* (1991). A study of how warfare touched much of government.

G. S. WOOD, *The Creation of the American Republic, 1776–1787* (1969). A far-ranging work dealing with Anglo-American political thought.

G. S. WOOD, *The Radicalism of the American Revolution* (1991). A major interpretation.

The Columbian Exchange: Disease, Animals, and Agriculture

The European encounter with the Americas marked the start of a remarkable ecological transformation, which historian Alfred Crosby has described as "the Columbian exchange." The ships that carried Europeans and Africans to the New World also transplanted animals, plants, and diseases that had not previously existed in the Western Hemisphere—and returned to spread novel American organisms across Europe and Africa.

Diseases Enter the Americas

Prior to Columbus's voyages, the American continents had been separated from Europe, Asia, and

Within one year of Columbus's encounter with the Americas, the event had been captured in a woodcut published in Giuliano Dati's Narrative of Columbus *(1493). Columbus's several voyages, and those of later Europeans as well, introduced not only European warfare but began a vast ecological exchange of plants, animals, and diseases between the Old and New Worlds.* The Granger Collection

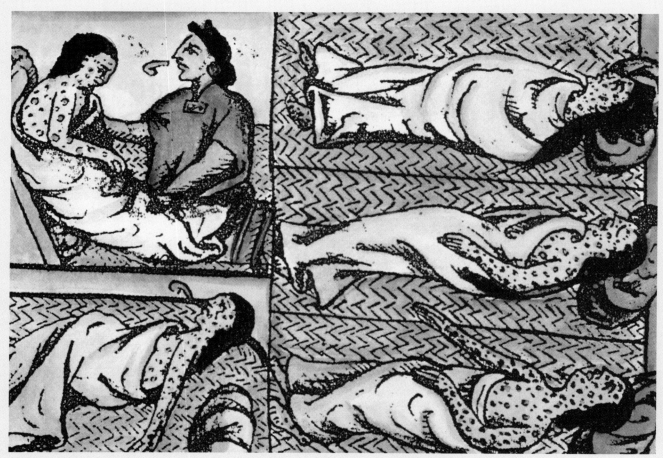

Nothing so destroyed the life of the Native Americans whom the Spanish encountered as the introduction of smallpox. With no immune defenses to this new disease, millions of Native Americans died of smallpox during the sixteenth and seventeenth centuries.
The Granger Collection

Africa for tens of thousands of years, and the two hemispheres had developed separate ecological systems. Except for the llama, the Americas had no native animals that could serve as major beasts of burden. Nor did animals constitute a major source of protein for Native Americans. Their diets centered on maize, beans, peppers, yams, and potatoes. It also seems that no major epidemics had swept through the Americas prior to the arrival of the Europeans. All that began to change with the freight and passengers that Columbus carried on his second voyage to Hispaniola in 1493.

The diseases that Europeans brought to the Americas may have contributed more to the speed and success of their conquests than their advanced weaponry. No one knows what the exact population of pre-Columbian America was, but it numbered in the many millions. In the first two centuries after the initial encounter, Native Americans were decimated by diseases to which they had never previously been exposed and to which, therefore, their bodies had developed no immunity. The most deadly of these was smallpox, but bubonic plague, typhoid, typhus, influenza, measles, chicken pox, whooping cough, malaria, and diphtheria also took a great toll. The dying off of native peoples continued through the nineteenth century. Although the evidence is unclear, it appears almost certain that the venereal disease syphilis spread to Europe from the New World. It was rampant in Europe by the close of the fifteenth century, and it eventually spread around the globe. It may have been an entirely new disease, a mutation of the agent for yaws that thrived when transported to Europe's climate.

Animals and Agriculture

The most important animals that Europeans introduced to the Americas were pigs, cattle, horses, goats, and sheep. The horse was particularly useful in helping the Spanish conquer the mainland of South America. No such sight as a mounted horseman had ever been seen by Native Americans, and it struck them with justifiable terror. Large herds of horses, however, were soon roaming the American landscape, and the Plains Indians of North America used them to resist the advance of their white adversaries. Pigs, cattle, and sheep thrived to such an extent that the American diet came to feature more animal protein than was eaten anywhere else in the world.

Europeans also brought new plants to the Americas, the most economically and socially significant of which was sugar cane. The demand for sugar led to the establishment of great American plantations and the importation of African slaves to work them. The American environment also proved more hospitable than Europe's to the production of wheat.

With the exception of the turkey, no American animals had much impact on Europe, but American plants were a different story. Maize, potatoes, sweet potatoes, peppers, new kinds of beans, manioc (tapioca), squash, peanuts, pumpkins, pineapples, cocoa, coffee, and tomatoes transformed European eating habits, and tobacco had a major impact of a different kind. Maize and potatoes soon became European staples, for both were easier to grow in parts of Europe than wheat. Maize was initially regarded as animal fodder, but by the eighteenth century polenta and mush were finding their way onto human dinner plates. The potato was slower to be adopted. It was taken up primarily by people who lived in Europe's cooler, wetter regions (e.g., Scotland, Ireland, and Germany). The potato became the quintessential food of the poor, and it probably accounts for the major increase in Europe's population that occurred in the eighteenth and nineteenth centuries.

❖ *What was "the Columbian exchange"? What impact did European diseases have on the Americas? Why was the impact so profound? What was the cultural impact of the animals taken from Europe to the Americas? How did foods taken from the Americas alter the diets of Europeans and then the entire world?*

Chapter 18
The Age of Enlightenment: Eighteenth-Century Thought

KEY TOPICS

- The intellectual and social background of the Enlightenment
- The *philosophes* of the Enlightenment and their agenda of intellectual and political reform
- Efforts of "enlightened" monarchs in central and eastern Europe to increase the economic and military strength of their domains
- The partition of Poland by Prussia, Russia, and Austria

The modern world's faith in the possibility and desirability of change is one of its key intellectual inheritances from the eighteenth century, the self-proclaimed Age of Enlightenment. The leaders of the Enlightenment were convinced that human reason could comprehend the processes of nature and manipulate them to create a better world. They believed that the rational order that the Scientific Revolution had discovered in the physical universe should also exist in human societies. They assumed that reason provided them *with the means to conduct a radical critique of all traditional beliefs and institutions and that this critique would inevitably inspire innovation and improvement. Some of the era's monarchs caught its spirit and centralized political authority in order to implement a rational restructuring of their subjects' lives. This led to a form of government called enlightened absolutism.*

The *Philosophes*

The writers and critics who championed the Enlightenment were called *philosophes*. Their ranks included Voltaire, Montesquieu, Diderot, Rousseau, Hume, Gibbon, Smith, Bentham, Lessing, Kant, and many lesser figures. These men were activist philosophers who viewed change favorably. They advocated the use of reason and common sense to reform the major institutions and social practices of their day. A few of them were university professors, but most were free agents who could be found in London coffeehouses, Edinburgh pubs, the salons of fashionable Parisian ladies, the country houses of reform-minded nobles, and the courts of monarchs.

The *philosophes* were not part of an organized movement and did not all advocate the same things. The chief bond among them was a common desire to reform intellectual attitudes, society, and government to enhance human liberty. They were intellectuals, but intellectuals who were interested in practical innovations (e.g., in agriculture, economics, and politics) that would transform everyday life. During the Reformation and era of the religious wars, writers used the printed word to

Philosopher, dramatist, poet, historian, and popularizer of scientific ideas, Voltaire (1694–1778) was the most famous and influential of the eighteenth-century philosophes. His sharp satire and criticism of religious institutions opened the way for a more general critique of the European political and social status quo. Nicolas de Largilliere. Portrait of Voltaire at age 23, bust length, 1728. Private Collection, Musée de la Ville de Paris, Musée Carnavalet, Paris, France. Giraudon/Art Resource, NY

debate the proper mode of faith in God. The *philosophes* of the Enlightenment employed print to proclaim a new faith in the capacity of humankind to improve itself without the aid of God.

Many of the *philosophes* were born into the middle class, whence they drew the bulk of their readership. Members of the middle class had sufficient income and leisure to buy, read, and discuss the *philosophes'* works. Although the writers of the Enlightenment did not consciously champion the goals or causes of the middle class, they did create an intellectual ferment that undermined traditional institutions that the middle class found restrictive. They taught middle-class readers how to pose pointed, critical questions, and they supported developments that were enlarging the middle class (i.e., programs that promoted the phenomenal economic growth of the eighteenth century).

The earliest exponents of the Enlightenment were individuals who did what they could on their own to popularize the rationalism and scientific ideas of seventeenth-century thinkers. By the middle of the eighteenth century, they had succeeded in awakening widespread interest in reform and in creating a kind of intellectual community. They began to correspond among themselves, to write for each other (as well as for the general public), and to defend one another from attack by political and religious authorities. During the second half of the century, the *philosophes* were sufficiently safe that they could afford to quarrel among themselves, and their attention switched from the theoretical to the practical. Politics was of more interest to them than religion. Having convinced Europeans that change was a good idea, they began to suggest exactly what changes were most desirable. Although they were hopeful that improvements could be made in human society, their optimism was more a tempered hopefulness than a glib certainty. They were aware that history did not support unbridled confidence in the goodness of human nature.

Formative Influences on the Enlightenment

Ideas of Newton and Locke

Two Englishmen, Isaac Newton (1642–1727) and John Locke (1632–1704), were the forerunners of the Enlightenment. The theory of gravitation that Newton developed brought a long scientific search to a triumphant conclusion. It answered questions that had been raised by the discoveries of Copernicus, Kepler, and Galileo and provided a coherent, unified explanation for the behavior of astronomical bodies. Although Newton was a Christian, he insisted that scientists avoid supernaturalism. His work demonstrated that the human mind could discover truth without the help of revelation. All that the search for truth required was the use of reason to formulate theories that could be confirmed by empirical observation.

Newton's suggestion that the universe operated like a rationally designed machine led his contemporaries to speculate that human nature and human society might also be explained mechanistically. In *An Essay Concerning Human Understanding* (1690), John Locke had argued that every human being is born with a mind that is a *tabula rasa*, a blank page. Personality is created when an individual's senses expose his or her formless mind to experiences of the external world. This means that human nature is the product of environment—and that, therefore, human nature can be engineered by controlling the environment that shapes it. Locke's psychology rejected the Christian doctrine that humans are permanently flawed by sin and in need of divine grace to change their lives. He insisted that the means were at hand for people to redesign themselves.

The Example of British Toleration and Stability

Newton and Locke created a rationale for a reformist approach to society, and their stable homeland, Great Britain as it was organized after the Glorious Revolution of 1688, furnished a test case that encouraged others to pursue reform. It seemed to be a society in which enlightened programs benefitted everyone. England tolerated all religions except Unitarianism and Roman Catholicism, and even they were not actually persecuted. The English press and speech were relatively free. The power of England's monarchy was limited, for political sovereignty resided in Parliament. English courts protected citizens from arbitrary action by government officials, and the nation's army was small. England was freer than any other European state, and far from

Joseph Wright, An Experiment on a Bird in the Air-Pump: Science in the Drawing Room

In the 1650s, Robert Boyle perfected a pump that drew air out of a spherical glass jar to create a vacuum. For a century this instrument for exploring the qualities of air and air pressure was the preeminent symbol of experimental science. In 1768 Joseph Wright painted a scene showing such an instrument in action. Wright counted among his friends people who were promoting science and industrialization in England. His painting documents the interest the upper classes took in experimental science and the apprehension some individuals felt about its practices. The man who operates the pump sacrifices the life of a beautiful bird to advance the progress of science. The faces of the witnesses to his experiment register emotions that range from dismay to stoic acceptance.

Wright's painting is a specimen of a genre known as the *conversation piece,* but it departs from convention by choosing a scientific experiment instead of a less serious activity as its subject. Wright also innovates by lighting his composition with the dramatic contrasts that were traditional for religious paintings—perhaps implying that science could perform some of the functions of religion by providing a new source of light to combat the darkness of ignorance and superstition.

Sources: David H. Solkin, *Painting for Money: The Visual Arts and the Public Sphere in Eighteenth-Century England* (New Haven, CT: Yale University Press, 1993); Steven Shapin and Simon Schaffer, *Leviathan and the Air-Pump: Hobbes, Boyle, and the Experimental Life* (Princeton, NJ: Princeton University Press, 1985).

Joseph Wright of Derby, *An Experiment on a Bird in the Air-Pump* (1768). National Gallery, London, Great Britain. The Bridgeman Art Library.

producing disorder, its liberal policies had nurtured a loyal, prosperous citizenry.

Need for Reform in France

If Great Britain illustrated the potential for social reform, France demonstrated its necessity. Louis XIV's policies—an absolute monarchy, a large standing army, heavy taxation, and religious persecution—rendered his people so miserable that many celebrated when he died. Unfortunately, his successors further curtailed freedoms. Critics of their regimes were subject to arbitrary arrest. State regulation hampered economic growth, and aristocrats gloried in a culture of wasteful militarism. The manifest need for change in France motivated French intellectuals to make their homeland the Enlightenment's intellectual center.

One of the earliest and most influential of the French *philosophes* was François Marie Arouet, known simply as Voltaire (1694–1778). During the 1720s, some of Voltaire's writings offended the French authorities, and he was briefly imprisoned. In 1733, after a visit to England, he indicted French society in a book *(Letters on the English)* that lauded England for its intellectual openness and political freedom. In 1738 his *Elements of the Philosophy of Newton* popularized the thought of the great English scientist and established Voltaire's reputation as an important writer. Thereafter, he lived either in France or just across the French border near Geneva, where the royal authorities could not harass him.

Voltaire's essays, histories, plays, stories, and letters made him Europe's literary arbiter. Using wit and sarcasm, he assaulted the evils of his day. His most famous satire, *Candide* (1759), ridiculed war, religious persecution, and sentimental confidence in the goodness of human nature. Like most *philosophes*, Voltaire believed that improvement of human society was necessary, but he doubted that a perfect society could ever be created.

The Emergence of a Print Culture

Although printed materials contributed greatly to the success of the Protestant Reformation, the Enlightenment was the first major movement in Europe's history to flourish in a cultural environment created by the printed word. Books were costly, but the information they contained could be widely disseminated. Private and public libraries were founded, and thinkers spread their ideas through inexpensive newspapers and journals. The volume of printed material increased dramatically during the eighteenth century, and print became—and remained—the chief vehicle for the communication of ideas until the invention of the electronic media of our own day.

The growing audience for the printed word affected the choice of issues discussed in print. During the Middle Ages, when the clergy were the dominant literate class, literature dealt mostly with religion. But as ordinary men and women acquired the ability to read, the secular and material concerns of their lives began to be explored in print. In the seventeenth century, half the books published in Paris had religious themes; by the 1780s only 10 percent of them did.

Increasingly, members of the aristocracy and the middle class were expected to be familiar with books and secular ideas. Periodicals such as Joseph Addison's and Richard Steele's *The Spectator* (founded in 1711) provided vehicles for communicating with a wide public. People gathered in private homes or met in places such as coffeehouses for serious discussions. Secret societies, such as the movement of Freemasons that began in Britain at this time, promoted reading and debate.

The expanding market for printed matter made it possible for writers to earn a living from their work. For the first time, authorship became an occupation and authors celebrities. Parisian ladies sought out popular writers as honored guests for parties in their fashionable salons, and some writers (notably Alexander Pope and Voltaire) earned fortunes.

A division soon emerged between high and low literary culture. The most successful authors addressed themselves to, and were accepted into, the upper levels of society. Other writers survived more precariously, writing for whatever newspaper or journal would pay for their pages. Many of these people were hacks who blamed their lack of success on society. They often carried Enlightenment ideas to radical extremes and transmitted them in an embittered form to a lower-class audience.

The spread of secular printed materials created a new and increasingly influential social force: public opinion. Such a phenomenon seems not to have existed before the middle of the eighteenth century. A book or newspaper could reach thousands of readers and persuade them to a single point of view. Authors were accountable only to the readers to whom they marketed their works, and the information they channeled to the public meant that governments could no longer operate in secret or disregard the opinions of their subjects. They, as well as their critics, had to explain and discuss policies openly.

Continental European governments sensed the political power of the new print culture and saw that it threatened their traditional authority. Consequently, they censored books and newspapers and imprisoned offending authors. The spread of the print culture revealed the importance of the freedom of the press as an instrument for maintaining political accountability.

The *Encyclopedia*

At midcentury, one of the greatest monuments of the Enlightenment began to appear. It was the *Encyclopedia* edited by Denis Diderot (1713–1784) and Jean le Rond d'Alembert (1717–1783). The first of its seventeen volumes of text and eleven volumes of plates (i.e., illustrations) was issued in 1751; the last, in 1772. About 16,000 copies of various editions were sold before 1789.

All the major French *philosophes* were invited to contribute to the *Encyclopedia*, and it was the product of a collaboration among more than 100 authors. Since it brought together the most advanced ideas of its day (especially critiques of religion, government, and philosophy), it served as a collective plea for reform. This annoyed the French government, which made attempts to censor it and to halt its publication. But contributors to the *Encyclopedia* learned to avoid censure by hiding controversial ideas in obscure articles or by cloaking them with irony.

The project was designed to secularize learning and undermine the intellectual assumptions that lingered from the Middle Ages and the Reformation. Articles on politics, ethics, and society ignored divine law and concentrated on issues affecting human well-being. Classical antiquity had more influence than Christianity in shaping the ideas advanced by the *Encyclopedia*. Its authors implied that the future welfare of humankind lay not in pleasing God or following divine commandments but in developing the resources of the Earth and in living at peace with

neighbors. The good life was a life on Earth characterized by the application of reason to human relationships. The *Encyclopedia* diffused this Enlightenment faith throughout the continent.

The Enlightenment and Religion

Many *philosophes* believed that Europe's churches were the chief impediment to the improvement and happiness of its people. They condemned almost all varieties of Christianity and especially Roman Catholicism, for they believed that piety and authoritarianism hindered the scientific study of nature and the pursuit of a life guided by reason. Both Protestant and Catholic versions of the doctrine of original sin stated that human nature was fundamentally flawed and could not be improved. Both faiths taught that people could not better themselves unless God chose to bestow the gifts of grace on them. Both diverted attention from reforming this world to preparing for the world to come. The *philosophes* also found plenty of historical evidence to support their argument that churches promoted intolerance and bigotry and that quarrels over obscure points of doctrine drove religious enthusiasts to acts of torture and war.

The *philosophes'* critique of religion was not just an attack on a set of ideas. It was an assault on some of Europe's most significant institutions. The churches were essential to the power structure of the Old Regime. They owned large amounts of land. The upper clergy were usually sons of aristocratic families who took an active part in politics. Membership in a nation's predominant denomination was often a requirement for admission to its political life and for full protection under its laws. Clergymen condemned political disobedience as a sin against God and provided intellectual justification for the social and political status quo.

Deism

The *philosophes* were not opposed to all religion. What they wanted was a religion without fanaticism and intolerance, a faith that would not substitute the authority of tradition for the authority of human reason. Newton's studies of physics implied that the universe was a rational structure, and this persuaded the *philosophes* that the God who had made the universe had to be a rational being who was best worshiped by honoring reason. The religion of reason is called *deism* to distinguish it from a faith based on revelation.

John Toland, in *Christianity Not Mysterious* (1696), was among the first to articulate the principles of deism. Deists claimed that authentic religious faith was a product of reason and ordinary experience, not of supernatural or mystical communications. Deism understood God to be a kind of divine watchmaker who created the mechanism of nature, set it in motion, and then ceased to interfere with it. Newton, the hero of the deists, disagreed. He clung to the traditional belief that God interfered with the natural order to produce miracles.

The deists were not atheists. They thought that the existence of God and the precepts of God's will could be established empirically by observing natural phenomena. An ordered universe implied the existence of a rational Creator, and a rational God would want human beings to behave rationally. Since a rational code of behavior required that good be rewarded and evil punished (something that was not always the case in life), the deists claimed that justice implied the necessity of a life after death when rewards and punishments would be meted out.

Since Deism was empirical, tolerant, reasonable, and capable of encouraging virtuous living, the deists hoped that their faith would replace traditional Christianity and end fanaticism, persecution, and rivalry among sects. They also hoped that this would eliminate the clergy, a profession they held responsible for fomenting much of the strife that had plagued European history. Once people realized that each rational individual could on his or her own arrive at the essentials of religion (i.e., the arguments for God's existence and for the necessity of moral conduct), there would be no need for clergy and no reason to prefer one of the world's traditional religions to another. All could be seen as embodying the crucial elements of divine truth.

Toleration

The *philosophes*, whose homelands were just emerging from the era of Europe's wars of religion, insisted that commitment to religious toleration was an essential precondition for the conduct of a virtuous life. Behind this belief lay an assumption that life on Earth and human relationships should not be subordinated to religion but that secular values and considerations were more important than religious ones. In 1763 a controversial trial and execution of a Huguenot inspired Voltaire to pen a *Treatise on Toleration* to protest France's long-standing battle between Protestants and Catholics. In 1779 Gotthold Lessing wrote an influential play (*Nathan the Wise*) to make a case for an even more generous spirit of toleration. It challenged traditional European prejudices against Judaism and claimed that all faiths, not just varieties of Christianity, deserved toleration.

Radical Enlightenment Criticism of Religion

Some *philosophes* were not content with proposing a rational religion as an alternative to faith based on revelation. They went on the offensive against traditional beliefs. Voltaire's *Philosophical Dictionary* (1764) pointed out inconsistencies in the biblical texts and humorously described the immoral behavior of various biblical figures. The Scottish philosopher David Hume (1711–1776), in a chapter of his *Inquiry into Human Nature* (1748), argued that there was no empirical evidence for the belief in divine miracles that was central to much of Christianity. In *The Decline and Fall of the Roman Empire* (1776), the English historian Edward Gibbon (1737–1794) credited the rise of Christianity to natural causes, not divine intervention. A few *philosophes* went further and embraced positions very near to atheism and materialism, but theirs was a minority opinion. Most sought not the abolition of religion but its transformation into a humane force encouraging virtuous living. As the title of a book by the German philosopher Immanuel Kant put it, they sought *Religion within the Limits of Reason Alone*.

Jewish Thinkers in the Age of Enlightenment

Despite their pleas for toleration, the *philosophes'* critiques of traditional forms of religion often led them to attack Judaism more vehemently than Christianity. Some viewed Judaism as a more primitive faith than Christianity and were openly contemptuous of much of the material in the Hebrew Scriptures. The Enlightenment sometimes, therefore, made things worse for Jews as they struggled to come to terms with Europe's dominant Christian culture.

Two major Jewish intellectuals, one at the start and the other near the end of the Enlightenment, made major contributions to the era's discussion of the issue of religious toleration. These were Baruch Spinoza (1632–1677) who lived in the Netherlands and Moses Mendelsohn (1729–1786) who resided in Germany.

Spinoza was powerfully influenced by the new science of the mid-seventeenth century, and like his contemporary Descartes, he thought that all traditional beliefs should undergo rational critique and reformulation. He believed that the origin of religion could be explained in thoroughly naturalistic terms and that sacred scriptures should be subjected to the same kinds of rational interpretation as all other ancient texts. In his most famous book (simply entitled *Ethics*) he so closely identified God with nature that there was little distinction between them. His pantheistic position seemed to eliminate the need for revelation and Scripture by deducing all knowledge of God from the scientific study of natural phenomena. By reducing all existence to the natural order (which is governed by the mechanistic laws of physics), he seemed also to leave no room for free will, the exercise of human moral responsibility, and the survival of the individual soul after death. Both Jews and Christians accused him of being an atheist, and at the age of 24 he was excommunicated by his synagogue. The *philosophes* regarded him as one of reason's martyrs, but his example encouraged them to advocate opening up European society to fuller participation by Jews while continuing to regard Judaism with contempt.

Moses Mendelsohn also hoped to win entry for Jews into modern European life but on grounds that would not compel them to abandon Judaism. In his most influential book, *Jerusalem, or, On Ecclesiastical Power and Judaism* (1783), he made a case for religious diversity within nations and urged governments to maintain neutrality on religious issues. He presented Judaism as just one of many paths leading to knowledge of God. He claimed that different groups of believers found different sets of rituals and laws conducive to promoting ethical behavior, but that these provided no basis for denying civil rights to some of them. Not only should different faiths tolerate each other in the civil community, but each should tolerate a wide diversity of opinions within its own ranks and rely on the fundamental rationality of human beings to work things out.

The Enlightenment and Society

The *philosophes* believed that a rational examination of society would reveal that there were laws for human relationships similar to those that governed physical nature. Although the term did not appear until later, the idea of *social science* originated with the Enlightenment. *Philosophes* hoped to end human cruelty by discovering the laws that made societies function. But like most people, the *philosophes* had blind spots. When they contemplated social reforms, they assumed a male world and thought mostly about men. With few exceptions, they had little interest in increasing social or intellectual opportunities for women.

Beccaria and Reform of Criminal Law

The work of Cesare Beccaria (1738–1794), author of *On Crimes and Punishments* (1764), was typical of the *philosophes'* approach to social reform. Beccaria argued that crimes should be defined as transgressions of the laws of nature and not of someone's concept of God's will. The intent of punishment should also not be vengeance but the deterrence of further crime. He rigorously opposed both torture and capital punishment. The purpose of law, Beccaria maintained, was not to impose a divinely mandated standard of conduct but to secure the greatest happiness for the greatest number of people. A utilitarian philosophy that sought to maximize happiness in this life shaped most of Enlightenment thought about social reform.

The Physiocrats and Economic Freedom

Mercantilist principles, which recommended the use of legislation to protect a country's trade from foreign competition, determined the economic policies pursued by most European nations in the eighteenth century. Many *philosophes* viewed economics from a quite different perspective.

In France, the reform-minded economists were called *physiocrats*. Their leaders, François Quesnay (1694–1774) and Pierre Dupont de Nemours (1739–1817), argued that government intervention in the economy should be limited to protecting property and permitting its owners to use it freely. They did not, however, advocate radical individualism. They believed, for instance, that for reasons of efficiency small peasant holdings should be consolidated into large, scientifically managed farms.

Adam Smith on Economic Growth and Social Progress

Adam Smith's *Inquiry into the Nature and Causes of the Wealth of Nations* (1776) was the Enlightenment's most important contribution to the field of economics. Smith believed that freedom was essential to a natural economic system, and he urged the abolition of mercantilism's navigation acts, bounties, tariffs, trade monopolies, and laws regulating labor and manufacture. These policies were designed to increase the wealth of one nation by confiscating the riches of others, but Smith insisted that their effect was to hinder economic growth for everyone.

The mercantilists assumed that Earth's resources were limited and that one nation could acquire wealth only at the expense of others. Smith challenged this dogma. He claimed that the resources of nature were boundless and that they existed to be exploited for the enrichment of humankind. Poverty could be abolished, he maintained, if individuals were unleashed to pursue their self-interest. Smith argued that each individual could find a way to prosper if he or she was liberated to do whatever it took to meet the needs of others in the marketplace. The innovation this would stimulate would create an economy that expanded and provided greater resources for everyone. Although Smith is often labeled a *laissez-faire* economist, he was not opposed to all government intervention in economic activity. The state, he believed, should provide schools, armies, navies, and roads, and it should undertake commercial ventures that

were desirable but beyond the means of private enterprise.

When Smith wrote, the population of the world was smaller, its people poorer, and the quantity of undeveloped resources per capita much greater than now. For Smith and his contemporaries in the eighteenth century, improvement of the human condition seemed both to demand and to justify the uninhibited exploitation of nature. Not until recently has concern for the environment forced a rethinking of this position.

The Wealth of Nations helped to ground another assumption that later generations of Europeans came to question. Smith endorsed the *four-stage theory*, a view of human social and political development that was widely shared in his day. The theory claimed that all societies were destined to pass through four stages of economic development, each of which was associated with a level of civilization. Nomadic hunters and gatherers were the most barbarous. Herding societies were somewhat more civilized, for they recognized the concept of private property. Farming societies were superior to herders, but the ultimate level of development was reached only by commercial societies that practiced extensive manufacture and trade. The four-stage theory provided Europeans with a scale by which to rate the progress of all other peoples on earth. Since it assumed that the European form of commercial life was the highest manifestation of civilization, it encouraged Europeans to look down on everyone else and to assume that it was their mission to "civilize" the world by imposing Europe's values and institutions on it. This provided an excellent justification for colonial exploitation.

Political Thought of the *Philosophes*

Most *philosophes* found something to criticize in the political institutions of their homelands, but none had more reason to be unhappy than the French. The most important political debates of the Enlightenment, therefore, took place in France, but they produced no consensus. The French *philosophes* advocated everything from a reformed aristocracy, to a democracy, to an absolute monarchy.

Montesquieu and *Spirit of the Laws*

Charles Louis de Secondat, Baron de Montesquieu (1689–1755), was a lawyer, a noble of the robe, a member of a provincial *parlement*, and a fellow of the Bordeaux Academy of Science. Although he was comfortably ensconced within the bosom of the French establishment, he believed that reform was needed. In 1721 he denounced the cruelty and irrationality of European society in *The Persian Letters*, a collection of satirical epistles purportedly written by two Persian tourists to explain European behavior to their friends at home.

In 1748 he published *Spirit of the Laws*, perhaps the single most influential book of the century. To research it, Montesquieu used the empirical method advocated by the Enlightenment. He analyzed the political institutions of both ancient and modern nations. From these he concluded that there could be no single set of laws that applied to all peoples at all times and in all places. Numerous variables had to be taken into account to determine the best political system for a particular country. Size, population, social and religious customs, economic structures, traditions, and climate all helped determine whether a land should have a monarchy or a republic or something else. Montesquieu anticipated by a century the discipline that is now known as sociology.

Montesquieu believed that France would be served best by a limited monarchy, a government in which groups of citizens had rights that curtailed the power of their ruler. Montesquieu pointed to the *parlements*, the aristocratic courts, as an example of the kind of political associations he thought could do the best job of protecting the rights of Frenchmen. In championing these aristocratic bodies, he appeared to endorse political conservatism, but he turned to them as the most effective available instruments for reforming a monarchy whose absolute authority had become oppressive and inefficient.

One of Montesquieu's most influential ideas was that power ought to be divided among branches of a government. The British constitution was the source of this insight. It vested executive power in a king, legislative power in Parliament, and judicial power in courts. Montesquieu thought that any two of these branches could check the actions of the third. He failed, however, to understand how patronage and electoral corruption allowed a handful of aristocrats to dominate the government of Great Britain. He was also unaware of the emerging cabinet system that subordinated the British executive to Parliament.

Montesquieu's description of the British system was not accurate, but it did suggest how constitutional limits might be placed on monarchs by independent legislatures with the power to formulate laws. Having set out to defend the French aristocracy, Montesquieu actually inspired the formation of a succession of liberal democracies.

Rousseau: A Radical Critique of Modern Society

Jean-Jacques Rousseau (1712–1778) was a troubled genius who was at odds with the other *philosophes*. They believed that life would improve if people produced more goods and con-

Jean-Jacques Rousseau (1712–1778) raised some of the most profound social and ethical questions of the Enlightenment. This portrait is by Maurice Quentin.
Maurice Quentin de la Tour, "Jean Jacques Rousseau", ca. 1740. Original: Genf, Musée d'Art et d'Histoire. Bildarchiv Preussischer Kulturbesitz

sumed more of the fruits of the earth. Rousseau raised the more fundamental question of the meaning of life: Was humankind created only to consume?

Rousseau had contempt for societies in which commerce and industry were regarded as the most important human activities. In his *Discourse on the Moral Effects of the Arts and Sciences* (1750) he declared that Europe's materialistic civilization had corrupted human nature, and in his *Discourse on the Origin of Inequality* (1755) he traced society's problems to the tendency of commerce to produce an uneven distribution of property.

In politics as well as economics, Rousseau's thought was a radical assault on the popular ideas of his day. Most eighteenth-century political theorists assumed that society was merely a collection of individuals pursuing personal, selfish goals. The reforms the *philosophes* wanted were aimed at liberating individuals from undue restraint by government. Rousseau picked up the stick from the other end. In *The Social Contract* (1762) he argued that society is more important than its individual members, for it determines their options. Only a relationship to a larger community creates the moral environment in which individuals are capable of significant action. The true task of a reformer, therefore, is to create the kind of community that allows people to achieve the highest morality.

Contemporary European society, which was an aggregate of competing individuals who each sought selfish independence, was not, in Rousseau's opinion, an ideal community. He envisioned a world in which each individual found personal freedom by serving the interests of the group. He tried to reconcile the ends of the individual and the group by defining freedom as obedience to democratically enacted laws that represented the general will. Rousseau believed that the will of the majority of informed citizens was always right and always marked the path of true freedom. This argument led him to the notorious conclusion that some people might have to be forced to be free. Rousseau's ideal state was a direct democracy that took collective action against dissidents.

Because Rousseau rejected the eighteenth-century cult of the individual and the fruits of selfishness, his impact on his contemporaries was slight. Too many people were either making

or hoping to make money to appreciate his criticism of commercial values. Rousseau proved, however, to be a figure to whom later generations returned. Many leaders of the French Revolution were inspired by him, and he influenced most of the writers of the nineteenth and twentieth centuries who were critical of the general tenor and direction of Western societies.

Women in the Thought and Practice of the Enlightenment

Aristocratic women, especially in France, arranged gatherings in their salons (i.e., drawing rooms) that were crucial to the careers of *philosophes*. Politically well-connected women, such as Madame Geoffrin, Mademoiselle de Lespinasse, and Madame Tencin, helped *philosophes* make useful contacts. Association with a fashionable salon brought a *philosophe* social status that added luster to his ideas and sales to his books. Sometimes his patroness also provided him with money or protection from persecution. Madame de Pompadour, the mistress of Louis XV, countered attacks on *philosophes* and helped defeat efforts to censor the *Encyclopedia*.

Despite their ties with learned women, few *philosophes* were feminists. Many advocated broader educations for women and rejected the ascetic views of sexuality that were part of the traditional religious training given girls. Montesquieu's *The Persian Letters* devoted considerable space to condemning by implication the restrictions European society placed on women. Montesquieu believed that women were in no way naturally inferior to men and should have a wider role in society. But in *Spirit of the Laws*, while supporting the right of divorce and opposing laws that directly oppressed women, he still recommended a dominant role for the husband in marriage and firmly upheld the ideal of chastity for women.

Although the *Encyclopedia* suggested some ways to improve women's lives, women's issues did not feature on the agenda of its reforms. The Encyclopedists were almost all male, and most of the articles that discussed women emphasized their physical weakness and inferiority—liabilities usually attributed to menstruation or child bearing. Women were viewed primarily in a family context in roles as daughters, wives, and mothers, and child rearing was represented as their chief occupation. The sexual double standard was never questioned, and some contributors opposed granting women social equality. The *Encyclopedia*'s articles convey a general sense that women were reared to be frivolous and unconcerned with important issues. But the *Encyclopedia*'s illustrations show many women engaged in vital economic activities. Many of these were working-class women, a group largely ignored in the *Encyclopedia*'s articles.

Rousseau, the most radical of the Enlightenment political theorists, took a very conservative position on gender issues. His novel *Émile* (1762) stressed the differences between males and females and recommended that women's educations center on duties relating to the bearing and rearing of children. Rousseau excluded women from public affairs and confined them to the home. He considered women to be inferior to men in all respects except the capacity for feeling and loving, and he argued that their chief duty was to make themselves pleasing to men.

Paradoxically, in spite of these views and in spite of his own ill treatment of the many women who bore his many children, Rousseau won a vast female following. Women responded to his appreciation of their feelings and his proclamation of the importance of their vocations as wives and mothers. He accorded them a degree of dignity in the domestic sphere that they were denied in public life. The praise he showered on female nurturing motivated thousands of upper-class women to lay claim to a significant social role by breast-feeding their children rather than putting them out to wet-nurses.

MARY WOLLSTONECRAFT AND WOMEN'S RIGHTS In 1792 *A Vindication of the Rights of Woman*, by Mary Wollstonecraft (1759–1797), indicted Rousseau and the *philosophes* for their failure to follow through on the Enlightenment's commitment to the rational reform of society. Wollstonecraft (who, like so many women of her day, died of puerperal fever) argued that to confine women to the home because of their supposed physical limitations was to condemn them to sexual slavery and make them victims of male tyranny. She insisted that the progress

of all humanity was impeded when women were denied good educations. By demanding for women the liberty that *philosophes* had been claiming for men for more than a century, Wollstonecraft broadened the reform agenda of the Enlightenment to include rights for women as well as men.

Enlightened Absolutism

Most of the *philosophes* rejected Montesquieu's reformed aristocracy and Rousseau's direct democracy as unrealistic. They believed that it was necessary to work with monarchies as they currently existed. Voltaire, Diderot, and others were monarchists who, rather than limiting the power of rulers, wanted to use that power to rationalize economic and political structures and to liberate intellectual life. *Philosophes* were not opposed to power if they could guide the powerful. The *enlightened absolutism* of Frederick II of Prussia, Joseph II of Austria, and Catherine II of Russia was declared by many *philosophes* to be the ideal form of government, for these rulers centralized their governments in order to enact reforms with maximum efficiency.

The Enlightenment's intellectuals often had less influence in shaping public policy than they realized. Monarchs such as Frederick II and Catherine II corresponded with the *philosophes*, hosted them at court, and made a show of referring to their ideas. But enlightened absolutists were motivated by more than a *philosophe*'s zeal for humanitarian reform. They were engaged in struggles with competing nations. They pursued the rational economic and social integration of their realms because it increased their military strength. It was a search for new revenues and for a more strongly solidified political base that prompted many of the enlightened reforms carried out by the monarchs of Russia, Prussia, and Austria. Their rational reforms were driven by a militarism that the *philosophes* considered irrational.

Frederick the Great of Prussia

Frederick II, "the Great" (r. 1740–1786), was prepared to do whatever was necessary to make his small country a leading European power. To that end he was eager to rationalize his government,

Frederick II, the Great (r. 1740–1786), sought to create prosperity for all parts of the Prussian economy and would make personal visits to factories and shops to inspect the goods being made and sold in his kingdom. Here, as portrayed in a late nineteenth-century painting, he visits a fashionable shop. Gemalde von Albert Baur, ca. 1901. *Frederick II, the Great, the house von der Leyen in Krefeld, on June 10, 1763.* Bildarchiv Preussischer Kulturbesitz

no matter what the human costs. Frederick liked to describe himself as "the first servant of the State." The phrase suggests that the medieval concept of personal monarchy was fading and the modern understanding of the state as an impersonal governmental apparatus separate from the monarch was taking its place.

The impetus for Prussia's economic development came from the state, for the state enjoyed most of the benefits. High taxes siphoned off much of the income of the productive classes, the peasants and townspeople. Silesia, which Frederick seized from Austria in 1740, was developed as a manufacturing district, while Prussia itself was reorganized to improve agricultural production. Under state supervision, swamps were drained, new crops (e.g., potatoes and turnips) were introduced, and peasants were compelled to migrate where they were needed.

Economic reality encouraged Frederick, a Lutheran, to practice religious toleration. Prussia needed manpower and had to attract immigration. Although the higher governmental and military offices were usually reserved for Protestants, both Catholics and Jews were protected under Prussian law. The laws themselves were recodified. By making the legal system more efficient, by eliminating regional peculiarities, and by reducing aristocratic influence, Frederick extended the power of the throne.

Joseph II of Austria

No eighteenth-century ruler so embodied rational, impersonal force as Joseph II of Austria (r. 1765–1790), Maria Theresa's son and co-ruler with her from 1765 to 1780. He was an austere, humorless person who prided himself on an ascetic lifestyle and a passionless, rational approach to life. Despite his cold personality, Joseph II sincerely wanted to improve the lot of his people and was, unlike his colleagues who ruled Prussia and Russia, neither a political opportunist nor a cynic. Despite his good intentions, however, the reforms he autocratically decreed spawned rebellions by both aristocrats and peasants throughout his domains.

CENTRALIZATION OF AUTHORITY The empire led by the Austrian Habsburgs was the most diverse of the great European states of the eighteenth century. Its subjects spoke many languages and had few ties in common. The throne could not depend on the aristocracy for much support, for in order to preserve the monarchy during the War of the Austrian Succession (1740–1748) Maria Theresa had granted the aristocrats (especially those in Hungary) extensive freedom.

Maria Theresa strengthened the power of the crown outside of Hungary by increasing the size of the empire's administrative bureaucracy. Her efficient tax collectors forced even the clergy and the nobles of Austria and Bohemia to pay. She established central councils to handle various kinds of problems, and she brought education under state control to ensure her government a sufficient supply of trained officials. Her concern for schools extended to increasing opportunities for primary education at the local level. She also tried to protect peasants and serfs by using the royal bureaucracy to enforce limits on the amount of labor noble landowners could demand from their tenants. Her concern was not solely humanitarian; it served her need to ensure a good pool from which to draw military recruits.

Joseph II followed the path blazed by his mother. But he was even more determined to have his way, and his projected reforms were more wide-ranging. Although he wanted to add territory belonging to Poland, Bavaria, and the Ottoman Empire to the Habsburg domain, his strongest desire was to increase his authority over his various domains. His strategy was to reduce the pluralism of the Habsburg holdings by imposing central authority in places that Maria Theresa had wisely chosen to ignore. In particular, Joseph sought to rein in the nobility of Hungary. To avoid having to guarantee their existing privileges or promise them new ones at the time of his coronation, he refused to have himself crowned king of Hungary. He reorganized local governments in Hungary to increase the authority of his officials and required the use of German in all transactions. The Magyar nobility protested, and in 1790 Joseph backed down.

ECCLESIASTICAL POLICIES The church, too, was subject to Joseph's program for establishing royal absolutism. Since the Reformation of the sixteenth century, the Habsburgs had been the single most important dynasty championing Roman Catholicism. Maria Theresa had adamantly opposed religious toleration, but refused to allow the church to limit her authority. She also adopted the enlightened policy of discouraging the more extreme forms of Roman Catholic popular piety (e.g., public flagellation as penance for sin).

Joseph II was a practicing Catholic, but both enlightenment and pragmatic politics urged him to pursue a policy of toleration. In October 1781, Joseph issued a Toleration Patent (i.e., decree) that extended freedom of worship to Lutherans, Calvinists, and the Greek Orthodox. These groups were allowed to establish places of worship, to sponsor schools, to enter skilled trades, and to hold academic appointments and positions in public service. Later, Joseph relieved the Jews of certain taxes and signs of personal degradation and extended to them the right of private worship. These actions benefitted the Jews but fell short of granting them full equality with other Habsburg subjects.

Joseph brought various Roman Catholic institutions directly under royal control. He forbade direct communication between his bishops and the pope. Viewing religious orders as unproductive, he dissolved and confiscated the endowments of the more than 600 monasteries that did not contribute to society by running schools or hospitals. He used funds confiscated from the monasteries to create new parishes in places where there was a shortage of priests. He closed the established seminaries, accusing them of instilling in priests too great a loyalty to the papacy and too little concern for their parishioners. He replaced these schools with eight new seminaries where training emphasized parish duties. *Josephinism*, the emperor's ecclesiastical policy, subjected the Roman Catholic Church to state control and made its priests state employees.

ECONOMIC AND AGRARIAN REFORM Like Frederick of Prussia, Joseph tried to expand the economy by using the powers of government. He abolished many internal tariffs and encouraged road building and the improvement of river transport. He personally inspected farms and factories. He reconstructed the judicial system to make laws more uniform and rational. National courts with power over the local courts of landlords were set up. All these things were intended to unify the state and increase the taxes paid to the imperial treasury.

Over the course of Joseph's reign, he introduced a series of reforms relating to serfdom that altered the structure of rural society. He did not abolish the authority of landlords over their peasants, but he did try to lessen it and make it accountable to royal officials. He ended serfdom as a legally sanctioned servile condition. He granted peasants a wide array of personal freedoms—including rights to marry, to engage in skilled work, and to have their children trained for such trades without the permission of their landlords. He reformed the procedures of the manorial courts and created avenues for appeal to royal officials. He encouraged landlords to change land leases to make it easier for peasants to inherit them or to transfer them to other tenants. The intent of his reforms was to make the peasants more productive and industrious farmers by reducing their traditional burdens.

In 1789, near the end of his reign, Joseph proposed a new and daring system of land taxation. He ended aristocratic immunity from taxation and decreed that all proprietors of the land be taxed regardless of social status. No longer were the peasants alone to bear the burden of taxation. The *robot* (i.e., the forced labor required of peasants) was commuted to a monetary tax, part of which was to go to the landlord and part to the state.

Although the nobility blocked the implementation of Joseph's tax reforms and his death in 1790 ended efforts to enforce them, they and his earlier reform proposals created turmoil throughout the Habsburg realms. Disputes over the interpretation of the new rights granted to the peasants prompted them to rebel, and the Magyars forced Joseph to rescind his centralization measures in Hungary. When Joseph's brother, Leopold II (r. 1790–1792), inherited the throne, he had to repeal the most controversial of Joseph's decrees. He retained Joseph's religious policies and maintained political centralization to the extent he thought possible. But expediency and conviction drove him to return much political and administrative authority to local nobles.

Catherine the Great of Russia

Joseph II took the claims of royalty to autocratic authority too literally. He never grasped the practical necessity of forging political constituencies to support his reforms. Catherine II (r. 1762–1796), a German princess who became empress of Russia, understood only too well the fragility of her Romanov dynasty's base of power. Tsar Peter the Great (d. 1725) had exercised vast power, but after his death the court nobles and the soldiers, who controlled the succession to the throne, chose rulers who dissipated the authority of the monarchy. Peter was followed by his wife, Catherine I (r. 1725–1727), and then his grandson, Peter II (r. 1727–1730).

Catherine the Great ascended to the Russian throne after the murder of her husband. She tried initially to enact major reforms, but she never intended to abandon absolutism. She assured nobles of their rights and by the end of her reign had imposed press censorship. The Granger Collection

The crown then devolved on Anna, his niece. Ivan VI, who was less than a year old, became nominal tsar in 1740, until Peter's daughter, Elizabeth, took control in 1741. Political and romantic intrigues made a shambles of her court, and at her death in 1762 she was succeeded by a nephew, Peter III, whose mental stability was doubtful. He exempted the nobles from compulsory military service and precipitously reversed Russia's foreign policy in the Seven Years' War. Inspired by adolescent hero worship for Frederick the Great, Peter refused to continue to cooperate with Austria and France in containing Prussia. That decision may have saved Prussia, but it was of no benefit to Russia. The one achievement of Peter's life was his marriage in 1745 to a young German princess born in Anhalt Zerbst, the future Catherine the Great.

For almost twenty years Catherine endured a precarious, miserable life at Elizabeth's court.

But she was a shrewd woman who honed her survival skills by studying a palace seething with rumors, intrigue, and conspiracy. She befriended important nobles and read widely in the works of the *philosophes.* Her demented husband inspired neither affection nor respect. A few months after his accession as tsar, she acquiesced to his murder and seized his throne (1762).

Catherine's study of the Enlightenment and the culture of western Europe taught her how backward Russia was, and it suggested to her the reforms that were needed to sustain her nation as a great power. She understood that reform would not succeed unless it had widespread support and that she—a foreign woman who had acquired the throne in a palace coup—was not secure enough to act unilaterally.

In 1767 Catherine charged a Legislative Commission representing all sectors of Russian society with responsibility for proposing changes in Russia's laws and government, and the empress provided the commission with a set of *Instructions* drawn from the political works of the *philosophes.* A year later, Catherine dismissed the commission before several of its key committees had reported, but the commission was not a useless exercise. It gathered vast amounts of information about local administration and economic life, and the debates of its delegates suggested that most Russians saw no alternative to an autocratic monarchy. This consensus created support for Catherine's exercise of enlightened absolutism.

LIMITED ADMINISTRATIVE REFORM Catherine's reforms made a virtue of necessity. She knew that the Moscow nobles and the military men who had given her the throne could take it away. She also knew that she had too few educated subjects to staff an independent bureaucracy and that her treasury could not on its own sustain the cost of an army. Catherine, therefore, had no choice but to rely on the nobles for help in running and defending her empire. In 1777 she reorganized local government to solve problems discovered by the Legislative Commission, and she appointed nobles to most of the offices responsible for local affairs. In 1785 she issued a Charter of the Nobility that secured many of the rights and privileges of the aristocracy.

ECONOMIC GROWTH Catherine followed the example of Peter the Great in promoting economic development. She removed internal barriers to trade. Exports of grain, flax, furs, and naval stores were greatly increased. The small Russian urban middle class, which was vital to trade, was protected. And Catherine befriended and corresponded with *philosophes* in order to promote Russia's image in western Europe as a progressive nation.

TERRITORIAL EXPANSION Catherine's program for the development of Russia, like Peter the Great's, called for the acquisition of warm-water ports through which Russia could maintain contact with Europe. The ports she wanted belonged to the Turks. In 1769 the Ottoman Empire obliged her by declaring war on Russia, and Russia occupied the Ottoman provinces on the Danube River and the Crimean coast of the Black Sea. In 1774 the Treaty of Kuchuk-Kainardji ended hostilities by granting Russia access to the Black Sea, navigation rights on that sea, and free passage through the Bosporus to the Mediterranean. The province of the Crimea became an independent state that Catherine had no difficulty annexing in 1783.

The Partition of Poland

Russia's victories along the Danube River were most unwelcome to Austria, for Austria had hoped to expand in the same region. The Ottoman Empire was also alarmed by Russia's aggression, and it pressed Frederick the Great of Prussia for help. He devised a means to exploit the situation for his own advantage while restoring peace among the central European powers. He suggested that Russia agree to abandon the conquered Danubian provinces if Austria and Prussia compensated it by helping it annex a large part of Poland. Prussia claimed for itself a stretch of Polish land between East Prussia and Prussia proper that would link together some of Frederick's scattered territories. Austria was to be given Galicia and other parts of Poland.

Since the Polish aristocracy had prevented the development of a strong centralized monarchy for their country, they lacked the leadership necessary to defend themselves. In September 1772, they ratified the loss of nearly a third of their territory. This humiliation inspired a revival of national feeling and an attempt to create a stronger government in what was left of Poland. This

MAP 18–1 EXPANSION OF RUSSIA, 1689–1796 *The overriding aim of the Russian monarchs of the eighteenth century was to acquire ports that were navigable year-round for their country. Peter the Great pushed through to the Baltic Sea and Catherine the Great to the Black Sea.*

MAP 18–2 PARTITIONS OF POLAND: 1772, 1793, 1795 *The eradication of Poland from the map displayed eighteenth-century power politics at its most extreme. Having no strong central government, Poland fell victim to neighboring states that had centrally organized.*

proved, however, to be too little too late. The partition of Poland made it clear that a nation that had not established a strong monarchy, bureaucracy, and army could not compete as a European state.

Russia and Prussia partitioned Poland again in 1793. When in 1795 they did so for the third time, it disappeared from the map of Europe for more than a century. Each time the great powers carved up Poland, they contended that they were doing so to prevent the outbreak of war in Europe. They claimed that squabbles among the Poles could spread to neighboring states and spark a general war. In reality, Poland's political weakness made it irresistibly tempting to plunderers who would not have hesitated, had Polish

land not been so easily available, to resort to war to settle their rivalries.

The End of the Eighteenth Century in Central and Eastern Europe

As the eighteenth century waned, enlightened absolutism became increasingly conservative and repressive. Frederick the Great, who grew remote during his old age, allowed the Prussian aristocracy the freedom to abuse their military and administrative offices, and a reaction to Enlightenment ideas also set in among Prussia's intellectuals. When the Austrian nobility called for an end to Joseph II's innovations, the Habsburg government resorted increasingly to censorship and intimidation by a secret police. In Russia, the Pugachev peasant rebellion (1771–1775) raised fears of social upheaval that Catherine the Great never fully laid to rest—and when the French Revolution broke out in 1789, the nervous empress censored books based on Enlightenment thought and sent offensive authors into Siberian exile. By the close of the century, fear of and hostility to change permeated the ruling classes of central and eastern Europe, and monarchs who had pursued enlightened absolutism increasingly repudiated the humanity and liberalism of the Enlightenment.

From 1763 to 1789, however, the rulers of both western and eastern Europe had been the major agents of institutional change. In every case, their programs provoked resistance and resentment from some of their subjects. George III of Britain fought for years with Parliament and lost the colonies of North America. Frederick II of Prussia succeeded with his reforms only because he allowed his nobles increased authority. Catherine II of Russia had survived by coming to terms with Russia's aristocrats. Joseph II, on the other hand, did not compromise with his nobles, and this threw his domains into turmoil. The drive toward royal absolutism was met by aristocratic resistance in France also, but there the monarchy and aristocracy lost control of the situation their quarrel created and opened the way for revolution.

In Perspective

The philosophes *who promoted the Enlightenment charted a new path for Western nations. They prospered in a print culture that mobilized a new form of popular power: public opinion. Brilliant advances in the physical sciences by men such as Newton encouraged the* philosophes *to apply rational, scientific methods of analysis to social problems. They were not extreme rationalists. They accepted passions and feelings as essential parts of human nature and recommended moderation in the conduct of life. Most of them advocated religious toleration and opposed dogmatic faiths—particularly Roman Catholicism. They hoped to create a science of society with the means to discover ways to maximize human productivity*

and material happiness. Rousseau went further than most philosophes. He insisted that enhanced consumption was not enough and that true social reform required the promotion of virtue.

Dramatically different implications were drawn from these ideas by political leaders. The founding fathers of the American republic found inspiration in them, as did liberal reformers throughout Europe. The revolutionaries in France honored them, and the autocratic monarchs of eastern Europe believed that Enlightenment ideas would help them rule more efficiently. This diverse response to the Enlightenment suggests that its thought cannot be reduced to a simple formula. It was an outlook that championed change and reform and focused on human beings and their welfare on Earth rather than on God and the hereafter. But it dictated no single path to, or vision of, the world it was determined to perfect.

REVIEW QUESTIONS

1. How did the Enlightenment change basic Western attitudes toward reform, faith, and reason? What were the major formative influences on the *philosophes?* How important were the contributions of Voltaire and the *Encyclopedia* to the success of the Enlightenment?

2. Why did the *philosophes* consider organized religion their greatest enemy? What were the basic tenets of deism? What criticism might a deist direct at traditional Christianity? What would a deist do to improve on Christianity?

3. What were the attitudes of the *philosophes* toward women? What was Rousseau's view of women? What were the separate spheres he imagined men and women occupying? What were Mary Wollstonecraft's criticisms of Rousseau's view?

4. How did the arguments of the mercantilists differ from the theories developed by Adam Smith in *The Wealth of Nations?* How did each side in this debate view Earth's resources? Why might Smith be regarded as an advocate of the consumer?

5. What political views were held by Montesquieu and Rousseau? Was Montesquieu's description of the situation in England ac-

curate? Was Rousseau a child of the Enlightenment, or was he its opponent? Which did Rousseau value more, the individual or society?

6. Were the enlightened monarchs true believers in the ideals of the *philosophes* or was their "enlightenment" merely a pose or veneer? Was their power really absolute? What motivated their reforms?

SUGGESTED READINGS

G. J. BARKER-BENFIELD, *The Culture of Sensibility: Sex and Society in Eighteenth-Century Britain* (1992). A broad exploration of the role of women in society and literature in the age of Enlightenment.

C. B. A. BEHRENS, *Society, Government, and the Enlightenment: The Experiences of Eighteenth-Century France and Prussia* (1985). A wide-ranging comparative study.

R. CHARTIER, *The Cultural Origins of the French Revolution* (1991). A wide-ranging discussion of the emergence of the public sphere and the role of books and the book trade during the Enlightenment.

D. GOODMAN, *The Republic of Letters: A Cultural History of the French Enlightenment* (1994). Concentrates on the role of salons.

J. B. LANDES, *Women and the Public Sphere in the Age of the French Revolution* (1988). An extended essay on the role of women in public life.

I. DE MADARIAGA, *Russia in the Age of Catherine the Great* (1981). The best discussion in English.

S. NADLER, *Spinoza: A Life* (1999). The best recent biography.

C. ORWIN and N. TARCOV, eds., *The Legacy of Rousseau* (1997). Essays on the major themes in Rousseau's work.

D. ROCHE, *France in the Enlightenment* (1998). A brilliant work relating the society and government of eighteenth-century France to the Enlightenment agenda.

D. SPADAFORA, *The Idea of Progress in Eighteenth Century Britain* (1990). A major study that covers many aspects of the Enlightenment in Britain.

L. WOLFF, *Inventing Eastern Europe: The Map of Civilization on the Mind of the Enlightenment* (1994). A remarkable study of the way in which Enlightenment writers recast the understanding of this part of the continent.

Chapter 19

The French Revolution

KEY TOPICS

- The financial crisis that persuaded the French monarchy to convene a meeting of the Estates General

- The transformation of the Estates General into the National Assembly, the Declaration of the Rights of Man and Citizen, and the reconstruction of the political and ecclesiastical institutions of France

- The second revolution, the end of the monarchy, and the turn to more radical reforms

- The war of France against Europe

- The Reign of Terror, the Thermidorian Reaction, and the establishment of the Directory

By the late 1780s the French monarchy was confronting a major financial crisis. It could not collect adequate taxes from its commoner subjects, and the nobility refused to give up their immunity from taxation. In the spring of 1789, the struggle between the king and the nobles of France precipitated a political crisis. Unlike earlier disputes at the top of society, this one spread and produced universal social upheaval. The result was a revolution that changed France and Europe forever.

The Crisis of the French Monarchy

The problems that produced revolution in France were common to most late eighteenth-century states. France emerged from the Seven Years' War (1756–1763) deeply in debt. Its decision to continue to try to weaken Great Britain, its traditional enemy, by sending aid to England's rebellious American colonies worsened its financial situation. Given the economic vitality of France, its national debt was neither overly large nor disproportionate to the debts of other European powers, but the French monarchy could not tap the wealth of the nation through taxes to service and repay the debt. France was a paradox: a rich nation with an impoverished government.

The Monarchy Seeks New Taxes

To resolve its financial difficulties, the French monarchy would have had to bring the aristocracy under tighter control, but each royal minister who tried to devise a tax scheme to tap the wealth of the nobility was blocked by opposition from the aristocratic courts, the *parlements.* Both Louis XV (r. 1715–1774) and Louis XVI (r. 1774–1792) lacked the strength of character needed to wage a determined campaign. They hesitated, retreated, and tried deception.

In 1770 Louis XV's chancellor, René Maupeou (1714–1792), pushed him to take drastic action. Maupeou abolished the *parlements,* exiled their

Well-meaning but weak and vacillating, Louis XVI (r. 1774–1792) stumbled from concession to concession until he finally lost all power to save his throne. Joseph Siffred Duplessis, *Louis XVI,* Versailles, France. Giraudon/Art Resource, NY

members to different parts of the country, and began to reorganize government to increase efficiency. It was Louis's death in 1774 and not aristocratic resistance that doomed Maupeou's program. The new king, Louis XVI, restored the *parlements* in hopes of winning support.

France's plan to humiliate Great Britain by underwriting the American Revolution was a political triumph and a fiscal disaster. In 1781 Jacques Necker (1732–1804), a Swiss banker who became France's director-general of finances, published a budget that was intended to quiet the nation's fears. He claimed that when the expenditures for the American war were discounted, the budget was in surplus, and he revealed that a large portion of royal expenditures went to pensions for aristocrats and court favorites. His exposé mobilized the court against him, and he was driven from office. His questionable budget survived, however, to make it difficult for later government officials to claim a need to raise taxes.

In 1786 Charles Alexandre de Calonne (1734–1802), the minister of finance, proposed another reform. He hoped to promote growth of the economy by encouraging internal trade, lowering some taxes, and transforming peasants' services to money payments. Calonne's most significant proposal was a new tax on land to be paid by all landowners, regardless of social class. Calonne intended to set up local assemblies to approve the land taxes. In these assemblies, voting power was to depend on the amount of land one owned rather than on one's social status. The new assemblies were designed to undermine the *parlements*, the bases for the political power of the French aristocracy.

The Aristocracy and the Clergy Resist Taxation

In 1787 Calonne sought support for his plan by convening an Assembly of Notables representing the higher-ranking aristocrats and clergy. Although the creditors were at the door and the treasury was nearly empty, the assembly adamantly refused to cooperate. Instead, it called for the reappointment of the optimistic Necker and insisted that it had no right to consent to new taxes. That authority was said to be vested in a medieval institution that had not met since 1614, the Estates General.

Since aristocrats and clergy had always dominated the Estates General, the king was not willing to risk convening such a meeting. Instead, Louis XVI replaced Calonne with Étienne Charles Loménie de Brienne (1727–1794), archbishop of Toulouse and Calonne's chief opponent at the Assembly of Notables. In office, Brienne found, to his astonishment, that the situation was as bad as Calonne had said it was, and Brienne became a convert to the idea of a land tax. The *Parlement* of Paris blocked action by insisting that only the Estates General had the authority to approve such an innovation. In desperation, Brienne appealed to the Assembly of the Clergy for extra help in meeting a payment on the national debt. The clergy not only refused; they reduced the contributions they had been making to the government.

As pressures on the government mounted, from both the Notables and the *parlements* and estates of the provinces, the king agreed to convene an Estates General in 1789. Brienne resigned, and Necker was returned to office. In the country of its origin, royal absolutism had been defeated.

The Revolutions of 1789

Historians have proposed many explanations for what happened as the meeting of the Estates General in 1789 escalated into revolution. Some believe that the revolution was the culmination of an old class conflict—of a struggle between the bourgeoisie and the aristocracy. Others claim that there was a great deal of social mobility that blurred the lines between aristocratic and bourgeois families. Both opposed the clumsy absolutism of the monarchy, and many simply wanted the government of France to better represent the wealthy, no matter what their social origin. When disagreements divided the propertied classes, some of the bourgeoisie turned to the tradespeople and working classes for support. But when the revolution became too radical, the upper and middle classes joined forces to protect rights to private property. Class conflict was not, some historians believe, the cause of the revolution, but a strategy that its leaders occasionally used to further their objectives.

The power vacuum created by the faltering monarchy created an unprecedented opportunity for new kinds of leaders to emerge. The development earlier in the century of the print culture had produced a reading public and troops of hungry authors seeking audiences to sustain them. This encouraged political debate on a wider scale than ever before in Europe's history, and it produced a new political culture. Print communication enabled the concerns of articulate individuals to prevail over those of groups.

To some extent, the explanations that are offered for the French Revolution depend on which years, or even months, of its development one has in mind. No single theory may adequately explain the whole event. Different groups opposed and cooperated with each other at different times. Individual leaders shifted their positions frequently. There was enormous confusion, and political situations varied from city to city and region to region.

The Estates General Becomes the National Assembly

Three groups (i.e., estates) were represented in the Estates General: The First Estate was the clergy; the Second, the nobility; and the Third, everyone else. In reality, the Third Estate represented members of the commercial and professional middle classes. The fact that the Estates General was an assembly of men of property did not ensure cooperation among its members. The estates had different interests over which they clashed from the start.

DEBATE OVER ORGANIZATION AND VOTING   A debate about the organization of the Estates General split the aristocracy and the Third Estate before the meeting convened. The aristocrats demanded an equal number of representatives for each estate, and in September (1788) the *Parlement* of Paris ruled that each estate, not each delegate, should have one vote. This ensured that the aristocratic First and Second Estates could always outvote the Third Estate. Spokesmen for the Third Estate charged the aristocrats with hypocrisy for accusing the crown of transgressing on the liberties of French citizens while they were pursuing the same course of action.

The royal council decided that the Third Estate would be its best ally in the fight for fiscal reform. In December 1788, the council granted the Third Estate twice as many representatives as the nobles and clergy. This meant that the Third Estate could dominate the Estates General if voting were allowed by head rather than by order. It was correctly assumed that some liberal nobles and clergy would support the Third Estate, for all the estates had some interests in common. The king did not decree the method of voting until the Estates General had gathered at Versailles.

THE *CAHIERS DE DOLÉANCES*   The men who assembled at Versailles in May 1789 brought the king a list of grievances (i.e., *cahiers de doléances*) compiled by the citizens who had elected them to the Estates General. The voters were upset about government waste, indirect taxes, church taxes, corrupt clergy, and the hunting rights of the aristocracy. They wanted periodic meetings of the Estates General, more equitable taxes, more local control of administration, unified weights and measures, a free press, and equality of rights among all the king's subjects.

Unresolved procedural problems prevented the Estates General from immediately taking up issues of substance, and things ground to a halt when the Third Estate refused to obey the king and convene as a separate group. On June 1, the Third Estate took things into its own hands. It invited the clergy and the nobles to join it in dissolving the Estates General and setting up a new legislative body. On June 17 the Third Estate, with the support of some of the lower clergy, declared itself the National Assembly.

THE TENNIS COURT OATH   Three days later, members of the National Assembly took an oath not to disperse until they had given France a constitution. (Since they had accidentally been locked out of their usual meeting place and moved to a nearby tennis court, this came to be known as the Tennis Court Oath.) Although Louis XVI ordered the assembly to desist, within a few days it had recruited a majority of the clergy and a large group of nobles. On June 27, the king capitulated and formally requested the First and Second Estates to meet with the National Assembly and to vote by head rather than by order.

The National Assembly, which renamed itself the National Constituent Assembly, was composed of men from all three estates who shared liberal hopes for the reform of France. They succeeded in their campaign to end government by privileged hereditary orders but at the cost of a revolution extending over a century.

Fall of the Bastille

Many members of the National Constituent Assembly wanted to create a constitutional monarchy, but Louis's refusal to cooperate thwarted them. By choosing to oppose the diverse groups that were converging against him, the king helped unite them. His efforts to nip the revolution in the bud only spurred it on.

Queen Marie Antoinette, the king's brothers, and the most conservative nobles urged him to use force to break up the National Constituent Assembly, and he did try to intimidate it by mustering royal troops in the vicinity of Versailles and Paris. On July 11, he demonstrated his intent to ignore the assembly by abruptly dismissing Necker, the minister of finance, without informing the assembly.

The mustering of royal troops created anxiety in Paris, where there had recently been bread riots. The Parisians who had met to elect representatives to the Third Estate continued to meet after the elections were over, and in June they formed a citizen militia. A few weeks later, Louis's dismissal of Necker convinced them that the king intended to mount an offensive against Paris and the National Constituent Assembly.

On July 14, somewhat more than 800 people—mostly simple working folk—marched to a Parisian fortress called the Bastille to demand weapons for the city's militia. The governor of the Bastille lost control of the situation, and his troops fired into the crowd. Ninety-eight people died, and many others were wounded. The enraged crowd stormed the fortress, gained entrance, released seven prisoners, and killed the governor and some of his soldiers. They found no weapons.

On July 15, the militia of Paris—calling itself the National Guard—offered its command to a hero of the American Revolution, the marquis de Lafayette. He suggested the guard's insignia: red and blue stripes, the colors of Paris, separated by a white stripe, the emblem of the king. This design became the cockade (i.e., badge) of the revolution and eventually the flag of France.

The attack on the Bastille was the first of many acts by the people of Paris that determined the course of the revolution. It revealed that the National Constituent Assembly was not in control of all the forces that were to determine the destiny of France. As word of the Bastille's fall spread, mobs in the provincial cities took to the streets to assault other governmental institutions. In an effort to gain the upper hand, Louis XVI decided to court the allegiance of the Parisian rioters. He donned a revolutionary cockade and went to Paris to authorize the National Guard and to recognize the electors' organization as the city's legitimate government.

The "Great Fear" and the Surrender of Feudal Privileges

The urban disturbances spawned a rumor that royal troops were to be sent to occupy the countryside, and this caused a few scattered peasant revolts, which had erupted that spring, to blossom and spread. As the "Great Fear" swept the countryside, chateaux were burned, public records and documents destroyed, and feudal dues repudiated. The peasants took possession of scarce food supplies and of land that they had lost to the "aristocratic resurgence" during the last quarter-century.

On the night of August 4, 1789, aristocrats in the National Constituent Assembly carried out a maneuver designed to undercut the motivation of the rebellious peasants and restore order to the countryside. Several liberal nobles and churchmen rose in the assembly to renounce their feudal rights, dues, and tithes. Their emotional speeches led other members of the assembly to divest themselves of their privileges. In a sense, these men gave up what they had already lost and what they could not have regained without civil war. Most also had enough political influence to see to it that they were compensated. Nonetheless, their act of renunciation meant that henceforth all French citizens were subject to the same and equal laws. That dramatic session of the assembly paved the way for the legal and social reconstruction of France.

The rioters who stormed through city streets and roamed the countryside had more on their minds than the political issues being debated at

Versailles. Harvests in 1787 and 1788 had been poor, and food prices in 1789 were higher than they had been for almost a century. Wages had not kept up with rising prices. The winter of 1788–1789 had been unusually cold, and many people had suffered severely from hunger. Political, social, and economic grievances combined in sections of the nation to make the revolution cataclysmic. The National Constituent Assembly exploited the fear created by these popular uprisings to intimidate the king and the conservative aristocrats. But when the various elements of the assembly began to quarrel among themselves, factions turned for support to the masses. The shopkeeping and artisan classes were best organized to respond, and they knew the price they wanted for their cooperation.

The Declaration of the Rights of Man and Citizen

On August 27, 1789, the National Constituent Assembly approved the Declaration of the Rights of Man and Citizen, a statement of the political principles that would guide its writing of a new constitution. It affirmed that all men were born free and equal with inalienable rights to liberty, property, and personal safety. Governments were said to exist to protect those rights, and all citizens were guaranteed equal protection before the law and equal opportunity of admission to public office—commensurate, of course, with their abilities and characters. Due process of law, presumption of innocence until proof of guilt, and freedom of religion were affirmed. Taxation was to be apportioned according to ability to pay, and property was declared a right ordained by God. The declaration was an indictment of the abuses of the absolutist monarchy, and it served as the death certificate of the Old Regime.

It was not accidental that the declaration focused on the rights of men and made no mention of women. Many of the Enlightenment's political theorists assigned men and women separate spheres. Men were said to be suited for public service (i.e., citizenship) and women for

The women of Paris marched to Versailles on October 5, 1789. The following day the royal family was forced to return to Paris with them. Henceforth, the French government would function under the constant threat of mob violence. France, 18th c., *To Versailles, to Versailles. The Women of Paris going to Versailles, 5 October, 1789.* Musée de la Ville de Paris, Musée Carnavalet, Paris, France, Giraudon/Art Resource, NY

the domestic duties of motherhood and home-making. Nonetheless, in the charged atmosphere of the summer of 1789, many French women hoped that a new constitution would improve their legal situation—particularly with respect to property, inheritance rights, family, and divorce. Some believed that the declaration might eventually extend full citizenship to women.

The Royal Family Forced to Return to Paris

Since Louis XVI delayed ratification of both the declaration and the aristocrats' renunciation of feudalism, suspicion grew that he was again contemplating military action. On October 5, a crowd of about 7,000 Parisian women (armed with pikes, guns, swords, and knives) marched to Versailles to demand relief from a bread shortage. Intimidated, the king agreed to sanction the decrees of the assembly, but the Parisians were deeply suspicious of him. They insisted that the royal family move to Paris where its conduct could be monitored. Louis had no option, and on October 6, 1789, his carriage followed the crowd into the city to the palace of the Tuileries. The women's march was the first mass insurrection to use the language of popular sovereignty against a monarch.

The Reconstruction of France

The National Constituent Assembly followed the royal family to Paris, and the situation remained relatively peaceful until the summer of 1792. In Paris the assembly set about reorganizing France as a constitutional monarchy. It endorsed a policy of unregulated free trade and promised protection of property. Its religious views were anticlerical. On all these issues, the aristocracy and the middle-class elite stood united. Although championing civic equality before the law, the assembly spurned social equality and radical democracy. It intended to leave control of the nation in the hands of propertied men.

Political Reorganization

ACTIVE AND PASSIVE CITIZENS The Constitution, which the assembly issued in 1791, established a unicameral Legislative Assembly as the chief political authority for the nation. The monarch was granted a veto that could delay, but not halt, legislation. An elaborate system of indirect election was created to diminish pressure on the government from the masses. France's citizens were divided into two categories: active and passive. Active citizens were men who paid annual taxes equal to three days of local labor wages. Only they could vote to choose the electors who chose the members of the legislature. Since there were higher property qualifications for service as an elector or a member of the legislature, only about 50,000 of France's 25 million people could hold office. No women were enfranchised.

These constitutional arrangements made wealth rather than birth the basis of political power, and they made no distinctions among forms of wealth—aristocratic estates or commercial property. They recognized the changes that were taking place in French society by allowing the newly emerging economic interests to have a voice in governing the nation.

Some women tried to fight the laws that gave them no right to vote and hold office. In 1791 Olympe de Gouges, a butcher's daughter from Montauban, published a Declaration of the Rights of Woman. By revising the Declaration of the Rights of Man and Citizen to include the word *woman* in each clause relating to men, it demanded that a woman be regarded as a citizen in her own right, not as a dependent of a citizen family. Olympe de Gouges argued for property rights and improved education for women and for equality between wives and husbands in marriage. She also wanted to compel men to recognize the paternity of all their children. By campaigning for a list of rights for men, the National Assembly had established a set of values against which its own conduct could be measured. This prompted those to whom it had not extended full liberties to ask why they had been shut out and to claim that the revolution would not be complete until they were included.

DEPARTMENTS REPLACE PROVINCES The national Constituent Assembly used the rational methods of Enlightenment science to reorganize local government and the judiciary. It replaced the provinces that had evolved as part of medieval France's feudal system with eighty-three *départements* of approximately equal size, subdivided into

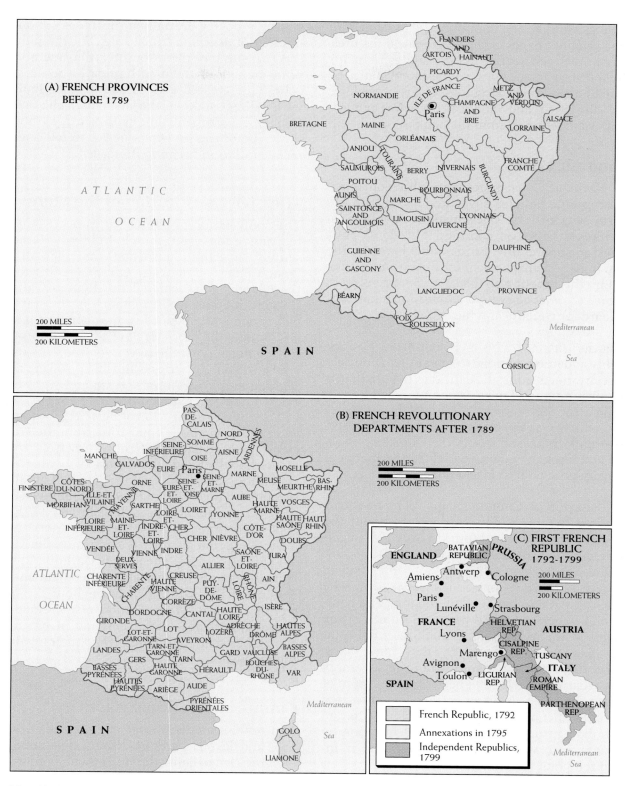

(A) FRENCH PROVINCES BEFORE 1789

FLANDERS AND HAINAULT
ARTOIS
PICARDY
NORMANDIE
ÎLE DE FRANCE
Paris
CHAMPAGNE AND BRIE
METZ AND VERDUN
LORRAINE
ALSACE
BRETAGNE
MAINE
ORLÉANAIS
ANJOU
TOURAINE
BERRY
NIVERNAIS
BURGUNDY
FRANCHE COMTÉ
SAUMUROIS
POITOU
BOURBONNAIS
AUNIS
MARCHE
SAINTONGE AND ANGOUMOIS
LIMOUSIN
AUVERGNE
LYONNAIS
GUIENNE AND GASCONY
DAUPHINÉ
BÉARN
LANGUEDOC
PROVENCE
FOIX
ROUSSILLON

ATLANTIC OCEAN

SPAIN

Mediterranean Sea

CORSICA

200 MILES
200 KILOMETERS

(B) FRENCH REVOLUTIONARY DEPARTMENTS AFTER 1789

PAS-DE-CALAIS
NORD
SEINE INFÉRIEURE
SOMME
AISNE
ARDENNES
MANCHE
CALVADOS
EURE
OISE
Paris
SEINE-ET-MARNE
MARNE
MEUSE
MOSELLE
BAS-RHIN
CÔTES-DU-NORD
FINISTÈRE
ORNE
SEINE-ET-OISE
EURE-ET-LOIRE
AUBE
MEURTHE
VOSGES
HAUT-RHIN
ILLE-ET-VILAINE
MAYENNE
SARTHE
LOIRE-ET-CHER
LOIRET
YONNE
HAUTE MARNE
HAUTE SAÔNE
MORBIHAN
MAINE-ET-LOIRE
INDRE-ET-LOIRE
CHER
NIÈVRE
CÔTE-D'OR
DOUBS
LOIRE INFÉRIEURE
VENDÉE
VIENNE
INDRE
SAÔNE-ET-LOIRE
JURA
DEUX-SÈVRES
ALLIER
AIN
CHARENTE INFÉRIEURE
HAUTE VIENNE
CREUSE
PUY-DE-DÔME
RHÔNE
CHARENTE
CORRÈZE
LOIRE
ISÈRE
GIRONDE
DORDOGNE
CANTAL
HAUTE LOIRE
ARDÈCHE
DRÔME
HAUTES ALPES
LOT-ET-GARONNE
LOT
AVEYRON
LOZÈRE
LANDES
TARN-ET-GARONNE
GARD
VAUCLUSE
BASSES ALPES
GERS
TARN
HÉRAULT
BOUCHES-DU-RHÔNE
VAR
BASSES PYRÉNÉES
HAUTE GARONNE
BASSES PYRÉNÉES
HAUTES PYRÉNÉES
ARIÈGE
AUDE
PYRÉNÉES ORIENTALES

ATLANTIC OCEAN

SPAIN

Mediterranean Sea

GOLO
LIAMONE

200 MILES
200 KILOMETERS

(C) FIRST FRENCH REPUBLIC 1792–1799

ENGLAND
BATAVIAN REPUBLIC
PRUSSIA
Amiens
Antwerp
Cologne
Paris
Lunéville
Strasbourg
FRANCE
Lyons
HELVETIAN REP.
AUSTRIA
CISALPINE REP.
TUSCANY
Avignon
Marengo
ITALY
Toulon
LIGURIAN REP.
ROMAN EMPIRE
SPAIN
PARTHENOPEAN REP.

Mediterranean Sea

200 MILES
200 KILOMETERS

French Republic, 1792
Annexations in 1795
Independent Republics, 1799

MAP 19–1   FRENCH PROVINCES AND THE REPUBLIC   *In 1789 the National Assembly redrew the map of France. The ancient provinces (A) were replaced with a larger number of new, smaller departments (B) in an effort to create a more rational administrative system for the country. The borders of the republic (C) changed as the French army conquered new territory.*

districts, cantons, and communes, and named for rivers, mountains, or other geographical features. The various seigneurial courts and *parlements* were replaced by a uniform court system staffed by elected judges and prosecutors. Court procedures were simplified, and the most degrading punishments were removed from the books.

Economic Policy

The National Constituent Assembly continued the economic policies advocated by Louis XVI's reformist ministers. These usually involved removing restraints on commerce by doing such things as suppressing guilds and liberating the grain trade. An enthusiasm for the rationalism of the Enlightenment also inspired the assembly to endorse the metric system as a uniform national standard for weights and measures.

WORKERS' ORGANIZATIONS FORBIDDEN The assembly's determination to create a "natural" economy freed from all restraints meant that it was unsympathetic to any attempt by workers to organize for their own protection. The Chapelier Law, which was enacted on June 14, 1791, forbade workers' associations (i.e., unions). Peasants and workers were to be left to the mercy of a largely unregulated marketplace.

CONFISCATION OF CHURCH LANDS The assembly inherited the job of doing something about the financial crisis that had forced Louis XVI to call its predecessor, the Estates General. The assembly did not, as governments sometimes had in the past, simply repudiate the royal debt. The debt was owed to bankers, merchants, and commercial traders who had powerful voices in the assembly. Instead, old and much-resented indirect taxes were replaced by new land taxes. When these proved insufficient, the assembly took what may well have been, for the future of France, its most decisive action. It confiscated and sold the property of the nation's Roman Catholic Church. This step caused inflation by putting more wealth in circulation, and it invited religious schism and civil war.

THE *ASSIGNATS* In December 1789, the assembly authorized the issuance of *assignats*, government bonds whose value was backed up by the revenue that was to be generated from the sale of church property. Initially a limit was set on the number of *assignats* to be sold, but the public's eagerness to buy them tempted the assembly to print enough of them to liquidate the national debt. This created a large body of bondholders with a direct stake in the survival of the revolutionary government, but within a few months the value of the *assignats* began to fall and the rate of inflation began to increase.

The Civil Constitution of the Clergy

The confiscation of church lands necessitated a reorganization of the church. In July 1790 the assembly, without consulting the pope or the French clergy, issued the Civil Constitution of the Clergy. This declared the Roman Catholic Church in France to be a branch of the state. Its bishoprics were reduced in number from 135 to 83 to make the dioceses of religious administrators conform with the new *départements* of the civil government. Priests and bishops were made salaried employees of the state and were to be elected like other state officials.

The Civil Constitution of the Clergy was a major blunder. Vigorous opposition from the French clergy provoked the assembly unwisely to demand that all clergy take an oath of loyalty to the state. Only seven bishops and about half the clergy complied. Those who did not were removed from their ecclesiastical offices. In February 1791, the pope condemned not only the Civil Constitution of the Clergy but also the Declaration of the Rights of Man and Citizen. The Roman Catholic Church launched an offensive against liberalism and the revolution that continued throughout the nineteenth century. Many French people suddenly found themselves in the position of having to choose between their religion and their loyalty to the revolution.

Counterrevolutionary Activity

The revolution had other enemies besides the pope and devout Catholics. Many aristocrats, the *émigrés,* fled to countries on France's borders and set up bases for counterrevolutionary activity. The king's younger brother, the count of Artois (1757–1836), was among them. In 1791 he and the queen persuaded Louis XVI to attempt to flee France.

FLIGHT TO VARENNES On the night of June 20, 1791, Louis and his immediate family, disguised as servants, left Paris hoping to reach Metz. At Varennes the king was recognized and prevented from going farther. On June 24, a company of soldiers brought the royal family back to Paris. The leaders of the National Constituent Assembly, who wanted to save the constitutional monarchy, announced that the king had not fled but been abducted. This public fiction failed, however, to cloak the fact that the nation's most prominent counterrevolutionary was now seated on its throne.

DECLARATION OF PILLNITZ Two months later, Marie Antoinette's brother, Leopold II of Austria, and Prussia's King Frederick William II issued the Declaration of Pillnitz. The two monarchs promised to intervene in France's affairs to protect the royal family and to preserve the monarchy if the major European nations supported them. This provision rendered their threat meaningless, for Great Britain would not have endorsed a move on their part that would have upset the continental balance of power. France's revolutionaries, however, concluded that they were surrounded by hostile monarchists, and their anger increased the precariousness of the royal family's situation.

A Second Revolution

The National Constituent Assembly dissolved itself in September (1791). One of its last acts forbade any of its members to seek election to the Legislative Assembly that took its place. This new assembly, which convened on October 1, faced immense problems. Louis XVI had reluctantly accepted the establishment of a constitutional monarchy, but many French aristocrats resented their loss of position and plotted against the new government. In western France, peasants resisted the revolutionary changes, especially as they affected the church. On the other hand, radical members of the assembly sided with groups of Parisian workers and women who believed the revolution had not gone far enough. Abroad, various nations were concluding that the French Revolution was becoming a threat to their interests. By the spring of 1792, all these pressures had begun to unravel the original political settlement and to encourage implementation of a second series of revolutionary changes that were far more radical.

End of the Monarchy

Factionalism plagued the Legislative Assembly throughout its short life (1791–1792). During meetings of the Estates General, deputies from the Third Estate had established clubs to bring together persons with similar political philosophies. The Jacobins, who took their name from the Dominican (i.e., Jacobin) monastery in Paris where they met, were the best organized of these groups. They embraced the most radical of the Enlightenment's political theories and urged the National Constituent Assembly to establish a republic rather than a constitutional monarchy. The events of the summer of 1791 increased their following.

A group of Jacobins called Girondists (from the department of the Gironde that many of them represented) or Brissotins (from their spokesman in 1792, Jacques-Pierre Brissot) assumed a leadership role in the Legislative Assembly. To defeat the forces of counterrevolution, they passed measures confiscating the property of *émigrés* who refused to return to France and deprived refractory clergy of state pensions. The king vetoed these laws, but he did not oppose all Girondist legislation.

On April 20, 1792, the Girondists persuaded the Legislative Assembly to declare war on Austria, now governed by Francis II (r. 1792–1835), and on Prussia. The Girondists believed that the war would solidify domestic support for the revolution and make the revolution more radical. Paradoxically, Louis XVI favored the war, for a need for strong leadership during a war usually rallies a nation's people behind its chief executive. Louis may also have felt that he had nothing to lose, for defeat of the revolutionary armies could have hastened restoration of the Old Regime.

The king was to be disappointed and the Girondists delighted. The war radicalized the revolution and led to a second revolution that overthrew the constitutional monarchy and established a republic. To defend the nation, the government had to mobilize all its resources. Its need for support persuaded it to lend a sympathetic ear to appeals for rights from patriotic

Jacques-Louis David Champions Republican Values: Lictors Bringing to Brutus the Bodies of His Sons

Jacques-Louis David (1748–1825) was the foremost French painter of the revolutionary era. He was a proponent of a movement called *neoclassicism*, which drew its inspiration from classical themes and models. His paintings sometimes resemble a static tableau and were often meant to be more didactic (i.e., morally instructive) than emotional in their impact. David was an opponent of the Old Regime, and his paintings on ancient republican themes were indictments of his country's corrupt monarchy.

David began *Lictors Bringing to Brutus the Bodies of His Sons* in 1789 before that year's revolutionary events but did not finish it until the National Assembly was proclaimed. The painting depicted a decisive moment in the life of Brutus, a noble Roman who had helped drive out Rome's last king and who had become one of the new Roman Republic's first consuls. When Brutus learned that his sons were conspiring to restore monarchy to Rome, he did his duty as a republican official and ordered their execution. His decision to put duty to the state above family interests turned him into a heroic symbol of selfless republican patriotism.

David's design divides the painting into separate male and female spheres, which correspond to Rousseau's theories about gender and ancient societies. On the left males demonstrate reason and control as they fulfill their civic responsibilities and unflinchingly carry out their duties under the law. On the right the women of the household exhibit, by their extreme emotional distress, a lack of self-control that suggests that women are incapable of honoring civic virtue above private family feeling. David's belief that loyalty to the republic's abstract political principles should transcend human sympathies revealed its bloody dark side during the years of the Terror, but David himself survived the upheavals of the revolutionary era to serve a new French monarch, the emperor Napoleon.

Source: Robert Rosenblum and H. W. Janson, *Nineteenth-Century Art* (Englewood Cliffs, NJ and New York: Prentice Hall: Harry N. Abrams, Inc., 1984), pp. 24–50; Albert Boime, *Art in an Age of Revolution, 1750–1800* (Chicago: University of Chicago Press, 1987, pp. 417–421); Norman Bryson, *Looking at the Overlooked: Four Essays on Still Life Painting* (Cambridge, MA: Harvard University Press, 1900), pp. 156–158; and Thomas Crow, *Emulation: Making Artists for Revolutionary France* (New Haven, CT: Yale University Press, 1995).

Jacques-Louis David (1748–1825), *Lictors bringing to Brutus the bodies of his sons.* 1789. Oil on Canvas, 323 × 422 cm—Inv. 3693, Louvre, Paris, France, Erich Lessing/Art Resource, NY

groups that had previously been excluded from politics. As early as March 1792, a group of women led by Pauline Léon petitioned the Legislative Assembly for the right to bear arms and to fight for the revolution. Once the war began, a number of French women enlisted in the army and served with distinction.

The war went badly, and suspicion of the king's loyalty increased when the Prussians threatened dire consequences if the royal family was harmed. On August 10, 1792, a large crowd of Parisians invaded the Tuileries palace and forced Louis XVI and Marie Antoinette to take refuge in the Legislative Assembly. The crowd fought with the king's Swiss guards, and several hundred of the soldiers and a large number of Parisians were killed. The royal family was imprisoned in comfortable quarters, and the king was prohibited from exercising his political functions. The constitutional monarchy began to ignore its monarch.

The Convention and the Role of the *Sans-culottes*

In July radicals from the working class had designated Paris a commune and turned the city's government over to a committee composed of representatives from the municipal wards. Two months later the Paris Commune ordered the "September Massacres." Many of the approximately 1,200 people who were executed were aristocrats or priests, but the majority were simply common criminals who, because they were being held in the city's jails, were assumed to be counterrevolutionaries.

The Paris Commune then compelled the Legislative Assembly to decree universal male suffrage and call an election for a new assembly to write a democratic constitution. The Convention, which was named for the American Constitutional Convention of 1787, met on September 21, 1792, a day after the French army halted the Prussian advance at the Battle of Valmy in eastern France. The victory of democratic forces at home was confirmed by victory on the battlefield, and the Convention's first act was to declare France a republic—a nation governed by an elected assembly without a king.

GOALS OF THE *SANS-CULOTTES* The second revolution was the work of two groups: a faction of Jacobins who were more radical than the Girondists, and Parisians called *sans-culottes*. The term meant

"without breeches," and it referred to long trousers that working men wore in place of the knee breeches favored by court aristocrats. The *sans-culottes* were shopkeepers, artisans, wage earners, and factory workers who had been ignored by the Old Regime and victimized by the economic policies of the National Constituent Assembly. To win the war the revolutionary government needed their cooperation, and between the summers of 1792 and 1794, they were the dominant force determining the course of the revolution.

The *sans-culottes* knew what they wanted: immediate relief from food shortages, government-imposed limits to end rising prices, and an end to social inequality. They were intensely hostile to aristocrats and suspected the original leaders of the revolution of aspiring to become a new aristocracy. Their campaign against inequality did not entail the abolition of private property. They envisioned a nation of small property owners who all enjoyed the same political rights. They were antimonarchical and strongly republican but distrustful of representative government. The *sans-culottes'* political experience had been gained in meetings of the Paris wards that, like New England town meetings, were run as direct democracies, and the economic hardship of their lives made them impatient and unwilling to trust their fates to anyone but themselves.

THE POLICIES OF THE JACOBINS The goals of the *sans-culottes* were not wholly compatible with those of the Jacobins, for Jacobins wanted representative government and favored an unregulated economy. After Louis XVI's flight to Varennes, however, the more extreme Jacobins (called "the Mountain" from their seats at the top of the assembly hall) sided with leaders of the Parisian *sans-culottes* in an effort to win the war and end the monarchy.

EXECUTION OF LOUIS XVI In December 1792, Louis XVI was put on trial for conspiring against the liberty of the people and the security of the state. The Girondists tried to spare his life, but the Mountain won his conviction. On January 21, 1793, Louis, now stripped of his title and officially known as "Citizen Capet" from the name of the ancestor who had founded his dynasty, was beheaded.

The execution of the king increased pressure on the government. The Prussians renewed their offensive and drove the French out of Belgium.

Louis XVI was executed on January 21, 1793. Execution of Louis XVI. Aquatint. French,
18th century. Musée de la Ville de Paris, Musée Carnavalet, Paris. France. Giraudon/Art Resource, NY

Every major European power declared its opposition to the revolution, and the Convention declared war on Great Britain, Holland, and Spain. In March 1793, a royalist revolt erupted in western France and began to spread. In light of all this, the Mountain concluded that the Girondists, who had led the country into the war, were incapable of defending the nation from either its foreign or its domestic enemies.

Europe at War with the Revolution

Not all Europeans were initially opposed to the French Revolution. Some reformers hoped that the revolution would rationally reorganize a corrupt and inefficient government. Some nations were pleased that the revolution would prevent France from taking much part in European affairs for several years. But by 1792, the European monarchies were alert to the danger of both French ideas and French aggression. The Declaration of the Rights of Man and Citizen was a highly exportable document applicable to the rest of Europe, and to prevent the spread of its revolutionary ideology one government after another instituted repressive domestic policies.

Edmund Burke Attacks the Revolution

In 1790 *Reflections on the Revolution in France* by Edmund Burke (1729–1799), a British statesman, outlined the position that was to be taken by Europe's emerging conservative political parties. He rejected Enlightenment rationalism as a realistic program for reform and predicted disaster for any government that failed to recognize the historical realities of a country's political evolution—or that failed to accommodate the complexities of human social relations. He forecast turmoil as inexperienced people tried to lead France, and events there unfolded much as he predicted.

Suppression of Reform in Britain

Prime Minister William Pitt the Younger (1759–1806), who had supported moderate reform of Parliament during the 1780s, turned against both reform and popular political movements. His government suppressed the London Corresponding Society, a working-class reform group, and drove the chemist Joseph Priestley (1733–1804), a radical political thinker, out of the country. Early in 1793, Pitt secured parliamentary approval for acts that suspended *habeas corpus* and broadened the definition of treason to include not just actions but writings of which the government disapproved. Pitt had less success curbing freedom of the press, but all political groups that opposed him risked being indicted for sedition.

The End of Enlightened Absolutism in Eastern Europe

By sullying the idea of reform, the revolution brought an end to enlightened absolutism's experiments in eastern Europe. Francis II (r. 1792–1835), second heir to Joseph II's Habsburg empire, became a major leader of the counterrevolution. In Prussia, Frederick the Great's nephew and successor, Frederick William II (r. 1786–1797), turned to the conservative Lutheran church and the aristocracy for help in suppressing popular uprisings. Catherine the Great burned the works of Voltaire, her former friend, and exiled Alexander Radishchev (1749–1802) whose *Journey from Saint Petersburg to Moscow* described the grim social conditions prevailing in Russia. In 1795 the eastern powers announced that a constitutional monarchy that had been established in Poland in 1791 was dangerously revolutionary, and this provided them with an excuse to annex sections of the country. Poland disappeared from the map of Europe until after World War I.

War with Europe

The success of France's revolution set back reform movements in the rest of Europe. In November 1792, after French armies occupied the Austrian Netherlands, the Convention alarmed Europe's heads of state by declaring that it would aid all peoples who wished to cast off the burdens of aristocratic and monarchical oppression. The British, whose commerce was directly threatened, were on the point of declaring war on France when the Convention beat them to it (February 1793). By the time the Mountain took charge of France's government in April 1793, France was at war with Austria, Prussia, Great Britain, Spain, Sardinia, and Holland.

The Reign of Terror

The task of mobilizing for war in 1793 changed the way the French revolutionaries thought about themselves. They were engaged, they believed, not in a struggle over national borders but in the defense of a bold new ideology: a republican political and social order that the world was determined to destroy. To protect the revolution, the government considered it necessary to employ extreme measures.

The Republic Defended

THE COMMITTEE OF PUBLIC SAFETY In April 1793, the Convention increased its efficiency by establishing powerful committees to serve as a collective executive. The Committee of General Security and the Committee of Public Safety handled most duties of government. The latter, which was led by Jacques Danton (1759–1794), Maximilien Robespierre (1758–1794), and Lazare Carnot (1753–1823), acquired almost dictatorial power. Each of its leaders was a committed republican and an opponent of the Girondists. They believed that it was their duty to save the revolution from mortal enemies at home and abroad. To that end, they found it expedient to court the *sans-culottes* of Paris and to suppress many of the rights the revolution claimed to protect. Chief among these was the right to life. France's precarious international situation intensified anxiety about national security and prompted a rigorous search for internal enemies. The search quickly got out of hand.

THE *LEVÉE EN MASSE* In early June (1793) the Parisian *sans-culottes* invaded the Convention, expelled the Girondists, and established the radical Mountain in control. On June 22, the Convention approved a fully democratic constitution but delayed its implementation until the end of the war. On August 23, Carnot issued a *levée en masse,* an order for the total military mobilization of the nation—both its men and its goods. On September 17, the ceiling on prices the *sans-culottes* demanded was instituted. Never before had Europe seen a nation organized in this way—nor one defended by a citizen army.

The Reign of Terror that the new republic promptly inflicted on itself did nothing to persuade the nations of Europe that they could risk reform and revolution. The spate of quasi-judicial bloodletting that began in the autumn of 1793 and extended into midsummer 1794 constitutes the revolution's most infamous episode. It can be understood only in the context of a foreign war on one hand and pressure from the Convention and the *sans-culottes* for a rapid transformation of society on the other.

The "Republic of Virtue"

The threat of foreign armies closing in on France made it easy to dispense with legal due process, but the revolution's leaders did not see their actions simply as expedients required by war. They believed they had created something new in world history, a "republic of virtue" where concern for the common good had replaced aristocratic corruption. Every aspect of society was now to be transformed for the benefit of the masses. Streets were renamed to memorialize the egalitarian vocabulary of the revolution. A republican style of dress was adopted patterned after the ordinary clothing of the *sans-culottes* or the imagined garb of the Roman republic. Plays whose themes were not sufficiently republican were suppressed. Special efforts were made to fight crimes such as prostitution that were supposedly characteristic of aristocratic societies.

THE SOCIETY OF REVOLUTIONARY REPUBLICAN WOMEN During these impassioned months, women organized to fight the internal enemies of the revolution. In May (1793) Pauline Léon and Claire Lacombe founded the Society of Revolutionary Republican Women. It filled the galleries of the Convention with women who came to hear the debates and cheer their favorite speakers. It also developed a radical political agenda: stricter controls on the price of food and other commodities, persecution of food hoarders, and the indictment of working women who were insufficiently revolutionary.

By October (1793) the Convention had begun to fear the turmoil the society was causing, and a campaign to suppress women began. The deputies used Rousseau's argument that nature intended separate spheres of activity for men and women to make it illegal for women to organize for political purposes. Olympe de Gouges, author of the *Declaration of the Rights of Woman,* opposed the Terror, accused certain Jacobins of corruption, and was guillotined in November 1793. That year women were excluded from serving in the army and shut out of the galleries of the Convention. In the republic of virtue, men were to handle duties of citizenship while women cared for the home.

DE-CHRISTIANIZATION The most dramatic sign of the republic of virtue's determination to break with a past it regarded as corrupt was its attempt to de-Christianize France. In October 1793, the Convention decreed a new chronology that chose the day on which the Republic was established, not the birth of Christ, as history's pivotal point of reference. The calendar year was to consist of twelve months of thirty days with names (e.g., Thermidor, Floreal) derived from the seasons. Every tenth day, rather than every seventh, was a holiday. In November the Convention declared the Cathedral of Notre Dame in Paris a "Temple of Reason," and officers were dispatched to the provinces to close churches, persecute believers, and force priests to marry. This policy roused much opposition and drove a wedge between the provinces and the revolutionary government in Paris. In May 1794, the government abandoned the worship of reason as too abstract for most people and endorsed the "Cult of the Supreme Being." This was Rousseau's vision of a deistic civic religion designed to promote public morality.

ROBESPIERRE During the crucial months of late 1793 and early 1794, the chief figure on the Committee of Public Safety was Robespierre. He and those who supported his policies were the first in a long line of secular ideologues of the left and the right who, in the name of humanity, occasioned much suffering over the next two centuries.

Robespierre was a complex, controversial figure. He was utterly selfless and committed to the republic, but he was also a shrewd and sensitive politician. He had opposed the war in 1792 because he feared it might strengthen the monarchy, and he argued against de-Christianization as a political blunder. For him, the "republic of virtue" entailed renunciation of selfish gains from political life. This was a noble thought, but his confidence in his own selflessness enabled him to overlook issues of morality and view the Terror as nothing more than an instrument of swift, republican justice.

Progress of the Terror

During the summer of 1793, the Convention established tribunals to search out the enemies of the republic. Much hinged on the definition of *enemy*, which shifted as the months passed. Ultimately, the term was applied to staunch republicans who made the mistake of opposing the will of the dominant faction in their government.

The tribunals began in October by executing Marie Antoinette, other members of the royal family, and some aristocrats. Certain Girondist politicians then followed. By the early months of 1794, the search for enemies of the revolution had spread to the provinces and had begun to involve members of every social class—including the *sans-culottes*. Thousands died.

REVOLUTIONARIES TURN AGAINST THEMSELVES Late in the winter of 1794, Robespierre began to manipulate the Terror to remove anyone who threatened him—on both the left and the right. On March 24, he executed some leaders of the *enragés, sans-culottes* extremists who were pressing for more price regulation, social equalization, and de-Christianization. Robespierre then accused some conservative republicans of a lack of commitment to the war, of profiting, and of rejecting the link between politics and moral virtue. On June 10, he secured passage of the Law of 22 Prairial, which increased the murderous efficiency of the tribunals by permitting them to convict suspects without hearing substantial evidence.

FALL OF ROBESPIERRE On July 26, Robespierre made an ill-tempered speech in the Convention, declaring that unnamed leaders of the government were conspiring against the revolution. This vague but potent threat caused the members of the Convention, who feared becoming his

next victims, to act on their instinct for self-preservation. The next day, the ninth of the month of Thermidor, they shouted him down when he rose to make another speech. That night they arrested him, and the next day he was executed. Robespierre had destroyed rival leaders without creating any followers of his own.

The Thermidorian Reaction

By the late summer of 1794, uprisings in the provinces had been crushed, and the foreign war was also going well. A growing sense of security and a spreading conviction that the revolution had become too radical persuaded the revolutionaries to end the Terror. Despite the fact that the largest number of its over 25,000 victims had been peasants and *sans-culottes*, the events that followed suggest that the public had begun to fear that the *sans-culottes* had become too powerful.

The End of the Terror

The Thermidorian Reaction, which began in July 1794, inaugurated a new constitutional regime. Wealthy middle-class and professional people replaced the *sans-culottes* as the voices the government heeded. The Convention allowed the Girondists who had been in prison or hiding to return to their seats, and there was a general amnesty for political prisoners. The power of the Committee of Public Safety was greatly reduced, and the notorious Law of 22 Prairial was repealed. Some of the people responsible for the Terror were removed from public life. Some leaders of the Paris Commune and certain deputies were executed. The Paris Commune itself was outlawed, and the Paris Jacobin Club was closed. There was also a bloody reaction known as the "white terror." People who had been involved in the Terror were attacked and often murdered. Jacobins were executed with little more due process than they had extended to their victims. Some of this was spontaneous mob action, but some was approved by the Convention.

The republic of virtue yielded, if not to vice, at least to pleasure. Well-to-do people gave up the affectation of dressing like the poor. Theaters presented new plays. Prostitutes returned to the streets. Families of victims of the Terror gave parties in which they appeared with shaved necks (like prisoners prepared for the guillotine) banded by blood-red ribbons. The Convention allowed Catholic services to be held. Priests returned, and there was a marked resurgence of Catholic piety.

The Thermidorians and their successors had seen enough of proposals for political and social reform. The stability of traditional institutions attracted them, and among the things they wanted was a return to family life as it had been before the revolution. Consequently, French women may have had somewhat less freedom after 1795.

Establishment of the Directory

The fully democratic constitution adopted in 1793 had never gone into effect, and the Convention now replaced it with the Constitution of the Year III. This provided for a bicameral legislature: a Council of Elders composed of married or widowed men over forty years of age, and a Council of Five Hundred consisting of married or single males at least thirty years old. The executive branch was a five-person Directory chosen by the Elders from a list submitted by the Council of Five Hundred. Property qualifications determined which civilians could vote, but all soldiers were enfranchised.

The Directory moderated, but did not try to reverse, the revolution. By 1795 permanent changes had taken place in France. Assumptions of civic equality had replaced traditional distinctions of rank and birth, and social status was determined by property ownership. Some people who had never been allowed any political power now had it—at least to a limited degree. Representation had been established as a principle of government, but it was not yet clear which new groups would be permitted representation. The post-Thermidorian course of the French Revolution

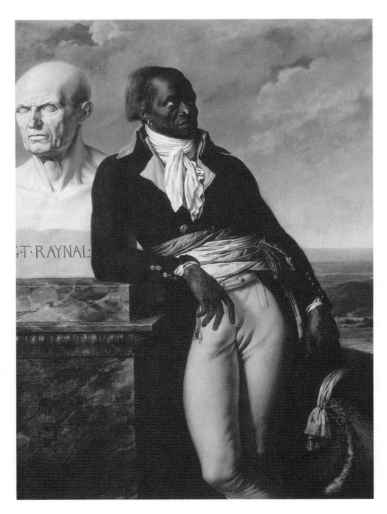

Jean-Baptiste Belley was a Senegalese African born in Gorée in 1747 and later taken to Saint-Domingue as a slave. In February 1794, he was seated in the Convention along with two other people as representatives of citizens of Saint-Domingue. He had joined the French army there to resist counterrevolutionary forces, and once the representatives from Saint-Domingue were seated, the Convention abolished slavery in the French colonies. Belley remained active in French revolutionary politics at least as late as 1797. He was one of several people of color from the Caribbean who served in either the Convention or the institutions of the Directory. Girodet de Roussy-Trioson Anne-Louis (1767–1824). *Portrait de Jean-Baptiste Belley*, depute de Saint Dominique a la Convention (1747–1805). Chateaux de Versailles et de Tranon. © Photo RMN

The French Revolution

1789

May 5	The Estates General opens at Versailles
June 17	The National Assembly is declared
June 20	The Tennis Court Oath
July 14	Fall of the Bastille
August 4	Surrender of feudal rights
August 27	Declaration of the Rights of Man and Citizen
October 5	Parisian women march on Versailles

1790

July 14	Louis XVI accepts constitutional monarchy

1791

June 20	The royal family attempts to flee
October 1	Formation of the Legislative Assembly

1792

April 20	France declares war on Austria
September 2	The September Massacres
September 21	The Convention meets; monarchy is abolished

1793

January 21	Louis XVI is executed
February 1	France declares war on Great Britain
April	Formation of the Committee of Public Safety
June 22	Adoption of the Constitution of 1793
August 23	*Levée en masse* proclaimed
October 16	Marie Antoinette is executed
November 10	The Cult of Reason and the revolutionary calendar

1794

March 24	Execution of *sans-culottes* leaders
May 7	Cult of the Supreme Being proclaimed
June 10	The Law of 22 Prairial is adopted
July 27	Ninth of Thermidor, the fall of Robespierre

1795

August 22	Constitution of the Year III and the Directory

was a victory for holders of property. The property that won the day was not industrial wealth but the middle-class wealth stemming from commerce, the professions, and land. The largest new propertied class to emerge from the revolutionary turmoil was the peasantry.

Removal of the *Sans-culottes* from Political Life

With the war effort succeeding, the Convention severed its ties with the *sans-culottes*. The Thermidorians repealed price controls and returned to an unregulated economy. As a result, the winter of 1794–1795 brought the worst food shortages of the period. Royalist agents tried to take advantage of the discontent, and on October 5, 1795 (13 Vendémiaire), they inspired rioting in Paris against the Convention. A general named Napoleon Bonaparte (1769–1821) commanded the cannon that dispersed the crowd.

In March 1795, the Convention concluded peace with Prussia and Spain and took steps to prevent extreme democrats and royalists from winning seats in the Council of Five Hundred. The next year the Directory again beat back the radicals by executing Gracchus Babeuf (1760– 1797), the leader of a "Conspiracy of Equals" that advocated radical democracy and greater equality of property. The Directory lacked a broad base of political support, but it survived because the army was willing to sustain it while France was at war with Austria and Great Britain. The instability of the Directory and the deepening involvement of the army in its politics were, however, to have profound consequences not only for France but for the entire Western world.

In Perspective

The French Revolution, the central political event of modern European history, unleashed forces that determined the course taken by Europe and much of the rest of the world for the next two centuries. The revolution started as a clash between the monarchy and the nobility. But once the Estates General gathered, the Third Estate, in all of its diversity, acquired control of the government. At first, the middle class dominated, but quite soon the people of Paris and the peasants of the countryside made their voices heard.

The revolution transformed the social as well as the political life of France. The nation soon found itself at war with itself (during the Reign of Terror) and at war with virtually all of the rest of Europe. Nobles surrendered social privileges. The church's property was confiscated. Vast amounts of land changed hands, and France became a nation of peasant landowners.

A desire for stability and a determination to defeat the foreign enemies of the revolution finally helped France to reorganize itself and eventually to export revolutionary ideals. This worked to the advantage of the army and, particularly, of a brilliant young officer named Napoleon Bonaparte.

REVIEW QUESTIONS

1. What is meant by this statement: "Paradoxically, France was a rich nation with an impoverished government"? How did the financial weaknesses of the French monarchy pave the way for the revolution of 1789?
2. What role did Louis XVI play in the French Revolution? What were his most serious mistakes? Had Louis been a more able ruler, could the revolution have been avoided? Would a constitutional monarchy have succeeded? Or did the revolution ultimately have little to do with the competence of the monarch?
3. How was the Estates General transformed into the National Assembly? Which social and political values associated with the Enlightenment are reflected in the Declaration of the Rights of Man and Citizen? How were France and its government reorganized in the early years of the revolution? Why has the Civil Constitution of the Clergy been called the greatest blunder of the National Assembly?
4. Why were some political factions dissatisfied with the constitutional settlement of 1791? What was the revolution of 1792? Why did it take place? Who were the *sans-culottes?* How did they acquire political influence? How influential were they, particularly during the Reign of Terror? What initially drew the *sans-*

culottes and the Jacobins together? What ended their cooperation?
5. Why did France go to war with Austria in 1792? What were the benefits and drawbacks for France of fighting an external war while in the midst of a domestic political revolution? What were the causes of the Terror? How did the rest of Europe react to the French Revolution and the Terror?
6. In what ways did the French Revolution both live up to and betray its motto: "equality, liberty and fraternity"? Did French women benefit from the revolution? Did French peasants benefit from it?

SUGGESTED READINGS

K. M. BAKER, *Inventing the French Revolution: Essays on French Political Culture in the Eighteenth Century* (1990). Important essays on political thought before and during the revolution.

K. M. BAKER and C. LUCAS, eds., *The French Revolution and the Creation of Modern Political Culture*, 3 vols. (1987). A splendid collection of important original articles on all aspects of politics during the revolution.

C. BLUM, *Rousseau and the Republic of Virtue: The Language of Politics in the French Revolution* (1986). An exploration of the role of Rousseau's political ideals in the debates of the French Revolution.

R. COBB, *The People's Armies* (1987). The best treatment in English of the revolutionary army.

F. FEHÉR, *The French Revolution and the Birth of Modernity* (1990). A wide-ranging collection of essays on political and cultural facets of the revolution.

J. GODECHOT, *The Counter-Revolution: Doctrine and Action, 1789–1803* (1971). An examination of opposition to the revolution.

P. HIGONNET, *Goodness beyond Virtue: Jacobins during the French Revolution* (1998). An outstanding work that clearly relates political values to political actions.

E. KENNEDY, *A Cultural History of the French Revolution* (1989). An important examination of the role of the arts, schools, clubs, and intellectual institutions.

D. G. LEVY, H. B. APPLEWHITE, and M. D. JOHNSON, eds. and trans., *Women in Revolutionary Paris, 1789–1795* (1979). A remarkable collection of documents on the subject.

S. E. MELZER and L. W. RABINE, eds., *Rebel Daughters: Women and the French Revolution* (1992). A collection of essays exploring various aspects of the role and image of women in the French Revolution.

M. OZOUF, *Festivals and the French Revolution* (1988). A pioneering study of the role of the public festivals in the revolution.

R. R. PALMER, *The Age of Democratic Revolution: A Political History of Europe and America, 1760–1800*, 2 vols. (1941). An impressive survey of the political turmoil in the transatlantic world.

R. R. PALMER, *Twelve Who Ruled: The Committee of Public Safety During the Terror* (1959, 1964). A clear narrative and analysis of the policies and problems of the committee.

C. PROCTOR, *Women, Equality, and the French Revolution* (1990). An examination of the manner in which ideas of the Enlightenment and the attitudes of revolutionaries affected the legal status of women.

A. SOBOUL, *The Parisian Sans-Culottes and the French Revolution, 1793–94* (1964). The best work on the subject.

D. G. SUTHERLAND, *France, 1789–1815: Revolution and Counterrevolution* (1986). A major synthesis based on recent scholarship in social history.

T. TACKETT, *Becoming a Revolutionary: The Deputies of the French National Assembly and the Emergence of a Revolutionary Culture (1789–1790)* (1996). The best study of the early months of the revolution.

D. K. VAN KLEY, *The Religious Origins of the French Revolution: From Calvin to the Civil Constitution, 1560–1791* (1996). Examines the manner in which debates within French Catholicism influenced the coming of the revolution.

Chapter 20
The Age of Napoleon and the Triumph of Romanticism

KEY TOPICS

- Napoleon's rise, his coronation as emperor, and his administrative reforms
- Napoleon's conquests, the creation of a French Empire, and Britain's enduring resistance
- The invasion of Russia and Napoleon's decline
- The reestablishment of a European order at the Congress of Vienna
- Romanticism and the reaction to the Enlightenment

The French Revolution created many new property owners, particularly among the peasantry. By the late 1790s, large numbers of these people were losing confidence in the ability of the unstable Directory to protect the gains they had made. The citizens' army, which had successfully defended the revolution, seemed better able to maintain order.

Napoleon Bonaparte was the most politically astute of the army's generals. Once in power, he consolidated many of the achievements of the revolution but ultimately overthrew the republic and declared himself emperor. Napoleon turned France's army into an instrument for conquest, and he waged offensive war for more than a decade. Europe's old political and social order was overturned, but a fierce new nationalism was born. This patriotic fervor created alliances among Napoleon's enemies that enabled them eventually to overwhelm him.

The Napoleonic era saw the flowering of the romantic movement, a new phase in the history of European culture. Some romantic ideas (e.g., nationalism) sprang from the French Revolution; others, such as respect for history and religion, had been opposed by the revolutionaries.

The Rise of Napoleon Bonaparte

The chief danger to the Directory came from royalists who believed that the restoration of the Bourbon monarchy offered the best hope for restoring stability to France. In the spring elections of 1797, constitutional monarchists and their sympathizers won the majority of offices. To preserve the republic, the Directory staged a *coup d'état* on 18 Fructidor (September 4, 1797). Men loyal to the Directory took control of the

Napoleon Bonaparte used his military successes to consolidate his political leadership as First Consul and later as Emperor of France. In this heroic image, Jacques-Louis David portrays Napoleon as a force of nature conquering not only the armies of the enemies of France but also the Alps. On the rocks in the foreground his name follows those of Hannibal and Charlemagne, other great generals who had led armies over the Alps. Bildarchiv Preussischer Kulturbesitz

legislature; imposed censorship; exiled some of their enemies; and asked Napoleon Bonaparte, the officer who had put down the riots spawned in 1795 by the Thermidorian Reaction, to protect the government once again.

Napoleon Bonaparte was born in 1769 on the Mediterranean island of Corsica. France's annexation of Corsica a year earlier made it possible for him to go to French schools and obtain a commission as a French artillery officer (1785). Although his family was impoverished minor nobility, he was a fiery Jacobin who strongly supported the revolution. During the Thermidorian Reaction, this radical background threatened his career, but his successful defense of the Directory from attack by the Parisian mob on October 5, 1795, won him a promotion and a command in Italy.

Early Military Victories

Prussia and Spain made peace with France in 1795. But when Britain and Austria refused to accept France's annexation of Belgium, France put pressure on them by sending Napoleon into Italy to take the provinces of Lombardy and Venetia from Austria. Napoleon quickly crushed the Austrians and, on his own initiative, concluded the Treaty of Campo Formio (October 1797). It took Austria out of the war and acknowledged France's domination of Italy and Switzerland.

Napoleon did not think that it was possible to invade Britain directly from France. Instead, he proposed undermining Britain by weakening its control over its empire. By taking Egypt from the Ottomans, Napoleon hoped to acquire bases that would enable him to drive the British fleet from the Mediterranean and cut Britain's communications with India. The French overran Egypt, but Napoleon's plan failed because England's admiral, Horatio Nelson (1758–1805), destroyed the French fleet at Abukir (August 1, 1798). Napoleon was stranded in Egypt, and his campaign there frightened Russia, Austria, and the Ottomans into joining Britain in the Second Coalition, an alliance against France. By 1799 France was facing invasion.

The Constitution of the Year VIII

As confidence in the Directory faded, one of the directors (the Abbé Siéyès) orchestrated a plot to establish a new government with an executive strong enough to ignore the whims of the electorate. Since military support was essential to the success of the coup, Napoleon spotted an opportunity. He deserted his doomed army in Egypt and returned to France in October 1799. Some people thought that he deserved a court-martial, but Siéyès needed the military assistance Napoleon could offer. On 19 Brumaire (November 10, 1799), troops commanded by Napoleon dispersed the legislature and cleared the way for Siéyès's faction to propose a new constitution.

Siéyès wanted to vest executive authority in three consuls, a title borrowed from the Roman Republic. But Napoleon swept him aside and in December (1799) issued the Constitution of the Year VIII. Behind a screen of democratic and republican gestures, this document vested full authority in a magistrate called the First Consul, the office claimed by Napoleon. Napoleon anticipated the dictators of the twentieth century by combining military force and the popular rhetoric of revolution and nationalism to mobilize a nation for imperial expansion.

The Consulate in France (1799–1804)

The French Revolution ended with Napoleon's Consulate. From the perspective of most members of the Third Estate, it had achieved its goals. Hereditary privilege was abolished. Obstacles to the careers of professionals and merchants had been removed. The peasants were satisfied with the land they had acquired and the termination of their feudal duties. The propertied classes were politically influential and profoundly conservative, and they did not want to imperil their new privileges or share them with the lower social orders. Since they believed that Napoleon would provide the best defense for the status quo, they overwhelmingly approved his constitution in a national plebiscite.

Suppressing Foreign Enemies and Domestic Opposition

Napoleon pleased his supporters by making peace with France's enemies. Russia had already left the Second Coalition, and a French victory at Marengo, Italy, in 1800 induced Austria to end hostilities. Britain, abandoned by its allies, came to terms in 1802 and signed the Treaty of Amiens.

Having secured the nation externally, Napoleon set about restoring peace internally. He courted his enemies, issued a general amnesty, and provided employment for people of all political persuasions. He found offices for those who had led the Reign of Terror, those who had fled it, those who favored constitutional monarchy, and those who had been agents of the Old Regime. Napoleon valued loyalty to his person above ideology, and he was ruthless and efficient in eliminating his enemies. He created a highly centralized administration and employed secret police. He stamped out a royalist rebellion in the west and, for the first time in years, brought Brittany and the Vendée under the control of the central government.

Napoleon seized on every opportunity to destroy potential threats to his regime. In 1804 his soldiers even violated the sovereignty of the German state of Baden by invading it to capture the Bourbon Duke of Enghien. The duke was accused of leading a royalist plot and put to death even though Napoleon knew him to be innocent. Because the episode turned other nations against France, Charles Maurice de Talleyrand-Périgord (1754–1838), Napoleon's foreign minister, later branded it "worse than a crime—a blunder."

Concordat with the Roman Catholic Church

Religion was a source of tensions that threatened to create problems for Napoleon's government. Some Roman Catholic clergy were in favor of a counterrevolution, and many pious laypeople were unhappy with the secular nature of the society the revolution had created. Napoleon understood religion's value as an instrument of social control, and he was determined to harness it for the benefit of the state. In 1801 he shocked his anticlerical supporters by concluding a concordat with Pope Pius VII. The agreement acknowledged "Catholicism to be the religion of the great majority of French citizens." This restored the official status of the Roman Catholic Church, but Napoleon did not grant the church any power or independence. Its clergy had to swear an oath of loyalty to the state. The state named all its bishops. It paid their salaries, and it provided financial support for one priest in each

of its parishes. In exchange, the church gave up claims to the property it had lost to the revolution. In 1802, the Organic Articles declared the supremacy of the state over the church. The influence of Roman Catholicism was further countered by extending privileges to Protestant and Jewish groups.

The Napoleonic Code

In 1802 a plebiscite granted Napoleon the office of consul for life. He then revised the constitution to give himself supreme power and further centralized authority by issuing a new codification of French law. The Civil Code of 1804—the so-called Napoleonic Code—safeguarded property and the established social order. It confirmed the abolition of privileges based on birth. State offices were no longer to be sold, but appointments were to be made on the basis of merit. Conservative regulations affecting labor and women were issued. Workers' organizations were forbidden. Fathers were granted extensive control over their children and men over their wives. Laws of primogeniture were rejected in favor of a system that distributed an estate among all a decedent's children—including females. Married women, however, could dispose of their property only with the consent of their husbands, and divorce remained more difficult for women than for men. Since the Napoleonic Code superseded a patchwork of earlier legal customs that had differed from region to region, women could no longer protect their interests, as they had previously, by exploiting confusions within the law.

Establishing a Dynasty

In 1804 a failed assassination attempt gave Napoleon an excuse to end the republic and declare himself emperor. He argued that the establishment of a dynasty would, by creating a recognized heir, secure the future of the government and make attempts on his life pointless. Yet another constitution was promulgated and overwhelmingly ratified in a plebiscite. Napoleon invited the pope to the cathedral of Notre Dame to witness his coronation, but not to crown him. Napoleon I placed the crown on his own head. He had no intention of allowing anyone to think that his authority depended on the church.

Napoleon's Empire (1804–1814)

Between his coronation as emperor in 1804 and his defeat at Waterloo in 1815, Napoleon conquered most of Europe. His campaigns astonished the world, redrew political borders, and unleashed the powerful forces of nationalism. The weapon that Napoleon wielded so effectively was a French nation that had been militarily mobilized by its revolution. He could muster as many as 700,000 soldiers at a time, risk as many as 100,000 in a single battle, endure heavy losses, and return to fight again. No single enemy could match his resources, and even coalitions failed—until Napoleon made mistakes that led to his own defeat.

Conquering an Empire

The Peace of Amiens (1802) between France and Great Britain was merely a truce, for Napoleon's ambition convinced his neighbors that they could not live with him. When he sent an army to recover Haiti from rebels, the British assumed that this would be only the first stage in a campaign to win back France's American empire. His interventions in the Dutch Republic, Italy, and Switzerland, and the role the Treaty of Campo Formio (1797) had given him in the reorganization of Germany created even greater anxiety. As Austria's influence in Germany had declined, newly augmented states had developed in western Germany, and all were dependent on Napoleon.

BRITISH NAVAL SUPREMACY   In May 1803, Britain declared war on France. William Pitt the Younger returned as prime minister in 1804 and organized a new alliance, the Third Coalition. Russia and Austria again joined Britain in opposing France's aggression. On October 21, 1805, a great naval victory raised the allies' hopes. The British admiral, Horatio, Lord Nelson, destroyed the combined French and Spanish fleets at the Battle of Trafalgar. The victory cost Nelson his life, but it ended the fear of a French invasion of Britain and guaranteed British control of the sea for the rest of the war.

NAPOLEONIC VICTORIES IN CENTRAL EUROPE   On land the story was different. Before Trafalgar, Napoleon had marched down the Danube River to attack his continental enemies. In mid-October, at Ulm, he forced a large Austrian army to surrender, and this enabled him to occupy Vienna. On December 2, 1805, in perhaps his greatest victory, he defeated a combined Austrian and Russian army at Austerlitz. In the Treaty of Pressburg that followed Austria agreed to withdraw totally from Italy and leave Napoleon in control of everything on the Italian peninsula north of Rome. In July 1806, Napoleon set up the Confederation of the Rhine and removed most of the western German principalities from the Austrian Habsburgs' Holy Roman Empire. Francis II of Austria then ceded the end of that empire and assumed the title Emperor of Austria.

When Prussia, which had remained neutral up to this point, declared war, Napoleon crushed its famous army at the battles of Jena and Auerstädt (October 14, 1806). Two weeks later he was in Berlin. On June 13, 1807, he defeated the Russians at Friedland and moved on to Königsberg, the capital of East Prussia. The emperor of France had become the master of Germany and was now able to threaten Britain's economy by closing continental ports to British traders.

TREATY OF TILSIT   Unable to fight another battle, Tsar Alexander I (r. 1801–1825) made peace. On July 7, 1807, he signed the Treaty of Tilsit and confirmed France's territorial gains. Alexander was able to save Prussia from extinction but at the cost of the loss of half its territory.

Napoleon disposed of the lands he conquered as if they were the private property belonging to his family. He, as head of a Corsican clan, ruled a great French empire, which he surrounded with satellite states governed by his relatives. His stepson ruled Italy. Three of his brothers and his brother-in-law became kings. (Only his brother Lucien, whose wife Napoleon disliked, was denied a kingdom.) This aggrandizement of Napoleon's family was unpopular, and it created the potential for serious resistance.

The Continental System

The Treaty of Tilsit isolated Britain as the only major power still opposed to France. Since Napoleon was unable to compete with the British navy, he resorted to economic warfare. By cutting off Europe's trade with Britain, he hoped to cripple the British economy and cause domestic unrest that would culminate in revolution. In 1807 he issued the Milan Decree to intimidate the neutral nations still remaining on the Continent and force them to take part in France's boycott of British goods.

Napoleon's Continental System backfired. It hurt the European economies more than the British, for Britain had access to growing markets in North and South America and the eastern Mediterranean. Napoleon refused to help things by establishing free trade within his empire, and he imposed tariffs that favored France. This reduced the willingness of merchants elsewhere to cooperate with the boycott of Britain, and it encouraged smuggling. It was in part to prevent smuggling that Napoleon invaded Spain in 1808 and began the campaign that led to his ruin.

European Response to the Empire

Napoleon's policies were intended first and foremost for his own glory and that of France, but his conquests also spread Enlightenment reforms and the ideals of France's revolution. Wherever he ruled, the Napoleonic Code was imposed, hereditary social distinctions were abolished, feudal dues disappeared, peasants were freed from serfdom, the guilds and oligarchies that had long dominated urban life were deprived of power, churches were subordinated to the state, and policies of religious toleration replaced church monopolies. These reforms outlasted Napoleon's regime. With the addition of a demand for the kind of representative, constitutional government originally envisioned by the French revolutionaries, they formed the program for which later generations of European liberal reformers fought.

German Nationalism and Prussian Reform

Napoleon had a dramatic effect on the German states. There had never been a unified Germany, and the great German writers of the Enlightenment (e.g., Immanuel Kant, Friedrich von Schiller, and Gotthold Lessing) were neither politically active nor nationalistic. Nationalism was a new idea associated with the romantic movement that arose in Germany early in the nineteenth century.

In the beginning, German nationalists simply celebrated the uniqueness of German culture, which they said sprang from the special history of the German people. But Napoleon's humiliation of Prussia at Jena in 1806 changed their message. They began to promote nationalism as a safeguard for German culture. They warned that conquest by France endangered the independence and achievements of the German-speaking peoples, and they argued that these peoples had to unite if they hoped to survive the French onslaught. France had become powerful by appealing to the patriotism of all its people, and the German nationalists hoped that something similar could guarantee a future for Germany.

After Tilsit, only Prussia was in a position to indulge patriotic feelings. Other German states were either under Napoleon's thumb or actively collaborating with him. German nationalists from other states, therefore, fled to Prussia, where they called for unification and reform—ideas that were anathema to Prussia's ruler, Frederick William III, and to the Junker nobility. After its losses at Jena, however, Prussia had no choice but to reform and reorganize. The reforms that were implemented were the work of Baron von Stein (1757–1831) and Count von Hardenberg (1750–1822). Neither man wanted to reduce the autocratic power of the Prussian monarch or weaken the Junkers who staffed the state bureaucracy and the army officer corps. Their intent was to fight France by imitating what it had become: that is, a democracy led by a strong monarchy. To this end, Stein ended the Junker monopoly of landholding and abolished serfdom. But the Junkers did not permit as clean a sweep of medieval customs as was achieved in the western principalities of Germany. Prussian peasants were allowed to leave the land if they chose, but those who stayed continued to owe manorial labor. The end of serfdom was progressive politics, but it did nothing to solve Prussia's social and economic problems. These were due to a population explosion that enlarged the country's landless labor force.

Prussia's loss at Jena had made it clear that its army of serfs and mercenaries commanded by incompetent nobles was not the equal of France's companies of free patriots led by officers chosen for merit rather than birth. To remedy the situation, Prussia's reformers abolished inhumane punishments, nurtured patriotism, gave merit

Francisco Goya Memorializes a Night of Executions: The Third of May, 1808

In 1807 Spain allied with France against Portugal, and Napoleon sent troops into Spain. By 1808, the Spaniards had come to view the French as an army of occupation and to resent their presence. Revolts broke out, the French exiled the members of Spain's Bourbon dynasty, and confirmed their hold on Spain by seating Napoleon's brother Joseph on its throne.

Early in May 1808, the French responded to riots in Madrid by ordering retaliatory executions.

Goya y Lucientes, Francisco de Goya. *The Third of May, 1808.* 1814–1815. Oil painting on canvas. Museo del Prado, Madrid, Spain. Scala/Art Resource, NY

No trials were held to discover the identity of the rioters. A number of Spaniards were simply randomly seized and shot. Popular outrage at the slaughter inaugurated a grass-roots campaign to drive the French from Spain. When the Bourbon monarchy was finally restored in 1815, Francisco Goya (1745–1828) commemorated Spain's liberation with the painting illustrated here.

The Third of May, 1808 is one of the earliest works dedicated to the victims of the kind of ideologically motivated combat that has dominated modern warfare. Goya interpreted the Madrid executions as a confrontation between two types of military power: that of the scientifically equipped soldier who kills efficiently and mechanically; and that of the impassioned civilian guerilla (a term coined in Goya's era) who fights however he can. The latter symbolized the heroism of the ordinary citizen whose pride in himself as a patriot was fundamental to the nationalism promoted by the romantic movement. Goya equated the victims of the new national wars of liberation with the religious martyrs of earlier ages. The pose of the central figure in the painting is meant to conjure up thoughts of Christ's crucifixion. Spain's conservative monarchs, however, would have had no sympathy with popular uprisings and would have seen Goya's subjects less as men dying for liberty than as loyal subjects sacrificing themselves in defense of their rightful sovereigns.

Sources: Alfonso E. Perez Sanchez and Eleanor A. Sayre, *Goya and the Spirit of Enlightenment* (Boston: Museum of Fine Arts, 1989); Albert Boime, *Art in an Age of Bonapartism 1800–1815* (Chicago: University of Chicago Press, 1990), pp. 210–212, 297–300; Janis A. Tomlinson, *Goya in the Twilight of Enlightenment* (New Haven: Yale University Press, 1992), pp. 131–149; Robert Rosenblum and H. W. Janson, *19th-Century Art* (Englewood Cliffs, New Jersey: Prentice-Hall, Inc. and New York: Harry N. Abrams, Inc, Publishers: 1984), pp. 55–56.

promotions, admitted commoners to the officer corps, and organized war colleges to modernize strategy and tactics. These measures began to restore Prussia's standing as a military power, but Napoleon imposed a limit on the size of the Prussian army. The Prussians evaded his ceiling of 42,000 active troops by raising a new group of recruits each year and assigning those who were completing their training to the reserves. In 1813, after Napoleon's retreat, Prussia introduced universal conscription, and by 1814 it had an army of 270,000 men.

The Wars of Liberation

SPAIN   Resentment of French occupation was stronger in Spain than elsewhere in Europe. In 1807 a French army was allowed to enter the Iberian Peninsula to help Spain put pressure on Portugal, England's ally. The army stayed in Spain to protect lines of supply, and in 1808 Napoleon deposed the Spanish Bourbon dynasty and made his brother Joseph king of Spain. Subsequent attacks on the privileges of the church increased public outrage, and the peasants, urged on by the lower clergy and the monks, rose in a general rebellion.

Napoleon faced a new kind of warfare in Spain. Instead of massed armies, small guerilla bands cut his communication lines, killed stragglers from his forces, destroyed isolated garrisons, and disappeared into the mountains before he could organize a response. The British eventually sent an army commanded by the future duke of Wellington, Sir Arthur Wellesley (1769–1852), to aid the Spanish insurgents. This began a long campaign that drained French soldiers from other European fronts and contributed to Napoleon's eventual defeat.

AUSTRIA   France's troubles in Spain tempted Austria to renew the war. Austria wanted to avenge German losses at Austerlitz, but it seriously miscalculated. The help Austria counted on from German princes did not materialize, and Napoleon's difficulties elsewhere were not as great as had been assumed. Napoleon defeated the Austrians at the battle of Wagram and forced them to agree, in the Peace of Schönbrunn, to surrender territory containing over 3.5 million people. Among the other spoils Napoleon claimed was Marie Louise, the Austrian em-

Napoleon's second wife, Marie Louise (1791–1847), bore him a son. It was clear that Napoleon hoped to establish a new imperial dynasty in France. Marie Louise (1791–1847) and the King of Rome (1811–73) (oil on canvas) by Francois Pascal Simon Gerard, Baron (1770–1837). Chateau de Versailles, France/Bridgeman Art Library, London/Giraudon

peror's daughter. Napoleon's wife, Josephine de Beauharnais, was forty-six and had borne him no children. His desire to found a dynasty linked with Europe's most regal lines prompted him to divorce Josephine and marry the eighteen-year-old Habsburg princess.

The Invasion of Russia

The Franco-Russian alliance concluded at Tilsit was unpopular with Russia's nobles. They disliked France's liberal politics, and Napoleon's Continental System interfered with their timber sales to Britain. Tsar Alexander I also had a long list of grievances against Napoleon. Russia received no

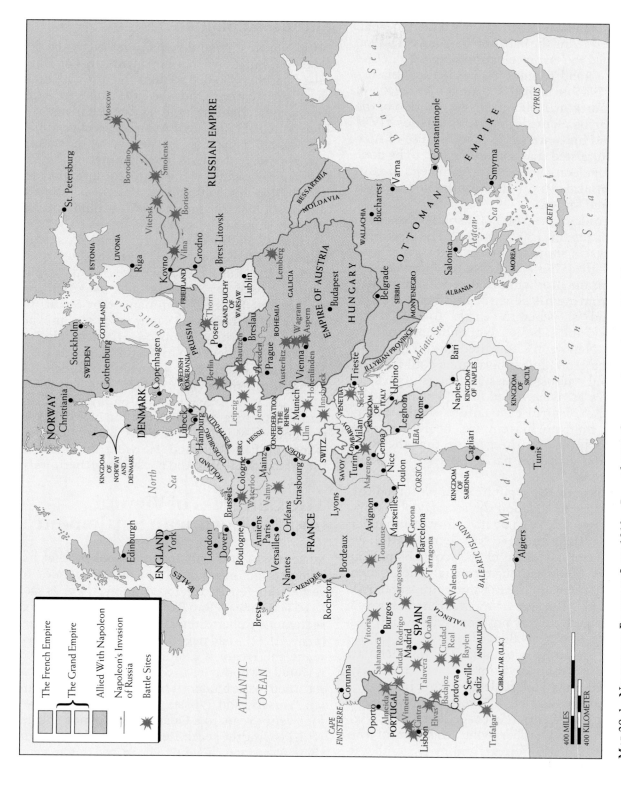

Map 20–1 Napoleonic Europe in Late 1812   By mid-1812 the areas shown in peach had been incorporated into France and most of the rest of Europe was controlled by or allied with Napoleon. Russia had, however, withdrawn from the Continental System, and Napoleon's decline was about to begin.

The French Empire
The Grand Empire
Allied With Napoleon
Napoleon's Invasion of Russia
Battle Sites

400 MILES
400 KILOMETER

help from France in its struggle with the Ottoman Empire. Following the battle of Wagram, Napoleon had annoyed the tsar by creating a French satellite state (the Grand Duchy of Warsaw) on Russia's doorstep. Napoleon had violated the Treaty of Tilsit by annexing Holland. His recognition of the French Marshal Bernadotte as King Charles XIV of Sweden and his marriage to Marie Louise of Austria also suggested that something had to be done to curb Napoleon's ambitions. At the end of 1810 Russia withdrew from the Continental System and prepared for war.

Napoleon gathered 600,000 soldiers to crush Russia's army of 160,000 men. His preferred strategy was a short campaign determined by a decisive battle, but the Russians deprived him of that option. Knowing that it was foolish to risk confronting his superior numbers, they retreated and "scorched the earth" to deprive his men of food and supplies. Not enough remained to enable Napoleon's so-called Grand Army to live off the land, and supply lines could not be maintained across Russia's huge expanse. Napoleon's advisers urged him to abandon the venture. But, fearful that failure would undermine his hold on his empire, he refused. He staked his future on the gamble that the Russians would give him battle rather than abandon Moscow.

In September 1812, public opinion forced the Russian army to abandon the strategy of victory through retreat devised by its canny commander General Kutuzov and give Napoleon a battle. At Borodino, not far west of Moscow, Napoleon fought his bloodiest engagement. The French lost 30,000 men and the Russians almost 60,000. But since the Russian army was not destroyed and Napoleon gained nothing substantial, his victory was the equivalent of a defeat. The Russians set fire to Moscow and left Napoleon to face a fierce winter far from home with a badly diminished army and inadequate supplies.

Napoleon made several overtures to Alexander offering to negotiate a peace, but the tsar ignored him. By October what was left of the Grand Army had to retreat, and by December it was clear that the Russian fiasco was raising plots against Napoleon at home. He left the remnants of his army to struggle westward, and he hastened to Paris. Only 100,000 of the Grand Army's 600,000 soldiers may have survived to describe their terrible ordeal.

European Coalition

Napoleon weathered the crisis created by the disaster. He put down his opponents in Paris and raised another 350,000 soldiers. Neither the Prussians, the Austrians, nor the Russians were eager to continue fighting, and Prince Klemens von Metternich (1773–1859), Austria's foreign minister, wanted Napoleon to survive with enough power to prevent Russia from dominating Europe. Napoleon, however, refused to compromise, for he felt that his self-made dynasty—lacking the support of history and tradition—would not survive if it showed any sign of weakness.

The last and most powerful coalition against Napoleon formed in 1813. Assisted by British money, the Russians drove westward to join armies raised by Prussia and Austria, and Wellington, Britain's commander in Spain, invaded France. Napoleon's new army was inexperienced and poorly equipped. His generals had lost some confidence in him, and they were tired. Napoleon himself was worn out and sick. He managed one more victory at Dresden, but in October he was decisively beaten by the allied forces at Leipzig ("the Battle of the Nations"). By the end of March 1814, Paris had fallen, and Napoleon had abdicated. He went into exile on the island of Elba off the coast of northern Italy.

The Congress of Vienna and the European Settlement

Since it was primarily fear of Napoleon that had held the victorious coalition of his enemies together, differences developed among them as soon as he was gone. Before Paris fell, the British foreign secretary—Robert Stewart, Viscount Castlereagh (1769–1822)—had negotiated a preliminary agreement: the Treaty of Chaumont (March 9, 1814). It restored the Bourbons to the throne of a France that returned to the borders it had in 1792. Britain, Austria, Russia, and Prussia committed themselves for twenty years to a Quadruple Alliance charged with keeping the peace. Remaining problems—and there were many—were to be ironed out at a conference to be held in Vienna.

Territorial Adjustments

The Congress of Vienna met from September 1814 until November 1815. The great powers

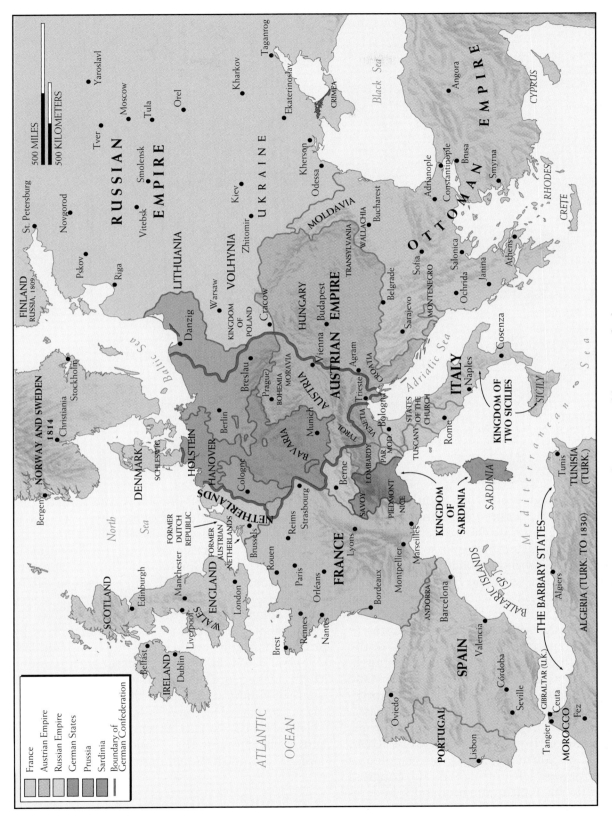

MAP 20–2 EUROPE AFTER THE CONGRESS OF VIENNA IN 1815 *The most notable territorial adjustments agreed to at the Congress of Vienna concerned areas along France's borders (i.e., the Netherlands, Prussia, Switzerland, and Piedmont), Poland, and northern Italy.*

In this political cartoon of the Congress of Vienna, Tallyrand simply watches which way the wind is blowing, Castlereagh hesitates, while the monarchs of Russia, Prussia, and Austria form the dance of the Holy Alliance. The king of Saxony holds onto his crown and the republic of Geneva pays homage to the kingdom of Sardinia. Bildarchiv Preussischer Kulturbesitz

found it easy to agree on what should be done about France. None wanted any single state to dominate Europe, and all were determined that France should not attempt to do so again. The restoration of the Bourbon monarchy, which was temporarily popular with the French, and a fair boundary settlement succeeded in keeping France calm.

The powers also established border states to block future French expansion: a kingdom of the Netherlands (including Belgium) in the north, and a combined Genoa and Piedmont in the south. Austria resumed control of parts of northern Italy. On France's eastern frontier, Prussia, which had already expanded into eastern Europe, was given new territories along the Rhine River. In the rest of Germany, most of Napoleon's arrangements were left untouched. The congress endorsed rule by legitimate monarchs and rejected the French Revolution's republican and democratic ideologies.

Most difficult for the congress was the reorganization of eastern Europe. Alexander I of Russia wanted all of Poland. Prussia was willing to give it to him if it received all of Saxony. But Austria refused to surrender its share of Poland, and it did not want to see Prussia grow and to allow Russia to penetrate deeper into central Europe. The congress came to a standstill, and a new war might have developed had France not provided a way out. Talleyrand, who represented France at Vienna, suggested that an agreement supported by Britain, Austria, and France might intimidate Alexander. When news of a secret treaty among them leaked out, the tsar accepted a smaller share of Poland and Frederick William III of Prussia only a part of Saxony. Talleyrand's strategy restored France's status as one of Europe's great powers by showing that France still mattered as a player in international politics.

The Hundred Days and the Quadruple Alliance

News that the allies in Vienna were fighting among themselves encouraged Napoleon to escape from Elba and return to France (on March 1, 1815). The French army had remained loyal to him, and many French people believed him to be a stronger protector than the Bourbon monarchy. Napoleon was quickly restored to power, promising a liberal constitution and a peaceful foreign policy. The allies were not convinced. They declared Napoleon an outlaw (a new possibility under international law) and sent armies to crush him. On June 18, 1815, Wellington, aided by the Prussians under Field Marshal von Blücher, defeated Napoleon at Waterloo, Belgium. Napoleon again abdicated and was exiled to Saint Helena, a tiny Atlantic island off the coast of Africa. He died there in 1821.

The Hundred Days, as the period of Napoleon's return is called, frightened the great powers into imposing harsher terms on France. These included minor territorial losses, a war indemnity, and an army of occupation. Tsar Alexander, under the personal influence of an increasingly mystical religious faith, proposed a "Holy Alliance" of monarchs who agreed to act together in accordance with Christian principles. Austria and Prussia signed; but Castlereagh thought it absurd, so England abstained. The Quadruple Alliance of England, Austria, Prussia, and Russia was renewed on November 20, 1815.

The Congress of Vienna negotiated a settlement that allowed Europe to avoid general war for a hundred years. The leaders of Europe had learned from past failures that the purpose of a treaty should not be to claim victory but to secure peace. Their goal was not to punish France but to make arrangements that would guarantee future stability. This necessitated the creation of a balance of power and a process for negotiating adjustments as conditions changed. Politicians abandoned the simple proposition that a nation's strength depended on maintaining a trade surplus (i.e., the belief that one people could prosper only at the expense of another). They began to operate on the assumption that general growth in agriculture, commerce, and industry could help all states thrive.

The diplomats at Vienna have been criticized for failing to recognize the great nationalistic and democratic movements that would stir the nineteenth century. Their chief concern, however, was to cure past ills. To anticipate problems that had yet to manifest themselves, they would have had to be more than human.

Significant Dates from the Era of Napoleonic Europe	
1797	The Treaty of Campo Formio
1798	Nelson defeats the French navy
1799	The Consulate is established in France
1801	Concordat between France and the papacy
1802	Treaty of Amiens
1803	War renewed between France and Britain
1804	Execution of the Duke of Enghien
	Napoleonic Civil Code issued
	Napoleon crowned emperor
1805	Nelson wins at Trafalgar (October 21)
	Battle of Austerlitz (December 2)
1806	Battle of Jena
	Continental System imposed (November 21)
1897	Treaty of Tilsit
1808	Spain revolts against Napoleon
1809	Battle of Wagram
	Napoleon marries Marie Louise of Austria
1810	Russia leaves the Continental System
1812	Invasion of Russia, battle at Borodino
1813	Leipzig ("Battle of the Nations")
1814	Treaty of Chaumont and the Quadruple Alliance
	Congress of Vienna convenes (September)
1815	Napoleon returns from Elba (March 1)
	Battle of Waterloo (June 18)
	Holy Alliance formed (September 26)
	Quadruple Alliance renewed (November 20)
1821	Napoleon dies on Saint Helena

The Romantic Movement

During the French Revolution and Napoleon's reign an important new intellectual movement called *romanticism* took root in Europe. It was, in part, a reaction to the Enlightenment. Romantic writers objected to what they considered to be the narrowness of the eighteenth-century *philosophes'* search for truth. They accused the

In A Philosopher in a Moonlit Churchyard, *the British artist Philip James de Loutherbourg captured many of the themes of the romantic movement. The painting suggests a sense of history, a love of Gothic architecture, a sense of the importance of religion, and a belief that the world is essentially mysterious.* Philip James de Loutherbourg (RA) (1740–1812), *A Philosopher in a Moolit Churchyard*, signed and dated 1790. Oil on canvas, 34 × 27 in. (86.3 × 68.5 cm). B1974.3.4. Yale Center for British Art, Paul Mellon Collection.

latter of holding everything to a narrow scientific standard (i.e., of trying to reduce everything to geometrical and mathematical models). Romantic thinkers refused to conceive of human nature as primarily rational. They insisted on the importance of human feelings and imagination. For them inspiration, as well as reason, was a means to knowledge.

During the Age of Romanticism (1780–1830), unique and often independent romantic movements flourished in Germany, England, and France. Despite national differences, each reacted to the Enlightenment by championing the imagination or some other intuitive intellectual faculty. Unlike the *philosophes,* the romantics valued the art, literature, and architecture of the Middle Ages, and many urged a revival of medieval Christianity. They were deeply interested in folklore, folk songs, and fairy tales. They were fascinated by dreams, hallucinations, sleepwalking, and all phenomena that suggest that there is a world beyond the reach of empirical observation, sensory data, and discursive reasoning.

Romantic Questioning of the Supremacy of Reason

Many historical streams fed the romantic movement: the individualism of the Renaissance and the Reformation, the pietism of the seventeenth century, England's Methodist revival in the eighteenth century, the eighteenth century's sentimental novels (e.g., Samuel Richardson's *Clarissa*), the so-called *Sturm und Drang* ("storm and stress") period in German literature, and German idealist philosophy. Two writers closely associated with the Enlightenment, Jean-Jacques Rousseau and Immanuel Kant, also helped to lay intellectual foundations for romanticism by casting doubt on the *philosophes'* rationalistic assumptions.

Rousseau and Education

Though sharing in the reformist spirit of the Enlightenment, Jean-Jacques Rousseau opposed many of its other facets. Romantic writers were especially drawn to Rousseau's claim that society and wealth had corrupted human nature. Rousseau theorized that the first human beings were happy, innocent creatures who lived in a state of equilibrium with nature. To become happy again, he argued, humankind had to be true to its natural state while developing the moral values essential for social life. His *Social Contract* (1762) was a prescription for reforms of political institutions that he believed would achieve that goal.

Rousseau set forth his theories about human development in a novel entitled *Émile* (1762). In *Émile* he described stages in the human maturation process and urged that each child be allowed to grow freely and individually—learning by trial and error what reality is and how best to deal with it. Parents or teachers could help most by providing the basic necessities of life and warding off manifest harm. Beyond that, Rousseau believed that adults should stay out of the way, letting nature take its course. He insisted that a child's sentiments as well as its reason should be allowed to flourish, and he claimed that his unguided method of education would result in a society dictated by the needs of nature, not distorted by human artifice. From this, the romantics concluded (1) that the uniqueness of each individual ought to be valued, and (2) that the individual, nature, and society are organically interrelated.

Kant and Reason

Immanuel Kant (1724–1804) wrote the two greatest philosophical works of the late eighteenth century: *The Critique of Pure Reason* (1781) and *The Critique of Practical Reason* (1788). They were products of an ambitious attempt to reconcile the rationalism of the Enlightenment with belief in human freedom, immortality, and the existence of God.

Kant rejected the opinion of Locke and other philosophers that knowledge was rooted in sensory experience alone. He claimed that the human mind did not simply reflect the world around it like a passive mirror. It actively imposed itself on the world of sensory experience using tools it generated itself. He called these tools "forms of sensibility" and "categories of understanding." In other words, he believed that the human mind perceives the world as it does because of its own techniques of perception. Human knowledge is not the product of an active world imposing itself on a passive mind but of an interaction between sensory experience and the mind's activity.

Kant differentiated between "pure reason," which dealt with the phenomenal world of sensory experience, and "practical reason," which intuited a "noumenal" world of ethics and aesthetics. The sphere of reality accessible to pure reason was quite limited. It could not produce evidence to support belief in transcendental things such as the existence of God, eternal life, and ultimate rewards and punishments for personal conduct. These were truths belonging to the realm of practical reason.

Kant thought that all human beings possessed an innate sense of moral duty, which he called a *categorical imperative*—an inner command to act in every situation as one would have other people act in that situation. Kant saw the existence of this imperative (of the conscience) as proof that we are endowed by nature with personal freedom. It follows logically that if we are not free, then conscience has no use or purpose; that is, we would not have the power to let conscience guide our actions. This insight gave Kant a starting point for exploring transcendental realities. Whether the romantics called it "practical reason," "fancy," "imagination," "intuition," or simply "feeling," they believed, with Kant, that human understanding was a creative act, not just the passive reception of sensory data that Hobbes, Locke, and Hume had imagined. Most romantics assumed that poets and artists possessed this creative ability in particular abundance.

Romantic Literature

The term *romantic* appeared in England and France as early as the seventeenth century as a description of literature that was judged to be unreal, sentimental, or excessively fanciful. In both England and Germany, *romantic* came to be applied to all literature that failed to observe classical forms and rules and that gave free play to the imagination. Most folk tales and much of the art of medieval Europe fell into this category. In the early nineteenth century, August Wilhelm von Schlegel (*Lectures on Dramatic Art and Literature, 1809–1811*) began to use *romantic* as a term of praise, not approbation. To him it indicated an exciting alternative to the predictable, lifeless work produced by authors who merely imitated classical models. He associated Dante, Petrarch, Boccaccio, Shakespeare, the Arthurian legends, Cervantes, and Calderón with romanticism.

The romantic movement had peaked in Germany and England before Madame de Staël (1766–1817) and Victor Hugo (1802–1885) made it a major force in France. So powerful was the classical tradition in France that no French writer openly claimed to be a romantic until 1816. The first was Henri Beyle (1783–1842) who wrote very successful novels under the pseudonym Stendhal.

The English Romantic Writers

Lockean psychology, which regarded the mind as a passive receptor of sensory data, explained poetry as an exercise of "wit" mechanically guided by prescribed rules. The English romantics disagreed. They saw poetry as proof of the mind's ability not just to respond, but to create truth. When so conceived, poetry could not be dismissed as idle play. It became the highest of human acts, the fulfillment of humanity's unique ability to transcend the level on which other sentient creatures operated.

BLAKE William Blake (1757–1827) considered the poet a seer and poetry to be a translation of visions. In the 1790s he suffered a deep depression brought on by his inability to reconcile his vision of a world of innocence and beauty with the harsh realities of experience. The more one studied the world with the tools of reason, the more the life of the imagination and its spiritual values seemed to recede. Blake was deeply troubled by a strong sense of contradiction between the poet's childlike, inspired vision of the world's glory and the harsh view of the world that emerged from daily life. He blamed the discordance on the materialism and injustice of English society.

COLERIDGE Samuel Taylor Coleridge (1772–1834) contributed to the development of romantic literary criticism and theory, but he is best remembered for his Gothic poems of the supernatural: "Christabel," "Kubla Khan," and "The Ancient Mariner." "The Ancient Mariner" tells the story of a sailor cursed for killing an albatross, an act that symbolizes crimes against nature and God. The poem explores guilt, punishment, and the redemptive possibilities of humility and penance. In the end, the mariner grasps the unity and beauty of all things, repents, and is delivered from the curse of having the dead albatross hung around his neck.

WORDSWORTH Coleridge's closest friend was William Wordsworth (1770–1850), with whom in 1798 he published a manifesto (*Lyrical Ballads*) calling for a new kind of poetry that rejected the rules endorsed by eighteenth-century critics. Wordsworth's "Ode on Intimations of Immortality" (1803)—written in part to console Coleridge during a personal crisis—is among his most important later works. It deals with the loss of poetic vision. Nature, which he had worshiped, had ceased to speak to him, and he feared that it might never speak again. He had lost what he believed all human beings necessarily lost as they matured—their childlike vision and original intimacy with spiritual reality.

For both Wordsworth and Coleridge, childhood was the bright period of creative imagination. Wordsworth believed that the soul had a preexistence in a celestial state before its appearance on earth. Children, being closer in time to this experience of the eternal and being undistracted by knowledge of the world, recollect the supernatural much more easily than adults. Age and urban life corrupt and deaden the adult imagination, making inner feelings and the beauty of nature seem less important. Wordsworth's book-length poem, *The Prelude* (1850), illustrated this theory by detailing a long autobiographical account of the development of the poet's mind.

LORD BYRON Most of Britain's romantic writers distrusted and disliked the greatest rebel their movement produced: Lord Byron (1788–1824). Outside England, however, his rejection of tradition and his advocacy of personal liberty caused him to be regarded as the embodiment of the "new person" of the age of the French Revolution. An unconventional love life contributed to this reputation.

Byron had little sympathy for theories about imagination, and he was outrageously skeptical and mocking even of his own beliefs. His *Don Juan* (1819), for instance, described—with ribald humor—nature's cruelty as well as its beauty, and the poem expressed an unfashionable admiration for urban life.

The German Romantic Writers

Almost all the major German romantics wrote both novels and poetry. Their novels tended to be highly sentimental. They often borrowed material from medieval romances, and they intended their characters to be interpreted as symbols more than descriptions of real individuals. They avoided purely naturalistic description.

The first German romantic novel was Ludwig Tieck's *William Lovell* (1793–1795), the story of a young man who lives for love and imagination and avoids the cold rationality that leads others to unbelief, misanthropy, and egoism. In the end, Lovell is ruined when two women, whom he naively loves, infect him with philosophy, materialism, and skepticism.

SCHLEGEL *Lucinde* (1799), by Friedrich Schlegel (1767–1845), demonstrates how the romantics became involved in the social issues of their day. The novel attacked the assumption that women could be nothing more than lovers and domestics. Lucinde is the hero's perfect companion (and an unsurpassed sexual partner). The book was considered shocking for its frank discussion of sex and its description of Lucinde as the equal of the male protagonist.

GOETHE Towering above all German writers is Johann Wolfgang von Goethe (1749–1832). He was both a romantic and a critic of the excesses of romanticism. A novel, *The Sorrows of Young Werther* (1774), first brought him to the public's attention. It depicted, through an exchange of letters, the sentimental emotions of a youth in love with another man's wife. When the correspondence ceases, grief drives Werther to suicide. The book was much admired because of its insistence on the importance of feeling and its call for people to transcend the conventions of polite society.

As Goethe aged, erotic themes yielded to ethical ones, and he began to explore relationships between morality and sensuality. *Faust*, a long dramatic poem, was his masterpiece. In Part I, published in 1808, Faust, a world-weary scholar, promises his soul to the Devil in exchange for knowledge. Faust seduces and abandons a young woman named Gretchen. When she dies, disgraced on Earth but judged worthy of heaven, he struggles with grief and guilt. In Part II of the poem, completed in 1832 (the year of Goethe's death), Faust has strange adventures with witches and mythological characters. When he finally dedicates his life to the improvement of humankind, commitment to an altruistic goal brings him peace and a knowledge of life's meaning that annuls his pact with the Devil. *Faust* was a criticism of the shallowness of much romantic thought and a description of the serious spiritual problems that faced Europeans as their commitment to the values of traditional Christianity faded.

Religion in the Romantic Period

Methodism

Enlightenment writers tried to derive religion from reason, but the romantics, like medieval mystics, saw it as an expression of deep human emotion. Methodism, a movement begun in England by John Wesley (1703–1791), an Oxford-educated Anglican priest, presented religion not as a set of concepts but as a "method" for living. In 1735 Wesley came to America as a missionary and made the acquaintance of the Moravians, a sect of German pietists. He concluded that their faith, based on unquestioning trust in God, was much stronger than his. In 1739 he had a conversion experience that assured him of his salvation and sent him forth to preach a message of simple trust. Thousands of humble people responded to his call for repentance and good works, and by the late eighteenth century Methodism had become a church with a wide following in Britain and, especially, America.

New Directions in Continental Religion

Methodism stressed inward, heartfelt religion and the duty to strive for Christian moral perfection in this life. It accepted enthusiastic emotional experience as fundamental to Christian conversion and worship. Similar religious movements also appeared on the continent. After the Thermidorian Reaction, there was a strong Roman Catholic revival in France. Viscount François René de Chateaubriand (1768–1848) argued, in *The Genius of Christianity* (1802), that the essence of religion was "passion," the emotion that doctrines and sacraments inspired in the hearts of Christians. A similar point of view was articulated by a Protestant scholar, Friedrich Schleiermacher (1768–1834). His *Speeches on Religion to Its Cultured Despisers* (1799) defined religion as a feeling of absolute dependence on an infinite reality.

Romantic Views of Nationalism and History

Romanticism, in all its forms, glorified individuality—both in persons and in cultures. German idealism provided romanticism's philosophic underpinning by arguing that the world was a projection of the subjective ego of the individual. J. G. Fichte (1762–1814) identified the individual human ego with the absolute creative power that underlies all existing things. The world is what it is, he argued, because certain human beings (e.g., Napoleon) have conceived of it in a particular way and imposed their wills on it.

Herder and Culture

Johann Gottfried Herder (1744–1803), who resented the preponderance of French culture in Germany, led Germans on a search for the roots of their identity as a "folk" (i.e., an ethnic people). Herder urged the collection of distinctive German songs and sayings. The Grimm brothers, Jakob (1785–1863) and Wilhelm (1786–1859), rose to the challenge by assembling their famous collection of fairy tales. Believing that each language and culture were the unique expressions of a people, Herder opposed the Enlightenment's advocacy of universal, rational institutions such as the Napoleonic Code. His insistence on the importance of uniqueness revived the study of history and ultimately stimulated Europe's interest in world cultures. A flood of brilliant work in comparative literature, religions, and philology resulted.

Hegel and History

Georg Wilhelm Friedrich Hegel (1770–1831), one of the most difficult and important philosophers in the history of Western civilization, exerted the most powerful romantic influence on the writing of history. He claimed that a historical period is shaped by the ideas that the people who live through it hold true. History, therefore, evolves like ideas evolve—through a process of contradiction, conflict, and resolution. The ideas that hold sway over a generation constitute a "thesis." This thesis is eventually challenged by conflicting ideas, an "antithesis." Ultimately, a "synthesis," a new consensus, emerges. It then becomes a new thesis, and the cycle begins all over again. Because each stage in the process is necessary to the one that follows it, all periods of history are of almost equal value and all cultures are important because each contributes to the clash of ideas by which humankind evolves.

In Perspective

Romanticism contributed to the emergence of nationalism, one of the strongest historical forces of the nineteenth and twentieth centuries. The Enlightenment had generally promoted a cosmopolitan outlook, while romantic thinkers stressed individuality and the worth of each separate group of people. A shared language, history, homeland, and customs were posited as the defining characteristics of a people, and the romantics assumed that each people, ethnic group, or nation ought to be an independent political entity. Only then could each protect its unique character.

The French, who under their revolutionary government and Napoleon had demonstrated the power of nationhood, inspired other peoples similarly to assert themselves. Napoleon, by toppling ancient institutions such as the Holy Roman Empire, necessitated the political reorganization of Europe. The Congress of Vienna, which undertook this task in 1815, was able to ignore popular pressure for change, but later statesmen had to deal with a hunger for reform that swept Europe from Ireland to the Ukraine.

REVIEW QUESTIONS

1. How did Napoleon rise to power? What groups supported him? What were the stages by which he eventually made himself emperor? What were his major domestic achievements? Did his rule more nearly fulfill or betray the ideals of the French Revolution?

2. What regions made up Napoleon's realm? Did each have equal status within it? How did Napoleon rule his empire? Which of his policies strengthened the empire? Which ones undermined it?

3. Why did Napoleon decide to invade Russia? Why did his campaign fail? Could you justify calling Napoleon a military genius? To what extent was his brilliance a reflection of the ineptitude of his enemies?

4. Who were the principal personalities at the Congress of Vienna? What were the most significant problems they addressed? What was the long-term significance of the Congress?

5. How does the role romantic writers assigned to feelings compare with the role Enlightenment writers claimed for reason? What questions did Rousseau and Kant raise about reason?

6. Why did poetry become important to romantic writers? How did the romantic concept of religion differ from Reformation Protestantism and Enlightenment deism? What significance did romantics see in history?

SUGGESTED READINGS

M. H. ABRAMS, *The Mirror and the Lamp: Romantic Theory and the Critical Tradition* (1958). A standard text on romantic literary theory that looks at English romanticism in the context of German romantic idealism.

M. H. ABRAMS, *Natural Supernaturalism: Tradition and Revolution in Romantic Literature* (1971). A brilliant survey of romanticism across western European literature.

F. C. BEISER, *Enlightenment, Revolution, and Romanticism: The Genesis of Modern German Political Thought, 1790–1800* (1992). The best recent study of the subject.

L. BERGERON, *France Under Napoleon* (1981). An in-depth examination of Napoleonic administration.

E. CASSIRER, *Kant's Life and Thought* (1981). A brilliant work by one of the major philosophers of this century.

D. G. CHANDLER, *The Campaigns of Napoleon* (1966). A good military study.

K. CLARK, *The Romantic Rebellion* (1973). A useful discussion that combines both art and literature.

O. CONNELLY, *Napoleon's Satellite Kingdoms* (1965). The rule of Napoleon and his family in Europe.

H. HONOUR, *Romanticism* (1979). The best introduction to the subject in terms of the fine arts.

G. N. IZENBERG, *Impossible Individuality: Romanticism, Revolution, and the Origins of Modern Selfhood, 1787–1802* (1992). Explores the concepts of individualism in Germany, England, and France.

H. KISSINGER, *A World Restored: Metternich, Castlereagh and the Problems of Peace, 1812–1822* (1957). A provocative study by an author who became an American secretary of state.

G. LEFEBVRE, *Napoleon*, 2 vols., trans. by H. Stockhold (1969). The fullest and finest biography.

R. MUIR, *Tactics and the Experience of Battle in the Age of Napoleon* (1998). A splendid account of the experience of troops in battle.

H. NICOLSON, *The Congress of Vienna* (1946). A good, readable account.

B. M. G. REARDON, *Religion in the Age of Romanticism: Studies in Early Nineteenth-Century Thought* (1985). The best introduction to this important subject.

C. TAYLOR, *Hegel* (1975). The best one-volume introduction.

J. M. THOMPSON, *Napoleon Bonaparte: His Rise and Fall* (1952). A sound biography.

T. ZIOLKOWSKI, *German Romanticism and Its Institutions* (1990). An exploration of the manner in which institutions of intellectual life influenced creative literature.

Chapter 21
The Conservative Order and the Challenges of Reform (1815–1832)

KEY TOPICS

- The challenge of nationalism and liberalism to the conservative order in the early nineteenth century
- The domestic and international politics of the conservative order from the Congress of Vienna through the 1820s
- The wars of independence in Latin America
- The revolutions of 1830 on the Continent and the passage of the Great Reform Bill in Britain

Reactionary movements that supported monarchy and aristocracy dominated European politics for the decade following the Congress of Vienna. But nationalism and liberalism, two new ideologies, challenged the traditional belief that a state was nothing more than the properties belonging to a royal dynasty. Nationalists believed that ethnicity was the true basis for statehood; they wanted to redraw the map of Europe to reflect boundaries among ethnic groups. Liberals urged states to implement moderate political reforms and establish freer economic markets.

The Challenges of Nationalism and Liberalism

The Emergence of Nationalism

The nineteenth century was the great age of *-isms*: for example, liberalism, nationalism, republicanism, socialism, and communism. Nationalism was the most powerful of the political ideologies of the era. It promoted a belief in popular sovereignty that called into question the royalist assumptions that had guided the Congress of Vienna. It held that a nation should be defined by the identity of its inhabitants, not by claims rulers made to jurisdiction over certain properties.

CREATING NATIONS   During the first half of the nineteenth century, small intellectual elites fostered the birth of nationalist identities in various parts of Europe by generating enthusiasm for the study of the histories and languages of their countrymen and women. Scholars wrote histories of their homelands and collected folk literatures. Schoolteachers spread the fruits of this work abroad to nurture the development of national languages and cultures. This won mass support for the nationalist political movements that flourished in the second half of the century.

Nationalists put a great deal of emphasis on the language used in schools and government offices. In France and Italy, official versions of the national language replaced local dialects in the schools. In parts of Scandinavia and eastern Europe, nationalists tried to revive earlier, "purer" versions of a national language. These resurrected tongues were often the inventions of modern linguists, but they served to bring people together. Standardization of speech was further aided by the increased availability of printed materials (e.g., books, journals, magazines, and newspapers) that fixed language in a permanent form. In many regions, a national printed language augmented local spoken dialects and won acceptance as the preferred instrument for serious thought and political debate. Europe developed far more linguistic uniformity than at any earlier time in its history, but there was still a great deal of variety. By 1850 less than half the people of France spoke official French.

MEANING OF NATIONHOOD   Nationalists explained nationhood, and argued for it, in different ways. But their greatest difficulty was deciding which ethnic groups had the right to be considered nations with claims to territory and political autonomy. In practice, recognition as a nation has usually been based on possession of (1) a population large enough to support a viable economy, (2) a history of significant cultural association, (3) an educated elite that spreads a national language, and (4) a capacity to defend oneself or conquer other peoples. Much domestic unrest has been created by small ethnic groups that have tried, but failed, to fulfill these criteria.

REGIONS OF NATIONALISTIC PRESSURE   During the nineteenth century, Europe dealt with continuing nationalistic upheavals on six fronts. By bringing Ireland under direct rule in 1800, England created an "Irish problem" that continues to complicate Britain's politics to this day. German nationalists, in an effort to unify all German-speaking peoples, challenged the Austrian Empire and pitted Prussia and Austria against each other. Italian nationalists tried to drive the Austrians off the Italian peninsula. Polish nationalists struggled to free their land from Russian domination. A host of eastern European groups—Hungarians, Czechs, Slovenes, and others—sought either recognition within the Austrian Empire or independence from it. And in southeastern Europe, Serbs, Greeks, Albanians, Romanians, and Bulgarians fought the Ottoman and Russian empires. Since nationalist activities ebbed and flowed in each of these areas, their rulers often thought they needed only to ride things out until stability returned. Over the course of the century, however, nationalists changed Europe's map and political culture.

Early Nineteenth-Century Political Liberalism

POLITICAL GOALS   The word *liberal*, as applied to political activity, entered the West's vocabulary during the nineteenth century. Its meaning has changed over the years, and its current use in America has little or nothing to do with what it originally signified. The liberal political program derived from the Enlightenment, from England's customary liberties, and from the so-called principles of 1789 embodied in the French Declaration of the Rights of Man and Citizen. Liberals favored equality before the law for all citizens, religious toleration, and freedom of the press. They wanted constitutional political machinery that would prevent governments from arbitrarily using their powers against the persons or property of individuals. They tended to believe that government derived its legitimacy from the freely given consent of the governed as expressed through elected, representative, or parliamentary bodies. And they insisted that ministers of state be responsible to the representatives of the people, not to a monarch.

Although the aspirations of liberal reformers were limited (and nothing like the constitutional governments the West now takes for granted existed in Europe in the early nineteenth century), conservatives did not share the liberal confidence in constitutions. They associated constitutions with the upheaval that followed the French Revolution, and they did not believe that all the political arrangements a people might need could be prescribed in a document.

Liberals tended to be educated, prosperous people who had been excluded in some way from the existing political system. They were often academics, members of the professions, or people involved in the increasingly important commercial and manufacturing segments of the economy. The monarchical, aristocratic regimes that were restored by the Congress of Vienna often failed to recognize the status achieved by these people and to provide for their economic, professional, and social aspirations.

Although liberals wanted broader political participation, they did not advocate democracy. They favored expansion of representation for the propertied classes. Second only to their hostility for aristocrats was their general contempt for the poor. Liberals wanted to reinterpret the eighteenth century's concept of aristocratic privilege by using wealth, not birth, to determine the political rights to which an individual was entitled. This drove a wedge between them and the rural and urban working classes that was to have important consequences.

ECONOMIC GOALS The economic policies favored by nineteenth-century liberals erected another barrier between them and working people. The commercial classes generally accepted the theories of Adam Smith, the Enlightenment economist who advocated the abolition of the trade restraints enacted by mercantilists and the regulated economies managed by absolutist monarchs. Liberals wanted to manufacture and sell goods freely, and they opposed paternalistic governments or guilds that regulated wages or labor practices. For them, labor was simply a commodity to be bought and sold at the price it would bring on the free market. They believed that if people were set free to exploit whatever opportunities they had to enrich themselves, the result would be more and cheaper goods and services for everyone.

RELATIONSHIP OF NATIONALISM TO LIBERALISM
The reforms associated with liberals varied according to where they lived. In Great Britain and France, the problem for liberals was to protect civil liberties, to define the respective powers of the monarch and the elected representative body, and to expand the electorate moderately while avoiding democracy. The situation in German-speaking Europe was different. There monarchs and aristocrats offered stiffer resistance to liberal ideas, and German liberals had fewer opportunities to participate in government. The aristocratic landowning class staffed government bureaucracies and army officer corps and looked down on the small commercial and industrial middle class that had no role to play in government. Most German liberals wanted to unite Germany and believed that either Austria or Prussia would be the instrument for its unification. Consequently, they were more tolerant of strong state and monarchical power than other liberals. Plans for a freer social and political order were deferred until after unification.

There was no logical link between liberalism and nationalism. Indeed, nationalism sometimes opposed liberal reform. Some nationalists wanted their own ethnic group to dominate the other peoples resident in their homelands. Some refused to cooperate with groups they regarded as their cultural inferiors or historical enemies. But liberalism and nationalism could compliment each other, for people who were fighting for representative government, civil liberties, and economic freedom in one nation readily identified with those engaged in similar struggles elsewhere.

Conservative Governments: The Domestic Political Order

Conservative Outlooks

Despite the challenges mounted by liberalism and nationalism, conservative institutions demonstrated remarkable staying power. Their influence did not fade until after World War I. Conservative governments were products of an alliance among monarchies, landed aristocracies, and established churches. Traditionally, these groups had been competitors for power, but the upheavals of the French Revolution and the Napoleonic era turned them, if sometimes reluctantly, into friends.

The fate of Louis XVI convinced most monarchs that the only persons who could be trusted with political power were aristocrats, the very wealthiest members of the middle class, and some professionals. Aristocrats and others who profited from the status quo believed that their property and influence would not be safe under any form of genuinely representative government. Most clergy also assumed that it was their duty to defend traditional institutions against the critical rationalism unleashed by the Enlightenment. These conservative factions retained their customary arrogance but lost the confidence on which it had been grounded. They knew they could be driven from power, and they understood that revolution in one country could spill over into another. They were determined, therefore, to deal firmly with all potential sources of unrest.

Considerable unrest was generated by the difficulty of reorganizing societies that, for a quarter century, had been militarily mobilized. It was hard to refit them for an era of peace. Economies that had been fueled by war had to be restructured. Employment had to be found for soldiers and sailors, and young people faced futures that were no longer dominated by military concerns. Conservative governments dealt with the domestic unrest this situation produced by resorting to differing degrees of repressive action.

Liberalism and Nationalism Resisted in Austria and the Germanies

DYNASTIC INTEGRITY OF THE HABSBURG EMPIRE Prince Metternich (1773–1859) of Austria epitomized conservatism more than any other early nineteenth-century statesman. A devoted servant of the Habsburg emperor, he and Britain's Viscount Castlereagh (1769–1822) were the architects of the agreements ratified at the Congress of Vienna.

The Congress of Vienna replaced the defunct Holy Roman Empire with a German Confederation. It consisted of thirty-nine states, each more or less autonomous but recognizing Austrian leadership. Austria was determined to prevent any movement toward constitutionalism in these states, for the future of the Habsburg Empire depended on its ability to prevent the German Confederation from becoming a German national state. The Habsburg Empire was more threatened by liberalism and nationalism than most states, for it was nothing but a collection of diverse ethnic groups. The only thing that held it together was the fact that each of these groups recognized the emperor as its hereditary ruler. Metternich feared that any attempt at representative government would lead to internal squabbling among the component parts of the empire. This would paralyze Austria and make it impossible for it to wield international influence.

DEFEAT OF REFORM IN PRUSSIA Prussia joined Austria in holding the line against nationalism and liberalism. In 1815 Frederick William III (r. 1797–1840) was carried away by the excitement that followed the "War of Liberation" (Germany's last battles with Napoleon) and promised Prussia a constitutional government. Instead, in 1817, he created a new Council of State that improved administrative efficiency but issued no constitution.

In 1819 a major disagreement over the organization of the army led to the resignation of the king's reform-minded ministers and their replacement with hardened conservatives. In 1823 Frederick William III created eight provincial assemblies. These advisory bodies, dominated by the Junkers, reaffirmed the old bonds among Prussia's monarchy, army, and landholders and created a conservative alliance opposed to German nationalism.

STUDENT NATIONALISM AND THE CARLSBAD DECREES In bids to win broad bases of support, the rulers of three southern German states (Baden, Bavaria, and Württemberg) had issued constitutions following the events of 1815. None recognized popular sovereignty, and all defined political rights as gifts from the monarch. Many young Germans, whose nationalism had been inflamed by the war against Napoleon, were unhappy with this. The best-organized youth were the university students whose *Burschenschaften*, like student groups today, served many functions. One of their effects was to diminish old provincial loyalties and generate enthusiasm for a united Germany.

In May 1820, Karl Sand, a German student and a member of a Burschenschaft, *was executed for his murder of the conservative playwright August von Kotzebue the previous year. In the eyes of many young German nationalists, Sand was a political martyr.*
Bildarchiv Preussischer Kulturbesitz

In 1817 a student club in Jena organized a large celebration of the fourth anniversary of the Battle of Leipzig and the tercentenary of the posting of Luther's Ninety-five Theses. More than 500 people gathered for the bonfires, songs, and processions. Since some professed republicans were involved, the event made the government nervous. Two years later a *Burschenschaft* member, Karl Sand (d. 1820), was executed for assassinating a conservative dramatist, August von Kotzebue (1761–1819). When some nationalists proclaimed Sand a martyr, Metternich decided that the time had come to suppress student clubs and other liberal groups.

In July 1819, Metternich persuaded the German states to endorse the Carlsbad Decrees. These dissolved the *Burschenschaften* and provided for university inspectors and press censors. The next year, the German Confederation promulgated the Final Act. It limited what might be discussed by the constitutional assemblies of Bavaria, Württemberg, and Baden, and affirmed their monarchs' right to oppose constitutionalists. For many years thereafter, the secret police of the various German states harassed anyone who sought even moderate social or political change.

Postwar Repression in Great Britain

LORD LIVERPOOL'S MINISTRY AND POPULAR UNREST
The years 1819 and 1820 were also a peak period

for enacting repressive conservative policies in Britain. Two years of poor harvests and the widespread unemployment that followed the end of the Napoleonic wars created problems with which the Tory ministry of Lord Liverpool (1770–1828) was unprepared to deal. Its response was to protect the wealthy and abandon the British ruling class's paternalistic tradition of caring for the poor. The government had already outlawed labor unions by the Combination Acts of 1799, and during the war it ended protection for wages. In 1815 Parliament passed a Corn Law that maintained high prices for domestically produced grain by imposing duties on imports. The next year, Parliament replaced income taxes with sales taxes, which weighed much more heavily on the poor than on the rich. Many of the well-off also called for the abolition of the poor law that provided public relief for the destitute and unemployed. It is hardly surprising that the lower social orders responded by calling for reform of Parliament. Mass meetings were held, reform clubs were organized, and radical newspapers were founded.

Government ministers regarded the organizers of the protest as demagogues who seduced the people away from allegiance to their natural leaders. Memories of *sans-culottes* crowds hanging French aristocrats from lampposts were still vivid, and Britain's leaders had no intention of letting the rabble get out of hand. In December

1816, an unruly mass meeting at Spa Fields near London gave Parliament an excuse to pass the Coercion Act (March 1817), which temporarily suspended *habeas corpus* and extended existing laws against seditious gatherings.

"PETERLOO" AND THE SIX ACTS Threats of repression and an easing of socioeconomic conditions because of improved harvests produced a period of calm. But by 1819 the people were again restive. In the industrial north, well-organized mass meetings demanded reform. On August 16, 1819, a large gathering in Manchester, at Saint Peter's Fields, ended disastrously. The troops that were on hand to ensure order caused the crowd to panic. At least eleven people were killed and scores injured. In a mocking reference to Wellington's victory at Waterloo, the event was dubbed the Peterloo massacre.

The responsibility for Peterloo lay with the local Manchester officials. Lord Liverpool's cabinet felt that it had to support these authorities and that the time had come for decisive action. Most of the radical leaders were incarcerated, and in December 1819, a few months after the German Carlsbad Decrees, Parliament passed the Six Acts. These (1) forbade large unauthorized, public meetings, (2) raised the fines for seditious libel, (3) speeded up the trials of political agitators, (4) increased newspaper taxes, (5) prohibited the training of armed groups, and (6) allowed local officials to search homes in certain counties.

Bourbon Restoration in France

Napoleon's abdication in 1814 opened the way for a restoration of the Bourbon monarchy that had been unseated by the revolution. The new king, Louis XVIII (r. 1814–1824), was Louis XVI's brother. (Louis XVI's son, whom royalists regarded as Louis XVII, had died uncrowned in prison.) Twenty years in exile had made Louis XVIII a political realist. He knew he could not turn back the clock, for France had changed irreversibly. Consequently, he agreed to a constitutional monarchy, but under a constitution of his own making.

THE CHARTER Louis XVIII's constitution, the Charter, combined a hereditary monarchy with a bicameral legislature. The monarch appointed the upper house; the lower house, the Chamber of Deputies, was elected, but only men with substantial property qualified to vote. The Charter guaranteed most of the rights enumerated by the Declaration of the Rights of Man and Citizen. It designated Roman Catholicism France's official religion but promised toleration for other faiths. Most important for many citizens of all classes, the Charter promised not to challenge the rights of current owners of land that had been confiscated from aristocrats and the church. Louis XVIII hoped this would encourage those who had benefitted from the revolution to accept his regime.

ULTRAROYALISM Louis XVIII's conciliatory mood was not shared by many of his royalist supporters whose families had suffered from the revolution. Led by the count of Artois (1757–1836), who was more royalist than the king, they demanded revenge. Following Napoleon's defeat at Waterloo, royalists in the south and west of France launched the White Terror, an attack on the supporters of the revolution and Napoleon. The king could do little or nothing to halt the bloodshed. The Chamber of Deputies, the elected house, was similarly extreme in its royalist sentiment. The majority elected in 1816 was so dangerously reactionary that the king dissolved the chamber and called for another election.

Years of give and take, during which liberals made moderate advances, ended in February 1820, when the duke of Berri, Artois's son and, after his father, heir to Louis's throne, was assassinated. The ultraroyalists persuaded Louis that liberal politicians were to blame, and the king responded with repressive measures. Electoral laws were revised to give wealthy men two votes. Press censorship was imposed, and rules protecting people from arbitrary arrest were relaxed. In 1821 the government turned secondary education in France over to the Roman Catholic bishops. The government's aura of constitutionalism faded as liberals were driven out of politics.

The Conservative International Order

The Congress of Vienna closed with an understanding that the major powers (Russia, Austria, Prussia, and Great Britain) would hold postwar meetings to consult on matters affecting Europe as a whole. This agreement, called the Concert of Europe, aimed at coordinating foreign policies and preventing any nation from acting without the assent of the others. The purpose of the Concert of Europe was to defend a balance of power that was endangered by Russia's military might and the possibility of renewed French aggression.

The Congress System

The first Concert of Europe assembly was convened at Aix-la-Chapelle in 1818. The four major powers agreed to remove their troops from France and restore France's standing among European nations. Britain, however, rejected a proposal by Tsar Alexander I (r. 1801–1825) that the Quadruple Alliance pledge to defend the borders and governments that then existed in all European countries. Debate of this issue remained academic until a series of revolutions began in southern Europe in 1820.

The Spanish Revolution of 1820

After Napoleon's fall, Ferdinand VII (r. 1814–1833), heir to the earlier Bourbon dynasty, ascended the Spanish throne. Once in power, he ignored a pledge he had made to issue a written constitution, dissolved Spain's parliament (the *Cortes*), and ruled alone. In 1820 a group of army officers, who were about to be sent to suppress revolution in Spain's Latin American colonies, rebelled and frightened Ferdinand into accepting a constitution. About the same time, a revolt in Naples forced the king of the Two Sicilies to endorse a constitution. There were other similar but unsuccessful uprisings elsewhere in Italy.

Metternich wanted to intervene, for he feared that disturbances in Italy might spread into the Habsburg lands. Britain opposed joint intervention by the major powers in either Italy or Spain. But when the Congress of Troppau met in late October 1820, Tsar Alexander persuaded Russia's colleagues in the Holy Alliance (Austria and Prussia) to issue the Protocol of Troppau. It declared that stable governments could intervene to restore order in countries experiencing revolution. The decision to authorize Austrian intervention in Italy, however, was delayed until January 1821, when the Congress of Laibach met. Austrian troops then marched into Naples and restored monarchy and non-constitutional government to the Two Sicilies. Metternich hoped to win local support for this move by proposing policies to improve governmental administration.

The final postwar congress took place in October 1822 at Verona. Once again Britain balked at joint action to deal with the situation in Spain. Its new foreign minister, George Canning (1770–1827), in effect withdrew Britain from the Continent's affairs. Austria, Prussia, and Russia agreed to allow the French to send an army into Spain in April 1823. The Spanish revolution was suppressed within a few months, but the purge of liberals that followed was one of the century's bloodiest manifestations of reactionary politics.

What did not happen in Spain was as important for the new international order as what did happen. France's intervention did not become an excuse to expand French territory or power. All the interventions of the period were motivated not by a desire for territorial conquest, but for the maintenance of the stable international order established at Vienna.

George Canning used the Spanish situation to further Britain's commercial interests. He prevented Europe's reactionary governments from intervening in the affairs of Spain's colonies in Latin America. The colonies had rebelled against Spain, and Canning exploited their revolutions to end Spain's colonial monopoly and win Britain access to Latin American trade. This was the reason why Britain accepted the Monroe Doctrine of 1823, which declared the United States' opposition to further European colonization and intervention in the Americas. Canning's policy allowed Britain to dominate the commerce of Latin America for the rest of the century.

The Greek Revolution of 1821

While conservative governments were being restored in Italy and Spain, a famous revolution erupted in Greece. It attracted the support of illustrious liberal literary figures who, seeing their hopes crushed across Europe, hoped that Greece's revolt heralded the return of democracy to the land that gave it birth. Philhellenic societies flourished in most countries, and Lord Byron one of the era's famous poets, went to Greece. He died there fighting for the cause of liberty in 1824.

The Greeks were struggling to free themselves from the Ottoman Empire, whose slow deterioration threatened the international balance of power. Most of Europe's great nations had keen interests in Ottoman holdings in the eastern Mediterranean. Russia and Austria wanted parts of the Balkans. France and Britain wanted commercial access to the empire and control of key naval posts in the Mediterranean. Christians of all nations wanted access to the shrines in the Holy Land.

The goals of the great powers often conflicted with the desire many of the Ottoman Empire's subjects had for independence. For several years, suspicion of rebels and of nationalistic movements delayed direct intervention in Greek affairs by European nations. Eventually, however, Britain, France, and Russia concluded that Greek independence would promote their strategic interests without threatening their domestic security. In 1827 they issued the Treaty of London, which demanded Turkish recognition of Greek independence, and they sent a joint fleet to support the Greek revolt. In 1829 Russia conquered and annexed the Ottoman territory known today as Romania. The Treaty of Adrianople, which ended that campaign, also stipulated that the Turks allow Britain, France, and Russia to decide Greece's future. In 1830 a second Treaty of London declared Greece an independent kingdom, and Otto I (r. 1832–1862), son of the king of Bavaria, was chosen to found a new Greek dynasty.

Serbian Independence

The year 1830 also saw the establishment of a second independent state on the Balkan peninsula. Serbia had been seeking independence from the Ottoman Empire since the late eighteenth century. From 1804 to 1813, a remarkable leader, Karageorge (1762–1817), fought a guerilla war, which, although unsuccessful, helped publicize the cause and build a sense of national identity. In 1815 and 1816 a new leader, Milos (1780–1860), won increased autonomy for part of Serbian territory. But a majority of Serbs lived outside the borders of this district. In 1830 the Ottoman sultan granted independence to Serbia, and by the late 1830s the major powers had extended it recognition.

The structure of the new nation remained in doubt for many years. Milos, who became its

hereditary prince, persuaded the Ottomans to extend its borders in 1833. The new boundaries held until 1878, but continuing agitation for land created problems with Austria. Questions about the status of minorities, particularly Muslims, also generated considerable internal tension. In the 1820s Slavic Russia, although separated from Serbia by Austrian territory, declared itself the protector of the Slavs of Serbia. In 1856 the great powers established a collective protectorate, but Russia continued to claim a special relationship with the Serbs.

The Wars of Independence in Latin America

The Napoleonic era marked the end of Europe's 300-year domination of Latin America. A slave revolt begun in 1794 by Toussaint L'Ouverture (1743–1803) and Jean-Jacques Dessalines (1758–1806) won Haiti its independence in 1804. Haiti's revolution was unusual in that it was a popular uprising of a repressed social group. Generally

Toussaint L'Ouverture (1743–1803) began the revolt that led to Haitian independence in 1804. Corbis

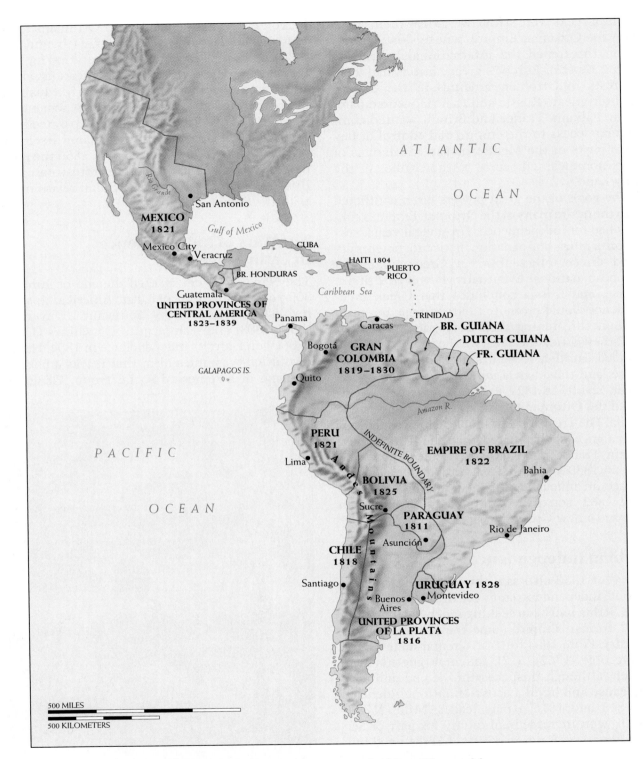

MAP 21–1 LATIN AMERICA IN 1830 *By 1830, Latin America had been liberated from European government. This map illustrates the early borders of the states of the region with the dates of their independence.*

speaking, the drive for liberty on the South American continent was led by the Creole elite (i.e., by merchants, landowners, and professional people of Spanish descent). Very few Indians, blacks, mestizos, mulattos, or slaves became involved in the fight or benefitted from it. The Haitian slave revolt haunted the Creoles, as did the memory of an earlier rebellion by Indians in the Andes (1780—1781). The Creoles were determined that their struggle for independence should not diminish their privileged position in society. (Revolutionaries often see no inconsistency in denying to others the liberties they claim for themselves.)

CREOLE DISCONTENT Creole discontent had many sources. Latin American merchants wanted to trade more freely within their region and with North America and Europe. They wanted commercial regulations that would benefit them rather than a European motherland. Creoles in Spanish districts deeply resented the favoritism shown *peninsulares* (i.e., whites born in Spain) when appointments were made to offices in the colonial governments, the church, and the army.

The Creoles drew inspiration for their revolutions from the works of the Enlightenment *philosophes* and from the American Revolution, and Napoleon gave them the impetus to act when he toppled the monarchies of Portugal in 1807 and of Spain in 1808. The Portuguese royal family fled to Brazil and established a government in exile. Spain's Bourbon monarchy, however, disappeared—leaving a political vacuum throughout Spanish Latin America. The Creole elite feared that Napoleon's puppet monarchy in Spain would impose reforms incompatible with their interests and drain them of money to fund France's wars. Between 1808 and 1810, therefore, various Creole *juntas* (i.e., political committees) assumed responsibility for governing different regions of Latin America. Spain was never able to restore its authority over the continent.

SAN MARTÍN IN RIO DE LA PLATA Vast size, geographical barriers, regional differences, and the absence of an integrated economy meant that different parts of Latin America took different routes to independence. The first region to assert itself was that of the Rio de la Plata, modern Argentina. The center of revolt was Buenos Aires.

In 1810 its *junta* not only thrust off Spanish authority but also sent armies of liberation into Paraguay and Uruguay. They were defeated, but they cost Spain control of both areas. Paraguay asserted its independence, and Brazil absorbed Uruguay.

The Buenos Aires government then set about liberating Peru, the most loyal royalist stronghold on the continent. José de San Martín (1778–1850), the most prominent general among the Rio de la Plata forces, created a disciplined army and led it on a daring march over the Andes Mountains. By early 1817, he had occupied Santiago, Chile, where a local rebel, Bernardo O'Higgins (1778–1842), was established as dictator. San Martín constructed a navy at Santiago, and in 1820 he launched it against Peru. A year later, he drove the royalist forces from Lima and declared himself Protector of Peru.

SIMÓN BOLÍVAR'S LIBERATION OF VENEZUELA What San Martín did for the south, Simón Bolívar (1783–1830) did for the north. In 1810 Bolívar, the son of a rich aristocratic family, helped organize a republican *junta* in Caracas, Venezuela. Civil war erupted, and from 1811 to 1814 the fledgling republic was assaulted by royalists on the one hand and slaves and *llaneros* (i.e., cowboys) on the other. Bolívar was forced into exile, but in 1816 the president of Haiti helped him renew his fight for a republican Venezuela. He captured Bogota, capital of New Granada (a viceroyalty that encompassed modern Colombia, Bolivia, and Ecuador), and used it as a base for war in Venezuela. By the summer of 1821, he had taken Caracas and been named president.

A year later, Bolívar and San Martín cooperated in liberating Quito, the capital of Ecuador. San Martín opposed Bolívar's republicanism and urged the establishment of monarchies in Latin America. But San Martín soon gave up the struggle, retiring from public life and exiling himself to Europe. Without San Martín's guidance, the political situation in Peru deteriorated. In 1823 Bolívar marched in and took control. On December 9, 1824, at the battle of Ayacucho, he gave the royalist forces the defeat that ended their campaign to retain an empire in America for Spain.

INDEPENDENCE IN NEW SPAIN The campaign for independence in New Spain (the viceroyalty that encompassed modern Mexico, Texas, California, and the southwestern United States) best illustrates the conservative nature of the Latin American revolutions. The local governing *junta* that here, as elsewhere, was organized to lead the revolt quickly lost the initiative. A Creole priest, Miguel Hidalgo y Costilla (1753–1811), proposed a program of sweeping social reform and incited the Indians of his parish to rise up. They and other repressed groups (e.g., black and mestizo urban and rural workers) responded enthusiastically, and soon Father Hidalgo had an army of 80,000. They captured several major cities and marched on Mexico City itself. Atrocities were committed on both sides, and in July 1811, Hidalgo was captured and executed. Leadership of his movement passed to José María Morelos y Pavón (1765–1815), a mestizo priest who was far more radical than Hidalgo. He called for substantial land reforms and an end to forced labor. He kept the revolt alive for five more years until he, too, was captured and executed in 1815.

The revolt had the effect of uniting Mexico's conservatives, both Creole and Spanish. Since they opposed any reform that might lessen their privileges, they worried when the Bourbon monarch, Ferdinand VII, was restored to the Spanish throne. He had been forced to accept a liberal constitution, and conservative Mexicans feared that his government might impose liberal reforms on Mexico. The revolution they launched was intended to defend their conservative principles. In 1821 a former royalist general, Augustín de Iturbide (1783–1824), declared Mexico's independence and proclaimed himself emperor. His regime was short-lived, but it established persons opposed to social reform in control of an independent Mexico.

BRAZILIAN INDEPENDENCE   Brazil's independence came relatively simply and peacefully. In 1807 the Portuguese royal family and several thousand government officials and members of the court took refuge from Napoleon in Brazil. Their arrival transformed Rio de Janeiro into a royal city. The prince regent, João, addressed many local complaints and in 1815 he declared Brazil a kingdom independent of Portugal. In 1820 a revolution in Portugal allowed João VI (r. 1816–1824) to return to Lisbon, and his son, Dom Pedro, became regent for Brazil. In 1822 Dom Pedro declared himself emperor of Brazil in order to block attempts by a revolutionary government in Portugal to regain control of its former colony. Thus, unlike most other Latin American nations, Brazil won its independence without an internal fight that disrupted established institutions. This was a mixed blessing. Elsewhere, wars of independence encouraged the abolition of slavery, but not in Brazil.

CONSEQUENCES OF LATIN AMERICAN INDEPENDENCE Latin America emerged from its wars for independence economically exhausted and politically unstable. Only Brazil, which had little internal adjustment to make, prospered immediately. In other places, the fight for independence had produced civil wars in which disaffected populations challenged new governments. Economies contracted until overall production in 1830 was lower than it had been in 1800. The situation provided Britain a great opportunity, for Britain was able to offer grateful Latin American governments and businesses protection, markets, and capital investment.

The Conservative Order Shaken in Europe

During the first half of the 1820s, Europe's restored conservative governments successfully resisted the forces of liberalism. The only liberal victories (the Greek revolution and the Latin American Wars of Independence) occurred on the periphery of the European world. In the middle of the 1820s, things changed as conservative regimes began to be assaulted by new waves of discontent. Russia responded with suppression; France, with revolution; and Britain, with accommodation.

Russia: The Decembrist Revolt of 1825

UNREST IN THE ARMY   When the Russian army pursued Napoleon across Europe and occupied France, some of its aristocratic officers became aware of how backward their homeland was. Many of them had been exposed to the ideas espoused by the French Revolution and the Enlightenment, and they developed reformist sympathies that were not shared by their tsar. Both at home and abroad, Alexander I had taken the lead in suppressing liber-

When the Moscow regiment refused to swear allegiance to Nicholas, he ordered the cavalry and artillery to attack them. Although a total failure, the Decembrist Revolt came to symbolize the yearnings of all Russian liberals in the nineteenth century for a constitutional government. *The Insurrection of the Decembrists at Senate Square, St. Petersburg on 26th December, 1825 (w/c on paper) by Russian School (19th century). Private Collection/Bridgeman Art Library, London/Novosti*

alism and nationalism. While he lived, there could be no challenge to tsarist autocracy.

Some of the officers who were interested in politics formed small secret societies to discuss reform, but they evolved no single, coherent program. Some advocated representative government and the abolition of serfdom. Some called for democracy and limited independence for Poland. Some favored constitutional monarchy but wanted protection for the aristocracy. All agreed that Russia's government had to change, and sometime during 1825 they began to plan a coup.

DYNASTIC CRISIS Alexander I suddenly and unexpectedly died in late November 1825. He left no direct heir, and a peculiar dispute broke out over the succession. His brother Constantine, who would have been next in line for the throne, had disqualified himself by marrying a woman who was not of royal blood. Furthermore, Constantine did not want the crown. Alexander had left secret instructions naming a younger brother, Nicholas (r. 1825–1855), as the new tsar. But Nicholas was not confident of the legality of this arrangement. He, therefore, acknowledged Constantine as tsar, and Constantine acknowledged him. This muddle continued for about three weeks, until the army command warned Nicholas of a conspiracy in the officer corps. Much to the relief of the exasperated Constantine, Nicholas overcame his scruples and declared himself tsar.

A number of junior officers had plotted to rally the troops under their command to the cause of reform. On December 26, 1825, when the army was to take the oath of allegiance to Nicholas, the Moscow regiment—whose officers, surprisingly, were not secret society members—refused. They called for a constitution and the coronation of Constantine, who was personally more popular than Nicholas and politically less conservative. Nicholas ordered the cavalry and the artillery to attack the insurgents, and more than sixty people were killed. Nicholas himself then presided over a commission appointed to investigate the Decembrist Revolt and the army's secret societies. Five plotters were executed and more than a hundred exiled to Siberia. Although the Decembrist Revolt failed, it produced martyrs who, for a century, symbolized the yearnings of Russia's small clique of liberals.

THE AUTOCRACY OF NICHOLAS I Although Nicholas was neither an ignorant nor a bigoted reactionary, he feared that any tinkering with Russia's traditional institutions—such as serfdom, which he admitted to be an evil—might cause the nation's nobles to overthrow the monarchy. Consequently, he turned his back on reform and became the most extreme kind of nineteenth-century autocrat. He employed a large secret police, imposed censorship, and did little to ensure the efficiency and honesty of his administration. The only reform he carried out was a codification of Russian law in 1833.

OFFICIAL NATIONALITY To undercut calls for reform, Nicholas instituted an educational program called Official Nationality. Its slogan, published repeatedly in government documents, newspapers, journals, and schoolbooks, was "Orthodoxy, Autocracy, and Nationalism." The Russian Orthodox faith was to provide the basis for morality, education, and intellectual life. (The church, through control of the schools, was to teach young Russians to accept their places in life and to spurn social mobility.) The autocracy of the tsar was declared to be the only authority strong enough to hold the huge Russian state together and guarantee its prosperity and influence. Nationalism was glorified to convince the Russians that their religion, language, and customs were the source of a unique wisdom that protected them from the moral corruption and political turmoil of the West.

REVOLT AND REPRESSION IN POLAND   Poland had remained under Russian domination after the Congress of Vienna, but the tsar had granted it a constitutional government. Both Alexander I and Nicholas appointed their brother, the Grand Duke Constantine (1779–1831), to govern Poland. Although both tsars frequently infringed on Poland's constitution and quarreled with the Polish Diet, this arrangement lasted through the 1820s.

In late November 1830, news of recent revolutions in France and Belgium reached Poland and inspired a small insurrection among soldiers and students in Warsaw. The disturbances spread throughout the country, and on December 18, the Polish Diet declared the revolt to be a nationalist movement. When the Diet voted to depose Nicholas as ruler of Poland, the tsar sent in troops to suppress the uprising. In February 1832, Nicholas issued the Organic Statute and claimed Poland as an integral part of the Russian Empire. The Polish uprising confirmed all of Nicholas's worst fears and persuaded him to become the *gendarme* of Europe, a monarch ever ready to provide troops for the suppression of liberal and nationalist movements.

Revolution in France (1830)

THE REACTIONARY POLICIES OF CHARLES X   Poland's revolt was one of several disturbances inspired by the overthrow of France's Bourbon dynasty in July 1830. Charles X (r. 1824–1830), Louis XVIII's brother and successor, was a firm believer in the divine right of kings. His first action as king

was to order France's Chamber of Deputies to indemnify aristocrats who had lost lands in the revolution. He raised the money that was needed by lowering the rate of interest the government paid on its bonds. This alienated members of the middle class who were bondholders. Charles restored primogeniture as a legally mandated system of inheritance, and he enacted a law that punished sacrilege against the Roman Catholic Church with imprisonment or death.

In the elections of 1827, liberals, who had been angered by the king's actions, gained enough seats in the Chamber of Deputies to force him to compromise. He appointed a less conservative ministry. Laws restraining the press and allowing the government to dominate education were eased. Liberals, however, wanted much more. They wanted a genuinely constitutional regime. In 1829 the king decided that a policy of accommodation had failed, and he replaced his moderate ministers with a group of ultraroyalists headed by the Prince de Polignac (1780–1847).

THE JULY REVOLUTION   In 1830 Charles X called new elections, and the liberals scored a stunning victory. Instead of accommodating the new Chamber of Deputies, the king tried to destroy it. In June 1830, Polignac had sent a naval expedition against Algeria, and reports of its victory—which inaugurated a French empire in North Africa—reached Paris on July 9. Charles X hoped that the euphoria created by his military venture would enable him to stage a royal *coup d'état*. On July 25, 1830, he issued the Four Ordinances. They (1) limited freedom of the press, (2) dissolved the recently elected Chamber of Deputies, (3) restricted the franchise to the wealthiest people in the country, and (4) called new elections under the new royalist franchise.

Reaction was swift and decisive. Liberal newspapers called on the nation to reject the monarch's actions, and the working class of Paris, which was suffering from a downturn in the economy, took to the streets. The king called out troops, and more than 1,800 people died battling in the city. On August 2, Charles X accepted defeat, abdicated, and went into exile. The Chamber of Deputies named a new ministry, composed of constitutional monarchists, and ended the Bourbon dynasty by proclaiming Louis Philippe (r. 1830–1848), the liberal duke of Orléans, king of France.

MONARCHY UNDER LOUIS PHILIPPE   A fundamental political and social tension underlay the new monarchy. The Revolution of 1830 might have failed if Charles X had provided himself with sufficient troops to maintain order in Paris, and had the aristocratic and middle-class liberals who favored constitutional monarchy not acted quickly, the workers of Paris might have tried to form a republic. Liberals, however, feared popular revolution and had no desire to see another *sans-culottes* regime. An alliance between France's hard-pressed laborers and its prosperous middle class won the struggle in 1830, but these groups had different objectives that made it hard for them to stay united.

Politically, the so-called July Monarchy was more liberal than the restoration government of the Bourbons. Its new constitution was regarded as a recognition of the rights of its people, not just a concession from their monarch. Catholicism was described as the religion of the majority but not the official religion. Censorship was abolished. The franchise broadened somewhat but remained restricted. The king had to cooperate with the Chamber of Deputies and could not dispense with laws on his own authority.

Socially, the new order created by the Revolution of 1830 was quite conservative. The hereditary peerage was abolished in 1831, but the power of the landed oligarchy was not challenged. Money was the major source of influence in a government noted for corruption. The Paris workers in 1830 had called for protection of jobs, better wages, and the preservation of the traditional crafts, but the monarchy took little interest in the plight of the lower classes. The kind of economic regulation they wanted was inconsistent with the political liberalism of Louis Philippe's government, which tended to view the working classes primarily as a source of trouble.

Late in 1831 troops suppressed a workers' revolt in the city of Lyons, and in July 1832, a funeral for a popular Napoleonic general sparked another uprising in Paris. Again the government called out troops, and over 800 people were killed or wounded. In 1834 a large strike by Lyons silk workers was crushed. This temporarily smothered expressions of discontent, but there would be no lasting peace until France acquired a government that was prepared to address its serious social and economic problems.

Belgium Becomes Independent (1830)

The skirmish that established France's July Monarchy ignited revolutionary fires in neighboring Belgium. In 1815 the Congress of Vienna had created a problem by joining Belgium, the former Austrian Netherlands, to the kingdom of Holland. Since the two countries differed in language, religion, and economy, the Belgian upper classes were never reconciled to the arrangement.

Their impetus to organize and to assert their independence came on August 25, 1830. When a disturbance erupted in Brussels following the performance of an opera with a revolutionary theme, the municipal authorities and propertied classes formed a provisional national government to restore order. Attempts at compromise with the Dutch failed, and William of Holland (r. 1815–1840) invaded. The Dutch were defeated by November 1830, and a few months later a national congress issued a liberal constitution for Belgium. The revolution in Belgium

Significant Dates from the Era of Political Reaction and Reform	
1814	Louis XVIII, Bourbon monarchy restored in France
1815	Holy Alliance (Russia, Austria, and Prussia)
	Quadruple Alliance (Russia, Austria, Prussia, and Britain)
1819	Carlsbad Decrees
	Peterloo Massacre
	The Six Acts passed in Great Britain
1820	Spanish revolution
1821	Greek revolution
1823	France intervenes to crush the Spanish revolution
1824	Charles X becomes king in France
1825	Decembrist Revolt in Russia
1829	Catholic Emancipation Act passed in Great Britain
1830	Charles X abdicates; Louis Philippe proclaimed king
	Belgian revolution
	Polish revolution
1832	Great Reform Bill passed in Great Britain

upset the boundaries established by the Congress of Vienna, but the major powers were not inclined to intervene. Russia, Austria, Prussia, and other German states were busy suppressing various disturbances elsewhere. France favored an independent Belgium, which it expected to dominate, and Britain was prepared to tolerate a liberal Belgium so long as it was not the pawn of another nation.

In December 1830, Lord Palmerston (1784–1865), the British foreign minister, gathered representatives of the powers in London and persuaded them to acknowledge Belgium as an independent, neutral state. In July 1831, Leopold of Saxe-Coburg (r. 1831–1865) was crowned king of the Belgians. Belgium's neutrality was recognized by the Convention of 1839 and respected until 1914. In that year, a German invasion of Belgium brought Britain into World War I.

The Great Reform Bill in Britain (1832)

George IV's death in 1830 and the accession of a new king, William IV (r. 1830–1837), necessitated the calling of a parliamentary election for the summer that witnessed France's July revolution. Although the new House of Commons proposed the first major reform of Parliament, it does not seem to have been influenced by events in France. The Great Reform Bill (1832) was the result of an accommodation between the forces of conservatism and reform that was unique to Britain.

POLITICAL AND ECONOMIC REFORM   The inclination to accommodate that was characteristic of British politics had several sources. Since the commercial and industrial classes were larger in Britain than in other countries, every British government recognized that the nation's prosperity depended on guarding the economic interests of those classes. Britain's aristocratic Whig liberals believed in constitutional liberty and advocated successive moderate reforms—not revolution. Britain also had a long tradition, supported by law and public opinion, of respect for civil liberties.

CATHOLIC EMANCIPATION ACT   Repressive conservative government reached a peak under Lord Liverpool when the Tory minister tried to stifle calls for reform by issuing the notorious Six Acts (1819). In 1820, however, Liverpool shuffled his cabinet and created a government more disposed to accommodate changing conditions. It expanded economic freedoms and repealed earlier restraints imposed on labor organizations.

England's relationship with Ireland brought about another change. In 1800, fearful that Irish nationalists might rebel (as they had in 1798) and offer Ireland to Napoleon as a base for a French invasion of England, William Pitt the Younger persuaded Parliament to pass the Act of Union. Ireland was granted 100 seats in the House of Commons, but only Irish Protestants were permitted to stand for election. During the 1820s, Irish nationalists organized the Catholic Association to agitate for Catholic emancipation, and in 1828 they challenged the law by

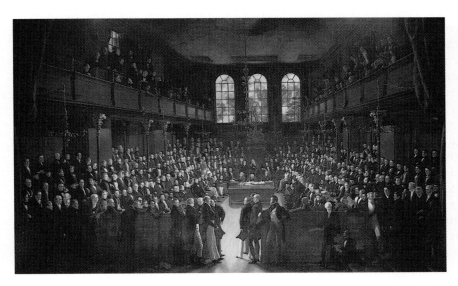

At the first meeting of the House of Commons following the passage of the Great Reform Bill, most seats were still filled by the gentry and the wealthy. But the elimination of "rotten boroughs" and the election of members from the new urban centers began to transform the House into a representative national body.
National Portrait Gallery, London

Art & the West

John Constable's Harmonious Landscapes in Unstable Times

$\mathcal{T}$he English artist, John Constable (1776– 1837), was as staunchly conservative as his French contemporary, the revolutionary Jacques-Louis David, was radical. David's neoclassicism celebrated France's political and social innovations by cloaking them in the dignity of Greek and Roman antiquity. Constable's romanticism, on the other hand, countered Britain's changing social order with a medieval vision of stability and harmony between nature and humankind. The painter tried to fix fleeting moments in nature's panorama to call attention to a traditional way of life, which he feared was endangered by the changes that the liberal reformers of his day were promoting. Constable did not idealize the English landscape. He carefully described real places and real people engaged in ordinary tasks. He did, however, view rural England through the lens of an idealized medieval past characterized by organic stability and religious reverence.

Salisbury Cathedral from the Meadows, which Constable painted in 1831, employs the characteristic techniques of the romantic artist (e.g., lavish application of paint) to convey the atmosphere of a severe storm. The turbulent sky, which is the primary subject of the painting, poses no threat, however, to the order of nature, the ancient cathedral, nor the humble laborer whose horses drink from the stream in the foreground. All the components of the picture are parts of an integrated, stable order framed by a rainbow, a symbol of divine blessing. The peaceful, orderly rural world that Constable described here exhibits none of the disruptive effects of the enclosures, mechanized farming techniques, and fluctuating world markets that were inflicting enormous suffering on England's farmers. Constable believed that such developments were modern threats to the natural order that God had ordained, and he accused the liberals whom he held responsible for them of being in league with the devil.

John Constable (1776–1837), *Salisbury Cathedral, from the Meadows*, 1831. Oil on canvas, 151.8 × 189.9. © The National Gallery, London

Sources: Ann Bermingham, *Landscape and Ideology: The English Rustic Tradition, 1740–1860* (Berkeley, CA: University of California Press, 1986); Michael Rosenthal, *Constable: The Painter and His Landscape* (New Haven, CT: Yale University Press, 1983); John Barrell, *The Darker Side of Landscape* (Cambridge, U.K.: Cambridge University Press, 1980).

electing one of their leaders, Daniel O'Connell (1775–1847), to a seat he could not legally occupy. To head off civil war, the British ministry (led by the duke of Wellington and Robert Peel) persuaded Parliament to seat Catholics by passing the Catholic Emancipation Act (1829). This, with an earlier repeal of restrictions against Protestant nonconformists (1828), ended the Anglican Church's monopoly of British political life.

Catholic emancipation was a liberal measure intended for a conservative purpose: the preservation of order in Ireland. Its passage alienated many of Wellington's Anglican Tory supporters and split the Tory Party. An election in 1830 seated a Parliament disposed to reform, and Wellington's ministry fell. King William IV asked Earl Grey (1764–1845), leader of the Whigs, to form the next government.

LEGISLATING CHANGE   The Whig ministry quickly sent the House of Commons a major reform bill. It proposed replacing "rotten" boroughs with new districts that increased representation for cities and manufacturing areas, and it extended the franchise. When the House of Commons rejected the bill, Grey called for a new election (1831). The new Commons passed the bill, but the House of Lords refused to concur. Mass protest meetings were held throughout the country, and riots broke out. Finally, William IV agreed to create enough new peers to give a third reform bill a majority in the House of Lords. The Lords yielded to this pressure and passed the measure (1832).

The Great Reform Bill expanded the size of the English electorate, but it did not create a democracy. It increased the number of voters by about 50 percent, but it maintained the property qualification for the franchise. It ignored women, and some members of the working class actually lost the right to vote. What the bill achieved was representation in the House of a wider variety of propertied people. This reconciled previously unrepresented economic interests to the political institutions of the country. By admitting people who wanted change to the legislative process, it undercut the need for revolution in Britain.

In Perspective

In the fifteen years that separated the Congress of Vienna from the Revolution of 1830, the Congress System restrained revolutionary and nationalistic activity in Europe. Nonetheless, during the 1820s, political liberalism made inroads into the dominant conservative order, and in 1830 revolutionary and reform movements reappeared. The French replaced the Bourbon monarchy with a more liberal government. Belgium achieved independence under a liberal government, and Great Britain moved slowly toward a more liberal position. The pace of change in Europe was slow, but new political ideas and forces were coming to the fore.

REVIEW QUESTIONS

1. What is nationalism? What were the goals of the nineteenth-century nationalists? What were the difficulties they confronted in realizing their goals? Why was nationalism a special threat to the Austrian Empire? What parts of Europe saw significant nationalist movements between 1815 and 1830? Which of these movements were successful? Which failed?

2. What were the tenets of liberalism? What effects did liberalism have on political developments during the early nineteenth century? What relationship does liberalism have to nationalism?

3. What difficulties did the conservatives in Austria, Prussia, and Russia face in the years after the Napoleonic wars? How did they respond on both national and international levels? What were the aims of the Concert of Europe? What did it accomplish and why did Britain withdraw?

4. What political changes took place in Latin America between 1804 and 1824? What were the main reasons for Creole discontent with Spanish rule? To what extent were Creole leaders influenced by Enlightenment political

philosophy? Who were the major leaders in the fight for Latin American independence? Why did they succeed?

5. What kind of constitution was decreed for the restored monarchy in France? Was the new government truly constitutional? What did Charles X hope to accomplish? How much support did he have? What were the causes of the Revolution of 1830? What did this revolution achieve? What was its cost?

6. How do you explain the fact that although prior to 1820 Britain was moving down the same reactionary road as the other major European powers, events arrived at a different outcome in Britain? What was the purpose of the Great Reform Bill? What did it achieve? Is it correct to call it a "revolutionary" document?

SUGGESTED READINGS

M. BERDAHL, *The Politics of the Prussian Nobility: The Development of a Conservative Ideology, 1770–1848* (1988). A major examination of German conservative outlooks.

R. J. BEZUCHA, *The Lyon Uprising of 1834: Social and Political Conflict in the Early July Monarchy* (1974). An excellent discussion of the tensions in France after the Revolution of 1830.

A. BRIGGS, *The Making of Modern England* (1959). Remains the best survey of English history during the first half of the nineteenth century.

M. BROCK, *The Great Reform Act* (1974). The standard work.

G. A. CRAIG, *The Politics of the Prussian Army, 1640–1945* (1955). A splendid study of the conservative political influence of the army on Prussian development.

J. DROZ, *Europe Between Revolutions, 1815–1848* (1967). An examination of Europe as created by the Vienna settlement.

E. J. HOBSBAWM, *The Age of Revolution, 1789–1848* (1962). A comprehensive survey emphasizing the social ramifications of the liberal democratic and industrial revolutions.

E. J. HOBSBAWM, *Nations and Nationalism since 1780: Programme, Myth, Reality*, rev. ed. (1992). The best recent introduction to the subject.

S. HOLMES, *Benjamin Constant and the Making of Modern Liberalism* (1984). An outstanding study of a major liberal theorist.

C. and B. JELAVICH, *The Establishment of the Balkan National States, 1804–1920* (1977). A standard, clear introduction.

J. LYNCH, *The Spanish American Revolutions, 1808–1826* (1973). An excellent one-volume treatment.

C. A. MACARTNEY, *The Habsburg Empire, 1790–1918* (1971). An outstanding survey.

A. PALMER, *Alexander I: Tsar of War and Peace* (1974). An interesting biography that captures much of the mysterious personality of this ruler.

P. PILBEAM, *The 1830 Revolution in France* (1991). An account that emphasizes the restoration accommodation to various interest groups.

N. V. RIASANOVSKY, *Nicholas I and Official Nationality in Russia, 1825–1855* (1959). A lucid discussion of the conservative ideology that made Russia the major opponent of liberalism.

The Abolition of Slavery in the Transatlantic Economy

The greatest achievement of the liberal reformers of the eighteenth and nineteenth centuries was the antislavery movement. Chattel slavery (i.e., the ownership of one human being by another) had existed in the West and elsewhere in the world since ancient time, and many justifications had been provided for it. Greek philosophers argued that slavery was part of the natural order, and early and medieval Christian authors tended to follow their lead. In the middle of the eighteenth century, however, (and for the first time in world history) questions began to be raised about the legitimacy of slavery. Efforts were made to abolish it, and by 1888 these efforts had succeeded in Europe and the Americas. Slavery succumbed to a variety of different kinds of influences: Christian ethics, Enlightenment ideals, slave revolts, American and European revolutionary wars, economic dislocations of slave-based economies, and civil war in the United States.

Slavery Spreads to the Americas

Although there was a vast slave trade throughout the medieval Mediterranean world, by the fifteenth century slavery had ceased to be an important factor within the European economy. Europe's encounter with the Americas changed that, for a huge market developed in Europe for American products—chiefly sugar, cotton, and tobacco. From Maryland south to Brazil agricultural entrepreneurs brought great tracts of land under cultivation, created plantations, and worked them with unfree labor. Some Native Americans were enslaved, but the chief solution to the problem of labor shortages in these regions was the importation of slaves from Africa.

This was encouraged by that fact that about the same time that Europeans made contact with the Americas, they were establishing ties with areas of West Africa where slavery already existed. West Africa became the chief source for the slaves that were shipped to the Western Hemisphere, and its economy became dependent on slavery as the volume of the trade increased.

The spread of slavery to the Americas is not surprising. Slavery has existed at most times and places in human history. But American slavery took on a unique characteristic. Since the persons enslaved in America were either Native Americans or Africans, there were obvious racial differences between slaves and masters. Racial theories, therefore, were soon invented to justify the social hierarchy of the plantation economy.

The Crusade Against Slavery

Given the antiquity and universal presence of slavery, one of the West's more remarkable achievements was the creation, about 1760, of an international movement to abolish chattel slavery in the transatlantic economy. Several things inspired this original reform. Enlightenment reasoning steadily eroded the traditional defenses of slavery—particularly the assumption that an unchanging social hierarchy was a fact of nature. The rhetoric of the Enlightenment politicians who preached equality was at odds with slavery, as was the thought of the period's economists who advocated free labor and free markets. Literary figures also promoted a new view of the populations from which slaves were drawn. Traditionally, Europeans had regarded primitive peoples as backward and rebellious, but eighteenth-century authors tended to idealize them and depict them as noble exemplars of natural virtues that civilized people had lost. The empathetic attitudes fostered by the romantic movement encouraged Europeans to sympathize with the enslaved and to view them as people who had been betrayed and robbed of their innocence. The old view that slaves were inherently inferior beings who deserved their condition began to change as some people concluded that

After 1807 the British Royal Navy patrolled the West African coast attempting to intercept slave-trading ships. In 1846 the British ship HMS Albatross *captured a Spanish slave ship, the* Albanoz *and freed the slaves. A British officer depicted the appalling conditions in the slavehold in this watercolor.* The Granger Collection, New York

slavery was a monstrous injustice inconsistent with the values of Western civilization.

Religious movements did the most to launch the antislavery campaign. In 1774, Methodism's founder, John Wesley, published *Thoughts on Slavery.* Evangelical preachers such as Wesley believed that salvation depended on a conversion experience that led to a change of heart. The repudiation of slavery by a plantation owner was described as one such sign of saving grace, and some slavers came to see slavery as a threat to their souls' salvation. One such was John Newton, author of the hymn "Amazing Grace." English Quakers, a small but influential sect, took the lead in organizing protests against slavery. In the early eighteenth century some Quakers owned slaves or profited from the trade, but the hardships created by the Seven Years' War (1756–1763) convinced some of them that the world was being punished for its sins, the chief of which was the enduring presence of slavery.

This inspired them to try to purge its evil from their lives, their congregations, and ultimately from society as a whole. Quakers on both sides of the Atlantic joined forces to publish exposés of the horrors of the slave trade and the brutality of slave owners. They set up organizations to assist slaves and founded societies to work for the legal abolition of slavery.

The values for which the patriots of the American Revolution fought increased sympathy for the antislavery movement. Most of the northern states in the new American republic endorsed emancipation, and in 1787 the Continental Congress decreed that slavery should not extend into the newly organized Northwest Territory. These were important achievements, but it was Great Britain that led the international campaign against slavery. During the 1780s, British activists decided to attack the slave trade rather than the institution itself. It was easier to grab the public's attention by calling attention to atrocities committed by slavers than by arguing the moral issues involved in slavery. An attack on slavery might have been regarded by the public as a radical attack on rights of private property, and this could have produced an unfortunate backlash against the movement. Slave owning also seemed a less overtly criminal activity than slave trading, and it was hoped that an end to the trade would require slave owners to treat their remaining slaves more humanely. At the end of the 1780s, English Quakers and evangelical Christians joined forces to form the Society for the Abolition of the Slave Trade, and in 1807 the legislation for which they campaigned was finally passed.

Slave Revolts

Slaves were not passive in the fight for emancipation. In some places they took matters into their own hands. Their greatest success was on the island of Saint-Domingue (Haiti), France's wealthiest colony. In 1794, Toussaint L'Ouverture and Jean-Jacques Dessalines raised a successful slave rebellion, and in 1805 Haiti won its independence. Other revolts were to follow: in

The Slave Revolt on the French Island of St. Dominique achieved the largest emancipation of slaves in the eighteenth century. In this print Toussant L'Ouverture leads the revolt. Corbis

British Demarra in 1823 and 1824, in Jamaica in 1831, and in the United States (Gabriel Prosser's in Virginia in 1800, Nat Turner's in Virginia in 1831, and Denmark Vesey's in south Carolina in 1822). Each of these was brutally suppressed.

Economic Pressures

During the second half of the eighteenth century the influence of the West Indies sugar planters in the British parliament began to decline. Soil exhaustion, the development of new sources of supply from the French colonies, and a glut of sugar on the market led the planters to moderate their position on slavery. They came to view the abolition of the slave trade as a strategy for depriving their French competitors of the labor they needed to expand production. In 1807 Parliament forbade slave trading from any British port, and Britain tried to persuade its allies to follow its lead. The British navy patrolled the West African coast to intercept slave traders. The French and Americans cooperated but with less commitment. In 1824, however, the American Congress did declare slave trading a capital offense.

The struggles with Napoleon that began to preoccupy the Spanish government in 1808 set the stage for wars of independence to break out in Latin America. The leaders of these revolutions were inspired by Enlightenment ideals, and they sought to win the support of enslaved elements in their countries by promises of emancipation.

They also needed to court abolitionist Britain to obtain essential economic support. Although emancipation was quickly proclaimed, the actual freeing of slaves took some time. With the exception of Brazil, however, by midcentury slavery had ended in the independent nations of Latin America.

Abolishing Slavery in the New World

In 1823 British reformers launched a campaign for the gradual emancipation of all slaves. By 1830 they had become more radical and were demanding an immediate end to slavery. In 1833, they carried the day, and Parliament abolished the right of all British subjects to hold slaves. This liberated 750,000 people in the British West Indies.

Other colonial powers were much slower to follow the British example. Portugal ended slavery in its American possessions in 1836, but this had no effect on Brazil, which had, by then, won its independence. Sweden outlawed slavery in 1847 and Denmark in 1848. The Dutch followed in 1863. France did not end slavery in its West Indian possessions until the revolution of 1848.

During the opening decades of the nineteenth century, support for slavery actually revived, and slavery spread to new regions in the transatlantic world. Cotton promoted it in the southern United States. Coffee growing led to its popularity in Brazil, and Cuba relied on it for the cultivation of sugar. World demand for these products continued to make slavery so economically profitable that campaigns for emancipation had little effect.

In the 1830s the example set by the British reinvigorated the fight for the abolition of slavery in the United States. Abolitionists such as William Lloyd Garrison kept the issue alive, but it was the disposition of the new lands that the United States had won in the Mexican War of 1847 that made the future of slavery a matter for urgent, impassioned debate. The subject increasingly divided the nation, and in 1860 the election of President Lincoln precipitated the events that culminated in the outbreak of the Civil War in the spring of 1861. In 1862 Lincoln's Emancipation Proclamation ended slavery in the combatant states, and in 1865 the Thirteenth Amendment to the Constitution abolished it in the United States. In the Western Hemisphere, only Cuba and Brazil still practiced slavery. Political agitation and a declining economy led Cuba to abandon slavery in 1886, and two years later Brazil followed suit. The end of slavery in the transatlantic economy did not, however, mean a rapid transition to equality and social justice for all peoples. Slavery bequeathed a legacy of problems for the nations that had once supported it.

Africa and the End of Slavery

The transatlantic slave trade had adverse affects on Africa. It caused a vast loss of population, and the internal trading in slaves it stimulated undermined African society. The trade also drew Europeans—both as traders and as abolitionists—deeply into Africa's affairs. Those Westerners who opposed the trade hoped to end it by promoting "Christianity and Civilization" or "Christianity and Commerce" in Africa. They believed that slavery could be discouraged by converting Africans to European ways and encouraging them to cultivate tropical products for trade with Europe and America. There was also a drive to return slaves or the descendants of slaves to Africa. In 1787 Britain established a colony for free blacks from Britain in Sierra Leone. The French attempted something similar at Libreville in Gabon, but the most famous and lasting of these efforts was the establishment of Liberia in 1817 by the American Colonization Society. Liberia became an independent republic in 1847.

In 1841 Britain's African Civilization Society sent an ill-fated expedition up the Niger River in the hope of establishing a new basis for trade with Africa. The intent was to exchange European manufactured goods for African agricultural products and, thus, wean the African economy from dependence on slavery. Disease defeated this first attempt, but the impulse to penetrate Africa persisted. As the West African slave trade declined, attention shifted to ending the slave trade in East Africa and the Indian Ocean. The drive against slavery and the slave trade within Africa provided a rationale for the European interventions in Africa that led to the establishment of the nineteenth century's colonial empires.

The fight against slavery is not yet over, for the institution still exists, as do little publicized antislavery societies. But the abolition of slavery in the transatlantic world stands as one of the great achievements of the West's Age of Enlightenment and of the revolutions that established the West's democratic governments.

✤ *What justifications were offered for slavery prior to the eighteenth century? What religious and intellectual developments led some Europeans and Americans to question the legitimacy of slavery? Why did the antislavery movement first concentrate on ending the slave trade rather than slavery itself? How did slavery and the attempts to end it lead Westerners to become more deeply involved with Africa? How did that involvement change between 1600 and 1870?*

Chapter 22
Economic Advance and Social Unrest (1830–1850)

K E Y   T O P I C S

- ⟳ The development of industrialism and its effects on the organization of labor and the family
- ⟳ The changing role of women in industrial society
- ⟳ The establishment of police forces and reform of prisons
- ⟳ Early developments in European socialism
- ⟳ The revolutions of 1848

By 1830 Great Britain had become an industrialized nation, and the rest of Europe was soon to resound with the pounding of machinery and the grinding of railway engines. Between 1825 and 1850, the groups that opposed industrialism made their final protests, and intellectuals articulated major creeds that both supported and criticized the emerging society. These were years of uncertainty, a period of self-conscious transition leading to an unknown future. They culminated in 1848 with a continent-wide outbreak of revolution.

Toward an Industrial Society

Industrialism and the urban growth that accompanied it, no less than the political upheavals that derived from the French Revolution, overturned the Old Regime. The slow but steady conversion of Europe's economy to industrial manufacturing during the first half of the nineteenth century reorganized society. In unprecedented numbers, people migrated to cities to find work in the new factories. There they faced radically different conditions of life.

Britain's Industrial Leadership

The Industrial Revolution, led by textile manufacturing, began in Great Britain in the eighteenth century. Britain had advantages (e.g., natural resources, capital, technology, food supply, relative social mobility, and strong foreign and domestic markets) that gave it an edge in developing its productive capacities. It also profited from the fact that for two decades the French Revolution and the Napoleonic wars disrupted economic activity on the Continent and weakened France as a competitor for Atlantic trade. Both the United States and Canada were rich markets for British goods. The Latin American Wars of Independence opened South America to British merchants, and from bases in India Britain dominated the trade of southern Asia.

The wealth that Britain acquired through various industries (e.g., textile weaving, ironmaking, shipbuilding, china production, etc.) was invested in the development of global networks that enabled Britain to dominate the world scene in the nineteenth century. British textile mills, for example, bought cotton produced by slaves on the plantations of the southern United States and turned it into finished cloth that was shipped to India. At each stage in the process, the trade moved along sea lanes protected by the British navy.

By the 1830s, Belgium, France, and Germany were headed down the same path as Britain. They had a growing number of steam engines in use. They were substituting coke for charcoal in iron and steel production (and, thus, stimulating mining in the coal fields of the Ruhr and the Saar basins). Large districts of concentrated manufacturing, comparable to the British Midlands, did not yet exist. There were some pockets of production in cities such as Lyons, Rouen, Liège, and Lille, but most manufacturing still took place in the countryside where new machines were integrated into the existing system of domestic production. By midcentury, peasants and urban artisans were still more politically influential than industrial factory workers.

Population and Migration

As industrialization spread, the population explosion that had begun in the eighteenth century continued. Between 1831 and 1851, France grew from 32 million to 35 million; Germany, from 26 million to 33 million; and Britain, from 16 million to 20 million. Increasingly, Europeans lived in cities. By midcentury, half the population of England and Wales was urban—as was a quarter of the population of France and Germany. Eastern

Cities all across the continent grew during the first half of the nineteenth century. Some developed with little planning into bewildering places. Others—as this Berlin street scene suggests—developed in ways more congenial to their residents, with neighborhoods that continued to combine workshops, stores, and residences. Bildarchiv Preussischer Kulturbesitz

Europe, however, remained overwhelmingly rural and little industrialized.

The sheer numbers of human beings exhausted the physical resources of cities. Housing, water, sewers, food supplies, and lighting could not be improved quickly enough to deal with migration from the countryside. Indescribably filthy slums appeared where disease, especially cholera, ravaged the population. Crime became a way of life for some, and human misery and degradation seemed to contemporary observers to have no bounds.

The situation in the countryside was scarcely better. Liberal reformers had hoped that the changes in land ownership that followed the French Revolution and the emancipation of serfs in Prussia, Austria (1848), and Russia (1861) would turn peasants into progressive, industrious farmers. Instead, possession of land made most of them cautious and conservative. Having too little land to support themselves in an increasingly commercialized agrarian economy, few had additional capital to invest in it to make it more productive. By midcentury, the revolution in landholding was improving agricultural production, but it did so by driving small farmers from the countryside into cities and from Europe into the outside world.

If emancipation movements did little for agrarian economies, they did assist industrialization. In England, France, and the Low Countries, they freed a labor force to move between country and town as needed. In Germany, eastern Europe, and Russia, however, such migration remained difficult even after emancipation. Consequently, from Germany eastward, the pace of industrialization was slow.

Europe continued to be haunted by the specter of poor harvests. The century's worst agricultural disaster was the famine Ireland endured from 1845 to 1847. A disease that blighted the nation's potato crop caused about 500,000 Irish peasants to starve to death and hundreds of thousands to emigrate.

Railways

Industrial development in the 1830s and 1840s was driven by the construction of Europe's railway system. The Stockton and Darlington Line opened in England in 1825. The first French company began to operate in 1832, although serious expansion of France's rail system waited until the 1840s. Belgium had begun to run trains by 1835—as had Germany. By midcentury, Britain had 9,797 kilometers of track; France, 2,915; and Germany, 5,856.

Railways epitomized the character of the industrial economy of the second quarter of the nineteenth century—an economy that stressed investment in capital goods more than consumer goods. The construction of railways speeded industrialization in several ways. Trains were the most dramatic application of the steam engine, and the construction of railroads sharply increased demand for iron and steel and for skilled laborers. Increased manufacturing capacity at forges meant that more iron and steel became available to construct other things (e.g., ships and machines). As the vast fortunes created by the capital industries were invested to inaugurate other enterprises, industrialism grew on itself.

The Labor Force

The emphasis on capital goods rather than consumer production meant that the working class often found little to purchase for the wages it earned in the new industries. The early nineteenth-century labor force was extremely diverse: factory workers, urban artisans, cottage industry craftspeople, household servants, miners, rural peddlers, farm workers, and railroad navvies. Some workers were reasonably well off, enjoying steady employment and decent wages. Others constituted a class of "laboring poor" (i.e., people who had jobs that paid little more than subsistence wages). Some of these (e.g., the women and children who worked naked in the mines of Wales) endured conditions that shocked Europe when they were described by a parliamentary report in the early 1840s.

During the first half of the century, only the textile manufacturing industry became thoroughly mechanized and concentrated in factories. Industrial factory workers were still vastly outnumbered by the skilled artisans who lived in cities or small towns. Industrialization, however, threatened to make the skills of many artisans useless and to deprive them of control over their trades. All workers faced possible unemployment with little or no provision for their security. All were aware of the dissolution of the

J. M. W. Turner, Rain, Steam, and Speed—The Great Western Railway

Railway systems, in the construction of which Britain took the lead, were the most powerfully transforming technology of the nineteenth century. Both the building and the operation of railways disrupted rural landscapes and traditional rural ways of life. The Great Western Railway, which was featured in a canvas that Joseph Mallord William Turner painted in 1844, was the largest rail system of its day. Stretching from London into England's western counties, it was both an agent and a symbol of the new industrial age.

Turner enhanced the tendencies found in some romantic art to emphasize light and color more than line. This enabled him to create luminous canvases that seemed to be translucent and to glow with their own inner light. His revolutionary techniques of painting were well adapted to celebrating the revolutionary industrial technologies of his day. His paintings produce powerful, visceral experiences that suggest that mere human individuals are insignificant when compared with the great forces of nature, history, and technology, which, during his lifetime, were moving the West into a radically new age.

Sources: Michael Freeman, *Railways and the Victorian Imagination* (New Haven, CT: Yale University Press, 1999); Gerard Finley, *Angel in the Sun: Turner's Vision of History* (Montreal, and Kingston, ON: McGill–Queen's University Press, 1999); Martin Butlin & Evelyn Joll, *The Paintings of J. M. W. Turner*, rev. ed. (New Haven, CT: Yale University Press, 1984).

Joseph Mallord William Turner, 1775–1851, *Rain Steam, and Speed—The Great Western Railway*, 1844. Oil on canvas, 90.8 × 121.9. © The National Gallery, London.

traditional social ties that had been maintained by custom and community.

Proletarianization of Factory Workers and Urban Artisans

During the century, both artisans and factory workers underwent a process of *proletarianization*. That means that they lost ownership of the means of production (i.e., tools and equipment) and lost control of their trades. They became wage earners. This occurred whenever people with capital constructed factories and purchased what was needed to run them: labor as well as machinery and raw materials. The process spread beyond the factory system when inventions, such as mechanical printing presses, took over the work of artisans. Factory workers, unlike self-employed artisans, had to submit to a kind of discipline that was unpopular and difficult to maintain. The needs of machines determined what was expected of their human operators, and threats and punishments were used to compel laborers to match the pace and consistent performance of the cables, wheels, and pistons of the mechanisms with which they worked.

Factory conditions were difficult, but workers in textile factories were better off than competitors who resisted the factory mode of production. English hand-loom weavers who continued to work in their homes slipped into ever-deepening poverty as they struggled to match the output of power looms.

Urban artisans were proletarianized more slowly than factory workers, and machinery was only one contributor to the process. Factories did not necessarily harm urban artisans, some of whom prospered from them. The construction and maintenance of machines, for instance, increased demand for metalworkers, the erection of factories and subsequent expansion of cities benefitted the building trades, and lower prices for machine-made textiles reduced the cost of raw materials for tailors and hatters. It was the change in the organization of production inspired by the factory model that threatened the skills and livelihood of urban artisans.

In the eighteenth century, as earlier, a guild system had organized production in Europe's urban workplaces. A master (i.e., guild member) owned a workshop and the larger pieces of equipment. He trained apprentices who, when they became journeymen, acquired their own tools.

Ultimately, they expected to be admitted to the guild as masters and be permitted to set up shops of their own. The guild system gave workers control over labor recruitment, training, pace of production, quality of product, and price. In the nineteenth century, however, it became increasingly difficult for guilds to control trades. France had outlawed guilds during the French Revolution, and elsewhere in Europe, liberals worked to ban labor and guild organizations on the theory that they limited economic freedom. Guild masters also faced increasing competition as machine production invaded craft-dominated industries. In response, many workshops tried to increase efficiency by what was known in France as *confection*, production of standard sizes and styles rather than special orders for individual customers. This practice increased the division of labor, for each of a shop's artisans produced only a part of a more or less uniform final product. Consequently, less skill was required and the value of skills diminished.

Masters also tried to increase production and reduce costs by lowering the wages paid for piecework. This often led to work stoppages or strikes. But immigration from the countryside guaranteed a surplus of relatively unskilled workers who were willing to work for lower wages or under less protected conditions than traditional artisans. This made it difficult for urban journeymen to ascend the ladder and become masters with their own shops. More and more of them were forced to spend their lives as wage laborers whose skills were simply bought and sold according to their fluctuating value in the marketplace.

Working-Class Political Action: The Example of British Chartism

In the 1830s artisans, who were proud of their skills and frustrated by their diminishing opportunities for advancement, began to organize movements to protect their social and economic interests. By the middle of the century, they had become the most radical element in the European working class.

In 1836 William Lovett (1800–1877) joined with other London radical artisans to form the London Working Men's Association. In 1838 the group issued the Charter, a call for six specific reforms. The Six Points of the Charter were universal male suffrage, annual election of the

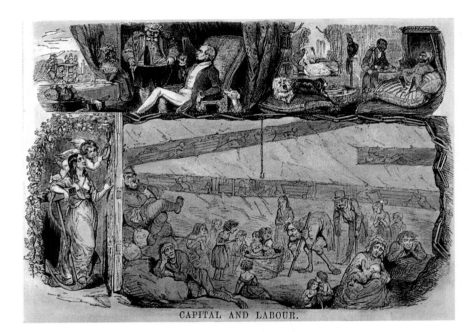

CAPITAL AND LABOUR.

A parliamentary report in the early 1840s revealed the deplorable conditions of women and children working underground in Welsh mines. The report had published illustrations of those conditions. This contemporary political cartoon draws upon those illustrations by portraying the wealthy and comfortable classes living a life based on the foundation of the misery of workers. The Granger Collection, NY

House of Commons, the secret ballot, equal electoral districts, abolition of property qualifications for members of Parliament, and payment of salaries to members of the House of Commons. The Chartists agitated for their reforms for over a decade. On three occasions the Charter was presented to Parliament, which refused to pass it. Petitions with millions of signatures were sent to the House of Commons. Strikes were called, and a newspaper, *The Northern Star*, was published.

The Chartists had some success in local government. But Chartism failed to cohere as a national movement because it split between members who favored violence and those who wanted to use peaceful tactics. The return of prosperity following a depression in the late 1830s and early 1840s also caused many working people to lose interest in the issues Chartism advocated. Nevertheless, as the first large-scale political movement organized by the working class, Chartism provided a model and inspiration for workers throughout Europe who sought some way to improve their situation.

Family Structures and the Industrial Revolution

The European working-class family of the early industrial age is difficult to describe in general terms, for industrialism developed at different rates across the continent. More is known about the family in Great Britain in this period than elsewhere, and many British developments foreshadowed those in other countries.

The Family in the Early Factory System

Before England's revolution in textile production in the late eighteenth century, the individual family was the chief unit of textile manufacture. In the domestic system of the family economy, father and mother worked with children as a family unit. They trained and disciplined their children at home, and their home and work lives were closely intertwined. Early textile inventions, such as the spinning jenny, did not alter that situation, for these machines could be used at home.

It was the mechanization of weaving that led to major changes. A father who became a machine weaver was employed in a factory, and his work was separated from his home. Still, the adoption of machinery and factory production did not destroy the working-class family, for the organization of early English factories allowed the father to preserve some of his traditional family roles. Early factory owners allowed men to employ their wives and children as their assistants. This made it possible to transfer parental training and discipline from the home to the factory, but it did not forestall changes in family life caused by the discipline required for factory work.

A major shift in Britain's family and factory structures took place between the mid-1820s and mid-1830s when spinning and weaving came under one roof, and factories and machinery grew larger. The new machines required fewer skilled operators but many relatively unskilled attendants. Machine tending became the work of unmarried women and children, for they accepted lower wages and were less likely than men to form labor organizations.

CONCERN FOR CHILD LABOR The children who stayed in factories were often the children of economically depressed hand-loom weavers. Wages for skilled adult male factory workers were high enough to allow them to support their families. They could keep their wives at home and send their children to school. The familial links that had organized the work force in the British textile factory for over a quarter-century faded when the women and children who worked there began to be supervised by men who were not their relatives.

Once parents ceased to be present to watch over their children in factories, public concern developed for the child laborer. In 1833 the English Factory Act forbade the employment of children under age nine, limited to nine hours the workday of children below the age of thirteen, and required that these children be given two hours of education a day at company expense.

The effect of reform legislation was to further divide work and home life. Adult males and older teenagers worked twelve-hour days, and younger children worked in relays of four or six hours. This diminished parent-child contact and passed on to schools the responsibility for some of the nurturing and training that traditionally had been done in the home. After the English Factory Act was passed, many of the British working class demanded shorter workdays for adults. Since they no longer had a relationship with their children at work, they wanted more time to spend with them at home. In 1847 Parliament mandated a ten-hour day.

CHANGING ECONOMIC ROLE FOR THE FAMILY In the British textile industry by the middle of the 1840s, men of the working class had evolved distinct roles as breadwinners, fathers, and husbands. What occurred in Britain happened elsewhere as industrial capitalism and public education spread. The European family ceased to be an important unit of both production and consumption and became only a consumer. The family did not stop performing as an economic unit, but its members now lived by sharing wages derived from different sources rather than by sharing work in a home or factory. Families linked only by wages might be less closely bound than those that worked together. Wages could be sent over long distances, so children could live and work away from home. But it was also true that some children might stay home longer to accumulate the savings needed to marry and begin their own households.

Women in the Early Industrial Revolution

The concerns reformers raised about working conditions for women arose in part from a spreading societal conviction that woman's place was in the home, not the factory or even the field.

Opportunities and Exploitation in Employment

The industrial economy had an immense impact on the lives of women. By taking virtually all productive work out of the home and allowing many families to live on the wages of the male spouse, it created a new understanding of gender-determined roles. Women were associated with domestic duties: housekeeping, food preparation, child rearing and nurturing, and household management. Men were linked, almost exclusively, with breadwinning. The domestic division of labor into separate spheres for males and females that had existed only for the small middle class and the gentry came, during the nineteenth century, to characterize the working class as well.

WOMEN IN FACTORIES Women's factory work required fewer skills than the work expected of men, and it was more poorly paid. Paradoxically, factories created new jobs for women but diminished the level of their skills. The women who sought factory work were young single women or widows. When a woman married or certainly when she had a child, she usually gave up her job. Her husband was expected to support her, and employers did not want to accommodate her needs as a wife and mother. The loss of a husband and, therefore, the family income often sent such women back into the factories.

WORK ON THE LAND AND IN THE HOME In France the largest group of employed women worked the land. In England domestic servants constituted the majority of female laborers. All were poorly paid, relatively unskilled, and subjected to harsh working conditions. Desperation and need drove many to prostitution. The situation was not new, but what was new was the increased numbers of women who found themselves in positions of vulnerability.

Changing Expectations in Working-Class Marriage

Many traditional practices associated with the family economy survived into the industrial era. Most women expected to marry as soon as possible, and they sought employment so that they could earn dowries. A girl born in the country often migrated to a nearby town or city for a job as a domestic, sometimes with a relative. If a girl became a factory worker, she might live in a supervised dormitory. Factory owners established these to recruit young workers from families that feared for their safety.

Female workers in nineteenth-century cities faced challenges known to few women of earlier generations. Movement to cities and entrance into the wage economy increased their freedom in the choice of marriage partners. Since there were fewer family and community ties, parents made fewer arranged marriages. There were also more available young men in cities than in rural villages. But since these men had greater mobility in terms of employment, their relationships with women may have been more fleeting. Cohabitation during courtship seems to have been common, and the number of illegitimate births increased. Since marriage usually meant that a woman left the work force to live on her husband's earnings, it might improve her situation. But if her husband became ill or died or deserted her, she returned to the labor market to face harder competition from younger women.

Reliance on industrial wages diminished marriage's function as an economic partnership and created a new set of gender relationships. By separating the workplace from the home, industrialization made it difficult for women to combine domestic duties with wage employment. When married women worked, it was usually because of dire family necessity. Since children were sent out to work more often than wives, children became an economic asset. This encouraged higher birthrates.

The domestic duties of working-class women were unpaid but essential to their family's wage-based economy. While most members of a family worked abroad, someone had to maintain the home front. The separation of home life from the workplace made homemaking a distinct occupation with great economic significance. Since a female homemaker was primarily responsible for the purchases that provided her family's food and maintained its shelter, she often took charge of its finances.

Problems of Crime and Order

The revolutions Europe had experienced at the turn of the century made its propertied classes anxious about social upheaval at a time when the processes of industrialization and urbanization were already dislocating many communities. Thousands of people migrated from the countryside to the towns and cities, where they encountered poverty, disappointment, and frustration. For the first sixty years of the nineteenth century, crime increased slowly but steadily until it reached a plateau.

New Police Forces

The ruling classes developed two strategies for containing crime: improved policing and prison reform. Police forces did not exist until the early nineteenth century, when Europe invented the concept of a permanent police force distinct from an army. Police are a paid, trained group of civilian professionals charged with enforcing law, keeping order, protecting property and lives, investigating crime, and apprehending offenders. Their function is partly preemptive, that is, to prevent crime by merely being visible. Theoretically, at least, they have no involvement with politics. The powers and organization of police forces differed from one country to another, but their creation was fundamental to the establishment of an orderly society in Europe.

Professional police forces appeared in Paris in 1828. The same year, the British Parliament authorized police for London's streets. The Londoners came to be called "bobbies" after Sir Robert Peel (1788–1850), sponsor of the bill that created them. Police on the Continent were armed; those in Britain were not. All were distinguished by an easily recognizable uniform.

Prison Reform

Before the nineteenth century, Europe had several kinds of prisons: local jails, state prisons such as Paris's Bastille, and prison ships. Some Mediterranean nations forced prisoners to work out their terms of incarceration as rowers on galleys. All prisoners lived under wretched conditions. Men, women, and children were housed together. Those who had committed minor offenses were mixed with those guilty of the most serious crimes. Late in the eighteenth century, the British government began to transport serious offenders to foreign colonies (notably, to New South Wales in Australia). The practice continued until the middle of the nineteenth century, when some colonies began to raise ob-

jections. Britain then established public works prisons to house long-term prisoners.

Reformers, such as John Howard (1726–1790) and Elizabeth Fry (1780–1845) in England and Charles Lucas (1803–1889) in France, exposed the horrendous conditions in prisons and demanded change. But since there was little sympathy for criminals and less popular support for taxes to construct new prisons, governments were slow to respond. In the 1840s, however, both the French and the English launched some bold initiatives. On the theory that crime was the result of character flaws in criminals, reformers tried to design modes of imprisonment that would correct the criminal psyche. The result was an exceedingly repressive system.

All the popular experiments implemented ideas that spread to Europe from the United States. They involved separating prisoners from each other in individual cells. In the Auburn system (named for a prison in New York State), prisoners were confined alone during the night but worked together during the day. The Philadelphia system kept prisoners rigorously isolated at all times. In the Pentonville Prison near London, no prisoner was ever allowed to speak to or even see another one. Each wore a mask when in the prison yard, and each had a separate stall in the chapel. The point of the system was to turn the prisoner's mind in on itself and to force it to con-

In many prisons, treadmills like these were the only source of exercise available to English prisoners. Bildarchiv Preussischer Kulturbesitz

front its criminal tendencies. The intense isolation often triggered mental collapse.

Prisoners were supposed to be trained in some kind of trade or skill while in prison so that they could reemerge as reformed, productive citizens. Those who failed rehabilitation were dealt with very harshly. In 1885 the French government began to send repeat serious offenders to places such as the infamous Devil's Island off the coast of South America. The idea was to excise from society the criminal elements that could not be saved.

Classical Economics

Nineteenth-century attitudes toward commerce were shaped by the *classical economists*, the disciples of Adam Smith who advocated economic growth through competitive free enterprise. Their ideal society was one in which individuals competed on their own to meet the demands of consumers in the marketplace. They distrusted government intervention in economic processes and believed that government's functions ought to be limited to maintaining a sound currency, enforcing contracts, protecting property, and keeping tariffs and taxes low.

Malthus on Population

Classical economic theory, as developed by Thomas Malthus (1766–1834) and David Ricardo (1772–1823), maintained that the condition of the working class could not be improved. Malthus's *Essay on the Principle of Population* (1798) claimed that population must eventually outstrip the supply of food, for population grows geometrically and food production arithmetically. If wages were raised, this would only speed up the process by encouraging workers to have more children. The only hope for improving the lot of the poor, Malthus believed, lay in persuading the working class to spend its wages on consumer goods and have fewer children. Employers welcomed Malthus's theories as justifications for low wages and opposition to trade unionization.

Ricardo on Wages

David Ricardo's *Principles of Political Economy* (1817) derived an "Iron Law of Wages" from Malthus's work. If wages were raised, more children would be produced. When they entered the labor market, the increased number of workers would lower wages. As wages fell, working people would have fewer children. When a labor shortage then developed, wages would again rise—and the process would start all over again. The effect, in the long run, was to keep wages at a minimum level.

Government Policies Based on Classical Economics

The major classical economists were British, as was the utilitarian philosopher Jeremy Bentham (1748–1832). Bentham proposed a "principle of utility" (i.e, the greatest happiness for the greatest number) as a scientific standard to guide government decisions. In his *Fragment on Government* (1776) and *The Principles of Morals and Legislation* (1789), he argued that the application of the principle of utility would sweep aside the special interests of privileged groups and the legal clutter that obstructed justice. Bentham's disciples combined his ideas with those of classical economics and persuaded the House of Commons, in 1834, to pass a new Poor Law. It was premised on the idea that if people did not work, they must be lazy, and it set up a Poor Law Commission to make sure that the poor were motivated to embrace self-discipline and hard labor. Government poor relief was disbursed only in workhouses, where living conditions were intentionally very unpleasant.

The second British monument to applied classical economics was the repeal of the Corn Laws in 1846. For years, an Anti–Corn Law League, organized by manufacturers, had tried to persuade the government to abolish tariffs protecting the domestic price of grain. That change, they argued, would lead to lower food prices, which would allow them to cut wages for their workers. This would reduce costs for British manufactured goods and enhance their competitive position in the world market. The need to open Britain's ports to foreign grain to counteract the effects of the Irish potato famine also encouraged Parliament to act, and its repeal of the Corn Laws began an era of free trade that lasted until late in the century.

Early Socialism

The socialist movement (either in the form of communism or social democracy) was one of the major political forces in twentieth-century

Europe, but 150 years ago it had no significant following. Early socialists were often fans of industrialization because of its great productive capacity, but they did not believe that the free market could adequately manage the production and distribution of goods. An unregulated industrial system, they believed, resulted in mismanagement, low wages, poor distribution, and widespread suffering. Socialists wanted society to function as a humane community, not an aggregate of atomistic, selfish individuals.

Utopian Socialism

Early critics of industrialism were dubbed *utopian socialists* by their opponents, for their visionary programs often involved the creation of ideal communities with noncapitalistic values. Almost all such proposals involved radical changes in society's attitudes toward sexuality and the family. People who were sympathetic with their economic ideas were often alienated by their advocacy of free love and open family relationships.

SAINT-SIMONIANISM   Count Claude Henri de Saint-Simon (1760–1825) was the earliest of the socialist pioneers. A liberal French aristocrat, he fought in the American Revolution and welcomed the French Revolution. By Napoleon's day, he had become a writer and social critic. Saint-Simon was convinced that modern society required thoroughly rational management. His ideal government was a board of directors that achieved harmony by coordinating the activity of individuals and groups. In a sense, he was the ideological father of technocracy. He believed that expert management of wealth, not its redistribution, would alleviate poverty and suffering.

OWENISM   The first major British advocate of socialism was Robert Owen (1771–1858), a self-made industrialist. In his early twenties, Owen became a partner in a cotton factory in New Lanark, Scotland, one of Britain's largest mills. Owen believed in the environmentalist principles of Enlightenment psychology: that is, that human characters could be improved by improving their surroundings. Owen also believed that a company could provide humane working conditions and still make a profit.

Owen tested his theories at New Lanark. Its workers were provided with good quarters. They

had abundant opportunities for recreation, and schools were set up for their children. Although Owen himself was a notorious freethinker on matters of religion and sex, he tolerated churches. Incentives were offered to encourage good work, and the workers vindicated Owen's faith in them by making a fine profit for his company.

Visitors flocked from all over Europe to see what Owen had accomplished through enlightened management. In numerous articles and pamphlets, and in letters to influential people, he pleaded for a general organizational reform of industry. Finally, he sold his New Lanark factory and, during the 1820s, toured the United States. At New Harmony, Indiana, he founded another model community. It failed, but he was not discouraged. He returned to Britain to promote the Grand National Union, a unification of all the British trade unions. It collapsed in the early 1830s.

FOURIERISM   In France, Charles Fourier (1772–1837) developed ideas similar to Owen's, but he was less successful financially and in attracting public attention. Fourier believed that the industrial order erred in ignoring the emotional side of human nature, the natural human desire for things in which to take delight. He advocated the construction of communities called phalanxes, where liberated customs would dispel the dullness of factory life.

Agrarian rather than industrial production was to predominate in Fourier's phalanxes. Sexual activity was to be relatively free, and marriage was to be delayed until later in life. Fourier urged that no person be required to perform the same job for an entire day. He argued that people would be happier and more productive if they moved from one task to another. Fourier's discussion of the problem of boredom highlighted one of the key difficulties of modern economic life.

Saint-Simon, Owen, and Fourier expected governments to implement their ideas, but they failed to confront the political difficulties of radical social transformation. Others paid more attention to practical politics. In the Organization of Labor (1839) Louis Blanc (1811–1882) called for an end to competition but not for a wholly new social order. He believed that giving the vote to workers would adequately empower them to use the political process to reform the system. A state controlled by its working class would set up workshops to employ the poor, and in time, such shops might replace private enterprise and reorganize industry to ensure jobs for everyone. The state could become the great employer, an employer that was kept true to the mission of improving the conditions of labor by the laborers themselves.

Anarchism

A few social critics of the 1840s were called *anarchists* because they opposed any cooperation with organized industries or governments. Some believed that violence and terrorism would be needed to force society to change; others trusted in peaceful means.

Auguste Blanqui (1805–1881), a major advocate for terror, sought the abolition of both capitalism and the state. His ideas for a new society were vague, but his strategy for achieving it—the development of a revolutionary vanguard professionally equipped to attack capitalism—foreshadowed Lenin's program for managing the Russian Revolution. Pierre Joseph Proudhon (1809–1865), author of *What Is Property?* (1840), was a peaceful anarchist who wanted society to be organized on the basis of mutualism. He believed that a system of small businesses peacefully cooperating and exchanging goods would make the state redundant. Proudhon influenced the French labor movement, which was less political than comparable movements in Britain and Germany.

Marxism

Too often European socialism is seen as developing naturally or necessarily into Marxism. Nothing could be further from the truth. At midcentury the opinions of Karl Marx were simply one ingredient among many in the heady mixture of ideas discussed by critics of emerging industrial capitalist society. Marxism differed from its competitors primarily in its claim to a scientific foundation and in its insistence on reform through revolution. Marx also set the rise of industrialized societies in the context of a theory about the processes of historical development, and from this he drew sweeping political conclusions.

Karl Marx (1818–1883) was the son of a German-Jewish family that converted to Lutheranism. He was trained at the University of Berlin,

Karl Marx's socialist philosophy eventually triumphed over most alternative versions of socialism in Europe, but his monumental work became subject to varying interpretations, criticisms, and revisions that continue to this day. Bildarchiv Preussischer Kulturbesitz

where Hegelian philosophy and radical politics, not Judaism, shaped his education. When editorship (1842–1843) of a radical newspaper (the *Rheinische Zeitung*) caused him to be exiled from his native land, he moved to Paris, then to Brussels, and finally, after 1849, to London.

PARTNERSHIP WITH ENGELS In 1844 Marx met Friedrich Engels (1820–1895), another young middle-class German, but one whose father owned a textile factory in Manchester, England. The next year, Engels published *The Conditions of the Working Class in England*, a devastating picture of industrial life. Late in 1847 Engels and Marx were asked to write a pamphlet explaining the philosophy of a newly organized (and short-lived) secret society, the Communist League. The league embraced the name *communist* because it was more radical than socialist. Communism implied the outright abolition of private property rather than socialism's less thorough re-organization of economies. The *Communist Manifesto,* though only about fifty pages long, was to become the most influential political document in modern European history. The recent collapse of the Soviet Union and the communist governments in eastern Europe make it difficult for many people now to grasp the power that Marx's vision had for so many for so long.

SOURCES OF MARX'S IDEAS   Marx drew his theories from German Hegelianism, French socialism, and British classical economics. Hegel had explained intellectual progress as a historical process by which a thesis and an antithesis clash until they form a synthesis. What Hegel saw in the history of thought, Marx saw in the history of societies. That is, he claimed that conflicts between dominant and subordinate groups led to the rise of a new dominant group for a society—and that this group then became the source of new discontents and conflicts that led to yet further development.

The socialists helped make Marx aware of the significance of property distribution in the formation of classes, and the classical economists provided the analytical tools with which he carried out an empirical, scientific examination of industrial capitalist society. He came to the conclusion that the new industrial work force, the proletariat, was the most potent force in contemporary history. Marx equated the fate of the working class with the fate of humanity itself. He argued that a universal utopian society would emerge as the proletariat succeeded in liberating itself from bondage to the capitalist mode of industrial production.

REVOLUTION THROUGH CLASS CONFLICT   In *The Communist Manifesto,* Marx and Engels contended that reason provided a simple explanation for the whole of human history: History is fundamentally the story of humankind's struggle with the physical world to obtain the goods needed for survival. The structures, values, and ideas of a society are a function of the economy that sustains it. History is driven, Marx claimed, by a conflict between the classes who own and control the means of production and the classes who work for them. Conflict between these groups is not an accidental by-product of mismanagement or bad intentions. It is inherent in the structures of production. Consequently, piecemeal reforms cannot eliminate social and economic evils. A radical transformation of society is required, and Marx believed that the natural development of capitalism would inevitably bring about a revolution that would achieve this.

Marx and Engels believed that class conflict had, early in the nineteenth century, become a simplified struggle between the bourgeoisie and the proletariat—between the middle class and the workers. The nature of capitalism ensured that the struggle would intensify. Capitalist competition and large-scale industrial production would steadily increase the size of the unpropertied proletariat by forcing both traditional and smaller industrial producers into its ranks. As business structures grew ever larger, competitive pressures would reduce the size of the middle class and generate a larger, more miserable proletariat. Eventually these suffering workers, Marx contended, would be driven to foment revolution and overthrow the few remaining owners of the means of production. For a time, the workers would then manage the means of production through a dictatorship of the proletariat, but this would eventually give way to a propertyless, classless communist society—the end product of the Hegelian dialectic process that governed history. Although the class conflict that would bring the proletariat to power resembled earlier social clashes, it differed in a significant respect. The victorious proletariat, by its very nature as a huge majority, could not become a new oppressor class. Having no significant group to oppress, it would automatically function for the good of all.

Marx's prediction of the collapse of capitalism in the later part of the nineteenth century proved to be wrong. Nor did the middle class become proletarianized, as Marx had expected. Rather, more and more people benefitted from the capitalist industrial system. Nonetheless, Marxist doctrines thrived. The utopian vision of ultimate human liberation they projected appeared to be based on the empirical evidence of hard economic fact. For people of the late nineteenth century, who were fascinated by all things scientific, the scientific aura of Marxism enhanced its credibility. Within a generation, Marxism had captured the imagination of many socialists (especially in Germany) and large segments of the working class.

1848: Year of Revolutions

A series of revolutions erupted across the continent in 1848. They had no single cause, but the conditions that encouraged them were the same in many places: severe food shortages, economic depression, widespread unemployment, overburdened poor relief systems, wretched living conditions in cities, and increasing frustration and discontent among the artisan and laboring classes.

The agents of change in 1848 were not workers but political liberals from the middle classes who were agitating for more civil liberties, better representative government, and an unregulated economy. Although they preferred to pursue their objectives by peaceful means, they put pressure on governments by appealing for support from the urban working classes. The workers had little interest in liberal political reform. They wanted improved working and economic conditions, and they were prepared to use violence to get them. Everywhere but in France nationalism also played a part in the uprisings.

The 1848 revolutions were stunning, for never in a single year had Europe known so many major uprisings. Yet, without exception, the revolutions failed because their supporters fragmented. Nationalistic groups turned against each other, and differences in goals soon divided middle-class revolutionaries from those who came from the working classes.

France: The Second Republic and Louis Napoleon

Now as before, the tinder of revolution was first ignited in Paris. During 1846 and 1847 France's economy went into decline, and the regime of Louis Philippe and his minister Guizot seemed adept only at corruption. Liberal opponents of the monarchy organized a series of banquets to rally support for increasing the political privileges of the middle class, and angry workers were eager to back any movement critical of the government. When the king tried to silence his opponents by forbidding the political banquets (February 21, 1848), a crowd of disgruntled Parisian workers took to the streets. The government quickly lost control, and within a few days Louis Philippe had abdicated and fled to England (February 24, 1848).

THE NATIONAL ASSEMBLY AND PARIS WORKERS Led by the poet Alphonse de Lamartine (1790–1869), the liberals set up a provisional government to organize an election for a new National Assembly and to write a new republican constitution. Various Parisian working-class groups wanted more—a social as well as a political revolution. They demanded posts in the cabinet for their leader, Louis Blanc, and two of his compatriots. These men forced the government to fund public works and relief programs.

On April 23, an election based on universal male suffrage chose the new National Assembly. Moderates and conservatives won most of the seats, for electors in the provinces were not as inclined to radical socialist reform as the workers of Paris. When the new government began to trim back public works projects and relief programs, crowds of unemployed Parisians rioted, and late in June, they began to erect barricades across some city streets. The government then ordered General Cavaignac (1802–1857) to call in troops from the conservative countryside to restore order. Over 400 people were killed in two days of combat, and another 3,000 were subsequently hunted down.

EMERGENCE OF LOUIS NAPOLEON The so-called June Days ended the drive for social revolution and confirmed dominance of French politics by men who wanted safety for small property. The conservatives were further strengthened when, late in 1848, Louis Napoleon Bonaparte (1808–1873), nephew of the former emperor, won election to the presidency. The voters associated the name of Bonaparte with stability and greatness.

The election of the "Little Napoleon" doomed the Second Republic, for Louis Napoleon was dedicated to his own fame, not to republican ideals. He was the first of the modern dictators, a man who ruled by manipulating unstable political situations and exploiting the insecurity of the masses. He opposed the National Assembly, claiming that he, not it, represented the will of the nation. When the assembly refused to amend the constitution to allow him to run for reelection, he used soldiers to disperse it—on December 2, 1851, the anniversary of his uncle's victory at Austerlitz. Over 200 people died resisting his coup, and more than 26,000 were arrested. About 10,000 of these were ultimately transported to

Algeria. A plebiscite was scheduled for December 21, 1851, and only about 600,000 voters protested Louis Napoleon's actions. A year later, another plebiscite approved his decision to proclaim himself Emperor Napoleon III. For the second time in just over fifty years, France had turned from republicanism to Caesarism.

FRENCH WOMEN IN 1848   Following the collapse of the July Monarchy and Louis Philippe's abdication, numerous political clubs sprang up. Some, particularly in Paris, mobilized women who wanted to work for women's rights. A radical group called the *Vesuvians* (after Italy's volcano) demanded full equality between men and women in the home, the right of women to serve in the military, and similarity in dress for both sexes. Feminism of this kind remained a politically naive fringe phenomenon, but a more conservative women's movement won some support in the National Assembly. By lauding the importance of the traditional family and motherhood, it defended itself against the charge that feminists wanted to destroy marriage and family life.

Some Parisian feminists moved quickly to use the liberal freedoms that had suddenly become available to promote their cause. They founded a daily newspaper, the *Voix des femmes* (*The Women's Voice*), to demand that special attention be given to women's interests. It pointed out that reforms that improved things for men did not necessarily liberate women. A society with the same name as the newspaper was created to work with male political groups. It cleverly appealed to the conservatives' faith in the importance of the family to make a case for women's rights. Because motherhood and child rearing were so important to society, the *Voix des femmes* argued that women needed educations, employment, economic security, civil and property rights, and the vote.

Feminists met the same fate as the workers who helped launch the revolution of 1848: total defeat. Women, as well as men, were hurt when the conservative National Assembly cut back relief and public works projects. A subsequent crackdown on political clubs destroyed the arena in which they worked for reform, and soon they were specifically forbidden to participate in any political clubs. The *Voix des femmes* tried to skirt this law by creating labor organizations dedicated to helping working-class women. But

two leaders of this movement, Jeanne Deroin (d. 1894) and Pauline Roland (1805–1852) were arrested, tried, imprisoned, and exiled. By the time of Louis Napoleon's triumph in 1852, the feminist movement that had sprung up in 1848 had been eradicated.

The Habsburg Empire: Nationalism Resisted

France's revolution of 1848 shook the Habsburg domains, where the frustrations of liberals and nationalists were building to dangerous levels. The imperial regime was suddenly confronted by revolts in Vienna, Prague, Hungary, and Italy, and its stability was adversely affected by disturbances that broke out in Germany.

THE VIENNA UPRISING   The Habsburg troubles began on March 3, 1848, when Louis Kossuth (1802–1894), a Magyar nationalist and member of the Hungarian Diet, called for the independence of Hungary. His speeches inspired students to riot in Vienna. When the army failed to restore order, Metternich resigned and fled the country—leaving his feeble-minded emperor, Ferdinand (r. 1835–1848), to try to restore order by promising a moderately liberal constitution. Radicals among the students were not satisfied with this and formed democratic clubs to press the revolution further. On May 17, the emperor and his court fled to Innsbruck and surrendered Vienna to a committee composed of about 200 people. The committee's chief concern was to address the plight of Viennese workers.

What the Habsburg government feared most was not an urban worker rebellion but an uprising of the serfs. There had already been isolated instances of serfs invading manor houses and burning records. Almost immediately after the Vienna revolt, the imperial government emancipated the serfs in much of Austria, and the Hungarian Diet followed suit and abolished serfdom in March 1848. These actions headed off the most serious potential threat to order in the empire, and the end of serfdom was among the most important permanent achievements of the revolutions of 1848.

THE MAGYAR REVOLT   The Vienna revolt encouraged dissident Hungarians to take action. The Magyar leaders were primarily liberals backed by nobles who wanted to protect their aristocratic privileges against infringement by the Habsburg government. The Hungarian Diet's reform program, which was spelled out in the March Laws, demanded equality of religion, jury trials, the election of a lower chamber, a relatively free press, and payment of taxes by the nobility. Emperor Ferdinand, who had little choice, acquiesced.

The Magyars also wanted a nearly autonomous Hungarian state within the Habsburg domains. The partially independent nation they envisioned required them to annex Transylvania, Croatia, and neighboring parts of the Habsburg Empire. That brought Romanians, Croatians, and Serbs under their control, and these groups resisted Magyarization (particularly through the imposition of the Hungarian language). The minority populations concluded that their chances for ethnic survival were better under the Habsburg government. In late March, the Vienna government sent Count Joseph Jellachich (1801–1859) to assist the rebels who were rebelling against the Hungarian rebels. By early September 1848, he was invading Hungary with the strong support of the opponents of Magyarization.

CZECH NATIONALISM In the middle of March 1848, with Vienna and Budapest in revolt, Czech nationalists demanded that Bohemia and Moravia be recognized as an autonomous Slavic state within the empire. Conflict immediately developed between the Czechs and the Germans who inhabited these regions.

The Czechs convened a meeting of representatives of the Slavic peoples (i.e., Poles, Ruthenians, Czechs, Slovaks, Croats, Slovenes, and Serbs) in Prague early in June. Francis Palacky (1798–1876), leader of this first Pan-Slavic Congress, issued a manifesto calling for the national equality of Slavs within the Habsburg Empire and protesting the repression of the Slavic peoples who were under Habsburg, Hungarian, German, and Ottoman domination. The document envisioned a vast Slavic nation or federation extending from Poland south and eastward through Ukraine. Such a state never came into being, but the dream of a unified, independent Slavic people was a useful political tool. Russia invoked Pan-Slavism to win the support of nationalist minorities in eastern Europe and the Balkans and to bring pressure against Austria and Germany.

On June 12, the day the Pan-Slavic Congress closed, an insurrection erupted in Prague. By June 17, General Prince Alfred Windischgraetz (1787–1862) had put it down. The middle class was happy to see the radicals suppressed, and resident Germans approved the smothering of Czech nationalism. A policy of "dividing and conquering" had worked.

REBELLION IN NORTHERN ITALY In addition to the Hungarian and Czech revolts, the Habsburg government faced war in northern Italy. On March 18, 1848, a revolution began in Milan, and five days later General Count Joseph Wenzel Radetzky (1766–1858), the Austrian commander, withdrew from the city. King Charles Albert of Piedmont (r. 1831–1849), whose kingdom was in Lombardy (the province of which Milan is the capital), aided the rebels. In July Radetzky, reinforced by new troops, defeated Piedmont and suppressed the revolution.

The emperor returned to Vienna in midsummer. A newly elected assembly was struggling to write a constitution while dealing with radicals who pressed for ever more concessions. When a new insurrection broke out in October, the imperial government reacted strongly. Its army bombarded Vienna and crushed the revolt. On December 2, Emperor Ferdinand, now clearly too feeble to govern, abdicated in favor of a young nephew, Francis Joseph (r. 1848–1916). By January 5, 1849, Austrian troops had occupied Budapest, and by March they had imposed military rule in Hungary. The Magyar nobles attempted one last revolt, but in August, the Austrian army—reinforced by 200,000 soldiers happily furnished by Tsar Nicholas I of Russia (r. 1825–1855)—crushed the Hungarians. Divisions among the empire's enemies and a determination to use military force had enabled it to survive the gravest internal challenges.

Italy: Republicanism Defeated

The brief Piedmont-Austrian war of 1848 was only the first stage in Italy's revolution. After King Charles Albert of Piedmont was defeated by the Austrians, Italy's nationalists pinned their hopes for the unification of their country on their liberal pope, Pius IX (r. 1846–1878). Unfortunately, however, political radicalism got out of control in Rome. On November 15, 1848, a democratic extremist assassinated Count Pelligrino Rossi (1787–1848), the liberal minister of the Papal States. The next day, popular demonstrations forced the pope to appoint a radical ministry, and shortly thereafter he fled to Naples. In February 1849, the radicals proclaimed Rome a republic, and nationalists from all over Italy—most prominently Giuseppe Mazzini (1805–1872) and Giuseppe Garibaldi (1807–1882)—flocked to the city. They hoped to use Rome as a base of operations to unite Italy under a republican government.

In March 1849, radicals in Piedmont forced Charles Albert to renew the war against Austria. Prompt defeat led to his abdication in favor of his son Victor Emmanuel II (r. 1849–1878). Piedmont's surrender meant that the Roman Republic was left to defend itself alone. Since France wanted to prevent the rise of a strong nation on its southern border, it decided to enter the fray. In early June 1849, 10,000 French soldiers laid siege to Rome. The Roman Republic dissolved, and on July 3, Rome fell to the French, who remained in Italy to protect the pope until 1870. These events ended Pius IX's flirtation with liberalism. The pope became an archconservative, and Italy's nationalists had to look elsewhere for a leader to unify their homeland.

Germany: Liberalism Frustrated

Revolutionary contagion spread rapidly through the German states of Württemberg, Saxony, Hanover, and Bavaria. The rebels demanded liberal governments and greater national unity. The most serious disturbances took place in Prussia.

REVOLUTION IN PRUSSIA   Since Frederick William IV (r. 1840–1861) preferred to believe that foreign agitators were to blame, he refused to turn his troops on the Berliners who rioted on March 15, 1848. When the royal government failed to overcome its own internal confusion and restore order, the king agreed to convene a constituent assembly to write a Prussian constitution. He also implied that he would work for German unification. For all practical purposes, the Prussian monarchy capitulated.

Frederick William IV appointed a cabinet headed by David Hansemann (1790–1864), a respected moderate liberal. However, it found that it could not work with the radical democrats

The Revolutionary Crisis of 1848–1851

1848
February 22–24	Abdication of Louis Philippe
March 3	Kossuth demands freedom for Hungary
March 13	Revolution in Vienna
March 15	Habsburg emperor accepts the March Laws
March 18	Frederick William IV promises a constitution Revolution in Milan
March 22	Piedmont declares war on Austria
April 23	Election of the French National Assembly
May 17	Emperor Ferdinand flees Vienna
May 18	The Frankfurt Assembly gathers
June 2	Pan-Slavic Congress convenes in Prague
July 24	Austria defeats Piedmont
September 17	General Jellachich invades Hungary
October 31	General Windischgraetz pacifies Vienna
November 16	Revolution in Rome
November 25	Pope Pius IX flees Rome
December 2	Francis Joseph becomes Habsburg emperor
December 10	Louis Napoleon and the Second French Republic

1849
January 5	General Windischgraetz occupies Budapest
February 2	The Roman Republic proclaimed
March 12	War resumes between Piedmont and Austria
March 2	Piedmont is defeated, Victor Emmanuel II crowned
March 28	German crown offered to Frederick William IV
June 18	Frankfurt Parliament dispersed
July 3	Collapse of the Roman Republic
August 9–13	Austria defeats Hungarian forces

1851
December 2	*Coup d'état* of Louis Napoleon

seated in the constituent assembly. The king, in frustration, replaced his liberal ministry with a conservative one and, in April 1849, dissolved the assembly and proclaimed a constitution of his own. All adult males were given the vote, but they were divided into three classes (according to the taxes they paid) and limited to voting for representatives from their class. This meant that the major taxpayers—about 5 percent of the population—elected one-third of the Parliament. The ministry reported to the king alone, and the Prussian army swore direct loyalty to him.

THE FRANKFURT PARLIAMENT On May 18, 1848, representatives from all the German states gathered in Saint Paul's Church in Frankfurt to reorganize the German Confederation. The Frankfurt Parliament intended to write a moderately liberal constitution for a united Germany, but the assembly's liberalism alienated conservatives and members of the working class. Conservatives resented any challenge to the existing political order, and workers and artisans disliked liberalism's commitment to free trade (i.e., liberalism's hostility to the protections the guild system offered labor). At Frankfurt a split developed between liberals and workers, which German conservatives were able to exploit for the rest of the century.

The Frankfurt Parliament also floundered in its discussions of unification. Members could not agree on whether to include Austria in a united Germany. The *kleindeutsch* (small German) faction prevailed over the *grossdeutsch* (large German) party when Austria rejected the whole notion of unification. Austria took this stance because the numerous nationalities resident within the Habsburg domains feared German domination.

Austria's opposition to unification strengthened support for Prussian leadership of Germany. On March 27, 1849, the parliament produced a constitution and offered the crown of a united Germany to Frederick William IV of Prussia. He rejected the offer, asserting that kings ruled by the grace of God, not with permission from man-made constitutions. His refusal caused the Frankfurt Parliament to collapse and gave German liberals a blow from which they never recovered. In the end, all the various revolutions accomplished was an extension of the franchise in some of the German states and the establishment of conservative constitutions.

In Perspective

During the first half of the nineteenth century, Europeans confronted unprecedented social challenges. The emerging industrial economy was transforming virtually all their institutions, and the societal tensions this caused generated political strife. The liberal revolution that began in France in 1789 peaked as the uprisings of 1848 were suppressed and conservatives seized the political initiative. After 1848 the European middle class ceased to be revolutionary and became increasingly concerned with protecting its property. In particular, it feared radical movements associated with socialism and, eventually, with Marxism.

REVIEW QUESTIONS

1. What inventions were particularly important in the development of industrialism? What changes did industrialism make in society? Why were the years covered in this chapter so difficult for artisans? What is meant by "the proletarianization of workers"?

2. In what ways did the industrial economy change the working-class family? What roles and duties did various family members assume? How did the role of women change in the new industrial era?

3. What were the goals of the working class in the new industrial society? How did they differ from middle-class goals? How do you explain the separation of working-class and middle-class goals?

4. How did police change in the nineteenth century? Why were new systems of enforcement instituted? In what ways were prisons improved? How do you account for the reform movement that led to the improvements?

5. How would you define *socialism*? Were Karl Marx's ideas different from those of the socialists?

6. Why did revolutions break out in so many places in 1848? Were circumstances essentially the same or were they different in the various countries? Why did the revolutions fail? What roles did liberals and nationalists play in them? Did they always agree?

SUGGESTED READINGS

I. BERLIN, *Karl Marx: His Life and Environment* (1948). An excellent introduction.

P. BROCK, *The Slovak National Awakening* (1976). A standard work.

J. COFFIN, *The Politics of Women's Work* (1996). Examines the situation in France.

W. COLEMAN, *Death Is a Social Disease: Public Health and Political Economy in Early Industrial France* (1982). One of the first works in English to study this problem.

I. DEAK, *The Lawful Revolution: Louis Kossuth and the Hungarians, 1848–1849* (1979). The most significant study of the topic in English.

J. ELSTER, *An Introduction to Karl Marx* (1985). The best volume to provide a discussion of Marx's fundamental concepts.

T. HAMEROW, *Restoration, Revolution, and Reaction: Economics and Politics in Germany, 1815–1871* (1958). Traces the forces that worked toward the failure of revolution in Germany.

J. F. C. HARRISON, *Quest for the New Moral World: Robert Owen and the Owenites in Britain and America* (1969). Now the standard work.

G. HIMMELFARB, *The Idea of Poverty: England in the Early Industrial Age* (1984). A major work covering the subject from the time of Adam Smith through 1850.

M. IGNATIEFF, *A Just Measure of Pain: The Penitentiary in the Industrial Revolution, 1750–1850* (1978). An important treatment of early English penal thought and practice.

D. LANDES, *The Unbound Prometheus: Technological Change and Industrial Development in Western Europe from 1750 to the Present* (1969). The best one-volume treatment of technological development in a broad social and economic context.

R. MAGRAW, *A History of the French Working Class*, 2 vols. (1992). A major overview based on the most recent literature.

J. M. MERRIMAN, *The Agony of the Republic: The Repression of the Left in Revolutionary France, 1848–1851* (1978). A major study of the manner in which the Second French Republic and popular support for it were suppressed.

H. PERKIN, *The Origins of Modern English Society, 1780–1880* (1969). A provocative attempt to look at the society as a whole.

I. PINCHBECK, *Women Workers and the Industrial Revolution, 1750–1850* (1930, reprinted 1969). A pioneering study that remains of great value.

P. ROBERTSON, *An Experience of Women: Pattern and Change in Nineteenth-Century Europe* (1982). A useful survey.

D. SORKIN, *The Transformation of German Jewry, 1780–1840* (1987). An examination of the decades of Jewish emancipation in Germany.

E. P. THOMPSON, *The Making of the English Working Class* (1964). An influential and controversial work.

L. A. TILLY and J. W. SCOTT, *Women, Work, and Family* (1978). A useful and sensitive survey.

D. WINCH, *Riches and Poverty: An Intellectual History of Political Economy in Britain, 1750–1834* (1996). A superb survey from Adam Smith through Thomas Malthus.

H. ZEHR, *Crime and the Development of Modern Society: Patterns of Criminality in Nineteenth-Century Germany and France* (1976). An examination of crimes against property in urban society.

Chapter 23

The Age of Nation-States

KEY TOPICS

- The unification of Italy and Germany
- The shift from empire to republic in France
- The emergence of dual monarchy in Austria-Hungary
- Reforms in Russia, including the emancipation of the serfs
- The emergence of Great Britain as the exemplary liberal state and its confrontation with Irish nationalists

Although the revolutions of 1848 collapsed and authoritarian regimes spread across Europe in the early 1850s, within a quarter of a century many of the objectives of early nineteenth-century liberals and nationalists had been realized. Italy and Germany were each unified under constitutional monarchies. The Habsburg emperor accepted a constitution and granted liberties to the Magyars of Hungary. Russia's tsar emancipated the serfs. France again became a republic. Liberalism and even democracy flourished in Great Britain. Paradoxically, most of this liberal agenda was enacted while conservatives were in power.

The Crimean War (1854–1856)

At midcentury the impetus for political change in Europe was the Crimean War (1854–1856), a product of a long-standing rivalry between Russia and the Ottoman Empire. Russia had both material and spiritual motives for beginning the conflict. It wanted to annex the Ottoman provinces of Moldavia and Walachia (modern Romania), and the tsar felt he had a duty to protect Orthodox Christians resident within the Ottoman Empire. Europe's other great powers soon became involved. France and Great Britain both had extensive naval and commercial interests in the eastern Mediterranean, and they did not want to see Russia increase its power in that region. Austria and Prussia chose to remain neutral. The Austrians had ambitions of their own in the Balkans, and Prussia decided to follow Austria's lead.

Both sides conducted the conflict ineptly. Their ill-equipped and poorly commanded armies bogged down along the Crimean coast of the Black Sea. In September 1855, the Russian fortress of Sevastopol finally fell to the French and British, and in March 1856, Russia came to terms. The Treaty of Paris required Russia to surrender territory near the mouth of the Danube River, to recognize the neutrality of the Black Sea, and to renounce claims of protection over Christians in the Ottoman Empire. Austria had already forced Russia out of Moldavia and Walachia. The aura of invincibility that Russia had enjoyed since defeating Napoleon was dispersed.

Also shattered was the Concert of Europe, the arrangement whereby nations were to consult on foreign policy issues in order to maintain the balance of power established by the Congress of Vienna. Napoleon III favored redrawing the map of Europe to recognize nationalities. The Austrians wanted more influence within the German Confederation. Prussia did not want its interests in Germany subordinated to Austria's. Russia, although it was the chief defender of the Vienna settlement, was determined to compensate itself for the humiliation inflicted on it by the Treaty of Paris. Britain, having stumbled through the Crimean War, was loath to risk any military involvement on the Continent.

Since the suppression of the 1848 revolutions had increased the confidence of nations in their ability to control domestic affairs, many were now more willing to embark on aggressive foreign policies to achieve their ends. Their ambition was limited only by the extent of their military and diplomatic resources. The most significant achievements of the era's political maneuvers were the unifications of Italy and Germany—developments that transformed Europe's international politics.

Italian Unification

Romantic Republicans

Nationalists had long wanted to fuse the small principalities of the Italian peninsula into a single state, but opinion differed about what should be done. Following the Congress of Vienna, the "romantic republicans" took the lead in rallying nationalistic sentiment. They organized secret societies throughout Italy and declared the unification of Italy to be a divine mission, a duty to God and to humanity.

In 1831 Giuseppe Mazzini (1805–1872), the most important nationalist leader in Europe, founded the Young Italy Society. It was dedicated to driving Austria from the peninsula and establishing a republic in Italy. During the 1830s and 1840s, Mazzini and his fellow republican, Giuseppe Garibaldi (1807–1882), led insurrections. Both were involved in the ill-fated Roman Republic of 1849, and throughout the 1850s they conducted what amounted to guerilla warfare. They spent much time in exile, and their travels took them to the United States where they and their cause became well known.

More moderate Italians wanted to end Austrian domination but not establish a republic. For a time, they proposed the papacy as a vehicle for unification. That plan foundered after Pius IX's disastrous experience with the Roman Republic in 1849. However, an alternative moderate liberal plan succeeded. Camillo Cavour (1810–1861), the prime minister of Piedmont, pursued a Machiavellian strategy (combining military force with secret diplomacy) to unify Italy under a constitutional monarchy.

Cavour's Policy

Piedmont in northwestern Italy was the most independent of the Italian states. The Congress of

Vienna had restored it to create a buffer between the French and the Austrians. During 1848 and 1849, King Charles Albert of Piedmont twice fought Austria. Following his second defeat, he abdicated in favor of his son, Victor Emmanuel II (r. 1849–878). In 1852 the new king appointed Count Camillo Cavour prime minister.

Cavour began political life as a conservative but gradually moved toward a moderately liberal position. A practical man deeply imbued with the ideas of the Enlightenment, classical economics, and utilitarianism, Cavour made a fortune investing in railroads, reforming agriculture on his estates, and editing a newspaper. He had no respect for Mazzini's romantic ideals or for republicanism. Believing that the unification of Italy was necessary for its economic and material progress, Cavour worked for free trade, railway construction, credit expansion, and agricultural improvement. Although he felt that material and economic bonds, not fuzzy romantic yearnings, would bring Italians together, he tried to win the support of nationalists of all kinds. To this end, he founded the Nationalist Society, which established chapters in other Italian states to press for unification under the leadership of Piedmont. Cavour also solicited help from France.

FRENCH SYMPATHIES Cavour used the Crimean War to establish a role for Italy in European politics. In 1855 Piedmont sent 10,000 troops to assist France and Britain. Participation in the war gave Cavour a seat at the Paris peace conference and an opportunity to raise the Italian question. He left Paris with no firm commitments, but he impressed the other diplomats and won Napoleon III's sympathy. For the rest of the decade, he courted international respectability by opposing Mazzini's various nationalist uprisings. Cavour's strategy was to depict Piedmont as a moderate liberal alternative to both republicanism and reactionary absolutism.

In January 1858, an Italian named Orsini tried to assassinate Napoleon III. The incident persuaded the French emperor to take a stronger interest in the Italian issue. He liked the idea of continuing his famous uncle's efforts to liberate the peninsula, and he wanted Piedmont as an ally against Austria. In July 1858, Cavour and Napoleon III met at Plombières in southern France and agreed to provoke a war in Italy that would give them a chance to defeat Austria. In exchange for its help, France was to receive French-speaking Nice and Savoy from Piedmont.

WAR WITH AUSTRIA When Austria objected to Piedmont mobilizing its army early in 1859, Piedmont claimed that Austria was provoking war. France joined in, and Austria was defeated at Magenta on June 4 and at Solferino on June 24. These victories encouraged revolutionaries who wanted union with Piedmont to seize control in Tuscany, Modena, Parma, and the Romagna provinces of the Papal States. This alarmed Napoleon III and prompted him to make a separate peace with Austria. Although Cavour felt betrayed, Austria had been driven from most of northern Italy, and Piedmont was able to annex Lombardy. Soon Parma, Modena, Tuscany, and the Romagna voted to become part of the Piedmontese kingdom.

GARIBALDI'S CAMPAIGN At this point, the romantic republicans pressured Cavour into completing the unification of northern and southern Italy. In May 1860, Garibaldi landed in Sicily with more than a thousand soldiers who had been outfitted in the north. He captured Palermo and prepared to invade the mainland. By September he controlled the kingdom of Naples.

Garibaldi wanted a republican Italy, but Cavour forestalled him by sending Piedmontese troops into the south. They conquered the remaining Papal States—except for the area around Rome, which the French preserved for the pope. Faced with the choice of sacrificing either republicanism or hope for national unity, Garibaldi unhappily accepted Piedmontese domination. Late in 1860 Naples and Sicily voted to join Piedmont's northern union.

The New Italian State

In March 1861, Victor Emmanuel II was proclaimed king of Italy, and three months later Cavour died. This was unfortunate, for the new state needed the skills of a consummate diplomat. Italy had been more nearly conquered than united. The republicans resented Piedmont's treatment of Garibaldi, and clerical factions resented its conquest of the Papal States. Furthermore, the economies of north and south were incompatible. The south was rural, poor, and

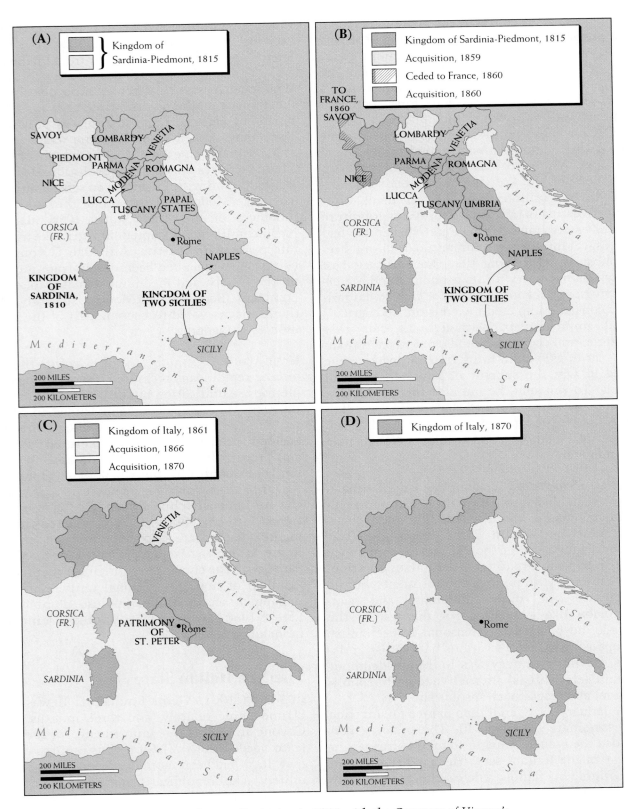

(A)

Kingdom of
Sardinia-Piedmont, 1815

SAVOY
LOMBARDY
PIEDMONT
PARMA
VENETIA
NICE
MODENA ROMAGNA
LUCCA
TUSCANY
PAPAL STATES
CORSICA (FR.)
• Rome
NAPLES
KINGDOM OF SARDINIA, 1810
KINGDOM OF TWO SICILIES
SICILY
Adriatic Sea
Mediterranean Sea
200 MILES
200 KILOMETERS

(B)

Kingdom of Sardinia-Piedmont, 1815
Acquisition, 1859
Ceded to France, 1860
Acquisition, 1860

TO FRANCE, 1860 SAVOY
LOMBARDY
VENETIA
NICE
PARMA
MODENA ROMAGNA
LUCCA
TUSCANY UMBRIA
CORSICA (FR.)
• Rome
NAPLES
SARDINIA
KINGDOM OF TWO SICILIES
SICILY
Adriatic Sea
Mediterranean Sea
200 MILES
200 KILOMETERS

(C)

Kingdom of Italy, 1861
Acquisition, 1866
Acquisition, 1870

VENETIA
CORSICA (FR.)
PATRIMONY OF ST. PETER
• Rome
SARDINIA
SICILY
Adriatic Sea
Mediterranean Sea
200 MILES
200 KILOMETERS

(D)

Kingdom of Italy, 1870

CORSICA (FR.)
• Rome
SARDINIA
SICILY
Adriatic Sea
Mediterranean Sea
200 MILES
200 KILOMETERS

MAP 23–1   THE UNIFICATION OF ITALY   *Beginning in 1815 with the Congress of Vienna's decision to combine the kingdom of Sardinia with Piedmont, Italian unification was achieved through the expansion of Piedmont (primarily between 1859 and 1870).*

backward. The north was industrializing and developing links to the rest of Europe. Large landholders and peasants peopled the south, while an urban working class emerged as the dominant group in the north. The south resorted to arms to delay the imposition of a Piedmontese-style administration until 1866.

The political machinery the monarchy set up to govern Italy was inadequate. Piedmont's constitution of 1848 provided for a conservative constitutional monarchy with a Parliament of two houses: a Senate appointed by the king and a Chamber of Deputies elected on a narrow franchise. Since ministers reported to the king and not to Parliament, Parliament had little power. Its leaders often simply avoided problems and kept themselves in power by *transformismo* (i.e., the use of bribes to "transform" enemies into friends). Italian politics became a byword for corruption.

Many Italians also believed that their nation would be incomplete until it acquired Venetia and Rome. Italy won the former in 1866 by supporting Prussia in the Austro-Prussian War. In 1870 the Franco-Prussian War forced the French to withdraw the troops that had been guarding Rome since 1849. The Italian state promptly annexed the city and declared it the nation's capital. The Vatican retained its independence, but the papacy remained hostile to the Italian state until 1929 when the two sides negotiated the Lateran Accord.

By 1870, of the lands Italians thought of as theirs, only the province of Trent and the city of Trieste remained under foreign domination (i.e., Austria's). A patriotic desire to liberate *Italia Irredenta* ("Unredeemed Italy") helped persuade the Italians to support the Allies against Austria and Germany during World War I.

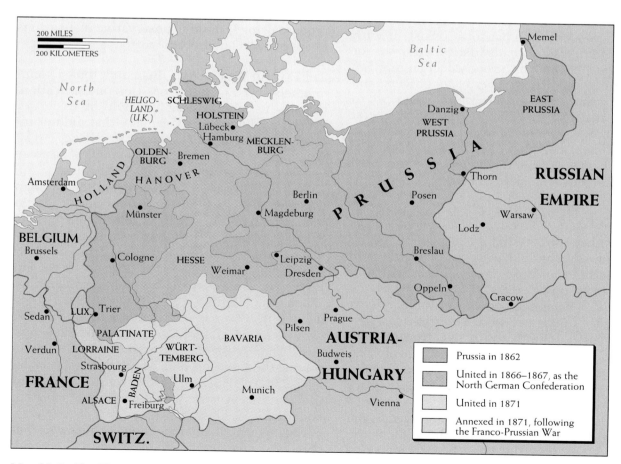

MAP 23–2 THE UNIFICATION OF GERMANY *Under Bismarck's leadership and with the strong support of its royal house, Prussia used diplomatic and military means, on both the German and international stages, to force unification on the German states.*

German Unification

The most important political development in Europe between 1848 and 1914 was the unification of Germany. German unity had been sought by two generations of liberals, but it was the product of moves conservatives made to outflank liberals.

Although the major German states were linked by trade agreements and railways, their unification seemed remote throughout the 1850s. Liberal nationalists were in retreat after the suppression of the revolts of 1848 and 1849. Frederick William IV of Prussia had quickly given up thoughts of leading the unification movement, and Austria opposed any union that might lessen its influence.

Prospects for unification suddenly improved, however, when Prussia's internal situation altered. In 1858 Frederick William IV was adjudged insane, and his brother William became his regent and then his successor. William I (r. 1861–1888) was less idealistic than his brother and more of a Prussian patriot. Consistent with Hohenzollern tradition, his first concern was for his troops. In 1860 he proposed enlarging the army, increasing the number of its officers, and extending the period of conscription from two to three years. The Prussian Parliament's liberal leaders, however, wanted to avoid increasing the power of the monarchy. They refused to approve the necessary taxes, and for two years monarch and Parliament were deadlocked.

Bismarck

In September 1862, William I turned for help to the person who, more than any other single individual, determined the course of Europe's history for the next thirty years: Otto von Bismarck (1815–1898). Bismarck came from Junker stock. He attended university, joined a *Burschenschaft* (i.e., one of the politically active student societies), and took an interest in German unification. During the 1840s he was elected to the provincial diet. Although he was so reactionary as to disturb even the king, he made his mark as a politician. From 1851 to 1859, he served as the Prussian delegate to the Frankfurt Diet of the German Confederation. Later he became Prussia's ambassador to Russia. He had just been named ambassador to France when William I decided to make him prime minister of Prussia.

Over the years, Bismarck mellowed into a conservative. He opposed parliamentary government but favored a strong monarchy under a constitution. He understood the importance to a nation of a strong industrial base, and he was, above all, a pragmatic politician, a believer that change was wrought more by power and action than by the discussion of ideas.

As soon as Bismarck became prime minister in 1862, he moved against the liberal Parliament. He contended that the Prussian constitution granted the government the power to impose the taxes it needed to carry out its regular functions. Therefore, the taxes required to expand the army could be collected despite the current Parliament's refusal to vote them. The army and most of the bureaucracy supported Bismarck's interpretation of the constitution, but in 1863 new elections sustained the liberal majority in the Parliament. Bismarck had to find a way to undercut the liberals and solicit popular support for the monarchy and the army. His strategy was to propose using Prussia's conservative institutions as a basis for German unification.

THE DANISH WAR (1864)   Bismarck took a *kleindeutsch* (small German) position on unification; that is, he believed that it would be easier for Prussia to dominate a Germany that did not include Austria. Since Austria was not likely to favor such an arrangement, Bismarck's strategy was to provoke and win a war with Austria.

A quarrel between Denmark and the German Confederation gave him an opportunity to begin maneuvering. The two northern duchies of Schleswig-Holstein had long been ruled by Denmark, but they were not part of Denmark. Holstein's population was more German than Danish, and it belonged to the German Confederation. When the Danish parliament annexed both duchies in 1863, the smaller states of the German Confederation clamored for war. Bismarck proposed that Prussia and Austria cooperate in resolving the situation, and Denmark was easily defeated. In August 1865, the Convention of Gastein declared that Austria would administer Holstein and Prussia, Schleswig.

Meanwhile, Bismarck gained Russia's friendship by supporting its suppression of a revolt in Poland in 1863, and he persuaded Napoleon III to promise neutrality in the event of a future Austro-Prussian conflict. In April 1866, Bismarck

Prince Otto von Bismarck (1815–1898) was the most important statesman of the second half of the nineteenth century. He used warfare and shrewd diplomacy to lead Prussia to unify Germany. Having achieved this goal, he worked for the rest of his career to keep the peace. Franz von Lenbach (1836–1904) *Prince Otto von Bismark in uniform with Prussian helmet.* Canvas. Kunsthistorisches Museum, Gemaeldegalerie, Vienna, Austria. (c) Photograph by Erich Lessing. Art Resource, NY

concluded a treaty with Italy, promising that Italy would get Venetia if it joined Prussia in an attack on Austria.

THE AUSTRO-PRUSSIAN WAR (1866) Austrian and Prussian forces clashed frequently in Schleswig and Holstein, for Bismarck ordered his men to provoke the Austrians by being as obnoxious as possible. On June 1, 1866, Austria appealed to the German Confederation against Prussia. Bismarck responded by claiming that this action violated Prussia's treaties with Austria, and he launched the Seven Weeks' War.

Austria was decisively defeated at Königgrätz in Bohemia. The only territory the subsequent Treaty of Prague forced Austria to surrender was Venetia, but loss of the war deprived the Habsburgs of the role they had

previously played in German affairs. Prussia emerged as the only major power among the German states.

THE NORTH GERMAN CONFEDERATION In 1867 Prussia annexed the German states (Hanover, Hesse, Nassau, and Frankfurt) that had allied with Austria during the war and created a confederation that united all of Germany north of the Main River. Each state retained its own local government, but all military forces were placed under federal control. Prussia's king was granted the presidency of a German federation that was to be governed by a bicameral legislature. One house, the *Bundesrat*, was composed of men appointed by the governments of the states; the members of the other, the *Reichstag*, were elected by universal male suffrage.

The constitution of the North German Confederation (which after 1871 became the constitution of the German Empire) looked more liberal than it was. The *Reichstag,* which was chosen by all male citizens, had little power. Government ministers were responsible only to the monarch, and only the king's chancellor could initiate legislation. Bismarck, in effect, subjected Germany to a military monarchy. His liberal opponents acquiesced because, in the end, their desire for national unity proved greater than their commitment to liberal principles.

The Franco-Prussian War and the German Empire (1870–1871)

Events in Spain gave Bismarck an excuse to bring the south German states into Prussia's confederation. In 1868 the corrupt Bourbon queen of Spain, Isabella II (r. 1833–1868), was deposed. Two years later the Spaniards offered their crown to Prince Leopold of Hohenzollern-Sigmaringen, a Catholic cousin of Prussia's William I. Leopold's father, fearing that France would attack Prussia to prevent the Hohenzollerns from establishing themselves in Spain, renounced his son's candidacy (July 12, 1870). William I was relieved that he had not been required, as the French had urged him, to order Leopold to renounce the Spanish throne.

The matter might have rested there had it not been for the impetuosity of the French and the guile of Bismarck. On July 13, the French government instructed its ambassador to Prussia, Count Vincent Benedetti (1817–1900), to ask William I for assurances that he would tolerate no future Spanish candidacy for Leopold. The king refused and sent Bismarck, who was in Berlin, a telegram describing the meeting. Bismarck, who wanted war with France in order to bring the remaining German states into the Prussian federation, used the king's telegram to incite the war the king hoped to avoid. He released an edited version of the dispatch that made it appear that William I had insulted the French ambassador.

Everything developed as Bismarck expected. France was goaded into declaring war on July 19, and once the conflict erupted, the south German states rallied to Prussia's side. On September 1, at the Battle of Sedan, the Germans beat the French army and captured Napoleon III. Paris was besieged in late September. On January 18, in the Hall of Mirrors at the Palace of Versailles, the German Empire was proclaimed. On January 28, 1871, Paris capitulated, and at the peace conference France ceded control over Alsace and part of Lorraine to Germany.

German unification changed the face of Europe by creating a powerful new state that was far stronger than Prussia had been alone. A humiliated France returned to republican government, and the beleaguered Habsburgs hastened to come to terms with their unruly Magyar subjects. Liberals everywhere were alarmed, for conservative politics now had the backing of the strongest state on the Continent.

France: From Liberal Empire to the Third Republic

Historians divide the reign of Emperor Napoleon III (r. 1851–1870) into halves to mark a shift in the year 1860 from authoritarian to more liberal government. Initially, Napoleon III controlled the legislature, censored the press, and harassed political dissidents. He relied on the army, the Catholic clergy, property owners, and businessmen. His supporters wanted a government strong enough to guarantee security for property, the papacy, and commerce.

Late in the 1850s Napoleon III began to suffer reverses abroad that forced him to change his domestic policy. His influence faded in Italy as Piedmont pursued unification, and he had little choice but to stand by passively while Prussia reorganized Germany. He was further humiliated when France intervened against the Spanish in Mexico and the man the French army helped to the Mexican throne, the Archduke Maximilian of Austria (r. 1864–1867), was speedily overthrown and executed.

To shore up support at home for a government weakened by these foreign policy failures, Napoleon III began to make liberal concessions. In 1860 he granted the legislature greater freedom of debate. He concluded a free trade treaty with Britain. He relaxed the laws limiting the press and forbidding labor unions. In 1870 he accepted a ministry formed by moderates in the legislature, and he approved a liberal constitution that made ministers of state responsible to the legislature.

Napoleon III began the Franco-Prussian War hoping that the struggle would consolidate support for his Second Empire, but the result was quite the opposite. The Prussians captured the French emperor at the Battle of Sedan on September 1, 1870, and when the news reached Paris, the French government repudiated the monarchy and proclaimed a republic. A Government of National Defense was organized, and the Prussians besieged Paris. Most of France was ready to sue for peace long before Paris surrendered in January 1871.

The Paris Commune

The new French National Assembly, which was elected in February, accepted Prussia's terms for peace and signed the Treaty of Frankfurt. France promised to pay a large indemnity, to permit occupation by Prussian troops until the indemnity was paid, and to surrender Alsace and part of Lorraine. Napoleon III was exiled to England where he died in 1873.

Many Parisians, who had suffered from the Prussian siege of their city, felt betrayed by the National Assembly's capitulation. On March 28, 1871, they installed the Paris Commune, a municipal government that pledged to administer Paris separately from the rest of France. The National Assembly quickly surrounded Paris with an army and, on May 8, ordered bombardment. On May 21, the day on which the treaty with Prussia was signed, the assembly's forces broke through the city's defenses. About 20,000 Parisians were killed before order was restored.

The short-lived Paris Commune quickly became a legend throughout Europe. Marxists claimed that it was a genuine proletarian government suppressed by the bourgeoisie, but they were wrong. The goal of the commune was not a worker's republic but a nation of relatively independent democratic enclaves. Its suppression was the triumph, not of the middle over the lower class, but of a centralized national government over an alternative form of political organization. In Italy and Germany armies pulled nations together; in France an army prevented a nation from coming apart.

The Third Republic

The National Assembly was dominated by monarchists who backed it into endorsing a republican form of government. The monarchists were divided between support for the House of Bourbon and for the House of Orléans. This problem could have been resolved by appointing the Bourbon claimant, the Count of Chambord. He had no children and was willing to make the Orléanist heir his successor. But Chambord refused to be king if France retained the tricolor flag of the revolution. Since restoration of the white flag of the Bourbons was too politically reactionary even for the most conservative of the monarchists, negotiations stalemated.

In 1873 the indemnity France owed Prussia was paid, and the Prussian military occupation of French territory ended. The new president of the assembly, Marshal MacMahon (1808–1893), favored restoration of the monarchy—if an acceptable king could be found. But in 1875 the National Assembly, frustrated by the inability of the monarchists to unite, decreed a different form of political organization: a Chamber of Deputies elected by universal male suffrage, a Senate chosen indirectly, and a president elected by the two legislative houses. This Third Republic proved much more durable than many expected. It defended itself against the maneuvers of General George Boulanger (1837–1891), who campaigned for a stronger executive authority, and it survived a number of scandals (e.g., sales of awards of the Legion of Honor and bribes paid politicians by a company constructing a canal in Panama).

The Dreyfus Affair

The Third Republic's greatest trauma was the Dreyfus affair. On December 22, 1894, a French military court found Captain Alfred Dreyfus (1859–1935) guilty of passing information to the German army. But after he was sent to the notorious prison on Devil's Island, secrets continued to flow to the Germans. In 1896 a new head of French counterintelligence reopened the case and found that evidence against Dreyfus had been forged. Suspicion centered on a different officer, but a military court quickly acquitted this man of all charges.

Dreyfus was Jewish, and the near-hysterical public debate over his case revealed the extent of French anti-Semitism. The army, the French Catholic church, conservative politicians, and certain newspapers vehemently contended that

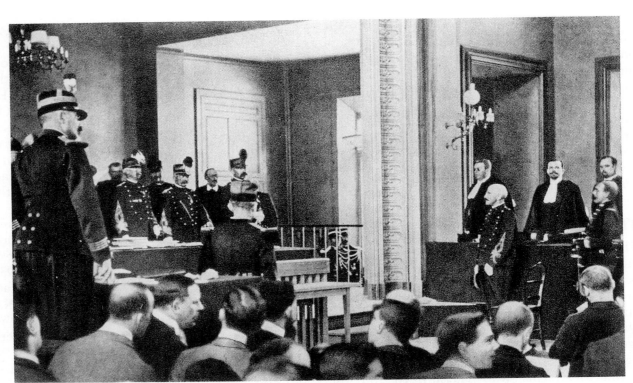

The prosecution of Captain Alfred Dreyfus, who is shown here standing on the right at his military trial, provoked the most serious crisis of the Third Republic. Corbis

Dreyfus was guilty. In 1898 the novelist Émile Zola countered with a newspaper article: *J'accuse* (*I Accuse*). He contended that the army had consciously denied due process to Dreyfus and had plotted to suppress or forge evidence. The government's response was to convict Zola of libel and sentence him to a year in prison. Zola fled to England, but the political left—liberals, radicals, and socialists—took up Dreyfus's cause. They were eager to embarrass the conservative government by proving that it had denied Dreyfus the rights belonging to all citizens of the republic. They also wanted to humble the military by showing that it had offered up Dreyfus to protect guilty parties in its own ranks. In August 1898, further evidence of forged material came to light, and the officer responsible committed suicide in jail. When a second military trial refused to acquit Dreyfus, the president of France stepped in and pardoned him. In 1906 a civilian court set aside the verdicts of both military tribunals.

The Dreyfus case had long-lasting political repercussions. It put conservatives on the defensive, for they had persecuted an innocent man, falsified evidence to protect themselves, and em-

braced violent anti-Semitism. Support for Dreyfus helped bring the radicals, republicans, and socialists of the left closer together. But divisions and suspicions growing out of the Dreyfus affair continued to divide the Third Republic until France's defeat by Germany early in World War II (1940).

The Habsburg Empire

After 1848 the Habsburg Empire became a problem to itself and to the rest of Europe. The Habsburg response to the revolts of 1848 to 1849 had been the reassertion of absolutism. Consequently, in an age characterized by national states, liberal institutions, and industrialism, the Habsburg domains remained dynastic, absolutist, and agrarian. Francis Joseph, emperor from 1848 to 1916, was honest and hardworking but unimaginative. He reacted to events but rarely commanded them.

During the 1850s his ministers tried to impose a centralized administration on the empire using an army and bureaucracy consisting largely of German-speaking Austrians. Internal tariffs in

Édouard Manet, A Bar at the Folies-Bergère: *Painting Modern Life*

Édouard Manet (1832–1883) was probably the most influential painter of the second half of the nineteenth century. *Impressionism,* a new style that transformed the art of the Western world, flowered in Paris during his lifetime. Manet did not consider himself an Impressionist, but his last painting, *A Bar at the Folies-Bergère,* suggests that the Impressionists were having an influence on him. Impressionism sought to paint the light that made things visible more than the things themselves. By using brilliant, prismatic colors, it captured the visual "impression" of a passing moment. Impressionist art was not didactic. The Impressionists avoided subjects laden with religious and mythological symbols or political commentary. They preferred instead to catch fleeting moments from the lives of ordinary people. Their favorite themes were the leisure-time activities of members of the urban middle and lower middle classes.

Although *A Bar at the Folies-Bergère* overtly deals with a very prosaic subject (a young woman standing behind a bar listening to a customer who is glimpsed only as a reflection in the big mirror behind her), it invites reflection. The Folies-Bergère was Paris's leading music hall. It was a place where audiences could enjoy singers, instrumentalists, dancers, gymnasts, and animal acts. The scene in the mirror suggests an exciting, perhaps raucous, show—the legs of a trapeze artist can be seen at upper left. Yet the barmaid has a blank expression that is at odds with her busy environment. Women in her situation were often forced into prostitution. Manet may have intended her to be seen less as a person than as an object. Like the bottles of champagne and spirits and the fruits and flowers on the bar, she is merely another one of the pleasant consumer items the music hall offered well-heeled patrons from the middle class.

Édouard Manet (1832–1883), *A Bar at the Folies-Bergère, 1882.* Oil on canvas, 96 × 130 cm. Signed, dated. Courtauld gift 1932. Courtauld Institute of Gallaries, London.

Sources: T. J. Clark, *The Painting of Modern Life: Paris in the Art of Manet and His Followers* (Princeton, NJ: Princeton University Press, 1984); Anne Coffin Hanson, *Manet and the Modern Tradition* (New Haven, CT: Yale University Press, 1977); Robert L. Herbert, *Impressionism: Art, Leisure, and Parisian Society* (New Haven, CT: Yale University Press, 1988); Bradford R. Collins, ed., *Twelve Views of Manet's Bar* (Princeton, NJ: Princeton University Press, 1996).

the empire were abolished. Hungary was divided into military districts. The Roman Catholic Church took control of education. National groups, such as the Croats and Slovaks, who had helped the empire defeat the Hungarian rebels of 1848, got nothing in recognition of their loyalty. The government's "neoabsolutism" provoked resentment and opposition, and setbacks in foreign affairs led to its fall.

Austria's refusal to support Russia in the Crimean War cost the Habsburgs Russia's help in Hungary. This removed an external prop for their power there on which they had relied for half a century. This, together with Austria's loss of territory to Piedmont in 1859, necessitated radical changes in domestic policy, and for seven years Austria's leaders struggled to construct a viable system of government.

Formation of the Dual Monarchy

In 1860 Francis Joseph issued the October Diploma. It proposed a federated government for the states and provinces of the empire and vested authority in a single imperial parliament and local diets dominated by the landed classes. When the Magyar nobility of Hungary rejected the plan, the emperor responded with the February Patent (1861). It established a bicameral imperial parliament (the *Reichsrat*), with an upper chamber appointed by the emperor and an indirectly elected lower chamber. Government ministers reported to the emperor, not the *Reichsrat*. Civil liberties were not guaranteed. Armies could be levied and taxes raised without parliamentary consent. And when the *Reichsrat* was not in session, the emperor could rule by decree. Although the Magyars again refused to cooperate, the February Patent

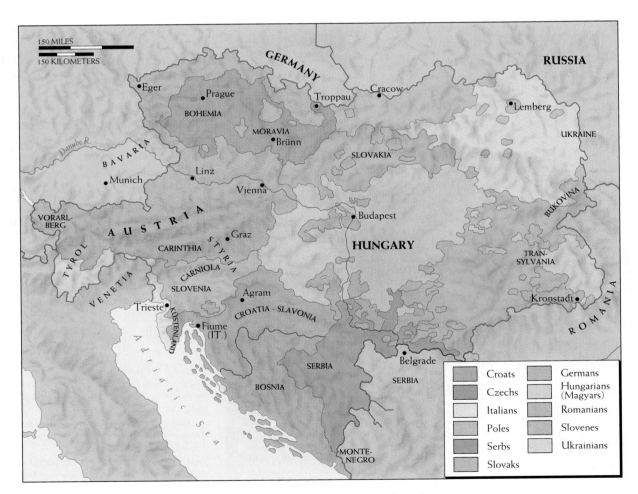

MAP 23–3   NATIONALITIES WITHIN THE HABSBURG EMPIRE   *The patchwork appearance reflects the unusual problem the Habsburgs had of trying to unite numerous ethnic groups to form a modern national state. Only the Magyars were recognized in 1867, leaving nationalist Czechs, Slovaks, and the others chronically dissatisfied.*

established the system that governed the empire for six years and Austria until World War I.

Secret negotiations between the emperor and the Magyars produced no concrete result until 1866 when Prussia defeated Austria and excluded it from German affairs. This forced Francis Joseph to come to terms with the Magyars. The result was the *Ausgleich* (i.e., compromise) of 1867. The empire was reorganized as a dual monarchy. Except for a common ruler and a few shared ministries (e.g., foreign affairs, defense, and finance), Austria and Hungary functioned as separate states. Every year sixty parliamentary delegates from each kingdom met to discuss mutual interests. Every ten years, Austria and Hungary renegotiated their trade relationship. This cumbersome machinery, unique in European history, reconciled the Magyars to Habsburg rule by giving them the free hand they had long wanted in Hungary.

Unrest of Nationalities

By acceding to the nationalistic desires of the Hungarians, the Compromise of 1867 increased tensions within the empire. Many peoples—including the Czechs, the Ruthenians, the Romanians, and the Croatians—opposed the compromise because it permitted German-speaking Austrians and Hungarian Magyars to dominate other nationalities. Since the Hungarians had received a government on their own terms, various ethnic groups believed that the time had come for them too to demand political reforms.

The Czechs of Bohemia were most insistent in demanding recognition as a separate kingdom (like Hungary) within the empire. Francis Joseph was willing, but the Magyars objected. They were afraid that his example would force them to make similar concessions to minorities residing in Hungary. Germans resident in Bohemia also resisted the plan, for they were convinced that it would lead to the Czech language being imposed on them. For over twenty years the emperor placated the Czechs with generous patronage, but in the 1890s Czech nationalists again became strident. In 1897 Francis Joseph made Czech and German equal official languages in various localities. When angry Germans in the Austrian *Reichsrat* protested by disrupting its meetings, the Czechs did the same. This paralyzed the *Reichsrat* and forced the emperor to rule by decree. By 1914 constitutionalism was a dead issue

in Austria. It survived in Hungary, but only because the Magyars were allowed to preserve their political supremacy over other nationalities.

Nationalism seems to have become stronger during the last quarter of the nineteenth century and lines between groups more clearly drawn. Language was believed to be the most important defining attribute of a nation. But racial ideologies, which taught that there was a genetic basis for ethnic identities, were also popular. Austria's dominant population was German speaking and loyal to the emperor, but a significant faction yearned to be part of Bismarck's united Germany. These nationalistic Austro-Germans often hated the non-German subjects of the empire, and many of them were anti-Semites. Their prejudices shaped an Austrian who in the twentieth century became Germany's leader: Adolph Hitler.

Strife among the diverse nationalities that were subject to the Habsburg Empire created political instability in central and eastern Europe. Both foreign and domestic policy issues were involved, for nationalists wanted self-determination within the empire and unification with fellow nationals outside the empire. Groups such as Ukrainians, Romanians, Italians, and Bosnians saw themselves as potentially linked to Russia, Romania, Italy, Serbia, or to a yet to be established south Slavic or Yugoslav state. The significance of nationalist unrest within the late nineteenth-century Austrian Empire and its neighboring states can hardly be overestimated. It helped bring on World War I, World War II, and the recent bloodshed in the former Yugoslavia.

Russia: Emancipation and Revolutionary Stirrings

Russia changed remarkably during the second half of the nineteenth century, for foreign policy reversals (e.g., defeat in the Crimean War and the humiliation of the Treaty of Paris) compelled the Russian government to reconsider its domestic policies.

Reforms of Alexander II

Nicholas I's son and heir, Alexander II (r. 1855–1881), was well trained for his duties as tsar. Travel within his nation and experience in its government gave him a sense of the difficulties that Russia faced. The debacle of the Crimean War made reform both necessary and possible, and

Life in Russian villages during the 1870s was very difficult. Tsar Alexander II abolished serfdom in 1861, but peasants were required to pay compensation to the government for 49 years and living standards remained dismal. This painting shows peasants waiting patiently outside a government office while officials inside take their time over lunch.
Bildarchiv Preussischer Kulturbesitz

Alexander II seized the opportunity. He attempted the most extensive restructuring of Russian institutions since the days of Peter the Great.

ABOLITION OF SERFDOM   A profound cultural gap separated Russia from the rest of Europe. Nowhere was this more apparent than in the survival of serfdom in Russia at a time when it had been abandoned by all other European states. Among Western nations, forms of involuntary servitude were maintained only in Russia, Brazil, and certain portions of the United States.

Serfdom was economically inefficient and a constant source of social unrest. In March 1856, at the conclusion of the Crimean War, Alexander II announced his intention to abolish it. He claimed that its abolition was necessary to allow Russia to exploit its human and natural resources efficiently. For more than five years government commissions wrestled with the problem of how to implement the tsar's wish. Finally, in February 1861—over opposition from the nobility and the landlords—Alexander II promulgated the emancipation statute.

Former serfs were disappointed by the tsar's legislation, for freedom was not accompanied by land. They were required to purchase (with payments spread out over a period of forty-nine years) plots of land, which were often too small to support them. These payments were made to the government, which had immediately reimbursed landlords for the losses the decree caused them. The procedures imposed on the peasants for paying their debt (and its interest charges) were so complicated and the benefits so limited that many serfs believed that real emancipation was still to come. Poor harvests worsened a bad situation by making it impossible for many peasants to keep up with the government's payment schedule. They fell increasingly behind, and the situation was not remedied until a widespread revolutionary upheaval in 1905 persuaded the government to cancel the remaining debt.

REFORM OF LOCAL GOVERNMENT AND THE JUDICIAL SYSTEM   The abolition of serfdom required the reorganization of local government and the judicial system. Village communes replaced land-lords as the authorities keeping peace among the peasants, but the nobles were given a larger role in other aspects of local administration. They sat on provincial and county *zemstvos* (councils) that oversaw things such as bridge and road repair, education, and agricultural improvement. The arrangement was not very successful. Since the councils received inadequate funds, they never developed much vigor.

In 1864 Alexander II promulgated a statute that addressed abuses and inequities in the judiciary. Western European legal principles (e.g., equality before the law, impartial hearings, uniform procedures, judicial independence, and trial by jury) became, for the first time, part of Russian practice. Judges were, however, not genuinely independent, for the tsar could change the sentences they handed out. Also, certain offenses (e.g., those involving the press) were not tried before a jury. Nonetheless, the new courts improved the efficiency and honesty of law enforcement.

MILITARY REFORM   Russia maintained the largest army on the Continent. Villages had to meet quotas for recruits, and serfs were often seized from their homes and impressed into service. Once in the army, men rarely saw their families again. Soldiers remained on active duty for twenty-five years, and Russian military life was harsh.

Poor performance in the Crimean War prompted the government to enact some reforms. In the 1860s the period of military service was reduced to fifteen years, and discipline was slightly relaxed. In 1874 the enlistment period was lowered to six years of active duty followed by nine years in the reserves.

REPRESSION IN POLAND   In 1863 Polish nationalists tried to end Russian dominance of their homeland, and Alexander II responded by trying to "russify" Poland. In 1864 he punished the politically restive nobility by emancipating their serfs. Russian law, language, and administration were imposed throughout Poland, and, until the close of World War I, Poland was treated as a Russian province.

Alexander II entertained no reforms that would limit his autocracy, and his programs earned him little gratitude from his subjects. The serfs felt that their emancipation was inadequate. The nobles and the wealthier, educated segments of society resented his refusal to allow them a meaningful role in government. Although Alexander II came to be known as the Tsar Liberator, he was never popular. After an attempt was made on his life in 1866, the tsar grew increasingly close-minded and reactionary, and Russia evolved into a police state. The tsar's repression fueled the activities of political radicals.

Revolutionaries

One of the most prominent critics of the tsarist regime was an exile, Alexander Herzen (1812–1870), who published a newspaper called *The Bell*. Students who were disenchanted with the pace of reform in Russia drew on the ideas of Herzen and other radicals to organize a movement known as *Populism*. It proposed using the communal life of the Russian peasants as a model for rebuilding Russian society.

In the early 1870s hundreds of young Russians, male and female, took their revolutionary message into the countryside. They intended to live with the peasants, to gain their trust, and to teach them about the peasant role in the coming revolution. The bewildered and distrustful peasants turned most of them over to the police. In the winter of 1877–1878 almost 200 were tried. Most were acquitted or given light sentences, for the court believed that a display of mercy would lessen public sympathy for the revolutionaries.

The tsar made it known that he favored heavy penalties for anyone involved in revolutionary activity, and this convinced the revolutionaries that they had to attack the tsarist regime directly. Their strategy was terrorism. In January 1878, Vera Zasulich tried to assassinate the military governor of Saint Petersburg. When the jury acquitted her because of her intended victim's reputation for brutality, the verdict encouraged other terrorists.

In 1879 Land and Freedom, the most radical of the revolutionary organizations, split. The faction that advocated educating the peasants soon dissolved. The other, known as People's Will, focused on the overthrow of the autocracy and the assassination of the tsar. After several attempts failed, they finally succeeded on March 1, 1881, in planting a bomb that killed Alexander II. Four men and two women were sentenced to death for the deed.

The result of the assassins' act was to bring Alexander III (r. 1881–1894) to the throne, a tsar who confirmed all the evils that the revolutionaries

Tsar Alexander II (r. 1855–1881) was assassinated on March 1, 1881. The assassins first threw a bomb that wounded several Imperial guards. When the tsar stopped his carriage to see the wounded, the assassins threw a second bomb, killing him. Bildarchiv Preussischer Kulturbesitz

saw as inherent in autocratic government. Alexander dedicated his reign to rolling back his father's reforms. He favored government by centralized bureaucracy, not local councils (the *zemstvos*). He built up the secret police and increased press censorship. He bequeathed his son, Nicholas II (r. 1894–1917), a legacy of reactionary policies that hastened the destruction of Russia's monarchy.

Great Britain: Toward Democracy

Great Britain was the model of the confident liberal state endowed with stable political institutions and equipped to handle all difficulties and domestic conflicts. Several things contributed to its success. Parliament admitted new groups and interests to the political process. The general prosperity of the third quarter of the century mit-

igated social tensions, and all classes in British society shared a belief in competition and individualism.

The Second Reform Act (1867)

During the early 1860s pressure began to build to widen the franchise. In 1866 a Liberal ministry introduced a reform bill. It was defeated. A Conservative ministry led in the House of Commons by Benjamin Disraeli (1804–1881) then assumed office and surprised everyone by introducing legislation to expand the electorate beyond the limits earlier proposed by the Liberals. It nearly made Britain a democracy. Disraeli's motive was political self-interest. He believed that reform was inevitable and that the Conservatives' best strategy was to take credit for it. He expected grateful voters of the working class to support Conservative candidates if they

Consolidation of States (1854–1900)	
1854–1856	The Crimean War
1855	Alexander II becomes tsar
1859	Piedmont and France fight Austria
1860	Garibaldi invades southern Italy
1861	Austria issues the February Patent
	Proclamation of the Kingdom of Italy (March 17)
	Russia abolishes serfdom
1862	Bismarck becomes prime minister of Prussia
1863	Russia suppresses the Polish Rebellion
1864	Danish-Prussian War
1866	Austro-Prussian War
	Venetia ceded to Italy
1867	North German Confederation formed
	Formation of the Dual Monarchy: Hungary and Austria
	Britain's Second Reform Act
1868	Gladstone becomes prime minister of Britain
1870	Franco-Prussian War begins (July 19)
	Third Republic proclaimed in France (September 4)
	Italian state annexes Rome (October 2)
1871	The German Empire proclaimed (January 18)
	Paris Commune (March 28–May 28)
	Treaty of Frankfurt between France and Germany (May 1)
1872	Introduction of the secret ballot in Britain
1874	Disraeli becomes prime minister of Britain
1880	Gladstone's second ministry
1881	Alexander II assassinated; Alexander III succeeds
1884	Britain's Third Reform Act
1886	Lord Salisbury becomes prime minister of Britain
1892	Gladstone's third ministry
1894	Nicholas II becomes tsar

showed themselves responsive to social issues, and he thought that the growing suburban middle class would become increasingly conservative. He was generally correct. The Conservative Party dominated British politics for much of the twentieth century.

Gladstone's Great Ministry (1868–1874)

The voters in the election of 1868 disappointed Disraeli by choosing a prime minister whose term in office (1868–1874) marked the culmination of British liberalism: William Gladstone (1809–1898). Gladstone opened to people from all classes and of all faiths the institutions that had been the preserve of the aristocracy and the Anglican Church. In 1870 competitive examinations for the civil service replaced patronage. In the same year the government passed the Education Act and assumed responsibility for establishing and running elementary schools. In 1871 the practice of purchasing officers' commissions in the army was abolished, and Anglican religious requirements for admission to the faculties at Oxford and Cambridge universities were removed. The Ballot Act of 1872 introduced voting by secret ballot.

All of these reforms were typically liberal in that they ended abuses without destroying existing institutions. They enabled all citizens to compete on the grounds of ability and merit. They confronted the danger an illiterate citizenry poses to a democratic state, and they created new bonds of loyalty to the nation by abolishing sources of discontent.

Disraeli in Office (1874–1880)

Disraeli succeeded Gladstone as prime minister in 1874. The two men had stood on different sides of most issues for over a quarter-century. Whereas Gladstone looked to individualism, free trade, and competition to solve social problems, Disraeli believed in paternalistic legislation and state action to protect the weak. Disraeli talked much but had few specific programs or ideas. The significant social legislation of his ministry was the work of his Home Secretary, Richard Cross (1823–1914). The Public Health Act and the Artisans' Dwelling Act (both 1875) improved conditions for the working classes, and by expanding protection for trade unions the government empowered laborers to fight for additional reforms.

The Irish Question

From the late 1860s onward, Irish nationalists sought home rule—by which they meant Irish control of Ireland's local government. Gladstone responded with two major pieces of legislation. In 1869 he disestablished the branch of the Anglican Church in Ireland so that Roman Catholics were not taxed to support Protestant clergy. In 1870 a land act was passed to provide compensation for evicted Irish tenants and loans for those who wished to purchase land. The Irish question, however, continued to fester throughout the 1870s, and land was at the heart of the problem. An Irish Land League agitated for change and intimidated landlords, who were often English. In 1881 Gladstone strengthened tenant rights but also issued the Coercion Act, a set of regulations intended to restore law and order to Ireland.

By 1885 Charles Stewart Parnell (1846–1891) had organized eighty-five Irish members of the House of Commons into a tightly disciplined party that often voted as a bloc. In the election of 1885 their votes had the power to decide whether the English Liberals or Conservatives would take office. When Gladstone announced his support for home rule, Parnell helped him form a Liberal ministry. The home rule issue split the Liberal Party, and in 1886 some Liberals joined the Conservatives to defeat Gladstone's Home Rule Bill.

Gladstone's Conservative successor, Lord Salisbury (1830–1903), tried a combination of public works, administrative reform, and coercion to reconcile the Irish to English government. In 1892 Gladstone returned to power and proposed a second Home Rule Bill, which passed the House of Commons but was defeated in the House of Lords. In 1903 the Conservatives carried out the final transfer of land to ownership by former tenants, and Ireland became a country of small farms. In 1914 a Liberal ministry took advantage of limitations imposed on the upper house (the House of Lords Act of 1911) to pass the third Home Rule Bill, but its implementation was suspended for the duration of World War I.

Political divisions spawned by the "Irish question" made it difficult for the government to re-solve other issues. By the turn of the century, frustration with the inability of the two traditional parties to enact reforms created an opportunity for a third group, the Labour Party, to attract a significant following and enter British politics.

In Perspective

Between 1850 and 1875 the contours were drawn for the political systems that dominated Europe until World War I. The concept of the nation-state had triumphed. Support for governments no longer stemmed from loyalty to dynasties but from ethnic, cultural, linguistic, and historical bonds and a sense of participation in the duties of citizenship. The major sources of discontent were unsatisfied aspirations to political power by subject nationalities and by laborers. These forces ultimately undermined the political structures that had been erected during the third quarter of the nineteenth century.

REVIEW QUESTIONS

1. Why was it so difficult to unify Italy? What groups were urging unification? Who was Camillo Cavour? How did he succeed where others had failed? What were Garibaldi's contributions to Italian unification?

2. Who was Otto von Bismarck? Why did he want to unify Germany? What attempts at unification had preceded his? Why did they fail? What was his plan for German unification? Why did it succeed? What effect did the unification of Germany have on the rest of Europe?

3. How did France's Second Empire (under Napoleon III) become its Third Republic? Why did the Second Empire fall? What problems faced the new republic? Why did the Paris Commune become a legend throughout Europe? What effect did the Dreyfus affair have on the politics of the Third Republic?

4. What changes in government took place in Austria after 1848? What unique problems did Austria have? Were they solved? Why was nationalism a more pressing problem for Austria than for any other nation?

5. What reforms were instituted by Tsar Alexander II? Did he solve some of Russia's domestic problems? Can he be regarded as a "visionary" reformer? Why or why not?

6. How did the politics of the British Liberal and Conservative parties evolve in the period from 1860 to 1890? Who were their leaders? What problems did they confront? What solutions did they favor? How did British politicians handle the "Irish question"? Are there similarities between England's situation with Ireland and the Austrian Empire's struggles with its nationalities?

SUGGESTED READINGS

M. BENTLEY, *Politics Without Democracy, 1815–1914* (1984). A well-informed survey of British development.

D. BLACKBOURN, *The Long Nineteenth Century: A History of Germany, 1780–1918* (1998). An outstanding survey based on up-to-date scholarship.

R. BLAKE, *Disraeli* (1967). The best biography.

J. BLUM, *Lord and Peasant in Russia from the Ninth to the Nineteenth Century* (1961). A clear discussion of emancipation in the later chapters.

G. CHAPMAN, *The Dreyfus Affair: A Reassessment* (1955). A detached treatment of a subject that still provokes strong feelings.

G. CRAIG, *Germany, 1866–1945* (1978). An excellent survey.

S. ELWITT, *The Making of the Third Republic: Class and Politics in France, 1868–1884* (1975). An excellent introduction.

E. HOBSBAWM, *The Age of Empire, 1875–1914* (1987). A stimulating survey that covers cultural as well as political developments.

R. A. KANN, *The Multinational Empire*, 2 vols. (1950). The basic treatment of the nationality problem of Austria-Hungary.

G. KITSON KLARK, *The Making of Victorian England* (1962). The best introduction.

A. J. MAY, *The Habsburg Monarchy, 1867–1914* (1951). Narrates in considerable detail and with much sympathy the fate of the dual monarchy.

C. C. O'BRIEN, *Parnell and His Party* (1957). An excellent treatment of the Irish question.

O. PFLANZE, *Bismarck and the Development of Germany*, 3 vols. (1990). A major biography and history of Germany for the period.

A. PLESSIS, *The Rise and Fall of the Second Empire, 1852–1871* (1985). A useful survey of France under Napoleon III.

D. M. SMITH, *The Making of Italy, 1796–1870* (1968). A narrative that incorporates the major documents.

F. VENTURI, *The Roots of Revolution* (trans. 1960). A major treatment of late nineteenth-century revolutionary movements.

J. WERTHEIMER, *Unwelcome Strangers: East European Jews in Imperial Germany* (1987). Examines the difficult position of Jews in Wilhelminian German.

T. ZELDIN, *France: 1848–1945*, 2 vols. (1973, 1977). Emphasizes the social developments.

Chapter 24
The Building of European Supremacy: Society and Politics to World War I

KEY TOPICS

- The transformation of European life by the second Industrial Revolution
- Urban sanitation, housing reform, and the redesign of cities
- The condition of women in late-nineteenth-century Europe and the rise of political feminism
- The development of labor politics and socialism in Europe to the outbreak of World War I
- Industrialization and political unrest in Russia

The growth of industrialism between 1860 and 1914 increased Europe's productive capacity to unprecedented levels. As goods and capital flowed out of Europe and across the globe, Europe's political, economic, and social institutions assumed many of their current characteristics. Nation-states with centralized bureaucracies, large electorates, and competing political parties emerged. Business developed huge corporate structures.

Labor organized trade unions. The number of white-collar workers increased. Urban life predominated. Socialism became a major political force. Foundations were laid for welfare states and for vast military establishments, and taxation increased accordingly.

Confident in their prosperity, Europeans failed to realize how dependent they were on the resources and markets of the world. Their assumption that European supremacy was natural and enduring was challenged as the twentieth century unfolded.

Population Trends and Migration

In 1900 Europe was home to about 20 percent of the world's people—a greater proportion than ever before or since. Its population rose from about 266 million in 1850, to 401 million in 1900, to 447 million in 1910. Thereafter, growth declined or stabilized in advanced nations and began to increase in less developed countries.

In addition to its size, Europe's population was more mobile in the second half of the century than ever before. Emancipation of peasants removed legal blocks to migration. Railways, steamships, and better roads increased access to transportation. Offers of cheap land and better wages, which accompanied economic development in Europe, North America, Latin America, and Australia, provided motivation for people to move.

Europeans left their continent in record numbers—more than 50 million between 1846 and 1932. Most went to the United States, Canada, Australia, South Africa, Brazil, or Argentina. At midcentury Great Britain (especially Ireland), Germany, and Scandinavia produced the most emigrants. After 1885 migration from southern and eastern Europe dominated. The exodus solved some of Europe's domestic problems, and relocation of its peoples contributed, along with trade and industry, to the Europeanization of the world.

European emigrants from eastern Europe wait to board a ship that will carry them to the United States. Between 1846 and 1932, more than 50 million Europeans immigrated to the United States, Canada, South America, Australia, and South Africa. Bildarchiv Preussischer Kulturbesitz

Events in the Formation of the Early Twentieth Century

1848	Britain's Public Health Act
1851	France's Melun Act
1857	Bessemer steel manufacturing process invented
1864	Meeting of the First International
1869	John Stuart Mill publishes *The Subjection of Women*
1875	German Social Democratic Party founded
1876	Telephone invented
1879	Electric light bulb invented
1882	England's Married Woman's Property Act
1884	Britain's Fabian Society founded
1887	Automobile invented
1889	Establishment of the Second International
1895	Invention of wireless telegraphy
1900	Lenin leaves Russia
1902	Formation of the British Labour Party
1903	British Women's Social and Political Union founded
	Lenin creates the Bolsheviks
	The Wright brothers begin the age of aviation
1904–1905	Russo-Japanese War
1905	Saint Petersburg's Bloody Sunday
	Russia's October Manifesto
1907	Norway, first nation to grant women the vote
1909	Henry Ford begins mass production of automobiles
1910	British suffragettes adopt radical tactics
1911	Stolypin assassinated
1914	World War I begins
1918	Some British women acquire the vote
1918	Constitution of the Weimar Republic gives women the vote
1928	British women acquire same voting rights as men

Not since the sixteenth century had European civilization had such an impact on other cultures.

The Second Industrial Revolution

The first Industrial Revolution centered on textiles, on iron, and on applications of steam power. The second, which began after 1850, stimulated economic growth by adding production of steel, chemicals, electricity, and oil.

New Industries

In the 1850s an English engineer, Henry Bessemer (1830–1898), discovered a process for manufacturing large quantities of steel cheaply. Production in Great Britain, Belgium, France, and Germany rose from 125,000 tons in 1860 to 32,020,000 tons in 1913. The chemical industry also came of age. The Solway process of alkali production allowed more chemical by-products to be recovered and increased production of sulfuric acid and laundry soap. New dyestuffs and plastics were developed. Formal scientific research played an important role in the growth of the chemical industry, and chemists established the modern world's alliance between science and industrial development. Germany took the lead in this process and in fostering scientific research and education.

The most significant changes for industry and daily life resulted from the application of electrical energy to production. Electricity was the most versatile and most transportable source of power ever discovered. It could be delivered almost anywhere to run almost anything, making factory location more flexible and factory construction more efficient. The first major public power plant was constructed in Great Britain in 1881. Soon electric poles, lines, and generating stations dotted the European landscape, and electricity began to be marketed to homes.

The internal combustion engine was invented in 1886. A year later Gottlieb Daimler (1834–1900), a German engineer, put it on wheels and created the automobile. The car remained a novelty that only the wealthy could afford until 1909, when Henry Ford (1863–1947), an American entrepreneur, developed production techniques that made autos cheap enough for ordinary people to purchase.

The automobile and new industrial and chemical uses for petroleum had, by the turn of the century, created the first significant demand for oil and the first great oil companies: Standard Oil of the United States, British Shell Oil, and Royal Dutch. Then as now, Europe depended largely on imported supplies.

Economic Difficulties

Industry and agriculture boomed from 1850 to 1873, but in the last quarter of the nineteenth century economic advance slowed. Bad weather and foreign competition created problems for European agriculture that put a drag on the economy. This motivated much of the immigration of the period. Many of the emigrants who left Europe during these years came from rural areas or from countries where industrialization was least advanced.

Several large banks failed in 1873. The rate of capital investment slowed, and some industries stagnated for a twenty-year period that many contemporaries regarded as a depression. Over all, however, the second half of the nineteenth century produced improvements in standards of living in industrialized nations. Real wages generally held firm or, in some countries, rose. Many workers still lived and labored in abysmal conditions, however, and there were pockets of *unemployment* (a word that was coined during this period). Labor unrest promoted the growth of trade unions and socialist political parties.

By the end of the century, expansion of consumer demand had revived the economy. Lower food prices allowed all classes to spend more of their income on other kinds of consumer goods. The new industries produced new products, and urbanization created larger markets. New approaches to sales (e.g., department stores, chain stores, packaging techniques, mail-order catalogs, and advertising) stimulated consumer demand. Imperialism also generated new consumers for European products abroad.

The Middle Classes in Ascendancy

The sixty years before World War I were the age of the middle classes. The London Great Exhibition of 1851 (housed in a huge solarium called the Crystal Palace) was a monument to the material comforts that industrialization provided for middle-class life. The middle classes, as the largest group of consumers, were the arbiters of taste. Prosperity also made them defenders of the status quo and diminished the enthusiasm some members of the middle class had shown for revolution in 1848. As issues of social equality and political rights were raised, owners of property, small as well as large, worried that socialists and other working-class groups might deprive them of their possessions.

Social Distinctions Within the Middle Classes

The middle classes had never been perfectly homogeneous, and during the nineteenth century they grew increasingly diverse. In the lead were a few hundred families, the owners and managers of great businesses who could afford to live in a splendor beyond the reach of many aristocrats. Behind them were the comfortable small entrepreneurs and professionals—people who could afford private homes, large quantities of furniture (including luxuries such as pianos, pictures, books, and journals), education for their children, and vacations. With this group might also be numbered people with smaller holdings or lesser educations but with respected nonmanual employment (e.g., shopkeepers, schoolteachers, and librarians). Last was a wholly new element: white-collar workers who formed a lower middle class or petty bourgeoisie (e.g., secretaries, retail clerks, and lower-level bureaucrats). Many of these people had working-class origins. Some belonged to unions, but all had middle-class aspirations and consciously distanced themselves from the lifestyle of the lower classes. They actively pursued educational opportunities and career advancement, especially for their children. They spent a considerable portion of their disposable income on consumer goods in order to keep up a middle-class appearance.

Significant tensions and anxieties marked relations among the groups composing the middle class. Small shopkeepers resented competition from the department stores and mail-order catalogs belonging to the great capitalist merchants. Professions grew overcrowded, and those who struggled into the middle class feared being forced out by economic hard times. Nonetheless, during the decades leading up to World War I, the middle class had sufficient cohesion to set society's values and goals.

Late-Nineteenth-Century Urban Life

Between 1850 and 1911 the portion of France's population living in cities increased from 25 percent to 44 percent; in Germany the shift was from 30 percent to 60 percent. Other western European countries experienced similar, unprecedented growth in urbanization.

Migrants to cities from rural areas were uprooted from traditional social ties and condemned to poor housing, social anonymity, and, often, unemployment. Different ethnic groups found it difficult to get along when thrown together—particularly when they were competing for jobs. The migration of thousands of Russian Jews to western Europe's cities prompted an outbreak of anti-Semitism that became a factor in politics in the latter part of the century.

The Redesign of Cities

Migration to cities increased demands on their resources and transformed patterns of urban life. During the second half of the century, governments redesigned many European cities. Central areas, which had been home to large numbers of people from all social classes, became business districts with government offices, large retail stores, and theaters. Residents moved to the peripheries of cities as commerce, trade, government, and entertainment came to dominate urban centers.

THE NEW PARIS   The greatest transformation of a major city occurred in Paris. Like most European cities, Paris had evolved with little or no planning. Lavish public buildings and squalid hovels were jumbled together. Streets were narrow, crooked, and crowded. The River Seine, which ran through the center of town, was little more than an open sewer and an obstacle to traffic. In 1850 the government did not even have a complete, correct map of Paris. This was particularly worrisome, for the city's streets had for sixty years provided battlegrounds for insurrec-

tions that, as recently as 1848, had toppled French governments.

Napoleon III decided to redesign Paris, and he appointed Georges Haussmann "prefect of the Seine" (from 1853 to 1870) to oversee a vast urban reconstruction program. Whole districts were destroyed to make room for broad boulevards and streets. The wide vistas were beautiful, but they were also, from the government's point of view, functional. They allowed for the quick deployment of troops to put down riots, and they eliminated the narrow passages where barricades could be erected. The project was politically astute for a second reason. It created thousands of government-funded jobs and employment in the private industries that support public works projects.

Rebuilding continued under the Third Republic. Many department stores, office complexes, and apartment buildings for the middle class were constructed. By the late 1870s, mechanical trams were operating, and in 1895 construction of the "Métro" (i.e., subway) began. New railway stations were erected toward the close of the century. These improvements in transportation linked the refurbished central city to its expanding suburbs.

DEVELOPMENT OF SUBURBS   Redesign of cities displaced many of their residents and raised land values and rents. As both the middle classes and the working class sought alternative housing, suburbs sprang up around cities. They housed families whose breadwinners commuted by the new transportation systems to the town centers or urban factories. European suburbs, unlike those that developed in the United States, often consisted of apartment buildings or closely huddled private houses with small lawns and gardens. Suburban life meant that for hundreds of thousands of Europeans, home and work were more physically separated than ever before.

Urban Sanitation

The growing conservativism of the middle classes stiffened government's resolve to maintain public order. This led to improvements in health and housing for the poor, for it was believed that the well-being of the middle class and the stability of political systems depended on easing the effects of poverty.

IMPACT OF CHOLERA The great cholera epidemics of the 1830s and 1840s drove this lesson home. Many common deadly diseases touched only the poor, but cholera struck all classes. Before the development of the bacterial theory of disease late in the century, physicians and sanitary reformers believed that cholera and other illnesses were spread through infection from miasmas in the air. Miasmas were identified by their foul odors and were believed to arise from filth. The only way to rid cities of dangerous, foul-smelling air was to clean them up.

NEW WATER AND SEWER SYSTEMS During the 1840s physicians and government officials began to publicize the dangers posed by human overcrowding and the wastes from some industries. The solution to the health hazard was said to be cleanliness achieved through new water and sewer systems. These facilities were constructed slowly, and some major urban areas did not have good water systems until after the turn of the century. The Parisian sewer system was one of the most famous parts of Haussmann's rebuilding program.

EXPANDED GOVERNMENT INVOLVEMENT IN PUBLIC HEALTH Concern for public health led to an expansion of governmental power on various levels. Britain's Public Health Act (1848), France's Melun Act (1851), various laws in the still-disunited German states, and additional later legislation introduced new restraints on private life and enterprise. Medical officers and building inspectors were allowed to enter homes and other structures in the name of public health. Private property could be condemned for posing health hazards. Private land could be excavated for the construction of sewers and water mains, and building codes increasingly restrained the activities of private contractors. At the close of the century, acceptance of the bacterial theory of disease (which was developed by Louis Pasteur in France, Robert Koch in Germany, and Joseph Lister in Britain) increased concern for sanitation and opened the way for even greater government intervention in the lives of citizens.

Housing Reform and Middle-Class Values

The wretched dwellings of the poor, which were monuments to bad sanitation, came to be viewed as health hazards for the general public. Middle-class reformers and bureaucrats were shocked by reports describing the domestic arrangements of the lower classes and worried by suggestions that revolutions, such as those of 1848, could be caused by the pressures of overcrowded housing. Reformers looked to housing reform to solve all kinds of medical, moral, and political problems. Proper, decent housing was expected to foster a good home life that would create a healthy, moral, happy, and politically stable community. It was also believed that the saving and investment required for owning a home would motivate members of the working class to adopt the thrifty habits of the middle classes.

The goal of housing reform was to make it possible for the working class to enjoy family lives much like those of the middle classes. At the minimum, this necessitated a dwelling of several rooms with a private entrance and toilet. Private philanthropy made the first attack on the problem. Companies operating on low profit margins or making low-interest loans encouraged construction of housing for the poor. Firms such as the German Krupp armaments manufacturers tried to ensure a contented, healthy, and stable workforce by constructing model communities for their employees.

By the mid-1880s migration into cities had made housing a political issue. In 1885 England lowered the interest rates for the construction of cheap housing. Soon thereafter, government authorities began public housing projects. Similar action, initiated by local municipalities, followed in Germany, and in 1894 France made inexpensive credit available for constructing housing for the poor. By 1914 the housing problem had been fully recognized if not yet adequately addressed.

Varieties of Late-Nineteenth-Century Women's Experiences

Social Disabilities Confronted by All Women

Like men, women in the late nineteenth century led lives that reflected their social ranks. Yet within each rank, the experience of women was distinct from that of men. Women, no matter what their class, were always economically dependent and legally inferior. Virtually all European women were handicapped with respect to property rights, family law, and education, but by the end of the century improvements had been made in each of these areas.

WOMEN AND PROPERTY In most European countries, until the last quarter of the century, married women of all classes could not own property in their own names. At marriage, any property a woman owned, inherited, or earned came under the control of her husband. She had no independent standing before the law. Her legal identity was subsumed in his. (The theft of her purse was, for instance, regarded as a theft of his property.) Because European society was based on private property and wage earning, these disabilities put women at a great disadvantage.

Reform of women's property rights came very slowly. Great Britain passed a Married Woman's Property Act in 1882. It allowed wives to own property as individuals. But in France, a married woman could not even open a savings account in her own name until 1895, and married women were not granted possession of the wages they earned until 1907. In 1900 Germany allowed a woman to take a job without her husband's permission, but except for her wages, her husband retained control of most of her property. Similar laws prevailed elsewhere in Europe.

FAMILY LAW Divorce was difficult to obtain, and most nations did not permit termination of a marriage by mutual consent. Expensive court trials were required, and these were beyond the means of women who had no control over their own property.

French law forbade divorce altogether from 1816 to 1884. Thereafter, the chief legal grounds for divorce were acts of cruelty and injury that could be proven in court. In Germany, only adultery or serious mistreatment were recognized as reasons for divorce. In England prior to 1857, divorce required an act of Parliament. Thereafter, divorce could be gained—with difficulty—through the Court of Matrimonial Causes. Adultery was the usual cause for granting a divorce in Britain, but everywhere on the continent a double standard prevailed. A husband's extramarital sexual relations were tolerated much more than a wife's.

Legal codes required wives to obey their husbands, and the Napoleonic Code and the remnants of Roman law still in effect throughout Europe designated women the legal equivalents of minors. In cases of divorce and separation, husbands were usually given custody of children. The authority of fathers over children was extensive. A father could take children away from their mother and give them to someone else for rearing. Only a father, in most countries, could permit a daughter to marry, and in some countries he could force his daughter to wed the man of his choice.

The sexual and reproductive rights of women were seldom discussed in the nineteenth century. Both contraception and abortion were illegal well into the twentieth century, and laws punishing rape worked to a woman's disadvantage. Wherever victims turned for help (e.g., to physicians or lawyers), they confronted a world controlled by men.

EDUCATIONAL BARRIERS Throughout the nineteenth century, women had less access to education than men. Most were given only enough schooling to permit them to do their duties as wives and mothers. Not surprisingly, there were more illiterate women than men, and the absence of a system of private or public secondary education prevented women from acquiring the qualifications needed to enter university.

Universities and professional educations were closed to women until at least the third quarter of the century. The University of Zurich admitted women in the 1860s. Women's colleges were founded at Oxford and Cambridge during the last quarter of the century, but women who passed examinations at those universities were not awarded degrees until 1920 (at Oxford) and 1921 (at Cambridge). Women were not admitted to lectures at the Sorbonne in Paris until 1880. Not until the end of the century did universities and medical schools in the Austrian Empire allow women to matriculate. Prussian universities did not admit women until after 1900. Russian women did not attend universities before 1914 but could study at other degree-granting institutions. Italian universities were more open to female students and instructors than comparable institutions elsewhere.

Restriction of a woman's access to secondary and university education was justified as a defense of her traditional gender roles and a way to shield her from political radicalism. There was one career, however, that provided an exception to the general assumption that women needed little education. Because elementary teaching was associated with child nurturing, it was thought of as a female job. It provided a haven for intellectually inclined women, but the schools that trained women for this work were regarded as inferior to universities.

A few women did enter professions, particularly medicine. Most nations refused to allow women to practice law until after World War I, and many of the American women who founded or taught in the first women's colleges in the United States had to go to Europe to acquire their educations. Female pioneers in these fields faced grave social obstacles, personal humiliation, and outright bigotry. They and their male allies called into question a recently acquired article of middle-class faith, namely, that males and females had distinctly separate spheres of activity. Women were often so acculturated to their roles that they were reluctant to campaign for their own liberation. They, as well as men, feared that their family responsibilities were incompatible with feminism.

New Employment Patterns for Women

The Second Industrial Revolution featured two developments that had a major impact on the economic lives of women. The first was an expansion in the variety of jobs available apart from the learned professions. The second was the reduction of the number of married women in the workforce.

AVAILABILITY OF NEW JOBS Although the kinds of industrial occupations that women had filled in the middle of the nineteenth century (especially in textile and garment making) shrank, expansion of governmental bureaucracies, large-scale business organizations, and retail stores created new employment opportunities for women. Government-mandated compulsory education increased the need for elementary schoolteachers, and new inventions, such as typewriters and telephones, fostered employment of females.

Employers paid low wages to women in these jobs. The work required low-level skills, and society assumed, quite often knowing better, that women did not need a living wage. They were supposed to be lifetime dependents for whom fathers or husbands provided support. A woman could rarely find an adequately paying job or earn as much as a man for comparable work. Men were paid more, for they were assumed to have primary responsibility for the maintenance of women and children.

WITHDRAWAL FROM THE LABOR FORCE Most of the women filling the new service positions were young and unmarried. After marriage, or certainly after the birth of a child, a woman usually

Women working in the London Central Telephone Exchange. The invention of the telephone opened new employment opportunities for women.
Mary Evans Picture Library

withdrew from the labor force. She either did not work or worked at something that could be done at home. Employers in offices and retail stores often limited openings to unmarried women without family responsibilities that might interfere with work schedules.

Many changes discouraged married women from working outside their homes. As wages paid to males increased, the importance of a wife's second income diminished. Improving health conditions meant that as more men lived longer, fewer widows were forced back to work. Smaller family sizes decreased the need for supplementary wages. Working children stayed home longer and contributed longer to the family's wage pool. The cultural dominance of middle-class values (i.e., the ideal of the wife as full-time homemaker) also created social expectations that eased women out of the workforce. The more prosperous a working-class family became, the less suitable it seemed for its women to be earning money.

Working-Class Women

The assumption that a woman's proper work pertained to the home degraded the economic situation for women who had to work outside the home. Because their wages were expected merely to supplement those of their husbands, they were treated as casual workers who could be hired and fired according to the whims of the moment.

Poverty and Prostitution

Most nineteenth-century cities had a surplus of working women who had to support themselves, not merely supplement their families' incomes. Economic vulnerability and consequent poverty drove many of them into prostitution. Prostitution had always been a way for very poor women to find some income, but in the late nineteenth century it was closely related to the difficulty they had making their way in an overcrowded female labor force. On the Continent, prostitution was often legalized and regulated by governments (led by men). Great Britain preferred generally to ignore its existence.

Most prostitutes were active on the streets for a very few years, usually from their late teens to about age twenty-five. Thereafter, they moved into the regular workforce or married. Very poor

women who had recently migrated from nearby rural areas were most likely to become prostitutes. Their trade flourished in cities with large army garrisons or naval ports or, like London, large transient populations. Fewer prostitutes worked in manufacturing towns where there were more opportunities for steady employment and where community life was more stable.

Women of the Middle Class

A vast social gap separated working-class women from their middle-class counterparts. As their fathers' and husbands' incomes permitted, middle-class women responded to the increasing preoccupation with domestic comfort. Their purchases helped feed a rapid growth in consumerism in the late nineteenth and early twentieth centuries. They and their numerous domestic servants moved into fashionable new houses constructed in the rapidly expanding suburbs. They filled these homes with manufactured items—clothing, china, furniture, carpets, drapery, wallpaper, and prints. They profited from the improvements that sanitation made in urban life, and they enjoyed the new conveniences provided by electrical power.

THE CULT OF DOMESTICITY   During the first half of the nineteenth century, a middle-class husband expected his spouse to be involved in his business—frequently to handle accounts or correspondence. She often had little to do with rearing their children, a task that was left to nurses and governesses. By the end of the century, things had changed. Middle-class women, if at all possible, did not work for wages. They were limited to the roles of wives and mothers. They often enjoyed great domestic luxury but at the cost of circumscribed lives, talents, ambitions, and intellects. Their duties reflected society's belief that the home was a man's retreat from the stresses of business and the marketplace. Scores of women's journals urged wives to make their homes comfortable, peaceful and private oases where their husbands could find refuge from the pressures of the male world.

Marriages were usually arranged for some kind of family economic benefit. (Romantic marriage was viewed as a danger to social stability.) Middle-class women married young and, since the rearing of children had become their chief

Family was central to the middle-class conception of a stable and respectable social life. This portrait of the Bellelli family is by Edgar Degas. Notice that the husband and father sits at his desk, suggesting his association with business and the world outside their home, whereas the wife and mother stands with their children, suggesting her domestic role. Giraudon/Art Resource, NY

task, began to have babies immediately. Women received no training for any role other than that of dutiful daughter, wife, and mother.

Within the home, a middle-class woman had weighty duties. She was in charge of a household that could be very large. She oversaw all domestic management and child care. She handled most purchases for her family (which is why so much advertising began to be directed toward women). But there were strict limits set to her initiative. A woman's conspicuous idleness was an important symbol of her father's and then her husband's worldly success.

RELIGIOUS AND CHARITABLE ACTIVITIES Churches promoted the cult of domesticity, for it endorsed religion as a suitable activity for women. Women

were expected to attend public worship frequently, to arrange religious instruction for their children, and to see that their families observed domestic religious disciplines and rituals. Prayer was urged as a daily activity for women, and they were encouraged to internalize the aspects of Christian faith that stressed meekness and passivity.

Middle-class women were also expected to engage in charitable work, which was a form of the nurturing to which females were said to be innately disposed. Middle-class women oversaw clubs for poor youth, societies to protect poor young women, schools for infants, and societies for visiting and relieving the poor. Charity of this kind was supposed to inspire the poor to emulate character traits exemplified by middle-class women. Charity work did give women an opportunity to expand their spheres of activity. By the end of the century, some were becoming social workers for private, ecclesiastical, and government organizations.

SEXUALITY AND FAMILY SIZE   Recent studies have called into question older theories about sexual repression in the nineteenth century. Diaries, letters, and early sex surveys indicate that sexual enjoyment, not inhibition, characterized middle-class marriages. Much of the anxiety about sexuality stemmed from the dangers of childbirth, not from a disapproval of sex.

A major change in the sexual behavior of married people took place during the second half of the century. Many couples were eager to limit the number of their offspring in order to maintain a relatively high level of material consumption. The children of the middle class had become much more expensive to rear at a time when expectations for standards of living were also rising. Family sizes declined as new contraceptive devices became available and acceptable to middle-class couples.

The Rise of Political Feminism

Liberal reforms did not automatically benefit women, particularly in the political arena. Liberal leaders feared that women would be unduly susceptible to the religious influences that conservatives would try to use to manipulate their votes. Conservatives, on the other hand, were opposed to the break with tradition that would have been needed to put this theory to the test.

OBSTACLES TO ACHIEVING EQUALITY   Women themselves were often reluctant to support feminist causes or particular feminist organizations. For some, other issues took precedence over those relating to gender (e.g., patriotic struggles for national independence). Among feminists, there were disagreements about which goals for improvement in women's conditions were most important and about which tactics were appropriate for use in the pursuit of reforms. Except in England, it was often difficult for working-class and middle-class women to cooperate.

Although liberal society and law confronted women with obstacles, they also provided feminists with intellectual tools. As early as 1792, Mary Wollstonecraft (*A Vindication of the Rights of Woman*) had cited the revolutionary declarations that asserted rights for men in her arguments for extending comparable rights to women. In 1869 John Stuart Mill (1806–1873) and Harriet Taylor, his wife, published *The Subjection of Women*. It applied the logic liberals used to undermine tyranny to critique woman's place in European society. Socialists often, but by no means always, indicted capitalist societies for their treatment of women.

The fact that early statements of feminist positions were often linked with unorthodox opinions about sexuality, family life, and property made it difficult for feminists to enlist widespread public support. Everywhere in Europe, including Britain, the feminist cause was badly divided over both goals and tactics.

VOTES FOR WOMEN IN BRITAIN   Europe's most advanced women's movements were in Great Britain. Millicent Fawcett (1847–1929) founded a moderate National Union of Women's Suffrage Societies that, by 1908, could organize rallies of half a million women. Fawcett's husband was an economist who had served as a Liberal Party cabinet minister, and her tactics were those of English Liberals. She believed that Parliament would give women votes when women demonstrated that they would be respectable, responsible participants in politics.

Emmeline Pankhurst (1858–1928) advocated a much more radical approach. Her husband, who died near the close of the century, had fought for labor and for Irish home rule. Irish nationalists employed numerous disruptive political tactics to promote their cause, and early labor leaders also had confrontations with police over the right to hold meetings. In 1903 Pankhurst and her daughters, Christabel and Sylvia, founded the Women's Social and Political Union. Derisively dubbed "suffragettes," they spent years lobbying for votes for women. By 1910, having failed to move the government, they turned to violent tactics. They organized marches on Parliament and resorted to arson, window breaking, and sabotage of postal boxes. The Liberal government of Herbert Asquith imprisoned demonstrators, force-fed those who staged hunger strikes in jail, and steadfastly refused women the franchise. In 1918 gratitude for women's contributions to the war effort finally won the vote for some British women.

POLITICAL FEMINISM ON THE CONTINENT   Although Norwegian women were voting on national issues by 1907, the rest of the Continent lagged far behind them and behind the pace set by Britain's feminists. In France, when Hubertine Auclert (1848–1914) began campaigning for the vote in the 1880s, she stood virtually alone. Almost all French feminists opposed violence in any form, and they were never able to organize mass rallies. Their leaders believed that the vote could be achieved by appeal through legal channels. In 1919 the French Chamber of Deputies passed a bill granting the vote to women, but the French Senate defeated the bill in 1922. It was not until after World War II that French women were granted votes.

Political feminism was even more underdeveloped in Germany, where laws actually barred women from participation in political activities. But since no group in the German Empire enjoyed extensive political rights, German women were not particularly sensitive to their situation. Calls for rights for women were suspected of being subversive not only of the state, but of society. In 1894 the Union of German Women's Organizations (BDFK) was founded. It was primarily concerned with improving women's social conditions, access to education, and various protections, but by 1902 it was supporting a call for the right to vote. The German Social Democratic Party endorsed women's suffrage, but the party was so disdained by the German authorities and German Roman Catholics that its support increased opposition to suffrage proposals. Women received the vote in Germany in 1918, when defeat abroad and revolution at home influenced the constitution written for the Weimar Republic.

Jewish Emancipation

Until the late eighteenth century, Europe's Jews generally lived apart from Christians in ghettos or villages where they were regarded as resident aliens, not citizens. The ideals of the Enlightenment called this custom into question and motivated some reforms.

Differing Degrees of Citizenship

In 1782 Joseph II gave the Jews of the Habsburg Empire more or less the same standing before the law as Christians. The National Assembly of France recognized Jews as citizens in 1789, and,

during the turmoil of the Napoleonic wars, Jews and Christians mixed on a relatively equal footing in Italy and Germany. Steps toward the political emancipation of Jews were, however, subject to repeal whenever governments changed.

Russia's tradition of harsh discrimination against Jews continued until World War I. The Russian government undermined Jewish community life, limited publication of Jewish books, restricted areas where Jews might live, required internal passports for Jews, banned Jews from forms of state service, and excluded Jews from many institutions of higher education. The police and others conducted *pogroms*—riots organized to disrupt Jewish communities. Hundreds of thousands of Jews fled Russia and eastern Europe for western Europe and the United States. There they encountered prejudice on the personal level, but their legal position was more secure.

Broadened Opportunities

Following the revolutions of 1848, the situation for Jews in western Europe improved. Germany, Italy, the Low Countries, and Scandinavia granted Jews full citizenship. After 1858 Jews could be elected to Great Britain's Parliament, and Austria-Hungary extended full legal rights to Jews in 1867. Jews entered politics and won the highest offices. Politically, they tended to be liberals or, especially in eastern Europe, socialists.

From 1850 to 1880 there was little overt prejudice toward Jews, and many entered professions and occupations previously closed to them. They participated fully in literary and cultural life and became leaders in science and education. The process of their acculturation was encouraged when prohibitions against intermarriages were repealed during the last quarter of the century.

Prejudice against Jews did not, however, disappear. Anti-Semites openly accused Jewish bankers and financial interests of causing the economic stagnation of the 1870s. In the 1880s, organized anti-Semitism erupted in Germany and France. This caused some Jews called Zionists to work for the establishment of an independent Jewish nation, but most believed that the revival of old prejudices would be temporary and that the liberal legal protections they had acquired over the course of the century would protect them. They were disastrously betrayed by that faith.

Labor, Socialism, and Politics to World War I

The industrial expansion that took place in the late nineteenth century increased the size and changed the nature of the urban proletariat. For the first time, factory wage earners outnumbered artisans and highly skilled workers. Workers had always had to look to themselves to improve their lot, but after the failed revolutions of 1848 European laborers changed their strategy. They stopped rioting in the streets and trying to revive paternalistic guild systems and embraced new institutions and ideologies (e.g., trade unions, democratic political parties, and socialism).

Trade Unionism

Trade unionism flourished during the second half of the century as governments recognized the right of workers to organize. Unions were legalized in Great Britain in 1871 and allowed to picket in 1875. Napoleon III, his power waning in 1868, allowed weak labor associations, and France's Third Republic legalized unions in 1884. Drives for unionization in Germany met little resistance after 1890.

At midcentury, unions concentrated on organizing skilled workers and improving wages and working conditions. By the close of the century, industrial unions for unskilled workers were also being established. These large unions of thousands of members met intense opposition from employers and frequently had to wage long strikes. A majority of Europe's labor force was still not unionized in the decade leading up to World War I.

Democracy and Political Parties

With the exception of Russia, all the major European states established broad-based, if not perfectly democratic, electoral systems in the late nineteenth century. Great Britain passed its second voting reform act in 1867 and its third in 1884. Bismarck decreed universal male suffrage for the German Empire in 1871. The French Chamber of Deputies was democratically elected. Universal male suffrage was adopted in Switzerland in 1879, in Spain in 1890, in Belgium in 1893, in the Netherlands in 1896, in Norway in 1898, and in Italy in 1912.

The broadened franchise fundamentally changed politics. It meant that politicians could not ignore workers and that workers no longer had to go outside institutions of government to voice their grievances. Instead of staging revolts against political authorities, they could hold them accountable at the ballot box. But when European states had narrow electoral bases, most voters were people of property who knew what they had at stake in politics. They were a fairly cohesive group that did not require much party organization. The expansion of the electorate brought into the political processes many voters whose level of political awareness and interest was quite low. The political party—with its workers, newspapers, offices, social life, and discipline—was created to mobilize this new electoral force.

The democratization of politics and growing political awareness of workers presented socialists with greater opportunities to challenge the traditional ruling classes. The major question for late-century socialist parties throughout Europe was whether the lot of the working class could be improved by democratic reform or whether revolution would be necessary. This issue sharply divided socialist parties, most especially those whose leadership adhered to the intellectual legacy of Karl Marx.

Marx and the First International

In 1864 a group of British and French trade unionists founded the International Working Men's Association, which became known simply as the First International. It encompassed a vast array of radical political types. Although Karl Marx believed that the capitalist system was beyond reform, in his inaugural address to the International he approved efforts by labor to work within existing political and economic processes. His private writings, which criticized such reformist activity, were not made public until after his death.

The violence associated with the doomed Paris Commune of 1871, which Marx had praised as a genuine proletarian movement, cast a pall over socialism. France suppressed socialist activities, and British trade unionists, who received legal protections in 1871, wanted to avoid being associated with supporters of the Commune. Faced with declining interest, the First International held its last European congress in 1873. It then moved its offices to the United States and dissolved in 1876.

Although short-lived, the First International had a great impact on the future of European socialism. Throughout the late 1860s, the organization gathered statistics, kept labor groups informed of mutual problems, provided a forum for the debate of socialist doctrine, and extravagantly proclaimed its own influence over contemporary events. These activities helped Marxism triumph over other brands of socialism. The apparently scientific character of Marxism also made it attractive to an age that was enthralled with the progress science had been making.

Great Britain: Fabianism and Early Welfare Programs

Neither Marxism nor any other form of socialism made significant progress in Great Britain, the most advanced industrial society of the day. British trade unions usually supported Liberal Party candidates. In 1892 Keir Hardie became the first independent working man to be elected to Parliament, but the socialist Independent Labour Party, which was founded a year later, attracted little support.

Until 1901 labor took little part in politics. But that year, when the House of Lords removed the legal protection accorded union funds (the Taff Vale decision), the Trades Union Congress responded by launching the Labour Party. In the election of 1906 the new party sent twenty-nine members to Parliament. Trade unionists were not yet advocates of socialism, but they were becoming more militant. There were scores of strikes in the years leading up to the war, and the government assumed a greater role as mediator.

British socialism was primarily the preserve of non-Marxist intellectuals. Britain's most influential socialist group was the Fabian Society. Founded in 1884, it took its name from Q. Fabius Maximus, a Roman general famous for defending Rome by refusing directly to confront Hannibal, a Carthaginian invader. The name symbolized the society's gradualist approach to social reform. Its leading members, Sidney (1859–1947) and Beatrice (1858–1943) Webb, H. G. Wells (1866–1946), Graham Wallas (1858–1932), and George Bernard Shaw (1856–1950), hoped to convince their country of the rational wisdom of so-

cialism. They believed that collective ownership, often at the municipal level, could solve the problems of industry and that the expansion of ownership and state direction of production could be achieved gradually, peacefully, and democratically.

The British government and the major political parties slowly responded to pressures from labor. In 1903 Joseph Chamberlain (1836–1914) split the Conservative Party by waging an unsuccessful tariff-reform campaign intended to finance social reform through higher import duties. After 1906 the Liberal Party, led by Sir Henry Campbell-Bannerman (1836–1908) and by Herbert Asquith (1852–1928) after 1908, pursued a two-pronged policy. Fearful of losing seats in Parliament to the new Labour Party, they restored the former protection of the unions. Then, after 1909, with Chancellor of the Exchequer David Lloyd George (1863–1945) as its guiding light, a Liberal ministry enacted a broad program of social legislation. This included the establishment of labor exchanges, the regulation of sweatshop trades (e.g., tailoring and lacemaking), and the National Insurance Act (1911), which provided unemployment benefits and health care.

Proposals to finance these programs created conflict between the House of Commons and the Conservative-dominated House of Lords. This led to the enactment in 1911 of the Parliament Act, which allowed the Commons to override the legislative veto of the upper chamber. The new taxes and social programs (which were not yet enough to content labor) meant that in Britain, the home of nineteenth-century liberalism, the state was expanding its role in the lives of its citizens.

France: "Opportunism" Rejected

At the turn of the century, Jean Jaurès (1859–1914) and Jules Guesde (1845–1922) led opposing factions of French socialists. Guesde repudiated Jaurès for attempting to work with France's governing ministries. He insisted that socialists could not cooperate with a bourgeois government that they were dedicated to overthrowing. The Dreyfus affair brought the quarrel to a head when, in 1899, Prime Minister René Waldeck-Rousseau (1846–1904) tried to unite Dreyfus's supporters by finding a socialist willing to serve in the French cabinet. Alexander Millerand (1859–1943) accepted the appointment.

Georges Seurat and Giuseppe Pellizza da Volpedo: European Society in Conflict

*M*any late-nineteenth-century Europeans viewed society as divided into hostile political and social factions. Socialism tried to mobilize the recently enfranchised working class while the propertied middle class subscribed to liberalism. The art of the period recognized this division.

A Sunday on La Grande-Jatte–1844 by Georges Seurat (1859–1891) depicted members of the Parisian middle class enjoying a leisurely summer outing in a parklike setting. Seurat's interest in scientific studies of light and vision led him to develop a technique for painting called

Georges Seurat, (French, 1859–1891), *A Sunday on La Grande-Jatte–1884.* Oil on canvas, 1884–86, 207.6× 308 cm. Helen Birch Bartlett Memorial Collection, 1926.224. Photograph © 1999, The Art Institute of Chicago. All rights reserved.

Giuseppe Pellizza da Volpedo, *Il Quarto Stato (The Fourth Estate)*, 1901. Oil on canvas, 283 cm × 550 cm. Civica Galleria d'Arte Moderna–Milano. Photo by Marcello Saporetti

pointillism. By constructing a picture like a mosaic composed of tiny "points" of pure color, Seurat invited the viewer's eye to do the work of blending dots of pigment into tints and shadows. The mood of Seurat's painting seems more somber than its subject would suggest. Deep shadows imply that all is not sunny for these prosperous people. Their rigid postures make them look like the mannequins in the fashionable new department stores where they fed their insatiable appetites for consumer goods. They seem bored stiff and perhaps troubled by their comfortable lives.

The Fourth Estate, which Giuseppe Pelliza de Volpedo (1868–1907) painted (1898–1901) using Seurat's pointillist technique, was intended to make a socialist statement. Pelliza belonged to a school of artists who developed a style called *social realism.* They eschewed nostalgic, sentimental depictions of rural peasants in favor of studies of the harsh realities that faced modern industrial and agricultural laborers. The painting's title was an allusion to the socialist faith that the traditional three estates (i.e., clergy, aristocracy, and commoners) would eventually be displaced by a fourth estate—a solidarity of the world's workers. The strong, determined men and women in Pelliza's composition form a united front as they stride forward, confident in their power to overcome all obstacles and to demand a place in their viewers' world.

Sources: T. J. Clark, *The Painting of Modern Life: Paris in the Art of Manet and His Followers* (Princeton: Princeton University Press, 1984); Robert Rosenblum and H. W. Janson, *19th-Century Art* (Englewood Cliffs, N.J.: Prentice Hall and New York: Harry N. Abrams, 1984).

Cabinet participation was part of a political strategy that socialists termed *opportunism.* In 1904 the Amsterdam Congress of the Second International (a group founded in 1889 to coordinate various national socialist parties and trade unions) condemned opportunism and ordered France's socialists to form a single party. Jaurès acquiesced; by 1914 Socialist Party members were the second-largest group in the Chamber of Deputies. Socialists did not, however, serve in a French cabinet until the Popular Front Government of 1936.

French workers tended to vote socialist, but their unions, unlike those in Great Britain, avoided direct participation in politics. The Confédération Générale du Travail, founded in 1895, saw itself as an alternative to socialist parties. Its leaders embraced the doctrines of syndicalism expounded by Georges Sorel (1847–1922) in *Reflections on Violence* (1908). They believed that the general strike, not the political process, was the tool workers should use to demand reform. Strikes often conflicted with socialist efforts to use the machinery of the state on behalf of workers. Strikes, some of which the government used troops to suppress, were common between 1905 and 1914.

Germany: Social Democrats and Revisionism

The Marxist-dominated German Social Democratic Party, or SPD, was consistently hostile to all nonsocialist governments. The SPD emerged in 1875 in response to the work of Ferdinand Lasalle (1825–1864), a labor agitator who wanted to win a role for the working class in German politics. Since Marxists who opposed reformist politics—particularly Wilhelm Liebknecht (1826–1900) and August Bebel (1840–1913)—helped organize the party, it was, from the start, divided between those who advocated reform and those who trusted only in revolution.

BISMARCK'S REPRESSION OF THE SPD   Bismarck, the so-called "Iron Chancellor," opposed socialism. Although no socialists were involved in an 1878 assassination attempt on William I, Bismarck exploited the event to steer laws through the *Reichstag* that suppressed the organization, meetings, newspapers, and other public activities of the SPD. The legislation proved politically

counterproductive. From the early 1880s onward, the SPD steadily polled more and more votes in elections to the *Reichstag.*

When repressive laws failed to wean German workers away from socialism, Bismarck designed social welfare legislation to provide a paternalistic, conservative alternative to socialism. In 1883 the German Empire adopted a health insurance measure. A year later, it created accident insurance. In 1889 Bismarck sponsored a plan for old-age and disability pensions. Since these programs were funded by contributions from both workers and employers, they constituted a state-organized system of social security that did not require any change in ownership of property or in politics. Germany became the first major industrial nation to enjoy this kind of welfare program.

THE ERFURT PROGRAM   After Bismarck's forced resignation, Emperor William II (r. 1888–1918) tried to win support from the working class by allowing the antisocialist legislation to expire. The lifting of the repressive laws, which had never prevented members of the SPD from sitting in the *Reichstag,* forced the party to ponder what attitude it ought to assume toward the German Empire.

The SPD's stand, called the Erfurt Program of 1891, was formulated by Bebel and by Karl Kautsky (1854–1938). In good Marxist fashion, the party declared its faith in the imminent doom of capitalism and the necessity of socialist ownership of the means of production, but it pledged to pursue these goals through legal political participation, not revolution. Consequently, although in theory the SPD was hostile to the German Empire, in practice it worked within the system.

The SPD's dilemma prompted the most important rethinking within socialist circles of the orthodox Marxist critique of capitalism. Eduard Bernstein (1850–1932), a socialist thinker who had been exposed to Fabianism in Great Britain, questioned Marx's confident prediction that the inadequacies of capitalism would make revolution inevitable. In *Evolutionary Socialism* (1899), Bernstein pointed to recent developments that did not support orthodox Marxist predictions—primarily, a rising standard of living in Europe and sales of stocks that broadened ownership of capitalist industry. These things increased the size of the middle class instead of forcing it, as Marx had predicted, into the ranks of the proletariat. Moreover, the extension of the franchise to the working class meant that revolution might not be necessary to achieve social change.

THE DEBATE OVER REVISIONISM Although a heated debate led German socialists to condemn Bernstein's doctrines (which were dubbed "revisionism"), the SPD pursued a course of action consistent with Bernstein's views. Its trade union members, who were prospering, did not want revolution, and its leaders did not want to provoke the kind of persecution they had experienced under Bismarck. Subsequently, by working for electoral gains, membership expansion, and short-term reform, the SPD succeeded in becoming one of the most important political organizations in imperial Germany.

Russia: Industrial Development and the Birth of Bolshevism

During the last decade of the nineteenth century, Russia entered the industrial age and encountered many of the problems that more advanced nations had experienced fifty or seventy-five years earlier. Alexander III (r. 1881–1894) and his successor, Nicholas II (r. 1894–1917), believed that Russia had to become an industrial power to maintain its international influence. To Sergei Witte (1849–1915), the finance minister appointed in 1892, fell the task of devising a program. He was the epitome of the nineteenth-century modernizer—trusting to planned economic development, protective tariffs, high taxes, the gold standard, efficient management, and the development of heavy industries.

In Russia, as elsewhere, industrialism created considerable social discontent. Landowners resented the profits foreign investors took out of the country. Peasants objected to being taxed to sustain development that did not improve their lives, and a small but significant industrial proletariat protested abysmal working conditions.

Emancipation of the serfs in 1861 had not improved Russian agriculture. Peasants were handicapped by redemption payments, excessive taxes, and falling grain prices. Many owned land communally through a *mir* (i.e., village) and farmed it inefficiently. Many had too little land to support themselves and had to work for the

nobility or the *kulaks* (prosperous peasant farmers). To make things worse, between 1860 and 1914, Russia experienced a population explosion: increasing from 50 million to 103 million.

Social discontent motivated the formation of new political parties. The Social Revolutionary Party, founded in 1901, adopted the Populists' agenda of the 1870s. This involved opposition to industrialism and advocacy of an idealized version of the communal life of the Russian peasantry. In 1903 the liberal Constitutional Democratic Party (known as the Cadets) was formed to work for the establishment of a new regime utilizing ministries, guaranteeing civil liberties, and promoting progressive economic policies—all under the guidance of a parliament. A socialist Social Democratic Party appeared in 1898, but its leaders were soon driven into exile.

LENIN'S EARLY THOUGHT AND CAREER Since Russia had a small working class and no representative institutions, its socialists, unlike socialists elsewhere, despaired of working through established political channels. Their commitment to revolution inclined them to a brand of Marxism developed by two exiled leaders: Gregory Plekhanov (1857–1918) and his disciple Vladimir Illich Ulyanov (1870–1924), known as Lenin.

Lenin's father was a high-ranking bureaucrat whose elder son was executed in 1887 for plotting against Alexander III. In 1893 Lenin, while studying in Saint Petersburg, became involved with revolutionary factory workers. He was arrested in 1895 and sent to Siberia. In 1900 he left Russia and spent most of the next seventeen years in Switzerland in the company of the exiled Russian Social Democrats.

Unlike the backward-looking Social Revolutionaries, the Social Democrats were Marxists and modernizers. They favored industrial development, and most believed that Russia had to create a large proletariat before the revolution could begin. Like other socialist groups, they split over the issue of working to reform the system or to overthrow it. Lenin, in *What Is to Be Done?* (1902), condemned any accommodations, such as those practiced by the German SPD. He maintained that revolutionary consciousness would not arise spontaneously from the working class. Only a small, tightly organized, elite party could sustain adequate revolutionary fervor and resist penetration by police spies. He rejected Kautsky's

In this photograph taken in 1895, Lenin sits at the table among a group of other young Russian radicals from Saint Petersburg.
Corbis

claim that revolution was inevitable and Bernstein's faith that it would arrive democratically. For Lenin, the social transformation Marx predicted would be the work of a small party of professional revolutionaries, not the proletariat.

In 1903, at its London Congress, the Russian Social Democratic Party split. Lenin emerged the leader of a very slim majority of its members, a faction calling itself the *Bolsheviks* ("majority"). Their more moderate opponents were the *Mensheviks* ("minority"). In 1912 the Bolsheviks organized separately.

In 1905 Lenin published a program for revolution in Russia: *Two Tactics of Social Democracy in the Bourgeois-Democratic Revolution.* He grasped better than any other revolutionary the profound discontent in the Russian countryside and argued for an alliance between workers and peasants to overthrow the tsarist regime. In November 1917, his Bolsheviks seized power, but only after other political forces had toppled the government.

The Revolution of 1905 and Its Aftermath
Industrialization, not Lenin, was the source of Tsar Nicholas II's problems. In 1903 he dismissed Witte from office. In 1904 he declared war on Japan, hoping to generate a wave of patriotism. Instead, Russia was defeated, and a political crisis ensued. On "Bloody Sunday" (January 22, 1905), the tsar's troops fired into a crowd of workers in Saint Petersburg who were trying to present a petition to the tsar asking him to improve industrial conditions. The incident sparked revolutionary disturbances throughout Russia. Sailors mutinied, peasants revolted, the tsar's uncle was assassinated, the liberal Constitutional Democratic Party demanded political reform, students staged strikes, and Social Revolutionaries and Social Democrats stirred up urban workers. Early in October 1905, strikes broke out in Saint Petersburg, and worker groups, called *soviets*, took control of the city. Nicholas II responded with the October Manifesto, a pledge to institute constitutional government in Russia.

Early in 1906 Nicholas II announced elections for a bicameral representative body, the Duma, but he reserved to himself ministerial appointments, financial policy, military matters, and foreign affairs. When the April elections returned a very radical assembly, the tsar again discharged Witte, whom he had recalled, and chose a new adviser, P. A. Stolypin (1862–1911). After only four months, Stolypin persuaded him to dissolve the Duma. A new assembly, which was elected in February 1907, lasted only into June. By limiting the franchise, the government finally won election of a more pliable third Duma in late 1907.

Since Nicholas II appeared to have recaptured much of the ground he had conceded, Stolypin set about repressing rebellion and rallying support from property owners. In November 1906, the government canceled payments for land that peasants still owed under the terms of the Emancipation Act of 1861. Peasants were encouraged to assume individual management of their holdings and to abandon the communal system associated with the *mirs*. This, combined with a program offering instruction in farming methods, helped stimulate agricultural production. Moderates approved of the land measures, and many people were eager to compromise with the government to avoid further revolutionary disturbances.

When the unpopular Stolypin was assassinated in 1911, Nicholas II failed to find a competent adviser to replace him. The situation at court was complicated by the increasing influence of Grigory Efimovich Rasputin (1871?–1916), a strange, uncouth monk who claimed to be able to heal the tsar's hemophilic heir. As social malcontents demanded and conservatives rejected further liberal reforms, the domestic situation became increasingly unmanageable. The tsar again began to hope that a bold move on the diplomatic front might rally the popular support he so desperately needed. World War I loomed just ahead.

In Perspective

Between 1860 and 1914, two apparently contradictory developments occurred in European social life: the lifestyle of the property-owning urban middle classes became the model to which much of society aspired, while socialists and labor unions demanded a broader redistribution of property. The working class was not alone in seeking change. Women began to demand a political role and to protest the gender inequalities embedded in law and family life. Their demands, as much as the theories of socialists, would in time raise questions about the adequacy of the much admired late-nineteenth-century middle-class lifestyle.

REVIEW QUESTIONS

1. How was European society transformed by the Second Industrial Revolution? What new industries developed? Which do you think had the greatest impact in the twentieth century? How do you account for European economic difficulties in the second half of the nineteenth century?

2. What were living conditions like in European cities during the late nineteenth century? Why were European cities redesigned during this period? How were they redesigned? Why were housing and health key issues for urban reform?

3. What was the status of European women in the second half of the nineteenth century? Why did they grow discontented with their lot? What factors led to change? To what extent had they improved their position by 1914? What tactics did they use in effecting change? Was the emancipation of women inevitable? How did women approach their situation differently from country to country?

4. What forms did the emancipation of Jews take in the nineteenth century?

5. What was the status of the proletariat in 1860? Had it improved by 1914? What caused the growth in trade unions and organized mass political parties? Why did socialist parties debate "opportunism" and "revisionism"?

6. How important was industrialism for Russia? Were the tsars wise to attempt to modernize their country? Would they have been better off leaving it as it was? How did Lenin's view of socialism differ from that of the socialists in western Europe?

SUGGESTED READINGS

I. M. Aronson, *Troubled Waters: The Origins of the 1881 Anti-Jewish Pogroms in Russia* (1990). The best discussion of this subject.

J. Auerbach, *The Great Exhibition of 1851: A Nation on Display* (1999). Explores the most influential exhibition of manufactured goods of the nineteenth century in its larger cultural and natural setting.

C. M. Cipolla, *The Economic History of World Population* (1962). A basic introduction.

S. P. Frank, *Crime, Cultural Conflict and Justice in Rural Russia, 1856–1914* (1999). An extensively documented study of the interaction of Russian peasants and the Czarist state during the decades of the abolition of serfdom.

S. C. HAUSE, *Women's Suffrage and Social Politics in the French Third Republic* (1984). A wide-ranging examination of the question.

G. HIMMELFARB, *Poverty and Compassion: The Moral Imagination of the Late Victorians* (1991). The best examination of late Victorian social thought.

E. J. HOBSBAWM, *The Age of Capital* (1975). Explores the consolidation of middle-class life after 1850.

T. HOLPEN, *The Mid-Victorian Generation, 1846–1886* (1998). The most extensive treatment of the subject.

S. S. HOLTON, *Feminism and Democracy: Women's Suffrage and Reform Politics in Britian, 1900–1918* (1986). An excellent treatment of the subject.

S. KERN, *The Culture of Love: Victorians to Moderns* (1992). A major discussion of the manner in which Europeans have thought and behaved in regard to love, family, and sexuality.

D. LANDES, *The Unbound Prometheus: Technological Change and Industrial Development in Western Europe from 1750 to the Present* (1969). Includes excellent discussions of late nineteenth-century development.

G. L. MOOSE, *German Jews Beyond Judaism* (1985). Sensitive essays exploring the relationship of Jews to German culture in the nineteenth and early twentieth centuries.

P. G. NORD, *Paris Shopkeepers and the Politics of Resentment* (1986). An examination of the political attitudes of Paris shopkeepers in the wake of the redesign of the city.

D. H. PINKNEY, *Napoleon III and the Rebuilding of Paris* (1958). A classic study.

H. ROGGER, *Russia in the Age of Modernization and Revolution, 1881–1917* (1983). The best synthesis of the period.

C. E. SCHORSKE, *German Social Democracy, 1905–1917* (1955). A brilliant study of the difficulties of the Social Democrats under the empire.

B. G. SMITH, *Ladies of the Leisure Class: The Bourgeoises of Northern France in the Nineteenth Century* (1981). Emphasizes the importance of the reproductive role of women.

N. STONE, *Europe Transformed* (1984). A sweeping survey that emphasizes the difficulties of late nineteenth-century liberalism.

F. M. L. THOMPSON, *The Rise of Respectable Society: A Social History of Victorian Britain, 1830–1900* (1988). A major survey.

J. TOSH, *A Man's Place: Masculinity and the Middle-Class Home in Victorian England* (1999). A pioneering work.

A. B. ULAM, *The Bolsheviks: The Intellectual and Political History of the Triumph of Communism in Russia* (1965). Early chapters discuss prewar developments and the formation of Lenin's doctrines.

A. M. VERNER, *The Crisis of Russian Autocracy: Nicholas II and the 1905 Revolution* (1990). A major study of this crucial event.

E. WEBER, *Peasants into Frenchmen: The Modernization of Rural France, 1870–1914* (1976). An important and fascinating work on the transformation of French peasants into self-conscious citizens of the nation-state.

Chapter 25
The Birth of Modern European Thought

The New Reading Public
Advances in Primary Education
Reading Material for the Mass Audience

Science at Midcentury
Comte, Positivism, and the Prestige
of Science
Darwin's Theory of Natural Selection
Science and Ethics

Christianity and the Church Under Siege
Intellectual Skepticism
Conflict Between Church and State
Areas of Religious Revival
The Roman Catholic Church and the
Modern World

Toward a Twentieth-Century Frame of Mind
Science: The Revolution in Physics
Literature: Realism and Naturalism
Modernism
Friedrich Nietzsche and the Revolt
Against Reason
The Birth of Psychoanalysis
Retreat from Rationalism in Politics
Racism
Anti-Semitism and the Birth of Zionism
Science, Racial Thought, and the
Non-Western World

Women and Modern Thought
Antifeminism in Late-Century Thought
New Directions in Feminism

K E Y   T O P I C S

- The dominance of science in the thought of the second half of the nineteenth century
- The conflict of church and state over education
- The effect of modernism, psychoanalysis, and the revolution in physics on intellectual life
- Racism and the resurgence of anti-Semitism
- Late-nineteenth and early-twentieth-century developments in feminism

The political systems, industrialized economies, and middle-class lifestyles that emerged in the late nineteenth century were accompanied by intellectual developments that shaped a "modern" mind. The new intellectual orientation was rooted in the Enlightenment (which contributed confidence in reason and science and a tolerant, cosmopolitan outlook) and the romantic movement (which fostered respect for feeling, imagination, artistic insight, and the value of individuals). Most of the West's traditional assumptions about nature, religion, and social life were subjected to radical reexamination. As a result, at the turn of the century European intellectuals were more daring than ever *before but less certain about where their work might lead. Fading confidence in the reliability of traditional points of view helped some disadvantaged groups, such as women, win liberating social reforms.*

The New Reading Public

Advances in Primary Education

Fifty percent of Europeans were illiterate in 1850, and many of those who technically could read and write did so poorly. State-financed education changed that, and during the next half-century Europe developed its first mass reading public. Hungary led the way, providing elementary education in 1868; Britain, in 1870; Switzerland, in 1874; Italy, in 1877; and France, between 1878 and 1881. After 1871, Prussia's superior educational system was extended in various ways throughout the German Empire. By 1900 the literacy rate in Britain, France, Belgium, the Netherlands, Germany, and Scandinavia was 85 percent. Italy, Spain, Russia, Austria-Hungary, and the Balkans achieved rates of 30 to 60 percent.

The educational crusade embodied the Enlightenment rationalist faith that right knowledge would lead to right action. Both liberals and conservatives believed that literacy would enable newly enfranchised voters to use political power responsibly and that it would help the poor to help themselves by making them a more productive labor force. Once the masses were given a taste for education and realized its benefits, demands for schooling increased. Having already established systems for primary education, during the World War I era the major nations began to provide secondary education. A generation later, democratic university instruction was under development.

Reading Material for the Mass Audience

Advances in technology lowered publication costs just as the expanding literate population developed an appetite for new kinds of reading materials. The number of monthly and quarterly journals designed for particular groups of subscribers increased. Cheap mass-circulation newspapers, such as *Le Petit Journal* of Paris and the *Daily Mail* and *Daily Express* of London, enjoyed their first heydays.

Because many of the new readers were marginally literate and relatively unsophisticated, the materials produced for them were often mediocre. Newspapers, in particular, exploited stories of sensational crimes and political scandals and carried pages of advertising that made extravagant, unsubstantiated claims. Despite the low level of public taste, the new literacy was the intellectual equivalent of the railroad and the steamship. It enabled people to explore new intellectual territory and to take the initiative in improving their skills and deepening their understandings. Governments and political leaders quickly discovered the power of newspaper editorials to influence voters.

Science at Midcentury

The link between science and technology in the Second Industrial Revolution made the public more aware of science than ever before, and during the first half of the nineteenth century science gained ground as the model for all human knowledge. The dominant world view remained Newton's—a rational universe that operated according to observable mechanical principles.

Comte, Positivism, and the Prestige of Science

Auguste Comte (1798–1857), building on the Enlightenment's faith, claimed that science was the culmination of human intellectual development. In *The Positive Philosophy* (1830–1842), Comte argued that human understanding evolved in three stages: the theological (where natural events are credited to the action of spiritual beings), the metaphysical (where abstract principles, not personified entities, are thought to control nature), and the positive (where natural phenomena are explained by referring them to each other, not to unobservable forces). Comte believed that physical science had entered the positive stage first and that other fields would eventually follow. His argument helped establish the idea that knowledge of all subjects must resemble the kind of knowledge common to the natural sciences. Comte is remembered, in particular, as the father of sociology, for he predicted that laws, such as those of physics, would be found to explain social behavior.

During the third quarter of the century, talk emerged of a religion of science that would explain all nature without resort to supernaturalism. Men such as Thomas Henry Huxley (1825–1895) in Britain and Ernst Haeckel (1834–1919) in Germany interpreted scientific advances for the general public, while proclaiming their belief that science held the answer to all the questions of life. They advocated government support for scientific research and the inclusion of science in the curricula of schools and universities.

Darwin's Theory of Natural Selection

In 1859 Charles Darwin (1809–1882) published *The Origin of Species.* The book is one of the seminal works of Western thought, the equivalent in biology of Newton's contribution to physics and Copernicus's to cosmology. Darwin's work has been much misunderstood. He did not originate the concept of evolution, which had been discussed widely before his time. His contribution was a theory proposing a mechanical process to explain how evolution operated: the principle of natural selection. Working independently, his contemporary, Alfred Russel Wallace (1823–1913), came up with the same idea.

Building on one of Malthus's insights, Darwin and Wallace contended that more organisms come into existence than can survive in their environment. Those that have a unique trait that gives them a marginal advantage in the struggle for existence change the nature of their species by reproducing more successfully than their competitors. Since the fittest survive to pass on their unique characteristics, a mechanistic process of "natural selection," not divine choice, shapes the design of living things. Neither Darwin nor anyone else at the time could explain the origin of the chance variations that gave certain individuals advantages over others of their species. Only after 1900, when work on heredity by an Austrian monk named Gregor Mendel (1822–1884) began to circulate, did the mystery of those variations begin to be unraveled.

The theory of evolution by natural selection removed a need for a guiding purpose in nature. It explained a species' traits as the result of its past struggles with the environment, not a de-

In two works of seminal importance, The Origin of Species *(1859) and* The Descent of Man *(1871), Charles Darwin articulated the theory of evolution by natural selection and applied that theory to human beings. The result was a storm of controversy that affected not only biology but also religion, philosophy, sociology, and even politics.* Bildarchiv Preussischer Kulturbesitz

ity's plan for its destiny. It called into question a literal interpretation of the biblical narrative of Creation and undermined the deistic argument for God as the author of a rationally designed universe. No God was needed if the universe had no design. And if there was no design, no fixity in nature—nothing but flux and change—might not the same thing also be true of society, values, customs, and beliefs? What did "truth" mean in such a world?

In 1871 Darwin published *The Descent of Man* and spelled out the implications of natural selection for the human species. He contended that not only the human frame but human conscience and religious intuition evolved naturalistically as part of a survival strategy. No God was needed to provide an image for humanity. Not since Copernicus had removed the earth from the center of the universe had human pride received so sharp a blow. With so much at stake, Darwin's theories were slow to win support. By the end of the nineteenth century scientists widely accepted evolution, but not natural selection. Support for the latter within the scientific community dates to the 1920s and 1930s when developments in modern genetics began to solve some of the puzzles Darwin's theory had created.

Science and Ethics

Debates about *Darwinism* inevitably raised questions about the implications for society of the kind of science it represented. The phrase "survival of the fittest," which Darwin used, was coined earlier by classical economists to affirm the healthiness of competition. Some philosophers hastened to suggest that it might also apply to ethics and human relationships.

A British philosopher, Herbert Spencer (1820–1903), was the most famous of the thinkers who applied evolutionary analogies to ethics. He advocated individualism and asserted that competition was essential if society was to progress. The strong had a kind of ethical imperative to subdue the weak, for attempts to spare the weak only served (by perpetuating their inferior traits) to undermine the species. Spencer's arguments were used to justify neglect of the poor and the working class, exploitation of colonial peoples, and aggressive competition among nations.

Social Darwinism of this kind came close to claiming that might makes right, but Thomas Henry Huxley (1825–1895), a vigorous defender of Darwin's ideas, rejected it. He argued that the process of evolution in the physical world was at odds with the development of ethical awareness in human beings. The struggle in physical nature was not the same as the struggle within human nature. Many admirers and practitioners of science disagreed with him. During the second half of the century, they confidently spoke as if they had discovered nearly all that might be discovered and as if the future would do nothing but refine and extend their insights. They confidently expected every human thought, sooner or later, to conform to their current understanding of science.

Christianity and the Church Under Siege

As might be expected—given the intellectual attitudes that were in the ascendancy—the nineteenth century was one of the most difficult for organized Christianity. Many intellectuals left the faith. Nation-states, under liberal leadership, curtailed the influence of the church. The expansion and migration of population and the growth of cities challenged traditional forms of ecclesiastical organization. Yet the churches, Protestant and Catholic, made considerable headway among the masses.

Intellectual Skepticism

HISTORY The *philosophes* of the Enlightenment had delighted in pointing out contradictions in the Bible, and the historical scholarship of the nineteenth century brought intellectual rigor to the analysis of these texts. In 1835 David Friedrich Strauss (1808–1874) published a *Life of Jesus* that questioned whether the Bible contained any genuinely historical information about Jesus. Strauss explained the story of Jesus as a myth reflecting the aspirations of the people of first-century Palestine.

During the second half of the century, Julius Wellhausen (1844–1918) in Germany, Ernst Renan (1823–1892) in France, and William Robertson Smith (1847–1894) in Great Britain showed how human authors had written and revised various books of the Bible with the problems of the societies in which they lived in mind. Like the Homeric epics, the Bible reflected the concerns of primitive human communities. The doubt these scholars cast on the literal truth of the Bible as a text dictated by God caused a crisis of faith for many literate individuals.

SCIENCE Enlightenment theologians had tried to ground the Christian religion in science, but the scientific discoveries of the nineteenth century had the effect of undermining faith. Darwin's theory cast doubt on the doctrine of the Creation. Anthropologists, psychologists, and sociologists suggested that religious sentiments were nothing but natural phenomena. The geology of Charles Lyell (1797–1875) demonstrated that Earth was much older than the biblical records implied, and by finding natural causes for floods, mountains, and valleys, Lyell also removed the miraculous hand of God from the physical processes shaping Earth.

MORALITY In addition to questions about Christianity's historical validity and congruence with science, its worth as a moral force was also questioned. The colorful behavior of certain biblical figures, particularly from the Old Testament, had long embarrassed Christians, but now the Bible's image of God Himself was subjected to critical comment. Liberals considered the Old Testament depiction of God as a whimsical, vindictive deity to be unworthy of the progressive, tolerant, rational values that they associated with divinity. The morality of the New Testament view of God—as a being who, for his own satisfaction, sacrificed the only perfect man ever to walk the earth—was similarly suspect.

During the last quarter of the century, a different kind of attack was made on Christian ethics. Friedrich Nietzsche (1844–1900), a German philosopher, described Christianity as a religion for sheep—a glorification of weakness instead of the vigor of a full-blooded human life. Christianity was said to demand useless, debilitating sacrifices of the flesh and spirit and not to encourage heroic living.

Theological skepticism was confined largely to the upper levels of educated society, but it cost Christianity much of its intellectual respectability. Fewer educated people joined the clergy, and many were content to lead their lives with little or no reference to organized Christianity.

The increasing secularism of Western (particularly urban) societies was as harmful to faith as direct attacks on it. Cities expanded faster than ecclesiastical institutions and services. Whole generations of the urban poor grew up with little or no experience of the church or training in Christian doctrine.

Conflict Between Church and State

For centuries, religious orders or denominations had run most of Europe's schools. But the governments of the major nations of the late nineteenth century were secular organizations that were often suspicious or resentful of the church. Consequently, a heated debate over religious education erupted in the last quarter of the century.

GREAT BRITAIN   Great Britain's Education Act of 1870 provided for the construction of state-supported schools run by elected school boards in districts where religious organizations had failed to provide satisfactory educational opportunities. Problems had been created in some

places by intense local hostility among competing religious groups. (They cooperated only to oppose educational reforms that increased the costs of their schools.) In 1902 another Education Act attempted to ensure the quality of all schools by providing state support for and by imposing the same educational standards on both religious and nonreligious institutions.

FRANCE   The church-state conflict in Britain was far less intense than in France. France had a dual system of Catholic and public schools, but the Falloux Law of 1850 mandated Catholic religious instruction (under the tutelage of a local priest) in public schools. Increasing hostility between the Third Republic and the conservative clergy of the French Catholic church led to the enactment, between 1878 and 1886, of educational reforms sponsored by Jules Ferry (1832–1893). The Ferry Laws increased the number of public schools, replaced their religious instruction with civic training, and barred members of religious orders from their faculties. After the Dreyfus affair, the radical government of Pierre Waldeck-Rousseau (1846–1904) punished the French clergy for their reactionary politics by suppressing the religious orders; in 1905 the termination of the Napoleonic Concordat separated church and state.

GERMANY   The most extreme example of church-state conflict was the *Kulturkampf* ("cultural struggle") that Bismark waged in Germany during the 1870s. When Germany was unified, its Catholic hierarchy wanted freedom for the churches guaranteed in the constitution. Bismarck originally left the matter to the discretion of each federal state, but he soon concluded that the Roman Catholic Church and the Catholic Center Party were a threat to the unity of the German Empire. In 1870 and 1871 he brought Prussia's educational system under state management and prohibited clergy (both Catholic and Protestant) from overseeing schools.

Secularization of education began a concerted attack on the independence of Germany's Catholic church. The May Laws of 1873, which applied to Prussia but not to the German Empire at large, transferred to the state the disciplinary power over the clergy traditionally exercised by the pope and the church. Priests were required to be educated in Germany, to pass state examinations, and to seek state ratification for their appointments to church offices. When many of the clergy refused to obey these laws, Bismarck resorted to force. In 1876 he either arrested or drove from Prussia all the Catholic bishops. This was the greatest blunder of his career. Persecution created martyrs and increased resistance. By the end of the 1870s, the chancellor had abandoned his attack. He had gained state control of education and civil laws governing marriage, but at the price of provoking long-lasting resentment of the German state among Catholics.

Areas of Religious Revival

The intense hostility of religion's enemies resulted in part from its persistent vitality. The second half of the nineteenth century witnessed the final great effort to Christianize Europe. In Great Britain, both the Anglican Church and the nonconformist denominations grew considerably. In Ireland, the 1870s saw a widespread Catholic devotional revival. France's defeat by Prussia resulted in mass pilgrimages by penitents who believed that their sins had caused their nation's defeat. (The famous cult of the miracle of Lourdes grew during these years.)

The evangelical programs of all denominations were well organized, well led, and well financed—and they paid particular attention to the urban poor. When they fell short, it was not from want of effort but because the population of Europe outstripped the resources of the churches.

The Roman Catholic Church and the Modern World

The papacy struggled to chart a course through the turmoil of a period marked by skepticism and religious revival. The liberal sympathies of Pope Pius IX (r. 1846–1878) vanished on the night in November 1848, when he fled the revolution that tried to restore the Roman republic. Further embittered by the process of Italian unification, he waged a counteroffensive against liberalism. In 1864 he issued the *Syllabus of Errors*, a condemnation of modern thought that declared that the Roman Catholic faith was incompatible with contemporary science, philosophy, and politics. In 1869 he summoned the First Vatican Council, and a year later, despite opposition from numerous bishops, he promulgated the doctrine of pa-

pal infallibility. His assertion that in matters of faith and morals the pope's pronouncements could not be questioned was the most sweeping claim ever made for monarchical papal authority. Pius had been helpless to prevent the new Italian state from stripping the papacy of all its territory, save for the Vatican City in Rome. He believed that the Roman Catholic Church, having been deprived of political and temporal power, could sustain itself in the modern world of nation-states only by enhancing the spiritual authority of the papacy.

Leo XIII (r. 1878–1903), Pius IX's successor, tried to be more accommodating of the modern age and to address its great social questions. In the philosophical tradition of Thomas Aquinas (1225–1274), he believed that the claims of faith and reason could be reconciled. His encyclicals of 1885 and 1890 permitted Catholics to participate in the politics of liberal states. His most important encyclical, *Rerum Novarum* (1891), defended private property, religious education, and religious control of marriage law. It condemned socialism and Marxism, while affirming the right of workers to organize unions and to demand just treatment from employers. He supported laws and regulations to protect labor and urged that modern society pursue goals benefitting all citizens. He hoped that a corporate model derived from medieval social organization would provide an alternative to both socialism and unrestrained capitalism. Leo XIII's endorsement of Catholic participation in politics led to the establishment of democratic Catholic parties and Catholic trade unions throughout Europe.

Pius X (r. 1903–1914), who has been proclaimed a saint, was not enthusiastic about Leo XIII's social policies, and he set the church squarely against the intellectual currents of his day. He urged the rejection of modern thought and the revival of traditional devotional life. In 1910 he required all priests to take an oath to oppose Catholic Modernism, a movement that accepted the results of modern textual criticism of the Bible.

Toward a Twentieth-Century Frame of Mind

During the last quarter of the nineteenth century and the first decade of the twentieth century, the kind of fundamental reassessment that

Darwin's work made necessary in biology began to occur in other disciplines. New concepts challenged the presuppositions of mid-nineteenth-century science, rationalism, liberalism, and bourgeois morality.

Science: The Revolution in Physics

By the late 1870s, some members of the scientific community were voicing concern about the excessive realism of traditional science. They warned that the mechanistic model of Newtonian physics—solid atoms moving in absolute time and space—was only a model, not a definitive description of reality. Ernst Mach (1838–1916), in *The Science of Mechanics* (1883), urged scientists to think of their concepts as reports not about the physical world but about their sensations as observers. All that investigators can know, he warned, is how their senses are responding to the world. They cannot know the physical realities that produce their sensations. Henri Poincaré (1854–1912), a French scientist, agreed. He claimed that scientific concepts were hypothetical constructs made by the human mind, not literal descriptions of the true state of nature. By World War I, few scientists believed any longer that they could portray the "truth" about physical reality. Their task was to record observations and devise useful hypothetical or symbolic models of nature.

X-Rays and Radiation Laboratory work soon confirmed the provisional nature of scientific knowledge. In December 1895, Wilhelm Roentgen (1845–1923) announced the discovery of X-rays, a form of energy that penetrated various opaque materials. When major steps in the exploration of radioactivity followed within months of the publication of his paper, the comfortably "complete" explanation nineteenth-century physicists thought they had for the world vanished.

In 1896 Henri Becquerel (1852–1908), building on Roentgen's work, discovered that uranium emitted a form of energy resembling the X-ray. A year later, J. J. Thomson (1856–1940) of Cambridge University's Cavendish Laboratory formulated the theory of the electron. The interior of the supposedly indivisible atom suddenly became a new frontier for human exploration. In 1902 Ernest Rutherford (1871–1937), who had been Thomson's assistant, suggested that radiation was

Marie Curie (1869–1934) and Pierre Curie (1859–1906) were two of the most important figures in the advance of physics and chemistry. Marie was born in Poland but worked in France for most of her life. She is credited with the discovery of radium, for which she was awarded the Nobel Prize in Chemistry in 1911.
Bildarchiv Preussischer Kulturbesitz

caused by the disintegration of the atoms of certain materials and speculated that immense stores of energy were present within atoms.

Theories of Quantum Energy, Relativity, and Uncertainty The discovery of radioactivity was followed by revolutionary theories that made the certainties trusted by the previous generation of physicists problematic. In 1900 Max Planck (1858–1947) articulated a quantum theory of energy, which describes energy as a series of discrete quantities or packets rather than a continuous stream. In 1905 Albert Einstein (1879–1955) published his first epoch-making papers on relativity. He contended that time and space exist as a combined continuum whose measurement depends as much on the observer as on the entities being measured. In 1927 Werner Heisenberg (1901–1976) stated the uncertainty principle. It postulated that the behavior of subatomic particles is a matter of statistical probability—that it cannot be traced with the certainty of a cause-and-effect encounter between solid objects.

The mathematical complexity that substantiates the theories of modern physics makes it impossible for most people to comprehend much science. But the highly visible transformation that science—applied as technology—has worked in daily life has made scientists the best supported and most respected group among Western intellectuals.

Literature: Realism and Naturalism

Between 1850 and 1914, the moral certainties of learned and middle-class Europeans underwent modifications no less radical than their concepts of the physical universe. The *realist* movement in literature tried to observe and describe human beings with scientific objectivity. It rejected the romantic idealization of nature, poverty, love, and polite society, and portrayed the hypocrisy, the physical and psychic brutality, and the dullness that underlay bourgeois life.

In the preceding generation, writers such as Charles Dickens (1812–1870) and Honoré de Balzac (1799–1850) had vividly depicted the cruelty of industrialized societies that focused simply on the pursuit of money. Authors such as George Eliot (born Mary Ann Evans, 1819–1880) had paid close attention to the details of their scenes and characters. There had always been room, however, in the works of this period for imagination, fancy, and artistry—and a hope that the world could be improved by human efforts and the application of Christian values. The major figures of late-century realism were less certain that a better life was possible. They saw human beings as animals, subject to passions, to Marx's materialistic determinism, and to the pressures of Darwin's struggle for survival. Society itself seemed designed to perpetuate evil.

FLAUBERT AND ZOLA The novel that signaled the advent of realism was *Madame Bovary* (1856) by Gustave Flaubert (1821–1880). It is a story of colorless provincial life and a woman's hapless search for love within and beyond her marriage. It views human existence as devoid of heroism, purpose, or even simple civility.

Émile Zola (1840–1902) articulated the rationale for literary realism. He asserted that human events were as much the products of determinism as events in the physical world and that, therefore, writers should observe and report the characters and actions in their novels as scientists record the course of laboratory experiments. Zola suggested that literature model itself on medical texts such as Claude Bernard's (1813–1878) *An Introduction to the Study of Experimental Medicine* (1865).

IBSEN AND SHAW The Norwegian playwright Henrik Ibsen (1828–1906) wrote stark, unsentimental dramas depicting crises in domestic life. His intent was to peek beneath the cloak of respectability that middle-class morality tried to drape over the family. His most famous play, *A Doll's House* (1879), describes the awakening of Nora, the spouse of a narrow-minded middle-class man who will not grant her any independence of character or thought. The play ends as she comprehends her situation and leaves him, slamming the door behind her. In *Ghosts* (1881), a respectable middle-class woman must deal with the shame and guilt of passing syphilis, unknowingly contracted from her husband, to her son.

George Bernard Shaw (1856–1950), an Irish playwright who spent most of his life in England, was one of Ibsen's greatest admirers and imitators. His *Mrs. Warren's Profession* (1893) was long censored in England for its blunt treatment of prostitution. In *Arms and the Man* (1894) and *Man and Superman* (1903), Shaw heaped scorn on the romantic era's idealization of love and war. In *Androcles and the Lion* (1913), he pilloried Christianity. Shaw made sure that no one missed the point of his plays by attaching long prefaces to them to spell out the social criticism they intended.

Advocates of realism believed that artists ought to portray reality and the commonplace. By dissecting the "real" world and refusing to let public opinion dictate what they wrote, they attempted to change the moral perception of the good life. By forcing audiences to consider unmentionable things, they sought to strip away the veneer of hypocrisy that prevented discussion of important issues. They tried to compel the public to confront reality by destroying all social and moral illusions. Few of the realist writers who vividly described problems had, however, any solutions to suggest for them. They stripped society of old values and offered no new ones.

Modernism

Beginning in the 1870s, a new movement emerged to shape Western arts: *modernism.* Like realism, modernism criticized middle-class society and traditional morality. But modernism's concern was not social reform as much as aesthetics—the production of an artistic experience for its own sake.

In all the arts, modernists abandoned traditional canons of beauty and tried to create new forms. (Many observers ridiculed the new forms as formless.) Modernists also believed that each of the arts should influence the others. Painters gave pictures musical titles—such as James Abbott McNeil Whistler's (1834–1903) "Nocturnes." Musicians drew material from many sources. Igor Stravinsky's (1882–1971) notorious ballet, *The Rite of Spring* (1913), combined jazz rhythms, dissonance, and anthropological theory. Pablo Picasso (1881–1973) and other artists were inspired by primitive masks they saw in anthropological museums. England's practitioners of "New Sculpture" mixed materials, and some rejected traditional forms entirely. For all these artists, the immediate aesthetic experience of a work of art overrode all other concerns.

Among the chief proponents of modernism in England were the members of the Bloomsbury Group: authors Virginia (1882–1941) and Leonard Woolf (1880–1969), artists Vanessa Bell (1879–1961) and Duncan Grant (1885–1978), historian and literary critic Lytton Strachey (1880–1932), and economist John Maynard Keynes (1883–1946). Bloomsbury was determined to expose the inadequacy of what it regarded as "Victorian" values, particularly an allegedly repressive Victorian sexual morality.

Strachey, in *Eminent Victorians,* produced a series of biographical sketches less to write history than to heap contempt on famous Victorians. Grant and Bell followed the lead of modernist Continental artists. Keynes challenged nineteenth-century economic theory. But no one charted the changing sensibilities of the time with more care and eloquence than Virginia Woolf. Her novels *Mrs. Dalloway* (1925) and *To the Lighthouse* (1927) portrayed a world that had lost most of the social and moral certainties of the nineteenth century.

Continental literary modernism is well illustrated by Marcel Proust (1871–1922). His seven-volume novel, *In Search of Time Past* (issued from 1913 to 1927), used a stream-of-consciousness format that allowed him to explore memories. He would concentrate on a single experience or object and then allow his mind to wander through all the thoughts it evoked. Germany's Thomas Mann (1875–1955) wrote a series of novels—including *Buddenbrooks* (1924) and *The Magic Mountain* (1927)—to explore the social experience of middle-class Germans as they attempted to come to terms with the intellectual heritage of the nineteenth century. In *Ulysses* (1922), James Joyce (1882–1941), an Irish author who spent much of his life on the Continent, wholly transformed both the novel and the structure of the paragraph.

Literary modernism flourished in the atmosphere of turmoil and social dislocation created by World War I. The war destroyed many of the political and social systems modernism opposed, and, after war's appalling violence, readers were much less shocked by anything artists could do or say.

Friedrich Nietzsche and the Revolt Against Reason

The legacy of the Enlightenment had been supreme confidence in the power of reason, but, during the second half of the nineteenth century, philosophers began to argue that rational thought had severe limitations. Friedrich Nietzsche (1844–1900), a German philologist, was the most inflammatory of these thinkers. He wanted to tear away the masks of respectable life, but also to discover how human beings made these masks.

In *The Birth of Tragedy* (1872), Nietzsche claimed that the nonrational aspects of human nature were as important and noble as the rational. He insisted that instinct and ecstasy were vital functions and that to limit the human to the rational was to diminish it. In Nietzsche's view, the strength that produced heroes and great artists sprang from something beyond reason. In later works, such as the prose poem *Thus Spake Zarathustra* (1883), Nietzsche criticized democracy and Christianity for empowering the mediocrity of the sheepish masses. He proclaimed the death of God and the rise of the *übermensch* (the

Cubism Changes the Shape of Painting

*C*ubism, a term a contemporary critic coined to describe the work of Pablo Picasso (1881–1973) and Georges Braque (1882–1963), was the most important innovation in twentieth-century Western art. For over 500 years Western painters had sought to reproduce the appearance of things, but at the end of the nineteenth century this began to change. Reacting to the Impressionists' concentration on light, which produced luminous, insubstantial images, French painter Paul Cezanne returned form and solidity to painting. Europeans such as Paul Gauguin also began to study the work of non-Western artists and to adapt to their unique styles of viewing and representing reality.

In 1907 Picasso and Braque started to produce paintings that rejected the traditional view of a painting as a window on the world. They argued that paintings should be ends in themselves, that is, that they should create, not recreate, visual experiences. In a break with the past, both artists worked in two dimensions and reproduced on the same flat surface a number of views of their subject from different perspectives. This dismantled the shapes of objects and created a sense of dislocation.

Braque's *Violin and Palette* illustrates the Cubists' approach to creating a nonimitative vision of the world. Portions of the violin and the palette are recognizable, but as shapes, not objects. The violin and the palette are not so much the subjects of the painting as they are objects that are taken apart and reassembled to create a painting that has a reality that is entirely its own.

Sources: Max Kozloff, *Cubism/Futurism* (New York: Charterhouse, 1973); Edward F. Fry, *Cubism* (New York: McGraw-Hill Book Company, 1966); Douglas Cooper, *The Cubist Epoch* (New York: Paidon, 1970); Christopher Green, *Cubism and Its Enemies* (New Haven: Yale University Press, 1987); Christine Poggi, *In Defiance of Painting: Cubism Futurism, and the Invention of Collage* (New Haven: Yale University Press, 1992); Marilyn Stokstad, *Art History* (Englewood Cliffs, N.J.: Prentice Hall and New York: Harry N. Abrams, 1999).

Friedrich Nietzsche (1844–1900) became the most influential German philosopher of the late nineteenth century. His books, which challenged existing morality and values, exerted a powerful influence on twentieth-century literature and philosophy. Detail from a portrait by Kurt Stoeving, 1904. Bildnis Friedrich Nietzsche *von Kurt Stoeving, 1904; Original: Staatliche Museen zu Berlin–Preussischer Kulturbesitz National-galerie. Photograph: Klaus Goken, 1992. Bildarchiv Preussischer Kulturbesitz*

"Overman"), the embodiment of a heroic humanity free to seek its own fulfillment without illusions. The term was often misunderstood as a reference to a superman or superrace, but Nietzsche was no racist or anti-Semite. He idealized a heroism he associated with the Greeks of the Homeric age, a people who had not been exposed to the emasculating influences of Christianity and bourgeois morality.

Two of Nietzsche's most profound works, *Beyond Good and Evil* (1886) and *The Genealogy of Morals* (1887), explore the idea that morality is a human convention that has no grounding in external reality. Good and evil, he claimed, do not exist on their own. They are human projections onto the world. Human beings have to forge from their own inner will the truth and values that are to exist in their world. Nietzsche did not condemn morality, but he challenged human beings to ponder its worth and purpose. He urged them to reject the values of Christianity, utilitarianism, and middle-class respectability because he

believed that these things were life-denying. He insisted that people could, if they wanted, create a new moral order based on life-affirming values such as pride, assertiveness, and strength.

The Birth of Psychoanalysis

All the major figures of late-nineteenth-century science, art, and philosophy were driven to probe beneath the surfaces of things—of atoms, of reason, of codes of respectability, and of human relationships. Their work dispelled smugness and complacency, but it also undercut self-confidence. Such was the effect of psychoanalysis.

DEVELOPMENT OF FREUD'S THEORIES Sigmund Freud (1856–1939), the founder of psychoanalysis, was the son of an Austrian Jewish family. In 1886 he opened a medical practice in Vienna. He continued to work there until driven out by the Nazis in 1938. Freud's earliest interests were psychic disorders. In 1885 he went to Paris to observe

Jean-Martin Charcot's (1825–1893) use of hypnosis to treat hysteria. In 1895 he and another Viennese physician, Josef Breuer (1842–1925), published *Studies in Hysteria*.

In the mid-1890s Freud abandoned hypnosis and allowed his patients to talk freely and spontaneously about themselves. Repeatedly, they associated their neurotic symptoms with experiences that brought to mind earlier experiences going back to childhood. Freud also observed that his patients' problems were often connected with sex, and for a time he wondered if sexual abuse during childhood accounted for their illnesses.

By 1897 Freud had moved beyond this view to a theory of infantile sexuality that scandalized many contemporaries. He claimed that human beings were sexual creatures from birth, that sexual drives and energy do not simply emerge at puberty but exist in infants. This cast doubt on the innocence of childhood and forced people to face up to issues of sexuality and mental health that, in his day, they preferred not to discuss.

In 1900 Freud published his most important book, *The Interpretation of Dreams*. It combined his theory of infantile sexuality with another idea: the psychic significance of dreams. As a rationalist, Freud believed that apparently irrational phenomena, such as dreams, must have reasonable, scientific explanations. He concluded that dreams are expressions of unconscious wishes, desires, and drives that waking consciousness suppresses. While awake, the mind censors certain thoughts fundamental to an individual's psychological makeup, but during sleep it expresses them cloaked in symbols. Freud claimed that these unconscious drives and desires were clues to explanations of certain conscious behaviors.

In later works, Freud defended the importance of the human unconscious and developed a model to explain its role in the mind. He saw the mind as an arena where three entities struggled: the *id*, the *ego*, and the *superego*. The id consists of innate, amoral, irrational drives for sexual gratification, aggression, and sensual pleasure. The superego internalizes the moral imperatives that society and culture impose on the personality. The ego mediates between the impulsive id and the self-denying superego. Personality, as expressed in everyday behavior, is the product of the ego's efforts to repress impulses of the id and

satisfy the demands of the external world embodied in the superego.

Freud never claimed that humankind ought to liberate the id and free itself of all repression. While he believed that excessive repression could lead to mental disorders, he said that civilization and the survival of humankind were impossible without some repression of sexuality and aggression. Freud saw human beings as attaining rationality, not as being inevitably endowed with it. He wanted civilization to prevail. But he warned that an immense sacrifice of instinctual drives was required to maintain civilized behavior, and he revealed previously unsuspected obstacles that lay in the way of rationality. Freud believed that the sacrifices that had to be made in order to become a humane being were worthwhile, but he was pessimistic about civilization's prospects.

DIVISIONS IN THE PSYCHOANALYTIC MOVEMENT
By 1910 Freud had attracted followers, some of whom eventually broke with him. Chief among these was Carl Jung (1875–1961), a Swiss whom Freud regarded as his most promising student. Freud was firmly rooted in the rationalism of the Enlightenment, but Jung shared the religious mysticism of the romantics. He questioned the primacy of sexual drives in the formation of human personality and of mental disorders. He believed that the subconscious was a soul formed by personal experiences and "collective" memories inherited from one's ancestors. Illness, he claimed, was caused by alienation from useful collective memories.

Although the psychoanalytic movement had fragmented by the 1920s, it had tremendous influence on modern intellectuals—affecting work in psychology, sociology, anthropology, religious studies, history, and literary theory. The explanations psychoanalysis offered for human behavior have recently been questioned and its future is in doubt, but there is no question about the contribution it made to the development of the modern mind.

Retreat from Rationalism in Politics

WEBER Nineteenth-century liberals and socialists believed in the rationality of human beings. They thought that if given votes and properly educated, individuals would see to their own rational self-interest. German sociologist Max Weber (1864–1920) regarded the development of reason as humanity's major achievement, for reason laid the foundations for civilization (i.e., scientific knowledge and bureaucratic organization). Where Marx saw capitalism as the driving force in modern society, Weber saw *bureaucratization*. Bureaucratization is the process whereby labor is divided and individuals acquire a sense of personal identity by finding roles for themselves in large organizations. Also unlike Marx, Weber believed that noneconomic factors account for history's major developments. Weber's *The Protestant Ethic and the Spirit of Capitalism* (1905) traced capitalism itself to the ascetic religious doctrines of Puritanism. The Puritans, he argued, sought worldly success less for its own sake than to assure themselves that they were God's elect.

THEORISTS OF COLLECTIVE BEHAVIOR Many of Weber's colleagues were less sanguine about human rationality than he was. Gustave LeBon (1841–1931) was a psychologist of mob behavior who pointed out that reason's power faded when people gathered in crowds. In *Reflections on Violence* (1908), Georges Sorel (1847–1922) argued that people were motivated less by reason than by collectively shared ideals. Émile Durkheim (1858–1917) and Graham Wallas (1858–1932) insisted that instinct, habit, and affections had more power than reason to direct human social behavior. All of these theorists suggested that when people made political decisions, they operated not as rational individuals but as defenders of the groups that gave them their senses of identity.

Racism

The common human tendency to sacrifice the individual to the group, which social theorists noted, manifested itself in theories of race. Racial thinking has had a long history, but the prestige associated with biology and science in general provided the racists of the late nineteenth century with what they believed were materialistic, scientific bases for their belief that peoples could be arranged on a hierarchy from inferior to superior.

GOBINEAU Count Arthur de Gobineau (1816–1882), a reactionary French diplomat, presented the first detailed arguments to support what became an increasingly popular theory—namely that race is the major determinant of human history. His four-volume *Essay on the Inequality of the Human Races* (1853–1854) blamed the failings of Western civilization on the degeneration of an original white European race he called the Aryans. (Linguists of the late eighteenth century had postulated the existence of Aryans to account for a vanished language that was the common ancestor of most European tongues and Sanskrit.) Gobineau claimed that intermarriage with inferior yellow and black races had weakened modern Europeans by diluting their superior Aryan blood.

CHAMBERLAIN Initially, Gobineau's essay had little influence, but racial thinking was encouraged by trends in nineteenth-century science. Anthropologists and explorers adapted Darwin's theory of the survival of the fittest to explain cultural differences, and in 1899 Houston Stewart Chamberlain's (1855–1927) *Foundations of the Nineteenth Century* advanced a theory of biological determinism to integrate information drawn from many different fields. Gobineau had assumed that the "degeneration" of the human race was irreversible, but Chamberlain suggested that careful attention to genetics might enable scientists to breed a new super race.

Chamberlain's work had alarming political implications, for he accused the Jews of being the major threat to Europe's racial regeneration. His opinion was shared by Paul de Lagarde (1827–1891) and Julius Langbehn (1851–1907) who both declared the Jews to be a racial and cultural threat to Germany. By linking racism with nationalism, they set Europe on a perilous path.

LATE-CENTURY NATIONALISM Nationalism had begun as a movement among scholars and liberals who cherished national languages and wanted the map of Europe to acknowledge ethnic identities. From the 1870s onward, however, nationalism became a well-financed, well-organized mass movement that equated nationality with race. It opposed the internationalism advocated by liberals and socialists and worked to create solid, homogeneous states commanding unquestioned loyalty from all their citizens. Nationalism sometimes became a secular religion evangelized by state-supported schools. It promoted major conflicts in the early twentieth century, and it has experienced a resurgence following the recent collapse of most of Europe's communist regimes.

Anti-Semitism and the Birth of Zionism

The rationalism of the Enlightenment had helped dispel some of Europe's traditional religious prejudice against Jews. In the first half of the nineteenth century, Jews won political rights and social acceptance in Britain, France, and Germany. But during the last third of the century, the economic pressures created by rampant capitalism revived anti-Semitism, particularly among members of the lower middle class.

Anti-Semitic crusades led by Karl Lueger (1844–1910) as head of Austria's Christian Socialist Party, by Germany's Adolf Stoecker (1835–1909), and by the prosecutors of France's Captain Dreyfus convinced many Jews that assimilation was no guarantee of permanent acceptance. Their racist enemies insisted that the problem with Jews was not objectionable conduct that could be unlearned but the ineradicable defects of inferior blood.

If Jews were unacceptable as citizens of European nations, their only safety lay in establishing a nation of their own—or so argued Theodor Herzl (1860–1904), founder of the Zionist movement. In 1896 Herzl published *The Jewish State* to make a plea for an independent Jewish country where the Jews of the world would be assured of the rights that should have been theirs in the liberal states of Europe. Herzl, an Austro-Hungarian, directed his appeal to the impoverished Jews of eastern Europe's ghettos and western Europe's slums. His Zionism linked opposition to anti-Semitism with socialism.

Science, Racial Thought, and the Non-Western World

Europe's focus on science during the nineteenth century affected relationships between the West and the rest of the world. Many scientists traveled outside of Europe and did much of their fieldwork in foreign lands. This was true of scientists (such as naturalists, anthropologists, and astronomers) whose interests were pure research, but it was also true of geologists who explored for resources, engineers who built railroads, and agronomists who experimented with new agricultural techniques.

The power of European science and technology was often used to justify European economic and political dominance of non-European peoples. Europeans saw themselves as bringing the benefits of modern civilization to "backward" regions. Some assumed that it was their mission to bring non-European societies up to European standards. But others assumed that Europe's technological superiority was evidence of European racial superiority and that other peoples were destined to remain subservient to their European colonizers.

Women and Modern Thought

Many of the new ideas advanced in the late nineteenth century seemed to confirm old gender stereotypes, representing women as weaker and less able than men. Whatever changes were to be wrought through science, significant reorganization of the home and of male-female relationships was not among them.

Antifeminism in Late-Century Thought

Late Victorian biologists and anthropologists tended to lump women with nonwhite races as inferior members of the human family. T. H. Huxley, the popularizer of science, gave lectures presenting what he claimed was scientific evidence of female inferiority. Karl Vogt (1817–1895), a prominent German anthropologist, advanced similar views. Darwin drew on their work for his *The Descent of Man*. He, like Huxley, believed that women's opportunities for education should be improved, but neither man advocated admitting women to the scientific community. Male scientists insisted that codes of decency prohibited women from discussing certain subjects, and many claimed that women's limited intellects would depress the level of debate in learned societies.

Freud and his followers were trained as medical doctors at a time when medical education assumed the inferiority of women. Many of Freud's theories were developed using case histories of female patients, but his view of the female psyche is controversial. Some critics argue that Freud portrayed women as incomplete human beings, flawed males who were destined for mental problems. He claimed that they needed motherhood (particularly the nurturing of sons) to fulfill themselves. Distinguished female psychoanalysts, such as Karen Horney (1885–1952) and Melanie Klein (1882–1960), have challenged Freud's ideas and attempted to establish a psychoanalytic basis for feminism, but the psychoanalytic profession and academic psychology remain dominated by men. Psychology's influence on child-rearing practices has given men, ironically, an impact in the one area of social activity that had always been dominated by women.

Virtually all of the early sociologists took a conservative view of marriage, the family, child rearing, and divorce. Auguste Comte, drawing on Rousseau, portrayed women as biologically and intellectually inferior to men. Herbert Spencer advocated improving women's lot while accepting as fact their inability to be men's equals. Émile Durkheim described women as creatures motivated by feeling more than intellect. Max Weber favored improvements in social conditions for women, but not changes in their social roles.

The Swedish feminist Ellen Key maintained that motherhood was so crucial to society that the support of mothers and children should be a government responsibility. Hulton Getty/Liaison Agency, Inc.

New Directions in Feminism

At the close of the nineteenth century, feminist thought revived in Europe and began to raise issues that would not be more fully and successfully explored until after World War II. Many women's organizations concentrated on achieving the vote for women, but consciousness was growing of a broader need to redefine women's relationships to men and society at large—primarily, to challenge the double standard of sexual morality and the traditional male-dominated family.

SEXUAL MORALITY AND THE FAMILY Demands for women's rights often began with campaigns to abolish prostitution, a fate to which poverty drove many lower-class women. Between 1864 and 1886 the English Parliament passed the Contagious Diseases Acts. It gave police in cities

with naval or military bases the power to force women suspected of prostitution to undergo immediate examinations for venereal disease. Without legal recourse, those infected were locked up for months in special hospitals. These laws angered middle-class women, for they literally assigned control over women's bodies to men—as customers, physicians, and police. By denying poor women the freedoms and protections that all men enjoyed in English society, they implied that all women were less than fully human. Also, they decreed no penalties for prostitutes' customers. The purpose of these laws was, after all, the protection of such men.

Thanks to a campaign waged by Josephine Butler (1828–1906), head of the Ladies' National Association for the Repeal of the Contagious Diseases Acts, the laws were suspended in 1883 and repealed in 1886. The English movement became a model for other nations struggling with the issue of police regulation of prostitution. During the 1890s, the General Austrian Women's Association, led by Auguste Ficke (1833–1916), fought the introduction of legalized prostitution. In Germany, women's groups divided between those who wanted to penalize prostitutes and those who saw prostitutes as victims of male society.

By opposing laws that punished prostitutes and let their customers go free, feminist groups were challenging society's sexual double standard and, by extension, the traditional relationship of men and women in marriage. Virtually all turn-of-the-century feminists advocated greater sexual freedom for women and access to contraception. Arguments for contraception were bolstered by appeals to social Darwinism. It was claimed that limiting the number of children ensured that those who were born would be better cared for and grow up to be healthier and more intelligent.

WOMEN DEFINING THEIR OWN LIVES The European feminist movement hoped to end male-dominated society and create a world in which women were as free as men to determine their destinies. Many feminists were attracted to socialism, for they assumed that a classless society would liberate women. Socialist parties tended to have male leaders who—like Lenin, and, later Stalin—were intolerant of feminist demands for changes in family life or in sexual codes, but they were willing to support feminist efforts to improve women's economic situation.

It was within literary circles that feminists most successfully articulated the problems confronting women. Distinguished female writers functioned on a more or less equal footing with men—leading some to wonder whether simple equality was the real issue. In *A Room of One's Own* (1929), Virginia Woolf produced a fundamental text for twentieth-century literary feminism. It described the difficulties that gifted women encounter in being taken seriously as intellectuals, and it argued that a woman who wished to write required complete independence: an income and a room of her own. Woolf also established a new stance for feminist writers. She challenged the idea that women should write like men and insisted that all writers, male

as well as female, should be able to share the sensitivities of both sexes. This encouraged people to ponder definitions of gender.

By World War I, feminism in Europe was associated in the popular mind with socialism, political radicalism, and attacks on traditional gender roles and morality. As a result, when extreme conservative political movements arose between the world wars, feminism faced stiffened opposition—even in communist societies.

In Perspective

By the opening of the twentieth century, European thought had achieved its current contours. Science had revolutionized the way Westerners thought about the world and themselves. Western intellectuals, having rejected the idea that human beings were a special divine creation, were compelled to seek a rational, scientific basis for ethics and morality. This spawned conflicts between faith and reason and ultimately raised questions that promoted a loss of faith in the power of reason. Political theorists doubted that a thoroughly rational basis for social life could be developed, and racial theorists claimed that characteristics carried in the blood were the primary determinants of human behavior.

REVIEW QUESTIONS

1. Why did science dominate thought in the second half of the nineteenth century? What were some of the major changes in scientific outlook that occurred between 1850 and 1914? What advances took place in physics? How would you define *positivism*? What was the theory of natural selection proposed by Darwin and Wallace? What effect did it have on theories of ethics, on Christianity, and on European views of human nature?

2. Why did Christianity come under attack in the late nineteenth century? What form did the attack take? What political agendas were pursued by popes Pius IX, Leo XIII, and Pius X? Why was Leo XIII regarded as a liberal pope? How do you account for the resilience of the papacy during this period of attack on the church?

3. How were changes in society reflected in the literature of the late nineteenth century? What was the significance of the explosion of literacy material? What was literary *realism?* How was it influenced by science? How did the realists undermine middle-class morality? How did literary modernism differ from realism?

4. How did Nietzsche and Freud challenge traditional middle-class and religious morality? Was Freud a product more of the Enlightenment or of the romantic movement?

5. How do you account for the fear and hostility many late-nineteenth-century intellectuals displayed toward women? What was Freud's view of women? What were some of the social and political issues that especially affected women in the late nineteenth and early twentieth centuries? How did reformers confront them? What new directions did feminism take?

6. What forms did racism take in the late nineteenth century? How did it become associated with anti-Semitism? What was Zionism? Why did Herzl develop it?

SUGGESTED READINGS

C. ALLEN, *The Human Christ: The Search for the Historical Jesus* (1998). A broad survey of the issue for the past two centuries.

S. AVINERI, *The Making of Modern Zionism: The Intellectual Origins of the Jewish State* (1981). An excellent introduction to the development of Zionist thought.

P. BOWLER, *Evolution: The History of an Idea* (1989). An outstanding survey of the subject.

O. CHADWICK, *The Secularization of the European Mind in the Nineteenth Century* (1975). The best treatment available.

C. M. CIPOLLA, *Literacy and Development in the West* (1969). Traces the explosion of literacy in the past two centuries.

F. J. COPPA, *The Modern Papacy since 1789* (1999). A straightforward survey.

A. DANTO, *Nietzsche as Philosopher* (1965). A helpful and well-organized introduction.

A. DESMOND and J. MOORE, *Darwin* (1992). A brilliant biography.

P. GAY, *Freud: A Life for Our Time* (1988). The new standard biography.

P. GAY, *Pleasure Wars* (1998). An expansive analysis of changing tastes among the upper middle class.

R. HELMSTADTER, ed., *Freedom and Religion in the Nineteenth Century* (1997). Major essays on the relationship of church and state.

J. KATZ, *From Prejudice to Destruction: Anti-Semitism, 1700–1933* (1980). An excellent and far-reaching analysis.

W. LACQUER, *A History of Zionism* (1989). The most extensive one-volume treatment.

G. L. MOSSE, *Toward the Final Solution: A History of European Racism* (1978). A sound introduction.

L. POLIAKOV, *The Aryan Myth: A History of Racist and Nationalist Ideas in Europe* (1971). The best introduction to the problem.

F. STERN, *Einstein's German World* (1999). An exploration of German science from the turn of the century to the rise of Hitler.

F. M. TURNER, *Contesting Cultural Authority: Essays in Victorian Intellectual Life* (1993). Essays that deal with the relationship of science and religion and the problem of faith for intellectuals.

D. VITAL, *A People Apart: The Jews of Europe 1789–1939* (1999). A remarkably broad and deeply researched volume.

A. N. WILSON, *God's Funeral* (1999). Explores the thinkers who contributed to religious doubt during the nineteenth and twentieth centuries.

Chapter 26

Imperialism, Alliances, and War

KEY TOPICS

- The economic, cultural, and strategic factors behind Europe's New Imperialism in the late nineteenth and early twentieth centuries
- The formation of alliances and the search for strategic advantage among Europe's major powers
- The origins and progress of World War I
- The Russian Revolution
- The peace treaties ending World War I

During the second half of the nineteenth century, Europe wielded unprecedented worldwide influence. Massive immigration turned North and South America, Australia, and New Zealand into extensions of European nations that were simultaneously dividing up Africa into colonies and dictating terms to the countries of Asia. Europe's dominance created a single world economy that might have increased general prosperity. Instead, competition among the great powers led to a terrible war that undermined Europe's strength and global influence. The peace settlement that followed humiliated Germany and provoked its desire for revenge. The United States also made the fateful decision to withdraw into disdainful isolation from world affairs.

Queen Victoria (r. 1837–1901) works on state papers in 1893. Note the Indian attendant. The Queen was also Empress of India, which was by far the most important possession in the British Empire. Hill & Sanders/National Portrait Gallery, London

Expansion of European Power and the New Imperialism

Europe's power was based on the progress it made during the nineteenth century in science, technology, industry, agriculture, transportation, communications, and military weaponry. These things enabled a few Europeans (and Americans) to impose their wills on peoples many times their number. The growth of nation-states, a Western phenomenon, also permitted Europeans to exploit their advantages to maximum effect. Confidence in the superiority of their civilization made Europeans energetic, if self-righteous, expansionists.

The New Imperialism

Imperialism is a policy of expanding a nation's power by seeking hegemony over an alien people. Imperialism in earlier ages involved seizing land and settling it with the conqueror's people or establishing trading centers to exploit the resources of a dominated area. The New Imperialism employed these devices and introduced others.

A European nation often began by investing capital in a "backward" country to develop its mines and agriculture, to build railroads, bridges, harbors, and telegraph systems. These ventures employed great numbers of its people, and European states safeguarded their investments by lending local rulers money or by intimidating them into making favorable concessions. As a result, native economies and cultures were transformed.

If these arrangements proved inadequate, the dominant power would take direct control. Sometimes this meant annexation, or it could result in protectorate status whereby a local ruler became a figurehead for European military occupation. A European state might also establish a "sphere of influence" in which it enjoyed commercial and legal privileges without overt political control.

Motives for the New Imperialism: The Economic Interpretation

A need for markets and raw materials is not an adequate explanation for the New Imperialism. Although some European businessmen and politicians hoped that colonial expansion might cure the great depression of 1873–1896, colonies were usually not important markets for imperial nations. It is not even certain that colonialism was profitable. Some individuals and companies made great profits from particular ventures, but the people who did so had minimal influence on national policy. Economic interests were involved, but a full understanding of the New Imperialism requires consideration of other motives.

Cultural, Religious, and Social Interpretations

Advocates of imperialism justified it in various ways. Some argued that European nations had a duty to extend the benefits of their superior civilization to "backward" peoples. Churches demanded that governments furnish political and military support for Christian missions. Some politicians, particularly in Germany, hoped that imperialism might deflect public interest from domestic problems. Joseph Chamberlain (1836–1914),

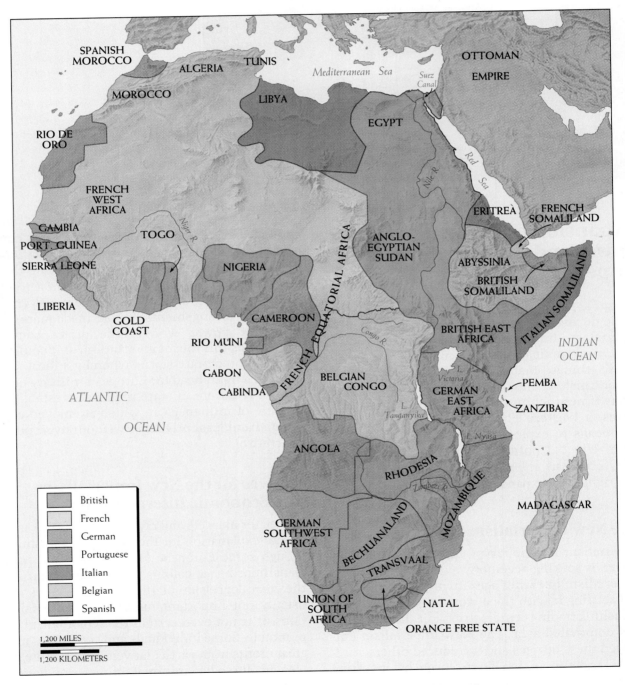

MAP 26–1   PARTITION OF AFRICA, 1880–1914   *Before 1880, the European presence in Africa was largely the remains of early exploration by old imperialists and did not penetrate the heart of the continent. By 1914, the occupying powers included most large European states, and only Liberia and Abyssinia remained independent.*

Britain's colonial secretary from 1895 to 1903, argued that Britain might finance a program of domestic reform and welfare from the profits of empire, but most imperial expansion was over by the time he advanced this idea. Some social reformers hoped to use colonies to relieve population pressures in Europe, but most emigrants went to places not controlled by their homelands (e.g., North and South America and Australia).

Strategic and Political Interpretations: The Scramble for Africa

The New Imperialism may have owed more to strategic considerations and national pride than to economics. On the eve of the scramble for Africa, Britain was the world leader, and other nations coveted the strategic advantages and status it derived from its extensive overseas holdings.

GREAT BRITAIN The completion of the Suez Canal in 1869 stimulated British interest in Africa, for Britain's shortest route to its Indian empire was now through Egypt. In 1875 Disraeli's ministry purchased a major, but not controlling, interest in the canal. In the 1880s, when Egypt's internal stability was threatened, the British intervened. They then moved into the Su-

dan to protect their position in Egypt. In the 1890s Britain also imposed its will on Zimbabwe and Zambia to prevent expansion by other nations from imperiling its other route to India around the Cape of Good Hope.

FRANCE AND SMALLER NATIONS A raid on pirates based in the city of Algiers brought the French to North Africa in 1830. By the 1880s France was in full control of Algeria, which was attracting thousands of European immigrants. In 1882 France took over Tunisia to prevent it from falling into Italy's hands, and it annexed much of West Africa, the Congo, and the island of Madagascar. Small states such as Belgium, Portugal, Spain, and Italy were soon seeking to enhance their prestige by acquiring new African colonies or expanding old ones.

GERMANY In 1884 and 1885 Germany declared protectorates over Southwest Africa (Namibia), Togoland, the Cameroons, and East Africa (Tanzania). None of these places was of much value or strategic importance, and Bismarck had no interest in them for themselves. His concern was for Germany's exposed position in Europe between Russia and France. He hoped that African colonies could be used as bases to put pressure on Britain and to provide outlets for France's hostility.

In the Spanish–American War of 1898, Spain was driven from the Western Hemisphere and Cuba came under U.S. influence. This lithograph shows the Ninth and Tenth Cavalry Regiments, composed of black Americans, engaged in the Battle of Quasimas, near Santiago, Cuba, on June 24, 1898. The Granger Collection

The Irrational Element

Germany's annexations started a wild scramble for African territory among European nations, and by 1890 almost all of the continent had been parceled out. There were few sound economic or political justifications for this. It was driven by the desire to appear powerful.

In Asia the emergence of Japan as a great power frightened the Europeans who were interested in China. The Russians were building a railroad across Siberia to Vladivostok, and they were worried by Japanese threats to Manchuria. Consequently, they joined the French and Germans in forcing Japan out of north China's Liaotung Peninsula. In 1899 the United States, fearing that concessions granted to European nations would close China to American trade, proposed the Open Door Policy. British support won endorsement from all the powers except Russia for the policy's pledge that there would be no attempts at annexation of Chinese territory or acquisition of special trade advantages.

The United States was only beginning to emerge as a force in international affairs, for until the end of the nineteenth century, its people were focused on westward expansion across the North American continent. Cuba's bid for independence from Spain sparked the United States' interest in international affairs. The Monroe Doctrine of 1823 had proclaimed the Western Hemisphere an American protectorate, and sympathy for the Cuban cause—as well as concern for American investments in Cuba and for the island's strategic importance in the Caribbean—persuaded the Americans to declare war on Spain. The Spanish-American War of 1898 won the United States an empire in the Caribbean and the Pacific. The United States assumed an informal protectorate over Cuba and annexed Puerto Rico. Spain was also forced to sell the Philippine Islands and Guam to the United States. The Americans and the Germans divided Samoa between them, and Germany bought Spain's other Pacific islands. The remaining islands in the Pacific were snapped up by France and Britain. Hawaii, which had been under American influence for some time, was annexed in 1898.

Emergence of the German Empire and the Alliance Systems (1873–1890)

By defeating Austria and France and uniting Germany in 1871, Prussia revolutionized European diplomacy. The appearance of a vast new nation of great and growing population, wealth, industrial capacity, and military might endangered the balance of power that had existed in Europe since 1815 and the Congress of Vienna.

Britain and Russia (though the latter had been weakened by the Crimean War) remained formidable. But Austria, struggling with the disintegrating forces of nationalism, was in decline. France, its prestige damaged by the Franco-Prussian War and the subsequent surrender of Alsace-Lorraine to Germany, had lost its traditional position as the dominant nation in western Europe.

Bismarck's Leadership (1873–1890)

Bismarck, who hoped to avoid provoking a conflict that might undo his achievements, insisted after 1871 that Germany wanted no more territory. He tried to placate the French, while developing a strategy to isolate them in case he failed. To this end, he sought treaties with Austria and Russia. The Three Emperors' League that he formed in 1873 collapsed in 1875, when the Russo-Turkish War pitted Russia against Austria in the Balkans.

The tottering Ottoman Empire was an invitation to disorder in the Balkans, but it survived because the European powers could not agree on how to divide it up. When, however, Slavs in Bosnia and Herzegovina revolted against Turkish rule and Slavs in Serbia and Montenegro came to their aid, a rebellion spread to Bulgaria, and Russia entered the fray. The Ottoman Empire quickly sued for peace, and the resulting Treaty of San Stefano (March 1878) was a triumph for Russia. Slavs in the Balkans were liberated from Ottoman control. Russia annexed territory and won a large monetary indemnity. These developments, however, alarmed other nations. Austria feared growth of Russian influence in the Balkans. The British worried that Russia might seize the Dardanelles, alter the European balance

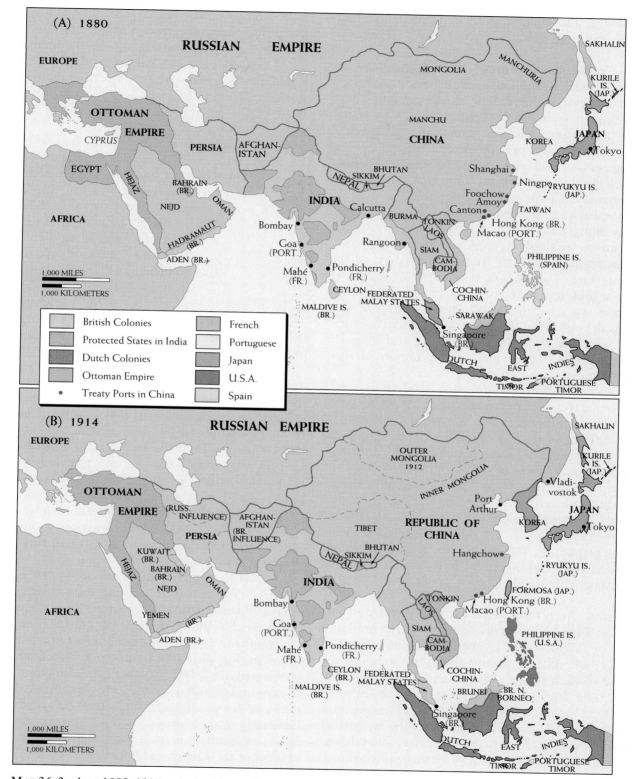

MAP 26–2 ASIA 1880–1914 *As in Africa, the decades before World War I saw imperialism spread widely and rapidly in Asia. Two new powers, Japan and the United States, joined the British, French, and Dutch in extending their control and exploiting an enfeebled China.*

of power, and even imperil Britain's control of the Suez Canal.

THE CONGRESS OF BERLIN   Britain and Austria forced Russia to agree to an international conference to review the Treaty of San Stefano. Bismarck's insistence that Germany had no territorial aspirations made him an acceptable international arbiter, and in June–July 1878, a congress met in Berlin under his presidency. Bismarck dubbed himself an "honest broker," and he earned the title.

Bismarck's chief aim was to prevent Germany from being drawn into a war between Austria and an increasingly aggressive Russia. The congress dealt a blow to Russia by depriving its client state, Bulgaria, of two-thirds of its territory and of access to the Aegean Sea. The great powers also compensated themselves for the lands they allowed Russia to keep. Austria-Hungary was authorized to "occupy and administer" Bosnia and Herzegovina, which remained formally under Ottoman rule. Britain took Cyprus, and France was urged to occupy Tunisia.

Although Germany asked for nothing, its role in the congress earned it Russia's resentment. The Balkan states were also annoyed. Romania wanted Bessarabia, which Russia kept; Bulgaria wanted the borders originally granted it by the Treaty of San Stefano; and Greece wanted a share in the Ottoman spoils. Serbia and Montenegro deeply resented Austria's occupation of Bosnia and Herzegovina, as did many of the natives of those provinces. These lingering south Slavic issues and the estrangement between Russia and Germany threatened Europe's peace.

GERMAN ALLIANCES WITH RUSSIA AND AUSTRIA
Russia's hostility drove Germany closer to Austria. In 1879 a secret treaty created the Dual Alliance, whereby Germany and Austria agreed to come to each other's aid if either were attacked by Russia. Each was also to stay out of the other's conflicts with other nations. The treaty remained in force until 1918 and was the anchor of German policy. In retrospect, it may have been an error. It linked Germany's fortunes with those of the troubled Austro-Hungarian Empire, and by isolating the Russians, it pushed them to seek new alliances in the West.

Bismarck never allowed the alliance to drag Germany into Austria's Balkan quarrels. He also made it clear to the Austrians that the alliance was purely defensive and that Germany would never be a party to an attack on Russia. Bismarck believed that monarchical, reactionary Russia would not seek ties with republican France or democratic Britain. In fact, he expected news of Austro-German negotiations to frighten Russia into reconciling with Germany.

In this he was correct. By 1881 he had renewed the Three Emperors' League on a firmer basis. Germany, Austria, and Russia pledged neutrality if any of them were attacked by a fourth power. Austria was granted the right to annex Bosnia-Herzegovina and promised help in closing the Dardanelles to all nations in case of war. The league allayed German fears of a Russian-French alliance and Russian fears of a German-Austrian alliance. It also safeguarded Russia from British plots to win Austria's support for allowing the British fleet into the Black Sea. Most important, the agreement hoped to keep peace in the Balkans between Austria and Russia.

THE TRIPLE ALLIANCE   In 1882 Italy crowned Bismarck's policy with triumph. Seeking to strengthen its defenses against France, it asked to join the Dual Alliance. As a result, Germany had treaties with three of the great powers and friendly relations with the one that held aloof from all alliances, Great Britain. France was thus isolated and neutralized. Bismarck's challenge now was to maintain the complicated system of secret treaties in the face of rivalries among his allies. He succeeded until a change in the German monarchy upset things.

In 1888 Kaiser William II (r. 1888–1918) came to the German throne. At age twenty-nine, he was ambitious, impetuous, imperious, and a believer in the divine right of kings. An injury at birth left him with a physical defect (a withered left arm) for which he overcompensated by vigorous athletic activity, military bearing, and embarrassingly bombastic rhetoric. Like many Germans of his generation, William II believed that Germany was destined to lead Europe. At the least, he wanted Britain, under the rule of his grandmother Queen Victoria, to acknowledge Germany its equal. To win a "place in the sun" for Germany, he coveted a navy and colonies like Britain's. This, of course, ran counter to Bismarck's limited continental policy. When Bismarck opposed William's attempts to build up the German navy, William used a disagreement over domestic policy to dismiss him (1890).

With Bismarck in power, Germany had been secure and had earned respect as the guardian of peace in Europe. Germany could not have exercised its leadership role without its great military power. But control of this power required consummate statesmanship, a willingness to exercise restraint, and a clear understanding of the nation's true self-interest—things in which the young kaiser was lacking.

Forging of the Triple Entente (1890–1907)

FRANCO-RUSSIAN ALLIANCE Bismarck's retirement led to the immediate collapse of his system of alliances. His successor, General Leo von Caprivi (1831–1899), doubted his ability to manage Bismarck's complicated policy and hoped to secure Germany by the simpler strategy of drawing closer to Britain. The results were unfortunate. Britain remained aloof, and Russia was alienated.

Diplomatic isolation and the need for foreign capital drove the Russians into the arms of the French, and the French, who were even more isolated than the Russians, were delighted to find any friend who promised to help them against Germany. In 1894, despite their inconsistent political philosophies, France and Russia formed a defensive alliance against Germany.

BRITAIN AND GERMANY Britain held the key to the international situation, and initially it was disposed to favor Germany. Colonial rivalries pitted the British against the Russians in Central Asia and against the French in Africa. Britain had also long opposed Russian control of Constantinople and the Dardanelles and French dominance of the Low Countries. However, despite all this and despite Britain's long history of friendly relations with Germany, within a decade of William II's accession most Britons had come to think of Germany as the greatest threat to their national security. They had been alarmed by the foreign and naval policies Germany embraced as a consequence of William II's envy of Britain's colonial empire and fleet. At first the emperor tried to win the British over to the Triple Alliance. When Britain chose instead to maintain its "splendid isolation," his strategy

changed. He decided to demonstrate Germany's importance as an ally by making trouble for Britain. Germany blocked British attempts to build a railroad from Capetown to Cairo. It openly sympathized with the Boers of South Africa, who were fighting British expansion. And in 1898 William began to implement plans for a great German navy. He ordered construction of nineteen battleships, and two years later he doubled that number.

The architect of the new navy was Admiral Alfred von Tirpitz (1849–1930). He explained that Germany's naval policy was to build a fleet strong enough, not to defeat Britain, but to do sufficient damage to make the British navy inferior to that of other nations. The plan was absurd, for the British, who had greater financial resources than the Germans, could add enough new ships to maintain their advantage over Germany. The main achievement of the policy was to waste German resources by challenging Britain to an arms race.

Initially, Britain was not unduly concerned, but the steady growth of the German navy gradually persuaded the British to abandon their isolationist policy. Widespread international disapproval of Britain's Boer War (1899–1902)—an unequal struggle in which the great empire crushed a rebellion by South African farmers—also convinced the government to seek some treaties of friendship. Between 1898 and 1901 Joseph Chamberlain, the colonial secretary, made several approaches to Germany. But the Germans, who were confident that a British alliance with France or Russia was impossible, spurned him in the expectation of forcing greater concessions in the future.

THE ENTENTE CORDIALE The first breach of Britain's isolation came in 1902 when Britain concluded an alliance with Japan to defend British interests in the Far East from Russia. Next, Britain overcame its traditional antagonism to France and, in 1904, established the Entente Cordiale. This was not a formal treaty with military provisions but a coordination of the colonial ambitions of the two nations. Britain gave France a free hand in Morocco in return for French recognition of British control over Egypt. The Entente Cordiale was a long step toward the alignment of Britain with one of Germany's great potential enemies.

Britain's new relationship with France was surprising, but even more so was Britain's emerging sympathy for Russia. A humiliating defeat in the Russo-Japanese War (1904–1905) and the experience of countering a revolution sparked by that war in 1905 had sufficiently weakened Russia to dispel Britain's fear of the nation's expansion. Britain worried instead that Russia might drift into the German orbit.

THE FIRST MOROCCAN CRISIS   At this point, Germany tested the new relationship between Britain and France. In March 1905, William II landed at Tangier, made a speech in favor of Moroccan independence, and implied that Germany had a role in determining Morocco's destiny. This was a challenge to France that Germany hoped would reveal the weakness of France and of Britain's commitment to France. The Germans demanded an international conference, a forum for a more dramatic demonstration of their power.

At the conference, which met at Algeciras in Spain in 1906, the Germans overplayed their hand. Austria sided with Germany, but Spain, Italy, and the United States voted with Britain and France. The Germans received trivial concessions, and France's position in Morocco was confirmed. German bullying had succeeded only in driving Britain and France closer together. Sir Edward Grey, the British foreign secretary, authorized the British and French general staffs to discuss what they might do if Germany attacked France. By 1914, French and British military and naval plans had become so mutually dependent that the two countries were effectively, if not formally, allied.

BRITISH AGREEMENT WITH RUSSIA   As Britain grew closer to France, it grew closer to France's ally, Russia. Germany's expanding navy and its ambitions in the Middle East (reflected in a plan to build a railroad from Berlin to Baghdad) prompted Britain to conclude an agreement with Russia (1907) much like the Entente Cordiale. Russo-British disputes in Central Asia were resolved and wider cooperation was promised. A Triple Entente, an informal, but powerful, association of Britain, France, and Russia, gradually emerged to oppose the Triple Alliance of Germany, Austria-Hungary, and Italy. (Since Italy was an unreliable ally, this made Germany and Austria-Hungary feel increasingly threatened by encirclement.)

The equilibrium that Bismarck had worked so hard to achieve in Europe began to disintegrate. Britain ceased to help Austria block Russia's ambitions in the Balkans, and Germany was unwilling to restrain Austria for fear of alienating its most important ally. The new alliances had increased the risk of conflict and made the Balkans a flashpoint. Thanks to William II and his ministers, Bismarck's nightmare of a two-front war with France and Russia was in danger of becoming a reality—a conflagration made even more horrible than Bismark had imagined by involving Britain.

World War I

The Road to War (1908–1914)

The Ottoman Empire was weak, but it still held a vital corridor of land running across the Balkan peninsula from Constantinople to the Adriatic. The technically Ottoman, but in reality autonomous, states of Romania, Serbia, and Bulgaria lay to the north and Greece to south. The territory on the Adriatic coast north of Serbia was part of the Austro-Hungarian Empire. It included Croatia and Slovenia and, since 1878, an "occupied and administered" Bosnia and Herzegovina.

Except for the Greeks and the Romanians, most of the inhabitants of the Balkans spoke variants of the same Slavic language and felt a kinship with one another that had been strengthened by centuries of foreign domination—Austrian, Hungarian, and Turkish. The nationalistic movements that swept across Europe in the late nineteenth century fanned desires for independence, and the more radical among the Balkan leaders longed to unify the south Slavic (i.e., Yugoslav) peoples. Serbia was to be the center of a new nation that would liberate all the Austrian Empire's Slavic provinces, especially Bosnia. Serbia dreamed of uniting the Slavs as Piedmont had united the Italians and Prussia the Germans.

THE BOSNIAN CRISIS   In 1908 a group of modernizing reformers (the "Young Turks") launched a revolution in the Ottoman Empire. Austria and Russia, which planned to partition that empire, were suddenly alarmed that the revolutionaries might succeed in breathing new life into it. They acted quickly. Russia consented to Austria's annexation of Bosnia and Herzegovina in return for Austria's support in opening the Dardanelles to Russian warships. Austria declared the annexation but did nothing for Russia when the British and French helped the Turks maintain their hold on the Dardanelles. The Russians were humiliated, for they, a Slavic nation, had let down their "little brothers," the Slavic Serbs who believed that Bosnia belonged to them, not to Austria.

The Austrians had given the Germans no warning before they seized Bosnia. Germany was upset, for as Austria's chief ally, its relations with Russia were strained by the coup. But Germany was so dependent on the Dual Alliance that it had to allow its foreign policy to be made in Vienna. The Triple Entente was, however, similarly strained. The refusal of Britain and France to allow Russia to move into the Dardanelles meant that they had to acquiesce to some future Russian demand if they wanted to retain Russia's friendship.

THE SECOND MOROCCAN CRISIS In 1911 a second crisis involving Morocco drove France and Britain closer together. When France sent an army to Morocco to put down a rebellion, Germany sent a gunboat named the *Panther* to the Moroccan port of Agadir—allegedly to protect German residents. The British, anticipating the worst, wrongly believed that the Germans meant to seize Agadir and develop it into a naval base on the Atlantic. In 1907 Germany had built its first "dreadnought," a version of a new type of battleship that Britain had launched in 1906. In 1908 Germany had passed still another naval law to accelerate development of its fleet. Negotiations failed to persuade the Germans to slow naval construction, and Britain concluded that the security of its island kingdom was at stake.

The Moroccan dispute was resolved when France yielded some insignificant bits of the Congo in exchange for German recognition of France's protectorate over Morocco. The chief effect of the crisis was to increase Britain's fear of Germany and to forge stronger links between Britain and France. Although there was no formal treaty, German naval construction and the threat to Agadir turned the Entente Cordiale into a de facto alliance.

WAR IN THE BALKANS The second Moroccan crisis provoked another crisis in the Balkans. Italy,

which wanted to achieve status as a colonial power, planned to take Libya from the Turks. Fearing that the recognition of the French protectorate in Morocco would encourage France to move into Libya before it could, Italy hastened to attack the Ottoman Empire and to force the Turks to cede it control over Libya and some islands in the Aegean. This encouraged the Balkan states to try their luck against the Ottomans. In 1912 Bulgaria, Greece, Montenegro, and Serbia jointly defeated the Turks. Following this "First Balkan War" the victors quarreled over the division of Macedonia, and in 1913 a "Second Balkan War" enabled Turkey and Romania and the other states to strip Bulgaria of much of what it had won in 1878 and 1912.

The First Balkan War alarmed the Austrians who were determined to prevent the Serbs from entering Albania and gaining a port on the Adriatic. When the Russians backed the Serbs, Britain sponsored an international conference to resolve the matter (1913). It called for an independent kingdom of Albania. Austria, however, felt humiliated by the airing of Serbia's demands, and the Serbs defied the agreement by staying in Albania until Austria forced them to withdraw. When the Serbs returned in September 1913, after the Second Balkan War, Austria issued an ultimatum. Again Serbia withdrew. Many Austrians favored an all-out attack on Serbia that would decisively end its threat to their empire, but Russia was committed by its allegiance to Pan-Slavic solidarity to helping the Serbs. Britain, France, Italy, and Germany cooperated in restraining both parties, but both worried that by holding back they might appear too reluctant to help their friends.

The crisis of 1913 shaped the response the European nations made to the events of 1914 that finally precipitated world war. The Russians' allies, having urged them to back down in 1913 as in 1908, were reluctant to restrain them again. The Austrians, having discovered that they got better results from a threat of force than from humiliating debates at international conferences, lost interest in negotiating.

Sarajevo and the Outbreak of War (June–August 1914)

THE ASSASSINATION On June 28, 1914, a young Bosnian nationalist shot and killed the heirs to the Austrian throne, Archduke Francis Ferdinand and his wife, as they drove through the Bosnian capital of Sarajevo. The assassin was a member of a terrorist organization called Union or Death (popularly known as the Black Hand). The chief of intelligence on the general staff of Serbia's army had helped plan the crime. His role was not known at the time, but the glee with which the Serbian press reported the event led many Europeans to assume that Serbian officials had been involved.

GERMANY AND AUSTRIA'S RESPONSE Since the assassination was condemned everywhere in Europe except Serbia, Austrians who favored military action against Serbia as a solution to the empire's Slavic problem believed that the time had come to declare war. Conrad von Hötzendorf, chief of the Austrian general staff, urged an attack, but Count Stefan Tisza, representing the Hungarian portion of the Dual Monarchy, resisted. Count Leopold von Berchtold, the foreign minister, knew that German help was needed to sway the Hungarians to war and that German support would be required in the likely event that Russia intervened to protect Serbia. The ultimate decision, therefore, was Berlin's.

William II and Chancellor Theobald von Bethmann-Hollweg (1856–1921) readily promised German support for an attack on Serbia. They urged the Austrians to move swiftly while the other powers were still angry. The Austrians hoped that Germany's protection would discourage intervention by other states and allow them to fight Serbia alone. They were, however, prepared to risk a general European conflict. The Germans, too, recognized the risk of a broader war but believed they could contain the fight. Although the German decision to support Austria made war difficult if not impossible to avoid, there is no evidence that Germany had long been plotting a war. The subsequent conduct of its leaders suggests that they were reacting to events, not implementing some master plan.

The emperor and his chancellor alone, without consulting their advisers, made the fateful commitment to Austria. William II was motivated by violent passions. He had been the archduke's friend, and he was outraged by an attack on royalty. Bethmann-Hollweg, the chancellor, was less emotionally involved, but he was reluctant flatly to oppose the emperor and to appear

"soft" to the military establishment. Moreover, he, like many other Germans, feared for the future. The time had come to take a "calculated risk." Russia was recovering its strength. The Triple Entente was growing more powerful, and Austria was Germany's only reliable ally. While it was dangerous to support Austria, it might have been even more dangerous to withhold support. If Austria failed to crush Serbia, Slavic nationalism could disrupt the empire and invite Russian intervention and expansion.

Bethmann-Hollweg hoped that the Austrians would strike swiftly and present the powers with a *fait accompli*. He believed that fear of Germany

Above: The Austrian Archduke Francis Ferdinand and his wife in Sarajevo on June 28, 1914. Later in the day the royal couple were assassinated by young revolutionaries trained and supplied in Serbia, igniting the crisis that led to World War I. Below: Moments after the assassination the Austrian police captured one of the assassins. Brown Brothers

would keep Russia from becoming involved. But if not, he was prepared for war with France and Russia. In that case, he convinced himself that he could persuade Britain to remain neutral—despite the fact that Germany continued to provoke the British with its naval arms race.

The Austrians did not act quickly, and the Serbians returned so soft and conciliatory an answer to the ultimatum that was meant to provoke war that even the mercurial German emperor concluded that there were no longer grounds for hostilities. The Austrians, however, were determined not to turn back. On July 28, they declared war on Serbia, even though their army could not be mobilized before mid-August.

THE TRIPLE ENTENTE'S RESPONSE The Russians responded angrily to Austria's treatment of Serbia. Conservative elements within the Russian government opposed war, fearing that it would lead to revolution. But nationalists, Pan-Slavs, and the majority of the politically conscious classes demanded action. The government ordered a partial military mobilization that was intended to dissuade Austria from attacking Serbia.

Mobilization of any kind was dangerous. It was generally seen as an act of war, and Russia's mobilization was particularly alarming to the German general staff. Germany's strategy, the Schlieffen Plan, called for an attack on France before Russia could get itself organized to enter the war, and Germany now concluded that it had no choice but to ready its forces. Perceptions of military necessity began to escalate pressures on nations.

France and Britain were not eager for war. France's president and prime minister were on their way home from a visit to Russia when the crisis flared on July 24. Had they been in Paris, they might have tried to restrain the Russians, but France's ambassador to Russia gave the Russians the same assurances that Germany had given the Austrians. The Austrians, smarting from the humiliation of the London Conference of 1913, rejected a British proposal for another conference. Germany privately supported Austria while making conciliatory public statements to court British neutrality. Soon, however, Bethmann-Hollweg realized what he should have known from the first. If Germany attacked France, Britain would fight. After July 30, when

Austria ordered mobilization against Russia, Germany's sham appeals for Austrian restraint became sincere. It was, however, too late for Austria to back down without a massive loss of face.

Bethmann-Hollweg resisted enormous pressure to call up the army, not because he hoped to avoid war but because he wanted Russia to act first and appear to be the aggressor. Only then would the German people support a war. Minutes before Germany was set to initiate mobilization, news arrived that Russia had begun. The Schlieffen Plan was put into effect. On August 1, the Germans occupied Luxembourg. An invasion of Belgium two days later violated Belgian neutrality, which Britain had promised to protect in a treaty of 1839. This united the British people against Germany, and when Germany proceeded to invade France, Britain entered the war (August 4). As Sir Edward Grey, the British foreign secretary, put it, the lights were going out all over Europe. When they came on again, Europe was a different place. Debate continues today on the causes for the "Great War," but common opinion holds that it was German ambition (fanned by Kaiser William II) to win a higher place in the international order that did most to upset the status quo.

Strategies and Stalemate (1914–1917)

There was jubilation throughout Europe as the decision to fight released the tensions created by the repeated crises of recent years. No general war had been fought since Napoleon's day, and few anticipated the horrors of modern combat. The dominant memory was of Bismarck's swift, decisive campaigns whose costs were light and rewards great. Both sides expected to take the offensive, force a battle on favorable ground, and win a quick victory. The "Allies" (the Triple Entente nations) had superior numbers and financial resources and command of the sea. The "Central Powers" (Germany and Austria) had the advantages of internal lines of communication and of launching the first attack.

Germany's war plan had been developed a decade earlier by Count Alfred von Schlieffen (1833–1913), chief of the German general staff from 1891 to 1906. The German army was to outflank the French defenses by sweeping through Belgium to the English Channel. Then,

John Singer Sargent, Gassed: The Horrors of Modern War

In 1918, the British War Memorials Committee commissioned the American painter, John Singer Sargent (1856–1925), to create a huge picture commemorating American-British military cooperation. Sargent, who was best known for his society portraits and Impressionist landscapes, was a surprising choice for such a project, and he produced a surprising painting. Although his canvas recalls ancient Greek friezes, where their sculptors celebrated the heroism of a warrior's suffering and death, Sargent focused on the horror of battle. His decision to do so was appropriate, for the "Great War" of 1914–1918 was the testing ground for a raft of terrible new weapons: machine guns, tanks, airplanes, barbed wire, and poison gasses. Sargent's picture shows a line of men, temporarily blinded by mustard gas, being led from the front.

Sources: John Keegan, *The First World War* (New York: Alfred A. Knopf, 1999); Martin Gilbert, *The First World War* (New York: Henry Holt and Co., 1994); Radcliff Carter, *John Singer Sargent* (Abbeville Press, 1982); Website, Imperial War Museum, London.

John Singer Sargent, *Gassed*, 1918–1919. Imperial War Museum, London

wheeling to the south and east it was to envelop the French and crush them against German fortresses in Lorraine. The key to the plan lay in making the right wing of the advancing German army immensely strong while deliberately weakening the left, opposite the French frontier. The weakness of the left was meant to draw the French into attacking there while the war was decided by the German right. In the East, the Germans planned simply to defend against Russia until France was crushed. That was expected to take only six weeks.

Helmuth von Moltke (1848–1916), the nephew of Bismarck's most effective general, was given command of the campaign. He, however, lacked the courage to heed Schlieffen's warning that it was necessary to risk Germany's frontier and depend entirely on the strength of the right wing. Moltke added divisions to the left wing and even weakened the Russian front to get them. As a result of his hesitant strategy and of mistakes by commanders in the field, the Schlieffen Plan failed—narrowly.

THE WAR IN THE WEST The French, like the Germans, put their faith in an offensive but with less reason than the Germans. They badly underestimated the numbers and effectiveness of the German reserves and overestimated the importance of the courage and spirit of their own troops. Courage and spirit could not prevail against machine guns and heavy artillery. The French attack on Germany's western frontier failed totally, but defeat proved to be better than partial success. It freed troops for use against the main German army and helped the French and British stop the German advance on Paris at the Battle of the Marne (September 1914).

Thereafter, the war in the West bogged down. Both sides dug in behind a wall of trenches and barbed wire that stretched from the North Sea to Switzerland. Strategically placed machine-gun nests made assaults difficult and dangerous. Both sides, nonetheless, attempted massive attacks preceded by artillery bombardments of unprecedented force. Sometimes assaults that cost hundreds of thousands of lives produced advances measured in mere hundreds of yards. The development of poison gas increased casualties but not victories. In 1916 the British invented the tank as an effective counter to the machine gun, but the Allied command was slow to grasp its

significance for new offensive strategies. For three years, the western front moved only a few miles in either direction.

THE WAR IN THE EAST In the East, the war began auspiciously for the Allies. The Russians advanced into Austrian territory and inflicted heavy casualties, but Russian incompetence and German energy soon reversed the situation. A junior German officer, Erich Ludendorff (1865–1937), under the command of the elderly General Paul von Hindenburg (1847–1934), destroyed or captured an entire Russian army at the Battle of Tannenberg and defeated another one at the Masurian Lakes. In 1915 the Central Powers drove into the Baltic states and Russian Poland and inflicted over 2 million casualties in a single year.

As the battle lines hardened, both sides sought new allies. In 1916 Romania joined the Allies but was quickly defeated and driven from the war. Turkey, which was hostile to Russia, and Bulgaria, which was Serbia's enemy, joined the Central Powers. In the Far East, Japan honored its alliance with Britain by overrunning the German colonies in China and the Pacific—and using the opportunity to improve its position with respect to China. Both sides in the war bid for Italy's support. The Allies won by promising the Italians more of what they wanted—namely, spoils from Austria's empire. In a secret treaty of 1915 the Allies agreed to give Italy most of *Italia Irredenta* (i.e., the South Tyrol, Trieste, and some of the Dalmatian Islands), colonies in Africa, and a share of the Turkish Empire. By the spring of 1915, Italy was engaging Austrian armies. The campaign weakened Austria and forced the Germans to divide some of their troops, but Italy's help failed to achieve anything significant for the Allies.

Each side tried to stir up trouble for the other by appealing to nationalistic movements in its opponent's territory. The Germans supported the Irish against Britain, the Flemings in Belgium, and the Poles and the Ukrainians in their opposition to Russia. They tried to persuade the Turks to lead a Muslim uprising against the British in Egypt and India and against the French in North Africa. The Allies had greater success appealing to nationalists who wanted to break free from the Austrian Empire: Czechs, Slovaks, southern Slavs, and Poles. A movement for Arab independence from Turkey, which was coordinated by

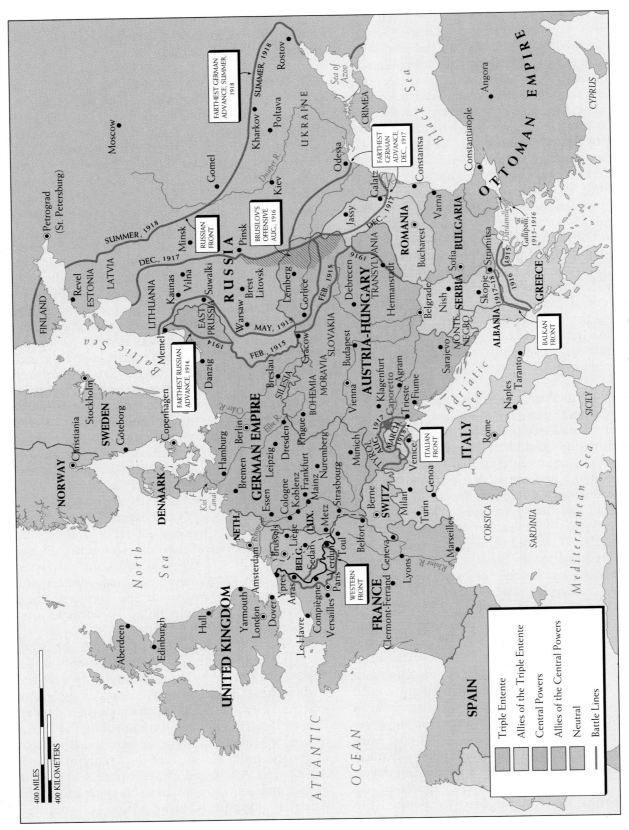

MAP 26–3 WORLD WAR I IN EUROPE *Despite the importance of military action in the Far East, in the Arab world, and at sea, the main theaters of activity in World War I were in Europe.*

FARTHEST GERMAN ADVANCE, SUMMER, 1918

SUMMER, 1918

FARTHEST GERMAN ADVANCE, DEC., 1917

BRUSILOV'S OFFENSIVE AUG., 1916

RUSSIAN FRONT

SUMMER, 1918

DEC., 1917

FARTHEST RUSSIAN ADVANCE, 1914

WESTERN FRONT

ITALIAN FRONT

BALKAN FRONT

Moscow

Petrograd (St. Petersburg)

Rostov

Kharkov

Poltava

Gomel

Dnieper R.

Kiev

Odessa

Galatz

Constantsa

Angora

Constantinople

CYPRUS

OTTOMAN EMPIRE

Black Sea

Sea of Azov

CRIMEA

UKRAINE

Minsk

Pinsk

Jassy

DEC., 1917

RUSSIA

RUSSIAN FRONT

Brest Litovsk

Lemberg

Gorlice

FEB. 1915

Debrecen

9161

Varna

Bucharest

ROMANIA

Hermanstadt

TRANSYLVANIA

Sofia

Nish

SERBIA

BULGARIA

Strumitsa

Skopje

1917–18

Dardanelles

Gallipoli, 1915–1916

1915

1916

GREECE

Revel

ESTONIA

LATVIA

FINLAND

Kaunas

Vilna

LITHUANIA

Suwalki

Memel

Danzig

EAST PRUSSIA

Warsaw

MAY, 1915

FEB., 1915

1914

Cracow

SLOVAKIA

MORAVIA

BOHEMIA

Budapest

AUSTRIA-HUNGARY

Vienna

Klagenfurt

Agram

Fiume

Trieste

Caporetto

MARCH 1918

AUG. 1917

Belgrade

Sarajevo

MONTE-NEGRO

ALBANIA

Adriatic Sea

BALKAN FRONT

Stockholm

Christiania

SWEDEN

Göteborg

Copenhagen

DENMARK

Breslau

SILESIA

Berlin

Oder R.

Leipzig

Dresden

Prague

Elbe R.

GERMAN EMPIRE

Hamburg

Bremen

Essen

Cologne

Koblenz

Frankfurt

Mainz

Nuremberg

Strasbourg

Munich

TIROL

Venice

ITALY

Rome

Naples

Taranto

SICILY

Mediterranean Sea

SARDINIA

CORSICA

NORWAY

North Sea

Baltic Sea

Kiel Canal

NETH.

Amsterdam

Brussels

BELG.

LUX.

Liège

Sedan

Metz

Verdun

Toul

Belfort

Berne

SWITZ.

Geneva

Milan

Turin

Genoa

Lyons

Rhône R.

Marseilles

FRANCE

Clermont-Ferrand

Versailles

Compiègne

Paris

WESTERN FRONT

Ypres

Arras

Le Havre

Dover

London

Yarmouth

Hull

Edinburgh

Aberdeen

UNITED KINGDOM

ATLANTIC OCEAN

SPAIN

Rhine R.

Triple Entente

Allies of the Triple Entente

Central Powers

Allies of the Central Powers

Neutral

Battle Lines

400 MILES

400 KILOMETERS

502

British tanks moving toward the battle of Cambrai in Flanders late in 1917. Tanks were impervious to machine-gun fire. Had they been used in great numbers they might have broken the stalemate in the west. Bildarchiv Preussischer Kulturbesitz

Colonel T. E. Lawrence (1888–1935) "of Arabia," was especially important later in the war.

In 1915 Winston Churchill (1874–1965), first lord of the British admiralty, suggested a plan to break the deadlock on the western front. He proposed an attack on the Dardanelles and Constantinople. This was to knock Turkey out of the war, relieve the Balkan front, and ease communications with Russia—all at minimal risk. Thanks to British naval superiority and the element of surprise, a naval action alone was deemed sufficient to force the straits and capture the city. If it failed, the fleet could escape with little loss. Success, however, depended on timing, speed, and daring leadership, and the attackers had none of these. Troops were landed, and as Turkish resistance continued, more were added. Before the project was abandoned, the Allies had lost almost 150,000 men and diverted three times that number from more useful occupations.

RETURN TO THE WEST   In 1916 both sides turned their attentions back to the West. General Erich von Falkenhayn (1861–1922), who had succeeded Moltke in September 1914, attacked the French stronghold of Verdun. His goal was not to take the fortress but to inflict enormous casualties on the French who would have to defend it against superior firepower coming from several directions. The French, however, held Verdun with comparatively few men and inflicted almost as many casualties as they suffered. Verdun's commander, Henri Pétain (1856–1951), became a national hero.

The Allied initiative was a major offensive along the River Somme. Aided by a Russian attack in the East that drew off some German strength and by an enormous artillery bombardment, the Allies hoped at last to break through the German line. But once again, enormous casualties on both sides brought no one a decisive advantage.

THE WAR AT SEA   As the war dragged on, control of the sea became increasingly important. The British ignored international laws that protected ships carrying peaceful cargo and imposed a strict blockade to starve out their enemies. The Germans responded with submarine warfare. By threatening all shipping, they hoped in their turn to starve Britain. The policies of both nations offended neutrals—especially the United States, which conducted extensive trade in the Atlantic.

In 1915 the British liner *Lusitania* was torpedoed by a German submarine, and 118 Americans were among the 1,200 of its passengers who drowned. When President Woodrow Wilson (1856–1924) warned Germany that a repetition would have grave consequences, the Germans tried to avoid incidents that might bring America into the war. The German fleet that had cost so much money and caused so much trouble ultimately played no significant part in the war. Its only battle, fought at Jutland in the spring of 1916, resulted in a standoff that confirmed British domination of the surface of the sea.

AMERICA ENTERS THE WAR   In December 1916, Woodrow Wilson tried to mediate a peace, but neither side was willing to renounce aims that the other found unacceptable. The war seemed likely to continue until exhaustion felled one or both.

Two events early in 1917 altered the situation. On February 1, the Germans resumed unrestricted submarine warfare. This led the United States to break off diplomatic relations and, on April 6, to declare war on the Central Powers. The decision to enter the war was made easier by an unexpected event that took place in March. Wilson, who could justify war only as an idealistic crusade "to make the world safe for democracy," had been reluctant to join the Allies in defending autocratic tsarist Russia. But in March 1917 the Russian Revolution overthrew the tsarist regime.

The Russian Revolution

Russia's March Revolution was neither planned nor led by any political faction. It resulted from the collapse of the monarchy's ability to govern. Tsar Nicholas II was weak and incompetent, and the demands the war put on the resources of his country and government were too great. Military and domestic mismanagement produced massive casualties, widespread hunger, strikes by workers, confusion in the army, and peasant uprising. In 1916 the tsar alienated all political factions by adjourning the Duma, Russia's parliament, and proceeding to rule alone.

The Provisional Government

Strikes and worker demonstrations erupted in Petrograd (Saint Petersburg) early in March 1917. When the ill-disciplined troops stationed in the city refused to fire on the demonstrators and restore order, the tsar abdicated (March 15). The Duma reconvened to form a provisional government that was composed chiefly of Constitutional Democrats (Cadets) sympathetic to the West.

Outside the provisional government, various socialists, including both Social Revolutionaries and Social Democrats of the Menshevik wing, organized *soviets* (i.e., councils of workers and soldiers). As relatively orthodox Marxists, the Mensheviks believed that Russia had to pass through a bourgeois stage of development before the revolution of the proletariat could be launched. Consequently, they were willing to work, temporarily, with the Constitutional Democrats in a liberal regime. The provisional government was doomed, however, by its decision to continue the war against Germany, for the war perpetuated the suffering and discontent that had brought down the tsar. When Russia's last offensive collapsed in the summer of 1917, military discipline disintegrated and mass disillusionment undermined loyalty to the government.

Lenin and the Bolsheviks

Opposition to the provisional government by the Bolshevik wing of the Social Democratic Party suggested a scheme to the Germans for subverting order in Russia. They smuggled V. I. Lenin, a brilliant Bolshevik leader, in a sealed train from Switzerland across Germany to Petrograd.

Lenin believed that an opportunity was at hand to realize a key piece of Marxist theory: a political alliance between workers and peasants (using the *soviets* that the Bolsheviks controlled). Lenin attempted a coup following 1917's failed military offensive. When it collapsed, he fled to Finland, and his chief collaborator, Leon Trotsky (1877–1940), was imprisoned. The failure of a right-wing countercoup then gave the Bolsheviks a second chance. Trotsky was released from prison, and Lenin returned. On November 6, Trotsky, leader of the powerful Petrograd *soviet,* staged an uprising that concluded with an armed assault on the provisional government. Almost as much to their own astonishment as to that of the rest of the world, the Bolsheviks became Russia's rulers.

The Communist Dictatorship

In an election the provisional government had called for late November to select a Constituent Assembly, the Social Revolutionaries won a large majority over the Bolsheviks. The assembly convened in January, but it met for only a day before the Bolsheviks' Red Army dispersed it. In November and January the Bolshevik government nationalized land ownership and turned it over to peasant proprietors. Factory workers were put in charge of their plants. The debt of the tsarist government was repudiated. Banks were seized by the state, as was the church's property.

The Bolshevik government signed an armistice with Germany in December 1917. On March 3, 1918, by the Treaty of Brest-Litovsk, Russia surrendered claims to Poland, the Baltic states, and the Ukraine. Some territory in the Transcaucasus region went to Turkey, and the Bolsheviks agreed to pay a heavy war indemnity. The price for peace was terribly high, but Lenin had no choice. Russia was incapable of renewing the war effort, and the Bolsheviks needed time to establish control over a devastated, chaotic Russia. Besides, Lenin believed that the war and Russia's example would soon spark communist revolutions across Europe.

Resistance to the Bolshevik takeover continued within Russia until 1921. It took the form of a civil war between "Red" Russians who supported the revolution and "White" Russians who opposed it. In the summer of 1918, the Bolsheviks murdered the tsar and his family. Loyal army officers, with help from the Allies, continued to fight until Trotsky's Red Army finally established Lenin in firm control.

The End of World War I

The collapse of Russia and the Treaty of Brest-Litovsk marked the zenith of German success. Control over eastern Europe and its resources freed Germany to concentrate its forces on the western front. This might have tipped things decisively in favor of Germany had not America intervened.

It took about a year for American troops to arrive in significant numbers, and in the interim the bloody deadlock continued. When an Allied offensive in the West failed disastrously, the French army mutinied. The Austrians defeated the Italians at Caporetto and threatened to overrun Italy. They were checked with the aid of Allied troops.

Germany's Last Offensive

In 1918 Germany decided to gamble everything on one last offensive. Its army again advanced as far as the Marne, where lack of reserves and exhaustion caused it to bog down. The Allies, bolstered by the arrival of American troops, launched an irresistible counteroffensive. The Austrian fronts in the Balkans and Italy collapsed, and the German high command realized that the end was imminent.

Ludendorff was determined that peace should be made before the German army was thoroughly defeated and that civilians should take responsibility for ending the war. President Wilson refused to deal with any German government but a democracy that claimed to speak for the German people. Consequently, Ludendorff had Prince Max of Baden establish such a government and sue for peace on the basis of the Fourteen Points that President Wilson had articulated as America's goals in the war. These idealistic principles included self-determination for nationalities, open diplomacy, freedom of the seas, disarmament, and establishment of a league of nations to keep the peace.

German Republican Government Accepts Defeat

The disintegration of the German army forced William II to abdicate on November 9, 1918. The Social Democratic Party then proclaimed a republic in order to block formation of a soviet government by a Leninist faction. Two days later Germany signed the armistice. The German people were not aware of the dimensions of their defeat, for no foreign soldiers occupied their land. Most expected a mild settlement, and many refused to believe that Germany had been beaten. They claimed it had been tricked by the enemy and betrayed by republicans and socialists at home.

There was little cause for either side to rejoice. Battle casualties alone amounted to 4 million dead and 8.3 million wounded among the Central Powers and 5.4 million dead and 7 million wounded on the opposing side. In addition, millions of civilian deaths were directly and indirectly attributable to the war. The economic and financial resources of the European states had been badly strained, and the old international order was destroyed. Russia was ruled by a Bolshevik dictatorship fomenting world revolution. Germany was in chaos. The Austro-Hungarian, Russian, and Turkish empires disintegrated into gaggles of small states. Europe's hold on its overseas colonies weakened, and the United States began to intervene in European affairs in a major way. Europe was no longer the center of the world, and its nineteenth century's optimism—its confidence in the inevitability of progress through reason, science, and technology—yielded to severe disillusionment. Worst of all, it is widely agreed that World War I was mother to World War II and most of the horrors that were to plague the twentieth century.

The Settlement at Paris

Representatives of the victorious states gathered at Versailles early in 1919. The "Big Four" were Wilson of the United States, David Lloyd George (1863–1945) of Britain, Georges Clemençeau (1841–1929) of France, and Vittorio Emanuele Orlando (1860–1952) of Italy. Japan also took an important part in the discussions.

At Versailles, as in Vienna in 1815, diplomats faced the challenge of restoring world order after long, costly wars. The delegates to the Congress of Vienna had the advantage of being able to confine their attention to Europe. Unswayed by public opinion, they were free to draw a new map along practical lines determined by realities of

Significant Dates from the Era Culminating in World War I	
1871	Creation of the German Empire
1873	The Three Emperors' League
1875	The Russo-Turkish War
1879	The Dual Alliance (Germany and Austria)
1882	The Triple Alliance (Germany, Austria, and Italy)
1888	William II becomes the German emperor (kaiser)
1899–1902	Boer War
1890	Bismarck is dismissed
1894	The Franco-Russian alliance
1898	Germany begins to build a battleship navy
1902	The British alliance with Japan
1904	The Entente Cordiale (Britain and France)
1904–1905	The Russo-Japanese War
1905	The first Moroccan crisis
1908–1909	The Bosnian crisis
1911	The second Moroccan crisis
1912–1913	The First and Second Balkan Wars
1914	(August) Germans attack in the West (August–September) First Battle of the Marne (September) Battles of Tannenberg and the Masurian Lakes
1915	(April) Dardanelles campaign (May) Germans sink British ship *Lusitania*
1916	(February) Germans attack Verdun (May–June) Battle of Jutland
1917	(February) Germans declare unrestricted submarine warfare (March) Russian Revolution (April) United States enters war (November) Bolsheviks seize power
1918	(March) Treaty of Brest-Litovsk; German offensive in the West (November) Armistice

power and softened by compromise. The negotiators at Versailles in 1919 were less fortunate. They represented generally democratic governments accountable to public opinion, and surging nationalistic sentiments meant that Europe's many ethnic groups would not remain quiet while the great powers distributed them about the map. Propaganda, much of it American, had turned World War I into a moral crusade, and this made compromise very difficult.

Wilson's idealistic Fourteen Points declared the right of nationalities to self-determination, but the map of Europe could not be drawn to match ethnic groups perfectly with homelands. Wilson also had to contend with many secret treaties made before and during the war. The British and French electorates had been promised that Germany would be made to pay for the war. Russia had been promised Constantinople in return for recognizing France's claim to Alsace-Lorraine and Britain's control of Egypt. Romania had been promised Transylvania at the expense of Hungary. Italy and Serbia had competing claims to the islands and shores of the Adriatic. The British had encouraged Arab hopes of an independent Arab state carved out of the Ottoman Empire, although that contradicted the Balfour Declaration (1917), which supported Zionist claims to a Jewish homeland in Palestine. These plans conflicted with an Anglo-French agreement to divide up the Middle East.

The national interests of the victors defeated Wilson's idealistic plan for a "peace without victors." France wanted permanently to weaken Germany. Italy still wanted *Italia Irredenta*. Britain pursued its imperial objectives. Japan had aspirations in Asia, and the United States insisted on freedom of the seas and on the Monroe Doctrine.

The peacemakers of 1919 faced a world still in turmoil. Fear of Germany was intense, and Bolshevism created a new source of anxiety. The Allies landed small armies at several places in Russia to help overthrow the Bolshevik regime, but they failed to halt the spread of revolution. Communist governments were established in Bavaria and Hungary, and there was a communist uprising, led by the "Spartacus group," in Berlin.

The Peace

Liberals and idealists who expected a new kind of international order to be achieved in a new and better way were disillusioned. The notion of a peace without victors was jettisoned when the Soviet Union (as Russia was now called) and Germany were excluded from the peace conference. Terms were dictated to the Germans, and the principle of national self-determination was fre-

quently and unavoidably violated. Wilson, who received undeserved adulation on his arrival at the conference, gradually became the object of equally undeserved scorn.

THE LEAGUE OF NATIONS Wilson made unpalatable compromises in the hope that injustices could be corrected by a new international organization he insisted on establishing, the League of Nations. The league was not an international government but a group of sovereign states, which agreed to consult and submit differences to arbitration. The league had no armed forces of its own, but it planned to enforce its edicts by economic sanctions and by military interventions sponsored by its members. Any action by it, however, required the unanimous consent of a council with permanent seats for Britain, France, Italy, the United States, and Japan, and temporary seats for four other states. The exclusion of Germany and the Soviet Union from the league undermined its claim to evenhandedness.

Colonial areas were placed under the "tutelage" of one or another of the great powers and encouraged to advance toward independence. This provision had no teeth, and little progress was made. Disarmament agreements were equally ineffective. Members of the league remained fully sovereign and fully committed to their own national interests.

GERMANY Although a united Germany was less than fifty years old, no one seems to have thought of undoing Bismarck's work and dividing it into its component parts. To protect France against a resurgent Germany, France received Alsace-Lorraine and the right to work the coal mines of the Saar for fifteen years. A belt of land extending from the frontier fifty kilometers east of the Rhine was declared a demilitarized zone. Allied troops were to be stationed west of the Rhine for fifteen years. Britain and the United States promised to defend France if it were again attacked by Germany, and Germany was permanently disarmed.

THE EAST Poland was reestablished and connected to the sea by a corridor that cut East Prussia off from the rest of Germany. The Austro-Hungarian Empire was broken up into five small successor states. Most of its German-speaking

MAP 26–4   WORLD WAR I PEACE SETTLEMENT IN EUROPE AND THE MIDDLE EAST   *The map of central and eastern Europe, as well as that of the Middle East, underwent drastic revision after World War I. The enormous territorial losses suffered by Germany, Austria-Hungary, the Ottoman Empire, Bulgaria, and Russia led to gains for France, Italy, Greece, and Romania and the appearance, or reappearance, of at least eight new independent states. The mandate system for former Ottoman territories outside Turkey proper laid foundations for several new, mostly Arab, states in the Middle East.*

people were gathered into the republic of Austria, cut off from the Germans of Bohemia, and forbidden to unite with Germany. The Magyars retained a much-reduced kingdom of Hungary. The Czechs of Bohemia and Moravia joined with Slovaks and Ruthenians to form Czechoslovakia—which was also home to Poles, Magyars, and several million unhappy Germans. The southern Slavs formed the Kingdom of Serbs, Croats, and Slovenes (Yugoslavia). Italy gained the Trentino and Trieste. Romania acquired Transylvania from Hungary and Bessarabia from Russia. Bulgaria lost territory to Greece, Romania, and Yugoslavia. Finland, Estonia, Latvia, and Lithuania established their independence from Russia.

The Ottoman Empire disappeared. Constantinople became the capital of a republic of Turkey approximately equivalent to Asia Minor. The British established a "mandate" over Palestine and Iraq. The French did the same in Syria and Lebanon. Britain, France, Belgium, and South Africa divided Germany's African colonies. Its Pacific possessions went to Australia, New Zealand, and Japan. In theory, the "advanced nations" were to govern their "mandates" in the interests of native peoples until the latter were ready to govern themselves. In practice, "mandates" were treated as colonies. Twenty years after the signing of the Versailles treaty, not one had achieved independence.

REPARATIONS   The most controversial part of the peace settlement dealt with reparations for the damage Germany did during the war. The American estimate was between $15 billion and $25 billion, an amount Germany could pay. France and Britain, however, worrying about their own debts to the United States, wanted Germany to pay everything—including pensions to veterans and their dependents. Realistically, it was acknowledged that Germany could not pay such a huge sum, whatever it might be. So it was agreed that Germany was to pay $5 billion annually until 1921, when a final figure would be set that would have to be paid off in thirty years. To justify these huge reparation payments, the Allies declared that the Germans were solely responsible for the war.

The Germans, of course, bitterly resented the charge and the blight on their future. They had already lost territories containing badly needed natural resources, and now they were presented with an apparently unlimited reparations bill. Germany's prime minister, Philipp Scheidmann (1865–1939), described the treaty as the imprisonment of the German people, but he had no recourse. The Weimar government that ruled Germany until 1933 never overcame the stigma of accepting the Treaty of Versailles.

Evaluation of the Peace

Few peace settlements have been as severely criticized as the one negotiated in Paris in 1919. Both the defeated and the victorious parties found it wanting. Many criticisms of the Treaty of Versailles are, however, unjustified. It did not dismember or ruin Germany, which, until the worldwide depression of the 1930s began, was recovering its prosperity. The terms the Germans imposed on Russia at Brest-Litovsk (and Germany's plans for Europe, had it won) were far harsher than anything enacted at Versailles. The peace Versailles decreed was, however, unsatisfactory. Dismemberment of the Austro-Hungarian Empire was economically disastrous, for it separated raw materials from manufacturing areas and producers from markets. Realignments of national borders also exacerbated ethnic conflicts. The Germans believed that they had been cheated rather than defeated, and they remained unreconciled to the outcome of the war. The Allied position was not enhanced by rhetoric professing a higher morality than that reflected in the terms of the treaty.

The great weakness of the peace treaty was its failure to acknowledge reality. Germany and Russia, although destined inevitably to play important roles in Europe, were excluded from the settlement and from the League of Nations. The treaty also created no machinery to enforce its terms. The Treaty of Versailles was, therefore, neither conciliatory enough nor harsh enough to create a stable world order.

In Perspective

The outburst of European imperialism in the last part of the nineteenth century spread Western influence around the globe, but the world order created by the New Imperialism did not endure. A conflict in the Balkans spread to become a war involving all of Europe, and that war affected people under Europe's colonial rule. The principles of nationalism and self-determination, which Europeans invoked to justify the war, inspired Europe's colonies to seek independence and nationhood. A glance at the new map of the world could give the impression that the old imperial nations, especially Britain and France, were more powerful than ever, but that impression would be misleading. The European states had been weakened by the enormous price they had paid in lives, money, and will during the war. By denying their colonies the "universal" rights that they claimed to defend in the war, they burdened themselves with new sources of political instability.

REVIEW QUESTIONS

1. To what areas of the world did Europe extend its power after 1870? How did European attitudes toward imperialism change after 1870? Why? What features differentiate the New Imperialism from previous imperialistic movements? What features did they have in common?
2. What role in the world did Bismarck envisage for the new Germany after 1871? How successful was he in realizing his vision? What was Bismarck's attitude toward colonies? Was he wise to tie Germany to Austria-Hungary?
3. Why, at the turn of the century, did Britain abandon its policy of "splendid isolation"? By what stages did it engineer the change? Were the policies it pursued wise ones? Should it have followed a different course?
4. How did developments in the Balkans lead to the outbreak of World War I? What was Serbia's role? Austria's? Russia's? What was Germany's objective in July 1914? Did Germany want a general war?
5. Why did Germany lose World War I? Could Germany have won, or was victory never a possibility? What were the benefits to Europe of the Treaty of Versailles? What were its drawbacks? Was the settlement too harsh or too conciliatory? Could it have secured lasting peace in Europe? How might it have been improved?
6. Why was Lenin successful in establishing Bolshevik rule in Russia? What role did Trotsky play? Was it wise policy for Lenin to take Russia out of the war?

SUGGESTED READINGS

M. BALFOUR, *The Kaiser and His Times* (1972). A fine biography of William II.

V. R. BERGHAHN, *Germany and the Approach of War in 1914* (1973). A work similar in spirit to Fischer's (see later) but stressing the importance of Germany's naval program.

R. BOSWORTH, *Italy and the Approach of the First World War* (1983). A fine analysis of Italian policy.

N. FERGUSON, *The Pity of War* (1999). An analytic study of important aspects of World War I with controversial interpretations.

D. K. FIELDHOUSE, *The Colonial Experience: A Comparative Study from the Eighteenth Century* (1966). An excellent study.

F. FISCHER, *Germany's Aims in the First World War* (1967). An influential interpretation that stirred an enormous controversy by emphasizing Germany's role in bringing on the war.

O. J. HALE, *The Great Illusion 1900–1914* (1971). A fine survey of the period, especially good on public opinion.

M. B. HAYNE, *The French Foreign Office and the Origins of the First World War* (1993). An examination of the influence on French policy of the professionals in the foreign service.

H. HERWIG, *The First World War: Germany and Austria, 1914–18* (1997). A fine study of the war from the loser's perspective.

J. KEEGAN, *The First World War* (1999). A vivid and readable narrative account.

W. L. LANGER, *European Alliances and Alignments*, 2nd ed. (1966). A splendid diplomatic history of the years 1871 to 1890.

D. C. B. LIEVEN, *Russia and the Origins of the First World War* (1983). A good account of the forces that shaped Russian policy.

Z. STEINER, *Britain and the Origins of the First World War* (1977). A perceptive and informed account of the way British foreign policy was made before the war.

S. R. WILLIAMSON JR., *Austria-Hungary and the Origins of the First World War* (1991). A valuable new study of a complex subject.

Imperialism:
Ancient and Modern

The concept of empire has fallen out of favor, and imperialism (i.e., the forcible domination and exploitation of one state by another) is now generally considered one of the worst acts a nation can commit. The last great empire of the traditional kind was the one dominated by Russia prior to the collapse of the USSR.

The modern disdain of empires is something new in history. The change of attitude may owe something to Christianity's deprecation of power and worldly glory, but for much of its history the Christian religion has been quite comfortable with the empires that have endorsed its faith. The rise of democracy and nationalism during the last two centuries has probably had more influence on current concepts of imperialism. Both these movements are premised on the belief that people have rights to freedom of association and autonomy. The greatest influence on popular opinion, however, has probably been fear of the horrors inflicted by modern warfare and the awareness that competition for empire has often led to war.

Earlier generations viewed things quite differently. The first empires were established by the Mesopotamians and Egyptians four thousand years ago. Empires arose somewhat later in China, Japan, India, Iran, and Central and South America. In all these cases no one seems to have questioned the propriety of one people conquering and exploiting another. Empires were assumed to be part of the order of things.

The Greeks: Ambiguities of Power

The Greeks generally shared the attitudes of other ancient peoples toward power, conquest, and empire. They even assumed that their gods had won sway over the universe by defeating earlier deities. The Greeks' national epics glorified warrior heroes who earned honor and fame by subduing other peoples, and Greek culture promoted the view that life was an intense competition that brought glory to winners and shame to losers.

The rise of the *polis* shifted some of the emphasis from competition between individuals to competitions between communities of citizens. The historian Thucydides claims that the Athenians believed that it was natural and inevitable that the stronger states should try to dominate the weak. There was, however, an aspect of Greek experience that ran counter to the imperialistic impulse. Greek culture was the product of small, independent city-states that considered freedom to be a natural right for their citizens, and these citizens held their free, autonomous *poleis* to be superior to the greatest empires of their day. When one city triumphed militarily over another, it usually annexed some border land, but it did not enslave or try to assume total control over its opponent. Greek attitudes were different, however, when it came to dealings with non-Greeks. Greeks viewed themselves as naturally free, but persons who had not grown up in free Greek communities and who had been content to live as subjects of a ruler were assumed to be slaves by nature. Dominating them was perfectly acceptable. (Sometimes the Greeks made exceptions to this rule: For example the *Helots* whom the Spartans enslaved were native Greeks.)

The Greeks shared another belief that made them uncomfortable with the kind of excessive power represented by empires. They thought that any human good pursued to excess resulted in *hubris,* an inclination to acts of wanton violence that arises from an arrogant belief in one's own greatness. The gods were assumed to be offended when a person presumed to exceed the limits the gods had established for human conduct, and the gods were assumed to punish acts of *hubris* that upset the just order of things by inflicting *nemesis,* divine retribution. This was the explanation the Athenians gave for the remarkable failure of the Persian emperors to conquer Greece, and it

Exile of the Israelites. In 1722 B.C.E. the northern part of Jewish Palestine, the kingdom of Israel, was conquered by the Assyrians. Its people were driven from their homeland and exiled all over the vast Assyrian empire. This wall carving in low relief comes from the palace of the Assyrian king Sennacherib at Nineveh. It shows the Jews with their cattle and baggage going into exile. Erich Lessing/Art Resource, NY

made them uneasy about their own conduct as empire builders. Alexander the Great's campaign for the conquest of Persia, however, seems to have converted the Greeks to the generally prevailing, positive attitude toward imperialism.

The Romans: A Theory of Empire

The Romans had few doubts about the desirability of imperial power. They evolved from a nation of small farmers who were accustomed to hard work and subordination to authority. They venerated military virtues and valued the glory and responsibilities of leadership. They believed that their empire was justified by the benefits it brought its subjects: prosperity, justice, the rule of law, and peace. There was some truth in this, else the Roman Empire could not have survived, as it did, for over half a millennium.

Muslims, Mongols, and Ottomans

A new kind of imperialism, energized by religious zeal, appeared with the rise of Islam in the seventh

The philosopher-emperor Marcus Aurelius was compelled to spend much of his time fighting against tribal invaders on Rome's northern frontiers. This relief from the triumphal arch dedicated to him in Rome (176–180) shows him mounted, on campaign.
Nimatallah/Art Resource

century C.E. Bursting out of Arabia, recently converted and passionately faithful Muslim armies quickly won control of most of the Persian Empire, North Africa, and Spain. In the twelfth and thirteenth centuries, the Mongols, many of whom converted to Islam, built a huge empire that dominated Eurasia from the Pacific to central Europe. They ruled Russia for two centuries, controlled China and parts of India, and at their peak held sway over much of the Islamic world.

In the fourteenth century the Ottoman Turks of Asia Minor began to construct yet another great Islamic empire. Their conquest of Constantinople in 1453 brought an end to the ancient Byzantine Empire and opened the way for them to dominate southeastern Europe and threaten Austria and western Europe with invasion. They surged around the Black Sea and across the eastern and southern rim of the Mediterranean as far as Morocco. Their power extended east as far as Kurdistan and Georgia. Toward the end of the seventeenth century the Ottoman Empire entered a slow period of decline that by the end of the nineteenth century had turned it into "the sick man of Europe."

European Expansion

For most of the Middle Ages Europe was politically fragmented and subject to threats of invasion. Late in the 1400s, however, it began the economic and political expansion that culminated by 1900 in its virtual dominance of the planet. The first phase in this process involved the conquest and exploitation of the Americas. Superior naval and military technologies helped with this, but so did the economic dynamism created by European capitalism and the freedom that European states had to compete among themselves for wealth and power.

Spain and Portugal took the lead in founding Europe's colonial empires. Spain quickly overthrew and absorbed the native American empires of the Aztecs and Incas and used their resources to support its imperialistic ambitions elsewhere. Tiny Portugal acquired a huge territory in Brazil and in the East Indies. By the seventeenth century, the Dutch, British, and French were also expanding into the Americas, the Indian subcontinent, and the East Indies. Some of the British colonies proved of lasting significance, for they were outposts for permanent overseas settlement by Europeans, not mere colonial exploitation. Toward the end of the eighteenth century, France lost or retreated from many of its foreign outposts, and this left Britain in sole possession of Europe's colonial establishments in North America and India. The empire that Britain steadily acquired circled the globe and became the largest, most populous in history.

Scholars have argued about the degree to which colonialism actually profited the Euro-

The period in which the European imperial powers were compelled to abandon their colonies was sometimes difficult and painful for both sides. The French departure from Algeria, under French control for more than a century, was especially agonizing. This picture shows the Rue Michelot, one of Algiers's chief shopping streets, patrolled by armed troops in 1962. AFP/Archive Photos

pean nations, but it is clear that it rewarded the British more than anyone else. Britain imported great quantities of natural resources from its colonies and dominated much of their trade. Some of the components of its empire were self-governing states such as Canada, Australia, New Zealand, and South Africa. They were ruled by emigrants from Britain who remained loyal and supported their motherland in its European wars. India, with a population of 300 million, was an immense source of imperial profit. At the height of its imperial power in the mid-nineteenth century, Britain managed to maintain its global position with a remarkably small military. The British army was the smallest in Europe, and Britain supported it and a great navy with a much tinier percentage of its gross national product than other European states spent on their armed forces.

After the Napoleonic wars, France resumed the pursuit of a colonial empire, especially in North Africa and Southeast Asia, and toward the end of the nineteenth century, Germany and Italy entered the race to acquire foreign possessions. The European powers partitioned Africa and extended their authority throughout Asia. Japan followed their example and developed imperialist aspirations of its own. The result of all of this was the establishment of a single global economy in which events in any corner of the world could have wide-ranging repercussions. The jockeying for position within this economy helped to bring on the great war that opened the twentieth century.

Toward Decolonization

The strains of World War II weakened the European colonial powers and began the process of decolonization. Colonies had proved to be of less economic advantage than had been anticipated, and the postwar European states had neither the means nor the incentive to try to reestablish control over them. Surging nationalist movements, which were inspired in the colonies by European ideas and examples, would have made any such attempts costly and unpleasant, and the example of Nazi Germany had discredited the racist arguments that had been used to justify European imperial dominance. Some colonial powers (e.g., the French) hung on longer than others, but by the 1970s a postcolonial world had emerged to condemn the very idea of empire.

❖ *Describe the prevailing attitudes about empire among ancient peoples. What are the modern attitudes? What accounts for the differences? How have modern peoples justified and explained imperialism? How valid are their arguments? Are ancient and modern motives for imperialism fundamentally different?*

Chapter 27

Political Experiments of the 1920s

Political and Economic Factors After the Paris Settlement
New Governments
Demands for Revision of the Paris Settlement
Postwar Economic Problems
New Roles for Government and Labor

The Soviet Experiment Begins
War Communism
The New Economic Policy
Stalin Versus Trotsky
The Third International

The Fascist Experiment in Italy
The Rise of Mussolini
The Fascists in Power

Joyless Victors
France: The Search for Security
Great Britain: Economic Confusion

Trials of the Successor States in Eastern Europe
Economic and Ethnic Pressures
Poland: Democracy to Military Rule
Czechoslovakia: Successful Democratic Experiment
Hungary: Turmoil and Authoritarianism
Austria: Political Turmoil and Nazi Conquest
Southeastern Europe: Royal Dictatorships

The Weimar Republic in Germany
Constitutional Flaws
Lack of Broad Popular Support
Invasion of the Ruhr and Inflation
Hitler's Early Career
The Stresemann Years
Locarno

KEY TOPICS

- Economic and political disorder in the aftermath of World War I
- The Soviet Union's far-reaching political and social experiment
- Mussolini and the fascist seizure of power in Italy
- French determination to enforce the Versailles treaty
- First Labour government and general strike in Britain
- The development of authoritarian governments in all the successor states to the Austrian Empire except Czechoslovakia
- Reparations, inflation, political turmoil, and the rise of Nazism in the German Weimar Republic

The economic and military provisions of the Paris (or Versailles) peace treaties created problems throughout Europe. By the close of the 1920s, support was building for the brutally authoritarian, territorially aggressive governments that sought to dominate Europe in the 1930s and 1940s. These regimes were not inevitable. They were responses to failures to secure democratic systems, stable international relations, and economic prosperity.

Political and Economic Factors After the Paris Settlement

New Governments

Following World War I numerous experiments in government were conducted in Europe. Many countries embraced liberal democracy, and for the first time in Europe's history the politicians who handled diplomatic and economic matters found themselves accountable to mass electorates. Too often, however, nations lacked the will and the political skill to make their new systems of government work.

Demands for Revision of the Paris Settlement

Throughout the 1920s politicians discovered that they could win votes by appealing to various nationalistic concerns and resentments created by the Paris peace treaties. Germany had been humiliated. Various national groups in the successor states of eastern Europe felt that they had been treated unjustly, and France encouraged the victorious powers in the belief that the provisions of the treaty were not being adequately enforced.

Postwar Economic Problems

Europeans shared the dream of returning to the economic prosperity of the prewar years, but after 1918 it proved impossible to turn back the clock and restore what American President Warren Harding termed "normalcy" to economic life. During the Great War, Europeans had turned the vast physical power that they had created in the previous century against themselves, and this had devastated the economic foundations of their civilization. More than 750,000 British soldiers had perished. The combat deaths for France and Germany were 1,385,000 and 1,808,000, respectively. Russia had lost no fewer than 1,700,000 troops. Hundreds of thousands more from other nations had also been killed, and still more millions had been wounded. These casualties represented not only a waste of human lives and talents but also a loss of producers and consumers.

At the start of the war, Europe was the financial and credit center of the world. At its end, European states were deeply in debt to each other

and to the United States. The Paris settlement imposed heavy financial obligations on the defeated parties. The Bolsheviks simply repudiated the debt of the tsarist government, much of which was owed to France. The United States did not seek any reparations from Germany, but it did demand repayment of the loans that it had made to its allies. Reparations and debt structures meant that no nation retained full control over its own economic affairs. Furthermore, the lack of any means for negotiating international economic cooperation encouraged individual states to believe that they had to develop selfish, nationalistic strategies to promote economic recovery.

Market and trade conditions after the war no longer resembled those that had prevailed before 1914. In addition to the unprecedented loss of life, Europe's infrastructure (i.e., transportation systems, mines, industries, etc.) had been damaged or destroyed. Russia all but withdrew from participation in the European economy. The division of eastern and central Europe into a multitude of small states broke up a trade region that had been unified by Germany and Austria-Hungary, and the new political boundaries separated raw materials from the factories that used them. Railway systems were subjected to management by two or more nations, and customs barriers appeared where none had been before.

Patterns of international trade also changed. The United States had become less dependent on European production and begun to compete with Europe's industries. In the markets of Europe's colonies and former colonies decline and slowed postwar growth further lessened demand for European goods. Since the combatant nations had financed the war by selling many of their foreign investments, European influence on the world economy diminished, and the United States and Japan began to penetrate markets in Latin America and Asia that European producers and traders had previously dominated.

New Roles for Government and Labor

In every country, labor unions had supported wartime production by ensuring that workers cooperated with government. The loyalty of union members had been rewarded with higher wages and the admission of their union leaders to government councils. The links established between organized labor and various national governments dispelled the aura of internationalism that had characterized the prewar labor movement. These ties also made it impossible for government ever again to ignore labor's demands. This was one of the more significant political changes wrought by the war.

Since conditions for workers seemed to improve while those of the middle class stagnated or declined, the middle class grew suspicious of labor's new role and of socialist political parties. Once the vanguard of the liberal revolution, the middle classes became conservative and worked throughout the 1920s to fend off advances by the working classes. The new conservatism of the middle class deepened as fear of Bolshevism spread across the Continent.

The Soviet Experiment Begins

Russia's Bolshevik Revolution established the most extensive and durable of the twentieth-century authoritarian governments that came to power in the wake of World War I. The Soviet Union's Communist Party, the greatest single factor shaping the history of Europe in the twentieth century, retained power from 1917 until the end of 1991. It was neither a mass party nor a nationalistic one. In its early days, its membership rarely exceeded 1 percent of the Russian population, and for years following 1917 it faced widespread domestic opposition.

Communists regarded their revolution in Russia not as an event confined to that nation's history

Anxiety over the spread of the Bolshevik Revolution was a fundamental factor of European politics during the 1920s and 1930s. Images like this Soviet portrait of Lenin as a heroic revolutionary conjured fears among people in the rest of Europe of a political force determined to overturn their social, political, and economic institutions. Gemalde von A. M. Gerassimow, *Lenin as Agitator*/Bildarchiv Preussischer Kulturbesitz

but as the beginning of a new epoch in the history of humanity. The leaders of the Soviet Union believed they had a duty to export the ideology and doctrines of communism, and opposition to their efforts shaped the foreign policies of other Western nations for most of the century.

War Communism

The Red Army, under the guidance of Leon Trotsky (1879–1940), eventually overcame the internal and foreign military opposition that was mounted to Russia's communist government. The White Russian armies, which opposed communism's Red Army, failed to organize themselves adequately, and the Allies gave them insufficient help. The military threat the White Army posed, however, helped the Bolsheviks justify authoritarian policies. A new secret police, the Cheka, was established, and Lenin declared that the Bolshevik Party was empowered as a "dictatorship of the proletariat." Political and economic administration became highly centralized, and all major decisions were made at the top. This resulted in an economic policy called War Communism that called for the revolutionary government to take over banks, the transportation system, and heavy industries. The state also confiscated grain from peasants to feed soldiers and urban workers. Resistance to these moves was vigorously suppressed.

War Communism helped the Red Army triumph and the revolution survive, but the policy generated domestic opposition to the Bolsheviks. In 1920 the party numbered only about 600,000 members. When many Russians balked at making the sacrifices demanded by central party bureaucrats, the alliance of workers and peasants the Bolsheviks claimed to represent began to break down. In 1920 and 1921 there were large strikes at many factories, peasants resisted the requisition of their grain, and in March 1921, the Baltic fleet mutinied at Kronstadt. The Red Army crushed the revolt with grave loss of life.

If the Russian proletariat resisted the Communist Party's idea of a proletariat dictatorship, by late 1920 it was also apparent that working classes in the European nations were not responding to Bolshevik invitations to join the revolution. For the time being, the Soviet Union was to be a vast island of revolutionary socialism in a global capitalist sea.

The New Economic Policy

Acknowledging reality, Lenin made a crucial strategic retreat. In March 1921, following the Kronstadt mutiny and faced with continuing peasant resistance, Lenin issued the New Economic Policy (i.e., the NEP). The government authorized private economic enterprise except in fields involving banking, heavy industry, transportation, and international commerce. The NEP was designed to court the peasants (whom Lenin believed held the key to the success of the revolution) by permitting them to sell surplus grain on the open market.

After 1921 the countryside quieted down, and a more secure food supply seemed assured for the cities. Free enterprise flourished in light industry and domestic retail trade, but there were virtually no consumer goods for entrepreneurs to buy with the money they made. By 1927 the NEP had restored industrial production to its 1913 level, but it had also transformed Russia into a land of discontented small family farmers, private shop owners, and businesspeople.

After the Bolshevik Revolution there were many shortages in the cities of the new Soviet Union. This painting shows citizens buying and selling goods in a Moscow street market in the early 1920s. Alfredo Dagli Orti/Bildarchiv Preussischer Kulturbesitz

Stalin Versus Trotsky

The NEP caused sharp disputes within the Politburo, the Communist Party's highest governing committee. Some members saw it as a partial return to capitalism and, therefore, a betrayal of Marxist principles. So long as Lenin was in control, unity was maintained. In 1922, however, he suffered the stroke that led to his death in 1924.

The power vacuum created by his disappearance invited an intense struggle for leadership within the party. Two factions emerged—one led by Trotsky and the other by Joseph Stalin (1879–1953), general secretary of the party since 1922. Lenin had voiced reservations about both men but was especially critical of Stalin. Stalin, however, had attracted a large following within the party and won control of its day-to-day management.

The issue between Trotsky and Stalin was leadership of the party, but it was cast as a dispute about Russia's path toward industrialization and the future of the communist revolutionary movement. Trotsky, representing a left wing, urged rapid industrialization financed through the expropriation of farm production. He wanted to collectivize agriculture and make the peasants pay for industrialization. He also argued that the revolution in Russia could succeed only if similar revolutions took place elsewhere, for Russia needed the help of sympathetic nations to expand its economy. As Trotsky's influence waned, he also became a late, if self-interested, convert to principles of free speech. He demanded that party members be allowed to criticize government and party policies.

Stalin led the right-wing faction that opposed Trotsky, and Nikolai Bukharin (1888–1938), the editor of the official party paper, *Pravda (Truth)*, formulated its ideology. Given the uncertain economic outlook of the mid-1920s, Stalin's people recommended continuation of Lenin's NEP: that is, relatively slow industrialization, decentralized economic planning, and tolerance of modest free enterprise and small landholdings.

Stalin, the son of a poor family, had not spent time in western Europe as had other early Bolshevik leaders. He was much less intellectual and internationalist in his outlook than they, and he was much more brutal. As commissar of nationalities, his treatment of recalcitrant groups within Russia after the revolution had shocked Lenin—though not enough for Lenin to dismiss him. As the party's general secretary, a post many of his colleagues disdained as a clerical position, Stalin was able to build a power base within the party's bureaucracy. He was not a brilliant writer or an effective public speaker, but he was a master of the crucial, if dull, details of party structure. His control of admission to the party and promotion within it won him the support of the lower levels of the party apparatus in his fights with other leaders.

In 1924, in opposition to Trotsky, Stalin articulated the doctrine of "socialism in one country." It stated that socialism could be achieved in Russia without support from revolutions elsewhere. Stalin, thus, nationalized what had been an international Marxist movement while cunningly using his control of the Central Committee to edge out Trotsky and his supporters. By 1927 Trotsky had been expelled from the party and exiled to Siberia. In 1929 he left Russia for Mexico and was murdered there—presumably by Stalin's agents—in 1940. Trotsky's defeat left Stalin in unchallenged control of the Soviet state, but it remained to be seen where he would take it.

The Third International

The Bolshevik Revolution posed a challenge to the socialist parties in western Europe. Most of them were Marxist in ideology, but not revolutionary. They believed that the lot of the proletariat would be improved gradually by evolutionary means, and they were willing to take part in parliamentary governments. The Bolsheviks rejected this and forced the west European social democrats to rethink their place in the world of international socialism.

In 1919 the Soviet communists founded the Third International (known as the *Comintern*) to coordinate the European socialist movement and bring it under Bolshevik control. The Comintern aimed at making Lenin's version of socialism the rule for all socialist parties outside the Soviet Union. In 1920 the Comintern imposed something called the Twenty-one Conditions on any socialist party that wished to join its organization. The conditions required acknowledgment of leadership from Moscow, rejection of revisionist socialism, repudiation of previous socialist leaders, and adoption of the Communist Party name. Their intent was to put an end to democratic socialism and its accommodation of gradual reform and parliamentary government.

Debate about the conditions split socialist ranks and led to the rise of separate communist and social democratic parties in many European countries. Communist parties modeled themselves after the Soviet party and took orders from Moscow. The social democratic parties retained their independence and pursued reform agendas by adopting the strategies of liberal parliamentary politics. Throughout the 1920s and early 1930s, the communists and socialists fought each other more intensely than they fought either capitalists or political conservatives.

The Comintern unintentionally helped fascist and Nazi parties recruit supporters. It is difficult to exaggerate the fear aroused in Europe in the 1920s and 1930s by Soviet rhetoric and Communist Party activity, and it was to the advantage of conservative and right-wing political groups to stir up as much popular anxiety as possible. The communist parties that were active in Western nations gave right-wing politicians a convenient target that they could justly accuse of seeking to overthrow the governments of their respective homelands. Right-wing politicians could also cast suspicion on democratic socialist parties as allies of communist insurgents. On the other side, the divisions that existed in Europe's leftist political parties diminished their power to fight back and oppose extreme right-wing groups.

The Fascist Experiment in Italy

It was in Italy that fear of Bolshevism produced the first western European experiment in political authoritarianism: fascism. The term derives from the *Fasci di Combattimento* ("Bands of Combat"), which were founded in 1919 in Milan by Benito Mussolini (1883–1945). Although a number of the right-wing dictatorships that appeared in Europe between the wars have been labeled *fascist,* authorities find it hard to formulate a precise definition for the word. Most fascist states were antidemocratic, anti-Marxist, antiparliamentary, often anti-Semitic, and usually intensely nationalistic. They opposed the spread of Bolshevism and claimed to want to make the world safe for the small property owners of the middle class. Fascists rejected parliamentary politics, for they believed that political parties sacrificed national interests to achieve in-

dividual petty objectives. By uniting citizens in pursuit of some great national project, fascists hoped to transcend Marxism's class conflicts and liberalism's party struggles. Fascist governments were usually single-party dictatorships that employed terrorism and police surveillance to guarantee absolute loyalty to the state. Unlike the small Communist Party's role in leading the Soviet Union, mass political movements empowered fascist states.

The Rise of Mussolini

Mussolini recruited his first followers among Italy's war veterans, many of whom believed that the Paris peace conference had cheated Italy—particularly by denying it control of the city of Fiume at the northern end of the Adriatic Sea. These people also suffered economically from the effects of postwar inflation, and they feared the spread of socialism.

Mussolini was born the son of a blacksmith, and he worked as a schoolteacher and a day laborer before entering politics. He was initially drawn to socialism, and by 1912 he was editor of the movement's newspaper *Avanti* (*Forward*). In 1914, however, he broke with the socialists to support Italy's entry into the war on the side of the Allies. He established his own paper, *Il Popolo d'Italia* (*The People of Italy*), served in the army, and was wounded. In effect, he switched from the socialist fight for the betterment of the proletariat to the nationalist struggle to strengthen Italy's ineffective liberal government.

By 1919 Mussolini had become simply one among many politicians, and his *Fasci* organization was one among many small groups jockeying for position in Italy. Mussolini was, however, a gifted opportunist, and he changed his ideas and principles to suit every new occasion. He considered action more important than thought or ideology, and his chief objective was political survival.

POSTWAR POLITICAL TURMOIL   Postwar Italian politics was a muddle. The Italian Parliament had virtually ceased to function during the war, and many Italians were disillusioned with their government—believing that it had failed at the Paris peace conference to win for Italy the respect and land it deserved. In 1919 a band of Italian nationalists, led by author Gabriele D'Annunzio (1863–1938), showed how a private military force could succeed where government failed. They occupied the disputed city of Fiume, and the Italian army that finally drove them out seemed to many people to be less patriotic than D'Annunzio and his men.

Between 1919 and 1921 Italy experienced considerable internal turmoil. There were industrial strikes. Workers occupied factories, and peasants seized uncultivated land from large estates. The nation's Parliament demonstrated no capacity for dealing with the situation. It was dominated by two parties that both claimed to represent the working and agrarian classes: a Socialist Party (the split between socialists and communists had not yet taken place) and a new Catholic Popular Party. Since neither group would cooperate with the other, Parliament deadlocked. Many Italians feared that the combination of social upheaval and political paralysis would result in a communist revolution.

EARLY FASCIST ORGANIZATION At first, Mussolini endorsed factory occupations and land seizures. But when he realized that Italians of the upper and middle classes, who were pressured by inflation and fearful of losing their property, were more concerned about order than vague concepts of social justice, he reversed himself. He and his fascists stepped in and took charge wherever the government failed to act. They formed local squads of terrorists who disrupted Socialist Party meetings, beat up socialist leaders, and intimidated socialist supporters. They attacked strikers and farm workers and protected strikebreakers. Conservative land and factory owners were grateful, and officers and institutions of the law simply ignored crimes committed by fascist squads. By early 1922 intimidation had won fascists control of local governments in much of northern Italy. In the election of 1921 Italian voters sent Mussolini and thirty-four of his followers to the national Chamber of Deputies.

In October 1922, the fascists, dressed in their characteristic black shirts, led a march on Rome. King Victor Emmanuel III (r. 1900–1946), fearing a confrontation, ensured a fascist seizure of power by refusing to sign a decree authorizing the army to intervene. The cabinet resigned in protest, and on October 29, the monarch asked Mussolini to become prime minister. The next day Mussolini took the train from Milan to Rome, and by the time his marchers arrived, he was the head of the government.

Although Mussolini technically had acquired office by legal means, his party did not hold a majority of votes in the government. His appointment was the result of months of terrorist intimidation. The politicians of opposing parties, whose ineptitude had given Mussolini his chance, were not alarmed. He had developed allies within the political system, and many of his opponents assumed that his ministry, like others since 1919, would be brief. They failed to comprehend what he was.

The Fascists in Power

Mussolini owed his success to the impotence of his rivals, his effective use of his office, his power over the masses, and his sheer ruthlessness. He employed propaganda to great effect to build a cult of personality. His intelligence and oratorical skill enabled him to hold his own with large crowds and prominent individuals, and many responsible Italians credited him with saving Italy from Bolshevism. On November 23, 1922, the king and Parliament commissioned him to restore order and granted him dictatorial authority for one year. Mussolini used this opportunity to put fascists in as many offices as possible.

REPRESSION OF OPPOSITION In 1924 Mussolini had Parliament change the election law to end the confusion created by weak coalition governments. Previously, a party's representation in the Chamber of Deputies reflected the portion of the popular vote it had won. The new election law gave the party that had the largest popular vote (if at least 25 percent) two-thirds of the seats. In the election of 1924, the fascists took control of the Chamber of Deputies and used their majority to end parliamentary government and authorized Mussolini to rule by decree. In 1926 all other political parties were dissolved, and Italy became a single-party dictatorial state.

PARALLEL STRUCTURE OF PARTY AND GOVERNMENT Mussolini strengthened his regime by creating a party organization to correspond with each government institution. By the late 1920s the Grand Council of the party, which Mussolini controlled, had become the organ of the state that

In October 1922, Mussolini's fascist followers staged a highly publicized march on Rome. Although Mussolini had been asked to form a government shortly before the arrival of his followers, fascists created a myth that their march was what had put him into office. This picture, taken from the Victor Emmanuel monument in Rome, shows the gathering of the fascists at the base of the monument. Once in power Mussolini would often make speeches from a balcony in this square.
Hulton Getty/Liaison Agency, Inc.

decided who could stand for election to the Chamber of Deputies and which issues the chamber could vote on. The outlawing of other political parties forced citizens to look to the fascists in their community for political favors.

Fascists also made sure people knew the risk of opposition. Fascist terrorist squads became a government militia. Late in 1924 they murdered Giacomo Matteotti (1885–1924), a prominent noncommunist socialist member of Parliament who had criticized Mussolini and exposed the criminality of the fascist movement. In protest, most opposition deputies withdrew from the Chamber of Deputies. That tactic only gave Mussolini a freer hand.

ACCORD WITH THE VATICAN   In the 1860s seizure of papal lands by Italy's armies of unification had opened a rift between church and state, and from 1870 on the popes had remained secluded in the Vatican. Mussolini negotiated the Lateran Accord of February 1929 to lend respectability to his authoritarian regime by healing the long-standing breach between the church and the Italian state. The pope was recognized as the temporal ruler of Vatican City. The state agreed to compensate the papacy for the territory it had confiscated. Catholicism was recognized as the religion of the nation. Church property was exempted from taxes, and the church was given legal jurisdiction over marriage.

Joyless Victors

France and Great Britain (with the help of the United States) had won the war. Britain had suffered almost no physical damage. France had, but still emerged as the strongest military power on the Continent. Both nations had lost vast numbers of young men. Their economies had been weakened and their power overseas diminished. Unlike Russia and Italy, neither experienced a revolution or a shift to authoritarian government, but both faced problems.

France: The Search for Security

In France the 1920s were marked by frequent changes of ministries and drift in domestic policy. Between the end of the war and January 1933, France was governed by no fewer than twenty-seven different cabinets. For five years following the Paris settlement, France's policy was to keep Germany weak by enforcing clauses in the Versailles treaty and by building a system of eastern alliances to replace France's prewar tie with Russia.

NEW ALLIANCES   In 1920 and 1921 three eastern states that feared revision of the Versailles treaty—Czechoslovakia, Romania, and Yugoslavia—formed the Little Entente. France allied with them and with Poland, whose independence also depended on the Paris settlement. This new system of eastern pacts was far weaker than the old Franco-Russian alliance, for the new states were no match for Russia and were neither united nor reliable. Poland and Romania were more concerned about Russia than France's enemy, Germany, and fear of Hungary primarily drove the Little Entente. If Germany threatened any one of these allies, it was unlikely that the endangered state could depend on the others for help.

Despite its weakness, the formation of this alliance heightened anxieties in the two excluded powers, Germany and the Soviet Union. In 1922, while the European states were holding an economic conference at Genoa, the Russians and the Germans met at nearby Rapallo to sign a treaty of their own. Although the treaty had no secret political or military clauses, the Germans did agree to help train the Russian army (thus giving German soldiers an opportunity to improve their skills in the use of tanks and planes). The treaty increased suspicions about Germany's intentions and prompted France to take action.

QUEST FOR REPARATIONS   Early in 1923 the Allies declared Germany to be in technical default of its reparations payments, and Raymond Poincaré (1860–1934), France's nationalistic prime minister, decided to teach the Germans a lesson. On Jan-

uary 11, 1923, he sent a French army to occupy the Ruhr mining and manufacturing district until the reparations were paid. The German government responded by ordering a general strike. Poincaré then recruited French civilians to run the mines and railroads, and France ultimately prevailed. Germany paid, but so did France. The English were alienated by France's heavy-handed policy and developed increased sympathy for Germany, and the cost of the Ruhr occupation vastly increased inflation and hurt the economies of both France and Germany.

In 1924 Poincaré's conservative ministry yielded to a coalition of leftist parties, the *Cartel des Gauches* led by Edouard Herriot (1872–1957). The new cabinet recognized the Soviet Union and adopted a more conciliatory policy toward Germany. Aristide Briand (1862–1932), foreign minister for the remainder of the decade, championed the League of Nations and urged the French not to think that their military power gave them the ability to control foreign affairs throughout Europe.

When the value of the franc fell sharply in 1926, Poincaré and the conservatives returned to office, and for the rest of the 1920s, the conservatives remained in power. France's economy flourished until 1931, a longer period of prosperity than enjoyed by any other nation.

Great Britain: Economic Confusion

World War I changed Britain's politics but not its political system. In 1918 Parliament increased the electorate by extending the vote to men at age twenty-one and to women at age thirty. (It was ten more years before women won equal treatment.) The war helped dispel the radical image of the Labour Party, for the war effort was directed by a coalition cabinet that included Labour alongside Liberal and Conservative ministers. Liberal Prime Minister Herbert Asquith (1852–1928) had presided over the cabinet until 1916, when disagreements over management of the war caused him to be ousted by fellow Liberal David Lloyd George (1863–1945). Lloyd George decided to maintain coalition government until the tasks of peacemaking and domestic reconstruction were finished.

The British economy was depressed throughout the 1920s. Unemployment never dipped below 10 percent and often hovered near 11 percent (meaning that at least a million people were always without work). Government assistance to the unemployed and to widows and orphans increased, but there was no expansion of the number of jobs available. From 1922 onward, life on the "dole" with little hope of employment became the fate of thousands of poor British families.

THE FIRST LABOUR GOVERNMENT   In December 1923, King George V (r. 1910–1936) asked Ramsay MacDonald (1866–1937) to form the first Labour ministry in British history. The Labour Party was socialistic in its platform but democratic and distinctly nonrevolutionary. MacDonald's version of socialism owed little, if anything, to Marx. He advocated social reform, not nationalization of industry. He also understood that the most important task facing his government was proving to the nation that the Labour Party was responsible. His nine months in office achieved that, and the respect he won for Labour led to the decline of the Liberal Party. The Liberal Party continued to exist, but the bulk of its voters drifted into either the Conservative or the Labour camps.

THE GENERAL STRIKE OF 1926   The Labour government fell in the autumn of 1924, and the Conservatives governed until 1929. The stagnant economy remained the nation's chief concern. Business and political leaders believed that all would be well if they could restore prewar conditions of trade. This, they believed, required a return to the gold standard, which the government decreed in 1925. By setting the conversion rate for the pound too high against other currencies, however, they raised the price of British goods to foreign customers.

The managers of Britain's industries tried to restore the competitiveness of their products on the world market by cutting wages to lower production costs. Trouble erupted first in the coal industry, which was inefficient and poorly managed and had a long history of unruly labor relations. Negotiations soon broke down, and the coal miners went on strike. Sympathetic workers in other industries supported them with a general strike that lasted for nine days in May 1926. In the end the workers capitulated, for high levels of unemployment weakened the bargaining positions of their unions. After the strike, the government courted labor by erecting new housing and reforming the poor laws. Despite the economic difficulties of these years, the standard of living of most British workers, including those receiving government assistance, improved.

EMPIRE   World War I modified Britain's role as an imperial power. The right of self-determination, which Britain had claimed to be defending during the war, made it difficult to oppose liberation movements in its colonies.

The growing popularity of Mohandas Gandhi's (1869–1948) Congress Party forced the British to consider eventual self-government for India. During the 1920s India acquired the right to impose tariffs to favor its industries rather than to protect British manufacturers. British textile producers' access to the Indian market was also limited.

IRELAND   In 1914 the Irish Home Rule Bill had passed Parliament, but its implementation had been postponed until after the war. When the war dragged on, Irish nationalists decided they could not wait. On Easter Monday, 1916, they rose up in Dublin. Theirs was the only revolt staged by a national group against any government in wartime. The British suppressed it within a week but made a grave tactical blunder by executing its leaders. Overnight the rebels became national martyrs, and leadership of the nationalist cause shifted from the Irish Party in Parliament to an extremist group, *Sinn Fein* ("Ourselves Alone"). In the election of 1918 the Sinn Fein Party won all but four of the Irish parliamentary seats outside Ulster (i.e., Northern Ireland). They refused to join the Parliament at Westminster, constituted themselves as the *Dail Eireann* (i.e., Irish Parliament), and on January 21, 1919, declared Ireland's independence. The military wing of Sinn Fein established the Irish Republican Army (IRA), and a vicious guerilla war soon broke out between it and the British army.

In December 1921, secret negotiations between the two governments resulted in a treaty establishing the Irish Free State as one of the dominions of the British Commonwealth. The six counties of Ulster were granted home rule and allowed to remain part of what was now called the United Kingdom of Great Britain and Northern Ireland. But no sooner had the treaty been signed than a new civil war broke out. Moderates supported the treaty; diehards wanted a totally independent republic. The second civil war continued until 1923. In 1933 the Dail Eireann abolished the oath of allegiance to the British monarch, and the Irish Free State professed neutrality during World War II. In 1949 it declared itself the wholly independent republic of Eire.

Trials of the Successor States in Eastern Europe

France and Great Britain had much experience with democratic government. But in Germany, Poland, Austria, Czechoslovakia, and the other successor states that replaced the German, Austro-Hungarian, and Russian empires, parliaments had never exercised genuine political power. It remained to be seen whether they could handle responsibility and whether conservative groups (particularly the military) would cooperate with them.

Economic and Ethnic Pressures

It had been an article of faith among nineteenth-century liberals sympathetic to nationalism that only good could come from the demise of Austria-Hungary, the restoration of Poland, and the establishment of nation-states throughout eastern Europe. The right to self-determination was expected to guarantee popular support for the new states and make them buffers against the westward spread of Bolshevism. From the beginning, however, they were in trouble, for none of the new states had strong economies such as France and Germany had developed in the course of the nineteenth century.

The collapse of the empires that had once imposed restraint on the conduct of ethnic groups freed those groups to demand political self-determination. Majorities in the populations of the new countries refused to make compromises with minorities lest they undermine the identities of their nations, and many minorities wanted independence or union with a nation other than the one that claimed them. The recent breakup of Yugoslavia and Czechoslovakia and the present turmoil in the former Soviet Union are a continuation of this struggle—a struggle that in the period between the world wars led to the rise of authoritarian governments in all the states but Czechoslovakia.

Poland: Democracy to Military Rule

Poland, divided up by its neighbors, had disappeared from the map late in the eighteenth century. Its restoration, which was something Woodrow Wilson had urged in the Fourteen Points, proved a disappointment to liberals. The Poles' sense of national identity was too weak a bond to overcome disagreements stemming from differences in class, region, and economic self-interest. Sections of the new Poland had been governed for over a century by Germany, Russia, and Austria. Each had its own laws, administration, economy, and history of experience with electoral institutions. A vast number of tiny political parties made it difficult to form a stable parliament, and the constitution gave the executive too little power. In 1926 a military takeover led by Marshal Josef Pilsudski (1857–1935) ended the confusion. At his death, the government passed into the hands of a group of his officers.

Czechoslovakia: Successful Democratic Experiment

Czechoslovakia was the only central European nation to avoid self-imposed authoritarian government. It had unique advantages: a strong industrial base, a substantial middle class, and a tradition of liberal values. During the war Czechs and Slovaks had learned to work together, and in the person of Thomas Masaryk (1850–1937) they had a gifted leader of immense integrity and fairness. His government broke up large estates in favor of small peasant holdings and gave the country the chance to become a viable modern nation. Some of Czechoslovakia's smaller ethnic groups were, however, unhappy. Chief among these were the Germans of the Sudetenland who found themselves, thanks to the Paris peace settlement, inside the Czech borders. Rather than cooperate with the Czech Parliament, they called for German intervention.

Hungary: Turmoil and Authoritarianism

Hungary's defeat in the First World War cost it land, but Hungary achieved something it had long sought: separation from Austria. In 1919 Bela Kun (1885–1937), a communist, established a short-lived Hungarian Soviet Republic. The

Allies responded by authorizing an invasion by Romania to remove the communists. Kun's government collapsed, thousands of Hungarians were executed or imprisoned, and Hungary's landowners established a regency government headed until 1944 by Admiral Miklós Horthy (1858–1957).

Austria: Political Turmoil and Nazi Conquest

Austria's economy barely functioned, but union with Germany, which would have created a more viable economic unit, was prohibited by the Paris settlement. Throughout the 1920s the leftist Social Democrats and the conservative Christian Socialists contended for power. Both groups built small armies with which to terrorize their opponents and impress their followers.

In 1933 a Christian Socialist, Engelbert Dollfuss (1892–1934), became chancellor. He tried to steer a course between the Social Democrats and the newly emerging Nazi Party. In 1934, he outlawed all political parties except the Christian Socialists, the agrarians, and the paramilitary groups that composed his "Fatherland Front." He was shot later that year during an unsuccessful Nazi coup. Kurt von Schuschnigg (1897–1977), his successor, presided over Austria until Hitler annexed it in 1938.

Southeastern Europe: Royal Dictatorships

Yugoslavia—which, until 1929, was known as the Kingdom of the Serbs, Croats, and Slovenes—had been founded by the Corfu Agreement of 1917. Throughout the interwar period, Serbs dominated its government and clashed violently with the Croats. The Croats tended to be Roman Catholic, better educated, and accustomed to reasonably uncorrupt government. The Serbs were Orthodox, somewhat less well educated, and considered (by the Croats) to be corrupt administrators. Though each group had regions of the country that it dominated, each also had isolated enclaves in other parts of the nation for which it was concerned. In addition, Bosnia-Herzegovina had a significant Muslim population, and Slovenes, Muslims, and other minorities often played the Serbs and the Croats off against each other. Each of the political parties (except for a small Communist Party) repre-

sented an ethnic group, not the nation as a whole. In 1929, King Alexander I (r. 1921–1934), a Serb, tried to impose order by outlawing political parties, jailing popular politicians, and declaring a royal dictatorship. He was assassinated in 1934, but authoritarian government continued under a regency for his son.

Elsewhere in the Balkans, other royal dictatorships were imposed. King Carol II (r. 1930–1940) of Romania and King Boris III (r. 1918–1943) of Bulgaria endeavored to control rival ethnic groups and prevent seizure of power by extremist movements. Greece's parliamentary monarchy was plagued by military coups and calls for a republic until 1936, when General John Metaxas (1871–1941) instituted a dictatorship and dispersed Parliament.

The Weimar Republic in Germany

The Weimar Republic (which was named for the city in which its constitution was proclaimed in August 1919) embodied the hopes of German liberals. It was headed by the Social Democrats, the party that assumed power following the abdication of Kaiser William II (November 1918). The republic's acceptance of the terms of the Versailles Treaty spared Germany Allied invasion, but that won it little gratitude from the German people. They associated the republic with the disgrace and the economic hardship imposed by the treaty.

Throughout the 1920s the republic, which was responsible for implementing the Paris settlement, became an easy target for the very nationalists and military factions whose policies had caused the war. These groups blamed the republic and the socialists for Germany's defeat and the grievous consequences. All Germany's politicians shared a desire to revise the treaty, but they differed about the means. The degree of loyalty they felt to the Weimar constitution depended upon the extent to which they wanted to alter the Paris settlement with which Weimar was associated.

Constitutional Flaws

The Weimar constitution was in many respects a highly enlightened document. It guaranteed civil liberties and provided for universal suffrage and direct election of the Reichstag and the president. However, the Weimar Republic had crucial structural flaws that allowed its liberal institutions to be overthrown. A system of proportional representation made it easy for small parties to win seats in the Reichstag. Ministers were responsible to the Reichstag, but the republic's president could appoint or remove its chancellor—and in an emergency the president could declare a temporary dictatorship.

Lack of Broad Popular Support

The Weimar Republic had not been established by a popular revolution, and it failed to inspire loyalty in many Germans. Some would have preferred a constitutional monarchy. Civil servants, schoolteachers, and judges, who had previously been the Kaiser's devoted agents, distrusted the Social Democrats who dominated republican politics. The officer corps, which profoundly resented the military provisions of the Paris treaty, perpetuated the myth that the German army had surrendered on foreign soil only because it had been stabbed in the back by civilians—particularly by those who had founded the republic.

In March 1920, the right-wing *Kapp Putsch* (i.e., an armed insurrection) erupted in Berlin. Led by a civil servant and supported by army officers, the coup failed, but only after the government had fled the city and German workers had staged a general strike. When later in the month workers in the Ruhr struck, the government sent in troops. Throughout the early 1920s there were numerous assassinations or attempted assassinations of important republican leaders, and in May 1921, the Allies humiliated the republic by threatening Germany with occupation if it did not accept a preposterous reparations bill of 132 billion gold marks.

Invasion of the Ruhr and Inflation

Borrowing to finance the war and deficit spending after the war created disastrous inflation. As government bonds came due, printing presses poured forth paper money to redeem them. The general strike that German workers staged to counter France's invasion of the Ruhr in January 1923 accelerated economic decline. By November 1923, an American dollar was worth more than 800 million German marks. Money was literally not worth the paper it was printed on.

Stores refused to sell goods, and farmers withheld produce from market.

The great inflation of 1923 devastated the lives of many Germans. Middle-class savings, pensions, and insurance policies were wiped out—as were investments in government bonds. The ease with which debts and mortgages could be paid off led to speculation in land, real estate, and industry that made great fortunes for some. Union contracts allowed workers to keep up with rising prices, and farmers and food store proprietors could resort to barter. But many members of the middle and lower-middle classes were caught in the squeeze. Their desire for order and security at almost any cost contributed to Hitler's rise.

Hitler's Early Career

Adolf Hitler (1889–1945), the son of a minor Austrian customs official, originally hoped to become an artist. As a young man, he sought his fortune in Vienna. There he was supported by his widowed mother, an Austrian orphan's allowance, postcards he painted, and work as a day laborer.

During a Nazi Party rally in Nuremberg in 1927, Adolf Hitler stops his motorcade to receive the applause of the surrounding crowd. In the late 1920s, the Nazi movement was only one of many bringing strife to the Weimar Republic. Heinrich Hoffman/Bildarchiv Preussischer Kulturbesitz

George Grosz Satirizes Germany's Social and Political Elite

George Grosz, *Pillars of Society*, 1926. Bildarchiv Preussischer Kulturbesitz.

In 1926, when George Grosz painted *Pillars of Society*, the Nazi Party was small and discredited, but Grosz accurately foresaw how it would lead Germany to disaster by pandering to the greed and irrational patriotism of the nation's conservative classes. Grosz had reluctantly volunteered for service in World War I and was critical of the role Germany's government had played in provoking that conflict. Following the war he joined the Communist Party but soon became disillusioned with it and fearful of the direction in which the Weimar Republic was headed.

Grosz's painting was an indictment of Germany's political and social elites. The elderly soldier who brandishes a sword at the top of the canvas represents the imperialism of the old military aristocracy. Beneath him a leering clergyman preaches the gospel of resurgent German patriotism. At his back, the flag-bearing figure with the socialist pamphlet in his pocket represents nationalism. (The top of his head is cut off to reveal a pile of excrement where his brain should be.) At his side, the pacifist with the palm branch and the chamber pot hat is revealed to be a hypocrite by the nationalistic newspapers he carries. The most menacing figure is at the bottom of the painting, a Nazi who sports a swastika on his tie and brandishes a sword. His beer stein reminds the viewer of Hitler's abortive Beer Hall *Putsch* (Munich, 1923), but the mounted soldier who leaps from his head suggests the future into which the Nazi Party hoped to lead Germany. Late in 1932, when the Nazis were on the brink of taking power, Grosz fled to the United States, and in 1937 the Nazis featured Grosz's work in an exhibit of what they declared to be "degenerate" art.

Sources: Richard Cork, *A Bitter Truth: Avant-Garde Art and the Great War* (New Haven: Yale University Press, 1994); Bärbel Schrader and Jürgen Scheber, *The "Golden" Twenties: Art and Literature in the Weimar Republic* (New Haven: Yale University Press, 1988).

There he also became acquainted with Mayor Karl Lueger's (1844–1910) Christian Social Party, a fount of anti-Semitic ideology.

During World War I, Hitler fought in the German army, was wounded, was promoted to corporal, and was awarded the Iron Cross for bravery. The war gave him his first sense of purpose. He became a rabid German nationalist and an extreme anti-Semite. Hatred for Jews led him to oppose everything associated with Karl Marx.

After the war, Hitler settled in Munich and joined a small, nationalistic, anti-Semitic political party. In 1920 it adopted the name National Socialist German Workers' Party, which was shortened phonetically as "Nazi." The group paraded under a red and white banner with a black swastika, an ancient symbol supposedly representing Germany's "original" Aryan race. The party's platform (the *Twenty-five Points*) called for repudiation of the Versailles Treaty, unification of Austria and Germany, exclusion of Jews from German citizenship, agrarian reform, prohibition of land speculation, confiscation of war profits, state administration of giant economic cartels, and replacement of department stores with small retail shops.

Originally, the Nazis tried to compete with Marxist political parties for workers' votes by calling for nationalization of industries. When this tactic failed, the Nazis began to redefine socialism. In their minds it meant not state ownership of the means of production but subordination of all economic enterprise to the welfare of the state. The Nazis grew by appealing to every economic group that was under pressure and by tailoring their message to their audiences. Economically beleaguered war veterans were particularly responsive to their appeals.

Soon after the promulgation of the Twenty-five Points, Captain Ernst Roehm (1887–1934) created a paramilitary organization to serve the party, the *Sturmabteilung* (i.e., storm troopers) or SA. In the mid-1920s the SA adopted the uniform that caused it to be known as the "brown shirts." Until the Nazis won control of the government, the SA was their chief instrument for intimidating socialists, communists, and other opponents. A private army was a way to skirt the rearmament limitations imposed by the Paris peace settlement and to bring down the Weimar Republic. The republic had no way to control it and the similar paramilitary organizations set up by competing political groups.

On November 9, 1923, Hitler and a band of followers attempted unsuccessfully to stir up a *Putsch* at a meeting held in a beer hall in Munich. When local authorities crushed the coup, sixteen Nazis were killed and Hitler was arrested and tried for treason. The trial gave him a national forum for airing his opinions about the republic, the Versailles Treaty, the Jews, and the weakened condition of his adopted country. Sentenced to five years in prison, he served only a few months before being paroled. He passed the time dictating a book—*Mein Kampf (My Struggle)*—and devising a plan to seize political power by legal methods.

Although *Mein Kampf* was not taken seriously at the time, it outlined the key political ideas from which Hitler never swerved. Chief among these was a conviction that Germany had to expand eastward to acquire adequate "living space." This applied to central and eastern Europe (and to groups opposing Hitler within Germany) foreign policy goals and racial attitudes that had previously been promoted by German imperialism. Hitler emerged from prison still a regional politician but one who was convinced that it was his destiny to restore his nation to greatness.

The Stresemann Years

Gustav Stresemann (1878–1929), who became chancellor in August 1923, gave new life to the Weimar Republic. He abandoned the expensive policy of passive resistance in the Ruhr, and with the aid of a banker named Hjalmar Schacht (1877–1970) he introduced a new German currency. He also helped crush Hitler's abortive *Putsch* and various small communist disturbances.

In 1924 the Allies agreed to a new system of reparation payments, the Dawes Plan (named for the American banker Charles Dawes). It lowered annual payments and pegged them to fluctuations of the German economy. When the last French troops left the Ruhr in 1925 and foreign capital began to flow into Germany, employment started to rise. That year, the election to the presidency of a conservative monarchist and war hero, Field Marshal Paul von Hindenburg (1847–1934), suggested that increasing political and economic stability were reconciling conservatives to the republic.

In late November 1923, Stresemann resigned as chancellor to become foreign minister. In this

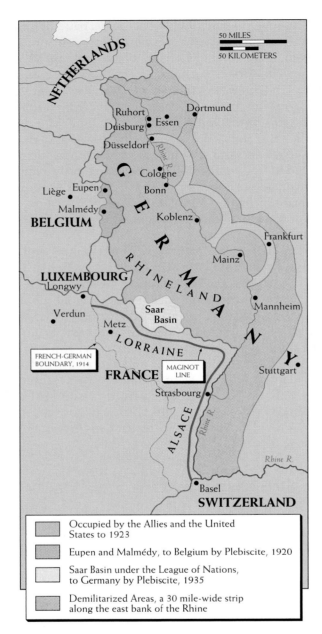

MAP 27–1 GERMANY'S WESTERN FRONTIER   *The French-Belgian-German border area between the two world wars was sensitive. Despite efforts to restrain tensions, there were persistent difficulties related to the Ruhr, Rhineland, Saar, and Eupen-Malmedy regions that necessitated strong defenses.*

role, he sought both to fulfill and to revise provisions of the Paris settlement. His goal was to recover German-speaking territories lost to Poland and Czechoslovakia and to join Austria to Germany. He hoped that a policy of accommodation would restore the respectability and the eco-

nomic stability Germany needed to win acceptance by the community of nations.

Locarno

In a spirit of conciliation, foreign secretaries Austen Chamberlain (1863–1937) for Britain and Aristide Briand (1862–1932) for France accepted Stresemann's proposal for a fresh start. This led to the Locarno Agreements of October 1925. France and Germany accepted the western frontier established by the Versailles Treaty. No agreement was reached about Germany's eastern border, but the Germans signed treaties of arbitration with Poland and Czechoslovakia. France supported German admission to the League of Nations and agreed to withdraw from the Rhineland five years ahead of schedule (i.e., in 1930).

The Locarno Agreements raised hopes across Europe. Chamberlain and Dawes received the Nobel Peace Prize in 1925 and Briand and Stresemann in 1926. In 1928 the leading European nations, Japan, and the United States signed the

Kellogg-Briand Pact, renouncing "war as an instrument of national policy."

This much optimism was not justified. France had merely acknowledged that it could not coerce Germany without help, and Britain had revealed its unwillingness to uphold the Paris settlement in the East where Germany disputed its frontiers. Many in France and Germany also opposed conciliation. When the Dawes Plan ran out in 1929, it was replaced by the Young Plan (named for American businessman Owen D. Young). Although the Young Plan lowered reparation payments, limited the term for such payments, and removed outside supervision of Germany, there was an intense outcry in Germany against the continuation of any reparations.

The Germans were far from accepting their situation, but another war was not inevitable. Europe, aided by American loans, was recovering its prosperity. A growing economy and further diplomatic adjustments might have rallied the German people behind the Weimar Republic and moderate revisionism. But the Great Depression of the 1930s turned Europe onto a quite different path.

In Perspective

At the close of the 1920s Europe appeared to be emerging from the difficulties created by World War I. Resentments over the peace settlement were apparently abating, and the major powers were cooperating. The economic and political stability that seemed to be emerging proved illusory, however, for the world was about to enter the deepest economic depression in modern history. As governments responded to the economic collapse, the search for liberty gave way to the search for security. The decade of the 1920s was a time for political experimentation—and the 1930s, for political tragedy.

REVIEW QUESTIONS

1. How did the Bolshevik Revolution pose a challenge to the rest of Europe? Why did Lenin institute the New Economic Policy? Was it successful? Could the Russian Revolution have succeeded without Lenin? How did Lenin's policies lead to divisions among Western socialist parties?

2. How did Joseph Stalin come to power? How did he overcome Trotsky's opposition?

3. What is fascism? How did the fascists succeed in obtaining power in Italy? To whom did they appeal? To what extent does Mussolini deserve the credit for his success? How did Mussolini's right-wing fascist dictatorship compare with Stalin's left-wing communist dictatorship?

4. Why were Britain and France "joyless victors" after World War I? What weakness did each have? How did World War I change British politics? What caused the decline and fall of the Liberal Party? How successful was the general strike of 1926? By what stages did Ireland win its independence?

5. What foreign policy problems did France face after the signing of the Versailles Treaty? What was the best way to guarantee security for France? Was the invasion of the Ruhr wise? Should France have signed the Locarno pact?

6. Why did all but one of the successor states in eastern and central Europe fail to establish viable democracies?

7. Could the Weimar Republic have taken root in Germany, or was its failure inevitable? Between 1919 and 1929, what were the republic's greatest strengths and weaknesses? To what extent did its fate depend more on personalities than on trends in politics and society? Why did the Versailles Treaty loom so large as an issue in Germany's domestic politics?

SUGGESTED READINGS

I. BANAC, *The National Question in Yugoslavia: Origins, History, Politics* (1984). An outstanding treatment of the reorganization of eastern European political life.

R. BESSEL, *Political Violence and the Rise of Nazism: The Storm Troopers in Eastern Germany, 1925–1934* (1984). A study of the uses of violence by the Nazis.

K. D. BRACHER, *The German Dictatorship* (1970). A comprehensive treatment of both the origins and the functioning of the Nazi movement and government.

A. BULLOCK, *Hitler: A Study in Tyranny*, rev. ed. (1964). The best biography.

L. FISCHER, *The Life of Lenin* (1964). A sound biography by an American journalist.

S. FITZPATRICK, *The Russian Revolution, 1917–1932* (1994). An excellent brief introduction.

F. FURET, *The Passing of an Illusion: The Idea of Communism in the Twentieth Century* (1995). A brilliant account of the manner in which communism shaped politics and thought outside the Soviet Union.

P. GAY, *Weimar Culture: The Outsider as Insider* (1968). A sensitive analysis of the intellectual life of Weimar.

N. GREENE, *From Versailles to Vichy: The Third Republic, 1919–1940* (1970). A useful introduction to a difficult subject.

B. HAMANN, *Hitler's Vienna: A Dictator's Apprenticeship* (1999). Probing study of the politics and society of Vienna as experienced by the young Hitler.

J. HELD, ed., *The Columbia History of Eastern Europe in the Twentieth Century* (1992). Individual essays on each of the nations.

B. JELAVICH, *History of the Balkans*, vol. 2 (1983). The standard work.

P. KENEZ, *The Birth of the Propaganda State: Soviet Methods of Mass Mobilization, 1917–1929* (1985). An examination of the manner in which the communist government inculcated popular support.

B. KENT, *The Spoils of War: The Politics, Economics, and Diplomacy of Reparations, 1918–1932* (1993). A comprehensive account of the intricacies of the reparations problem of the 1920s.

I. KERSHAW, *Hitler, 1889–1936: Hubris* (1998). The best treatment of Hitler's early life and rise to power.

B. LINCOLN, *Red Victory: A History of the Russian Civil War* (1989). An excellent narrative account.

A. MARWICK, *The Deluge: British Society and the First World War* (1965). Full of insights into both major and more subtle minor social changes.

J. F. POLLARD, *The Vatican and Italian Fascism 1929–32: A Study in Conflict* (1985). Provides the background to the Lateran Pacts.

D. P. SILVERMAN, *Reconstructing Europe After the Great War* (1982). Examines the difficulties confronted by the major powers.

Z. STERNHELL, *The Birth of Fascist Ideology: From Cultural Rebellion to Political Revolution* (1994). A controversial examination of the roots of Mussolini's ideology.

A. J. P. TAYLOR, *English History, 1914–1945* (1965). Lively and opinionated.

R. TUCKER, *Stalin as Revolutionary, 1879–1929: A Study in History and Personality* (1973). A useful and readable account of Stalin's rise to power.

E. G. WALTERS, *The Other Europe: Eastern Europe to 1945* (1988). An excellent introduction to the problems in the region.

T. WILSON, *The Downfall of the Liberal Party, 1914–1935* (1966). A close examination of the surprising demise of a political party in Britain.

R. WOHL, *The Generation of 1914* (1979). An important work that explores the effect of the war on political and social thought.

Chapter 28
Europe and the Great Depression of the 1930s

KEY TOPICS

- Financial collapse and depression in Europe
- The emergence of the National Government in Great Britain and the Popular Front in France in response to the political pressures caused by the depression
- The Nazi seizure of power, the establishment of a police state, and the imposition of racial laws in Germany
- Planned industrialism, agricultural collectivization, and purges in the Soviet Communist Party and army under Stalin

Europe did not share the economic boom that made the 1920s a "roaring" decade for the United States, for the economies of the European nations did not fully recover from World War I. The Great Depression that began when the boom ended in 1929 was the most severe slump ever experienced by capitalist nations. Business and political leaders despaired at the failure of the market's mechanisms to restore prosperity, and Marxists rejoiced that the downfall of capitalism was at hand.

Toward the Great Depression

Three factors heightened the severity and duration of the Great Depression: (1) the financial difficulties created by World War I and the subsequent peace settlement, (2) a crisis in production and distribution of goods on the world market, and (3) a failure of the United States and its European trading partners to cooperate.

The Financial Tailspin

The debts European nations incurred during World War I inflated their currencies, and the demand for consumer and industrial goods that the return of peacetime unleashed drove prices still higher. Price and wage increases subsided after 1921, but nations found it difficult to maintain the value of their currencies. The German financial disaster of 1923 and its specter of uncontrolled inflation explain why most governments refused, when the depression struck, to try to stimulate their economies by running budget deficits.

REPARATIONS AND WAR DEBTS   French and American politics regarding reparation payments and international war-debt settlements complicated the international economic scene. France had paid reparations following its defeats in 1815 and 1871, and now that it was a victor it wanted reparations to finance its postwar recovery. The United States was no less determined to be repaid for the loans it had made to its allies, who were also indebted to one another. Most of the Allies hoped to discharge these obligations by demanding that Germany pay them as reparations.

Reparations obligations and war debts impeded capital investment and thereby hindered business expansion and international trade. Since the volatile situation encouraged currency speculation that siphoned off more of the capital needed to fund productive enterprises, governments placed controls on their currencies. They also imposed high tariffs to curtail importation of foreign goods. An unfavorable balance of trade meant that a nation was losing money it needed to pay its war debts. The financial muddle that resulted from all these policies hurt trade, production, and employment.

AMERICAN INVESTMENTS   In 1924 the Dawes Plan renegotiated the sums demanded from Germany as reparations and smoothed debt repayments to the United States. Private American capital then began to flow to Europe (especially to Germany), and this created a short burst of prosperity in Europe after 1925. In 1928, however, the booming New York stock market began

to siphon money away from European investments, and virtually unregulated financial speculation led to Wall Street's crash in October, 1929. U.S. banks had lent customers large amounts of money to invest in the stock market. When the crash made it impossible for banks to recover these loans, banks failed and all kinds of credit diminished or disappeared. Little American capital remained for investment in Europe, and a shortage of capital prevented renewal of loans already made to Europeans.

THE END OF REPARATIONS   The shortage of American loans contributed to a financial crisis in Europe. In May 1931, a major bank, the Viennese Kreditanstalt, collapsed. Government intervention saved Germany's banking system, but Germany could not make its next scheduled reparation payment.

In June 1931, American President Herbert Hoover announced a one-year moratorium on payments of all international debts. This struck a blow to France's economy, which relied on German reparations, but France had little choice but to go along. Germany's economy had all but collapsed, and it was clear that Germany could not pay. In the summer of 1932 the Lausanne Conference ended the era of reparations. Debts owed the United States were settled either through small token payments or declarations of default. This did not, however, restore stability.

Problems in Agricultural Commodities

Turmoil in the financial markets was accompanied by a downturn in production and trade. In the 1920s Europe's capacity to produce goods began to exceed the market for them. This led to factory closings and unemployment. As improved methods of farming, new crop species, expanded tillage, and better transportation increased the world supply of grain, wheat prices also fell to record lows. Initially consumers benefitted, but the collapse in grain prices meant lower incomes for European farmers at a time when higher wages were raising the cost of the industrial goods they used. Farmers curtailed purchases and began to have difficulty paying off their mortgages and annual business loans.

Countries tried to protect their domestic grain markets by imposing tariffs on imports. This disrupted trade and may have made things worse. As production outstripped demand and prices plummeted, governments tried to sustain farming by buying agricultural commodities. Government-held reserves soon rose to record levels, and farmers in underdeveloped nations in Asia, Africa, and Latin America could not compete and make enough money to buy finished goods from industrial Europe.

Turmoil in the international agricultural and money markets caused Europe's industries, which depended on foreign customers, to stagnate. Unemployment spread from heavy industries to those producing finished goods. Persistent unemployment in Great Britain and Germany during the 1920s meant that domestic markets in those countries were already shrinking. Attempts to restrain spending by governments whose tax bases were declining further weakened domestic demand. All these factors interacted to deepen and extend the Great Depression.

Depression and Government Policy

During the Great Depression people with work always well outnumbered the unemployed, and there was economic expansion—particularly in new industries, such as automobiles, radios, synthetics, and service fields. But the general downturn made everyone feel insecure. People in

nearly all walks of life feared that it was only a matter of time before they faced poverty or reduced circumstances.

The governments of the late 1920s and the early 1930s were not well suited to deal with these problems. Orthodox economic theory called for governments in this situation to cut spending to prevent inflation and to wait for market mechanisms to regulate the economy and restore prosperity. In 1936 John Maynard Keynes's (1883–1946) *General Theory of Employment, Interest, and Money* challenged this view and argued that governments could spend their way out of the Depression. But even before that idea took hold, governments across Europe had begun to respond to demands from their electorates to interfere with the economy as never before.

Confronting the Great Depression in the Democracies

Great Britain: The National Government

The Great Depression ended the business-as-usual attitude that had characterized politics in Great Britain and France during the late 1920s. In 1929 a second minority Labour government,

Crowds gathered on Wall Street in New York on October 29, 1929, the day the stock market crashed. The Great Depression in the United States dried up American capital previously available for investment in Europe. Brown Brothers

Art & the West

René Magritte, The Human Condition, Exploring Illusion and Reality

*T*he *Human Condition*, which René Magritte (1898–1967) painted in 1933, is a product of the surrealist movement in modern art. Surrealist painters depict things realistically but place those things in unreal relationships. Surrealist art functions much like a dream in that it provides an encounter with an unreal reality that stirs the viewer's subconscious. It confounds rational analysis. In *The Human Condition* a painting of a landscape stands before a window looking out on the scene the painting depicts. The borders between the painting and the landscape are so problematic that it is impossible to decide where reality lies. The painting within the painting functions as a window within a window presenting a view of a world where it is impossible to decide what is image and what is reality.

Magritte's work was influenced by Freudian psychoanalytic theory and reflects the general loss of confidence in absolutes and certainties that began to spread throughout Western societies in the early twentieth century. His painting seems to imply that uncertainty itself—ignorance of what is reality and what is illusion—is the fundamental human condition.

René Magritte (Belgian, 1898–1967), *The Human Condition, (La Condition Humaine)*, 1933 Oil on canvas, 1.000 × .810 × .016. © 2000 Board of Trustees, National Gallery of Art, Washington 1933, Gift of the Collectors Committee © 1998 C. Herscovici, Brussels/Artists Rights Society (ARS), New York

headed by Ramsay MacDonald, took office. As the number of Britain's unemployed passed 2.5 million in 1931, the ministry split over what to do. MacDonald believed that the budget should be slashed, government salaries reduced, and unemployment benefits cut. This was a bleak program for a Labour government, and many government ministers resisted. The prime minister responded by requesting the resignation of the entire cabinet.

MacDonald arranged for a meeting with King George V, at which he was expected to announce the fall of his government. But instead of resigning, MacDonald agreed to form a coalition cabinet (the National Government) that included Labour, Conservatives, and Liberals. The facade of a coalition created the impression that there was a political consensus, and this helped the government impose unpleasant measures.

The National Government devised three programs to fight the Depression. It tried to balance its budget by raising taxes, cutting benefits to the unemployed and the elderly, and lowering government salaries. In September 1931, it took Britain off the gold standard and let the value of the pound fall about 30 percent. (This was expected to stimulate exports by lowering the price of British goods abroad.) In 1932 Parliament passed the Import Duties Bill. It required that importers of goods that originated outside the empire pay a 10 percent *ad valorem* tariff (i.e., not a fixed import fee but a charge of 10 percent of the value of each item brought into the country). The hallmarks of a century of British commercial policy—the gold standard and free trade—were abandoned.

The National Government's program had some success. Great Britain avoided the banking crises that hit other countries. Government efforts to keep interest rates down encouraged borrowing for home mortgages and fostered the largest private housing boom in British history. This created a market that helped related industries. In 1934 Britain became the first nation to restore and exceed its 1929 level of production, and by 1937 the number of its jobless had fallen to just below 1.5 million.

Although Britain's economy was stagnant at the start of the Great Depression and remained so after the crisis had passed, Britain's political system was never seriously challenged. There were demonstrations by the unemployed, but social insurance kept them from becoming too desperate. The National Government placated the populace by seeming to steer a middle course between the extremes of both the Labour and the Conservative parties.

France: The Popular Front

France's Great Depression began later but lasted longer than Britain's. The economic slide did not affect the French economy until 1931. Although wages then went down, unemployment was not a major problem. Rarely were more than 500,000 French workers without jobs, but relations between labor and management were nonetheless tense. The government raised tariffs to protect French goods and French agriculture. These measures sustained the domestic market, but they did little to combat industrial stagnation.

The first political fallout from the Great Depression was the election of another Radical coalition government in 1932. The earlier Radical government's policies had allowed rampant inflation to erupt in 1924. This administration decided to pursue a deflationary program, but in the same year that the new ministry took office, the reparation payments upon which the French economy depended stopped. As the economic crisis mounted, the political situation became increasingly difficult.

RIGHT-WING VIOLENCE In addition to the legitimate government represented by the Chamber of Deputies, right-wing groups with authoritarian tendencies forced themselves onto the political scene. These included the *Action Française*, founded in the wake of the Dreyfus affair, and a veterans' organization, the *Croix de Feu* ("Cross of Fire"). More than 2 million people joined these and similar groups. Some advocated monarchy; others wanted military rule. All opposed parliamentary government, socialism, and communism. Their eagerness to end party politics and unite all citizens in pursuit of glory for their nation suggests a certain sympathy with the spirit of the fascists and Nazis.

On February 6, 1934, a large demonstration by right-wing groups was staged in Paris. When the crowd attempted to march on the Chamber of Deputies, violence erupted. Fourteen demonstrators were killed; scores were injured. This was the largest disturbance in Paris since the Commune of 1871, and it brought down the Radical ministry of Édouard Daladier (1884–1970). A national coalition government composed of all living former premiers was formed, but the demonstration served chiefly to warn the parties of the left that a right-wing coup might succeed in France.

EMERGENCE OF SOCIALIST-COMMUNIST COOPERATION   Between 1934 and 1936, the French left worked at making peace within its own ranks. In 1920 the Comintern had split the French Socialists, who were led by Léon Blum (1872–1950), from French Communists. Stalin's fear of Hitler, however, made cooperation between the two groups possible. In July 1935 the left-wing parties overcame their mutual suspicions and united to form the Popular Front. Its purpose was to preserve the republic and press for social reform.

The election of 1936 gave the Popular Front a majority in the Chamber of Deputies and, for the first time in France's history, enabled the Socialists, as the largest single party, to form a cabinet. Léon Blum, who assumed the premiership on June 5, was a Jewish intellectual and humanitarian who opposed the communist version of socialism. He believed that socialism was compatible with democratic, parliamentary government.

Before the Popular Front came to power, strikes had begun to spread throughout French industry, and the Blum government was immediately challenged by spontaneous work stoppages. Over 500,000 workers staged sit-ins at their factories. These were the most extensive labor disturbances in the history of the Third Republic, and they alarmed a conservative business community that had already been frightened by the Popular Front's election.

Blum moved swiftly. On June 8, he announced an accord that restructured relations between labor and management. Wages were raised 7 percent to 15 percent, depending on the job involved. Employers were required to recognize unions and accept collective bargaining. The forty-hour week was established, and workers got annual two-week paid vacations. Blum hoped that better labor-management relations would reduce worker hostility to France's social and political institutions and help the economy by increasing domestic consumer demand.

Blum also raised the salaries of civil servants and instituted a program of public works. Government loans were extended to small industry.

Spending on armaments was increased, and some armament industries were nationalized. A National Wheat Board was set up to manage the production and sale of grain. In the autumn of 1936, international monetary pressure forced Blum to devalue the franc, and he did so again in the spring of 1937. This enraged the conservative banking and business community, and in March 1937, they pressured the ministry to end Blum's reform program. The following June, Blum resigned. The Popular Front ministry held on until April 1938, when it was replaced by a Radical ministry under Daladier.

French industrial production did not return to 1929 levels until 1939, and citizens from all walks of life had reason to wonder if the republic was worth preserving. Business leaders accused it of being inefficient and too subject to socialist pressures. The left remained divided in its opinion, and the right hated republics in principle. When the time came to defend the republic in 1940, too many French citizens doubted whether it was worth the trouble.

Germany: The Nazi Seizure of Power

Germany's Nazi (National Socialist) Party was the most important of the political movements to emerge from the turmoil of the Great Depression. In the late 1920s, the Nazis were a small group that could not seriously contend for power in the Weimar Republic. The change in their political fortunes was wrought by their successful exploitation of fears created by the Depression.

Depression and Political Deadlock

The prosperity of Weimar Germany was undermined when supplies of foreign (especially American) capital dried up in 1928. The coalition of center parties and Social Democrats that headed the republic that year was broken up by disputes over economic policy. Social Democrats wanted spending on unemployment insurance and social programs, while conservative parties, frightened by memories of 1923's rampant inflation, insisted on cuts to balance the budget. President von Hindenburg appointed Heinrich Brüning (1885–1970) chancellor to break the deadlock in the Reichstag, and Brüning governed through emergency presidential decrees, as authorized by Article 48 of the Weimar constitution. Since divisions among parties prevented Parliament from overriding his orders, the Weimar Republic became an authoritarian regime.

As unemployment rose (from 2,258,000 in March 1930 to over 6 million in March 1932) and as government succumbed to gridlock, the desperate masses turned to extremist leaders. In the election of 1928, the Nazis had won only 12 Reichstag seats and the Communists 54, but by 1930 the Nazis held 107 seats and the Communists 77. The Nazis pursued power by legally campaigning for office while simultaneously resorting to terror and intimidation. The unemployed hastened to join the storm troopers (SA), who grew from 100,000 in 1930 to almost 1 million in 1933. The SA destroyed decency and civility in political life by viciously attacking opposition parties. The Nazis staged mass rallies resembling religious revivals to recruit a following. Their appeal to the pride and frustration of the German nation won them the support not just of the people in the streets, but of intellectuals and the leaders of business, the military, and the media.

Hitler Comes to Power

Brüning survived in the chancellor's office for two years. But when the economy did not improve, Hitler seized the opportunity to contest his control of the government by challenging Hindenburg for the presidency. In the election of 1932, Hitler got 30.1 percent of the vote—enough to force a runoff. In the second election, he polled 36.8 percent. Hindenburg survived in office but decided to replace Brüning. His new chancellor, Franz von Papen (1878–1969), was one of a small group of extremely conservative advisers on whom the 83-year-old president had become dependent. Given the continuing paralysis in the

Hitler's mastery of the techniques of mass politics and propaganda—including huge staged rallies like this one in 1938—was an important factor in his rise to power.
Bildarchiv Preussischer Kulturbesitz

Reichstag, these men virtually controlled the government.

Since the Nazis were the only party with mass support, Papen wanted to win Hitler's cooperation but avoid giving him any real power. He hoped to convince Hitler that the Nazis could not succeed without the help of the Hindenburg circle. He removed the ban on Nazi meetings that Brüning had imposed and called a Reichstag election for July 1932. When the Nazis won 230 seats (37.2 percent of the vote), Hitler demanded appointment as chancellor. Hindenburg refused and called another election in a bid to wear down the Nazis' financial resources. The Nazis lost 34 seats, and their popular vote dipped to 33.1 percent.

In November 1932, Papen resigned, and his successor, General Kurt von Schleicher (1882–1934), tried to head off civil war between the left and the right by building a broad-based coalition of conservatives and trade unionists. This alarmed Hindenburg's advisers, who did not trust Schleicher's motives, and they persuaded Hindenburg that Hitler was the lesser evil. On January 30, 1933, Hitler was appointed chancellor and Papen returned as vice chancellor. It was assumed that Papen and a cabinet filled with conservatives would be able to keep Hitler under control.

Since Hitler had obtained office legally, the civil service, the courts, and the other agencies of government could support him in good conscience. He headed a rigidly disciplined party structure, and he was a master of techniques of mass propaganda. He knew how to touch the raw nerves of the electorate, and he won support across the social spectrum—not just from the lower middle class. In some rural areas and small towns, Roman Catholic voters opposed him. But his following was strong among farmers, war veterans, and the young whose hopes for the future were imperiled by the Great Depression. Hitler promised them a defense against communism and socialism, effective government in place of petty party squabbles, and an inspiring nationalist vision of a strong, restored Germany.

Big business once received much of the credit for the rise of Hitler, but there is little evidence that contributions from business leaders made a crucial difference to the Nazi campaign. Hitler's supporters were often suspicious of business and giant capitalism. They wanted a simpler world in which small property would be safe from the consolidation threatened by both socialism and capitalism. The Nazis won out over other conservative nationalistic parties because they better addressed the fears of the German people.

Hitler's Consolidation of Power

Once in office, Hitler quickly consolidated control by winning full legal authority, crushing alternative political groups, and purging rivals within his own party. His opportunity came on February 27, 1933, when a mentally ill Dutch communist set fire to Berlin's Reichstag building. The Nazis claimed that the fire was a prelude to a communist assault on the government, and under Article 48 of the Weimar constitution, Hitler issued an emergency decree suspending civil liberties. The decree remained in effect for as long as Hitler ruled Germany.

In early March 1933, there was another Reichstag election. The Nazis received only 43.9 percent of the vote (288 seats), but the removal of all Communist deputies and the political fear aroused by the fire enabled Hitler to get the legislation he wanted. On March 23, 1933, the Reichstag passed an Enabling Act authorizing Hitler to rule by decree. Since this lifted all legal limits on his power, he never found it necessary formally to repeal or amend the Weimar constitution.

Hitler knew that he and his party had not been swept into office by destiny. He had worked to get where he was, and he worked to protect his position. He outlawed or undermined any German institution that might have become a rallying point for his opponents. In early May 1933, the Nazi Party, acting like a branch of government, seized the offices, banks, and newspapers of the free trade unions and arrested their leaders. In July of that year, the National Socialists were declared the only legal party in Germany. The Nazis then moved against the governments of the individual federal states in Germany, and by the end of 1933, all their opponents had been silenced.

Hitler's final step was to consolidate his hold on the Nazi Party. His chief concern was his strongest potential rival, Ernst Roehm (1887–1934), commander of the SA, the party's private army of 1 million storm troopers. On June 30, 1934, Hitler ordered the murders of Roehm and key SA officers. By July 2 more than 100 SA leaders had been killed, including the former chancellor General Kurt von Schleicher and his wife. The regular German army, the only institution that might have prevented the slaughter, was delighted by the destruction of the leadership of a group that it saw as trespassing on its territory. On August 2, Hindenburg died, and Hitler claimed the offices of both chancellor and president—making himself sole ruler of Germany and its Nazi Party.

The Police State and Anti-Semitism

Hitler set up a police state under the surveillance of the SS, the *Schutzstaffel* (i.e., "protective force"), commanded by Heinrich Himmler (1900–1945). This group had originated in the mid-1920s as Hitler's bodyguard, and it had evolved into a more elite paramilitary organization than the huge SA. (By 1933 it had about 52,000 members.) It carried out the bloody purges of the party in 1934, and by 1936 Himmler, its leader, was second only to Hitler in Germany.

Hitler's police state bore down most heavily on Germany's Jews, for anti-Semitism was a key plank in the Nazi program. It was not motivated by religious feeling but by biological theories of race that were rooted in late-nineteenth-century science.

There were three stages in the Nazi attack on the Jews. In 1933, shortly after assuming power, the Nazis excluded Jews from the civil service and tried, ineffectively, to persuade the public to boycott Jewish businesses. In 1935 a series of measures known as the Nuremberg Laws robbed Jews of rights of citizenship. Professions and key occupations were closed to them. Marriage and sexual intercourse between them and non-Jews were prohibited, and an elaborate attempt was made to establish a legal standard for deciding who was and who was not a Jew. The third assault on the Jews began in November 1938, when Jewish businesses were outlawed. Under orders from the Nazi Party, thousands of Jewish stores and synagogues were sacked on what came to be known as *Kristallnacht* (i.e., "glass night," from the sound of breaking windows). By these means and other acts of public humiliation, the Nazis persuaded the masses to accept the idea that Germany should be "cleansed" of everyone who was not a descendant of the "master race," the legendary Aryans. Germany was reconciled to the "final solution," the extermination of Europe's Jews.

Nazi Economic Policy

Hitler was more effective than any other European leader at dealing with economic problems, and his success ensured loyalty to his tyrannical regime. His strategy for engineering economic recovery was to create jobs by mobilizing his nation for a war of aggression. In the process he sacrificed all political and civil liberties, destroyed trade unions, prevented the private exercise of capital, and ignored consumer demand.

Hitler endorsed private property and capitalism but subordinated all economic enterprise to the needs of the state. He instituted a massive program of public works and spending, much of which was related to rearmament. Workers were often assigned jobs rather than being allowed freely to choose them. The government handled labor disputes through compulsory arbitration, and it enrolled workers and employers in the "Labor Front," a propaganda campaign that fostered worker loyalty to the state.

In 1935 Germany renounced the military provisions of the Versailles Treaty and began openly to rearm. In 1936 Hitler commissioned Hermann Göring (1893–1946), head of the air force, to develop a Four-Year Plan to prepare Germany economically and militarily for war. This essentially restored full employment while pandering to the desire of the German people for national vindication.

Italy: Fascist Economics

In Italy, the Fascists substituted discipline for economic policy and creativity. During the 1920s Mussolini undertook vast public works, such as draining the Pontine Marshes near Rome. The government subsidized the shipping industry and introduced protective tariffs. Mussolini desperately tried to make Italy self-sufficient, but he was unable to stave off the effects of the Great Depression. Production, exports, and wages fell.

Syndicates

The Fascists sought to steer an economic course between socialism and a liberal laissez-faire system. Their policy, known as corporatism, organized major industries as syndicates of labor and management. These syndicates were to cooperate in designing a planned economy. The government stepped in when necessary to settle labor disputes, but labor and management were urged to look beyond their private interests to the greater goal of productivity for the nation.

Corporations

After 1930 industrial syndicates were further organized into entities called corporations. A corporation united all the people who contributed anything—from raw materials through finished products and distribution—to a particular kind of productive work (e.g., agriculture or metallurgy). Twenty-two corporations encompassed Italy's whole economy. In 1938 Mussolini replaced the Chamber of Deputies with a Chamber of Corporations. Instead of increasing production, however, this vast organizational framework spawned bureaucracy and corruption.

Italy's experiment with corporatism did not last long. In 1935 Italy, like Germany, began to restructure its economy to support military mobilization. When Italy revealed its imperialistic intentions by declaring war on Ethiopia, the only response from the League of Nations was the imposition of ineffective economic sanctions. Taxes rose, and the government imposed a forced loan on the citizenry (i.e., property owners were required to buy government bonds). Wages fell, and as international tensions mounted, the state assumed ever greater control over the economy.

Fascism brought order to Italy, but it was not the order of prosperity.

The Soviet Union: Central Economic Planning and Party Purges

While Western capitalist systems suffered through the Great Depression, the Soviet Union made tremendous economic progress. But Russia achieved its stunning growth during the 1930s only at the cost of, or the degradation of, millions of lives.

The Decision for Rapid Industrialization

Lenin's New Economic Policy (NEP) remained in effect until 1927. It encouraged private enterprise in rural districts to ensure the adequate production of food for urban workers. Although the NEP had succeed by 1927 in restoring industrial production to 1913's prewar level, the Party Congress, under Stalin's leadership, decided in that year to abandon it and to push for more rapid industrialization.

Stalin's strategy was to create a series of Five-Year Plans overseen by *Gosplan*, the State Planning Commission. The goal was to strengthen Russia by quickly overtaking the productive ca-

An enormous propaganda effort accompanied the Soviet five-year plans. This poster proclaims, "For the betterment of the Soviet people we are building an electricity plant." Bildarchiv Preussischer Kulturbesitz

pacity of its opponents, the capitalist nations. The emphasis was on the development of heavy industries and the nation's infrastructure, not consumer goods. This was to be achieved by massive central planning that set goals for production and coordinated every step in the process. This proved to be an immensely complicated undertaking that promoted the growth of centralized agencies that frequently worked at cross-purposes. The work force was increasingly regimented, and workers were compelled to live in deplorable conditions that were worse than anything that Marx and Engels had decried in the nineteenth century. Russia maintained full employment of its people throughout the Depression but compelled them to accept an astoundingly low standard of living and a total loss of political liberties. To elicit their cooperation, the government and the Communist Party undertook a vast program of propaganda lauding the five-year plans, the heroism of devoted workers, and the alleged success of the system. Anyone who presumed to differ with the official point of view was accused of political opposition.

By the close of the 1930s the results of the three five-year plans were truly impressive. Russia's economy grew more rapidly than that of any other Western nation during any comparable time period. By conservative Western estimates, Soviet industrial production rose about 400 percent between 1928 and 1940. Industries that had not previously existed in Russia began to challenge and, in some cases, surpass counterparts elsewhere. Large new industrial cities had been built and populated, but the social and human costs of these developments were astounding.

The Collectivization of Agriculture

The pursuit of rapid industrialization had enormous consequences for Soviet agriculture. The *kulaks*, cultivators of relatively large farms (less than 5 percent of farmers), prospered under the NEP. They, however, were discontented, for there were few consumer goods for them to buy with the cash they earned. Throughout the 1920s they repeatedly organized movements to withhold grain from the market, and the possibility that this might cause food shortages and prompt urban uprisings alarmed the government.

Following months of difficulty beginning in 1928 and extending into 1929, Stalin came to the decision that agriculture had to be collectivized. His goals were to end upheavals in the farm sector of the economy, to produce sufficient grain for domestic consumption and export, and to free some peasants to work in the factories of the expanding industrial sector. Stalin basically embraced Trotsky's earlier economic position and unleashed a second Russian revolution of unprecedented violence.

In 1929 Stalin blamed the *kulaks* for grain shortages and set about eliminating them as a class. Peasants and farmers of all kinds, however, resisted collectivization and joined forces to sabotage it. Between 1929 and 1933 they slaughtered more than 100 million horses and cattle, and the countryside erupted in open warfare. In March 1930, Stalin—claiming "dizziness from success"—called a brief halt to the process.

The drive to collectivize the farms was soon renewed with vehemence. Even with the recent opening of the Russian archives, it is difficult to estimate how many peasants were killed. The number was probably in the millions. The turmoil that this created in rural areas caused agricultural production to fall and famine to spread in 1932 and 1933. Stalin persisted, however, in uprooting peasants and moving them to thousand-acre collective farms. The state's monopolistic control over the seed and machinery needed to farm made it very difficult for anyone to resist.

Collectivization dramatically changed Russian farming. In 1928 small peasant holdings accounted for approximately 98 percent of Russia's farms. Ten years later, over 90 percent of the land had been collectivized, and the amount of farm produce handled by the government had risen 40 percent. The government had won control of the food supply and, thus, deprived farmers of the power to influence it by threatening to cause unrest in the cities. Stalin's policy failed, however, to achieve its second crucial objective: the expansion of grain production. That difficulty continued to plague the Soviet Union until its collapse in 1991 and remains a problem for the new Commonwealth of Independent States.

Foreign Reactions and Repercussions

Many foreigners were naively enthusiastic about the Soviet economic experiment, for while the capitalist world languished, the Soviet economy

Significant Dates from the Era of the Great Depression	
1928	Russia's First Five-Year Plan
	Nazis win first seats in the Reichstag
1929	(October) Wall Street crash
	Britain's second Labour government
	Collectivization of Russian agriculture
1931	(May) Collapse of Kreditanstalt in Vienna
	Britain goes off the gold standard
1932	Lausanne Conference ends reparations
	(April 10) Hindenburg defeats Hitler for presidency
1933–1934	Stavisky Affair in France
1933	(January 30) Hitler appointed chancellor
	(February 27) Reichstag fire
	(March 23) Enabling Act passed
	(July 14) Nazis declared Germany's only legal party
1934	(June 30) Murder of SA leadership
	(August 2) Death of von Hindenburg
	(December 1) Assassination of Kirov
1935	Passage of Nuremberg Laws
1936	Stalin begins the Great Purge
	(June 5) Popular Front government in France under Blum
1937	Neville Chamberlain becomes British prime minister
1938	Radical ministry in France
	(November 9) *Kristallnacht*

grew at a pace never realized in the West. These observers ignored the shortages in consumer goods, the poor housing, and the social cost of the Soviet achievement. The full extent of human suffering and loss during those years will probably never be known, but it far exceeded the price of Europe's nineteenth-century industrialization that had so appalled Marx and Engels.

The internal upheaval created by collectivization and industrialization and the fear (by 1934) that Russia might be left alone to face aggression by Nazi Germany prompted Stalin to make a shift in foreign policy. He reversed the Comintern policy established by Lenin in 1919 as part of the Twenty-one Conditions and permitted communist parties in other countries to cooperate with noncommunist groups against Nazism and fascism.

The Purges

Stalin's programs aroused internal opposition. In 1929 he forced Nikolai Bukharin, a fervent supporter of the NEP, off the Politburo. Not much is known about continuing resistance at lower levels in the party, but by 1933 Stalin was afraid that he was losing control. Whether the threat to him was real or imagined, it resulted in the Great Purges, one of the most mysterious and horrendous political events of the twentieth century.

On December 1, 1934, Sergei Kirov (1888–1934), a member of the Politburo, was assassinated. In the wake of the shooting, thousands of people were arrested. Many others were expelled from the party and sent to labor camps. At the time, it was believed that Kirov had been murdered by opponents of the regime, for Stalin accused many of his victims of complicity in the crime. Some have assumed that Stalin himself ordered Kirov's assassination to remove a potential rival, but the available documentary evidence is inconclusive.

Between 1936 and 1938, a series of spectacular show trials were held in Moscow. High Soviet leaders confessed to political crimes they had not committed and were convicted and executed. Other party members were tried in private and shot. Many people received no trials at all, and no one can explain why some were executed while others were sent to labor camps and still others were left unmolested. After the civilian party members had been purged, the prosecutors turned against the army. Officers, including heroes of the civil war, were shot. Hundreds of thousands of members of the party were expelled, and applicants for membership were removed from the rolls. The exact numbers of executions, imprisonments, and expulsions are unknown, but certainly they ran into the millions.

Two things may help to explain the purges. One was a power struggle between factions within the Communist Party. The purges enabled the central Moscow leadership to enhance its control over the lower levels of the

By the mid-1930s Stalin's purges had eliminated many leaders and other members from the Soviet Communist Party. This photograph of a meeting of a party congress in 1936 shows a number of the surviving leaders with Stalin, who sits fourth from the right in the front row. To his left is Vyacheslav Molotov, long-time foreign minister. The first person on the left in the front row is Nikita Khruschev, who headed the Soviet union in the late 1950s and early 1960s. Itar–Tass/Sovfoto/Eastfoto

party in the far-flung regions of the Soviet Union. Stalin also used the purges to remove members of the party elite whom he distrusted, and lower-ranking officials of the party followed his example—producing a flurry of accusations, imprisonments, and executions.

The second motive for the purges may have been Stalin's determination to create a new party structure that was totally loyal to him. The purges weeded out the "old Bolsheviks" of the October Revolution who knew how far Stalin was departing from Lenin's policies. The newcomers who replaced them in the party's leadership knew only the world that Stalin had shaped for them.

In Perspective

By the middle of the 1930s, dictators of the right and the left had established themselves across Europe. Political tyranny was not new, but these rulers were unique. They were supported by well-organized political parties rooted in nationalism, driven by fear of the Great Depression, and eager for schemes that promised to transform the social and political order. They monopolized mass communications and used armies, police forces, and party machines to terrorize their opponents. Thanks to the technologies of the Second Industrial Revolution, they had unprecedented destructive power at their disposal.

REVIEW QUESTIONS

1. What caused the Great Depression of the 1930s? Why was it more severe and longer lasting than previous depressions? Could it have been avoided?
2. How successful, respectively, were Britain's National Government and France's Popular Front in dealing with their nations' economic problems? How would you account for the differences? Why did France's Third Republic have so few supporters?
3. How did the Great Depression affect Germany? How did Hitler rise to power between 1929 and 1934? Was his dictatorship inevitable? Which played the larger role in his successful seizure of power, his personality or his politics?
4. What were Hitler's economic policies? Why did they work? How does his economic program compare with the economic policies put in place in Britain, Italy, and France? Why were some nations more successful than others in addressing the Great Depression?
5. What are the characteristics of a police state? What is the role of terror and intimidation in the consolidation of an authoritarian regime? Are they necessary to its survival? How did Hitler, Mussolini, and Stalin use terror to achieve their goals? What were the particular characteristics of Nazi racial policy?
6. Why did Stalin decide that Russia had to industrialize rapidly? Why did this require the collectivization of agriculture? What obstacles stood in the way of collectivization? How did Stalin overcome them? What caused the purges in the Soviet Union? What groups were the special targets of the purges? Why?

SUGGESTED READINGS

W. S. ALLEN, *The Nazi Seizure of Power: The Experience of a Single German Town, 1930–1935*, rev. ed. (1984). A classic treatment of Nazism in a microcosmic setting.

N. BRANSON and M. HEINEMANN, *Britain in the Nineteen Thirties* (1971). Primarily considers the social and economic problems of the day.

R. CONQUEST, *The Great Terror: Stalin's Purges of the Thirties* (1968). Remains the most useful treatment of the subject to date.

R. CONQUEST, *The Harvest of Sorrow: Soviet Collectivization and the Terror-Famine* (1986). A study of how Stalin used starvation against his own people.

B. EICHENGREEN, *Golden Fetters: The Gold Standard and the Great Depression, 1919–1939* (1992). A remarkable study of the role of the gold standard in the economic policies of the interwar years.

R. GELLATELY, *The Gestapo and German Society: Enforcing Racial Policy, 1933–1945* (1990). A discussion of how the police state supported Nazi racial policies.

J. A. GETTY and O. V. NAUMOV, *The Road to Terror: Stalin and the Self-Destruction of the Bolsheviks, 1933–1939* (1999). A major collection of newly available documents revealing much new information about the purges.

J. JACKSON, *The Politics of Depression in France, 1932–1936* (1985). A detailed examination of the political struggles prior to the Popular Front.

J. JACKSON, *The Popular Front in France: Defending Democracy, 1934–1938* (1988). The best recent treatment.

H. JAMES, *The German Slump: Politics and Economics, 1914–1936* (1986). A difficult but informative examination of the German experience of the Great Depression.

C. KINDLEBERGER, *The World in Depression, 1929–1939* (1973). An account by a leading economist whose analysis is comprehensible to the layperson.

D. J. K. PEUKERT, *Inside Nazi Germany: Conformity, Opposition, and Racism in Everyday Life* (1987). An excellent discussion of life under Nazi rule.

D. SCHOENBAUM, *Hitler's Social Revolution: Class and Status in Nazi Germany* (1966). A fascinating analysis of Hitler's appeal to various social classes.

D. M. SMITH, *Mussolini's Roman Empire* (1976). A general description of the fascist regime in Italy.

A. SOLZHENITSYN, *The Gulag Archipelago*, 3 vols. (1974–1979). A major examination of the labor camps under Stalin by one of the most important contemporary writers.

J. STEPHENSON, *The Nazi Organization of Women* (1981). Examines the attitude and policies of the Nazis toward women.

L. YAHIL, *The Holocaust: The Fate of the European Jewry, 1932–1945* (1990). A major recent study of this fundamental subject in twentieth-century history.

*Reference should also be made to the works cited in chapters 27, 29, and 31.

Chapter 29

World War II

KEY TOPICS

- ⊚ The origins of World War II
- ⊚ The course of the war
- ⊚ Racism and the Holocaust
- ⊚ The impact of the war on the people of Europe
- ⊚ Relationships among the victorious Allies and the preparations for peace

Idealistic survivors of the First World War hoped that it would be "the war to end all wars," but only twenty years after its conclusion a second and even more terrible global conflict erupted. In Europe and Asia, democracies fought for their lives against militaristic, nationalistic, authoritarian, and totalitarian states. The victory that they ultimately won did not bring world peace but a Cold War in which the European states were subordinated to two partially or fully non-European superpowers: the Soviet Union and the United States.

Again the Road to War (1933–1939)

World War I and the Versailles Treaty contributed only marginally to the world depression of the 1930s, but after payment of war reparations fueled vast inflation in Germany in 1923, Adolf Hitler was able plausibly to denounce the peace settlement as the root of all his nation's ills. The Nazi Party succeeded, in part, because it appealed to German nationalism and attended to Germany's social problems. Once Hitler became chancellor in January 1933, the nation's foreign policy also focused on these issues.

Hitler's Goals

From his first published manifesto, *Mein Kampf (My Struggle)*, the book he wrote in jail in 1924, to his suicide in his underground bunker in Berlin in 1945, Hitler's thoughts centered on race. He considered the *Volk* (i.e., the German people) to be a race, and he was determined to extend Germany's boundaries to take in all the Germanic parts of the old Habsburg Empire—including Austria. He believed, however, that a virile, growing Germany would need even more *Lebensraum* ("living space"), and this was to be acquired by conquering Poland and Ukraine, land occupied by Slavs—a "race" that Hitler considered fit only for servitude. The Jews, another "race" the Nazis regarded as inferior, were to be removed completely from German territory. Hitler's book and subsequent policy statements developed no blueprint for action. He owed his success less to planning than to his gifts as an improviser. He kept his goals clearly in sight and simply exploited opportunities as they arose.

GERMANY REARMS   When Hitler came to office, Germany was far too weak simply to take the land he wanted. It had first to break the fetters imposed by the Versailles Treaty so that it could rebuild its formidable military power. In October 1933, Germany—claiming that other powers had not honored their promises to disarm—withdrew from an international disarmament conference and from the League of Nations. The following January, Germany signed a nonaggression pact with Poland, an eastern enemy that France had hoped would prevent Germany from risking another war on its western front. In March 1935, Hitler formally renounced the disarmament provisions of the Versailles Treaty. He then created a German air force and reinstated conscription to build an army of 500,000 men.

THE LEAGUE OF NATIONS FAILS   In September 1931, two years before Hitler became Germany's chancellor, a Japanese invasion of Manchuria had sent China fleeing to the League of Nations for help. A British diplomat, the Earl of Lytton (1876–1951), wrote a report condemning the Japanese action, but the league failed to do anything about it. Japan simply withdrew from the league and continued to occupy Manchuria.

The league's manifest weakness convinced Hitler that it was safe to rearm Germany, and, as he expected, his decision was condemned but unopposed. France and Britain, having themselves reneged on promises to disarm, were not in a strong position to object, so they tried intimidation. In June 1935, they formed the Stresa Front, a pact with Mussolini to cooperate in using force to maintain the status quo in Europe. This arrangement failed as each nation pursued its own interests. Britain, which was desperate to maintain its superiority at sea, sacrificed France's security by making a separate naval agreement with Hitler. The treaty authorized a German fleet 35 percent as large as the British navy. Italy's ambitions in Africa caused further friction among the Allies, and their inability to work together guaranteed Hitler a free hand.

Italy Attacks Ethiopia

Mussolini attacked Ethiopia in October 1935 to avenge a humiliating defeat that Italy had suffered in 1896 and to distract the Italians from domestic problems by invoking memories of the glory days of the ancient Roman Empire. The League of Nations' limp response to his act of imperialist aggression advertised its impotence and the timidity of the Allies. France and Britain hoped to offset the growing power of Germany by courting help from Mussolini, but Italy's aggression so outraged public opinion that their governments were compelled at least to appear to resist. For the first time, the League of Nations voted sanctions—imposing an arms embargo on Italy and limiting any loans, credits, and trade that might assist Mussolini's government. Anxiety about alienating Mussolini, however, led Britain and France to refuse to embargo oil, the one thing that could have prevented Italy's victory. The British fleet also allowed Italian troops and munitions passage through the Suez Canal. This totally discredited the League of Nations and its commitment to collective security. It also failed to prevent an offended Mussolini from defecting to Hitler's camp. By November 1, 1936, there was open talk of a Rome-Berlin "Axis."

Remilitarization of the Rhineland

The Ethiopian affair lessened Hitler's respect for the Western powers, and on March 7, 1936, he probed their resolve by sending a small armed force into the demilitarized Rhineland. This breached the Versailles Treaty and the Locarno Agreements and removed a key guarantee of French security. France and Britain had every right to resist. Yet neither power did anything but register a feeble protest with the League of Nations. British opinion was opposed to backing France, and the French would not act alone. Both countries were weakened by a spreading pacifist sentiment. In retrospect, it is clear that on this occasion the Allies lost a great opportunity to stop Hitler before he became a serious menace. His move into the Rhineland was taken against the advice of his generals, and its failure might have led to his overthrow. At the least, it would have made German expansion to the east dangerous or impossible. The Germans themselves later admitted that the French army could easily have routed the tiny force they sent into the Rhineland.

A rearmed Germany with a defensible western frontier changed the diplomatic game in Europe and prompted the Allies to devise a policy of "appeasement." It was based on beliefs that Germany's grievances were real and Hitler's goals limited. Horror at the memory of the last war increased public pressure on governments to make concessions to preserve peace, and development of a firmer policy would have required a rapid rearmament that British leaders particularly hoped to avoid. They feared its expense and believed that it had been an arms race that had led to World War I. Britain simply hoped for the best, while Germany armed and France huddled behind a newly constructed defensive wall, the Maginot Line.

The Spanish Civil War

The polarization of Europe between democracies and fascist states was made clear when a civil war erupted in Spain in 1936. In 1931 the Spanish monarchy had collapsed, and Spain had become a democratic republic. The republic's program of moderate reform antagonized landowners, the Roman Catholic Church, nationalists, and conservatives—without satisfying peasants, workers, Catalan separatists, or radicals. In February 1936, the Spanish Popular Front (a coalition of moderate republicans, communists, and anarchists) triumphed at the polls, but losers in the election, especially the Falangists (Spain's fascists), refused to accept defeat. In July, an army led by General Francisco Franco (1892–1975) invaded from bases in Spanish Morocco and began a civil war that lasted almost three years. The conflict turned Spain into a practice arena for World War II. Germany and Italy sent troops, airplanes, and supplies to Franco, and the Soviet Union aided the republicans—as did many American and European volunteers.

The civil war brought Germany and Italy closer together and led to the Rome-Berlin Axis Pact of 1936. The Axis powers were joined that year by Japan in the Anti-Comintern Pact, an alliance designed, ostensibly, to oppose international communism. Western Europe, especially France, was eager to prevent Spain from falling into the hands of a fascist regime allied with Germany and Italy, but their appeasement continued. Although international law permitted the sale of munitions to Spain's legitimate republican government, France and Britain forbade the export of war materials to either side, and the United States declared neutrality. A half a million lives were lost before Spain succumbed to Franco early in 1939.

Austria and Czechoslovakia

In 1934 Nazis had assassinated Austria's prime minister and tried to seize power. They failed, however, for Mussolini, who was not yet allied with Hitler, quickly moved an army to the Austrian border. The threat this implied prevented Germany from intervening to complete the coup. In 1938, Hitler, who was now Mussolini's friend, made a second bid for control of Austria. The Austrian chancellor, Kurt Schuschnigg

Picasso's Guernica

*T*he twentieth century's most famous painter may have been the Spaniard, Pablo Picasso (1881–1973). In 1937 he accepted a commission to produce a mural for the Spanish pavilion at the Paris World's Fair. The subject he chose was an event from the civil war that had erupted in Spain in July of the previous year.

Picasso's mural interpreted an infamous atrocity that took place shortly after the Spanish Republic offered him his commission: the bombing of the Basque town of Guernica by the German Condor Legion on April 26, 1937. This was the most thorough aerial attack on a city up to that time, and its purpose was simply to terrorize the civilian populace. Picasso's surrealistic nightmare of a painting illustrated the plight of the bombers' innocent, defenseless victims, and it was extraordinarily effective in focusing the public's attention on the outrage and winning Western support for the republican cause.

Sources: H. W. Janson and Anthony F. Janson, *History of Art*, rev. 5th ed. (Upper Saddle River, NJ: Prentice Hall, 1997), p. 82; R. O. Paxson, *Europe in the Twentieth Century* (New York: Harcourt, Brace, 1975), pp. 289–398; Paul Johnson, *Modern Times* (New York: Harper and Row, 1983), pp. 321–337; Marilyn Stokstad, *Art History* (New York: Harry N. Abrams, 1999), p. 109.

Pablo Picasso, *Guernica*, 1937. Oil on Canvas. 11'5 1/2 × 25'5 3/4. Museo Nacional Centro de Arte Reina Sofia/ © 1998 Estate of Pablo Picasso/Artists Rights Society (ARS), New York.

(1897–1977), refused, however, to be intimidated by German threats. He declared that the Austrian people would decide the question of union with Germany for themselves and scheduled a plebiscite for March 13. To forestall this, Hitler sent his army into Austria on March 12, and this time Mussolini stood quietly by as Hitler entered Vienna amid the cheers of Austrian sympathizers. This *Anschluss* (i.e., union of Germany and Austria) was a clear violation of the Versailles Treaty, but no nation stepped forward to oppose it. This was alarming, for the process of German expansion was not likely to stop with Austria. Czechoslovakia, a French ally at Germany's back that was supposed to help guarantee France's security, was now surrounded on three sides by the new Germany.

Hitler was affronted by the very existence of a democratic Czechoslovakia allied to France and Russia. The nation had been created partly as a check on Germany, and about 3.5 million Germans lived as a resentful minority in Czechoslovakia's Sudetenland district. When a Nazi leader, Konrad Henlein (1898–1945), persuaded them to agitate for autonomy within the Czech state, Hitler claimed that his duty to protect the German people necessitated intervening in Czech affairs. The Czechs tried to stave him off by making concessions, but Hitler increased his demands in order to force a confrontation that would destroy Czechoslovakia.

In May 1938, the Czechs reacted to rumors of invasion and mobilized their army. France, Britain, and Russia warned that they would defend the Czechs, and Hitler, who was not yet prepared to attack, was forced to deny that he had designs on Czechoslovakia. Infuriated by this public humiliation, he put his troops on alert. This frightened France and Britain. Neville Chamberlain (1869–1940), the British prime minister who was willing to agree to almost anything in order to keep Britain out of war, pressed the Czechs to make further concessions. Nothing short of surrender, however, could be enough.

On September 12, 1938, Hitler made a speech at a Nazi Party rally in Nuremberg that prompted rioting in the Sudetenland. When the Czechs responded by declaring martial law, German intervention seemed imminent. Between September 15 and 29, Chamberlain made three flights to Germany to negotiate with Hitler, and on September 15, Chamberlain forced the Czechs (who were defenseless without the support of their Western allies) to separate the Sudetenland from Czechoslovakia. A week later, Hitler insisted on German military occupation of the Sudetenland within three days.

Munich

At the last moment, at Chamberlain's request, Mussolini proposed a conference representing Germany, Italy, France, and Britain. The meeting, which took place in Munich on September 29, granted Hitler almost everything he wanted. The Sudetenland became part of Germany. It was recognized that this deprived the Czechs of the ability to defend themselves, but Hitler calmed fears by claiming that he had no further territorial ambitions. Chamberlain returned to England to announce that he had made a "peace with honour."

Munich taught Europe that fear of war can bring on war. By giving Germany a hunk of Czechoslovakia, the Munich agreement encouraged Poland and Hungary to lay claims to other parts of that nation, and its Slovak residents demanded recognition of their region as a separate state. On March 15, 1939, Hitler swept all this aside by breaking his promise and occupying Prague. If the French and the British had attacked Germany from the west while the Czechs fought in the east, Hitler might have been stopped. A war begun in October 1938 would at least have forced him to fight before he had promises of neutrality and material assistance from the Soviet Union and before he gained control of the resources of eastern Europe.

Poland was Germany's next target. In the spring of 1939 Hitler demanded that Poland restore the formerly German city of Danzig and allow a railroad and a highway through the Polish Corridor to connect East Prussia with the rest of Germany. When the Poles refused, tension began to mount. On March 31, Chamberlain announced a Franco-British guarantee of Polish independence, but Hitler did not take him seriously. Hitler knew that Britain and France were not prepared materially or emotionally for war and that they had no means of getting effective help to the Poles. To defend Poland, England and France needed help from Russia, but there were obstacles to such an alliance. The French and the British opposed communism, and Stalin's purge of the Red Army raised doubts about Russia's current military effectiveness. The Russian army could also not help Poland without being given permission to enter Poland and Romania, and both nations had good reasons based on previous experience to deny this.

The Nazi-Soviet Pact

The Russians feared, quite rightly, that the Western powers meant them to bear the burden of a war with Germany. Consequently, they opened negotiations with Hitler, and on August 23, 1939, a Nazi-Soviet nonaggression pact was announced. Its secret provisions, which were soon carried out, divided Poland between the two powers and allowed Russia to occupy the Baltic states and Bessarabia.

The West had offered the Russians danger without prospect of gain, and Hitler had countered with an offer of gain without prospect of danger. Stalin was not about to allow ideological disputes to interfere with rational self-interest. Communist parties in the West immediately reversed themselves, ceasing to advocate resistance to Hitler and calling for peace. On September 1, 1939, the Germans invaded Poland. Two days later, Britain and France declared war on Germany.

World War II (1939–1945)

The German Conquest of Europe

Using a new military strategy, the *Blitzkrieg* (i.e., "lightning warfare"), in which airplanes supported fast-moving armored columns, Germany quickly defeated Poland. The speed of the German victory astonished the Russians, who hastened to grab parts of Poland for themselves before Hitler took it all. Stalin's territorial gains enabled him to encircle the Baltic countries. He sent in the Red Army, and by 1940 Estonia, Latvia, and Lithuania had become puppet states within the "Soviet Union," the USSR (i.e., the Union of Soviet Socialist Republics). In June 1940, the Russians forced Romania to cede Bessarabia, and in November of that year they invaded Finland. The Finns resisted fiercely for six months but finally yielded territory to Russia in exchange for guarantees of independence. Russia's

German troops march down the Champs-Elysées in Paris in September 1940 after the rapid collapse of French defenses. Roger-Viollet/Liaison Agency, Inc.

expansionism and the poor performance of its army in Finland may have persuaded Hitler to turn against Stalin. In June 1941, just twenty-two months after conclusion of the Nazi-Soviet pact, Germany invaded Russia.

While Hitler and Stalin swallowed Poland and the Baltic states, France remained entrenched behind the Maginot Line and Britain hastily rearmed. In April 1940, without warning, the Germans invaded and quickly subdued Denmark and Norway. This secured Hitler's northern front and gave him air and naval bases closer to Britain. A month later he struck at Belgium, the Netherlands, and Luxembourg. The Dutch surrendered in a few days and the Belgians, despite French and British aid, less than two weeks later. The British and French armies in Belgium fled to the English Channel and gathered on the beaches at Dunkirk. Hundreds of heroic Britons manning small boats rescued over 200,000 British and 100,000 French soldiers, but losses of men and equipment were high.

The Maginot Line ran from Switzerland to Belgium, and the French had expected the Belgians to continue it along their part of the German border. But when France failed to oppose Hitler's remilitarization of the Rhineland in 1936, the Belgians lost faith in France as an ally and declared neutrality. By overrunning Belgium, Hitler was able, therefore, to sweep around the left flank of France's main line of defense. The French army was poorly led by aged generals who did not understand tanks and planes, and it soon collapsed. Mussolini then saw a chance for a safe, easy conquest, and on June 10 he invaded southern France. Less than a week later, a new French government headed by the elderly hero of the Battle of Verdun, Marshal Henri Philippe Pétain (1856–1951), asked for an armistice. Hitler had accomplished in two months what his predecessors in the previous war had failed to achieve in four years of hard fighting.

The Battle of Britain

The fall of France left Britain isolated, and Hitler expected the British to come to terms. In exchange for allowing Britain to retain its empire, he wanted a free hand for Germany on the Continent. If there was any chance that the British would consider such terms, it disappeared when

Winston Churchill (1874–1965) replaced Chamberlain as prime minister in May 1940. Churchill had been an early critic of Hitler, the Nazis, and the policy of appeasement. His sense of history, his confidence in Britain, his hatred of tyranny, and his love of freedom made him reject any thought of compromise with Hitler.

The situation looked hopeless for Britain. Hitler and his allies, including the Soviet Union, controlled all of Europe. Japan was advancing in Asia, and the United States was awash in isolationist sentiment and determined to remain neutral. Churchill, however, used his skill as an orator and an author to inspire his people with the courage and determination to fight. In addition to that, his most important achievement may have been the close relationship he established with the American president, Franklin D. Roosevelt (1882–1945). Roosevelt found ways to help Britain despite strong opposition in Congress. In 1940 and 1941 "neutral" America traded military supplies and badly needed warships for leases on British naval bases. The United States even convoyed ships across the Atlantic to help Britain survive.

As weeks passed and Britain remained defiant, Hitler was forced to contemplate invasion. That required control of the air. The first strikes by the *Luftwaffe*, the German air force, were on airfields in southeastern England in August 1940. If Germany had stuck with this strategy, it might have won control of the air and a chance for a successful invasion. But in early September, the *Luftwaffe*, eager to avenge British bombing raids on German cities, switched its attention to London. For two months, London was bombed nightly. Much of the city was destroyed, and about 15,000 people were killed.

Strategists who had argued that victory could be achieved through air power alone were proved wrong. Casualties were much less than expected, and Britain's morale was not shattered. In fact, the bombings united the British people and made them more resolute, while the Royal Air Force (RAF) inflicted heavy losses on the *Luftwaffe*. Aided by a new invention called radar and an excellent system of communications, the British Spitfire and Hurricane fighter planes destroyed more than twice as many German aircraft as the RAF lost. The Battle of Britain was won in the air, and it forced Hitler to abandon his plans for invasion.

The German Attack on Russia

Hitler had always believed that the conquest of Ukraine was necessary to provide *Lebensraum* ("living space") for the German people. In December 1940, while the bombing of England continued, he ordered his generals to prepare to invade Russia by May 15, 1941. He may have thought that a *Blitzkrieg* victory in the East would undermine Britain's will to fight. Operation Barbarossa, the code name for the invasion of Russia, was designed to destroy Russia before winter set in. Success required an early start, but Hitler's Italian alliance held him up.

Mussolini's invasion of France turned into a fiasco, and he hoped to avenge this humiliation by attacking the British in Egypt. Encouraged by initial success, he also invaded Greece from a base that he had seized in Albania in 1939. The British counterattacked in North Africa and drove the Italians back into Libya. When the Greeks, aided by Britain, pushed into Albania, Hitler was forced to intervene on behalf of this Italian ally. General Erwin Rommel (1891–1944), "the Desert Fox," was sent to Africa to force the British out of Libya, and an army was dispatched to crush Greek resistance and occupy Yugoslavia. These preparations delayed the start of Hitler's Russian campaign by six weeks.

Operation Barbarossa was launched on June 22, 1941, and it almost succeeded. Despite a later claim by the Russians that the Nazi-Soviet pact was a diversion intended to give them time to prepare for war with Germany, Hitler took them by surprise. Stalin had not fortified his frontier, and he was so panicked that he failed to orchestrate an orderly retreat for his military forces. In the first two days, 2,000 Russian planes were destroyed on the ground, and by November, Hitler had advanced farther into Russia than Napoleon. The German army reached the gates of Leningrad, the outskirts of Moscow, and the Don River. Of the 4.5 million troops with which the Russians had begun the fight, they had

Mussolini inspecting Italian troops at the Florence train station in October 1940 as he awaits a visit from Hitler. Mussolini's military reverses in North Africa and the Balkans would divert German resources in 1941 and delay the beginning of Hitler's planned invasion of Russia. Popperfoto/Archive Photos

MAP 29–1 AXIS EUROPE, 1941   *On the eve of the German invasion of the Soviet Union, a combination of annexations, occupations, and alliances had created a German-Italian Axis that bestrode most of western Europe—from Norway and Finland in the north to Greece in the south and from Poland in the east to France in the west. Britain, the Soviet Union, a number of insurgent groups, and, finally, America faced the prospect of a long struggle to conquer the Axis's "fortress Europe."*

lost 2.5 million, and of their 15,000 tanks, only 700 were left. German victory seemed imminent.

The Germans failed, however, to deliver a decisive blow. The Nazi general staff wanted to concentrate on taking Moscow before winter. Although this had not worked for Napoleon, it might have worked now, for Moscow had become the hub of Russia's transportation system. Hitler chose, instead, to divert a large part of his army to the south. By the time he was ready for an offensive near Moscow, it was too late. German soldiers, who lacked appropriate dress and equipment, were devastated by the onslaught of winter. This gave Stalin a respite, which he used to construct defenses for the city and to call in troops from Siberia. The Russians counterattacked, and the Germans began to have Napoleon's nightmares.

Hitler's Plans for Europe

Hitler often spoke of the "new order" that would be established in Europe by the Nazi's Third Reich. The earlier Reichs (i.e., German empires) were those of Charlemagne (in the ninth century) and Bismarck (in the nineteenth century). Hitler claimed that his, unlike those, would last for a thousand years. Hitler seems to have had no single plan for governing either Germany or Europe. He relied on intuition and pragmatism to create patchwork organizations in the lands he conquered. Some districts were annexed by Germany; some were administered directly by German officials; some remained nominally autonomous under puppet governments.

Hitler's regime was probably unmatched in history for its studied use of terror and its active cultivation of inhumanity. The *Lebensraum* he sought for Germans was to be won by dispossessing people he deemed inferior. In Poland, German colonists evicted natives from their land or used them as cheap labor. A similar fate on a grander scale was planned for Russia. The Russians were to be driven into central Asia and Siberia and kept in check by frontier colonies settled by German war veterans. European Russia was then to be settled by Germans.

In addition to colonization a process of cultural "Germanization" was to be employed to build the Reich. People who were racially akin to the Germans (e.g., the Scandinavians, the Dutch, and the Swiss) were to be reeducated, purged of dissenting elements, and absorbed into the German nation. Selected individuals from lesser races might also be assimilated. A half-million Ukrainian girls were, for example, to be dispatched to Germany as servants and potential wives for German men. (About 15,000 were actually sent.)

In practice, Hitler plundered wherever he conquered. Eastern Europe was stripped of everything useful, including entire industries. Russia and Poland offered only land for confiscation, but the Western nations the Germans occupied were forced to support their armies of occupation at a rate several times above real costs. Germans used the excess to buy up everything they desired, stripping defeated populations of most necessities. The Nazis frankly admitted their eagerness to exploit, to enslave, and to destroy—all to advance their dream of German glory.

Racism and the Holocaust

The worst abuses of Nazi power were the result not of military or economic policies but of Hitler's racial doctrines. The Slavs were among the many nationalities labeled *Untermenschen* (i.e., "subhumans" who did not need to be treated as full human beings). In parts of Poland the upper and professional classes were entirely exterminated—jailed, deported, or killed. Polish schools and churches were closed; the birthrate was kept down by limiting the right to marry; and harsh living conditions were imposed. Things were even worse in Russia, where Hitler characterized the Russian campaign as a war of extermination. Heinrich Himmler, head of the elite SS, had plans to eliminate 30 million Slavs to make room for Germans. Six million Russian prisoners of war and deported civilian workers may have died under Nazi rule.

Hitler had a special fate in mind for Jews. He intended to make Europe *Judenrein* ("purified of Jews"). At first, he thought he might send them to the African island of Madagascar, but he ultimately decided on extermination—his "final solution." The Nazis built camps in Germany and Poland where sophisticated technology was developed to kill millions of men, women, and children with maximum efficiency. Before the war was over, 6 million Jews may have died in the Holocaust. About 1 million inmates of the Nazi concentration camps survived, mostly in pitiable condition.

The meaning of the Holocaust is hotly debated. Some commentators see it as just one more manifestation of a destructive tendency that is a normal part of human nature. They note that the twentieth century witnessed purges by Stalin and Mao that accounted for more deaths than Hitler's persecution of Jews. Others argue, however, that the Holocaust was unique in its effort to eradicate an entire people simply because of their identity. They claim that the roots of the horror are to be found in flaws in German culture and in the effects of Hitler's perverse character.

Some reasons for the choice of the Jews as the Nazi's target are obvious. Germany, as a Christian nation, was influenced by the persistent strain of anti-Semitism that has plagued Christianity throughout its history. The pseudo-scientific racist theories that emerged during the Enlightenment also seemed to some to provide confirmation of ancient socioreligious prejudices.

These are some of the dead at the Nordhausen concentration camp, which was liberated by the American army in April 1945. The Nazis set up their first concentration camps in Germany in 1933 to hold opponents of their regime. After the conquest of Poland, new camps were established there as part of the "final solution," the extermination of the Jews. About 6 million Jews were murdered in these camps. Even in those camps not dedicated to extermination— in which political prisoners and "undesirables" such as Gypsies, homosexuals, and Jehovah's Witnesses were held—conditions were brutal in the extreme, and tens of thousands died. The crimes of the Nazi regime have no precedent in human history.
National Archives

This seemed to be the most powerful influence on Hitler himself, but there were other cultural influences that helped mobilize support for his racist agenda. One was the intense nationalism that had rooted itself in the European psyche during the nineteenth century. This divided the world into two camps: one's fellow nationals versus everyone else. The need to defend the national "fatherland" made it easy to justify atrocities against those who were defined as its opponents. The Enlightenment's claim that social engineering could create a perfect society was also seductive, particularly when modern media technology was employed to persuade people to commit themselves to the pursuit of such a utopian dream. All these things together help explain the rise of a totalitarian state that committed itself to mass murder on the unprecedented scale of the Holocaust.

World War II was unmatched for the cruelty of its combatants on all sides. When Stalin's armies conquered Poland and entered Germany, they avenged themselves by raping, pillaging, and deporting millions. The British and American bombing of Germany killed thousands of civilians, and the dropping of atomic bombs on Japan inflicted terrible casualties on noncombatants. The Western allies obviously became convinced that Nazi atrocities justified virtu-

ally any act that would bring the war to a successful conclusion.

Japan and the United States Enter the War

The assistance that Roosevelt gave Britain would have justified a German declaration of war, but Hitler held back in the hope that America would distance itself from the European conflict. Isolationist sentiment might, indeed, have kept the United States out of the war in the Atlantic if war had not been forced on the Americans in the Pacific.

Japan's conquest of Manchuria in 1931 caused the United States to regard it with suspicion. When fighting broke out in Europe and the Japanese accelerated their drive to dominate Asia, relations between Japan and the United States further deteriorated. The Japanese allied themselves with Germany and Italy, made a treaty of neutrality with the Soviet Union, exploited France's weakness by moving into Indochina, continued their war in China, and planned to take Malaya and the East Indies from Britain and the Netherlands. The United States was the only thing standing in their way.

The Americans had delayed cutting off vital supplies of oil and other materials to Japan for fear of provoking an attack on Southeast Asia and Indonesia. But when Japan occupied Indochina in July 1941, the United States froze Japanese assets and cut off oil supplies. The British and Dutch did the same. The Japanese then decided that to continue their expansion, they had to acquire Indonesia for its oil and Malaya for its rubber and tin.

In October 1941, a pro-war faction led by General Hideki Tojo (1885–1948) came to power in Japan. A little over a month later, on Sunday morning, December 7, 1941, while Japanese representatives were discussing a settlement in Washington, Japan launched an air attack on America's chief naval base in the Pacific, Hawaii's Pearl Harbor. The Americans were taken by surprise and lost much of their fleet and many airplanes. For the time being, their capacity to wage war in the Pacific was negated. A day later, the United States and Britain declared war on Japan, and three days later, Germany and Italy declared war on the United States.

The Japanese swiftly captured Guam, Wake Island, and the Philippines. By the spring of 1942, they had won control of Hong Kong, Malaya, Burma, Indonesia, and the Southwest Pacific as far as New Guinea. They then began positioning themselves to invade Australia. The Germans, in the same year, almost reached the Caspian Sea in a drive toward Russia's oil fields. In Africa, Rommel closed in on the Suez Canal, pushing the British back to El Alamein, only seventy miles from Alexandria. The German submarines that roamed the Atlantic made it difficult for allies to keep Britain supplied.

The Tide Turns

The future looked bleak, but more than twenty nations around the world joined forces to oppose the Axis powers. Great Britain, the Soviet Union, and the United States took the lead. The Russians accepted all the aid they could get, but they did not trust their allies. Complaining of inadequate help, they demanded that the democracies open a "second front" on the mainland of Europe.

Although the United States' potential power was enormous, America was not yet prepared to contribute to an invasion of Europe. Conscription had been introduced in 1940, but the American army was tiny, inexperienced, and ill supplied. American industry was not geared for war, and German submarines made the Atlantic unsafe for shipping troops to Europe. Not until 1944 would conditions be right for an invasion. In the meantime, however, there were developments that forecast doom for the Axis.

The Allies' first victory in the Pacific, a battle in the Coral Sea, came in the spring of 1942. The ships Japan lost diminished the likelihood that Australia would be invaded. A month later, the United States defeated the Japanese in a fierce air and naval battle off Midway Island. This minimized the risk of another assault on Hawaii and did enough damage to halt Japan's advance. American Marines then landed on Guadalcanal in the Solomon Islands and began to reverse the momentum of the war. The fight in the Pacific was far from over, but Japan was sufficiently contained to allow the Allies to concentrate their efforts in Europe.

ALLIED LANDINGS IN AFRICA, SICILY, AND ITALY After stopping Rommel at El Alamein, British Field Marshal Bernard Montgomery (1887–1976) began a drive to the west. In November 1942, an Allied force landed in French North Africa, and the American general, Dwight D. Eisenhower (1890–1969), pushed eastward through Morocco and Algeria. By crushing the Germans between them in Tunisia, the two armies won control of the Mediterranean and opened the way for an invasion of Europe from the south.

In July and August 1943, the Allies completed the conquest of Sicily and drove Mussolini from power. A new Italian government, led by Marshal Pietro Badoglio (1871–1956), joined the Allies, but Italy did not prove as easy to occupy as the Allies had hoped. Hitler deployed the German army to defend Italy despite the fact that the fierce fighting strained Germany's thinning resources.

BATTLE OF STALINGRAD The Russian campaign heated up in the summer of 1942 when the Germans launched offensives on all fronts. Stalingrad was a key point on the flank of the German army in the south, and Hitler was as determined to take it as Stalin was to defend it. The battle of Stalingrad raged for months. More Russians died in this one campaign than did Americans in the entire war. In the end, Russia prevailed. Hitler, however, overruled his generals and refused to retreat—sacrificing an entire German army.

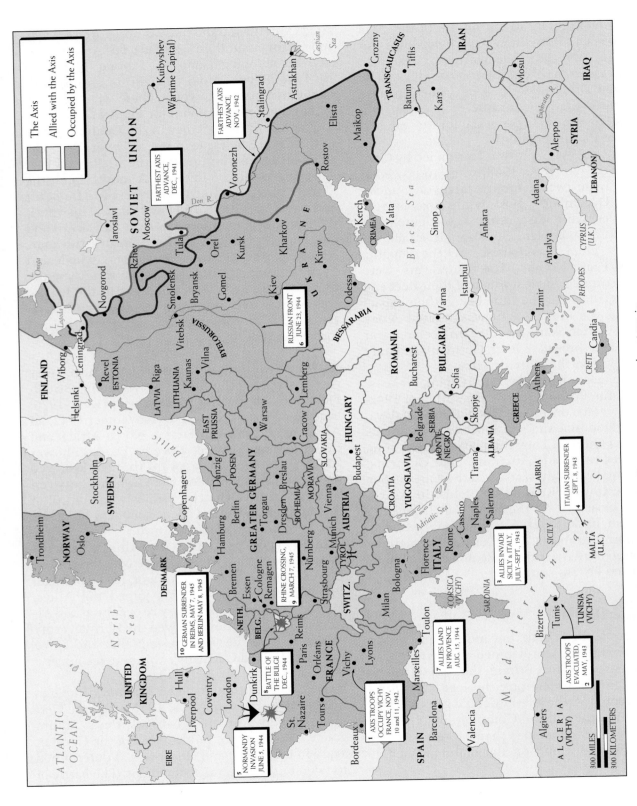

MAP 29–2 DEFEAT OF THE AXIS IN EUROPE, 1942–1945 *Here we see some major steps in the progress toward Allied victory against the Axis powers. From the south through Italy, the west through France, and the east through Russia, the Allies gradually conquered the continent to bring the war in Europe to a close.*

Stalingrad was the turning point in the war for Russia. America provided some material help, but increased production from Russian industries that had been moved to or built up in the safe central and eastern regions of the USSR allowed the Soviets to gain and keep the offensive. As Germany's resources dwindled, Russia advanced inexorably westward.

STRATEGIC BOMBING In 1943 the industrial might of the United States began to tell. New technology and tactics greatly reduced the submarine menace, and American and British air forces began a massive bombardment of Germany that continued night and day. The Americans, who favored a strategy of "precision bombing" limited to military and industrial targets, preferred day missions. The British, who believed that precision bombing was impossible, chose to fly at night for maximum security and to practice indiscriminate "area bombing" in order to undercut German morale. Neither approach was very effective until 1944, when the Americans introduced long-range fighters that could protect bombers and increase the accuracy of daylight missions.

By 1945 the skies were virtually cleared of German planes, and the Allies could bomb at will. Attacks on industrial targets helped to shorten the war, but terror bombing also continued—even though it seems to have had little effect. An air raid on Dresden in February 1945 was especially savage. It was much debated within the British government at the time, and it continues to raise moral questions. Whatever else the aerial war over Germany accomplished, it took a heavy toll of the German air force and diverted resources from other military purposes.

The Defeat of Nazi Germany

On June 6, 1944 (D-Day), American, British, and Canadian troops under the Allied commander, Dwight D. Eisenhower, landed on the heavily fortified coast of Normandy. Despite the fact that the German coastal defenses were very strong and amphibious assaults are especially vulnerable to wind and weather, the Allies established a beachhead and began to advance. In mid-August they landed in southern France, and within a few weeks France was liberated.

THE BATTLE OF THE BULGE In December the Germans launched a counterattack through Belgium's Ardennes Forest and dented the Allied line—making a "bulge" that gave the battle its name. The Allies suffered heavy losses, but the Battle of the Bulge was Germany's last Western offensive. The Allies recovered their momentum and crossed the Rhine in March 1945. As German resistance crumbled in this war, unlike the first one, no German could doubt that their country was being defeated on the battlefield.

THE CAPTURE OF BERLIN In the East, the Russians overcame fierce German resistance to advance swiftly on Berlin. Since the Allies refused any terms but unconditional surrender, the Germans fought on as long as possible. Finally, on May 1, 1945, Hitler committed suicide in an underground bunker in Berlin, and the Russians, with the consent of their allies, occupied the city. Instead of the millennium Hitler had promised, the Third Reich had survived for a mere twelve years.

Fall of the Japanese Empire

The war in Europe ended on May 8, 1945, and by then victory over Japan was also in sight. The longer the war lasted, the more American superiority in industrial production and population began to tell.

AMERICANS RECAPTURE THE PACIFIC ISLANDS In 1943, the American forces, which were still relatively small, began a campaign of "island hopping." Its goal was not to recapture every island Japan held but to gain strategic sites along the enemy's supply line. Starting from the Solomon Islands, the Americans moved northeast toward Japan. In June 1944, they won the Mariana Islands from which bombing raids could be launched on the Philippines, China, and Japan itself. The Philippines were recaptured in October, forcing the Japanese fleet to retreat to its home waters. In 1945 Iwo Jima and Okinawa fell, giving the Americans more bases for bombers whose missions devastated Japan's industry and disabled its navy.

THE ATOMIC BOMB When the Japanese government, which was dominated by a military clique,

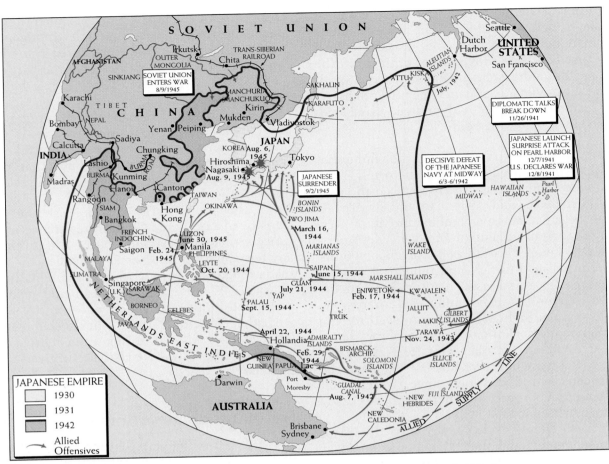

MAP 29–3 WORLD WAR II IN THE PACIFIC   *As in Europe, the Pacific war involved Allied recapture of areas that had been quickly seized by the enemy. The enormous region represented by the map shows Japan's initial expansion across half the Pacific and its islands and huge sections of eastern Asia.*

refused to surrender, the Americans made plans for a frontal assault on the Japanese mainland. A million American casualties and greater Japanese losses were anticipated, but at this point science provided the Americans with another option. A secret program had been in progress since the start of the war. Staffed in part by refugee scientists who fled Hitler, it was set up to explore military uses for atomic energy.

On August 6, 1945, an American plane dropped an atomic bomb on the Japanese city of Hiroshima. More than 70,000 of the city's 200,000 residents were killed. Two days later, the Soviet Union declared war on Japan and invaded Manchuria, and the next day a second atomic bomb destroyed Nagasaki. The Japanese cabinet wanted to fight on, but unprecedented intervention by Japan's Emperor Hirohito (r. 1926–1989),

who by tradition took no part in politics, forced the generals to offer terms on August 14. Although the Allies had insisted on unconditional surrender, Harry S Truman (1884–1972)—who became president after Franklin D. Roosevelt died in office on April 12, 1945—agreed to Japan's request to keep its emperor. The war ended with the signing of a treaty aboard the USS *Missouri* in Tokyo Bay on September 2, 1945.

Some analysts claim that the bombings were unnecessary to defeat Japan and that their main purpose was to frighten the Russians into respecting America after the war. Others have suggested that the decision to use the bomb was almost automatic once the nation had committed to its development. At the time, however, the choice was simple. The bomb promised to end the war swiftly and, thus, bring a halt to the loss of American lives. Its employment was conscious, not automatic, and it required no ulterior motive.

The Cost of War

World War II was the most terrible war in history. About 15 million military personnel died, as did at least as many civilians. Deaths from disease, hunger, and other causes indirectly linked to war raise the number of its victims to 40 million. Most of Europe and significant parts of Asia were devastated.

At so terrible a cost, the war bought little peace of mind. It inaugurated the Atomic Age with the concomitant knowledge that another conflict could extinguish humanity. Human survival depended on achieving a stable peace, but even as the fighting ended, tensions among the victors made prospects for a lasting peace doubtful.

The Domestic Fronts

Germany: From Apparent Victory to Defeat

Hitler had expected the techniques of the *Blitzkrieg* to win him a quick victory that would not require Germany to alter its social or economic life in order to prevail in the war. For the first two years of the war, few sacrifices had been demanded from the German people. Spending on domestic projects continued, and food was plentiful. Things changed, however, when the assault on the Soviet Union bogged down. Food imports from the East declined, and Germany had to mobilize for total war.

In 1942 Germany began a push to expand its army and increase military production. Albert Speer (1905–1981), minister for armaments and munitions, diverted the economy from production of consumer goods to production of military supplies. The output of military products tripled between 1942 and 1944, but productivity began to decline after a growing manpower shortage forced the government to start drafting workers. Shortages of everyday products became serious, and the standard of living of German workers fell. Prices and wages were controlled, and food rationing was implemented in April 1942. Shortages became severe until Germany began to confiscate food from occupied countries. The Nazis tried to preserve their home front by passing its suffering on to the lands Germany had occupied.

By 1943 labor was also in short supply. Teenagers, retired men, and increasing numbers of women were recruited into the work force. The Germans closed retail businesses, raised the age for women eligible for compulsory service, shifted non-German domestic workers to wartime industries, closed theaters, moved artists and entertainers into military service, and reduced basic public services such as mail and railways. The Nazis also compelled thousands of people from conquered lands to do forced labor in Germany.

Women had a special place in Hitler's war effort. Propaganda depicted them as mothers and wives who loyally sent sons and husbands off to war. Their other wartime activities were said to be natural extensions of their maternal roles. As air raid wardens, they protected their families. As factory workers, they aided their men on the front lines. As farm laborers, they provided food for soldier sons and husbands. As housewives, their frugal management conserved supplies needed to win the war. And, most important, as chaste wives and daughters, they guarded the purity of the German race.

Hitler and other Germans genuinely believed that a lack of support from the home front had led to Germany's defeat in World War I, and they devised a propaganda campaign of unique intensity to make sure this did not happen again. Propaganda Minister Josef Goebbels (1897–1945) exploited radio and films to boost the Nazi cause at home, and the same mass media were used to control occupied lands. The ministry broadcast exaggerated claims of Nazi victories. And when Germany's armies were finally checked on the battlefield, propaganda stiffened resistance by spreading alarm about the consequences of defeat. Allied bombing raids that, after May 1943, began devastating one German city after another may have played into the hands of the Nazis. They seemed to confirm propaganda that branded Germany's enemies as ruthless.

The war effort increased the power of the Nazi Party by bringing everything in Germany under its control. During the war, there was virtually no serious opposition to Hitler. In 1944 a few army officers did try to assassinate him, but their failed attempt elicited few signs of popular approval. A radically different nation was to

The Allied campaign of aerial bombardment did terrible damage to German cities. This photograph shows the devastation it delivered to the city of Cologne on the Rhine.
UPI/Corbis

emerge from the utter defeat of the Nazis and the consequent devastation of Germany.

France: Defeat, Collaboration, and Resistance

The truce Hitler had made with the French on June 22, 1940, gave the Germans the right to occupy more than half the country, including the Atlantic and English Channel coasts. To prevent the French from turning their fleet over to Britain and continuing to fight in North Africa, Hitler left southern France unoccupied until November 1942. Marshal Pétain set up a dictatorial regime in the city of Vichy and collaborated closely with the Germans in the hope of preserving as much autonomy as possible.

Many conservatives and extreme rightists hoped that the Vichy government would end what they considered to be the corrupting influences of liberalism. The Roman Catholic Church supported Pétain, who restored religious instruction in state schools and increased financial support for Catholic institutions. Vichy also endorsed the church's views on family and spiritual values—making divorce difficult and subsidizing large families. The Vichy regime encouraged intense, chauvinistic nationalism and exploited long-standing prejudice against foreigners working in France. Its chief victims were France's Jews. Even before 1942, when Hitler undertook his "final solution," the French were driving Jews from influential posts in government, education, and publishing. In 1941 the Germans began to intern the Jews who lived in occupied France. In the spring of 1942, they started to deport them, and over 60,000 were ultimately sent to extermination camps in eastern Europe. The Vichy government had no part in these decisions, but it did not protest them.

A few French fled to Britain after their homeland surrendered to the Nazis. There, under the leadership of General Charles de Gaulle (1890–1969), they organized the French National

Committee of Liberation, the Free French. The Vichy government retained control of French North Africa and France's navy until the end of 1942, but the Free French established a base in central Africa and waged propaganda offensives from London. A serious internal resistance movement did not begin to develop until late in 1942, and the number of its members was small—less than 5 percent of the adult French population.

In early 1944, when it became clear that the Allies were winning, active resistance began on a large scale. General de Gaulle, from his base in London, urged the French to fight their conquerors and the Vichy administration. From Algiers on August 9, 1944, the Committee of National Liberation repudiated the legitimacy of the Vichy government, and French soldiers joined in the liberation of Paris. On October 21, 1945, France voted to end the Third Republic and adopt a new constitution that established the Fourth Republic. Bitter quarrels over who had done what during the occupation were to divide the French for decades.

Great Britain: Organization for Victory

On May 22, 1940, the British Parliament gave the government emergency powers to enable it to institute compulsory military service, food rationing, and economic controls. All Britain's political parties joined forces in a government led by Winston Churchill.

The nation's most pressing military need was for airplanes to fight the Battle of Britain. Lord Beaverbrook, one of Britain's most important newspaper publishers, oversaw their production. A massive campaign to reclaim scrap metal was launched, the first of many appeals to support the war effort to which the civilian population enthusiastically responded. Factory hours were extended. Women were brought into the work force in great numbers, and unemployment disappeared. By the end of 1941, Britain's production had already surpassed Germany's.

Germany's "blitz" air raids during 1940 and 1941 provided the British people with their most dramatic war experiences. Thousands were killed and many left homeless. Families sent children to the countryside for safety. Gas masks were issued to city-dwellers, who sought shelter from the bombs in London's subways. Hitler

needed most of his air force on the Russian front after the spring of 1941, but he managed to continue bombing Britain. Bombs killed more than 30,000 Britons before the war ended, and Allied bombers took a much greater toll on the Germans. In Germany, as in England, however, bombing—far from breaking people's spirits—seems to have increased their determination to resist. The British people made many sacrifices. Transportation facilities strained to carry enough coal for domestic heating and fueling factories. Food and clothing were in short supply, and the government imposed strict rationing. Every scrap of land was farmed, increasing tillage by almost 4 million acres. And since gasoline was scarce, private vehicles almost vanished.

Like the Germans, the British used propaganda to further the war effort. The British Broadcasting Company (BBC) urged resistance to the Nazis in programs transmitted abroad in all the European languages. At home, radio serials and Churchill's famous speeches helped bring the nation together.

The Soviet Union: "The Great Patriotic War"

No nation suffered greater losses of life and property during the war than the Soviet Union. About 16 million of its people were killed, and vast numbers of its soldiers suffered imprisonment. Hundreds of cities and towns and well over half the nation's industrial and transportation facilities were devastated. Thousands of Soviets became forced laborers in German factories, and Germans confiscated the Soviet Union's grain, mineral resources, and oil.

In the decade leading up to the war, Stalin had made the Soviet Union a highly centralized state that was permanently on something resembling a wartime footing. Stalin worried that the army might siphon power away from the Communist Party, and his purges in the late 1930s had eliminated many officers whose loyalty he doubted. As the war continued, the army did acquire a degree of independence, and generals ceased to be subservient to party commissars. The military was, however, still constrained by Stalin's power and by the nature of Soviet government and society.

Soviet propaganda differed from that of other nations. Distrustful of the loyalty of its citizens, the government confiscated radios to shield

Significant Dates from the Era Culminating in World War II

1919	(June) The Versailles Treaty
1931	(Spring) Onset of the Great Depression in Europe
1933	(January) Hitler comes to power
1935	(March) Hitler renounces disarmament
	(October) Mussolini attacks Ethiopia
1936	(March) Germany remilitarizes the Rhineland
	(July) Outbreak of the Spanish Civil War
	(October) Formation of the Rome-Berlin Axis
1938	(March) *Anschluss* with Austria
	(September) Munich Conference; partition of Czechoslovakia
1939	(August) The Nazi-Soviet pact
	(September) Germany and the Soviet Union invade Poland; Britain and France declare war on Germany
	(November) The Soviet Union invades Finland
1940	(April) Germany invades Denmark and Norway
	(May) Germany invades Belgium, the Netherlands,Luxembourg, and France
	(June) Fall of France
	(August) Battle of Britain begins
1941	(June) Germany invades the Soviet Union
	(July) Japan takes Indochina
	(December) Japan attacks Pearl Harbor; United States enters war
1942	(June) Battle of Midway
1942	(November) Battle of Stalingrad begins; Allies land in North Africa
1943	(February–August) Allies take Sicily, land in Italy
1944	(June) Allies land in Normandy
1945	(May) Germany surrenders
	(August) Atomic bombs dropped on Hiroshima and Nagasaki
	(September) Japan surrenders

them from German and British propagandists. In cities, the government communicated with the people using loudspeakers, not radios, and it appealed to patriotism, not Marxist class theory, to marshal support for the war. Stalin even made peace with the Russian Orthodox Church in an effort to win support at home and improve the image of the Soviet Union in regions of eastern Europe where the church was strong.

Since the German army advanced so quickly that thousands of Soviet soldiers were stranded behind German lines, an active resistance movement quickly developed in the western Soviet Union. Many soldiers were captured and shipped to Germany as prisoners of war, but others escaped to become guerilla fighters. In addition to causing trouble for the Germans, these partisans helped keep peasants, who resented the Soviet government's policy of collectivization, from collaborating with the enemy. As the Soviet army moved westward at the end of the war, the partisans rejoined the regular units.

Although Stalin had entered the war reluctantly, he emerged a major winner. The Soviet Union established itself as a world power second only to the United States, and the feelings of patriotism and self-sacrifice the war inspired in Russia's people consolidated support for Stalin and the Communist Party more effectively than any strategy they could have devised.

Preparations for Peace

The split that quickly developed between the Soviet Union and its allies came as no surprise. The Soviet Union was dedicated to the overthrow of capitalist nations, and those nations were no less open about their hostility to communism. Only the emergency of the war had forced them to put their ideological differences temporarily aside.

Cooperation against a common enemy and effective propaganda did improve attitudes toward the Soviets in the West, but Churchill was determined to halt a Soviet advance into Europe. Roosevelt's hope that the Allies could work together after the war had already begun to fade by 1945, and any expectation for a mutually satisfactory peace settlement upheld by continued cooperation was quickly disappointed.

The Atlantic Charter

In August 1941, before the Americans went to war, Roosevelt and Churchill met on a ship off Newfoundland to negotiate the Atlantic Charter. It was intended, in the spirit of Wilson's Fourteen Points, to provide a theoretical basis for the peace they sought. On the other hand, the alliance that Russia, the United States, and Britain formed in January 1942 was purely military. At the time, both powers chose to ignore significant political issues.

Tehran: Agreement on a Second Front

The leaders of the USSR, Britain, and the United States (the so-called Big Three) first met in Tehran, the capital of Iran, in 1943. Britain and the United States agreed to open a second front in France, and Stalin promised to join the war against Japan once Germany had been defeated. The most important decision reached at Tehran was the choice of Europe's west coast rather than the Mediterranean as the place to begin the Allied offensive. Britain and the United States failed to consider that this might lead to Soviet forces occupying eastern Europe. In 1943 the Russians were still fighting far behind their own frontiers, and immediate military objectives overrode all long-range considerations.

By 1944 the situation had changed. In August, Soviet armies reached Warsaw. Expecting imminent liberation, its residents rose up against the Germans. But the Russians turned south into the Balkans and allowed the Poles to be annihilated. They occupied Romania and Hungary and realized the dreams of centuries of expansionist tsars. Churchill was alarmed, and in October he went to Moscow to meet with Stalin. They agreed to split up the Balkans. The Soviets were to dominate Romania and Bulgaria, the West was to control Greece, and the two sides were to share influence equally in Yugoslavia and Hungary.

GERMANY The Americans were reluctant to agree to enforce such spheres of influence. But the three powers easily agreed on plans for Germany—its disarmament, denazification, and division into four zones of occupation: one for each of the Big Three and France. Churchill balked at Stalin's demand for $20 billion in reparations and the requisition of forced labor from all the zones, especially since Stalin claimed half of all this for Russia.

EASTERN EUROPE The settlement of Eastern Europe was a thorny problem. Everyone agreed that the Soviet Union deserved friendly neighbors, but the Western allies insisted that they be independent, autonomous, and democratic. Western leaders were not eager to see Eastern Europe fall under Russian domination, and they were committed to democracy and self-determination. Stalin knew, however, that independent, freely elected governments in Poland and Romania could not be counted on to be friendly to Russia. In Poland, Stalin established a puppet government, although there was already a Polish government-in-exile in London. Fearful that the Allies would betray him by making a separate peace with Germany, he made all kinds of conciliatory promises to win Allied acceptance of his arrangements. He added some people friendly to the West to Poland's government and signed a Declaration on Liberated Europe that promised self-determination and free democratic elections for all liberated states. Once the war was over, he ignored these agreements.

Yalta

The Big Three held their next meeting at Yalta in the Crimea in February 1945. Western armies had yet to cross the Rhine, but the Soviets were within a hundred miles of Berlin. Roosevelt, faced with the prospect of invading Japan with heavy losses, was eager to bring the Russians into the Pacific war. To encourage their participation, he and Churchill made extensive concessions to Russia in Sakhalin, the Kurile islands, Korea, and Manchuria. Roosevelt suspected Churchill of maneuvering to maintain the British Empire and disapproved of efforts to set up British spheres of influence in Europe. He saw these as invitations to the Russians to do the same and as sources of future conflicts. Roosevelt, like Wilson, pinned hopes for peace on a united-nations organization. Soviet support for this seemed well worth the concessions he was asked to make.

Potsdam

The Big Three met for the last time in the Berlin suburb of Potsdam in July 1945. President Truman replaced the deceased Roosevelt, and Clement Attlee (1883–1967), leader of the Labour Party, had defeated Churchill at the polls. Previous agreements were reaffirmed, but progress on new issues was slow. Russia's western frontier was moved far into what had been Poland and German East Prussia. Poland was compensated by a grant of authority over the rest of East Prussia and Germany east of the Oder-Neisse river line. This, in effect, accommodated the Soviet Union by moving Poland about a hundred miles into Germany. A Council of Foreign Ministers was established to negotiate peace terms with Germany's allies, and Germany was divided into occupation zones. It was not completely reunited until 1990.

The war was slow to come to an official end. Italy, Romania, Hungary, Bulgaria, and Finland did not sign peace treaties until February 1947. The Russians rejected the treaty that the United States made with Japan in 1951 and signed their own agreement with the Japanese in 1956. Potsdam had left much unresolved.

In Perspective

Since World War II was a response to the resolution of World War I, the two wars might be considered one continuous conflict interrupted by a brief, uneasy truce. The second war was not, however, inevitable. It was caused by failures of judgment and will on the part of the Western democracies. The United States, potentially the strongest nation in the world, had made the mistake of withdrawing into short-sighted isolation and failing to respond promptly when ambitious dictators appeared in Europe. Britain and France, for their part, also refused to face up to the threat posed by the Axis powers until war was unavoidable.

In Europe, where World War II began, it ended not—as World War I had—with unsatisfactory peace treaties but with no treaties at all. Instead two hostile camps emerged (headed respectively by the United States and the Soviet Union) and began to wage what has been characterized as a "Cold War." Competition between the two superpowers complicated life for the Third World of developing nations that emerged in part from Europe's crumbling colonial empires. Both the Soviet Union and the United States competed

for their support, and the generous postwar treatment the Allies accorded both Germany and Japan was due in large part to their eagerness to build alliances that would contain the spread of communism. As a result Japan and Germany quickly recovered to build two of the world's greater economies.

REVIEW QUESTIONS

1. What were Hitler's foreign policy aims? Was he bent on conquest in the East and dominance in the West, or did he simply want to return Germany to its 1914 boundaries?
2. Why did Britain and France adopt a policy of appeasement in the late 1930s? What were its main features? Did the appeasers buy the West valuable time to prepare for war by their actions at Munich in 1938?
3. How was Hitler able to defeat France so easily in 1940? Why was his air war against Britain a failure? Why did Hitler invade Russia? Why did the invasion ultimately fail? Could it have succeeded?
4. Why did Japan attack the United States at Pearl Harbor? What was the significance of American intervention in the war? Why did the United States drop atomic bombs on Japan? Did President Truman make the right decision when he ordered the bombs to be used?
5. What impact did World War II have on the civilian population of Europe? How did experiences on the domestic fronts differ in Great Britain, Germany, and France? What impact did the "Great Patriotic War" have on the people of the Soviet Union? Did participation in World War II solidify Stalin's hold on power?
6. What was Hitler's "final solution" for Europe's Jewish population? Why did Hitler want to eliminate Slavs as well as Jews? Was the twentieth century the century of Holocaust as well an age of great progress?

SUGGESTED READINGS

A. ADAMTHWAITE, *France and the Coming of the Second World War, 1936–1939* (1977). A careful account making good use of the newly opened French archives.

E. R. Beck, *Under the Bombs: The German Home Front, 1942–1945* (1986). An interesting examination of a generally unstudied subject.

A. Bullock, *Hitler: A Study in Tyranny*, rev. ed. (1964). A brilliant biography.

J. L. Gaddis, *We Now Know: Rethinking Cold War History* (1998). A fine account of the early years of the Cold War, making use of new evidence emerging since the collapse of the Soviet Union.

M. Gilbert, *The Holocaust: A History of the Jews of Europe During the Second World War* (1985). The best and most comprehensive treatment.

A. Iriye, *Pearl Harbor and the Coming of the Pacific War* (1999). Essays on how the Pacific war came about.

J. Keegan, *The Second World War* (1990). A lively and penetrating account by a master military historian.

M. Knox, *Mussolini Unleashed* (1982). An outstanding study of fascist Italy's policy and strategy in World War II.

S. Marks, *The Illusion of Peace* (1976). A good discussion of European international relations in the 1920s and early 1930s.

R. Overy, *Why the Allies Won* (1997). An analysis of the reasons for the victory of the Allies with special emphasis on technology.

M. Sherwin, *A World Destroyed: The Atomic Bomb and the Grand Alliance* (1975). An analysis of the role of the atomic bomb in the years surrounding the end of World War II.

H. Thomas, *The Spanish Civil War*, 3rd ed. (1986). The best account in English.

P. Wandycz, *The Twilight of French Eastern Alliances, 1926–1936* (1988). A well-documented account of the diplomacy of central and eastern Europe in a crucial period.

G. L. Weinberg, *A World at Arms: A Global History of World War II* (1994). A thorough and excellent narrative account.

G. Wright, *The Ordeal of Total War 1939–1945* (1968). An excellent survey.

Chapter 30
Faces of the Twentieth Century: European Social Experiences

KEY TOPICS

- Social impact of state violence on women, Russian peasants, and Polish Jews
- Migration in twentieth-century Europe
- Changing status and role of women in Europe
- New cultural forces and continuing influence of Christianity
- The impact of computer technology

World War II marked the great political divide for the twentieth century. It signaled the end of the era of European world dominance and the beginning of the Cold War competition between the superpowers, the United States and the Soviet Union. In the field of social history, however, the war was only one enormously destructive event in a century that witnessed the unleashing of numerous military and political forces that repeatedly reshaped the lives of Europeans.

State Violence in Twentieth-Century Europe

Prior to the twentieth century, governments tended to have relatively modest impacts on the lives of their citizens. As the century unfolded, however, two developments vastly increased the power of government to influence the options and opportunities available to ordinary men and women.

The first of these developments was the military mobilization of Europe that began with World War I and continued through the Cold War. For most of the twentieth century, Europe was an armed camp. To maintain military preparedness, the power of government to tax and to command resources—both human and material—was greatly expanded. In addition to the tens of millions who were killed, the hopes and expectations of most Europeans were altered in numerous ways by the experience of war and the need to contribute to defense efforts.

The second political development that affected social life was the prevalence of ideologies (e.g., communist, fascist, national socialist, democratic socialist, and democratic welfare) that supported the belief that centralized governments should develop social and economic policies to reshape the lives of their citizens. Democratic socialism and welfare legislation were often based on the belief that help offered to the needy would safeguard capitalism and democracy from the threat posed by more radical social agendas. Communism, fascism, and national socialism, on the other hand, aspired to rapid, total transformations of whole societies—even at the cost of relocating or eradicating certain categories of people.

The governmental authority that was enhanced to wage wars and campaigns to implement political ideologies was greatly strengthened by the technological revolutions of the twentieth century. Technology gave governments enormous destructive power that could be employed for acts of war and for economic and industrial projects that had comparably high human and environmental costs. The ability of the new technologies to make positive improvements in health and living conditions also made the dream that some leaders had of radically transforming society seem genuinely possible for the first time. The groups whose lives were most dramatically affected by these developments were women, Soviet peasants, and central and eastern European Jews.

Women in Early Twentieth-Century Authoritarian Regimes

The opening decades of the twentieth century were marked by expanded opportunities for women. Universities and professions opened to women of the upper classes, and office work and public school systems provided new opportunities for the employment of others. The manpower drain created by World War I enabled many women to enter the work force as substitute laborers, and their contributions to the war won them support for their campaign to win full admission to the political arena. These developments and the dislocations of war altered attitudes toward sex and family life and enabled women to imagine themselves as something other than wives and mothers.

In the Soviet Union and fascist Italy and Germany the state intervened to impose new constraints on the lives of women while also giving them some paternalistic protections. Often, however, the roles that political ideology said that women should play were quite different from the roles the realities of daily life imposed on them.

Women and the Family in the Early Soviet Union

The Soviet Union claimed to be committed not only to reengineering civilization but to creating new kinds of human beings: the "Soviet Man" and the "Soviet Woman." Nowhere, however, did women face greater contradictions between rhetoric and reality.

During the upheavals of the collectivization of farming, starvation in the Soviet countryside was not uncommon. The Soviet government used famine against political enemies, and collective farms that failed to meet their quotas might see their own food rations reduced. Here, a woman and her son search for food. Hulton Deutsch Collections/Corbis

EARLY SOVIET UTOPIANISM REGARDING WOMEN AND THE FAMILY Communist theory held that the traditional family embodied the middle-class capitalist values that the revolution of the proletariat would overthrow. Communism, some of its advocates believed, was destined to produce a utopian state of complete equality between men and women. The chief proponent of this view was Alexandra Kollontai (1872–1952), the author of *Communism and the Family* (1918). She predicted the dawning of a new era of sexual freedom, of shared domestic tasks between husbands and wives, and of loving families free of exploitative relationships. Her vision was not widely shared even among communists, but at a time when few outsiders knew what was going on inside the Soviet Union, many of the country's foreign sympathizers imagined that Kollon-

tai was describing developments that were actually taking place. Fascists and Nazis were eager to distance their traditionalist view of women from what was alleged to be this radical communist agenda.

FAMILY LEGISLATION FROM REFORM TO REPRESSION Shortly after taking power in 1917, the Bolsheviks issued a number of laws affecting women and family life. Marriage ceased to be sanctified by religious ceremony, divorce became easier, children born inside and outside marriage were given equal legal standing, abortion was legalized (1920), and women were accorded special protections within marriage and in the workplace. Some women advanced to high rank in the Communist Party, and voting by women steadily increased.

These legal reforms had some unfortunate unintended consequences, and war, property confiscations, shifting economic policies, political repression, collectivization of agriculture, housing shortages, purges within the Communist Party, and the general reordering of Soviet society contributed to the dislocation of family life. Domestic violence was prevalent. Divorce made it easier for husbands to abandon wives. Birthrates fell, and the numbers of abortions and abandoned children increased. In 1937 the state reversed itself on some issues. Abortion (except for medical reasons) was outlawed, and divorce was made more difficult. During World War II divorce became virtually impossible, and common-law marriages were no longer recognized.

In the 1920s educational opportunities for women did begin to improve. Some advanced to positions of leadership in the party and on collectivized farms. Yet working women—even professionals—were still expected to do housework. They were paid less than men, and little provision was made for child care. This, combined with the chronic shortage of consumer goods, which required women to spend long hours waiting in line to shop for their families, imposed enormous stresses on women and on family life.

Motherhood for the Nation in Fascist Italy

Italian fascist social policy combined Roman Catholic traditionalism with campaigns to promote the growth of the nation. The male role was held to be that of wage earner and the female role that of mother and homemaker. The chief motive for promoting conformity to these gender roles was to aggrandize the nation by growing Italy's population.

THE CULT OF MOTHERHOOD Mussolini wanted women to have more children and to stay home to raise them. To encourage this, he provided maternity leaves, insurance, subsidies for large families, and education in child rearing. Contraception and abortion were outlawed, and publication of information about human biology was limited to make it more difficult for women to limit the size of their families. Since Italian wages were so low, government agencies provided benefits for mothers and children. This made them dependent on the state and brought the home under some state control.

WOMEN IN THE ITALIAN WORK FORCE Despite the claim that families should be supported by their male members, 25 percent of the Italian work force was female. The fascist government discouraged women from working outside the home and tried to keep them in lower-skilled jobs. In 1938, for example, the government decreed that no more than 10 percent of the employees of a governmental or private office could be female. Laws that were designed to protect women from exploitation also had the effect of limiting their access to the labor market. The result of fascist policy was a general degradation of woman's work.

Radical Ideology and the Lives of Women in Nazi Germany

Like Italy's fascists, Nazi writers portrayed women as wives and mothers. Hitler claimed that men were naturally suited for the world of action and women for the home and that these gender roles should not overlap. During periods of high unemployment, men found this an appealing idea for it discouraged women from competing for jobs. Movements for women's liberation were dismissed as symptoms of cultural decline and weakness.

The Nazi Party did vow to protect the jobs of working women, for it understood that the depression of the 1930s compelled many women to seek employment. It urged women, however, to confine themselves to tasks that were said to be consistent with their femininity (e.g., teaching, nursing, domestic service, social service, and farm work). The Nazis claimed that women, as caretakers and educators of the young, had unique opportunities to protect and transmit German cultural values. They were also expected to use their power as the homemakers who shopped for families to support German stores and German-made products.

There were a few Nazi feminists—mostly professional women who were concerned about protecting their place in society. They argued that the earliest documented phase in German history proved that gender equality was a characteristic of the original, authentic German social order, and they insisted that the Nazi social vision could only be achieved by granting women broad latitude for action. None of this had any influence on the major Nazi leaders.

The Italian fascists' policies regarding women were simply designed to increase Italy's population. The Nazis wanted to do this, but they also wanted to guard Germany's "racial" purity. They insisted that women, by their choice of mates, had a duty to preserve German blood unmixed and that a woman's highest calling was to bear healthy sons and daughters for the state. Childbirth was for women what military service was for men—the prime demonstration of one's patriotic willingness to sacrifice self-interest for the good of the nation. It followed from this that the Nazis favored motherhood only for women who were considered pure Germans. Females from groups that the Nazis branded inferior (e.g., Jews, Slavs, and Gypsies) were discouraged from breeding, and during the Holocaust plans for exterminating the Jews particularly targeted Jewish women. Attempts were also made to weed out elements from the German population that the Nazis considered undesirable (e.g., those Germans who had mental or physical defects that might be hereditary).

To encourage favored women to bear children, the Nazis promoted early marriage and provided tax breaks for families with children and child allowances for the poor. These subsidies were sent to husbands, not wives, in order to make family life seem more appealing to men than bachelorhood. Nazi population policy had a profound effect on the lives of everyone in Germany but particularly on women.

The Social Experience of Stalinism

The Communist Party claimed to be rescuing Soviet society from backwardness and to be leading it to a bright socialist future. This often necessitated the transformation of even the smallest details of life. Collectivization of agriculture, rapid industrialization, and political purges touched everyone—and often intimately.

The Social Experience of Collectivization

During the 1920s Lenin's New Economic Policy tried to expand the urban food supply by encouraging farmers and shopkeepers to be ambitious and entrepreneurial. This allowed a lot of small-scale commerce to flourish, and farmers responded eagerly on the assumption that they were doing what was expected of them. In 1929, however, the state suddenly reversed itself. Stalin decreed the collectivization of Soviet agriculture and set about destroying the *kulaks,* the prosperous farmers who opposed him. Over 2 million people were evicted from their homes for resettlement or confinement in prison camps. Because the government controlled the press, few people were aware of the extent of what was happening. Stalin's demonization of the *kulaks* was so severe that discrimination extended to their descendents, who were assumed to be political subversives.

The Attack on Religion

The Soviet Communist Party was officially atheistic, and it used the drive for collectivization to weaken the Russian Orthodox Church. Priests were attacked, and church buildings were confiscated for secular uses. The Orthodox faith was not the state's only target. Similarly harsh treatment was accorded to Catholics, Muslims, and Jews.

Life on the Collective Farm

In many regions the peasants actively resisted collectivization by destroying livestock and crops. The result was widespread famine in 1932 and 1933, which the Soviet government—through its control of food supplies—sometimes manipulated for its own ends. The peasants who worked the farm collectives were supervised by party officials who set production quotas for them. Farms that failed to meet their quotas were subjected to collective punishment (e.g., reduction in food allotments). Village communities became divided between those who wanted to win favor with the communist authorities by increasing output and those who wanted to subvert the system. Under these circumstances, there was little privacy or protection from malicious informants. Living conditions were extremely poor and contrasted shockingly with the image of the happy socialist peasant that appeared in government propaganda. Conditions did not improve much until the government raised prices for farm goods in the 1970s. Still, standards of living in the countryside remained lower than in cities, and many peasants viewed collectivization as the reimposition of serfdom. Collectivization did, however, improve rural education and literacy.

Flight to the Soviet Cities

Collectivization sparked an enormous migration of peasants who fled the land seeking better lives in cities. Between 1928 and 1932, about 12 million peasants left the countryside, and in the 1930s the number of peasant households declined by 20 percent. Between 1939 and 1980 the proportion of the Soviet population living on the land fell from two-thirds to one-third. Since young males were most likely to migrate, women and the elderly were left behind to struggle with enormous poverty.

Urban Consumer Shortages

The rapid pace of urban migration created severe housing shortages. In some of the newer cities, barracks were built for workers. Elsewhere families huddled in tiny apartments and shared baths and toilets with their neighbors. Cramped quarters created arguments that sometimes turned into political denunciations and fodder for purges.

Housing was not the only thing in short supply. Food, clothing, and basic consumer items were scarce. Throughout the 1930s Russians consumed less food annually than they had before the revolution. The goods that did appear were often funneled to specialty shops reserved for the patronage of party members. Sharp inequality distinguished the small minority of party members from the general population.

Urban infrastructures were also grossly inadequate. Transportation systems were too small for the populations they served. As late as the mid-1930s some major cities lacked sewer systems, and some of the newer towns had little running water and few paved and lighted streets.

In order to survive, people turned to the black market, raised food on private plots, and developed informal systems of exchange that sidestepped government controls. Through it all, the Soviet people were sustained by their belief that the hardships they endured were required to defend their homeland and achieve the glorious future that socialism promised. Their faith proved to be misplaced.

The Destruction of the Polish Jewish Community

The largest Jewish community in Europe prior to World War II consisted of 3 million people who lived in Poland. Only about 10 percent of them survived the Nazi Holocaust that ended not only their way of life but that of Jews in many other central and eastern European regions.

Polish Jews at the End of World War I

Although Jews resided in Poland for centuries, a persisting climate of anti-Semitism made life difficult for them. For their own protection, most chose to live in separate villages or in their own urban neighborhoods. During the nineteenth century Jews in the rest of Europe found that barriers to their participation in society began to crumble, but such was not the case in Poland. Following the Congress of Vienna, most Polish territory had come under Russian control, and the tsars hoped to consolidate their lands by promoting allegiance to Russian Orthodox Christianity. Thus, the Jews became, in the opinion of the government, a religious minority that was to be made unwelcome by discriminatory legislation. In 1919, when the treaties that ended World War I reestablished Poland as an independent state, a surge of Polish nationalism once again marginalized the Jews and defined them as outsiders.

Polish Jewry Between the Wars

As the most religiously observant Jews in Europe, Poland's Jews developed customs that sharply distinguished them from Poland's dominant Catholic culture. They wrote in Hebrew, spoke Yiddish, often adopted distinctive dress, and ate food that differed from that of other Poles. Most resided in cities, in districts that they dominated, but they were among the poorest people in Poland. They tended to be self-employed merchants, peddlers, and craftspersons. They were particularly active in the textile, clothing, and paper-making industries. By the nature of their employment, few belonged to trade unions, and they were particularly vulnerable to the economic turmoil of the 1920s and 1930s.

Polish Anti-Semitism

During the interwar years the Polish government enacted legislation that severely handicapped Jewish workers. Some industries were nationalized and forbidden to hire Jews. Work rules made it difficult for Jews to keep their jobs or do business while being true to their religion's prohibition against working on the Sabbath. Businesses were compelled to display the names of their owners so that customers could choose to avoid patronizing Jewish establishments, and civil service jobs were closed to Jews.

Many Jewish leaders during the nineteenth century had urged their people to assimilate and enter into the mainstream of the cultures in which they lived. Some Polish Jews did try to fit in by adopting the social customs, dress, and language of the Polish majority, but they were not accepted. They were regarded as more modern Jews but still as outsiders.

Political Alternatives for Polish Jews

The constitution that reestablished Poland did not create a government friendly to the Jews, but it did guarantee them the right to participate in political life. Different factions of Polish Jews advocated doing this in different ways. The Zionists

Art & the West

Cultural Divisions and the Cold War

Despite dramatic contrasts that make them look like products of different ages, *Bread* by the Soviet artist Tatjiana Yablonskaya and *One (Number 31, 1950)* by the American Jackson Pollock were painted only one year apart. The differences between them mirror the cultural conflicts of the Cold War. *Bread* (1949) is a monumental example of Socialist Realism, an artistic style that remained dominant in the communist world until Khrushchev liberalized Soviet cultural policy at the end of the 1950s. *Bread* is an optimistic depiction of a happy, hopeful scene from a future socialist society in which prosperity and worker solidarity reign. The reality of life in the Soviet Union under Stalin was quite different.

Tatjiana Yablonskaya, *Bread*, 1949. Ria Novosti/Sovfoto/Eastfoto

If Yablonskaya's painting described a dream, Pollock's, on the other hand, accurately documented the energy of postwar life in America. Pollock placed his canvases on the floor and created looping skeins of paint by flinging pigment at them from sticks and brushes. His exuberant "drip" paintings are interpreted as embodiments of American cultural freedom—the products of an artistic "cowboy" who rejected the kinds of stilted conventions that governed Socialist Realism. Yablonskaya and Pollock illustrate the two poles of twentieth century art: realism and abstraction.

Sources: Matthew Cullerne, *Art under Stalin.* Oxford: Phaidon, 1991. Bowlt, John E. (ed.) *Russian Art of the Avant-Garde: Theory and Criticism 1902–1934.* New York: Viking Press, 1976. McAuley, Alastair, *Women's Work and Wages in the Soviet Union.* London: Allen & Unwin, 1981. O'Conner, Francis V. *Jackson Pollock.* New York: Museum of Modern Art, 1967. Varnedoe, Kirk and Pepe Karmel, *Jackson Pollock.* New York: Museum of Modern Art, 1998.

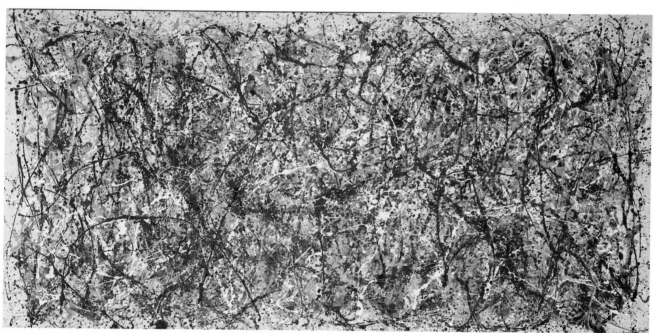

Jackson Pollock, *One (Number 31, 1950).* Oil and enamel on unprimed canvas, 8 ft. 10 in. × 17 ft. 5 5/8 in. (269.5 × 530.8 cm). The Museum of Modern Art, New York. Sidney and Harriet Janis Collection Fund (by exchange). Photograph © 2000 The Museum of Modern Art, New York. 00007.68 © 2000 Pollock-Krasner Foundation/Artists Rights Society (ARS), NY.

urged Jews to take an active part in Polish life until such time as they could emigrate to a Jewish state that the Zionists hoped to establish in Palestine. Another group, the *Bund*, combined Marxism with Jewish nationalism. These secularized Jews regarded Poland as their homeland and pinned their hopes for their people on an alliance between the Jews and the Polish working class. There were also traditionalist Jewish leaders who urged their followers to retreat to the shelter of their separate communities, maintain their distinctive religious practices, and preserve their faith. All of these groups assumed that an independent Poland would continue to exist and be key to any plan to improve the lot of the Jews. The Nazi conquest of Poland in 1939 confronted them with quite a different situation.

The Nazi Assault on the Jews of Poland

The total Jewish population of Germany was not much more than the number of Jews who lived in the single Polish city of Warsaw. When the Nazis occupied Poland, they seized what they considered to be the chief breeding ground of European Jewry, and in pursuit of their racist agenda, they set about destroying it.

The Nazis' original plan was to herd all of the Jews in their occupied territories into the Lublin region of Poland. By the early 1940s, the Nazis were confining Jews to ghettoes, walled neighborhoods with entrances controlled by Nazi guards. The ghettoes were governed by Jewish councils that struggled with the difficult task of mediating between their people and the Germans. The personal property and businesses of the Jews who were driven into the ghettoes were confiscated, and families were allowed to support themselves by sending some of their members out to work as contracted laborers. By 1941, all the Polish Jews had been deprived of their civil rights and their property and crowded into unhealthy, segregated communities. Malnutrition and disease began to decimate their ranks, and about 20 percent of the residents of the ghettoes in Warsaw and Lodz died. From the Nazi point of view, however, this was not enough.

Germany and the Soviet Union had cooperated in overrunning Poland, but in June 1941, war broke out between the former allies. The German forces that advanced into Soviet territory killed tens of thousands of Jews in 1941 and hundreds of thousands more the following year. German propaganda encouraged the masses to associate Jews with the Bolsheviks, and this prepared the way for acceptance of the Nazi government's decision (during the second half of 1941) to exterminate the Jews. From 1941 to 1944, German authorities in Poland sent Jews from the ghettoes to camps established at Kulmhof, Belzen, Sobibor, Treblinka, Birkenau, and Auschwitz, where they were systematically murdered. The Nazis declared this to be the "final solution" to the problem posed by the existence of Jews in their midst. Sadly, the end of the war did little to improve the lot of the handful of Jewish survivors. Anti-Semitism flourished in a Soviet-dominated Poland,

A member of the German SS supervises the boarding of Jews from the Krakow ghetto onto box cars that will carry them to one of the several concentration camps in eastern Europe where millions perished.   [Left] United States Holocaust Memorial Museum.

persuading many Jews to forsake their homeland for the new state of Israel. Only a few thousand remained of a community that had once numbered in the millions.

The Twentieth-Century Movement of Peoples

The forced relocations of peasants by the Soviets and of Jews by the Germans were dramatic, but they were not the only mass migrations of the twentieth century. War and the economic transformation of Europe that followed World War II worked profound changes in patterns of residency. The most persistent trend was the migration of people from the country to the city. In western Europe today about 75 percent of the population lives in an urban setting.

Displacement Through War

World War II created a vast flood of refugees that numbered in the tens of millions. Bombing and fighting destroyed cities and drove people from their homes. The Nazis brought hundreds of thousands of foreign workers into Germany to staff their wartime industries. Hundreds of thousands of soldiers were taken as prisoners of war. Shifting political borders forced some ethnic groups to relocate. Immediately following the war, anti-German feeling in Poland, Czechoslovakia, and Hungary compelled the German minorities that had long lived in these regions to flee to Germany. (This affected about 12 million Germans.) The Soviets also relocated hordes of peoples of various nationalities in the lands they occupied.

External Migration

Between 1945 and 1960 about half a million Europeans left Europe each year, the largest outflow of people since the economic difficulties of the 1920s. Decolonization, on the other hand, led many European and non-European residents of former colonies to relocate to Europe. This created an ethnic diversity that has become a persistent source of social tension and open conflict. Resentment of non-European immigrants has in some places sparked the resurgence of right-wing movements preaching racist ideologies.

Economic Growth and Internal Migration

The Soviet Union made it difficult for the citizens of its subject nations in eastern Europe to emigrate, but many of the younger and more mobile managed to move to the West in pursuit of better, freer lives. Before the Berlin Wall went up, about 3 million East Germans migrated to West Germany.

Political factors were not the only things that encouraged internal migration. The expansion of the European economy that began in the 1950s brought increasing prosperity to the nations of northern and western Europe and created a need for more workers. People from the poorer parts of the continent were eager for employment, and some countries negotiated deals to facilitate the migration of workers—a process that was helped by the establishment of the European Economic Community in 1957. Most of Europe's so-called "guest workers" were welcomed in the countries where they sought employment during periods of prosperity, but they were resented whenever an economic downturn created a threat of unemployment for the citizens of a host nation. In Germany in the early 1990s workers whom the government had originally invited in began to be threatened with violence.

Thousands of people wanted to flee the communist-dominated states of Eastern Europe. This contributed to the fall of their governments in 1988 and 1989, an event which freed more immigrants to seek their fortunes in Western Europe. Wars, such as the recent conflicts in Yugoslavia, also continue to dislocate populations and create refugees in Europe.

The Welfare State

The Great Depression and the mobilization required to fight World War II changed the way many Europeans thought about issues of social welfare. Prior to the war, there had been two basic models for social legislation in Europe—one German, and the other British. In the 1880s Bismarck had introduced some forms of social insurance to Germany in an effort to deprive the Social Democratic Party of its appeal to the masses. By granting German workers some security, he undercut their motivation to agitate for expanded political rights. In Britain, where the working class had full access to the political system, social insurance tended to be provided only for the very poor. In both countries, it was accepted that workers should be insured to help them with the problems created by disease, injury, and old age, but unemployment was not considered something that called for a legislative solution. People higher up on the social scale, who could generally look out for themselves, viewed unemployment as a short-term problem that workers often created for themselves.

After World War II, the belief spread that social insurance against predictable risks was a right that should be accorded all citizens. Universal coverage obviously appealed to socialists, but even conservatives thought that it was a good idea. They assumed that by providing medical care, old-age pensions, and other benefits they could diminish popular pressure for more radical redistributions of income from the rich to the poor.

Great Britain was the first European nation to create a welfare state. The ground work for it was laid by the Labour Party during the ministry (1945–1951) of Clement Attlee (1883–1967). The centerpiece of Attlee's program was the creation of the National Health Service. In the 1970s, France and Germany followed Britain's example and passed similar health care legislation. The Cold War created an environment that encouraged the growth of welfare programs—particularly unemployment insurance. Since communist nations promised their people enormous social security and full employment, capitalist states believed that they had to offer their citizens competitive deals. The communists promised, however, more than they could deliver.

Western European attitudes toward the welfare state have fluctuated with the European economy. While Europe was recovering from the war and experiencing economic growth, Europeans placed their confidence in the government's ability to intervene in and effectively manage a mixed economy. In the 1970s, however, an era of inflation, slow growth, and high rates of unemployment set in and persisted through the 1990s. This diminished faith in government intervention in the economy and persuaded many people that free markets should (within limits) be allowed to regulate themselves. Resistance also developed to the idea that

governments owe their citizens as many benefits as had been promised by Europe's welfare states. In order to afford the costs of their welfare systems, Europe's nations need growing populations and low unemployment. The welfare burden is only bearable when the number of employed, younger workers (who pay the bills) is much greater than the number of older people (who draw the benefits). Europe's population growth has, however, leveled off, and unemployment rates have remained uncomfortably high for two decades. Governments across the continent (including those of the left) have, therefore, begun to limit the growth of the welfare state and to curtail some benefits. The golden age of welfare states may have passed, and in the future societies may have to develop new approaches to dealing with issues of social welfare.

New Patterns in the Work and Expectations of Women

Although the decades following World War II witnessed changes that enabled more women than ever before to reach positions of leadership in business, politics, and the professions, traditional patterns of family and economic life have persisted to perpetuate gender inequality in European societies.

Feminism

European feminism has been less well organized than American feminism, but it has become an influential force. After the collapse of communism undercut confidence in the social critiques proposed by the socialists, feminist (and environmentalist) groups assumed chief responsibility for critically evaluating the European way of life. Feminism should be understood, therefore, as an important manifestation of Western civilization's characteristic tendency to engender self-criticism.

Prior to World War II, the goal of feminists was to gain legal and civil equality with men. Early feminism was primarily a movement that campaigned for specific political rights. Since the war, however, the feminist agenda has broadened to offer a more general critique of European culture and to pursue issues that are particularly important to women (e.g., spousal abuse). The more radical European feminists argue that society, as currently organized, inherently represses women, and they hold all political parties—the left as well as the right—equally guilty for failing to address women's issues.

The most influential feminist thinker of the postwar period was the French intellectual, Simone de Beauvoir (1908–1986). In 1949 she published *The Second Sex*, an analysis of the difference it had made in her life to be born female rather than male. Although she enjoyed privileges as a member of the French intellectual elite, she and other feminist commentators explained how gender imposed social, legal, and economic disadvantages on women of all classes.

Modern European Household Structure

Prior to World War II, a significant number of women remained single all their lives. Since the war, the proportion of married people in the population has increased, and far fewer women now remain single. Over all, people tend to marry at younger ages than ever before in European history, and traditional assumptions about married life have also changed. Family size fell and divorce rates rose during the twentieth century, and in the Scandinavian countries, more children were born to parents who chose to live together but not to marry. Government-sponsored programs providing aid for children helped to make such arrangements and single motherhood more economically feasible.

More Married Women in the Work Force

One aspect of women's lives that has changed significantly is the sharp increase in the number of married women who work outside the home. During the twentieth century, both middle-class and working-class women have sought such employment in unprecedented numbers. Because birthrates were low in the 1930s, the numbers of single women in the work force after World War II were few, and married women entered the job market to replace them. Consumer conveniences and alterations in work schedules have gradually made it easier for married women to work outside the home, but responsibilities for the care of children still compel many women to accept only part-time employment.

Unlike earlier periods in history, children in the modern West are no longer expected to contribute substantially to their families' support. If a family needs more income than one parent can provide, the other seeks work, and their children spend years in compulsory education. It is also true that many mothers choose to work outside their homes for reasons of personal fulfillment, not economic necessity.

New Work Patterns

Careers and wage-paying jobs have come to occupy a much larger part of a woman's life in the twentieth century than they did in the nineteenth. Where single women used to drop out of the work force following marriage, this is no longer the case. A married woman may temporarily leave her employment to care for young children but return to her job once her children enter school. Increasing life spans have also made work outside the home more important to women. When women died relatively young, bearing and rearing children consumed most of their time. But since modern women can anticipate many years of vigorous life after their children are grown, work has taken on a new significance for them. Interest in careers persuades some women to limit the size of their families, to postpone childbearing, or to forgo it altogether. The age at which women begin to bear children has risen to the early twenties in Eastern Europe and to the late twenties in Western Europe.

Controversy over abortion has recently increased in Europe. Prior to the formation of the European Union, each nation had its own legislation governing abortion, but negotiations for union forced the states to move toward the establishment of a common policy. By the 1990s, abortion was legally (if not equally conveniently) available everywhere in western Europe except Ireland. Abortion was legalized in Eastern Europe during the era of communist domination, and in the Soviet Union following the death of Stalin. The freeing of political debate that followed the collapse of communism in these countries has allowed renewed public discussion of the issue.

Women in the New Eastern Europe

The collapse of the communist regimes has created special problems for women in Eastern Europe.

Under communism well over 50 percent of women were in the work force, and they enjoyed social equality and many government-financed benefits. There were no "women's movements," for communist authorities regarded all independent associations with suspicion.

The governments that have replaced the communists face serious economic challenges, and they have shown little concern for how their economic policies may impact the lives of women. Many of the health and welfare programs that benefit women and children face cutbacks, and in order to be competitive with free-market economies, the states of Eastern Europe will probably shorten the lengthy maternity leaves to which female workers were formally entitled. Women will also probably find themselves more poorly paid than men, and during economic downturns they may be subject to earlier layoffs and later rehires.

Transformations in Knowledge and Culture

Cultural and intellectual life has been transformed in Europe during the twentieth century. An explosion of educational institutions has made learning available to a wider and more diverse student body than ever before, and this has acquainted more people with intellectual movements that challenge traditional attitudes. Concern for the environment has raised new issues for debate, and Europe's traditional Christian faith has struggled to assimilate all this and to remain relevant.

Communism and Western Europe

Following the Russian revolution, the socialist movement in western Europe split between independent democratic socialist parties and Soviet-dominated communist parties that supported the agenda of the Third International. Throughout the 1920s and 1930s these groups were generally opposed to each other.

THE INTELLECTUALS   During the 1930s, as the Great Depression caused liberal democracies to flounder and right-wing regimes to spring up, some people concluded that communism provided the best hope for defending humane, liberal values. Many students and older intellectuals from across Europe affiliated with the Communist Party and visited the Soviet Union. For some of them communism almost became a religion, and they were willing to ignore or justify Stalin's terrorism.

Four events contributed to the eventual disillusionment of most European intellectuals with Soviet communism: the purges of the late 1930s, the Spanish Civil War (1936–1939), the 1939 alliance between Russia and Germany, and the 1956 Soviet invasion of Hungary. Disillusionment with the Soviet Union's system did not, however, necessarily entail a loss of confidence in communism itself. Some social critics pinned their hopes for the realization of their visions for society on non-Soviet communist governments. Yugoslavia was one such, and in the late 1950s there was a surge of interest in China.

Some people hoped that a uniquely European form of communism would evolve and that communist parties could win power democratically. Toward this end, efforts were made to adapt Marxism to midcentury European thought. During the 1930s the abstract, philosophical writings of the "young Marx" (i.e., those that preceded the *Communist Manifesto* of 1848) were published. They made Marx appear more a humanist than a revolutionary, and they allowed some people to believe that they could sympathize with Marxism without condoning revolution or supporting the Soviet Union. Given the collapse of the Soviet Union and of eastern Europe's communist governments, the future of a European Marxism and of its influence on European intellectual life is unclear.

Existentialism

The intellectual movement that was most characteristic of mid-twentieth-century European culture was existentialism. It was not a unified movement. Existentialist philosophers disagreed on major issues, but in general they continued the nineteenth century's revolt against rationalism.

ROOTS IN NIETZSCHE AND KIERKEGAARD   The forerunners of existentialism were Friedrich Nietzsche (see Chapter 25) and Søren Kierkegaard (1813–1855), a Danish author who received little attention until after World War I. Both men rejected the dominant Hegelian philosophy of their

Jean-Paul Sartre (1905–1980) and Simone de Beauvoir (1908–1986) were two leading midcentury French intellectuals. His was a major voice in the existentialist movement, and she wrote extensively on the social position, experience, and psychology of women. Bildarchiv Preussischer Kulturbesitz

day and its confidence that life could be explained in abstract, rational terms. Kierkegaard opposed the same shallow tendency in organized religion. In *Fear and Trembling* (1843), *Either/Or* (1843), and *Concluding Unscientific Postscript* (1846) he argued that Christian truth could not be captured in creeds, doctrines, and ecclesiastical organizations. It could only be grasped when people faced extreme challenges. Passion, he claimed, was the sole human faculty capable of comprehending truth.

It was the intellectual and ethical crises created by World War I that brought Kierkegaard's thought to the fore and revived interest in Nietzsche's critique of reason. The war raised doubts about the ability of human beings to control their destinies and to make historical progress. Its destructiveness undercut faith in the redemptive power of reason, for the war's most terrible weapons were the products of rational technology. One of the casualties of war was the nineteenth century's sunny faith in orderly human development.

QUESTIONING OF RATIONALISM   The major existential writers were two Germans—Martin Heidegger (1889–1976) and Karl Jaspers (1883–1969)—and two Frenchmen—Jean-Paul Sartre (1905–1980) and Albert Camus (1913–1960). Although they disagreed

on many things, they all, in one way or another, questioned the primacy of reason and scientific understanding as approaches to comprehending the human situation. The Enlightenment tradition claimed that analysis—the division of human experience into its component parts—was the path to understanding. But existentialists argued that the human condition was greater than the sum of its parts and could only be grasped as a whole. The romantics of the early nineteenth century had also questioned reason but much less radically. They believed that truth could be grounded in imagination and intuition. The existentialists focused primarily on the obliterating extremes of human experience: death, dread, fear, and anxiety. They claimed that confrontations with such ultimate challenges compel human beings to formulate ethical values for themselves. They insisted that traditional religion, rational philosophy, intuition, or social customs cannot help people when they stare into the abyss. At such times each person discovers that he or she is endowed with the dreadful freedom to create value for himself or herself.

The attraction of existentialism, like communism, was very much a response to a mood that existed in Europe before and just after World War II. During the 1960s, however, the turmoil created by the Vietnam War and the youth rebellion redirected the intellectual interests of Europeans.

Expansion of the University Population and Student Rebellion

At the turn of the twentieth century, no more than a few thousand people were enrolled in universities in any major European country. But by the 1980s, even though university education was less common in Europe than in the United States, that figure had risen to hundreds of thousands. Higher education is now available to people from a wide variety of social and economic backgrounds and, for the first time, to significant numbers of women.

The great intellectual developments of the seventeenth, eighteenth, and nineteenth centuries thrived primarily outside the university, but beginning with the twentieth century, most intellectuals have sought a university home. The expanding population of university-educated people has, not surprisingly, transformed social, political, and intellectual life in Europe. Millions of citizens have been trained in skills of critical thinking that once were the preserve of small, literate elites, and television has given them access to the arguments of reformers and social critics. More scientists, historians, economists, literary critics, and other professional scholars have been produced during the last seventy-five years than have existed in total in all of human history.

One unexpected result of the ballooning population of students and intellectuals was a rebellious student movement that began in the United States in the early 1960s and then spread to Europe and other parts of the world. Since it thrived on opposition to the war in Vietnam, it was usually associated with antimilitarism and a radical critique of American politics. In Eastern Europe, the Soviet Union was the target of some of its resentment. The movement also rejected middle-class values and sexual mores and traditional family life.

The student movement reached its peak in 1968—a year in which American students demonstrated against U.S. involvement in Vietnam, French students at the Sorbonne in Paris instigated a serious challenge to the government of Charles de Gaulle, and students in Czechoslovakia backed a drive to establish a more liberal form of socialism. These protests failed to alter the policies of the governments at which they were directed, and by the early 1970s the era of the student rebellion seemed to have passed. European students continued to oppose nuclear weapons (particularly the basing of American missiles in Europe), but from the middle of the 1970s, students maintained a generally radical political stance without engaging in the kinds of disruptive protests that marked the 1960s.

Nothing has so characterized both student and youth culture in the second half of the twentieth century as rock music, which first appeared in the 1950s. Rock has become so common a feature of contemporary life that lyrics of songs by the Beatles, the British rock group of the 1960s, may be the most widely dispersed poetry in world history. Despite the enormous popularity of the Beatles and some European pop musicians, rock music originated in the United States and is part of a greater wave of postwar American popular culture that has inundated Europe.

The Americanization of Europe

During the past half-century, Western Europe has been enormously influenced by the United States. Following World War II, Europe's economy was rebuilt by the Marshall Plan and its defense provided by NATO—both American initiatives. Over the years, hundreds of thousands of Americans have spent time in Europe on military service, as students, as businesspeople, and as tourists. This has had an influence on European cultures that Europeans much discuss and frequently lament. They call it "Americanization." The shopping centers and supermarkets that Americans pioneered are displacing Europe's traditional sales districts. American television programs and movies are readily available everywhere. Fast-food restaurants, such as McDonald's, line the streets of European cities from Dublin to Moscow, and American clothing styles (e.g., blue jeans) are wildly popular throughout Europe. Thanks to the influence of the media and the power of American corporations, American English also seems to be emerging as the common language for Europe's business and academic communities.

Rock Music and Political Protest

One of the more significant effects of Americanization on the lives of Europeans is the impact that American rock music has had as a vehicle for conducting an ongoing critique of the European political and social orders. In the 1960s rock trumpeted Western youth's discontent with the values of older generations, and it contributed greatly to efforts to mobilize opposition to the Vietnam War. In the 1970s and 1980s, it began to provide people in Eastern Europe and the Soviet Union with an instrument with which to agitate for social and political change in their homelands. They came to regard the rock stars who attacked communist governments and defended subjectivity and individualism as heroes, and the lyrics of rock songs helped to raise the passions that contributed to the collapse of communist regimes at the end of the 1980s.

A Consumer Society

During the past half-century, the economy of Western Europe has differentiated itself from that of Eastern Europe by its emphasis on the manufacture of consumer goods. The Soviet bloc's economic planners, on the other hand, continued to concentrate on capital investments and military needs, and, consequently, people in communist countries witnessed a steady decline in the quantity and quality of food and consumer items. Since the early 1950s, Europeans have seen their food supply steadily improve, and they have enjoyed an expanding array of consumer goods and services: automobiles, household appliances, entertainments, clothing, "disposable" conveniences, and vacations—all the appurtenances of the leisured lifestyle.

This development has had dramatic political repercussions. Through the limited number of radios, television, movies, and videos available to them, Eastern Europeans became aware of the discrepancy between their circumstances and those of Westerners. They intuited the link between Western consumerism and democracy, between free societies and economic policies that minimize government planning. Although Western consumerism has been deplored by Western commentators and Christian moralists, it helped generate the discontent in Eastern Europe that brought down its communist governments.

Environmentalism

The shortage of consumer goods in the West after World War II created the demand that fueled the West's economic expansion through the 1960s. During this period, the public paid scant attention to the ethical implications of growth and its effect on the environment. Concern for the environment emerged in the 1970s, and by the 1980s environmentalism had acquired real political clout. Among the most important of the politically active environmental groups were the Club of Rome (founded in 1972) and the German Greens. In 1979 the Greens formed a political party that immediately became an electoral force. Governments outside of Europe and United Nations agencies also began to take up environmental issues.

Several developments lay behind the increasing concern for the environment. The 1973–1974 Arab oil embargo alerted Europeans to the degree to which their lifestyle was dependent on imports of natural resources that were in limited supply. At the same time, the dire environmental consequences of three decades of economic expansion were becoming impossible to ignore. Fish were disappearing from major river systems because of industrial pollution, and acid rain was killing forests. The anxiety created by the Cold War's nuclear threat and descriptions of the nightmares that would follow accidents at nuclear reactors also began to have an effect on voters.

The German Green movement shared the views of the radical student groups of the late 1960s from which it recruited many of its members. It was anticapitalistic—holding business responsible for pollution. It was peace oriented—opposing nuclear arms. But unlike the earlier

Pollution of waterways poses danger to human health in many parts of Europe and has been one of the conditions giving rise to the European environmental movement. Here, a German factory pours its refuse and chemicals into a river. Such pollution has been a particular problem in the former Soviet bloc nations.
Frischmuth/Argos/SABA Press Photos, Inc.

student groups, the Greens chose to compete in the electoral process rather than to resort to mass demonstrations to agitate for changes in government policies. The Greens had modest success, winning seats in the West German Parliament and on some local councils.

The 1986 meltdown of nuclear reactors at Chernobyl in the Soviet Union raised environmental issues that no government in Europe could ignore. There were many deaths and injuries, and the Soviet authorities had to relocate tens of thousands of people. Clouds of radioactive fallout spread across Europe, posing a threat to the health of people and to food supplies. Chernobyl demonstrated that environmental issues transcend national borders, and it prompted governments in both the East and the West to take action. Environmental groups now command a significant share of votes, and as the European Economic Community solidifies, it will likely impose environmental regulations on business and industry. The nations of Eastern Europe face a particularly daunting challenge. They must clean up vast areas that have been polluted while simultaneously trying to catch up economically with their Western neighbors.

The Christian Heritage

Christianity has been hard-pressed during the twentieth century. Material prosperity, political ideologies, environmentalism, gender politics, and simple indifference have replaced religious faith for many people, but Europe's Christian churches still exercise considerable influence. In Germany, during World War II, churches were among the few major institutions not wholly subdued by the Nazis. After the war, in Poland and elsewhere in Eastern Europe, the Roman Catholic Church kept opposition to communism alive. In Western Europe, religious affiliation still provides a basis for the construction of Christian democratic parties. Churches everywhere have also heightened concern about such issues as colonial exploitation, nuclear weapons, human rights, and ethics.

Neo-Orthodoxy

The rational optimism that characterized intellectual life in the nineteenth century encouraged liberal theologians of that era to soften the concept of sin and to portray human nature as not far removed from divinity. The horror of World War I destroyed that illusion, and the "neo-Orthodox" movement responded by emphasizing the importance of Christian insights that liberals had neglected (namely, the power of evil and the human potential for self-destructive behavior).

Karl Barth (1886–1968), a Swiss pastor and theologian, produced the most influential neo-Orthodox Christian reflection on the lessons of war. In *A Commentary on the Epistle to the Romans* (1919), Barth claimed that Christian faith sprang from a sense of God's transcendence and humanity's dependence. Under Kierkegaard's influence, Barth returned to the Reformation theology of Martin Luther. He described God as the "wholly other" who is encountered in the extreme moments of life when people are forced to confront their insufficiencies.

Liberal Theology

Neo-Orthodoxy did not end the liberal tradition in Christian theology. Its strongest defender was a German American named Paul Tillich (1886–1965). Where Barth saw God as dwelling outside humankind, Tillich believed that evidence for the divine was to be found in human nature and culture. Similarly, Rudolf Bultmann (1884–1976) produced a brilliant analysis of the development of the Christian Scriptures that rejected supernaturalism as a basis for Christian faith. His work was popularized by Anglican bishop John Robinson's *Honest to God* (1963), and another British liberal Christian, the literary scholar C. S. Lewis (1878–1963), attracted millions of readers with amusing and accessible explications of doctrine. His best-remembered work is *The Screwtape Letters* (1942). In recent years, Europe has produced few major Protestant voices.

Roman Catholic Reform

The most significant postwar changes in institutionalized Christianity have been developments within the Roman Catholic Church. In 1959, Pope John XXIII (r. 1958–1963) called the twenty-first ecumenical (i.e., universal) council, popularly known as Vatican II. By 1965, under the guidance of his successor, Paul VI

(r. 1963–1978), the council had carried out the most extensive reform of Catholicism that has taken place, some would say, since the sixteenth century. Catholic liturgy was rewritten, and the Latin mass gave way to celebrations in the vernacular. The pope permitted freer relations with other Christian denominations, gave more power to bishops, and made the church more representative of the world at large by appointing cardinals from former European colonies.

While granting these liberal reforms, Pope Paul VI and his successors have rejected others. They have firmly upheld celibacy for priests, maintained prohibition of contraception, and opposed ordination for women. These policies have increased resentment among the laity and made it difficult for the church to recruit people for the priesthood and the religious orders.

Paul VI's successor, John Paul I, reigned for only thirty-four days. He was followed by the youngest pope to be elected in more than a century, Karol Wojtyla, the former archbishop of Cracow. Wojtyla, who took the name John Paul II, has defended traditional positions stressing the authority of the papacy and limiting doctrinal and liturgical experimentation. He has pursued expansion of the church in the non-Western world and insisted on the need to fight for social justice, but he has also ordered priests to limit their political activism.

John Paul II's opposition to communism strengthened the demands for freedom in Eastern Europe that contributed to the fall of its communist regimes. As a Polish cardinal archbishop, he had clashed with Poland's communist government, and after his election to the papacy his visit to Poland bolstered the *Solidarity* movement. His encouragement of popular resistance to Eastern Europe's communist governments during the 1980s opened a new chapter in the relationship between church and state in modern Europe.

Late Twentieth-Century Technology: The Arrival of the Computer

During the twentieth century, technology, like popular culture, freely crossed international borders, and it contributed greatly to the impact that America had on Europe. No single American technological achievement, however, promises to exert a greater influence on life everywhere than the computer.

The Demand for Calculating Machines

Although computers are relatively recent inventions, they have roots stretching back to the seventeenth century. The giants of the Scientific Revolution (e.g., Kepler, Galileo, Descartes, and Newton) maintained that mathematics held the key to understanding and controlling nature. This inspired some of their contemporaries to try to construct mechanisms that could assist scientists with the labor of mathematical calculation. In 1644, the French mathematician, Blaise Pascal, built a machine that could add and subtract. Demand for such inventions increased during the nineteenth century as nation-states consolidated their power and confronted administrative tasks that involved collecting and managing vast amounts of data. The growth of private businesses created another market that was vastly expanded by the development of electronic communications (i.e., the telephone, telegraph, and wireless). The complex electrical circuitry that made these things possible also made calculating machines a technical feasibility. By the late 1920s, major companies had been established to manufacture a variety of such machines to serve the needs of business.

Early Computer Technology

Military developments did much to spur the invention of calculator technology. Following World War I and during World War II, the major powers developed bombers and long-range guns that needed precise ballistic calculations in order to strike their targets. The people who worked on techniques for decoding messages made more advances, and the Cold War persuaded governments to invest heavily in the research that ultimately produced the modern computer.

The first machine that might legitimately be considered a digital computer was up and running by 1946. Called ENIAC (Electronic Numerical Integrator and Computer), it was designed and built at the University of Pennsylvania. It was an enormous piece of equipment that utilized 1,500 electric relays, 18,000 vacuum tubes, and thousands of punch cards.

For the first decade of their existence, computers were largely invisible to the general public. They were so big and costly that it seemed their use would be reserved to government agencies and the largest corporations. Few people understood the potential of computers—that is, that they were far more than calculating machines and could store, sort, transmit, manage, and transform all kinds of information if that information was described numerically.

The nature of computers began to change in the 1950s following the invention of the transistor. By miniaturizing electronic circuitry and making vacuum tubes obsolete, transistors reduced the size of computers and increased their dependability. Nevertheless, throughout the 1950s and 1960s, computers continued to be reserved for the use of the government, the military, and large corporations. They were still large, unconnected "mainframes" that were programmed with difficult computer languages.

The Development of Desktop Computers

During the 1960s, computing technology was transformed yet again. First, direction for the control of the computer was transferred to a bitmap covering the screen of a monitor, and in 1964 the "mouse" was invented to ease the movement of the cursor around the computer's screen. The bitmap on the screen hid a complicated computer language behind simple images that a user could manipulate with the mouse. This made it possible for people who were not elaborately trained experts to learn to operate computers.

Second, the microchip—the heart of all future computers—was invented by a California start-up company called Intel Corporation. The microchip was itself a miniature computer (a microprocessor) that allowed computer technology to abandon mainframe design for smaller units. This downsizing was key to extending the computer's use, multiplying its applications, and generating a new vision for the role it might play in society.

Xerox Corporation was the first to devise a small computer controlled by a mouse, but the machine's commercial potential was not exploited. By 1982 IBM (International Business Machines Corporation) had also produced a small computer, but in marketing its invention it lagged behind a company called Apple Computer Corporation. In 1984 the Apple engineers adapted the Xerox design to create the Macintosh, a highly accessible computer that would fit on a desktop in a home or office. IBM then reengineered its machine and produced the PC (i.e., the personal computer). By the mid-1980s ordinary people, for a modest cost, could acquire computers that were more powerful than the great mainframes of the 1950s and 1960s, and as these computers became more and more common, everyday life underwent radical transformations. The development of the World Wide Web during the 1990s enhanced the computer's impact by making it the portal for immediate access to rapid communications and the largest store of information in human history. This, in turn, has spawned a development that promises to have major economic implications: e-commerce.

The Social Impact of the Computer

Computer literacy, like reading, is not an end in itself. It is a skill that opens up all kinds of possibilities. The access to information that the computer supplies through the Web, for instance, advances personal freedom and democratization at the dawn of the twenty-first century much like the mobility created by affordable automobiles did in the early part of the twentieth century. Computers have transformed work and workplaces. The industrial revolution forced workers to labor in a factory setting, but the computer now allows many of them again to work from their homes. Education is being revolutionized as students access courses via the computer rather than by gathering on college campuses. Computers touch daily life in a myriad of ways—communications, banking, travel, shopping, and as hidden components of automobiles and dozens of household appliances and gadgets. They are, of course, essential to government administration, and they have transformed warfare. But they have also created a unique forum for private individuals to assert themselves by launching their ideas and opinions into cyberspace.

Access to computer technology has given new meaning to the old distinction between society's "haves" and "have-nots." Computers, for good and ill, give their users the ability to do things that nonusers cannot do. People who do not have the opportunity to master them will be severely handicapped in the world's increasingly computerized economies. Nations whose governments and businesses are not fully integrated into the world of computers will compete at a serious disadvantage. The possession of computers and the ability to use them is, in many arenas, the key to the future.

In Perspective

The twentieth century was the most destructive in human history. Wars took the lives of millions, as did the policies of authoritarian governments. The Soviets sacrificed human rights and innumerable lives in order to experiment with economic schemes such as the collectivization of agriculture. The Nazis deliberately slaughtered millions of Jews in the service of a racist ideology.

The defeat of national socialism and fascism allowed Western Europe to evolve more peacefully in the second half of the twentieth century. Migration reshaped societies, as did powerful economic and cultural forces originating in America. Welfare systems provided increased security for individuals and families. Women were granted greater freedoms. Opportunities for education expanded, and computers launched Europeans into an era of technological revolution. By the start of the twenty-first century, Western Europeans were enjoying high standards of living under liberal governments, but regions that had been part of the former Soviet Union and its empire were still struggling with social, political, and economic difficulties that were a legacy from their communist pasts.

REVIEW QUESTIONS

1. What are the major examples of state-initiated violence in twentieth-century Europe? What impact did this violence have on social life?
2. What were the differences and similarities in ideas and policies affecting women that were advanced by the communists, fascists, and Nazis?
3. What was the impact on peasant life of Stalin's policy of collectivization? How did this policy affect city dwellers? What effect did shortages of consumer goods have on daily life in the Soviet Union?
4. What was Polish Jewish society like between the world wars? What were the major developments that contributed to its destruction?
5. How did migration affect twentieth-century social life in Europe?
6. In what ways was Europe "Americanized" in the second half of the twentieth century? How do you account for the trend toward a consumer society?
7. How did women's social and economic roles change in the second half of the twentieth century? What problems have new patterns of work created for women? How has the political instability of Eastern Europe affected women in that region?
8. How did the pursuit and diffusion of knowledge change during the twentieth century? What are the effects of the revolutions in communications and of the increased access to university educations? Has intellectual life in the West become more unified or less so? Why?
9. What did Nietzsche and Kierkegaard contribute to existentialism? What did Sartre mean when he said that existentialism is a philosophy of anguish and despair? In what sense was existentialism a response to the crises of the twentieth century?
10. What were the major stages in the development of the computer? What are the major fields to which computers have been applied? What changes are computers most likely to bring in the next decade?

SUGGESTED READINGS

G. AMBROSIUS and W. H. HUBBARD, *A Social and Economic History of Twentieth-Century Europe* (1989). The best one-volume treatment of the subject.

B. S. ANDERSON and J. P. ZINSSER, *A History of Their Own: Women in Europe from Prehistory to the Present*, vol. 2 (1998). A broad-ranging survey.

A. APPLEBAUM, *Between East and West: Across the Borderlands of Europe* (1995). A travelogue recounting the state of numerous regions of Europe in the aftermath of the collapse of communism.

E. BRAMWELL, *Ecology in the 20th Century: A History* (1989). Traces the environmental movement to its late-nineteenth-century origins.

S. FITZPATRICK, *Everyday Stalinism, Ordinary Life in Extraordinary Times: Soviet Russia in the 1930s* (1999). A major study based on newly available materials.

H. H. GOLDSTINE, *The Computer from Pascal to von Neuman* (1972). A clear history of the technological development of the computer.

C. S. HELLER, *On the Edge of Destruction: Jews of Poland between the Two World Wars* (1994). A probing examination of the subject.

THOMAS K. LANDAUER, *The Trouble with Computers: Usefulness, Usability, and Productivity* (1997). An informed skeptical commentary on the impact of computers.

R. MALTBY, ed., *Passing Parade: A History of Popular Culture in the Twentieth Century* (1989). A collection of essays on a topic just beginning to receive scholarly attention.

G. MONTEFIORE, *Philosophy in France Today* (1983). A good introduction to one of the major centers of contemporary thought.

D. VITAL, *A People Apart: The Jews in Europe, 1789–1939* (1999). A major survey with excellent discussions of the interwar years.

Chapter 31
The Cold War Era and the Emergence of the New Europe

KEY TOPICS

- The origins of the Cold War and the division of Europe into eastern and western blocs following World War II
- Decolonization and the conflicts in Korea and Vietnam
- Political and economic developments in Western Europe during the Cold War
- Polish protests against Soviet domination of Eastern Europe
- *Peristroika* and *glasnost* in the Soviet Union
- The collapse of communism in Eastern Europe and the Soviet Union
- The civil war in Yugoslavia
- Europe in the twenty-first century

From 1945 (the end of World War II) until 1989 to 1991 (the collapse of the Soviet Union), Soviet and American nuclear-armed superpowers waged the Cold War. Europe's nations divided and chose sides, forming NATO (North Atlantic Treaty Organization) with the United States and the Warsaw Pact with the USSR.

The active role that the United States began to play in world affairs was a major departure from its traditional isolationism. It reflected a lesson that the nation had learned from the world wars: that is, that it was risky to assume that American security was unrelated to developments abroad. The greatest challenge that now faced the West was the expansion of Soviet power and communist influence. To counteract these, the United States promoted Europe's economic recovery and stability with the Marshall Plan and NATO. The Cold War quickly became globalized, however, as the nations of Europe relinquished their colonial empires and the two superpowers began to compete for the allegiance of Europe's former colonies. Superpower intervention aggravated local conflicts on every continent, and the United States became embroiled in bitter wars in Korea and Vietnam. Harsh disagreements emerged between the Soviet Union and other communist nations (most notably the People's Republic of China), and the leaders of the Soviet Union failed to build lasting support for their policies either internally or among their Eastern European dependencies.

The Emergence of the Cold War

Basic differences of ideology and self-interest lay behind the split that developed between the United States and the USSR. At the end of World War II, the Soviet Union's drive to expand westward into central Europe and the Balkans and southward into the Middle East was a continuation of policies established by tsarist governments. Traditionally, it had been Britain's role to block Russian moves in these regions, but in the wake of the war only the United States was strong enough to contain the Soviets. Despite the facts that American military forces were at their historical peak, American industrial power was unmatched, and the United States had exclusive possession of atomic weapons, the United States made no attempt to roll back the Soviets and began instead to withdraw its troops from Europe. Within a year of the war's end, the United States had reduced its forces in Europe from 3.5 million to 500,000.

The American plan for peace reflected American principles and served American interests. The United States supported self-determination, autonomy, and democracy in the political arena and free trade, freedom of the seas, and unrestrained investment opportunities in the economic sphere. As the strongest industrialized power remaining in the world, the United States had much to gain from the kind of international order it envisioned.

From the Soviet perspective, the USSR had to extend its borders and dominate the formerly independent states of Eastern Europe in order to guarantee its own security and to obtain the compensation due its people for their fearful losses in the war. The Soviets saw American opposition to their expansion as a threat to their legitimate national interests and claims, while the United States viewed the activities of communist parties in countries friendly to the United States as evidence of a Moscow-led plot for the worldwide subversion of capitalism and democracy. Not long after the war concluded the former allies began openly to manifest mutual hostility. In February 1946, Stalin and his foreign minister, Vyacheslav Molotov (1890–1986), declared the Western democracies enemies of the Soviets, and a month later Churchill, in a speech in Fulton, Missouri, announced that an "Iron Curtain" had descended on Europe, dividing a free and democratic West from a totalitarian East.

"Containment" in American Foreign Policy

In 1947 American foreign policy adopted containment as a method for countering the communist threat. The plan was to resist the spread of Soviet influence until internal difficulties caused the collapse of the Soviet Union. This strategy was ultimately successful but it forced the United States to make the kinds of military and financial commitments abroad that it had traditionally avoided.

THE TRUMAN DOCTRINE   In a speech to Congress on March 12, 1947, President Truman set forth what came to be called the Truman Doctrine. It affirmed America's willingness to support all free peoples who were determined to resist subjugation by armed minorities or takeovers by foreign powers. Truman had in mind immediate aid for Greece and Turkey as they struggled to fend off communist aggressors, but his statement implied America's willingness to help others who were similarly besieged anywhere in the world.

THE MARSHALL PLAN   Following the war, the peoples of Western Europe were faced with poverty and hunger. The United States undercut

the appeal that communist solutions might have had for desperate electorates by instituting the European Recovery Program. This Marshall Plan (as it came to be called after George C. Marshall, the secretary of state who introduced it) provided broad economic aid to European states, conditional only on their working together for their mutual benefit. The Soviet Union and its clients were invited to apply to it for help. Czechoslovakia and Finland were willing, and Poland and Hungary expressed interest, but the Soviets forbade them to take part. It feared that American aid would draw them out of its orbit. The Marshall Plan was a great success. The tremendous economic growth that it helped to create in postwar Europe sapped the strength of communist parties in the West.

Soviet Assertion of Domination of Eastern Europe

The West believed that communism was inherently aggressive and that the policy of containment was, therefore, justified. From the Soviet perspective, however, the West's efforts at containment looked like attacks on Russia's legitimate interests in Eastern Europe. Tsarist Russia had governed Poland for over a century and, at the request of the Austrian Empire, had intervened in Hungary in 1848 to put down a revolution. Russia had a long-standing interest in the area around the Black Sea, and European powers had, after all, invaded Russia once in the nineteenth century (under Napoleon) and twice in the twentieth. Given this history and the extraordinary losses the Russian people had suffered in World War II, it is not surprising that Soviet leaders believed that they needed Eastern European satellites to protect their frontiers.

Behind the Iron Curtain that separated Russia's allies from the West Stalin replaced multiparty governments with thoroughly communist regimes completely under his control. In the autumn of 1947 he called a meeting in Warsaw of all communist parties around the world. There, the former Comintern was reborn as Cominform (the Communist Information Bureau), an organization dedicated to spreading revolutionary communism throughout the world. Communist leaders in the West who favored working within the political system were replaced by hard-liners dedicated to sabotaging it.

In February 1948, Stalin brutally displayed his new policy. Communists expelled the democratic members of what had been a coalition government in Prague and murdered Jan Masaryk (1886–1948), foreign minister and son of Czechoslovakia's founder, Thomas Masaryk (1850–1937). President Edvard Beneš (1884–1948) was forced to resign, and Czechoslovakia was brought under Soviet rule. The Soviet Union forced subject governments in Eastern Europe to adopt Stalinist policies: that is, one-party political systems, close military cooperation with the Soviet Union, collectivization of agriculture, Communist Party domination of universities and schools, and discouragement of religion.

The Postwar Division of Germany

DISAGREEMENTS OVER GERMANY The Allies had no clear plan for dealing with Germany after its defeat. Although Churchill worried that dismemberment of the nation would encourage Soviet expansion, the Allied armies established separate occupation zones. The Soviets quickly dismantled the factories in their eastern zone and then laid claim to all the industrial equipment left in Germany as reparations for their losses in the war. The Western powers refused to agree to this. The United States did not want to assume financial responsibility for Germany or cause resentment that communist politicians might exploit. It proposed instead to help Germany become self-sufficient by restoring its industrial capacity. This alarmed the Soviets who had reason to fear the resurgence of Germany.

BERLIN BLOCKADE In 1948 the Western powers issued a separate constitution and currency for the western sectors of Germany. The Soviets protested and withdrew from the joint Allied Control Commission. Berlin, which was under the jurisdiction of all four powers despite being well within the Soviet zone, immediately became a point of contention. The Soviets, who feared that foreign currencies circulating in Berlin would undercut their own, decided to seal the city off by closing the railroads and highways that connected it with West Germany. Their hope was to drive the other occupying armies out of Berlin.

The West countered the Berlin blockade by airlifting supplies for almost a year. In May 1949, the Soviets yielded and restored access to Berlin. The incident, however, hastened the separation of Germany into two states. In September 1949, West Germany became the German Federal Republic (GFR), and a month later, the eastern region became the German Democratic Republic (GDR). Berlin remained a divided city isolated in the new communist GDR. No one had anticipated this as the outcome of the war.

NATO and the Warsaw Pact

The USSR became increasingly isolated as the Marshall Plan promoted greater cooperation among the Western nations. In March 1948, Belgium, the Netherlands, Luxembourg, France, and Britain signed the Treaty of Brussels, which spelled out terms for economic and military cooperation. In April 1949, they joined Italy, Denmark, Norway, Portugal, Iceland, Canada, and the United States in a mutual defense pact called the North Atlantic Treaty Organization (NATO). West Germany, Greece, and Turkey also soon signed on. For the first time in history, the United States had committed itself to defend allies outside the Western Hemisphere.

In 1949 the states of Eastern Europe formed the Council of Mutual Assistance (COMECON) to integrate their economies. Unlike NATO, the eastern alliance was directly dominated by its superpower member, the Soviet Union. The Warsaw Pact of May 1955, which committed Albania, Bulgaria, Czechoslovakia, East Germany, Hungary, Poland, Romania, and the Soviet Union to cooperate in their mutual defense, merely recognized a system that already existed. The formal division of Europe between two antagonistic alliance systems clearly defined sides for the Cold War but did not limit the confrontations of that war to the European arena.

The Creation of the State of Israel

Following World War I, Great Britain had become the dominant power in the Middle East, but after World War II nationalists who wanted self-determination for their homelands began to challenge British authority. The postcolonial struggles that erupted here and elsewhere

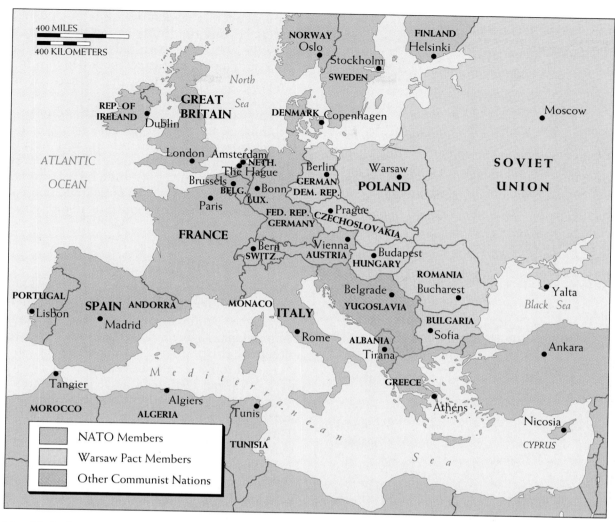

MAP 31–1 MAJOR EUROPEAN ALLIANCE SYSTEMS *The North Atlantic Treaty Organization includes both Canada and the United States and stretches as far east as Turkey. By contrast, the Warsaw Pact nations were limited to the contiguous communist states of Eastern Europe, with the Soviet Union as the dominant member.*

invited interventions by combatants in the Cold War.

BRITISH BALFOUR DECLARATION Crises in the Middle East centered on relations between Jews and Arabs. In 1897 Theodore Herzl had founded the Zionist movement to push for the creation of a homeland for the world's Jews. Between the world wars, thousands of Jews, mainly from Europe, immigrated to the British mandate of Palestine. There they created an organized Jewish community (the *Yishuv*) with political parties, a press, labor unions, and schools. In 1917 the Balfour Declaration promised British support for a Jewish state in Palestine, and Britain tried, un-

successfully, to mediate the frequent clashes that took place between the native Arabs and the Jewish settlers.

The Nazi persecution of Jews rallied support for the Zionist ideal of a Jewish state in Palestine, and following the war the Allies concluded that Jewish refugees from Nazi concentration camps had some sort of moral claim on the international community. In 1947, the British referred the problem of working out a relationship between Palestinian Arabs and Jews to the United Nations, and over opposition from some Arab groups, the United Nations suggested dividing Palestine between Jews and Arabs. The Palestinian Arabs resented the influx of new settlers who

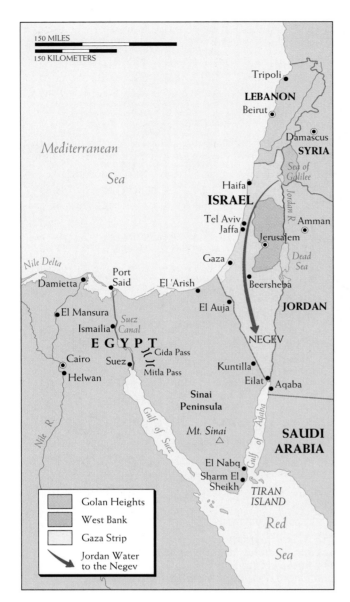

MAP 31–2 ISRAEL AND ITS NEIGHBORS IN 1949   *The territories gained by Israel in 1949 did not secure peace for the new nation. In fact, the disposition of these lands and the fate of Arab refugees constitute the core of the region's current difficulties.*

displaced many of them from their lands and turned them into refugees.

ISRAEL DECLARES INDEPENDENCE   In May 1948, the *Yishuv* declared the existence of an independent Jewish state called Israel and chose David Ben-Gurion (1886–1973) as prime minister. The United States quickly recognized the new nation. During 1948 and 1949, Israel fought a war of independence against the Arabs and pushed its borders beyond the limits set by the United Nations. By 1949, it had secured its existence, but it had not won diplomatic recognition from the Arab states. Its peace was, therefore, little more than an armed truce.

Many Israelis had emigrated from Europe, and both Europe and the United States are dependent on oil from Arab countries. It was not long, therefore, before the Arab-Israeli conflict drew in the superpowers. By 1949 the United States had committed itself firmly to Israel, and the Soviet Union had begun to ingratiate itself with the Arab states.

The Korean War

The Japanese occupied Korea in 1910 and held it until their defeat in 1945. The United States and the Soviet Union, which had been cooperating against Japan, agreed to divide Korea temporarily along the thirty-eighth parallel. The nation was supposed to be reunited eventually, but by 1948 its halves had coalesced as separate states: the Democratic People's Republic of Korea in the north, and the Republic of Korea in the south. The Soviet Union backed the former and the United States the latter.

In late June 1950, North Korea invaded the south. A Soviet boycott of the United Nations gave the United States an opportunity to win a mandate from the United Nations authorizing international intervention. Great Britain, Turkey, and Australia joined the United States in providing support for what was termed a UN "police action" to halt aggression. The United States, however, viewed the Korean conflict as a vital part of its effort to contain the spread of communism.

Late in 1950, when UN forces approached the Chinese border, China intervened on behalf of the North Koreans. China had been governed since 1949 by a communist regime under Mao Tse-tung (1893–1976), and U.S. policy makers leapt to the conclusion that Mao was simply executing orders from Moscow. No one at the time knew of the tensions that existed between the USSR and China. The Chinese initially pushed the Americans back, but eventually the war bogged down, and on June 16, 1953, an armistice was signed restoring the thirty-eighth parallel as the border between a north and a south Korea. The American government claimed success for its policy of containment. The conflict had, however, turned the Cold War into a global struggle and committed the United States to maintaining troops in Korea indefinitely.

The formation of NATO and the police action in Korea capped the first round of the Cold War, which came to an end in 1953 with Stalin's death and the Korean armistice. For a while tensions appeared to ease. Early in 1955 the Soviets withdrew their army of occupation from Austria, and it became a neutral country. Later that year, France, Great Britain, the Soviet Union, and the United States met in Geneva to discuss nuclear weapons and the future of Germany. Despite public displays of friendliness, the meeting produced few substantial agreements, and the polemics of the Cold War soon resumed.

The Khrushchev Era in the Soviet Union

The Last Years of Stalin

No nation suffered greater losses during World War II than the Soviet Union, whose people hoped that their sacrifices would win them freer, more comfortable lives. They were disappointed, for Stalin tolerated few modifications of the regime he had created. Until his death on March 6, 1953, he continued to centralize authority, purge opponents, and favor heavy industry over production of consumer goods.

For a time, no single leader replaced Stalin. The presidium (the renamed politburo) governed the nation as a group, but power gradually devolved on the party secretary, Nikita Khrushchev (1894–1971). He formally became premier in 1956, but he never enjoyed Stalin's extraordinary power.

Khrushchev's Domestic Policies

The Khrushchev era (1956–1964) retreated from Stalinism but not from authoritarianism. An attempt was made to reform the Soviet system in ways that would not threaten the dominance of the Communist Party. Intellectuals were gradually permitted somewhat greater freedom of expression. Although Boris Pasternak (1890–1960),

author of *Dr. Zhivago*, was ordered not to accept the Nobel Prize for Literature in 1958, in 1963 Aleksandr Solzhenitsyn (b. 1918) was permitted to publish another novel (*One Day in the Life of Ivan Denisovich*) critical of the Soviet system. Khrushchev tried to improve production of consumer goods and allowed some modest decentralization of economic planning. Recognizing that collectivization had not created an agricultural system capable of feeding his people, he removed many restrictive regulations on private farming and made hundreds of thousands of additional acres available for wheat cultivation. Initially, grain production set records, but poor farming techniques caused soil erosion and led to declining yields. The Soviet Union had ultimately to resort to importing vast quantities of grain from the West.

THE SECRET SPEECH OF 1956 In February 1956, at the Twentieth Congress of the Communist Party, Khrushchev broke with Soviet tradition and made a secret speech (later published outside the Soviet Union) denouncing Stalin. There was shock and consternation in party circles, but this opened the way for limited internal criticism of the Soviet government and the gradual removal of the strongest supporters of Stalinist policies from the presidium. Communist leaders in Eastern Europe took Khrushchev's speech as a signal that they could retreat, if not from communism, from the Stalinist policies that had been required of them since the late 1940s. The result was a series of crises that made 1956 one of the key years in the Cold War.

The Three Crises of 1956

The Suez Intervention

In 1952 Gamal Abdel Nasser (1918–1970) won control of Egypt's government, and in July 1956 he ended the hold that Anglo-French interests had on the Suez Canal. Egypt's nationalization of the canal endangered Britain's and France's access to Persian Gulf oil supplies. Therefore, when war broke out between Egypt and Israel later in that year, Britain and France were eager to intervene. Israel quickly occupied the Sinai, and France and Britain hastened to reoccupy the canal zone—claiming that it was necessary to separate the combatants. The operation succeeded militarily but foundered on the shoals of diplomacy. The United States refused to support their venture, and the Soviet Union vigorously protested on behalf of its Arab allies. The Anglo-French forces had to withdraw and return control of the canal to Egypt, and a year later Israel evacuated the Sinai and the Gaza Strip.

The Suez incident proved that without U.S. support, the nations of Western Europe could no longer use military force to impose their will on the rest of the world. It also demonstrated that the United States and the Soviet Union could restrain their allies from ventures that might lead to wider conflicts. For Israel the conflict had the unfortunate effect of widening the breach between it and its Arab neighbors by creating the impression that the new state was nothing but an agent for the old imperialistic powers.

Poland's Efforts Toward Independent Action

Erroneous readings of the meaning of Khrushchev's secret speech attacking Stalin led to important developments in Eastern Europe. In 1956, a few months after the delivery of the speech, Wladyslaw Gomulka (1905–1982) became Poland's leader. Resentment of the rigidly disciplined communist regime had prompted a workers' uprising and forced the resignations of hardline Stalinist officials. Gomulka, a communist whom Stalin had imprisoned, was acceptable to both the Polish communists and the Soviets. He promised the latter that he would continue Poland's membership in the Warsaw Pact. For the former, he proposed an end to the collectivization of Polish agriculture and an improvement in relations between the government and the Roman Catholic Church. Since Gomulka's compromise appointment made it appear that the Soviets were now willing to allow Poland to chart its own course under the leadership of its Communist Party, another Eastern European country was inspired to seek similar autonomy.

Uprising in Hungary

In late October 1956, demonstrations in Budapest in support of Poland escalated into street fighting, and the Hungarian Communist Party created a new ministry headed by former premier Imre Nagy (1896–1958). Although he was a communist, Nagy wanted Soviet troops withdrawn from Hungary. He also favored neutrality for Hungary and withdrawal from the Warsaw Pact. This was wholly unacceptable to the Soviets. In early November, they invaded, deposed Nagy (who was later executed), and made Janos Kadar (1912–1989) premier.

The events of 1956 in the Middle East and Eastern Europe taught the nations of Europe what they could expect from the Cold War era. The Western European states could chart their own courses in dealing with one another, but they were prevented by the superpowers from taking independent action on the broader international scene. The Eastern European countries had no autonomy in either the domestic or the international spheres.

Later Cold War Confrontations

Collapse of the 1960 Paris Summit Conference

The Soviets made advances after 1956 that allowed them to feel more secure and, thus, able to contemplate "peaceful coexistence" with the United States. Their successful launch in 1957 of the earth's first satellite (*Sputnik*) confirmed their belief that they had achieved technological superiority over the West, and in 1958 they began to negotiate limits on the testing of nuclear weapons with the United States. Tempers flared that year when the Soviets demanded that Allied occupation forces evacuate West Berlin, but by 1959 tensions had eased enough for several Western leaders to visit Moscow and for Khrushchev to tour the United States. A summit meeting was scheduled for May 1960. Just before the Paris Summit Conference was to convene, however, the Soviets shot down an American U-2 aircraft that was flying reconnaissance over their territory. Eisenhower accepted responsibility for ordering the surveillance but refused to apologize to the Soviets. Khrushchev decided to retaliate by scuttling the summit. This gave him a chance to refute charges, particularly from the leaders of communist China, that the Soviet Union was softening its attitude toward the capitalist world.

The Berlin Wall

The abortive Paris conference inaugurated the most difficult period in the Cold War. In 1961 the newly elected American President John F. Kennedy and Premier Khrushchev met in Vienna, and Kennedy left wondering if the two nations could avoid war. Throughout that year thousands of refugees from East Germany had also been crossing into West Berlin, to the chagrin and economic detriment of the East. In August 1961, the East Germans, with Soviet approval, erected the Cold War's starkest symbol: a concrete wall dividing East from West Berlin. Crossing from one part of the city to the other became possible only at designated checkpoints and only for people with proper papers. The United States protested and sent Vice President Lyndon Johnson to Berlin to reassure its citizens. But when nothing was done to force the wall's removal, doubt spread about U.S. commitments to West Germany.

The Cuban Missile Crisis

The most dangerous days of the Cold War occurred during the Cuban missile crisis of 1962. In 1957 Fidel Castro (b. 1926) launched a revolution that in 1959 made Cuba, an island nation less than 100 miles from the United States, a communist country and a Soviet ally. This greatly alarmed the United States, and its worst fears were realized in 1962 when Khrushchev decided to build bases for nuclear missiles in Cuba. America responded with a blockade and a demand for their removal. After a tense week of exchanging threats, the Soviets backed down. Khrushchev's retreat weakened his support at home and raised doubt among non-European communist states about the Soviet Union's reliability as an ally. The People's Republic of China began to exercise greater influence in international communist circles, and the Soviet military concluded that it had to undertake a major buildup to strengthen its forces.

In 1963 international tensions eased somewhat when the United States and the Soviet Union concluded a Nuclear Test Ban Treaty.

Many Russians, however, feared that Khrushchev had tried to do too much too soon—and had done it too poorly. On October 16, 1964, a defeat in the Central Committee of the Communist Party prompted his resignation and brought Alexei Kosygin (1904–1980) and then Leonid Brezhnev (1906–1982) to power.

Brezhnev and the Invasion of Czechoslovakia

Although the Soviet Union had demonstrated in Poland and Hungary in 1956 that it would not tolerate independent action by its Eastern European neighbors, in 1968, during an episode known as the "Prague Spring," Alexander Dubcek (1921–1992) experimented with liberalizing communism in Czechoslovakia. When he expanded freedom of discussion and intellectual rights (at a time when they were being curtailed in the USSR), the Soviets responded by invading Czechoslovakia and installing leaders more to their liking. Brezhnev also articulated what came to be called the "Brezhnev Doctrine," a claim that the Soviet Union had the right to interfere in the domestic politics of communist countries. The invasion of Czechoslovakia proved, however, to be the last major Soviet military intervention in Europe related to issues surrounding the Cold War.

The European Retreat from Empire

One of the most significant postwar developments was the decolonization movement that engineered the retreat of the European nations from their empires. The desire of the newly liberated nations to avoid aligning themselves with either of the superpowers led to them being called members of a Third World. Both the United States and the USSR, however, worked hard to win their support.

The Effects of World War II

World War II encouraged decolonization in several ways. Soldiers that had been stationed in the colonies were recalled to fronts in Europe, and the Japanese drove the Europeans out of some parts of Asia. The dislocations caused by the war and the postwar economic collapse deprived European nations of the resources needed to maintain empires, and it was difficult for them to justify continued colonial dominance. They had fought to oppose tyranny at home, and colonists based their appeals for freedom on European political ideology. Nonetheless, colonial masters did not generally surrender their foreign possessions willingly or without resistance.

Major Areas of Colonial Withdrawal

The decolonization process that reshaped the global map proceeded in different ways—sometimes with systematic preparation and sometimes as hasty retreat. India and Pakistan separated when Britain withdrew in 1947. In 1948 Burma and Sri Lanka (formerly Ceylon) became independent. During the 1950s Britain tried to prepare some of its other colonies for self-government. Ghana (formerly the Gold Coast) and Nigeria—which became self-governing in 1957 and 1960, respectively—enjoyed planned decolonization. But in areas such as Malta and Cyprus, the British retreat was less orderly and hastened by militant nationalist movements.

The smaller colonial powers often had no options. The Dutch were forced from Indonesia in 1950. In 1960 great turmoil led to independence for the Belgian Congo (now Zaire). France maintained its position in Southeast Asia until 1954 and in Algeria until 1962. President de Gaulle then conducted referendums on independence for the rest of France's colonial possessions. By the late 1960s only Portugal was still a traditional colonial power, but following a revolution in 1974, it relinquished its African colonies of Mozambique and Angola. The newly independent states of Africa have subsequently experienced political instability and poverty, while former colonies in Asia have achieved stability and remarkable economic growth.

France, the United States, and Vietnam

Problems relating to decolonization helped transfer Cold War rivalries from Europe to other continents. France's retreat from Southeast Asia, in particular, led directly to American military involvement in Vietnam.

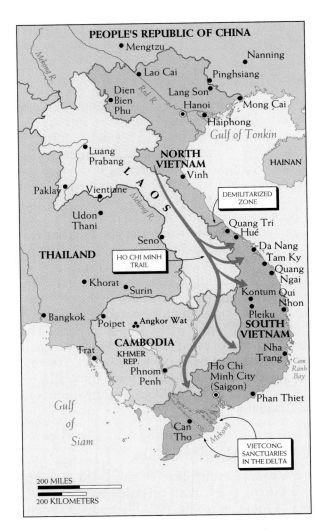

MAP–31-3 VIETNAM AND ITS NEIGHBORS *The map identifies important locations in the long and complex struggle centered in Vietnam.*

Resistance to French Colonial Rule

France's occupation of Laos, Cambodia, and Vietnam had begun in the nineteenth century, but by the time the Korean conflict broke out, the opponents of French colonialism (the leaders of the Viet Minh nationalist movement) were igniting another war in Indochina.

HO CHI MINH'S LEADERSHIP By 1930 Ho Chi Minh (1892–1969) had turned the opposition to French colonial rule into an Indochinese Communist Party. Throughout the 1930s the French were able to suppress most communist activity in their colony, but World War II created an opportunity for Ho Chi Minh. When France's Vichy government angered the people of Vietnam by collaborating with the Japanese invaders of their country, Ho Chi Minh's support increased. His popularity was based less on his communism than the nationalistic role he played as a leader of the resistance. As a communist, he was also careful to avoid identification with Vietnam's traditional enemy, China.

In September 1945, Ho Chi Minh declared the independence of Vietnam under the Viet Minh, a coalition of nationalists that the communists dominated. In 1946 France and the Viet Minh declared an armistice, but full-fledged war broke out a year later. Until 1949, the United States paid little attention to these developments. But the establishment of the Communist People's Republic of China in that year dramatically changed the American outlook. France's campaign to defeat Ho Chi Minh now appeared to be a front within the Cold War. For the time being, however, the United States offered the French only financial support and decided against military intervention.

The Geneva Settlement and Its Aftermath

In the spring of 1954, while a conference was convening in Geneva to negotiate terms for concluding the Indochina war, the French stronghold at Dien Bien Phu fell to the Viet Nimh. By late June an unsatisfactory peace accord had been negotiated.

NORTH AND SOUTH VIETNAM The Genevan agreement temporarily divided Vietnam at the seventeenth parallel and set 1956 as the date for elections to reunify the country. Meanwhile, the north was to be administered by the Viet Minh from the city of Hanoi and the south by the French from the city of Saigon. In order to campaign for the elections, each was to have access to the territory of the other. Geneva hoped, in this way, to turn a military conflict into a political one.

The United States was not happy with the Geneva solution, for it assumed that a North Vietnamese government would, like the government of North Korea, be a communist puppet state. To block the spread of communism, it established the Southeast Asia Treaty Organiza-

tion (SEATO), a security agreement similar to NATO. It consisted of the United States, Great Britain, France, Australia, New Zealand, Thailand, Pakistan, and the Philippines.

THE UNITED STATES AND THE DIEM GOVERNMENT As French troops withdrew from South Vietnam, the United States stepped in with offers of aid for Ngo Dinh Diem (1901–1963), a strong noncommunist nationalist who had not collaborated with the French. Unfortunately, because America had been France's ally, its support for Diem caused many Vietnamese to view him with suspicion.

In October 1955, Diem established a Republic of Vietnam in the south and announced that he would not hold the reunification elections agreed to at the Geneva meeting. The United

U.S. armed forces patrol in Vietnam. At the war's peak, more than 500,000 American troops were stationed in South Vietnam. The United States struggled in Vietnam for more than a decade, seriously threatening its commitment to Western Europe. C. Simonpietri/Corbis Sygma Photo News

States, which had not signed the Geneva documents, supported him. Diem then launched an anticommunist campaign that escalated into a program of political repression, and by 1960 his opponents had united to form the National Liberation Front. It pledged to overthrow him, unify the country, reform the economy, and oust the Americans. It was anticolonial, nationalist, and communist, and its military arm, the Viet Cong, received assistance from the government of North Vietnam. Diem's response was further repression.

The U.S. Involvement

The Eisenhower and Kennedy administrations demanded that Diem reform his government, but they continued to support him. The American military presence in Vietnam quickly grew from 600 troops in 1961 to 16,000 in 1963. On November 1, 1963, Diem was murdered in an army coup that the United States may have encouraged in the hope that a new government, headed by Nguyen Van Thieu (b. 1923), would enjoy greater popular support.

In August 1964, the U.S. Congress responded to an attack on an American ship in the Gulf of Tonkin by authorizing the bombing of North Vietnam. Bombardment continued, with only brief pauses, from February 1965 until early in 1973, and a land war escalated until more than 500,000 American military were stationed in South Vietnam. In 1969 President Nixon initiated "Vietnamization," a policy of gradual withdrawal from Vietnam and shifting of more responsibility for the fighting to the South Vietnamese. In January 1973, a cease-fire was arranged. Early in 1975, however, an evacuation of South Vietnamese troops from the northern part of their country turned into a rout, and on April 30, 1975, the city of Saigon fell to the Viet Cong and the North Vietnamese army.

This war in the East had a major impact on the West. For a decade it diverted the attention of the United States from Europe. American prestige suffered, and American commitments to Europe were questioned. Many young Europeans—and not a few Americans—came to see the United States not as a protector of liberty but as a cruel champion of defunct colonialism.

Western European Political Developments During the Cold War

Following World War II, most of the nations of Western Europe endorsed principles of liberal democracy. (The exceptions were Portugal and Spain, where dictatorships survived into the mid-1970s.) The experience of the Great Depression and the events leading up to the war had made it clear that stable democracies required sound social and economic bases as well as political structures. Most Europeans concluded that it was, therefore, the duty of government to ensure economic prosperity and social security. This was the only way to stave off the kind of turmoil that fostered tyranny and war and might lead to communism.

Christian Democratic Parties

Except for the British Labour Party, democratic socialist parties did not prosper during the Cold War. The policies Europeans embraced were usually devised by coalition governments headed by various Christian Democratic parties. These groups were a major new development in postwar politics. Although they were largely Roman Catholic, they differed from the Catholic parties that had thrived from the late nineteenth century through the 1930s. Those had been very conservative—opposing communism but proposing few positive programs. The postwar Christian Democratic parties of Germany, France, and Italy welcomed non-Catholic members and fought for democracy, social reform, and economic growth.

Economic Concerns Within Western Europe

Everywhere but in France the economy was the dominant political concern in the years following the war. The most remarkable recovery was the "economic miracle" that brought unprecedented prosperity to West Germany. In Great Britain a Labour ministry under Clement Attlee (1945–1950) introduced the welfare state and nationalized a number of major industries. From the

1960s through the 1970s, there were frequent clashes between labor and business interests. When Margaret Thatcher (b. 1925), Britain's first female prime minister, took office in 1979, she moved against the unions and fought for a freer market economy. In 1997, the Labour Party returned to power but on a platform advocating much less state intervention in the economy than it had previously sought. At the end of the century parties of the left were winning elections throughout Europe but trimming back their traditional support for welfare programs and government activism.

Toward Western European Unification

Postwar Europe's greatest political success story is the progress that has been made toward economic cooperation and unity. This was driven in part by American encouragement, fear of Soviet expansion, and awareness of Europe's declining influence in the global arena.

Postwar Cooperation

European unification could be approached by three paths: political, military, or economic. The economic route was the easiest, for it entailed little loss of political sovereignty and produced material benefits that won popular support for cooperative efforts. The first step toward economic cooperation was the formation in 1951, by France, West Germany, Italy, and the "Benelux" countries (i.e., Belgium, the Netherlands, and Luxembourg), of the European Coal and Steel Community. Its success in promoting the growth of production did much to allay suspicions politicians and business leaders had about economic integration.

The European Economic Community

The diplomatic isolation of France and Britain that followed their unsuccessful Suez intervention persuaded many Europeans that unified action was necessary to maintain Europe's independence of the superpowers. In 1957 the six members of the Coal and Steel Community signed the Treaty of Rome, a pledge to form a new organization called the European Economic Community (EEC). The members of the "Common Market," as the EEC soon came to be called, wanted to eliminate tariffs, guarantee unimpeded flow of capital and labor, and establish similar wage scales and social benefits in all member states.

The Common Market was stunningly successful during its early years. By 1968, well ahead of schedule, all tariffs among the six members had been abolished. Trade and labor migration grew steadily, and other countries had begun to copy the community or consider joining it. In 1959 Britain, Denmark, Norway, Sweden, Switzerland, Austria, and Portugal formed the European Free Trade Area, and by 1961 Great Britain had decided to seek Common Market membership. Twice, in 1963 and 1967, France, under de Gaulle, vetoed British membership, claiming that Britain was too closely tied to the United States to support the EEC wholeheartedly. In 1973 Great Britain, Ireland, and Denmark were finally admitted, but from the late 1970s through the 1980s the growth of the EEC slowed. Norway and Sweden, whose economies were relatively strong, declined to join. In 1982 Spain, Portugal, and Greece applied for membership and were eventually admitted, but sharp disagreements and a sense of stagnation hampered the work of the EEC.

The European Union

Early in 1988 the leaders of the EEC ended a decade of drift by announcing an important decision. They targeted the year 1992 for achieving a virtual free-trade zone throughout the community. In 1991 the Treaty of Maastricht proposed creation of a unified currency and a central bank. A number of states submitted the treaty to referendums. It was rejected by Denmark and only narrowly passed in France and Great Britain—making clear that it could not be enforced without wider popular support. When the treaty took effect in 1993, the EEC was renamed the European Union. Its most ambitious undertaking to date has been the launching, in 1999, of the Euro, the first step toward the creation of a single currency for its member states.

The European Union (EU) faces a number of challenges. It must decide on its relationship with the newly independent and generally weak states of Eastern Europe. It must cope with the fear that its most populous member (Germany) may acquire excessive influence over its affairs, and it must see how the Euro and the new European Parliament, seated in Strasbourg, evolve. At the start of the twenty-first century the EU faced an unexpected test when a coalition government containing suspected Nazi sympathizers came to power in Austria. The EU demonstrated sufficient solidarity to take steps to isolate the Austrian government on the grounds that it was violating the implicitly liberal values on which the EU is based.

The Brezhnev Era in the Soviet Union and Eastern Europe

While Western Europe progressed toward unity, democracy, and prosperity, the Soviet Union seemed, under Brezhnev, to revert to Stalinism and become more repressive. Brezhnev made no attempt to recruit young blood for the party or for service in his government. Although the Communist Party never accounted for a large percentage of the population, membership did increase. Party members enjoyed special privileges and a variety of perks. Such favoritism, however, encouraged corruption, and in some of the Soviet republics ethnic groups won control of the party organization and began to undermine its unity.

The terrorism of the Stalinist era was not restored, but police surveillance increased. Novelist Aleksandr Solzhenitsyn was expelled in 1974, and the government began to harass Jewish citizens and to place obstacles in the path of their emigration to Israel. The government's repressive measures gave rise to a dissident movement, and a few prominent citizens, such as the Nobel-prize-winning physicist Andrei Sakharov (1921–1989), accused their government of violating international agreements on human rights. Brezhnev responded by cracking down even more.

The United States and *Détente*

Brezhnev tried to reach some accommodation with the United States while also working to expand Soviet influence. Although he sided with North Vietnam in its war with the United States, his support was limited. He and President Nixon pursued a policy of *détente* (i.e., agreement) designed to increase trade and reduce strategic arms deployments. During Gerald Ford's presidency, the United States and the Soviet Union both signed the Helsinki Accords (1975). These recognized the Soviet sphere of influence in Eastern Europe but also acknowledged that both nations had a duty to safeguard the human rights of all their citizens. When President Carter, a strong advocate of human rights, sought to induce the Soviet Union to live up to these commitments, relations between the two countries cooled.

Détente did not persuade the Soviet Union to abandon its activist foreign policy. It poured resources into conflicts in Angola, Mozambique, Ethiopia, Nicaragua, and Vietnam. It provided arms to Arab enemies of Israel, and in order to restore its prestige after the Cuban missile it built the largest armed force in the world and achieved virtual nuclear parity with the United States.

Invasion of Afghanistan

It is not clear why the Brezhnev government felt it had to invade Afghanistan to support its client Afghan government, but the decision had long-range consequences for the future of the Soviet Union. The U.S. Senate protested by refusing to ratify a second Strategic Arms Limitation Agreement and embargoing American grain shipments to the Soviet Union. The United States boycotted the 1980 Olympic Games in Moscow and sent aid to the Afghan rebels. China also condemned the invasion.

The Soviet forces could not defeat the Afghan guerilla fighters who, as the war dragged on, slaughtered approximately 2,000 Soviet troops each year. The morale and prestige of the Soviet army plummeted, and the conflict had a demoral-

In August 1980, Polish workers struck the shipyard at Gdansk, demanding the right to be represented by their own independent union. Solidarity. *Here, strikers display the* Solidarity *banner.* Liaison Agency, Inc.

izing effect on the Soviet Union comparable to that which the Vietnam war had on the United States.

Communism and *Solidarity* in Poland

At a time when the Soviet government was becoming increasingly rigid and preoccupied by its war in Afghanistan, it found its authority and that of the Polish Communist Party challenged by developments in Poland. Following the crisis of 1956, the Polish Communist Party, which governed Poland, had yielded to Soviet domination, and the result had been chronic mismanagement of the economy and persistent food shortages. In 1978 the election to the papacy of the cardinal archbishop of Cracow, Karol Wo-

jtyla, elevated to a position of great public visibility an outspoken Polish opponent of communism. The new pope received a tumultuous welcome when he visited his homeland in 1979. In July of the following year, the Polish government sparked hundreds of protest strikes by decreeing an increase in meat prices. On August 14, workers occupied the Lenin shipyard at Gdansk, and the strike spread rapidly to other facilities connected with the shipbuilding industry. The strikers' leader, Lech Walesa (b. 1944), refused to negotiate through the old government-controlled unions, and the strike did not end until the government allowed the workers to organize *Solidarity*, an independent union. The new union and Poland's Catholic clergy also won access to the news media.

During the summer of 1981, remarkable changes took place within the Polish Communist Party. For the first time ever in a European communist state, secret elections for a party congress were held. Poland remained governed by a single party, but that party permitted real debate. This extraordinary experiment ended late in 1981, when General Wojciech Jaruzelski (b. 1923) became party head and declared martial law. A number of *Solidarity*'s leaders were arrested, and martial law continued until late in 1983. None of this did anything to help Poland deal with its economic problems.

By the time of Brezhnev's death in 1982, the Soviet system had grown rigid and seemed incapable of meeting the needs of its people or conducting a successful foreign policy. But no observers expected rapid change in either the Soviet Union or its satellites. It was assumed that the political situation that had lasted forty years would endure. Almost no one anticipated that vast changes were imminent.

Relations with the Reagan Administration

Early in his first term, American President Ronald Reagan relaxed America's grain embargo and decreased emphasis on campaigns for human rights. He chose instead to intensify Cold War rhetoric, increase U.S. military spending, slow arms limitation talks, deploy a major new missile system in Europe, and propose a new

Strategic Arms Defense Initiative. This program, which was dubbed "Star Wars" by the press, aimed at developing a high-technology, space-based defense system to protect the United States from nuclear attack. The Star Wars proposal and the Reagan defense buildup forced the Soviet Union to increase military expenditures when it could ill afford to do so. This worsened economic problems that contributed to the collapse of the Soviet regime, but there were no signs during Reagan's first term that major transformations were in the offing.

The Collapse of European Communism

The end of Soviet influence in Eastern Europe and the collapse of the Soviet Union are the most important events of the second half of the twentieth century. Military defeats or domestic revolutions are the common explanations for the fall of governments, but the Soviet Union essentially imploded from within.

Gorbachev Redirects the Soviet Union

Brezhnev died in 1982. His immediate successors, Yuri Andropov (1914–1984) and Constantin Chernenko (1911–1985), died within thirteen months of each other—clearing the way for a reformer, Mikhail S. Gorbachev (b. 1931), to rise to power. Gorbachev inherited a government whose authority was being undercut by a stagnating economy, corruption, and a lingering war in Afghanistan. He was impatient with the inefficiencies of the Soviet system and disappointed in the Communist Party's failure to be true to its socialist ideals. He believed in the original Bolshevik vision and thought that it had not failed but had been undermined by party corruption and a reign of political terror. He expected to be able to reform the Soviet system, but the policy changes he implemented unleashed forces that soon overwhelmed it.

ECONOMIC *PERESTROIKA* Gorbachev's primary goal was to raise his country's standard of living. To do this, he embarked on a strategy called *perestroika* (i.e., "restructuring"). This involved, among other things, reducing the size and importance of centralized economic ministries. When a strike by Siberian coal miners in July 1989 threatened the Russian economy, Gorbachev acceded to their demands for better wages and greater political freedom, and by 1990 he was abandoning Marxist ideology and promoting private ownership of property and an economy governed by free market mechanisms.

Gorbachev's inspiration may have been Lenin's New Economic Policy of the early 1920s, but in the Soviet context his approach was genuinely radical in its willingness to attack the effectiveness of centralized planning and the efficiency of the party bureaucracy. This, however, proved not to be enough to stimulate the growth of the Soviet economy. Shortages of food, consumer goods, and housing became chronic, and Gorbachev instituted political reforms to distract attention from the failure of his economic programs.

GLASNOST Gorbachev announced a policy of *glasnost* (i.e., "openness") that permitted extraordinary public discussion and criticism of Soviet history and the Communist Party. The reputations of some of the figures whom Stalin had purged were rehabilitated. Censorship was relaxed. Dissidents were released from prison. Workers were allowed to criticize the government's economic policies, and the Communist Party congress of 1988 witnessed real debate.

The Soviet Union was a vast empire composed of subject peoples who had been conquered either by the tsars or by Stalin, and *glasnost* allowed these national minorities to voice their discontent with Soviet rule. Gorbachev badly underestimated the amount of such internal unrest, and this became clear when he advanced from mere *glasnost* to *perestroika* in the political arena. When in 1988, he issued a new constitution that permitted openly contested elections, real political campaigning won seats for former dissidents in the Congress of People's Deputies.

PERESTROIKA AND THE ARMY The army was perhaps the Soviet Union's single most important national institution. Its victory in World War II had won it great prestige, and it was the sole institution that bridged the ethnic diversity of the Soviet Union. The Soviets had always showered abundant resources on their armed forces, but Gorbachev concluded that military expenditures had to be reduced to permit investment in projects that would raise the civilian standard of living. So much of the Soviet economy was based on military enterprises, however, that when Gorbachev began to retreat from the Afghan war and to cut back the military budget, there were massive dislocations in the economy. Between 1986 and 1991 a confused and demoralized military was called on to put down domestic unrest—caused either by ethnic groups fighting among themselves or national minorities challenging the Soviet Union's central government. Since the media was now free to publicize these clashes between Soviet soldiers and Soviet citizens, the status and self-confidence of the military were further eroded.

As Gorbachev's massive military cuts (which he hoped would be matched by the West) reduced the size of the army, the Soviet Union began to withdraw its forces from Eastern Europe. Some Soviet republics responded by setting up armies of their own—a step toward establishing their national autonomy. Respect for the Soviet army declined and resistance to conscription led to some republics failing to provide their quota of recruits. The army's unintended disintegration meant that when a political vacuum developed in the early 1990s, it had lost the power to hold the nation together.

1989: Year of Revolution in Eastern Europe

SOLIDARITY REEMERGES IN POLAND   In the early 1980s Poland's government relaxed martial law and eventually released all the members of the *Solidarity* labor union whom it had imprisoned. In 1988 a spate of new strikes erupted, and this time the communist government under General Jaruzelski failed to reimpose control. *Solidarity* was legalized and its founder, Lech Walesa, mediated between it and the government.

With the tacit consent of the Soviet Union, Jauzelski promised free elections to a parliament with increased powers. In the elections of 1989 the communists lost overwhelmingly to *Solidarity* candidates. Jaruzelski, unable to find a communist who could form a majority coalition,

turned to *Solidarity's* representatives for help and Poland chose its first noncommunist prime minister since 1945. Gorbachev approved this development.

Throughout 1989, one Soviet-dominated state after another in Eastern Europe moved toward independence. When Hungary opened its border with Austria, a breach opened in the Iron Curtain that permitted thousands of East Germans freely to emigrate to the West via Hungary. That same year Janos Kadar, the president of the Hungarian Communist Party, whom the Soviets had installed following their intervention in 1956, was deposed. The party changed its name to the Socialist Party, permitted opposition parties to organize, and promised free elections.

In the autumn of 1989, mass demonstrations were staged in several of East Germany's cities, and the Soviet Union informed the East German Communist Party that it would not intervene to suppress them. The East German government then resigned, and in November a new government ordered the opening of the Berlin Wall. Tens of thousands of East Berliners crossed into the western sector to visit relatives and to shop. The way was suddenly open for the reunification of Germany, a development which by February 1990 was accepted as inevitable by the United States, Great Britain, France, and the Soviet Union.

The breach in the Berlin Wall was followed by a revolution in Czechoslovakia. In December 1989 popular pressure forced its communist government to apologize for the Soviet invasion of 1968 and to resign. A new parliament was seated, and Vaclav Havel (b. 1936), a well-known playwright and long-term opponent of the communist regime, was elected president.

The only revolutionary violence to erupt in 1989 was in Romania. There, in mid-December, forces loyal to President Nicolae Ceausescu (1918–1989), who had controlled the country since 1965, fired on crowds of protesters. Bucharest was soon in full revolt, and Ceausescu and his wife attempted to flee. They were captured, tried, and shot.

THE SOVIET STANCE ON REVOLUTIONARY DEVELOPMENTS   None of the revolutions of 1989 would have succeeded if the Soviet Union had not refused

The collapse of Communist Party governments in Eastern Europe and the Soviet Union is the most important political event of the closing years of the twentieth century. It was accompanied by the destruction of the public symbols of those governments. Throughout the region gigantic statues of Communist Party leaders were torn down. Here, Hungarians explore a toppled statue of Lenin. Corbis Sygma Photo News

to intervene militarily to prop up the old-line communist governments and parties of Eastern Europe. In October 1989, however, Gorbachev formally renounced the Brezhnev Doctrine, leaving the peoples of Eastern Europe free, for the first time since the end of World War II, to choose their own political destinies. Thousands took to the streets to denounce Communist Party domination and to call for democracy. The Soviet army was suddenly compelled to organize a hasty withdrawal from Eastern Europe. This and the poverty to which its troops returned at home contributed to a further decline of its influence.

The peaceful character of the Eastern European revolutions may have owed something to the shock that much of the world felt in the spring of 1989 when China violently suppressed prodemocracy protesters in Beijing's Tiananmen Square. The Communist Party officials of Eastern Europe and the Soviet Union clearly decided at some point in 1989 that they could not risk offending world opinion by behaving in a similar manner.

The Collapse of the Soviet Union

Gorbachev ended support for the communist governments of Eastern Europe because he believed that the Soviet Union could no longer afford the expense of upholding their regimes. He also could not endorse repressive measures abroad that were inconsistent with the political restructuring he was attempting to engineer at home.

RENUNCIATION OF COMMUNIST POLITICAL MONOPOLY
Early in 1990 Gorbachev proposed to the Communist Party's Central Committee that it relinquish the party's monopoly of power. After intense debate, it concurred. Gorbachev did not want to abandon communism (at least not socialism), but he did want to open the political process to competition. He was determined, however, to preserve the Soviet Union as a strong state with a powerful central government.

NEW POLITICAL FORCES   By 1990, Gorbachev was facing challenges from three sources. One consisted of groups considered conservative in the Soviet context. They wanted to rely on traditional Soviet instruments of control to deal with the country's economic stagnation and social turmoil. In 1991 Gorbachev added some of these people to his government to help him deal with opposition from a second group. Its leader, Boris Yeltsin, pushed for more rapid progress toward a market economy and a more democratic form of government. In 1990, Yeltsin became president of the Russian Republic, the largest and most important of the Soviet Union's constituent units. This gave him a strong base from which to challenge Gorbachev.

MAP 31–4   REPUBLICS OF THE FORMER SOVIET UNION   *In December 1991 the Soviet Union broke up into the fifteen republics that are now loosely associated as the Commonwealth of Independent States.*

The third problem that faced Gorbachev in 1989 was increasing regional unrest in some of the Soviet Union's republics. This was not new, but in the past it had been suppressed by military and Communist Party action. Initially, the strongest outcries came from the three Baltic republics: Estonia, Latvia, and Lithuania. They had been independent until the eve of World War II when the Soviet-German Nonaggression Pact assured Stalin that Hitler would not stand in the way of their annexation by the USSR. During 1989 and 1990 the parliaments of the Baltic republics sought to increase their independence from the Soviet Union, and Lithuania actually declared independence. Gorbachev turned to the army for help in opposing these developments, but unrest also developed in the Soviet Islamic republics in central Asia. Riots broke out in Azerbaijan and Tadzhikistan. Throughout 1990 and 1991 Gorbachev tried to negotiate new constitutional arrangements between the republics and the central government, and the failure of his proposals may be the most important reason for the Soviet Union's rapid collapse.

THE AUGUST 1991 COUP   In August 1991, the conservative forces that Gorbachev had brought into the government attempted a coup. Armed forces occupied Moscow, and Gorbachev was placed under house arrest while on vacation in the Crimea. On the day of the coup, Boris Yeltsin, from the top of a tank stationed in front of the Russian Parliament building, denounced the reactionaries and called on the world to help maintain movement toward democracy in the Soviet Union.

The coup collapsed within two days, and what may have been the largest demonstration in Russia's history erupted in Moscow to celebrate its failure. Gorbachev returned to Moscow, humiliated and victimized by men he had brought into the government. The Communist Party, compromised by its role in the coup, lost its effectiveness as a political force as Yeltsin's following increased. Constitutional arrangements between the central government and the individual republics were revised, and on December 25, 1991, Gorbachev left office. The Soviet Union ceased to exist, and the Commonwealth of Independent States came into being.

The Yeltsin Decade

As president of Russia, Boris Yeltsin headed the largest, most powerful state in the new commonwealth. Initially, he enjoyed great popularity in Russia and throughout the commonwealth, but by 1993 he was facing serious economic and political problems. Opposition to Yeltsin, personally as well as to his reforms, developed in the Russian Parliament, which was heavily populated by former communists. Relations between the Parliament and the president soon reached an impasse, and in September 1993, Yeltsin suspended Parliament. It responded by deposing him and trying to provoke popular uprisings against him. The military backed Yeltsin, surrounded the Parliament building with troops, and on October 4, 1993 (after pro-Parliament rioters had rampaged through Moscow), employed tanks to crush the revolt.

This consolidated Yeltsin's position and authority, and all the major Western powers, which were deeply concerned by the turmoil in Russia, declared support for him. In December 1993, Russians elected a new Parliament and approved a new constitution that granted the president extensive powers. In 1994, however, a war erupted between the central government and the Islamic province of Chechnya. Inability to bring it to a quick conclusion and to improve relations with

\multicolumn{2}{c}{**Significant Dates from the Era of the Cold War**}
1945	Yalta Conference; founding of the United Nations
1946	Churchill's Iron Curtain speech
1947	(March) Truman Doctrine (June) Announcement of Marshall Plan
1948	Communist takeovers in Czechoslovakia and Hungary; State of Israel proclaimed
1948–1949	Berlin blockade
1949	NATO founded; East and West Germany emerge as separate states
1950–1953	Korean conflict
1953	Death of Stalin
1955	Warsaw Pact founded; Austria established as a neutral state
1956	(February) Khrushchev's secret speech denouncing Stalin (October) Suez crisis and the Hungarian uprising
1957	*Sputnik* launched
1961	Berlin Wall erected
1962	Cuban missile crisis
1963	Test Ban Treaty (Soviet Union and the United States)
1964	Gulf of Tonkin Resolution, America in Vietnam
1967	Six Days' War, Arab-Israeli conflict
1968	Soviet invasion of Czechoslovakia
1972	Strategic Arms Limitation Treaty
1973	Yom Kippur War
1975	Saigon falls to North Vietnam; Helsinki Accords
1978	Camp David Accords
1979	Soviet invasion of Afghanistan
1981	*Solidarity* founded in Poland
1982	Israel Invades Lebanon; Death of Brezhnev
1985	Israel withdraws from Lebanon
1987	Arab uprising on the West Bank commences
1988	PLO accepts Israel's right to exist
1993	Israel and PLO agree to phased self-rule in the West Bank and Gaza
1995	Israeli Prime Minister Rabin assassinated

other Islamic republics discredited the military and raised questions about the effectiveness of the central government. This led to a resurgence of the Communist Party in the elections of late 1995.

Although Yeltsin's popularity was waning, he managed to defeat the Communist Party candidate for the presidency in the summer of 1996. This did little, however, to clarify the situation in Russia. President Yeltsin suffered from poor health and seemed unable to do much about his country's faltering economy. In 1998, Russia defaulted on it international debt repayments, and growing unrest finally persuaded Yeltsin to resign the presidency. His premier, Vladimir Putin, became acting president and was elected to the presidency in March 2000. Putin successfully courted popular support by vigorously renewing the war in Chechnya where victory had become a matter of national pride. No one can predict what the future holds in store for Russia, but it may face decades of uncertain political stability and economic difficulty.

THE UNITED STATES AND THE COLLAPSE OF THE SOVIET UNION. It fell to George Bush, who won the American presidency in 1988, to guide the United States as it adjusted to the changes taking place in the Soviet Union and Eastern Europe. The close diplomatic relationship with the leadership of the new Russia that Bush developed proved useful in the fall of 1990 when Iraq invaded Kuwait. President Bush ordered the largest mobilization of American troops since the Vietnam war, and he used the United Nations as a forum to forge a worldwide coalition to counter Iraq's aggression. Russia joined America's traditional allies in this effort, and early in 1991 Operation Desert Storm forced Iraq out of Kuwait.

In 1992 the American presidency passed to William Clinton, governor of Arkansas, and he retained it in the 1996 election. During his two terms, President Clinton continued the difficult task of building a relationship with the Commonwealth of Independent States. He also pushed for the expansion of NATO to accommodate the security concerns of some of the former Warsaw Pact members. The Clinton administration steadfastly supported Yeltsin as the best hope for reform in the former Soviet Union, but it remains to be seen what U.S. policy will be now that Vladimir Putin is president.

The Collapse of Yugoslavia and Civil War

The communist government of Yugoslavia had long been distinct from those of the other eastern bloc nations dominated by the Soviet Union. The country's leader, Marshal Tito, had acted independently of Stalin in the late 1940s. Thereafter, Yugoslavia pursued a foreign policy that was independent of the Soviet Union. After Tito's death in 1980, Yugoslavia became increasingly unstable until it broke apart in civil war.

Yugoslavia was created after World War I by combining six national groups: Serbs, Croats, Slovenes, Montenegrins, Macedonians, and Bosnians. They have quarreled for centuries, and each has staked historical claims to a particular region: Serbia, Croatia, Slovenia, Montenegro, Macedonia, and Bosnia-Herzegovina. These regions, which were separate republics within Yugoslavia, have mixed populations. Many Serbs, for instance, live outside Serbia.

Tito, the communist leader of Yugoslavia, muted ethnic differences by complex power-sharing arrangements and by a cult of personality that made loyalty to him the linchpin for a nation. After Tito's death in 1980, Yugoslavia had serious economic problems that undermined its central government, and in the late 1980s the old ethnic differences flared up. Nationalist leaders came to power—most notably Slobodan Milosevic (b. 1941) in Serbia and Franjo Tudjman (b. 1922) in Croatia. The Serbs contended that Serbia was not powerful enough within the Yugoslav federation and that Serbs living in other parts of Yugoslavia suffered discrimination (especially from Croats). The Croats and Slovenes, for their part, created tension by pushing hard for rapid movement toward a market economy. During the summer of 1990, in the wake of the upheaval in the former Soviet bloc, Slovenia and Croatia seceded from Yugoslavia and won recognition from the European Community.

From this point on, violence escalated steadily. Serbia was determined to maintain a united Yugoslavian state under Serbian control. Croatia was equally determined to secure independence. Croatian Serbs, who demanded pro-

MAP 31–5   THE NATIONS IN THE CENTER OF EUROPE   *The rapid changes in Eastern Europe at the end of the 1980s allowed long-standing ethnic tensions to reemerge. This map shows national and ethnic borders and major ethnic enclaves within areas dominated by a single ethnic group.*

tection, provided the Serbian army with a pretext to attack Croatia, and in June 1991 war erupted between the two republics. The struggle took a new turn in 1992, when Croatian and Serbian forces decided to divide Bosnia-Herzegovina. The Muslims in Bosnia were caught between the opposing forces, and the Serbs, in particular, began a process of "ethnic cleansing," a euphemism for the murder or dispossession of large numbers of Bosnian Muslims. Unremitting Serbian bombardment of Sarajevo, the capital of Bosnia-Herzegovina, brought the Yugoslavian civil war to the attention of the world, and the United Nations tried, unsuccessfully, to mediate an end to the conflict.

Early in 1990 the bombing of a marketplace in Sarajevo prompted NATO to threaten retaliation against Serbian military positions if the Serbs did not withdraw their artillery from Sarajevo. This was the first such action in NATO history, and it was successful. In 1995 NATO strategic air strikes finally persuaded the leaders of the warring factions to meet in Dayton, Ohio, to work out a peace agreement. The terms of the complex agreement were to be enforced by NATO troops.

Toward the end of the 1990s, Serbian aggression again drew NATO into Yugoslav affairs. Employing techniques similar to those they had used in Bosnia, the Serbs began to drive ethnic Albanians from the province of Kosovo. NATO responded with an air campaign, the largest military operation in Europe since the end of World War II. The Serbs withdrew, and NATO troops were sent in to restore the Albanians to their homes. Many tensions remain unresolved, and the future of the region threatens to be troubled.

The opening of the Berlin Wall in November 1989, more than any other event, symbolized the collapse of the communist governments in Eastern Europe.
R. Bossu/Corbis Sygma Photo News

Problems in the Wake of the Collapse of Communism

The collapse of communism in Eastern Europe and the former Soviet Union means that nations in those areas have a chance to restore civil liberties and develop standards of living comparable to those in Western Europe. But the problems facing the communist successor states are enormous. Unemployment is widespread. Existing plants and factories are obsolete, and some are causing the worst environmental pollution in the world. Hundreds of thousands of people have migrated from Eastern to Western Europe to find work. There, like immigrants from the Third World, they have often been met with resentment, opposition, and

Architecture and Internationalism: Guggenheim Museum Bilbao, Spain

The Guggenheim Museum Bilbao, Spain, the work of architect Frank Gehry (b. 1929), was hailed as a masterpiece upon its completion in 1997. It is one of five museums that the Solomon R. Guggenheim Foundation has established across the globe for the display of modern art. Like Frank Lloyd Wright's 1959 Guggenheim Museum in New York City, it marks an architectural milestone. The Bilbao building would have been impossible without the help of advanced computer-aided design techniques and sophisticated titanium metal alloys.

Bilbao, Spain's fourth largest city, is an unlikely location for such a monument. It is a shipping and industrial community plagued by the violence of separatist Basque politics. (Terrorists attempted to plant explosives near the building shortly before its opening.) The museum owes its existence to the foresight of Bilbao officials who developed an urban renewal plan for their city. Their vision included a museum, but having no art collection with which to fill it, they entered into a partnership with the Guggenheim Foundation.

Gehry, the Canadian-American architect who received the commission, developed a reputation for utilizing unconventional materials to create whimsical forms that test the limits of architecture. The building he designed to serve Bilbao as a museum has itself become an attraction that draws millions of visitors to the city. It signals what can be achieved as Europe enters a new millennium in which international partnerships are replacing Cold War divisions and the West will seek to reconcile diversity and unity under the banner of pluralistic democracy.

Frank O. Gehry. *Guggenheim Museum Bilbao, Spain,* 1997. Javier Bauluz Stringer/AP/Wide World Photos.

Sources: Bruggen, Coosje van. *Frank O. Gehry: Guggenheim Musem Bilbao.* New York: Guggenheim Museum Publications, 1997. Forster, Kurt Walter. *Frank O. Gehry: Guggenheim Bilbao Museum.* Stuttgart and London: Edition Axel Menges, 1998. Muschamp, Herbert. *The Miracle in Bilbao. New York Times* (September 7, 1997), section 6, p. 54. Reid, T. R. *The Art of Rejuvenation. Washington Post* (March 31, 1999), p. A16.

violence. The nations of Western Europe are also grappling with the issue of how the former communist economies can be related to the European Economic Community without threatening Europe's prosperity.

The freedom made possible by the fall of communist governments has, thus far, been used to pursue ethnic goals that almost inevitably stir up domestic political turmoil. In 1993 disagreements between Czechs and Slovaks led them to split Czechoslovakia into separate states. With exceptions (e.g., Austria, Romania, Bulgaria, and Greece), all of the nations between Germany and the Commonwealth of Independent States have existed as distinct political units with their present borders only since World War I. Between World War I and 1989, all of them spent time under either fascist or communist governments. After World War II, only Germany and Austria developed strong democracies. The key question is whether the young democratic governments in the former communist states can cope with disorder, economic stagnation, and competing ethnic claims—or whether they will succumb to an authoritarian alternative.

The collapse of European communism has ended the era, which began in the 1870s, during which Marxism has dominated socialist thought. Marxist socialism has been discredited by the collapse of the states and economies that were founded on it, and socialism itself seems to have lost much of its appeal. The primary inspiration for future social critics may emerge from new movements such as feminism and environmentalism.

Meanwhile, however, international relations within Europe must be adjusted to accommodate the situation created by the collapse of European communism. The demise of the Warsaw Pact raised questions about the future of NATO whose primary function had been to deter a Soviet attack on Western Europe. Many have argued that NATO should now become an instrument to preserve international order, but the lingering problem in Yugoslavia raises doubts about its effectiveness in such a role. NATO's heavy reliance on American aircraft during the Yugoslav conflict has also persuaded some European leaders that their nations need to build up their own militaries to avoid excessive dependence on the United States. Much debate in the future will center on the admission of former members of the Warsaw Pact to NATO. Poland, the Czech Republic, and Hungary have already joined despite Russia's protests. At present it appears that NATO will continue to expand while working to allay Russia's concerns.

Europe at the Opening of the Global Century

In 1900 the major European nations reached the apex of developments that began with the commencement of the era of European exploration at the end of the fifteenth century. Economically and militarily they influenced the lives of millions on every continent and provided the models accepted everywhere to guide industrial development, economic life, and the practice of high culture's arts and sciences. In short, they dominated the world.

The twentieth century, however, held in store massive, unanticipated problems for Europe, and today no European power can dream of world dominion. What that means for Europe's future is not entirely clear, but there are some likely developments. Europeans have begun, for instance, to see themselves as part of a global culture and economy in which they play a major, but not dominant, role. Electronic technology contributes to this, but global integration involves more than economic and technological developments. Religious life is also affected. Christianity, which at the start of the twentieth century was largely a European religion, has become a global phenomenon that now thrives much more vigorously abroad than in Europe. In Europe, on the other hand, immigration has given Islam more visibility than some Christian denominations.

In order to cope with all their changed relationship with the wider world, the European nations will doubtless continue to pursue greater economic and perhaps political integration. Language barriers, ethnic prejudices, and the forces of nationalism will create problems, but greater coordination of activities will occur as the Continent ponders a new vision of itself as a single community. It remains to be seen to what extent Europeans want unity and what they might be willing to pay to achieve it. The most significant divisions on the Continent may prove to be those between its richer and poorer regions, and hovering in the background is the perennial question of Russia's place in European civilization.

It is highly likely that the traditional features of European life will endure—concern for constitutional government, tension between religion and politics, pursuit of science, inclination toward rationalism, and a penchant for self-criticism. These things have not always guaranteed that Western civilization will choose the moral high road, but they have protected its ability to question its actions and to correct and redirect its conduct. Perhaps the best transmitters of Western civilization into the new century are those who embrace it while criticizing it and demanding that it justify its existence.

REVIEW QUESTIONS

1. How did Europe come to be dominated by the United States and the Soviet Union after 1945? Through what stages did the Cold War pass? What was crucial about the years 1956 and 1962?

2. How would you define the policy of containment? What were some of the global events in the period from 1945 to 1982 that were influenced by this American policy?

3. How did Khrushchev change the Soviet state that had been created by Stalin's repression? Why did many people inside and outside the Soviet Union regard Khrushchev as reckless?

4. How did the nations of Western Europe move toward political unity following World War II while restoring their economic prosperity and preserving their liberal democratic governments?

5. Why did the nations of Europe give up their empires? How was the process of decolonization carried out? How did the United States become involved in Vietnam? What was the effect of the Vietnam War on Europe?

6. What internal political pressures did the Soviet Union experience in the 1970s and early 1980s? What did the Soviet government do to

silence protest? What did Gorbachev's reforms contribute to the collapse of the Soviet Union?

7. What were the major events in Eastern Europe that contributed to the collapse of communism? What was Poland's role in this process?

8. What are the major economic and political challenges that face Europe as it enters a new century?

SUGGESTED READINGS

F. ANSPRENGER, *The Dissolution of Colonial Empires* (1989). A broad survey.

I. BANAC, ed., *Eastern Europe in Revolution* (1992). Excellent articles on the events of 1989 and afterward.

E. BOTTOME, *The Balance of Terror: Nuclear Weapons and the Illusions of Security, 1945–1985* (1986). An examination of the role of nuclear weapons in the Cold War climate.

M. ELLMAN and V. KONTOROVICH, *The Disintegration of the Soviet Economic System* (1992). An overview of the strains that the Soviet Union experienced during the 1980s.

R. EMERSON, *From Empire to Nation: The Rise to Self-assertion of Asian and African Peoples* (1960). An important discussion of the origins of decolonization.

B. B. FALL, *The Two Vietnams: A Political and Military Analysis*, rev. ed. (1967). A discussion by a journalist who spent many years on the scene.

H. FEIS, *From Trust to Terror: The Onset of the Cold War, 1945–1950* (1970). The best general account.

J. L. GADDIS, *The United States and the Origin of the Cold War, 1941–1947* (1992). The most important recent discussion.

L. JOHNSON, *Central Europe: Enemies and Neighbors and Friends* (1996). Examines the various nations of central Europe with an eye to the recent changes in the region.

J. KEEP, *Last of the Empires: A History of the Soviet Union, 1945–1991* (1995). An outstanding one-volume survey.

F. LEWIS, *Europe: Road to Unity* (1992). A discussion of contemporary Europe by a thoughtful journalist.

L. P. MORRIS, *Eastern Europe Since 1945* (1984). Concentrates on the political and economic organization of the Soviet-dominated states.

D. OBERDORFER, *The Turn: How the Cold War Came to an End: The United States and the Soviet Union, 1983–1990* (1992). A major narrative by a Washington journalist.

L. SCHAPIRO, *The Communist Party of the Soviet Union* (1960). A classic analysis of the most important institution of Soviet Russia.

H. A. TURNER, *Germany from Partition to Reunification* (1992). The best brief introduction.

A. ULAM, *The Communists: The Story of Power and Lost Illusions: 1948–1991* (1992). The best account to date of the days of communist strength and collapse.

M. WALKER, *The Cold War and the Making of the Modern World* (1994). A major new survey.

Energy and the Modern World

Throughout recorded history no technological factor has done more to determine the destiny of a society than its relationship with energy. The degree to which a state has access to sources of energy—and efficient technology for its use—dictates the standard of living of its citizens and the extent of its international influence.

Animals, Wind, and Water

Technology advances by finding ways to apply energy to the performance of tasks. The energy source exploited by the earliest civilizations was animal power. It was used extensively everywhere but in the Americas. Before Columbus, there were no indigenous species in the Western Hemisphere comparable to the oxen, water buffalo, and horses that were the chief sources of animal power elsewhere in the world.

Wind and water were also harnessed, and well into the eighteenth century most machinery was powered by these sources of energy. Wind and water-driven mills ground grain and had other important applications, but wind and water were variable power sources that were not consistent-ly or universally available. Winds could die down, droughts could reduce the flow of the streams that turned waterwheels, and mills could be constructed only in those places that had strong prevailing winds or substantial water courses.

The economic and political developments that have radically transformed society during the past two and a half centuries would not have been possible if animals, wind, and water had remained the civilized world's chief sources of power. Modern life has been shaped by technologies that have allowed us to exploit two additional sources of energy: fossil fuels and, later, electricity. Until the second half of the eighteenth century fossil fuels (i.e., coal, petroleum, and natural gas) were little used. A series of inventions was required before the heat they can produce could be turned into mechanical energy.

Steam Power and the Age of Coal

People who lived near coal deposits had long used coal as a household fuel, but there was no industrial demand for it until James Watt patented the steam engine in 1769. Steam engines had myriads

Until the eighteenth century sailing ships were powered by wind alone. In this fourteenth-century manuscript illustration, sailors navigate with the help of an astrolabe. Bridgeman Art Library International

Cancel distance & conquer weather

The woman who drives her own Ford Closed Car is completely independent of road and weather conditions in any season.

It enables her to carry on all those activities of the winter months that necessitate travel to and fro—in or out of town. Her time and energy are conserved; her health is protected, no matter how bitterly cold the day, or how wet and slushy it is underfoot.

A Ford Sedan is always comfortable—warm and snug in winter, and in summer with ventilator and windows open wide, as cool and airy as an open car.

This seasonal comfort is combined with fine looks and Ford dependability; no wonder there is for this car so wide and ever-growing a demand.

FORD MOTOR COMPANY, DETROIT, MICHIGAN

TUDOR SEDAN, $580   ·   FORDOR SEDAN, $660
COUPE, $530   ∴   ALL PRICES F. O. B. DETROIT

CLOSED CARS

Until 1924, Henry Ford had disdained national advertising for his cars. But as General Motors gained a competitive edge by making yearly changes in style and technology, Ford was forced to pay more attention to advertising. This ad was directed at "Mrs. Consumer," combining appeals to both female independence and motherly duties. Ford Motor Company

of applications that increased the demand for coal, and they provided the means for pumping water from mines so that coal production could be increased. Coal-fueled steam power utterly transformed human existence in the nineteenth century, and coal has maintained its importance into the twenty-first century as the energy that drives many of the turbogenerators that produce the electricity on which civilized life depends.

Steam engines have many advantages over wind and water mills. They can be built in any size to match any job. The larger ones generate far more power than wind or water mills. They can be located anywhere to provide energy to places that are not served by wind and water. And so long as they are supplied with coal, they provide continuous, unvarying streams of power around the clock day in and day out. Steam engines made the Industrial Revolution's factory mass-production system possible, and they powered the trains and ships that distributed factory goods to a world market. The increased consumption that this distribution made possible set up a cycle that promoted economic growth. Expanding markets stimulated the construction of larger factories (and the increased utilization of coal and steam) to make more goods. Steam engines also had military applications, producing steel for weapons and powering the massive propellers that drove steel-hulled naval vessels.

The age of steam was the age of coal, and the nations that had large coal deposits dominated nineteenth-century economic life. For much of that period, Great Britain held the lead in the production and delivery of coal. Late in the century, the United States, Russia, and China began to compete. The United States remained largely dependent on coal until after World War I. Europe's dependency continued through World War II, and coal is still the primary fuel used in China.

Coal elevated the standard of living in the West, but it also created serious social problems. For much of the nineteenth century, working conditions in coal mines were shockingly bad. Half-naked women and small children were employed as draft animals pulling carts through underground tunnels, and thousands of people died in mining disasters. Work in the mines injured the health of miners, but the health of the general public was also adversely affected by the pollution that coal fires in homes and factories spewed into the air. By the early twentieth century, some notice began to be taken of the environmental damage being done by coal mining and burning.

The Internal Combustion Engine: The Age of Oil

As with coal, interest in petroleum as a power source was prompted by the invention of some machinery. Initially, oil was used primarily for producing kerosene which, by 1900, was the chief fuel used for lighting in most parts of the world. The invention of the internal combustion engine by Rudolf Daimler in 1882 and the diesel engine by Rudolf Diesel in 1892 vastly expanded demand for oil-based products. As a fuel and lubricant for internal combustion engines, oil increased social mobility by revolutionizing transportation. It powered machines that transformed farming and greatly increased global food supplies. It also affected residence patterns—encouraging the movement of redundant farm laborers to cities and permitting people who worked in cities to commute to homes in suburbs.

Fuel oil was not cheaper than coal, but it burned more efficiently and cleanly and was easier to store and transport. Initially, it tended to be used by industrialized countries that could produce it domestically and that did not need, therefore, to import it from distant suppliers. Until the end of World War II, the United States was the leading oil-producing and consuming nation.

Electricity Increases the Demand for Oil

Automobiles, planes, and trains greatly increased consumption of oil, but it was the application of electricity to the needs of daily life that put the greatest pressure on oil supplies. Electricity was the twentieth century's most flexible and versatile source of energy, and its generation constituted the single greatest source of demand for both coal and oil. Hydroelectric and wind-driven generators were also developed, and they represented innovative new uses for the ancient power sources of water and wind.

Michael Farady's studies of electromagnetic induction paved the way for the invention of uses for electrical energy. In 1831, he demonstrated that mechanical energy could be converted into electrical energy, which could then be turned back into mechanical energy. This meant that electricity could be produced mechanically in one place, distributed by wire to a different location, and used there to power machines. During the second half of the nineteenth century a whole host of inventors (e.g., Thomas Alva Edison) worked on methods to generate and use electricity. In the twentieth century access to electricity became the key factor determining standards of living. The extension of electrical lines into the countryside was one of the major achievements of Franklin Roosevelt's New Deal.

Electrical power transformed the workplace, but its effects on home life were even more wide-ranging. It made possible a wide array of labor-saving appliances and devices. It provided light for homes and streets. It linked the home to the wider world through the telephone, the radio, and television. It spawned new industries (e.g., movie studios), and it allowed industrial complexes to be built wherever electrical lines could be run. Access to electrical power became the best indicator of a region's or a nation's level of economic achievement.

All of this, of course, came at a cost. Ever-expanding electrification immensely increased the demand for coal and oil to power generating stations. To meet growing needs, producers developed increasingly intrusive methods for finding and extracting fossil fuels, and that had major geopolitical and environmental consequences.

Oil and Global Politics in the Twentieth Century

At the start of the century, the United States was the major producer and exporter of oil, but by the 1920s, both the U.S. and British governments had begun to worry about diminishing oil supplies. They encouraged oil companies to enter into agreements with Middle Eastern countries for developing and exporting their petroleum resources. The arrangements that were negotiated reflected the informal colonialism that characterized the period between the world wars. After World War II, global oil consumption increased as Western Europe, the Soviet Union, the nations of the Warsaw Pact, and eventually Japan switched from coal to oil to power their economic growth. By 1947, the United States was importing more oil than it was producing, and the stage was set for access to oil supplies to become a major compli-

In 1989, when a supertanker spilled 35,000 tons of crude oil into Alaska's Prince William Sound, rescue workers struggled to save the lives of sea birds and animals. Nevertheless, thousands died.
Ron Levy/Liaison Agency, Inc.

cation in the international politics of the Cold War.

Just as the world's industrialized economies were growing dependent on oil imported from the Middle East, nationalistic leaders were emerging in that region who deeply resented the West's former colonial domination of their homelands. They rejected relationships with the West and with Israel, a new nation populated by Jewish refugees and immigrants on land to which many Middle Easterners believed the Jews had no right. In 1960 many of the oil-exporting countries banded together to form OPEC (Organization of Pe-

troleum Exporting Nations). They were determined that they and not their former colonial masters would control their oil resources. By setting production quotas they could regulate the supply of oil on the world market, and this gave them considerable political clout. In 1973, while Israel waged the Yom Kippur War with its Arab neighbors, OPEC curtailed oil supplies to drive up prices for the Western governments that were generally viewed as pro-Israeli. The West reacted by searching for new oil reserves in politically safe places (e.g., the North Sea and Alaska). In 1979, when a revolution in Iran overthrew a government supported by the United States, OPEC again cut off oil shipments to the West. The recent Persian Gulf war was motivated in part by the West's concern to secure the Middle Eastern oil supply.

In addition to fluctuations in the supply of oil that periodically cause serious economic dislocations and inspire political conflicts, the industrial world's reliance on imported oil has had severe environmental consequences. Since the places where oil is produced and where it is used are now generally widely separated, oil must be transported over long distances. Crude oil is shipped to refineries on enormous tankers. When accidents inevitably happen, there are massive oil spills that have very adverse impacts on ecosystems.

The Promise and Danger of Nuclear Energy

In the 1940s scientists working for the military unlocked the power of the atom. The result was a weapon of unprecedented destructive power but also the possibility of a remarkably abundant new source of energy for generating electricity. Atomic science (and breeder reactors that produced their own fuel) promised to provide the world with virtually infinite quantities of energy. The production of this energy, however, necessitated the construction of the most complicated machinery ever devised to generate electricity. France and Great Britain took the lead in developing nuclear reactors in the 1950s. The United States, the Soviet Union, and various European nations followed in the 1960s. The shocks to the oil market during the mid-1970s created a surge of enthusiasm for nuclear energy, but the economic slowdown of the late 1970s and early 1980s retarded the construction of new reactors. The technology of nuclear energy production also proved to be exceedingly dangerous. Reactors produce waste that remains dangerously radioactive for many centuries, and the potential damage from nuclear accidents (such as the one at Pennsylvania's Three Mile Island plant in 1979) is enormous. The potential threat that reactors pose became real in 1986 when the Chernobyl nuclear generating plant in the Soviet Union spewed radioactivity over an immense area. A related threat from nuclear energy springs from the fact that the scientists who master its technology can, as they have in India and Pakistan, apply what they know to the production of atomic weapons.

Nuclear technology has produced far less power than was initially anticipated, and as the world enters the twenty-first century, the problems posed by energy supplies and use remain. Environmental pollution, nuclear proliferation, and political struggles for control of diminishing oil supplies constitute major challenges that the nations of the world will be hard-pressed to meet.

❖ *What changes in technology took place as the West moved from wind and water power to petroleum? How did coal transform the industrial and military might of the West? What effect did the internal combustion engine have on consumption of energy? Why did the rise of electrical power increase the need for petroleum? What opportunities and dangers has nuclear energy posed?*

Glossary

absolutism Term applied to strong centralized continental monarchies that attempted to make royal power dominant over aristocracies and other regional authorities.

Acropolis (ACK-row-po-lis) The religious and civic center of Athens. It is the site of the Parthenon.

Act of Supremacy The declaration by Parliament in 1534 that Henry VIII, not the Pope, was the head of the Church in England.

agape (AG-a-pay) Meaning "love feast." A common meal that was part of the central ritual of early Christian worship.

Agricultural Revolution The innovations in farm production that began in the eighteenth century and led to a scientific and mechanized agriculture.

Albigensians (Al-bi-GEN-see-uns) Thirteenth-century advocates of a dualist religion. They took their name from the city of Albi in southern France. Also called Cathars.

Anabaptists Protestants who insisted that only adult baptism conformed to Scripture.

anarchism The theory that government and social institutions are oppressive and unnecessary and that society should be based on voluntary cooperation among individuals.

Anschluss (AHN-shluz) Meaning "union." The annexation of Austria by Germany in March 1938.

anti-Semitism Prejudice, hostility, or legal discrimination against Jews.

appeasement The Anglo-French policy of making concessions to Germany in the 1930s to avoid a crisis that would lead to war. It assumed that Germany had real grievances and that Hitler's aims were limited and ultimately acceptable.

Areopagus The governing council of Athens, originally open only to the nobility. It was named after the hill on which it met.

Arete (AH-ray-tay) Manliness, courage, and the excellence appropriate to a hero. It was considered the highest virtue of Homeric society.

Arianism (AIR-ee-an-ism) The belief formulated by Arius of Alexandria (ca. 280–336 C.E.) that Jesus was a created being, neither fully man nor fully God, but something in between. It did away with the doctrine of the Trinity.

aristocratic resurgence Term applied to the eighteenth-century aristocratic efforts to resist the expanding power of European monarchies.

Arminians (are-MIN-ee-ans) A group within the Church of England who rejected Puritanism and the Calvinist doctrine of predestination in favor of free will and an elaborate liturgy.

Asia Minor Modern Turkey. Also called Anatolia.

asiento (ah-SEE-ehn-tow) The contract to furnish slaves to the Spanish colonies.

assignants (as-seen-YAHNTS) Government bonds based on the value of confiscated Church lands issued during the early French Revolution.

Atomists School of ancient Greek philosophy founded in the fifth century B.C.E. by Leucippus of Miletus and Democritus of Abdera. It held that the world consists of innumerable, tiny, solid, indivisible, and unchangeable particles called atoms.

Attica (AT-tick-a) The region of Greece where Athens is located.

Augsburg (AWGS-berg) **Confession** The definitive statement of Lutheran belief made in 1530.

Augustus (AW-gust-us) The title given to Octavian in 27 B.C.E. and borne thereafter by all Roman emperors. It was a semireligious title that implied veneration, majesty, and holiness.

Ausgleich (AWS-glike) Meaning "compromise." The agreement between the Habsburg Emperor and the Hungarians to give Hungary considerable administrative autonomy in 1867. It created the Dual Monarchy or Austria-Hungary.

autocracy (AW-to-kra-see) Government in which the ruler has absolute power.

Axis The alliance between Nazi Germany and Fascist Italy. Also called the Pact of Steel.

banalities Exactions that the lord of a manor could make on his tenants.

baroque (bah-ROWK) A style of art marked by heavy and dramatic ornamentation and curved rather than straight lines that flourished between 1550 and 1750. It was especially associated with the Catholic Counter-Reformation.

beguines (bi-GEENS) Lay sisterhoods not bound by the rules of a religious order.

benefice Church offices granted by the ruler of a state or the Pope to an individual. It also meant "fief" in the Middle Ages.

bishop Originally a person elected by early Christian congregations to lead them in worship and supervise their funds. In time bishops became the religious and even political authorities for Christian communities within large geographical areas.

Black Death   The bubonic plague that killed millions of Europeans in the fourteenth century.

blitzkrieg (BLITZ-kreeg)   Meaning "lightning war." The German tactic early in World War II of employing fast-moving, massed armored columns supported by airpower to overwhelm the enemy.

Bolsheviks   Meaning the "majority." Term Lenin applied to his faction of the Russian Social Democratic Party. It became the Communist Party of the Soviet Union after the Russian Revolution.

boyars   The Russian nobility.

Bronze Age   The name given to the earliest civilized era, c. 4000 to 1000 B.C.E. The term reflects the importance of the metal bronze, a mixture of tin and copper, for the peoples of this age for use as weapons and tools.

Bund   A secular Jewish socialist organization of Polish Jews.

Caesaro-papism (SEE-zer-o-PAY-pi-zim)   The direct involvement of the ruler in religious doctrine and practice as if he were the head of the Church as well as the state.

cahiers de doleances (KAH-hee-ay de dough-LAY-ahnce)   Meaning "lists of grievances." Petitions for reforms submitted to the French Crown when the Estates General met in 1789.

caliphate (KAH-li-fate)   The true line of succession to Muhammad.

capital goods   Machines and tools used to produce other goods.

carbonari (car-buh-NAH-ree)   Meaning "charcoal burners." The most famous of the secret republican societies seeking to unify Italy in the 1820s.

categorical imperative   According to Emmanuel Kant (1724–1804), the internal sense of moral duty or awareness possessed by all human beings.

Catholic Emancipation   The grant of full political rights to Roman Catholics in Britain in 1829.

catholic   Meaning "universal." The body of belief held by most Christians enshrined within the Church.

censor   Official of the Roman Republic charged with conducting the census and compiling the lists of citizens and members of the Senate. They could expel senators for financial or moral reasons. Two censors were elected every five years.

Chartism   The first large-scale European working-class political movement. It sought political reforms that would favor the interests of skilled British workers in the 1830s and 1840s.

chiaroscuro (kyar-eh-SKEW-row)   The use of shading to enhance naturalness in painting and drawing.

civic humanism   Education designed to promote humanist leadership of political and cultural life.

civilization   A form of human culture marked by urbanism, metallurgy, and writing.

classical economics   The theory that economies grow through the free enterprise of individuals competing in a largely self-regulating marketplace with government intervention held to a minimum.

clientage (KLI-ent-age)   The custom in ancient Rome whereby men became supporters of more powerful men in return for legal and physical protection and economic benefits.

Cold War   The ideological and geographical struggle between the United States and its allies and the USSR and its allies that began after World War II and lasted until the dissolution of the USSR in 1989.

collectivization   The bedrock of Stalinist agriculture, which forced Russian peasants to give up their private farms and work as members of collectives, large agricultural units controlled by the state.

coloni (CO-loan-ee)   Farmers or sharecroppers on the estates of wealthy Romans.

Commonwealthmen   British political writers whose radical republican ideas influenced the American revolutionaries.

Concert of Europe   Term applied to the European great powers acting together (in "concert") to resolve international disputes between 1815 and the 1850s.

Conciliar Theory   The argument that General Councils were superior in authority to the Pope and represented the whole body of the faithful.

condottieri (con-da-TEE-AIR-ee)   Military brokers who furnished mercenary forces to the Italian states during the Renaissance.

Congress System   A series of international meetings among the European great powers to promote mutual cooperation between 1818 and 1822.

conquistadores (kahn-KWIS-teh-door-hez)   Meaning "conquerors." The Spanish conquerors of the New World.

conservatism   Support for the established order in church and state. In the nineteenth century it implied support for legitimate monarchies, landed aristocracies, and established churches. Conservatives favored only gradual, or "organic," change.

Consulate   French government dominated by Napoleon from 1799 to 1804.

consuls (CON-suls)   The two chief magistrates of the Roman state.

consumer revolution   The vast increase in both the desire and the possibility of consuming goods and services that began in the early eighteenth century and created the demand for sustaining the Industrial Revolution.

containment   The U.S. policy during the Cold War of resisting Soviet expansion and influence in the expectation that the USSR would eventually collapse.

Convention French radical legislative body from 1792 to 1794.

Corn Laws British tariffs on imported grain that protected the price of grain grown within the British Isles.

corporatism The planned economy of fascist Italy that combined private ownership of capital with government direction of Italy's economic life and arbitration of labor disputes. All major areas of production were organized into state-controlled bodies called corporations, which were represented in the Chamber of Corporations that replaced the Chamber of Deputies. The state, not consumers and owners, determined what the economy produced.

corvée (cor-VAY) A French labor tax requiring peasants to work on roads, bridges, and canals.

Council of Nicaea (NIGH-see-a) The council of Christian bishops at Nicaea in 325 C.E. that formulated the Nicene Creed, a statement of Christian belief that rejected Arianism in favor of the doctrine that Christ is both fully human and fully divine.

Counter-Reformation The sixteenth-century reform movement in the Roman Catholic Church in reaction to the Protestant Reformation.

coup d'état (COO DAY-ta) The sudden violent overthrow of a government by its own army.

creed A brief statement of faith to which true Christians should adhere.

creoles (KRAY-ol-ez) Persons of Spanish descent born in the Spanish colonies.

Crusades Religious wars directed by the church against infidels and heretics.

culture The ways of living built up by a group and passed on from one generation to another.

cuneiform (Q-nee-i-form) A writing system invented by the Sumerians that used a wedge-shaped stylus, or pointed tool, to write on wet clay tablets that were then baked or dried ("cuneus" means wedge in Latin). The writing was also cut into stone.

Curia (CURE-ee-a) The papal government.

Cynic (SIN-ick) **School, The** A fourth-century philosophical movement that ridiculed all religious observances and turned away from involvement in the affairs of the *polis*. Its most famous exemplar was Diogenes of Sinope (ca. 400–325 B.C.E.).

deacon Meaning "those who serve." In early Christian congregations, deacons assisted the presbyters, or elders.

deism A belief in a rational God who had created the universe, but then allowed it to function without his interference according to the mechanisms of nature, and a belief in rewards and punishments after death for human action.

Delian (DEE-li-an) An alliance of Greek states under the leadership of Athens that was formed in 478–477 B.C.E. to resist the Persians. In time the league was transformed into the Athenian Empire.

deme (DEEM) A small town in Attica or a ward in Athens that became the basic unit of Athenian civic life under the democratic reforms of Clisthenes in 508 B.C.E.

demesne (di-MAIN) The part of a manor that was cultivated directly for the lord of the manor.

divine right of kings The theory that monarchs are appointed by and answerable only to God.

Domesday (DOOMS-day) **Book** A detailed survey of the wealth of England undertaken by William the Conqueror between 1080 and 1086.

domestic system of textile production Method of producing textiles in which agents furnished raw materials to households whose members spun them into thread and then wove cloth, which the agents then sold as finished products.

Donatism The heresy that taught that the efficacy of the sacraments depended on the moral character of the clergy who administered them.

Duma (DOO-ma) The Russian parliament, after the Revolution of 1905.

electors Nine German princes who had the right to elect the Holy Roman Emperor.

émigrés (em-ee-GRAYS) French aristocrats who fled France during the Revolution.

empiricism (em-PEER-ih-cism) The use of experiment and observation derived from sensory evidence to construct scientific theory or philosophy of knowledge.

enclosure The consolidation or fencing in of common lands by British landlords to increase production and achieve greater commercial profits. It also involved the reclamation of waste land and the consolidation of strips into block fields.

encomienda (en-co-mee-EN-da) The grant by the Spanish Crown to a colonist of the labor of a specific number of Indians for a set period of time.

ENIAC Electronic Numerical Integrator and Computer. The first genuine modern digital computer, developed in the 1940s.

Enlightenment The eighteenth-century movement led by the philosophies that held that change and reform were both desirable through the application of reason and science.

Epicureans (EP-i-cure-ee-ans) School of philosophy founded by Epicurus of Athens (342–271 B.C.E.). It sought to liberate people from fear of death and the supernatural by teaching that the gods took no interest in human affairs and that true happiness consisted in pleasure, which was defined as the absence of pain. This could be achieved by attaining *ataraxia*, the freedom from trouble, pain, and responsibility produced by withdrawing from business and public life.

equestrians (EE-quest-ree-ans) Literally "cavalrymen" or "knights." In the earliest years of the Roman Republic those who could afford to serve as mounted warriors. The equestrians evolved into a social rank of well-to-do businessmen and middle-ranking officials. Many of them supported the Gracchi.

Estates General The medieval French parliament. It consisted of three separate groups, or "estates:" clergy, nobility, and commoners. It last met in 1789 at the outbreak of the French Revolution.

Etruscans (EE-trus-cans) A people of central Italy who exerted the most powerful external influence on the early Romans. Etruscan kings ruled Rome until 509 B.C.E.

Eucharist (YOU-ka-rist) Meaning "thanksgiving." The celebration of the Lord's Supper. Considered the central ritual of worship by most Christians. Also called Holy Communion.

Euro The common currency created by the EEC in the late 1990s.

European Economic Community (EEC) The economic association formed by France, Germany, Italy, Belgium, the Netherlands, and Luxembourg in 1957. Also known as the Common Market.

European Union (EU) The new name given to the EEC in 1993. It included most of the states of Western Europe.

excommunication Denial by the church of the right to receive the sacraments.

Existentialism The post–World War II Western philosophy that holds that human beings are totally responsible for their acts and that this responsibility causes them dread and anguish.

Fabians British socialists in the late nineteenth and early twentieth centuries who sought to achieve socialism through gradual, peaceful, and democratic means.

family economy The basic structure of production and consumption in preindustrial Europe.

fascism Political movements that tend to be antidemocratic, anti-Marxist, antiparliamentary, and often anti-Semitic. Fascists were invariably nationalists and exhalted the nation over the individual. They supported the interests of the middle class and rejected the ideas of the French Revolution and nineteenth-century liberalism. The first fascist regime was founded by Benito Mussolini (1883–1945) in Italy in the 1920s.

fealty An oath of loyalty by a vassal to a lord, promising to perform specified services.

feudal (FEW-dull) **society** The social, political, military, and economic system that prevailed in the Middle Ages and beyond in some parts of Europe.

fief Land granted to a vassal in exchange for services, usually military.

foederati (FAY-der-ah-tee) Barbarian tribes enlisted as special allies of the Roman Empire.

folk culture The distinctive songs, sayings, legends, and crafts of a people.

Fourteen Points President Woodrow Wilson's (1856–1924) idealistic war aims.

Fronde (FROHND) A series of rebellions against royal authority in France between 1649 and 1652.

Gaul (GAWL) Modern France.

German Confederation Association of German states established at the Congress of Vienna that replaced the Holy Roman Empire from 1815 to 1866.

ghetto Separate communities in which Jews were required by law to live.

glasnost (GLAZ-nohst) Meaning "openness." The policy initiated by Mikhail Gorbachev (MEEK-hail GORE-buh-choff) in the 1980s of permitting open criticism of the policies of the Soviet Communist Party.

Glorious Revolution The largely peaceful replacement of James II by William and Mary as English monarchs in 1688. It marked the beginning of constitutional monarchy in Britain.

gold standard A monetary system in which the value of a unit of a nation's currency is related to a fixed amount of gold.

Golden Bull The agreement in 1356 to establish a seven-member electoral college of German princes to choose the Holy Roman Emperor.

Great Depression A prolonged worldwide economic downturn that began in 1929 with the collapse of the New York Stock Exchange.

Great Reform Bill (1832) A limited reform of the British House of Commons and an expansion of the electorate to include a wider variety of the propertied classes. It laid the groundwork for further orderly reforms within the British constitutional system.

Great Schism The appearance of two and at times three rival popes between 1378 and 1415.

Green Movement A political environmentalist movement that began in West Germany in the 1970s and spread to a number of other Western nations.

grossdeutsch (gross-DOYCH) Meaning "great German." The argument that the German-speaking portions of the Habsburg Empire should be included in a united Germany.

guild An association of merchants or craftsmen that offered protection to its members and set rules for their work and products.

hacienda (ha-SEE-hen-da) A large landed estate in Spanish America.

Hegira (HEJ-ear-a) The flight of Muhammad and his followers from Mecca to Medina in 622 C.E. It marks the beginning of the Islamic calendar.

heliocentric (HE-li-o-cen-trick) **theory** The theory, now universally accepted, that the Earth and the other planets revolve around the Sun. First proposed by Aristarchos of Samos (310–230 B.C.E.). Its opposite, the geocentric theory, which was dominant until the sixteenth century C.E., held that the Sun and the planets revolved around the Earth.

helots (HELL-ots) Hereditary Spartan serfs.

heretic (HAIR-i-tick) A person whose beliefs were contrary to those of the Catholic Church.

hieroglyphics (HI-er-o-gli-phicks) The complicated writing script of ancient Egypt. It combined picture writing with pictographs and sound signs. Hieroglyph means "sacred carvings" in Greek.

Holocaust The Nazi extermination of millions of European Jews between 1940 and 1945. Also called the "final solution to the Jewish problem."

Holy Roman Empire The revival of the old Roman Empire, based mainly in Germany and northern Italy, that endured from 870 to 1806.

home rule The advocacy of a large measure of administrative autonomy for Ireland within the British Empire between the 1880s and 1914.

Homo sapiens (HO-mo say-pee-ans) The scientific name for human beings, from the Latin words meaning "Wise man." *Homo sapiens* emerged some 200,000 years ago.

honestiores (HON-est-ee-or-ez) The Roman term formalized from the beginning of the third century C.E. to denote the privileged classes: senators, equestrians, the municipal aristocracy, and soldiers.

hoplite phalanx (FAY-lanks) The basic unit of Greek warfare in which infantrymen fought in close order, shield to shield, usually eight ranks deep. The phalanx perfectly suited the farmer-soldier-citizen who was the backbone of the *polis.*

hubris (WHO-bris) Arrogance brought on by excessive wealth or good fortune. The Greeks believed that it led to moral blindness and divine vengeance.

Huguenots (HYOU-gu-nots) French Calvinists.

humanism The study of the Latin and Greek classics and of the Church Fathers both for their own sake and to promote a rebirth of ancient norms and values.

humanitas (HEW-man-i-tas) The Roman name for a liberal arts education.

humiliores (HEW-mi-lee-orez) The Roman term formalized at the beginning of the third century C.E. for the lower classes.

Hussites (HUS-Its) Followers of John Huss (d. 1415) who questioned Catholic teachings about the Eucharist.

iconoclasm (i-KON-o-kla-zoom) A heresy in Eastern Christianity that sought to ban the veneration of sacred images, or icons.

id, ego, superego The three entities in Sigmund Freud's model of the internal organization of the human mind. The id consists of the amoral, irrational instincts for self-gratification. The superego embodies the external morality imposed on the personality by society. The ego mediates between the two and allows the personality to cope with the internal and external demands of its existence.

Iliad (ILL-ee-ad) **and the** *Odyssey* (O-dis-see), The Epic poems by Homer about the "Dark Age" heroes of Greece who fought at Troy. The poems were written down in the eighth century B.C.E. after centuries of being sung by bards.

imperator (IM-per-a-tor) Under the Roman Republic it was the title given to a victorious general. Under Augustus and his successors it became the title of the ruler of Rome meaning "Emperor."

imperialism The extension of a nation's authority over other nations or areas through conquest or political or economic hegemony.

imperium (IM-pear-ee-um) In ancient Rome the right to issue commands and to enforce them by fines, arrests, and even corporal and capital punishment.

indulgences Remission of the temporal penalty of punishment in purgatory that remained after sins had been forgiven.

Industrial Revolution Mechanization of the European economy that began in Britain in the second half of the eighteenth century.

insulae (IN-sul-lay) Meaning "islands." The multistoried apartment buildings of Rome in which most of the inhabitants of the city lived.

intendents (in-TEN-duhnts) Royal officials under the French monarchy who supervised the provincial governments in the name of the king.

Intolerable Acts Measures passed by the British Parliament in 1774 to punish the colony of Massachusetts and strengthen Britain's authority in the colonies. The laws provoked colonial opposition, which led immediately to the American Revolution.

Investiture Struggle The medieval conflict between the church and lay rulers over who would control bishops and abbots, symbolized by the ceremony of "investing" them with the symbols of their authority.

Ionia (I-o-knee-a) The part of western Asia Minor heavily colonized by the Greeks.

Islam (IZ-lahm) Meaning "submission." The religion founded by the prophet Muhammad.

Italia Irredenta (ee-TAHL-ee-a ir-REH-dent-a) Meaning "unredeemed Italy." Italian-speaking areas that had been left under Austrian rule at the time of the unification of Italy.

Jacobins (JACK-uh-bins) The radical republican party during the French Revolution that displaced the Girondins.

jacquerie (jah-KREE) Revolt of the French peasantry.

Jansenism A seventeenth-century movement within the Catholic Church that taught that human beings were so corrupted by original sin that they could do nothing good nor secure their own salvation without divine grace. (It was opposed to the Jesuits.)

Judah (JEW-da) The southern Israelite kingdom established after the death of Solomon in the tenth century B.C.E.

Julian calendar The reform of the calendar by Julius Caesar in 46 B.C.E. It remained in use throughout Europe until the sixteenth century and in Russia until the Russian Revolution in 1917.

July Monarchy The French regime set up after the overthrow of the Bourbons in July 1830.

junkers (YOONG-kerz) The noble landlords of Prussia.

jus gentium (YUZ GEN-tee-um) Meaning "law of peoples." The body of Roman law that dealt with foreigners.

jus naturale (YUZ NAH-tu-rah-lay) Meaning "natural law." The Stoic concept of a world ruled by divine reason.

Ka'ba (KAH-bah) A shrine in the city of Mecca that became Islam's holiest place.

Keynesian economics The theory of John Maynard Keynes (CANES) (1883–1946) that governments could spend their economies out of a depression by running deficits to encourage employment and stimulate the production and consumption of goods.

kleindeutsch (kline-DOYCH) Meaning "small German." The argument that the German-speaking portions of the Habsburg Empire should be excluded from a united Germany.

Kristallnacht (KRIS-tahl-NAHKT) Meaning "crystal night" because of the broken glass that littered German streets after the looting and destruction of Jewish homes, businesses, and synagogues across Germany on the orders of the Nazi Party in November 1938.

kulaks (koo-LAKS) Prosperous Russian peasant farmers.

Kulturkampf (cool-TOOR-cahmff) Meaning the "battle for culture." The conflict between the Roman Catholic Church and the government of the German Empire in the 1870s.

laissez-faire (lay-ZAY-faire) French phrase meaning "allow to do." In economics the doctrine of minimal government interference in the working of the economy.

latifundia (LAT-ee-fun-dee-a) Large plantations for growing cash crops owned by wealthy Romans.

Latium (LAT-ee-um) The region of Italy in which Rome is located. Its inhabitants were called Latins.

League of Nations The association of sovereign states set up after World War I to pursue common policies and avert international aggression.

Lebensraum (LAY-benz-rauhm) Meaning "living space." The Nazi plan to colonize and exploit the Slavic areas of Eastern Europe for the benefit of Germany.

levée en masse (le-VAY en MASS) The French Revolutionary conscription (1792) of all males into the army and the harnessing of the economy for war production.

liberal arts The medieval university program that consisted of the trivium (TRI-vee-um): grammar, rhetoric, and logic, and the quadrivium (qua-DRI-vee-um): arithmetic, geometry, astronomy, and music.

liberalism In the nineteenth century, support for representative government dominated by the propertied classes and minimal government interference in the economy.

Lollards (LALL-erds) Followers of John Wycliffe (d. 1384) who questioned the supremacy and privileges of the Pope and the church hierarchy.

Lower Egypt The Nile delta.

Luftwaffe (LUFT-vaff-uh) The German air force in World War II.

Magna Carta (MAG-nuh CAR-tuh) The "Great Charter" limiting royal power that the English nobility forced King John to sign in 1215.

Magna Graecia (MAG-nah GRAY-see-a) Meaning "Great Greece" in Latin, it was the name given by the Romans to southern Italy and Sicily because there were so many Greek colonies in the region.

Magyars (MAH-jars) The majority ethnic group in Hungary.

mandates The assigning of the former German colonies and Turkish territories in the Middle East to Britain, France, Japan, Belgium, Australia, and South Africa as de facto colonies under the vague supervision of the League of Nations with the hope that the territories would someday advance to independence.

mannerism A style of art in the mid- to late sixteenth century that permitted the artist to express his or her own "manner" or feelings in contrast to the symmetry and simplicity of the art of the High Renaissance.

manor   Village farms owned by a lord.

Marshall Plan   The U.S. program named after Secretary of State George C. Marshall of providing economic aid to Europe after World War II.

Marxism   The theory of Karl Marx (1818–1883) and Friedrich Engels (FREE-drick Eng-ulz) (1820–1895) that history is the result of class conflict, which will end in the inevitable triumph of the industrial proletariat over the bourgeoisie and the abolition of private property and social class.

Mein Kampf (MINE KAHMFF)   Meaning "my struggle." Hitler's statement of his political program published in 1924.

Mensheviks   Meaning the "minority." Term Lenin applied to the majority moderate faction of the Russian Social Democratic Party opposed to him and the Bolsheviks.

mercantilism   Term used to describe close government control of the economy that sought to maximize exports and accumulate as much precious metals as possible to enable the state to defend its economic and political interests.

Mesopotamia (MEZ-o-po-tay-me-a)   Modern Iraq. The land between the Tigris and Euphrates Rivers where the first civilization appeared around 3000 B.C.E.

Messiah (MESS-eye-a)   The redeemer whose coming Jews believed would establish the kingdom of God on earth. Christians considered Jesus to be the Messiah (Christ means Messiah in Greek).

Methodism   An English religious movement begun by John Wesley (1703–1791) that stressed inward, heartfelt religion and the possibility of attaining Christian perfection in this life.

millets   Administrative units of the Ottoman Empire that were not geographic but consisted of ethnic or religious minorities to whom particular laws and regulations applied.

Minoans (MIN-o-ans)   The Bronze Age civilization that arose in Crete in the third and second millenia B.C.E.

missi dominici (MISS-ee dough-MIN-ee-chee)   Meaning "the envoys of the ruler." Royal overseers of the king's law in the Carolingian Empire.

mobilization   The placing of a country's military forces on a war footing.

modernism   The movement in the arts and literature in the late nineteenth and early twentieth centuries to create new aesthetic forms and to elevate the aesthetic experience of a work of art above the attempt to portray reality as accurately as possible.

moldboard plow   A heavy plow introduced in the Middle Ages that cut deep into the soil.

monophysitism (ma-NO-fiz-it-ism)   A Christian heresy that taught that Jesus had only one nature.

monotheism   The worship of one, universal God.

Mycenaean (MY-cen-a-an)   The Bronze Age civilization of mainland Greece that was centered at Mycenae.

"mystery" religions   The cults of Isis, Mithra, and Osiris, which promised salvation to those initiated into the secret or "mystery" of their rites. These cults competed with Christianity in the Roman Empire.

nationalism   The belief that one is part of a nation, defined as a community with its own language, traditions, customs, and history that distinguish it from other nations and make it the primary focus of a person's loyalty and sense of identity.

natural selection   The theory originating with Darwin that organisms evolve through a struggle for existence in which those that have a marginal advantage live long enough to propagate their kind.

naturalism   The attempt to portray nature and human life without sentimentality.

Nazis   The German Nationalist Socialist Party.

Neolithic (NEE-o-lith-ick) **Revolution**   The shift beginning 10,000 years ago from hunter-gatherer societies to settled communities of farmers and artisans. Also called the Age of Agriculture, it witnessed the invention of farming, the domestication of plants and animals, and the development of technologies such as pottery and weaving. The earliest Neolithic societies appeared in the Middle East about 8,000 B.C.E. "Neolithic" comes from the Greek words for "new stone."

Neoplatonism (NEE-o-play-ton-ism)   A religious philosophy that tried to combine mysticism with classical and rationalist speculation. Its chief formulator was Plotinus (205–270 C.E.).

New Economic Policy (NEP)   A limited revival of capitalism, especially in light industry and agriculture, introduced by Lenin in 1921 to repair the damage inflicted on the Russian economy by the Civil War and War Communism.

New Imperialism   The extension in the late nineteenth and early twentieth centuries of Western political and economic dominance to Asia, the Middle East, and Africa.

nomes   regions or provinces of ancient Egypt governed by officials called nomarchs.

oikos (OI-cos)   The Greek household, always headed by a male.

Old Believers   Those members of the Russian Orthodox Church who refused to accept the reforms of the seventeenth century regarding church texts and ritual.

Old Regime   Term applied to the pattern of social, political, and economic relationships and institutions that existed in Europe before the French Revolution.

optimates (OP-tee-ma-tes)   Meaning "the best men." Roman politicians who supported the traditional role of the Senate.

orthodox   Meaning "holding the right opinions." Applied to the doctrines of the Catholic church.

Ottoman Empire   The imperial Turkish state centered in Constantinople that ruled large parts of the Balkans, North Africa, and the Middle East until 1918.

Paleolithic (PAY-lee-o-lith-ick) **Age, The**   The earliest period when stone tools were used, from about 1,000,000 to 10,000 B.C.E. From the Greek meaning "old stone."

Panhellenic (PAN-hell-en-ick) Meaning "all-Greek." The sense of cultural identity that all Greeks felt in common with each other.

Panslavism   The movement to create a nation or federation that would embrace all the Slavic peoples of eastern Europe.

papal infallibility   The doctrine that the Pope is infallible when pronouncing officially in his capacity as head of the church on matters of faith and morals, enumerated by the First Vatican Council in 1870.

Papal States   Territory in central Italy ruled by the Pope until 1870.

parlements (par-luh-MAHNS)   French regional courts dominated by hereditary nobility. The most important was the *Parlement* of Paris, which claimed the right to register royal decrees before they could become law.

patricians (PA-tri-she-ans)   The hereditary upper class of early Republican Rome.

Peloponnesian (PELL-o-po-knees-ee-an) **Wars**   The protracted struggle between Athens and Sparta to dominate Greece between 465 and Athens final defeat in 404 B.C.E.

Peloponnesus (PELL-o-po-knee-sus)   The southern peninsula of Greece where Sparta was located.

peninsulares (pen-in-SUE-la-rez)   Persons born in Spain who settled in the Spanish colonies.

perestroika (pare-ess-TROY-ka)   Meaning "restructuring." The attempt in the 1980s to reform the Soviet government and economy.

Pharisees (FAIR-i-sees)   The group that was most strict in its adherence to Jewish law.

pharoah (FAY-row)   The god-kings of ancient Egypt. The term originally meant "great house" or palace.

philosophes (fee-lou-SOPHS)   The eighteenth-century writers and critics who forged the new attitudes favorable to change. They sought to apply reason and common sense to the institutions and societies of their day.

Phoenicians (FA-nee-shi-ans)   The ancient inhabitants of modern Lebanon. A trading people, they established colonies throughout the Mediterranean.

physiocrats   Eighteenth-century French thinkers who attacked the mercantilist regulation of the economy, advocated a limited economic role for government, and believed that all economic production depended on sound agriculture.

plantation economy   The economic system stretching between Chesapeake Bay and Brazil that produced crops, especially sugar, cotton, and tobacco, using slave labor on large estates.

plebeians (PLEB-bee-ans)   The hereditary lower class of early Republican Rome.

plenitude of power   The teaching that the Popes have power over all other bishops of the church.

pogroms (PO-grohms)   Organized riots against Jews in the Russian Empire.

polis (PO-lis) (plural, poleis)   The basic Greek political unit. Usually, but incompletely, translated as "city state," the Greeks thought of the *polis* as a community of citizens theoretically descended from a common ancestor.

polytheism (PAH-lee-thee-ism)   The worship of many gods.

pontifex maximus (PON-ti-feks MAK-suh-muss)   Meaning "supreme priest." The chief priest of ancient Rome. The title was later assumed by the Popes.

Popular Front   A government of all left-wing parties that took power in France in 1936 to enact social and economic reforms.

populares (PO-pew-lar-es)   Roman politicians who sought to pursue a political career based on the support of the people rather than just the aristocracy.

Positivism   The philosophy of Auguste Comte that science is the final, or positive, stage of human intellectual development because it involves exact descriptions of phenomena, without recourse to unobservable operative principles, such as gods or spirits.

Pragmatic Sanction   The legal basis negotiated by the Emperor Charles VI (r. 1711–1740) for the Habsburg succession through his daughter Maria Theresa (r. 1740–1780).

predestination   The doctrine that God had foreordained all souls to salvation (the "elect") or damnation. It was especially associated with Calvinism.

Presbyterians   Scottish Calvinists and English Protestants who advocated a national church composed of semi-autonomous congregations governed by "presbyteries."

presbyter (PRESS-bi-ter)   Meaning "elder." A person who directed the affairs of early Christian congregations.

proconsulship (PRO-con-sul-ship)   In Republican Rome the extension of a consul's imperium beyond the end of his term of office to allow him to continue to command an army in the field.

Protestant Ethic   The theory propounded by Max Weber in 1904 that the religious confidence and self-disciplined activism that were supposedly associated with Protestantism produced an ethic that stimulated the spirit of emergent capitalism.

Ptolemaic (tow-LEM-a-ick) **System**   The pre-Copernican explanation of the universe, with the Earth at the center of the universe, originated in the ancient world.

Punic (PEW-nick) **Wars**   Three wars between Rome and Carthage for dominance of the western Mediterranean that were fought from 264 B.C.E. to 146 B.C.E.

Puritans   English Protestants who sought to "purify" the Church of England of any vestiges of Catholicism.

Qur'an (kuh-RAN)   Meaning "a reciting." The Islamic bible, which Muslims believe God revealed to the prophet Muhammad.

racism   The pseudo-scientific theory that biological features of race determine human character and worth.

raison d'état (RAY-suhn day-TAH)   Meaning "reason of state." Concept that the interests of the state justify a course of action.

realism   The style of art and literature that seeks to depict the physical world and human life with scientific objectivity and detached observation.

Reformation   The sixteenth-century religious movement that sought to reform the Roman Catholic Church and led to the establishment of Protestantism.

regular clergy   Monks and nuns who belong to religious orders.

Reichstag (RIKES-stahg)   The German parliament, which existed in various forms, until 1945.

Reign of Terror   The period between the summer of 1793 and the end of July 1794 when the French Revolutionary state used extensive executions and violence to defend the Revolution and suppress its alleged internal enemies.

relativity   The scientific theory associated with Einstein that time and space exist not separately but as a combined continuum whose measurement depends as much on the observer as on the entities that are being measured.

Renaissance   The revival of ancient learning and the supplanting of traditional religious beliefs by new secular and scientific values that began in Italy in the fourteenth and fifteenth centuries.

reparations   The requirement incorporated into the Versailles Treaty that Germany should pay for the cost of World War I.

revisionism   The advocacy among nineteenth-century German socialists of achieving a humane socialist society through the evolution of democratic institutions, not revolution.

robot (ROW-boht)   The amount of labor landowners demanded from peasants in the Habsburg Monarchy before 1848.

Romanitas (row-MAN-ee-tas)   Meaning "Romanness." The spread of the Roman way of life and the sense of identifying with Rome across the Roman Empire.

romanticism   A reaction in early nineteenth century literature, philosophy, and religion against what many considered the excessive rationality and scientific narrowness of the Enlightenment.

SA   The Nazi paramilitary forces, or storm troopers.

sans-culottes (SAHN coo-LOTS)   Meaning "without kneebreeches." The lower-middle classes and artisans of Paris during the French Revolution.

Schlieffen (SHLEE-fun) **Plan**   Germany's plan for achieving a quick victory in the West at the outbreak of World War I by invading France through Belgium and Luxembourg.

Scholasticism   The method of study based on logic and dialectic that dominated the medieval schools. It assumed that truth already existed; students had only to organize, elucidate, and defend knowledge learned from authoritative texts, especially those of Aristotle and the Church Fathers.

scientific induction   Scientific method in which generalizations are derived from data gained from empirical observations.

Scientific Revolution   The sweeping change in the scientific view of the universe that occurred in the sixteenth and seventeenth centuries. The new scientific concepts and the method of their construction became the standard for assessing the validity of knowledge in the West.

Second Industrial Revolution   The emergence of new industries and the spread of industrialization from Britain to other countries, especially Germany and the United States, in the second half of the nineteenth century.

secular clergy   Parish clergy who did not belong to a religious order.

Sejm (SHEM)   The legislative assembly of the Polish nobility.

serfs   Peasants tied to the land they tilled.

Shi-a (SHE-ah)   The minority of Muslims who trace their beliefs from the caliph Ali who was assassinated in 661 C.E.

Sinn Fein (SHIN FAHN)   Meaning "ourselves alone." An Irish political movement founded in 1905 that advocated complete political separation from Britain.

Social Darwinism   The application of Darwin's concept of "the survival of the fittest" to explain evolution in nature to human social relationships.

Sophists (SO-fists) Professional teachers who emerged in Greece in the mid-fifth century B.C.E. who were paid to teach techniques of rhetoric, dialectic, and argumentation.

soviets Workers and soldiers councils formed in Russia during the Revolution.

spinning jenny A machine invented in England by James Hargreaves around 1765 to mass-produce thread.

SS The chief security units of the Nazi state.

Stoics (STOW-icks) A philosophical school founded by Zeno of Citium (335–263 B.C.E.) that taught that humans could only be happy with natural law. Human misery was caused by passion, which was a disease of the soul. The wise sought *apatheia*, freedom from passion.

Sturm und Drang (SHTURM und DRAHNG) Meaning "storm and stress." A movement in German romantic literature and philosophy that emphasized feeling and emotion.

suffragettes British women who lobbied and agitated for the right to vote in the early 20th century.

summa (SUE-ma) An authoritative summary in the Middle Ages of all that was allegedly known about a subject.

Sunna (SOON-ah) Meaning "tradition." The dominant Islamic group.

symposium (SIM-po-see-um) The carefully organized drinking party that was the center of Greek aristocratic social life. It featured games, songs, poetry, and even philosophical disputation.

syncretism (SIN-cret-ism) The intermingling of different religions to form an amalgam that contained elements from each.

syndicalism French labor movement that sought to improve workers' conditions through direct action, especially general strikes.

Table of Ranks An official hierarchy established by Peter the Great in Imperial Russia that equated a person's social position and privileges with his rank in the state bureaucracy or army.

tabula rasa (tah-BOO-lah RAH-sah) Meaning a "blank page." The philosophical belief associated with John Locke that human beings enter the world with totally unformed characters that are completely shaped by experience.

taille (TIE) The direct tax on the French peasantry.

"ten lost tribes" The Israelites who were scattered and lost to history when the northern kingdom of Israel fell to the Assyrians in 722 B.C.E.

tertiaries (TER-she-air-ees) Laypeople affiliated with the monastic life who took vows of poverty, chastity, and obedience but remained in the world.

tetrarchy (TET-rar-key) Diocletian's (r. 306–337 C.E.) system for ruling the Roman Empire by four men with power divided territorially.

Thermidorean Reaction The reaction against the radicalism of the French Revolution that began in July 1794. Associated with the end of terror and establishment of the Directory.

thesis, antithesis, and synthesis G. W. F. Hegel's (HAY-gle) (1770–1831) concept of how ideas develop. The thesis is a dominant set of ideas. It is challenged by a set of conflicting ideas, the antithesis. From the clash of these ideas, a new pattern of thought, the synthesis, emerges and eventually becomes the new thesis.

Third Estate The branch of the French Estates General representing all of the kingdom outside the nobility and the clergy.

Third Reich (RIKE) Hitler's regime in Germany, which lasted from 1933 to 1945.

Thirty-nine Articles (1563) The official statement of the beliefs of the Church of England. They established a moderate form of Protestantism.

three-field system A medieval innovation that increased the amount of land under cultivation by leaving only one-third fallow in a given year.

transportation The British policy from the late eighteenth to the mid-nineteenth centuries of shipping persons convicted of the most serious offenses to Australia as an alternative to capital punishment.

transubstantiation The doctrine that the entire substances of the bread and wine are changed in the Eucharist into the body and blood of Christ.

tribunes (TRIB-unes) Roman officials who had to be plebeians and were elected by the plebeian assembly to protect plebeians from the arbitrary power of the magistrates.

ulema (oo-LEE-mah) Meaning "persons with correct knowledge." The Islamic scholarly elite who served a social function similar to the Christian clergy.

Upper Egypt The part of Egypt that runs from the delta to the Sudanese border.

utopian socialism Early-nineteenth-century theories that sought to replace the existing capitalist structure and values with visionary solutions or ideal communities.

vassal A person granted an estate or cash payments in return for accepting the obligation to render services to a lord.

vernacular The everyday language spoken by the people as opposed to Latin.

vingtième (VEN-tee-em) Meaning "one twentieth." A tax on income in France before the Revolution.

Vulgate　The Latin translation of the Bible by Jerome (348–420 C.E.) that became the standard bible used by the Catholic Church.

Waldensians (wahl-DEN-see-ens)　Medieval heretics who advocated Biblical simplicity in reaction to the worldliness of the church.

War Communism　The economic policy adopted by the Bolsheviks during the Russian Civil War to seize the banks, heavy industry, railroads, and grain.

water frame　A water-powered device invented by Richard Arkwright to produce a more durable cotton fabric. It led to the shift in the production of cotton textiles from households to factories.

Weimar (Why-mar) **Republic**　The German democratic regime that existed between the end of World War I and Hitler's coming to power in 1933.

White Russians　Those Russians who opposed the Bolsheviks (the "Reds") in the Russian Civil War of 1918–1921.

Zionism　The movement to create a Jewish state in Palestine (the Biblical Zion).

Index